AF600252

The Papers of

HENRY CLAY

The Papers of
HENRY CLAY

Robert Seager II
Editor

Melba Porter Hay
Associate Editor

Volume 9
THE WHIG LEADER
January 1, 1837-
December 31, 1843

THE UNIVERSITY PRESS OF KENTUCKY

"My ambition is that we may enter a new and larger era of service to humanity."

Dedicated to the memory of
JOSIAH KIRBY LILLY
1861 - 1948
President of Eli Lilly and Company
Founder of Lilly Endowment, Inc.

Whose wisdom and foresight were devoted to the service of education, religion, and public welfare

ISBN: 08131-0059-3
Library of Congress Catalog Card Number: 59-13605

Scholarly publisher for the Commonwealth, serving Bellarmine College, Berea College, Centre College of Kentucky, Eastern Kentucky University, The Filson Club, Georgetown College, Kentucky Historical Society, Kentucky State University, Morehead State University, Murray State University, Northern Kentucky University, Transylvania University, University of Kentucky, University of Louisville, and Western Kentucky University.

Editorial and Sales Offices: Lexington, Kentucky 40506-0024

CONTENTS

Preface vii

Symbols & Abbreviations viii

THE PAPERS OF HENRY CLAY 1

Calendar of Unpublished Letters 904

Name & Subject Index: Volume 9 919

PREFACE

The editors must gratefully acknowledge the contributions made to Volume 9 of *The Papers of Henry Clay* by the staff who have given unstintingly of their time, energy, and skills. In this regard, Mackelene G. Smith has continued her work as senior research and editorial assistant. Joining her in this task since October, 1983, is Anna B. Perry. Those who have assisted, primarily in proofreading and typing, are Margaret Spratt-Wyatt, Shannon Cox, Susan Brothers, and Kimberly Montgomery. The dedication of these people has contributed much to the production of this volume.

The editors have again employed the editorial philosophy and methodology outlined in Volume 7 (*see* 7: vii–viii) and amended in Volume 8 (*see* 8: vii–viii). This will not be repeated except to reemphasize three points: (1) while not all persons mentioned in passing have been identified, a serious attempt has been made to identify all of Clay's correspondents; (2) letters used as notes to other letters have been included in the To and From sections of relevant Index entries; and (3) documents summarized are almost entirely those of Clay's speeches and his incoming mail and are employed to provide a thorough historical context for his outgoing mail. Again, a calendar of marginal and peripheral Clay material has been provided.

Once more the editors sincerely thank the Lilly Endowment, Inc., for its support of the early volumes. We also wish to thank the National Historical Publications and Records Commission, the University of Kentucky Research Foundation, and the University Press of Kentucky for the financial support which has made possible the editing and publishing of this volume.

Robert Seager II
Melba Porter Hay
June, 1987

SYMBOLS & ABBREVIATIONS

The following symbols are used to describe the nature of the originals of documents copied from manuscript sources.

AD	Autograph Document
AD draft	Autograph Document, draft
ADI	Autograph Document Initialed
ADS	Autograph Document Signed
AE	Autograph Endorsement
AEI	Autograph Endorsement Initialed
AES	Autograph Endorsement Signed
AL	Autograph Letter
AL draft	Autograph Letter, draft
ALI	Autograph Letter Initialed
ALI copy	Autograph Letter Initialed, copy
ALI draft	Autograph Letter Initialed, draft
ALS	Autograph Letter Signed
ALS draft	Autograph Letter Signed, draft
AN	Autograph Note
AN draft	Autograph Note, draft
ANI draft	Autograph Note Initialed, draft
ANS	Autograph Note Signed
Copy	Copy not by writer (indicated "true" is so certified)
D	Document
DS	Document Signed
L	Letter
L draft	Letter, draft
LI draft	Letter Initialed, draft
LS	Letter Signed
N	Note
N draft	Note, draft
NS	Note signed

The following, from the *Symbols Used in the National Union Catalog of the Library of Congress* (9th ed., rev.; Washington, 1965), indicate the location of the original documents in institutional libraries of the United States.

CSmH	Henry E. Huntington Library and Museum, San Marino, California
CtY	Yale University, New Haven, Connecticut
DCU	Catholic University of America Library, Washington, D.C.
DLC	Library of Congress, Washington, D.C.

DLC-HC	Library of Congress, Henry Clay Collection
DLC-TJC	Library of Congress, Thomas J. Clay Collection
DNA	United States National Archives Library, Washington, D.C. Following the symbol for this depository, the letters A. and R. mean Applications and Recommendations; M, Microcopy; P. and D. of L., Publication and Distribution of the Laws; R, Reel; and RG, Record Group.
IaU	University of Iowa, Iowa City, Iowa
ICH	Chicago Historical Society, Chicago, Illinois
ICN	Newberry Library, Chicago, Illinois
ICU	University of Chicago, Chicago, Illinois
IHi	Illinois State Historical Library, Springfield, Illinois
In	Indiana State Library, Indianapolis, Indiana
InHi	Indiana Historical Society, Indianapolis, Indiana
InU	Indiana University, Bloomington, Indiana
KHi	Kansas State Historical Society, Topeka, Kansas
Ky	Kentucky Library and Archives, Frankfort, Kentucky
KyBgW	Western Kentucky University, Bowling Green, Kentucky
KyHi	Kentucky Historical Society, Frankfort, Kentucky
KyLoF	The Filson Club, Louisville, Kentucky
KyLxT	Transylvania University, Lexington, Kentucky
KyU	University of Kentucky, Lexington, Kentucky
MB	Boston Public Library, Boston, Massachusetts
MCM	Massachusetts Institute of Technology, Cambridge, Massachusetts
MdBP	Peabody Institute, Baltimore, Maryland
MeHi	Maine Historical Society, Portland, Maine
MH	Harvard University, Cambridge, Massachusetts
MH-BA	Harvard University, Graduate School of Business Administration Library
MHi	Massachusetts Historical Society, Boston, Massachusetts
MiU	University of Michigan, Ann Arbor, Michigan
MiU-C	University of Michigan, William L. Clements Library
MnHi	Minnesota Historical Society, St. Paul, Minnesota
MoSHi	Missouri Historical Society, St. Louis, Missouri
MoU	University of Missouri, Columbia, Missouri
MWA	American Antiquarian Society, Worcester, Massachusetts
MWalk	John F. Kennedy Memorial Library, Waltham, Massachusetts
NBuHi	Buffalo Historical Society, Buffalo, New York
Nc-Ar	North Carolina State Department of Archives and History, Raleigh, North Carolina
NcD	Duke University, Durham, North Carolina
NcU	University of North Carolina, Chapel Hill, North Carolina
NhD	Dartmouth College, Hanover, New Hampshire
NhHi	New Hampshire Historical Society, Concord, New Hampshire
NHi	New-York Historical Society, New York City
NIC	Cornell University, Ithaca, New York
NjHi	New Jersey Historical Society, Newark, New Jersey
NjMD	Drew University, Madison, New Jersey

NjMoHP	Morristown Edison National Historical Park, Morristown, New Jersey
NjP	Princeton University, Princeton, New Jersey
NN	New York Public Library, New York City
NNC	Columbia University, New York City
NNS	New York Society Library, New York City
NRU	University of Rochester, Rochester, New York
NWattJHi	Jefferson County Historical Society, Watertown, New York
ODa	Dayton and Montgomery County Library, Dayton, Ohio
OCHP	Historical and Philosophical Society of Ohio, Cincinnati, Ohio
OClW	Western Reserve University, Cleveland, Ohio
OHi	Ohio State Historical Society, Columbus, Ohio
PCarlD	Dickinson College, Carlisle, Pennsylvania
PHC	Haverford College, Haverford, Pennsylvania
PHi	Historical Society of Pennsylvania, Philadelphia, Pennsylvania
PLF	Franklin and Marshall College, Lancaster, Pennsylvania
PPPrHi	Presbyterian Historical Society, Philadelphia, Pennsylvania
PU	University of Pennsylvania, Philadelphia, Pennsylvania
PWW	Washington and Jefferson College, Washington, Pennsylvania
RHi	Rhode Island Historical Society, Providence, Rhode Island
RPB	Brown University, Providence, Rhode Island
Sc	South Carolina State Library, Columbia, South Carolina
ScU	University of South Carolina, Columbia, South Carolina
THi	Tennessee Historical Society, Nashville, Tennessee
USlC	Church Historian's Office, Church of Jesus Christ of Latter Day Saints, Salt Lake City, Utah
ViHi	Virginia Historical Society, Richmond, Virginia
ViU	University of Virginia, Charlottesville, Virginia
ViW	College of William and Mary, Williamsburg, Virginia
WHi	State Historical Society of Wisconsin, Madison, Wisconsin
WvU	West Virginia University, Morgantown, West Virginia

The following abbreviations are used in the footnotes of this volume:

AH	*Agricultural History*
BDAC	*Biographical Directory of the American Congress 1774–1961.* Washington: United States Government Printing Office, 1961.
BDGUS	*Biographical Directory of the Governors of the United States 1789–1978.* Robert Sobel and John Raimo, eds. Westport, Ct.: Meckler Books, 1978.
CAB	*Cyclopedia of American Biography.* James G. Wilson and John Fiske, eds. New York: D. Appleton & Company, 1888.
CHR	*Canadian Historical Review*
CWH	*Civil War History*
DAB	*Dictionary of American Biography.* Allen Johnson, ed. New York: Charles Scribner's Sons, 1927, 1964.

DH	*Delaware History*
DNB	*Dictionary of National Biography*. Sir Leslie Stephen and Sir Sidney Lee, eds. London: Oxford University Press, 1917.
FCHQ	*Filson Club History Quarterly*
GHQ	*Georgia Historical Quarterly*
HM	*Historical Magazine*
HRDUSA	*Historical Register and Dictionary of the United States Army 1789–1903*. Reprint. Urbana: University of Illinois Press, 1965.
IMH	*Indiana Magazine of History*
JNH	*Journal of Negro History*
JPE	*Journal of Political Economy*
JW	*Journal of the West*
LH	*Lincoln Herald*
LHQ	*Louisiana Historical Quarterly*
MHM	*Maryland Historical Magazine*
MPP	*A Compilation of the Messages and Papers of the Presidents 1789–1902*. James D. Richardson, comp. 10 vols. Washington: Bureau of National Literature and Art, 1904.
MVHR	*Mississippi Valley Historical Review*
NAR	*North American Review*
NCAB	*National Cyclopedia of American Biography*. New York: James T. White & Company, 1898.
NEHGR	*New England Historical and Genealogical Register*
NF	*Niagara Frontier*
PMHB	*Pennsylvania Magazine of History and Biography*
PSQ	*Presidential Studies Quarterly*
QJE	*Quarterly Journal of Economics*
RKHS	*Register of Kentucky Historical Society*
SCHGM	*South Carolina Historical and Genealogical Magazine*
SCHM	*South Carolina Historical Magazine*
THQ	*Tennessee Historical Quarterly*
TQHGM	*Tyler's Quarterly Historical and Genealogical Magazine*
USMA, *Register*	*Register of Graduates and Former Cadets, United States Military Academy*. West Point: The West Point Alumni Foundation, Inc., 1960.
VMHB	*Virginia Magazine of History and Biography*
WMH	*Wisconsin Magazine of History*
WMQ	*William and Mary Quarterly*

The Papers of
HENRY CLAY

From Rezin D. Shepherd, Baltimore, January 1, 1837. Instructs Clay to "make any arrangement you please" for selling the cattle, so long as he disposes of the three heifers. Mentions that he is anxious about stock which he is having shipped from England, because "the Ship has beene out 110 days & the weather on the coast has beene intensely severe." Hopes by spring to have some cattle in shape to send to Kentucky. Promises that "The moment my Stock arrives, I will inform you its situation and give you particulars about it." ALS. DLC-TJC (DNA, M212, R14). See 8:804-5, 834-836, 841.

Remark in Senate, January 2, 1837. Presents petition of Col. Anthony Gale. Referred to Committee on Naval Affairs. *Cong. Globe*, 24 Cong., 2 Sess., 67.

From John F. May, Richmond, Va., January 5, 1837. Reports that the "people of Petersburg" have elected him to the Virginia house of delegates and that, as a result, he has resigned his judicial office. Notes that "Tired & disgusted as I have been, for some years, with the politics & influences which predominate in our state; I had almost ceased to trouble myself about any thing connected with the government. From this cause, or because I have grown older, I distrust, very much, my opinions on any political question."

Proceeds to ask, "in perfect confidence," Clay's opinion on the subject of slavery. States that in his own opinion "I regard the continuance of this union as utterly hopeless, unless something can be done to repress the abolitionists of the North; and to prevent the irreparable mischiefs which their fanaticism must inflict, on the whole South, and especially this state We are so near the Northern cities; the facilities of communication are so numerous & so expeditious; our slaves, especially in & about our towns, are so intelligent; and the means of intercommunication between them & their northern allies are so easy; that we in Va. will suffer, more & sooner, than any other state, from their machinations." Feels that "we have no means of resisting" the activities of the abolitionists, and yet if a foreign country behaved in such a manner, "we should make war against them."

Suggests a constitutional amendment "to secure, not only our property, but our peace." Encloses a sketch of the amendment [not found] saying, "If we cannot procure it now, we never can; and the sooner we ascertain the fact, the better." Thinks this will be a good test of the sincerity of the "dominant [Democratic] party" which professes "the most amicable views towards us, in this matter." Continues: "I am aware of the disposition of the Northern Whigs on the subject; and I regret it; but they are now a small minority; destined probably to annihilation; and I do not perceive that the proposition can have an injurious effect on them." On the other hand, "In the South, I should think that it must operate favourably for our party, especially coming from *us*; for it is of vital importance to all the South." Concludes by again asking for Clay's views on the matter. ALS. DLC-HC (DNA, M212, R5). For May (1784-1858), an oft-time member of the Virginia house of delegates and a judge of the general court from 1829 to 1836, see *WMQ* (Series 2), 3:202-3; and Landon C. Bell, *The Old Free State*, 2 vols. (Richmond, Va., 1927), 2:313. The nature of the amendment proposed by May is not known.

Remark in Senate, January 6, 1837. In the absence of Sen. Thomas Ewing (Ohio), moves for further consideration of the joint resolution repealing the Treasury Department order [Specie Circular] of July 11, 1836 [8:860-61], which designated only "gold and silver and certificates of deposites signed by the Treasurer of the United States" as acceptable currency for payment for public lands, effective August 15, 1836. Notes that the question is now on the substitute resolution offered by Sen. William C. Rives (Va.) on December 22, 1836, which would permit payment for public lands with specie or bank notes of less than five dollars denomination (until June 30, 1839), not less than ten dollars denomination (July 1, 1839-June 30, 1841), and not less than twenty dollars denomination (July 1, 1841 and after). *Register of Debates*, 24 Cong., 2 Sess., 8, 123, 326. For Rives's resolution and his explanation of it, see *Cong. Globe*, 24 Cong., 2 Sess., 44, 61, 127; *ibid.*, Appendix, 36-37, 100-105; see also Speech in Senate, January 11, 1837; Comment in Senate, March 7, 1838.

Earlier this day, Clay presented a petition of John McLane, a Virginian, asking that he be permitted to purchase an island in the Mississippi River lying off riverfront property he owns in Illinois. *Cong. Globe*, 24 Cong., 2 Sess., 76.

From Reuben G. Beasley, Havre, France, January 8, 1837. Sends certificates for two jacks and six jennies which have "arrived here in good condition." States that they will be sent to Clay in a few days "on board the American ship New Orleans."

Mentions that the "late attempt upon the King's [Louis-Philippe] life here will serve to strengthen his government." Adds that "The message of our President [Jackson] has been received & is highly spoken of by all parties in England & France." Notes also that "The difficulty in money matters in England is not so great as it was a few weeks ago, it has never been seriously felt in France." ALS. Josephine Simpson Collection, Lexington, Ky.

On December 27, 1836, a young Frenchman, called Meunier, had attempted to shoot Louis-Philippe while he was crossing the Quai des Tuileries on his way to open a session of the French Chamber. See Thomas E. B. Howarth, *Citizen-King, The Life of Louis-Philippe King of the French* (London, 1961), 243-44. The "message of our President" to which Beasley refers is Jackson's Eighth Annual Message. See *MPP*:236-60, espec. 236. The "difficulty in money matters in England" had resulted from a specie drain caused, in part, by a low rate of exchange. By mid-1836 the Bank of England began raising the rediscount rate to correct this problem and subsequently denied the rediscount privilege to merchants and bankers who continued to accept bills of exchange drawn by Americans. The deflationary pressures generated by this action contributed to the banking crisis in the United States in the spring of 1837. See Thomas P. Govan, *Nicholas Biddle, Nationalist and Public Banker 1786-1844* (Chicago, 1959), 305-6; Bray Hammond, *Banks and Politics in America* (Princeton, N.J., 1957), 457-59.

On January 18, 1837, Beasley wrote Clay that the *New Orleans* sailed on the 14th with "seven Jannetts & two Jacks for you to the address of Mr. [Rezin D.] Shepherd." States that "They are Insured against all risks at 13 PCent." ALS. Josephine Simpson Collection, Lexington, Ky.

Beasley sent Clay on January 21 an "Account of cost and expenses . . . on 9 Asses" he had shipped to Clay, amounting to a total of £14,814.70. DS. Courtesy of M.W. Anderson, Lexington, Ky.

Remark in Senate, January 9, 1837. Moves for further consideration of the joint resolution rescinding the treasury order [Specie Circular] of July 11, 1836 [Remark in Senate, January 6, 1837]. *Register of Debates,* 24 Cong., 2 Sess., 327.

Remark in Senate, January 10, 1837. Announces that as the hour is late he will postpone until tomorrow his speech on the treasury [Specie Circular] order [Remark in Senate, January 6, 1837]. *Register of Debates,* 24 Cong., 2 Sess., 360.

Speech in Senate, January 11, 1837. Says he has lately expressed his opinion [8:860-61] on the treasury order [Specie Circular] of July 11, 1836, and that "what I uttered I sincerely believed. I believed it then, I believe it now; and I reaffirm it with all sincerity here in my place, as my settled opinion." Compliments Sen. William C. Rives (Va.) for an "able speech" on the subject yesterday, especially in making his point that in demanding specie payments for public lands, "The Treasury order proceeds on the principle of requiring specie only in payment for one of the most important branches of the public revenue." Mentions his difficulty in understanding Rives's argument that public land might best be purchased with "mixed currency." Notes that another of Jackson's loyal supporters (Benton) holds, on the contrary, that "precious metals alone are to form the currency," whereas Jacksonian Rives calls for a "mixed currency, consisting in part of specie, and in part of the notes of specie-paying banks." Asks: "Which of these friends of the administration are we to credit?" Points out that the central principle found in the Specie Circular was "put down by an almost unanimous vote" during the past session only to reappear in the treasury order promulgated "almost immediately on the rising of Congress." Wonders where Jackson himself stands on the paper money versus specie issue, since he seems to have shifted his ground since 1829 from a "mixed currency" stance to advocacy in 1835 of an "exclusive specie circulation." Affirms his support of Sen. Daniel Webster's basic idea of "increasing and strengthening the metallic basis of our paper currency" in part by "restricting issues of bank notes below prescribed denominations." The problem with this approach, however, is having to rely "on the voluntary action of a thousand banks, and of twenty-six State sovereignties operating on those banks." Such reliance on voluntary self-controls cannot and will not work, even if we assume the highest patriotic motives on the part of the banks and the states; and even though "We of the opposition" have for "four or five years" now sought to "widen the metallic foundation of the currency by a prohibition of small bank notes."

Repeats that few states have shown the "enlightened patriotism" necessary to effect such controls. Indeed, only a national bank could have made such a policy work; but "From the moment that the Bank of the United States ceased to exist [8:443, 552-53, 639-41], you gave up the rudder of the National currency." Shows that lacking a national bank, or the patriotic self-discipline of all the nation's bankers, there can be no workable way to prevent state and private banks from issuing profit-making "small notes." Develops this point at length. Criticizes the folly of Congress in not rechartering the Bank of the United States. Reminds the Senate that "We told you that the moment you destroyed a Bank of the United States there would immediately spring up innumerable local banks; that banking capital would then be greatly extended, and that the change might lead to the destruction of all confidence in the circulating paper medium." Asks: "Are not these predictions in a rapid progress of fulfilment?" Fears a sharp increase in paper money, the possibility of great depression, a substantial reduction in the price of Southern cotton, the sale of American stocks by their European holders, the resulting flow of specie from America to Europe, and, finally, "such a run upon the banks as May cause a general suspension of specie payments, if not the bankruptcy of many of the banks."

Predicts "a general panic throughout the country," a calamity that was "foretold" by those who supported recharter of the Bank of the United States. Believes that the broad effect of the Specie Circular will be to create such a demand for specie that it will be hoarded and will disappear from circulation. Does not believe that British banking and currency policies cited by Rives in support of his dual currency proposal pertain to the U.S. economic situation. Reviews the condition of the U.S. currency in 1816 and the relation of specie vs. bank notes to currency circulation problems existing at that time. Claims that the recreation of the Bank of the United States in 1816 brought currency order out of disorder by providing for the restoration of specie payments. Admits, however, that the bank cannot now be revived. Moreover, "I have not the least expectation of any effort being made by my friends to re-establish it. They have no such purpose." Adds, on the other hand, that the pending "experiment . . . as to the power of local banks in meeting the wants of the community" is doomed to failure. Cites the incorporation of the United States Bank of Pennsylvania [Biddle to Clay, February 21, 1837] in this regard. Asserts, further, that the secretary of the treasury has no "authority to require only specie, or to exclude entirely any of the four specified funds in payments to Government." The behavior of Secretary Levi Woodbury in this regard is essentially a "question of power." Even if the treasury circular conforms to "the letter of the law, I should still argue against its gross injustice." Affirms that the circular has thrown the banking community into great confusion and disorder. "The moment the order appeared, there was an instant pressure for specie, especially in the West and Southwest. The banks were called upon, and specie in all quarters was put in requisition, for the purpose of paying for the public lands. The pressure upon the banks in Kentucky was great." Argues that specie has thus been "transported from the seaboard, from the Western and Southwestern banks, from the theaters of business, where it might have been constantly and advantageously used, and taken into the interior, to banks of very limited business. And even there they were afraid to use it, lest it might be suddenly called for." Charges that the end result of this "iniquitous order" is rank discrimination against the West and Southwest. Only Ohio Sen. Thomas Ewing's resolution flatly to rescind the treasury order can abolish "this odious distinction, and [place] all parts of the community and every branch of the revenue, upon a footing of perfect equality."

Maintains that to rescind the treasury order implies no act of censure of President Jackson. Recalls, in this regard, that he has long fought against "the complete ascendency of executive power." Continues: "But, sir, its march has been steady, onward, and, I lament to say, triumphant. It is now practically the supreme power in the State. Every branch of the Government bends beneath its sway. . . . It is a monarchy in disguise." Merely issuing censures of such power will do no good. "We must not presume to censure them. We must bear, in silent and dutiful submission, whatever ills the acts of the Executive may bring on the country." Blames the treasury order of July 11 last not on the weak Secretary Levi Woodbury but on the powerful Jackson. Equates the president's order to Woodbury with his earlier order to Roger B. Taney to remove the deposits [8:583-84, 684-85], noting that Woodbury and "the whole cabinet" had opposed it. Chides Sen. Rives for a speech which "from beginning to end was directed against that order, which he says we must not repeal, lest we censure the President." Lauds Sen. Ewing's resolution to rescind as "open, direct, manly, but not offensive." Remarks, however, that he is willing to abandon Ewing's resolution to rescind outright and to accept instead the Rives amendment to it that would permit the purchase of public land with either specie or the notes of specie-paying banks. "That will sufficiently accomplish our purpose, and accommodate the measure to the delicate and nervous sensibility of any friend of the administration. That is all concerning which I feel any solicitude, and with this I will be content." Discusses difficulties in adopting such a solution; mainly the problem of Rives's additional proviso that the secretary of the treasury shall be empowered to determine what kinds of notes the deposit banks shall accept in payment for public lands. Thinks that a compromise solution to this problem can be worked out by accepting Alexander Hamilton's contention that "the bank notes of specie-paying banks are equivalent to specie, being in fact the representatives of specie." Such notes are not "paper money," Clay argues. Develops this point at some length. Has no real objection to the last clause in the Rives amendment "which requires the suppression of small notes (though I believe that, in practice, it will prove perfectly nugatory, that it will effect just nothing), I am quite willing to indulge him with the experiment. Nothing, I am persuaded, will come out of it; but try it." Points out, however, that "We passed an act at the last session prohibiting the use of notes below $10" and the government disbursing bank in Washington has paid no attention whatever to the law. Fears entrusting either the secretary of the treasury or the government's deposit banks with the power to determine the acceptability of notes. The test of acceptability should be this: "When a bank note is presented to a collector in payment of a debt to the Government, if, at the place such payment is made, it is at par, that is, equal to so much specie, the collector shall be obliged to receive it; if it is not, then he shall be at liberty to reject it. . . . The place of payment is what I would adopt as the test of all bank notes offered to us. If they are equal to specie there, they ought to be received." Asks that Rives "insert in his amendment a clause making the place of payment the test of the notes." With this addition, "we shall then have some rule which all can understand. All parties concerned will know whether the notes offered are at par at the place where payment is made. . . . otherwise, no one can know but the Secretary." *Register of Debates*, 24 Cong., 2 Sess., 360-76; see also *Cong. Globe*, 24 Cong., 2 Sess., Appendix, 295-99; and Remark in Senate, January 6, 1837. For Rives's approach to a modification of the Specie Circular, see his speeches of December 22, 1836, and January 10, 1837, in *Cong. Globe*, 24 Cong., 2 Sess., Appendix, 36-37, 100-105; also Comment in Senate, March 7, 1838. For the relationship that had existed between the state banks in the various sections and the B.U.S., see Jean A. Wilburn, *Biddle's Bank, The Crucial Years* (New York, 1967), 31-45.

On December 12, 1836, Sen. Thomas Ewing (Ohio) introduced a resolution to rescind the Specie Circular and to make uniform the currency receivable for the public revenue. After much debate the resolution was defeated and replaced by a bill designating and limiting the funds receivable for the revenues of the United States. This bill was reported by the Committee on Finance on January 27, 1837, and passed the Senate on February 10 by a vote of 41 to 5. It passed the House on March 1 by a 143 to 59 vote only to be pocket vetoed by Jackson. *Register of Debates*, 24 Cong., 2 Sess., 31, 106, 133, 146, 569; U.S. Sen., *Journal*, 24 Cong., 2 Sess., 235; U.S. H. of Reps., *Journal*, 24 Cong., 2 Sess., 556; Glyndon G. Van Deusen, *The Life of Henry Clay* (Boston, 1937), 288-89. The Specie Circular thus remained in effect until its repeal on May 30, 1838. See Comment in Senate, May 2, 1838; Remark in Senate, May 25, 1838; James C. Curtis, *The Fox at Bay, Martin Van Buren and the Presidency, 1837-1841* (Lexington, 1970), 130-31; Charles W. Wiltse and Harold D. Moser (eds.), *The Papers of Daniel Webster, Correspondence*, 7 vols. (Hanover, N.H., 1974-), 4:293, 301-4. For the act rescinding it, see 5 *U.S. Stat.*, 310. Benton had submitted a resolution on April 22, 1836, calling for "nothing but gold and silver . . . to be received in payment for public lands." After much debate the measure was dropped without having a vote taken. *Register of Debates*, 24 Cong., 1 Sess., 1254-77.

Clay's prediction of a panic and depression was soon realized. By March, 1837, business in New Orleans had come to a virtual standstill, and failures of business houses had become quite common. The full force of the panic was felt when New

York banks suspended specie payment on May 10, and banks throughout the country followed suit the next day. For a discussion of the causes, effects, and results of the panic and depression, see Curtis, *The Fox at Bay*, 64-151; Van Deusen, *Henry Clay*, 301-5; Govan, *Nicholas Biddle*, 299-338; Reginald C. McGrane, *The Panic of 1837, Some Financial Problems of the Jacksonian Era* (Chicago, 1924), *passim*. For a revisionist view of Jackson's fiscal policies, arguing his blamelessness in thought, word, and deed for the Panic of 1837, see Peter Temin, *The Jacksonian Economy* (New York, 1969), 113-47, *passim*.

From William Clay, "Fulwell Lodge," Twickenham, England, January 12, 1837. Sends "a pamphlet I have recently published.—which may not be wholly without interest to You—as it relates to a question of great interest as well in the United States as in England." Adds: "I trust—that by accepting this trifling work—you will permit me to consider myself not wholly a stranger to one who has conferred such celebrity on the name I bear." ALS. DLC-HC (DNA, M212, R5). Printed in Calvin Colton, *The Life, Correspondence, and Speeches of Henry Clay*, 6 vols. (New York, 1864), 4:409-10. For William Clay, see *DNB*. His pamphlet was *Speech on Moving for a Committee to Inquire into the Act Permitting the Establishment of Joint Stock Banks*. 2nd ed., London, 1837.

Remark in Senate, January 12, 1837. Moves that the administration's bill proposing "an entire change in the whole land system of the country" not be brought up until Sen. Thomas Ewing (Ohio), the only member of the Committee on Public Lands who is opposed to the bill, returns to Washington. Explains that Ewing's absence is due to the illness of his wife. *Register of Debates*, 24 Cong., 2 Sess., 377. The "entire change" proposed was in the form of an amendment, dated December 14, 1836, by Sen. Robert J. Walker, chairman of the Committee on Public Lands, to Clay's land bill [8:873] that completely replaced Clay's bill with one that would "limit the sales of public lands, except to actual settlers, and in limited quantities." *Ibid.*, 204. On February 7, 1837, Walker's substitute bill, freighting several amendments, was passed to a third reading 24 to 16. Clay's vote was not recorded. *Ibid.*, 726-37. On February 9, 1837, the bill passed the Senate 27 to 23. Clay was recorded in the negative. In the House, it was tabled on March 1, 1837. *Ibid.*, 777, 2091.

Later this day, Clay withdrew his motion to delay discussion of Walker's bill. *Ibid.*, 380. Walker's substitute land bill of December 14, 1836, permitted the purchase of from 40 acres to 1,280 acres (two sections) of public land at $1.25 per acre, if purchased for one's own use and for actual settlement and not for sale or speculation. Such land and its purchase price would be subject to forfeiture unless, within five years, a dwelling house had been built on it and at least one-eighth of it had been cleared and cultivated. Automatic preemption rights would be extended to "actual settlers" who occupied as little as a quarter of an acre, if such plot had also been cultivated prior to December 1, 1836; no patent would be issued such settlers until five years after application and their land would be forfeited unless they could prove "actual occupancy" within that period. Owners of farms or plantations abutting public land could buy up to one section (640 acres) of such land. All public land could be subdivided for sale down to 40-acre lots; and all future public land sales would be subject to taxation by the state in which the land was situated. In the amended version, which the Senate passed on February 9, 1837, three significant changes appeared. The clearing and cultivation requirement of one-eighth of the amount purchased was reduced to one-tenth; a parent could enter land claims for his children, up to a total of two sections, the patent to be issued only when the child attained his majority; and preemption rights would extend to an applicant who had resided on any tract of the public land and had cultivated any part of it within the year 1836. For summaries of the Walker bill, original and amended, see the Memphis (Tenn.) *Enquirer*, February 4 and March 4, 1837. For a comparison of Walker's December 14, 1836, bill with his earlier land bill of March 31, 1836 [8:839], see *Cong. Globe*, 24 Cong., 1 Sess., 309. Walker's remarks and parliamentary maneuvers in the Senate on January 14, 20, and February 1, 2, 3, 7, 1837, reveal his effort to provide potential and actual settlers on public land with preemption rights to more land at a lower price; he also sought minimal requirements for size of initial claim, length of occupancy, extent of cultivation, and necessity of the construction of a habitation; also fewer and lower legal barriers to eventual preemption. See *Register of Debates*, 24 Cong., 2 Sess., 419-28, 529, 668, 679, 695-96, 726, 731. For Walker's own speculation in public lands see James P. Shenton, *Robert John Walker: A Politician from Jackson to Lincoln* (New York, 1961), 13-17, 25-26.

Remark in Senate, January 13, 1837. Says there are several topics on which he hopes to speak. *Register of Debates*, 24 Cong., 2 Sess., 418.

Remark in Senate, January 14, 1837. Says he is "gratified" to learn from Sen. Robert J. Walker (Miss.), chairman of the Committee on Public Lands that "the Treasury order of July, 1836 [8:860-61] would, in some way be dispensed with." Asks when the committee will report on this subject. *Register of Debates*, 24 Cong., 2 Sess., 428. For the legislative history of the bill to rescind the Specie Circular, see Speech in Senate, January 11, 1837.

To THE GENERAL ASSEMBLY OF THE STATE OF KENTUCKY — Washington, January 16, 1837

His excellency the Governor of the State [James Clark] has done me the honor to transmit to me the official evidence of my election to the Senate of the United States,[1] for the constitutional term commencing on the 4th of March next. I have received this distinguished proof of the continued confidence and attachment of the General Assembly with sentiments of profound respect.

A considerable time prior to its present session, before the event of recent political elections,[2] and without regard to whatever might have been their issue, I had repeatedly both publicly announced and privately expressed, my sincere wish and intention to retire from the Senate of the United States. This must have been well known to every member of the General Assembly. Nevertheless it has done me the high honor of re-electing me to the Senate, not only unsolicited, but without knowing whether I would accept the appointment or not. On the one hand, this spontaneous and flattering expression of the favorable opinion of me, entertained by the General Assembly, has excited in my breast feelings of gratitude which no language can adequately portray, whilst, on the other, it has occasioned me distressing embarrassment in determining what ought to be the line of my duty.

Much the largest portion of a life, now not short, has been spent in the service of the State and the Union. It is upwards of thirty years since I was first honored by an election to the Senate of the United States. During that period, with short intervals, I have been in the councils of the General Government. I have thought that my long public service gave me some title to repose, of which I feel most sensibly great need. It also appeared to me not unreasonable to dedicate some time to the care of my private interests and duties which heretofore have had so little of my attention.

If therefore I were to consult exclusively my personal wishes and inclination, I should not hesitate a moment in declining to accept the appointment. But when I reflect upon the great and numerous obligations which I am under to the people of Kentucky, and upon the command implied, in my recent election, of the General Assembly to remain at the post assigned to me, I feel that there is no sacrifice which I ought not to make. I should have less reluctance in renouncing, or at least postponing, the gratification of my private wishes, if I did not fear that, constituted as the Senate now is and is likely to be, I can render no public services corresponding with the expectations of the General Assembly or with my own anxious desire. All that I dare promise, then, is that the same zeal and fidelity which have heretofore actuated me shall continue to be exerted in advancing the honor and welfare of our common country.

Copy. Printed in Ky. Sen., *Journal* . . . 1836-1837, pp. 239-40. 1. See 8:871. 2. See 8:782-85.

From Francis S. Latham, Memphis, Tenn., January 16, 1837. Thanks Clay for sending him a pamphlet which he will publish "in two or three several numbers of my paper . . . as early as may be expedient." Adds: "I am aware, sir, of the extreme delicacy of your position, and of the positive necessity of your future passiveness, with which even it will be impossible for you to escape the wiles and traductions of the enemy. But you are well aware of the great importance of securing this state to your interests; of which I have no doubt, although to make 'assurance doubly sure' we must not sleep. It is a great change for a people to make in 3 or 4 years,—to support one whom they so lately ejected or suffered not to claim the least share of their kind regard but they have *turned from their idol,* and this *alone* could be convincing that they have and will embrace the one [Clay] whose principles of polity are antipodes to those of Gen. Jackson."

Asks to be furnished with "any and all intelligence that may bear upon the great question on behalf of our common country." Notes that his paper, the Memphis *Enquirer,* has "great effect in North Mississippi and Arkansas." ALS. DLC-HC (DNA, M212, R5). For Latham and his newspaper, see John P. Young (ed.), *Standard History of Memphis, Tennessee* (Knoxville, 1912), 445-46. The editors have not been able to determine which, if any, of the articles in Latham's paper came from the pamphlet supplied by Clay.

From James Prenter, Dromore, Ireland, January 16, 1837. Thanks Clay for a draft he recently received for fifty-one pounds, two shillings, and nine pence sterling. Notes that apparently James Weir "is giveing you all the Annoyance in his power as regards the division of the property" of his late uncle, James Weir [1:189] of Lexington. Is glad Clay was able to get the former division of property set aside, and hopes "you will soon be Enabled to have a New and More beneficial one Made." Mentions that he has informed his granddaughter, Eliza Jane Weir, of Clay's opinion that she should move to Lexington, but "she Cannot think of leaving her friends here." Emphasizes that he has spent "a Considerable sum of Money in advance for the Education of Eliza," and wants Clay to "Send me another Remittance as Soon as in your power to do so." ALS. KyLxT. For Clay's involvement in acting as guardian in America of Eliza Jane Weir who had inherited part of the estate of her great-uncle James Weir, see 8:718-20.

On June 27, 1837, Prenter again wrote asking that a remittance be sent via

James Stuart in Philadelphia. Notes that "money is very scarce here," and he is "now Considerably in advance" for Eliza Jane's expenses as well as the cost "of a Long and troublesome lawsuit with the Wier [*sic*, Weir] famiely." ALS. KyLxT.

Eliza Jane wrote Clay on August 2, 1838, saying she has heard from her grandfather that Clay has "had a great deal of trouble and received much annoyance on my account for which I am extremely sorry and lose no time in acknowledging my deep sense of all the kindness I have received and obligations I am under to you for the protection of my rights." Asks again that money be sent to her grandfather "as soon and as fully as in your power." *Ibid.*

Thomas Dunlap, acting cashier of the United States Bank of Pennsylvania, wrote Clay on October 6, 1838, that he had "invested your Check for $500 in a Sterling Bill at the rate the Bank is now drawing and remitted the same . . . to Dromore Ireland." ALS. *Ibid.*

An agreement, concluded October 25, 1838, between Clay, acting as guardian for Eliza Jane, and James Weir, acting as "administrator and one of the Heirs of James Weir deceased," provided for the redivision of the Weir estate. In the new division Eliza Jane received nine slaves in lieu of a house and lot on Mulberry Street and James Weir agreed to hire the nine slaves in addition to the five slaves previously allotted her. ADS. *Ibid.*

In a receipt, dated October, 1838, Clay indicated he had received two notes from James Weir; one for $470 for the hire of five slaves allotted to Eliza Jane in the first division for the year 1835 and the other for $250 for the rent for a house and lot on Mulberry Street for 1835. These notes were received "in consequence of a redivision." DS. *Ibid.*

A document, dated October, 1838 and called "List of Negroes in the possession of J. Weir at his death," lists 67 slaves, mostly men, which commissioners valued at $26,002.50, three slaves having died before the evaluation took place. Included also is a list of the nine slaves, valued at $4,000 as of 1838, allotted to Eliza Jane in lieu of the house and lot on Mulberry Street. An additional notation indicates that ten slaves were either sold or died before the division of the estate, two became free before the division, while three died and four were sold after the division. *Ibid.*

Another document, dated November, 1838, lists the fourteen slaves owned by Eliza Jane after the redivision. The skilled slaves included one rope spinner, two hacklers, two weavers, two chain spinners, and two felling spinners. AD. DLC-HC (DNA, M212, R5).

On November 14, 1838, Clay concluded an agreement with Woolson Cutter & Co. thereby leasing Eliza Jane's house on Main Street for three years for the sum of $600 per annum, to be paid quarterly. ADS. KyLxT.

A.O. Newton, secretary of the Lexington Fire, Life and Marine Insurance Co., gave Clay on November 20, 1838, a receipt for $29.80 paid as premium for an insurance policy of $4,550 for one year on the Main Street house belonging to Eliza Jane. *Ibid.* A copy of the policy, *ca.* November 20, 1838, is in *ibid.* Endorsements on verso of policy certify the continuance of coverage "to November 20, 1840 and 1841, upon receipt of $27.30 on November 20, 1839, and $34.12½ on November 20, 1840."

On December 7, 1838, James Prenter wrote Clay thanking him for his letter of September 28 and for the money, "being the proceeds of the 500 Dollars you Mentioned which is placed to the credit of my wards account." Is glad to hear the final settlement of the estate may come soon. ALS. *Ibid.*

Clay wrote "The Cashr. of the B.U.S." in Philadelphia on April 29, 1839, asking him to remit $500 "to James Prenter, guardian of Eliza Jane Weir . . . and charge the same to my account." ALS. PPL.

On May 6, 1839, A. Lardner, assistant cashier of the B.U.S., notified Clay that the money had been drawn on his account and would be sent to Prenter by packet sailing on May 8. ALS. KyLxT.

Prenter wrote on June 29, 1839, saying he had received $500 and deposited it to Eliza Jane's account. Adds that "the arrangements you have with so Much trouble and attention got effected with her property are Most Satisfactory and all her friends here Join me in thanking you Most heartily for the Valuable Services rendered her—" *Ibid.*

Eliza Jane, in a letter from Dromore dated July 12, 1839, also acknowledged receipt of the $500 and thanked Clay "for all the trouble you have taken with my affairs, and which you have brought to such a very satisfactory termination." In addition, thanks him for "still continuing to take charge of and promote my interests." *Ibid.*

In November, 1839, Clay paid $42.00 Lexington city tax and $5.25 fire tax for Eliza Jane. John Wirt to Clay, account and receipt. ADS. *Ibid.*

On January 1, 1840, A.D. Hunt gave Clay a receipt for $92.10 paid on behalf of Eliza Jane's estate. The payment included: $22.85 for 12 pairs of shoes for her slaves; $1.75 "for Dabney per order"; $5.00 for "1 Truss for Tom"; and $62.50 for "Loss of Andersons time who died 26th June." *Ibid.*

On March 27, 1840, Clay wrote the cashier of the U.S. Bank of Pennsylvania saying that "last Spring" he obtained a remittance of $500 to Dromore, Ireland, and "I want to make a similar remittance." Asks how much it will cost in current funds to make the remittance "through your Bank." Copy. Printed in Swann Galleries Catalogue, *Autographs and a Private Collection of Printed & Manuscript Americana* (New York, 1986), item 248. Auction, November 6, 1986.

Joseph Cowperthwait, cashier of the United States Bank of Pennsylvania, wrote Clay on March 30, 1840, saying that he is sending a bill via the *British Queen* to James Prenter in Ireland, and that the "cost of the Bill $500 is charged to your ac[coun]t." ALS. KyLxT. For Cowperthwait, see Govan, *Nicholas Biddle*, 322, 350, 378, 405.

On April 1, 1840, Clay wrote Cowperthwait thanking him for sending the draft to James Prenter and enclosing a check on the U.S. Bank of Pennsylvania to cover "the advance you have been good enough to make for me." ALS. PP.

James Prenter wrote Clay on May 16, 1840, acknowledging receipt of a draft to Eliza Jane for $500. States that she herself would have written if she had not been ill with smallpox. Notes she is now recovered and will write soon. ALS. KyLxT.

Eliza Jane Weir wrote Clay from Dromore on July 15, 1840, expressing "my gratitude for the protection afforded me, and the great trouble you have taken to substantiate my rights," but says she cannot leave her elderly grandfather and grandmother to come to America. Notes that she will "not be 21 years of age until the 29th July 1841, and am so happy and comfortable that I have no wish to make any change in my life whatever." *Ibid.*

On November 10, 1840, Clay paid John Wirt, the city tax collector, $45.56½ for Eliza Jane's city tax. ADS. *Ibid.*

On November 20, 1840, Clay received a receipt from Thomas Baxter of the Lexington Fire, Life and Marine Insurance Company for $34.12½ he had paid for insuring Eliza Jane's three-story brick building on Main Street for the sum of $4,550. *Ibid.*

James Prenter wrote on August 5, 1841, acknowledging receipt of a bill for £100 Sterling which Clay had sent Eliza Jane who "Came of age 29th. Last month." ALS. *Ibid.* See also Lewis to Clay, July 2, 1841.

On August 28, 1841, Eliza Jane also acknowledged receiving the money. States that although she came of age last July 29, "As yet I have not made up my mind respecting my property nor can I until I hear from you." *Ibid.*

Eliza Jane wrote Clay on October 6, 1841, saying she had not heard from him and asking that he send all the money due her so that she could have it by December. Asks also for "the full particulars of what my property consists & also the supposed value." *Ibid.*

After receiving a letter from Clay, dated September 14 [not found], Eliza Jane wrote again on November 15, 1841, saying that "as you in a former letter intimated that in consequence of your getting advanced in life you were anxious to get rid of the charge of my affairs & as I do not like to have property in a country distant from where I reside, [I] think it better for me to have all sold in January first." States that she is "getting power of attorney prepared to have sent out . . . & will feel grateful by your having all in readiness to prevent delay." *Ibid.*

On November 20, 1841, Clay received a receipt from Thomas B. Baxter, Sr., of the Lexington Fire, Life & Marine Insurance Co. for $28.44 received as premium for insuring Eliza Jane's brick buildings on Main Street in Lexington for a twelve month period. ADS. *Ibid.*

As guardian for Eliza Jane, Clay received a bill and receipt from Garland Christy, dated January 1, 1842, for $19.50. Of this sum, $18.00 was Christy's fee "for hiring out 12 negro men for this year" and $1.50 was "Cash paid for advertising." *Ibid.* Christy was an auction and commission merchant in Lexington at 1 E. Main Street at corner of Jordan's Row. Julius P.B. MacCabe, *Directory of the City of Lexington . . . 1838 & '39* (Lexington, 1838), 44.

Clay received another bill and receipt from Garland Christy, dated only "Lexington 10th. 1842," for $6.50. Of this sum, $5.00 was "My fee for Selling Negro Man Bob" and $1.50 was "for advertising Same for Sale." ADS. KyLxT.

On January 10, 1842, Clay received a letter from Alexander Brown & Sons of Baltimore, enclosing "our bill on Brown Shipley & Co of Liverpool for £561.14.7 in favour of Mis[s] Eliza Jane Weir." They also acknowledged receipt of a letter from Clay of January 8, 1842, together with checks on New York and Philadelphia for $27.64. ALS. *Ibid.*

Eliza Jane wrote Clay from Belfast on February 23, 1842, acknowledging receipt of the £561:14:7 bill sterling. States that she reached the age of 21 on "the 29th July last & have since got my discharge from the guardianship of the court here." Says she will send her power of attorney by an uncle who will be coming to the United States in March and who will also bring a letter instructing "you fully in what way I wish my affairs arranged." *Ibid.*

On May 20, 1842, Eliza Jane wrote again acknowledging receipt of three bills "for which I feel much obliged." Mentions that her uncle has been delayed in his trip to the United States but now plans to come in June or July. She will send the power of attorney with him "& will likewise write you by June how I wish the property in Kentucky disposed of." *Ibid.*

Eliza Jane wrote Clay on August 29, 1842, introducing her uncle, John Hoy of Belfast, "who visits the U. States on business." States that she has given her uncle "authority to dispose of" her property, and that she is "convinced you will give him all the advice & assistance in your power, so as to enable him to sell to the best advantage." *Ibid.*

On August 30, 1842, Clay wrote James Harlan in Frankfort, Ky., concerning appeal of the *Weir* v. *Weir* case. Notes that the "division of the real Estate and of the Slaves has been effected and nothing remains to be done with that." Feels the "main object[s] now to be accomplished" are: to settle the administrator's account; "to resist the iniquitous demand for wages"; to charge the administrator for the slaves which he sold without authority and to make him liable for interest. Adds that "The most important item is the claim for Wages, and what is it? Three or four poor Irish boys are brought or come from Ireland and are taken under the care of their uncle who supports them. No contract for wages ever existed. He dies

& they inherit all his estate, or nearly all. And now they trump up large—enormously large—accounts for wages, in order to diminish the distributive share of their niece [Eliza Jane Weir]!" ALS. KyHi.

On November 12, 1842, Madison C. Johnson, gave to Clay as guardian of Eliza Jane, a receipt for $100 paid for his professional services rendered in the lawsuit with her uncles. DS. KyLxT.

Accounts and receipts, bearing as their last date November 18, 1842, show Clay giving to John Hoy, Eliza Jane's "attorney in fact," a check on the Northern Bank of Kentucky for the sum of $4,794.41. Also, Hoy received notes from Clay amounting to $1,385 "due at the end of this year for the hire of Eliza Jane Weirs twelve negroes this year." D. *Ibid.*

On November 23, 1842, John Hoy acknowledged the receipt of $1,558.39 from Clay, "being the bal. in full . . . of the hire of Miss Weirs negroes for the year 1841." Hoy promises, "as the agent of Miss Weir," to pay certain outstanding bills. ADS. *Ibid.* Receipt is accompanied by an account showing the origin of the $1,558.39.

Speech in Senate, January 16, 1837. Observes that since he was responsible for the resolution of March 28, 1834 [8:684-85, 708], censuring Jackson for the removal of deposits, he feels "it to be his duty to say something on this expunging resolution [8:735]." Had begun to doubt "whether there existed any serious intention of ever putting it to the vote." Reviews at length the historical and legal background of the resolution of censure which had, in turn, produced Sen. Thomas H. Benton's recurring efforts physically to expunge it from the pages of the Senate *Journal.* Discusses fully the unconstitutional dimensions of Jackson's dismissal in 1833 of secretaries Louis McLane and William J. Duane for their refusals to sign an order removing the government deposits from the Bank of the United States. Asserts, further, that "the charges of insecurity and insolvency of the bank were without the slightest foundation. And time, that great arbiter of human controversies, has confirmed all that we said. The bank, from documents submitted to Congress by the Secretary of the Treasury at the present session, appears to be able not only to return every dollar of the stock held in its capital by the public, but an addition of eleven per cent. beyond it." Defends the Senate's right and duty to censure Jackson for his violation of the constitution, specifically his abuse of executive power. Discusses the importance of the Senate's role in monitoring the actions of the president within the framework of the balance of power structure ordained by the constitution. Calls particular attention to its impeachment power in this regard. Notes, however, that the Senate's power to censure and its power to impeach stem from quite different constitutional roots. Asserts that there was never any intention in 1834 to impeach Jackson "whether the President merited impeachment or not." Declares that his censure resolution implied no presidential guilt of the sort or magnitude requiring impeachment. "It simply affirmed that he had 'assumed upon himself authority and power not conferred by the constitution and laws, but in derogation of both.' It imputed no criminal motives." Criticizes the friends of the president for introducing the constitutional impeachment issue in order to confuse the censure question. Points out that Jackson's supporters argue that since the "resolution neither affirmed his innocence, nor pronounced his guilt. It amounts then . . . to nothing." "Not so," Clay insists. The Senate must, he continues, "in language the most inoffensive and respectful, remonstrate against any executive usurpation, whatever may be its degree or danger. . . . I believe the resolution of March, 1834, to have been true; and that it was competent to the Senate to proclaim the truth." Addresses also the constitutionality of the proposed act of physical expunction. "In what article," he inquires, "is contained your power to expunge what they [your predecessors] have done? And may not the precedent lead to a perpetual code of defacement and restoration of the transactions of the Senate? . . . Are you not only destitute of all authority, but positively forbidden, to do what the expunging resolution proposes? The injunction of the constitution to keep a journal of our proceedings is clear, express, and emphatic. It is free from all ambiguity: no sophistry can pervert the explicit language of the instrument, no artful device can elude the force of the obligation which it imposes." Asks the expungers: "Can an unconstitutional act of that [1834] Senate, supposing it to be so, justify you in performing another unconstitutional act?" Cites at length historical examples of expunction, one from the France of Louis XIII, another from the Pennsylvania of 1816 to answer his own question in the negative. Dismisses the contentions of the expungers as speculative, largely beside the constitutional points involved, and factually inaccurate.

Asks, not without sarcasm, why Sen. Judah Dana of Maine, newly appointed by his governor to fill a three-month vacancy, spends so much of his brief time in Washington supporting the expunging resolution, and, in so doing, inundates "the Senate with a torrent of fulsome and revolting adulation poured on the President." Why not seek to accomplish "some great measure fraught with general benefit to the whole Union" while you are here, Clay asks. That not being of interest to you, why not at least do something for Maine? Suggests that Dana might "dedicate his time to an investigation into the causes of an alien jurisdiction being still exercised over a large part of the territory of the State which he represents"; or find out "why the American carrying trade to the British colonies, in which his State was so deeply interested, has been lost by a most improvident and bungling arrangement?" Concludes with the lengthy observation that passage of the expunging resolution can serve no "patriotic purpose" whatever; and that the whole expunging business can be traced to the ego and ambition of President Andrew Jackson who "exercises uncontrolled the power of the State. In one hand he holds the purse, and in the other brandishes the sword of the country. Myriads of dependants and partisans, scattered over the land, are ever ready to sing hosannas to him, and to laud to the skies whatever he does. He has swept over the Government, during the last eight years, like a tropical tornado. Every department exhibits traces of the ravages of the storm. Take as one example the Bank of the United States. No institution could have been more popular with the people, with Congress, and with State Legislatures. None ever better fulfilled the great purposes of its establishment. But it unfortunately incurred the displeasure of the President; he spoke, and the bank lies prostrate. And those who were loudest in its praise are now loudest in its condemnation. What object of his ambition is unsatisfied? When disabled from age any longer to hold the sceptre of power, he designates his successor [Van Buren], and transmits it to his favorite! What more does he want? Must we blot, deface, and mutilate, the records of the country, to punish the presumptuousness of expressing an opinion contrary to his own?" Asks again what patriotic purpose is to be served by the expunging resolution: "Is it to appease the wrath and to heal the wounded pride of the Chief Magistrate? If he be really the hero that his friends represent him, he must despise all mean condescension, all grovelling sycophancy, all self-degradation and self-abasement. He would reject, with scorn and contempt, as unworthy of his fame, your black scratches and your baby lines in the fair records of his country. Black lines! Black lines! Sir, I hope the Secretary of the Senate [John Forsyth] will preserve the pen with which he may inscribe them, and present it to that Senator of the majority whom he may select, as a proud trophy, to be transmitted to his descendants. And hereafter, when we shall lose the forms of our free institutions, all that now remain to us, some future American monarch, in gratitude to those by whose means he has been enabled, upon the ruins of civil liberty, to erect a throne, and to commemorate especially this expunging resolution, may institute a new order of knighthood, and confer on it the appropriate name of the Knight of the Black Lines. . . . Proceed, then, to the noble work which lies before you, and, like other skilful executioners, do it quickly. And when you have perpetrated it, go home to the people, and tell them what glorious honors you have achieved for our common country. Tell them that you have silenced one of the noblest batteries that ever thundered in defence of the constitution, and bravely spiked the cannon. Tell them that, henceforward, no matter what daring or outrageous act any President may perform, you have forever hermetically sealed the mouth of the Senate." *Register of Debates*, 24 Cong., 2 Sess., 429-40. Printed in Colton, *Clay Correspondence*, 6:45-60. The *Cong. Globe* of this date did not carry this speech, noting only that Clay spoke against the expunging resolution "at great length." The speech, said Sen. James Buchanan (Pa.), just after Clay had resumed his seat, was an "able and eloquent display" that had "enchained the attention of his audience." *Register of Debates*, 24 Cong., 2 Sess., 440. Sen. Judah Dana's speech of January 13, 1837, in support of the expunging resolution is in *ibid.*, 391-96. Dana served in the Senate only from December 7, 1836, to March 3, 1837. The unresolved Anglo-American dispute over the Maine boundary, in which Maine had a large stake, and which Clay suggested Dana might want to investigate, is treated extensively throughout volumes 4, 5, 6, and 7 of the *Clay Papers*. See subject index, 7:673, 729-30; and espec. 1:1006; 4:181-82, 390, 677-78, 830-31, 851-52, 875, 910-11; 5:11, 43, 446-48, 508-12, 1058; 6:363-65, 609-10, 656, 1047-48, 1100-1101, 1201-2, 1272-74, 1282-84, 1321-22, 1348; 7:108-9, 168-69, 220, 233, 283-84, 361, 581-82; 8:552; see also Gallatin, Albert. For the alleged "bungling arrangement" with Britain by which the American carrying trade with the British colonies was being regulated in 1837, see 2:564-66; 3:729, note 21; 4:180; 5:632; 8:248, note 6, 379-80, 389, note 11; Clay to Kennedy, April 17, 1839, note 3; also, McLane, Louis in index.

To ROBERT P. LETCHER Washington, January 17, 1837

I yesterday addressed letters to the G. Assembly accepting the appointment which it has recently conferred on me.[1] I need not say to you, who know with what unaffected sincerity I desired to retire, that this decision has cost me the most painful sacrifices of feeling. And I shall hail with the greatest pleasure the occurrence of circumstances which will admit of my resignation, with satisfaction to my friends, and without dishonor to myself. The Senate is no longer a place for any decent man. It is rapidly filling with blackguards. Yesterday Benton's Expunging Resolution passed 24 to 19,[2] and the disgraceful work of drawing black lines around the Resolve of 1834 was executed at 9 OClock at night. The darkness of the deed and of the house was well suited to each other.

You will have heard that a bill for the relief of yourself and your good friend [Thomas P.] Moore has passed the House. The latter part of it will be a bitter pill, which I do not know that I can swallow.[3]

ALS. NcD. Copy in OHi. 1. See 8:871-72; Clay to General Assembly of Ky., Jan. 16, 1837. 2. See 8:735. See also *Register of Debates*, 24 Cong., 2 Sess., 504. 3. The act for the relief of Robert P. Letcher and Thomas Moore provided that each be paid $1,545 for travelling expenses and for the time from Dec. 2, 1833, to June 12, 1834, during which the House seat, claimed by each, was in dispute. The bill passed the House on Jan. 6, 1837, and the Senate on Jan. 23. It was signed by the president on Jan. 31. U.S. H. of Reps., *Journal*, 24 Cong., 2 Sess., 174; U.S. Sen., *Journal*, 24 Cong., 2 Sess., 153; 6 *U.S. Stat.*, 684. For the disputed election of 1833 between Letcher and Moore, see 8:638-39. The "bitter pill" for Clay apparently was the provision of the bill which provided for paying Moore, the eventual loser, as much as Letcher for travelling expenses.

Comment in Senate, January 18, 1837. Asks that consideration of Sen. Robert J. Walker's public land sales bill [8:873; Remark in Senate, January 12, 1837] be postponed. Says he opposes the bill "throughout," and asserts that he will "be able to demonstrate conclusively, that instead of preventing speculations in the public lands, and limiting the sales, it would increase the sales to a great degree, and operate as an encouragement to speculation [Comment in Senate, January 24, 1837]." *Register of Debates*, 24 Cong., 1 Sess., 512.

Later this day, Clay comments intermittently on a bill that would in effect lend public money to spoliation claimants on France and Naples at an interest rate of 4 percent. As explained by Sen. Silas Wright (N.Y.), sponsor of the bill, France, under the spoliation claims convention [8:448, 754] is scheduled to pay the U.S. government $1,666,000 in two instalments; one in May, 1837, the other in May, 1838. At the same time, the Kingdom of Naples will be paying off the final six instalments of its nine-instalment spoliation indemnity, a payment in the total amount of $1,123,000. These six instalments fall due annually in June, 1837, through June, 1842. "The result, therefore, of the present bill," says Wright, "would be the payment to our own citizens of about $2,800,000, and placing that sum at an interest of four per cent. until, by the gradual payment of the instalments, the whole should return to the Treasury." Clay flatly opposes this bill on the financial ground that to advance these public funds, secured only by future treaty instalment payment promises, at a four percent interest rate, is bad business. The proposed rate is well below the seven percent now being paid by several state governments and far below the ten to twenty percent rate "in the money market." The whole "arrangement seems to me extremely injudicious," especially since the treasury anticipates a deficit on January 1, 1838, "so great as to render it necessary to recall a part of the sums deposited with the respective States under the act of last session [8:813]." It discriminates in favor of those relatively few Americans, "the merchants of New York, or of Philadelphia," who happen to have spoliation claims against the governments of France and Naples. Believes, too, that the bill is unconstitutional. "On what ground, either of the constitution or of expediency, will you make these gratuitous donations?" he asks. The money should be paid out to these claimants as the instalments are paid into the treasury. "The Government of the United States should not be required to interpose in advance the public money at four per cent. to a few favored individuals, to whom it is worth six, ten, and fifteen per cent." Agrees with Wright that "there are no party considerations involved in this measure," but hints that among the beneficiaries will be many New Yorkers. If the commercial community needs the kind of financial relief this bill will afford, "let them repeal the Treasury order [Speech in Senate, January 11, 1837]. . . . Let the administration cease to make these ruthless attacks upon the currency, and the country will get a little quiet." Notes approvingly that a bill has been reported by the Committee on Public Lands [Remark in Senate, January 14, 1837] that would effect repeal of the treasury order [Specie Circular]. Concludes: "I think the bill involves a most important principle. If the precedent shall once be established of thus loaning the public money to individuals, no human being can foresee where it will go." *Ibid.*, 514-15, 517-19. Wright's bill passed the Senate 20 to 8 on February 28, 1837, Clay's vote not recorded. *Ibid.*, 1009. It was introduced in the House on March 2, 1837, but was not brought up for discussion or vote during the session. U.S. H. of Reps., *Journal*, 24 Cong., 2 Sess., 578.

For the treaty between the United States and Naples, see 4:367, 369; 5:103,

421-22; and Clive Parry (ed.), *The Consolidated Treaty Series*, 231 vols. (Dobbs Ferry, N.Y., 1969), 83:11-15.

Remark in Senate, January 20, 1837. Moves reconsideration of the amendment of Sen. Thomas Morris (Ohio) to Sen. Robert J. Walker's substitute public land bill [Remark in Senate, January 12, 1837]. The Morris amendment set varying prices on public lands related to the length of time such lands had remained unsold [Remark in Senate, January 24, 1837]. Specifically, the Morris amendment required that land ten years in the market would sell for 75¢ per acre; five to ten years in the market, $1.00 per acre; all other land, $1.25 per acre. Clay moves reconsideration because of "the avowed embarrassment under which it had placed several gentlemen," and because he himself had earlier been mistaken "as to the import of the amendment." *Register of Debates*, 24 Cong., 2 Sess., 529-30. The reconsideration motion carried 19 to 14.

The Morris amendment, to which, at the suggestion of Sen. Benton, was added the proviso that "no person should enter more than a quarter section at a reduced price," failed by a vote of 19 to 18, Clay voting in the negative. Faced with this defeat, Walker observed that since a "very important principle had been stricken from the bill," it should be recommitted to the Committee on Public Lands. He believed that in "its present form" his bill would fail. He also thought that some measure or other must be carried for "The purpose of reducing the public revenue," and he felt that his land bill was "the only one which could be adopted to prevent the accumulation of a dangerous surplus." *Ibid.*, 529.

Remark in Senate, January 21, 1837. Presents a petition from sundry citizens of Wirtsborough [*sic*, Wurtsboro], N.Y., objecting to Roman Catholic emigrants "brought in under the auspices of Popes, Cardinals, Bishops, &c." The petitioners argue the "impropriety and inexpediency of allowing so many persons to enter the country whose practice and tenets were avowedly and directly hostile to our republican institutions." They ask Congress to institute study commissions in various parts of the nation "to procure information and report on the subject." While Clay thinks the petitioners are "good and religious people," he argues that Congress has no power to grant their request. Believes that the only "proper subject of inquiry" within the power of Congress would be consideration of a "change in our laws of naturalization." *Register of Debates*, 24 Cong., 2 Sess., 533; see also *Cong. Globe*, 24 Cong., 2 Sess., 114.

To SAMUEL L. SOUTHARD Washington, January 22, 1837

I recd. your favor. Nothing has been done since you left us to occasion you any regret on account of your absence. We were on the Land bill ([Robert J.] Walker's) yesterday and today,[1] but only upon details. No general argument upon it has been yet opened. The bill will be laid over until monday, when the consideration of it will be resumed. I think if you are here by tuesday or wednesday, you will be in time to vote upon it.[2] Indications of an opposition to the bill have been given from unexpected quarters, unless the graduating principle is incorporated in the bill, which we put out of it yesterday.

Our mess are all well. [John] Calhoon has left us, in consequence of objections to his room. . . .[3]

ALS. NjP. Letter is headed "S. Chamber Saturday 3 OClock P.M." Since it is postmarked Jan. 21 and Saturday fell on the 21st, Clay erred in dating it Jan. 22. 1. For Walker's land bill in the 24th Congress, 1st Session, see 8:839; for the Walker bill in the 24th Congress, 2nd Session, see Remark in Senate, Jan. 12, 1837. 2. When Walker's bill finally came to a vote on Feb. 9 and was passed 27 to 23, Southard was present. He voted nay. He was not in Washington on Tuesday and Wednesday, Jan. 24-25. *Register of Debates*, 24 Cong., 2 Sess., 777. 3. Clay, John J. Crittenden, Samuel L. Southard, and John Calhoon (Ky.; not to be confused with John C. Calhoun) all resided at the house of M.A. Clements on Pennsylvania Avenue. Perry M. Goldman & James S. Young, *The United States Congressional Directories 1789-1840* (New York, 1973), 303.

Comment in Senate, January 24, 1837. Wants to hear some solid arguments in support of the Tipton amendment to the public land bill. (Sen. John Tipton's proposal, similar to the Morris amendment [Remark in Senate, January 20, 1837], was based on the principle of graduation in that it would reduce the price of land unsold for ten years from $1.25 to $1.00 per acre and land unsold for fifteen years to 75 cents per acre.) Says he cannot understand the logic behind reducing the price of "all the public lands, after having been in the market at the low price of $1.25, down to $1, and then to 75 cents." The complaint against the present bill [8:873; Remark in Senate, January 12, 1837] has been that the public domain was selling too fast and at prices so low that speculation, rather than occupation and cultivation, was increased. Since the remedy for this is to increase the price or remove land from the market, "In the name of Heaven, then, why reduce the price?" Presents statistics that dispute the argument that population growth in the new states has been too slow. "Even at the present rate of $1.25, twenty-five millions of acres [have] been sold within the last year; and now, should the price be reduced still lower, what must the effect be, but still further to enhance the temptation to monopoly?" Urges that the government hold the land the Tipton amendment would sell off for a dollar or for seventy-five cents an acre until the price rises. Argues that the unsold 125,000,000 acres at present in the market is unsold not because it is not worth a higher price, but because "the supply is so immensely beyond the demand. . . . Wait a little, but do not adopt so wild a plan as to reduce your price in order to force a sale." As population increases, the number of sales will increase. Sharply contests Tipton's contention that high public land prices in Ohio ($2.00 per acre) had retarded the growth and development of Ohio and the Northwest, that early settlers north of the Ohio River had thereby suffered unusual hardships, and that they had enjoyed little government assistance in subduing the wilderness. Itemizes the generosity of federal assistance to the Northwest, viz: the national road, public school subsidies, and tax exemptions to aid internal development. "And what have we in Kentucky got from the General Government?" No government-built road, no land subsidy for public school use, no "princely donations of land and money" for canal construction. Asks rhetorically: "Does the gentleman suppose we are incapable of feeling and of comparing? Yet what do we hear but one eternal demand for more! more! at the sacrifice of a compact made for the general benefit of the whole confederacy? I hope this amendment will not prevail. I hope that while our lands are already sold at a price the gentlemen themselves say is too low, we shall not, at their request, reduce the price still lower." *Register of Debates*, 24 Cong., 2 Sess., 550-51, 555-56. For the Tipton amendment, see *ibid.*, 535. The Tipton amendment was defeated 19 to 18. *Ibid.*, 556.

Later this day, Clay supported an amendment by Sen. Thomas Morris (Ohio), offered to test Senate opinion on the "pre-emptive feature" in the Walker bill. This feature, he noted, had become much modified by various amendments. Walker, in turn, protested with "great vehemence" that "if the two features of graduation and pre-emption were stricken out of the bill, he should abandon it at once." Senate adjourned without a vote. *Ibid.*, 557.

Remark in Senate, January 25, 1837. Participates in debate on a bill for the relief of the executrix of Richard W. Meade. *Register of Debates*, 24 Cong., 2 Sess., 557.

The bill passed on February 17, 1837. Clay again participated in a "long discussion" on the measure. *Ibid.*, 846. For the Meade case, see 8:857.

Remark in Senate, January 26, 1837. Supports an amendment to the public lands bill by Sen. Hugh L. White (Tenn.) permitting a purchaser of land to relinquish it within five years and recover his purchase money. Passed. *Register of Debates*, 24 Cong., 2 Sess., 559. Also supports an amendment to the land bill by Sen. James Buchanan permitting fathers or widows "to enter a section of land in the name of each child" for which they are responsible between the ages of 12 and 21, the actual patent to be issued when the child reaches age 21. Clay urges Buchanan to expand the coverage of his amendment to include grandchildren as well. *Ibid.*, 560.

Later this day, Clay asks that the bill to rescind the treasury order [Speech in Senate, January 11, 1837] be taken up, because "Every hour that order continued, it inflicted injury and degradation on the West." *Ibid.*, 562.

Remark in Senate, January 27, 1837. Presents a memorial from "a number of citizens" of the District of Columbia asking for a charter incorporating a chapter of the American Colonization Society. Mentions purpose of the society. *Register of Debates*, 24 Cong., 2 Sess., 564.

When Sen. Calhoun protests that presenting such a petition at this time can only stir up the slavery question, Clay retorts that "The day would come, he would venture to predict, when the people living in all portions of this vast continent would become converts to the American colonization scheme, and become convinced of its utility, and the humane principles by which it is characterized in striving to ameliorate the present condition of the African race." He also recalls that James Madison had supported the colonization society. *Ibid.*

When Sen. Robert J. Walker (Miss.) mentions that the society, once popular in Mississippi, is now quite unpopular because of the abolitionist movement, Clay agrees that "the acts of the abolitionists" have damaged the reputation of the society. He notes that the abolitionists "were just as much opposed to the Colonization Society as to the slaveholders of the South; denouncing it and imputing motives to it which did not exist, and in fact assailing it in every possible form." As for Calhoun's contention that the society was opposed by nine-tenths of the Southern people, Clay counters with the observation that "he was well assured that a majority of the people of Virginia, Maryland, Kentucky, and Tennessee, and North Carolina, were in favor of its objects. He did not know but that the people of South Carolina and Georgia were opposed to it, and he could not speak as to Alabama; but the Senator from Mississippi had just assured them that this society was highly popular in his State, until the excitement produced by the abolitionists had brought it into discredit." *Ibid.*, 565-66.

On the legal question involved, he frankly doubts "whether Congress had the power to pass an act of incorporation which should have powers beyond the District of Columbia." Explains to Sen. James Buchanan (Pa.) that the society's memorialists are not asking Congress "for any legalization of their operations . . . they could go on, as they had already gone on for twenty years past. They could fit out their vessels from Norfolk, New Orleans, and elsewhere, without coming to ask Congress for permission. . . . the memorialists asked Congress to grant them simply the power to receive and to hold property bestowed upon them by voluntary benevolence." *Ibid.*, 567-68. The memorial was tabled by a vote of 24 to 12.

Later this day, with reference to the bill for the reduction of the revenue, Clay wryly observes that it would be useful to determine at the outset the probable revenue to be received from taxes and the probable amount of the public expenditure. The Finance Committee, in reporting this bill, provides nothing but "uncertain conjectures." Does not believe, as does Sen. Silas Wright, that "there can exist a redundant revenue" and that a surplus would be "an evil so great as to call for the legislation of Congress." Announces he will oppose any adjustments in the tariff schedules to reduce revenue. "I shall oppose, so far as my voice and my vote can go, this disturbance of the compromise arrangement made in March, 1833 [8:604, 621-22, 626-27], under which the country has flourished in an unparalleled degree, and on which all parties have reposed as being durable and permanent." Discusses specifically proposed reductions of the existing tariffs on salt, spirituous liquors, and coal, "all articles covered by the compromise," and asks "what security, what guarantee, can the country possess that the work of reduction is to stop at that point? Will not the process, ere long, reach to cotton and to woollens?" Urges Congress not to disturb the 1833 tariff compromise. Concludes: "I have now discharged what I believe to be a duty. You have the power, both in this House and the other; you can do in this matter as you think proper. Go on, then. Disturb, distract the country; reagitate the community; reopen its wounds, just closed; do this, if it seems to you good; take upon yourselves the awful responsibility; but you shall never do it with my consent, nor without my solemn protest." *Ibid.*, 575-76. See Comment in Senate, February 21, 1837.

Still later this day, in reaction to newspaper charges that some of the members of the Electoral College who had voted in the recent presidential election also "held offices under the General Government," in violation of article II, section 1, paragraph 2, of the constitution, Clay moves "to inquire into the expediency of ascertaining whether any votes were given at the recent election, contrary to the prohibition contained in the second section [*sic*] of the second article of the constitution. And if any such votes were given, what ought to be done with them; and whether any, and what, provision ought to be made for securing the faithful observance, in future, of that section of the constitution." Motion adopted. *Ibid.*, 617. On February 4, a Senate Select Committee—Felix Grundy (Tenn.), Henry Clay (Ky.), Silas Wright (N.Y.)—reported that while four or five presidential electors had indeed held government jobs, in violation of the Constitution, the number was not sufficient to change either the national electoral result or the electoral outcome in any state. The committee resolved to designate Wednesday, February 8, 1837, as the date of the meeting of a joint session of the Congress formally to count the electoral votes for president and vice president. It resolved also that if either counting or not counting the votes of Michigan (which had entered the Union on January 16, 1837) "shall not essentially change the result of the election," the final votes by Congress for president and vice president should be reported both with and without the Michigan tally. Clay defended the resolution on how best to count and report Michigan's vote as one designed by the select committee to avoid "doing any thing which would have the effect of creating excitement . . . on Wednesday next," when the Senate would have to choose a vice president. While he personally had some objections to this procedure, "under all the circumstances connected with this matter, it would be better to take the course recommended by the committee." *Ibid.*, 700-701. For the controversial and unique Senate vote of Wednesday, February 8, which broke the deadlock between vice presidential candidates Richard M. Johnson (Ky.) and Francis Granger (N.Y.) in the Electoral College ballot (Johnson had polled 147, which was not a majority, Granger-77, John Tyler (Va.)-47, William Smith (Ala.)-23), see *ibid.*, 738-39; Leland W. Meyer, *The Life and Times of Colonel Richard M. Johnson* (New York, 1932), 425-29. The final Senate vote was Johnson-33, Granger-16. Both of the new Michigan senators, Lucius Lyon and John Norvell, voted for Johnson; Kentucky senators Clay and Crittenden voted for Granger.

To HENRY CLAY, JR. Washington, December [*sic*, January] 28, 1837

I have at length received from Mr. [Reuben G.] Beasley the enclosed letter; and presume I shall shortly receive another from him informing me of the arrival of the Asses at Havre and their shipment to N. Orleans.[1] I hope that his confidence in the man he has selected to make the purchase has not been misplaced; and that the animals will correspond with our wishes. He has gone to our highest limits in the prices.

The scenes transpiring here are calculated to add to the regret which I felt from being as I thought under the necessity of accepting the office of Senator.[2] You will have seen an account of the degradation to which the Country has been brought by the passage of the Expunging resolution, and the execution of the process.[3] Other occurences of a similar character, showing the arrogance and the ascendancy of Jackson, are too frequent here. He has recently sent to Mr. [Henry A.] Wise's Investigating Commee. a most outrageously insulting letter, which I suppose will soon be published.[4] The only encouraging circumstance which has happened of late is a schism in the party about Hard money, and Bank notes. [Thomas H.] Benton heads the Hard money faction, and Reeves [*sic*, William C. Rives] the other.[5] It may lead to some good results.

Santa Anna goes from Norfolk to Mexico in a public vessel & has probably sailed. . . .[6]

ALS. Henry Clay Memorial Foundation, Lexington, Ky. 1. Beasley to Clay, Jan. 8, 1837. 2. See 8:871-72; Clay to General Assembly of Ky., Jan. 16, 1837. 3. See 8:735. 4. Wise's committee was appointed to investigate whether there had been abuses in the management of the executive departments during Jackson's administration; specifically, the propriety of the public deposit banks having hired a special agent (Reuben M. Whitney) to help them transact their business with the Treasury Department. The committee also wanted to know the character of the agent, the compensation he received, and who paid him. The majority report of the committee contained five resolutions on the question of an agent of or to the Treasury Department, concluding that the department itself had not employed or paid an agent but that some individual deposit banks had indeed employed Reuben M. Whitney as their agent to the department. The report was tabled on March 1, 1837. *House Reports*, 24 Cong., 2 Sess., no. 193, pp. 1-636, espec. 16. The majority report on the investigation of the executive departments found "no just cause of complaint" in their management. The minority report dissented strongly from this finding. Both reports, however, were tabled on March 3, 1837. *Ibid.*, no. 194, pp. 1-318, espec. 1-23. For a complete discussion of Whitney's role in this and related banking matters, see John M. McFaul & Frank Otto Gatell, "The Outcast Insider, Reuben M. Whitney and the Bank War," *PMHB* (April, 1967), 91:115-44. For Jackson's letter to Wise, see John Spencer Bassett (ed.), *Correspondence of Andrew Jackson* (Washington, D.C., 1926-35; reprint, New York, 1969), 5:452-55; and *Niles' Register* (Feb. 11, 1837), 51:370-71. See also *Register of Debates*, 24 Cong., 2 Sess., 1252, 1399-1400, 1410, 2076-77, 2094; and Claude Bowers, *Party Battles of the Jackson Period* (New York, 1922), 457-61. 5. For the developing split in the Democratic party between those "Conservatives" who favored the state banks and "soft" money—led by William C. Rives and Nathaniel P. Tallmadge—and those who supported the administration and the "hard" money policy employed in the Specie Circular, see Howard Braverman, "The Economic and Political Background of the Conservative Revolt in Virginia," *VMHB* (April, 1952), 60:266-87; also Curtis, *The Fox at Bay*, 74, 100, 102, 105, 107-9, 111, 124, 132-33, 144, *passim*; and Thomas Hart Benton, *Thirty Years' View; or, A History of the Working of the American Government for Thirty Years, From 1820 to 1850*, 2 vols. (New York, 1858), 1:694-703. 6. For Santa Anna's journey to Washington and back in Nov., 1836-Feb., 1837, following his defeat, capture, and signing of the peace and independence treaties with Texas, see Oakah L. Jones, *Santa Anna* (New York, 1968), 71-75.

From Peter Dudley, Frankfort, Ky., January 30, 1837. States that on December 28, 1836, he had transmitted to Secretary of War Benjamin F. Butler an abstract of the muster rolls of a regiment of volunteers "organised in this State for the service of the United States, with a letter requesting you to make application to Congress for indemnity for the losses they sustained in equipping themselves." Although he requested that these documents "be handed to you," he is "fearful they have not been received," since he has neither heard from Clay nor seen anything on the subject in the Senate Journal. ALS. DLC-John J. Crittenden Papers, vol. 5, item 901. Dudley was Kentucky's adjutant general. This letter is addressed jointly to Clay and Crittenden.

When Mexico moved troops into Texas during the summer of 1836, General Edmund P. Gaines had issued a requisition for militia forces to the governors of Kentucky, Tennessee, Mississippi, and Alabama. Jackson countermanded this action and ordered the troops to be mustered and discharged. See Bassett, *Jackson Correspondence*, 5:415-18, 420-21. The bill "to make payment and compensation to militia and volunteers of Kentucky, Tennessee, Alabama, and Mississippi, called into service and discharged before marching" was introduced in the Senate on January 25, 1837, and passed on February 16. It did not pass the House. U.S. Sen., *Journal*, 24 Cong., 2 Sess., 159, 259.

Remark in Senate, January 30, 1837. Moves to take up the memorial for incorporation in the District of Columbia of the American Colonization Society [Remark in Senate, January 27, 1837]. Motion defeated 25 to 16. *Register of Debates*, 24 Cong., 2 Sess., 636.

Later this day, Clay moves to strike out section 4 of the public land bill [Remark in Senate, January 12, 1837], including the entire preemption clause, and asks for yeas and nays. He and Calhoun "spoke with warmth against the unlimited pre-emptive rights conferred by the bill." Senators Robert J. Walker and Ambrose H. Sevier (Ark.) upheld section 4. *Ibid.*, 645. Senate adjourned prior to vote on Clay's motion.

Comment in Senate, January 31, 1837. Moves to amend the [Walker] public land bill [Remark in Senate, January 12, 1837] to provide that "the right of pre-emption shall not apply to any lands prior to their being surveyed." Motion lost, 23 to 23. Supports an amendment by Nathaniel P. Tallmadge (N.Y.) to continue the operation of the bill only to June 30, 1842, because the "Congress was entering on an untried experiment," even though he doubts it will have any practical effect. "Pass this bill, (cried Mr. C.) and the national domain is gone. By the year 1842, it will require a search-warrant and corps d'armee to find any part of it. A few men would settle on the woods, surround a prairie, and would at once get command of the whole prairie. . . . The public lands would be gone. They were now going. What had the Senate heard from the Senator [Sevier] from Arkansas? That gentleman, it seemed, had received an assurance that when his friends should come into power, all manner of good things were to be done for him in regard to the public lands. . . . The country ought to know more about this matter. They had a right to know what these arrangements were which were to be fulfilled so soon as the dominant party got the control of both Houses of Congress." *Register of Debates*, 24 Cong., 2 Sess., 662-63.

Later this day, Clay explains that much of the public land to be sold off under the provisions of this bill are lands initially ceded to the nation by Virginia "for the benefit of the entire Union, and not of eight or nine States only." Wonders why Sen. William C. Rives (Va.) has not protested the purposes of this measure. In partial response to Rives's support of the bill, Clay notes that under it even the

Virginians, who had conveyed the land to the nation, did not enjoy advantages thereupon "conferred on the people of the new States." Charges further that Rives "advocated this bill as a measure to restrict the sales of the public land, and prevent a surplus in the Treasury; and what did it do by way of restriction? It threw open to the occupancy of pre-emptioners 180 millions of acres of land, now beyond their reach, in addition to the 120 millions now in the market." *Ibid.*, 663-65.

Remark in Senate, February 1, 1837. Moves to amend a resolution by Sen. Robert C. Nicholas (La.) asking the secretary of the treasury to provide information on "alleged frauds on the public lands" in Louisiana. Clay would expand the resolution to cover "frauds in preëmption floats" in other states and territories as well. Motion passed. *Register of Debates*, 24 Cong., 2 Sess., 666-67; *Cong. Globe*, 24 Cong., 2 Sess., 145.

Later this day, Clay proclaims he will vote against Sen. Robert J. Walker's land bill even "if no one else did." Attacks again the principle and practice of unregulated preemption. Demands that preemption be based on "actual cultivation and possession," the latter of at least "a six months' residence," as was the "intention of the old pre-emption laws." *Ibid.*, 668.

Comment in Senate, February 2, 1837. Presents and supports a petition from "certain living authors of Great Britain" who "represent that, owing to the want of legal protection in the United States, they are deprived of the benefit here of their literary property; that their works are published without any compensation being made to them for their copy-rights; that they are frequently altered and mutilated, so as to affect injuriously their reputations; and that an arrangement which they, or some of them, had made with booksellers in the United States, to secure a fair and just remuneration for their labors, had been defeated by the practice of other American booksellers. They therefore request the passage of a law, by which their right of property may be protected." Points out that British copyright laws cover foreigners, and notes that "when we reflect what important parts of the great republic of letters the United States and Great Britain are, and consider their common origin, common language, and similarity of institutions, and of habits of reading, there seems to me to be every motive for reciprocating between the two countries the security of copy-rights. Indeed, I do not see any ground of just objection, either in the constitution or in sound policy, to the passage of a law tendering to all foreign nations reciprocal security for literary property." *Register of Debates*, 24 Cong., 2 Sess., 670.

The memorial was referred to a special committee composed of Senators William C. Preston, Henry Clay, James Buchanan, Daniel Webster, and Thomas Ewing. There was no further action on it during the 24th Congress, 2nd Session. The question of the need for an international copyright law continued intermittently until 1891 when a bill, providing for reciprocity agreements between countries, was finally passed by Congress. For the history of this movement in the United States, as well as Clay's role in it, see James J. Barnes, *Authors, Publishers and Politicians, The Quest for an Anglo-American Copyright Agreement 1815-1854* (Columbus, Ohio, 1974), 61-77, 87, 90, 94, 117, 136, 217, 252, 272-74; Richard R. Bowker, *Copyright, Its History and Its Law* (New York, 1912), 37-38, 341-72; Aubert J. Clark, *The Movement for International Copyright in Nineteenth Century America* (Washington, 1960), 24-83. For the 1891 statute, see 26 *U.S. Stat.*, 1106-8.

Remark in Senate, February 3, 1837. Demands yeas and nays on Sen. John Ruggles's amendment to James Buchanan's amendment to the public land bill [Remark in Senate, January 26, 1837]. Buchanan's amendment, now section 8 of the revised bill, assured the rights of certain children to eventual ownership of public lands purchased in their names by a surviving parent. The Ruggles amendment would limit this provision to male children only. *Register of Debates*, 24 Cong., 2 Sess., 693. Ruggles's amendment was defeated 38 to 3, Clay voting with the majority.

Later this day, in the midst of debate on proposed amendments to the public land bill, Clay moved adjournment. Defeated 24 to 22. *Ibid.*, 695.

Comment in Senate, February 4, 1837. Submits the names of additional British authors who are petitioning for a U.S. copyright law [Comment in Senate, February 2, 1837] that would protect their literary property rights. Also submits the names of "sundry American authors" who support the British authors, "owing to the fact that booksellers in this country can possess themselves of and publish new works as they issue, from time to time, from the British press, without any charge on account of the copy-right, American authors of similar works are unable to obtain for their copy-rights a fair compensation. They therefore pray that a just security may be given by law to British authors." Explains how the republishing business works in the United States. Points out, in response to an observation by Sen. John M. Niles (Conn.), "that the whole object was to put foreign authors on the same footing on which our own authors are in England." Does not think new U.S. copyright legislation will add to the cost of books. *Register of Debates*, 24 Cong., 2 Sess., 696-97. An undated copy of the entry in the *Register of Debates* for February 4, 1837 (pp. 696-97), dealing with the copyright question, in Clay's hand, is in NcD.

Later this day, Clay commented on the recent Electoral College vote for president and vice president. See Remark in Senate, January 27, 1837.

To ENOCH COBB WINES Washington, February 4, 1837

I recd. your favor of the 29h. Ulto. The decision of the question of my son John [Morrison Clay] accompanying you to Europe must depend upon a family consultation, after my return home. In making it, the consideration of Expence will have some influence. And I think it best that such a sum should be specified as will cover your own charges, and leaving nothing to contingencies.

I feel an inclination to favor my son's being of your party; but I cannot now make any positive assurances.[1] Upon my return home, and after you have fully weighed the whole matter I shall be glad to hear from you. . . .

ALS. KyU. 1. There is no evidence that John accompanied Wines to Europe. For Wines, see 8:753.

To HENRY CLAY, JR. Washington, February 6, 1837

I received your last favor, and regretted to find from it that you had not heard from your Mares. I received information of their safe arrival at N. Orleans, and that they were very much admired. I am afraid that they were detained on the river by the ice, but hope they have reached you by this time, in safety. I have heard nothing further from Mr. [Reuben G.] Beasley. If our Asses were shipt, as he wrote me they would be, at Havre, in the month of Decr. they ought by this time to be at or near N. Orleans.[1]

On the subject of Russia Hemp, the result of my enquiries is that altho' there is some there is not any very great increase in the production. But Manilla Hemp answers many of the purposes of Russia Hemp, altho' there are some of the uses of Russia Hemp to which the Manilla can not be applied. Manilla Hemp is admitted free, or with a duty merely nominal. And there has been a great increase in the amount of Manilla Hemp imported.

The real cause however of the fall in the price of K. Hemp is the fall in the price of the articles into which it is manufactured. And the late high price of bagging (which I always thought unfortunate) has led to the establishment of other manufactures of that article, out of Hemp, flax &c and tended to reduce the price.

I will make further enquiries on this subject.

Majr. [Thomas] Smith has sold my Jack, and I must let him have my Poitou Jack, if he arrives. Would it not be best for your's to stand at Mansfield?[2]

My love to Julia [Prather Clay], and embrace Henry [Clay III] for me.

ALS. Henry Clay Memorial Foundation, Lexington, Ky. 1. Beasley to Clay, Jan. 8, 1837. 2. See 8:843.

To DEMETRIUS A. GALLITZIN Washington, February 8, 1837

I received your friendly letter and thank yon [*sic*, you] for calling my attention to the newspaper paragraph which it enclosed. The petition which it refers to was forwarded by mail to me, why, I did not know. I saw that it was from very ignorant persons. It prayed for one object, an alteration in the naturalization laws, on which congress had power to act. They had a *right* to petition, and without sharing their prejudices, their very ignorance made me more anxious to fulfil[l] the duty of presenting their petition. I neither wished nor expected that they would obtain their object, and accordingly the committee reported against it.[1]

Such, my dear sir, is a true account of this matter. You do me no more than justice in supposing me incapable of any feelings of prejudice, or entertaining any spirit of intolerance towards the Catholic religion. I have, on the contrary, the highest respect for it, and count among its members some of my best and truest friends.

I am mortified and grieved that any one should have misconceived me. . . .[2]

Copy. Printed in *Niles' Register* (March 25, 1837), 52:51; reprinted from the *Catholic Herald*. For Gallitzin, see 6:133. 1. Remark in Senate, Jan. 21, 1837. 2. This letter was published with the following explanation: "Many of our Catholics in reading the Herald of February 9th, have been filled with indignation against the hon. Henry Clay for presenting a certain petition against Roman Catholics; and much more so in reading a paragraph in a Pittsburgh paper, which represents the said H. Clay as combining with Maria Monk & Co. for the destruction of Catholics. The respect and friendship I felt for Mr. Clay, founded in part on gratitude for some particular favors I received from him when he was secretary of state prompted me to send him the said paragraph enclosed in a letter, to which I received the following answer." For Maria Monk, an imposter who contributed to anti-Catholic feelings by telling horrible stories about the nunnery from which she had allegedly escaped, see *CAB*.

From Edwin Harriman, Mobile, Ala., February 8, 1837. States that he has been sending and will continue to send Clay the newspaper he edits, the Mobile *Mercantile Advertiser*, in order to show "the high esteem and regard we entertain for you as a public man and a private citizen." Explains that he "published a Weekly journal in Massachusetts from 1831 to 1835," and that he always used its pages "to advocate the claims of Henry Clay to the Presidency." Adds that he also served as a correspondent and assistant editor of the Baltimore *Patriot* before moving to Mobile a year ago.

Gives his explanation of why Clay was not chosen president in 1836. First, it was due to the failure of the Maryland legislature to nominate Clay in December, 1834, or January, 1835, and second "because Duff Green kept his meddlesome ding-dong agoing against you in the [Washington *United States*] Telegraph, which set others of that kidney throughout the South in similar motion, and thus prevented the Southern Whigs as a body coming heartily into your support. Had you been nominated by the Maryland Legislature, at the time I have mentioned, that nomination would have been seconded by the Legislature of Kentucky, and Mr. Webster would not have received the nomination of his own State Legislature. The result of all would have been your election."

Suggests that Clay write "a friendly, line" to Henry King, a trader in Mobile and a former Kentuckian who is an "old and true-hearted supporter of yours." ALS, manuscript torn. DLC-HC (DNA, M212, R5). Harriman and Sol Smith had purchased the Mobile *Mercantile Advertiser* about the year 1836 and operated it at the corner of Dauphin and Dearborn. Henry King was a merchant at the corner of Dauphin and Hamilton streets. He died on April 23, 1837, and was buried in Mobile. Information supplied by the City of Mobile Museum Department and the 1837 *Mobile Directory*.

Comment in Senate, February 9, 1837. A discussion of the public land bill [Remark in Senate, January 12, 1837], which occupied the Senate for the entire day, includes intermittent observations by Clay on various aspects of the proposed legislation.

Repeats the fact of his opposition to the administration's (Walker's) bill. Also announces his opposition to Calhoun's proposal of February 7 that unsold public lands be ceded to certain of the states in which they lie. Defends again the land bill he himself had introduced in 1832 [8:539-41], claiming that while the president had then vetoed it, "a decided majority of the people of the United States, were, notwithstanding, in its favor." Views the Walker bill as a clever attempt "to wrest these lands from the common benefit of the Union, and appropriate them to the use either of a small portion of the States or of speculators." Hopes that his colleagues will not "allow a matter of this weight and moment to be made an object of party politics," but wonders if "the party now dominant in the country" will seek to conciliate the favor of the new states on the public land issue in an attempt to "perpetuate itself in power." *Register of Debates*, 24 Cong., 2 Sess., 730-31, 741-42; *Cong. Globe*, 24 Cong., 2 Sess., Appendix, 156.

Later this day, Clay intervenes in a bitter confrontation between Jackson and Calhoun in which the president, in a letter dated February 7, accused the senator of "fabrication" and "calumny" in a February 4 speech that linked Jackson to speculation in public lands. Clay brands Jackson's letter of protest, which included a demand for a public retraction and apology, "most extraordinary," one that "has filled me with the deepest regret and mortification." Argues that its very tone and language has reduced the Senate of the United States "to a state of degradation in which we all feel and know it now to be." Adds: "That this letter is a palpable breach of the privileges appertaining to this body by the constitution, is beyond all controversy. It has not been denied, and cannot be denied." Notes, however, that no member of the majority party rises to "vindicate the privileges which belong to the Senate," and reports that Calhoun intends to make no motion relative to Jackson's letter, but would "leave it to the Senate to protect its own rights." *Register of Debates*, 24 Cong., 2 Sess., 753-57, 759-60. See also Charles M. Wiltse, *John C. Calhoun: Nullifier, 1829-1839* (Indianapolis, 1949), 303-4; Clyde N. Wilson (ed.), *The Papers of John C. Calhoun*, 14 vols. to date (Columbia, S.C., 1959-), 13:376-83, 403-5.

Still later this day, Clay calls attention to the history of land speculation in the United States and the "three different epochs at which speculation had raged"—1792-96, 1816-19, and the present one. Believes it is a "disease" leading to disaster. Reviews the provisions of the Walker land bill which is designed, ostensibly, "first to reduce the revenue, and then to suppress speculation." Wonders how "gentlemen could give their assent to this bill, if they saw the constitutional objections as he did. What power had Congress thus to dispose of the public lands? This bill supposed that Government had some power over the land, beyond and after its disposition"; but "that when they had sold the land their power was exhausted." Further, "the constitution of the United States declared that the judicial power created by this Government should be vested in a Supreme Court of the United States and such inferior courts as Congress should establish. But by this bill was not this power vested in the registers and receivers of the public lands? They were to examine evidence and decide on the rights of property. And, further, between two preemptioners they were to decide without appeal, without trial by jury, without revisal." Sees also "insuperable objections" to the bill, on the ground of affidavits. Explains some of these objections. Argues anew the point that the bill would benefit land speculators and increase the level of speculation. Discusses at length the preemption clause which will produce "settlers in hordes" who would "take possession of the public land; and they would come here [Washington] with all the power they could exert, to procure the passage of pre-emption laws. Pass it, and such laws would be as regular as the general appropriation bill." The bill can only project future public land sale legislation more deeply into politics and lead to even a more rapid disappearance of the public land. *Register of Debates*, 24 Cong., 2 Sess., 741-42, 759-60, 774-77. As soon as Clay took his seat, the final vote on the Walker bill, as amended, was taken. It passed 27 to 23, Clay opposing. *Ibid.*, 777; *Cong. Globe*, 24 Cong., 2 Sess., 172.

To John Howard Payne, February 9, 1837. Feels that "on the subject of Copyright. . . . it will hardly be practicable to do anything at this Session, or, if any thing, more than to provide prospectively for the security of literary property in such works as may *hereafter* be published by foreign authors [Comment in Senate, February 2, 1837]." Adds that "As to Dramatic works, there will be more difficulty"; for example, "There is much equity in exacting from the Managers of Theatres a fair compensation for the publication of a play which takes place in its public exhibition; but, then, suppose they have purchased some half a dozen copies, charged with the Copy right, for recitation, preparation, &c. Can the law rightfully restrain the oral use which they make of the property which they have acquired in those Copies?" Notes that he has "not yet seen Mr. Bulwer's law" which may have "justly reconciled the interests of Authors and the rights of the Theatre." Copy. Printed in *HM*, 2nd ser. (November, 1867), 2:288.

For Edward George Earle Lytton Bulwer (1803-73)—novelist, dramatist, and member of parliament—see *DNB*. "Mr. Bulwer's law" probably refers to the dramatic copyright act of 1833 which attempted to clear up confusion as to whether or not public performance of a work constituted publication. Bowker, *Copyright*, 181-82. See also Comment in Senate, February 2, 1837, and Remark in Senate, January 6, 1840.

To FRANCIS T. BROOKE Washington, February 10, 1837

I received your favor of the 8th, as I did the preceding one to which it refers, and which I postponed answering until I had something worth communicating. There is indeed some highly interesting occurrence here almost daily, but the papers generally notice it. You will have seen the letter of the President to the [Henry A. Wise] Committee of Investigation.[1] Yesterday, a still more extraordinary one was presented to the Senate by Mr. Calhoun, in which the President, in the harshest and most offensive language animadverts upon a speech made by that Senator in the Senate.[2] The majority was reminded that they alone possessed the power to vindicate the privileges of the Senate against the Executive encroachments. But they all remained mute; not one venturing to offer any motion. Such is the degradation to which Congress is reduced!

You congratulate me on my acceptance of the new appointment recently conferred on me to the Senate.[3] I think you ought to have condoled and sympathized with me, because, by the force of circumstances, I was constrained to remain in a body, in the humiliated condition in which the Senate now is. I shall escape from it as soon as I decently can, with the same pleasure that one would fly from a charnel-house.

Mr. [Daniel] Webster retires positively, Mr. [Thomas] Ewing is ousted, and [Benjamin W.] Leigh, and [John M.] Clayton, and [Willie P.] Mangum, and [Alexander] Porter, are gone.[4] What good can I do, what mischief avert, by remaining?

I should be delighted to see you, but in the month of March the Cumberland route offers advantages so superior to any other, that I must follow it to Kentucky. Would to God it were for the last time!

Can you not come to Ashland from Lewisburg, when you are attending the Court there? It is an affair of but two or three days, and we should be rejoiced to have you, and Mrs. Brooke, too, if she would accompany you, under our roof. . . .

Copy. Printed in Colton, *Clay Correspondence*, 4:410-11. 1. Clay to Henry Clay, Jr., Jan. 28, 1837. 2. Comment in Senate, Feb. 9, 1837. 3. See 8:871-72; Clay to General Assembly of Ky., Jan. 16, 1837. 4. Webster had planned to retire, but Massachusetts and New York Whigs rallied behind him, and he was persuaded to remain in the Senate. Wiltse, *Papers of Daniel Webster Correspondence*, 4:181. For Leigh's resignation, see 8: 819-20. Clayton had resigned from the Senate in 1836 to become chief justice of Delaware. He was replaced by Whig Thomas Clayton. *DAB*; *BDAC*. Thomas Ewing (Ohio) had been defeated in 1836 by William Allen, a Democrat. *BDAC*. Willie P. Mangum (N.C.) resigned the Senate on Nov. 26, 1836, and was replaced by Democrat Robert Strange. *Ibid*. The vacancy caused by Alexander Porter's (La.) resignation was filled by Alexander Mouton, a Democrat. *Ibid*.

Remark in Senate, February 10, 1837. Moves that the secretary of the treasury submit his correspondence with John Pope, commissioner of the General Land Office and late governor of Arkansas, dealing with ten sections of public land granted to the territory of Arkansas for the erection of a public building in Little Rock. Motion adopted. *Cong. Globe*, 24 Cong., 2 Sess., 176.

Later this day, Clay complains that the bill "to designate and limit the kinds of funds receivable for the public revenue" still leaves "the Treasury order [Speech in Senate, January 11, 1837; Remark in Senate, January 14, 1837] unrescinded." Offers an amendment, "that would reconcile him to the bill." The amendment prohibits the secretary of the treasury from making "any discrimination in the funds so receivable as public revenue." *Register of Debates*, 24 Cong., 2 Sess., 778. Amendment adopted unanimously. Bill as amended passed 41 to 5.

Remark in Senate, February 13, 1837. Notes that the volume of Dutch trade with the United States in 1835 showed an increase. *Register of Debates*, 24 Cong., 2 Sess., 801.

Remark in Senate, February 14, 1837. Moves to amend the Cumberland Road bill so as to strike out provision for four superintendents of the road, each with two assistants. Motion passes 26 to 17. *Cong. Globe,* 24 Cong., 2 Sess., 193-94.

Clay then moves an amendment to the Cumberland Road bill that would prohibit the section in Illinois from being stoned and gravelled "unless at a cost not exceeding the average expense of doing it in Ohio and Indiana." Motion adopted. *Register of Debates,* 24 Cong., 2 Sess., 803-4.

Later this day, Clay supports an amendment to reduce the appropriation for the Cumberland Road in Indiana from $150,000 to $50,000. *Cong. Globe,* 24 Cong., 2 Sess., 194.

Remark in Senate, February 15, 1837. Urges that the provisions of the trade reciprocity act of 1824 with the Netherlands [4:116, 644] be applied to Belgium now that the political union of the Netherlands and Belgium has ended. Notes that the Dutch have departed from the "principle of entire and perfect reciprocity" built into the act, and argues that such departure explains the decline in U.S. trade with Holland in 1834-36 and the concomitant rise in Dutch trade with the United States during that period. Nevertheless, supports the bill which puts Holland and Belgium "on the same footing" insofar as the reciprocity act of 1824 is concerned. *Register of Debates,* 24 Cong., 2 Sess., 806.

Later this day, Clay moves to reduce the proposed Cumberland Road appropriations to Ohio, Indiana, and Illinois by substantial amounts. *Cong. Globe,* 24 Cong., 2 Sess., 197; *Register of Debates,* 24 Cong., 2 Sess., 806.

Remark in Senate, February 16, 1837. During the debate on the bill to increase the size of the U.S. Army, asks Sen. William C. Preston (S.C.) if he believes that "an increase of the army on paper would secure an actual increase of its numbers in the field?" Observes that if "the army, when nominally containing but 6,000 men, could not be recruited, how was it likely to be filled up when nominally 12,000?" *Register of Debates,* 24 Cong., 2 Sess., 839. The bill was passed 26 to 13, Clay voting nay.

Later this day, Clay moves the adoption of a bill to provide copyright protection to foreign authors [Comment in Senate, February 2, 1837]. *Cong. Globe,* 24 Cong., 2 Sess., 201.

Remark in Senate, February 17, 1837. Participates in a discussion of N.Y. Sen. Silas Wright's bill to "remit the duties upon certain goods destroyed by fire at the late conflagration in the city of New York [8:816-18]. Suggests adding a proviso to limit to $500,000 the total amount of money to be paid in duty remission and other damage claims, but agrees to Wright's counter-suggestion that the limit be set at $600,000. *Register of Debates,* 24 Cong., 2 Sess., 848-49. The bill passed by voice vote on February 18. *Cong. Globe,* 24 Cong., 2 Sess., 218. The bill did not come before the House during this session. It was reintroduced during the special (first) session in the fall and passed the Senate on September 27, 1837; however, again it was not considered by the House. U.S. Sen., *Journal,* 25 Cong., 1 Sess., 46.

To G.H. WELCH Washington, February 18, 1837

I have recd. your letter requesting me to communicate an account of the proceedings in the Senate on the petition which I presented from the A. Colonizn. Society for an act of Incorporation.[1]

I have but little to add in reply to the published account. The object of the petition was opposed, and it was laid on the table. This result I attribute to two causes 1st. the excitement prevailing in regard to Abolition which produces an unwillingness to touch the African subject in any of its forms. And 2dly. the policy of the V. Buren party to impress the South with the belief that it is friendly to Southern interests.

In the mean time the Colonizn. Society will attain its object probably by the aid of some of the State Legislatures and I trust go on prosperously.

ALS. MWalK. 1. Remark in Senate, Jan. 27, 1837.

Remark in Senate, February 20, 1837. Presents a memorial from a "very large number of persons who stated themselves to be American authors and friends of literature" calling for a copyright law [Comment in Senate, February 2, 1837] that would protect foreign authors. Supports the need for such legislation. *Register of Debates*, 24 Cong., 2 Sess., 857-58.

Later this day, Clay announces he will vote "with the greatest readiness and pleasure" for a resolution authorizing the purchase, for $30,000 of certain James Madison manuscripts [8:868-70], leaving to Mrs. Madison "the right to use copies of the said manuscript[s] in foreign countries as she may think fit." *Ibid.*, 871-72.

From Martin Ruter, Meadville, Pa., February 20, 1837. Praises the selection of Clay as president of the American Colonization Society [8:874], and asks for a position as "an agent for the Society, during the ensuing Summer, provided I should find it convenient." Notes that he now holds the position of president of Allegheny College, "But as I dislike the climate, I have determined on going farther South, perhaps to Kentucky or Indiana." Believes that as an agent for the American Colonization Society, "I might form numerous aux. Societies and be successful in raising funds. The prospects of the Society are manifestly improving. We have formed an auxiliary in this place—others will be formed in the vicinity." ALS. DLC-Records of the American Colonization Society (DNA, M212, R20). Ruter apparently never served as an agent for the colonization society. He resigned from Allegheny College in 1837, moved to Texas to superintend mission work, and died there in May of 1838. *DAB*.

From Nicholas Biddle, Philadelphia, February 21, 1837. Reports that a letter he wrote previously "to thank you in the name of the Country for your determination to remain in public life. . . . was accidently mislaid, but the acknowledgment now, tho' more tardy, is not less sincere [Clay to General Assembly of Kentucky, January 16, 1837]." Writes, however, primarily "because the report of the Secretary of the Treasury presents so entirely erroneous a view of the conduct of the Bank that we deem it necessary to correct it by a Memorial . . . of which I inclose a Copy." States: "The truth is that this question of settlement with the Bank has been studiously kept open for the sake of the elections. It was my intention to have paid the money in full before Jany. last, but the embarrassments brought on by the Govt. during the last summer were such as would not permit the additional payment of So large a debt by the Community—and instead of asking them for repayment we were obliged to increase our loans. Even now nothing prevents the immediate payment but the necessity of sustaining the Community. On the footing upon which it is now placed we shall be able to pay a high price for the Stock with a high interest, and a certainty of payment on a day fixed." Copy. DLC-Nicholas Biddle Papers (DNA, M212, R20).

When the charter of the Bank of the United States expired in early 1836, the bank continued operation under a Pennsylvania state charter and was renamed the United States Bank of Pennsylvania. It was decided that the new bank would buy the U.S. government's stock in the old bank. Agents appointed by Biddle and

Secretary of the Treasury Levi Woodbury could not reach an agreement on the price to be paid. Woodbury, in his annual treasury report in December, 1836, blamed the old bank for this failure. Biddle and the directors of the bank defended their actions in a memorial to Congress, in effect blaming Woodbury for the lack of an agreement, and offering to pay $115.54 per share. Congress directed Woodbury to accept the offer which was to be paid in four annual installments. Govan, *Nicholas Biddle*, 283-88, 304-5; Hammond, *Banks and Politics in America*, 439-40. For Woodbury's report, see *House Exec. Doc.* 4, 24 Cong., 2 Sess., pp. 7-8. For the bank memorial and related documents, see *Sen. Docs.*, 24 Cong., 2 Sess., nos. 201, 208.

Comment in Senate, February 21, 1837. Asks Sen. Silas Wright (N.Y.) whether the administration's tariff reduction bill is intended to pass in its "present shape" or whether protected articles are to be "stricken from it." Says he believes "the Senate generally would agree to a reduction of the duties on all except protected articles." Will vote to take up the bill if Wright and other senators "intended to preserve the general policy of the [1833 tariff] compromise [8:604, 621-22, 626-27]." Explains to Sen. James Buchanan (Pa.) that the compromise act of 1833 permitted either reductions or elevations of the tariff on articles below the 20% level if necessary to rectify deficiencies or excesses in the federal revenue; and notes that the schedules in this bill, "with the exception of three or four articles," are in "entire accordance with the compromise act." Believes the bill "beneficial" to the "manufacturing interest." Speaks for and votes for placing a number of chemicals on the free list, "with the exception of calomel, salts, and quinine." Points out the importance of a protective tariff policy to American industrial development, and urges that there be no tampering with the 20% protective shield until 1842, as provided by the 1833 legislation. Notes also that the compromise tariff act, when passed, "had every where been received with plaudits and the utmost demonstration of joy." Asserts that the nation expects that compromise to be adhered to with the same firmness as the "sacred" constitutional compromise of 1787 or the Missouri Compromise of 1820-21 [8:786-88]. Asks if the South would foolishly work to repeal either the Missouri Compromise or the 1833 tariff compromise. States that the latter is "the salt which had preserved our body politic from dissolution. It was the bond of peace and reconciliation between the North and the South." As for the specific tariff on china and porcelain, "if it paid a duty of 20 per cent. or above," he would not disturb it. Indeed, "he would not, for the sake of doing so, disturb any of the great principles of the compromise law." *Register of Debates*, 24 Cong., 2 Sess., 872-74, 882-83. The bill to alter, adjust, and amend the several acts imposing duties on imports passed the Senate 27 to 18 on February 25, 1837. It was not taken up by the House. U.S. Sen., *Journal*, 24 Cong., 2 Sess., 169, 247, 272, 274, 278, 280, 286.

To HENRY CLAY, JR. Washington, February 22, 1837

I have at length recd. the enclosed letter from Mr. [Reuben G.] Beasley.[1] The Asses I hope have by this time reached N. Orleans or near it. The Groom will be an acquisition, if he does not too soon get spoiled.

As I am now in your debt, on account of this purchase you may retain the $500, as part of it, which I advanced you before I left home; and on my arrival there I will pay the residue.

I think we shall not be detained more than one or two days by the call of the Senate,[2] and I shall hasten home afterwards with as little delay as practicable.

The belief here is that Mr. V. Buren will retain in place all the present

Secretaries;[3] and it is rumored that the Department of War has been offered to Mr. [Joel R.] Poinsett of So. Carolina.[4] But I feel very little interest in these matters.

I gained the cause of the Commonwealths Bank.[5]

Give my love to Julia [Prather Clay], and tell her that I pray for her happy Accouchement.[6]

ALS. Henry Clay Memorial Foundation, Lexington, Ky. 1. Probably the letter of Jan. 8 or Jan. 18. See Beasley to Clay, Jan. 8, 1837. 2. The 24th Congress, 2nd Session adjourned on March 3, 1837. 3. Van Buren retained the following Cabinet members from the preceding administration: State—John Forsyth; Treasury—Levi Woodbury; Attorney General—Benjamin F. Butler; Postmaster General—Amos Kendall; and Navy—Mahlon Dickerson. See Joseph N. Kane, *Facts About the Presidents* (New York, 1974), 60; Curtis, *The Fox at Bay*, 52-59. 4. Butler, who had served as interim secretary of war in the previous administration, in addition to his duties as attorney general, was replaced in the War Department by Joel R. Poinsett on March 7, 1837. *Ibid.* 5. *Briscoe* v. *The Bank of the Commonwealth of Kentucky*. 11 Peters 257-350. 6. A daughter, Anne Clay, was born in 1837.

Speech in Senate, February 25, 1837. Blames his relatively inactive role in the debate on the tariff bill on "the prevailing influenza, which disables me from attending at night, on account of the state of atmosphere produced by the multitude of lights in the chamber." Believes that the administration's bill, as it now stands, violates in several respects the compromise tariff act of 1833 [8:604, 621-22, 626-27], especially insofar as some articles protected by a duty above 20% are slated to have their levels of protection reduced. Complains that there are those senators present who care little about the 1833 compromise. Concludes that "it is the purpose of the administration to strike every vestige of the protective system from the statute book." Argues that "The present signal prosperity of our country is attributable to two causes: the success of the cotton interest at the South, and of manufactures in the Northern and Middle States. These interests are intimately blended. If the manufacturing interest at the North could be annihilated, there would be a destruction of the demand for three hundred and fifty thousand bales of the cotton of the South; and if that quantity were thrown upon the foreign market, the inevitable effect would be a ruinous reduction in the price of that staple. As to the policy which has produced this state of prosperity, my convictions have been long since formed, and still remain unshaken. When I look at the diversified interests and pursuits of our people, and the impossibility of the largest portion of them supplying themselves with foreign articles of manufacture, for want of those necessary exchanges which alone can bring them into the country, it has always appeared to me, and still does appear, necessary to protect the industry of our own country." Points out that when the Jackson administration came into power, "it made warm professions of friendship to those who were the advocates of this policy; while, at the same time, it held out hopes to those on the other side of a complete subversion of the system." At the present time, however, it seems ready to abandon the protective policy. Reviews at length his role in designing the "healing and tranquillizing" 1833 compromise tariff which sought to head off civil war and, simultaneously, to preserve aspects of the protective policy. Explains that "At the time of its conception he was not in the city, but in Philadelphia, whither he had retired for three weeks. While there, he was called upon by a committee of manufacturers, who disclosed to him their apprehensions of the imminent danger to which the tariff system was exposed, and who asked, with anxiety, what was to be done; whether no measure could be devised to save the manufacturing interests from the ruin with which they were threatened. It was to these individuals, and not to his friends in Congress, that he first applied to know whether, in their apprehension, a long lease of the protective policy, even though on a lower scale, would not be better than the uncertain state with regard to it in which they then were. To this question not a single man (and he put it to the most intelligent individuals) hesitated for a moment to reply in the affirmative. He afterwards conferred with other manufacturers, and found that they concurred in the same view. He then communicated with his friends in both Houses of Congress; and among these he found a diversity of sentiment." Discusses the sectional dimensions of that diversity, noting, however, that "All that has been said about its having been concocted by the joint efforts of the Senator from South Carolina [John C. Calhoun] and myself is absolutely without one particle of truth. My first communication, as I have stated, was with the manufacturers; I then submitted the plan to the late Mr. [Josiah S.] Johnston, of Louisiana, and to the Senator from Massachusetts [Mr. Webster]. The former, on consideration, gave his assent to it; the latter never did; but I was so supported by those who thought themselves well acquainted with the wishes and the interests of the manufacturers, that I felt it my duty to bring forward the measure." Explains in detail the provisions of his 1833 compromise tariff proposal, emphasizing the gradual biennial reduction by 10% of all duties over 20% until December 1, 1841, and the more rapid rate of reduction in 1842 and after. Points out how successful the whole thing has been. Admits that while Congress has the power to amend or repeal the 1833 legislation, it would be "exceedingly indiscreet" for it to do so, as illadvised as it would be were Congress to repeal or alter the 36° 30′ provision of the Missouri Compromise. Believes that most senators, "by general agreement," regard the "act of 1833 as of binding authority." Insists that the integrity of the 1833 act must be maintained. Confesses, however, that "although I should have no objection to a reduction of duty on one or two articles in the bill, which are now over 20 per cent., yet I cannot consent, for the sake of reaching this object, to hazard the whole arrangement." Insists that the "protective system is an entire system. All its parts are to be regarded in their mutual connexion and dependence. The moment you touch one of them, although with the utmost possible caution, there is no saying when or where you will stop." Pleads with the administration not to destroy the 1833 tariff compromise piecemeal. "I conjure gentlemen to let this subject alone. Is it not enough that they have tampered with the currency? Is our domestic industry also to be made the subject of experiment? . . . Are all the great interests of the country to be dragged into the service of mere party politics?" Adds: "There are some things too dear to be dragged into the vortex of political contest, and made the objects of party calculation. Let the protective policy remain where it has happily flourished for these four years past. There are yet but four years more, till we shall reach the expiration of the term limited by the compromise bill; and all parts of the country will acquiesce in its provisions, if they shall not now be rashly disturbed. But if this bill shall become a law, from that moment I shall hold myself absolved from all obligation to observe that compromise, and shall be ready, according as my sense of the public wishes shall point out my duty, to augment the rate of protection to any point which they may require." Moves to recommit this bill to the Committee on Finance "with instructions to strike from it all those articles on which there is now levied a duty of 20 per cent. or over." Does this for "no purpose of embarrassment," but to "test the opinion of this body as to the obligation of the compromise act of 1833." Says he is particularly interested in testing Senate opinion on the tariffs on foreign spirits and cotton bagging, both important to Kentucky, and both slated for sharp reduction. Notes that the duty on foreign spirits (brandy) is slated to be reduced from 66⅔ cents to 33⅓ cents, "a sum exceeding the average price of the American article which is the rival of the foreign." Hopes that the Senate will not "reopen again this source of eternal contention—the tariff question." *Register of Debates*, 24 Cong., 2 Sess., 967-75. Clay's motion to recommit was defeated 25 to 24. Later in the day the administration bill, as amended, was passed 27 to 18, Clay voting in the negative. *Ibid.*, 975, 981. See also *Cong. Globe*, 24 Cong., 2 Sess., Appendix, 300-302.

To NICHOLAS BIDDLE Washington, February 26, 1837

I think I was entitled to your condolence and sympathy, rather than the kind thanks expressed in your letter of the 21st. inst. on account of my remaining in the Public Councils.[1]

I am glad the Bank has presented the Memorial.[2] It presents the case fairly and honorably. And the ground it takes about the damages must be sustained.

I regret that it will not be in my power to see my good friends in Philada. this Spring. Wherever I shall be they will have my affectionate wishes; and none more of them than yourself. . . .

ALS. James Biddle, The Biddle Family Papers, Andalusia, Pennsylvania. 1. See 8: 871-72; Clay to General Assembly of Ky., Jan. 16, 1837. 2. Biddle to Clay, Feb. 21, 1837.

To EDWIN HARRIMAN[1] Washington, February 27, 1837

. . . I think with you that it is highly probable that, but for the prejudices excited at the south against me. . . . after the passage of the compromise act,[2] my name would have been more acceptable in that quarter, and it is possible that it might have been successfully presented to the American people as a candidate for the presidency [in 1836]. But I do not complain. That high office never possessed any charms in my sight which could induce me to seek it by unworthy means, or to desire it but as the spontaneous grant of those who alone had the right to bestow it. I shall be happy if the government of my country, by whomsoever administered, shall wisely and justly employ its powers to promote the interest and happiness of the people. As to myself, personally, I only regret that I am restrained by circumstances[3] from seeking in retirement that repose of which I feel so much need. . . .

Copy, fragment. Printed in *Niles' Register* (April 22, 1837), 52:115; reprinted from the Mobile *Mercantile Advertiser*. 1. The editors have determined that this letter, in all probability, was written to Edwin Harriman, editor of the Mobile *Mercantile Advertiser*. See Harriman to Clay, Feb. 8, 1837. 2. See 8:604, 621-22, 626-27. 3. See 8:871; Clay to General Assembly of Ky., Jan. 16, 1837.

Speech in Senate, February 27, 1837. Believes that the U.S. controversy with Mexico is not of the sort to justify "a resort to war or for the issuing of reprisals." Thinks the case made out against Mexico in the report by the Committee on Foreign Relations was "rather stronger . . . than the correspondence of the Government with that country justified," and that "the departure of our representative [Powhatan Ellis] from Mexico, under the circumstances, was harsh, abrupt, and unnecessary." Thinks Ellis in some measure precipitated his own departure. Had he not left so abruptly, he "would have heard what they thought of the letter from our Secretary of State [John Forsyth] relative to the final disposition of our Government in regard to the occupation of the Mexican territory near the Sabine, and which occasioned so much unpleasantness." Refers to his experiences at Ghent in 1814 to illustrate the need for cautious and careful deliberation when nations are involved in delicate matters of diplomacy. Notes, in this regard, the satisfactory conclusion of America's recent crisis with France [8:448, 754-55]. Admits that the conduct of Mr. [Manuel Eduardo de] Gorostiza in publishing his controversial pamphlet "was decidedly wrong, and highly reprehensible; but . . . it was not . . . an offence justifying war. The pamphlet had produced no impression, and had done no mischief." Argues that Secretary Forsyth should not have made the pamphlet "the subject of communication" to the Mexican government. Announces his support of the resolution of the Committee on Foreign Affairs which asks the Mexicans for a redress of grievances, leaves the manner of securing this redress to the discretion of the president, and promises "further measures" by Congress to uphold "the honor of the nation and the rights of our injured fellow-citizens." *Register of Debates*, 24 Cong., 2 Sess., 982-83.

When he was sent to Mexico in January, 1836, Ellis was instructed to press for immediate settlement of American claims against the Mexican government. Failing to receive a satisfactory reply from the Mexicans, he demanded his passport and left Mexico City on December 27, arriving in Washington on February 1, 1837. Another issue in the controversy involved the sending of U.S. troops under General E.P. Gaines to enforce neutrality along the Mexican frontier—to prevent either Mexico or Texas from using U.S. territory in their war, as well as to prevent Indian hostilities in the area. When Gaines moved his command into territory south of the Sabine River, claimed by both Texas and Mexico, Gorostiza, the Mexican minister to the U.S., protested it as an invasion of Mexican soil. Failing to receive an apology, he asked for his passport in October, 1837. Before leaving Washington, however, he published a pamphlet containing correspondence between himself and the U.S. State Department on the troop-movement controversy. In a letter of December 10, 1836, Secretary Forsyth attempted to explain to Mexico, through Ellis, the march of General Gaines south of the Sabine. He concluded the letter with a complaint about Gorostiza's pamphlet. Ellis did not stay in Mexico long enough to receive a reply to this letter. For a complete discussion of these problems and their resolutions, see James M. Callahan, *American Foreign Policy in Mexican Relations* (New York, 1932), 82-99; George L. Rives, *The United States and Mexico 1821-1848*, 2 vols. (New York, 1913), 1:372-88, 420-29; Curtis R. Reynolds, "The Deterioration of Mexican-American Diplomatic Relations, 1833-1845," *JW* (April, 1972), 11:213-24. Forsyth's letter of December 10, 1836, is in William R. Manning (ed.), *Diplomatic Correspondence of the United States, Inter-American Affairs 1831-1860*, 12 vols. (Washington, 1932-39), 8:71-75. For Gorostiza's pamphlet and relevant correspondence, see *House Exec. Doc.* 190, 25 Cong., 2 Sess., pp. 61-120.

Speech in Senate, February 28, 1837. Addresses the question of whether there will or will not be a treasury surplus as of January 1, 1838. Says that the existence of a surplus largely depends on how the House now handles its various appropriation bills. Argues, for instance, with specific reference to the U.S. Army appropriation bill, that much could be cut out of it. "There is, in my opinion, no emergency which renders so great an increase of our military establishment at all necessary." Holds also that there is no "justification for the expenditure of the public money on a long list of useless fortifications." Notes that if there is a treasury surplus, it should be distributed to the states as provided for by the amendment (section two) of the Senate's fortification bill. Does not want that money to sit long in the government's deposit banks. Hence, asks for its distribution before the next session of Congress meets. "If there is no surplus, the amendment can do no injury; if there is, we shall gain a year." Points out that the House of Representatives, the more democratic and less aristocratic branch of the legislature, has a distribution section in its final version of the fortification bill; also that the last distribution bill passed by Congress [8:813] was "hailed with acclamation. Not a single State has been found which will venture to refuse its quota of the deposites." In Kentucky, the distribution of the surplus was considered a "beneficent measure, and eminently calculated to advance the public good." Attacks the argument of Sen.

James Buchanan (Pa.) that "if we pass this amendment, the effect will be to check the necessary appropriations of the public money for purposes of the General Government," and his related contention that in the event of war the surplus funds proposed to be distributed to the states will be needed. If war comes, Clay counters, Congress will surely do its patriotic duty and provide the funds necessary to fight it. *Register of Debates*, 24 Cong., 2 Sess., Supplemental Speeches, 2188-90.

Clay's remarks on the floor on this issue, as reported in the main columns of the *Register of Debates* on this day, February 28, vary substantially in length, substance, and tone from the above version. He begins by asking whether a treasury surplus is indeed expected and whether, if there is one, the Finance Committee intends to leave it in the government's deposit banks at 2% interest or put it in the hands of the states where it would yield 6%. When Sen. Silas Wright (N.Y.) interrupts to say that no surplus can be expected, Clay nevertheless pushes ahead, reminding his colleagues that section two of the pending, amended fortification bill provides for the distribution to the states of the surplus in the treasury as of January 1, 1838. He therefore urges all those administration senators who had voted for the distribution bill in the last session [8:812-13] now to "rally round their own principles and oppose the striking out." He also suggests "by way of compromise" on the distribution matter, the adoption of his land bill, which had been tabled on February 23 [8:873], and the distribution concept it contains. *Register of Debates*, 24 Cong., 2 Sess., 993. It is estimated that Kentucky received nearly $1.5 million in the 1837 distribution. For a table depicting the amount received by all states, see Edward G. Bourne, *The History of the Surplus Revenue of 1837* (New York, 1885; reprint ed., 1968), 143.

During the evening session this day, a motion to strike out section two of the Senate's fortification bill passed by a 26 to 19 vote. Clay was not recorded as present or voting. *Register of Debates*, 24 Cong., 2 Sess., 1008.

Earlier this day, Clay asks whether there are historical precedents having to do with the specific roles played by the House and the Senate in the inauguration of presidents. Wonders why the "Senate had the exclusive care of administering the oath." *Ibid.*, 992. In actual fact the U.S. Senate had not had "exclusive care of administering the oath." Inaugurations had been held in the Senate chamber, in the House chamber, and outside the Capitol building, depending on the choice of the president-elect and the prevailing weather. Beginning in 1787, the oath was administered to the president by the Chief Justice of the United States. See Glenn D. Kittler, *Hail to the Chief; The Inauguration Days of Our Presidents* (Philadelphia, 1965), *passim*.

Remark in Senate, March 1, 1837. Asks whether the resolution by Sen. Robert J. Walker (Miss.) to recognize the independence of the state of Texas [8:838-39, 848] is to be followed by any legislative action and, if so, what? Complains that the resolution covers "not only the legislative but also the executive functions of the Government." Hopes the question of Texas independence can be delayed "a little longer," but states that if it be put to him so that he has to say yes or no, he will, "in conformity with the principles on which he had always acted in reference to the South American states [2:343-44, 385-86, 517, 520, 529, 548-51, 572-73], give an affirmative answer." Notes, however, that on "the very grave and important question of Texas annexation," he will "at present express no opinion. They are entirely different questions; and a vote on the one would not commit any man on the other." *Register of Debates*, 24 Cong., 2 Sess., 1012.

During the evening session on this day, at which Clay was not present, the resolution to recognize the independence of Texas came to a vote and was passed 23-19. When the vote was announced, it "called forth some applause from the gallery, which was promptly checked by the Chair." *Ibid.*, 1013. On March 2, 1837,

Clay voted against a resolution to reconsider the previous evening's affirmative vote on Texas independence. The resolution to reconsider failed, 25 to 23. *Ibid.*, 1019. For Texas annexation and the coming of the Mexican War, see Justin H. Smith, *The War with Mexico.* 2 vols., New York, 1919; Otis A. Singletary, *The Mexican War.* Chicago, 1960; Rives, *The United States and Mexico.*

From Nicholas Biddle, Philadelphia, March 2, 1837. Regrets that "you will not be able to make a visit to Phila., for . . . independent & patriotic men desire to know the opinions of experienced statesmen as to the future prospects of the country." Adds that the U.S. Bank of Pennsylvania "did not wish to make" discounts to "Mr [John] Black & Mr [Rice] Garland the other day," but did so because of "the interest you felt in their success." Notes that "we charged a rate of exchange less certainly than the loans could have been obtained for anywhere else," yet it amounted to three percent plus interest. Continues: "Formerly the Bank did this for one per cent at most, so that in this single transaction, Mr Garland loses $300; and Mr Black $140, being an actual tax of that amount, as much as if an Assessor had appraised their estates & levied that tax. In that event, we should have thought it an oppression. Now it is only that necessary alloy to the happiness of possessing a Chief Magistrate who regulates our currency & his own temper so admirably." Copy. DLC-Nicholas Biddle Papers (DNA, M212, R20). For the increase in discount rates, see Walter B. Smith, *Economic Aspects of the Second Bank of the United States* (Cambridge, Mass., 1953), 183-85.

On February 20, 1837, Clay had written Biddle introducing "Rice Garland of the H. of R. from Louisiana" and saying that Garland would be in Philadelphia to negotiate a bill of exchange with "John Black of the Senate" as one of his endorsers. Adds that he has "no hesitation in expressing my conviction of the entire security of the bill." ALS. PHi.

To Thomas Bowman *et al.*, Carlisle, Pa., March 2, 1837. States that he has received the invitation from "the Belles Lettres Society, to pronounce the annual discourse, before the Literary Associations of Dickinson College, at the commencement in July next." Although receiving "with great satisfaction this testimony," regrets "that I cannot comply with the appointment . . . without too great sacrifices." ALS. PCarlD. For Bowman, who graduated from Dickinson College in 1837 and subsequently became a Methodist Episcopal bishop, educator, and chaplain of the U.S. Senate, see *DAB*.

Comment in Senate, March 2, 1837. States that it pleases him to learn that the land bill [Remark in Senate, January 12, 1837] has been rejected by the House of Representatives. Thinks this will insure a "large surplus in the Treasury," especially if other large-expenditure bills "follow the fate of the land bill." Urges the Senate to "look ahead . . . to provide for the future," by returning the surplus to the states rather than leaving it in the government's deposit banks. Calls favorable attention to "the distribution clause inserted by the other House in the fortification bill, rather than leave the money in the deposite banks." Asserts that the nation owes "its thanks to the other House for what it had recently done" and rejoices "to see light breaking out in that glorious quarter, so immediately related to the people." Asks if it is possible for a majority of the Senate now to "oppose the ascertained popular will in relation to the disposition of the surplus revenue," and wonders whether his colleagues still "insist on leaving the public money in the hands of the deposite banks." *Register of Debates*, 24 Cong., 2 Sess., 1020.

On the following day, March 3, the House informed the Senate that it could not accept the Senate's action in striking out the amendment to the fortification bill that provided for distribution of the surplus revenue [Remark in Senate, February 28, 1837] and called for a Senate-House conference on the issue. The conference produced no compromise. *Ibid.*, 1021-22.

Comment in Senate, March 3, 1837. Favors restoring section two of the fortifications bill [Remark in Senate, February 28, 1837; Comment in Senate, March 2, 1837] as insisted upon by the House of Representatives in its version of the legislation. Repeats his arguments of February 28 and March 2 in favor of distributing the treasury surplus to the states, if there indeed is a surplus, rather than leaving it in the deposit banks. Attacks the deposit banks as "so many mere political machines." Praises the "democratic" action of the House in retaining the distribution clause in the fortifications bill and notes wryly that on this issue the Jacksonian senators who had brought about the deletion of section two of that bill on February 28 had acted the part of aristocrats. Asks them: "will you oppose the democracy of the country? Will you withstand the people's will?" Calls on the "majority of this Senate who, at the last session, thought it unwise to leave the public money in the deposite banks [8:813], to rally around their own principles, to stand by their democratic friends in the other House, and to take the money of the nation out of the hands of these deposite banks, and distribute it among the people of the States, on the principles advocated by themselves last year." Suggests to Jacksonian leader Sen. Silas Wright (N.Y.) "by way of a compromise, that he consent to the [Clay] land bill [8:873]. This is a middle measure; it disposes of two great interests at once. Is it possible to conceive of a better disposition both of the question of the surplus and the question of the tariff? If the honorable gentleman will consent to that, I will agree with him; but I entreat the majority of this body not to lend themselves to the plan of retaining this surplus revenue in a few banks, to be selected by the administration." *Register of Debates*, 24 Cong., 2 Sess., 1024-25. Later this day, by a vote of 27 to 23, the Senate upheld its February 28 decision to delete section two (the distribution of surplus section) of the fortifications bill. Clay voted with the minority. *Ibid.*, 1034.

At the end of this day, March 3, the 24th Congress adjourned *sine die*. The Senate of the 25th Congress was called into extra session by President Jackson on Saturday, March 4, 1837, at 10:00 a.m. for the purpose of swearing in new members and, in executive session, to act upon the various nominations of President Van Buren. It adjourned *sine die* at 10:00 a.m. on Friday, March 10. *Ibid.*, 1035-38.

To NOAH NOBLE Washington, March 4, 1837

I recd. with much satisfaction your friendly letter of the 10h. ulto. but should have much more in shaking you by the hand as the Senator from Indiana.[1]

I have seen Mr. [Oliver H.] Smith. He talks well, and I hope will act well. He can hardly do more than his predecessor.[2]

We have strong hopes of the next H. of R. if you can *Keep right* in Indiana.[3]

Jackson played the tyrant to the last. Knowing that the Currency bill would be passed if he exercised his veto against it, he pocketed the bill![4]

The H. of R. during the few last days of its existence displayed much spirit and independence. . . .[5]

Copy. Printed in *IMH* (June, 1926), 22:211-12. 1. Noble, a Whig, had been defeated for the U.S. Senate by Oliver H. Smith, also a Whig, by a vote of 79 to 63. Dorothy Riker and Gayle Thornbrough, *Indiana Election Returns, 1816-1851* (Indiana Historical Bureau, 1960), 131. 2. Smith's predecessor was William Hendricks, who only received 1 vote for senator in the 1837 election. *Ibid.*; *BDAC*. 3. The Whigs had won a majority of both houses of the state legislature in 1836. See Clay to Noble, June 20, 1837. In the 1837 Indiana elections David Wallace, a Whig, was elected governor over John Dumont, also a Whig, by a vote of 46,067 to 36,915. David Hillis, a Whig, was elected lieutenant governor over Alexander S. Burnett, a Democrat, by 49,535 votes to 22,829. Although the precise margin of their victory in the state legislative elections cannot be determined, the Whigs continued to control both houses. In the U.S. House elections, one Democrat and six Whigs were chosen. Riker and Thornbrough, *Indiana Election Returns*, 94-97, 145-47, 168-70, 235-36, 239. 4. Speech in Senate, Jan. 11, 1837. 5. For example, the House laid on the table a resolution to investigate the banks, the administration's land bill, and several appropriation bills. In addition, the House refused to accept a Senate amendment to the fortification bill concerning distribution of the treasury surplus. *Register of Debates*, 24 Cong., 2 Sess., 2078, 2096-99, 2141, 2146, 2150, 2154. See also 8:873; Remark in Senate, Jan. 12, 1837; Speech in Senate, Feb. 28, 1837.

To O.T. Reeves *et al.*, Chillicothe, Ohio, March 6, 1837. Acknowledges receipt of their letter of December 24, 1836 [8:874], and expresses appreciation "for the friendly feelings and sentiments towards me which it expresses." Notes that he has accepted reappointment as U.S. senator [8:871; Clay to General Assembly of Ky., January 16, 1837]. Is pleased to know "that the people in your neighborhood regard with approbation my public services generally." Adds: "I shall be happy if, during the time I may continue to remain in the public councils, I shall be so fortunate as to deserve the same favorable judgment." Copy. Printed in *Niles' Register* (April 22, 1837), 52:119; reprinted from the Cincinnati *Daily Gazette*.

To UNKNOWN RECIPIENT Washington, March 6, 1837

I owe you an apology for not earlier answering your favor of the 19h. Jan. which consists in the extent of my correspondence, and the pressure of business. And now I must be brief.

If you intend removing to Kentucky or any other part of the Western Country, my earnest advice to you would be to make a previous visit. It is impossible that any written or verbal account should supply the place of personal observation.

Our climate in K. is upon the whole a good one, but is nevertheless subject to much variation. The thermometer neither rises so high nor falls so low as in corresponding latitudes on this side of the mountains. I have not by me here any regular observations which have been taken and recorded upon it. Frosts generally cease in March and April, and do not return in severity until the last of Novr. or early in Decr. But there are exceptions in both cases. Generally we have but little snow in winter, and when it falls it does not remain long. It very seldom remains a fortnight. Corn Rye grass, hemp and tobacco are the crops most cultivated. Labor is chiefly performed by slaves, but it is not discreditable for the whites to work and many of them do very hard. We have no U. States lands. In the part of the State in which I reside (the region about Lexington) the price of the best lands is from $40 to $80 per acre, and it is rising. In other parts of the State it commands from $5 to $20 per acre. There is no prevailing autumnal fever in my neighbourhood, nor any other *prevailing* disease. The Country is healthy, and the maladies are those which usually occur in healthy Countries. Northern and Eastern constitutions bear our climate as well as any others.

Having[1]

AL, incomplete. NWattJHi. Copy in KyU. 1. Manuscript ends here.

To FRANCIS T. BROOKE Washington, March 7, 1837

I recd. your favor. This day the ex President [Jackson] left this City, and the President [Van Buren] for the first time sent in a batch of nominations.[1] [Joel R.] Poinsett for the War Dept. [George M.] Dallas for Russia, [William H., Jr.] Haywood of No. Carolina for Belgium &c The three mentd. was confirmed.[2] [William] Smith of Alabama, and Cahon [*sic*, John Catron] of Tennessee were nominated by Jackson for Judges of the Supreme Court under the new law. And what Judges they will make! They are not yet confirmed.[3] Labranche [*sic*, Alcee LaBranche] of Louisiana was also nominated by Jackson for Texas, and has been confirmed, as Chargé des Affaires.[4]

You ask if I can communicate any consolation to you for the future as to public affairs. I lament to say not much. Hopes are entertained, and with some probability, that there will be a majority in the H. of R. at the next session, against the Admon.[5] And if there were more concert, and an union as to the ultimate object, among the Opposition there would be better prospects. I think there is a tendency to union among them, but it is not yet produced. Mr. [John C.] Calhoun now, as heretofore, stands in the way.

The City has been filled with strangers. The crowd from N. York has been as great as it was from Scotland, when James ascended the throne of England. . . .[6]

ALS. DLC-TJC (DNA, M212, R14). Copy in DLC-HC (DNA, M212, R5). Printed in Colton, *Clay Correspondence*, 4:412. Addressed to Brooke in Richmond, Va. 1. For Van Buren's Cabinet, see Clay to Henry Clay, Jr., Feb. 22, 1837. 2. For William H. Haywood, Jr., who declined the appointment and who later served as U.S. senator from North Carolina, see *Who Was Who in America*, 3 vols. (Chicago, 1963), historical vol.:243; also *BDAC*. Virgil Maxcy (see *DAB*) later received the appointment to Belgium. 3. The Judiciary Act of 1837, passed on the last day of Jackson's term, increased the court from seven to nine members. Jackson immediately named John Catron and William Smith to the seats. Smith was confirmed by a vote of 23 to 18 and Catron 28 to 15. Smith, however, declined the appointment. *Congressional Quarterly's Guide to U.S. Supreme Court* (Washington, D.C., 1979), 664, 813, 946; U.S. Sen., *Journal*, 24 Cong., 2 Sess., Appendix, 353. For the Judiciary Act of 1837, see 5 *U.S. Stat.*, 176-78. 4. For LaBranche, see James T. White & Co. (eds.), *Notable Names in American History* (Clifton, N.J., 1973), 438. 5. In the 25th Congress the Democrats held 108 seats in the House to 107 for the Whigs, with 24 seats held by others. Richard Morris (ed.), *Encyclopedia of American History* (New York, 1953), 406. Professor Thomas B. Alexander, analyzing voting patterns, finds in the House 128 Democrats and 112 Whigs. Thomas B. Alexander, *Sectional Stress and Party Strength* (Nashville, 1967), 25. In the Senate the Democrats held 30 seats to 18 for the Whigs and 4 by others. McKee counts 117 Democrats, 115 Whigs, and 10 Independents in the House; 31 Democrats, 18 Whigs, and 3 Independents in the Senate. Thomas H. McKee, *National Conventions and Platforms of All Political Parties, 1789 to 1905; Convention, Popular and Electoral Vote* (New York, 1906; reprint ed., 1971), 39. Those designated "others" and "independents" in both houses include a variety of States' Rights Democrats, States' Rights Whigs, Unionists, Nullifiers, Anti-Masons, Anti-Jacksonians, Federalists, Anti-Federalists, and a few for whom no party designation can be determined. However, in the House it appears that about 13 so-called "Conservatives" [Clay to Henry Clay, Jr., Jan. 28, 1837] within the Democratic party occasionally held the balance of power between the Van Buren Democrats and the Whigs. For example, James K. Polk was elected Speaker of the House by a majority of 13 votes with Conservatives and Democrats voting together. Later, Van Buren's subtreasury bill was defeated in the House by 13 votes when Conservatives joined their votes with those of the Whigs. Speech in Senate, Sept. 25, 1837; White, *Notable Names in American History*, 82-83; John Niven, *Martin Van Buren: The Romantic Age of American Politics* (New York, 1983), 421-24. 6. On March 24, 1603.

From Henry S. Fox, Washington, March 8, 1837. States that if it is convenient, Clay may "draw upon me a draft for the 1180 dollars which I am in your debt, at ten days date from the present." Adds that "if agre[e]able to you, the draft can be sent to me for acceptance, at that date, before your departure; or you can inform me in whose hands you leave it." ALS. DLC-HC (DNA, M212, R5). Printed in Colton, *Clay Correspondence*, 4:412-13. For Fox, who became the British minister to the United States in 1835, see *DNB*.

To DANIEL WEBSTER Lexington, March 28, 1837

I should like to know at what time we may expect the pleasure of seeing you in Kentucky, as I do not wish to be absent on that interesting occasion. I have no intention of leaving home during the Spring, or before August, except to make an excursion to Missouri to visit a young son [James Brown Clay] that I have established there.[1] Without being bound to any specific time for this trip, I wish to make it towards the last of May; but, of course, will be regulated by your movements if I can know them.[2]

ALS. DLC-Daniel Webster Papers (DNA, M212, R22). Printed in George T. Curtis, *Life of Daniel Webster*, 2 vols. (New York, 1870), 1:562. 1. Clay did not visit Missouri in 1837. See Clay to Logan *et al.*, June 17, 1837. 2. Webster, his wife Caroline LeRoy Webster, and daughter Julia, arrived in Lexington on May 19, 1837, and stayed at the Phoenix Hotel for about five days. Lexington *Kentucky Gazette*, May 25, 1837.

To JAMES ERWIN Lexington, March 30, 1837

I received yesterday your favor of the 19h. inst. communicating the arrival at N.O. of my Asses,[1] and that you had procured a passage for the survivors to Louisville in the N. America. I shall send down to assist the Groom in bringing them from Louisville.

I am glad that you have taken measures to make the Underwriters pay for the three Asses that died on the passage. The insurance provided expressly against the contingency which has happened of death at Sea; and I hope that you will see that the Protest and other papers to charge the Underwriters are in due form and sent to Mr. [Reuben G.] Beasley. The insurance was at a high rate, and if recovered we shall be completely indemnified.

Mr. R[ezin]. D Shepherd has sent from Balto. to the care of his brother Mr. James Shepherd three hair Mattrasses that were made for me in that City.[2] I will thank you to see, on their arrival, that they are duly forwarded to Hill & Co. of Louisville Mr. J Shepherd will not know who to forward them to.

I am rejoiced to learn that you will not suffer by any of the late failures in N. Orleans.[3] You must have been very fortunate to escape all injury. The pressure in the money market at the Eastward seems to continue very severe.

Your children are all in excellent health.[4]

You have not informed whether you recd. the orders sent by Mr [John J.] Crittenden and myself on Mr B[enjamin] Story for our fees in his unfortunate Suit.[5]

ALS. CtY. 1. Beasley to Clay, Jan. 8 and Feb. 7, 1837. 2. For James H. Shepherd (1790-1837), a commercial merchant in New Orleans, see Samuel G. Smyth, *A Genealogy of the Duke-Shepherd-Van Metre Family* (Lancaster, Pa., 1909), 245; see also 8:804-5. 3. For a discussion of bank failures in New Orleans and the northeast, see Memphis *Enquirer*, April 8, 15, 22, 1837; Govan, *Nicholas Biddle*, 306-7; Albert Fossier, *New Orleans, the Glamour Period 1800-1843* (New Orleans, 1957), 72-75. 4. Erwin's three younger children—Andrew Eugene, Lucretia, and Charles Edward—were being reared by the Clays. Part of the time James Erwin kept his two oldest children—James, Jr., and Henry Clay—with him, and part of the time they lived with the Clays. See 8:807-8, 866; Clay to Hughes, June 18, 1837. 5. For the case of *Edward Livingston* v. *Benjamin Story* in which the Supreme Court ruled in favor of Livingston, see 11 Peters 351-418.

To R. PETERS[1] Lexington, April 21, 1837

I recd. your favor of the 13h. inst. transmitting a letter for Mr. [James] Erwin respecting the Monument and its appendages intended for my lamented daughter [Anne Brown Clay Erwin].[2] They will on their arrival at New Orleans find him there, in all probability; but I will reserve your letter for him when he joins us here. I feel, as I have no doubt that he does, greatly indebted to you for your kind attention to this melancholy commission.

I hope that the severe pressure felt in the Eastern Cities will speedily abate.[3] It has not been much experienced with us but we cannot expect to escape entirely.

ALS. NcD. 1. Probably Richard Peters, Jr., of Washington, D.C. 2. See 8:808-9. 3. Speech in Senate, Jan. 11, 1837; Clay to Erwin, March 30, 1837.

From Alexander W. Stow, Louisville, Ky., April 22, 1837. Apologizes for not writing sooner, explaining that "I have been confined to my room . . . with a diseased limb." Despite this impediment and the fact that "I now know but little more of this state, and its men & institutions, than I did on my arrival last autumn, yet my favourable impressions are on the whole confirmed, and I believe I shall make it my permanent residence."

Notes, especially, that "on the important subject of slavery my views have undergone an entire change—effected, probably, quite as much by your opinions as by my own observation." States that "though I have no conception of how it is to be brought about, I now long to see our Country ridded of its slave population. I hope I need not add that I am as far as ever from approving of the schemes and doings of the northern abolitionists." Gives the latter "but little credit for even honesty of purpose."

Comments also on the "sad condition of the cotton region and Atlantic cities . . . which must soon be felt to a considerable degree throughout the whole country [Speech in Senate, January 11, 1837; Clay to Erwin, March 30, 1837]." Predicts that, as a result of this situation, if Andrew Jackson lives a few years longer, "I have no doubt he will behold himself as bitterly cursed as he has been blindly worshiped" and that the "great man to whom the country is indebted for all its useful legislation from the commencement of the war [of 1812] to the present day, will be by common consent acknowledged, not only as its mother spirit, but as its greatest benefactor. Long may you live, my Dear Sir, to enjoy the triumph!" AL. WHi.

Frank A. Flower of Washington, D.C., who donated this letter to the State Historical Society of Wisconsin in 1907, attributed its authorship to Alexander W. Stow. For Stow, a lawyer in Rochester, N.Y., and later the first chief justice of the Wisconsin supreme court in 1848-53, see *NCAB*, 12:513. See also Clay to Stow, April 26, 1837.

To JAMES ERWIN Lexington, April 26, 1837

I recd. your letter of the 9h. inst. and was rejoiced to learn by it that you had not, on your own account, nor that of others, lost one dollar, in consequence of the recent failures.[1] I was very uneasy until I received your letter, especially after the failure of the Messrs. Dicks,[2] and the rumor, as a consequence of it, of the failure of Yeatman Woods & Co.[3] I sincerely hope this rumor is unfounded. But if it should be true how much will Mrs. [John] Bell regret not having taken our advice to discontinue business after the death of Mr Yeatman![4]

Here, there is no considerable pecuniary distress yet, nor do I apprehend there will be much. Property may fall, as hemp has and slaves will. I think land not much.

I wrote you requesting your assistance to Martin [Duralde] to sell Tom Balto. & his wife. If they could be sold on a credit for undoubted paper, I should prefer it to a cash sale, at the price that this would bring.

I think you cannot fail to do well with your purchase of Sugar, if you will hang on to it & not sell too soon. I should think too that the price of good Cotton at 8 or 8½ Cents was very tempting. If however the fall in Europe proceeds from an excess of supply beyond demand, and not from pecuniary embarrassments there, it will be hazardous to engage in it. Most probably both causes have contributed to produce the fall in Europe. And when the effect of our American embarrassments shall reach and be felt in England, we may expect a further reduction of price. Another consideration should not be overlooked: Our distresses in the U. States will lessen the demand for British Cotton manufactures, and that probably will affect the raw material. Upon the whole, it seems to me that it would not be wise for you to embark largely in the purchase of Cotton, especially if you should not be able to keep it on hand some time.

I think after this year, I will withdraw my funds from below, and pay off the [Transylvania] University.[5] Indeed, during this year I may have occasion when you come up to draw six or seven thousand dollars. I have postponed building in town, for the present.

I am glad that Mr. [Richard] Chinn is engaged to assist in closing the business of Mr. [James] Browns Estate.[6]

I was engaged by N[athaniel]. Cox to appear for him in a suit of the U. States agt. him in the Supreme Court.[7] It was dismissed at the last term for want of jurisdiction, which was in effect a decision in favor of Mr. Cox. I will thank you to call on his Exor or Admor and receive $250 for me, which amt. I shall be satisfied with as a fee, since he was an old friend & it was a small & not very troublesome case. This letter will be sufficient authority to you to receive the sum.

Your children are all well. Lucretia [C. Erwin] was much pleased to get a letter from you yesterday. And we are all very anxious to see you. This month has been very cold dry and uncomfortable. P.S. Mrs. Clay wishes you to bring her a box of good fresh Macaroni. Mrs. J. Clay[8] perhaps had better select it.

ALS. NHi. Written to Erwin in New Orleans. 1. Speech in Senate, Jan. 11, 1837; Clay to Erwin, March 30, 1837. 2. N. & J. Dick & Co., commercial merchants at 87 Canal Street, New Orleans, did close temporarily, but they were back in business in 1838. Memphis *Enquirer*, April 22, 1837; John Gibson, *Gibson's Guide and Directory of the State of Louisiana and the Cities of New Orleans and LaFayette . . .* (New Orleans, 1838), 218. 3. Apparently a reference to Yeatman, Woods & Co., a leading bank in Nashville, Tenn., which did fail. However, Yeatman, Woods & Co., a commercial house in New Orleans, which had the same owners as the Tennessee bank of the same name, was still in business at Magazine Street, opposite Bank's Arcade, in 1838. Gibson, *Guide and Directory of . . . Louisiana*, 218; W.G. Sumner *et al.*, *A History of Banking in all the Leading Nations*, 4 vols. (New York, 1896), 1:269. 4. Jane Erwin Yeatman Bell was the sister of James Erwin and the wife of John Bell of Tennessee. Thomas Yeatman, her first husband, had died of cholera in 1833. Joseph H. Parks, *John Bell of Tennessee* (Baton Rouge, 1950), 114-15, 139-40. See also *National Banner & Nashville Whig*, June 17, 1833, for Yeatman's obituary; and W.W. Clayton, *History of Davidson County, Tennessee* (Philadelphia, 1880), 203. 5. See 7:413-14. 6. See 8:739-40, 768-69, 771-72. 7. For the case of *The United States* v. *Nathaniel Cox*, see 11 Peters 162-65. 8. Probably Julie Duralde Clay.

To ALEXANDER W. STOW Lexington, April 26, 1837

I was extremely sorry to learn by your letter of the 22d instant that you had been so long confined by a disabled limb. I was not at all aware of your situation until I received your letter. You have my fervent wishes for a speedy and effectual recovery.

The convictions to which you have brought your mind in regard to slavery do not surprize me. It is an institution of which our Country would be most happily rid, if it were practicable. In spite of the delusions of those who are directly interested in its preservation, and of the rash and impolitic interference of those who have no direct interest and no right to interfere about it, undoubtedly it is fraught with great mischiefs to both races, to say nothing of the injustice which it inflicts upon one of them. Their separation is the only remedy which has ever appeared to me to offer any practical advantages. Separation, by first Colonizing the free blacks, and afterwards with the consent of the Slave States, the class of slaves. But the success of this scheme is seriously affected by the indiscretion of the Abolitionists.

The intelligence from the South, as to our Commercial embarrassments, is dreadful.[1] The most alarming circumstance is the reduction in the price of Cotton. That, if it continues, must affect every interest and every part of our Country.

The measures of Government have beyond all doubt contributed largely to produce the present calamitous state of affairs. Whether the people will at last open their eyes remains to be seen. In Connecticut they appear to prefer darkness,[2] whilst in the great Capital of your State [New York][3] the people have broken loose from the chains of party.

Should you pass this way, on your return to N. York, we shall be happy to see you. . . .

ALS. ViU. 1. Speech in Senate, Jan. 11, 1837. 2. In the state elections in Connecticut on April 3, the Whigs lost all seats in the state house of representatives to the Democrats, won 5 seats and lost 6 in the state senate, and lost all other state offices. Henry W. Edwards, a Democrat, polled 53% of the vote for governor, defeating Whig candidate, William W. Ellsworth. Democrats also won all 6 Connecticut seats in the U.S. House. Connecticut *Courant*, April 22, 1837; *BDGUS*, 1:165; *Congressional Quarterly's Guide to U.S. Elections* (Washington, 1975), 568. 3. In the Albany city elections in April, 1837, the Whigs won all seats except one. Also in the spring elections in New York City, Whig candidate, Aaron Clark, won the mayor's race and the Whigs won 12 seats on the board of aldermen to 5 for the Democrats and 11 seats on the assistant board of aldermen to 6 for the Democrats. For the state elections in the fall of 1837, see Clay to Curtis, Oct. 25, 1837.

From J. Jones, Philadelphia, April 27, 1837. Writes as "a native citizen, and an author," concerning "the proposed International copyright law [Comment in Senate, February 2, 1837]!" Asserts first, "that there is a conspiracy formed by the booksellers throughout the union, against native authors, instigated by pecuniary interest"; second, that American publishers "by successful monopoly, have acquired despotic power in the controlment of the literature of the country," and that "They dictate to Americans, and maintain their supremacy, by piratical operations in another land"; third, that publishers "discriminate at pleasure, whatsoever principles they chose. . . . And the press, in some measure, is forced to enlist in their suicidal practices; for they pay a vast amt. of money for advertising." Adds that "This is the time to deal out justice." Details at length the difficulties facing a native author attempting to have his work published. Argues: "If our authors are not as able as those of other countries, it is not because the God of Nature has not endowed them with equal capacities. Give them a chance. When we depended soley on our own exertions, we could fight as well as other men—why not write?" ALS. DLC-HC (DNA, M212, R2). The writer of this letter was probably John Beauchamp Jones who later became co-editor of *The Madisonian* during the Tyler administration and author of such works as *Wild Western Scenes* (1841) and *A Rebel War Clerk's Diary* (1866). See *DAB*; also Richard A. Bland, "Politics, Propaganda, and the Public Printing: The Administration Organs, 1829-1849," Ph.D. dissertation, University of Kentucky, 1975, pp. 95-96.

From Harriet Martineau, Westminster, England, May 15, 1837. Thanks Clay "on behalf of many authors besides myself" for his "exertions on the Copyright business [Comment in Senate, February 2, 1837]." Notes that "We are exceedingly pleased with your Report, & have strong hope that our object may be attained next session." Believes that "Amer[ica]n newspapers seem to show a more & more favourable disposition towards our claim" and that "honourable Amer[ica]n publishers" understand "the injury we suffer."

Continues: "Have you seen what my New York publishers (who are English) have been doing, to obviate mutilation of my book? We fear we must submit to be pirated; but the risk of mutilation is much lessened by the work being divided into parts. The book has been published here only four days. I have had little hope of pleasing any body in either country with my work. I might have done so by merely copying my journal; but I felt the occasion to be too serious an one to be trifled with; & I have accordingly risked every thing by making an open avowal of principles which have no chance of being popular. I am very easy, now the thing is done. My conscience is discharged, & I really do not care much what becomes of me in name & fortune, while I cannot live without freedom of speech. This last can never now be taken from me."

Mentions also that "Your new President [Van Buren] seems to have succeeded in making himself gloriously unpopular at the very outset. I do not believe in his power of retrieving himself. We shall see. I hope you will never have another President who will venture to declare, on entering upon office, that under no circumstances will he, on a particular point, assent to a constitutional act which may become the will of the nation."

On English politics, explains: "We are in a critical state, & the tories may very likely have another short turn of office. The weakness of the sovereign, the incompleteness of the Reform Bill, & the difficulties thereby left in the way of the representation are too much for the present Ministry [of Lord Melbourne]. . . . We do not fear breach of the peace, but much political struggle." ALS. DLC-HC (DNA, M212, R5). Printed in Colton, *Clay Correspondence*, 4:413-14. Clay's report and bill on the copyright were presented on February 16, 1837. See *Sen. Docs.*, 24 Cong., 2 Sess., no. 179, pp. 1-3. Clay reintroduced the bill in the 25th Congress, 1st Session on December 13, 1837. Bowker, *Copyright*, 318-19. Martineau's *Society in America* (2 vols.), which was published in New York in 1837 by Saunders and Otley, expressed her strong anti-slavery views. Piercy and Reed in New York also published in 1837 her pamphlet entitled *Views of Slavery & Emancipation; from "Society in America."* Van Buren had stated in his inaugural address that he was opposed to the abolition of slavery in the District of Columbia unless the slave states approved. *MPP*, 3:318. For a discussion of British politics and weaknesses of the Reform Act of 1832, see J. Herbert Low, *English History . . .* (Chicago, 1928), 421-22.

From Reuben G. Beasley, Havre, France, May 16, 1837. Regrets learning that three of the female asses [Beasley to Clay, January 8, 1837] he had sent Clay died during the passage. Promises to "collect the loss & remit the amount to Messrs. Baring Brothers & Co. to the credit of your son [Henry Clay, Jr.] as you direct."

Notes that "Commercial embarrassment seems to have fallen like an avalanche over our Country [Speech in Senate, January 11, 1837]," but it is not unexpected "seeing, what was passing on this side the water some time past [Beasley to Clay, January 8, 1837]." Continues: "If the American houses in London, now supported by the Bank of England, should go by the board, those at Paris who have executed commissions to a large amount taking their reimbursement on them, must also go. The Paris Bankers have agreed to loan Havre 10 millions secured by Cotton at a low valuation, but this does not prevent the continued Protest of all bills from the U.S. which come to a large amount by every Packet." Concludes with a discussion of domestic political events in France, Spain, and Britain. ALS. Josephine Simpson Collection, Lexington, Ky.

From Daniel Huey, Pleasant Bowery, Ohio, May 24, 1837. States that "Although an entire stranger to you" and one who often differs in political sentiments, "I find there is one good and great cause you have espoused which I feel a deep interest in, viz. you have accepted the Presidency of the American Colonization Society [8:874]." Relates his personal background, saying he is a native of Pennsylvania who moved to Mississippi at age 22 with "two dollars in my pocket," and that last year he moved to Ohio. Before leaving Mississippi, reports that he offered his "African servants" a chance to colonize on the coast of Africa "at the age of 26 years on an average." However, "they declined my offer; all they wished was to choose a proprietor, and remain in the State. I gratified them in their desire." Continues: "Subsequently, I was desirous of doing something for the nation in Africa, or those free blacks who desire to go there. Some time last summer, I advertised in two public papers, and made the following proposition: If eleven others would join, I would make a donation of 400 acres of land to the American Colonization Society, out of my lands in the State of Illinois, and my intention was to form a society, and bind the American Colonization Society not to sell said land under six years. No person has come forward to meet this proposition; I have been determined to do my part, and am now ready to make a title of said 400 acres of land to the American Colonization Society." Asks "how to proceed in order to execute my designs." Also asks "if the labors of your Society are exclusively intended to operate only in Africa, as there has been something said about colonizing on the Northwest coast of America." Copy. Printed in Washington *Daily National Intelligencer,* August 26, 1837. Huey is identified in the *African Repository,* 12:284, as a resident of Reading, Ohio, formerly of Fayette, Miss. See also Clay to Huey, May 30, 1837.

To JAMES B. CLAY Lexington, May 26, 1837

Just as I was making preparations for my trip to St Louis and had resolved to start in a few days the proclamation of the President arrived calling Congress on the first of September.[1] I shall be obliged to leave home to reach Washington in time about the middle of August. Consequently I have only two months and a half to attend to my private affairs. If I were to go to St. Louis and examine my lands in Missouri[2] as I wished, it would absorb one half of that time, and not leave me enough to attend to necessary matters here. I am compelled therefore to abandon my contemplated journey for the present. I assure you, my dear Son, that I do it with great regret, for I wanted much to see you, and to see your place and the improvements you have made upon it.

As I cannot go to see you, you must come and see me. You will yourself judge of the most convenient time for you to leave home, and come here. By the first of July, I suppose your Crop will be laid by and the Season of your Jack will be over; and if you cannot come before then, you will be able to leave home at that time.

I wish you to say to Majr. [Richard] Graham how much I regret not being able to see him at his residence, as I expected and intended. I am sorry for it also on account of his suit, in which I wished to have rendered him any service in my power. But it is probable that, if his suit shall be tried at the time he expected, he may be able to engage the services of Mr. [Daniel] Webster, who left here on yesterday on his way to Louisville, and thence to St Louis, which place he will reach I suppose about the 6h. of June. His wife [Caroline LeRoy Webster] and his daughter [Julia] accompany him, and when they get there, I wish you to call and see them.

We have had a very dry Spring, in so much, that I have never seen the grass so low. But two days ago the rain began and we have had the most copious showers. Should the remainder of the Season prove good we shall be able, I trust, to make good Crops. I shall do better than I expected with Derby; and my two Jacks, Magnum Bonum, and Royale (the French Jack) have more to do than they can perform at ten dollars for mares, and 20$ & $25 for Jeanettes. If I had one or two more other Jacks, I believe they could get plenty of employment.

Henrys two mares from England have arrived, and both had Colts, but he had the misfortune to lose one of them. He had also imported Six Cows, two died on the passage, the other four arrived with four Calves. I have given him nine hundred dollars for one of the Cows and her Calf.

Should you want money to bring you home, you must inform me, or if there be not time to inform me, draw upon me.

The family are all well and join me in love to you.

ALS. DLC-TJC (DNA, M212, R10). Printed in Colton, *Clay Correspondence*, 4:414-15.
1. The special session of Congress ran from Sept. 4 to Oct. 16, 1837. 2. See 8:801.

To ALEXANDER HAMILTON Lexington, May 26, 1837

I have to thank you for the hearty laugh (which in these gloomy times is no small affair) which you afforded me by the Caricature which you did me the favor to send me.

I think that, altho' they are complicated, it would not be difficult to develope the causes which have led to the present unhappy state of our Country. But, as Congress will shortly be in Session, I shall reserve for that occasion an exposition of my views of them, and of the remedies which should be applied, if indeed there be any sure remedies.[1] I say this, in answer to your friendly suggestion that I should make a public statement of my views at this time.

In regard to the kind expression of your wish that I would consent to the use of my name for a particular office, I must say that I have seen no indications of any general desire that it should be so used; and that to allow myself to be forced upon the public attention is the last thing I should be willing to do.

Mr. Webster and his lady [Caroline LeRoy Webster] and daughter [Julia Webster][2] have passed a week with us. They left Lexington yesterday. Their reception has been very cordial and I hope satisfactory to him. P.S. As far as I have heard the suspension of Specie payments by the Banks in the West is general, without a single exception.[3]

ALS. ViU. For Hamilton—a lawyer and the son of President Washington's famous secretary of the treasury, Alexander Hamilton—see Rossiter Johnson (ed.), *The Twentieth Century Biographical Dictionary of Notable Americans. . . .* Boston, 1904. 1. He did so in his Speech in Senate, Sept. 25, 1837. *Cong. Globe*, 25 Cong., 1 Sess., 67-68. 2. Clay to Webster, March 28, 1837. 3. Speech in Senate, Jan. 11, 1837; Remark in Senate, Jan. 14, 1837.

To William Creighton, Jr., *et al.*, Lexington, May 28, 1837. Declines their invitation to a public dinner in honor of Thomas Ewing which is to be given by the Whigs of Ross County, Ohio. However, praises Ewing's "ability, his integrity, his indefatigable industry, and the soundness of his principles," and sees his recent "loss to the public service as one of the greatest which has been sustained in these disastrous times." Copy. Printed in Washington *Daily National Intelligencer*, June 23, 1837.

To DANIEL HUEY Lexington, May 30, 1837

I received the letter you did me the favor to address to me on the 24th instant, and I assure you that I perused with much interest the amount [*sic*, account] of your personal history which it contains. It is our lot to differ in opinion occasionally, but it should be the aim of all of us to prevent these differences from disturbing our amicable and social relations.

No man is infallible, and no one, therefore, should set up his own opinion as an unerring standard, to which all others must conform.

Whatever other differences exist betwixt you and me, I am happy to learn from you that we concur as to the utility of the American Colonization Society. I believe it to be an institution fraught with incalculable good, both to the United States and Africa; and that, with the help of Providence, it is destined ultimately to rid our country of the greatest evil that affects it, and to bestow on Africa the greatest blessing which it needs.

You inquire of me how you can effect your benevolent purpose of appropriating 400 acres in Illinois to the Society. Perhaps the best mode would be to convey it to the Rev. R. R. GURLEY, the Secretary, who resides at Washington city, in trust for the benefit of the Society. It was in that way Mr. [James] Madison recently made a donation to the Society.[1] It would be necessary that you should make a deed, and have it recorded in that county in Illinois in which the land lies. In the deed you could specify the trust on which the land is conveyed, and, among other things, you might provide that the land should not be sold within any term of years you might be pleased to specify.

You ask me if the Society contemplates the establishment of a colony on the western coast of America. It does not at present entertain any such view, but thinks it best to direct all its efforts to the colonies on the African coast. There ample scope exists for any number of colonies which the Society can send out. Depending, as it does, for pecuniary means almost entirely upon individual benevolence, the Society believes it would not be wise to engage in any different enterprise, at least whilst those means are so limited. It believes, also, that, looking to the great moral, religious, and political objects which it has in view, as well as to economy, Africa offers greater advantages than any other country. If, however, any other society, or individuals, should attempt to place a colony of the descendants of Africa upon our Northwest coast or elsewhere, the American Colonization Society, far from seeing their exertions with regret, would regard them with the best wishes for success and prosperity.

Should you visit this quarter of the country, I shall be happy to see you at Ashland; and, thankful for your kind wishes towards myself, I beg you to be assured that they are all cordially reciprocated. . . .

Copy. Printed in Washington *Daily National Intelligencer,* August 26, 1837. 1. See 8:871.

To ROBERT P. LETCHER Lexington, May 30, 1837

Your favor of the 28h confirms the impressions which had been previously made on my mind, as to the views of Mr. W[ebster]. I sincerely hope that your fears may not be realized as to a certain habit. I confess that I have been surprized at his exhibition of defective judgment in what concerns himself and his prospects. After the events of last fall[1] most men, who had been placed in a situation such as he was, would have recoiled instin[c]tively from a similar predicament. Perhaps however the mistake is with me, as none of us are infallible; and if he should be the Candidate of the Whig party,[2] I shall rejoice if I should prove to have been mistaken.

I hope you will not omit to perform your promise of spending a night with me prior to my departure for Washington.

ALS. KyLoF. 1. See 8:782-85. 2. On March 15, 1837, at Niblo's Saloon in New York City, Webster had delivered a lengthy speech to the "Whigs of New York." In this address he roundly criticized the Jacksonians and their "wrong-headed" policies which had brought the nation to near-collapse. He outlined, instead, his own "correct" views of the major issues of the day. He also explained the underlying political, economic, and constitutional principles that guided him in his opinions, and he called on his audience to join him in a pledge "to hold on to the last to our professed principles, to the doctrines of true liberty, and to the constitution of the country." As for himself, "Whether in public life or in private life, in the capitol or at home, I mean never to desert them." The speech was widely interpreted as the opening of his campaign for the presidency in 1840, and the points he had made were viewed as a possible platform for the Whig party. B.F. Tefft (ed.), *Speeches of Daniel Webster* (New York, n.d.), 281-329; Claude M. Fuess, *Daniel Webster,* 2 vols. (Boston, 1930), 1:60. For a discussion of Webster's strategy for the 1840 campaign, see Irving H. Bartlett, *Daniel Webster* (New York, 1978), 150-64. For Webster's "nomination" by New York Whigs, see Clay to Davis, July 3, 1837.

To Richard Graham, St. Louis, Mo., June 1, 1837. Reports that the proclamation summoning an "extra session" of Congress [25th Congress, 1st Session] to convene on September 4 [Clay to James B. Clay, May 26, 1837] causes him to cancel his plans "to visit my son [James Brown Clay]" and "to see you." Discusses the plat of the 572 91/100 acre farm he had bought for his son to work and some legal problems relating to its title [8:801]. Concludes on a political note saying that the "wretched condition" to which Van Buren "has brought our Country and its currency is enough to make [one] almost despair [Speech in Senate, January 11, 1837]." Nor is there a "disposition on the part of our Rulers or their party to correct past errors, by the application of any safe and sure remedy." ALS. MoShi.

To Stephen T. Logan, John M. Cabiness *et al.*, Springfield, Ill., June 17, 1837. States that "It had been my purpose to visit this summer my son [James B. Clay] established near St. Louis," but the "Call of an extraordinary Session of Congress [Clay to James B. Clay, May 26, 1837], by which I am left time barely sufficient to attend to my private affairs at home, deprives me of the pleasure of the excursion I intended to make." Declines, therefore, an invitation to visit Springfield, and thanks them for their "flattering and friendly Sentiments." Copy. IHi. ALS owned by James T. Hickey, Elkhart, Ill.

Logan (1800-1880) was born in Franklin County, Ky., and studied law in Glasgow, Ky. In 1832 he moved to Illinois where he became a circuit judge, a member of the state legislature, and a law partner of Abraham Lincoln. Newton Bateman (ed.), *Historical Encyclopedia of Illinois and History of Sagamon County*, 2 vols. (Chicago, 1912), 1:343. Cabiness (or Cabanis) was born in Virginia in 1783, moved to Kentucky in 1792 and to Springfield, Ill., in 1830. In the War of 1812 he commanded a company of Kentucky volunteers in the Battle of New Orleans. He was active in Whig politics for many years prior to his death on December 27, 1848. Springfield *Illinois Journal*, January 3, 1849.

To CHRISTOPHER HUGHES Lexington, June 18, 1837

This is a very rainy wet day and I have thought that I cannot employ a part of it better than to acknowledge the receipt of your favor of the 14h. April. I had heard, with much regret, of your depression of spirits of which it treats; and I rejoice to learn from you that they are now dissipated, and that "Richard is himself again." I thought you had more philosophy than to allow yourself to be affected by such a cause. Why should you? Few men have seen as much of the world as you have, or enjoyed more of it, or put more good things in and out of his mouth, or laughed more, or cracked more jokes. That, before you have passed fifty-five, you should have surrendered yourself to ennui is too bad. For shame! No more ennui, no relapses. They are unworthy of you.

I do not think that you need apprehend any recall. Mr. V[an]. Buren is too much pressed by difficulties to hazard the loss of any more friends, if indeed Genl. [Samuel] Smith[1] &c. are not regarded by him as no longer capable of injuring him. I heard nothing to induce me to suppose that they meant to bring you home. But if they were to recall you *from Sweden*, I suppose it would be no great calamity.[2]

The papers will have informed you of the Commercial and Currency Embarrassments of our Country.[3] They are dreadful and exceed all that you can imagine. Six months ago no Nation ever enjoyed more apparent prosperity; now none ever experienced a more sudden and sad reverse. It has been produced mainly by the measures of the last administration persevered in by the present. Congress is called the first monday in September,[4] but I much fear that it will be unable to devise any effectual remedy. None is conceivable which does not comprehend a Bank of the U.S.; and against the establishment of such an institution the dominant party has committed itself so often, so recently and so strongly that I do not see how they can decently or consistently agree to one.

Numerous changes among individuals have taken place; but their effect will not be known until after the elections of this summer. The Hero of the Hermitage [Jackson] has lived to hear himself cursed as bitterly and as lowdly as any of his Class of whom History treats.

I am here in the midst of tranquillity and abundance. I have around me every thing to render me comfortable and independent. One deplorable event alone continues to prey upon me. If my beloved daughter [Anne Brown Clay Erwin] had been spared me, I should have been more happy than most men at Sixty, which I have just reached.

We should be delighted to have you with us. And would not a change from the Court of Stockholm to my humble Court at Ashland be agreeable? You would get no outfit, nor salary, but we could give you here some of the good things which Salaries and Outfits command. Among others, I have, yet untaped, the Cask of S. Wine which you ordered for me, and which I received more than a year ago. And it shall remain unbroached until you come, if you will promise to come in some four or five years at farthest.

Mrs. [Lucretia Hart] Clay's health is much better than it was when you last saw her; and we now have the care of seven Grand Children, left by my two daughters.[5] Our house therefore has all the animation which it exhibited twenty years ago.

I have written you a very long letter *for me*—a proof of my esteem which I hope you will duly appreciate. I must conclude with assurances of my unabated friendship.

ALS. MiU. 1. U.S. senator from Maryland, and Hughes's father-in-law. 2. Hughes was chargé d'affaires at Stockholm from 1830 to 1842. 3. Speech in Senate, Jan. 11, 1837. 4. Clay to James Brown Clay, May 26, 1837. 5. Susan Clay Duralde's children were Martin Duralde III and Henry Clay Duralde. Anne Brown Clay Erwin's children were James Erwin, Jr., Henry Clay Erwin, Lucretia Erwin, Andrew Eugene Erwin, and Charles Edward Erwin. See Clay to Lucretia Hart Clay, March 6, 1840.

To NOAH NOBLE Lexington, June 20, 1837

I am sure that you will agree with me in thinking that the unfortunate Condition of our Common Country is such, at present, as to fill every patriotic bosom with the deepest solicitude and to animate to the greatest exertions to relieve it from its existing embarrassments. No time has ever occurred, within my knowledge, in which it was more evidently the duty of us all to repress individual aspiration or ambition and to dedicate our undivided energies to the rescue of the Country; the Constitution and the public Councils from the hands of those who have brought upon us our present difficulties and who are leading us rapidly to ruin.[1]

Whether any effective remedy for the disorders which prevail will be provided or not depends very much upon the Constitution of the approaching H. of R.[2] If the States which have now to elect members shall return the same number of Jackson or V. Buren delegates that they had in the last Congress, there will be, I think, no prospect of adopting any beneficial measure. In that event, it will be argued by the Administration party, and with much plausibility, that the People approve the past, and cling, for the future, to the same men whose policy has produced the present state of things.

In Kentucky we have a fair prospect of reducing the 4 members of the Jackson party, who were in the last Congress[3] to two, and perhaps one. Indeed there are some who are so sanguine as to believe that we shall not elect one. For myself, I would compromise at two.[4]

What are your prospects in Indiana? I hear, with regret, that in some of the Districts there is division among our friends, to such an extent as to endanger the result.[5] Can nothing be done to heal it, and to prevent such an inauspicious event. Can not, you, my dear Sir, to whom the Whigs are already so much indebted, do some thing, in the way of conciliation and harmony, to encrease their obligations to you?

I am told, particularly, that in the District lately represented by Genl [Jonathan] McCarty, if the existing divisions are not healed, a V[an]. B[uren]. member will be returned. Is it not possible to prevent that? Can not the strongest man of our party be run, and the others be prevailed upon to retire?[6] Whatever personal wishes any of us might have, in respect to the Candidates, ought to be unhesitatingly sacrificed to the good of our Country, which should be paramount.

Of Genl McCarty, I will say, without knowing what may be your feelings towards him, that when he was first elected to Congress, I regretted it; but that for the two or three last Sessions he has been a resolute, unflinching and highly useful opponent of the Administration. As he has ceased long since to be a Jackson man, we must suppose upon conviction and in all sincerity, good policy would point to his re-election, unless there be against it reasons of which I am unaware. If we discourage and discountenance Converts from the other party, we may long continue in the minority. Whilst uniform and consistent friends, who have been always faithful, ought not to be neglected, we should at the same time, in the spirit of our religion, hold out the hand of forgiveness and friendship to those erring men who sincerely repent and change. By doing so, we ultimately advance the interests of those very steadfast friends whom, for a moment, we may appear to overlook.

We have had great hopes of Indiana, arising out of the issue of your last fall election.[7] Do my dear Sir write me soon and write me, if you can, that these hopes will be realized.

ALS. In. Letter marked "(Confidential)." 1. Speech in Senate, Jan. 11, 1837. 2. Clay to Brooke, March 7, 1837. 3. The Jackson men from Kentucky in the 24 Congress, 2nd Session were: Linn Boyd, Albert G. Hawes, Richard French, and Richard M. Johnson. *BDAC* and Lexington *Observer & Kentucky Reporter*, August 12, 19, 1835. 4. In Kentucky's congressional elections of August, 1837, 1 Democrat, 11 Whigs, and 1 Independent (John Pope) were elected. *Guide to U.S. Elections*, 568. In elections for the Kentucky general assembly, 24 Whigs and 14 Democrats were elected to the senate, while 71 Whigs and 29 Democrats were elected to the house. Lewis Collins and Richard H. Collins, *History of Kentucky*, 2 vols. (Cynthiana, Ky., 1874; reprint ed., 1966), 1:42. 5. Clay to Noble, March 4, 1837. 6. In Indiana's 5th congressional district James Rariden, a Whig, defeated Jonathan McCarty, also a Whig, by the vote of 6,599 to 4,845. Riker and Thornbrough, *Indiana Election Returns*, 95-96. 7. In the Indiana general assembly elections in 1836, the Whigs had won 53 seats in the house to 43 for the Democrats, and 12 seats in the senate to 7 for the Democrats and 1 for whom no party affiliation is given. *Ibid.*, 229-35.

From Drs. Samuel M. Letcher & David Bell, Lexington, June 21, 1837. Receipt for $10.00 paid the two doctors "for Medicines & medical attendance on Negro man" named George. ADS. DLC-TJC (DNA, M212, R18). Letcher and Bell were partners with offices at 7 South Upper Street. MacCabe, *Directory of the City of Lexington . . . 1838 & '39*, p. 91. For Letcher, a graduate of Transylvania's medical school, see Robert Peter, *The History of the Medical Department of Transylvania University* (Louisville, 1905), 58, 146-47, 156. For Bell, see William H. Perrin, *History of Fayette County, Kentucky* (Chicago, 1882), 573. See also Richard L. Troutman, "The Emancipation of Slaves by Henry Clay," *JNH* (April, 1955), 40:179-81.

On April 26, 1837, Clay evidenced an interest in selling "Tom Balto. & his wife. . . . If they could be sold on a credit for undoubted paper, I should prefer it to a cash sale, at the price this would bring." See Clay to Erwin, April 26, 1837.

Clay purchased from John M. Garnett on June 17, 1839 "the following negro slaves to wit, Annis and her four children, Milton, Henry, Jane, and a young boy at the breast, which said Slaves I [Garnett] warrant to be sound, and do hereby warrant and defend the title of the said Slaves to the said H. Clay his heirs and assigns." DS, in Clay's hand. DLC-TJC (DNA, M212, R18). Endorsed on verso by Clay: "For Annis & her children." The purchase price was $1,000. Clay to cashier of the Bank of Kentucky, Lexington Branch. Payment order, June 17, 1839. ALS. Henry Clay Memorial Foundation, Lexington, Ky.

On July 30, 1840, the Rev. Edward McMahon, rector of St. Peter's Roman Catholic Church in Lexington, sold to Clay "the Negro Slave Charlotte and her son Ned for and in consideration of the sum of Six Hundred Dollars." The sale was attested by Garland Christy, local auction and commission merchant. Bill of Sale. ADS. DLC-TJC (DNA, M212, R18).

On September 5, 1840, Drs. Thomas P. Satterwhite and W.W. Whitney, Lexington physicians, submitted to Clay a bill for $197.00 for professional services rendered "Ashland" from January 11, 1837 through September 5, 1840. These included the costs of medical (including catheter insertions and bleeding), dental (extractions), surgical ("vivisection") and pharmaceutical (prescriptions) services to the white and slave residents of the plantation. The latter receiving such attention and listed by name were: Aaron, Adam, Amelia, Betsy, Bristo, Charles, Charlotte, Eliza, Giles, Lotty's daughter, Sibby, Sidney, Old Ron (at "Mansfield"), Tom, and Vesper. Other black patients treated at "Ashland" during this period are designated variously as "boy," "n[egr]o woman," "n[egr]o ch[il]d," "child," "woman," or "old N[egr]o. woman." Whites named and treated were: Miss [Sarah] Hall, housekeeper [1:309]—"vivisect[ion] & Med[icine]. [$]3.00," on January 25, 1838; one of the Duralde grandsons [Martin III or Henry C.], on January 11, 1837 for tooth extraction; and "Lady" [presumably Lucretia Hart Clay] for undesignated complaints. The cost of these services and prescriptions, $197.00, Clay paid in full on September 5, 1840. Account & Receipt. DS. DLC-TJC (DNA, M212, R18).

On October 12, 1840, in a Deed of Emancipation filed in Fayette County, Ky., Clay emancipated his slave Charlotte and her daughter, Mary Anne. He noted in the document that Charlotte had "nursed most of my children, and several of my grand Children." He specifically stated, however, that none of the children born either to Charlotte or Mary Anne prior to the date of the deed were included in the emancipation; indeed, such children remain "subject to me." Copy. Printed in Richard L. Troutman, "The Emancipation of Slaves by Henry Clay," *JNH*, (April, 1955), 40:181.

On November 9, 1840, Clay paid Garland Christy, local auctioneer and commission merchant, $3.00 as "fee & Commiss for Selling Negro man." Bill and Receipt. Clay to Christy. D. DLC-TJC (DNA, M212, R18).

In January, 1841, Clay successfully defended Robert Slaughter before the U.S. Supreme Court in the case, *Groves* v. *Slaughter*, which dealt with the validity of a promissory note in a slave purchase contract in Mississippi in 1836. See Slaughter & Ballard to Clay, January 9, 1841.

On February 1, 1841, Clay purchased from the Young & Stern store in Washington, for his body slave, Charles, a coat, pair of pants, and vest. Cost for all three garments was $34. Receipt. DS, by Young & Stern. DLC-TJC (DNA, M212, R19). Endorsed on verso by Clay: "Charless Clothes"

On June 23, 1841, in his capacity as president of the American Colonization Society, Clay executed the will (probated on September 24, 1840) of the late Alexander Watson of Charleston, S.C., by emancipating the five slave children of the more recently deceased Lizzy, also formerly a slave to Watson. Identifies the emancipated children (and their approximate ages) as Edward (2), Samuel (9), David (5), Mary (7), and Muryar (12). Copy (true). Sc. Clay to W. Thompson, County of Washington, District of Columbia, June 23, 1841. See also Clay to the State of South Carolina, February 23, 1841.

To SANFORD S. BENNETT Lexington, June 23, 1837

I have received your[1] favor of the 16h. June, and take pleasure in communicating any information in my power on the subject of it.

The best Jacks are obtained from Malta, from Spain and from the Balearic islands (Minorca & Majorca.) The first I think are in the highest repute. I understand that their price has risen in Malta, in consequence of the great demand for them within the last few years. The price now is about $250. The expences and charges of importation would amount to about $300 or $400 more. In Minorca and Majorca the price is about the same, but the charges would probably be less. What the price may be in Spain I do not know. They have no Asses in England that I would accept as a present.

I believe there are more good Asses now in Kentucky than in any other Country in the world. The price of good Jacks varies from $750 to $2000. One that I introduced into this State a few years ago has sold as high as $5000. He was the only Jack that I have ever seen that measured fifteen hands in height.[2] The ordinary height of the best Maltese Jacks is about 13½ hands. I sold three Maltese Jacks last year, one for $1000; and the other two for $1500 cash. The first was purchased by Mr. [Gwin] Tompkins and is stood by him and Mr. [Walter] Dun this year near Chillicothe.[3] After his purchase, he refused $2000 for him.

When at Louisville a few days ago, I saw 11 Asses (7 males and 4 females) which had just arrived from Malta via N. Orleans. They were a good lot, and I expect will be in the neighbourhood of Lexn. and for Sale. They were imported by a Company.

I have six Jennettes and three Jacks. The Jacks have done quite as much this Season as I wished them to perform, at $20 & $25 for Jennettes & $10 for mares. There is but one that I would sell. He is an uncommonly fine young Jack, not yet three years old, of the Maltese Strain, and about fourteen hands high. I think he will probably reach 14½. I would take $1800 for him. He is proved, and has served this year 90 mares & Jennettes.

The other two I imported this Spring from the interior of France. They cost me nearly $500 each there. I imported 2 Jacks & 7 Jennettes, but three of the latter died at Sea.[4] I do not desire to sell either of them until I have made a fair trial of them.

Considering the cost, the charges, the risk, & the uncertainty of a good selection, I should think it would be your interest to purchase here rather than to import. You would have to give a some what higher price, but then you would know what you bought, and avoid all risks & charges.

We have an annual fair or Stock Exhibition in Septr near Lexington, at which a great number of Asses is usually exhibited. That would be a good time for you to come over and look about you. I regret that I shall not then be at home; but if you choose to come prior to my departure for

Washington (about the middle of Augt.) I shall be happy to afford you any assistance in my power in selecting & purchasing.

ALS. Courtesy of Dr. Thomas D. Clark, Lexington, Ky. Addressed to Bennett in Marion, Marion County, Ohio. 1. For Bennett, an associate judge of the Marion County Court of Common Pleas and an owner of the mercantile firm of Bennett & Hardy, see John W. Jacoby, *History of Marion County, Ohio, and Representative Citizens* (Chicago, 1907), 97, 132, 139-40, 177, 215, 270; also, Leggett, Conaway & Co., *The History of Marion County, Ohio* . . . (Chicago, 1883), 300, 379, 382, 510, 522, 527. 2. Probably "Warrior." See 8:665. 3. See 8:835-36. 4. See 8:841.

From Jefferson Scott, Paris, Ky., June 26, 1837. States that the "bearer of this Chas. O'Neal [*sic*, Oneal] is the person who cured your Jack Ass at my house about two years since." Believes that "he deserves some compensation for his services and is willing to take whatever you are pleased to allow." Adds that Oneal's "avocation is that of a horse Doctor and he has some reputation in his line." ALS. DLC-TJC (DNA, M212, R18). For Scott, see *RKHS*, 37:25; 58:14. For Oneal, see *RKHS*, 44:135.

On June 29, 1837, Oneal gave Clay a receipt for $5.00 paid him "in full of the within demand." DS. DLC-TJC (DNA, M212, R18).

To David A. Hall, Washington, D.C., June 27, 1837. Thanks him for his letter and reports that "We have evidence, at a distance from Washington, in the distracted condition of the dominant party, that no plan has been devised at Head quarters for the relief of the Country, and the restoration of the soundness of the currency [Speech in Senate, January 11, 1837]. In the mean time the state of things is getting worse instead of improving. A gentleman who has just arrived here from N. Orleans informs me that as high as ten per Cent, in the local currency, was given for notes of the Bank of the U. States, as a medium of Exchange." ALS. NcD.

To MATTHEW L. DAVIS Lexington, July 3, 1837

I perceive that, in spite of your remonstrances, a meeting has been gotten up to publicly present Mr. Webster as a Candidate for the Presidency. They do not propose actually to *nominate* him but to *recommend* him for nomination. I do not think that there is much difference between the two forms. Either will be attended with the same effect of diminishing that prospect of harmony and concert, without which future, like past, efforts of the Whigs must be attended with disaster and defeat. They both equally expose the Whigs to the animadversion that their impatience will not allow them to wait until the fruit is ripe but prompts them to pluck it before it is mature. I perceive also that the wiser counsels of Col. [James Watson] Webb could not prevail, and that he was induced to compromise for a recommendation.[1] From which I infer that the feeling among the Whigs of N. York, at least in the City, is very strong or very active for Mr. Webster.

Col. Webb, I observe, recommends that the friends of other Gentlemen should, in like manner, *recommend* their favorites; and thus the National Convention, or the Whigs in Congress, will have before them evidence of the wishes of various portions of the Whig party. Fearing that the suggestion of Col. Webb may be acted upon, my object now in writing to you is to express the hope that you will exert yourself among my friends in the City to prevent any such recommendation of me at this time. I believe, as already intimated, that these recommendations, if they become general, will have all the injurious tendency, in preventing union and concert, that would be produced by positive nominations. And I wish nothing to be done by my friends, as certainly I shall myself do nothing, to prevent ultimate union and concentration upon some Candidate who may be acceptable to the great body of the Whigs. This forbearance on the part of my friends will be moreover entirely conformable with all that I have heretofore said and now think and feel in regard to the subject of the Presidency. It seems to me that we ought not, by premature action, to prevent the consummation of those changes which, it is presumable, have been wrought in the ranks of the dominant party by the absolute failure of the measures of the Administration. If, in the paroxism of the sufferings of the Country, produced by a disordered Currency and prostrated business,[2] in the first six months of a new administration, we initiate measures to determine the next Presidential election, do we not expose our patriotism to a charge of selfishness and insincerity? And shall we not drive back those of the other party who were coming out from it to oppose it or to join our standard?

I do not wish to be understood as censuring any thing that has been done in behalf of Mr. Webster. You know well my favorable opinion of him, and that I should be perfectly contented to see him at the head of our public affairs. In expressing contrary views from those which his friends entertain, as to the expediency of present action, I am far from being disposed to assume infallibility for myself or to pronounce theirs erroneous. It would be my wish only that *my* friends may concur with me as to the expediency of what concerns myself. Truth compels me to add that the cordial and distinguished reception of Mr. Webster at the West[3] (with which I have been greatly rejoiced) ought to be viewed as homage to his acknowledged ability rather than as indicating any general disposition to support him as a Candidate for the Presidency.

We are here still in the dark as to the purposes of the Admon in regard to measures for correcting the disorders of the Currency and Exchanges. My latest information from Washington is that they are not for a National bank, nor a treasury bank, but that their inclination is to cut all connexion with all banks and to collect and disburse the public revenue in specie only. I think finally they must abandon that scheme.[4] It would be a most singular spectacle to behold a hard-money Government and a paper money people. It would be base treachery on the part of the Government to lead the people into the mire and then to leave them sticking there. Under the operation of such a scheme, specie would cease altogether to circulate as money, and become exclusively a merchantable commodity; and finally the People would be unable to command it at any price to discharge their dues to the Government.

I expected that the Admon would promulgate some plan of relief prior to the approaching Elections. Their partizans are in great confusion for the want of a cue. It is perhaps better for us that they should remain in the dark.

ALS. PHi. Letter marked "(Confidential)." 1. For Webb, the editor of the *Morning Courier and New-York Enquirer*, see *DAB*. On June 28, 1837, a mass meeting of Whigs at the New York City Masonic Hall had urged the nomination of Webster. Allan Nevins (ed.), *The Diary of Philip Hone 1828-1851*, 2 vols. in 1 (New York, reprint ed., 1970), 265-66. 2. Speech in Senate, January 11, 1837. 3. Clay to Webster, March 28, 1837. 4. Speech in Senate, Sept. 25, 1837.

From John Greenleaf Whittier, New York, June 5 [*sic,* July 5], 1837. Addresses Clay "on the subject of human rights," because "thou canst not be indifferent to the condition of more than two millions of our fellow countrymen, deprived of all the rights, & shut out from all the glorious privileges & immunities of American citizens." States: "According to thy own emphatic declaration, '*Slavery is all wrong.*' " Asserts that many of the charges made against the abolitionists are false. Claims that "We are *not* the enemies of the slave=holder," but rather their hearts would go out to the slaveholder who would "throw off the shackles of a corrupt public opinion . . . & stand forth the fearless & the eloquent advocate of the rights of the *colored American*! How many prayers from the closet & around the fire-side of the free farmers of New England would arise for his welfare!"

Mentions that the number of abolitionist societies has "more than doubled during the past year," reaching a level of 1100. Believes that the subject of slavery "is fast becoming the all-enquiring one" and is bringing people of different political parties and different religious creeds together. "It is the conscience—the soul—the deep religious principle of the North that is speaking out on this subject," he says. Asks: "And will a cause, thus baptized in prayer, and associated with the holiest emotions of the soul, & the best feelings of humanity, fail of its great object? Believe it not. I will do thee the justice to believe that thou wouldst not wish it to fail."

On the subject of Texas annexation [Remark in Senate, March 1, 1837], remarks: "God grant that my fears may not be realized—but I confess I have little hope of anything else than such an annexation. I trust that *thy* voice will be raised against it." Adds that the Society of Friends would like "to entrust some petitions or remonstraces against the annexation of Texas to thy care could they be assured that thou wouldst sustain the petitions. I should be pleased to have a line from thee on the subject, as early as may suit thy convenience." ALS. DLC-HC (DNA, M212, R5). Printed in John B. Pickard (ed.), *The Letters of John Greenleaf Whittier*, 3 vols. (Cambridge, Mass., 1975), 1:241-43. For Whittier, see *DAB*. Whittier misdated the letter "6th. Mo" when it should have read the 7th month. See Clay to Whittier, July 22, 1837.

Sen. Benjamin Swift (Vt.) introduced a petition by New York and Vermont Quakers against the extension of slavery through the annexation of Texas. It was ordered to lie on the table on September 23, 1837. Clay did not introduce such a petition. U.S. Sen., *Journal*, 25 Cong., 1 Sess., 41.

From Moore, Morton & Co., Illinois Land Agency, Quincy, Ill., July 6, 1837. Report that a bookkeeping error caused them to delay paying his district tax for 1836 on section SW6. 14N. 10W. Will take care of the problem when paying the 1837 tax. "Please remit us Ten Dollars—and should there be a road tax, we will pay it in advance." ALS. DLC-TJC (DNA, M212, R12). Endorsed by Clay: "Transmitted $10 in a U[nited]. S[tates]. B[ank]. note the 28h. July 1837." See Moore, Morton & Co. to Clay, July 20, 1840.

To WADDY THOMPSON, JR. Lexington, July 8, 1837

I received your friendly letter of the 21st. Ulto. yesterday. I had expected the pleasure of hearing from you directly, as, if I am not mistaken, you promised to write to me, prior to our separation at Washington.

With the exception of one or two short excursions, I have remained at home since I reached it. Amidst my herds and flocks, and with the occupations incident to my farms, I have been quite tranquil and happy, and I regretted extremely the summons which is to take me from these quiet scenes to the turmoils of the Senate Chamber.[1] I shall be compensated for the privation of them in the pleasure, I hope, of meeting you and other friends; for I understand that, although you have resolved not again to offer for Congress, you will serve during the approaching Congress.[2] And I sincerely trust that you will revoke that resolution before it is carried into effect. We all, who serve in public life, must make sacrifices of private interests and comforts, and I hope that yours may not be too great to allow our Country to have the benefit of your services and counsels.

I received the paper, which you did me the favor to send me, containing Genl. [James] Hamilton's letter to Mr. [Nicholas] Biddle,[3] and I have attentively perused it. It is a manly production, written in excellent temper and spirit, and worthy of its high minded author. But I think nevertheless that the comments you make upon it are just. It acquits the Administration too much of blame for the existing disorders in the currency and business of the Country.[4] If the Bank Charter had not been refused to be renewed,[5] the deposites not removed,[6] the treasury Circular not issued,[7] and the Compromise [tariff] not threatened with violation,[8] I do not believe the present state of things would have existed, or would have existed in the aggravated condition which we find.

I will not burthen you with the proofs of these several propositions. But in regard to the non-renewal of the Charter, I will illustrate the remark by a statement of what took place in Kentucky. In 1832 we had no bank whatever (for I count as none the old Banks of the Comm[onweal]th. and of K. both of which were nearly wound up.) We were satisfied with the branches among us of the Bank of the U.S. We were entirely content with the currency which they and the parent institution supplied. We were reluctant to establish any local banks; but after the veto of 1832 our people could not resist the necessity, real or apparent, of having a substitute for the B. of the U.S. and the Legislature, in the three succeeding years, established three Banks whose aggregate Capital is ten millions of dollars![9] A similar augmentation of Banking Capital, in consequence of the overthrow of the B. of the U.S., took place in many if not in most of the States. Can it be doubted that these additional Banks threw out many of those facilities which occasioned the speculation and overtrading of which Genl. Hamilton treats?

And with regard to the Compromise [tariff] act, you South Carolina Gentlemen have much reason to be satisfied with your opposition to any violation of it. There cannot I think be a doubt that the constant threats to disturb it, which have been thrown out only by the Admon party, have discouraged manufacturing at home, and this has tended to swell our foreign debt by increasing the amount of our importations. And I should not be surprized to see, among the measures of relief which may be proposed, within a few years, a revival of the Protective system, in some such form as existed before the Compromise.

You ask what is to be done? No measure of relief can be conceived which does not comprehend a Bank of the U.S. and I see no prospect of establishing such an institution.[10] Undoubtedly if a declaratory amendment of the Constitution, or any other Amendmt. conveying the power to Congress to establish a Bank could be *certainly* adopted, for one I would cheerfully consent to it. But I apprehend that there will be a combination against such a measure of those who think the power already exists and those who believe, or affect to believe, in the dangers of a National institution.

I confess too that I have serious doubts whether a Bank of the U.S. aided by the Government can bring about speedily, if at all, a renewal of Specie payments. Our situation now is widely different from what it was in 1816. The financial power of the Government is less in consequence of the extinction of the public debt, and the reduction & repeal of duties. And the controlling influence of a Bank of the U.S. is less too in consequence of the multiplication of local banks.

But, my dear Sir, ought the Opposition, at the approaching Session, to bring forward any measures of relief? Ought they not to leave that duty to the party of the Administration? If indeed we should fortunately secure a majority in the H. of R.[11] then, perhaps, in *that house* it may be the duty of the Opposition to present a plan of relief. But if in both Houses the Admon posess the majority, I think we ought to profess a readiness to concur in any safe scheme for the extrication of the Country from its present embarrassments, and leave to the dominant party the performance of the duty of devising and presenting it.

The movements of Mr. Webster and his friends, in reference to the Presidential question, are to be regretted as premature.[12] Still, I think at some time or other during the next Session, that we ought to unite on some one Candidate, if possible. We shall otherwise repeat the error of delay and postponement, committed in the former canvass, and experience again defeat and discomfiture. We gave to that gentleman in the West a very cordial reception,[13] but it would be wrong to take this as evidence of a determination among the Whigs to support him for the Presidency, to the exclusion of all others. So far from being desirous that any movement should be now made for me, I have written to N. York with the express view of preventing it if I can.[14]

It is a great misfortune of the Opposition that they are not more united in respect to some one to oppose Mr. V. B. And I must say that I think this is more owing to the aspiration of individuals than to any real difference of opinion among the members of our party, in regard to public measures. Ambition has a powerful blinding effect. And I think Mr. Websters case is a shocking proof of it. Within less than six months after it had been demonstrated that he could get the vote of but one of 26 States against not a very popular Candidate, he commences a long and arduous tour with the evident purpose of becoming a Candidate again. Whilst I make this reflection, it is proper altho' perhaps unnecessary for me to say that I should greatly prefer him to Mr. V. Buren, and should think the Country safe with him at the head of our public affairs.

I think we shall reduce the 4 Jackson members from K. in the H. of R. to two possibly one.[15]

I was disappointed about my Stamboul poney intended for you; but I had taken up another which my homme des affaires has picked—a very pretty creature—the produce of an Indian mare, that I intended to send you. And I had even engaged Mr. Downing,[16] our great Horse trader, to take charge of the colt and deliver it at your house in August or Septr. But as you say that you will have no occasion for it, I shall decline sending it. Should you alter your views be pleased to say so to me and I will forward it with pleasure. It is only three years old, and will I think improve a good deal. . . . P. S. Do me the favor to make my best respects to your father.[17]

ALS. KyU. Copy printed in *The Collector* (May, 1909), 22:75-76. 1. Clay to James B. Clay, May 26, 1837. 2. For Thompson, who represented South Carolina in Congress from Sept., 1835, to March, 1841, see *BDAC* and *DAB*. 3. James Hamilton's letter to Biddle explained Hamilton's opinions of the causes of the current panic and advocated gradual elimination of the state-chartered banks and establishment of a new national bank in which the government would own only ⅛ interest. The letter was published in the Charleston *Mercury* on June 16, 1837. 4. Speech in Senate, Jan. 11, 1837. 5. See 8:434, 443, 558, 639-41. 6. See 8:583-84, 680-81, 684-85, 728. 7. See 8:860-61; Speech in Senate, Jan. 11, 1837; Remark in Senate, Jan. 14, 1837. 8. See 8:604, 621-22, 626-27. 9. For the veto of 1832, see 8:552-53, 558. The Louisville Bank of Kentucky was established by an act of Feb. 2, 1833. This bank was allowed no branches. Ky. Gen. Assy., *Acts* . . . 1832-1833, pp. 195-209. The Bank of Kentucky, which had its headquarters in Louisville and was allowed as many as six branches, was established by an act of Feb. 22, 1834. *Ibid.*, 1833-1834, pp. 618-34. The Northern Bank of Kentucky, with headquarters in Lexington, was allowed not less than three or more than four branches and was created by an act of Feb. 20, 1835. *Ibid.*, 1834-1835, pp. 166-181. 10. Comment in Senate, Sept. 26, 1837; Speech in Senate, May 21, 1838. 11. Clay to Brooke, March 7, 1837. 12. Clay to Letcher, May 30, 1837. 13. Clay to Webster, March 28, 1837. 14. Clay to Davis, July 3, 1837. 15. Clay to Noble, June 20, 1837. 16. Probably Richard W., Josiah, or Samuel Downing, a family of well-known farmers and horse traders. William A. Leavy, *A Memoir of Lexington And Its Vicinity* (written 1875; printed Lexington, 1944), 360. 17. For Waddy Thompson, Sr., see Johnson, *Twentieth Century Biographical Dictionary*.

To SAMUEL L. SOUTHARD — Lexington, July 11, 1837

I congratulate you on your recent appointment of President to the Morris Canal Bank, which I have heard with the more pleasure since it will not occasion your loss to the Senate, I understand.[1] Tell me how that is.

I begin to entertain hopes that there may be a majority in the next H. of R. opposed to the Admon.[2] Such a majority might prevent mischief if it could not effect good. In this State, I think we shall reduce the Jackson members to two, possibly one.[3] Govr [Noah] Noble writes me that in Indiana the Whigs will elect six, possibly all.[4] If we realize our hopes in Maryland & R. Island,[5] and do not lose else where, we may be able to secure a majority in the House.

Have you any information whether the Admon have formed any and what plan for the remedy of the disorders in the currency and business of the Country which the Executive has brought about?[6]

My family, with the exception of Mrs. [Lucretia Hart] Clay, are well. She has been ill, but is getting better. I hope this will find you and your's all well. . . .

ALS. NjP. 1. Southard held both the bank presidency and his Senate seat until his death in 1842. *BDAC*; *DAB*. 2. Clay to Brooke, March 7, 1837. 3. Clay to Noble, June 20, 1837. 4. Clay to Noble, March 4, 1837. 5. In Rhode Island two Whigs—

Robert B. Cranston and Joseph R. Tillinghast—were elected to the U.S. House. *Guide to U.S. Elections*, 568. In Maryland 5 Whigs and 4 Democrats were elected to the House. *Ibid.* 6. Speech in Senate, Jan. 11, Sept. 25, 1837.

From MATTHEW L. DAVIS New York, July 12, 1837

Your letter of the 16th ult was received in due course of mail; that of the 3d. Int was received this day. I owe you an apology for an apparent neglect in not acknowledging the receipt of the former at an earlier period, but I have been overwhelmed with various avocations.

Your friends here *have* acted; *are* acting, and *will* act, not only with discretion, but what is equally important, with *Effect*. All is well. Good is coming out of evil. The movement of Mr. Websters friends[1] have produced a feeling and an action among those who disapprove of the measure, that was not anticipated even by me. I repeat—*We are doing well.* Now for details.

Your friend, Governor [James T.] Morehead and several other gentlemen were present at a Scene between Mr [Hiram] Ketchum and myself, which gave rise to some excitement, and some animated, if not warm remarks. My fixed and solemn determination, if an attempt was made to *nominate* Mr Webster, was fully expressed. This interview contributed, probably, to a change of measures on the part of Mr Webster's friends, and induced a pledge that they would support the nomination of a Convention. This was a point gained; and while I considered a *recommendation* and a *nomination*, in effect the same thing, yet I deemed it most prudent (with the *pledge*) to let it pass sub silentio.

Mr. [James Watson] Webb thought, that in a Convention Daniel Webster had no chance of a nomination and therefore that he could, ultimately, render more Service in supporting the Convention nomination by the policy which he was about to adopt, than by attempting to breast the Storm. He entertained the opinion, also, that the friends of each Candidate ought to, and would recommend their man. Now, I differed with him on both these points; but he has pursued the bent of his own inclination, and will, in the sequel, go for that Individual who shall appear most likely to concentrate the Whig force.

I admit, and I urged as an objection to the recommendation of Mr Webster, by a public meeting, that it was calculated to create an impression abroad—"that the Whigs in the City of New York were very strong, or very active for him."[2] But this is not true, and the *effect* of the recommendation, in this particular will be counteracted. Means have already been adopted, and others are in progress, to meet the case. The first movement is, to *prevent*, as far as practicable, the Whigs in other parts of our State, such as Poughkeepsie, Hudson, Albany, Utica, Canandagua [*sic*, Canandaigua] Geneva Buffalo, &c. from responding to this recommendation. After which our attention will be turned to other States.

Some of your friends have had two meetings. About One hundred convened on Thursday Evening the 6th.[3] They appointed a Committee of *One* from Each Ward (seventeen Wards) to report a plan of organization. Some of the persons present were for a public meeting and recommending, as suggested by Col Webb, but the proposition was withdrawn, and the understanding was general, that no question should be pressed to a vote, when we were not *unanimous*. We meet again tomorrow night to receive the report of this Committee. Their report is not yet agreed upon. But my impressions are, that we shall have a General Committee of *One hundred and Seventy*. An Executive Committee of *two* or *three* from each ward say 34 or 51; and a Corresponding Committee of from seven to fifteen. The 170 will consist of electioneering men, taken from the mass of the Clay party. The Executive and Corresponding Committees, however, will be the efficient bodies.

Rest assured that I speak with sincerity when I say, that the force which we are now in a condition to call into action, if deemed Expedient, is at least *double* what I thought it was possible for us to command. The movement of Messrs Ketchum, [Joseph] Hoxie, [Rufus] King, Talman[4] & Co is considered as a species of *dictation*. In every stage of this proceeding, I have pronounced it high handed, impudent, and dictorial—worthy the Champions of the black cockade in 1798. These views were expressed in the presence of your Governor. I feel not the same charity for these men, that you appear to feel.[5] I declare before high Heaven, that I believe their motives to be selfish and mercenary, totally unconnected with a patriotic emotion. But they have awakened men who were slumbering at their posts, and the most beneficial consequences must follow.

If delegates were now to be chosen to attend a Convention, we should certainly carry *twelve* probably *thirteen*, possibly *fourteen* out of the *Seventeen* Wards. The friends of General [William H.] Harrison almost to a man, are acting in our ranks. I repeat, with Entire confidence, that a large majority of the Whigs in this City are with us.

I know not whether the fact has been communicated to you, but the letter which you received in May, signed by Stephen Wakeman, Charles Smith Junr. and J[eromus]. Johnson was a forgery. Mr Wakeman is a Jackson man. No such meeting as the letter refers to, was ever held. Wakeman called on Mr. [Mordecai M.] Noah and showed him your letter. As I knew through Noah, the contents of it, I did not call on Wakeman. The answer was such as I should have anticipated from you, and the more especially in a case where you could recognise none of the signatures.[6] No public attention has been made to it, and for the very good reason, I suppose, because nothing could be gained by it.

The division in the Regency ranks are rapidly Extending. The [Samuel] Beardsley's, with the Talmadges [*sic*, Nathaniel P. Tallmadge] are denounced by [Silas] Wright, [Azariah C.] Flagg & Co.[7] How much longer "the Spoils of Victory" will be sufficiently powerful to keep them together is a problem.

ALS. DLC-TJC (DNA, M212, R10). 1. Clay to Davis, July 3, 1837. 2. Quoted from *ibid.* 3. Clay to Committee of N.Y. City Whigs, August 8, 1837. See also Morris, "The New York Whigs, 1834-1842," Ph.D. dissertation, University of Rochester, 1970, p. 221. 4. It is unclear whether the Talman referred to is George F., James T., or John H. See Thomas Longworth, *Longworth's American Almanac, New York Register, and City Directory*. New York, 1836. 5. Clay to Davis, July 3, 1837. 6. Possibly a reference to a letter mentioned in Clay to Hamilton, July 18, 1837. 7. Clay to Henry Clay, Jr., Jan. 28, 1837.

From George S. Bryan, Charleston, S.C., July 14, 1837. States that the "Whigs in this quarter of the Country have been surprized and pained at the nomination of

Mr Webster in N.Y. as a Candidate for the suffrages of the Whig party throughout the Union [Clay to Davis, July 3, 1837]." Notes that "It does seem to us that they cannot have regarded his relationship to the South, in this unfortunate proceeding. He has never acted with the South: from the war [of 1812] down to the compromise [tariff of 1833], on every question of interest or feeling, he has been uniformly opposed to it. If he is to be the candidate of the Party, the South will be thrown by irresistible necessity into the arms of the President. He is the very man whom Mr Van Buren desires to *coop* the South for him. If I can infer any thing from the manner of his reception at the West, I would conclude, that he is not the first choice of that important section of the country. The homage is paid to talent, and is the offspring of respect and hospitality. Should the West take him up, the growing connection between the South and west will be rudely severed." Adds that although "Genl Harrison is held in greater personal kindness, it is my deliberate opinion that similar political results would flow from his being the candidate." Emphasizes that the "South looks to yourself as the only man in the Nation, whom abandoning her first choice [John C. Calhoun], she can support. In your history, position, character and principles, she finds something in common, and would cheerfully consent to accept of your name, as a fair Compromise. I hope you still continue a passive position and hold yourself at the disposal of the Nation. You will find that the Charleston Mercury has put you in nomination. It speaks the feeling and wish of our State."

Reports that "When Mr Calhoun passed thro' here, he spoke of you to me on terms of great Kindness and confidence—Mr [William C.] Preston with Enthusiastic regard and admiration." Mentions that "Mr [James L.] Petigru who is now on his way to the West has seperated himself from Mr [Joel R.] Poinsett," has "no confidence" in Van Buren, and is now "among your warmest admirers." Reports also that "Col [William] Cumming [5:234; 7:269] has abandoned the administration—and Come out for [George R.] Gilmer. They calculate Electing him by 5000 majority." ALS. DLC-HC (DNA, M212, R5).

For Bryan (1809-1905), a Charleston lawyer and later a federal judge, see Harold Chase *et al.* (eds.), *Biographical Dictionary of the Federal Judiciary* (Detroit, 1976), 34; and *SCHGM*, 49:222. On July 8, 1837, the Charleston *Mercury* had stated that Clay was "the only man" on whom the northern Whigs "can rally a conquering party." For Petigru, a Unionist Whig leader and law partner of James Hamilton, see *CAB*; *DAB*. George R. Gilmer, the states' rights candidate, defeated William Schley, the Unionist candidate, for the governorship of Georgia on October 2, 1837, by a vote of 34,178 to 33,417. *DAB*; *BDGUS*, 1:289-90.

From Matthew L. Davis, New York, July 15, 1837. Reports that the Clay Whigs in New York City "met on the Evening of the 13th. and compleated our organization [Davis to Clay, July 12, 1837], without a *dissenting voice* on any question that was presented. We appointed a General Committee of One hundred and seventy, of which Genl Robert Swartwout [5:28] was chosen chairman;—Ward Executive Committees of ten for each ward;—a General Executive Committee of seventeen;—a finance committee of *nine*, and a corresponding Committee of *nine*. The zeal which was evinced and the determination to act forthwith, so far as it is proper to act, leave no doubt on my mind, as to the character of the delegates which would be sent to a convention, if the Whigs were now called upon to make such appointments. I speak of the State, as well as of the City of New York."

Adds that "Mr. Websters friends, by their premature and indiscreet movements [Clay to Davis, July 3, 1837] have done us much good. I felt it my duty to *state*, not *read* to the meeting your feelings on the subject, so far as it applied to *yourself*, and did not omit noticing your liberality towards Mr. Webster's friends, but took occasion to add, that I did not concur in this sentiment. We have the rank and file with us; and the Effect of what has already been done, is to have brought into our ranks, some of the most active in the late proceedings." ALS. InU. Copy in OHi.

To ALEXANDER HAMILTON Lexington, July 18, 1837

The letter addressed by me to some Gentlemen in the City of N. Y.,[1] on the subject of the next Presidency, was in reply to one which I received from them, as a Commee. appointed by a preliminary meeting of some of my friends. I retained no copy of it, and regret therefore that I cannot comply with the request for a copy contained in your favor of the 29h. Ulto.

Further reflection has served to confirm my opinion that any public agitation of the question of the next President, at this time, is premature and unwise. The public mind is absorbed with the pecuniary embarrassments of the Country;[2] and all thoughts are now directed more to the means of the preservation than the future command of the Vessel of State. The Whigs, by stirring the Presidential subject, at this time, expose themselves to the danger of bringing the sincerity and disinterestedness of their patriotism into doubt. And I think, prior to the presentation of the name of any Candidate, whether in the form of recommendation, or a positive nomination, that a strenuous exertion should be made at Washington to bring about union and concert in behalf of some particular person. Without that every thing will be hazarded, if not lost.

The details for a Bank of the U. S. and in respect to proper denominations of Bank notes, suggested in your letter, will deserve serious consideration, after it shall be ascertained that a Nat. Bank *can* be established. For one, I must say, that I have constantly thought that there was no likelihood that such an institution would be formed during the Administration of Mr. V[an]. B[uren]. He and all his prominent friends stand too strongly committed against it; and I observe that the recent movements of the dominant party in your State continue to manifest a determined opposition to any Nat. Bank.[3] Several suggestions have been made of the expediency of an amendmt. of the Constitution conferring the power upon Congress to establish a Bank, in express terms; but I do not remark that any of these suggestions are made by prominent prints, or persons, of the V. Buren party.

Mr. [William M.] Gouge (the author of the work on banking,[4] paper money &c) has sent me a Copy of a pamplet lately published by him,[5] in which he endeavors to prove the practicability and expediency of the Governmt disconnecting itself from all banks. He thinks that it ought to demand and pay nothing but specie, and that its fiscal affairs may be safely managed by a system of Sub-treasuries,[6] properly located. If, as I have heard, he be an officer in the Treasury department,[7] this plan may have been put forward, with its sanction, and to feel the public pulse. But, if that be the real scheme of the Administration, it would imply a base and treacherous dereliction of the duty of Góvernment. It would, in effect be to say to the People, you have been brought into your present Calamitous condition by the measures of Government, and, now, the Government will take care of itself and leave you to emerge, as you may, from the ruinous embarrassments by which you are surrounded.

We shall so soon be called at Washington to deliberate on all these grave matters that I will now add nothing but assurances of the respect and regard of. . . .

ALS. DLC-Alexander Hamilton Papers (DNA, M212, R21). 1. Possibly Stephen Wakeman, Jeromus Johnson, and Charles Smith, Jr., mentioned in Davis to Clay, July 12, 1837. 2. Speech in Senate, Jan. 11, 1837. 3. For the shifting alignments of New York Democrats on the issue of whether to adopt a state bank, a national bank, or a subtreasury system, see James R. Sharp, *The Jacksonians versus the Banks: Politics in the States After the Panic of 1837* (New York, 1970), 297-305. 4. For Gouge, an uncompromising opponent of banks and paper money, see *DAB*. He had written *A Short History of Paper Money and Banking in the United States. . . .* Philadelphia, 1833. A second edition was published in New York in 1835. 5. Gouge had recently published *An Inquiry into the Expediency of Dispensing with Bank Agency and Bank Paper in Fiscal Concerns of the United States.* Philadelphia, 1837. 6. Clay to Davis, July 3, 1837. 7. Gouge was a clerk in the Treasury Department from 1834 to 1841. *DAB.*

To JOHN G. WHITTIER Lexington, July 22, 1837

I duly received your favor of the 5h. inst. and hope you will excuse me for writing very briefly on the several subjects of which it treats. I certainly do, as you suppose, feel great concern in regard to the condition of the African portion of our population. I have so often expressed my sentiments, in respect to Slavery, that it is not necessary now to repeat them. Without looking to the Religious aspect of the question, all my reflections have satisfied me that it is unjust, and injurious both to the Master & Slave.

But whilst I say this, candor obliges me to express my deep regret that the Abolitionists at the North have deemed it their duty to agitate the question of immediate emancipation. I will not impute to them bad motives, nor stop to examine their right to entertain and discuss the question. But I must say that I think their proceedings are highly injurious to the slave himself, to the master, and to the harmony of the Union. I believe that, instead of accelerating, they will retard, abolition, and, in the mean time, will check other measures of benevolence and amelioration. This, no doubt, was not intended, but it is nevertheless absolutely Certain.

I am not aware that the annexation of Texas to the U.S. will ever become a question for general consideration.[1] I learn that the desire of becoming a part of the U.S. is weakening in Texas. Should the question arise, it will be necessary to weigh, with great deliberation, all the probable consequences both of admission and exclusion. Slavery is only one of many considerations which will come up. I do not think that the question should be decided *exclusively* by that. Should there be a decided opposition by a large portion of the U.S. to the admission of Texas into our National family, that fact ought to have great, if not conclusive, influence in the determination of the question.

I think those Gentlemen at the South have been unwise who have expressed a wish for the incorporation of Texas *in order to strengthen the Slave interest*; and I should think it also unwise in Gentlemen at the North to avow the opposite ground, as a motive for action.

As for myself, I shall reserve my judgment for all the lights of which I can avail myself when the proposition of annexation shall be made, if it ever be made. It may become a matter of serious enquiry whether the spread of slavery and the introduction of Slaves from Foreign Countries may not be more successfully prevented by taking Texas in the Union than keeping her out of it.

ALS. Courtesy of Dr. John C. Hepler, Mount Pleasant, Michigan. Printed in John C. Hepler (ed.), "John G. Whittier Hears from Henry Clay," ***RKHS*** **(April, 1953), 51:171-72. Letter marked "(Private)."   1. Remark in Senate, March 1, 1837; Whittier to Clay, July 5, 1837.**

To Unknown Recipient, *ca.* late July, 1837. Thanks him for his "friendly wishes and feelings towards me." Continues: "If I have been, during my public career, sensible of great injustice having been done me, I have nevertheless had the consolation of knowing that I possessed the esteem and confidence of many good men." Says he will be happy if he can "outlive [the] calamities which have befallen" the country, calamities "which I have in vain struggled to avert. As for myself personally, I wish nothing, seek nothing, expect nothing from the public." Copy, extract. Printed in *Niles' Register* (August 12, 1837), 52:370.

From William E. Channing, Newport, R.I., August 1, 1837. This is a lengthy, widely publicized and circulated open letter to Clay summarizing the various arguments—historical, moral, theological, pacifist, isolationist, anti-slavery, and cultural—against the annexation of Texas by the United States; and arguing that the annexationist movement was a conspiracy of slaveowners seeking to augment their power in the Union. William E. Channing, *The Works of William E. Channing* (2 vols., Boston, 1853; 2 vols. in 1, reprint ed., New York, 1970), 752-81. See Remark in Senate, March 1, 1837. For Channing, see *DAB*. This letter furnished an important weapon for the anti-annexationists to use in their fight. See Madeleine Hooke Rice, *Federal Street Pastor, The Life of William Ellery Channing* (New York, 1961), 230-34. See also Frederick Merk, "A Safety Valve Thesis and Texan Annexation," *MVHR* (December, 1962), 49:414.

From Oliver Dangerfield, Georgetown, S.C., August 3, 1837. Reports that he has recently "traversed South Alabama Georgia & So. Carolina" and that "Every step I travel convinces me more and more that you ought to be a candidate at the next election for President." Is certain Alabama and Georgia will support Clay; however, "in Carolina it is not so certain, but to secure [John C.] Calhoun, [George] McDuffie and a few others gives you the State and this may be done." Believes Calhoun's "Nullification heresy . . . has postponed his pretensions for at least 8 years to come, and neither Webster, nor Harrison can get the Votes of Mississippi, Louisiana, Alabama, Georgia or So. Carolina," while Clay could carry these plus "all the States who would vote for Webster or Harrison." Therefore, urges him to begin organizing early "so as to let us know how our efforts are to be directed; the light troops should at least be in the field, and feel the enemy by skirmishing, in this part of the service I shall lead the Cossacks, and we shall charge with a hurrah!" AL. DLC-HC (DNA, M212, R5). Letter was sent under cover addressed to John Tilford, Lexington, with a note explaining that "in these squally times correspondence with certain characters is always subjected to the casualty of never reaching its destination."

To SAMUEL L. SOUTHARD   Lexington, August 3, 1837

I duly recd. your favor of the 25h. Ulto. and was highly gratified with the honorable manner of your recent appointment,[1] and especially with the reservation you made of your right to retain your Seat in the Senate.

I have made no arrangements respecting boarding for the next Session and shall make none until I reach the City. I should be very glad if we could all get together again.[2]

[John J.] Crittenden & family I believe are well.

We have just heard of our defeat at Balto. which I regret extremely.[3] I hope we shall be compensated by the result of elections elsewhere during this month.

My respects to the Ladies [Mrs. Southard and Virginia Southard]. I am sorry that I cannot prevail upon Mrs. [Lucretia Hart] Clay to meet them next winter.

ALS. NjP. 1. Clay to Southard, July 11, 1837. 2. During the 25th Congress, 1st Session, Clay, Southard, and John J. Crittenden boarded at Mrs. Handy's at the corner of Sixth and Louisiana Avenue. During the 2nd session, they moved to Mrs. S.A. Hill's, nearly opposite Gadsby's; during the 3rd session, the three men split up, with Clay, joined by five others, boarding at Mrs. Arguelle's which was also near Gadsby's. Goldman and Young, *United States Congressional Directories*, 317, 330, 345. 3. In the U.S. House elections in Baltimore in 1837, two Democrats and one Whig were elected. *Guide to U.S. Elections*, 568.

To ROBERT P. LETCHER Lexington, August 5, 1837

I should be very glad to be able to take the [excursion to Lancaster] as invited by your favor of the 4h. inst. independent of any public considerations; but I regret that it is not in my power. In a fortnight from tomorrow I expect to take my departure for Washn. and the intermediate time is too important to my private affairs to allow of my leaving home.

I should be very glad to see you here, if possible. I wish to let you know what has been done, and is doing, about bringing me out as a Candidate &c. I have several communications, letters &c. I have given no consent to the use of my name; and shall hesitate much before I do. They write me from N. York that, notwithstanding the recent movement there for Mr. W[ebster].[1] a decided majority of the Whigs are for me in that City.[2] But I think all public agitation of the question at present is premature.

ALS. ViU. 1. Letcher to Clay, May 30, 1837. 2. Davis to Clay, July 12, 1837.

To COMMITTEE OF NEW YORK CITY WHIGS[1] Lexington, August 8, 1837

I duly received the letter which you did me the honor to address to me on the 20th ult.[2] transmitting a copy of the proceedings adopted at preliminary meetings held by some of my friends in the city of New York, in relation to the next Presidential Election. And I have read them, as well as your letter, with respectful attention and interest. I now beg leave to communicate to you the impressions I entertain of the matters of which they treat.

On the question of the propriety of agitating the public at this time, by a discussion of the fitness of candidates for the Presidency, I entirely concur in the opinion expressed by you, that it would be altogether premature. Six months have not elapsed since the official termination of the last election, and more than three years and a half remain of the term which was then filled. The country is moreover suffering under a great calamity.[3] All minds are absorbed by the consideration in respect to measures of immediate relief. At such a moment, to divert or distract the public attention by introducing another exciting but remote topic, seems to me unwise. In expressing this sentiment, it is far from my purpose to convey any reproach or censure towards those who have taken a different view.[4] They have supposed, and it is quite likely that they were right in supposing, that the only adequate remedy which can be found for existing evils, will be a change of the rulers by whose agency they have been produced or continued. But the necessity of some earlier relief is so great, and the expediency of bringing to the consideration of it a spirit of moderation, forbearance and conciliation, is so obvious, that I think we should first direct our united exertions exclusively to this single object. We shall soon ascertain how far the Administration will co-operate with the country in the restoration of a sound state of things.

To guard against misconception, I ought to add that too much delay as well as too much precipitation should alike be avoided, in arrangements connected with the next election of a Chief Magistrate. Precipitation would expose the disinterestedness of our patriotism to animadversion; protracted delay to the danger of division and defeat.

I agree with you, gentlemen, entirely, in thinking, in regard to a candidate for the Presidency, that some mode should be adopted for collecting the general sense of those who believe that the purity of our institutions, and the preservation of our liberties require a change in the Executive, and none better appears to me to have been suggested [than] that of a National Convention.[5]

This will not supersede the previous employment of all proper means to produce union, harmony and concentration. A resort to such means is recommended by their tendency to prevent those unpleasant collisions in the choice of Delegates to the Convention, which might leave among the friends of the respective persons thought of as candidates a state of irritated feeling, unfavorable to that hearty co-operation in the final struggle, so essential to success.

It cannot be too strongly impressed upon our friends that the question of the selection of the particular individual to accomplish those patriotic purposes which we have in view, although not unimportant, is of subordinate consequence. It should never be allowed to become the paramount object, nor to divide more than is absolutely unavoidable, those who agree in the general principle.

Having said this much upon the general subject, suffer me now to add a few words in relation to myself personally. You are pleased to honor me with your confidence and attachment, to appreciate highly my public services, and to desire to place me in the highest station of the government. I am profoundly grateful to you and to all other friends who cherish towards me similar feelings and sentiments. For several years I have not looked to the event of my being placed in the office of Chief Magistrate, as probable. My feelings and inclinations having taken a different direction. Whilst I am not insensible of the exalted honor of filling the highest office in the gift of this great people, I have desired and sought retirement from the cares of public life; and although I have not been able fully to gratify this disposition, I am in the enjoyment of comparative repose, and looking anxiously forward to more. I should be extremely unwilling, without the strongest reasons, to hazard this tranquillity, and be thrown into the turmoil of a Presidential canvass. Above all, I am most desirous not to seem, as in truth I am not, importunate for any public office whatever; nevertheless, if I were persuaded that a majority of my fellow-citizens wished to assign me to their highest executive office, that sense of duty by which I have ever been guided, would prompt obedience to their will; candor, however, obliges me to say, that I have not seen sufficient evidence of such a wish.

Entertaining these feelings and sentiments, and having resolved to occupy a position of perfect passiveness, I think it best to adhere to that resolution. Should a National Convention of the friends of reform nominate any other person, he shall have my hearty wishes for his success, and my cordial support; and before the assembling of such a Convention, if one should be agreed upon, there may be such demonstrations of the popular will as clearly to trace the line of duty towards our common country. Requesting, gentlemen, you and all who participate[d] in the proceedings of the meetings forwarded to me, to accept my respectful and grateful acknowledgments. . . .

Copy. Printed in *The New Yorker*, Dec. 30, 1837, under date of August 8, and in Colton, *Clay Correspondence*, 4:415-17, under date of August 6 with minor variations in wording. 1. The committee consisted of Noah Cook, Horace Greeley, William A. Lawrence, A.R. Wyckoff, Willis Hall, Daniel Ullmann, Dudley Selden, Adoniram Chandler, Gulian C. Verplanck, and Matthew L. Davis. See also Davis to Clay, July 12, 1837. 2. The committee had written Clay from New York City on July 20, 1837, to report on the meeting held in their city on July 6 by Whig friends of Clay. They stated "that after much enquiry . . . they feel confident that a decided majority of them [Whigs] in this City are favorable to the nomination of Henry Clay, as a candidate for the presidency, and they have strong reason for believing, that those feelings and sentiments pervade the State of New York." Think also that the recommendation of Webster for president by some New York Whigs will have a "tendency . . . we fear to be mischievous if not disastrous"; because, "Any attempt, this early, to designate a presidential Candidate, we believe would expose us to the charge, however unfounded, of wanting patriotism, acting as mercenaries, and scrambling for 'the spoils of victory.' " Feel that "our undivided efforts should be devoted against the men who by misrule have brought unparalleled sufferings upon our common country," and conclude "that our present object is to write our Whig friends in favor of a General Convention, to limit our exertions to that, and ultimately to be governed by its recommendation." ALS. DLC-TJC (DNA, M212, R10). See also Clay to Letcher, May 30, 1837. 3. Speech in Senate, Jan. 11, 1837. 4. Clay to Letcher, May 30, 1837; Clay to Davis, July 3, 1837. 5. Porter to Clay, Nov. 14 and Dec. 30, 1837.

To PHILIP R. FENDALL Lexington, August 8, 1837

I recd. your favor of the 1st. inst. On the subject of the proposed publication of the Speeches[1] we will confer together and decide when I have the pleasure of seeing you at Washington, which I expect to have shortly.

I thank you for your friendly offer to procure Boarding for me.[2] It is a matter of so much consequence to one's personal comfort that I must defer making an engagement until I reach the City.

The rumor to which you refer can hardly be true. I do not see how it is possible for Mr. V[an]. B[uren]. to be in favor of a Nat. Bank as the Constitution now is.[3]

We are in the midst of our elections which as far as we have yet heard are going better than ever. It is even possible that Col. [Richard M.] Johnson may have a Whig successor.[4]

ALS. NjMoHP. 1. The only Clay speech recorded as having been published in Washington in 1837 was his Senate speech of Jan. 16, 1837. It was titled *Expunging Resolutions*. Washington, 1837. 2. Clay to Southard, August 3, 1837. 3. Speech in Senate, Sept. 25, 1837; Comment in Senate, Sept. 26, 1837; Speech in Senate, May 21, 1838. 4. Johnson, who was elected vice president in 1836, had previously been a member of the U.S. House. In his old district William W. Southgate, a Whig, defeated the Democrat, Jefferson Phelps, in 1837 by a margin of 4,457 votes to 4,116. *Guide to U.S. Elections*, 568.

To ALEXANDER HAMILTON Lexington, August 8, 1837

I recd. by the Express Mail your obliging letter of the 2d. inst. communicating the wish of yourself and other friends that I would consent to the publication of my letter addressed to you on the 18h. Ulto.[1] You will probably be surprized when I tell you that I kept no copy of that letter, and consequently I have no recollection of its precise language. It was written in the confidence and carelessness of private correspondence. It may possibly contain expressions which may bear, or may be construed to bear, injuriously on others.

Under these circumstances, I should be unwilling to consent to its publication.

I received your previous favor, and in the consideration of the important matters of which it treats, I shall avail myself of your reflections.[2]

We are in the midst of our general election; and from present appearances there is reason to hope that Kentucky will not send to the H. of R. more than one [Democrat], instead of four in the last Congress, friendly to the Administration.[3]

ALS. DLC-Alexander Hamilton Papers (DNA, M212, R21). 1. Clay to Hamilton, July 18, 1837. 2. Reference obscure, since the previous letter from Hamilton has not been found. 3. Clay to Noble, June 20, 1837.

To GEORGE D. PRENTICE Lexington, August 14, 1837

From numerous communications and circumstances, I think it probable, that, whatever may be my own inclination or disposition, I shall be again forced into the Presidential arena. It is right that I should put *you* in possession of some of the information which has reached me.

In the City of N. York, notwithstanding and subsequent to the movement there for Mr. Webster,[1] my friends spontaneously resolved to organize.[2] From all the Wards, a Comee. of 170 was formed, sub divided into other Comees. of Correspondence Finance &c. And they tell me that they have ascertained that a decided majority of the Whigs prefer me in that City. The Comee. has addressed me, and I have replied.[3] Perhaps my reply may be published. I take the ground of entire passiveness; that I do not wish my name used, unless there is reason to believe it is wanted by a majority of the Country &c

Col. [James W.] Webb of the [New York] Courier [*and Enquirer*] writes me that Mr. W[ebster']s. friends have utterly ruined his prospects; that I will be certainly elected; and that he is perfectly satisfied with it. He notifies me that in no event will the North go for Genl [William Henry] Harrison.

Genl. P[eter]. B. Porter assures me that in the West of N. York I am greatly prefered to all others and that Mr. W. is only a secondary choice.

From N. England they write me that I am prefered to any other Candidate, and I am assured that even in Massachusetts I should get a larger vote than Mr. W.[4]

Letters from So. Carolina, state an utter repugnance to Mr. W. less but still a decided aversion from Genl H. a preference for Mr. Calhoun, and next to him for me.[5]

In Louisiana, they speak with great confidence of its preferring me to all others.

I have reason to believe that both in Tennessee and in Georgia great progress has been made and is making in feelings and sentiments favorable to me.

A member of the Ohio Convention recently assembled assured me that there were not 13 members of that body who themselves preferred Genl. Harrison.[6]

Such is a general but rapid view of the information which has reached me.

Assuming the rumors to be true, which have come to us about the Elections in K.[7] Tennessee[8] and Indiana,[9] and arguing from the effect of known causes, the downfall of the present administration is inevitable.

As a necessary consequence some Whig must be elected, if we can unite in favor of any one.

I think,

First that a National Convention to designate a Candidate in any and every event is desirable.[10] If there be no previous agreement and understanding about a Candidate such a Convention is indispensible. If there be such an understanding then the Convention will be still necessary altho' its duties will be lighter.

But 2dly. That every exertion ought to be made during the approaching Session of Congress to produce concentration. With it, all will go well. Without it, it is to be feared that we shall, in the collisions to elect delegates to the N[ational]. Convention, have all the consequences and heart-burnings without the fruits of an election. And the parties, contending for their respective favorities, will be in a state of irritated feeling ill adapted to united exertion on the final struggle. Still, if there can be no union upon any one; and if different sections will persevere in pressing their peculiar choices, a N. Conventn. objectionable as it is, upon that supposition, will be the only remaining alternative.

I will now say a few words about myself. I have no wish, not the least wish, to be run without a high degree of probability of success. If there be a Convention, I shall most cheerfully acquiesce in its decision, be it what it may.

But I do not like to be run down by other Candidates or would be Candidates on our own side.

They talk of prejudices against me in the Jackson or V. Buren party, as if that party were to elect a *Whig* Presidt.! as if there were not prejudices against Mr. Calhoun more recent; against Mr. Webster of more strength and of longer standing! &c.

The truth is that if there be a Whig Presidt. elected it will be by the Whigs, consisting of the present Whig party, and of converts to it from the V. Buren party. These converts not only do not retain those prejudices against me but are anxious to atone for former injuries. Witness the present & known feelings of Louis McLane, Dudley Selden, Verplank [*sic*, Gulian C. Verplanck] &c &c.[11]

In all notices of the P. question, which the Whig Press should take, sound policy, as well as justice, requires that all who are spoken of as Candidates and their friends should be treated with the utmost delicacy, and in a spirit of true conciliation.

Without instituting invidious comparisons my friends may point to my services, to my sacrifices, to the calumnies of which I have been the object if not the victum, to my early prediction of the fatal effects of electing Genl Jackson, to the uniformity of my opposition to him, and to my denunciation of those measures which have spread bankruptcy and ruin throughout the Land.

I think it premature to hold public meetings now and publicly to discuss at large the P. question; but perhaps some such occasional notice of me as I have hinted may serve to counteract the efforts to put me aside or to put me down by the zealous partizans of other Candidates.

I send you enclosed some communications which I have recd. which you will be pleased to return by Mr. [James] Erwin; and if you do not wish to retain this letter (as I have kept no copy of it) be pleased to return that also.

I still think of and hope that arrangements may be made to make it your interest to go to Washn.[12]

ALS. DLC-TJC (DNA, M212, R10). Printed in Colton, *Clay Correspondence*, 4:418. Letter marked "(Strictly Confidential)." 1. Clay to Letcher, May 30, 1837; Clay to Davis, July 3, 1837. 2. Davis to Clay, July 12, 1837. 3. Clay to Committee of N.Y. City Whigs, August 8, 1837. 4. Reference obscure. 5. For example, see Bryan to Clay, July 14, 1837; Dangerfield to Clay, August 3, 1837. 6. Clay's optimism on this matter was somewhat misleading, because the Ohio Whig convention, which had met on July 4, 1837, had expressed Ohio's preference for William Henry Harrison. It had also advocated holding a national convention in Pittsburgh in June of 1838. Francis P. Weisenburger, *The Passing of the Frontier, 1825-1850*, vol. 3 in *The History of the State of Ohio*, Carl Wittke (ed.), 6 vols. (Columbus, Ohio, 1941-44), 387. 7. Clay to Noble, June 20, 1837. 8. The Whig party gained a sweeping victory in Tennessee in 1837, winning 10 of 12 seats in the U.S. House and also winning control of both houses of the state legislature. Also, Whig gubernatorial candidate Newton Cannon defeated Democrat Robert Armstrong by 51,341 votes to 33,944. Charleston *Mercury*, August 26, 1837; *BDGUS*, 4: 1471-72; Robert Cassell, "Newton Cannon and State Politics, 1835-1839," *THQ* (Dec., 1956), 15:317. 9. Clay to Noble, March 4, 1837. 10. Porter to Clay, Nov. 14 and Dec. 30, 1837. 11. Although McLane remained a Democrat, it was known that he disliked and distrusted Van Buren. John Munroe, *Louis McLane: Federalist and Jacksonian* (New Brunswick, N.J., 1973), 432-33, *passim*. Verplanck had switched from the Democratic to the Whig party in 1834 and remained a Whig thereafter. Jabez D. Hammond, *The History of Political Parties in the State of New York. . .*, 3 vols. (Syracuse, 1842-48), 3:183. Selden held no elected political office after he left Congress in 1834. *DAB*. 12. Prentice did not go to Washington, but remained a newspaper editor in Louisville, Ky.

To SETH WHEATLEY[1] Lexington, August 18, 1837

I duly recd your obliging letter requesting a Copy of the Pamphlet published by me some years ago,[2] in refutation of charges against me brought forward by Genl Jackson, in connection with the election of Mr. Adams.[3] I regret extremely that, after examining my own papers and searching in Lexington, I cannot find a single Copy. I think it was published in Niles's Register,[4] where alone it is probably permanently preserved. I am very thankful for the friendly motives which prompted you to desire the copy, and for the friendly purposes to which you intended to apply it.

I thank God that I have been permitted to live down those charges. They were never believed by those who originated them, and by few, if any, of those who circulated them. They deceived however, I dare say, many of the uninformed. They were contrived for political effect, and unfortunately accomplished their object. Our afflicted Country is now bleeding, in consequence of their success, and when its wounds will be healed God only knows. The author of all our present calamities, not satisfied with the desolation which he prepared for us whilst at Washington, is now, from his Hermitage, urging his successor upon new & fatal experiments, destined, if not arrested, to plunge the Country into still deeper distress and embarrassment. In the mean time, the result of Elections in Kentucky,[5] Tennessee[6] & Indiana,[7] during this month, justifies the hope that the People have at last awaked, and are resolved to put down all Experiments and Experimenters—That they may consummate that patriotic work, I sincerely pray.

ALS. Courtesy of Mrs. H.W. Hill, Mooresville, Ala. Copy in NcU. 1. For Wheatley, the one-time mayor of Memphis, see James P. Davis, *History of Memphis* (Memphis, 1873), 33. 2. See 6:1394-96; 7:339. 3. See 7:660-61, 716-17, 719. 4. Clay's address of Dec., 1827, was published in *Niles' Register* (Jan. 5, 1828), 33:296-315. That of June, 1828, was published in *ibid.* (July 5, 1828), 34:306-12. 5. Clay to Noble, June 20, 1837. 6. Clay to Prentice, August 14, 1837. 7. Clay to Noble, March 4, 1837.

To LUCRETIA HART CLAY White Sulphur Springs, Va. (W. Va.), August 27, 1837

We arrived here yesterday, having parted from Mr. [James] Erwin at Guyandotte, he proceeding up the Ohio river, and we taking the Land route by this place. I was concerned to learn from him that James [Brown Clay] became worse the day on which I left home, and it was necessary to call in a Physician. He assured me however that altho' threatened with a severe fever no danger was apprehended. I sincerely hope that this may prove to be the case, but as I shall feel very uneasy until I hear again from home, I wish he would write me to Washington as soon as you get this letter.

I wrote you from Maysville, and in that letter I mentioned most of the things to which I desired James[']s attention in my absence. I forgot to mention that I wished the Red Cow with a white face (an old Hereford that was put up last winter to be killed) fattened for beef for the family, and any other of the old Cows that he may think it well enough to kill. There is a little two year old at Mansfield (I believe she is an estray herfer, with a black nose) that might as well be slaughtered for early beef.

We shall leave here on wednesday morning at farthest for Washington. By that time I hope to recover from the fatigues of the journey. John [Morrison Clay] looks very serious, but has conducted himself very well.

ALS. DLC-TJC (DNA, M212, R10). Printed in Colton, *Clay Correspondence*, 4:418-19.

Remark in Senate, September 5, 1837. Has no objection to printing up to 15,000 copies of Van Buren's message of September 4 on the state of the economy and the proposed remedies therefore, but regrets that "the President, entertaining such views [Speech in Senate, September 25, 1837], and proposing such a plan of relief of the country, as he had presented, had deemed it his duty to call an extra session of Congress at this inconvenient period of the year." *Register of Debates*, 25 Cong., 1 Sess., 3. See Clay to Henry Clay, Jr., September 8, 1837.

Remark in Senate, September 6, 1837. Objects to appointing standing committees until the Senate meets at its usual time in December. Points out that the president has convened them for the single purpose of dealing with the nation's economic distress and that committee appointments should not be made until the Senate has before it the full scope of its business. *Register of Debates,* 25 Cong., 1 Sess., 3-4. In spite of Clay's plea, standing committee appointments were announced on September 8. *Ibid.,* 6.

Remark in Senate, September 7, 1837. Since the political "complexion of the Senate is well known," he thinks it a "waste of time" to elect the members of standing committees. Urges that the vice president simply appoint the committees, as he had done "at some times formerly." *Register of Debates,* 25 Cong., 1 Sess., 5.

To HENRY CLAY, JR. Washington, September 8, 1837

I reached here not very well on the evening of the third. I am now better.

The Message[1] (of which I send you a Copy) has disappointed every body, and leaves the Country nothing to expect for its relief from Congress. Such is the general apprehension. We shall see in future developements if any thing good can be done. The Conservatives[2] (for so they denominate themselves) are said to be resolved to make battle with their quondam friends; but then they take ground (the Local banks) on which they can not long stand.

Dr. [Stephen] Duncan writes me that we shall get 12 Cents for our Bale Rope.[3]

I go to day to Princeton with John [Morrison Clay],[4] and being busy preparing I write you briefly. My love to Julia [Prather Clay] and your children.

ALS. Henry Clay Memorial Foundation, Lexington, Ky. Written in "S. Chamber."
1. Van Buren's message of Sept. 4, 1837, to the Special or 1st Session of the 25th Congress. See *MPP,* 3:324-46, and *Cong. Globe,* 25 Cong., 1 Sess., 4-9. Van Buren had advocated in the message the independent or sub-treasury system to meet the financial crisis. See Speech in Senate, Sept. 25, 1837. 2. Clay to Henry Clay, Jr., Jan. 28, 1837. 3. For Stephen Duncan, see 8:16. On August 21-22, 1837, Clay had shipped 294 coils of bale rope, weighing 30,530 lbs., from Maysville, Ky., to Natchez, Miss., in the steamboat *North Star.* Total cost of drayage, storage, freight, and insurance came to $418.38. The steamboat operators refused payment for the freight costs ($305.30) in "Mississippi currency," so January & Huston in Maysville "made arrangement to pay in Kentucky paper" four weeks hence, or following safe delivery in Natchez. Some of the bale-rope shipment sold for 12½ and 13 cents per pound in Natchez ("your Rope is much approved of by our Planters, both as to regularity in size and quality," wrote Lambdin & Bennett from Natchez), the remainder for 12¢. W.H. Latham to Clay, Invoice, Maysville, August 21, 1837. D. DLC-TJC (DNA, M212, R18). January & Huston to Clay, Account and Receipt, Maysville, August 22, 1837. *Ibid.*; January & Huston to Clay, Maysville, August 31, 1837. ALS. *Ibid.* (R14); Lambdin & Bennett to Clay, Natchez, Sept. 25, 1837. *Ibid.* On Oct. 18, 1837, Lambdin & Bennett wrote from Natchez that they had sold all Clay's remaining rope, "about 70 coils of it at 13¢, the balance at 12½ payable 15th January 1838." Assure him that "these are the highest prices obtained in this market." Report that the "Yellow fever has been prevailing in Natchez," that they have left the city, and that they will settle Clay's account when they return. *Ibid.* Hemp bale rope was sold by the pound. A "coil" of bale rope weighed about 100 lbs. and was often shipped and/or sold by the coil. Hemp bagging was sold by the yard and was generally cut in 40" widths. A "piece of bagging" would measure from 50 to 75 yards. Unprocessed hemp was sold either by the hundred-weight or by the ton. It took about 6 yards of 40" wide bagging to wrap each 400 to 425 lb. bale of cotton. A bale was usually secured with 6 hemp ropes. See James F. Hopkins, *A History of the Hemp Industry in Kentucky* (Lexington, 1951), 112-50. 4. John was admitted to the sophomore class at Princeton University on Nov. 9, 1837.

Comment in Senate, September 15, 1837. Refers to the bill just passed by the Senate postponing payment of the fourth installment of surplus treasury funds to the states [Speech in Senate, September 25, 1837] and applying such funds to government operating needs. Asks if it is the intention of the Van Buren administration "to employ the funds in the [state-chartered private deposit] banks before being reduced in some way or other to a specie basis . . . such, for example, as a bankrupt law, to force the conversion of the funds now in the banks into metal, and then throw the sum thus obtained from the banks into the Treasury, there to lie without being used?" He failed to get what he considered to be a satisfactory answer to his question from Sen. Silas Wright (N.Y.), chairman of the Finance Committee, who informed him that the amount of government funds in the deposit banks would, by October 1, total between $2,500,000 and zero, probably the latter. Clay then inquired if the government money in these banks was to be used as bank notes, or whether the banks would be "compelled to pay them in specie," or if the funds were to "be left idle?" When Wright replied that the funds would not be used as bank notes, unless authorized by law, Clay responded: "Then it comes to this: we have passed a bill to take funds out of the hands of those who would have been glad to use them, to put them into the hands of others who refuse to acknowledge and make use of them. The States would have been glad to receive this money in the shape of bank-notes, and we have taken it from them." Further, since the government will not acknowledge these remaining deposits as funds, and will not pay them out to the states, it thus creates a deficit and "this deficiency is to be supplied by issuing Treasury notes, in order that Government may be able to get along. That is to say, Government will not receive the paper of the country, and is about to create a paper of its own, which the country is expected to receive! And thus, all the promises which have been made to us of the flowing of gold and silver all over the country—these promises of a better currency result in the issue of ten millions of paper money!" *Register of Debates*, 25 Cong., 1 Sess., 45-47. The bill to postpone the fourth installment passed by 28 to 17 on September 15, Clay voting in the negative. *Ibid.*, 7, 45. The bill authorizing the issuance of treasury notes in the amount of $10,000,000, and in denominations of no less than $100, and at interest rates of no more than 6% per annum, was passed by the House on October 9 and was promptly sent to the Senate where it was passed 25 to 6 on October 11, Clay voting against. *Ibid.*, 520-22, 1359-72. The president signed it on October 12, 1837. See 5 *U.S. Stat.*, 201-4. The notes were designed to perform the function of emergency federal currency.

To FRANCIS LIEBER Washington, September 16, 1837

I received today, and had appropriated this evening to a rapid glance at, the MSS. with the perusal of which you had favored me. I am deprived of that satisfaction by unexpected circumstances, beyond my control. And I find, my dear Sir, that, amidst the public duties which press upon me at this most critical moment of our public affairs, I shall be altogether unable, without a neglect of those duties which you would not allow, to give to your MSS. the deliberate consideration to which I am sure it is entitled. Thus unable to express any opinion of it, from actual examination, which would deserve the least weight, I must restrict myself to saying that, from my knowledge of you, of your principles, and of some of your literary labors, to which the world is already indebted, I am perfectly persuaded that your "Political Ethics,"[1] of which this MSS. forms only a part, will be found eminently worthy of the patronage of all who love truth, justice and civil liberty. I am happy to find myself fortified in this opinion, which I hesitate not to give in advance, by that of a judge so highly competent as Mr. [Joseph] Story,[2] who has been able to command that time for its deliberate inspection, which I am truly sorry is not now at my disposal. . . .

ALS. CSmH. For Lieber—political scientist, educator, and author—see *DAB*. 1. Lieber's *Manual of Political Ethics*. . . . was published in two volumes in Boston in 1838-39. 2. Story's favorable views are summarized (p. 3) in the 2nd edition of Lieber's *Manual* . . . , which was edited by Theodore D. Woolsey and published in Philadelphia in 1876.

Remark in Senate, September 18, 1837. Says he is "entirely in favor" of the objective of the so-called "Warehouse Bill" which would allow merchants to store imported goods and merchandise in government warehouses under certain conditions. Argues that the legislation "would be beneficial ultimately to the commerce of the country, and immediately to the manufacturing and other interests." *Register of Debates*, 25 Cong., 1 Sess., 10-11, 76. The bill was passed on October 12. A similar bill was introduced in the House on September 18, but never cleared committee. *Ibid.*, 550, 628. The Senate version of the bill is in *Cong. Globe*, 25 Cong., 1 Sess., 26-27. See Remark in Senate, October 9, 1837.

Remark in Senate, September 23, 1837. Senate adjourns on motion of Clay. *Register of Debates*, 25 Cong., 1 Sess., 250.

To William O. Niles, Washington, September 25, 1837. Thanks Niles for "the present of the Seal" which he will esteem "highly as proceeding from a member of a family which has ever enjoyed my greatest respect and consideration." Continues: "I should be most happy to continue and cherish towards you the same amicable relations which have ever existed between your excellent father and me. And I have every reason to hope and to anticipate their existence, from the acquaintance which I have already had the satisfaction of forming with you." ALS. KyU. Niles, the eldest son of Hezekiah Niles, had taken over editorship of *Niles' Register* in 1836 when his father became ill. He continued the task until the *Register* was sold in 1839. Hezekiah Niles died on April 2, 1839. Richard G. Stone, "H. Niles as an Economist," *The Johns Hopkins University Studies in Historical and Political Science*, no. 5 (Baltimore, 1933), 51:48.

Speech in Senate, September 25, 1837. In a three-hour speech, Clay attacks the Sub-Treasury bill [called also the Independent Treasury bill and/or the Divorce bill], as advocated and outlined by President Van Buren in his special message of September 4, 1837 [*Cong. Globe*, 25 Cong., 1 Sess., 4-9]. In that message, which Clay challenges point by point, Van Buren blamed the nation's currency crisis on three principal factors: on European (mainly British) economic policies which had first fueled a "spirit of reckless speculation" in the United States through credit expansion, and had then caused a drain of gold out of the United States when credit was contracted; on the Deposit Act of June 23, 1836 [5 *U.S. Stat.*, 53], section 5 of which prohibited the government from depositing its funds in private banks which had suspended specie payment [8:813]; and on the inability of the Pennsylvania-chartered United States Bank of Pennsylvania, successor of sorts to the B.U.S. [Biddle to Clay, February 21, 1837] to restrain the currency issues of less stable private banks. Van Buren's basic solution to the currency crisis and depression was to divorce government banking functions from involvement with state-chartered private banks, whether government-deposit banks or not, to center such functions exclusively in the U.S. Treasury, and to establish a national network of government banks (Sub-Treasuries) in and from which all government specie income would be deposited and disbursed. Notes issued by various state banks, whether backed by specie or not, would not be accepted in payment of government obligations by the Sub-Treasury branches. He asked also that the fourth installment of the deposit (distribution) of the treasury surplus with (to) the states (paid out on January 1, April 1, July 1; and due to be paid again on October 1, 1837), as provided by sections 13 and 14 of the Deposit Act of 1836 [8:813, 873-74] be postponed.

Clay commences his remarks with the observation that the nation clearly needs "some effectual plan . . . to correct the disorders in the currency, and to restore the prosperity of the country." This situation he attributes to the "overthrow of the Bank of the United States [8:434, 443, 552, 558, 640-41]." Charges that the demise of the B.U.S. undermined a strong currency system and produced inflation, speculation, and the suspension of specie payments [Speech in Senate, January 11, 1837] by numerous private banks in May, 1837. Asserts that Van Buren's explanation of specie-payment suspension as having been caused by the "indulgence of a spirit of speculation produced by bank and other facilities" is like arguing that a homicide perpetrated by gunshot is really caused by "the leaden ball, and not the man who levelled the piece." Calls special attention to the proliferation of weak, state-chartered private banks in Kentucky after Jackson vetoed the B.U.S. recharter bill [8:434, 443, 552, 558, 640-41]. Protests that it is not correct for the president to blame the national economic crisis on "the condition of Europe, and especially . . . Great Britain." Indeed, "In Great Britain a sound currency was preserved by a recharter of the Bank of England about the same time that the recharter of the Bank of the United States was agitated here." Notes also that "the recent embarrassments of Europe were the embarrassments of a creditor, from whom payment was withheld by the debtor, and from whom the precious metals have been unnecessarily withdrawn by the policy of the same debtor."

Lists five measures, attributable to the Jacksonians, that brought about the panic and depression of 1837, viz: 1) veto of the B.U.S. recharter bill [8:552, 558, 640-41]; 2) removal of government deposits from the B.U.S. [8:583-84, 681, 684-85, 728]; 3) the gold bill [Gold Coinage Act of 1834]; 4) "clumsy execution" of the deposit law by the Treasury; and 5) the Treasury Order [Specie Circular] of July 11, 1836 [8:861; Speech in Senate, January 11, 1837; Remark in Senate, January 14, 1837]. Explains the relationship of each of these actions and decisions by Jackson to the present crisis and charges, further, that the Jackson administration had even lately begun to tamper with the schedules in the Compromise Tariff Act of 1833 [8:603, 621-22, 626-27] in such a manner as to indicate "to the manufacturing interest that no certain reliance was to be placed upon the steadiness of the policy of the Government, no matter under what solemn circumstances it was adopted." Argues, too, that had his land bill [8:539-41] not been vetoed by Jackson [8:552], "it would have distributed gradually and regularly among the several States the proceeds of the public lands." Moreover, his land bill would have prevented the chain of events which began with a "vast surplus" in the Treasury and ended with the suspension of specie payments by the banks. Claims also that an underlying "cause of our present difficulties" can be traced to the despotic government, the one-man rule, created by Jackson and blindly supported by "the party in power." The "fatal error" of that party "has been to lend its sanction, and to bestow its subsequent applause and support upon Executive acts which, in their origin, it previously deprecated or condemned."

Attacks Van Buren's proposed Sub-Treasury bill as certain to "terminate in the total subversion of the State banks; and that they will be all placed at the mercy of the Federal Government. It is in vain to protest that there exists no design against them. The effect of these measures cannot be misunderstood. And why this new experiment or untried expedient? The people of this country are tired of experiments. Ought not the administration itself to cease with them? Ought it not to take warning from the events of recent elections?" Adds that "according to the latest expression of public opinion in the several States, the Senate is no longer a true exponent of the will of the States or of the people. If it were, there would be thirty-two or thirty-four whigs to eighteen or twenty friends of the administration."

Believes it undesirable to outlaw convertible paper currency which is time-saving and convenient to use and rely instead on "precious metals as the sole currency," given the "vast extent of varied business of this entire country." Expresses surprise that Sen. John C. Calhoun is now arguing "that a convertible paper would not answer for a currency, but that the true standard of value was to be found in a paper medium not convertible into the precious metals." Attacks this notion at considerable length, emphasizing instead the economic and commercial advantages of sound, specie-backed paper money, and illustrating his contention with references to the sad history, to date, of nonconvertible paper currency in the United States. Suggests, in addition, that since "the great mass of legislative authority abides with the States" an attack on state banks is an attack on the various and several states. "Their banks exist without us [the federal government], independent of us, and in spite of us. We have no constitutional power or right to put them down. . . . In making war upon the [state] banks . . . you wage war upon the people of the United States" who own them, use them, & rely on them. The government should therefore help sustain state-chartered private banks, not undermine them. Indeed, "Let us not be deluded by sounds. Senators might as well talk of separating the Government from the States, or from the people, or from the country. We are all—people—States—Union—banks, bound up and interwoven together, united in fortune and destiny, and all, all entitled to the protecting care of a parental Government. You may as well attempt to make the Government breathe a different air, drink a different water, be lit and warmed by a different sun from the people! A hard-money Government and a paper-money people!" Suggests a "mixed medium," perhaps two-thirds paper and one-third specie.

Wonders if it can be assumed that the collectors of the revenue, who would also serve as sub-treasurers, will be honest. Asks whether the safety of specie deposits in the sub-treasuries can be assured? Sees political patronage considerations infecting the operation of the proposed Sub-Treasury system. "Hundreds and thousands of new officers are to be created; for this bill is a mere commencement of the system, and all are to be placed under the direct control of the President." Attacks Calhoun's contention that since "the Executive is now weak . . . no danger is to be apprehended from its patronage." Adds: "I wish to God I could see the subject in the same light that he does." Asks which of Jackson's assumed powers of appointment, proscription, veto, treasury orders, and expunging acts "has the present Chief Magistrate disavowed? So far from disclaiming any one of them, has he not announced his intention to follow in the very footsteps of his predecessor?" Predicts: "Lastly, pass this bill, and whatever divorce its friends may profess to be its aim, that perilous union of the purse and the sword, so justly dreaded by our British and Revolutionary ancestors, becomes absolute and complete. And who can doubt it who knows that over the Secretary of the Treasury at Washington, and every sub-treasurer, the President claims the power to exercise uncontrolled sway? To exact implicit obedience to this will?" Says he is firmly convinced that Van Buren's "scheme of sub-treasuries . . . is destined to become, if it be not designed to be, a vast and ramified connexion of Government banks, of which the principal will be at Washington, and every sub-treasurer will be a branch."

Offers as an alternative to the Sub-Treasury system the possible creation of a new national bank [Remark in Senate, September 27, 1837], arguing that "I can conceive of no adequate remedy which does not comprehend a national bank as an essential part. It appears to me that a national bank, with such modifications as experience has pointed out, and particularly such as would limit its profits, exclude foreign influence in the government of it, and give publicity to its transactions, is the only safe and certain remedy that can be adopted. The great want of the country is a general and uniform currency, and a point of union, a sentinel, a regulator of the issues of the local banks; and that would be supplied by such an institution." Affirms that the constitutionality of such an institution is "a settled question," and urges Congress to push ahead with the establishment of a national bank even though Van Buren may veto the bill. Asserts, in this regard, that the election of Van Buren "ought not to be taken as evidence that the people are against a bank. . . . I firmly believe that if such a question were now submitted to them, the response of a vast majority would be in the affirmative." Discusses the functions, advantages, and capitalization of "a bank of the United States," and the circumstances under which it could stimulate the resumption of specie payments throughout the land and contribute to the return of prosperity. Contends that "If . . . the remedies which I have suggested were successful at a former period of our history, there is every reason to hope that they would again prove efficacious; but let me suppose that they should not, and that some unknown cause, which could not then, should now, thwart their operation, we should have, in any event, the consolation of knowing that we had endeavored to profit by the lessons of experience, and, if they failed, we should stand acquitted in the judgment of the people. They are heartily tired of visionary schemes and wild experiments. They wish to get out of the woods, into which they have been conducted, back to the plain, beaten, wide road, which they had before trodden."

Says he is not at this time proposing the "establishment of a national bank" because "constituted as the Congress now is, I know that such a proposition would be defeated; and that it would be therefore useless to make it." Thinks it would be "unwise even to propose a bank" until a conviction of its necessity "is deeply impressed upon the people, and clearly manifested by them [Comment in Senate, September 26, 1837]."

Believes that the scheme of Sen. William C. Rives (Va.) to create a "connexion of State banks" to serve as the fiscal agent of the government is impracticable [Comment in Senate, March 7, 1838]. But says he will vote for the Rives plan over that proposed by the Van Buren administration "because it is harmless . . . and looks to the preservation of the State banks; whilst the other is fraught with mischiefs . . . and tends . . . to the utter destruction of those institutions." Would prefer "in the first instance," however, to vote to postpone the bill until December as suggested by Sen. John P. King (Ga.). Concludes with the recommendation that Congress should wait until the will of the people be made manifest on how best the economic problems of the nation might be remedied. "In the mean time, let us go home and mix with and consult our constituents." *Register of Debates*, 25 Cong., 1 Sess., 251-69. Printed in Colton, *Clay Correspondence*, 6:61-86.

The fiscal legislative package sponsored by the Van Buren administration contained four main elements: 1) the establishment of the Sub-Treasury system, which was the principal bill in the package; 2) a national bankruptcy bill, aimed at all the state-chartered private banks, which authorized federal seizure of the effects [assets] of any of them that ceased specie payments, and also authorized the subsequent administration of seized assets under federal authority; 3) a bill prohibiting people and corporations (including banks) in the District of Columbia from circulating any paper currency not convertible into specie on demand; 4) a bill providing for the suspension of the payment of the fourth installment of the Treasury surplus to the states.

A related bill authorizing government issuance of Treasury notes in the amount of $10,000,000 became law [Comment in Senate, September 15, 1837] on

October 12, 1837. No bankruptcy law was passed by the 25th Congress, 1st Session. The bill "to force the banks of this District to resume specie payments, and to suppress the small paper currency of the District" was passed by voice vote in the Senate on October 12, but was tabled in the House the following day. *Register of Debates*, 25 Cong., 1 Sess., 525, 532-33, 550, 1541; *Cong. Globe*, 25 Cong., 1 Sess., 27-28. A bill to force District of Columbia banks to resume specie payments was introduced in the 25th Congress, 2nd Session but made no headway. *Ibid.*, 25 Cong., 2 Sess., 40, 42, 71, 128, 357. See Comment in Senate, December 21, 1837.

The main Sub-Treasury bill, however, passed the Senate during the 25th Congress, 1st Session by a vote of 26 to 20 on October 4, 1837 with Calhoun's legal-tender amendment (see below) incorporated; it passed again, 27 to 25 on March 26, 1838 with the Calhoun amendment omitted and the Cuthbert amendment [Remark in Senate, March 24, 1838] included. *Cong. Globe*, 25 Cong., 2 Sess., 250-51, 259, 264. The House tabled it, by a vote of 120 to 107, on October 14, 1837, and rejected it outright, 125 to 111, on June 25, 1838. *Register of Debates*, 25 Cong., 1 Sess., 511, 1683-86; *Cong. Globe*, 25 Cong., 2 Sess., 478. When the Democrats took control of the 26th Congress, the resurrected Sub-Treasury bill passed the Senate, 24 to 18, on January 23, 1840, and the House, 124 to 107, on June 30, 1840. It was signed by Van Buren on July 4, 1840. See 5 *U.S. Stat.*, 385-92. It was repealed by a Whig Congress on August 13, 1841. For a general overview of Van Buren's fiscal package and the political implications thereof, see Major L. Wilson, *The Presidency of Martin Van Buren* (Lawrence, Kan., 1984), 47, 54-56, 61-127, 133-39, 143. For the Independent Treasury (Sub-Treasury) legislation, its history, and its political ramifications, see *ibid.*; also David Kinley, *The Independent Treasury of the United States and Its Relations to the Banks of the Country* (Washington, D.C., 1910), 33-45; Niven, *Martin Van Buren*, 416-29, 448-61; Curtis, *The Fox at Bay*, 75-109, 117-33, 146-51; Govan, *Nicholas Biddle*, 314-18; Van Deusen, *Life of Henry Clay*, 301-7.

Calhoun's legal-tender amendment to the Sub-Treasury bill permitted the proposed Independent Treasury to accept obligations owed to and payable to the government in various fractional combinations of specie and the notes of specie-paying banks until 1841, viz: three-fourths in the notes of specie-paying banks (in 1838), one-half in such notes (in 1839), one-quarter (in 1840), and in specie only from 1841 on. See Wiltse, *John C. Calhoun: Nullifier*, 353-56; and *Register of Debates*, 25 Cong., 1 Sess., 495-97.

The Jackson administration's "gold bill" (Gold Coinage Act of June 28, 1834), on which Clay in part blamed the U.S. currency crisis and depression, was an attack on the paper-currency system of Biddle's Bank of the United States. It reduced the gold content of the dollar by 6.26% and changed the silver to gold ratio from 15:1 to 16:1 at a time when the world-market ratio was 15.7:1. It thus overvalued gold in relation to silver. This was done in an effort to reverse the trend whereby gold coins were disappearing from circulation because their mint value was less than their market value measured in terms of silver. The return of gold coins, it was hoped, would displace B.U.S. notes, especially those of smaller ($5, $10, $20) denominations. It did not. See Comment in Senate, March 7, 1838; Smith, *Economic Aspects of the Second Bank of the United States*, 58, 169; Sophonisba P. Breckinridge, *Legal Tender: A Study in English and American Monetary History* (Chicago, 1903), 91-92; 4 *U.S. Stat.*, 699-701.

Clay's main speech against the Sub-Treasury bill was delivered on February 19, 1838. See *Cong. Globe*, 25 Cong., 2 Sess., Appendix, 614-19. Calhoun's principal speech advocating the administration's proposed fiscal program was delivered in the Senate on September 18, 1837. See *Register of Debates*, 25 Cong., 1 Sess., 50-66; and Wilson, *The Papers of John C. Calhoun*, 13:546-72. The alternate fiscal proposal of Sen. William C. Rives (Va.), presented on December 22, 1836, January 10,

1837, and September 19, 1837, is in *Register of Debates*, 25 Cong., 1 Sess., 77-104; and his defense of various elements of it is found in *ibid.*, 185-86, 187, 247-50; also in *Cong. Globe*, 24 Cong., 2 Sess., 44, 61, 127; *ibid.*, Appendix, 35-36, 100-105. It was ultimately acceptable neither to Calhoun nor Clay. See Comment in Senate, March 7, 1838.

To SAMUEL L. SOUTHARD Washington, September 25, 1837

I made a Speech to day which occupied upwards of 3 hours in the delivery,[1] after which, without any reply, a question was taken on Mr. [John] King's proposition of postponemt. to the next Session, and the vote stood 19 for 27 against it, the conservatives[2] and Mr. [William C.] Preston voting agt. the postponement, and some of our friends being absent. Then the subject was laid by, and other matters taken up.

My opinion is that we shall not have the final question on the Sub. treasury scheme until friday next, that is on the passage of the bill;[3] but some of us will write you tomorrow.

ALS. NjP. 1. Speech in Senate, Sept. 25, 1837. 2. Clay to Henry Clay, Jr., Jan. 28, 1837. 3. On "friday next," Sept. 29, James Buchanan (Pa.) occupied most of the time speaking on the Sub-Treasury bill. The bill did not pass the Senate until Oct. 4. It was subsequently tabled in the House. *Register of Debates*, 25 Cong., 1 Sess., 351-406, 511, 1683-86. See Speech in Senate, Sept. 25, 1837, for the legislative history of the Sub-Treasury bill.

Comment in Senate, September 26, 1837. Sen. Silas Wright (N.Y.), in response to petitions from several quarters asking for a United States bank, offers a resolution "that the prayer of the petitioners ought not to be granted." Clay sees little "utility in acting on a negative resolution of this kind." As he said yesterday [Speech in Senate, September 25, 1837], he thinks it not "expedient to express any opinion on this subject at this time." Suggests that Wright's resolution be tabled; but if it is not to be tabled, he moves to amend it with the following substitute: "Resolved, That it will be expedient to establish a United States bank whenever it shall be manifested that a clear majority of the people of the United States are in favor of such an institution."

In the subsequent debate on this resolution, Clay explains that his motive in offering it is "that by the character of the vote the people might see what little chance there was of getting a United States bank." However, a substitute resolution by Sen. Nathaniel P. Tallmadge (N.Y.) to the point that since a "clear majority" of the people opposed such a bank, it is "inexpedient to grant the prayer of the petitioners," passes 29 to 14. Clay then argues that the only reason Van Buren opposes a national bank is because he thinks the people oppose it. Believes that the president "would go for a bank if the wishes of the people were decidedly expressed in favor of a bank." Therefore, since "a decided majority" of the people will be found to favor a national bank, his amendment to leave it up to the people is "absolutely necessary." *Register of Debates*, 25 Cong., 1 Sess., 270, 273. For Clay's description of the features of a new national bank, see Speech in Senate, May 21, 1838.

To FREDERICK FREEMAN[1] Washington, September 27, 1837

I received in this City a copy of your "Plea for Africa"[2] which you did me the favor to send me, with your obliging letter which accompanied it. I thank you for it. I have been prevented, by my public engagements, from giving it that attentive perusal which I have no doubt it deserves, but I have looked enough into it to perceive that you have treated your subject with interest, and in a manner calculated to produce favorable popular effect. I shall seize the first leisure at my command to examine it more deliberately.

Far from feeling that you have taken any unwarrantable liberty with my name, I feel honored by the use you have been pleased to make of it.

How much is it to be deplored that so many circumstances have occurred inauspicious to the cause of Colonization, since the Society was first organized! Among these, I regard the recent abolition movements as exerting the most unhappy influence. It is not for me to scrutinize the motives (doubtless in most instances good) of those who have originated or united in them; but that they have tended to affect injuriously that cause, and otherwise to retard the progress of improvement in the condition of the African race, in this Country, I do most sincerely believe.

That you may long live in health and strength to promote those great works of Benevolence which you have espoused with so much zeal and ability is the cordial wish of. . . .

ALS. KyU. 1. For Freeman, a Presbyterian minister who later became an Episcopal clergyman, educator, and author, see Oscar F. Adams, *A Dictionary of American Authors*. Boston, 1904. 2. *A Plea for Africa, Being Familiar Conversations on the Subject of Slavery and Colonization*. . . . 2nd ed., Philadelphia, 1837. This work had originally been published in 1836 under the title *Yaradee*.

To WILLIAM O. NILES Washington, September 27, 1837

In reply to your friendly note, I have to say that not one step is yet taken towards the preparation of the Speech, which I pronounced on monday.[1] When completed, I will bear in mind your application. . . .[2]

ALS. ViU. Written in "S. Chamber." 1. Speech in Senate, Sept. 25, 1837. 2. Gales & Seaton, not Niles, published Clay's speech attacking Van Buren's Sub-Treasury scheme under the title *Speech of Henry Clay, of Kentucky, on the Bill Imposing Additional Duties, as Depositories, in Certain Cases on Public Officers, in the Senate of the United States, September 25, 1837*. Washington, 1837. 19pp.

Remark in Senate, September 27, 1837. To the charge of Sen. Robert J. Walker (Miss.) that Clay in his speech of September 25 presented the national bank issue in terms of "union or disunion," Clay replies that his views have been misunderstood, that he only "expressed the opinion that the failure to establish a national bank, which alone could supply a sound and uniform currency, might endanger the Union." Assures Walker, further, that he has "not proposed the re-establishment of the present Bank of the United States." *Register of Debates*, 25 Cong., 1 Sess., 298.

From James Watson Webb, New York, September 29, 1837. Reports "a declaration of Mr. Webster [soon] after his return from the West," but uttered prior to Clay's letter to Webb [not found] "in reply to what I had written [to you] on the subject of the Webster [speech] here [Clay to Letcher, May 30, 1837]. I mentioned to him [Webster] that I had [written in a] letter to you, that Genl. [William H.] H[arrison]. was [out of the] question." Webster replied that the "success of the party" was the main concern and told me to say to Mr. Clay that "if he should receive the nomination" and decide to accept it, "I will commence a tour [around] the United States, and mount the stump in [ever]y Hamlet advocating his election, & not cease [exerti]ons until the contest is over." Thinks this statement shows Webster's "good feeling" toward and "harmony" with Clay. Believes that Clay will, without "a shadow of a doubt" receive the nomination of the "Whig Counties" in New York. Believes Webster might be willing to run on the same ticket with Clay as vice president if the matter could be arranged in such a way that it did not appear he was "answering [an of]fer" from Clay. Therefore, advises Clay to announce that he would accept either the presidential or vice presidential nomination by the Whig convention. Given this circumstance, maintains that Webster would "willingly adopt a similar course" and that "in doing so, he would be accepting [your nomi]nation for Vice President." Thinks this approach would secure to the nation the "invaluable services of the two ablest Statesmen" in America. Hopes that if Clay does not think this idea worthy of consideration he will "never let my temerity be know[n to anyone] but ourselves." Nor will Webb "proclaim my own folly" in the matter to anyone else. ALS. DLC-HC (DNA, M212, R5). Letter badly torn and language difficult to reconstruct.

From William B. Astor, New York, September 30, 1837. Reports that his father [John Jacob Astor] is ill and has asked him to acknowledge Clay's check for $600 for six months interest on his [$20,000] loan, due November 1 [8:763]. Also thanks him for his "promptness and liberality" in the matter, and remarks that his father "would very willingly have received the amount in Bank notes; indeed he has always been ready to make collection of dues in the paper medium." ALS. DLC-TJC (DNA, M212, R14). Copy in MH-BA.

To Charles Ingersoll, September 30, 1837. Discusses a lawsuit pending against the estate of the late James Brown. Approves allowing it to be tried by "Mr. Justice [Henry] Baldwin only" in the absence of his associate Judge Joseph Hopkinson. ALS. KyLxT. For James Brown's estate, see 8:309-10, 739-40, 768-69, 771-72.

On April 23, 1838, Clay wrote Ingersoll indicating his approval of the favorable outcome of the lawsuit against the Brown estate. Notes that Ann Hart Brown left five heirs, of whom Mrs. Clay is one. Although he has no authority to do so, states his willingness to receive and disburse the whole amount to all the heirs, and "to give the necessary bond & security to indemnify you for the whole." However, if Ingersoll does not think this proper, "I will thank you to prepare a bond for Mrs. Clays part only." ALS. KyLxT.

Clay wrote Ingersoll again on April 28, 1838, saying that "I have written to Josiah Randall Esqr. to superintend, in behalf of Mrs. Browns heirs, the settlement of your a/c. of the Admon of Mr. Browns Estate before the proper Court." Adds that "I should be glad that the matter could be brought to a close, without unnecessary delay." *Ibid.*

On May 21, 1838, Josiah Randall wrote Clay from Philadelphia that he expects to receive all the funds from Ingersoll "on the 15 June or thereabouts." ALS. DLC-TJC (DNA, M212, R14).

Henry Clay Hart wrote from Paris, Ky., on May 31, 1838, enclosing a power of attorney to allow Clay "to receive and do for me, what ever may be necessary" in "the business connected with Uncle Browns Legacy in Philadelphia." Asks that the money be deposited in the Bank of the United States of Pennsylvania. *Ibid.*

Clay replied to Hart on June 7, 1838, saying that he will send a check as soon as Ingersoll makes the distribution of the funds. ALS. MoSHi.

On June 13, 1838, Clay wrote Mason Brown saying he cannot meet him in Philadelphia on June 15 as Brown had requested, but that "Mr. Josiah Randall is authorized to represent the interests of the heirs of Mrs. Brown, in the distribution of your Uncle's Estate, which I suppose to be the object on which you desire to see me." ALS. CtY.

Again on June 18, 1838, Clay wrote Mason Brown, agreeing "to unite in a joint bond with you." Asks if his presence at the distribution is essential. *Ibid.*

Josiah Randall wrote Clay on June 28, 1838, informing him that the "whole matter will be closed in a day or two and the amount placed to your credit in the Bk of U.S. [United States Bank of Pennsylvania] as you desire." Adds that while he would "prefer making no charge" for his services, he will accept any sum "not exceeding $100." Points out also that the "fees . . . already paid are large" and have diminished the estate more than the heirs have expected. ALS. DLC-TJC (DNA, M212, R14).

On July 3, 1838, Randall wrote regretting a further delay based on the fact "that all the Stocks are not sold." Notes, however, that he has placed in the bank $3,000 to Clay's credit. "I did this of my own motion. . . . If there is any thing wrong in this impute to me the fail[in]g–." *Ibid.*

Randall wrote again on July 6, 1838, saying he had received Clay's letter of July 5th, and adding "I regret you did not–approve of the payt. of the $3000 I did not know but that some of the heirs might have drawn upon it, and I supposed it wd do no harm." States that he has "pressed" Ingersoll to sell the stocks, and "I hope by tomorrow Evg. to advise it is done." *Ibid.*

On July 7, 1838, Randall wrote that he had deposited to Clay's account $8,514.92 which he received from Ingersoll. Discusses further the selling of stocks. *Ibid.* On the same day, Clay received a notice from the U.S. Bank of Pa. that the money had been credited to his account. ALS. DLC-HC (DNA, M212, R5).

Randall continued discussion on the sale of the stocks in a letter on July 10. Adds that he was sorry to learn from Clay's letter of July 8 "that you sh[ould] have left Washn. under such unfavorable feelings." Adds that "Mr. Ing[ersol]l. course has not met my entire approbation, but a delay of 3 weeks in collecting the funds . . . I do not think very extravagant." ALS. DLC-TJC (DNA, M212, R14).

On August 2, 1838, Randall wrote in detail concerning various complications involved in settling the Brown estate. Notes that he himself has been very anxious to leave the city because of the "oppressive heat" and "the Summer Complaint" which nearly took his daughter's life. "I mention it now to satisfy, you were not the only one who was impatient at the delay," he concludes. *Ibid.*

Randall wrote on November 26, 1838, that he had deposited $29.77 to Clay's account in the United States Bank of Pennsylvania. This was the balance from the $144.27 paid Randall by Mason Brown from which Randall's fee of $100 and various legal fees amounting to $14.50 had been deducted. *Ibid.*

On January 14, 1840, Clay wrote Charles Ingersoll saying that Judge Henry Baldwin "tells me that he furnished you with a Copy of his opinion" in the case of *Keene* v. *Brown* when it was tried in Philadelphia. Asks Ingersoll "to send it to me," adding that "The Judge concurs in this request." ALS. KyLxT. On January 21, 1840, Clay again wrote Ingersoll sending "a note from Judge Baldwin giving directions where the opinion . . . may be found." *Ibid.* At this time Clay and John J. Crittenden were representing Isaac T. Preston, executor of James Brown's estate, in a case pending in the Supreme Court of the United States against Richard R. Keene. This case resulted from a petition Keene had filed against the Brown estate on May 15, 1838, in the Circuit Court of the United States for the Eastern District of Louisiana, alleging that James Brown and his brother Samuel had contracted on August 21, 1807, to convey and deliver to Keene a tract of land containing 7,200 square feet located on the Gravier batture in New Orleans. The Louisiana circuit court had decreed that the Brown estate must convey to the plantiff $35,500 or a tract of land on the batture valued at $31,500. Preston, as Brown's executor, appealed this decision to the U.S. Supreme Court. In its January, 1840, term the court reversed the decision of the Louisiana circuit court and dismissed Keene's petition. 14 Peters 133-40. Handwritten "Notes of Argument" and the printed argument by Clay and Crittenden are in DNA, RG267.

On February 1, 1840, Clay again wrote Charles Ingersoll asking him to make further enquiries into the location of Judge Baldwin's opinion in the *Keene* v. *Brown* case. If the opinion cannot be found, asks Ingersoll to "state briefly the grounds of his [Baldwin's] decision." ALS. KyLxT.

Clay wrote Ingersoll on May 7, 1840, saying that he had made inquiries concerning the debt owed Brown's estate by Col. George Bomford and is sorry the news "is not more encouraging." *Ibid.*

From George W. Morton, Lexington, October, 1837. Recalls that he had sold Clay 111 acres of land "adjoining Ashland" on December 7, 1830. Offers Clay herein security for one-fifth of that parcel, or that part of it acquired through his deceased wife, the daughter of John McNair, deceased, in the event of future claims on it by other McNair heirs. The security conveyed amounts to five shillings cash and the option to purchase from Morton 50 acres situated across Tates Creek Road from the tract purchased in 1830. In the event of no claim by the McNair heirs, these 50 acres will revert unincumbered to Morton, who also retains the right "to substitute other sufficient security against the claim which the said heirs may possibl[y] assert." ADS. DLC-TJC (DNA, M212, R17).

Remark in Senate, October 4, 1837. Considers the bill to regulate the level of fees that federal district attorneys in New York City might charge for the renewal of the custom-house bonds put up by merchants to secure credit extended them by collectors for payment of import duties. Opposes as excessive the five dollar fee being proposed for each renewal. Believes that attorney's fees in New York City for this service would total between twenty and thirty thousand dollars, "so numerous" are the "bonds to be renewed under existing emergencies [8:816-17, 818]." Suggests retaining the renewal business in the hands of the collector of customs at a lower fee, because the five dollar fee "would fall heavily on the class of small importers," many of whose bonds do not exceed fifty dollars. "Five dollars on that sum—ten per cent. on the whole amount—would be unreasonable." *Register of Debates*, 25 Cong., 1 Sess., 498. The bill passed the Senate on October 10, as amended by Clay in such manner as to put the bond-renewal function in the hands of the collectors of customs. It also passed the House on October 10. *Ibid.*, 513-14, 518, 1397-1401.

To THOMAS HART CLAY Washington, October 8, 1837

I received your letter of the 29h. Ulto. and was gratified with the account it contained of the progress of work at Ashland. I had received from James [Brown Clay] a letter communicating the illness of his Overseer, and I fear he has died.[1] I have myself been ill but I have gotten better, altho' I do not yet feel quite well.

Congress will adjourn on the 16h. and I hope to reach home by the 25h.

The Sub treasury bill[2] is before the House, and the general opinion seems to be that it will not pass at this session.

I presume this letter will find you married.[3] I sincerely hope that you may be happy and enjoy a long life. And I feel quite certain that you may be.

Give my love and my blessing to Mary [Mentelle Clay].

ALS. Courtesy of Mrs. William Pettit, Lexington, Ky. Letter on loan to "Ashland," home of Henry Clay. 1. Clay to James B. Clay, Oct. 19, 1837. 2. Speech in Senate, Sept. 25, 1837; Comment in Senate, March 7, 1838. 3. Clay to James B. Clay, Oct. 19, 1837.

Remark in Senate, October 9, 1837. Resumes his attack on the unreasonableness and unfairness of the attorneys' fees bill [Remark in Senate, October 4, 1837].

Thinks the proposed five dollar fee much too high for the modest legal service to be rendered in renewing custom-house bonds. Offers an amendment, passed 22 to 18, to keep the renewal of custom-house bonds in the hands of the collectors. *Register of Debates*, 25 Cong., 1 Sess., 513-14.

Later this day, in speaking again on the warehouse bill [Remark in Senate, September 19, 1837], Clay announces that he has changed his mind on the provision of the bill which seeks to abolish the extension of credit to importers for customs duties owed the government. He thinks such abolition "would be favorable to the manufacturing interest." While he still favors "the entire abolition of credit for duties," he believes now it violates the Compromise Tariff Act of 1833 [8:604, 621-22, 626-27] which permits such credit arrangements. Admits that the violations in this bill are relatively minor ones. Fears, however, that "if that part relating to the payment of duties were violated, it might be violated in every other respect." *Ibid.*, 516-17. Section 2 of the bill permitted postponement of the payment of duties on commodities landed and stored in warehouses under certain conditions; this, in effect, was a form of credit extension.

To Matthew L. Davis, October 10, 1837. Reports receiving Davis's letter of October 8, "transmitting a resolution unanimously adopted by the Clay Executive Committee of the seventh Ward in the City of N. York." Thanks the committee members for their kindness and confidence in him, and hopes that Providence will "deliver us from the misrule which is threatening our Land with ruin, and our Liberties with subversion." ALS. MH.

Remark in Senate, October 10, 1837. Objects to Sen. Calhoun's suggestion that importers be permitted either to avail themselves of the provisions of the Warehouse bill [Remark in Senate, September 19, 1837], or refuse to do so and conform instead to existing law. Thinks this option gives "too much latitude to commercial operations, to the injury of the domestic trade and manufactures." Opposes specific provisions of the bill. Notes that since the measure comes "in collision with the [1833 tariff] compromise [Remark in Senate, October 9, 1837]," and since the Senate should determine the views of those whose "interests would be most affected by its passage," he will move to postpone it until the December session. That motion failing, 22 to 17, warns his colleagues to proceed cautiously. "This is a new system; no one can tell its results." Attempts to amend specific changes into or out of the bill. *Register of Debates*, 25 Cong., 1 Sess., 518-20.

Later this day, Clay again attacks the Treasury note bill [Comment in Senate, September 15, 1837], arguing that the notes are "mere post notes, only differing from bank notes of that kind in giving the Secretary [Levi Woodbury] a power of fixing the interests as he pleases." As for the institution that will issue the notes [Speech in Senate, September 25, 1837], it is "a Government bank, issuing Government bank notes; an experiment to set up a Government bank. It is, in point of fact, an incipient bank. Now, if Government has the power to issue bank notes, and so to form indirectly and covertly a bank, how is it that it has not the power to establish a national bank? What difference is there between a great Government bank, with Mr. [Levi] Woodbury as the great cashier, and a bank composed of a corporation of private citizens? What difference is there, except that the latter is better and safer, and more stable, and more free from political influences, and more rational and more republican?" Charges that administration forces "resort to paper, which you profess to put down; you resort to a bank, which you pretend to decry and to denounce; you resort to a Government paper currency, after having exclaimed against every currency except that of gold and silver!" *Ibid.*, 520-21. Following Clay's protest, the Treasury note bill was passed, 25 to 6, Clay voting no. *Ibid.*, 522.

Remark in Senate, October 11, 1837. Requests postponement of the Warehouse bill [Remark in Senate, September 19, 1837] until the December session for various reasons, viz: the need of additional information, concern that foreign manufacturers might derive from the new system "undue advantages" over American manufacturers, the expense of building public warehouses, the belief that it violates the Compromise Tariff of 1833 [Remark in Senate, October 9, 1837], especially in its "abolition of credits" section, and the belief that the privilege of warehousing gives "great advantages to the great capitalists." After his motion to postpone fails 23 to 15, he expresses regret that he has been given neither the information nor the time necessary to offer "some amendments." A motion to engross for a third reading passes 28 to 5, Clay not voting. *Register of Debates*, 25 Cong., 1 Sess., 522, 524-25.

To JOHN HOWARD PAYNE Washington, October 12, 1837

Your favor of the 10h. inst. has reached me at the moment of my departure from this City, and I am compelled therefore to write briefly.

I do not think that the funds can be raised for the work you suggest a plan of.[1] And, as a political publication, I am inclined to think its success would be doubtful. Such a work addresses itself to the intelligent; but they are precisely the class that do not stand in need of information. What is wanted, to enlighten the public mind, is a cheap publication, or rather news papers, of extensive circulation, adapted to the understandings and the purses of the mass of the community.

I have heard nothing here of the D. Review.[2]

ALS. NcD. 1. The kind of publication which Payne was planning at this time is uncertain. However, in 1833-34 he had attempted to establish a weekly international literary magazine to be called *Jam Jehan Nima*, but he had been forced to abandon the project. Gabriel Harrison, *John Howard Payne, Dramatist, Poet, Actor* . . . (Philadelphia, 1885), 145-50. 2. *The United States' Magazine and Democratic Review*, which began in 1837 and continued intermittently until 1859, was published until 1840 by John L. O'Sullivan and S.D. Langtree. Bland, "Politics, Propaganda, and the Public Printing," Ph.D. dissertation, Univ. of Ky., 1975, p. 77. Payne contributed articles to the *Review* in early 1838. Harrison, *John Howard Payne*, 177.

Remark in Senate, October 13, 1837. Offers resolution requesting from the president information on the progress of Mexico's provisions to pay claims due American citizens. *Cong. Globe*, 25 Cong., 1 Sess., 137. The 25th Congress, 1st Session, ended on October 16, 1837. At this juncture, Joseph Gales's and William W. Seaton's, *Register of the Debates of Congress*, ceased publication [8:670], leaving the field solely to Francis P. Blair's and John C. Rives's, *The Congressional Globe*.

To DOLLEY MADISON CUTTS[1] Washington, October 17, 1837

I called about ½ after seven last night to receive the message with which you were charged to me, and to congratulate you on the passage through the Senate of Mrs. [Dolley Payne Todd] Madison's resolution;[2] but met with my usual bad fortune in finding no body at home.

If you will send me word by Charles[3] at what hour tomorrow between 11 and 4 OClock you will be at home, I will endeavor to call.

ALS. NcD. 1. For Dolley M. Cutts, the daughter of Anna Payne and Richard Cutts and niece of Dolley Madison, see Virginia Moore, *The Madisons, A Biography* (New York, 1979), 246. 2. A bill for the relief of Dolley Madison was reported to the Senate on Oct. 12 and passed the same day. It passed the House on Oct. 13 and was signed by the president on Oct. 14. *Cong. Globe*, 25 Cong., 1 Sess., 137-38; U.S. Sen., *Journal*, 25 Cong., 1 Sess., 62, 65-66, 71-72. The bill granted Mrs. Madison the right to publish, for her own benefit in foreign countries, her husband's manuscript of the debates in the federal constitutional convention [8:868-70] of 1787. She could not, however, take back the copies she had already conveyed to the government. 5 *U.S. Stat.*, 205. 3. Clay's slave and bodyservant.

To Citizens of Wheeling, Wheeling, Va. (W. Va.), October 19, 1837. Joins John J. Crittenden in declining an invitation to a public dinner because of "our anxiety to rejoin our families." Express their gratification "that the opposition which we were constrained, by a high sense of duty, to make to certain measures of the Administration, proposed at the last session of Congress, is approved by you." Note that they were "greatly disappointed" at the administration's proposals "and were compelled to believe that the principal one [Sub-Treasury] if it had been adopted, would have proved ruinous to the country, highly injurious to the rights and independence of the States, and would have tended vastly to augment the already overgrown power of the Executive branch of the Government [Speech in Senate, September 25, 1837; Remark in Senate, January 16, 1838]." Add that "it now depends upon the People themselves whether a measure, fraught, as we believe, with imminent hazard to our free institutions, shall be finally adopted or not." Copy, signed by Clay and John J. Crittenden. Printed in Washington *Daily National Intelligencer*, October 26, 1837.

After their boat was delayed, a dinner did take place at the hotel where Clay and Crittenden were staying. Clay accompanied the customary laudatory toasts with a short talk [not recorded] for which he received "enthusiastic cheers." *Ibid.*

To JAMES B. CLAY Wheeling, Va. (W. Va.), October 19, 1837

I have reached this place on my return home from Congress, a good deal jaded and not very well. Prior to my departure from Washington, I received your letter communicating the death of poor Russell,[1] which gave me sincere concern. I have been quite uneasy about you, but hope that you have escaped sickness. You ought to be very careful with yourself; for your Missouri fevers are very dangerous.

I am sorry to hear of the great loss you have sustained in Sheep; and I am now convinced more than ever that it is unwise for you to keep them, unless you have a number sufficiently large to pay the expence of a Shepherd to keep constantly with them. Under these circumstances, I think you had better fatten what remain and sell them for mutton.

I suppose that you have heard that your brother Thom: [Thomas Hart Clay] was to have been married, and I presume was married, last thursday was a week.[2] We shall see if that event will make him steady.[3] I sincerely hope it may.

I expect to remain at home until late in November, and then proceed again to Washington, altho' I am very tired of so frequently crossing the Mountains. I wish you to write me often and let me know all that concerns you. I send this by the boat that carries me to Maysville.

ALS. DLC-TJC (DNA, M212, R10). Printed in Colton, *Clay Correspondence*, 4:419. Addressed to James "near St. Louis Missouri." 1. The overseer on James's Missouri farm. See Clay to T.H. Clay, Oct. 8, 1837. 2. Thomas Hart Clay married Marie (Mary) Mentelle, daughter of Augustus Waldemarde and Charlotte Mentelle, on Oct. 5, 1837. See Johnson's *Twentieth Century Biographical Dictionary* entry on Thomas Hart Clay. 3. A reference to his drinking habits.

To JAMES B. CLAY Lexington, October 24, 1837

I reached home on the 22d. inst. and recd. your letter of the 17h. I found all well here, but it is said to be very sickly at Louisville and at Frankfort,[1] and we have been uneasy about you. I hope that you will escape being sick. I wrote you by the journey from Wheeling, and sent my letter by the Steamboat. I advised you in that letter to sell your Sheep, seeing that they are not safe from the dogs & wolves. Unless you had a number sufficiently large to justify keeping a Herdsman, it is useless to keep sheep.

You tell me that Land is still rising in Missouri. I wish you could sell at a fair price my small tract in Lincoln, and also the Alton tract, if you could get a good price for it. What could you sell your Land for? But I suppose that nothing could induce you to sell it and return to K. Mr. [Thomas] Smith tells me that Chaumiere, the residence of the late Col. [David] Meade [Sr.], is in market at $40 per acre, which is very low as land has sold here. It is very good land, having, I understand, about 400 acres in the tract. That would not be large enough without the purchase of some addition to it, which probably might be made. But if you are contented with your situation and prospects, you had better not think of purchasing it.

We will try and have your Cattle &c sent to you, as you desire. I am afraid that the River may be too low, altho' it is now raining. Thomas [Hart Clay] seems quite happy, since his marriage.[2]

ALS. DLC-TJC (DNA, M212, R10). Printed in Colton, *Clay Correspondence*, 4:419-20. Addressed to James at "Richland near St. Louis Missouri." 1. Probably a reference to a smallpox epidemic which took several lives in 1837. L.F. Johnson, *The History of Franklin County, Kentucky* (Frankfort, Ky., 1912), 100. 2. Clay to James B. Clay, Oct. 19, 1837.

To EDWARD CURTIS Lexington, October 25, 1837

[Asks Curtis to forward an enclosed letter. Continues:]

I reached home on the 22d. inst. and found my family well. I hope that you were equally fortunate in respect to your's.

Ohio has given a Whig majority in her Legislature of from 14 to 16 on joint ballot.[1] All eyes will now be directed to the Empire State.[2] God grant that she may act a part worthy of her high and commanding position.

ALS. CtY. For Curtis, see *DAB* and *BDAC*. 1. The Whigs won 12 seats in the Ohio senate and 39 in the house, while Van Buren Democrats won 6 senate seats and 30 house seats. Indianapolis *Indiana Journal*, Oct. 21, 1837. 2. In the legislative elections in New York in Nov., 1837, Whigs won 10 senate seats, Conservative Democrats won 12, and Loco-Foco Democrats captured 10. In the house, the Whigs won 101 seats to 27 for the Conservatives and Loco-Focos combined. This gave the Whigs a majority on joint ballot of 62. The Whigs had also carried all 13 New York City seats in the state assembly, while Gulian C. Verplanck, the Whig candidate, won election to the state senate by a majority of 2,873 votes. Albany *Daily Argus*, Nov. 18, 1837; Indianapolis *Indiana Journal*, Dec. 2, 1837. For the origin of the Loco-Foco faction of the Democratic party, see Morris, *Encyclopedia of American History*, 176-77.

To ALEXANDER HAMILTON Lexington, October 25, 1837

[Thanks him for his recent invitation to visit New York City; regrets his inability to accept. Continues:]

Ohio has secured a Whig majority in both branches of her Legislature amounting in the aggregate to from 14 to 16.[1] Now, all eyes will be directed to the Empire State.[2] May her response confirm the high hopes so confidently entertained among the Whigs!

You will learn through Mr. [Edward] Curtis, Mr. [Josiah Ogden] Hoffman[3] & other members what were the sentiments prevailing with the Whig members of Congress, as to the next President. At present a more pressing object was the establishment at Washington of another Whig paper, of an effective character[.] Measures were adopted, which I hope may prove successful, in supplying that highly needed auxiliary.[4]

ALS. Courtesy of J. Winston Coleman, Jr., Lexington, Ky. 1. Clay to Curtis, Oct. 25, 1837. 2. *Ibid.* 3. For Hoffman, a New York City lawyer and congressman, see *DAB* and *BDAC*. 4. Although no overtly Whig newspaper was established in Washington at this time, a new Democratic newspaper, *The Madisonian*, with Thomas Allen as editor, was established on August 16, 1837, as a rival to Francis Blair's Washington *Globe*. It supported the philosophy of the Conservative Democrats in opposing Van Buren's financial program, and it later became the organ of the Tyler administration. William E. Ames, *A History of the National Intelligencer* (Chapel Hill, 1972), 238-40, 263.

To MATTHEW L. DAVIS Lexington, October 30, 1837

I have to thank you for the favor of your letter of the 23d. instant, communicating the arrangements which have been made, in the City of New York, for the approaching Election to the Legislature. I shall be obliged by a communication of the particular results in the City[1] and the general result in the State[2] as soon as they are known. It would seem from your letter that the Conservatives, or a considerable portion of them, after all their threatened opposition to the Message[3] have given in their adhesion!

The opposition to it in the West is firm, increasing and inconquerable. You will have heard that Ohio[4] has fulfilled our hopes.

I am happy to inform you that Mrs. Clays health is very good, and I trust entirely re-established. She desires to be remembered to you.

ALS. ViU. 1. Clay to Curtis, Oct. 25, 1837. 2. *Ibid.* 3. For Van Buren's special message advocating the Sub-Treasury system, see Clay to Henry Clay, Jr., Sept. 8, 1837. For the "Conservatives," see Clay to Henry Clay, Jr., Jan. 28, 1837. 4. Clay to Curtis, Oct. 25, 1837.

From Beverley A. Hicks, November 3, 1837. Encloses a bill and receipt for $75.00 paid by Clay for the board and tuition of his grandsons, Henry Clay Duralde and Martin Duralde III, at Lafayette Seminary for the period September 1 to December 15, 1837. Notes that "Should my eyes improve, I shall resume my labors in School on" January 15, 1838, "when, if You are pleased, I shall take great pleasure, in receiving, & teaching Yr. grand sons." Describes the boys' conduct as "honourable & polite" and predicts that they "will make, in future, greater speed" now that they have finished "english grammar . . . & commenced arithemetic." ALS. DLC-TJC (DNA, M212, R10).

On August 1, 1837, Clay had received a receipt from Josiah Dunham for $62.31 which he had paid for board and tuition from May 8 to July 31, 1837, for the Duralde boys. ADS. *Ibid.* (R18).

He also received a receipt on August 9, 1837, from Othon Boudet for $100 paid for instruction of his grandsons. DS. *Ibid.*

On February 9, 1838, Clay wrote Martin Duralde III saying he was "gratified" with the progress he and his brother, Henry Clay Duralde, were making at Lafayette Seminary, especially in arithmetic and writing. ALS. ICHi.

On February 13, 1838, Hicks acknowledged receipt of $150 from Clay in payment of board and tuition for both of the Duralde boys at Lafayette Seminary for the session January 15 to July 1, 1838. ADS. DLC-TJC (DNA, M212, R10). Hicks, who owned a 200 acre farm about 4 to 4½ miles from Lexington on the Winchester Turnpike conducted Lafayette Seminary in his residence. MacCabe, *Directory of the City of Lexington . . . 1838 & '39*, p. 125; Thomas S. Erwin, "Clay and Erwin Families," *FCHQ* (October, 1928), 3:111-16.

From Stephen Duncan, Natchez, November 4, 1837. States that he has received letters of October 12 and 21 from Clay and that "In regard to your Proposal for a sale of your cordage . . . I would not myself—accede To your Terms. Nor do I believe any other responsible planters here would do so." Suggests instead a contract whereby he would purchase from Clay "15 Tons of cordage—deliverable at the Natches [*sic*, Natchez] Landing—between the 1st. of March & 1st. of July of each year—for the years 1838-39 & 40," and promises to pay the highest rate prevailing at the time of delivery for an article of similar quality. Emphasizes: "I would not agree to pay any stipulated price." Adds in a postscript: "The yellow fever, has almost disappeared—yet I fear a return of our inhabitants and a few warm days would cause it to re appear." ALS. DLC-TJC (DNA, M212, R14). See also Clay to Henry Clay, Jr., September 8, 1837; Duncan to Clay, December 11, 1837.

To JAMES BROWN CLAY Lexington, November 10, 1837

I was glad to find by your letter of the 29th ultimo, just received, that you were in good health and spirits, and your business prosperous. I started Orphan Boy, your cow, dog, and gun, on the 7th instant, for St. Louis viâ. Louisville and steamboat, under the care of William Nelson White,[1] a young man raised in this county, and recommended to me. He lost two days in the start by accident, as he says, and I sent Aaron [Dupuy][2] to look after him and the cattle. Aaron has returned this evening and reports that he saw the man with the cattle safely across the bridge at Frankfort and going on well. So that I hope no further mishap will occur. I send you a copy of the receipt which Mr. White gave me, from which you will perceive that I advanced him $20, was to pay all expenses of himself and the cattle, and to allow him half a dollar per day as a compensation. The two days that he lost ought to be deducted from his account. Although he started with the dog, he could not carry but left him. I have written to Mr. Wm. Prather[3] to advance the money for his freight, etc. He had charge of another calf which he was to leave between here and Louisville.

I will make arrangements in a few days to advance you the $100 which you desire.

I wrote you, on my way home, and again after my return, and advised the sale of the sheep.

I have been engaged all this week in getting in my corn. My hogs are sufficiently fat to kill when it is cold enough. Yesterday my new overseer, Mr. [Albert] Florea, came and entered on business to-day.

Your mother had made up her mind to go with me to Washington, but has finally declined it.

We are all well, and she and the children send their love to you. Mr. [James] Erwin has not yet returned.

Copy. Printed in Colton, *Clay Correspondence*, 4:420-21. 1. For White, who died in Christian County, Ky., in 1855 at age 53, see *RKHS*, 46:512. 2. A slave. 3. William Prather was the son of Thomas and Matilda Fontaine Prather of Louisville and brother of Julia Prather Clay. He married his first cousin, Penelope Pope, who was the daughter of Alexander and Martha Fontaine Pope. Kathleen Jennings, *Louisville's First Families, A Series of Genealogical Sketches* (Louisville, 1920), 37-38.

From PETER B. PORTER Black Rock, N.Y., November 12, 1837

I take great pleasure in being able to inform you that our State election,[1] which closed last Wednesday evening, has resulted unquestionably, in the total, and so far as regards its extent, most unexpected overth[r]ow of the Van Buren party. Our present information is too limited to enable us to speak with positive certainty. Yet the fact that the entire Whig tickets have succeeded in 18 out of the 20 counties from which alone we have yet heard, and which counties have about 50 members of the Assembly out of 128 of which that body is composed, there can hardly remain a doubt but that we shall have a handsome majority. As to our Senate, the members of which, as you know, are chosen, like those of the U. S. only once in four years and in classes, we cannot of course expect an entire regeneration in a single year.

Assuming that New York is revolutionized & becomes a Whig State, I take it for granted that the Jackson dynasty must end with Mr. Van Buren's four years, and that the next President will be a Whig, and for that office I know of but three prominent candidates—Mr. Webster, Gen. Harrison & yourself. Mr. Webster has, & he deserves them, many powerful friends in this State, but I think I cannot be mistaken in saying that your strength here is decidedly greater than his, as I trust the event will show. As to General Harrison, we anticipated much more annoyance from his name some time ago, than we feel at present. We supposed that Pennsylvania instead of New York was most likely to become the leading State in the Whig confederacy—and, if so, she would have had great influence in naming the candidate, and that candidate would probably have been General H.

The movements of this State on the subject of the Presidency, will, I think, be regulated by the Whig members of the Legislature at their approaching session. This has not been the case of late years, because their members have scarcely at any time exceeded twenty, & they all Anti-Masons, on whose opinions the most perfect reliance has not been placed.

[Concludes with comments on his children, nephews, and neighbors.][2]

Copy. OHi. 1. Clay to Curtis, Oct. 25, 1837. 2. His nephews, Peter B. Porter, Jr., and John Milton Holley, had just been elected to the New York state assembly from Niagara and Wayne counties respectively. His neighbor, Lewis F. Allen, represented Erie County in the assembly. Albany *Argus*, Nov. 18, 1837. For Holley, see *BDAC*.

From Nicholas Biddle, Philadelphia, November 14, 1837. In regard to the elections in New York, states: "I dare not trust myself with beginning to write on the subject of the late happy events in New York [Clay to Curtis, October 25, 1837] for I am too much occupied to enlarge on them. But all good & true men are rejoiced at the prospect of expelling from power the banditti who have so long abused it." Copy. DLC-Nicholas Biddle Papers (DNA, M212, R20).

From Peter B. Porter, Black Rock, N.Y., November 14, 1837. Reports that the Whig victory in New York [Clay to Curtis, October 25, 1837] is even larger than stated in his letter of November 12. Thinks that 110 or more of the 128 members of the new legislature are Whigs. "Van Burenism is absolutely expunged in this State." Asks Clay to be "forebearing . . . even kind" toward the Conservatives [Clay

to Henry Clay, Jr., January 28, 1837] in the U.S. Senate during the coming session. "They are the best portion of our political opponents. To them we owe a great portion of our increased strength, and they are much disposed to amalgamate with us. I may add, moreover, that in my various conversations with many of their most influential men, I discover that they are decidedly friendly to you personally & will probably give you their united support." Says that the Whigs still lack a majority in the N.Y. senate by four or five seats, but points out that "There are about that number of Conservatives among the Administration members, and from conversations I have had with many of their friends here, there is reason to believe they will act with the Whigs, at least on some of the most important measures." Concludes: "Our state has now taken a commanding position in the Whig ranks, and as she is the largest state in the Union, may without cause of offence, take a leading part in indicating the time, place and manner of holding a Presidential Convention. I think our Whig members will be disposed to move in this business pretty early, & they would be doubtless glad to know your views on the Subject." Copy. OHi.

On April 18, 1838, Whig members of the New York legislature met in caucus and passed resolutions which included a call for a national convention to nominate candidates for the 1840 election of president and vice president. No specific candidate was endorsed. On May 29, some 4,000 Whigs met at Masonic Hall in New York City, approved the call for a national nominating convention, endorsed Clay as the Whig presidential candidate, and expressed their "high respect" for the Conservatives [Democrats] who adhered to Whig principles. Meanwhile, the Whigs in Congress had announced on May 15 that they would hold a national nominating convention in Harrisburg, Pa., on the first Wednesday in December, 1839. Washington *Daily National Intelligencer*, May 14, 30, June 1, 2, 1838. In June, 1839 the Whig state legislators again met in caucus, chose delegates to the Whig national nominating convention in Harrisburg in December, 1839, but failed to endorse a specific presidential candidate. See Porter to Clay, December 30, 1837 and February 16, 1839. For other preconvention developments, as well as the Harrisburg convention itself, see Robert G. Gunderson, *The Log-Cabin Campaign* (Lexington, Ky., 1957), 41-77; and Porter to Clay, December 30, 1837. For more on New York Whig political activities, see John David Morris, "The New York Whigs, 1834-1842: A Study of Political Organization," Ph.D. dissertation, University of Rochester, 1970.

To Willie P. Mangum, "Red Mountain," N.C., November 17, 1837. States that "I receive, almost daily, gratifying proofs of attachment and confidence from all quarters," and finds in them "abundant consolation for all politi[c]al injuries which I have ever received." Continues: "I offer you cordial congratulations on the recent unprecedented triumph in N. York [Clay to Curtis, October 25, 1837]. I now hope that I shall live to see the Goths expelled [from] the Capitol, and honest faithful and competent men once more in the Administration of the Government. Who they may be, should be—with me, I say, most sincerely, it is,—a perfectly subordinate question." ALS, manuscript torn. DLC-Willie P. Mangum Papers (DNA, M212, R22).

To ROBERT SWARTWOUT Lexington, November 21, 1837

I had the satisfaction to receive your agreeable letter, and letters from several other friends, conveying the pleasing intelligence of the astonishing issue of the recent election in New York.[1] There are occasions, and I feel this to be one, when the heart is too full to admit an expression of its feelings by any language. The capture of Lord Cornwallis did not diffuse more joy and gladness throughout the Land than the great event which has just happened in your State will every where excite. The first consummated a Nation's Independence; the last has saved the Nation. And, what is most gratifying, I understand that the work of regeneration has been accomplished by the People themselves; and that, out of the City, there was no organization among the Whigs, no leaders, no hand bills, no runners to stimulate exertion, but that the People, with a spontaneous and enthusiastic rush to the Polls, resolved to rescue their Country from impending ruin. And they have rescued it, nobly rescued it. God bless them; God bless them forever. . . .

ALS. NN. 1. Clay to Curtis, Oct. 25, 1837.

To SAMUEL P. LYMAN Lexington, November 22, 1837

Yes, my dear Sir, you were right in stating, in your favor of the 12h. inst. that you were sure I would rejoice with you on account of the glorious issue of your recent election.[1] I do from the inmost recesses of my heart congratulate you on that great event. It inspires new hopes, & opens bright prospects for our Country and for the cause of Civil liberty. The capacity of Man, which some began to fear and to doubt, for self-government, stands triumphantly vindicated. And the right of N. York to be hailed as the Empire state is consecrated by conclusive proof that she deserves it. There, party organization was complete; the dominant party was in possession of all the power and the places of the State; they appeared invincible. Nevertheless the People in their majority and their might have risen, and spontaneously rushing to the Polls, have saved their Country and immortalized themselves. And I learn that this glorious achievement has been effected without organization among the Whigs, out of the City, without leaders, without any extraordinary immediate aid from the press, and without runners! How greatly does this enhance the glory of the victory!

Mr. Talmadge [*sic,* Nathaniel P. Tallmadge] must indeed feel happy to be so nobly sustained. And if his colleague, were susceptible of much feeling, what would be his mortification![2]

Exclusively occupied in the enjoyment of the glad tidings, I have not speculated upon the probable course of the Administration in the new circumstances under which it finds itself. I can see no retreat for Mr. V. B. To renew a proposal of the S. Treasury system[3] would be the extreme of folly. And he has cut himself off from a Bank of the U. S. or from a revival of the State Bank system. I do not see that he has any thing left but to hang himself.[4]

ALS. MiU. 1. Clay to Curtis, Oct. 25, 1837. 2. Apparently a reference to the fact that Tallmadge, a Conservative Democrat who opposed Van Buren's Sub-Treasury system, had cooperated in electing both Whigs and Conservative Democrats in New York State while his colleague, Sen. Silas Wright, had introduced and sponsored the Sub-Treasury bill in the Senate. Speech in Senate, Sept. 25, 1837; Ivor D. Spencer, *The Victor and the Spoils; a Life of William L. Marcy* (Providence, R.I., 1959), 93, 299; Dixon Ryan Fox, *The Decline of Aristocracy in the Politics of New York* (New York, 1919), 398-99. 3. Speech in Senate, Sept. 25, 1837. 4. On Dec. 5, 1837, in his First Annual Message, Van Buren again advocated the Sub-Treasury system. See Clay to Porter, Dec. 5, 1837; and *MPP*, 3:373-95.

From Buckner H. Payne, Mt. Sterling, Ky., November 23, 1837. Discusses in detail the accounts he has kept of Stamboul's stud services. States that he is about to set out for his plantation in Louisiana and that as soon as he reaches it, he will forward the remainder of the information which Clay desires concerning Stamboul [8:415]. Notes: "Considering myself to be personally benefitted by your public services, mutch, very mutch beyond any tax, that your patronage of Stamboul would amount to, I take pleasure in saying, that I shall be pleased that you should have the services of the horse, to any number of mares, you may be pleased to send free of any expence to you whatever."

As he plans to "be a planter in Louisiana for some time," asks for "the benefit of a letter or two from you, to some of your friends in New Orleans, should you deem me worthy." ALS. Josephine Simpson Collection, Lexington, Ky.

To PETER B. PORTER Lexington, November 24, 1837

On the eve of my departure for Washington, I have the pleasure to receive your favor of the 12h. instant, and I reciprocate with all my heart felicitations on the glorious issue of your recent election.[1] It is indeed a great and decisive triumph, and opens new hopes, and inspires fresh confidence for our Country. What renders it more gratifying is, as I understand, that it was the spontaneous work of the People, who, without Whig organization out of the Cities, rushed to the Ballot boxes and saved their Country! There will be no longer doubts or fears of any as to the capacity of the American People for self-Government.

The first great care of the Whigs of N. York will now be to strengthen and maintain the ground which they have so nobly won. To that object every thing else should bend.

I am glad to hear that you purpose spending several months of the ensuing winter at Albany and Troy. Do, my dear friend, let me hear often and fully from you.

The event in N. York will have two effects on the next Presidency. 1st. It will moderate the tone of the Anti Masons of Pennsa. And 2dly. it will strengthen the hopes of Mr. Webster, until he becomes sensible that the preference of the Empire State is for another.

But I have not time now for speculation. We should devote ourselves, for the present, exclusively to the enjoyment of the glorious event. . . .

ALS. NBuHi. 1. Clay to Curtis, Oct. 25, 1837.

To Unknown Recipient, November 24, 1837. Rejoices over the "decisive and overwhelming" victory of the Whigs in New York [Clay to Curtis, October 25, 1837] which "is beyond my most sanguine anticipations." Continues: "During the years of darkness and tyranny which have just passed, I experienced, I must own, moments of discouragement, but I had an abiding confidence that truth and sound principles would ultimately triumph. And I thank God that I have not been disappointed. May the events which have just happened lead to the restoration of the public prosperity and the perpetuity of our free institutions!" ALS. PHi.

From Thomas H. Shelby, Lexington, Ky., November 28, 1837. Reports that about November 1, 1835, "I employed Chester G. Metcalf as an agent, and gave him four thousand five hundred dollars, with instructions to proceed directly to the Mediteranian [*sic*, Mediterranean], and to invest the Amt. in the purchase of Jacks & Jennys in the Island of Malta or else where." Details the information he has obtained about Metcalf's subsequent travels, including the fact that he had drawn out 880 pounds sterling of the capital at his disposal and had applied for, and supposedly obtained, a royal order authorizing him to ship stock from Spain. "From all the circumstances," concludes that Metcalf "has been seized and impris[oned] for an attempt to Ship Stock from Spain, although [clo]athed with Royal Authority, and that he is now la[ng]uishing in a Spanish prison." Asks that an inquiry be made through the State Department. ALS. DNA, RG59, Misc. Letters.

On December 8, 1837, Clay wrote Secretary of State John Forsyth, enclosing Shelby's letter and asking that an inquiry be made "into [the] fortunes and condition of Mr. Metcalfe [*sic*]." *Ibid.*

Forsyth replied on December 12, 1837, that "In the correspondence of the Chargé d'Affaires of the U.S. at Madrid, which has been examined, no mention is found of the individual, in question." Promises, however, that "Instructions will be given as desired, to the Minister of the U.S. at Madrid, and to the consuls at Barcelona [Joseph Borras] and Bordeaux [George Strobel], on the subject." Copy. DNA, RG59, Dom. Letters, vol. 29, p. 253. Forsyth evidently referred to the correspondence of John H. Eaton, U.S. minister to Madrid, and his predecessor, Cornelius P. Van Ness, because the U.S. had no chargé in Madrid during the time in question.

On November 2, 1839, Eaton wrote Forsyth that inquiries concerning Metcalf's whereabouts had been fruitless. He stated that the consul at Barcelona knew Metcalf and had placed an advertisement in the papers there giving his description, but had learned nothing. He concluded that Metcalf must have died, because the amnesties granted in recent years would have freed him had he been in prison. ALS. DNA, RG59, Dip. Disp., Spain, vol. 32 (M31, R32).

To Philemon Dickerson, Trenton, N.J., December 4, 1837. On behalf of a friend, asks Dickerson to purchase "a pair of handsome blood bay horses" which Clay had seen in Trenton last September. States that "If the Horses *continue sound,*" the unnamed friend "wishes to purchase them, if they can be had for $500, or for any sum not exceeding $600." ALS. PHi. For Dickerson—a congressman, governor, and judge from New Jersey—see *BDAC*.

From Francis S. Latham, Memphis, Tenn., December 4, 1837. Identifies himself as the editor of the Memphis *Enquirer* and sends an issue of that newspaper "in which . . . I have nominated you as a candidate for the Presidency, to succeed the present incumbent." Adds: "I have been smothering my wishes to place your name before the People for a long time—and, anxiously watching every development of public opinion upon this most interesting question, and being satisfied that in every quarter of the Union the whig party alone gaze upon you as their great head and centre, I have broken ground boldly, and doubt not that I shall be successfully sustained. Tennessee—yes Tennessee—even the state of the *Usurper* will vote for any good whig in preference to a Jacksonian or a Van-ite—and you—let me assure you—are her choice."

States that his "main object in addressing you this, is to request of you for publication, a copy of the pamphlet published by you during your last canvass refuting the many slanders urged against you by your enemies." Explains that his defense [against the corrupt bargain charge] had not circulated in the Tennessee region, "lest the truth might be seen." Believes it would benefit Clay's chances if the "many who have only heard of your enemies' charges against you, could hear you in self-defense." Boasts that "I enjoy the heart-felt consolation of being the first editor in this state (I believe) who openly oposed the highhanded and unconstitutional measures of general Jackson." States that "I have lived to see [illeg. word] people of a state in whose affections he was embalmed, follow me in my opposition to his policy" and hopes to "live to see this same people now elevate you to" the presidency. ALS. DLC-HC (DNA, M212, R5). For Clay's defense against the corrupt bargain charge, see 6:1394-96; 7:339.

The first article in the Memphis *Enquirer* endorsing Clay probably appeared in either the December 3rd or 4th issue, neither of which is available. For Latham's continuing support of Clay, see the Memphis *Enquirer*, December 19, 1837.

Remark in Senate, December 4, 1837. Moves that the Senate adjourn. *Cong. Globe*, 25 Cong., 2 Sess., 1.

Comment in Senate, December 5, 1837. Delivers eulogy to Sen. Joseph Kent of Maryland who died on November 24, 1837, at age 69. *Cong. Globe*, 25 Cong., 2 Sess., 8.

To PETER B. PORTER Washington, December 5, 1837

Your favor of the 14h. Ulto. addressed to me at Lexn. followed me here. I had received and answered the previous one from that place.

I concur cordially with you in thinking that the Conservatives should be treated with the utmost kindness and even confidence.[1] We could not have succeeded without them;[2] and without them we cannot maintain the ground which has been won by joint forces. They risked every thing; and nothing but honest convictions in the general could have induced them to separate from the dominant and triumphant party. Both from principle and policy I shall give them the right hand of fellowship.

N. York has, as you suggest, a commanding, indeed almost a decisive position in the politics of the Country. The first care however at Albany should be to maintain the vantage ground *in N. York* which has been won. If a nomination of any one for the Presidency should hazard that, it ought not to be made. If it would not; if it would benefit you; or if it would be merely neutral, I think it ought to be made. If I were nominated the question would be settled, I think, beyond all doubt, *even if N. York were subsequently lost*. But on this and all other subjects I will write you at Albany, when I hear of your arrival there. I have just parted from D. B. Ogden,[3] now in this City. He seemed to be glad that you were to be at Albany, will want your advice and will be disposed to follow it.

The Message of today adheres to the Sub treasury scheme![4] Nothing more was needed to consummate the overthrow of the President.

ALS. NBuHi. 1. Clay to Henry Clay, Jr., Jan. 28, 1837. 2. Clay to Curtis, Oct. 25, 1837. 3. For David B. Ogden, see 4:267. 4. For Van Buren's First Annual Message which continued to support the Sub-Treasury scheme [Speech in Senate, Sept. 25, 1837], see *MPP*, 3:380-83.

To ALEXANDER HAMILTON Washington, December 6, 1837

I received your favor of the 17h. Ulto. at the moment of my departure from home for this City, and, for want of time, postponed an answer until my arrival here. In the first place, I must thank you for the friendly motives which prompted you to write it.

I did receive such a communication from the Corresponding Commee. of the North [*sic*, Native] American Association[1] as you describe, during the late Extra Session; and I laid it aside, intending to answer it but defered a reply partly from incessant engagements but principally from a desire to acquire more information than I possessed, as to the causes which led to its formation, and as to the objects which it was proposed to accomplish by it. In the hurry of that busy Session, and in preparations for my return home, I mislaid it and never got the information I wished.

In the interior where I reside, we experience no inconvenience from the influx of Foreigners. I suppose it is otherwise in the Cities but to what extent I do not know, nor am I able to say what should be the remedy. There are many evils which should be left to the natural cure of public opinion. Whether this requires a more vigorous prescription by legislative authority depends upon circumstances of which I have not adequate knowledge. My general preference of every thing native over every similar thing which is foreign, I presume is sufficiently known.

I frankly confess then that, in the actual state of my information, I was not desirous, at least precipitately, to transmit any reply. I had another objection. I have great repugnance to my name voluntarily appearing in the News papers, without a strong necessity for it, and I supposed it not unlikely that any answer which I might return would be published.

If, under these circumstances, an answer be still expected and desired, I will transmit one as soon as I receive a copy of the communication formerly received, and obtain the requisite information; but I would be very glad if my friends would waive any formal reply from me. You will oblige me by letting me know their wishes.

You seem to think that the Whigs may find it expedient to depart from their system of nonaction in Congress and bring forward measures adapted to the present state of derangement in the business and currency of the Country. But what can they do? After condemning and denouncing Experiments, you would not have them go to experimenting. And the public mind is not now, if it ever should be, prepared for a National bank.[2]

The Message,[3] you will see, adheres to the S. Treasury project, and that I think consummates Mr. V. Bs. overthrow. It throws out, as an alternative, a plan of Special deposites,[4] to catch the Conservatives,[5] but I think they will not be caught.

I incline to believe we had better still look on, and seize the first favorable opportunity to carry any measure for effectual relief that may present itself.

ALS. DLC-Alexander Hamilton Papers (DNA, M212, R21). 1. The Native American Association had been formed in 1837 by about 700 subscribers representing all political parties. Its main purpose was to secure repeal of the naturalization law and to exclude naturalized citizens from public office. *Niles' Register* (August 5, 1837), 52:361-62. 2. See Speech in Senate, May 21, 1838. 3. Clay to Porter, Dec. 5, 1837. 4. Van Buren had suggested that in addition to the Sub-Treasury, some state banks might be used for the temporary deposit of a portion of the public revenue. Curtis, *The Fox at Bay*, 117. 5. Clay to Henry Clay, Jr., Jan. 28, 1837.

Remark in Senate, December 6, 1837. Has no objection to Sen. Felix Grundy's (Tenn.) motion that the chairman [Vice President Richard M. Johnson] appoint the standing committees for the 25th Congress, 2nd Session. *Cong. Globe*, 25 Cong., 2 Sess., 9. The only committee to which Clay was appointed was Foreign Relations. *Ibid.*, 15.

From William Jones, Jr., New York, December 8, 1837. Informs Clay that because he is a public man, "you cannot escape the malignant attacks of an infatuated political enemy." Writes, therefore, "for the purpose of obtaining a Phamplet published by you in 1828 [7:339] containing an appeal to the people of the West on the subject of the election of Mr. [John Q.] Adams as President in 1825, together with the Affadavits of the entire Western delegation to congres[s] during that year, showing forth, that they were not in any way influenced by you in giving their votes for Mr. Adams." Remarks: "There are many here in our city, as well as elsewhere, with whom I often come in contact with, who are ever ready to apply the harsh epithets of—Bribery—Corruption &c. whenever the name of him—of whom all true Americans should be proud of,—Henry Clay is mentioned; and it is therefore for the purpose of putting to rest, these false and malignant Slanders, which have been so extensively circulated, as well as to fulfill a promise of my own that 'I could prove from their own Affidavits' (referring to the Western delegation) 'that they were not influenced by you, in giving their votes for Mr. Adams in 1825,' that I thus have written."

Mentions "the recent results of the elections in the 'Empire State' as well as elsewhere, which I consider as affording, pretty strong evidence, of the Popular Will, however much Mr. Van Beuren [*sic*, Van Buren] and his partizans, may charge it to 'Bank Influence.'" Continues: "The people, have at length, shaken off the shackles, with which, they have so long been bound, and declared their 'Uncompromising Hostility' to New York's 'Favorite Son'; and that Ball, which was first set in motion by Kentucky, and other states of the mighty west, shall continue to roll on from West to East and from North to South; until Kentucky's Noble & Patriotic son, shall be placed in that chair, so ably filled by the 'Father of his Country.'!" ALS. DLC-HC (DNA, M212, R5). Jones lived at 53 Hester St. in New York City. For the Whig victories in New York and Ohio, see Clay to Curtis, October 25, 1837; for Tennessee, see Clay to Prentice, August 14, 1837. Clay's pamphlet, *An Address of Henry Clay, to the Public Containing Certain Testimony in Refutation of the Charges Against Him, Made by General Jackson, Touching the Presidential Election in 1825*, was reprinted in 1837 by E. Bryant in the office of the Lexington *Intelligencer*.

To GULIAN C. VERPLANCK *et al.* Washington, December 8, 1837

The delay in acknowledging the receipt of your letter of the 16th ultimo[1] has arisen from the fact that it reached Kentucky after my departure for this city, where it followed, and has been received by me.

I cordially reciprocate the congratulations with which you have honored me, on the glorious triumph of principle and the People, achieved at the recent election in New York.[2] There were many brilliant affairs which preceded it, beginning in Kentucky,[3] Tennessee,[4] and Indiana,[5] in August, and including those in Maine,[6] Rhode Island,[7] Pennsylvania,[8] New Jersey,[9] and Massachusetts[10] in the autumn; but there was still one signal and decisive victory wanting to close the campaign, and put an end to the contest. That has been nobly won in the State in which Burgoyne and his army surrendered to the Whigs of the Revolution. The battles of Yorktown, of Leipsic [*sic*, Leipzig], and of Waterloo, did not more effectually conclude the respective wars out of which they sprung, than the great event in New York has settled our political controversy. I rejoice heartily with you, and the enlightened world and posterity will rejoice with us.

It is true, gentlemen, as suggested by you, that I have lived in an age of revolution and great events, at home and abroad, deeply affecting large portions of the human race. Those in our own country have naturally most interested us. We have been acting not for ourselves and posterity only, but all mankind are concerned in the successful issue of the great experiment of self-government confided to our care. I have watched, therefore, with intense anxiety, the progress and the development of our system. When I beheld, nine years ago, the People of this country, impelled by enthusiastic gratitude, placing their Executive Government in hands which had only been accustomed to wield the sword, I trembled for the fate of our free institutions. My worst fears were more than realized by the [Jackson] Administration which ensued. Blow after blow fell upon the Constitution; experiment succeeded experiment upon the business and prosperity of the People, and violence and intimidation, abuses and corruption, became the order of the day. I stood amazed at the lawless acts of the Executive. Taking courage from the impunity which attended its career, and proclaiming the fallacious doctrine that the successful issue of every election was a popular approval of all previous measures and previous opinions of the Executive, there seemed to be no end or bounds to its encroachments. The expressed will of the Representatives of the People and of the States was openly contemned; an important proceeding, of vital influence on the Constitution and the public welfare, was adopted near the commencement of a session of Congress, with the known purpose of preventing its legislative counteraction;[11] and bills which had passed both Houses with remarkable concurrence, have been withheld, there is too much reason to believe, with the motive of preventing the exercise of the salutary restriction in the Constitution upon the power of the veto.[12] Amidst all these arbitrary acts and proceedings, a few faithful Senators, annually diminished, lifted up their warning but unheeded voices. I did not indeed despair; but I confess that I felt greatly discouraged. It seemed as if all the cautious checks of the Constitution were subverted, and that the Republic was almost drawing to a close.

Another Administration [Van Buren] came. Justice and liberality required that it should be judged by its acts and measures; but, as if resolved to cut off all hopes from the People, the new President soon announced his purpose to be to follow in the footsteps of his immediate predecessor; and he has faithfully trodden in them! His eye and his ear appear to be directed more towards the Hermitage than turned to the People and their sufferings.

But our deliverance, thank God! is at hand. The People—the deceived, the abused, the betrayed People—have risen in their majesty, and, by demonstrations which cannot be misunderstood, or perverted, have pronounced in a voice of thunder the doom of Experiments and Experimenters. They have again signally vindicated their capacity for self-government, and marked the limit beyond which madness and folly dare not proceed.

Gratitude and thanks to the People! Most of all, gratitude and thanks to the People of New York! They have shown themselves worthy of the proud and prominent position which they hold in the American Confederacy.

Henceforward it should be our constant care to maintain and strengthen the ground which has been so gloriously won. Prudence and moderation should characterize our councils, and we should extend the hand of friendship and confidence to all who have co-operated with us. Actuated by a high sense of duty to our common country, they have shown that they love Rome more than Caesar. We should not even forget that the vanquished themselves are not enemies, but misguided brethren, who will sooner or later unite with us in rescuing our Government and institutions from the corruption and ruin to which they are rapidly tending....

Copy. Printed in Washington *Daily National Intelligencer*, Dec. 28, 1837. 1. On Nov. 16, 1837, a group of friends wrote Clay from New York expressing their "joy and exultation" at the great Whig victory in the New York state elections. They added: "Permit us to sympathize in the devout joy of your heart at this auspicious event which dissipates the misgivings and gloomy doubts which were gathering over the future. . . . Long may you live, sir, to enjoy the gratitude of a People who cannot look upon the blessings they enjoy and not remember you." Copy. Printed in Washington *Daily National Intelligencer*, Dec. 28, 1837. 2. Clay to Curtis, Oct. 25, 1837. 3. Clay to Noble, June 20, 1837. 4. Clay to Prentice, August 14, 1837. 5. Clay to Noble, March 4, 1837. 6. Speech in Senate, Feb. 19, 1838. 7. *Ibid.* 8. *Ibid.* 9. In the New Jersey state legislative election of Oct. 10, 1837, 10 Whigs and 6 Democrats were elected to the council (state senate), while 35 Whigs and 18 Democrats were elected to the state house of representatives. This gave the Whigs a majority of 21 on joint ballot, whereas the Democrats had had a majority of 10 to 12 on joint ballot following the 1836 election. Washington *Daily National Intelligencer*, Oct. 16, 1837. 10. In the 1837 gubernatorial election in Massachusetts, Edward Everett, the Whig candidate, defeated Marcus Morton, the Democratic candidate, by the vote of 50,656 to 33,089. *BDGUS*, 2:701. All 40 members elected to the state senate were Whigs. Washington *Daily National Intelligencer*, Nov. 20, 1837. 11. Probably a reference to Jackson's reappointment to office during the Senate's recess of persons whom the Senate had already refused to confirm. See, for example, 8:559-60, 727. Also, for Clay's views of Jackson's removals from office of persons confirmed by the Senate, see 8:703. 12. For instance, see 8:214 for Jackson's Maysville Road veto; 8: 434, 552, 558 for his bank veto; 8:610 for his veto of Clay's public land (distribution) bill.

To FRANCIS T. BROOKE Washington, December 10, 1837

I received your favor transmitting the inclosed. The piece in *The Arena*[1] expressed correctly the views which I entertain on the subjects to which it refers. In respect to Internal Improvements and the Tariff, my opinions are unchanged as to the *powers* of the General Government; but the expediency of the exercise of any given power with which that Government may be invested must depend upon and be regulated by circumstances.

1. As to the Tariff. I had supposed and hoped that the Compromise Act[2] settled and terminated all our unhappy disputes. By that Act, to which I have uniformly adhered, I have been and am willing to be governed. I wish it faithfully executed; and I have no purpose of disturbing its provisions.

And 2. As to internal improvements; considering how much each of the states has done for itself; and considering how much Congress did, by the passage of the Distribution Act,[3] I have no wish to see anything more done by the General Government, except to pass, at some suitable time, the Land Bill[4] which I formerly proposed. And *this* is not the time to press the passage of that Bill. These opinions may be collected from my public course, and especially from my speeches on the Land Bill and other subjects. This being the case, I cannot consent to the publication of anything *as coming from me or by my authority*, upon either of those subjects. And my objection to such publication is that I cannot consent to *seem* to propitiate any one for the purpose of advancing what may be thought to be an object personal to myself.

Poor Leigh![5] I hope that we shall not, but fear that we shall, lose him. My heart yet bleeds for my lamented friend Keat [*sic*];[6] and I trust that it may not soon be put to fresh trials.

I left Mrs. [Lucretia Hart] Clay in excellent health; and at one time she had made up her mind to accompany me; but domestic duties, she thought, required her to remain. My warm regard to Mrs. [Mary Champe Carter] Brooke.

Copy. Printed in *Tyler's Quarterly Historical and Genealogical Magazine* (Oct., 1950), 32:96. 1. The Fredericksburg (Va.) *Political Arena* was a Whig newspaper that supported Clay for president. It is unclear to which article Clay refers. Washington *Daily National Intelligencer*, Feb. 21, 1838. 2. See 8:604, 619-22, 626-27. 3. See 8:813, 873-74. 4. See 8:539-41, 609-10, 812-13, 846-47, 873-74. 5. Benjamin W. Leigh was very ill for several months and newspapers mistakenly reported his death several times. He recovered, however, and lived until 1849. *Niles' Register* (Dec. 9, 1837), 53:240. 6. Probably Sen. Joseph Kent (Md.) who died on Nov. 24, 1837, and for whom Clay delivered an eulogy in the Senate on Dec. 5, 1837. *Niles' Register* (Dec. 2, 1837), 53:209, 214.

From Stephen Duncan, Natchez, December 11, 1837. States that "we will 'try the experiment of the Rope for one year.' " Adds that "I expect to realise the funds for your Rope, on the 16th. Jany. [Clay to Henry Clay, Jr., September 8, 1837; Duncan to Clay, November 4, 1837]."

Turning to politics, notes that "The Whig victory in New York, was a glorious result [Clay to Curtis, October 25, 1837]. But there is much yet to be done—to make it profitable to the party & to the country." Believes also that "The act for the relief of the Deposite Banks—will afford considerable relief to the people, and especially to those in the West & South West." States that "We are in anxious expectations here, for the doings of the Bank convention at New York. I think they ought to adjourn to *meet again* in May,—& *then* adjourn to *meet again* in Decr.,—and *then* resolve, to resume specie payments on 1st. July 1839. . . . for it is very obvious the Southern Banks cannot resume, until their discounts & circulation are reduced, by the *full* proceeds of two good crops—and if the resumption should not be simultaneous with those of the North & East, our Bankes will decrease the specie from them in order to prepare to resume." Continues: "Now, I think, there are two other points—much more important, in this respect, 1st. There must be a general return of Confidence—and a removal of the present distrust of Banks & Bank notes. and 2d. The Sub Treasury system—must be completely annihilated [Speech in Senate, September 25, 1837]. It now existed will continue to exist—until some other depositories for the public funds are created.—It matters not whether it has the sanction of Law for its continuance." Believes that the nation must produce at least $10 million in coin or "create a national institution, that will give us a currency, to the same extent,—which will be equivalent to specie, before we can think of resuming specie payments. True, a reduction in the rate of Exchange would facilitate the import of specie. But this cannot be accomplished at all, out of the exports of the next year; and if it could,—its expediency would be doubtful." Concludes that "It is obvious, our Banks must greatly reduce their discounts,—in order to call in their circulation. . . . the process . . . must be gradual & slow." Insists, in the final analysis, that "We must have a National Bank—before we can resume, specie payments [Comment in Senate, September 26, 1837; Speech in Senate, September 25, 1837 and May 21, 1838]—if we hope & wish to resume—without involving the whole country in greater suffering than she has yet endured; & with hope of continuance.—" ALS. DLC-TJC (DNA, M212, R14).

The "Act for adjusting the remaining claims on the deposit banks," which was passed by resolution on October 14, 1837, and signed by Van Buren on October 16, authorized the secretary of the treasury to withdraw moneys from "the former deposite banks, in a manner as gradual and convenient to the institutions" as possible in order to meet the government's needs. 5 *U.S. Stat.*, 206. For more on the bill, see Kinley, *The Independent Treasury of the United States*, 35; Wilson, *The Presidency of Martin Van Buren*, 74.

On August 15, 1837, a general meeting of the officers of the banks in New York City met and passed a resolution calling for a bank convention to agree on a time for the New York and other banks to resume specie payments. Such a convention was held on November 27-December 2 in New York City with 141 delegates present representing 19 states. Although many wanted to set July 1, 1838, as the date of resumption, they were unable to agree and adjourned until April, 1838, at which time they were still unable to decide on a date. New York banks ultimately lead the way by resuming specie payments on May 10, 1838, with most other banks following suit during the summer and early fall. *Niles' Register* (September 2, 9, 1837), 53:6, 19; *ibid.* (December 2, 9, 1837), 53:209, 226; *ibid.* (July 28, 1838), 54: 337; Hammond, *Banks and Politics in America*, 478-81.

On December 30, 1837, Lambdin & Bennett supplied an account of "Sales of 294 Coils Rope . . . sold for account risk of Henry Clay Esqr. proceeds subject to the order of Dr S. Duncan" with the net amount of $3,592.33 due January 15, 1838. ADS. DLC-TJC (DNA, M212, R18).

Remark in Senate, December 11, 1837. On the cost of providing express mail service, asks how much the government contributes and how much comes from private individuals. *Cong. Globe*, 25 Cong., 2 Sess., 17.

From Caleb Emerson, Marietta, Ohio, December 12, 1837. Although admitting that he has merely met Clay and shaken hands with him, professes to have been "with Mr Clay in 1820 & forward in favor of the American System. . . . excepting the two compromises [2:669-70, 740-48, 775-78, 785-86; 3:15-22, 26-33, 46-50; 8:604, 619-22, 626-27]." Warns that there is a project underway "to revive the connection which existed thirty years ago, between the planting interest of the South and the ultra democracy of the North." Adds that "you, my dear Sir, are approaching a fearful test. Southern interest or Southern whims swayed our destiny from Washington downward till you broke the charm in 1825. Terrible was the penalty you were doomed to suffer for your defection. But a more decisive crisis is hastening, if it be not already come. That interest which so long swayed our destinies now demands that its power shall be made absolute & perpetual. The destinies of our country may now be said to be most emphatically within your grasp. You are the only political man of importance, within a certain portion of our country, who has had the moral courage to loose himself from the deathlike grasp of its ruling influence. . . . Let us be plain. Slavery must triumph or freedom must go down. . . . The time is coming—is come—to decide whether or not we, Anglo Americans are to be deemed the true sons and supporters of liberty, or are to be branded as a race of mercenary political hypocrites. Northern Liberty will not be surrendered without a fearful struggle. New England is mustering to the contest with portentous unanimity. When once in array, do not look for their receding. The New Englanders are not always easily moved; but on a subject like this they may—and will, I think—be aroused to feel & move as one man; and I have little doubt that the same impulse will pervade all the free states." Furthermore, opposes the compromises with the South, because "Every yielding to impertinent bravado invites its frequent and aggravated repetition."

Notes that "I regretted & condemned the first movements of the abolitionists as injudicious & ill timed. Yet I accorded with their principles and respected their motives." Has come to believe that "the contest is not now between the Anti-Slavery Society and the Slaveholders: It is between Southern arrogance and the cause of liberty—and it will not end till one or the other shall be triumphant." Continues: "Would to God that Kentucky, Virginia & Maryland, instead of forging fetters for Missouri, had, long ago, set herself to demolish her own! How would the free hand of industry have embellished and enriched these regions so favored by nature—so cursed by man! . . . No men had ever a more fearful responsibility—no men can have more sublime proffers of enduring fame & everlasting gratitude—than men of influence in the Slave States.—Let Kentucky & Virginia come to the rescue—let them discard, at once & forever, the cause of Slavery & range themselves with the free—and the contest, now & forever—will be ended. Their own best interest—their very safety, demands it.—If they falter—if they miss this 'tide of fortune' they may rue it in misery, in bloodshed, in ruin." ALS. DLC-HC (DNA, M212, R5). For Emerson, an Ohio lawyer, see Thomas J. Summers, *History of Marietta* (Marietta, O., 1903), 130, 133, 164, 271.

Speech to American Colonization Society, Washington, December 12, 1837. Addresses the 21st annual meeting of the society in his capacity as its new president. Mentions at the outset that the society, in its twenty-year history, has acquired an extensive territory in Africa where it has established "eight flourishing settlements and towns" that abound in civilization and in "temples erected to the ever-living God." Is convinced that with proper support from state and federal governments the "colonization of the decendants of the African race may be effected to any desirable extent." Reminds his audience that the society was founded only "to colonize, with their own voluntary consent, the free persons of color in the United States." It does not exist to perpetuate slavery; nor does it exist to "abolish slavery forthwith, and to let loose the untutored and unprepared slaves upon society." Says that the members of the society consider slavery a "deplorable evil." The society and the abolitionists perform entirely different functions. "We deal only with free persons of color; their efforts are directed towards the slave. We seek to better the condition of the free persons of color; they the slave." Defends the society against the charge that the slave population now numbers two or three millions and that in twenty years "we have been able to colonize only a few thousand." Says the society should not be judged by a comparison of such figures, only "by the standard of our own promises and pledges." Explains that the society never claimed it "could separate the two classes of the American population, and colonize the African portion of it. . . . We have thought, and we have said, that we believed that the *principle* of colonization was susceptible of being applied to the extent of a total separation of the two races. But we have not attempted it. We have left that to the care and the judgments of those who alone can rightfully and constitutionally decide the matter. We promised only to be the pioneer, and to show the practicability of the principle." Believes, however, that it might take "near two centuries" to restore the Africans "to the parent country, with all the blessings of law and liberty, religion and civilization. A sudden and instantaneous separation of the two races, if it were possible, would be good for neither." Concludes with the proud observation that "There stand the colonies, on the shores of Africa planted under its [the society's] auspices. With but little or no further aid from this country, they now possess inherently the power of sustaining themselves and protecting their existence. The practicability of colonization is forever demonstrated." Copy. Printed in *Niles' Register* (December 23, 1837), 53:264-65.

To WILLIAM E. CHANNING Washington, December 13, 1837

I received both your favors,[1] that of the 16h. Ulto. and the previous one to which it refers. The great pressure of my correspondence, and my public engagements oblige me to avail myself of your kind permission to abstain from answering them at large. But you may be perfectly assured that there will be no violation by me of the confidence which is implied in a private correspondence even on public affairs. Your suggestions will always receive attentive and respectful consideration, even when I have the misfortune to differ from you. Like yourself, I seldom preserve copies of any letters that I write.

I am afraid that the desire to put down parties, which you express, has more of humanity then practicability in it. They can only, I apprehend, be extinguished, by extinguishing their cause, free Government, a free press, and freedom of opinion. The effort of the wise and the good should be rather directed to moderate their asperity.

ALS. RHi. 1. Neither found, but see Channing to Clay, August 1, 1837.

Remark in Senate, December 13, 1837. Introduces bills for the benefit of the executrix of the late R.H. Lee and to amend the several acts relating to the extension of copyrights to foreigners [Comment in Senate, February 2, 1837]. Asks also that a bill from the Committee on Finance inquiring into "the condition of the currency of the District of Columbia" be read in full since he wants to know "why this devoted District was to be thus doomed." Moves also to print a communication from the president on the diplomatic status of U.S. claims against Mexico, this in response to the Senate resolution of October 13 [Remark in Senate, October 13, 1837]. *Cong. Globe,* 25 Cong., 2 Sess., 20-21. For the prior history of unsuccessful legislation designed to force District banks to resume specie payments and suppress their issuance of notes of small denomination, see Speech in Senate, September 25, 1837. For the failure of similar legislation in the 25th Congress, 2nd Session, see *Cong. Globe,* 25 Cong., 2 Sess., 40-42, 50, 71, 128, 357. See also Comment in Senate, December 21, 1837.

From PETER B. PORTER Black Rock, N.Y., December 15, 1837

We are in the midst of a revolution!—surrounded by armed men, drums, trumpets and all the pomp and circumstance of glorious war.

About a week ago a parcel of giddy and ambitious young men, among whom is a son [Rensselaer Van Rensselaer] of Solomon Van Rensselaer, commenced beating up for volunteers in Buffalo, and collecting arms, &c., for the avowed purpose of crossing to Canada to assist the Patriots.[1] In this they were too openly encouraged by some of our most respectable citizens who attended their nightly meetings at the Theatre, made exhilerating speeches, &c. Night before last, having collected about 200 recruits, they invaded the Court House, took about 200 stand public arms and marched to Black Rock, bringing with them a field piece and about 400 muskets, and took up their quarters at a tavern adjoining the ferry to Canada.

This, with their previous movements, created a prodigious panic among the Canadians, who by yesterday morning had 500 men already assembled on the opposite shore, and 1000 men on their march from Toronto and other places, to repel the invasion.

Yesterday it became necessary for the sober and considerate citizens to interfere. We sent a messenger across the river to quiet the fears of the Canadians by informing them of the true state of things; in consequence of which their advancing troops were remanded—and most of those *on this side* dispersed in the course of the day.

The revolution in Upper Canada, which, under able leaders, might have been affected with the greatest ease, is now indefinitely postponed. [William Lyon] McKenzie, *who is a poor chief*,[2] undertook to attack Toronto with a few hundred men, wholly undisiplined and unprovided. The consequence was that he was beaten, about 30 of his men killed and the remainder dispersed, and he fled to Buffalo, where he now is, openly preaching sedition to our own citizens. A reward of $4000 is offered for him by the Gov. of Canada [Sir George Arthur], and I think it very probable he will be taken. [John] Rolph and [Marshall S.] Bidwell,[3] members of Parliament and reformers, are also here. They are very respectable and considerate men, have taken no part in the military movements on either side, and propose soon to return to Toronto.

I have received your two letters of the 24th Nov. and 8th Dec'r, and thank you for they contain the renewed indications of friendship on the revival of our correspondance, which had been for some time interrupted. I intend to be at Troy so as to spend the Christmas holy-days (which will be their vacation) with my children. Should you write me, please to direct me to that place, until otherwise advised.

Mr. Van Buren's Message[4] has had no other effect here than to confirm the unfavourable impressions which his late political course had created.

Yesterday Mr. Noah Cook[5] of New York, whom I believe you must know as a sensible and efficient politician, a member of the Corresponding Clay Committee, and a warm friend of yours, spent the day at my house. He has just returned from Ohio, where, as well as in several other Western States, he is extensively acquainted. His information in the political statisticks of the day is more ample than that of anyone I have lately met—and he *demonstrates* that not only New York, but a large majority of the States, will be for you, provided we can effect, as I have no doubt we can, in some unexceptionable way, an expression of a majority of the Whigs of this State in your favour. He informs me, what I did not know before, that three fourths of the present Assembly delegates from the City of N. York will be with us. I am glad you saw David B. Ogden. I have not seen him of late, but from what I have heard I think he will go with us, notwithstanding his personal intimacy with Mr. Webster, and if so he can do much toward securing the cooperation of the Webster men in the city.

I have just learnt that several new squads of recruits for Canada came into Buffalo in the course of last night, bringing two field pieces, and that they attempted again to take the public arms which had been restored to Court House, but were defeated in their purpose. I will pick up some papers in the course of the day and send them by this evening's mail to give you the latest accounts from the seat of war, which seems to have been transferred from Canada to our own shores.

Copy. OHi. 1. For Rensselaer Van Rensselaer's involvement in attempting to aid the revolutionary forces in Canada, see Catharina V. Van Rensselaer Bonney, *A Legacy of Historical Gleanings*, 2 vols. (Albany, N.Y., 1875), 2:64-105, 115-16, 123-27. For the causes, course, and consequences of the Canadian uprising for constitutional reform, as well as American involvement, see Albert B. Corey, *The Crisis of 1830-1842 in Canadian-American Relations*. New Haven, 1941; Douglas Frank, "The Canadian Rebellion and the American Public," *NF* (Winter, 1969), 16:96-104; Wilson P. Shortridge, "The Canadian-American Frontier During the Rebellion of 1837-1838," *CHR* (March, 1926), 7:13-26. See also Comment in Senate, Jan. 5, 1838. 2. For MacKenzie, leader of the Canadian revolt, see *DNB* and David Flint, *William Lyon MacKenzie, Rebel Against Authority*. Toronto, 1971. 3. For Rolph, see *DNB* and William Kingford, *History of Canada*, 10 vols. (Toronto, 1898), 10:224-25. For Bidwell, see *DNB* and Flint, *William Lyon MacKenzie*, 106, 122, 125-26, 132. 4. Clay to Porter, Dec. 5, 1837. 5. Cook was a forwarder, located at "108 Broad c. Watch h. 140 Amity" in New York City. Longworth, *American Almanac: New-York Register, and City Directory*, 169.

From **JAMES WATSON WEBB** New York City, December 15, 19, 1837

Your kind favour of the 27th October came to hand in the midst of our rejoicing upon the result of the contest with the Loco Focos in this State [New York].[1] That result so unexpected even to our friends, if achieved almost without an effort on the part of the Whig leaders, demonstrating as it does, the safety of relying upon the people, is however, attended with some consequences which it will become your duty in connexion with Mr. Webster to avert. The overwhelming strength of the Whig party—or rather I should say, the confident reliance upon its overwhelming strength hereafter, has rendered many of our politicians imprudently anxious to take the lead in exhibiting attachment to you, or to Mr. Webster as their feelings on the apparent strength of either might seem to render *politic*. For myself I have nothing to ask—nothing to expect—nothing to wish for from either you or Mr W. Should you be elected—and that one of you could be, is placed beyond the shadow of doubt in my mind, unless we are guilty of some more than ordinary imprudence. During our Whig Jubilee,[2] Mr. [Francis] Granger was here and we were both struck with the warm indications in your favour which most of the Baltimore & Philadelphia Delegates exhibited. This lead [*sic*, led] us and many others, to converse often & much upon the consequences & tendency of such preferences at this early day; and he satisfied my mind, that if *you* and Mr. *Webster* had it in your power definitely to arrange the succession at this time, it would be death to our hopes if you were to do so.

You appear to be perfectly familiar with the pertinacity of General [William Henry] Harrison looking upon the union of the Whigs last fall upon him as an indication of his strength and great popularity.[3] Never was a man more deceived. His was a reflected strength—reflected from the eminations of the great minds which have so nobly contended for, & so justly endeared Whig Principles to the people. He has no influence east of the Mountains except in the Anti-Masonic Districts, and there he has a strength which neither you nor Mr. W. possess, and which we must treat with a great deal of *apparent* respect. Mr. Granger thinks, and I certainly agree with him, that if either Mr. W. or yourself should retire from the field now, or if you should suffer your friends to take such means as would indicate a clear preferance for either of you, Anti-Masonry would raise its head on the instant and Vermont, Pennsylvania, & this state, be irretrievably lost to the Whig cause. With the defection of Mr. Calhoun,[4] & no man glories more in his [passing?] than I do—we cannot afford to lose the states named. It surely becomes us then, to take such measures, as shall keep our party united under the banner of "Principles" as long as possible, and only proclaim our ultimate determination at the very latest period that the nature of the contest renders practicable.

I may conscientiously say, and that without any assumption on my part, that there are few—very few men in this country, so thoroughly disinterested on this question as I am. The doctrines which I aver in my columns, are the honest convictions of my mind, and I shall never permit any other question but the success of our party to enter into my calculations of the result. I have therefore, strongly urged that there shall not be a National Convention till the Spring of 1840,[5] and I have inculcated the necessity of your friends & those of Mr. *Webster* abstaining as much as possible from all canvassing. I am happy to add that since Mr. *Webster* came here, nearly three weeks since, in all his public & private expressions of his sentiments he has strongly urged this course. Of you & your friends, both in public & private, he has expressed the highest opinion. For you he has declared his respect, his friendship, & esteem in unqualified terms—and in your principles and devotion to the Country he has both publicly & privately reiterated his confidence & the pleasure it will give him to unite in your support should you be selected by the deputations of the Whig Party as their candidate. But his language has uniformly been—"Let the question of the succession be kept as much as possible out of sight—let us in recruiting—recruit for the whig cause & whig principles—let us unite all who are, or may be opposed to the administration, in support of the Constitution & the Laws—& then, when the time for action arrives, let us abide the decision of the National Convention and look upon the Whig candidate whoever he may be, not as the particular friend of any section of our party, but as the representative of one and all of us—as embodying the very essence of all those Constitutional doctrines for which the Whigs as a party are contending.["] This in substance, has been the tenor of his public speeches & private conversations. These are my doctrines & they are as well known to every Whig who reads the Courier & Enquirer a[s] they are to you. True, I go further than some, & contend that the Country cannot afford to lose the services of either of you, & that if one should be nominated for the Presidency and the other for the Vice Presidency, the People may insist upon your serving them.

Tuesday Night Decr 19th

This letter has been laying unfinished on my table since friday night. Mr. W. left here on Saturday m[ornin]g, & for the reasons herein named, I said not a word in relation to his retiring in your favour. But I did say to him that if the people should nominate him for the V.P. he would be compelled to serve, & that in *my opinion* it was the road by which he is to reach the Presidency. It is said that some of your friends will attempt "to draw the lines" in our General Committee on the occasion of electing its chairman.[6] If so, I have no doubt that much mischief will be the Consequence. A word for you through our friend [Matthew L.] Davis would prevent this, if you should look upon the efforts of such a course in the same light that I do.—I am more than ever satisfied, that there exists not a reasonable doubt but *you* will receive the nomination of the Convention by acclamation; but we must not lose sight of Anti-Masonry.

ALS. DLC-HC (DNA, M212, R5). Letter marked "(Private)." 1. Clay to Curtis, Oct. 25, 1837. 2. For a detailed account of the Whig Jubilee, held at Masonic Hall in New York City on Nov. 22, 1837, see *Niles' Register* (Dec. 2, 1837), 53:211-13. 3. Apparently a reference to Harrison's strong showing in the presidential election of 1836. See Gunderson, *The Log Cabin Campaign*, 41-42. 4. Speech in Senate, Feb. 19, 1838. 5. Porter to Clay, Nov. 14 and Dec. 30, 1837. 6. Probably R.C. Wetmore, chairman of the General Committee of Whig Young Men. New York *Morning Herald*, April 2, 1838.

To Francis Lieber, Columbia, S.C., December 16, 1837. Asks where he can procure a copy of Lieber's "Essay on Political interpretation and construction." Turning to politics, comments: "Late political events are well worthy of the congratulations which you so kindly tender [Clay to Prentice, August 14, 1837; Clay to Curtis, October 25, 1837]. I believe they will lead to important results. I cannot see how it should be otherwise. From all that I can learn, the administration will not profit by them. It means to persevere in its fatal Subtreasury project [Speech in Senate, September 25, 1837]. What infatuation! How rare is it for men or for parties, long intoxicated with success, to adapt themselves to a radical change in public opinion!" ALS. CSmH. Lieber published the essay under the title *Legal and Political Hermeneutics; or, Principles of Interpretation and Construction in Law and Politics....* Boston, 1837. Reprinted from the *American Jurist* for Oct., 1837.

To JAMES B. CLAY Washington, December 18, 1837

I received today your favor of the 6h. inst. but have not received your previous letter, to which you refer, in which you made an offer of the Alton Land[1] to Mr. Tigert. I had however before I left home submitted the matter of the Sale of that land to you, and I shall be content with whatever you may do, being sure that your intentions will be to do the best for us all.

With respect too to your project of having Wood cut from it for the supply of the consumption of St Louis, I leave that affair to your judgment. If it be well attended to, I have no doubt that it may be rendered profitable; but recollect that it will depend altogether upon the degree of attention paid to it. It will have the effect of repressing trespasses upon the Land.

I am sorry to hear of the loss of your Heifers, but we must expect occasional losses, and increase our diligence to repair them

Your resolution to study and to begin with History is a good one, and I hope you will persevere in it.

Gillies Greece, with Plutarch's lives.
Gibbons Rise & Fall of the Roman Empire.
Tacitus.
Hume, with the continuation
Russells Modern Europe.
Hallam's Middle Ages.
Robertson, Charles the 5h. Indies &c.
Marshalls life of Washn.
Botta's History of the American Revolution.[2]

These books and others may be read with advantage. And you should adopt some systematic course, as to time, that is to read so many hours out of the 24.

Give my respects to Majr. [Richard] Graham.

ALS. DLC-TJC (DNA, M212, R10). Printed in Colton, *Clay Correspondence*, 4:421-22. Addressed to James at "Richland near St. Louis Missouri." 1. Clay's land, 680 acres of it, lay in the forks of the Mississippi and Missouri rivers, across the rivers from Alton, Ill. See Clay to James B. Clay, Oct. 30, 1840. 2. John Gillies, *The History of Ancient Greece...*, 4 vols., New York, 1814; John & William Langhorne, *Plutarch's Lives, Translated From the Original Greek; With Notes Critical and Historical, and a Life of Plutarch*, 3rd ed., 6 vols., Philadelphia, 1822; Edward Gibbon, *The History of the Decline and Fall of the Roman Empire*, 5th Am. ed., 6 vols., New York, 1836; *The Historical Annals of Cornelius Tacitus*. Philadelphia, 1829 (many other editions); David Hume, *The His-*

tory of England . . . Designed As a Continuation of Mr. Hume's History. London, 1785; William Russell, *The History of Modern Europe . . . to . . . 1763*, 6 vols., Philadelphia, 1800-11; Henry Hallam, *History of Europe During the Middle Ages*, 3 vols., Paris, 1820-21; William Robertson, *The History of the Reign of Charles the Fifth, Emperor of Germany*, 3 vols., Philadelphia, 1770; John Marshall, *The Life of George Washington*, 5 vols., Philadelphia, 1804-7; Carlo Botta, *History of War of Independence of the United States of America*. Translated by George A. Otis. 3 vols., Philadelphia, 1820-21.

Comment in Senate, December 18, 1837. Asks for the withdrawal of a motion to table the petition of 115 ladies of Gloucester County, N.J., asking for the immediate abolition of slavery in the District of Columbia. Says that his opinions on the subject are well known [8:817, 833], and that he has "no hesitation" in saying that Congress should not do what the petitioners request without the consent of the people of the district. Asks Sen. Garret D. Wall (N.J.) whether "abolition in the abstract" is growing there and elsewhere, or whether it is becoming "mixed up with other matters," such as a belief that the "sacred right of petition" has been "assailed." Argues that these abolitionist petitions should be referred to the Committee for the District of Columbia or some other committee "that would elicit all the facts, reason coolly and dispassionately" and present "the subject in all its bearings to the citizens of non-slaveholding States, and in a manner worthy of the great subject." In response to a statement by Sen. William C. Preston (S.C.) that these petitions are simply stirring up national excitement and therefore should not be received, Clay maintains that it is "much more important that the country should be quiet than the Senate." Believes that the excitement can be reduced were the Senate able to separate the "two classes of petitioners." The separation would deprive the abolitionists "of the advantage of mixing their peculiar objects" with those who support the "great republican right of petition." The Senate must thus go further than the "cold, simple act of reception, followed by an instant rejection," a practice which gives "color to the charge that it is a substantial denial of the right of petition." It must refer the abolitionist petitions to committee and let them be disposed of there, so that those who are "described as fanatics" will be separated from those who believe that the right of petition is being assailed. In reply to Sen. John C. Calhoun's charge that Clay's proposal would increase national excitement by converting the halls of Congress into a place for the discussion of abolition, and that continued firm resistance to the encroachments of abolitionist petitioners would serve best to preserve the Union, Clay remarks that he has "no fears for the Union," but that he does have "a desire to tranquilize every part." Notes, too, that the question is "not the same as to slavery in the District and slavery in the States." Repeats that his object is "merely to preserve the Union in its true spirit; and separate fanaticism from those . . . capable of listening to reason." Points out that Calhoun relies on "extreme cases" in illustrating the presumed dangers to the Union from abolitionist petitions; and asserts that in a realistic sense the actual abolition of slavery in the district is about as likely to occur as the abolition of the Christian religion. Concludes that the power of Congress to abolish slavery in the district is believed to exist; also that Congress has decided it is "right to receive petitions on the subject." Given these facts, his object is "to discover a healing measure." *Cong. Globe*, 25 Cong., 2 Sess., 34, 37-38. See also William L. Van Deburg, "Henry Clay, the Right of Petition, and Slavery in the Nation's Capital," *RKHS* (April, 1970), 68:132-46.

To George Getz, Washington, December 18, 1837. States that he has received "the Prospectus of the new paper which you propose to publish," and requests "you to consider me as one of your subscribers." Cautions, however, that "you should not embark in your enterprize without just reasons to expect that the expences of your establishment will be sustained. Good as I believe the cause is in which I have been so long struggling, I always feel concerned, when I hear of any new undertaking, such as you contemplate, lest it should not obtain the requisite public patronage." Continues: "Brighter prospects are opening to our Country; and I hope yet to live to see its Government once more placed in honest, competent and faithful hands. I shall be content whoever they may be. My friends tell me that the current of public feeling is taking a strong and decided direction towards me. For myself, I have resolved not to allow any personal feelings or wishes of my own to be enlisted in the future contest, but to leave the public judgment, uncontrolled by any personal efforts of my own, to settle down as it may think proper." ALS. InU. Apparently Getz did not establish such a newspaper. See 6:1175.

To FRANCIS T. BROOKE Washington, December 19, 1837

I recd. your favor of the 17h. Mr. [James] Madison's Journal is not yet ordered to be printed;[1] and, without any such object in the delay, it may tend to the benefit of Mrs. [Dolley Payne Todd] Madison, by allowing the sale and diffusion of her European edition of the work.[2] When printed by Congress, I will recollect your wish to obtain a Copy.

[Thomas] Ritchie has discovered a Mare's nest in the fact that the Whigs are making arrangements to establish a new paper here.[3] They do not propose to establish it by resorting to the Public crib, from which his and other papers are maintained, but by voluntary contributions raised among an abused and betrayed People. There is no occasion to conceal the object. The Whigs mean to beat the Administration party, and the Public press will be one of their instruments. The design is to establish a new paper to espouse and advance *the cause* generally, without reference at present to any particular Candidate.

The Comee. charged with the business have under consideration the selection of suitable Editors &c. I mentioned several days ago to one of the Comee Mr. Blackford[4] as one whose qualifications deserved attention. They will be doubtless duly weighed; but it will be best not to excite expectations, or to stimulate any direct application from him. I think very highly of his principles and his ability. I have no doubt however that whatever decision may be finally made will be the result of the best intentions.

My best respects to Mrs. [Mary Champe Carter] Brooke; and my hearty congratulations on your recent acquisition of a daughter.[5]

ALS. DLC-TJC (DNA, M212, R10). Copy in DLC-HC (DNA, M212, R5). Printed in Colton, *Clay Correspondence*, 4:422. Addressed to Brooke at "St Julien near Fredericksburg Va." 1. See 8:868-70. 2. Clay to Cutts, Oct. 17, 1837. 3. Although Clay and his supporters hoped to start a new Whig newspaper in Washington to rally support, no such paper materialized at this time. Ames, *History of the National Intelligencer*, 238. 4. Probably William M. Blackford, editor of the Fredericksburg (Va.) *Political Arena* and later (1842-44) chargé to Colombia. *NCAB*, 19:186. 5. Probably a reference to the marriage of Brooke's youngest son, Francis E., to Ella Ambler; less likely is the possibility that the reference is to the marriage of son Robert to his second wife, Margaret Lyle. Robert's first wife had died in 1834. Francis T. Brooke, *A Family Narrative of A Revolutionary Officer* (Richmond, Va., 1849), 107, 110.

Remark in Senate, December 19, 1837. Asks that Sen. Benjamin Swift (Vt.) withdraw a memorial from the Vermont legislature opposing, on anti-slavery grounds, statehood for Texas and asking for the abolition of slavery in the District of Columbia. *Cong. Globe*, 25 Cong., 2 Sess., 39-40. For the memorial, see *House Exec. Doc.* 182, 25 Cong., 2 Sess., pp. 1-4.

To NICHOLAS BIDDLE Washington, December 20, 1837

The Vice President [Richard M. Johnson] informs me that he is desirous of effecting a negotiation of some paper, for the amount of Eight or Ten thousand dollars to which the names of Mess Joel and Henry Johnson are attached,[1] and he is inclined to apply to your [United States] Bank [of Pennsylvania] to effect it.

I take pleasure in stating that both of these gentlemen (brothers of the Vice President) are gentlemen of large fortunes, of honor, probity and high respectability. And I should consider any paper which bears their names perfectly solid.

It is a bad time, I suppose, to obtain accommodations at any Bank; but I should be happy to hear that the V. P. should obtain that which he seeks.[2]

ALS. DLC-Nicholas Biddle Papers (DNA, M212, R20). 1. For Joel and Henry Johnson, see 7:462. 2. For the on-going financial problems of the Johnson brothers, see Meyer, *Richard M. Johnson*, 337-38, *passim*.

Comment in Senate, December 21, 1837. Doubts the expediency of trying to force banks in the District of Columbia to resume specie payments by May 1, 1838, on pain of revocation of their charters [Speech in Senate, September 25, 1837; Remark in Senate, December 13, 1837]. They cannot be expected to do this until other banks generally do the same. Recommends postponement of the district resumption bill until there is evidence of resumption in New York, Baltimore, and Richmond, Va.; and also because the holy days are approaching, "a period when Congress was not presumed to be subject to any very grave legislation." Also thinks it unwise to attempt to suppress the issuance of small bills by district banks because there is "no silver to supply the vacuum" in Washington and even congressmen have "found this small money very convenient on many occasions," such as paying waiters and hackmen. In fact, "business could not progress" without these notes. Says he now has in his purse small notes ranging from one dollar down to six cents which he picked up at various places along the way on his recent trip to Washington from Kentucky. Tells Sen. Silas Wright (N.Y.), chairman of the Committee on Finance, that he will support the elimination of small-denomination notes in the district if only Wright will "throw into the district a sufficient supply of silver change." *Cong. Globe*, 25 Cong., 2 Sess., 40-41. Clay's motion to postpone action on this bill was defeated, 27 to 14, and an amendment was added to it making it unlawful for district banks to issue notes of less than five dollars after April 10. *Ibid.*, 45. It was thought by hard-money advocates that if small notes were somehow driven out of circulation, specie would fill the vacuum thus created.

From JAMES G. BIRNEY New York, December 22, 1837

I notice, with a great deal of concern, the proceedings in Congress in relation to the abolition-question in all its ramifications.[1] It is now, and it will be, I am well satisfied, the *great* question in this country, till it is settled definitively, by the abolition of Slavery in the District of Columbia.

I am now residing in New-York, as Cor. Sec. of the American Anti-Slavery Society. My situation necessarily makes me well acquainted with the progress of the Anti-Slavery movement in all parts of the country. This letter is dictated, not only be [*sic*, by] the great regard I have for the honor and happiness of our country, but by that which I entertain for you—The friendly and respectful feelings that I have in former times cherished for you, have not been diminished by the difference that, I suppose, exists between us on the question of Slave-emancipation. I trust, that to you this will be a sufficient apology for asking your attention to this communication—

From a remark of yours in the Senate on Tuesday last,[2] I apprehend, you have not bestowed much attention on the progress of the Anti-Slavery cause. That you may have the best information on the subject, I do myself the pleasure of transmitting to you, by mail, today, the last 'Annual Report'[3] of the Am. A. S. Society. Since it was published, there has been an increase in the number of Societies of, I think, not less than from 300 to 400. The Societies will average one hundred members each. They are composed, as I believe, of the most effective men in the community—both in the Churches and out of them.

Mr. [Henry] Hubbard[4] remarked (according to the newspaper reports) that there was no abolition among the people or politicians of N. Hampshire. You will think it strange, that he would hazard such a remark, after you have seen the list of A. S. Societies in that State. And I can assure you, Sir, that the progress of Anti-Slavery principles in N.H. is, at this moment, rapid—and promises to be, in a little time, resistless.

Vermont is an abolition-State. Massachusetts is fast hastening to the same position—and, if I mistake not, will be found ready, at the next Session of her Legislature, to insist on the *immediate* emancipation of the Slaves in the District of Columbia.[5] All the N. England States are advancing rapidly to what abolitionists consider the proper point on this subject. But I will not detain you with particulars

I do not think that our politicians—even the most distinguished of them—are at all aware of the impregnation of nearly all the free States, with the abolition-principles. So effectually have these principles been impressed on their population, that I entertain no doubt, that the Slavery of this country will go out with the present discussion. The frenzy and the folly of the South may bring it to an end in blood and desolation to themselves—but that Slavery will go out, it seems to me beyond all question.

Can it be, Sir, that Kentucky will be so unwise as to go with the *planting* South in any measure to which the rashness of its leaders may impel it? Would it not be *infatuation* in her to do so? If Kentucky were to give up all her slaves *tomorrow*, I believe, that, in less than two years, the rise in the value of her lands would more than repay the loss.

I cannot close this letter without saying, that I have always cherished a hope, that you would be found in the stress to which the country is coming, the friend of Human Liberty. Most sincerely do I believe, that *you* could bring slavery to a speedy peaceful and happy termination throughout our country. *You* (and would not Mr. [John J.] Crittenden be with you?) could lead Ky.—and if K. or any other Slave state South of Delaware gave way, the final result would be certain—and glorious too to yourself and your country.—If you have confidence in me, and think I can render you any service in this matter, I should be pleased to have a reply to this, Whilst neither the Society that I represent, nor *I*, as an individual, have any thing in relation to the Anti Slavery movement to keep secret, we are careful as to the wishes of our correspondents as to a disclosure of their names or their views.

If you think it worth while, you can shew this letter to Mr. Crittenden with whom I have long had the pleasure of a personal acquaintance—or to Judge [Joseph R.] Underwood or Mr. [James] Harlan[6]—or indeed to any other gentleman who would desire the information it contains.

ALS. InU. 1. Comment in Senate, Dec. 18, 1837. 2. *Ibid.* 3. *American Anti-Slavery Society; Annual Report. . . .* New York, 1836. 4. For Hubbard, a U.S. senator from N.Y., see *BDAC.* 5. Although both houses of the Massachusetts legislature passed resolutions against the existence of slavery and the slave trade in the District of Columbia, the lower house specifically rejected an amendment calling for immediate abolition in the district. Boston *Daily Advertiser,* April 18, 1838; Charles F. Adams (ed.), *Memoirs of John Quincy Adams,* 12 vols. (Philadelphia, 1876), 9:535-38. 6. For Harlan, see 6:295.

Speech in Senate, December 22, 1837. Continues, from the previous day, his opposition to the bill to force District of Columbia banks to resume specie payments and discontinue the issuance of small-denomination (less than five dollar) notes [Remark in Senate, December 13, 1837]. Repeats and expands his arguments of December 21. Asks if the word "individuals" in the bill, as used to designate violators (those attempting to pass small-denomination notes or other paper) and the legal penalties applicable to such violators, includes slaves. Observes that when "terms so general as these were used, it certainly did appear to him that people of color were comprised in their meaning. But suppose for a moment they were not included in this description, then a dilemma arose in his mind; for, if they were included, here was a species of trial affecting only free persons, and altogether inapplicable to them, imposing a pecuniary mulct which slaves who had no property could not pay. On the other hand, if they were *not* included, then what would be the use of the bill, since it was chiefly by and among them that these notes were circulated, either instrumentally or directly?" Other likely violators chiefly affected by this bill, and liable to its "pains and penalties," would be the "minors—little boys and girls—children—the very beggars we meet on the avenue!" Thinks it unrealistic that this peculiar law can be enforced with any success "on this little spot [District of Columbia] of ten miles square" and have no applicability in nearby Virginia or Maryland. Why "Make this unfortunate District the scape-goat for an offence which is committed throughout the whole Union. . . . Under its operation any person, any member of Congress, may be put upon his oath to say if ever he has passed a sixpence of this currency." Urges his colleagues to "spare, oh! spare the little game," the poor, the women and children, "the market people" who "*must* take money in some shape. . . . Attack more noble game." Pleads the case of "the miserable, the wretched portion of the community," the slaves, negroes, beggars, infants, women, and children that this bill will mainly affect. *Cong. Globe,* 25 Cong., 2 Sess., Appendix, 18-19.

To PETER B. PORTER Washington, December 24, 1837

I received your favor of the 14h. [*sic,* 15] instant, with the papers accompanying it, respecting the movement at Buffalo to favor the cause of the Canadian Revolt.[1] I think the course pursued by yourself and others was marked by sound discretion and a just sense of the duties of peaceable Citizens. It is a monstrous spectacle to behold our Government at peace and our people at War. That at least I trust is one of those serious matters about which there will be no divorce of Government and People.

No lover of his Country can fail to be afflicted by the too numerous manifestations of personal violence and lawless proceedings of which our Country is the theatre. They throw obloquy on our free institutions. They ought to be put a stop to. How much of the spirit, in which they originate, is to be attributed to those fatal words, pronounced by the late President, "I take upon myself the responsibility" &c!

The exhibitions of public feeling, in regard to the next Presidency, which daily reach us from almost every quarter of the Union are as astonishing as they are gratifying to me. They evince that a rapid and enthusiastic concentration is taking place. Universal dissatisfaction seems to prevail with the present order of things and the present men in power. And, as is not difficult to comprehend, People are passing from one extreme to the other.

The friends of Mr. Webster are not unaware of this state of things and of the progress of events. I believe they are *almost* ready to withdraw his name, and to yield to what they feel to be a resistless current.

As to a movement in Albany,[2] whilst I think it would settle *absolutely* the question, as to the Candidate, I think it ought not to be taken without a deliberate consideration of its consequences upon your own State. If a nomination of me would jeopard[ize] our cause in N. York it ought not to be made. If it would add strength to it, then its effects every where else would be to produce immediate union & harmony. All these are however matters which you and other friends are much more competent than I am to judge of and decide.

We have been much excited here about Abolition—that is some Southern Ultras, who are quite as mischievous as the Abolitionists, have been.[3] I hope and believe that it will pass off without much harm.

ALS. NBuHi. Letter marked "(Confidential)." 1. Porter to Clay, Dec. 15, 1837; Comment in Senate, Jan. 5, 1838. 2. Porter to Clay, Nov. 14 and Dec. 30, 1837. 3. Comment in Senate, Dec. 18, 1837; Birney to Clay, Dec. 22, 1837.

Comment in Senate, December 26, 1837. Attacks a bill authorizing the states to tax lands sold by the United States within their boundaries, claiming it is "only another attempt to disturb the land system." Points out that such a law would "take away the great inducement the honest purchaser had to settle on the public lands—exemption from taxation for the period of five years." Criticizes the squatters who "had gathered in great numbers, and seized on the public lands, organizing themselves into companies, and threatening destruction to any man who might choose to purchase, thus taking from the Union the public property." Calls attention to a law in existence which authorizes the government "to use a military force to drive off these intruders." Wishes that senators "who had the poor so much in their mouths, would have their true interest more at heart." Adds, further, that the pre-emption law has led to "the most infamous speculation" and has helped produce "a spirit of lawlessness and violence abroad" that he would like to see "suppressed." *Cong. Globe,* 25 Cong., 2 Sess., Appendix, 15-17. For his more forceful condemnation of squatters, see Comment in Senate, January 26 and January 27, 1838; and Remark in Senate, January 9, 1839. This bill, introduced by Robert J. Walker (Miss.) on December 7, 1837, did not emerge from committee. *Cong. Globe,* 25 Cong., 2 Sess., Appendix, 15. See also Remark in Senate, January 23, 1838; Clay to Speed, March 2, 1838.

On this same day, Clay regrets that Sen. Silas Wright (N.Y.) has taken personally his recent attack on the bill to restrain District of Columbia banks from issuing small notes [Comment in Senate, December 21, 1837; Speech in Senate, December 22, 1837]. Says he objects to the bill because it is evident that it is "intended to have a much broader influence" than only in the district; and that it is also designed to discourage the circulation of small-denomination notes "in the surrounding country." *Cong. Globe*, 25 Cong., 2 Sess., Appendix, 32.

From Joseph Vance, Columbus, Ohio, December 29, 1837. Reports that "the timber is being very much destroyed on your land [in Ohio] by the persons in the Neighbourhood," and suggests that Clay should "give it into the care of some person who may reside near it [8:657]." As to politics, states that the Ohio legislature may "pass Resolutions in favor of the principles of your Land Bill [8:539-41, 609-10, 812-13, 846-47, 873-74], and against the Sub Treasury scheme [Speech in Senate, September 25, 1837], but this is by no means certain."

Says virtually all agree that "it would be unwise at present to make any move on the Presidential question." Notes that "Our old friend Judge [Jacob] Burnet & one or two others were here from Cincinnati to get up a Harrison fever, but they returned without doing any thing" after finding the current too strong against an early committment. Promises that "Ohio . . . will take no step that can by possibility prejudice the great cause of the country and of sound principles." Continues: "A very divided majority of the active & intelligent politicians of this State prefer you to any other man now being as the Whig candidate, and this feeling is growing daily. A few days ago a meeting was called at Maumee without distinction of party for to nominate H. Clay—& very many of those who have heretofore voted for Mr Van Buren now came forward & boldly say that they will vote for you but not for Harrison & I am well advised on the most authentic and undoubted authority that this is also the fact in the State of Indiana—In this State we have nothing to fear in the coming contest but this distracting question of abolition if that excitement could be al[l]ayed all would be well, but I confess that I sometimes fear that it is to distroy not the party, but the Union of these states." ALS. DLC-TJC (DNA, M212, R14).

For the land bill Clay had sponsored in the 24th Congress, 2nd Sess., see especially 8:839, 873-74. Resolutions from the Ohio general assembly regarding public lands were presented to the Senate on February 12, 1838. U.S. Sen., *Journal*, 25 Cong., 2 Sess., 214-15. Also in February, the Ohio legislature instructed its senators to vote against the Sub-Treasury, but they refused. Weisenburger, *The Passing of the Frontier*, 356. Also, the meeting at Maumee, held on December 30, 1837, by the "friends of Henry Clay" nominated Clay for president. Columbus *Ohio State Journal and Political Register*, February 2, 1838.

Vance enclosed a receipt for $8.22 which he had paid on Clay's behalf for taxes on 400 acres of land in Ohio. John L. Doran, clerk, in the office of the auditor of Ohio to Clay, December 27, 1837. ADS. DLC-TJC (DNA, M212, R18).

From PETER B. PORTER Troy, N.Y., December 30, 1837

[Writes to say that he has arrived in Troy and that he expects to go to Albany tomorrow and see the New York City legislative delegation. Continues:]

As far as my observations have yet extended, the best possible spirits are prevailing among the Whigs of our State. All seem fully impressed with the necessity of acting in concert, & to this end, of sacrificing personal predilections. It seems to me, indeed, that if the Whig members of our Legislature can bring themselves to act with harmony and discretion, they may accomplish almost anything they desire in regard to the presidential election in this State, & create, moreover, an important influence on the elections of other States. I do not know what their plan of operations will be, but I have sketched one in my own mind, without however entertaining any sanguine hopes that it will be adopted, which it seems to me would be a prudent course and calculated to consolidate the Whig strength. The following are its outlines:

As soon after the commencement of the Session, as the members shall have had an opportunity, by private intercourse, to ascertain each others sentiments or views, let a general caucus be called of all the Whig members of the Legislature, including as many of the Conservatives,[1] if any, as may be disposed to attend. Let this caucus appoint a special committee to propose and report at a subsequent meeting, the most eligible plan for ascertaining the sentiments of the Whigs of this State & giving efficiency to their vote on the Presidential question.[2] They might also, with due modesty, venture to recommend the same course of proceeding to the Whigs of other States.

As to the details of their report, let them recommend say—

1st. that the Whig candidate for the Presidency shall be selected by a national Convention to be held at some convenient time & place (both the time and place to be indicated in their report).[3]

2d. The Convention to be composed of delegates from the different states, corresponding in numbers with the aggregate of the members of the House of Reps and Senators to which each State and Territory is entitled; and these delegates to be elected or appointed in such manner as the Whigs of each State may deem most proper.

3d. That every delegate from each State, whatever may be his personal preferences, shall support before the convention the candidate most acceptable to a majority of the delegates of his State, so long as there is any reasonable prospect of his success; after which each delegate shall be at liberty to consult exclusively his own opinions & feelings in the selection of any other candidate. That the candidate ultimately agreed upon by a majority of the Convention, shall thereafter receive the individual support of every member of the Convention.

These preliminaries being settled, let the caucus prescribe the mode of choosing delegates for this State as follows:

4th Let the Whig electors of each congressional district choose one delegate in such manner as they may deem most convenient and proper.

5th Let the two supernumerary delegates be chosen by the same Legislative caucus, as being most likely to express the general sentiment of the Whigs throughout the State.

Although the sentiments of the caucus would be pretty clearly indicated by the known opinions of the two delegates whom they may appoint, yet I can conceive no impropriety in their making a direct & open declaration of their preference.[4]

Please let me know what you think of this course of proceeding.

I will write you again next week when I shall have learnt more of the composition of our Legislature. [P.S.] As the selection of a candidate for the Vice Presidency, will, and doubtless ought to be influenced more or less as well by the locality as the character of the Presidential candidate, would it not be well to leave the selection of the former entirely to the discretion of the Convention after they shall have agreed upon the latter? The Anti Masons will doubtless expect & perhaps ought to have the Vice Presidency.

Copy. OHi. 1. Clay to Henry Clay, Jr., Jan. 28, 1837. 2. Porter to Clay, Nov. 14, 1837. 3. *Ibid.* 4. In June, 1839, Whig members of the New York legislature adopted a resolution requesting the Whig State Central Committee to designate the proper mode and time for the appointment of delegates to a national nominating convention. The central committee, in turn, then recommended that the Whig electors in each congressional district meet in convention and appoint a number of delegates equal to the representation of such district in the U.S. House. When New York's Whig delegates met at the national convention in Harrisburg in early December, they were to choose two additional delegates from the state at large and fill any vacancies that had occurred. The central committee also recommended Nov. 19, 1839, as the date for the conventions in the congressional districts and strongly urged that such delegates be unpledged and uninfluenced by their personal preferences. In sum, there was no specific endorsement of Clay or any other candidate for the presidency by Whigs in the New York legislature. Washington *Daily National Intelligencer*, July 3, 1839. For the caucuses of New York State Whig legislators in April, 1838 and June, 1839 relative to a national Whig nominating convention and to the endorsement of a specific presidential candidate prior to the meeting of that convention, see also Porter to Clay, Nov. 14, 1837 and Feb. 16, 1839. For the proceedings of the Whig national convention, held at Harrisburg, Pa., Dec. 4-7, 1839, see Arthur M. Schlesinger, Jr., *History of U.S. Political Parties*, 4 vols. (New York, 1973), 1:401-10.

To NATHANIEL P. TALLMADGE Washington, *ca.* January, 1838

I am prevented by the badness of the day from calling to see you, as I intended.

I have thought that something, advantageous to the Conservatives[1] and to the common cause, may be derived from the allusion in the message to Local elections and to their cause.[2] Information may be called for. The allusion is undignified and insulting.

If a call be deemed expedient, would it not be best to be made in the House by some N. York member and a conservative, and in the Senate by you?[3]

What think you of it? If favorably, can you get any Conservative member from your State to present the resolution and who? Be pleased to favor me with a line.

ALS. WHi. Letter marked "(Confidential)." 1. Conservative Democrats. See Clay to Henry Clay, Jr., Jan. 28, 1837. 2. In his First Annual Message on Dec. 5, 1837, Van Buren maintained that Whig victories in several recent state elections, most notably New York, had not meant that the people were against his Independent Treasury system; rather, the elections had been determined by local interests, especially the large amount of bank capital in those states. *MPP*, 3:380-81. For the 1837 New York elections, see Clay to Curtis, Oct. 25, 1837. 3. On Feb. 8, 1838, Tallmadge delivered a lengthy Senate speech explaining the election results in New York and attacking Van Buren's annual message "which charged the result of those [state] elections to the influence of the banks." *Cong. Globe*, 25 Cong., 2 Sess., 619-21.

To Christopher Hughes, Baltimore, January 1, 1838. Sends Hughes "Compliments of the Season!" and thanks him for "your acceptable presents of Snuff and boxes." Wishes, however, he had learned "how to discontinue the use of that stimulant." ALS. MiU-C.

Remark in Senate, January 2, 1838. Has no objection to the postponement for further study of the bill for the relief of the executrix of Richard W. Meade, because "the more it was examined, the more would its justice become apparent." *Cong. Globe*, 25 Cong., 2 Sess., 70. For the nagging Meade claims case, first against Spain, and then against the United States under its treaty with Spain of February 22, 1819 (in which the U.S. government had assumed the claims of its citizens against Spain), see the Meade article in the *DAB*; also the more extensive account in *House Reports*, 22 Cong., 1 Sess., no. 316, pp. 1-213. The essence of the case was that Meade, an American merchant long resident in Spain who had served as agent for the U.S. Navy in Cadiz (1804-16), had furnished supplies and loans to the Spanish government in the amount of some $490,000 at the time of the French invasion of Spain in 1808. No payment for or repayment of these advances had been made, hence his claim.

From "Cadmus," Washington, D.C., n.d., *ca.* January 3, 1838. Submits observations on how the American printing and publishing business operates in order to show Clay that his recent advocacy [Comment in Senate, February 2, 1837] of "the (so called) international Copyright law" is misguided. Supports his criticism with evidence from the commercial history of Edward Lytton-Bulwer, called *Reinzi: The Last of the Roman Tribunes*, 2 vols. London, 1835. Notes that "thousands of copies" of it were sold at retail for fifty to seventy-five cents in the United States last year, and that the large volume of sale provided profit and employment to numerous publishers, printers, papermakers, booksellers, bookbinders and even "the very women and boys who folded and stitched the sheets." In England, however, the same book sold for a guinea, or about five dollars. Concludes that Clay's copyright bill would give Lytton-Bulwer the power to "make us pay for his book as he makes his own countrymen pay." Sees substantial economic injury to all Americans involved in the domestic book business if this sort of thing occurs. Argues that various republishing houses in the United States, by lowering the cost of foreign books, have "probably done more for the literature of this country . . . than all our native authors combined. It has been the entering wedge of a taste for reading with dozens and scores of your immediate constituents." Asks rhetorically: "Is it wise in Congress to check this growing taste for literature?" Believes that passage of the proposed copyright legislation will, in effect, "tax me for the encouragement of foreign authors" as well as destroy the U.S. book-publishing industry. Asks him to aid "those of your own citizens who have invested capital, labor and time in the business before you grant the protective duty to foreign booksellers, which is asked for under the plea of justice to foreign authors." Copy. Printed in Washington *Daily National Intelligencer*, January 3, 1838.

On this same day, the *National Intelligencer* published another open letter to Clay from "A Publisher" which also attacked the proposed international copyright legislation. The author, who identified himself as a publisher, held that "British literature would suffer but little if no American book were published in England; whereas, much the greater part of our literature is, and will continue to be, of British birth. . . . the benefits will chiefly be on the side of British writers." Asserting also that "I am a Southerner," he reminds Clay that "You know that public sentiment abroad, and especially in England, is at war with our institutions; I am opposed to your bill [Comment in Senate, February 2, 1837] because its inevitable consequence will be to place the greater part of our literature under the control of foreign publishers. . . . its tendency will be to make American writers more dependent upon foreign sentiment." Copy. Printed in Washington *Daily National Intelligencer*, January 3, 1838.

From Charles Kinsey, New Prospect [now Waldwick], Bergen County, N.J., January 3, 1838. Reports that when, "as a feeler," Webster was named at the New York City Whig Jubilee [Webb to Clay, December 15 and 19, 1837] as a possible presidential nominee, "it was feebly responded to—but when Harry of the West was named, a universal burst of unanimous soul cheering approbation pour[e]d forth from every heart." Contemplates working for the nomination of Clay by the New Jersey legislature, and asks his confidential opinion of the "propriety" of such an effort. Notes that as a Mason he pledges himself to hold Clay's answer "sacredly confidential." Remarks that while Theodore Frelinghuysen thinks a state convention for a Clay nomination "might be premature," he is, nevertheless, "decidedly favorable to you." Believes that various state nominations will do Clay more good politically "than a National one." Asks in conclusion: "Is not this violent opposition to the anexation of Texas and this unholy excitement of abolition got up purposely to keep you from the Presidency the same as . . . Misouri [*sic*] was [?]" ALS. NjP. See Clay to Southard, January 7, 1838. For Kinsey, see 3:839. The New Jersey legislature did not nominate Clay in 1838; nor did the New Jersey Whig convention, when it met in Trenton on September 5, 1838, make any recommendation concerning a national convention or express a preference for anyone as Whig presidential nominee for 1840. Washington *Daily National Intelligencer*, September 10, 1838; see also Michael Birkner, *Samuel L. Southard; Jeffersonian Whig* (Rutherford, N.J., 1984), 183-84, 241.

Comment in Senate, January 5, 1838. Asks for "some early action" on the seizure and destruction of the U.S. vessel *Caroline* by Canadian government militia on the American side of the Niagara River on the evening of December 29, 1837. Notes that the *Caroline* question is connected "to the vexatious and unsettled state of our Northern boundary," a situation which tends "to increase the danger" which now threatens the nation. Strongly supports Van Buren's neutrality proclamation of this date [January 5] and urges strict non-involvement by Americans in Canada's rebellion against Great Britain. Calls also for an examination of "whether or not the action of our citizens had not been limited to some disputed territory, or whether arms, munitions of war, or supplies, had been furnished" Canadian rebels by U.S. sympathizers. If this last "proved true, such conduct must be viewed by [the] Government as in the highest degree reprehensible." *Cong. Globe*, 25 Cong., 2 Sess., 79.

For the emotionally-charged *Caroline* incident, in which Amos Durfee, a U.S. citizen was killed, see Corey, *The Crisis of 1830-1842 in Canadian-American Relations*, 35-43; Kenneth R. Stevens, "The *Caroline* Affair: Anglo-American Relations and Domestic Politics, 1837-1842," Ph. D. dissertation, Indiana University, 1982, pp. 1-54; Paul A. Varg, *United States Foreign Relations, 1829-1860* (East Lansing, Mich., 1979), 98-100; the Alexander McLeod phase of the crisis in December, 1840-September, 1841 is treated in Corey, *op. cit.*, 130-45. For the Canadian revolt against Great Britain, see Porter to Clay, December 15, 1837. For the Maine-New Brunswick boundary crisis and so-called "Aroostook War" in that neighborhood, see Clay to Hamilton, February 24, 1839.

Later this day, Clay asks for more information on the circumstances surrounding a petition of two citizens for compensation for money they had lost in the U.S. mails. *Cong. Globe*, 25 Cong., 2 Sess., 80.

To PETER B. PORTER Washington, January 5, 1838

I recd. your favor of the 30h. Ulto. and was happy to hear of the harmony which prevails among the Whigs in N. York.

All your suggestions as to the organization of a N[ational]. Convention[1] are judicious and such as had occurred to me, and such as I believe will be *adopted* by the K. Legislature, or rather the Whig portion of it, now in Session.[2] Perhaps the third had better be so modified as to be left to the sense of the delegation from each State exclusively.

With respect to a Nat. Convention,[3] I ought to say to you that there is a strong if not invincible repugnance to it in the Southern & S.W States among the Whigs. This arises chiefly out of the policy which they thought it expedient to pursue in opposition to that which nominated Mr. V.B. It is possible that it may be overcome but is not certain. If they are not represented in the Convention, you can judge the effect as it respects me; for, beyond all question, I should obtain every vote in that quarter, looking to the present state of public opinion.

Still, I do not think that any friends of mine should shew any disinclination to the submission of my pretensions to the consideration of a Convention.

It is not, at the same time, to be disguised that if there is to be a warm contest for delegates to the Convention, any where, it may be [*sic*] lead to irritation unfavorable to subsequent hearty co-operation.

Hence the necessity of manifestations of the public preference, so as to prevent unpleasant collisions. I attach paramount importance to an expression of the preference of the Whig members at Albany.[4] I believe that it would be *decisive*. It ought not to be too exclusive, and in this respect the examples in Ohio[5] & Vermont[6] would furnish both examples and a justification of the proceeding. But if it will jeopard[ize] the preservation of the predominance which the Whigs have acquired in your State it should not be done.

Mr. Websters friends wish a late, Genl. Harrison's an early meeting of the Convention. Mine are indifferent as to time or place. I am inclined to think that it ought not to be earlier than next November.

How would it do for the Caucus at Albany to recommend the fixation of a time and place to the Whig members of Congress?

I write in haste, and will soon write again.

We have just heard the terrible event near Buffalo.[7]

ALS. NBuHi. Letter marked "(Confidential)." 1. Porter to Clay, Dec. 30, 1837. 2. The convention of Whigs in the Ky. legislature met in Frankfort on Jan. 12, 1838. They adopted resolutions calling for a national convention to be composed of delegates equal in number to the total number of senators and representatives in Congress from each state and recommended specific procedures for choosing such delegates. They also expressed a preference for Clay to be the nominee, although they promised to support anyone nominated by the national convention. For additional details, see Washington *Daily National Intelligencer*, Jan. 29, 1838. 3. Porter to Clay, Nov. 14 and Dec. 30, 1837. 4. *Ibid.* 5. Clay evidently referred to the fact that Ohio Whigs had called for a national convention and set forth procedures for choosing delegates. They had, however, in their convention of July 4, 1837, endorsed William Henry Harrison. See Clay to Prentice, August 14, 1837; Porter to Clay, March 8, 1838. In Feb., 1838 the Montgomery County, Ohio, Whigs endorsed both a national convention and Henry Clay. Subsequently, the 1838 Ohio Whig state convention reiterated the 1837 resolutions but added that they had great respect for both Clay and Webster and would support either if nominated by the national convention. Washington *Daily National Intelligencer*, March 6, June 6, 1838; Cincinnati *Daily Gazette*, March 1, 1838. 6. The Whigs in Vermont had already, in late 1837, appointed delegates to the national convention. Washington *Daily National Intelligencer*, Nov. 10, 1837. The convention of Whigs in the Vermont legislature, which met on Oct. 12, 1838, discussed endorsing either Clay, Webster, or Harrison for the 1840 nomination but could not agree. Lexington *Observer & Kentucky Reporter*, Nov. 14, 1838. In 1839 the Vermont Whigs, meeting on June 27, 1839, agreed to support whoever was nominated by the national convention in Harrisburg, but added that no one should be considered who would not pledge himself in advance to support the candidate named by a majority of the convention. Washington *Daily National Intelligencer*, July 10, 1839. 7. Porter to Clay, Dec. 15, 1837; Comment in Senate, Jan. 5, 1838.

Remark in Senate, January 6, 1838. Speaks to Calhoun's set of six resolutions on slavery, dated December 27, 1837. Asserts that if Sen. Richard A. Bayard (Del.) will word his amendment to the South Carolinian's resolution three [see below] in the light of historical fact, he will support it. "The historical fact," Clay explains, is that "the Constitution was adopted by the people of the several states, acting within their respective limits." Bayard declines to accept Clay's more nationalistic wording of his amendment and it is defeated 34 to 8. *Cong. Globe*, 25 Cong., 2 Sess., 80-81; *ibid.*, Appendix, 41. See also Speech in Senate, January 9, 1838.

Calhoun's six resolutions presented and upheld the following opinions and concepts: 1) the compact theory of the origin and structure of the constitution; 2) the importance of the reserved powers clause of the constitution, specifically as it sustains the sole and exclusive right of each of the several states to control its own domestic institutions and police; 3) the notion that the federal government is but an agent of the several states and cannot therefore be used as the instrument with which one state might attack the interests of another; 4) the proposition that domestic slavery is not to be attacked or interfered with in any way; 5) the contention that any effort to abolish slavery in the District of Columbia would be a dangerous assault on the institutions of all the slaveholding states; 6) and the insistence that any refusal, on antislavery grounds, to extend the territories of the nation or to admit new states to it would weaken the Union and discriminate among its members. During the debate on these resolutions, January 3-12, 1838, the first three were adopted (32-13, 32-9, 31-11); four and five were amended and adopted (35-5, 36-8) ; and six, also amended, was tabled (35-9). See *Cong. Globe*, 25 Cong., 2 Sess., Appendix, 21-32, 36-41, 53-65, 69-74; *Cong. Globe*, 25 Cong., 2 Sess., 73-74, 76, 80-81, 91, 96-98; U.S. Sen., *Journal*, 25 Cong., 2 Sess., 106-7, 117, 122, 127, 132, 136. See also William M. Wiecek, *The Sources of Antislavery Constitutionalism in America, 1760-1848* (Ithaca, N.Y., 1977), 187-88, 291-93.

There were numerous changes, proposed and effected, by amendment, by amendments to amendments, and by semantic shadings in the original language of Calhoun's six resolutions during the acrimonious debate that followed. For the final language in which they were voted upon by the Senate on January 12, 1838, see *Cong. Globe*, 25 Cong., 2 Sess., 98. Analyses of Calhoun's resolutions and Clay's counter-resolutions [Speech in Senate, January 9, 1838] are in Wiltse, *John C. Calhoun: Nullifier*, 369-73; Van Deusen, *Life of Henry Clay*, 314-17; Thomas Brown, *Politics and Statesmanship: Essays on the American Whig Party* (New York, 1985), 144.

To JAMES B. CLAY Washington, January 7, 1838

I recd. your letter of the 23d. Ulto. You complain of not hearing from me. I have written to you several times since I have [been] here and would have written oftener, if I had had any thing to commun[icate.] But my correspondence is very oppressive, and I find it impossible [to keep] up with it. You must not suppose that I feel any want of aff[ection] towards you. Far otherwise. You are constantly in my thoughts a[nd in] my hopes. I feel that you must be very loansome, and regret to hear you are not happy. You know, my dear Son, that I feared you would not be, separated as you are from all who love you, and that I reluctantly consented to your going to Missouri. I hope that you will endeavor to cultivate feelings of contentment, and I shall be most happy, on my return home, if we can make any arrangement by which you can come back to Kentucky and live in the midst of your friends.

The account you give me of your affairs is encouraging; and the account of you which I receive from others also gives me high satisfaction. What I would especially guard you against is every species of dissipation. And I own to you that I have feared your solitary condition might prompt you into it. But I sincerely hope that may not prove to be the case.

I suppose your offer of the Alton land was declined.[1] It is very important to protect it against trespasses and I trust you will take care of that. In a former letter I gave my assent to your having wood cut for the St. Louis market.

Should your pecuniary wants make it necessary, you may draw on me for $150 in the course of the Spring.

You do not tell me whether your Jack proved a sure foal getter.

I have no news. My friends are full of hopes and confidence about the next P[residential]. election.

ALS, manuscript torn. DLC-TJC (DNA, M212, R10). Printed in Colton, *Clay Correspondence*, 4:423. Addressed to his son at "Richland near St. Louis Missouri." 1. Clay to James B. Clay, Dec. 18, 1837.

To SALMA HALE Washington, January 7, 1838

I received your favor of the 1st. inst. with the accompanying News paper.[1] The resolutions to which you have called my attention appear to me to be characterized by good sense and sound discretion. If the expression of a preference for Mr. W[ebster]. had been made, it would have been quite natural, and would neither have surprized nor mortified me.[2]

The Seminole debate,[3] to which you refer, was the beginning of our political troubles. I wish we could see as distinctly the period of their termination. There is much reason to hope that it is nigh at hand. With proper concert and conciliation, I think that we may look forward with confidence.

I shall be most agreeably surprized if you succeed at your approaching contest.[4] The moral effect of your success would be very great and justifies the most strenuous exertions. These, I am sure, will be made, and I offer my fervent wishes for a triumphant issue. . . .

ALS. NhHi. 1. Not found. 2. The New Hampshire State Whig convention had assembled at Concord on Nov. 21, 1837. Hale had reported a series of resolutions—including one which pledged the support of the Whigs of New Hampshire to any candidate nominated by a national convention—which were subsequently adopted. At about this time Webster had visited in Concord. Clay seems to have thought that New Hampshire might endorse Webster because of his residence in an adjoining state. Richmond *Enquirer*, Dec. 1, 1837. 3. The Second Seminole War lasted from 1835 to 1842, costing the U.S. $40 to $50 million dollars and the lives of many soldiers. The causes and prosecution of the war became a subject of bitter partisan debate. Whigs, Clay among them, vigorously attacked the Van Buren administration with charges of duplicity in dealing with the Indians and ineptness in handling military operations against them. During the course of the conflict, various congressional investigations were initiated into the actions of U.S. field commanders in Florida—Edmund P. Gaines, Winfield Scott, and Thomas S. Jesup. Furthermore, the emotional problems of abolitionism, the recovery of fugitive slaves from the Florida Territory, and sectional tensions in general became increasingly involved in the debate. See John K. Mahon, *History of the Second Seminole War, 1835-1842* (Gainesville, Fla., 1967), *passim*; Edwin C. McReynolds, *The Seminoles* (Norman, Okla., 1957), 137-242; Niven, *Martin Van Buren*, 463-67; William and Ellen Hartley, *Osceola: The Unconquered Indian* (New York, 1973), 97-260. See also 8:823. 4. In the 1838 elections in New Hampshire, Isaac Hill, the Democratic candidate, was reelected governor over James Wilson, Jr., by a vote of 28,697 to 25,675. *BDGUS*, 3:953. Democrats won control of the New Hampshire senate, while Whigs won the house. *Niles' Register* (March 24, 1838), 54:49.

From Peter B. Porter, Saratoga Springs, N.Y., January 7, 1838. Reports that he was in Albany every day last week and found there "great unanimity and good feeling among the Whigs in the Legislature." Says that a decided majority of the members preferred Clay for president. Reveals that he had "several conversations with [Thurlow] Weed of the [Albany] Evening Journal, who is not only the most important man among the Anti-Masons, but has much influence with the Whigs proper. He says that you are decidedly the favorite of the Whig party and nothing can prevent your being their candidate. He told me that he had a very full and frank conversation with Mr. Webster on this subject about the 1st of Dec. when on his way to Washington. He told him frankly that he (Mr. W.) had been mislead by his own friends [Clay to Letcher, May 30, 1837; Clay to Davis, July 3, 1837]; that although he was greatly respected by the Whigs of this State, you were unquestionably their favorite, and would be their candidate. Mr. Webster, although evidently somewhat surprised, then said to him that as soon as he should become satisfied of this fact (and the truth of which he was not then prepared to question) he would immediately withdraw and give you a hearty support. Mr. D[avid]. B. Ogden also tells me that in a late interview with Mr. Webster at Washington he expressed to him the same feelings and intentions." Copy. OHi.

To Samuel L. Southard, Trenton, N.J., January 7, 1838. Encloses Charles Kinsey's letter of January 3. Comments: "I have answered [not found] the enclosed letter, declining personally to interfere in the matter to which it relates. You can appreciate the worth of the letter, which you may destroy after reading it. And you and other friends can best judge of the fitness of the movement at Trenton which the writer proposes." ALS. NjP.

From Stephen Duncan, Natchez, Miss., January 9, 1838. Reports the sale of Clay's bagging and rope and the deposit to his account of $3,592.33 which "will be invested the first opportunity." Says the Mississippi state legislature is now in session and that "if it were not for their unprincipled politicians the *Nullifiers*—Col. [Adam L.] Bingaman would go to the Senate of the U.S." Believes, however, that Judge [James Fisher] Trotter, the Democratic candidate, is a "smart amicable honest & upright man" and that if he is elected, "a little attention to him" might be a good idea. ALS. DLC-TJC (DNA, M212, R14).

Bingaman was several times a member of the Mississippi legislature, serving twice as speaker of the house and once as president of the senate. In 1839 he and Reuben Davis ran as the Whig candidates for Congress against Albert Brown and Jacob Thompson and lost. Harnett T. Kane, *Natchez on the Mississippi* (New York, 1947), 150-58; Dunbar Rowland, *History of Mississippi the Heart of the South*, 2 vols. (Chicago, 1925), 1:591-92, 610; *Guide to U.S. Elections*, 572. The latter incorrectly identifies Bingaman as "Benjamin." Trotter was elected to the U.S. Senate by the Mississippi legislature after the resignation of Sen. John Black. He served from January 22 to July 10, 1838, when he resigned. Washington *Daily National Intelligencer*, February 7, 1838; see also *BDAC* (which incorrectly states that he was appointed).

Speech in Senate, January 9, 1838. Says he cannot vote for either Calhoun's fifth or sixth resolution [Remark in Senate, January 6, 1838]. Points out that he has "voted without hesitation for the first resolutions" offered by the South Carolinian "after they were modified or amended, not from any confidence which I have in their healing virtues" but as "abstract propositions." As for the pros and cons of the compact theory, says "more importance is attached to it than it deserves." Explains that no matter how and why the constitution was created, whether it was the work of "the people of the United States collectively, or of the separate States composing the Confederacy," the powers it grants "are exactly the same." Cites the "historical fact" that it was framed by a convention of delegates appointed by state legislatures and then ratified in the states by conventions of delegates chosen by the people. Observes that Calhoun's resolutions, taken together, can only "increase and exasperate" the abolition of slavery issue, "particularly at the North." Sees, in this regard, "the unnecessary combination of the subject of abolition" with "the annexation of Texas to the United States, in the same series of resolutions, as particularly unfortunate," even though Texas is not specifically mentioned in the sixth and last of Calhoun's resolves. Calls attention, however, to the eagerness with which South Carolina's senators, Calhoun and William C. Preston, have embraced Texas annexation and attacks Preston's resolution of January 4 favoring such annexation. Argues that Calhoun's resolution six, "although abstract in form," is surely designed to "commit the Senate, in advance, to the annexation." Urges that "these two unhappy causes," abolition and annexation, be kept "separate and distinct." Notes Calhoun's statement that he offered his resolutions "to revive and rally the State rights party." Warns that the slaveholding states ought not "to place their peculiar interests in the exclusive safe-keeping of any party, however correct some of us may believe its principles to be. . . . Parties go up and down, but the Constitution remains a perpetual and sure bulwark against all attacks upon the rights of the slaveholding States." Makes it clear that while the slaveholding states may differ "on the degree of sensibility which we display . . . we are all firmly and unanimously resolved to defend and maintain our rights at all hazards; and should the hour of trial ever come, those who appear now the least agitated, will not be behind those who are foremost and loudest in proclaiming the existence of danger."

Maintains that the spirit of abolitionism is spreading in the North because the constitutional right of petition is perceived there to have been denied the abolitionists by the Congress. In support of this contention, reads into the record a lengthy extract from a letter he has "lately received" from a "highly intelligent and patriotic gentleman in Rhode Island." Asks, as he has in the past [Comment in Senate, December 18, 1837], that petitions to abolish slavery in the District of Columbia be received and referred, even "silently referred," to committee in order to "check the spirit of abolition"; and contends that the Senate must receive these petitions even though the petitioners are "misguided . . . and highly mischievous." Recommends that "what becomes us is to keep the Abolitionists separate and distinct from all other classes, standing out in bold and prominent relief; and the subject of Abolition separate and distinct from the right of petition, from Texas, and from all other subjects; let them stand alone, unmixed with the rest of the community, without the general sympathy, and exposed to the overwhelming force of the united opinion of all who desire the peace, the harmony, and the union of this Confederacy."

Expresses distress that "We allow ourselves to speak too frequently, and with too much levity, of a separation of this Union. It is a terrible word, to which our ears should not be familiarized. I desire to see in continued safety and prosperity *this* Union, and no other Union. I go for this Union as it is, one and indivisible, without diminution. I will neither voluntarily leave it, nor be driven out of it by force. Here, in my place, I shall contend for all the rights of the State which has sent me here." But adds that "if, contrary to all human probability, the rights and the security of the slaveholding States shall be assailed by any authoritative act emanating from the Capitol, a state of things for resistance, forcible resistance, will then occur. It will be time enough then to act."

Offers six resolutions of his own designed to solve the interrelated abolition and petition problems and allay the tensions generated by both. These maintain:

1) domestic slavery is subject to the exclusive control of the slaveholding states; 2) petitions touching the abolition of slavery in states where it exists shall be instantly rejected by the Senate; 3) abolition of slavery in the District of Columbia, which is within the constitutional power of Congress, cannot be effected without breaking faith with the two slave states, Virginia and Maryland, that ceded land to create the district; or without compensation to the proprietors of slaves, or without seriously alarming the South beyond any possible benefit in return; however, petitions for such abolition should be received and referred to committee; 4) the abolition of slavery in the territory of Florida (also within the constitutional power of Congress) would be highly inexpedient because the people there have not asked for it, will decide the slavery question for themselves when Florida is admitted to the Union, and because the "solemn" Missouri Compromise, "made at a memorable and critical period in the history of this country," prohibits slavery north of 36°30′, save in Missouri, while permitting it to areas south of that line; 5) the constitution delegates no power to Congress to prohibit the slave trade or movement of slaves in or between the slaveholding states; finally, 6) the attachment by the citizens of the United States to the Union is a sure bulwark of the safety, liberty and happiness of our people. Argues that "there is nothing abstract or metaphysical" in these six resolutions; but offers the two relating to the abolition of slavery in the District of Columbia and to the present and future status of slavery in the territory of Florida as "an amendment" to Calhoun's fifth resolution [Remark in Senate, January 6, 1838].

Does not agree with Calhoun's contention "that the abolition of slavery in the District of Columbia would be a *direct* and dangerous attack upon the institution of slavery in the States." Thinks that language is much too strong. As for Calhoun's additional observation that to concede the receipt and referral of abolitionist petitions is but to take the first step toward the breakdown of the entire slavery system, Clay counters with the observation that the only so-called "concession" built into the body of his resolutions is his acceptance of the fact that the constitutional right of petition to abolish slavery in the district clearly exists. Points out that before Calhoun can call this "a concession he ought to prove that there exists no such right. That, I think, he has failed to do." On the contrary, "the Constitution requires the Senate to receive such petitions." Notes, further, that "if a man were to present me a petition to grant him Ashland, (or Orozimbo! exclaimed some Senator—or Orozimbo [8:804-5] said Mr. CLAY, whose death I am sorry to announce to the Senate, and he was a great loss, public and private,) I would, without the least apprehension for the loss of my property, put it in my pocket, or lay it upon the table. Will not the Senator comprehend the difference between the act of receiving a petition, and the grant of the thing petitioned for?"

Explains the differences between Calhoun and himself on how best to protect the "just rights" of the slave states. "He goes for strong language, menacing tones, and irritating measures; I for temperate, but firm language, conciliation, and for obeying the injunction of the Constitution in respect to the right of petition." Concludes with a plea for national unity and the Union: "I cannot believe that it is prudent or wise to be so often alluding to the separation of the Union. We ought not to be perpetually exclaiming, wolf, wolf, wolf. We are too much in the habit of speaking of divorces, separation, disunion. In private life, if a wife pouts, and frets, and scolds, what would be thought of the good sense or discretion of the husband, who should threaten her with separation, divorce, disunion? who should use these terrible words upon every petty disagreement in domestic life? No man, who has a heart or right feelings, would employ such idle menaces. He would approach the lady with kind and conciliatory language, and apply those natural and more agreeable remedies, which never fail to restore domestic harmony. [A general burst of laughter, which continued for some time.]" *Cong. Globe*,

25 Cong., 2 Sess., Appendix, 57-60. See also Wiltse, *John C. Calhoun: Nullifier*, 372-73; Van Deusen, *Life of Henry Clay*, 314-17; Wiecek, *The Sources of Antislavery Constitutionalism in America*, 187-88.

On this same day, Clay refers to the seizure and destruction of the *Caroline* [Comment in Senate, January 5, 1837] as an "outrage committed on the soil of the United States, and on the lives of its citizens," an act "atrocious . . . in its character and consequences—wholly unjustifiable, and not in the slightest degree palliated by any thing which preceded it." Charges that the commander of the British forces [Col. Allan MacNab] surely knew of the planned attack and the fact that the *Caroline* was lying quietly at anchor in American waters. Regrets that "in our own history" there have been examples of similar behavior, but prefers not to avert to them "or to any recent occurrences." Does not want war with Great Britain, but does demand "that ample, prompt and full indemnity should be given us." Deplores war "as much as any man," but is certain that American resources, valor, and "achievements in former times" would be such that can have "no fear of the result." Indeed, in this instance "it would be a just war, and he would be ready to meet it." *Cong. Globe*, 25 Cong., 2 Sess., 87.

Comment in Senate, January 10, 1838. In a resumption of debate on Calhoun's fifth resolution [Remark in Senate, January 6, 1838; Speech in Senate, January 9, 1838], Clay regrets that Calhoun will not support his proposed amendments to that resolution dealing with slavery in the District of Columbia and in Florida. In response to Calhoun's criticism of his amendment attempt in this regard, seeks further to explain and clarify his intent. Notes particularly that the section of his amendment dealing with compensation to district slaveowners who emancipate their slaves has been misunderstood. Explains: "It simply says you cannot emancipate them without compensation. But whether you can do it at all or not, it does not assert. It says you cannot do it without compensation; but it does not say you can with compensation." Pushed further on the emancipation-compensation connection, agrees to strike that clause from his resolution. But asserts, on the question of abolition in general, that "You cannot abolish slavery without a breach of the public faith. Can any thing be stronger? It equals the Constitution itself." Agrees also to modify his resolution on the status of slavery in Florida to reflect the additional and broader view, supported by Calhoun, that abolition of slavery in the territories in general would be unjust to the inhabitants thereof, would excite "just apprehensions" among the slave states, and would be dangerous to their domestic institutions.

When asked to incorporate into the language of his resolution the provision in the U.S. treaty with Spain of February 22, 1819, that guarantees the right of private property in Florida, Clay replies that he was not aware of such a stipulation, but if it does exist he will "cheerfully insert it." Draws attention to Calhoun's intransigence, tough language, and general unwillingness to modify his own resolutions [Remark in Senate, January 6, 1838], even though he, Clay, has accepted and voted for the first four of them. Especially criticizes Calhoun for omitting from his fifth resolution the right of petition. In so doing he has omitted "the constitutional ground" from the issue of the abolition of slavery in the district. Asserts that his own moderate approach to the question raised by Calhoun's fifth resolution has been designed "to avoid creating enemies to the South by driving our friends into opposition to us, by any sort of violence or unreasonable exactions; in a word, not to render them opponents of the institutions of the South, by forcing them to abandon their principles . . . [or] leave them ground to stand upon." *Cong. Globe*, 25 Cong., 2 Sess., Appendix, 60-62. The initial vote on Clay's substitute amendment, as modified, to Calhoun's fifth resolution was 19 to 18 in favor. *Ibid.*, 62.

But since Clay's amendment to Calhoun's fifth resolution dealt both with the abolition of slavery in the District of Columbia and its future in Florida, a motion to reconsider the favorable vote on it was quickly introduced and carried. At this point Sen. James Buchanan (Pa.) offered an amendment to Clay's amendment that focused the question solely on slavery in the district and struck out, for the time being, the issue of the future of slavery in Florida. Buchanan's amendment, which incorporated Clay's views on the abolition of slavery in the district and the role of the right of petition in that process, passed 24 to 13. *Ibid.*, 63.

Following this vote, Clay reiterates his conviction that had Virginia and Maryland known in 1790 that their slavery institutions "would be ended" someday in the district, "they never would have made the cession." It would thus "be a breach of faith to abolish, while the ceding States retained that institution." Further, "when the cession was made there was an express reservation of the right of property," including "this kind [slave] of property."

After further clarification and discussion, a second vote was taken on "the first branch [slavery in the district] of Mr. Clay's substitute" to Calhoun's fifth resolution, as amended by Buchanan. It passed 36 to 9 (changed later to read 36 to 8). *Ibid.*, 63, 65.

As Clay soon discovered, there was in the U.S.-Spanish treaty of 1819 no provision specifically guaranteeing private property in Florida. *Ibid.*, 70; see also Comment in Senate, January 11, 1838.

To PETER B. PORTER Washington, January 10, 1838

I received this morning your favor of the 7h. inst. from Saratoga. As it does not contain an acknowledgement of the receipt of my letter,[1] in answer to a previous favor from you, I have feared that it has miscarried. It contained an expression of my concurrence in opinion with you as to the plan of operations which you had sketched.[2] Perhaps it will be best to put my letters for you under cover to some other person, and if you think so, and will suggest a name I will do so accordingly.

I am happy to hear of the good state of feeling which exists among the Whigs at Albany; and sincerely hope that nothing may occur to interrupt their harmony. They are right not to suffer the Presidential question to interfere with essential measures of Legislation.

Two traps have been set for me here by Mr. Calhoun to affect me at the South—one relating to Abolition,[3] and the other to Texas.[4] You will hear, with satisfaction, that he has totally failed as to Abolition; and that I have borne myself in such manner as to lose nothing neither at the South nor at the North. And I will equally disappoint him as to Texas.[5]

I continue to receive almost daily fresh evidences of the popular feeling concentrating on me. New papers hoisting my flag; public meetings in Ohio, Indiana, Tennessee &c &c. My friends here entertain the most undoubting confidence.

The Conservative movement at N. York appears imposing.[6] Will it take in the Interior? Or will they not lose their distinctive character and be absorbed by the Whigs?

ALS. NBuHi. Letter marked "(Confidential)." 1. Not found; apparently not the Clay to Porter letter of Jan. 5, 1838. 2. Porter to Clay, Dec. 30, 1837. 3. Comment in Senate, Dec. 18, 1837; Remark in Senate, Jan. 6, 1838. 4. Speech in Senate, Jan. 9, 1838. 5. *Ibid.* 6. Clay to Henry Clay, Jr., Jan. 28, 1837.

Comment in Senate, January 11, 1838. Participates in the resumption of debate on Calhoun's six resolutions of December 27, 1837 [Remark in Senate, January 6,

1838; Speech in Senate, January 9, 1838], specifically on his substitute for Calhoun's fifth resolution. This substitute, struck out on January 10, had been reinstated by the motion of Buchanan—a motion essentially encompassing Clay's views on the issue of the future of slavery in Florida Territory and in territories generally [Speech in Senate, January 9, 1838; Comment in Senate, January 10, 1838]. Clay asks at the outset that the question of slavery among the Florida Indian tribes ("these unfortunate beings") be omitted from the discussion since they had few if any slaves and since "The Abolitionists had not addressed to them any petitions on the subject." Also, he knew of no slaveholding Indian tribes residing north of the 36°30′ Missouri Compromise line. His motion to this effect is carried 31 to 10.

Clay is willing, however, to address the contention, contained in Buchanan's motion, that the abolition of slavery in Florida would, among other undesirable effects, violate "the treaty stipulation with Spain of 22d February, 1819, which guarantees the right of property." Informed that there was no such provision in the treaty with Spain, a surprised Clay asserts that the Louisiana Purchase treaty of 1803 with France certainly had such a provision, and that its omission from the Spanish accord in 1819 "could not have been by design, as the treaty was made in the administration of Mr. Monroe, when all his Cabinet was composed of gentlemen from the slaveholding States, who would not have assented to any omissions on this subject." Adds the argument that Congress under the Constitution has the "naked power" to abolish slavery in Florida, as well as in the District of Columbia, but that from various "high considerations" such power has not been exercised. Criticises Calhoun's objection that only the issue of slavery in Florida Territory is incorporated in Buchanan's resolution; also contests Calhoun's renewed insistence that to stem the tide of abolitionism the support and protection of slavery in any and all territories must be upheld. Calhoun responds that for Clay to suggest only that it would be "inexpedient to abolish slavery in Florida" is not enough, because such a geographically restricted stance would oppose no "obstacle to the assaults of the foe." To this criticism Clay replies, "what other Territory than Florida is there in which slavery exists? I framed the resolution as it is, because there is no other such Territory." Also attacks Calhoun for demanding tougher language in his [Clay's] Florida resolution: "Perhaps he [Calhoun] would say that, as slavery is represented as a moral evil, as sinful, we ought to take the opposite ground, and maintain that slavery is not sinful, but in conformity with religion; and he thus maintain the one side, and they the other. . . . Sir, suppose you should declare slavery accords with the Declaration of Independence, and that it is consistent with every high and holy principle, would it make any converts? Sir, I want to do nothing to aggravate this spirit at the North, and to increase the Abolitionists. I want to prevent the residue of the North from going over to join them. There lies our danger, and there, also, are we to look for safety. The Senator's resolutions are all sound; but there will nothing be gained by them of safety to the cause, or of permanency to the Union. These are great objections. It is well that our language should be firm, maintaining our rights; but let us avoid exasperating and irritating language." Further supports his defense of slavery in Florida Territory with specific invocation of the 36°30′ provision of the Missouri Compromise.

In response to an interrogative interruption by Calhoun about the Missouri Compromise, digresses to recount his own role in bringing about the second of "the two compromises"—that which was made necessary when Missouri, by a clause in her state constitution, sought to rid the state of "free persons of color," and in so doing created a new sectional crisis. It was that issue, Clay recalls, which "was the great point of difficulty which shook the Union with more alarm than any thing I have seen, from that day to this." Mentions that during the second Missouri crisis in 1821 the course followed by the late John Randolph of Virginia "came nearer hazarding the Union than any other event in our history. He was opposed to all compromises." Recalls that on one occasion, during House floor debate, Randolph proposed privately to Clay "a separation of the Southern delegation, retiring from Congress, and leaving the North in possession of the Government. . . . he urged me to make no compromise, even provided gentlemen would grant us every thing we wanted, in return for giving the North ground to stand on. We parted, promising to be friends in future; and to the end of the session he never spoke to me again. The two words (dough faces) with which that gentleman rated and taunted our Northern friends did more injury than any two words I have ever known."

On the suggestion of Sen. Henry Hubbard (N.H.), asserts his willingness to modify the language of his Florida amendment so as not to imply a "breach of faith, by abolition, with citizens who, with their slaves, settle in the United States Territories." To this end, Clay supports a variation in wording, proposed by Sen. Robert J. Walker (Miss.), "that any attempt of Congress to abolish slavery in any of the Territories would create serious alarm and just apprehension in the States sustaining that domestic institution," and would be "a violation of good faith toward the inhabitants of any such Territory who have been permitted to settle with, and hold slaves therein." *Cong. Globe*, 25 Cong., 2 Sess., Appendix, 69-72. The amendment in its final wording was passed this day 35 to 9, Clay and Calhoun voting in favor. *Ibid.*, 74. See also *Cong. Globe*, 25 Cong., 2 Sess., 96-97, in which the vote is given as 34 to 9. It was corrected on January 12 to read 35 to 9. *Ibid.*, 98-99. On January 12, Calhoun's sixth resolution, preempted in some measure by Clay's (Buchanan's) Florida substitute for his fifth resolution, was tabled by a vote of 35 to 9. *Ibid.*, 98.

Later in this day, January 11, Clay agrees to strike from his substitute bill the clause relating to the protection of property in Florida which he mistakenly thought had been provided for in the 1819 treaty with Spain. He also agrees to strike out clauses relating to slavery among the Indians "except in cases where, by their influence, the institution of slavery has extended north of the [Missouri] compromise line." *Ibid.*, 96.

To FRANCIS T. BROOKE Washington, January 13, 1838

The arrear which I am under in our correspondence has proceeded from my really having nothing of interest to communicate, and I need not tell you that my correspondence and public engagements are so oppressive that I am constrained to avoid writing, whenever I can. Even now I should not address you, but from my apprehension that you would misconstrue my silence.

We have been engaged in the Senate, during the last eight or ten days, in the most unprofatable discussion that ever engrossed the attention of a deliberative body. It was upon five or six as abstract resolutions as a metaphysical mind can well devise. They are at last disposed of.[1] Their professed object is Slavery—their real aim to advance the political interest of the mover and to affect mine. I am greatly deceived if in both respects he has not signally failed. He was caught in his own trap. You will see the series of counter-resolutions which I offered.[2] The two most important, after undergoing some modifications, with my assent, were adopted as substitutes for his. His Texas resolution was laid on the table yesterday by a vote of 35 to 9.[3] I think that when that subject comes up, I will turn the tables upon Mr Calhoun as much as I did on the affair of Slavery.[4]

There is not I think, the slightest ground of approaching war with G. Britian [*sic*], on account of Canada.[5] When the P[resident's]. message was recd. respecting the capture and destruction of the Caroline,[6] I thought it due to the occasion to reprehend in the strongest terms, the violation of our jurisdiction. My remarks are correctly published in the N. Intellr. and there only.[7] The [Washington] Globe habitually misreports me.[8]

Resolutions have been introduced in the K. Legislature recommending me as the next President.[9] Altho I presumed that something would be done at Frankfort. I anticipated nothing in this form, and I think it displays more zeal than discretion.

Copy. DLC-TJC (DNA, M212, R10). Printed in Colton, *Clay Correspondence*, 4:423-24. 1. Calhoun's six resolutions on slavery. See Remark in Senate, Jan. 6, 1838; Speech in Senate, Jan. 9, 1838. 2. *Ibid.* 3. *Cong. Globe*, 25 Cong., 2 Sess., 98. 4. Speech in Senate, Jan. 9, 1838; Clay to Porter, Jan. 10, 1838. 5. Porter to Clay, Dec. 30, 1837. 6. Comment in Senate, Jan. 5, 1838. 7. Clay's Comment in the Senate on Jan. 5, 1838, on the *Caroline* incident was reported in the Washington *Daily National Intelligencer* on Jan. 6, 1838. 8. The Washington *Globe* commented on and criticized Clay's remarks on the burning of the *Caroline* on Jan. 9, 1838. 9. The Frankfort *Commonwealth* reported on Jan. 10, 1838, that a resolution recommending Clay for president had been reported in the Ky. house of representatives and had been referred to a select committee. It was the Jan. 12 convention of Whigs in the Ky. legislature, however, which provided for choosing delegates to a national convention to nominate him. See Clay to Porter, Jan. 5, 1838.

To EPES SARGENT[1] Washington, January 13, 1838

I regret that I have not a single Copy left of the Copy Right bill[2] to send you, according to the request contained in your favor of the 9h. I concur with you in opinion entirely about the expediency of passing the bill. But the Booksellers, or rather some of them, are making efforts to defeat it by procuring signatures against it, and if they are not counter acted they may possibly succeed.

If I am to credit the information which almost daily reaches me, the same concentration which you describe as taking place, in Massachusetts in regard to the next P. Election, is going on, and perhaps more rapidly, elsewhere. It is the more gratifying, because it is without any personal exertion on my part to direct the current of public feeling towards me. I shall not deviate from the rule of absolute passiveness, which I have prescribed to myself. My greatest anxiety is that the mal-administration of the Government should be corrected, and I shall be content no matter under what auspices, or in whose name, that desirable object shall be accomplished. . . .

ALS. MCM. 1. Sargent, a prolific writer and editor of various newspapers in Boston and New York City, wrote *Life and Public Services of Henry Clay* in 1842. See *DAB*. 2. Comment in Senate, Feb. 2, 1837.

Remark in Senate, January 15, 1838. Presents a petition asking for a dry dock at the Philadelphia navy yard. *Cong. Globe*, 25 Cong., 2 Sess., 102.

Remark in Senate, January 16, 1838. Asks that more time be allowed for consideration of the administration's principal Sub-Treasury system bill [Speech in Senate, September 25, 1837], because it was a "measure of such momentous consequences." Thinks January 30 will be too soon to take it up, since the "details of the bill" are "numerous." Clay's motion for further delay was defeated. *Cong. Globe*, 25 Cong., 2 Sess., 112. The proposed bill, in 29 sections, was printed in full on this day. *Ibid.*, 110-12. It was taken up for debate on January 31. It was again reprinted, as amended, on March 26, 1838, the day it passed 27 to 25. *Ibid.*, 264-65. See also Speech in Senate, September 25, 1837; Speech in Senate, February 19, 1838.

To A. Wickham, January 17, 1838. In response to a question as to whether debating societies should deal exclusively with political questions, Clay remarks: "I think not. When I was myself a young man, I was a member of a Rhetorical Society, in which questions of history, philosophy, and political economy were discussed, and profitably to the members." ALS. KyU.

To Thomas Hart Clay, Lexington, January 18, 1838. Advises him on purchase of mules and hogs. Will go security on necessary loans involved. Reports that the "Sub-treasury project is again reported to the Senate, in a more odious form than ever." ALS. Henry Clay Memorial Foundation, Lexington, Ky.

On January 16, Sen. Silas Wright (N.Y.), chairman of the Committee on Finance, had introduced the administration's reworked Sub-Treasury bill. *Cong. Globe*, 25 Cong., 2 Sess., 109-12. See also Speech in Senate, September 25, 1837; Remark in Senate, January 16 and 18, 1838; Speech in Senate, February 19, 1838.

Remark in Senate, January 18, 1838. Supports Sen. William C. Preston's motion to reconsider yesterday's vote to take up the Sub-Treasury bill [Speech in Senate, September 25, 1837; Remark in Senate, January 16, 1838] on January 23, rather than on January 30 as the Senate had initially determined on January 16. Thinks this new date is much too soon to consider adequately "a measure more odious in itself than the far-famed alien and sedition laws." Asks why the bill has not been introduced in the House where it "properly belongs." *Cong. Globe*, 25 Cong., 2 Sess., 119. The motion to reconsider carried, and the date set to consider the Sub-Treasury bill was restored to January 30. *Ibid.*, 120. See also Speech in Senate, February 19, 1838; *Cong. Globe*, 25 Cong., 2 Sess., 109-12, 264-65.

From Peter B. Porter, New York, January 19, 1838. Acknowledges receipt of Clay's letters of January 5 and 10. Hopes that within "two or three weeks" an understanding can be reached among politicians that will "obviate the necessity of a national [Whig nominating] convention, which many are desirous of avoiding." Adds, further: "The admirable manner in which you have parried Calhoun's resolutions [Remark in Senate, January 6, 1838; Speech in Senate, January 9, 1838], has quieted (for a time at least) the disturbing question of abolitionism, and gained for you additional confidence and respect." Copy. OHi. See also Comment in Senate, January 10 and 11, 1838.

Remark in Senate, January 19, 1838. Asks Sen. John M. Niles (Conn.) to withdraw his amendment to the bill to provide relief to the executrix of the late Richard W. Meade so as not further to delay the long, drawn out measure [Remark in Senate, January 2, 1838]. *Cong. Globe*, 25 Cong., 2 Sess., 121.

From John Jacob Astor, New York, January 20, 1838. Expresses an interest in the U.S. treaty with the Chippewas at Fort Snelling soon to be laid before the Senate for ratification. Notes that "By this treaty a considerable amount is allowed to pay debts to Indian Traders; and I would recommend, in order to avoid the unjust division of dues so frequently complained of in similar cases, and as the only means occurring to me by which I and many others having rights under this treaty can expect to be fairly dealt with, that it be so amended before it pass the Senate, that the sum allowed to pay the Traders, shall be divided among them by a commissioner appointed for that purpose." Hopes that a similar provision can be inserted into the pending treaties with the Sioux, Winnebago, Sauk and Fox tribes if this has not already been done. Copy. MH-BA.

For the treaty with the Chippewas, signed at St. Peter in the Wisconsin Territory (present-day Minnesota) on July 29, 1837, and proclaimed June 15, 1838, see Parry, *Treaty Series*, 87:29-30. For the treaties with the Sioux, Sauk and Fox, and Winnebago Indians, all signed in Washington in late 1837 and proclaimed on February 21, 1838, see *ibid.*, 87:71-72, 111-15. All the treaties provided that Indian debts would be paid by the United States, but none specified the appointment of a U.S. commissioner.

To PETER B. PORTER Washington, January 21, 1838

I was glad to learn from your letter of the 19h. inst. that my two previous letters had been safely received by you.

We have just heard that a Caucus of the Whig members of the G. Assembly of K.[1] have 1st. concurred with the Ohio Convention[2] in recommending a Nat. Convention. 2dly. Expressed their preference. 3d. their determination to abide by the nomination of the Convention. 4h. Have appointed two delegates to the Convention, corresponding with the two Senators; and have recommended the people in the several Congressional districts to appoint 13 others. And 5h. Have recommended the Whig members of Congress to *fix* the time of the meeting of the Convention. Great unanimity prevailed. The proceedings will probably be received tomorrow or next day. I understand that similar proceedings will very soon take place in Maryland[3] & N. Jersey.[4]

I have sent you a Copy of the S. Treasury bill &c.[5] Will you not extend your visit to this place?

ALS. NBuHi. 1. Clay to Porter, Jan. 5 and Jan. 10, 1838. 2. Clay to Porter, Jan. 5, 1838. 3. The Baltimore *Chronicle* reported on Feb. 23, 1838, that the Whigs in the Maryland legislature, plus some other citizens, had met and endorsed Clay. They had also called for a state convention to choose delegates to a Whig national convention. Frankfort *Commonwealth*, March 7, 1838. 4. Kinsey to Clay, Jan. 3, 1838. 5. Printed in *Cong. Globe*, 25 Cong., 2 Sess., 109-12; see also Speech in Senate, Sept. 25, 1837, and Feb. 19, 1838.

To JAMES B. CLAY Washington, January 22, 1838

I received your letter of the 1st. inst.[1] this day, and the perusal of it gave me much concern. I had previously received from you a letter[2] complaining of your solitary condition, and stating that you were not happy. I answered it,[3] but as you do not acknowledge the receipt of my answer I suppose it had not reached you.

I desire most ardently, my dear Son, your happiness and that of every child I have. You know that I was not anxious for you to go to Missouri.[4] The very circumstances which now exist I anticipated. But you were confident, and I yielded. I have wished to see you happily married, under the hope that with a wife whom you loved and the prospects of a family you might be contented and happy. You tell me that you have not the means to go into Society. But you have not informed me what means you allude to. I have been very desirous that you should go much more into society than you have done; and why have you not? Do you want clothes? The slightest intimation of your wishes to me, on that subject, would have commanded them. I have refused you nothing that you have asked me. I have been, I own, exceedingly anxious that you should avoid all dissipation, but with that restriction I have not cared how much society you enjoyed, or rather I have wished that you should see much of it.

In my former letter I expressed a wish that you would attend diligently to your business, make yourself as happy as you can, and upon my return home I would see if we could not make some arrangement by which you should return to K. Of one thing you may be certain that you will be happy no where without constant employment. That is the great secret of human happiness.

I should be very glad to have you near us. Have you another Overseer? You have never informed me. If you have, I do not see why you might not at any time leave home for some weeks, go to Ashland or make a visit to see our Military lands or to your uncle Porter [Clay].

Of one thing you may be assured my dear Son that I not only feel the deepest interest in your welfare and happiness but that I am always willing to do any thing to promote it. I am the more concerned about you because John [Morrison Clay] has lately given me great pain, and I almost despair of him.[5] When you reflect how much inquietude several of my sons have given us,[6] I am sure that you will be stimulated to persevere in a course of regularity and propriety.

I have written to you frequently; but the mails are irregula[r.] I received two or three days ago your letter of Novr transmitting a Copy of that which you had addressed to your uncle Porter.

My friends are very sanguine about my Election to the next Presidency, and, with reason, if I am to credit the information which daily reaches me. But I strive to prevent my feelings being too much enlisted in the object.

ALS. DLC-HC (DNA, M212, R5). Apparently addressed to James at "Richland," near St. Louis, Mo. 1. Not found. 2. Probably that of Dec. 23, 1837, not found, mentioned in Clay to James B. Clay, Jan. 7, 1838. 3. Clay to James B. Clay, Jan. 7, 1838. 4. See 8:801. 5. Precisely what John had done at this particular juncture in his career to cause Clay pain is not known. But a year later, according to the Princeton University Faculty Minutes of Feb. 12, 1839, he "was suspended, for having gone to New York, and remained there several days, without permission." On March 4, 1839, the Faculty Minutes record that "John M. Clay, of the Junior Class, was dismissed, at his father's request." Information supplied by Princeton University Archivist, Earle E. Coleman. 6. See 8:213-14, 442-43, 670-71.

Remark in Senate, January 23, 1838. Asserts that this particular bill "to grant pre-emption rights to settlers on the public lands" is novel only in that it will "throw open the whole public domain to every man who will call himself a pre-emptioner." Is convinced that the Congress will receive applications for preemption laws "until the end of time," and that people will "go on choosing the best parcels of the public land, and applying to Congress for pre-emption rights until they reached the Pacific." This will not be the last such bill, Clay asserts. These claims will "never cease." *Cong. Globe*, 25 Cong., 2 Sess., 130. The 1838 preemption bill passed the Senate by a vote of 30 to 18 on January 30, 1838. *Ibid.*, 149. The House amended it and passed it 107 to 52 on June 14, 1838. *Ibid.*, 452-53. The Senate accepted the House version as amended by a vote of 42 to 2 on June 19, 1838. *Ibid.*, 462-63.

A Senate bill entitled "An Act to Grant Pre-emption Rights to Settlers on the Public Lands" had been introduced in 1829, passed by the Senate on January 13, 1830 (29 to 12), passed by the House on May 29, 1830, and signed by the president the same day. U.S. Sen., *Journal*, 21 Cong., 1 Sess., 43, 46, 50, 57, 61, 83, 344, 347,

350, 353-54; 4 *U.S. Stat.*, 420-21. An act supplementary to this act was signed into law on January 23, 1832. 4 *U.S. Stat.*, 496. An act to revive the preemption act of May 29, 1830, was reported in the Senate on December 17, 1833, and that day passed to second reading on motion by Clay. It passed the Senate (vote not recorded) on March 10, 1834, and the House, 124-53, on June 14 [Comment in Senate, January 30, 1838]. The president signed it on June 19, 1834. U.S. Sen., *Journal*, 23 Cong., 1 Sess., 46, 52, 91, 173, 177, 316, 320, 326, 328, 349; U.S. H. of Reps., *Journal*, 23 Cong., 1 Sess., 751-52; 4 *U.S. Stat.*, 678. A bill to extend the preemption act of May 29, 1830, was introduced in the Senate again in 1836 and was defeated by a vote of 23 to 17, Clay voting with the majority. U.S. Sen., *Journal*, 24 Cong., 1 Sess., 225, 242, 254-55, 350, 410, 416, 419. Thus, the 1830 act, as supplemented and extended in 1832 and 1834, died in 1836. It was soon revived, however, and was passed by the Senate, 30 to 18, on Jan. 30, 1838, amended by the House and passed, 107 to 52, on June 14, 1838. The Senate on June 19 approved, 42-2, the bill as amended by the House. *Cong. Globe*, 25 Cong., 2 Sess., 149, 452, 463; *ibid.*, Appendix, 143. The bill was signed by the president on June 22. For the 1838 preemption act, which resurrected the act of 1830 and extended it for two more years, see 5 *U.S. Stat.*, 251-52.

Remark in Senate, January 25, 1838. Challenges Mississippi Sen. Robert J. Walker's defense of the preemption bill [Remark in Senate, January 23, 1838]. Specifically, Clay attacks Walker's contention that even though large quantities of public land have been thrown on the market, the exercise of preemption rights upon it has reduced the price of such lands by not more than an average of two cents per acre, and that, in general, acts of preemption increase the value of the still unsold public land. Asks Walker if there are any figures showing the amount of public land sold at public sales at levels above the minimum price. Thinks Walker's average includes land sold at both public and private sales. Also raises questions about provisions of the bill, and proposed amendments to it, dealing with the problem of preemption rights by settlers on Indian lands prior to the extinguishment of the Indian titles. Wants the Indian titles carefully protected. Asks the secretary of the treasury, by resolution, for statistics on all public lands sold at public sale, the total sale price, and the average price of each acre sold. *Cong. Globe*, 25 Cong., 2 Sess., 136-37. For Walker's struggle with Clay on preemption and other public land policy issues, see 8:873-74; Remark in Senate, January 12, 1837; Remark in Senate, January 23, 1838.

Earlier this day, Clay presented two petitions from Philadelphia merchants asking for an appropriation to complete the U.S. Navy frigate *Raritan*, now on the stocks in Philadelphia. *Cong. Globe*, 25 Cong., 2 Sess., 135.

From Granville A. Sackett, Brooklyn, Long Island, N.Y., January 25, 1838. Says that while he is unknown to Clay, he wishes to take this opportunity to point out the advantages of reforming U.S. copyright laws so that literary piracy can be stamped out and encouragement rendered "original American works." Does this at great length. Also urges American participation in an international copyright convention [Comment in Senate, February 2, 1837]. ALS. DLC-HC (DNA, M212, R5). Sackett wrote poetry for a Brooklyn newspaper called the *Star*, signing his work "Alfred." Ralph F. Weld, *Brooklyn Village, 1816-1834* (New York, 1938), 175.

Comment in Senate, January 26, 1838. States he cannot vote for the administration's [Sen. Walker's] preemption bill [Remark in Senate, January 23, 1838] in any form, because in any of its aspects preemption is "a bounty, or a grant of the property of the whole people to a small part of the people; often the speculator." Introduces and quotes from various documents showing that preemption practices do not augment public revenue, as contended by the Jackson and Van Buren administrations, that they do not increase the value of unsold public land as claimed, and that fraud and scandal have long characterized the operation and administration of the preemption laws. Calls for "a fair, open, public sale" of government land if revenue augmentation and honesty are truly desired. Admits that from a political standpoint the debate on preemption is unequal and that a "number of senators from the new States were ever ready to spring up and eulogize the preemption laws." Denies Sen. Robert J. Walker's insistence that opposition to preemption is simply evidence of "the old States . . . grasping after the public lands." However, Clay says he will "take no part in the charge against the senator [Walker]" that he had personally speculated in preempted public lands. Copy. Printed in Colton, *Clay Correspondence*, 6:87-93.

A much shorter and somewhat different version, lacking excerpts from the numerous documents introduced and cited by Clay, is in *Cong. Globe*, 25 Cong., 2 Sess., 142-43. It includes, however, a controversial Clay statement, omitted by Colton, on the rapaciousness of squatters on the public lands. In this statement, later used against him in the 1844 election, Clay denounces "the whole system of pre-emption as a fraudulent, heartless, scandalous, abominable speculation" against which he would speak "as long as God gave him strength to do so." Specifically, he refers to land in Indiana recently acquired from the Miami Indians, and notes that these lands "worth from $10 to $40 per acre had been intruded upon by lawless men in violation of the rights of the Government; and yet these 'poor, honest settlers' were to have the rights of pre-emption. What right had these men to the public lands? By what power did they seize upon and rob the United States of their possessions? As well might they seize upon the dollars in the public Treasury; on the forts, arsenals, and public ships, as on the public lands." See also Comment in Senate, January 27, 1838; Remark in Senate, January 8, 1839; Clay to Estes, June 1, 1839.

Earlier this day, Clay had lectured Walker on the growing of corn in Kentucky and the excellent yields possible there. *Cong. Globe*, 25 Cong., 2 Sess., 140.

To PETER B. PORTER Washington, January 26, 1838

I duly recd. your favor of the 24h. We shall get today or tomorrow the proceedings of the K. Legislature, or rather the Whig Caucus, in respect to the Presidential question,[1] and I will forward them to you. If I am rightly informed, those of the Whigs of Maryland[2] and N. Jersey[3] will quickly follow.

On the subject of Texas, when [William C.] Preston's resolution is taken up,[4] I shall express my sentiments fully,[5] and I anticipate, with perfect confidence, your concurrence in every one of them. Shortly after the appearance of Dr. [William E.] Channings published letter addressed to me,[6] I wrote him,[7] and altho' my letter was confidential, it contained no opinion which I should be unwilling to see published.

I do not think that the question of annexation is one that ought to be considered or entertained at all, during the existence of War between Mexico and Texas. I would not for a moment consent to involve this Country in War to acquire that Country. Nor, if its independence were acknowledged by Mexico, and peace were established between them, would I concur in incorporating Texas in this Confederacy, against the decided wishes of a large portion of it. I think it better to harmonize what we have, than to introduce a new element of discord into our political partnership, against the consent of existing members of the concern.

These are briefly my views. But I do not wish publicity given to them, until they are announced by myself from my place in the Senate. I persuade myself that I shall in due time escape the Texas trap, set for me, as well as I did the Abolition trap.[8]

Can not our friends at Albany be induced to express their opposition to [Silas] Wrights S[ub]. Treasury bill?[9]

ALS. NBuHi. Letter marked "(Confidential)." 1. Clay to Porter, Jan. 5, 1838; Clay to Brooke, Jan. 13, 1838. 2. Clay to Porter, Jan. 21, 1838. 3. Kinsey to Clay, Jan. 3, 1838. 4. Sen. William Preston (S.C.) defended his Jan. 4, 1838, resolution to annex Texas in a lengthy speech on April 24, 1838. His motion was taken up on June 14 and was tabled by a vote of 24 to 14. *Cong. Globe*, 25 Cong., 2 Sess., 76, 319, 326, 453; *ibid.*, Appendix, 555-58. 5. In his Speech in Senate, Jan. 9, 1838, Clay attacked Preston's resolution favoring Texas annexation in conjunction with a broader attack upon Calhoun's sixth resolution on slavery [Remark in Senate, Jan. 6, 1838] which had broached the annexation issue in a less direct manner than had Preston. Clay did not again speak on Texas annexation during the session; but see Remark in Senate, March 1, 1837. 6. Channing to Clay, August 1, 1837. 7. Not found; but see Clay to Channing, Dec. 13, 1837, and Clay to Porter, Jan. 26, 1838. 8. Clay to Porter, Jan. 10, 1838. 9. Speech in Senate, Sept. 25, 1837; Remark in Senate, Jan. 16, 1838; Speech in Senate, Feb. 19, 1838.

Comment in Senate, January 27, 1838. Opposes Michigan Sen. Lucius Lyon's amendment to the preemption bill [Remark in Senate, January 23, 1838] that would exempt from the measure contested preemption claim certificates. Clay argues that such a proviso would "cover and protect cases of settlement by agent and attorney—a deceptive mode of obtaining pre-emption titles." Explains to Sen. James Buchanan (Pa.) how people are hired by speculators to occupy, claim, and hold land "for the purpose of getting these best portions of the public domains into their hands." Thanks Maryland Sen. William D. Merrick for his amendment to the preemption proposal that would limit future preemption rights to those who were citizens on December 1, 1837, thus "conferring the bounty of the Government to our own race, instead of holding out a general invitation to all the paupers of all the European Governments to come here, and compete with our own honest poor." Chides Buchanan, son of a naturalized foreigner, for his eulogy to immigrants, mainly those who had come to fight in the American Revolution: "Does he mean to compare the DeKalbs, the Steubens, the Lafayettes, the Pulaskis, with the hordes of foreign paupers that are constantly flooding our shores?" Does he include the Hessians in his eulogy? Would he grant preemptions to them? Following the defeat of Merrick's amendment, 28 to 15, Clay moves an amendment that would prohibit "all settlements upon the public lands" after December 1, 1837, and which would also authorize the president to remove violators. Claims this amendment is "strictly in accordance" with the "wise" recommendations on public land policy that were included in Van Buren's message of December 5, 1837. Calls for a vote on it "to see how many might, for the first time, run counter" to the president's position. Says that "in this instance" he will be "an Administration man for once," a comment leading to facetious banter with Buchanan.

His amendment having been defeated 27 to 17, Clay, on challenge from Sen. John Tipton (Ind.), repeats his opinion, expressed the previous day [Comment in the Senate, January 26, 1838], that "squatters on the public lands were a lawless rabble" who "might as well seize upon our forts, our arsenals, or on the public treasure, as to rush out and seize upon the public lands." *Cong. Globe*, 25 Cong., 2 Sess., Appendix, 129, 132-34. See also *Cong. Globe*, 25 Cong., 3 Sess., Appendix, 225, for what Clay later (January 8, 1839) said he had said about squatters on January 27, 1838. Also see Remark in Senate, January 8, 1839, and Clay to Estes, June 1, 1839. For Van Buren's December 5, 1837, remarks on public land policy, see *MPP*, 3:384-89. For Clay's recollection in 1843 of what he had said about squatters in 1838-39, see Clay to Mudd, Sept. 25, 1843.

From JOHN TYLER Williamsburg, Va., January 28, 1838

I owe you my acknowledgements for the pamphlet copy of your speech on Mr. Calhoun's resolutions.[1] I have read it with profound interest and have deriv'd profit from its perusal—It has restored me to the position which I occupied when agitation was first raised with some two or three years [?] ago on the abolition question, but from which I suffered myself to be jostled by the clamour of those around me—[2] If the petitions asking the abolition of slavery in the District had been silently referd Arthur Tappan & Co[3] would have made but slow progress in their dissorganizing schemes—We fell into the very snare which they design'd for us—[4] They wanted agitation and the South gave them agitation and now they constitute a formidable power in the States—I hope that your resolution will have the effect of rallying the sound-headed and sound-hearted to the North in favour of the Constitution and Union and that the dissorganizers will be left alone, as sould always be the fate of the plotters of iniquity—I need scarcely say to you that my opinion, the result of no passion, is that Congress have no right, with or without making remuneration to emancipate the slaves in the District without the consent of the owners—for if govt. can, under any pretext of public use, which mere fancy or speculation may suggest, confiscate an entire species of property held by its citizens, so may it confiscate every other species ad libitum—Its action at once degenerates into arbitrary, despotic and tyrannical, and that which was designed by the Constitution as a restraint upon its conduct, is converted into a sanction for grinding oppression—I think then that no plea of public use can any more justify the emancipation of slaves, than the forfeiture of lands and houses or the confiscation of any other article of personal property—But be this as it may, I think that every proper means should be adopted to allay excitement and to restore confidence to the Country—Wishing you all possible success in your efforts to accomplish this good work. . . .

ALS. DLC-HC (DNA, M212, R5). 1. Remark in Senate, Jan. 6, 1838; Speech in Senate, Jan. 9, 1838. Clay's speech of Jan. 9 was published under the title *Speech of Henry Clay of Kentucky on Certain Resolutions Offered to the Senate . . . in December, 1837 by Mr. Calhoun . . . Involving Principles of Interpretation of the Constitution of the United States. . . .* Washington, 1838. 2. Lyon G. Tyler, *Letters and Times of the Tylers.* 2 vols. (Richmond, Va., 1884, 1885), 1:579-82. 3. For Arthur Tappan, noted philanthropist and abolitionist and brother of Lewis Tappan, see *DAB*. 4. See 8:817-18.

Comment in Senate, January 29, 1838. Supports Sen. Calhoun's opposition to the preemption bill [Remark in Senate, January 23, 1838], noting that there has been much armed violence by squatters upon the public lands. Asserts that problems with the orderly disposition of the nation's land began with the first preemption law in 1830. This legislation was "one of the fatal series of experiments" which began in the Jackson administration but which "owing to the abuses and corruptions which sprung from it . . . came into general disrepute" and expired in 1836. Regrets that during the last session there was sentiment to revive preemption [8:839; Remark in Senate, January 12, 1837]. Explains the lack of any real need for such legislation, given the fact that there are 114,000,000 acres of surveyed land already on the market. Points out that settlement upon and preemption of the still unsurveyed lands have been made possible by "a combination . . . of the friends of the Administration, and the members from the [nine] New States," plus Sen. Daniel Webster. This combination has breathed political life into the current preemption bill. Argues that preemption must be "disconnected" from the nation's land system, but realizes "how vain any struggle of his was against the passage of this bill, two-thirds of the Senate voting for it." *Cong. Globe*, 25 Cong., 2 Sess., Appendix, 139.

Comment in Senate, January 30, 1838. Responds to Sen. Robert J. Walker's observation that he had voted for the preemption bill of June 19, 1834 [Remark in Senate, January 23, 1838]. Explains that he had voted for it in 1834 not to "change the principle of the sales" but "to put down combinations, and guard against violence as well as corruption." We knew of the "extent of the evil, of the number of squatters . . . on the public land, and the difficulty of removing them; and that therefore there was a necessity for passing this law, to give them the lands they . . . unjustly seized on." Asks why a squatter would not have the right to preempt part of the White House, since that too is public property. Says, further, that in 1834 senators were told that "the bill would only extend to a small number of settlers, who had not had the benefit of the former [1830] law; that it would embrace a few cases only." *Cong. Globe*, 25 Cong., 2 Sess., Appendix, 142-43.

Comment in Senate, January 31, 1838. Continues his opposition to the administration's Sub-Treasury [Independent Treasury] bill [Speech in Senate, September 25, 1837; Remark in Senate, January 16, 1838]. Emphasizes its excessive consolidation of financial power in the hands of the president. Asks that Senate discussion be postponed until the legislatures of several states now debating the concept are heard from. Complains that economic and financial matters, which should originate in the house "nearest the people," are more and more originating in the Senate. Suggests that it may be because the administration does not control the lower chamber. Asks that the Senate wait until the House as well as the state legislatures speak on the Sub-Treasury bill. Challenges, on tactical grounds, Sen. Calhoun's contention that the Senate should act now so that the arguments pro and con can be aired to the benefit of the state legislatures. No, Clay insists: "Let us not commit ourselves one way or the other, till we hear from our constituents." But says he is willing to push ahead if that is the will of the majority. "If the friends of this measure . . . will not wait for further information, let them come on; we are prepared for them, and ready to meet even their redoubtable champion from South Carolina. . . . [who] does not see that this measure can lead both to consolidation and disserverence." *Cong. Globe*, 25 Cong., 2 Sess., 151-52.

From Nicholas Biddle, Philadelphia, February 3, 1838. Reports his efforts to persuade the state legislature at Harrisburg to instruct Pennsylvania's legislators in Washington to oppose "this insane SubTreasury scheme [Speech in Senate, September 25, 1837; Remark in Senate, January 16, 1838; Speech in Senate, February 19, 1838]." Urges Clay "to keep up the debate in the Senate for a few days until the resolutions [of instruction] can reach you. I attach great importance to this measure as separating our state from these desperadoes." Copy. DLC-Nicholas Biddle Papers (DNA, M212, R20). Letter marked "(Confidential)" and dated "12 O clock Saturday night."

The Pennsylvania house passed a resolution on February 16 and the senate concurred on February 17, 1838, instructing their senators and representatives in Congress "to vote and use their influence for a postponement until the next session of congress" of the Sub-treasury bill and further instructed them to "vote at this session for no act of a similar nature. . . . And our senators are hereby further instructed and our members requested to vote for such a mode of receiving, keeping, and disbursing, the public moneys as will separate, as far as practicable, the banks from the government." However, the resolution also expressed "full confidence" in Martin Van Buren. Pennsylvania's two senators, Samuel McKean and

James Buchanan, mindful of the instructions, voted against the bill when it came before the Senate, but the state's Democratic representatives in the House voted in favor of it. *Niles' Register* (February 24, 1838), 53:385, 402; Henry R. Mueller, *The Whig Party in Pennsylvania* (New York, 1922), 46.

From Nicholas Biddle, Philadelphia, February 4, 1838. Says he wrote Clay "last night" and has since received "the enclosed resolution [Biddle to Clay, February 3, 1838]" of the Pennsylvania state legislature instructing Senators James Buchanan and Samuel McKean to vote against the administration's Sub-Treasury scheme [Speech in Senate, September 25, 1837; Remark in Senate, January 16, 1838; Speech in Senate, February 19, 1838]. Hopes that the instruction will force "the distinguished democrat [Buchanan] who represents us there . . . [to] follow the example of Mr. [William C.] Rives (Va.) & resign." Thinks it "very desirable" to force Buchanan "to express himself to that effect beyond the power of retreating before the resolution finally passes." Copy. DLC-Nicholas Biddle Papers (DNA, M212, R20). Letter marked "(Confidential)." Both Buchanan and McKean voted against the Sub-Treasury bill in its final form. *Cong. Globe*, 25 Cong., 2 Sess., 264.

Rives had resigned from the U.S. Senate in 1834 because of his unwillingness to comply with instructions of the Virginia legislature to vote for Jackson's censure. Robert Seager II, *And Tyler Too, A Biography of John and Julia Gardiner Tyler* (New York, 1967), 101.

To Nicholas Biddle, Philadelphia, February 5, 1838. Having "this moment recd. your letter," rejoices that legislative instructions against the Sub-Treasury bill are pending in Harrisburg, since "Buchanan told me that he would obey instructions. I hope they will come. They may be decisive of the fate of the atrocious measure." ALS. DLC-Nicholas Biddle Papers (DNA, M212, R20) . Letter dated "Sunday night 10 OClock." See Biddle to Clay, February 3 and February 4, 1838.

To NICHOLAS BIDDLE Washington, February 6, 1838

I received your favor of the 4th, & met Mr. B[uchanan]. last night at a small party given at the house at which I board. I rallied him on the subject of instructions, & he remarked to me, as he had done once or twice before, that if they came, he would obey or resign, intimating, I thought, a preference for the latter alternative.[1]

We are now in the midst of the debate on the Treasury Bank,[2] the denomination which should be given to it upon every occasion. [William C.] Rives began a very good speech, yesterday, which he will finish, today.[3] I do not know that an occasion will present itself, but if it does, I will embrace it, to draw from Mr. B. a more explicit declaration. We will run them to the girt in the Senate. If they carry their abominable measure, it will not be by a majority of more than two votes.[4] I am worked almost to death, & to relieve myself I have to engage the good offices of a young friend as an amanuensis—[5]

LS. James Biddle, The Biddle Family Papers, Andalusia, Pa. 1. Biddle to Clay, Feb. 3 and Feb. 4, 1838; Clay to Biddle, Feb. 5, 1838. 2. Speech in Senate, Feb. 19, 1838. See also Speech in Senate, Sept. 25, 1837. 3. On the Sub-Treasury proposal. For Rives's remarks on it, and Clay's reactions thereto, see Speech in Senate, Sept. 25, 1837; *Cong. Globe*, 25 Cong., 2 Sess., Appendix, 608-14; Comment in Senate, March 7, 1838. 4. It passed, as amended, by two votes (27 to 25) on March 26, 1838. *Cong. Globe*, 25 Cong., 2 Sess., 264. 5. Gales Seaton (1817-57), son of William W. Seaton. See Oren A. Seaton, *The Seaton Family with Genealogy and Biographies* (Topeka, Kan., 1906), 113, 118; Clay to Henry Clay, Jr., March 2, 1838.

Comment in Senate, February 6, 1838. Asks Sen. James Buchanan (Pa.) to explain why it is that those who in 1834 so enthusiastically supported the removal of government deposits from the Bank of the United States and the placement of those funds in selected private banks [8:583-84, 684-85] now claim that that arrangement was dangerous and corrupting and want to impose on the nation instead "the Sub-Treasury system, alias the *Government* Bank of the United States [Speech in Senate, September 25, 1837]." Points out that "having found that the system which they adopted three years ago has failed, they are now for giving us another of their prescriptions, which we must take from these same doctors." Is delighted to learn from Sen. Felix Grundy that the Tennessee legislature has instructed the state's senators to vote against the Sub-Treasury proposal. Says he supports the doctrine of instruction "with certain qualifications," and hopes that "those who hold to the doctrine act consistently." Predicts that Virginia too, like Tennessee, will declare against the Sub-Treasury scheme in the next election. Evokes laughter when he "pledge[s] his word" to vote against the Sub-Treasury proposal if the Kentucky legislature instructs him to do so. Calls attention to various discrepancies, contradictions, and points of confusion in the bill as it stands, and says his main interest now is to observe how the administration and its congressional supporters (its "household troops") can manage to achieve unity and consistency. *Cong. Globe*, 25 Cong., 2 Sess., 166-67.

From Reuben G. Beasley, Havre, France, February 7, 1838. Reports that "The Insurance on the Asses [Beasley to Clay, January 8, 1837] was specific," and "You will find a statement of the settlement of loss annexed."

Mentions that Clay has asked him for documents, "illustrating the practical operation of the French system of Revenue, including the mode of collection disbursemement &c." States that he "cannot do better than send you the last Budget" which will show "the total amount collected by each division or department of the Treasury & the number of receiving & disbursing officers with their salaries & other expenses attending the same."

In regard to banking in the United States, emphasizes his sorrow that the Bank of the United States has been abandoned and that the administration seems "likely to persist in the sub Treasy scheme [Speech in Senate, September 25, 1837]." Adds: "There is no doubt Banking has been greatly abused, the Bank of Pennsylvania & many other Banks have not only been dealing in Foreign Exchanges but the shipment of Produce—monopolizing as it were (to the destruction of our Merchants who cannot stand up against their large Capitals) the whole Trade of the Country. If there was no other reason, this would be sufficient with me for establishing a Bank of the U.S. which under proper regulations would keep all the rest on the *qui vive* & so prevent over issues of paper by them [Comment in Senate, September 26, 1837; Speech in Senate, May 21, 1838]." Believes that the capital of such a bank should be large, and it should be confined entirely to internal banking operations. Argues: "Leave to the merchants the exportation & importation of Specie & every other article of Commerce as also the Foreign Exchange business. It properly belongs to them—competition will keep that business on a proper footing." If this were done, he predicts that "we should very soon see the currency & Exchanges restored to a satisfactory state."

Mentions that "I do not apprehend any thing serious from the revolt in Canada [Porter to Clay, December 15, 1837; Comment in Senate, January 5, 1838]." ALS. Josephine Simpson Collection, Lexington, Ky. A statement, not in Beasley's hand, which is annexed to the letter indicates that the two jackasses being sent to Clay had been insured at a value of £2,800 each and the seven jennies at £1,400, for a total of £15,400.

Remark in Senate, February 7, 1838. Presents petition from Philadelphia asking for completion of the U.S.N. frigate *Raritan.* "The earlier the better," Clay adds. *Cong. Globe,* 25 Cong., 2 Sess., 168. Laid down in Philadelphia in 1820, launched and commissioned finally in 1843, the modified *Potomac*-class, ship-rigged frigate *Raritan* (32) was scuttled in Norfolk on April 20, 1861. K. Jack Bauer, *Ships of the Navy, 1775-1969* (Troy, N.Y., 1969), 18-19.

Moments later, in response to Missouri Sen. Louis F. Linn's introduction of a bill to occupy the Columbia River, establish a U.S. military presence in the Oregon country, and create an Oregon territory north of 42° N. Lat., suggests that the Committee on Military Affairs "would do well to make inquiries as to the stipulations of the present treaty with Great Britain and whether we could occupy this country now without giving cause of offence." Gives a brief account of past Anglo-American conflict in Oregon. *Cong. Globe,* 25 Cong., 2 Sess., 169. For the diplomatic background of the Anglo-American struggle for Oregon (1815-46), the joint occupation concept in the relevant treaties, and the peaceful settlement finally obtained in 1846 of the U.S.-Canadian boundary at 49° N.Lat., see Frederick Merk, *Albert Gallatin and the Oregon Problem.* Cambridge, 1950; J.S. Reeves, *American Diplomacy Under Tyler and Polk.* Baltimore, 1907; David M. Pletcher, *The Diplomacy of Annexation: Texas, Oregon, and the Mexican War.* Columbia, Mo., 1973; and the relevant bibliography in a standard text such as Thomas A. Bailey, *A Diplomatic History of the American People,* 10th ed. (Englewood Cliffs, N.J., 1980), 235-36, 1013-14. For earlier substantive references to this issue in these volumes, see 1:871-72; 2:611; 4:180-81; 5:449-51; 6:230-31, 859-60; also the numerous subject index references in 7:730.

Comment in Senate, February 8, 1838. Criticizes Van Buren for having mentioned in his annual message of December 5, 1837, the outcome of recent state elections in which his proposed Sub-Treasury plan was among the issues debated and sustained by the electorate. Says he was "shocked . . . at the President" for having "undertaken . . . to comment on the result of the local elections. It was unprecedented, and . . . undignified. It was the first example in which the President spoke of the elections, not of the General Government, but of the State Governments." Further, there was by the president "a direct insinuation of bank influence" in the New York elections [Clay to Curtis, October 25, 1837]. But in that state, Clay notes, "a great people moved by a sense of danger to preserve their interests" were prompted "to assert their rights against the madness, wickedness, and folly" of the Van Buren administration. *Cong. Globe,* 25 Cong., 2 Sess., 171-72. Van Buren's remark is in *MPP,* 3:380-81.

Remark in Senate, February 9, 1838. Presents four petitions from "sundry mechanics and others" in New York City and Brooklyn to appropriate funds to complete the U.S. Navy frigate *Raritan* [Remark in Senate, February 7, 1838]. *Cong. Globe,* 25 Cong., 2 Sess., 173.

To PETER B. PORTER Washington, February 10, 1838

I recd. your favor of the 5h. written after your return from Philada. as I had received that which you addressed to me before you went there. I delivered your letter to Mr. [John J.] Crittenden, who has transmitted an answer to our friend in N. York as advised by you.[1]

I am assured that Maryland, or rather the Legislature at Annapolis will certainly act on the Presidential subject in the course of the next week,[2] and that it will follow the example set by Kentucky.[3]

In reference to any movement at Albany,[4] I can only repeat what I have so often said that I hope nothing will be done to hazard the loss of the ground which has been won by the Whigs in that State. Whilst that principle should be, I think steadily kept in view, it should not be forgotten that the respective friends of Genl Harrison and Mr. Webster will naturally oppose any measure which is adverse to their particular wishes. That is a difficulty which must be encountered sooner or later; and the only question is when is the time when it can be overcome with the least prejudice. It must be remembered too that they, not my friends, were the first to begin to agitate this matter.

There are two courses which will come under consideration. 1st. To express a preference, with a recommendation to the [Whig] N. Conventn. of the person prefered, accompanied by a resolution to abide by the decision of the Convention.[5] Or, omitting to express any preference, 2dly. to appoint two delegates to the Convention, corresponding with the two Senators, whose opinions and wishes are well known, and to adopt other measures to secure the representation of the State in the Convention.

Of these two courses, the first beyond all doubt will have most influence out of the limits of the State of N. York; but that advantage, great as it is, should be made subordinate to the object of doing nothing to prejudice the Whig cause in that State. Upon the supposition of such prejudice it will be more prudent to adopt the second course.

We are anxiously hopeing that the Legislatures of Pennsa. and N. York will express their opposition to the Government Bank.[6] Should they do so, I think it will be defeated in the Senate.[7]

The dominant party displays here the desperation which it feels. But here, you know, its influence is most concentrated. We should have therefore all the distant aid that can be sent to us.

ALS. NBuHi. 1. Reference obscure since Porter to Clay of Feb. 5, 1838, has not been found. 2. Clay to Porter, Jan. 21, 1838. 3. Clay to Porter, Jan. 5, 1838. 4. Porter to Clay, Dec. 30, 1837. 5. Porter to Clay, Nov. 14 and Dec. 30, 1837. 6. For Pennsylvania's resolutions on the Sub-Treasury proposal, see Biddle to Clay, Feb. 3, 1838. New York also passed resolutions against the Sub-Treasury bill in Feb., 1838. Columbus *Ohio State Journal and Political Register*, Dec. 26, 1837. 7. Speech in Senate, Sept. 25, 1837, and Feb. 19, 1838.

To FRANCIS LIEBER Washington, February 12, 1838

I owe you many apologies for not having earlier addressed you. The delay has arisen from the multitude of my engagements, public & private, & from the great extent of a vast private correspondence. I wished too, to read your Political Hermeneutics[1] before I wrote to you, & have at last been fortunate enough to command leisure sufficient to run rapidly over them. Without being able to present you with any thing like a general review of the work, I take great pleasure in saying that I have derived much gratification from its perusal. It treats, I think, profoundly & philosophically, of the true principles which should govern in all cases of interpretation & construction. It may be thought by some, possibly, that two or three of your distinctions (that, for example, between a *transcendent* construction & an *extravagant* construction) are not sufficiently striking. But no one can come out of the perusal of the treatise without finding himself better prepared than he was before to expound any writing or instrument, which he may be called upon to consider. I have no hesitation in saying that there is more information & instruction embodied in your work, on the subject of which it treats, than I have met with in all the other books together which treat of the same subject.

I was particularly pleased with your chapter on Precedents. If I could have desired any change in it, it would have been that you should have insisted with more earnestness upon the obligation of the Legislative authority in a free country to conform to those expositions of its constitution which may have been often & deliberately made.[2] If considerations of security & stability to private rights require that judicial precedents should not be lightly departed from, the same considerations of stability & security, in respect to the rights of a whole nation, enjoin that fundamental principles, which have been deliberately settled in the administration of government, should not be too easily departed from. The present pecuniary embarassments of our country, mainly produced by the varying conduct of government, in regard to the power to establish a Bank of the U. States, illustrate the mischiefs which proceed from a disregard of an established interpretation of the Constitution, concurred in by all the departments of Government, & acquiesced in by the people of the U. States themselves

LS, revisions, closing signature, and subscription in Clay's hand. CSmH. 1. Clay to Lieber, Dec. 16, 1837. 2. This and other suggestions made by Clay were included by Lieber in a subsequent edition published in Boston in 1839. Frank B. Freidel, *Francis Lieber, Nineteenth-Century Liberal* (Baton Rouge, 1947), 177.

To JOSEPH CHILDS Washington, February 15, 1838

I duly received your letter of the 10th inst.[1] transmitting a copy of the resolutions adopted by the Whig Legislative Convention in Rhode Island, in relation to the nomination of a candidate for the Presidency.[2]

The support which I received for that office when my name was before the public in '32,[3] from that patriotic State, displayed its firm adherence to principle, under the most discouraging circumstances, and filled me with sentiments of the most profound gratitude. This new testimony of the attachment and confidence of Rhode Island towards me, adds to my obligations, and will be cherished in grateful recollection, whatever future results may be.

Having prescribed to myself a course of non-interference in respect to the designation of a the [*sic*] candidate for the next Presidency on the part of Whigs, it will not be expected that I should give or withhold any consent with respect to the use of my name, until the proper period arrives.

I congratulate you upon the prospect of a change in the policy of the government. The people of the United States have so generally manifested a dissatisfaction with the past course of the administration, that our rulers must change it or be themselves changed. We have now much reason to hope that the vast government project of a Treasury Bank will be defeated in one, if not both, Houses of Congress.[4] This fortunate result of that dangerous measure may be ascribed altogether to the intelligence and manifestation of the wishes of the people of the United States. . . .

Copy. Printed in Newark (N.J.) *Daily Advertiser*, Feb. 22, 1838. Childs was lieutenant governor of Rhode Island from 1838 to 1839. W. Strader Brady (ed.), *Rhode Island*

Manual. 1. Childs had written Clay on Feb. 10, 1838, enclosing "the Resolutions adopted by the Whig Legislative Convention" of Rhode Island in regard to the nomination of a presidential candidate. States that Rhode Island supported Clay in 1832 with her electoral votes while knowing they "would be of no avail." Adds: "She still retains her preference for you over all other candidates, and in all probability will, at the ensuing election (should the National Convention decide as it unquestionably will) choose electors favorable to you by an overwhelming majority." Copy. Printed in Newark *Daily Advertiser*, Feb. 22, 1838. 2. The Rhode Island Whigs in the legislature had met on Feb. 1, 1838, and had adopted five resolutions deploring the Van Buren administration, approving a national Whig convention, and nominating Clay for president. Joseph Childs was chairman of the convention. Washington *Daily National Intelligencer*, Feb. 8, 1838. 3. Rhode Island had cast all 4 of her electoral votes for Clay in 1832. 4. Speech in Senate, Sept. 25, 1837, and Feb. 19, 1838; Remark in Senate, Jan. 16, 1838.

Remark in Senate, February 16, 1838. Declares that because of poor health, he is not able to speak now on the Sub-Treasury proposal [Speech in Senate, September 25, 1837]. Asks that discussion of the bill be postponed. *Cong. Globe.*, 25 Cong., 2 Sess., 186.

From NICHOLAS BIDDLE Philadelphia, February 18, 1838

Knowing that Mr Lewis[1] was in Communication with you from Harrisburgh [*sic*, Harrisburg], I was unwilling to trouble you further—for the fate of the resolutions[2] was so uncertain that I feared to excite expectations which might not be realized. Our friends were anxious to amend the resolutions in the Senate, but with a vote so equally balanced in the House, it was dangerous to trust them there again, & therefore when applied to, I urged an instant passage of the resolutions as they had passed the House. This opinion did not reach our friends until Friday when the resolutions were passed, of which we have information to night. My idea was that the passage of the resolutions was opposition, no matter what their phraseology might be; & that the expressions of confidence in the midst of proofs of contempt would rather strengthen than impair their force. It would be well if you could do two things.

1st Extract a resignation[3] &

2d. Notice the incongruity of the resolutions, so as to destroy the apparent confidence they express. The idea of declaring their allegiance to Mr Van Buren while they denounce his only favorite measure of advising a separation from the Banks—while they negative the bill to effect that object, is an absurdity which you could show to infinite advantage. These resolutions have cost a great deal of trouble, owing to the peculiar position of parties here; but it is a pleasure to have succeeded at last. . . . [P.S.] Since writing the above, I have received a newspaper containing the explanatory resolutions of the Senate which I send herewith.[4]

Copy. DLC-Nicholas Biddle Papers (DNA, M212, R20). 1. Probably William Davis Lewis, a Philadelphia banker and friend of both Clay and Biddle. *DAB*. 2. Biddle to Clay, Feb. 3, 1838. 3. Biddle to Clay, Feb. 4, 1838. 4. Not found.

To CHILDREN OF UNIDENTIFIED FRIEND Washington, February 18, 1838

Having made the acquaintance of your father, and received from him many acts of kindness, I take great pleasure, in compliance with his wishes, in addressing these lines to you.

During a long life, I have observed that those are the most happy who love, honor, and obey their parents; who avoid idleness and dissipation, and employ their time in constant labor, both of body and mind; and who perform, with regular and scrupulous attention, all their duties to our Maker, and his only Son, our blessed Saviour.

May you live long and prove a blessing to your father and mother, ornaments to society and acceptable to God. Such is the hope of your father's friend, and although unknown to you, your friend.

Copy. KyU-Joel K. Lyle Scrapbook, Lyle Family Papers. Newspaper clipping from Richmond (Va.) *Penny Post* possibly reprinted in Paris (Ky.) *Western Citizen, ca.* July, 1854. Addressed to "My Dear Children" in Richmond, Va.

From Peter B. Porter, Troy, N.Y., February 19, 1838. Introduces him to "my friend" Thomas L. Ogden of New York City who is the agent for the Holland Land Company and part owner of some former Indian lands in New York state. The right to preempt these lands had been purchased "many years ago" by the company "subject to the native rights of the Indians." These native rights have recently been purchased by the company at "a treaty held at Buffalo" by authority of the U.S. government. Assures Clay this treaty is "most advantageous" to the Indians, and asks him to support its approval by the Senate. Copy. OHi. For the treaty signed with the tribes of St. Regis, Seneca, Cayuga, Onondaga, Oneida, and Tuscarora Indians on January 15, 1838, supplemented on February 13, 1838, and proclaimed on April 4, 1840, see Parry, *Treaty Series,* 87:332-48. See also Clay to White & Kennedy, May 22, 1840.

Speech in Senate, February 19, 1838. On the subject of the Sub-Treasury proposal [Speech in Senate, September 25, 1837], commences with the statement that he has never before spoken in Congress "upon any public measure, fraught with such tremendous consequences to the welfare and prosperity of the country, and so perilous to the liberties of the people, as I solemnly believe the bill under consideration will be." Speaks of the "sleepless hours reflection upon it has cost me," and of the "fervor and sincerity" with which "I have implored Divine assistance to strengthen and sustain me in opposition to it." Thanks God "that he has prolonged my life until the present time, to enable me to exert myself" against a project "far transcending in pernicious tendency" any he has ever before encountered. Also thanks God for his health, for a good sleep last night, and for today's bright sunshine.

Reviews in great length and detail the history of the monetary and financial policies of the two Jackson administrations. In so doing, quotes extensively from various of Jackson's messages to Congress and from his state papers to demonstrate the late president's unreasonable and unreasoning hostility to the Bank of the United States. This he does to develop and sustain the following five propositions:

"1st. That it was the deliberate purpose and fixed design of the late Administration to establish a Government bank—a Treasury bank—to be administered and controlled by the Executive Department.

"2d. That, with that view, and to that end, it was its aim and intention to overthrow the whole banking system, as existing in the United States when that Administration came into power, beginning with the Bank of the United States, and ending with the State banks.

"3d. That the attack was first confined, from considerations of policy, to the Bank of the United States; but that, after its overthrow was accomplished, it was then directed, and has since been continued, against the State banks.

"4th. That the present Administration, by its acknowledgments, emanating from the highest and most authentic source, has succeeded to the principles, plans, and policy, of the preceding Administration, and stands solemnly pledged to complete and perfect them.

"And 5th. That the bill under consideration is intended to execute the pledge, by establishing, upon the ruins of the late Bank of the United States, and the State banks, a Government bank, to be managed and controlled by the Treasury Department, acting under the commands of the President of the United States."

Develops each of these charges in a wide-ranging attack on those Jackson fiscal policies which had deprived the nation of the prosperity and happiness it had enjoyed in 1830 and reduced it to panic, depression, and despair by 1837. In developing his attack, Clay repeats relevant elements of his earlier arguments against Jackson's removal of government deposits from the Bank of the United States [8:684-85], the president's veto of the recharter of the B.U.S. [8:552-53, 558], the growth and extension of Jackson's power of removal from and appointment to office [8:703], and the stupidity of the Specie Circular [8:860-61]. Also repeats his attack on specific elements in Van Buren's Sub-Treasury bill [Speech in Senate, September 25, 1837]. Compares Jackson's ego and ambition with that of Bonaparte. Charges that under Jackson "Society has been uprooted, virtue punished, vice rewarded, and talents and intellectual endowments despised; brutality, vulgarism, and loco focoism upheld, cherished, and countenanced. Ages will roll around before the moral and political ravages which have been committed will, I fear, cease to be discernible. General Jackson's ambition was to make his administration an era in the history of the American Government, and he has accomplished that object of his ambition; but I trust that it will be an era to be shunned as sad and lamentable, and not followed and imitated as supplying sound maxims and principles of administration." Further, asserts that "War and strife, endless war and strife, personal or national, foreign or domestic, were the ailment of the late President's [Jackson] existence. War against the Bank, war against France, and strife and contention with a countless number of individuals. The wars with Black Hawk and the Seminoles were scarcely a luncheon for his voracious appetite. And he made his exit from public life, denouncing war and vengeance against Mexico and the State banks." Recounts his personal relations with Jackson prior to February, 1825 ("mutual respect and cordiality"), and the break in their relations when Clay had supported Adams in the House of Representatives vote for president, and Jackson had countered with cries of bargain and corruption [7:716-17]. Recalls that "All intercourse ceased between General Jackson and myself. We have never since, except once accidently, exchanged salutations, nor met except on occasions when we were performing the last offices towards deceased members of Congress or other officers of Government. Immediately after my vote, a rancorous war was commenced against me, and all the barking dogs let loose upon me. I shall not trace it during its ten years' bitter continuance. But I thank my God that I stand here, firm and erect, unbent, unbroken, unsubdued, unawed, ready to denounce the mischievous measure of his Administration, and ready to denounce this, its legitimate offspring, the most pernicious of them all."

Reviews Van Buren's personal relations with Jackson and his role in Jackson's administration. Condemns the new president as nothing but an unpatriotic "tool" of Jackson. Asks: Does Van Buren "promote the honor and advance the welfare of the people of the United States, and to add to the glory of his country? No, no; his country was not in his thoughts. Party, party, filled the place in his bosom which country should have occupied. He was the honored tool to carry out the principles and policy of General Jackson's administration; and . . . to tread in the footsteps of General Jackson—happy if he should be able to perfect the work which he had so gloriously begun."

Analyzes section 10 of the pending Sub-Treasury bill, pointing out the enormous concentration of financial power it places in the hands of the president and his treasury secretary; also calls attention to section 25 which is designed to "disguise the purpose of the vast machinery which we are about constructing." Wonders where the idea originated of having Sub-Treasury receivers of the nation's deposits. Thinks it might have come from Bonaparte's France, where it eventually provided jobs, after the restoration of the Bourbons, for some 100,000 employees. The Bourbons, of course, "were pleased with the immense patronage it gave them. They liked to have 100,000 dependents to add strength to the throne."

Concludes with an attack on Calhoun for shifting from his anti-Jackson states' rights stance of several years ago to a conspicuous advocacy of Van Buren's Sub-Treasury scheme. Recalls that Calhoun, not long ago, had even referred to Van Buren as an animal, crafty, skulking, and mean. Explains the motives behind the South Carolinian's desertion of the Whigs for "our common opponents," the Jacksonians. Contends that as of September 18 last, at the time Calhoun gave the speech in which he embraced Van Buren's Sub-Treasury plan, "The ardous contest in which we were so long engaged was about to terminate in a glorious victory. The very object for which the [anti-Jackson] alliance was formed was about to be accomplished. At this critical moment the Senator left us; he left us for the very purpose of preventing the success of the common cause. He took up his musket, knapsack, and shot-pouch, and joined the other party. He went, horse, foot and dragoon, and he himself composed the whole corps." Points out further that Calhoun "left us, as he tells us in his Edgefield letter, because the victory which our common arms were about to achieve, was not to enure to him and his party, but exclusively to the benefit of his allies and their cause. I thought that actuated by patriotism, (that noblest of human virtues,) we had been contending together for our common country, for her violated rights, her threatened liberties, her prostrate Constitution. Never did I suppose that personal or party considerations entered into our views."

Characterizes Calhoun's speech of September 18, 1837, in defense of the proposed Sub-Treasury system as being "plausible, ingenious, abstract, metaphysical, and generalizing," but says it has little to do with the real "business of human life." Critically analyzes various monetary illustrations and contentions in Calhoun's lengthy speech of that date. Returns to, and develops further, his argument of September 25, 1837, that "the true and only efficacious and permanent remedy, I solemnly believe, is to be found in a Bank of the United States, properly organized and constituted [Speech in Senate, September 25, 1837; Remark in Senate, September 27, 1837].

Confesses, near the end of his four and half-hour speech, his "exhausted strength" and "your more exhausted patience," but remains on his feet long enough to praise the voters of Maine, New York, Pennsylvania, Maryland, Ohio, Rhode Island, Mississippi, and Michigan for having "denounced the [Sub-Treasury] measure." Pleads with those senators instructed by their legislatures to oppose the Sub-Treasury bill to do their duty. Counts 35 votes against the bill. *Cong. Globe*, 25 Cong., 2 Sess., Appendix, 614-19. Printed in Colton, *Clay Correspondence*, 6:94-133.

Calhoun replied to Clay's attack on him on March 10, 1838, *Cong. Globe*, 25 Cong., 2 Sess., Appendix, 176-81; and Clay responded the same day. *Niles' Register* (May 26, 1838), 54:196-201. For an analysis of Calhoun's September 18, 1837, speech and his "Edgefield Letter" of November 3, 1837 (which asked the South and the States' Rights party there to abandon the Whigs and follow Van Buren), and Clay's angry reaction to both the speech and letter in his February 19 and March 10, 1838 speeches, see Wiltse, *John C. Calhoun: Nullifier*, 359-61, 378-82; Wilson, *Papers of John C. Calhoun*, 14:179-82, 191, 194-96, 198-99, 203-4; Wilson, *Presidency of Martin Van Buren*, 104-5. For Clay's view of the thrust of his February 19 speech and what he hoped to accomplish by it, see Clay to Biddle, February 20, 1838.

Soon after taking his seat Clay again took the floor briefly to reply to Calhoun's charge that he had misstated or perverted almost every argument he (Calhoun) had advanced and also to Calhoun's threat to retaliate. As to Calhoun's charge of perversion and misstatement, he "would appeal to a less partial judge—the Senate." As for Calhoun's threat of retaliation, he "was as ready to receive as the gentleman was to pay." While he "sought a contest with no man," he would "not avoid one with the Senator from South Carolina." *Cong. Globe.*, 25 Cong., 2 Sess., 191. For Calhoun's speech of September 18, 1837, see *Register of Debates*, 25 Cong., 1 Sess., 50-66, or *Cong. Globe*, 25 Cong., 1 Sess., Appendix, 32-37. For the political break between Calhoun and Clay manifested in part in this day's bitter confrontation, see Carl Schurz, *Life of Henry Clay*, 2 vols. (Boston, 1887), 2:144-51; Remark in Senate, June 28, 1838; Benton, *Thirty Years' View*, 2:91-93, 97-123. This speech was published under the title, *Speech of Mr. Clay, of Kentucky, Establishing a Deliberate Design on the Part of the Late and Present Executive of the United States . . . To Create . . . A Government Treasury Bank Under the Exclusive Control of the Executive; and in Reply To the Speech of Hon. J.C. Calhoun, of South Carolina, Supporting That Treasury Bank. Delivered in the Senate of the United States, February 19, 1838.* Washington, 1838.

In the September, 1837 elections in Maine, Edward Kent, the Whig candidate, was elected governor over Gorham Parks, the Democratic candidate, by a vote of 34,358 to 33,879. Whigs also won a majority of seats in both the Maine house and senate. *BDGUS*, 2:601; Washington *Daily National Intelligencer*, September 27, 1837. For the state legislative elections in New York and Ohio, see Clay to Curtis, October 25, 1837. In the Pennsylvania elections in 1837, the Whigs won 19 senate seats to 14 for the Democrats; however, the Democrats controlled the Pennsylvania house 56 to 44. *Niles' Register* (December 9, 1837), 53:225. In the Maryland house of delegates election, Whigs won 45 seats to 33 for the Democrats with two counties unrecorded. There was no senate election; however, the Whigs already held 100% of the senate seats. The legislature also reelected Thomas W. Veazey as governor. Washington *Daily National Intelligencer*, October 6, 1837; *BDGUS*, 2:661-62. Rhode Island, which in the previous election had given the Democrats a majority of 15 in the state house of representatives, in 1837 gave the Whigs a majority of 16 as well as electing Whigs for all congressional seats. Washington *Daily National Intelligencer*, September 5, 1837. In Mississippi, in the August, 1837 elections, the Democrats carried the state senate 17 seats to 13 for the Whigs and the house 53 to 37. *Niles' Register* (January 20, 1838), 53:321. In the governor's race, the Whig party, which had two candidates in the field, polled more votes than the Democrats. Alexander McNutt (Democrat), however, won the election with 12,936 votes to 4,974 for John Grimball (Whig) and 9,896 for Jacob B. Morgan (Whig). *BDGUS*, 2:807. The election of two members to the U.S. House for Mississippi was disputed; however, the Whig candidates, Thomas J. Word and Sergeant S. Prentiss, were eventually seated. *BDAC*. In the Michigan elections in November, 1837, 6 Democrats were elected to the state senate to 2 for the Whigs; in the state house, 30 Democrats and 20 Whigs were chosen. Although they did not win a majority, this was an increase for the Whigs. In the gubernatorial race Stevens T. Mason (Democrat) was reelected by a vote of 15,330 to 14,673 for Charles C. Trowbridge, his Whig opponent. Detroit *Daily Free Press*, November 30, December 2, 1837.

To NICHOLAS BIDDLE Washington, February 20, 1838

I have recd your favor of the 18h. The Resolutions from Harrisburg[1] have produced the effect of securing another vote in that of Mr Buckhanan [*sic*,

James Buchanan] agt the Govt. Bank. He presented them yesterday morning[2] and gave in his adhesion before I reached the Senate, from which I was detained half an hour, in consequence of a Speech which I had to deliver, and did deliver, against that measure.[3] It was wise in your Senate to pass the resolutions as they went from the House, notwithstanding the two exceptionable paragraphs.[4] The good in them more than counter balanced the bad, as the event has already proved. We now probably stand 26 against 26. One more vote would defeat the vile measure. We have a prospect of getting that by an instruction from Richmond to Mr. [William H.] Roane but it is not certain.[5] If it comes, he will obey it. Could it not be obtained from Trenton? Why could not a positive instruction (the Genl. Assembly *instructs* its Senators & requests its Representatives &c) emanate from that quarter? It would, I believe, decide Mr. [Garret D.] Wall. I think he would obey.[6] And as he acknowledges such an obligation, it might be given without justly wounding the sensibility of Mr. [Samuel L.] Southard.

My Speech yesterday satisfied my friends. I endeavored to prove a Conspiracy (without using that word) between the last & present Admon to destroy the whole Banking System of the U.S. beginning with the late U.S. Bank and ending with the Local banks. And I handled Mr. Calhoun without gloves. Of you & of the old Bank I spoke in terms such as my feelings prompted.

ALS. DLC-Nicholas Biddle Papers (DNA, M212, R20). 1. Biddle to Clay, Feb. 3 and Feb. 4, 1838. 2. Buchanan's speech of Feb. 19 announcing his opposition to the administration's Sub-Treasury bill is in *Cong. Globe*, 25 Cong., 2 Sess., 190-91. 3. Speech in Senate, Feb. 19, 1838. 4. Reference is to the statement expressing "full confidence in Martin Van Buren, and in the wisdom and intelligence of our democratic senators and representatives in congress"; and also the one requesting their senators and representatives "to vote for such a mode of receiving, keeping and disbursing the public moneys, as will separate as far as practicable, the banks from the Government." *Niles' Register* (Feb. 17, 1838), 53:385, 402. 5. The Whigs did not control the Virginia senate and, hence, could not mount a vote to instruct Roane to vote against the Sub-Treasury bill. Henry H. Simms, *The Rise of the Whigs in Virginia 1824-1840* (Richmond, Va., 1929), 129. Roane, a Democrat, thus voted for the bill. *Cong. Globe*, 25 Cong., 2 Sess., 264. 6. In the late fall of 1837 the New Jersey legislature had passed a series of resolutions condemning, among other things, the Sub-Treasury system and saying that "we declare our solemn conviction . . . that our representatives in both houses of congress will best conform their acts and votes to the wishes of their constituents by a faithful resistance to their adoption." *Niles' Register* (Nov. 25, 1837), 53:198-99. Clay evidently hoped for a direct instruction, which did not materialize. Sen. Samuel L. Southard (N.J.), who voted against the Sub-Treasury bill, cited these resolutions as an indication of his fidelity to the will of the people of New Jersey, saying that they needed "only the little word instruct to be instructions." On the other hand, Sen. Garret D. Wall (N.J.), who voted for the Sub-Treasury, claimed that "declaratory resolutions and instructions" were not the same. *Cong. Globe*, 25 Cong., 2 Sess., 264; *ibid.*, Appendix, 227-36.

Remark in Senate, February 21, 1838. Responds to issues raised in a motion that would allow the state of Indiana to preempt, at the $1.25 minimum price per acre, the roughly 215,000 acres of public land acquired recently by treaty with the Miami Indians. It was explained that this land was particularly valuable since much of it was situated near the Wabash-Erie Canal [4:543-44] route; and it was pointed out that the estimated $100,000 to be realized from the resale of this land would be used to complete the remaining Indiana segment of the canal. Joining the debate, Clay remarks that he is "entirely too unwell to enter into" this discussion, but that in general he favors Indiana's request on internal improvements grounds, though perhaps not at the $1.25 per acre minimum purchase price the state hopes to pay for it. Would suggest instead a compromise sum of $5.00 per acre. Also points out that he would rather see Indiana get the land for canal-construction purposes than have it preempted by squatters. *Cong. Globe*, 25 Cong., 2 Sess., 194. The motion was tabled. For the treaty between the United States and the Miami Indians—signed at the Forks of the Wabash on October 23, 1834, and proclaimed on December 22, 1837—see Parry, *Treaty Series*, 84:421-25.

From Thomas S. Wingate, Shelby County, Ky., February 22, 1838. Conveys the wording of six resolutions adopted February 15, 1838, at a meeting of the Clear Creek Polemic Society, held at Clear Creek Academy in Shelby County, 73 members present and voting. The resolutions laud Clay and Crittenden for their stances against the tyranny of Jacksonism, endorse "the late nomination of the Honble Henry Clay to the next Presidency" by the Kentucky General Assembly [Clay to Porter, January 5, 1838; Clay to Brooke, January 13, 1838], and promise "to exert all our energies to promote his Election." ALS. DLC-John J. Crittenden Papers (DNA, M212, R20). Addressed jointly to Crittenden and Clay.

To THOMAS HART CLAY Washington, February 23, 1838

I received your two last letters. As to the Va. mare, I wish her sent to Medoc, Col. [William] Bufords[1] horse. Are the imported mare and Allegrante in foal? What does Bertrand stand at?

As to the Duraldes,[2] I wish you and my dear Wife would consider what is best to be done for them. You have all the circumstances before you, and if you think it best that they should go to Mr. Smith's school,[3] let them be sent. I only regret that if they go the poor boys will be so far from us. Could not you and your wife let them live with and board with you, and go to Mr. [Beverley A.] Hicks?[4] I would pay a liberal price for their board.

My health is not good. I am worked to death almost. Last monday I spoke upwards of four hours.[5] I never was better satisfied with any Spe[e]ch I ever made.

I wish to know how many volumes of Niles's Register I have. I want to complete the set. . . .

ALS. NHi. Written in "S[enate]. Chamber." 1. For Buford, a well known stockbreeder near Versailles, Ky., see William E. Railey, *History of Woodford County* (Versailles, Ky., 1968), 91. 2. Clay's grandsons, Martin III and Henry Clay Duralde. 3. John P. and Robert N. Smith, brothers and teachers from Virginia, ran a boys' boarding school on Shelbyville Road about seven miles east of Louisville. *FCHQ*, 57:191. 4. Hicks to Clay, Nov. 3, 1837. On May 9, 1838, Clay paid $65 on an account of $79.50 from Robert N. Smith for Martin Duralde III's board, books, and tuition from May 9 to Nov. 24, 1838. Smith to Clay, May 9, 1838. AD. DLC-TJC (DNA, M212, R18). 5. Speech in Senate, Feb. 19, 1838.

From Henry Van Rensselaer Schermerhorn, Geneva, N.Y., February 25, 1838. Discusses the current political situation in "our unhappy country," wondering how it was, looking back on it, that "such a delusion" as Jacksonism "should have passed over such a land; that such a people as we boast ourselves to be should have been so long contented to be ruled by such miserable knaves and fools as now wield the destinies of the Nation." Thinks the result of elections this past year [Jones to Clay, December 8, 1837] indicate that "a better state of things is at hand." Supports a Whig national nominating convention [Porter to Clay, November 14 and December 30, 1837], but wants to see it postponed to 1839. Thinks such delay will benefit the Whigs in the coming elections in Pennsylvania and New York and increase Clay's presidential prospects. Credits Clay with warning the nation of the disastrous consequences of Jackson's election. "Alas you understood them but too well" and "too truly" saw "the evils they were to bring upon us." Is shocked by the "malice, hate and vindictivity with which they 'the rascally pack from fen & forest' have belied, abused & *attempted* to injure you." Says his congressman, Mark Hopkins Sibley ("a most noble and excellent fellow"), has written him of Clay's February 19 speech against the "Government Bank project" during which, in Sibley's words, "he used up Calhoun—body & bre[e]ches." Asks for a copy of the speech [Speech in Senate, February 19, 1838] when printed [Gales and Seaton to Clay, April 25, 1838]. Also asks Clay, as the "earliest and ablest friend of the American System," to support a bill, now before the House of Representatives, providing for a canal "around the falls of Niagara." Argues that such a canal would be commercially important, would afford advantages "in time of war with Great Britain," and would constitute "one of the noblest projects of the age." ALS. DLC-HC (DNA, M212, R5). Henry Van Rensselaer Schermerhorn was the nephew of Solomon Van Rensselaer. Bonney, *A Legacy of Historical Gleanings*, 2:162, 182.

In the New York governor's race in 1838, William H. Seward (Whig) defeated William L. Marcy (Dem.) by a vote of 192,882 to 182,461. Albert H. Tracy (Whig) defeated Luther Bradish (Dem.) for lieutenant governor by about the same margin. In New York City, Seward won 20,201 votes to 19,359 for Marcy, while Tracy won 19,548 to 19,206 for Bradish. The state assembly election in 1838 resulted in a Democratic majority of 4 in the state senate and a Whig majority of 34 in the house. In the election for the U.S. House, 21 Whigs and 19 Democrats were chosen. In New York City 8 Whigs and 8 Democrats were elected to the House with one seat undetermined. *BDGUS*, 3:1078; *Niles' Register* (November 17, 1838), 55:177; *Guide to U.S. Elections*, 570-71.

In the governor's election in Pennsylvania in 1838, David R. Porter (Dem.) defeated incumbent Joseph Ritner (Anti-Mason/Whig) by a vote of 127,821 to 122,325. *BDGUS*, 3:1304. In the state senate election, Whigs won 24 seats to 9 for Democrats, and in the state house of representatives the Whigs won 53 seats to 47 for the Democrats. *Niles' Register* (October 27, 1838), 55:129. In the U.S. House election in Pennsylvania, Democrats won 18 seats and the Whigs 10. The party affiliation is not given for one of the winners. *Guide to U.S. Elections*, 571. *Niles' Register* gives slightly different numbers for the gubernatorial race and for the U.S. House contest. For the October, 1838 state elections in Pennsylvania, especially the relationship between the Whig and Anti-Mason parties therein, see Mueller, *Whig Party in Pennsylvania*, 48-53.

A "Bill providing for the Niagara Ship Canal" had been reported in the U.S. House on January 25, 1838. It was read twice and referred to committee. On February 11, 1838, a resolution was introduced to take up the bill on February 21; however, it was not taken up again. It never reached the Senate. U.S. H. of Reps., *Journal*, 25 Cong., 2 Sess., 313, 517.

To WILLIAM W. HOPPIN[1] Washington, February 28, 1838

I received your friendly letter of the 22d inst. & beg you to accept my cordial thanks for the deep interest & anxious solicitude which you so kindly express respecting my personal safety & welfare. I have no reason to believe that that life on which you place a much higher value than it is worth, is exposed, or likely to be exposed, to any peril. Most certainly I shall expose it to no hazard, but under circumstances when I should not think it worth preserving. None such now exist, nor do I know that any will arise.

LS. RHi. 1. For Hoppin, later governor of Rhode Island, see *DAB*.

To HENRY CLAY, JR. Washington, March 2, 1838

I received your favor of the 22d. Ulto. and I avail myself of the occasion of the delivery of a very dull Speech in the Senate, on the Sub treasury bill,[1] to write to you. I thank you for the account of the proceedings of our Legislature[2] which you have communicated. They appear to be [to] me generally marked by sound discretion. I have heard from others, what gratified me much, that your own course and deportment were judicious and conciliatory.[3]

On the question whether, in the event of Mr. Hawes's retirement (of which by the by I have heard nothing here) you should not become a Candidate, I would advise no hasty or precipitate decision.[4] There is time enough to consider it. I need not say that it would afford me the highest satisfaction to see you in so distinguished a station. In the mean time, you can cultivate your popularity, maintain a cheerful and friendly intercourse with our fellow Citizens, and be in a position to avail yourself of favorable circumstances, just as well as if you were formally announced as a Candidate.

In regard to my being a Candidate for the Presidency, if I am to judge from information which daily, almost hourly, reaches me, there is *every where* an irresistable current setting in towards me. I believe that if the Election were to come on in Sixty days I should be elected by acclamation. But the Election is nigh three years off, great changes may take place, I may die, and therefore we should look to the future with all the uncertainty which hangs over it.

I have not received a letter from Julia [Prather Clay] this Session. Altho' I cannot promise to write to her, I should be very glad to hear directly from her. I am almost borne down by the weight of my labors, public & private. Company—Company—Correspondence—Correspondence, they are eternal & incessant. I have derived great assistance from young Gales Seaton acting as an Amanuensis for me. . . .[5]

ALS. Henry Clay Memorial Foundation, Lexington, Ky. Written in "S[enate]. Chamber." 1. By Robert Strange (N.C.). 2. Clay to Porter, Jan. 5, 1838; Clay to Brooke, Jan. 13, 1838. 3. Henry Clay, Jr., represented Fayette County in the Ky. general assembly. Frankfort *Commonwealth*, August 16, 1837. 4. Richard Hawes, Jr., held the seat in Congress for the district Clay had once represented. Henry Clay, Jr., did not run for Congress, and Hawes continued to serve until 1841. *BDAC*. Instead, Henry, Jr., ran for and won reelection to the Ky. house. Also elected for Fayette County were William Rhodes and Larkin B. Smith, also Whigs. John Curd, a Democrat, lost. Frankfort *Commonwealth*, August 15, 1838. 5. Clay to Biddle, Feb. 6, 1838.

To THOMAS SPEED Washington, March 2, 1838

I recd. your favor of the 21st. Ulto. as I did some former favors, which I did not acknowledge. The omission did not proceed from any diminution of the sincere friendship which I have long entertained for you; but from an oppressive correspondence which I am obliged to neglect or neglect my public duties.

I have always read with interest your suggestions and observations, as I have done those which are contained in your last letter. I wish I had time for a discussion of them.

I think that there is at present no danger of the passage of the Cession of the public lands proposed by Mr. Calhoun.[1]

The Senate is supposed to be equally divided on the Govt. bank or sub-treasury scheme. Our hopes are that if it should pass this body it will be defeated in the House.[2]

You will have heard of the lamentable issue of the duel in which our friend Mr. Graves was a party![3]

ALS. NhD. Written in "S[enate]. C[hamber]." 1. Calhoun's proposed amendment to Sen. Robert J. Walker's land bill, first introduced on Feb. 7, 1837, would cede all public lands in Ala., Miss., La., Ark., Mo., Ill., Ind., Ohio, Mich., and Tenn. See *Register of Debates*, 24 Cong., 2 Sess., 729-31. It was soundly beaten, 28 to 7, later that day, Clay not voting. *Ibid.*, 736. Nevertheless, Clay announced his opposition to the public land cession concept two days later. *Ibid.*, 741-42. See Comment in Senate, Feb. 9, 1837. On Feb. 9, 1837, Calhoun reintroduced his Feb. 7 amendment as a bill. It was laid on the table Feb. 11, 1837, by a vote of 26 to 20, Clay not voting. *Ibid.*, 739-40, 794. Calhoun introduced the same bill in the 25th Congress, 2nd Session on Feb. 5, 1838. It was tabled on June 16, 1838. U.S. Sen., *Journal*, 25 Cong., 2 Sess., 204, 475. 2. It passed the Senate 27 to 25 on March 26, 1838, and was rejected by the House 125 to 111 on June 25, 1838. See Speech in Senate, Sept. 25, 1837. 3. Rep. William J. Graves (Ky.), with Rep. Henry Wise (Va.) as his second, killed Rep. Jonathan Cilley (Me.), in a duel on Feb. 24, 1838. Rep. George W. Jones (Wisc.) had served as Cilley's second. The controversy arose when Graves attempted to deliver a note to Cilley from James Watson Webb which demanded an explanation of derogatory remarks Cilley had made about Webb and his newspaper in a speech in the House of Representatives. Cilley refused to receive the note, but Graves understood him to say that he held no antagonism toward Webb as a gentleman; however, when he subsequently asked Cilley to put the reasons for his refusal to receive the note in writing, Cilley refused and also repudiated Graves's version of his earlier verbal statements. Graves, viewing this as an attack on his own honor and veracity, then challenged Cilley to a duel which was fought with rifles across the Anacostia bridge in Maryland. On the third fire, Cilley fell. See William O. Stevens, *Pistols at Ten Paces, The Story of the Code of Honor in America* (Boston, 1940), 219-27. The duel caused a public outcry and a congressional investigation that resulted in the introduction of a bill to prohibit the giving or accepting of a challenge to fight a duel in the District of Columbia. The bill was introduced in the Senate on March 2, 1838, and passed on April 9 by a vote of 34 to 1, Clay voting in the affirmative. U.S. Sen., *Journal*, 25 Cong., 2 Sess., 260. On April 9 the bill went to the House where it died. U.S. H. of Reps., *Journal*, 25 Cong., 2 Sess., 735. In 1842, when Clay was again an acknowledged presidential candidate, Wise charged that Clay was the man primarily responsible for precipitating the duel. While admitting he had rewritten Graves's challenge to Cilley, Clay stated he had done so in an attempt to produce a version which would lead to an amicable settlement, and that at no time had he ever sought to promote a duel between the two men [Wise to Clay, Feb. 25, 1842; Clay to Wise, Feb. 25, 1842]. The editors have found no evidence beyond Wises's charge, either from the congressional investigation or from subsequent discussion or research, to prove Clay's culpability in the matter. Wise did not repeat the charge in his *Seven Decades of the Union. . . .* Philadelphia, 1872. See also Van Deusen, *Life of Henry Clay*, 370-71.

To PETER B. PORTER Washington, March 4, 1838

I am in arrear to you; but incessant business and having nothing important to communicate must be my excuse. I believe that I have acknowledged all your letters except that of the 14h. Ulto. I have no reason to believe that the P. Office has violated our correspondence.

Genl. R[obert]. Swartwout was here a few days ago, and left me resolved to see you. He can communicate much more than a letter, and some matters not proper for a letter.

At Trenton, they have been prevented from expressing their preference by the pulling-back policy now resorted to by those who were but the other day pushing-forward, I thought, prematurely.[1] But the preference of N. Jersey I understand is undoubted.[2] The Governor [William Pennington] and several members of the Legislature are now here. I suppose the same repressing game continues to be played at Albany.[3] Will it succeed? Or will there be any expression?

From Ohio I receive the most full & satisfactory accounts.[4] The Reserve (the great Whig District) knows scarcely any division, being all for me. And I have this moment received similar tidings from Dayton.

In the South & S. West our Cause continues to grow & widen. There no diversity of opinion exists. On that you may perfectly rely.

You will have heard from Boston,[5] and Maine.[6]

They will run us hard here about the S. Treasury project. In the Senate, I fear, it will be carried; and the House is very closely divided.[7] The Country has been too confident of its defeat. It had better continue to speak out more & more.

I will send you tomorrow my Speech;[8] and I wish when you have read it you would tell me truly what you think of it.

ALS. NBuHi. 1. For a discussion of the movements in Trenton for and against a Clay nomination, see Birkner, *Samuel L. Southard*, 183-84, 241; also Kinsey to Clay, Jan. 3, 1838. 2. Kinsey to Clay, Jan. 3, 1838. 3. Porter to Clay, Dec. 30, 1837. 4. Evidently a reference to the action of the Montgomery County Whigs in endorsing Clay. See Clay to Porter, Jan. 5, 1838. 5. In March, 1838, the Massachusetts Whig legislative convention, while expressing their "high confidence" in and "heartfelt gratitude" to Henry Clay, nominated Daniel Webster for president. However, they called for a national convention and promised to support whichever candidate was nominated, declaring that the triumph of the cause was more important than any individual. Washington *Daily National Intelligencer*, March 6, 1838; see also Clay to Otis, Dec. 13, 1838. 6. The Maine Whig legislative convention was held on March 8, 1838, at Augusta. They did not make a presidential nomination, but promised instead to abide by the decision of a national convention. Washington *Daily National Intelligencer*, March 12, 1838. 7. Speech in Senate, Sept. 25, 1837. 8. Speech in Senate, Feb. 19, 1838 (against the Sub-Treasury bill).

Remark in Senate, March 5, 1838. Presents petition of Jonathan Thompson, former collector of customs in New York, for restoration of his official bonds.

Also presents a petition from E.C. Watson of New York suggesting the creation of a "great national corporation to be called the United States Internal Improvement and Manufacturing Loan Office." Capitalized at $100,000,000, it would have custody of the public money and would issue bank notes from $5 to $1,000 in denomination.

Submits a petition from citizens in Hampshire County, Va. (W.Va.), complaining that the post office there demands specie for its services, at a time when there is little specie; it is thus "seeking to coerce the people to do what is physically impossible." They further charge that the local mail-route contractors "while they are exacting specie on their contracts from the country postmasters, are deluging the county with shin-plasters, redeemable only in current bank notes or stage fare." They ask relief. Clay remarks that he cares not to which committee the Hampshire County petition goes, although he thinks "the use of the term shin-plasters" might secure it a "favorable reception from certain quarters." *Cong. Globe*, 25 Cong., 2 Sess., 214. See Remark in Senate, March 27, 1838. The petition was referred to the Finance Committee.

Later this day, during discussion of a motion by Sen. James Buchanan (Pa.), chairman of the Foreign Relations Committee, to amend the Neutrality Act of April 20, 1818 [2:492-507], Clay comments on the new powers proposed to be given the president so that he might more effectively employ the armed forces to prevent Americans launching from U.S. soil, military expeditions by land or sea against nations with which the United States is at peace. Says that "the power of the Executive was probably too much extended by the bill," and "the right of the citizen to conduct foreign trade and commerce was too much abridged." But affirms his support for the proposed changes anyway. *Cong. Globe*, 25 Cong., 2 Sess., 215. The attempts to tighten and enforce better the existing neutrality laws of the nation following the Texas War of Independence got nowhere during the 25th Congress, 2nd Session. *Ibid.*, 216, 222-23.

To Thomas H. Clay, Lexington, March 6, 1838. Has learned that William Dunlap refuses to pay his note until he receives a deed to the land Clay sold him. Transmits power of attorney to Thomas. Authorizes Richard Pindell to prepare the necessary deed, and to sue Dunlap if he still declines paying the note. Adds: "tell Mr. Dunlap that I will receive nothing but Specie, if he puts me to a suit." ALS. Mary Clay Kenner Collection, Rogersville, Tenn. Written in "S[enate]. Chamber."

Remark in Senate, March 6, 1838. Moves that a bill to establish the office of surveyor general for Illinois be tabled for the present. Carried. Taken up again later in the day, Clay opposes the measure, because there is "a constant tending to an increase of Executive patronage in land offices, land surveyors, etc. which it [is] high time to check." Carried. *Cong. Globe*, 25 Cong., 2 Sess., 223.

To William Channing, March 7, 1838. Thanks him for sending "the projet of a Nat. Bank." Explains that there is a fixed majority in both houses against the "establishment of any N. Bank which shall be confided to a Corporate Government [Comment in Senate, September 26, 1837; Speech in Senate, May 21, 1838]." And since there is "no disposition to admit the general principle, all modifications of such a Bank (yours among others) are necessarily precluded." Concludes: "What we want therefore here most is *votes*—plans which shall change folly into wisdom, madness into sanity, and loco-foco legislators into rational Statesmen. If you can aid us in that conversion, you will render a most patriotic service. I know not what the Country will come to. If it be saved, the People must do it. I am sure that it will not be done by their present rulers." ALS. KyU. Channing has not been identified; not to be confused with William E. Channing.

Comment in Senate, March 7, 1838. Explains what he meant in his February 19 speech on the Sub-Treasury bill when he called attention to Calhoun's assertion (made in his September 18, 1837, speech) that there were but two choices on the bank question: either the Van Buren administration's Sub-Treasury proposal, which Calhoun favored, or the substitute proposed by Sen. William C. Rives (Va.). At that time, February 14, Clay had declared: "I do not concur in that statement of the case. There is another course embraced in neither branch of the Senator's [Calhoun] alternative; and that course is to do nothing: always the wisest when you are not certain what to do."

Points out now (March 7), however, that the Rives proposal "holds out to the banks, as a motive to resume specie payments, that the paper of such banks as shall resume by the first of July [1838], shall be received in the Treasury." Contrasts this with Calhoun's insistance that "the paper of all sound, safe, and unquestionable banks should be received at once for the dues of the Government, until, say the 1st of August [1838], at which time, if they did not resume [specie payment], then the Government shall no longer be under obligation to receive their paper." Believes that Calhoun's proposal would be viewed as but a "temporary measure of the Government" because of the administration's decision to issue $10,000,000 in treasury notes [Comment in Senate, September 15, 1837]. Asks: What are these treasury notes but "irredeemable paper . . . what is the difference between the irredeemable paper of the Government, and the temporary reception of the now irredeemable paper of the banks?" Asserts, further, that the state of the money market is such that "Government irredeemable paper is inferior to that of the banks, in the transaction of the business of the country, and the payment of debts." Concludes: "Under all the circumstances, it might be the most politic course to pursue, to do nothing, to propose nothing, but leave the responsibility where it rests, until there [is] a disposition evinced by the party in power to obey the public will." Urges, in the meantime, the "importance of receiving bank notes for the public dues, to enable the banks to resume specie payments, and of sympathising with the people, by making use of the common currency." *Cong. Globe*, 25 Cong., 2 Sess., 228-29. For the Rives proposal of September 19, 1837, see *Register of Debates*, 25 Cong., 1 Sess., 77-104.

On December 22, 1836, Rives had commenced his attack on the Specie Circular. Essentially, he suggested an end to Jackson's mandate that public land be paid for only with specie. Instead, his proposal would permit the Treasury to receive for all government obligations—"customs, public lands, taxes, debts, or otherwise"—either specie or large denomination "notes of banks which are payable and paid on demand in the said legal currency [specie]." He argued, also, that "the joint resolution of 1816 [Remark in Senate, March 24, 1838; Comment in Senate, May 2, 1838] ought to be remodeled, and adapted to the present condition of things." In his speech of January 10, 1837, on the subject, he outlined further a system whereby private state-chartered banks would be permitted to issue specie-backed notes of the higher denominations (above $20). These notes would be acceptable to the treasury in payment of all government obligations. By thus suppressing the issue of small-denomination state bank notes, specie would emerge from hoarding and hiding and would flow into the specie vacuum in the daily circulating currency now occupied by private bank notes below five, ten, and twenty dollar denominations. In essence, state-chartered private banks would assist the treasury in operating a dual specie and bank note circulating currency, the former for "the great mass of daily transactions" by farmers, artisans, and tradesmen, the latter "for the use and accommodation of the merchant, and for the larger operations of trade and business." As amended by Rives, the bill to repeal the Specie Circular [Remark in Senate, January 6, 1837; Speech in Senate, January 11, 1837; Remark in Senate, January 14, 1837] was passed by the Senate 41 to 5, on February 10, 1837, and by the House 143 to 59 on March 1, 1837. It received Jackson's pocket veto by fact of his leaving office on March 4 without having signed it. *Cong. Globe*, 24 Cong., 2 Sess., 44, 61, 127, 176-77, 272-73; *ibid.*, Appendix, 36-37, 100-105; also Wilson, *Presidency of Martin Van Buren*, 48-49. For Rives's views and activities on the specie and banking issues in the 25th Congress, see Ann Elizabeth Liston, "W.C. Rives: Diplomat and Politician, 1829-53," Ph.D. dissertation, Ohio State University, 1972, pp. 256-66, 271-72.

From Richard Haughton, Boston, March 7, 1838. States his belief that Clay could poll more votes for president in Massachusetts than Harrison and Van Buren tickets combined. Letter not found. Excerpt printed in Clay to Otis, September 24, 1838, below. Haughton was editor of the Boston *Atlas.*

From Peter B. Porter, Troy, N.Y., March 8, 1838. Reports that the partisans of William Henry Harrison in New York have been working diligently "to prevent any action by the present Legislature on the Presidential question [Porter to Clay, December 30, 1837]." Their object is "to prevent any movement in the States favorable to you, while they were secretly urging every possible demonstration of public sentiment in states supposed to be friendly to Gen. Harrison." Their argument has been that until the coming state and congressional elections have safely passed, there should be no "agitation" of the presidential issue. The "utmost harmony" among Whigs must be preserved. Thinks this tactic has been quite successful with Webster's followers, who still hope that "something might turn up favorable to their candidate." Fears, however, that the Harrison people have "made a considerable impression on many of your unsuspecting friends, who were bent on peace and conciliation." Adds: "In this state of things it was necessary to move with great caution." Says Mordecai Noah has informed him that a number of Webster men in New York City are "Very favorable to our views." Believes that "On the whole I think you are certainly gaining strength every day, both in the Legislature and among the people, and that there will be a Legislative caucus [Porter to Clay, November 14 and December 30, 1837] (probably one of their last acts) in which they will do all that we could wish—that is, follow the example of Rhode Island [Clay to Childs, February 15, 1838] & Massachusetts [Clay to Porter, March 4, 1838]." Also, "That you may know what is going on," encloses [not found] a "secret printed circular" signed by the chairman of the Harrison Corresponding Committee in Ohio which had mistakenly been sent to G.C. Verplanck. Asks that "it not be publicly known that it came from Verplank [*sic*]." Will show it "confidentially to several of our hesitating friends, & also to some of the most prominent friends of Mr. Webster." Concludes that "The Harrison men, as you will readily suppose, are composed of Anti Masons and Abolitionists, but by no means the whole of either sect. The leaders of the Anti Masons are a herd of office seekers, and they are so numerous that there are not offices enough in the State to satisfy them, & of course there are hard feelings, and an approaching break among them. [Albert H.] Tracy, [Francis] Granger, [John C.] Spencer &C are the principal Harrison men. Other leaders with a large proportion of the rank and file will, I think, go with us at all events. You perceive by the *circular* that they are calculating on a partial convention at Pittsburgh, in which they hope to get a majority [Clay to Brooke, April 14, 1838]. This project, however, may I think be easily defeated, as will another which they seem to have in contemplation, of running him whether nominated or not by a convention." Copy. OHi.

The Ohio Whig convention had met in Columbus on July 4, 1837, had declared for Harrison, and had called for a national convention to meet at Pittsburgh on the second Monday in June, 1838. The members of the Ohio Whig Corresponding Committee were: William Doherty, Joseph Ridgway, Jr., Lyne Sterling, Jr., John W. Andrews, and John L. Miner. This suggestion proved abortive, and when the Ohio Whig convention met in May, 1838, they again endorsed Harrison and called for a national meeting. The "secret circular" has not been found. *Niles' Register* (July 22, 1837), 52:328-29; Gunderson, *The Log-Cabin Campaign*, 50.

From Samuel Wood, Jr., Winthrop, Me., March 8, 1838. Reports that in the aftermath of the duel between Representatives Jonathan Cilley (Me.) and William J. Graves (Ky.), on February 24, 1838, in which Cilley was killed [Clay to Speed, March 2, 1838], Clay's suitability as the Whig presidential candidate is being sharply questioned by Maine "Locofocos" and "Tory party" members. This is because opposition to dueling is strong in Maine, and "It is known, sir, that you were once engaged in a duel [1:397-402; 5:208-12], and I believe if ever there was a duel which was justified that was the one [5:208-9]." Asks if there is truth in the report that Clay sought to prevent the Cilley-Graves duel. States that it is important politically that he condemn publicly the principle and practice of dueling and so reassure "many of the intelligent and moral portion of the Whig party in this community." Asks for a letter to that effect [Clay to Wood, March 22, 1838]. Copy.

DLC-Henry Clay Wood Papers (DNA, M212, R22). For Wood, who served for many years as town clerk in Winthrop, Me., and as a representative in the state legislature in 1842, see David Thurston, *A Brief History of Winthrop . . .* (Portland, Me., 1855), 37, 43-44, 162-63.

Speech in Senate, March 10, 1838. Responds at length to Sen. John C. Calhoun's speech of this date [*Cong. Globe*, 25 Cong., 2 Sess., Appendix, 176-81] which was an extension of his speech of September 18, 1837, in support of Van Buren's Sub-Treasury proposal. Calhoun's remarks today sharply attacked Clay's assault of February 19 on the administration's Sub-Treasury [or Independent Treasury] scheme [Speech in Senate, September 25, 1837; Remark in Senate, January 16, 1838; Speech in Senate, February 19, 1838]. Clay commences by insisting that Calhoun not interrupt him as he has in the past. Denies that he has misrepresented Calhoun's stance on particulars in the Van Buren proposal, and cites specific misconceptions in Calhoun's speech of September 18, 1837. As for his personal references to Calhoun in his (Clay's) February 19 speech, admits that "The duty which I had to perform in animadverting upon the public conduct and course of the senator from South Carolina was painful in the extreme; but it was, nevertheless, a public duty, and I shrink from the performance of no duty required at my hands by my country. It was painful, because I had long served in the public councils with the senator from South Carolina, admired his genius, and for a great while had been upon terms of intimacy with him. Throughout my whole acquaintance with him, I have constantly struggled to think well of him, and to ascribe to him public virtues. Even after his famous summerset at the extra session, on more than one occasion I defended his motives when he was assailed, and insisted that it was uncharitable to attribute to him others than those which he himself avowed. This I continued to do, until I read this most extraordinary and exceptionable letter: [Here Mr. *Clay* held up and exhibited to the senate the Edgefield letter, dated at Fort Hill, November 3, 1837:] a letter of which I cannot speak in merited terms, without a departure from the respect which I owe to the senate and to myself. When I read that letter, sir, its unblushing avowals, and its unjust reproaches cast upon my friends and myself, I was most reluctantly compelled to change my opinion of the honorable senator from South Carolina. One so distinguished as he is cannot expect to be indulged with speaking as he pleases of others, without a reciprocal privilege. He cannot suppose that he may set to the right or the left, cut in and out, and *chasser*, among principles and parties as often as he pleases, without animadversion. I did, indeed, understand the senator to say, in his former speech, that we, the whigs, were unwise and *unpatriotic* in not uniting with him in supporting the bill under consideration. But in that Edgefield [Speech in Senate, February 19, 1842] letter, among the motives which he assigns for leaving us, I understand him to declare that he could not 'back and sustain those in such opposition, in whose wisdom, firmness, and patriotism I have no reason to confide.' " Quotes from the Edgefield letter to cast scorn on Calhoun's contention therein that South Carolina's act of nullification [8:388-89, 473, 598, 603, 615] had effectively overthrown the protective tariff, ended the American system, and put a stop to congressional usurpation. States: "Nullification, Mr. President, overthrew the protective policy! No, sir. The compromise [tariff of 1833] was not extorted by the terror of nullification. Among other more important motives that influenced its passage, it was a compassionate concession to the imprudence and impotency of nullification! The danger from nullification itself excited no more apprehension than would be felt by seeing a regiment of a thousand boys, of five or six years of age, decorated in brilliant uniforms, with their gaudy plumes and tiny muskets, marching up to assult a corps of 50,000 grenadiers, six feet high. At the commencement of the session of 1832, the senator from South

Carolina was in any condition other than that of dictating terms. Those of us who were then here must recollect well his haggard looks and his anxious and depressed countenance. A highly estimable friend of mine, Mr. J.M. Clayton, of Delaware, alluding to the possibility of a rupture with South Carolina, and declarations of president Jackson with respect to certain distinguished individuals whom he had denounced and proscribed, said to me, on more than one occasion, referring to the senator from South Carolina and some of his colleagues, 'They are clever fellows, and it will never do to let old Jackson hang them.' Sir, this disclosure is extorted from me by the senator."

Explains and defends his compromise tariff legislation of 1833 [8:604, 619-22, 626-27] and the continuing support for it in Congress since passage. Characterizes nullification as a "strange, impracticable, incomprehensible doctrine, that partakes of the character of the metaphysical school of German philosophy, or would be worthy of the puzzling theological controversies of the middle ages." Defends also his American system, which "now so much derided, why I know not, unless it be because it be *American*, has advanced this country in the arts and in prosperity, at least half a century. I believed, and still believe it, eminently advantageous to all parts of the Union, and injurious really to none. In its origin it was denounced because it was alleged that it would dry up all the sources of our revenue from imports. Whoever will take the trouble to examine the early debates upon the subject, will find that to have been the prominent and strong ground of opposition. The prediction being falsified, its opponents changed their position, and charged it with being the parent cause of the late great surplus in the public revenue. That surplus was in fact chiefly produced by the operation of the land system, and if the land bill [8:494, 539-41, 609-10, 812-13, 846-47, 873-74] which I introduced some years ago had been passed (a bill by the bye to which the senator from South Carolina was opposed,) we should have avoided all perplexity in the disposal of that surplus, because there would have been none." Reminds the Democrats that President Van Buren had voted for the protectionist tariff bill of 1828 "after, as has been asserted, having advised such a concoction of it as to ensure its defeat, and having held out to the southern delegation the hope that it would be defeated."

Calls attention to the purely partisan political dimensions of Calhoun's Edgefield letter and his concurrent shift from the anti-Jacksonians to the Van Burenite Jacksonians [Speech in Senate, February 19, 1838]. "He quit us," Clay charges, "because he apprehended that he and his party would be absorbed by us. Well what is to be their fate in his new alliance? . . . Is there no danger that the senator and his party will be absorbed by the administration party?" Doubts that Calhoun's stated intention in his Edgefield letter to unite the entire south ("the plantation or staple states") for political leverage can possibly succeed, because he cannot explain which states fit the "plantation or staple" definition. Laughs at Calhoun's contention that "he has left no party, and joined no party! . . . Abandoned no party? Why this [Edgefield] letter proclaims his having quitted us, and assigns his reasons for doing it; one of which is, that we are in favor of that national bank which the senator himself has sustained about 24 years of the 27 that he has been in public life. Whatever impression the senator may endeavor to make without the senate upon the country at large, no man within the senate, who has eyes to see, or ears to hear, can mistake his present position and party connexion." Attacks Calhoun for his presumed reference to Clay's inconsistency in effecting a corrupt bargain [4:48, 53-54, 73-74, 80, 82, 84-85, 113-14, 144-50, 157-59] with John Q. Adams in 1825 and once again defends himself against that charge. "The senator has thought proper . . . without being very specific . . . to impute to me the charge of going over upon some occasion, and that in a manner which left my motive no matter of conjecture. If the senator mean[s] to allude to the stale and refuted calumny of George Kremer, I assure him I can hear it without the slightest emotion; and if he can find any fragment of that rent banner to cover his own aberrations, he is perfectly at liberty to enjoy all the shelter which it affords. In my case there was no going over about it; I was a member of the house of representatives, and had to give a vote for one of three candidates for the presidency. Mr. [William H.] Crawford's unfortunate physical condition placed him out of the question. The choice was, therefore, limited to the venerable gentleman from Massachusetts, or to the distinguished inhabitant of the hermitage. I could give but one vote, and, accordingly, as I stated on a former occasion, I gave the vote which, before I left Kentucky, I communicated to my colleague (Mr. Crittenden,) it was my intention to give in the contingency which happened. I have never for one moment regretted the vote I then gave. It is true, that the legislature of Kentucky had requested the representatives from that state to vote for General Jackson; but my own immediate constituents, I knew well, were opposed to his election, and it was their will, and not that of the legislature, according to every principle applicable to the doctrine of instructions, which I was to deposite in the ballot-box. It is their glory and my own never to have concurred in the elevation of Gen. Jackson. They ratified and confirmed my vote, and every representative that they have sent to congress since, including my friend, the present member has concurred with me in opposition to the election and administration of General Jackson." Charges Calhoun with apostasy for having withdrawn from the 1824 presidential canvass and subsequently joined both the Jackson and Adams tickets as vice presidential candidate. "What motives induced him . . . to unite in the election of General Jackson I know not. . . . I leave to the senator to settle that account with his own conscience and his country." As for myself, "I have no reproaches to make . . . and feel perfectly invulnerable to any attack from others, on account of any part which I took in the election of 1825. And I look back with entire and conscious satisfaction upon the whole course of the arduous administration which ensued." Continues: "Now, it is a part of my pride and pleasure to say, that I never in my life changed my deliberate opinion upon any great measure of national policy but once, and that was 22 years ago, on the question of the power to establish a bank of the United States [2:200-205, 216-19]. The change was wrought by the sad and disastrous experience of the want of such an institution growing out of the calamities of war. It was a change which I made in common with Mr. Madison, two governors of Virginia, and the great body of that republican party to which I have ever belonged." Notes the inconsistency inherent in Calhoun's shift on the national bank question, having supported it as constitutional since 1816 and now abandoning it as being unconstitutional. Also chides the South Carolinian for his shifts on internal improvements and on the protective tariff, both of which he once found constitutional but now finds unconstitutional. Wonders how Calhoun can possibly support the Van Buren administration and its noxious Sub-Treasury bank policy [Speech in Senate, September 25, 1837; Remark in Senate January 16, 1838; Speech in Senate, February 19, 1838] which can only produce "the perfect union of the sword and purse which all real patriots have ever so much dreaded." Recalls the days when he and Calhoun had worked on and voted together on various issues: "We began our public career nearly together; we remained together throughout the war and down to the peace. We agreed as to a bank of the United States—as to a protective tariff—as to internal improvements—and lately, as to those arbitrary and violent measures which characterised the administration of General Jackson. No two prominent public men ever agreed better together in respect to important measures of national policy. We concur now in nothing. We separate forever." Says he simply cannot agree with Calhoun that by passing Van Buren's Independent Treasury bill the national depression will end and all will be well again.

On the contrary, passing the bill is to risk a growth in executive power bordering on tyranny.

[At this point, Clay took his seat and Sen. William C. Preston (S.C.) took the floor. Preston proceeded to defend South Carolina's nullification policy in 1832-33, scorn Clay's having just made light of it, contest Clay's manipulation of history in his current claim that when he had seemed to compromise with South Carolina in 1833 on the tariff issue he was really attacking Jackson's tariff policy. Says Preston of Clay: "his declarations to-day show that he . . . prefers to have it known that his object was to drive a good bargain for the manufacturers; and that his views of peace did not extend beyond saving a good fellow or two from an ignominous death. That he did not believe that danger existed, or that South Carolina intended aught but child's play. The honorable senator has a right to establish the relation in which he stands to the transactions of that day, and to correct the history of them, which had falsely, as it now appears, assigned so different, and, in my judgment, so much nobler an attitude to the honorable senator. He now permits it to be understood, that when he seemed to compromise with South Carolina, it was, in fact, but securing the tariff against general Jackson; and that when he talked of the harmony of the union, and the peace of the land, he did not, in fact, consider either in the slightest danger. In all this he was totally mistaken; as much mistaken in regard to us, as we were to him. We were anxious to avoid, but not afraid to meet a collision." Following this, Clay regains the floor.]

He complains that Preston has misunderstood him and that he has the highest regard for the sincerity and gallantry that South Carolina displayed in 1832-33, even though the state was "eminently wrong in that memorable contest." Adds: "But the senator must excuse me for believing that South Carolina alone could not have beaten all the rest of the United States, and for thinking that, I justly described the inequality of such a contest in the parallel which I drew of the relative strength of the two parties. Nor did I, in the allusion which I made to what passed at the session of 1832-3, between my excellent friend (John M. Clayton) and myself, intend to intimate that the senator from South Carolina, (Mr. Calhoun,) or any of his colleagues, deserved the ignominious death with which they had been menaced. Neither of us thought they did; but we had heard the current reports of the threats of President Jackson to apply it to certain gentlemen in South Carolina, the senator from South Carolina himself (Mr. Calhoun) among them, and hence the remark of Mr. Clayton." Repeats and restates his motives in offering the compromise tariff proposal in 1833: "The motives for the passage of the compromise act were, 1st. to prevent a civil war, and to protect South Carolina from impending danger; 2d. to preserve the tariff, threatened with a total overthrow, which would have taken place at the next session, to insure stability, during a long term of years, to the policy of protection, and to save the manufacturers from the absolute ruin and prostration with which they were menaced; and, 3d. to avoid the necessity of placing a large army, and vast military resources, at the disposal of President Jackson, animated as he was by a spirit of resentment and vengeance towards South Carolina and some of her most prominent citizens. I had no confidence in the discretion of the President, and I was unwilling to see him invested with an immense military power, of the prudent use of which I saw no adequate security."

[At this point Calhoun rises to defend his Edgefield letter of November 3, 1837, and points out that he had expressed "those self-same sentiments just as strongly in 1834." Defends at length his record of consistency against Clay's charges of his inconsistency. Attacks Clay's insistence that his republican principles have remained those he held in 1798 with the observation that "if the gentleman has not changed *his principles*, he has most certainly changed *his company*; for, though he boasts of setting out in public life a republican of the school of '98, he is now surrounded by some of the most distinguished members of the old federal party."]

Clay resumes the floor, charging that Calhoun's Edgefield letter "took new ground" compared with his 1834 views in that "he denounced those with whom he had been acting as persons in whom he could have no confidence, and imputed to them the design of renewing a high tariff and patronizing extravagant expenditures, as the natural consequences of the establishment of a bank of the United States, and had presented this as a reason for his recent course." Adds: "the senator says, that if I have not changed principles, I have at least got into strange company. Why really, Mr. President, the gentleman has so recently changed his relations that he seems to have forgotten into what company he has fallen himself. [A laugh.] He says that some of my friends once belonged to the federal party. Sir, I am ready to go into an examination with the honorable senator at any time, and then we shall see if there are not more members of that same old federal party amongst those whom the senator has so recently joined, than on our side of the house. The plain truth is, that it is the old federal party with whom he is now acting. For all the former grounds of difference which distinguished that party, and were the great subjects of contention between them and the republicans, have ceased from lapse of time and change of circumstances, with the exception of one, and that is the maintenance and increase of executive power. This was a leading policy of the federal party. A strong, powerful, and energetic executive was its favorite tenet." Attacks, further, Calhoun's political inconsistency over the years.

[At this juncture, Calhoun rises again, "Hoarse as he was," to explain and defend his stance on the Bonus bill of 1816 (and the internal improvement implications in it) as well as his support of internal improvements for national defense purposes while serving as secretary of war in 1821-22. Admits that he had opposed the Sub-Treasury concept in 1834, because he "thought it not as safe as the system now before us. But it turns out that it was more safe. . . . I was then [1834] under the impression that the banks were more safe, but it proves otherwise."]

Clay again rises to repeat and further document his charge that Calhoun had clearly shifted from his 1834 position on the Sub-Treasury system. Concludes: "The distinguished senator from South Carolina (I had almost said my friend from South Carolina, so lately and so abruptly has he bursted all amicable relations between us, independent of his habit of change, I think, when he finds into what federal doctrines and federal company he has gotten, he will be disposed soon to feel regret and to return to us,) has not, I am persuaded, weighed sufficiently the import of the unkind imputations contained in his Edgefield letter towards his former allies—imputations that their principles are dangerous to our institutions, and of their want of firmness and patriotism. I have read that singular letter again and again, with inexpressible surprise and regret, more, however, if he will allow me to say so, on his own than on our account." Copy. Printed in *Niles' Register* (May 26, 1838), 54:196-201. Not printed in the *Cong. Globe.*

To CHARLES A. DAVIS Washington, March 11, 1838

I wish to God that I could execute any of the agreeable journeys which you have so kindly sketched out for me in your letter of the 9h. inst. But whilst you, merchants, know that *money* is the main spring of all your mercantile operations, you forget that *time* is that of the movements of politicians, and especially of us old politicians. We have, I assure you, upon my honor, wives and children, or grandchildren, homes, farms and business, to whom and to which we are some times inclined to go, whatever may be thought of us. I left all these in Novr. and feel most anxious to get back to them.

We are here yet in the midst of discussions and intrigues about the same Government Bank which occupied us when you were here.[1] I think that we have made a deep impression against that most unwise project; but the influence of party is strong and, I understand, that the Admon count upon carrying their measure, in both houses. The vote will undoubtedly be close in both. A N[ew]. Hampshire *breeze* would help us amazingly.

I was very sorry not to have seen my good friend Mrs. [Charles A.] Davis (to whom I pray you to present my best regards) before you ran away with that good lady from this City. The moment I was able to move out, I repaired to Gadsbys to see her, but you had fled with her.

ALS. Courtesy of Cassius M. Clay, Paris, Ky. 1. Speech in Senate, Sept. 25, 1837, and Feb. 19, 1838.

From Jonathan Roberts, Upper Marion, Pa., March 12, 1838. Congratulates Clay for his "splendid" speech against the Sub-Treasury bill [Speech in Senate, February 19, 1838]. Compares it with the pointed and forceful performance that was his speech of January 20, 1819, attacking Jackson's foray into Florida against the Seminoles [2:636-61]. Says his recent study of Phrenology and its view of man as a moral agent has supported his long-held opinion of Calhoun as wayward and inconsistent and Felix Grundy as lacking decisiveness ("Mr Grundy after aiding all in his power to get us into a war [1812] disappeared like a vapor"). Condemns Grundy's "penal bill against the U S Bank notes," ascribing "such folly as due to a malconformation of head." Sees no hope for national economic revival until the "pervirse men" who control Congress are "hurled" from their seats. "I always feared the fruits of Jacksonism would not ripen until he had retired & perhaps have been forgotten." On the complex question of "the nature of trade & credit," compliments Clay because "you very early took a ground the only ground in policy that can lead this country to its highest destinies—The constitution like the common law must[,] like an elastic mantle as Blackstone says[,] adapt itself to the state of things[;] a strict literal construction will not do, much less will that of specific grants—" Laments the death of Abner Lacock who told him "when we last met that Mr Web[ster ob]serv'd to him when in Pittsburg[h] that he now found in the last they had been all wrong [i]n supposing the executive too weak." Jackson has convinced Webster that he "is the government" if one were but to "take Judge [John] Marshall from the Bench & two or three votes out of the Senate." Considers Webster's statement to Lacock to be "a noble avowal," and hopes "he continues so to think and act." But remarks that little has been lately heard from Webster. Observes also that his role in supporting the Force bill in 1833 [8:615, 862] was a major blunder. Nonetheless, asks Clay to "make my compliments to Mr. Webster. He is among those to whom we must look to keep this union together notwithstanding his part in the force Bill." ALS. DLC-HC (DNA, M212, R5). Postmarked in Norristown, Pa. For Roberts, former representative and U.S. senator from Pa., see *BDAC*. For Grundy's bill, see Remark in Senate, April 17, 1838. For Lacock, a former Pennsylvania senator who died on April 12, 1837, see *BDAC*.

To PETER B. PORTER Washington, March 13, 1838

I have time only to acknowledge the receipt of your favor of the 8h. and to add a few words. I got a few days ago the [William Henry] Harrison Circular from another quarter.[1] That, and the abortive attempt made at Cincinnati to produce a separate popular nomination,[2] combined with a real want of confidence in his ability common with all the intelligent men of the Whig party, will ruin his prospects. He will give us no trouble six months hence. Mean time, I assure you that our Cause, even in Indiana and

Ohio, is daily acquiring strength and accession. At Dayton, you will have seen, that they have recommended me, in a large public meeting headed by the late member from that District.[3] And I continue to receive the most conclusive evidence from the Reserve (which you know is the great Whig District of Ohio) that I am greatly preferred there. In the entire sweep from the Potomac to Louisiana not another person but myself is thought or spoken of in opposition to Mr. V[an]. B[uren]. Every passing day brings fresh evidence of the growth of our cause. It may surprize you to learn that in Massachusetts[4] the mass of the Abolitionists are for me.

We are still engaged in debate in the Senate on Mr. [Silas] Wrights bill.[5] I still think it will pass there; but we have hopes of its defeat in the House. Let me hear from you when you reach home.

ALS. NBuHi. 1. Porter to Clay, March 8, 1838. 2. "A Great Meeting of the Citizens of Hamilton" County, Ohio, in favor of the nomination of Harrison for president had been held at the courthouse in Cincinnati on Jan. 16, 1838. They justified their nomination of Harrison on the grounds that the national convention had been postponed to a distant date, and they called for popular nominations rather than nominations by politicians or newspapers. They also pledged to stand by Harrison's nomination whether or not he was nominated by a national convention. Washington *Daily National Intelligencer*, Jan. 22, 1838; Louisville *Public Advertiser*, Jan. 18, 26, 1838. 3. Evidently a reference to the action of the Montgomery County Whigs in endorsing Clay; and to former U.S. Rep. Joseph H. Crane, a Whig from Dayton. See *BDAC*; and Clay to Porter, Jan. 5, 1838. 4. Clay to Porter, March 4, 1838. 5. Providing for the establishment of a Sub-Treasury system, which passed the Senate 27 to 25 on March 26, 1838, and was rejected by the House, 125-111, on June 25, 1838. See *Cong. Globe*, 25 Cong., 2 Sess., 109-12, 264-65, 478; see also Speech in Senate, Sept. 25, 1837, and Feb. 19, 1838.

To Edward Harden, March 14, 1838. Thanks him for his invitation, but regrets that he cannot visit Athens, Ga., to speak at the commencement of the college there next August, even though there are "favorable dispositions prevailing among the States right party in Georgia, in respect to myself, which you are desirous to strengthen and extend." Explains that because he is a presidential candidate, his visit to Georgia would be viewed in political terms. Has resolved to remain "perfectly passive" in his candidacy so that the "public judgment" on him can be formed "unaffected by any personal efforts of my own." Remarks, further, that the "lamented [William] Lowndes expressed a sentiment worthy of him and of the dignity of the Office of President of the United States, when he said that it was neither to be sought nor declined." Trusts that if he errs in his decision on this matter it is an error "on the safe side." Sends Harden a copy of a recent speech [probably that of February 19, 1838, against the Sub-Treasury bill]. ALS. NcD. For Harden, a member of the college's (the present day University of Georgia) board of trustees, see E. Merton Coulter, *College Life In the Old South* (Athens, Ga., 1928), 162.

To SAMUEL WOOD, JR. Washington, March 22, 1838

I received your letter of the 8th inst. and thank you for the friendly expressions towards myself in which it abounds. The unfortunate affair to which it relates[1] has given me great pain and profound regret. But you are perfectly right, sir in anticipating that my wishes and efforts were directed to prevent the unhappy catastrophe. I went so far with that view as to advise the interposition of the civil authority, but I lament it was unavailing. My opinion on the practice of dueling was expressed publicly thirteen years ago. If you will look into Niles' Register of the spring 1825, you will find in my address to my constituents the strongest language condemning it.[2] All my reflection since has tended to strengthen and confirm that opinion. Perhaps no man living has accommodated more differences and prevented more duels than I have.

I make this communication to you, my dear sir, for your own satisfaction, and not for publication. I cannot consent to notice calumnies so utterly unfounded as that which seeks to connect my name without the slightest foundation in a transaction, the issue of which has filled me with grief, as it has every other good man. . . .

Copy. DLC-Henry Clay Wood Papers (DNA, M212, R22). 1. The Cilley v. Graves duel. See Clay to Speed, March 2, 1838, and Wood to Clay, March 8, 1838. 2. Address to the People of the Congressional District, Washington, March 26, 1825, in 4:143-66, espec. 146. It was published in *Niles' Register* (April 2, 1825), 28:71-79. A year later, on April 8, 1826, Clay fought his celebrated duel with John Randolph. See 5:211-12.

To JAMES B. CLAY Washington, March 23, 1838

I received your favor of the 1st. inst. I have been a little unwell, and have been so much oppressed with business, correspondence and company, that I have been obliged to engage a young friend to act for me as Amanuensis,[1] and he wrote the letter to which you refer upon my dictation.

I return the enclosed Certificate with my signature. I am perfectly satisfied with the disposition you have made of your Cattle with Mr. Dorsey. I am sorry that the imported Cow does not breed, and I must give you another after a while. We will talk about the House which you wish to build, when I see you. But I still should be happy to have you back in Kentucky if we can make some arrangement, as I hope we can to that end. I have not yet procured the patent but I hope to get it for your Land to be issued in the name of Dr. [Coleman] Rogers.[2] I have been looking out for a wife for you, but I suppose you will have to select for yourself.

Besides the $150 which I have already authorized you to draw for, you may draw for another sum of $150 at any time after the 10h. Apl.

I hope, my dear Son, that you will continue to cultivate a cheerful disposition, and go into Society as often as you can.

ALS. DLC-TJC (DNA, M212, R10). Printed in Colton, *Clay Correspondence*, 4:426. Written in "S[enate]. Chamber." Addressed to son James at "Richland near St. Louis Missouri." 1. Gales Seaton. Clay to Biddle, Feb. 6, 1838. 2. See 4:407.

Remark in Senate, March 23, 1838. Speaking at great length for the administration's Sub-Treasury bill, Sen. Garret D. Wall (N.J.) pauses in mid-flight to assert that he can find in the Constitution no power to authorize the creation of a national bank. Asks Clay where he had found such power. Clay responds that he "found it in the late war and the necessities of the country." *Cong. Globe*, 25 Cong., 2 Sess., Appendix, 231.

Remark in Senate, March 24, 1838. Participates in debate (comments not recorded) on a motion to amend section 23 out of the Sub-Treasury bill. The motion passed, Clay voting with the majority. *Cong. Globe*, 25 Cong., 2 Sess., 259. Section 23 of the bill would gradually (beginning in 1839) prohibit the Government "from receiving bank notes at all."

On March 21, Sen. Alfred Cuthbert (Ga.) had moved to strike section 23 of the Sub-Treasury bill, replacing it with the Currency Resolution of 1816. This ancient legislation gave the treasury discretion to receive either specie or the notes of specie-paying banks in payment of all government obligations. It would again become the law of the land on the soft-money vs. hard-money question if and when the Specie Circular was repealed [Remark in Senate, January 14, 1837; Comment in Senate, May 2, 1838; Remark in Senate, May 25 and 29, 1838], as it finally was on May 30, 1838, and/or until new legislation specifically replaced it and ordered something other than the flexibility it provided on treasury acceptance of specie or specie-backed paper. The Cuthbert amendment passed 31 to 21 on March 24, Clay voting yea. Later that same day, the Sub-Treasury bill, with the Cuthbert amendment inserted, was ordered engrossed for a third reading by a vote of 27 to 25, Clay voting nay. Two days later, March 26, the measure was finally passed by the same margin, Clay again voting nay. *Ibid.*, 250-51, 259, 264. See also Speech in Senate, September 25, 1837. For the origin of Cuthbert's unexpected amendment, see Wilson, *Presidency of Martin Van Buren*, 106-7. For the tactical importance of the Currency Resolution of 1816 to both opponents and supporters of the Sub-Treasury bill, see *ibid.*, 75-76; and Comment in Senate, May 2, 1838.

From Willie P. Mangum, Red Mountain, Orange County, N.C., March 26, 1838. Since last writing Clay more than five months ago, when he felt "in the deepest gloom, in regard to public affairs," his mood has improved and he now thinks "the Administration may pretty certainly be displaced; & we think, we can throw the vote of this State against Mr Van Buren." Says that "the main object of this letter" is to inform him that North Carolina will send a delegation to the Whig national nominating convention to support Clay only if it is "perfectly sure" that he will be nominated there; if not a certainty, "we will decline being there." Explains that North Carolina Whigs have little use for the nominating convention approach, especially "when the body is formed by drumming up all the office holders." Reports that last fall and early winter he carried on an "extensive Correspondence with our friends in this State," and that there is perfect concurrence on the following points: "First, that we will not *make a ticket even* for any other than yourself, nominated or not, by the Convention—that we will make a ticket for you, & vote it, whether any other State in the Union shall join us or not. You will perceive the incompatibility of these views, with the idea of a Convention.—If we go into the Convention & fail, we should have to secede. . . . We feel, that the South owes you much, & if none other joins us, we shall regard the honor as still higher to give you our Vote.—Accordingly the Whig papers of this State, *almost* without impulse from leaders, have taken this ground." Thinks that support for Van Buren has steadily declined since the First Session ("Called Session") of the 25th Congress. Analyzes the relative strength of Van Buren, Calhoun, and Clay in North Carolina. Believes Clay can carry the state. Reports that a "fine spirit pervades the Whig ranks—I do not refer to the papers & leaders only, but I mean to include, the bone & sinew of our population—the substantial Country gentlemen & farmers.—With that portion of our population, that think & read, I have never known so strong an interest in the success of any Presidential Candidate as in your Case, with the exception perhaps, of that of Mr [William H.] Crawford.—" On the "propriety or probable necessity of No. Ca. going into the Convention," asks Clay to show this letter to John J. Crittenden and "request him to write me on this, & matters & things in general." Reports that he is presently running for the "lower & more numerous branch" of the state legislature as a candidate for one of the five Orange County seats. Thinks the Whig ticket in Orange is strong, and that "we shall carry the County," but doubts that the Whigs will capture control of the legislature from the Van Buren party. They do, however, expect to win the gubernatorial race. Congratulates Clay "for your great effort on the Sub: Treas: scheme [Speech in Senate, February, 19, 1838]. One of the greatest, if not the very greatest, because of its practical & useful tone & pitch of character, that you have made in my time.—A little too spicy, perhaps, towards Mr. C[alhoun]—For you ought to remember, that truth often hurts more than the worst calumny.—" ALS. InU. In the 1840 presidential election in North Carolina, Harrison defeated Van Buren by 46,376 to 34,218 and captured the state's 15 electoral votes.

North Carolina did send delegates to the Whig National Convention at Harrisburg on December 4, 1839. Mangum was not one of the delegates. In the 1838 state elections in North Carolina, Whig candidate for governor, Edward B. Dudley, defeated the Democratic candidate, John Branch, by a vote of 38,166 to 21,130. The Whigs also won control of both houses of the state legislature. They carried 27 seats in the senate to 23 for the Democrats; in the house of commons they won 65 seats to 53 for the Democrats with 2 doubtful. Eventually they claimed a joint-ballot majority of 14. Mangum was not elected to the house. Raleigh *Register and North Carolina Gazette*, September 10, 1838, December 14, 1839; *BDGUS*, 3:1128-29; *Niles' Register* (October 6, 1838), 55:82.

Remark in Senate, March 27, 1838. Reports that the people of Hampshire County, Va. (W.Va.), hearing it denied that one of the local mail-route contractors was "deluging the country with shinplasters [Remark in Senate, March 5, 1838]," have sent him one such shinplaster with the request that it be referred to the Committee on Finance to support the allegation in their petition. Clay so moves. Motion carried. *Cong. Globe*, 25 Cong., 2 Sess., 268. See *ibid.*, 214; Remark in Senate, March 5, 1838. The shinplaster in question, signed by Lucius W. Stockton, the local mail contractor, was for 25 cents and was good only for local stage fare.

Later this day, Clay participates (not recorded) in a discussion of the bill authorizing the continuation of the Cumberland Road through Ohio, Indiana, and Illinois. *Cong. Globe*, 25 Cong., 2 Sess., 268-69.

Remark in Senate, March 28, 1838. Supports bill for the relief of William R. Taylor, administrator of Jonathan Taylor, deceased. *Cong. Globe*, 25 Cong., 2 Sess., 271-72.

Remark in Senate, March 29, 1838. Urges postponement of a discussion of the bill "providing for the reduction and graduation of the price of the public lands." Identifies it as "one of the most important measures that could be brought before Congress, affecting the public domain to the amount of millions." Bill tabled with understanding it will be taken up on April 2. *Cong. Globe*, 25 Cong., 2 Sess., 274. The price reduction and graduation bill passed the Senate on April 13, 1838, by 27 to 16, Clay voting nay. *Ibid.*, 305. It was not brought to a vote in the House during the 25th Congress, 2nd Session, nor was it given any particular legislative priority there. *Ibid.*, 18, 92, 479, 498. For its fate in the 25th Congress, 3rd Session, see Remark in Senate, December 12, 1838.

To ROBERT SWARTWOUT Washington, April 2, 1838

I received your letter of the 21st ult. from Albany, with the memorandum enclosed.[1] Should our friends execute their intentions as communicated to you, it seems to me that every thing will be done that could be desired under actual circumstances. You will have seen that the friends of Gen. Harrison, in Pennsylvania, probably in despair of his obtaining the National nomination, propose a separate movement by a Convention of his peculiar friends, to be assembled at Pittsburg[h] on the 4th of July next.[2] Considering that the idea of a National Convention originated with his friends, the course which they now propose to take must excite both surprise & regret. It is not in conformity with that spirit of harmony, which is so desirable, which has been so constantly professed by every portion of the Whig party, & which is so essential to ultimate success. I think the course will be unavailing, & will finally meet with general rebuke. It is the more remarkable, because Pennsylvania, or rather a few persons in Pennsylvania, which against all our hopes & expectations has constantly yielded her support to the election of the late & present President U. S., assume a right to direct the course of the whole whig party throughout the Union.

On the several points on which you have done me the favor to consult me, I feel much repugnance to saying one word, even to so good & faithful a friend as I have ever found you to be. In regard to one of them, that of an expression of the popular sentiment, in opposition to the government Bank,[3] I have, however, no hesitation in saying, the more general & enthusiastic it is made, the better both for the common cause & for the defeat of that odious measure. As to the Florida war,[4] I think the sooner it can be honorably gotten rid of, the better. It is a source of most wasteful expenditure of public money, & the objects to be acquired by the most triumphant success are wholly inadequate to the exertions & expense which it calls for. It seems to me that it might be practicable, without affecting the National honor, to leave the Indians in the quiet possession of a portion of the Territory, which will never be occupied, or at least not occupied within a century, by the whites, & thus terminate a war in which no laurels are to be reaped.

With respect to popular expressions in the State of New York in my favor, I entreat that nothing may be done, if there be the least danger of its hazarding the whig cause, so important to be maintained in your state. If it would not have that effect, or if it would add strength to the cause, there cannot be a doubt that in other respects its influence would be salutary. These are matters, however, of which the friends of the cause in N. York are the best, & I wish them to be the exclusive, judges.

LS. NN. Letter marked "(Confidential)" in Clay's hand. 1. Neither found. 2. Porter to Clay, March 8, 1838. 3. Speech in Senate, Sept. 25, 1837 and Feb. 19, 1838. 4. Clay to Hale, Jan. 7, 1838.

To THOMAS HART CLAY Washington, April 3, 1838

I recd. your letter of the 26h. March. I hope that you will have received by this time the money from Mr. Dunlap, which I wish deposited to my credit in Bank when received.[1] I am glad to hear of the good turn out of your Crop of Hemp. If our two Crops together do not amount to 16 ton, whatever is deficient must be purchased of good hemp to make 16 ton of Bale Rope, which I am to deliver to Dr. [Stephen] Duncan. I want it completed, so as to be forwarded by the 25h. May to Maysville (before the river falls) to January & Huston, and thence shipt directly to Dr. Duncan at Natchez. It need not be sent earlier than the 15h. or 20h. of May.

I have written home requesting the Imported mare again to be sent to Bertrand. The [illeg. word] bay mare may be put to Royal or Perfect. The

Letcher mare may be put to some good cheap Saddle horse that may be selected by Mr. Downing.[2] How are the Jacks doing? Give my love to Mary [Mentelle Clay].

ALS. Mary Clay Kenner Collection, Rogersville, Tenn. 1. Clay to Thomas H. Clay, March 6, 1838. 2. Probably Samuel Downing or his son, Richard or Josiah. See Clay to Thompson, July 8, 1837.

To Whom It May Concern, April 4, 1838. Introduces Mr. Franklin Knight, the bearer, as a "respectable and intelligent gentleman" who is en route to the Western states to sell subscriptions to the *Christian Statesman.* Remarks that the paper is "highly worthy of support, & calculated to exercise a salutory influence." ALS. NjHi. Written in Washington. Subscription reads: "I concur in the above J.B. Anderson."

The weekly *Christian Statesman,* which was published from February 2, 1838 to January 25, 1839, claimed to be "Devoted to the promotion of just views in literature, humanity, liberty, politics, African colonization, and religion (American Colonization Society)." On July 2, 1838, Clay paid $3.00 for a subscription covering vol. I, no. 1 to no. 52. Clay to Etter & Bayne, July 2, 1838. ADS. DLC-TJC (DNA, M212, R18). Etter & Bayne were publishers of the *Christian Statesman,* and Ralph R. Gurley was the editor. See *African Repository* (May, 1838), 14:157.

Remark in Senate, April 9, 1838. Presents and supports a petition for a bridge across the Mississippi at "Des Moines, Illinois"; also for construction of a military road. *Cong. Globe,* 25 Cong., 2 Sess., 292. The "Des Moines, Illinois" referred to is probably to the river Des Moines which merges with the Mississippi River at the tip of Illinois.

Later this day, speaking to the Graduation bill [Remark in Senate, March 29, 1838], expresses his "utter aversion" to reducing the price of public land, "which is already low enough"; also holds that "all the tests of value" are "merely fallacious." Regrets that his indisposition prevents him from speaking now on the administration's graduation proposal, introduced by Sen. Robert J. Walker (Miss.), or the amendment to it by Felix Grundy (Tenn.). *Ibid.,* 293. Under the Grundy amendment, all public land in the nation remaining unsold for 5 years after September 30, 1838, after having been offered for sale at $1.25 per acre, would be offered for $1.00. All land offered for 10 years prior to September 30, 1838, and still unpurchased, would be sold for $1.00 per acre for 12 months after that date, at which time its price would be reduced to 75¢. All unpurchased land offered for 15 years would also be sold for $1.00 per acre for a 12-month period after September 30, 1838, at the end of which time it would be reduced to 75¢ for 12 additional months and, after 12 more months, reduced further to 50¢ per acre. *Ibid.* Grundy's amendment was approved *viva voce,* and, by general consent, inserted into the original text of the bill. *Ibid.* See also Speech in Senate, April 11, 1838.

Later this day, Clay asks for a delay of further consideration of the Graduation bill, "a measure the effect of which was to legislate away hundreds of millions," until more senators were present, there being only about two-thirds of them present today. Wants to "address the Senate on it when there was a full House." Postponed to April 11. *Cong. Globe,* 25 Cong., 2 Sess., 295.

A comment on this date on the bill to prevent dueling in the District of Columbia (*ibid.,* 292), attributed to "Mr. CLAY" in the index to volume 6 (25 Cong., 2 Sess.,) of the *Cong. Globe,* refers to a remark by Sen. Clement C. Clay of Alabama, not by Henry Clay.

To Thomas Allen, Washington, April 10, 1838. Encloses payment of $2.00 for "100 copies of Mr-Tallmadges Speech." ADS. DLC-TJC (DNA, M212, R18). Probably N.Y. Sen. Nathaniel P. Tallmadge's speech of February 8, 1838, attacking the Van Buren administration's Sub-Treasury bill. See *Cong. Globe*, 25 Cong., 2 Sess., Appendix, 619-21.

Speech in Senate, April 11, 1838. States his understanding of the Graduation bill [Remark in Senate, March 29, 1838] as it now stands with the Grundy amendment [Remark in Senate, April 9, 1838] incorporated into it. Notes that the rate of $1.25 per acre is "so low, so moderate, often so far below the actual value of the land, that every industrious man, however poor, may acquire a permanent home, and thousands are enriching themselves by purchasing from the public, and subsequently selling to individuals." Asserts that the current price graduation proposal applies immediately to 71,000,000 acres and reduces the value of those acres in the amount of $38,988,090. Supplies additional statistics to show that if the principle of reduction be applied to the remaining 240,000,000 acres of the public domain situated in the existing states and territories, land worth $300,000,000 at the $1.25 per acre level, the potential amount of additional loss to the people of the United States would be $180,000,000 if these acres were sold off at the 50¢ level. Points out that even such sharp losses as these do not take into account the losses inherent in selling the 750,000,000 acres presently located outside the limits of the present states and territories, "all of which would fall, beyond all doubt, within the scope" of the graduation policy. Asks why a graduation bill is necessary at a time when the "currency is disordered, the people are in debt; and yet, at such a period as this, we are asked to sanction a bill, which shall throw into the market an immense quantity of the common property of the people of the United States, and which must inevitably cripple their means, to disembarrass themselves from existing difficulties." Traces the history of public land policy and land-sale levels since 1820 to demonstrate that the amount of acreage "thrown into the market far [exceeds] the necessary wants of our growing population." Explains that this "inordinate supply has proceeded from the urgent demands upon the General Government, made by the new States, to bring more and more fresh lands into the market so they might attract new settlers." Cites Ohio as an example of prudent public land disposal. Repeats earlier warnings that past graduation policy and practice has mainly benefitted land speculators. Affirms that population is now increasing so rapidly in the new states that further reductions in land prices are no longer a necessary stimulant to continued population growth. Thinks the 1840 census will show these increases, just as had his 1832 study of comparative population growth in the new and old states between 1820 and 1830—a study he undertook in conjunction with his land bill [8:494, 539-41] of that year. Regrets that Van Buren in his message of December 5, 1837, has "become infected with the spirit of innovation, and joined in the cry for reduction and graduation. But there is some plausibility, if not much practicability, in the plan which he suggests. He proposes a previous valuation; in other words, that we should ascertain what the thing is worth before we fix a price upon it. But this bill, discarding all such idle and unnecessary knowledge, proposes arbitrarily and blindly to reduce prices without any sort of reference to values." Laments that "We glut the market by throwing into it vast quantities of fresh land of unsurpassed fertility. The powers of population and emigration, great and [surprising] as they are, we find incompetent to absorb the superabundant quantity. We violate or disregard all the laws of supply and demand; and, without waiting for the operation of natural causes; without stopping until the demands of our growing population shall ease the burdened market, we are called upon to reduce the price of what it was impossible to have sold, on the mere presumption, contrary to known facts, that it is not worth the extremely moderate price which the Government demands." Concludes that "this is not yet all. Once establish this principle of reduction, and who is to prescribe, or to see, the limits of its operation? Further and further, and lower and lower, reductions will be proposed. Politics—party politics—will mix themselves up in the question. In some of the new States, candidates for public office will present themselves upon the ground of securing other reductions in the price of the public lands, and will appeal to the popular suffrage. Other candidates will come out espousing still lower rates. It will become the leading and controlling object." And in the end "the common prosperity of all the States and the whole People shall be sacrificed at nominal prices, or be appropriated to a few, or be engrossed by speculators." *Cong. Globe*, 25 Cong., 2 Sess., Appendix, 563-64. As Clay took his seat, Grundy rose to amend the bill again; this time he sought to clean up a "misconception of it," i.e., "to make it operate only on lands that have been offered at public sale." Amendment agreed to. *Cong. Globe*, 25 Cong., 2 Sess., 301.

Earlier this dav, Clay speaks to Sen. James Buchanan's response to Sen. Robert J. Walker's resolution that "another demand ought to be made for the redress of our grievances from the Mexican Government." Concurs in Buchanan's inclination to move slowly on the claims issue with Mexico. Agrees also with Buchanan, chairman of the Foreign Affairs Committee, that the Senate should await the action of the House of Representatives on this matter since, if war were to ensue, the House under the Constitution would have to originate the revenue bills to prosecute it. Thinks, too, that "the present embarrassed state of the Treasury . . . should prevent, at least for the present, any resort to belligerent steps." Is it true, as he has heard, Clay asks Walker, that the U.S. minister plentipotentiary [Powhatan Ellis], "appointed last winter one year," has "never yet reached Mexico?" Remarks that the developing debate between Walker and Buchanan on the relative war-making powers of the Senate and House under the Constitution is "irregular and out of place." Explains that it would take considerable time for the Mexican minister for foreign affairs [Luis G. Cuevas] to examine the "large mass" of U.S. claims documents carried to Mexico by [Robert] Greenhow. They would have to be considered "one by one, admitting the justice of some, and rejecting others." Urges his colleagues to be patient and calm. *Ibid.*, 299.

A few minutes later in this debate, Clay interrupts Buchanan to interject the observation that Mexico had already admitted the justice of some of the claims. *Ibid.*, 300.

Powhatan Ellis had been commissioned chargé d'affaires to Mexico in January, 1836; but, failing to achieve anything in Mexico, he returned home in December, 1836. In March, 1837, he was nominated as U.S. minister to Mexico, "to be sent whenever circumstances will permit a renewal of diplomatic intercourse honorably with that power." Instead of sending Ellis back to Mexico immediately, Van Buren sent Robert Greenhow with documents detailing American claims. Although the Mexican government promised action, nothing was done. Ellis ultimately returned to Mexico as minister plenipotentiary in February, 1839. By that time the United States and Mexico had signed a convention agreeing to submit the claims to arbitration. Manning, *Diplomatic Correspondence . . . Inter-American Affairs*, 8:38, 84, 420, 422; Rives, *The United States and Mexico*, 1:422-31; 437; U.S. Sen., *Executive Journal*, 5:13, 23.

From Edward M. Samuel, Liberty, Mo., April 12, 1838. At Clay's personal request he has examined the land Clay owns "at the mouth of Grand River on the Mo River, in Carroll County." Reports that the property fronts about one-half mile on the Missouri and about one-quarter mile on the Grand, and that the town of Brunswick is situated one mile below the mouth of the Grand. Thinks Brunswick will become "a place of Considerable business" when the "Grand River Country becomes well settled, & the River be navigated, as it must be, by Steam Boats." Offers to buy Clay's land in whole or part "at a fair price . . . With a view of laying off a Town." Asks him to name a price, and the quantity he might want to sell. Adds: "I am Confident that the Mo River has taken off a Considerable portion of the land." Encloses a drawing [not found] of the site. Gives Kentucky Congressman William J. Graves ("He has known me from a Boy") as a character reference. ALS. DLC-HC (DNA, M212, R5). For Samuel, a Clay County, Mo., merchant who later moved to St. Louis and ran for Congress as a Whig candidate, see John V. Mering, *The Whig Party in Missouri* (Columbia, Mo., 1967), 90, 150.

Remark in Senate, April 13, 1838. Announces he will not vote for Michigan Sen. John Norvell's resolution that there should be no payment of the per diem allowance to a senator for those days he is absent from the Senate "unless detained from his seat by sickness." States that he is unwilling to admit "that absence from the Senate implie[s] neglect of public duties." Explains, further, that he himself "did infinitely more in his room than he did in the Senate chamber; for he was at work there night and day, either reading, digesting, or preparing matters connected with his public duties. This was the 32d year since his entrance into public life; and in all that period, he had lost less time from the public business, either by sickness, or from any other cause, than any man so long engaged in public life. In December, 1832 . . . he was absent; but it was while a highly important measure was to be brought about, in the prosecution of which he was as much engaged as though he had been present in the senate chamber. To presume a Senator, because not in his place, to be inattentive to his public duties, was what he could not admit; and he would go further, and say that the public business would be often expedited by attending more at home, or in the committee rooms." Resolution withdrawn by Norvell. *Cong. Globe*, 25 Cong., 2 Sess., 306. The December, 1832, absence of about 19 days resulted from his visit in Philadelphia preliminary to drawing up his Compromise Tariff Act of 1833 [8:604, 619-22, 626-27].

To FRANCIS T. BROOKE Washington, April 14, 1838

I should have written you more frequently but that I had nothing material to communicate, of which the papers would not inform you. I must add, too, that my labors, especially that of private correspondence, have greatly increased this session, from obvious causes.

In regard to the Presidential question, every thing is going on as well as my most zealous friends could desire. Public opinion every where, even in Indiana[1] and Ohio,[2] is rapidly concentrating as you could wish. The movement at Harrisburg for a separate nomination of General Harrison, is rebuked and discountenanced.[3]

The Whig members of Congress have had several consultations, as to the time and place of a National Convention. Their inclination, I understand, is to Harrisburg, and to a period between January and June of the next year.[4] They will probably definitely settle the matter the next week.

When do you return to St. Julien? I am very much jaded and fatigued, and have some thoughts of running somewhere for a few days. Possibly I may go to you, if I can be sure that I should meet only your family. . . .

Copy. Printed in Colton, *Clay Correspondence*, 4:426-27. 1. Earlier in the winter, the Indiana Whig convention, held in Indianapolis, had endorsed William Henry Harrison but had also passed a resolution praising Clay and promising to support him if he were nominated. Washington *Daily National Intelligencer*, Feb. 8, 1838. 2. Clay to Porter, Jan. 5, 1838. 3. A committee of Harrison supporters in Harrisburg had proposed that a national Harrison convention be held in Pittsburgh. A number of Whig newspapers, including the Washington *Daily National Intelligencer* and the Columbus (Ohio) *Journal and Register*, had soundly criticized this movement. Washington *Daily National Intelligencer*, April 20, 1838; see also Porter to Clay, March 8, 1838. 4. Porter to Clay, Nov. 14 and Dec. 30, 1837.

To PETER B. PORTER Washington, April 15, 1838

I received your favor of the 21st. Ulto. and should have written to you earlier but that I had nothing material to communica[te.]

There have been repeated meetings of the Whig members of Congress in consultation on the subject of the time and place of the meeting of the Nat. Convention. They have fixed upon Harrisburg, and their present inclination is June of the next year.[1] There was much diversity of opinion as to the *time*. Most of the N. York Whigs were for some period after your Election next year.[2] Some were for Feb. 1840; others for next Feb:; and others for next November. [Albert H.] Tracy and [Francis] Granger have both been here, but not together. They were both for delay; both decidedly against any expression of preference at Albany. Each has had a long conversation with me; and both profess to be uncommitted. They, of course, make strong professions for the success of the general cause. I infer that the desire for delay in the meeting of the N. Convention, manifested by the N. York Whigs, was their work. I know both these gentlemen well. The danger ahead is that if both Pennsa. and N. York should elect Anti Masonic Governors[3] (as seems probable, and as perhaps is desirable) it may render the Antimasons presumptuous, and they may underta[ke] to dictate in regard to the Presidency. I told Granger so; but he did not admit it. I think it probable that there will be a reconsideration of the time of the assembling of the Convention, and that it may be yet fixed for Feb. 1839.[4]

I do not learn that any thing has been done at Albany in respect to the Presidency, as you were induced to believe would be.[5] I think it probable that the efforts employed to prevent the expression of any preference, have been successfully directed also to defeat the Election of any delegates to represent the two Senators.[6]

I do not know that we have occasion to entertain any regrets about these delays. Our cause is daily gaining strength every where, whilst that of the other two gentlemen [Harrison and Webster] is certainly declining. Even in Indiana (the strongest supposed State for Harrison) I am satisfied from various sources of information that I am stronger there than he. Some of their papers have hauled down his flag and hoisted mine.

Granger expresses great apprehensions from the Abolitionists.[7] Do you think there is any foundation for them? From those of New England, I had much reason to believe that they prefered me to any person spoken of.

I learn that the Administration has not relinquished the hope of passing the Sub treasury bill, but even count upon carrying it. I think they are deceived. My belief is that it cannot pass.[8]

We have been much excited here about the Charter Election in N. York; and up to this moment are uncertain as to the Common Council.[9] The exertions of the Administration in that City shew that the greatest vigilance is still necessary to keep them down in your State.

Our intelligence is very satisfactory as to the probable issue of the Election in Mississippi.[10] And we have strong hopes of Virginia.[11]

ALS. NBuHi. 1. Porter to Clay, Nov. 14 and Dec. 30, 1837. The Whig convention convened in Harrisburg on Dec. 4, 1839. 2. For the 1838 state elections in New York, see Schermerhorn to Clay, Feb. 25, 1838. In the 1839 New York state elections, held the first Mon., Tues., and Wed. of November, the Whigs retained control of the lower house which they had won in 1838 and also gained control of the state senate. Clay to Sargent, Jan. 14, 1839; Glyndon G. Van Deusen, *Thurlow Weed: Wizard of the Lobby* (Boston, 1947), 106-8, 477-79. 3. For the election of William H. Seward, an Anti-Mason turned Whig, to the governorship of New York, and the defeat of the Anti-Masonic incumbent governor of Pennsylvania, Joseph Ritner, see Schermerhorn to Clay, Feb. 25, 1838. 4. Porter to Clay, Nov. 14, 1837. 5. Porter to Clay, Dec. 30, 1837. 6. *Ibid.* 7. Granger estimated the N.Y. State abolitionist vote at 20,000 in 1838 and predicted it would comprise 25% of the state's voters by the time of the presidential election in 1840. DeAlva Stanwood Alexander, *A Political History of the State of New York*, 2 vols. (New York, 1906), 2:25-26. 8. It did not until spring, 1840. See Speech in Senate, Sept. 25, 1837. 9. The Whigs were victorious in the New York City charter elections held on April 11-13, 1838. Aaron Clark (Whig) was elected mayor with a vote of 19,723 over Isaac Leggett Varian (Democrat) who polled 19,204 votes and Richard Riker (Conservative Democrat) who received 395 votes. In the common council the Whigs won 9 seats for alderman to 8 for the Democrats as well as winning 9 seats to 8 for assistant alderman. Melvin G. Holli & Peter d'A. Jones (eds.), *Biographical Dictionary of American Mayors, 1820-1980* (Westport, Conn., 1981), 67-68; New York *Morning Herald*, April 14, 1838. 10. A special election was held April 23-24, 1838, in Mississippi to settle the previous year's disputed U.S. House election [Speech in Senate, Feb. 19, 1838]. Whigs Sergeant S. Prentiss and Thomas J. Word won with 10,992 and 10,477 votes respectively against Democrats John F.H. Claiborne who polled 9,557 votes and James Davis who received 9,107. Washington *Daily National Intelligencer*, May 14, 1838. 11. The Whigs in Virginia won a total of 81 seats in the house and senate in the April, 1838 elections, up from the 60 they held in the 1837 general assembly; the Democrats captured 83 seats, down from their total of 103 in 1837. The Democrat seats included at least 14 held by so-called "Conservative Democrats [Clay to Henry Clay, Jr., Jan. 28, 1837]" who, led by U.S. Sen. William C. Rives, could be expected to vote with the Whigs on issues with states' rights implications. Howard Bravermen, "The Economic and Political Background of the Conservative Revolt in Virginia," *VMHB* (April, 1952), 60:282-84.

Remark in Senate, April 16, 1838. Presents petitions from William Warden and Leonard Stringer asking that arrearages in their pensions be paid. *Cong. Globe*, 25 Cong., 2 Sess., 311.

From Henry Shepherd, Shepherdstown, Va. (W. Va.), April 16, 1838. Forwards pedigree information pertaining to "the Bull Neptune & the White Bull Calf sent to Kentucky last winter," and asks Clay to forward the information to the purchasers. Explains that Neptune was got by Orozimbo [8:804]; White Bull Calf was got by Neptune, out of Maid of Baltimore, also sired by Orozimbo. ALS. DLC-TJC (DNA, M212, R14).

On May 10, 1838, Shepherd wrote from Shepherdstown to settle the account of this transaction. *Ibid.* For Henry Shepherd (1793-1870) a brother of Rezin D. Shepherd, see Smyth, *A Genealogy of the Duke-Shepherd-Van Metre Family*, 245.

Shepherd wrote again from Shepherdstown on June 2, 1838, saying he had received Clay's check for $150 for the White Bull Calf. Has concluded that Clay should not incur "any expense on the score of the Ayrshires.—all I desire to hear of them hereafter, is that the male is a sure producer of his Species . . . & that the female fills the largest pail in Mrs [Lucretia] Clays Dairy." ALS. DLC-TJC (DNA, M212, R14).

From Peter B. Porter, Rochester, N.Y., April 17, 1838. Reports "the increasing strength of the Whig party" in New York and the growth of sentiment there for Clay personally. Notes, however, that he does not know "that the Whigs in the Legislature have as yet done anything in regard to the Presidential question [Porter to Clay, November 14, and December 30, 1837]; but I take it for granted that they will before they adjourn hold a caucus, agree to a national convention, appoint the two senatorial delegates, as was pretty much agreed on before I left Albany." Regrets "extremely the disagreement that has occurred among the Banks, & especially the tone of Mr. [Nicholas] Biddle's letter to Mr. [John Quincy] Adams," and admits that the New York banks "may have been hasty & uncourteous toward their neighbors in resolving among themselves to resume" specie payments on May 10. Explains that resumption was dictated by the fact that the New York state senate was prepared to refuse to extend the suspension act and to "insist on a forfeiture of the [banks'] charters in case of failure to resume." Warns: "You perceive that Mr. Biddle's course has excited a good deal of feeling among the Whigs of this State who are offended, & not without reason, at the high and somewhat cavalier tone in which he has indulged towards them. You also perceive that the Regency are disposed to take advantage of this feeling for the purpose of injuring your personal popularity, by associating you with Mr. Biddle in this quarrel. I hope, my dear Sir, that you will keep aloof from this contest, and have nothing further to do with the question of resumption, than to endeavor to carry some measure through Congress, which will facilitate the return of specie payments, remove Mr. Biddle's objections, and thus relieve the distresses of the country. Will not the present State of the public mind justify such an attempt?" Copy. OHi.

Biddle, in a public letter to Adams, dated April 5, 1838, had condemned the New York banks and the Van Buren administration for not cooperating with him and the United States Bank of Pennsylvania on the resumption question, and for otherwise failing to contribute effectively to a permanent solution to the nation's monetary difficulties. So unpopular in New York was Biddle's attitude in this matter that Whigs there feared it would injure their party in the November, 1838 elections [Schermerhorn to Clay, February 25, 1838]. See Govan, *Nicholas Biddle*, 329-30; also Biddle to Clay, May 2, 1838.

Remark in Senate, April 17, 1838. Says he has no objection to postponing action on the administration's bill, introduced by Sen. Felix Grundy (Tenn.) on February 12, "to prevent the issuing and circulation of the bills, notes, and other securities of corporations created by Congress, which have expired"; but he eventually wants a vote "to see whether a majority of the Senate was prepared to assert the power claimed by it." *Cong. Globe*, 25 Cong., 2 Sess., 178, 313.

The bill in question was designed to prohibit the reissue and circulation of some ten million dollars worth of the notes of the late Bank of the United States by order of the directors of the successor United States Bank of Pennsylvania. Grundy's main speech in support of his bill to prevent the circulation of the so-called "Resurrection Notes," as well as to speak to "the late letter [Porter to Clay, April 17, 1838] of NICHOLAS BIDDLE to JOHN QUINCY ADAMS, recommending a non-resumption of specie payments by the banks," was delivered on April 16, 1838. *Cong. Globe*, 25 Cong., 2 Sess., Appendix, 299-304. Other attacks on the "Resurrection Notes" are in *ibid.*, 304-12. On April 20 the bill was ordered engrossed for a third reading by vote of 27 to 14, and on April 23 it was passed, 27 to 13, Clay voting nay on both occasions. *Cong. Globe*, 25 Cong., 2 Sess., 319, 324. It passed the House on July 6, 1838, and was signed into law the following day. *Ibid.*, 499. See 5 *U.S. Stat.*, 297.

Remark in Senate, April 18, 1838. Requests that the "Resurrection Notes" bill [Remark in Senate, April 17, 1838] be brought off the table. Speaks to a challenge by Sen. James Buchanan that he undertake a justification of the reissue and circulation of the notes of the old Bank of the United States, given the fact that its charter has expired. Replies only that "any justification" he might offer would not gratify Buchanan, and that all he seeks at this juncture is a vote on the issue. *Cong. Globe*, 25 Cong., 2 Sess., 315.

To ALEXANDER HAMILTON Washington, April 21, 1838

I received your letter of the 18th inst. By a vote taken in the Senate, yesterday, you will perceive that there is a large majority of that body in favor of Mr. [Felix] Grundy's Bill.[1] I have no means of knowing what its fate will be in the other house.[2] I do not see how it can operate injuriously upon the notes of the old Bank, now in circulation. It is limited to the object of preventing the reissue of notes of the old Bank by those who are charged with the duty of winding up its affairs. Its penalties are all directed against them, & do not extend to the rest of the community. The apathy in which you left Congress continues unabated. The prospect is that we shall do nothing, although some of the Administration party affect to believe that the Sub-Treasury Bill will pass.[3]

LS. NN. 1. Remark in Senate, April 17, 1838. 2. *Ibid.* 3. Speech in Senate, Sept. 25, 1837, and Feb. 19, 1838.

From Peter B. Porter, Black Rock, N.Y., April 22, 1838. Predicts that within the next 60 days the nation will experience "one of the most interesting and eventful crises that has ever occurred in the monetary affairs of our country." Thinks that the time has come for Clay to resolve the problem [resumption of specie payment] with his celebrated "judgment and tact" and win again the title "The Savior of your country." Believes that the administration's Sub-Treasury bill [Speech in Senate, September 25, 1837, and February 19, 1838] has been "virtually destroyed . . . by the rejection in your house of the specie clause, on which its whole superstructure was founded." Suggests that "A simple resolution by both houses (like the one of 1816 [Remark in Senate, March 24, 1838], excepting that it should be mandatory) directing the Secretary of the Treasury to receive (and to pay out again as far as it will be accepted) all the revenues of the Government in bills of specie paying banks of good standing, would enable all the banks instantly to resume [Comment in Senate, April 30, 1838], & within sixty days place the whole country in a state of prosperity equal to what it has ever enjoyed. This would leave the road open to the establishment of a National Bank [Speech in Senate, May 21, 1838] which I take it for granted we shall have after our next Congressional elections." Reports, in conclusion, that Whigs in the New York legislature seem to have "done nothing about the Presidency [Porter to Clay, November 14 and December 30, 1837]," probably because of "the confusion and ill temper which seemed to prevail in regard to several other exciting subjects." Copy. OHi.

Comment in Senate, April 23, 1838. On this day, Sen. James Buchanan (Pa.) spoke at length in favor of the administration's so-called "Resurrection Notes" bill [Remark in Senate, April 17, 1838], a speech that was recorded in the Appendix to the *Congressional Globe.* Clay answered him in a speech that was unrecorded and for which no manuscript version exists. Clay's answer was followed by "Mr. Buchanan's Reply to Mr. Clay," a lengthy document also printed in the Appendix to the *Globe.*

Given Buchanan's point by point refutation of Clay's remarks, those remarks can in part be reconstructed, viz:

Assures Buchanan that he had not planned to participate at all in this debate. Asks whether John Brockenbrough and Albert Gallatin could be constitutionally punished by Congress for reissuing the notes of the old Bank of the United States. Remarks facetiously that Buchanan "may hang Nick Biddle" if he pleases. Wonders why Buchanan chooses not to defend Nicholas Biddle, "a distinguished citizen" of the senator's own state. Points out that while the Bank of the United States no longer legally exists, its former officers continue as officers of the U.S. Bank of Pennsylvania ("a mere domestic institution of Pennsylvania"), and some of its branches continue to function. Argues that the bill is wholly unnecessary, and suggests that while the present United States Bank of Pennsylvania has no legal power to reissue the notes of the old Bank of the United States, reissue should be allowed "because these notes furnish the best and only universal currency in the Union." Argues further that the bill is unconstitutional, "the most enormous stretch of power he has ever known to be attempted"; shakes his head negatively when Buchanan charges that Clay's argument maintaining the unconstitutionality of the bill virtually denies that the government has the constitutional power to create another national bank. Given the fact that the Bank of the United States had assigned its property to individual trustees, asks whether Congress can force those trustees by law to wind up the institution's business. Maintains that while the power of Congress to create a national bank is a proper implied constitutional power, its power to terminate the bank's affairs demands embracing a second implied power; therefore, "to pass this bill would be piling implication upon implication . . . which cannot be done under the Constitution." Wonders if the Bank of England ceased to exist whether its agents in this country could reissue the institution's old notes without being punished. Inquires, "with a triumphant air," why it is that England and France are today prosperous "whilst we are embarrassed." Condemns the members of Van Buren's cabinet as men simply opposed to "the credit system of the country." *Cong. Globe*, 25 Cong., 2 Sess., 324; *ibid.*, Appendix, 309-10. Direct quotations herein are Buchanan's version of what Clay proportedly had said. For Albert Gallatin's strained relations with Biddle and his role in the resumption of specie payments issue and in the "Resurrection Notes" controversy, see Govan, *Nicholas Biddle*, 326-32.

Earlier this day, Clay presented evidence of the opposition of citizens of Cleveland, Ohio, to the Independent [Sub] Treasury bill [Speech in Senate, September 25, 1837, and February 19, 1838]. *Cong. Globe*, 25 Cong., 2 Sess., 323.

Remark in Senate, April 24, 1838. Presents a memorial from people of "all classes of society" urging the participation of the United States in an international copyright convention [Comment in Senate, February 2, 1837]. Asks his colleagues to move with dispatch on this proposal, since "everything that could be said or written on the subject had been exhausted." *Cong. Globe*, 25 Cong., 2 Sess., 326.

From JOSEPH GALES & WILLIAM W. SEATON Washington, *ca.*, April 25, 1838

1837

Feb.	18	To 100	Copies Mr. King's Speech[1]	$4.—
Oct.	7	" 25	do Nat[iona]l. Int[elligence]r. of date[2]	1.25
		To	Amount of inclosed bills	5.—
"	12	To 150	Copies own Speech[3]	4.50

1838					
Feb. 21	"	900	Cop. Speech Sub Treasury[4]		36.–
	"	350	" do Abolition[5]		8.75
Jan. 22	"	200	" Mr. Calhouns resolutions[6] 16 pges		20.–
	"	100	" Speech on abolition[7]—addl.		2.50
Mar. 15	"	200	" do on Sub Treasy[8]		8.–
	"	25	" Mr Johnsons Speech[9]		.62½
" 17	"	200	do Speech on Sub-Treas'y[10]		8.–
" 20	"	150	" ha[l]f Sheet N. Intr.[11]		3.75
" "	"	100	" Sub-Treasy Speech[12]		4.–
Apr 25	"	100	" do———do[13]		6.——
1837					
Mar–12	To Nat Int		from date to Mar 12. 1838.		$116.37½

AD. DLC-TJC (DNA, M212, R18). Bill for printing. Payment received by Thomas Donoho for Gales & Seaton. 1. Speech of John P. King (Ga.), Jan. 31, 1837, attacking the administration's public land (preemption) bill [8:873; Remark in Senate, Jan. 12, 1837]. *Cong. Globe*, 24 Cong., 2 Sess., 173-77. 2. The *Intelligencer* of Oct. 7, 1837, carried U.S. House speeches by Amasa J. Parker of N.Y. (in favor) and Waddy Thompson of S.C. (against) the "bill to postpone the fourth installment of the payment [of surplus revenue] to the States." 3. Probably Clay's speech of Sept. 25, 1837, attacking the administration's Sub-Treasury proposal. *Register of Debates*, 25 Cong., 1 Sess., 251-69. 4. Speech in Senate, Feb. 19, 1838. *Cong. Globe*, 25 Cong., 2 Sess., Appendix, 614-19. 5. *Speech of Henry Clay, of Kentucky, on Certain Resolutions Offered to the Senate of the United States in December, 1837, by Mr. Calhoun of South Carolina, Involving Principles of Interpretation of the Constitution of the United States; the Subject of the Abolition of Slavery in the District of Columbia and the Territories of the United States; and the Right of Petition on that Subject.* Washington, 1838. 6. Calhoun's six resolutions on various aspects of slavery. See Remark in Senate, Jan. 6, 1838. 7. See note 5. 8. See note 4. 9. Probably a reference to *Speech of William Cost Johnson . . . on Resolutions Which He had Offered Proposing to Appropriate Public Land for Educational Purposes, To All the States and Territories. Delivered in the House of Representatives . . . February, 1838.* Washington, 1838. 10. See note 4. 11. Probably a speech of Sen. William D. Merrick (Md.), carried in the *Intelligencer* on March 20, 1838, which highly praised Clay and vigorously opposed the Sub-Treasury bill. 12. See note 4. 13. *Ibid.*

Remark in Senate, April 25, 1838. Participates tangentially in debate on a bill to establish a board of commissioners to hear and investigate claims against the United States. Clay's comments are not recorded; but he voted against tabling the measure. *Cong. Globe*, 25 Cong., 2 Sess., 333-34. The bill, as amended, was passed 23 to 15 on April 26, Clay voting with the minority. It is printed in *ibid.*, 337.

To DAVID LEE CHILD Washington, April 28, 1838

In reply to your letter, I have to say that it is impossible to say beforehand whether Congress would or would not prolong the time allowed to foreigners to patent their inventions.[1] If you think proper to present a petition in behalf of Mr. Schuzenbach, it will afford me pleasure to offer it to the Senate, and to give to the Subject any attention in my power.[2]

I am obliged by your kind offer to communicate to me information respecting the new method of extracting Sugar from the Beet.[3] If I had leisure I should be glad to avail myself of it; but I must leave to those who have more youth enterprize and time to make these interesting experiments. They have my hearty good wishes for success; and from all I have seen & heard about the matter, I should think they will achieve it.

ALS. KyU. 1. Under the act of July 4, 1836, establishing the Patent Office, any alien who had resided in the U.S. for one year and who had declared his intention to become a U.S. citizen, as well as all persons who were already citizens, had to pay an application fee of $30 to file for a patent. However, subjects of Great Britain were charged a $500 fee and "all other persons" were charged $300. All patents were granted for a period of fourteen years with a possible extension of seven years. Also, "any citizen of the United States, or alien who shall have been resident in the United States one year next preceding, and shall have made oath of his intention to become a citizen thereof" could pay $20 for a caveat to protect an invention until he could perfect it. "And if application shall be made by any other person within one year from the time of filing such caveat, for a patent of any invention with which it may interfere," the commissioner of the Patent Office must notify the person who had filed the caveat. The person holding the caveat "shall, within three months after receiving the notice, if he would avail himself of the benefit of his caveat, file his description, specifications, drawings, and model." 5 *U.S. Stat.*, 117-25, espec. 121-22. 2. Clay presented no such petition. 3. Child, who had observed beet sugar production in France, sparked the effort in Northampton, Mass., in 1838 which produced the first beet sugar in the United States. The effort failed commercially, however, and the factory closed in 1841. U.S. Beet Sugar Association, *The Beet Sugar Story* (Washington, D C., 1959), 15.

To Thomas H. Clay, Lexington, April 29, 1838. Sends further instructions on shipping his hemp crop (bale rope) to Natchez via Maysville [Clay to Thomas H. Clay, April 3, 1838]. Asks for the results of the breeding of his jackasses. Adds in a postscript: "The news of the Virginia Elections so far is good [Clay to Porter, April 15, 1838]." ALS. DLC-HC (DNA, M212, R5).

To Nicholas Biddle, Philadelphia, April 30, 1838. Says "I want much to see you. I have a thousand things to say to you, most of them good, a few otherwise. I hope some how or some where to have the pleasure soon of meeting you." Reports that today in the Senate he presented a resolution that condemns discrimination "made as to the currency or medium of payment in the several branches of the Public Revenue, or in debts or dues to the Government"; it also requires the government's "reception and *disbursement*" of the notes of specie-paying private banks [Comment in Senate, April 30, 1838]. Remarks that "If it passes, it will afford you a fit occasion to resume [specie payments]. If rejected, it will cover your present position." ALS. James Biddle Family—Biddle Family Papers, Andalusia, Pa. Written in "S[enate]. Chamber."

From Damis L. Vigus, Lexington, April 28, 1838. As treasurer of Transylvania University, reports that "Our College drags heavily along with very slight prospects for improvement." Thanks him for his check for $300 "in full of Interest upon $10.000 (part of the Morrison fund) up to 1st. April 1838." Comments on Clay's "extreme punctuality in all pecuniary Matters," even though he is late with this payment. Notes that last December a committee of the Board of Trustees petitioned Congressman Richard Hawes of Winchester [Ky.] on the subject of a "donation of land to our institution," but nothing has come of it. Asks for a copy of Clay's speech on the Sub-Treasury issue [Speech in Senate, February 19, 1838] since the "detached parts" published in the local newspapers have been "unsatisfactory." Sees a good chance for a Whig victory in the next presidential election. ALS. DLC-TJC (DNA, M212, R14).

Comment in Senate, April 30, 1838. Reports that "Some of the banks in Boston and New York have in fact already resumed specie payments, and others are expected to follow that example in a few days." Asks Sen. Silas Wright (N.Y.), chairman of the Committee on Finance, if the administration has any intention to bring forth legislation, other than that already passed [Sub-Treasury bill] by the Senate [Speech in Senate, September 25, 1837, and February 19, 1838] and now lying in the House, "to aid and encourage the banks in that resumption." If not, and in the interest of aiding such banks, Clay offers the following just resolution:

"*Resolved by the Senate and House of Representatives of the United States of America in Congress assembled,* That no discrimination shall be made as to the currency or medium of payment in the several branches of the Public Revenue, or in debts or dues to the Government; and that, until otherwise ordered by Congress, the notes of sound banks which are payable and paid on demand in the legal currency of the United States, under suitable restrictions, to be forthwith prescribed and promulgated by the Secretary of the Treasury, shall be received in payment of the revenue and of debts and dues to the Government, and shall be subsequently disbursed, in course of public expenditure, to all public creditors who are willing to receive them." In response to a question from Sen. Felix Grundy (Tenn.) as to whether the resolution should not restrict the operation of such notes to banks in the vicinity in which they are to be received or disbursed, Clay remarks that this point is a "matter of detail" which the Senate can later discuss. Adds that his resolution does "not require the indiscriminate receipt of all notes," since in it the secretary of the treasury is given clear regulatory powers, and as a practical matter will receive only such notes "as the people [are] willing to accept in all parts of the country." *Cong. Globe*, 25 Cong., 2 Sess., 344. See also Comment in Senate, May 2, 1838. For the subsequent fate of Clay's April 30 resolution, see Remark in Senate, May 25 and 26, 1838. *Cong. Globe*, 25 Cong., 2 Sess., 411-13; also Clay to Southard, May 11, 1838.

Earlier this day, Clay presented a petition from the New York Peace Society, praying that an arbitrator be employed to adjust United States difficulties with Mexico; and asking that a congress of nations be established "for the purpose of settling difficulties which may arise among different nations, and for averting the evils of war." *Cong. Globe*, 25 Cong., 2 Sess., 344. The New York Peace Society (not to be confused with the one formed in 1815 and later disbanded) was formed in New York City in May, 1837, and for several months public meetings were held as often as once a week. About 150 persons joined. W. Freeman Galpin, *Pioneering for Peace: A Study of American Peace Efforts to 1846* (New York, 1933), 177-79, 187.

To JOEL R. POINSETT Washington, April 30, 1838

We are informed by letter from the Governor of Kentucky [James Clark] that the War Department now declines to comply with a contract, which, in March 1837, he, by the agency of Col. Richard M Johnson, and Major John Tilford, made with C[arey]. A. Harris Esq. Commissioner of Indian Affairs, for the sale of $250,000. of the Internal Improvement bonds of that State, to be paid for within the course of the next six months thereafter.

The failure of the Department to comply with that contract must be injurious to the State of Kentucky, and may probably arrest the prosecution of important works of internal improvements that are now in progress, and for the completion of which, this fund, among others, has been relied on and anticipated with certainty.

Under these circumstances the Governor feels greatly concerned, and has earnestly requested the undersigned to urge upon the department a fulfilment of its engagement with the State of Kentucky.

We persuade ourselves, Sir, that you will permit nothing Short of the most insuperable obstacles or objections to disappoint the just expectations of our State, or to prevent the faithful performance of the contract made with Her. Your answer,[1] we hope, will enable us to communicate to the Governor your assurance that it shall be complied with—[2]

LS. DNA, RG 75, Letters Received, Stocks, 1838, no. 643. Signed also by John J. Crittenden. 1. On May 8, 1838, Samuel Cooper, acting secretary of war, transmitted to Clay and Crittenden, in response to their letter of April 30, a report of the commissioner of Indian affairs on the issue "of carrying into effect the provisional arrangement made some time since by the Department, for the purchase of internal improvement bonds of the State of Kentucky." Copy. DNA, RG 75, Letters Sent, vol. 24, p. 163. 2. The Bureau of Indian Affairs was responsible for investing the trust funds which had been established by treaty for various Indian tribes, and they often used these funds to purchase state bonds. On March 9, 1837, C.A. Harris wrote Richard M. Johnson offering to buy $250,000 of Kentucky's bonds from Major John Tilford, the agent for the state; however on June 28, 1837, Harris notified the governor that "the general derangement of the pecuniary concerns of the country" had caused the War Department to be unable to fulfill this "provisional arrangement" made with Tilford. In October, Harris notified Tilford that the department might be able to fulfill its contract the following summer. On March 14, 1838, Gov. Clark gave James M. Bullock power of attorney to act as his agent in adjusting the sale with the War Department. When Bullock and Richard M. Johnson visited Harris on March 30, they were told that the department was still unable to complete the purchase due to a lack of funds. *Letterbook of Gov. James Clark 1836-1839*, pp. 27, 32-33, 35, 39-40, 59-60, 63-64, 65, 67-69, 129-30, 132-35, 150-51 in Ky. State Library & Archives. See also George D. Harmon, "The Indian Trust Funds, 1797-1865," *MVHR* (June, 1934), 21:23, 24, 27-28.

From Joseph Boulanger, American & French Restaurant, Washington, May 1, 1838. Submits four bills for food and drink, mostly drink, all dated May 1, viz: February 26, 1838: Dinner for sixteen ($80.), four bottles of sherry ($8.), four bottles of Madeira ($8.), six bottles of champagne ($12.), two bottles of claret ($4.), four decks of playing cards ($2.), three glasses of "Whiskey-Punches" (.37½), one dozen "Segars" (.37½). Total: $114.75. March 30: Dinner for twelve ($36.), eight bottles of champagne ($16.), two bottles of Madeira ($5.), two bottles of sherry ($4.), six decks of playing cards ($3.), tea (.50). Total: $64.50. AD. DLC-TJC (DNA, M212, R18). For two lesser bills of same date, see *ibid.*

On June 28, 1838, Senators Clay and William C. Preston (S.C.) were joint hosts of a dinner for 16, at which 8 bottles of champagne and 12 bottles of Madeira and Sherry were consumed. Total cost was $86.50, viz: 16 dinners @$3.00 each ($48) and the balance for drink. Boulanger to Clay and Preston, bill and receipt, June 29, 1838. AD. & ADS. *Ibid.*

From LEWIS TAPPAN New York, May 1, 1838

Without consulting with any individual I have thought it well to address a few lines to you about the presidential election. For ten years past I have abstained from all *partyism* in politics, and voted for those I deemed the best men irrespective of the party to which they belonged. The abolitionists will, I think, act on this principle generally. In order to obtain their votes the respective parties will be obliged to put up candidates they can conscientiously vote for. Acting independently, and being an increasing association, they will, ere long, decide the elections in the free States, without being a political party. Dr. [Eliphalet] Nott,[1] President of Union College, N.Y. told me a few days since, that in his opinion the abolitionists can now decide the elections in every county in this State West of Albany, & that the editors of the political papers know it. In Rhode Island the abolitionists recently decided the election.[2] They can decide the next election in this city.

I have no doubt a majority of the abolitionists prefer you to Mr Van Buren, in many respects, especially since the infamous pledge given by him in his inaugural speech,[3] but they will not, I believe, ever vote for a man, however distinguished in other respects, who is a slaveholder and the President of the Colonization Society, certainly not unless they are assured he will go for immediate emancipation in the District of Columbia, and relinquish all connexion with the Soc. mentioned. You will not be offended I am sure with this honest freedom of expression.

I respectfully submit these thoughts to you, for your consideration. The abolitionists throughout the country meet by their delegates in this city this week[4] & the begining of the next. They will discuss the proper action for them to take in the ensuing great election. If you deem it best to express any sentiments on the above subject I shall be happy to receive them under such restrictions as you see fit to impose.

In the great fire of Dec. 16/35[5] I lost all the letters received from you, which I regretted.

ALS. DLC-HC (DNA, M212, R5). 1. For Nott—educator, inventor, theologian, and abolitionist—see *DAB*. 2. In the Rhode Island gubernatorial election of April 18, 1838, William Sprague, the Whig candidate, defeated John B. Francis, the Democratic candidate, by a vote of 3,984 to 3,504. Joseph Childs (Whig) was elected lieutenant governor over Benjamin B. Thurston (Democrat) by 4,138 votes to 3,461. *BDGUS*, 4:1340. In the fall elections for the state legislature, the Whigs won all 11 senate seats and 46 house seats. The Democrats won 25 house seats and the conservatives 1. *Niles' Register* (Oct. 6, 1838), 55:82. 3. Van Buren had pledged that he would be an "uncompromising opponent of every attempt on the part of Congress to abolish slavery in the District of Columbia against the wishes of the slaveholding States, and also with a determination equally decided to resist the slightest interference with it in the States where it exists." *MPP*, 3:318-19. 4. The fifth annual meeting of the American Anti-Slavery Society met at the Broadway Tabernacle in New York City on May 2-3, 7-8, 1838. Lewis Tappan called the meeting to order. The chief source of debate was a proposal to amend the organization's constitution by deleting a clause in article 2 which stated "that each state in which slavery exists has by the Constitution of the United States, the exclusive right to legislate in regard to its abolition in that state." This proposal failed. The convention also appointed a political action committee which later in the year drew up a statement of abolitionist political principles. New York *The Emancipator*, May 10, 17, 1838; Betty Fladeland, *James Gillespie Birney: Slaveholder to Abolitionist* (Ithaca, N.Y., 1955), 178-79. 5. See 8:816-17.

From Nicholas Biddle, Philadelphia, May 2, 1838. Thanks him for his letter of April 30. Continues: "Your resolution [Comment in Senate, April 30, 1838] will do good if it fails—and more good if it succeeds. It would have certainly succeeded—and you would have had the fame of settling this question added to the glory of your former pacifications, but for this political defection in New York. While you were declaring, justly, in your place, that there could be no resumption until the Govt. changed its course—those who are regarded as your exclusive friends cross your path by announcing that they will resume whether the Govt. does or does not change its course. This seems to be an absolute unconditional surrender at discretion. It will require all your acknowledged skill to make these raw militia—these inconstant volunteers—stand against the discipline of their adversaries." Copy. DLC-Nicholas Biddle Papers (DNA, M212, R20). For Biddle's difficulties with New York bankers on the question of resumption of specie payments, see Porter to Clay, April 17, 1838.

Comment in Senate, May 2, 1838. Defends his resolution of April 30 [Remark in Senate, April 30, 1838] requiring the government to accept in payment from its debtors notes issued by sound [specie-paying] private banks. Opposes a motion by

Sen. Silas Wright (N.Y.), chairman of the Committee on Finance, to refer this resolution to his committee. Argues that referral is unnecessary because the principle of the resolution is "so simple that every Senator could comprehend it." States that the time has come to "signify to the whole country that there was no intention to persevere in a course of discrimination with regard to the money to be received in payment of the revenue." Responds to Wright's observation that the notes of the New York and Boston banks that have resumed specie payment are being accepted by collectors of customs and by post offices, and that Clay's resolution is therefore unnecessary. Explains that the New York banks have, under state law, no choice but to resume specie payments by May 10, regardless of "their ability to resume." But what the banks now need, he continues, "is some security in the shape of law, designating the medium in which the dues should be paid," rather than leaving this determination to the secretary of the treasury and postmaster general as provided by current law [Speech in Senate, January 11, 1837]. Notes that if customs collectors and postmasters are indeed accepting the notes of specie-paying banks, they are doing so outside the existing law, a situation his resolution seeks to correct.

Argues once again that "nothing but the establishment of a National Bank" can effectively "remedy the evils of a disordered currency." Points out that, save for a few banks in New York and New Jersey, no others have "admitted their readiness to resume"; claims that banks in Tennessee, Arkansas, and Mississippi "would not be ready under two years." Maintains that "under the present deposite system, without the agency of a United States Bank, if [some banks] did resume they could not continue for any length of time." Reaffirms his support for a Bank of the United States [Comment in Senate, September 26, 1837; Speech in Senate, May 21, 1838] and wishes it "so pronounced, so understood, that every man, woman, and child, should know it." Charges that referral to Wright's committee, "a majority of whom were known to be decidedly hostile, would be contrary to all parliamentary usage." *Cong. Globe*, 25 Cong., 2 Sess., Appendix, 294-96. The motion to refer passed 28-19, Clay voting nay. See also *Cong. Globe*, 25 Cong., 2 Sess., 352. For the resumption of specie payments by New York banks on May 10, as required by state law, and the subsequent repeal of the Specie Circular [Speech in Senate, January 11, 1837; Remark in Senate, January 14, 1837; Comment in Senate, March 7, 1838] on May 30, see *Cong. Globe*, 25 Cong., 2 Sess., 415-17, 421; Hammond, *Banks and Politics in America*, 489; Sharp, *Jacksonians Versus the Banks*, 287-88.

The "current law" under which the secretary of the treasury had discretion to determine the medium in which government debts might be paid was the act of April 30, 1816, called "A Resolution Relative to the More Effectual Collection of the Public Revenue." 3 *U.S. Stat.*, 343. The postmaster general had simply assumed the same right, since, legally, the Post Office Department was under the Treasury Department from its inception. John McLean, postmaster general from 1823-29, started the practice of reporting directly to the president. In 1829 Jackson made the postmaster general an official cabinet member, after which the Post Office Department was operated as a virtually autonomous institution. Gerald Cullinan, *The Post Office Department* (New York, 1968), 26, 28; Henry B. Learned, *The President's Cabinet; Studies in the Origin, Formation and Structure of an American Institution* (New Haven, 1912), 237, 249.

To JOHN AGG — Washington, May 4, 1838

I received your note, dated the 1st inst. & feel greatly obliged for the friendly sentiments towards me which it expresses. In respect to the new paper, to which you refer, I have, myself, nothing whatever to do. I know that it has been in the contemplation of our political friends, for some time past, to establish an additional paper at this place, & I believe such a purpose is still entertained. I understand that Mr. [William D.] Merrick, of the Senate, & Mr. [Rice] Garland, of Louisiana, are two of the Committee charged with attending to that business, but I am unadvised of what progress they have made.[1]

LS. ViU. 1. Clay to Hamilton, Oct. 25, 1837.

To JOHN M. CLAYTON Wilmington, [May 8, 1838]

I was greatly grieved, my dear friend, to hear which, for the first time, I did this morning, of the sad accident[1] which befel[l] you last night; and I could not but reproach myself with having been, in some measure, the cause, although the innocent cause of it. It would not have happened if I could have gone to New Castle, as I wished to have done, to see you, and as I should have done but for the indisposition under which I labored. The continuance of the same cause (for my cold is worse to day) prevents my presenting my regrets to you in person, and the expression, at the same time, of the high degree of satisfaction which I feel at your escape without any personal injury. I hope that your friends and your Coachman will soon recover from the slight injuries which I understand they received. The latter person feels his with more sensibility, no doubt, in consequence of some omission on his part to see that the Horses were properly harnessed.

I remain in the House today and have taken Medicine to try and get myself well enough to make tomorrow my excursion to Philada. On my return, or, if I am unable to go, prior to my return to Washn. I will make it a point to see you. . . .

ALS. ViU. Addressed to Clayton at New Castle, Del. 1. For the political conference between Clay and Clayton in Wilmington and the carriage accident Clayton suffered during his return to New Castle, see Richard A. Wire, "John M. Clayton and the Search for Order: A Study in Whig Politics and Diplomacy," Ph.D. dissertation, University of Maryland, 1971, pp. 134-35.

To THOMAS HART CLAY Wilmington, May 11, 1838

Your two letters of the 29h. & 30h. Ulto. found me here, whither I had come to pass a few quiet days to recover from fatigue and cold

I am truly surprized and disappointed as to the neglect of John [S.] Hart[1] to manufacture our hemp. I expected better things of John. It is very bad treatment. He has served me exactly as his brother Thomas[2] did, and in both cases it has been by putting aside my work to do their uncle Hunts.[3] I wish you to tell John how much I have been disappointed & mortified by him. I have made a positive contract to deliver the Rope at Natchez; and I wish you to go and see John and if there be any doubt about the manufacture of the Hemp by the 10h. of June or in a short time thereafter, I wish you to engage some other person to manufacture it and have the Hemp removed. If I am obliged to do this it is the *last* transaction I will ever have with John. I will not be trifled with again[4]

I am glad to hear that Allegrante has a filly foal. I have purchased from Govr [James] Barbour his interest in the Stock[5] at $500 to be paid for next Xmas. You may have it and pay for it out of your Bale Rope sold at Natchez. You may take the mare & Colt to keep at your place, or the yearling filly. I think I wrote to have her sent to Eclipse. Great care should be taken with her foal in sending her. The death of Bertrand adds value to it.

The Wickliffe mare may be sent to Woodpecker, whose owner has promised me a Season.

You may borrow of Ben Warfield[6] Hemp enough to make up the 16 tons if there be any deficiency in ours.[7]

My love to Mary [Mentelle Clay].

ALS. DLC-HC (DNA, M212, R5). 1. John S. Hart (1804-38), Lucretia Hart Clay's nephew, who was struck by lightning and killed on July 20, 1838. He had married Anna Marie Allee of Lexington on May 21, 1835. He was the son of Thomas, Jr., and Eleanor Grosh Hart. 2. Thomas Pindell Hart. 3. John Wesley Hunt, husband of Catherine Grosh Hunt who was sister to Eleanor Grosh (Mrs. Thomas Hart, Jr.). 4. On Sept. 24, 1838, Clay paid Richard Pindell, administrator of the estate of John S. Hart, his wife's recently deceased nephew, for the following hemp goods [Clay to Henry Clay, Jr., September 8, 1837] and services delivered on July 17, 1838: for spinning 12,136 lbs. of hemp @1.5¢ per pound—$182.04; for the purchase of 4,811 lbs. of rope @7.5¢ per pound—$350.82 [*sic*, $360.82]; for spinning 14,070 lbs. of rope from T.H. Clay @1.5¢—$210.05 [*sic*, $211.05]; for 100 lbs. of bale rope—$70.00. Total: $812.91 [*sic*, $823.91]. ADS. DLC-TJC (DNA, M212, R18). On October 5, 1838, January & Huston, forwarding merchants in Maysville, Ky., informed Clay that "the quantity of Rope recd the last Summer" from him was 308 coils. ALS. *Ibid.* For the financial details of the forwarding of Clay's coils to Natchez, see Clay's account with January & Huston, October 5, 1838, in *ibid.* 5. See 8:757. 6. See 1:305. 7. Clay to Thomas H. Clay, April 3, 1838.

To SAMUEL L. SOUTHARD Wilmington, May 11, 1838

I thank you for your letter, which I found here on my return yesterday afternoon from Philada. Without being confined, I have been quite unwell since I have been here with my cold which was increased by my journey hither. I feel better this bright morning than I have done since I left the City, and I think that one or two days more will restore my health. I shall therefore not return to Washington until monday. I suppose that the loss of two days by the death of Mr. Lawler[1] will have prevented much being done this week. I hope to learn by the mail to day whether Mr. [Silas] Wright has reported the Currency Resolution, and for what day it is assigned.[2] My best respects to the Ladies & Gentlemen of the Mess.[3]

ALS. NjP. 1. Joab Lawler, representative from Alabama, died on May 8. *Cong. Globe*, 25 Cong., 2 Sess., 357. 2. Comment in Senate, April 30, 1838. Clay's resolution of April 30 was read a second time on May 2 and was referred to Wright's Committee on Finance by a 28 to 19 vote, Clay voting nay. On May 16, Wright reported the bill back to the Senate without committee recommendation; and on May 25 and 26, during debate on on the issue, Clay sacrificed his resolution as part of a parliamentary maneuver by Webster that repealed the Specie Circular [Comment in Senate, May 2, 1838] instead. *Cong. Globe*, 25 Cong., 2 Sess., 352, 378, 411-13. 3. During the 25th Cong., 2 Sess., Clay lived at Mrs. S.A. Hill's boarding house. So too did Senators John J. Crittenden and Samuel L. Southard; also Representatives Thomas Corwin (Ohio), William Graves (Ky.), Richard Hawes (Ky.), William L. May (Ill.), and Richard H. Menifee (Ky.). Goldman and Young, *United States Congressional Directories*, 330.

To Fortescue Whittle, [probably Norfolk, Va.], May 15, 1838. Thanks him for his friendly letter. Says he has deplored for a long time "the infatuation and delusion which have sustained, so unfortunately, Genl. Jackson in his reckless course," but now sees brighter political prospects ahead. Adds: "I cordially congratulate you on the occasion [Porter to Clay, April 15, 1838]; and sincerely hope that we shall both live to witness our Government once more confided to honest and faithful hands. Whether I shall be called to the station or not, which your friendly wishes indicate, is a matter of subordinate consideration. On that question, I intend to take no part, but to remain in a perfectly passive position, content with whatever may be the pleasure of those who alone have a right to decide it." ALS. ViU. Fortescue Whittle, who had immigrated to the United States from County Antrim, Ireland and had opened an import/export business in Norfolk, was the father of Dr. Conway D. Whittle. Information supplied by personnel of the Alderman Library, University of Virginia.

From T.R. Newbold, Philadelphia, May 16, 1838. Writes in his capacity as secretary of the Executive Committee of the [Clay] Central Committee which his Philadelphia friends had formed on April 7. Asks Clay for any communication he may wish to send the committee. ALS. DLC-TJC (DNA, M212, R10). The author of this letter is probably Thomas Ross Newbold who in 1839 became the editor of the Philadelphia *North American*, a protectionist newspaper. *PMHB*, 64:345.

Remark in Senate, May 16, 1838. With reference to printing the Senate Finance Committee's "very voluminous report" on his resolution of April 30 [Comment in Senate, April 30, 1838], a report which "unfairly" cast his resolution aside, announces that he will nonetheless vote to print any number of the committee's report that the Senate desires. Criticizes Sen. Silas Wright (N.Y.), chairman of the committee, for his "unparliamentary" behavior in taking no specific action on his [Clay's] April 30 resolution. Charges the administration with thus attempting to suppress his resolution altogether, even though the "subject was one of such thrilling interest to the whole community." *Cong. Globe*, 25 Cong., 2 Sess., 378. A motion to print 30,000 copies of the Finance Committee report passed 23-19, Clay voting nay. A second motion, to debate Clay's April 30 resolution on May 21, also passed. *Ibid.*, 379.

Remark in Senate, May 17, 1838. Participates at several points in the debate on extending the charters of the private banks in the District of Columbia, as provided in the so-called District Bank bill [Remark in Senate, December 13, 1837; Comment in Senate, December 21, 1837]; his remarks were not recorded. Votes, however, to table the bill. *Cong. Globe*, 25 Cong., 2 Sess., 382.

To THOMAS HART CLAY Washington, May 18, 1838

I am greatly concerned about the Bale Rope. I would not on any account disappoint Dr. [Stephen] Duncan, or fail to comply with my contract.[1] I have received a letter from John [S.] Hart, but it is not satisfactory. I do not think that he has treated me well. He ought, when the Hemp was first delivered, to have said that he could not manufacture it, if he preferred working for his uncle Hunt,[2] or at least have said when he could do it, and then we could have made some other arrangement.

I wish you to do the best you can to have it speedily wrought up, and let me know on what I am to depend. If the Dr. is to be disappointed, I desire to let him know.

John [Morrison Clay] arrived the day before yesterday, and left me yesterday for Princeton.[3]

Is the white Cow that I sold to Blackburn likely to have a Ca[l]f or what is her condition?

My love to Mary [Mentelle Clay].

ALS. DLC-HC (DNA, M212, R5). 1. Clay to Thomas H. Clay, April 3, 1838. 2. John Wesley Hunt. See Clay to Thomas H. Clay, May 11, 1838. 3. Clay to Henry Clay, Jr., Sept. 8, 1837; Clay to James B. Clay, Jan. 22, 1838.

Remark in Senate, May 18, 1838. Questions the speed with which Silas Wright's Committee on Finance considered and reported the bill from the House authorizing "the issuing of Treasury notes to meet the current expenses of the Government [Comment in Senate, September 15, 1837; Speech in Senate, September 25, 1837]." Wonders whether Wright's committee "had authority from the Senate to meet while the Senate was in session." *Cong. Globe*, 25 Cong., 2 Sess., 384.

To LUCRETIA HART CLAY Washington, May 21, 1838

John [Morrison Clay] arrived here the wednesday after he left home and proceeded the next day to Princeton, in good health and spirits.[1] I am very happy to learn from Thomas [Hart Clay] that he conducted himself with perfect propriety, whilst at home, and I have endeavored to encourage him to persevere in the same way. He tells me that you will shortly be in want of money. I send you enclosed a check for $150 and if I should be detained here longer than I anticipate, I will before my return send you another. It is uncertain when Congress will adjourn; and the subjects, the definitive decision of which I thought would admit of my returning before the adjournment, are not yet finally acted upon.

I received a letter the other day from Lucretia [Clay Erwin] and from Mrs Smith.[2] She was quite well and in good spirits. Mrs. Smith speaks favorably of her in every respect, except the difficulty of her fixing her attention upon her studies. This I hope she will overcome.

I feel much anxiety to leave here and go home. The length of the Session has worn me down. Be assured my dear wife that I will join you as soon as I possibly can consistently with my public duties.

ALS. Courtesy of Mr. M. W. Anderson, Lexington, Ky. 1. Clay to Henry Clay, Jr., Sept. 8, 1837; Clay to James B. Clay, Jan. 22, 1838. 2. For Harriet Staples Douglas (Mrs. Benjamin Bosworth) Smith, who ran a school for young ladies on the premises of the Episcopal Seminary in Lexington, see Francis K. Swinford and Rebecca S. Lee, *The Great Elm Tree, Heritage of the Episcopal Diocese of Lexington* (Lexington, 1969), 102-3, 143. The reference to Lucretia is to Lucretia Clay Erwin (1830-66) who was the daughter of James and the deceased Anne Brown Clay Erwin. She is incorrectly referred to as Lucretia *Hart* Erwin in Zachary F. Smith and Mary Rogers Clay, *The Clay Family* (Louisville, 1899), 177, an error repeated herein in 7:591; 8:429, 434, 451, and 809. She later married Frederic Cowles. See Clay to Lucretia Clay Erwin, March 24, 1843.

Speech in Senate, May 21, 1838. Following the presentation of a citizens' petition to establish a Bank of the United States [Comment in Senate, September 26, 1837], Clay launches into a description of the features which a national bank should have if a new one were ever again to be chartered by Congress. Asserts that it should not simply be the U.S. Bank of Pennsylvania, with Nicholas Biddle at its head, reconstituted as the third Bank of the United States. The new bank must possess the power to establish branches; it should be capitalized at about $50,000,000; the stock should be divided between the "General Government, the States according to their federal population, and individual subscribers," the latter acquiring stock either at auction or by private subscription; non-resident foreigners should be prohibited from holding, directly or indirectly, any stock in the corporation or having any role in its administration; "an adequate portion" of its capital should be set apart in productive stocks and "placed in permanent security, beyond the reach of the corporation" so as to safeguard the integrity of its circulating paper bills and notes; full and open publicity about all aspects of its operation should be permitted, including regular "public inspection"; dividends must be limited to the amount necessary to "check undue expansions in the circulating medium, and restrain improper extension of business in the administration of the bank"; it should charge a rate of interest no higher than five to six percent; it should restrict to a maximum of one and a half percent the premium demanded on post notes and checks used for remittances; finally, there must be a complete separation of the bank and its executives from "interference in the popular elections," even though in the past there was no evidence of such interference by the old bank, save to "exercise the natural right of self-defense" in the face of unjust attacks.

Asserts at some length that the constitutional power to charter such a bank is above question. States, however, that he has no intention of offering any formal resolution to establish a national bank at this time. Indeed, "it would be an unnecessary waste of time to offer such a proposal." Believes that a majority of the people want a new national bank, but agrees that there is no "conclusive evidence" of this sentiment. Because this is so, "Let us wait until demonstrations of their will shall be clearly given." *Cong. Globe*, 25 Cong., 2 Sess., 396-97.

To JOHN LEEDS KERR Washington, May 22, 1838

I have received your[1] friendly letter of the 19h. inst. I share with you in the gratification which the course of late political events justly affords. We have great reason now to hope that the doom of the party in power is irrevocably fixed, and that better and brighter times are opening upon our Country. I rejoice in the prospect, and shall be most happy to see it realized, whatever may be my own personal fortunes. With these, as far as an opinion can be formed from numerous spontaneous indications, I have every reason to be satisfied and I am entirely satisfied.

After much consideration, I resolved to take a position of perfect passiveness in respect to the next Presidential election, without making any personal exertion to attract or fix public attention on myself. That resolution, I think is founded in principle. It would, you will perceive my dear Sir, be a departure from it, if I were to make any excursions with the object of meeting large portions of my fellow Citizens, however gratifying it might be to me personally. This observation is made in consequence of your suggestion that, if I could accept your kind invitation, I should have an opportunity of meeting a number of our friends in your quarter of Maryland. I am greatly obliged by your invitation, and should be most happy to be able to accept it; but I have recently returned from a visit of recreation which I made to Delaware, and I fear that my public duties will not allow me to enjoy a similar satisfaction; during the present Session. If, contrary to my present impressions, I shall have it in my power to visit you, I will do so with great pleasure, and, in that contingency, we will give you notice.

ALS. KyLoF. 1. For Kerr, see 8:726.

Remark in Senate, May 23, 1838. Asks if orders have been issued from the Post Office and Treasury departments "to receive for Government dues the notes of specie-paying banks [Comment in Senate, April 30 and May 2, 1838]." Offers a resolution requiring the treasury secretary and postmaster general to provide this information. If these two government agencies are accepting the notes of specie-paying banks, Clay wants to know under what specific instructions and by what authority. Resolution passes without dissent. *Cong. Globe*, 25 Cong., 2 Sess., 407. See also Remark in Senate, May 24, 1838.

To John Forsyth, Washington, May 24, 1838. States that the secretary of the Historical Society of Kentucky has asked him to "apply for any state papers or public documents to which that Institution may be entitled." Suggests that they be sent to Louisville in care of Dr. Edward Jarvis, librarian of the society. LS. DNA, RG59, Misc. Letters.

On May 28, Secretary of State Forsyth responded that he would need to know the date of incorporation of the society before forwarding copies of "such works as that Society may be entitled to." LS. PPPrHi.

On May 30, Clay wrote the secretary of the society in Louisville asking him to send along a copy of the act of incorporation of the organization. ALS. *Ibid.*

The Kentucky Historical Society had been started in Frankfort in 1836. The following year it was moved to Louisville and its incorporation by the legislature was approved on February 16, 1838. The corresponding secretary in 1838 was Leonard Bliss, Jr., and the recording secretary was Wilkins Tannehill [8:565]. It is unclear to which of these men Clay was writing on May 30. Willard Rouse Jillson, *A Sketch and Bibliography of the Kentucky Historical Society 1836-1943* (Frankfort, 1943), 9, 11; Ky. Gen. Assy., *Acts* . . . 1837-1838, pp. 269-71. For Edward Jarvis, a physician who practiced in Louisville from 1837 to 1843, see *DAB*.

Remark in Senate, May 24, 1838. In response to Clay's resolution, "recently offered [Comment in Senate, April 30, 1838]," the secretary of the treasury reports that his department's acceptance of bank notes stems from "previous orders, and of the resumption of specie payments by certain banks." The secretary specifically reveals that a letter to public officials in New York, dated April 23, 1838, sanctioned the receipt of notes from specie-paying banks "not issuing notes of less than $5, according to orders and instructions given previous to the suspension of specie payments [Speech in Senate, January 11, 1837]." Clay moves that this communication from Secretary Levi Woodbury be tabled and printed, as it was; adds that collectors of customs in New York are now receiving notes from specie-paying banks and that he has been informed that on the resumption of specie payments "the notes of specie-paying banks were to be received and disbursed in payment of the public dues." *Cong. Globe*, 25 Cong., 2 Sess., 409. For the repeal of the Specie Circular on May 30, 1838, see Comment in Senate, May 2, 1838; Remark in Senate, May 29, 1838.

From Peter B. Porter, New York, May 25, 1838. Reports that "your friends here are to hold a meeting on Tuesday next, to express their preference among the Presidential candidates, but submitting, at the same time, their wishes, to the ultimate decision of the national convention. The meeting will be held at Castle Garden, and, if I mistake not, will be a splendid affair—notwithstanding the efforts of the friends of the other candidates, first to put it down, and then to throw cold water on it—and will present to the whole country a warm and enthusiastic display of the public sentiment of this metropolis in your favour." Recalls that Webster's friends called a similar meeting a year ago [Clay to Letcher, May 30, 1837], discovered that public sentiment was not ready for the launching of Webster's candidacy, and "have ever since been systematically engaged in efforts to defer any expression of public opinion to the latest possible period—trusting to management or accident for a change more favourable to their views [Schermerhorn to

Clay, February 25, 1838]. These gentlemen combined for the purpose of preventing any expressions (and especially Legislative expressions in the States known to be friendly to you) in favour of any candidate, and in this they have but too well succeeded." Notes that the Webster people in New York City are "labouring to discourage the Castle Garden meeting and render it unpopular—not from any personal objection to you but because it will have a tendency to divide and distract the Whig party." Asks Clay his view on the "expediency" of meetings designed to advance his candidacy, but notes in the same breath that "it is perhaps best" that such views "not be publicly known." Says he himself will not attend the Castle Garden meeting on May 29. This is because he lives in a "remote part of the state" and does not want to be thought of as a "traveling partizan." Adds: "Meanwhile rest assured that your cause is constantly gaining ground in the State." Alerts him to the fact that his New York friends will soon invite him, John J. Crittenden, and "your other western friends" to a "*Barbecue* (in Southern style) in the neighborhood of the city, say in the 'Elysian Fields' at Hoboken." Urges them all to attend this "most splendid affair" if it is held, since it will accomplish much political good "particularly in this State and N. Jersey." Copy. OHi. Written to Clay from the Astor House in New York City.

The Clay meeting was held on May 29, 1838, not at Castle Garden, but at the Masonic Hall in New York City with Gulian C. Verplanck serving as its chairman. Resolutions were adopted calling for a national convention in Harrisburg in December, 1839, recommending Clay as the Whig candidate, opposing the Sub-Treasury system proposal, and praising the Conservative Democrats [Clay to Henry Clay, Jr., January 28, 1837] who also attended this convention. Washington *Daily National Intelligencer*, June 1, 2, 1838. Verplanck later wrote Clay inviting him to come to New York at the end of the congressional session, but Clay declined. There was, therefore, no barbecue in Hoboken's "Elysian Fields." See Clay to Verplanck, June 8, 1838.

Remark in Senate, May 25, 1838. In an unrecorded speech, supports "at length" his resolution of April 30 [Comment in Senate, April 30, 1838], as amended by Sen. Daniel Webster on May 16. The amendment, to which Clay assented, and which he supported, struck out the first clause of his [Clay's] resolution and substituted for it the following: "That it shall not be lawful for the Secretary of the Treasury to make, or to continue in force, any general order which shall create any difference between the different branches of revenue, as to the money or medium of payment, in which debts or dues, accruing to the United States, may be paid." Following the adoption of the language of Webster's amendment, which virtually repealed the Specie Circular [Comment in Senate, March 7 and May 2, 1838], Clay moves to strike out the last clause of his April 30 resolution. *Cong. Globe*, 25 Cong., 2 Sess., 411. See, further, Remark in Senate, May 26, 1838. For later disagreement between Clay and Webster over primary credit for having effected the repeal of the Specie Circular, see Clay to Porter, June 3 and 9, 1838.

Remark in Senate, May 26, 1838. Speaks [not recorded] to his motion of May 25 to strike out the last clause of his resolution of April 30, as amended [Comment in Senate, April 30, 1838; Remark in Senate, May 25, 1838]. Motion carried 44 to 1. Votes nay on Sen. Silas Wright's motion to strike out the second clause of his April 30 resolution, that section "which makes the reception of bank notes imperative." Motion carries 28 to 19. *Cong. Globe*, 25 Cong., 2 Sess., 412. Given these two actions, all that remained of Clay's April 30 resolution was Webster's May 25 substitute for its first clause, an amendment which in effect repealed the Specie Circular [Comment in Senate, May 2, 1838]. See Remark in Senate, May 25, 1838.

From Nicholas Biddle, Philadelphia, May 28, 1838. Remarks that "If Your resolution [Comment in Senate, April 30, 1838; Remark in Senate, May 26, 1838] passes, as I trust it will, even altho' limited to the virtual repeal of the Specie Circular [Comment in Senate, May 2, 1838; Remark in Senate, May 25 and 26, 1838], it will be very desirable that your friends should unite in urging it thro' the House as early as practicable." Believes its passage "will furnish sufficient motive for taking immediate steps for an early resumption [of specie payments]." Copy. DLC-Nicholas Biddle Papers (DNA, M212, R20). For the repeal of the Specie Circular on May 30, see Comment in Senate, May 2, 1838; Remark in Senate, May 29, 1838.

To ALEXANDER HAMILTON Washington, May 28, 1838

I have received several letters from you lately, which I did not acknowledge, because their contents did not seem to require a particular reply, and you know how much I am constantly occupied.

The object of this letter is to request you to obtain for me, in your own name, a copy of a late number of the Emancipator,[1] in which it avows its purpose to oppose me, if I should be a Candidate, and to support Mr. V. Buren, for the Presidency.

The Treasury Circular will be rescinded,[2] but the part of my resolution which directs the receipt of the notes of Specie paying Banks, in discharge of public dues, has been stricken out[3] by a strictly party vote.[4]

ALS. DLC-HC (DNA, M212, R5). Written in "S[enate]. Chamber." 1. New York *The Emancipator*, April 19, 1838. 2. Comment in Senate, May 2, 1838; Remark in Senate, May 26, 1838. 3. By a 28 to 19 margin. See Remark in Senate, May 26, 1838; also Comment in Senate, April 30, 1838. 4. On the back of Clay's letter, Hamilton wrote an undated comment: "A good autograph and an American endorsement of these inconsistencies of party principles. At the present moment it is worse than idle to talk of a speedy return to specie payments, the course of the treasury notes has to fix on some prospective progress of contraction, looking to the development of the progress of the future as the best guide—There should be no effort to force a system of results, the public mind must be kept at rest as the best almost the only way to inspire and preserve fiscal confidence—The establishment of any measures, tending to a sudden contraction, could not fail to be productive of injurious results in all our foreign and domestic financial relations; in self-defence, European capitalists would be compelled to withdraw their investments in our public funds &c &c."

To PETER B. PORTER Washington, May 28, 1838

I recd. your favor of the 26h. [*sic*, 25th] inst. You will have seen that the part of the resolution which I introduced,[1] in conformity with your views, relating to the receipt of the notes of Specie paying banks has been stricken out by a party vote.[2] Some of those who voted that way told me that they did so because they were confident that the very thing which I proposed would be done under the resolution of 1816.[3] It was in vain that I urged with all the force I could, that the matter ought not to be left to Executive discretion but should be regulated by positive law. We shall now see what they will do. The part of the resolution which regards the repeal of the Treasury Circular will, I anticipate, pass the Senate by a large majority.[4]

You will have seen that I threw out an idea in respect to a new Bank of the U.S.[5] My main object, in the movement, was to detach the Whig cause from Mr. Biddles bank. What has been the reception of it? I have been misunderstood in the supposition that I intended to indicate Mr. [Albert] Gallatin as the President of the new bank. I spoke of his financial skill without any such purpose. Our opponents have been chagrined that

I would not specify any place for the location of the Bank. I considered that a subordinate question, which belonged to the details of a bill, when one should be formally presented.

I have seen an account of the meeting of my friends which is intended to be held in the City tomorrow.[6] I have had, of course, nothing to do in originating or organizing it. I am quite sure of the friendly purposes with which it has been got up. There can be no doubt that the more there may be spontaneous demonstrations of popular feeling and opinion, on this subject, the greater will be the probability of ultimate union and co-operation, provided always that these meetings are conducted in a spirit not exclusive or intolerant. This is my judgment, whoever may be the object of the general preference.

Our cause has been making a steady and successful progress ever since the commencement of the Session, throughout the whole Union as far as I can judge. I do not believe that Mr V. Buren can, at this time, certainly count upon two States in the Union. There is not one Western, Southern, or South Western State that is not positively against him (as is the case with most of them) or strongly contested. And I have reason to be satisfied with the manifestations of the public confidence and attachment towards myself. They would have been more numerous but for the cause to which you advert.[7] The efforts of the friends of other Gentlemen, however, altho' successful in repressing an expression favorable to me at particular points, have not been able to prevent them at others.

I think that the separate movement which we were threatened with, for Genl Harrison, from Harrisburg, has been completely discountenanced and defeated.[8] They hold a State Convention at Columbus on friday next, at which I am confident they will pass a resolution to abide by the decision of a Nat. Convention.[9]

Should I receive the invitation to attend a Barbecue at N. York, I shall be obliged to decline it, upon a ground which I have resolved to occupy.[10] It will however furnish me a suitable occasion to explain that ground, which I trust and believe will prove satisfactory.

ALS. NBuHi. 1. Comment in Senate, April 30, 1838. 2. By a 28 to 19 margin. See Remark in Senate, May 26, 1838; *Cong. Globe*, 25 Cong., 2 Sess., 412. 3. For the 1816 resolution, see Comment in Senate, May 2, 1838. 4. It did, 34 to 9, on May 29; and in the House, by a vote of 154 to 29 on May 30. *Cong. Globe*, 25 Cong., 2 Sess., 416–17. See also Comment in Senate, May 2, 1838; Remark in Senate, May 26, 1838. 5. Speech in Senate, May 21, 1838. 6. Porter to Clay, May 25, 1838. 7. Reference obscure, but see Porter to Clay, May 25, 1838, for a discussion of the actions of Webster's friends in attempting "to defer" expressions of public opinion in favor of any candidate. 8. Porter to Clay, March 8, 1838. 9. *Ibid.*; Clay to Porter, Jan. 5, 1838. 10. Porter to Clay, May 25, 1838; Clay to Verplanck, June 8, 1838.

Remark in Senate, May 28, 1838. Calls for a vote on the resolution of Sen. Thomas Morris (Ohio) to repeal the joint resolution of 1816. Defeated 36 to 8, Clay voting nay. Following this vote, the question of ordering the engrossment of Clay's April 30 resolution, as amended [Remark in Senate, May 25 and 26, 1838], was passed 34 to 10, Clay voting yea. *Cong. Globe*, 25 Cong., 2 Sess., 415. For the joint resolution of 1816, see Comment in Senate, May 2, 1838.

From Richard Pindell, Lexington, May 29, 1838. Asks Clay to handle a financial matter for him. Reports that "the affairs of your place ["Ashland"] are managed pretty well, every thing seems to be in good order, though we have had the most backward spring Known for some years." Believes there is no opposition for the legislature save Larkin B. Smith who will get but a "slim vote" for the seat. ALS. DLC-TJC (DNA, M212, R14). For Larkin B. Smith, a Lexington attorney, who won election to the state legislature in 1838, see Collins, *History of Kentucky*, 2:170; *RKHS*, 48:75. See also Clay to Henry Clay, Jr., March 2, 1838.

Remark in Senate, May 29, 1838. Participates [not recorded] in the final debate on his resolution of April 30, 1838, as amended [Remark in Senate, May 25, 26, and 28, 1838]. Following this debate, the Senate voted 34 to 9 to pass it. *Cong. Globe*, 25 Cong., 2 Sess., 416. On May 30, the House also passed the measure, which effectively repealed the Specie Circular [Speech in Senate, January 11, 1837; Comment in Senate, May 2, 1838], by a vote of 154 to 29. *Ibid.*, 416-17.

To NICHOLAS BIDDLE Washington, May 30, 1838

I recd. your favor of the 28h. inst. You will have seen that the resolution, which had passed the Senate, rescinding the Specie Circular, has also passed the House this morning in less than three hours after it was recd. by a majority of more than five to one![1]

I sincerely hope that the condition of your Bank is such as to admit of your seizing of this occurrence to make an early resumption.[2] I am extremely anxious on *your* account as well as that of the public that your Bank shall continue to maintain its high character

You will have seen and *you* will comprehend the object and the benefits of the movement I made, in respect to a Bank of the U. S.[3] It will turn public attention to the subject in the abstract. It will suspend or render harmless malignant attacks on your Bank. And it may even reconcile the public ultimately to the grant of a National Charter to your Bank. I should be satisfied with either.

Altho' I did not think it right to allude to our conversation, in the few remarks I addressed to the Senate, I have to several friends said that Mr. Biddles elevated patriotism made him look above the interests of the particular institution with which he is charged to the welfare of his Country.

ALS. DLC-Nicholas Biddle Papers (DNA, M212, R20). 1. Comment in Senate, April 30 and May 2, 1838; Remark in Senate, May 29, 1838. 2. The United States Bank of Pennsylvania resumed specie payment in July, 1838. Hammond, *Banks and Politics in America*, 481. 3. Speech in Senate, May 21, 1838.

From Nicholas Biddle, Philadelphia, May 31, 1838. Announces that news of the passage of the resolution repealing the Specie Circular [Comment in Senate, May 2, 1838; Remark in Senate, May 25 and 29, 1838; Clay to Biddle, May 30, 1838] causes him "decidedly & instantly" to resume specie payments at the United States Bank of Pennsylvania. Since his letter of April 5 to John Quincy Adams [Porter to Clay, April 17, 1838] had defended non-resumption until "some change in the policy of the Government would justify" resumption, reports that he has again written to Adams, "not at all in a tone of triumph," but to explain his new position in the matter. Has had this letter published "so as to go by the English packet of to-day." Hopes it will "produce a beneficial effect abroad." Has also yielded "to a very general application from New York, for a renewal of its connection with the Bank. This was specially based upon the repeal of the Circular. So you see I have not been backward to seize this opportunity afforded by your resolution." Copy. DLC-Nicholas Biddle Papers (DNA, M212, R20).

Biddle wrote Adams on May 31, 1838, stating that he now sees in the repeal of the Specie Circular "the means of restoring the currency." States that he will now "cordially co-operate with the government by promoting . . . an early resumption of specie payments throughout the union." *Niles' Register* (June 9, 1838), 54: 226. See also Clay to Biddle, May 30, 1838.

To WILLIE P. MANGUM Washington, May 31, 1838

I placed the letter which you did me the favor some time ago to address to me[1] in the hands of Critt[en]den, as there were some parts of it on which you wished to hear from him. Judge my regret and surprize when he told me last night that he had not written to you! He is a good but a lazy fellow.

You will have seen that the Nat. Convention is fixed for Decr. 1839 at Harrisburg.[2] I understand that the day was made so distant in conformity with the urgent desire of members from N. York, Vermont, Pennsa. and Ohio. I think that if you can overcome your repugnance to Conventions in N. Carolina it would be desirable that you should be represented in it. The more general, fair and respectable the composition of the Convention may be the greater will be the influence of any recommendation that shall issue from it. And it is extremely important to prevent any cavilling, if there should exist any where a disposition to cavil, on the score of the Convention being partially constituted, and not being a full representative of all the States.

I am happy to tell you that our Cause every where is making sure and certain progress; and that my *particular* cause could hardly be improved. In Pennsa. some weeks ago a bad spirit was manifested in an effort to hold up and adhere to Harrison, without reference to the agency of a N. Convention;[3] but far from being seconded it has been generally rebuked, and I have no doubt will be abandoned, or rendered entirely impotent. A State Convention meets this day at Columbus in Ohio, and we are well assured here that it will pass a resolution to abide by the decision of the N. Convention.[4] In Pennsa. a better state of things exists, and if [Joseph] Ritner should be elected, we now believe that it will agree to the nomination [w]hich shall be made by the N. Convention.[5]

Webster is not in a good state of feeling. He thinks that he is not sufficiently appreciated, and perhaps thinks correctly; but that can not alter the case. He will be controll[ed] by his friends, or will submit to the force of circumstances.

I have heard nothing lately from your State. What is the prospect there of the general cause; what your own? I have lately transmitted some documents to your County, at the instance of Mr. Waddel & Mr. Stanley [*sic*].[6] I presume t[he] ridiculous charge against me of being an Abolitionist, prop[a]gated by the Calh[o]un School, can deceive no body. It is remarkable that whilst that charge is disseminated at the South, the Emancipator, the organ of the Abolit[ion]ists at the North, avows its preference for Mr. V. Buren, and its determination to oppose me, because the Slave interest will have in me a firm supporter.[7]

The Administration party professes to believe that it will yet carry the Sub treasury bill. We are not without fears, but we still think it must be defeated. . . .[8]

ALS. DLC-Willie P. Mangum Papers (DNA, M212, R22). Letter marked "(Confidential)." 1. Mangum to Clay, March 26, 1838. 2. Porter to Clay, Nov. 14 and Dec. 30, 1837. 3. A reference to a plan by Ohio Whigs to have a separate Harrison convention in Harrisburg, Pa. See Porter to Clay, March 8, 1838. 4. Porter to Clay, Jan. 5 and March 8, 1838. 5. For the 1838 Pennsylvania elections, see Schermerhorn to Clay, Feb. 25, 1838. The Pennsylvania Whigs did support Harrison when he won the nomination. Mueller, *The Whig Party in Pennsylvania*, 59-60. 6. For Edward Stanly, a North Carolina congressman, see *BDAC*; for Hugh Waddell, a North Carolina lawyer, see *CAB*. 7. Clay to Hamilton, May 28, 1838. 8. For the legislative history of the Sub-Treasury bill, see Speech in Senate, Sept. 25, 1837.

From Peter B. Porter, New York, May 31, 1838. Has heard that Clay has declined an invitation to visit New York State and urges him to reconsider his decision from a political standpoint [Porter to Clay, May 25, 1838; Clay to Porter, May 28, 1838].

Postscript. Friday morning, June 1. Adds: "I am delighted this morning with the appearance of Mr. Biddle's last letter to Mr. Adams [Biddle to Clay, May 31, 1838]. He had, I think, made an injudicious mar, & placed himself in an awkward position [Porter to Clay, April 17, 1838], from which I am glad to see him escape and with honor. He assumes, as I understand it, that the resolutions of 1816, are mandatory [Comment in Senate, May 2, 1838], and that the Treasury order being removed, the Government will be found, in good faith to receive the bills of specie paying banks, and this if I mistake not, is the instruction recently given to them by Mr. Calhoun. At any rate, after all that has passed, the Govt. will not dare to insist on specie in their receipts and expenditures." Copy. OHi.

It appears that Porter was confused respecting Calhoun's views. In the fall of 1837 Calhoun had, in fact, proposed an amendment to the Sub-Treasury bill which would have had the government temporarily accept the notes of specie-paying banks; however, on May 2, 18, 25, 26, and 29, 1838, he made speeches advocating that the government accept only specie. See Wiltse, *John C. Calhoun: Nullifier*, 354, 384-85; Wilson, *Papers of John C. Calhoun*, 14:282-86, 293-304, 306-18.

Remark in Senate, May 31, 1838. Presents two petitions, one from New York, another from Connecticut [Remark in Senate, June 12, 1838], praying for the establishment of a national bank [Speech in Senate, May 21, 1838], "that monster so frightful in the eyes of old maids, old bachelors, and old politicians." Notes that the petitioners are "the merchants, the manufacturers, and hardy yeomanry of the country, without respect to party." Recalls, facetiously, that the old Bank of the United States, "monstrous, and monster as it was, it afforded us the best currency that ever a nation was blest with." Notes that there is much sentiment for a new bank in the West, especially in Kentucky. In response to a critical question from "my namesake," Sen. Clement C. Clay (Dem., Ala.), identifies Jamaica, N.Y., as the source of one of the pro-bank petitions and assures the senator that if he went home to Alabama and "met his constituents in large bodies, at the Methodist or Baptist meeting houses, or would mix among them familiarly, take his chew of tobacco in his mouth, and tattle with his neighbors, he would find a much larger portion in favor of a bank than he was aware of." The petitions, he insists again, are signed by "persons of every party, Federal, Democratic, and . . . Conservative." Reminds Sen. John M. Niles (Dem., Conn.), critic of a new national bank, that the people of Connecticut had recently turned out of their state legislature "all those worthy Democrats," a development that was "to deprive the Senate of the benefit of the gentleman's [Niles] enlightened counsels." Perhaps this was because the song "sung by the Senator and his friends ever since the commencement of the session" had been "nothing but Sub-Treasury, Sub-Treasury." Having heard Niles's bitter explanation of his political defeat in Connecticut, Clay advises him "to retire from public life in a philosophical temper, and not give way to splenic and violent attacks on his own State." *Cong. Globe*, 25 Cong., 2 Sess., 418-20.

In the 1838 Connecticut elections, W.W. Ellsworth, the Whig gubernatorial candidate, defeated Seth Beers, a Democrat, by a vote of 27,115 to 22,986. In the election for the state senate, the Whigs won 28 seats to 1 for the Democrats. Approximately two-thirds of the 214 house seats also went to the Whigs. The legislature then chose Dennis Kimberly, a Whig, as U.S. senator over incumbent Democrat, John Niles, by a vote of 97 to 38. *BDGUS*, 1:167; *Niles' Register* (May 12 and 26, 1838), 54:176, 193.

From Gulian C. Verplanck *et al.*, New York, May 31, 1838. Report that at a meeting in Masonic Hall on the evening of May 29, a resolution was passed by the "vast and animated assemblage" present inviting Clay to pass through New York State on his way home to Lexington after Congress adjourns. Condemn the Van Buren administration for the "desolation brought upon our beloved country, by a bad administration of government," and assure Clay that New Yorkers wish to see and speak with one who has "taught us, by his precept and example, never to despair of the republic." Copy. Printed in *Niles' Register* (June 30, 1838), 54:277. Invitation signed also by Willis Hall, John L. Lawrence, Thomas L. Wells, Dudley Selden, Robert Swartwout. For Wells, a lawyer, see *Officers and Graduates of Columbia University, General Catalogue 1754-1900* (New York, 1900), 20, 115.

To ALBERT B. DOD — Washington, June 1, 1838

My son[1] writes me that he has been ill, and is threatened with a serious attack. He says that he has taken Calomel and was still not relieved. He complains of giddiness or Vertigo, to which he has been more or less liable since the serious illness which he had in this City two years ago. I have, therefore, my dear Sir, to request that you will let me know if he should be very unwell, as, in that case, I might feel it necessary to go to Princeton.

I presume that you safely received the small remittance I made.[2]

ALS. NcD. Written in "S[enate]. Chamber." For Dod, a mathematics professor at Princeton University, see *DAB*. 1. John Morrison Clay who was a student at Princeton University. See Clay to Henry Clay, Jr., Sept. 8, 1837; Clay to James B. Clay, Jan. 22, 1838. 2. On May 18, Clay had sent Dod $150. ADS. DLC-TJC (DNA, M212, R18).

To Thomas Hart Clay, Lexington, June 2, 1838. Asks him to search for and send him some legal papers relating to a New Madrid, Mo., land claim by Anthony Bonneau. Thinks they are on the table in his law office. Also asks him to attend to some details relating to the shipment of his bale rope to Mississippi. ALS. Henry Clay Memorial Foundation, Lexington, Ky.

For details of the Bonneau claim, which was complicated by the New Madrid earthquake destruction of December 16, 1811, see James Whitcomb to Clay, General Land Office, Washington, May 31, 1838. Copy. DNA, RG49, Letters Sent, Private Land Claims, Letterbook, vol. 4, pp. 252-54.

To George W. Featherstonhaugh, Washington, June 2, 1838. Shares his interest in copyright legislation [Comment in Senate, February 2, 1837], but doubts that it will clear committee during this session. LS. KyU.

To MARGARET BAYARD (Mrs. Samuel H.) SMITH — Washington, June 2, 1838

I share with you in all your sympathies with Mr. Pettrich,[1] and your wishes that I should sit again to him shall have the most friendly consideration. If his were the single application, I should have no difficulty, but I have already sat to two artists, and I have been obliged to refuse many others.

The bust which has been already taken of me by Mr. P. has been recently very much praised for its fidelity. I wished to see it again and will take some early opportunity to do so. If it would answer a further sitting would be unnecessary, and I should be able to economise my time at a period when I very much need it all. If it be condemned I will try and sit to him again at this or the next Session.

ALS. DLC-HC (DNA, M212, R5). 1. For Frederick August Ferdinand Pettrich (1798-1872), a German sculptor and painter, see George C. Groce & David H. Wallace, *The New York Historical Society's Dictionary of Artists in America 1564-1860* (New Haven, 1957), 503.

To PETER B. PORTER Washington, June 3, 1838

I recd. your favors of the 30h. and 31st. Ulto.

The proceedings at the recent public meeting[1] appear to me to have been highly judicious and marked by great discretion. They will have good effect out of N. York and I hope in that State.

I have received the invitation from the Comee. and mean to reply to it in a few days.[2] If I could yield the dictates of my most deliberate judgment, that of no friend would have more influence with me than yours; but after the fullest consideration, I am perfectly satisfied that it is best for me to make no journey which would wear the aspect of electioneering. It is right in itself, and it is the truest policy. I have already profited by my forbearance, and I have had abundant evidence of it. The dignity of the office of P. and, if it were fitting to electioneer for it, the impossibility of visiting all the important points to which one would be pressingly invited, appear to me to recommend standing still. Mankind are much more disposed voluntarily to grant an object which seems not to be sought with avidity. If I were to perform the proposed tour, on the whole route, I should receive the most urgent and earnest invitations to visit every town on either side of it. That would be impracticable and offense would be given. Then, the present position of the Whigs is peculiar. A canvass is going on among them, not against our common opponents, but to decide which of several persons shall be selected as the Candidate of the Whigs. In this contest, I think our party had better be left very much to itself to make its own unbiased choice. Efforts by any one of the persons in view, would excite jealousy and perhaps lead to alienation among the friends of the others. We already see signs of dissatisfaction; and it will require all the address and the sound discretion of the well disposed to prevent these breaking out into open discontent, if not worse consequences. I ought to be the last to make any efforts, as every thing every where is going on well. It is also encumbent upon me to bear in mind what I have heretofore said and done. I have on more occasions than one announced my desire to retire to private life, and my indifference to public station. That was the truth; and, if I continue in public life, it had better be believed to be, as would really be the case, from a sense of duty. I have moreover on more occasions than one written to friends, avowing my determination to remain passive and neutral. You see then, my dear Sir, how inconsistent I should appear, if I were to accept the invitation which I have received. It would be in vain to attempt to disguise the object. I am invited by a public meeting assembled to advance my pretensions to the Presidency to make a tour through the whole length of your State. No one would be deceived as to the purpose. I might proclaim a thousand times that I was *only* going to see your great Canal and other improvements &c. No body would believe me; and, what is worse, I should feel that I ought not to be credited.

I shall put some of these considerations in the reply to the Comee. which I purpose transmitting, and you will oblige me by using your influence in reconciling our friends to the course which seems to me most proper. Genl [Robert] Swartwout has written me a letter, strongly urging me to go. He has, I know, put his heart upon it. I wish you would negotiate with him for me. Tell him that I am bound to survey the whole ground, and look to the effect of a movement every where, and not merely at the point where it is made. We have every reason to be satisfied with the present condition of affairs; and there is more danger of my impairing than improving it, by the display of eagerness.

You will have seen enough around you to satisfy you that there is a morbid feeling among some of the friends of Mr. W[ebster]. Let me do nothing to justify or exasperate it. It was shewn in a little way in the effort to claim for him the parentage of the late resolution.[3] It was tweedle dum & tweedle dee, between his form and mine. Mine was indeed the more appropriate and more dignified shape for Legislation. And, then, the proposition itself to do away with all discrimination, was mine, made at the last (ordinary) Session, on the passage of the bill, which was called Mr. Reeves's [*sic*, William C. Rives].[4] But this competition about the resolution was unworthy of either of us.

You will have seen that the Secy [Levi Woodbury] has issued a new Circular admitting the receipt of Specie notes, under certain restrictions.[5] It will be attempted to do away with these restrictions, and if it should be accomplished, every object proposed, by my resolution, as originally offered, will have been attained, altho' in a mode somewhat different.

ALS. NBuHi. 1. Porter to Clay, May 25, 1838; Verplanck to Clay, May 31, 1838. 2. Verplanck to Clay, May 31, 1838; Clay to Verplanck, June 8, 1838. 3. Clay to Southard, May 11, 1838; Remark in Senate, May 25 and 26, 1838. 4. Speech in Senate, Jan. 11, 1837; Comment in Senate, March 7, 1838. 5. Remark in Senate, May 24, 1838.

To FRANCIS T. BROOKE Washington, June 5, 1838

I am extremely sorry to hear of the loss of your servant. It is a serious misfortune, and not easily repaired, independent of the distress which such an event must necessarily occasion to every feeling heart.

I can not understand from any inquiry which I have made here the exact value of your Military Land Warrant. Mr. [William] Allen, the Senator, from Ohio, thinks it worth seventy-five cents per acre; but recommends an application to William Creighton, Jr. (who is a man of honor and particular friend of mine), of Chillicothe, who resides in the heart of the county set apart for the army.

If the bill making further appropriations for land scrip, now pending in the House of Representatives should pass,[1] your warrant will be worth much more, perhaps $1 20 cents per acre. Although I can not vote for the bill, I think it very probable it will pass at this or another session, and you would probably do well not to part with it.

I should be most happy to see you here, and why can't you come? A few hours would put you in the Pennsylvania Avenue. If you visit us, come directly to Mrs. Hill's boarding-house, where I stay, and where you can be accommodated.[2] It is nigh Gadsby's.

Every thing has passed off admirably at the Ohio Convention.[3]

Copy. Printed in Colton, *Clay Correspondence*, 4:427. 1. The act "to extend the time for locating Virginia military land warrants, and returning surveys thereon to the General Land Office" passed the House on June 8, 1838, and was reported to the Senate on June 19. The Senate passed the bill on July 7, 1838, and the president signed it the same day. *Cong. Globe*, 25 Cong., 2 Sess., 435, 461; U.S. Sen., *Journal*, 25 Cong., 2 Sess., 569; 5 *U.S. Stat.*, 262. This bill, in effect, extended the time period for locating Virginia land warrants from Jan. 1, 1835, as established in the Script Act of 1830 [8:744-45], to August 10, 1840. For a discussion of this, see Benjamin H. Hibbard, *A History of the Public Land Policies* (New York, 1939), 116-26. 2. Clay to Southard, August 3, 1837. 3. Porter to Clay, Jan. 5, 1838.

From LEWIS TAPPAN New York, June 5, 1838

I cut the above from one of the Evening papers yesterday.[1] The facts disclosed appear to me exceedingly important, and I am anxious that influential planters in the U.S. should know the important results of emancipation in the West Indies.

The work of Thome & Kimball, entitled "Emancipation in the West Indies",[2] you may have seen. If you have not I will send you a copy if requested. Gov. [Edward] Everett of M[assachusett]s. and Gov. [William W.] Ellsworth of C[onnecticu]t. have written letters in which they honestly say that the success of emancipation in the W.I. settles the question in their minds of the safety, and utility of immediate emancipation. If safe and useful in the W.I. why not in the U.S.?

Have you read the printed Correspondence between Mr [Franklin H.] Elmore, on behalf of the S.C. Delegation in Congress, and James G. Birney, Esq. Cor-Sec of the American Anti-Slavery Society?[3] It unfolds the designs & measures of the abolitionists unreservedly, & demonstrates that they tend to the salvation of the country. "Whoso hath ears to hear let him hear."

It is strongly impressed upon my mind that an opportunity exists for you to render a service to your country and to mankind such as you have never known. In a political sense it is as true as in a religious sense that there are times when "he that would save his life shall lose it, and he that will lose his life shall save it." A politician may so shape his course as temporarily to save his political fame, but by the very act lose it, in the estimation of the wise at the time, and by the verdict of posterity. And he may, to superficial observers, lose his reputation by an act that really embalms it in the hearts of the judicious, and will command the applause of the historian.

If, Sir, you were one of those ephemeral statesmen whose highest object it is to win office, and the applauses of contemporaries, at all hazards, argument would be thrown away upon you: You might save your life, but would soon lose it. But if you desire to live in the hearts of the virtuous, of this and all succeeding ages, and have the respect of all men soon and forever, you will desire to do what is right.

The *opportunity* to which I have referred is this—by coming out against oppression in this land—making merchandise of men—wresting from them their wages & personal liberty—you can raise yourself to the very pinacle of earthly fame, confer an invaluable blessing upon all classes of your countrymen, & surround your name with associations that will embalm it in the breasts of the good in all future time. I know that there are higher considerations, such as ensure the approbation of God. But most men are less affected by these than those that operate upon their own happiness & supposed welfare.

To be *the man* who, at this junction, would nobly stand forth as the champion of human rights, would be a greater honor than any of our countrymen has yet attained. If I mistake not his contemporaries in his own country would soon acknowledge the wisdom of his course—certainly the wise & good in all lands would name him with gratitude—and success wd. attend his efforts. What is the reputation of a Jefferson, or Madison, or Franklin, compared with the reputation suc[h] a man would acquire?

Ky, if *you* should take the lead, would speedily go for immediate emancipation, and other states would rapidly follow her example. The real property of Ky would be doubled in value, & a spring would be given to her agriculture, trade & manufactures such as has never been witnessed. Look at Antigua & Barbadoes!—

As a friend to my country I lament that *she* did not set the high example to the world of giving liberty to her captives, and then following up the noble principles of liberty promulgated in the Dec. of Independence. But the U.S. allowed G. B[ritain]. to bear the palm. Let us not be slow in following such a bright example, lest other nations step in and bear away the honor that now awaits this country if she does her duty.

There is nothing connected with the politics o[f] this country, or its commercial or agricultural or manufacturing welfare that would give me so much real joy as to know that you had come out fearlessly and fully on the side of universal liberty.

ALS. DLC-HC (DNA, M212, R5). 1. Enclosure not found. 2. James A. Thome and Joseph Horace Kimball toured the West Indies in 1837 on behalf of the American Anti-Slavery Society in order to study the results of the 1834 emancipation of slaves there. Upon their return home, they published a pamphlet titled *Emancipation in the West Indies, or Six Months Tour in Antigua, Barbados, and Jamaica, in the Year 1837*. New York, 1838. For Kimball, see *CAB*. For Thome, see William H. and Jane H. Pease, *The Anti-Slavery Argument* (New York, 1965), 91; and Louis Ruchames, *The Abolitionists, A Collection of Their Writings* (New York, 1964), 149. 3. *Correspondence, Between the Hon. F.H. Elmore, One of the South Carolina Delegation in Congress, and James G. Birney, One of the Secretaries of the American Anti-Slavery Society*. New York, 1838.

Remark in Senate, June 6, 1838. With reference to establishing salary schedules for district judges in the proposed territory of Iowa, and the likely level of prosperity there, notes that the area is "one of the finest farming and grazing countries in the world." *Cong. Globe*, 25 Cong., 2 Sess., 435.

To GULIAN C. VERPLANCK *et al.* Washington, June 8, 1838

I have to acknowledge the receipt of a letter[1] which, as a committee appointed at a meeting of my political friends, recently convened in the city of New York, you addressed to me, transmitting a copy of their proceedings, and, in pursuance of one of their resolutions, inviting me to visit that city, and to pass through the state of New York to Buffalo, upon my return home, after the termination of the present session of congress.

I have perused the proceedings of the meeting with the liveliest feelings of gratitude; and I request you, gentlemen, to convey to those who composed it my cordial thanks, and respectful acknowledgments, for their friendly consideration of me. Whilst I feel highly gratified by the sentiments of attachment, confidence, and preference, with an expression of which the meeting has honored me, I think that it has wisely referred the designation of a suitable candidate for the office of president of the United States to the consideration and impartial decision of a national convention. Such an assemblage, representing all parts of the United States, and fairly constituted, will embody the opinions and best express the sense of the whole opposition to the present administration of the general government. It will reconcile differences, promote harmony, and secure hearty cooperation among those who are engaged in the patriotic cause of struggling to bring back the government to its former purity to heal the wounds in the constitution, and to restore the prosperity of the country.

I should be most happy to find myself under circumstances which would admit of my acceptance of the friendly invitation to visit your state. I am sure that every where, on a tour so agreeable, I should meet with the greatest kindness and hospitality, and behold in the virtue, intelligence, and enterprise of the people of New York, in the noble works of internal improvement which adorn its territory, and in the fruitful soil with which Providence has blessed it, abundant elements for repairing the temporary injuries inflicted by the errors and experiments of the federal executive. But I feel constrained to deny myself the satisfaction of contemplating these pleasing scenes. After an absence from my home, which has already extended to nigh eight months, I am naturally most anxious to rejoin my family without any unavoidable delay. I might content myself with the assignment of this simple reason, but I have other and higher motives, which candor requires I should communicate, for declining to accept your obliging invitation. Although I am not, in fact, a candidate for any office, I am aware that my name is freely used in connexion with the highest in the gift of the American people. Whilst it is thus a subject of consideration, I have thought that it best becomes me to remain in an attitude perfectly passive, doing nothing with the intention of attracting the current of public feeling to me, nothing to disturb or affect the exercise of the free and unbiassed judgment of the people. I have accordingly acted in strict conformity with this conviction of my duty. I have visited no place, and shall visit no place, with the view of promoting my own personal advancement. Considerations both of principle and convenience have induced me to adopt this resolution. I know that sentiments of personal esteem and regard for me, and for which I am very thankful, apart from political motives, have prompted the invitation with which you have favored me; but if I were to accept it, no matter under what protestations or professions, it would be believed, whether justly or not, that it had other objects besides social intercourse, and an examination of the inexhaustible resources of your great state. The same or similar reasons with which I might be induced to visit New York, would be urged to prevail on me to go to other portions of the union. How could I discriminate? What limit should I prescribe? There would be a physical impracticability to go to every important point of the union, which I might be pressed, or prompted by the impulse of my own feelings, to visit.

The office of president of the United States is of a nature so exhalted, and its functions so momentous, that it ought not to be, and, happily, never can be, reached by individual efforts to acquire it. It should only be bestowed by the free, spontaneous, and deliberate judgment of the people. When so conferred, it is more honorable to them and to the distinguished object of their choice. Thus receiving it, he will enter upon the career of its arduous duties, conscious that he has attained the elevated station by no low or unworthy arts, and overflowing with gratitude, will dedicate all his abilities, and his undivided energies, to the honor and the prosperity and the glory of his country.

Such, gentlemen, are the views which I should entertain if I were a formal candidate, and the sole candidate of the cause to which I am attached.—Far from being weakened, they appear to me to possess additional strength when we survey the actual state of the question to which they relate. The whigs have not yet determined on their candidate. They are now deliberating about it, consulting among themselves in their primary and other assemblies, as they have a right to do, and resolved to hold a great family consulation in December, 1839.[2] Other gentlemen, of eminent abilities, of distinguished services, and of acknowledged patriotism, are justly and properly and prominently in their view, and under their consideration. Whilst this preliminary question is in progress of an amicable adjustment, I feel that it would not be right for me to make any personal exertions, or even to be voluntarily placed in situations in which it might be supposed that I was making personal exertions, to withdraw from them the confidence, so justly due to them, of our common friends, and fix it exclusively upon myself. In announcing this rule of conduct for myself, it is foreign from my intention to mark out any course for others, or to intimate any dissatisfaction with whatever line they may consider it proper to pursue. . . .

Copy. Printed in *Niles' Register* (June 30, 1838), 54:277. 1. Verplanck *et al.* to Clay, May 31, 1838. 2. Porter to Clay, Nov. 14, 1837.

From Thomas P. Hart, Louisville, June 9, 1838. Encloses for Clay, his uncle, his power of attorney and that of John Hart in the matter of the division of the estate of James Brown. Announces that he opened his new home "on monday last with every prospect of success and the small mite coming to me will very much assist in furnishing our house with some articles which I have not the money to pay for." Says he is well satisfied with Louisville and with his prospects there. ALS. DLC-TJC (DNA, M212, R14).

To PETER B. PORTER Washington, June 9, 1838

I recd. your letter addressed to me from Philada.[1] I transmitted yesterday an answer to the invitation from N.Y. declining to accept it.[2] I hope that the reasons will prove satisfactory to my friends. I have a most perfect conviction of the propriety and the policy of the course which I have deliberately resolved to pursue. I should be glad that my answer should be published.

You ask why I gave up the provision in my resolution requiring the *disbursement* of Bank notes. It was, in consequence of an objection to that clause from Mr. *Webster* and one or two other friends, and my unwillingness to shew any state of division among our own friends. I thought, and still think, that the resolution was right as originally offered.[3]

The proceedings of the Ohio Convention are perfectly satisfactory.[4] I would not have them otherwise than they are.

Fears are entertained here, not without some foundation, of the Passage of the S.T. bill.[5] I think that it will not pass, but there is no absolute certainty.

ALS. NBuHi. Written in "S[enate]. Chamber." 1. Not found; but see Clay to Porter, June 3, 1838. 2. Verplanck to Clay, May 31, 1838; Clay to Verplanck, June 8, 1838. 3. Cf. wording of Clay's resolution of April 30, *Cong. Globe*, 25 Cong., 2 Sess., 344, with Webster's substitute language of May 16, *ibid.*, 378. See also Remark in Senate, May 25 and 26, 1838. 4. Clay to Porter, Jan. 5, 1838. 5. For the vote on the Sub-Treasury bill, see Speech in Senate, Sept. 25, 1837.

Remark in Senate, June 9, 1838. Presents a few petitions praying the establishment of a United States bank from "men of all parties . . . who have felt the pressure in their business from the present deranged state of the currency, particularly at the South and Southwest, where a large portion of their trade was concentrated." Believes their prayers will be "utterly unavailing," constituted as Congress now is [Clay to Brooke, March 7, 1837]. *Cong. Globe*, 25 Cong., 2 Sess., 444.

To ROBERT SWARTWOUT Washington, June 9, 1838

I was obliged to decline the invitation to visit N. York, as you will see from my reply to the Comee.[1] Whatever advantage if any might have resulted from it in your State would have been more than neutralized by injury elsewhere. Depend upon it I am right. I have received many strong testimonies of the good effects produced by my forbearance. Besides, every thing is moving on well for me every where. Should I not be satisfied? We cannot annihilate the 2½ years between now and the period of the Election. We must patiently wait their lapse. The proceedings in Ohio are all that we could wish.[2] I regard them as conclusive.

Impediments have been, and will continue to be interposed in the way of public expressions in my favor at the North. They can only operate for a short time; the popular feeling will burst forth, in due season, in spite of them all.

I should be glad that my reply may be published. It will save me the time of writing a multitude of answers which I might otherwise receive.

Give my best respects to our mutual friend Genl [Peter B.] Porter. . . .

ALS. NN. 1. Verplanck to Clay, May 31, 1838; Clay to Verplanck, June 8, 1838. 2. Clay to Porter, Jan. 5, 1838.

From Jonathan H. Jacocks, Durants Neck, N.C., June 11, 1838. Encloses counterfeit treasury bills, acquired during the settlement of an estate, which, he charges, are "living evidences" of the "corrupt and mad policy of the present *dominant party*." Hopes Clay can "make some use" of them. Reminds Clay that they have twice met, lauds his sound views over the years on the tariff and other issues, and remarks that "the great *leading principles* with you, has been the '*peace*' of your country & the caryíng out to the *last* and *forever* the intent, meaning & spirit which produced this great, and I fervently hope, lasting Confederacy." ALS. DLC-HC (DNA, M212, R5). For Jacocks, sometime member of the North Carolina legislature and the executor of a number of estates, see William P. Jacocks, "Descendants of Thomas Jacocks Who Died in 1692 in Perquimans Precinct, North Carolina." Typescript (1957) in N.C. Collection, University of North Carolina.

Remark in Senate, June 12, 1838. Presents a petition from sundry Connecticut citizens praying for establishment of a "Bank of the United States." Denies an allegation by Sen. John M. Niles (Conn.) that a similar petition from New Haven, Conn., presented a few days ago [Remark in Senate, May 31, 1838], was signed by some people not of the most respectable character. Niles replies that Clay misunderstood his criticism of that particular petition. *Cong. Globe*, 25 Cong., 2 Sess., 447.

To Thomas Hart Clay, Washington, June 14, 1838. Inquires as to nephew John Hart's bale rope production schedule [Clay to Thomas H. Clay, May 18, 1838], and the foaling and breeding of his [Clay's] jackasses at "Ashland." ALS. Henry Clay Memorial Foundation, Lexington, Ky.

To JOHN M. CLAYTON Washington, June 14, 1838

I recd. last night your favor of the 11h. and thank you for the information which it communicates.

The course of Mr. W[ebster]. and his friends is remarkable—They began to agitate the P. question, prematurely I think.[1] Well, the friends of others voluntarily put themselves in motion. The current of public feeling did not run to but from Mr. W; and now the whole effort of himself and some of his friends seems to be directed to the object of restraining demonstrations in favor of others. And, altho' I believe, from what has been communicated to me directly and indirectly, there were majorities of 4 or 5 to one for me at Trenton,[2] Albany,[3] Connecticut,[4] and Maine,[5] in their late legislatures. Mr. Ws. friends succeeded at each of those points to prevent the expression of the preference which was entertained for me. This was done by appealing to the timid, &c &c. I do not think it of much consequence; for it only retards; and the spontaneous bursts in other quarters will supply the place of those testimonies which might have been rendered at the points mentioned.

Your movement at Dover I regard as very important.[6] The State of Delaware has great moral power, much more than would be implied from the amt. of its population. Then, it went for Harrison at the last election. The declaration of its preference now will shew that it was the *cause* and not the *man* to which it was attached on that occasion.

I yesterday had a long interview and conversation with Mr. W. It was conducted throughout and terminated amicably; but he will do nothing at present, in regard to withdrawing from the contest I think he will ultimately be forced by his friends to adopt that course; but if he does he will embrace it slowly and sullenly. I shall avoid every thing on my part which might tend to produce a breach.

I invite your attention to a reply which I have recently made to an invitation to visit N. York, and which I presume is publis[h]ed.[7] I have announced in it a general rule of conduct for myself which I hope will meet with the approbation of my friends.

ALS. DLC-George P. Fisher Papers (DNA, M212, R21). 1. Clay to Letcher, May 30, 1837. 2. Kinsey to Clay, Jan. 3, 1838. 3. Porter to Clay, Nov. 14 and Dec. 30, 1837. 4. The Connecticut Whig convention in Feb., 1838, held for the purpose of nominating candidates for state office, had declined to endorse anyone for president. However, it did call for a national convention to choose a candidate for president and promised to support whoever was nominated. In June, 1839, Whigs in the Connecticut legislature met and endorsed Clay, although they still promised to support anyone nominated by a national convention. Washington *Daily National Intelligencer*, Feb. 21, 1838; June 14, 1839. 5. Clay to Porter, March 4, 1838. 6. The Whig delegates in the Delaware state assembly met in Dover on June 12, 1838, and called for a national presidential nominating convention. They also endorsed Clay as the best candidate. Washington *Daily National Intelligencer*, June 19, 1838. 7. Porter to Clay, May 25, 1838; Clay to Porter, May 28, 1838.

To JOHN M. CLAYTON Washington, June 15, 1838

I recd., my dear friend, your letter communicating the proceedings at your great Convention.[1] They have filled me with sentiments of the liveliest gratitude. I have been always proud of the attachment and confidence of your noble State. This last testimony of its friendly consideration overflows the measure of my thankfulness. What an encouraging moral spectacle has Delaware exhibited throughout all these times of trouble. Surrounded by the greatest influences to drive her from her principles, she has nevertheless firmly stood by them, with a courage and constancy worthy of the best days of Greece or Rome. I shall be most happy if, whilst I remain in public life, I shall be able to deserve and retain her affections.

Whatever others may think, I am fully convinced that all demonstrations of the public feeling and opinion, spontaneously made, in regard to the next Presidency, which tend to produce concentration, are wise and judicious. I should entertain this conviction, whether I was or was not the object of these demonstrations. Division is weakness, as Union is strength. Every movement therefore can but be salutary which diminishes the first and increases the last. In expressing this opinion, I mean, of course, such manifestations[2] as are voluntarily made by the People themselves, without any interested or artificial agency on the part of those who are spoken of as Candidates. As to them, the rule should be Hands off.

We are kept here in a state of anxious and feverish suspense about the S.T. bill.[3] I fear the truth is, that we have lost some two or three votes. On the other hand, we have probably gained some. I can but hope and believe that the measure will be defeated, altho' we must not be surprized if there should be a different result.

ALS. ViU. 1. Not found, but see Clay to Clayton, June 14, 1838. 2. Word "contingencies" is struck through and replaced by "manifestations." 3. Sub-Treasury bill. See Speech in Senate, Sept. 25, 1837; Speech in Senate, Feb. 19, 1838; *Cong. Globe*, 25 Cong., 1 Sess., 109-12, 264-65.

Remark in Senate, June 16, 1838. Opposes as "unnecessary" the creation of a surveyor general's office for the state of Michigan. *Cong. Globe*, 25 Cong., 2 Sess., 456.

To ISAAC WAYNE Washington, June 16, 1838

I thank you for the likeness of the late gallant General [Anthony] Wayne, which you did me the favor to transmit. It appears to me to be remarkably correct.

D[avid]. Trimble Esqr. whom you formerly knew in Congress, since he quit it, has been engaged in the Iron business, I believe successfully. His residence is Greenupsburg K[y].

You judge me rightly in supposing that I am most anxious for the termination of the present protracted Session of Congress. No day is yet fixed for it.

With friendly recollections of our service together in the H. of R. . . .

ALS. PU. Addressed to Wayne in Paoli, Pa. For Wayne, a lawyer who served in Congress from 1823 to 1825, see *BDAC*.

Remark in Senate, June 19, 1838. Listens to lengthy complaints by the two Ohio senators, Thomas Morris and William Allen, that they had been maligned by the Washington *Daily National Intelligencer* for asking why it was that over a two-year period only a paltry $30,000 (of a $1,000,000 goal) had been raised from the American public for construction of a monument in the District of Columbia to the memory of George Washington; and for implying, according to the newspaper, that the management of the Washington Monument Society, the private fund-raising agency involved in the appeal, was either inefficient, dishonest, or both. Interrupts Allen to state that personal complaints of this sort, based on nothing more consequential than "newspaper paragraphs," should be terminated at once by the Senate's presiding officer. If they were not, "What would it lead to? Look to his own case: he might, if he adopted that course, take up at least one third of the time of the Senate. . . . but this he would say, that no paper in this country was conducted with more regard to propriety, decorum, truth, and faithfulness of report than the National Intelligencer; and he could wish that the other journals of this city, and particularly the one connected with the Government [Washington *Globe*] would look more to this print for example." *Cong. Globe*, 25 Cong., 2 Sess., 461.

Later this day, Clay moves to table until tomorrow the bill "to abolish imprisonment for debt in certain cases" because of the apparent impracticality of implementing some of its provisions. Motion carried. *Ibid.*

Still later this day, Clay supports a Senate amendment to the House version of the Senate's "bill granting preëmption to settlers on the public lands [Remark in Senate, January 23, 1838]." This amendment, offered by Sen. Lucius Lyon (Mich.), would tighten the title-transfer regulations applicable to the resale of preempted land. After some discussion, however, Lyon agrees to withdraw it. Clay then calls attention to another amendment in the House version of the preemption bill which would subject to the provisions of the legislation "certain lands which had hitherto been always reserved from preëmption," especially land covered by valid Spanish or French claims. Because they were located near populous settlements, these lands "had now become very valuable." Specifies land of this kind near St. Louis which would sell "at once for ten dollars per acre." Moves to reject the House amendment. Motion carried 24 to 19, Clay voting yea. The vote was then taken on concurring with the amendments of the House as amended. Motion carried 42 to 2, Clay voting yea. *Ibid.*, 462-63.

Remark in Senate, June 20, 1838. With reference to a bill by Sen. Reuel Williams (Maine) "to provide for the survey and determination of the northeastern boundary of the United States according to the treaty of 1783," suggests that it be referred to the Committee on Foreign Relations, rather than to an impartial select committee as requested by Williams. *Cong. Globe*, 25 Cong., 2 Sess., 464-65. For the long and continuing Anglo-American dispute on the Maine-New Brunswick boundary question, see 2:147-48; 5:596-97; 6:265, 329-30; 7:729-30; and Henry S. Burrage, *Maine in the Northeastern Boundary Controversy* (Portland, Me., 1919), 231-46.

To ROBERT SWARTWOUT Washington, June 20, 1838

It affords me pleasure to learn through your favor of the 15h. inst. that you approve my declining to accept the invitation to visit your City. I have received the most abundant evidence of the propriety of the decision from all quarters.

Of the vital importance of success in your [New York] Fall elections[1] I am perfectly aware; and I can readily comprehend that the exertions and contributions of our friends in the City have almost exhausted their purses and their patience. You ask me if there is any prospect of obtaining assistance from members of Congress, if an application were made directly to them here? I scarcely need say that, on that subject, standing in the attitude in which I have been involuntarily placed, I have not deemed it proper to take any part in raising funds; but I know, in the general, that the members are very severely taxed, as they think, to supply means in aid of struggling Editors, and in the purchase and distribution of documents throughout the Union &c. The project of establishing a new press here has been under consideration, during the whole Session, and it has not been accomplished, but is postponed if not abandoned. One of the difficulties was the want of funds. There are very few of the members who are rich. Under all circumstances, I apprehend that not much could be obtained by an appeal to the members of Congress. The Cities are the places in which it is supposed most can be raised. Could you not draw upon Boston? I think that Abbot Lawrence would, if applied to, cause any reasonable amount to be supplied.

I should lament extremely the defeat of the Whigs in your State next fall. Our friends should reflect that the achievement of success in that election will probably relieve them from all future exertions. The Whig members from the interior of your State speak with increased confidence of Success.

I have addressed a letter to Philada. in behalf of your neighbour.[2] It was a sort of interposition which I did not much like, but I could not decline complying with your wishes.

ALS. NN. Letter marked "(Private)." 1. Schermerhorn to Clay, Feb. 25, 1838. 2. Reference obscure.

Comment in Senate, June 21, 1838. Responds to "gratuitous remarks" from Sen. John M. Niles (Conn.) that "political missionaries visited the State [Connecticut] last fall, one of whom was from Kentucky." Armed with Clay's frank, these men had "literally plastered over" Connecticut with printed Whig congressional speeches, "like the land of Egypt with frogs." Also reacts negatively to Niles's comparison of these political materials with the fertilizer made from white fish used by potato farmers in his state. Speaks, further, to references by Niles to the petitions from Connecticut for a new bank of the United States, petitions that Clay had presented to the Senate [Remark in Senate, May 31 and June 12, 1838].

To the claim by Niles that this was an action that had "interposed" Clay "between him and his constituents," Clay contends he had only done "for them what he would have done for any of the human kind." Denies that "political missionaries" from Kentucky had visited Connecticut to distribute printed Whig speeches. Such a charge, he says, was born in Niles's "own imagination." Notes also that both Connecticut senators, Niles and Perry Smith, have remarked that "on their vote hung the fate of the sub-Treasury bill [Speech in Senate, September 25, 1837]." Clay asserts his right, which they challenge, to raise again the question of the importance of the instructions of state legislators to U.S. senators, since both men have stated they will not obey the instructions of the Connecticut legislature on the Sub-Treasury vote. Calls on them to respect such direction because the "spirit" of Connecticut's instructions "pervade[s] the whole Union." To Sen. Perry Smith's statement that only from newspapers had he learned of a Kentucky political mission to Connecticut, Clay replies: "Then what must we think of a Senator who gets up in his place and asserts a fact, having no other authority than the newspapers?" *Cong. Globe*, 25 Cong., 2 Sess., 471-72.

Remark in Senate, June 25, 1838. Moves to postpone until tomorrow the joint resolution fixing July 9 as the date of adjournment.

Also criticizes a recent resolution requiring that original documents relating to private claims not be withdrawn from Senate files; instead, that claimants be required to pay a fee if they want copies of such papers made. Asserts that such a fee is "in the nature of a tax" and is thus beyond the constitutional power of the Senate to originate without the concurrence of the other house. Moves that the portion of the resolution having to do with the copying charge be rescinded. Motion carried 20 to 19. *Cong. Globe*, 25 Cong., 2 Sess., 478.

To HARRISON G. OTIS Washington, June 26, 1838

Altho' you kindly absolved me from the obligation of answering your favor of the 9h. March last, I cannot quit this City, which I hope in a few days to do, without making at least a brief acknowledgement of it, and expressing my thanks for the friendly feelings and sentiments towards me which it conveys. And I must offer you congratulations on the defeat of the S. T. bill which formed the topic of the Speech of which I transmitted you a copy.[1] It was consigned yesterday, by a decisive vote, to a repose which I trust will never be disturbed.[2]

Mr. Calhouns course, respecting which your reflections are just, has been most extraordinary. I believe in private life he is irreproachable; but I believe he will die a traitor or a madman. His whole aim, at least the tendency of all his exertions of late, is to sow the seeds of dissention between the different parts of the Union, and thus to prepare the way for its dissolution. His little clique, distinguished more by activity and paradoxes, than by numbers, is now busily endeavoring to propagate the notion that all the operations of the Fed. Government, from the commencement, have been ruinous to the South, and aggrandizing to the North! This, altho 40 years of the 48, during which the Governmt. has existed, have Southern men directed the course of public affairs!

I assure you, my dear Sir, that I share with you in an anxious desire for retirement; but we are not always allowed to follow our wishes, and that is my situation. I have however determined quietly to look on, with composure, and leave events to take their own course. Judging, from all I hear and see, there is much reason, I think, to anticipate that your friendly wishes about me will be realized. The admon party is, beyond all doubt, prostrated. Nothing can continue it in power but the division among the Whigs as to their Candidate for the Presidency. *Our* division now is *their* only remaining strength. The people appear to be likely to remove that obstacle, by concentrating on one individual. Much however remains to be done, and especially in *your* quarter of the Union. If Mr. W[ebster]. were to retire (and I think his retirement would add strength to the cause and to his own high pretensions) all other difficulties would speedily vanish. But I had forgotten that you are withdrawn from politics, and that I had promised to write briefly. I will therefore conclude with the fervent hope that you may long live in health & happiness, and witness the restoration of order, decency, and intelligence once more in our public councils. . . .

ALS. MHi. Letter marked "(Confidential)." 1. Speech in Senate, Feb. 19, 1838; see also Speech in Senate, Sept. 25, 1837. 2. The House of Representatives voted the bill down, 125-111, on June 25. *Cong. Globe*, 25 Cong., 2 Sess., 478.

Remark in Senate, June 26, 1838. Supports the bill for the relief of the heirs of Pierre Menard. *Cong. Globe*, 25 Cong., 2 Sess., 481. The bill was passed on June 27. *Ibid.*, 483. For Menard, see 6:845.

Remark in Senate, June 28, 1838. Participates in debate [not recorded] in opposition to James Buchanan's amendment to (or substitute for) Daniel Webster's bill of June 12 "making further provision for the collection of the public revenue." *Cong. Globe*, 25 Cong., 2 Sess., 485; *ibid.*, Appendix, 467. Webster's bill of June 12, 1838, undertook to amend section 5 of the Deposit Act of June 23, 1836, so as to qualify other than the so-called "Pet Banks" as depositories for government funds. The last clause of section 5 forbade government deposits in those banks which issued notes of less than five dollars denomination after July 4, 1836. Webster's bill sought to remove the small-bill limitation; it would also empower the government to deposit its funds in any state-chartered private bank, or in any bank currently in a specie-paying attitude even though that bank had had to suspend specie payments at some time after July 4, 1836. The first clause of section 5 required private banks of deposit to be specie-paying institutions after July 4, 1836. 5 *U.S. Stat.*, 52-57; *Cong. Globe*, 25 Cong., 2 Sess., 448. The chief features of Buchanan's amendment to Webster's proposal are outlined by the Pennsylvania senator in *ibid.*, Appendix, 466-67. It was defeated, 29 to 21, on June 29. *Cong. Globe*, 25 Cong., 2 Sess., 487.

Although Clay's speech of this date in support of Webster's bill and in opposition to Buchanan's amendment was not recorded, some indication of its thrust and scope may be inferred from Calhoun's angry answer to it. In the course of his remarks, Clay had apparently charged Calhoun with having become an administration man by virtue of his support of the Sub-Treasury bill and his opposition to Webster's bill of June 12. He had charged also that the centralizing tendencies of Van Buren's banking and currency policies threatened Southern sectional interests presumably dear to Calhoun, and he had further attacked Calhoun for belonging to a political faction not friendly to the continuation of the Union. Calhoun replied that Clay had severely wronged him. He was glad to see, however, that Clay "does not entirely deny the truth of the principles on which I act. He is at last compelled to admit, that Abolition is making greater progress than he had anticipated, and to acknowledge that the time may come when he shall be compelled to take a stand and lead against the fanatics." *Ibid.*, Appendix, 468. For the Clay-Calhoun split, see Speech in Senate, February 19, 1838; and Benton, *Thirty Years' View*, 2:97-123.

Comment in Senate, June 30, 1838. Clay is drawn into debate when Sen. Silas Wright (N.Y.) introduces a bill to "modify" the last clause of section 5 of the Deposit Act of 1836 [8:813; Remark in Senate, June 28 and July 4, 1838]. Wright's bill immediately received two readings by unanimous consent and was then taken up by the Senate sitting as a committee of the whole. As the debate opened, Webster offered an amendment to Wright's bill that was consistent with the provisions in his bill of June 12 relating to the liberalization of the qualifications required of government banks of deposit [Remark in Senate, June 28, 1838]. It was added to Wright's bill as section 2. Wright countered with an amendment to Webster's amendment calling for the repeal of sections 1 through 12 of the Deposit Act of 1836, "except so far as is above provided, and to enable the Treasury Department to collect any debts which may be due or owing from the late deposite banks."

At this point, Clay denounces Wright's counter-amendment to Webster's new section 2 "as monstrous in itself, in as much as it proposed to take the whole revenue of the country from its legitimate keeping and place it under the control of the Executive. As fast as that monster, the Sub-Treasury system [Speech in Senate, September 25, 1837], had been strangled by the people, it was sought to revive it." Clay argues further that the "original measure as introduced by Mr. Webster would have the most salutary effect," whereas the Wright amendment "would place the whole Treasury of the nation at the will of a single individual." Points out the utility to the poor of bank notes below $5 in denomination and defends the integrity of those banks that had been ordered to issue such notes by their state legislatures, because "the people had risen almost *en masse*, and asked the Legislatures to authorize these . . . small notes, as a relief measure to the country." Asserts that in the final analysis the only guarantor of a sound and healthy national currency is "a National Bank [Comment in Senate, September 26, 1837; Speech in Senate, May 21, 1838] such a one as had been destroyed to make room for the introduction of those wild and reckless experiments upon the currency, which had ended in one universal and wide-spread ruin of all the great leading interests of the country." *Cong. Globe*, 25 Cong., 2 Sess., Appendix, 456. Wright's amendment to Webster's amendment was accepted 26 to 21 and the bill to modify the Deposit Act of 1836 was ordered to be engrossed and read a third time. *Cong. Globe*, 25 Cong., 2 Sess., 488. Clay voted nay. On July 2, Wright's bill, as amended, was passed 27 to 22 and sent to the House. *Ibid.*, 491. Clay again voted nay. See also U.S. Sen., *Journal*, 25 Cong., 2 Sess., 513-14, 752. For the subsequent history of this bill, see Remark in Senate, July 4, 1838.

Also on this day Clay launched a personal attack on Sen. John M. Niles (Conn.) for not being particularly bright and for his slavish Jacksonism. Exults that Niles, defeated in the Connecticut legislature for reelection [Remark in Senate, May 31, 1838], is as "dead, dead, dead" as the Sub-Treasury scheme he has supported. "It is true he is not buried yet, but will be on the 3d of March, 1839. His epitaph is written, Here lies the body of ________________ (I will not name him . . . that would be unparliamentary,) lamented by his friends, especially his political friends! His course was marked by great ability and attachment to the tenets of the Jackson party!" *Cong. Globe*, 25 Cong., 2 Sess., 488; *ibid.*, Appendix, 456.

Earlier this day, Clay presented a petition asking that the good offices of the United States be used to settle the problem between Mexico and France. *Cong.*

Globe, 25 Cong., 2 Sess., 488. France and Mexico were engaged in the so-called "Pastry War" of 1838-39 in which France was attempting to collect the claims of her citizens against Mexico and to secure better treatment for French citizens living in Mexico. On April 16, 1838, the French announced a naval blockade of Mexico's gulf coast and in November the French took possession of the fortress at Veracruz. This culminated in a Mexican declaration of war against France. For a discussion of these events and the conclusion of the war, see Nancy N. Barker, *The French Experience in Mexico, 1821-1861; A History of Constant Misunderstanding* (Chapel Hill, 1979), 57-88; Rives, *The United States and Mexico*, 1:427-46.

Remark in Senate, July 3, 1838. Presents the memorial of a man who states he has discovered a method of preventing steamboat boiler explosions, and asks for legislation to provide for examining the value of his discovery and to compensate him for it "if it is found worthy of the patronage of Congress." *Cong. Globe*, 25 Cong., 2 Sess., 493.

Remark in Senate, July 4, 1838. Presents a petition from citizens of Westmoreland County, Va., opposing the adoption of the Sub-Treasury system and asking that a Bank of the United States be established. *Cong. Globe*, 25 Cong., 2 Sess., 496.

Later this day, Clay speaks to the House version of the Wright bill modifying the Deposit Act of 1836 as amended [Comment in Senate, June 30, 1838], noting that while he "had not obtained all that was desired, he should vote most cordially and heartily for the amendment. Without it, or at least in the shape the bill was sent from the Senate, it left all to Executive discretion; but, as it [now] was, it gave some semblance of legal control over the subject." *Ibid.*

The House version of the Wright bill, achieved after much give and take and compromise and amendment, was passed 173 to 31 on this same day, July 4 [Remark in Senate, June 28, 1838; Comment in Senate, June 30, 1838]. It dropped section 2 of Wright's bill (which struck out sections 1 through 12 of the Deposit Act of 1836). Instead, it confined itself to modifying the last clause of section 5 of the Deposit Act. Specifically, it provided that the U.S. Treasury accept in payment of obligations owed it the notes of banks which had been issued in denominations of less than five dollars after July 4, 1836; it went on to state, however, that the government would not accept the notes of those banks which continued to issue or reissue notes under five dollars in denomination after October 1, 1838. Specie-paying banks accepting this stricture would thus be qualified to serve as government depositories. The Senate accepted the House version on July 4 by a vote of 29 to 17, with Clay, Webster, and Wright all voting yea. Webster remarked that "It gave him the truest pleasure to learn that the House had rejected the second section of the bill, and that it had done so by so decisive a majority." On July 5, 1838, the president signed into law the "Act to modify the last clause of the fifth section of the deposite act" of June 23, 1836. *Ibid.*, 488, 491-92, 495-96; 5 *U.S. Stat.*, 255.

Still later this same day, Clay compliments Sen. James Buchanan (Pa.), chairman of the Foreign Relations Committee, for his "great ability" in bringing forth a resolution to settle the Northeast boundary issue by renewed negotiation and joint survey rather than by embracing Sen. Reuel Williams's bill to proceed with a unilateral survey and boundary determination under the provisions of the Anglo-American Treaty of Paris of 1783 [Remark in Senate, June 20, 1838]. On the related question of how many copies should be printed of the committee's accompanying report on the Maine boundary issue, Clay remarks that it is especially fitting that such Anglo-American problems be addressed on this particular day, July 4. *Cong. Globe*, 25 Cong., 2 Sess., 496-97.

Remark in Senate, July 5, 1838. Moves to table a proposed Senate rule change that would carry over to the next session all unresolved private bills, resolutions, and reports "as though an adjournment had not taken place." *Cong. Globe*, 25 Cong., 2 Sess., 498.

Remark in Senate, July 6, 1838. Learning that the secretary of the treasury had estimated government expenditures for the present year at "about $23,785,249," Clay asks if that figure includes funds for the maintenance and development of harbors. Also opposes an amendment to the harbor appropriation bill offered by Sen. Silas Wright (N.Y.) that would empower the president to "arrange" for the expenditure of all appropriated funds, aside from appropriations for "the regular, ordinary, annual expenses of the Government," in light of the actual "state of the Treasury." Amendment voted down. *Cong. Globe*, 25 Cong., 2 Sess., 500-501.

To LEWIS TAPPAN Washington, July 6, 1838

I hope that you will believe that my omission to answer earlier your last favor[1] has not proceeded from any intention to treat you with the slightest disrespect. The subject of your letter is one on which we unfortunately differ in opinion, and ascribing to you the same good motives which I claim for myself, I apprehend that there is no prospect of reconciling our conflicting opinions. I most conscientiously believe that the Northern agitation of the question of Abolition is productive of no good. I believe it injurious to the unfortunate black race and hazardous to the harmony, peace and union of the whites. I am sure that you can not view the matter in the same light. But with our opposite sentiments, it has not appeared to me profitable to enter upon a discussion, for which indeed I have no time, and which is not likely to lead to any useful result. . . .

ALS. DLC-Lewis Tappan Papers (DNA, M212, R22). 1. Not certain, but probably Tappan to Clay, June 5, 1838.

To HARRISON G. OTIS Washington, July 7, 1838

At the moment of my departure from this City, I am favored with your letter of the 2d. for which, as well as for the privilege of using it, altho'. I shall not probably avail myself of it, I am thankful.

The partiality for Mr. W[ebster]. and the admiration of his abilities, in your quarter, are quite natural. The same admiration extends every where. It is nevertheless perfectly manifest that he cannot be elected President at the next election. If I were withdrawn, [William H.] Harrison would sweep every thing before him.

I think then it is best for Mr. W. to retire from a position which, whilst it exhibits us divided and thereby encourages our opponents and discourages our friends, can lead to no issue favorable to himself. It is best for *him* and best for the common cause. It would be regarded as a measure of great magnanimity and his praises would be generally sounded. It could not fail to redound to his benefit hereafter.

As to the mode of retiring, there can be no difficulty in adopting a suitable one, when that course is resolved on. I think it would be more dignified on the part of Mr. W. and more conducive to harmony, that he should abstain from any indication of his preference. If he retire, the feelings at the North, now stifled, would burst forth, and Genl Hs. friends would perceive the utter hopelessness of his remaining in the field. In six months from Mr. Ws. retirement, the whole matter would be finally settled.

These are my views. It is not necessary to say, what is quite obvious, that I am not the most impartial judge, and that I am therefore liable to mistake.

In a long & friendly interview with Mr. W. I communicated them to him, of course not in the form of advice, but of suggestion This was three or four weeks ago, and the state of his mind then seemed to be, that he did not clearly see that he should abandon his position.[1]

Mr. [Stephen C.] Philips, Mr. [Nathaniel] Silsbee, I understand Mr. Abbott Lawrence, and I believe Mr. John Davis entertain views corresponding with those I have suggested.

He has no bad advisers in Massachusetts; but I think that it is otherwise in the City of N.Y.[2]

Already collisions have arisen between his friends and mine in that City which, if they be not suppressed, may jeopard[ize] the Fall election there.[3] Dissention is the inevitable consequence of our present respective positions; and it will increase with the progress of time and the natural zeal of ardent friends. In so much, that the energy and harmony, which should be reserved for the Locos', will be exhausted among ourselves, if not substituted by feelings of positive enmity, before the day of trial.

I write hastily. . . .

ALS. MHi. Letter marked "(Confidential)." 1. Webster reportedly "politely declined a personal appeal from Clay to drop out of the race." Bartlett, *Daniel Webster*, 156. 2. Clay to Letcher, May 30, 1837; Clay to Davis, July 3, 1837. 3. Schermerhorn to Clay, Feb. 25, 1838; Clay to Swartwout, June 20, 1838.

Remark in Senate, July 7, 1838. Moves to amend the harbor bill to include $20,000 for improvement of navigation on the Tennessee River above Nashville. Motion lost 19 to 12. Also joins [not recorded] the debate on a bill to extend the time for locating Virginia military land warrants and the amendment to it that would increase the amount of land set aside from 200,000 to 300,000 acres [8:744, 765]. *Cong. Globe*, 25 Cong., 2 Sess., 504-5. For the bill concerning the Virginia military land warrants, see Clay to Brooke, June 5, 1838.

During the evening session, Clay participates [not recorded] in a "long and earnest discussion" of an amendment to the fortifications bill that would appropriate $40,000 with which to secure land for Fort Delaware on Pea Patch Island in the Delaware River. Amendment defeated 19 to 14, Clay voting yea. *Cong. Globe*, 25 Cong., 2 Sess., 504-5.

From Stephen Duncan, Natchez, Miss., July 16, 1838. Reports he has received from Clay 90 or 95 coils of rope and presumes that the remainder is soon to arrive. Indicates that the price has not yet been settled between them. Adds that he "cannot agree" with Clay on his "Banke project [Comment in Senate, September 26, 1837; Speech in Senate, May 21, 1838]," but is inclined "to distrust my own opinion[s] when they come in conflict with yours on any subject." ALS. DLC-TJC (DNA, M212, R14).

From James W. Thomson, Wilmington, Del., July 21, 1838. Encloses receipt for $150 in payment for the Durham heifer "Lilly" purchased from Samuel Canby of Wilmington for Clay. Notes that Canby has agreed to keep Lilly until August,

1839, "if you determine to have her served by Maxwell." ALS. DLC-TJC (DNA, M212, R14).

For Thomson, a graduate of the University of Virginia Medical School and later president of the Medical Society of Delaware, see *DH*, 11:216-17; 16:339. Samuel Canby was a prominent farmer and breeder of Durham cattle in Castle County, Delaware. In fact, in 1840 Canby was gored by a Durham cow about to calve. He suffered a "*severe* cut on his head . . . and another on a very tender part which the doctors [Lewis D.P.] Bush and [James W.] Thompson [*sic*] sewed up." *Ibid.*, 16:79, 214, 216-17.

To JOHN B. DILLON Lexington, July 28, 1838

I recd. your letter expressing an opinion in favor of an amendment of the Constitution, and inviting an expression of mine You do not specify the kind of amendment which you think desirable, but I presume you allude to one which should limit the Presidential office to a single term, as that has been most frequently canvassed in late years. Without examining all the pros' and cons' (for which I have not time) I will briefly say that such an amendment, which should enlarge the present term to six years, and limit the incumbent to one term, would in my opinion be a great improvement of our present Constitution.

The public lands, of which your letter also treats, form a most interesting subject of Administration. You say large quantities of them are amassed, to the extent even of whole Townships, retarding settlement, and checking the progress of improvement. This species of speculation is greatly to be regretted. This is partly owing to the fact of unrestricted sales, which is perhaps unavoidable, and partly to the low price at which the Governmt. disposes of the public domain. Tempted, by that moderate price, individuals are induced to purchase more than they actually want, under the hope, which is almost sure to be realized, of obtaining a larger price. And yet, with all this experience before us, what ought we to think of that policy which recommends a graduation and further reduction of the price? Such a reduction would redound to the benefit of the speculator, and would be attended with but little advantage to the cultivator.[1]

My views of the best administration of the P[ublic]. lands have been so often laid before the Senate, that I will not dwell on this topic.[2] But I will take the occasion to say that language was attributed to me, during the last Session, when discussing the Preemption system, which I never used. To that system I was strongly opposed; but I never used the expressions "Land robbers or Land pirates."[3] Those which I did employ were substantially the same as those contained in the Presidents message. I considered the preemptioner a trespasser, and his occupation of the public lands, contrary to law, a trespass; and I contended that the property of the People of the U. S. ought to be protected and guarded as strictly and securely as that of individuals.

ALS. DLC-HC (DNA, M212, R5). Dillon had become editor of the Logansport (Ind.) *Canal Telegraph* in 1834. He later wrote a history of Indiana and served in various governmental offices such as state librarian and assistant secretary of state for Indiana. *IMH*, 1:4-8. 1. Remark in Senate, Jan. 23 and March 29, 1838; Speech in Senate, April 11, 1838. 2. *Ibid.*; see also 8:494, 539-41, 609-10, 671, 753, 812-13, 846-47, 873. 3. Comment in Senate, Dec. 26, 1837; Remark in Senate, Jan. 23, 1838; Comment in Senate, Jan. 26 and 27, 1838.

To RUFUS W. GRISWOLD Lexington, July 28, 1838

I have received your letter[1] informing me that at the Whig Convention lately held in Vermont,[2] some of the members who were friendly to me determined to cause an enquiry to be made of me whether, should it be deemed necessary at a Convention to be holden in the fall, to ask my sentiments on the Slavery question, I will answer, and permit the answer to be published? And the particular enquiries which you state it is desired to put to me are, Has Congress power over slavery in the District of Columbia? Has it power to regulate the Slave trade between the States &c?

I have, at the last Session of Congress, expressed in the Senate, my sentiments fully, on the subjects of your letter, in the form of a series of resolutions, and of Speeches,[3] which I addressed to that body. As to the Dt. of Col. I thought that Congress could not abolish slavery there, without a violation of good faith, and that Congress had no power to prevent the removal of slaves from one Slave state to another.

Having thus so recently publicly expressed my views, I confess that I do not perceive the necessity of any new expression of them. I will not say that I should not answer such a letter as you describe to be the intention of some of my friends to address to me; but I must think it not necessary.

It is remarkable that, at the very moment when I am replying to you, I have before me several letters from the South stating that I am charged there with being an Abolitionist.

ALS. MB. 1. For Griswold—journalist, anthologist, and Baptist minister—see *DAB*. 2. Clay to Porter, Jan. 5, 1838. 3. Comment in Senate, Dec. 18, 1837; Remark in Senate, Jan. 6, 1838; Speech in Senate, Jan. 9, 1838.

From John Van Ness Yates, Albany, N.Y., August 4, 1838. Introduces himself as the son of Robert Yates, "the writer of the secret debates in the convention of 1787," as well as "truly and legitimately a Whig." Also identifies himself as an enemy of Martin Van Buren and says of the president that "I never formed but one opinion of him, He was as adept in Intrigue and unprincipled in the means he adopted to obtain any proposed object—His whole aim in life was centered in *Self*—he never felt or entertained a single honorable or disinterested sentiment—Supple and full of tact, he knew all the most selfish and most depraved principles of human nature, and pursued the readiest avenues to them and through them to bring his views into successful operation—He never commanded the affections of a single human being (his immediate connections perhaps excepted)." Considers Clay's election to the presidency "certain" and asks him to appoint Robert C. Yates, his son, as U.S. consul in Rio de Janeiro. Explains Robert's qualifications for the post. Concludes that in the coming presidential contest, "The State of New York, Sir, will do you justice, The vote is yours." ALS. DLC-HC (DNA, M212, R5). Endorsed by Clay: "Answered, declining any Commitment." For Yates, see 5:114.

From George W. Lafayette, Paris, August 6, 1838. Presents to Clay, from the Lafayette family, a printed collection of the deceased general's memoirs and manuscripts. Thanks Clay for the attention and honor paid his father by Congress in 1824 [3:893-94, 899, 900]. ALS, in French. DLC-HC (DNA, M212, R5). Copy, printed in French, in Colton, *Clay Correspondence*, 4:427-28. Translated by Danielle Thompson. The six volumes of *Memoires, Correspondence et Manuscrits Du General Lafayette*, had been published in Paris by his family in 1836.

To ROBERT SWARTWOUT Lexington, August 10, 1838

I recd. your favor of the 28h. July. I must reserve your kind congratulations on the supposed escape of my Colleague and myself for some future occasion, as no disaster occurred to the Buffalo, in which we descended the Ohio river. Whig Boats do not founder. We took some Locofoco members off the wreck of the Detroit, the boat which met with an accident.[1] We shall I hope soon have to relieve others of them from the more important wreck which they have made of the Administration.

I thank you for the communication which you have made to me of the contingent plan of the Campaign of Mess. V. Buren and Calhoun. It won't do. Harrison has recently publicly declared, at a 4h. of July entertainment, that he will yield a hearty and honorable support to the Candidate nominated by the N. Convention, whoever he may be.[2] But, if he could be weak enough to allow himself to be a rallying point for the defeated Locofoco's, the only regret I should feel would be on his own account. He would, in such an event, lose all of the Whigs, and would be entirely unable to obtain the support of all the friends of the Administration. If I should be the Candidate such a russe de guerre would give me no concern. I had heard some thing of this plan, but it never excited the smallest apprehension.

Our State election for members to the General Assembly has just terminated. It is hardly necessary to say that the Whig cause has been fully sustained.[3] We are looking with anxiety for information from Illinois[4] and Missouri,[5] whose elections have also just closed. I think we shall receive from both those States encouraging news. But towards your great State our most anxious looks are directed.[6] I confess that I am not without fears for the City,[7] excited more from divisions among ourselves than from the strength of our adversary. I am particularly solicitous about the division between the friends of Mr. W[ebster]. and myself. It will require great discretion to prevent its producing mischief. I hope that no question will be made among our friends, as to [Josiah Ogden] Hoffman and [Edward] Curtis,[8] if otherwise it shall be deemed expedient to run them.

I am enjoying here comparative repose; but, as you may imagine, I have a good deal of Company.

ALS. NN. 1. The steamboat *Detroit*, bound to Cincinnati from Pittsburgh, had struck an obstacle in the river and had sunk. All the passengers were safely evacuated and were taken to Cincinnati on the steamboat *Buffalo*. The newspaper account erroneously stated that Clay and Crittenden had been on board the *Detroit*. Washington *Daily National Intelligencer*, July 23, 1838. 2. Harrison had made this statement in Massillon, Ohio, on July 4, 1838. Frankfort *Commonwealth*, August 29 and Sept. 12, 1838. 3. In the Kentucky general assembly elections in August, 1838, the Whigs won 65 seats in the lower house to 35 for the Democrats. In the state senate, the Whigs won 22 seats to 16 for the Democrats. Lexington *Observer & Kentucky Reporter*, Sept. 8, 1838. 4. In the 1838 gubernatorial election in Illinois, Thomas Carlin, a Democrat, won by a margin of 30,648 votes to 29,722 votes for Cyrus Edwards, the Whig candidate. *BDGUS*, 1:370. In the elections for the state senate, the Whigs won 22 seats to 16 for the Democrats and 2 for the Conservatives. The Whigs won 46 seats in the state house of representatives to 41 for the Democrats and 5 for the Conservatives. The Democrats won 2 seats in the U.S. House to 1 for the Whigs. Lexington *Observer & Kentucky Reporter*, Sept. 5, 1838; *Guide to U.S. Elections*, 570. 5. In the 1838 elections for the Missouri legislature, Democrats won 20 seats in the state senate to 13 for the Whigs, and 58 seats in the state house of representatives to 39 for the Whigs. The Democrats also won both seats in the U.S. House. Lexington *Observer & Kentucky Reporter*, Sept. 12, 1838; *Guide to U.S. Elections*, 570. 6. Schermerhorn to Clay, Feb. 25, 1838. 7. *Ibid.* 8. In the 1838 elections Hoffman and Curtis, both Whigs, ran for the U.S. House from New York's third district, which comprised two seats. Hoffman won with 20,577 votes; Moses Grinnell, also a Whig, won with 20,563 votes. Curtis lost, running third among the eight candidates. *Guide to U.S. Elections*, 570.

To NATHAN SARGENT Lexington, August 11, 1838

I duly received your friendly letter of the 18h. Ulto. and fully share in all your gratified feelings excited by the bright and encouraging prospects which have opened on our public affairs. The personal agency which I have had in them; the calumnies and ferocious attacks of which I have been the object; and the despair which, at one period of our troubles, had seized the better part of the public mind, and had almost reached my own, give to our present prospects peculiar delight. Still we have not yet overcome all difficulties; the adversary is in possession of the field, has two and a half years for operations, and the command of an almost boundless patronage to influence. If the approaching elections in both N. York[1] and Pennsa.[2] should terminate favorably for us, I think there will be an end of the whole controversy. If we lose either, our opponents will continue to struggle hard; and if we lose both, we should be in great danger of final defeat. In any and every event we should never, for a moment, cease to exercise great vigilance. Our greatest misfortune is the division which exists among our friends as to the next Presidency. That is our weakness and our adversary's strength. Knowing the zeal with which the friends of Mr. Webster and myself espouse the cause of their respective favorites in the City of New York, I entertain great apprehensions about the result there of the coming election.[3] It will require great discretion to prevent that division working injuriously, especially in that City.

Our elections for members to the General Assembly have just closed I scarcely need say that the Whig Cause has been fully maintained.[4] Indeed it has been only in a very few Counties that the friends of the Administration have made any effort. We are looking towards Illinois[5] and Missouri,[6] with the greatest anxiety. Our accounts of the probability of success in both of those States have been highly encouraging to the last. I shall be greatly disappointed if we do not succeed in Illinois, and somewhat if we fail in Missouri.

I am here enjoying some repose, and endeavoring to recruit from the fatigues of our late exhausting Session of Congress. But I see a great deal of Company, and my correspondence is not light.

ALS. ViU. 1. Schermerhorn to Clay, Feb. 25, 1838. 2. *Ibid.* 3. *Ibid.* 4. Clay to Swartwout, August 10, 1838. 5. *Ibid.* 6. *Ibid.*

To PETER B. PORTER Lexington, August 15, 1838

I am very sorry to have to inform you that the child of my son H. Clay junr. died this morning about 4 OClock.[1] I had hoped and supposed that it was better, but it seems we were mistaken. This event will deprive me of the pleasure of receiving you and other friends at dinner to day. My son, whom I saw on my return home yesterday, I am happy to tell you continued to be better; but the loss of his infant will afflict him very much.

I wish, my dear General, that you would any night after this, that suits your own convenience, come and tarry with me at Ashland. I have much to say to you, and if you would stay a night with me, we should not be exposed to any interruption from Company. I am always at home every afternoon and night.

ALS. NBuHi. Addressed to Porter at "Cabell's Dale," the Breckinridge family home near Lexington, Ky. 1. Probably the infant Martha, date of birth unknown.

From John A. Jones, Van Wert, Ga., August 16, 1838. Wants to purchase a half-Devonshire, half-Durham bull calf between 12 and 18 months old "to cross on the common cows of our country." Inquires what such an animal would cost in Kentucky. ALS. DLC-TJC (DNA, M212, R14). Endorsed by Clay: "[Blooded Cattle—Wrote him that he might have my Devon Calf & a yearling bull at $400 or either at $200 or the Ayshire at $250]."

To EDWARD C. DELAVAN Lexington, August 20, 1838

I duly received your favor of the 2d. inst. with the addresses on the subject of Foreign emigration to the U. States.[1] The object of guarding the emigrant against vicious practices and habits, upon his landing on our shores, must command the approbation of all good men. But may it not be doubted whether emigration to the U States is not already sufficiently great, without the employment of new incitements? And would it not be better, without disturbing its natural course, to direct the care of the Temperance Society[2] to the emigrants after their arrival in our ports? I am aware that that is already done to some extent, but would it not be more beneficial to employ the means which you can command at home instead of abroad?[3]

I adhere to the opinions which I briefly expressed, in regard to the operations of the Temperance Cause, at our interview in Washington. It has done great good; and will continue to do more as long as it employs only mild measures. Its means should only be those of persuasion. It will destroy itself whenever it resorts to coercion, or mixes in the politics of the Country. The misfortune in human affairs is that we convince ourselves of what we suppose to be right, and then we endeavor, as we ought to do, to persuade others; but if we fail to convince them, we then resort to force. Hence, religious intolerance, proscription, the stake &c. Now, it is generally admitted among us, that in Religion, the greatest of all our interests, every man should be left free to follow any or none, as he pleases. But if we may not compel men to be religious have we a right to oblige them to be sober? Have we a right to constrain them to eat or not to eat, to drink or not to drink, not as they please, but as we choose to think is best for them?

I know that you and I do not differ on this subject; but there is a constant tendency towards coercion, even in good institutions, against which the Temperance Society should guard itself.

I regret that I am so often appealed to for pecuniary contributions, for so many objects, that I cannot comply with your request for aid. If I were near you, I might present a trifle; but at this distance there is a difficulty in remitting a small sum. . . .

ALS. ICN. 1. For Delavan, who helped organize the New York State Temperance Society in 1829 and the American Temperance Union in 1836, see *DAB*. 2. For a history of the temperance movement, see August F. Fehlandt, *A Century of Drink Reform in the United States*. Cincinnati, 1904; Ernest H. Cherrington, *The Evolution of Prohibition in the United States of America*. Westerville, Ohio, 1920; Joseph R. Gusfield,

Symbolic Crusade: Status Politics and the American Temperance Movement. Urbana, Ill., 1963. 3. For the association between xenophobia and the temperance movement, which became even more pronounced in the late nineteenth century, see Thomas J. Curran, *Xenophobia and Immigration 1820-1930* (Boston, 1975), 22-26, 29-31; George Potter, *To the Golden Door, The Story of the Irish in Ireland and America* (Boston, 1960), 218-70; Jerome Mushkat, *Tammany, The Evolution of a Political Machine 1789-1865* (Syracuse, N.Y., 1971), 15-30.

To LEWIS F. ALLEN Lexington, August 21, 1838

I received your[1] favor of the 27h. Ulto. transmitting a stalk of grass which you supposed to be what is commonly called the Blue grass of Kentucky. But it is clearly not our blue grass, and I take it to be wild rye. I regret that it is too late in the season to send you a stalk of the blue grass, as it is gone to seed and the first growth is now dry. It goes to seed in June with us, although another crop springs up which continues to grow until we have a hard frost. It would now be knee high in some of my pastures, if it did not fall down and lye in swarth or masses upon the ground. If stock are removed from a Blue grass pasture on the first of July, it will grow up and, falling down in masses, will remain protected from the snow and frost during the winter; and nothing can be finer for young stock. I am afraid that you are too far North to derive that advantage from its cultivation. It scarcely ever requires renewal; the older the grass the richer it becomes.

Our blue grass is very different from the grass which is known by that name in Maryland and Virginia. It is the green sward or spear grass of England. When Kentucky was first settled small patches of it were found around our Salt-licks, carried there in the seed, no doubt, by the animals which resorted to them for salt, and it was sometimes called the English grass. As the Country opened and improved, its value became known, and it was extended and diffused, by being sown, and often by deposites made of the seed by Cattle and other stock. It is the same grass which is used in lawns, and yards, and I have no doubt that it is frequently to be met with in your State.

As I have been unable to send you a spire of the grass, I have made an arrangement with Genl [Peter B.] Porter (who is now with us) to forward to you some seed in the course of the fall. And you will find no better time to sow it, than to scatter it upon the snow in the month of March. Any moderate quantity of it can be procured in Lexington during the months of September and October. It is usually brought in, in chaff, and sells at one or two dollars per bushel. We consider it as making the best pastures by far of any other grass. It mixes well with timothy and clover but finally subdues both.

I hope that you will be successful in rearing Cattle of the improved breeds. I too have been long and largely en[g]aged in the same business. I have Durhams, Hereford Reds, Devons, Ayreshire, Kiloe,[2] and Holstein; but the Durhams are decidedly preferred by our breeders to all others. What price do your fullblooded Durhams command? Have you any Heifers of good and undoubted pedigrees which you wish to sell, and at what prices?

I am crossing my Devons with the Durhams, and, as far as I am yet able to jud[g]e, the experiment answers well. It has been said to have succeeded in England.

The results of our Western Elections have been encouraging. In Kentucky[3] and Indiana[4] the Whig cause has been fully maintained. We have not received intelligence of the final issue of the contest in Missouri[5] and Illinois,[6] but we have heard enough to be satisfied that it has been close, and that if the Administration has succeeded it has been by greatly diminished majorities.

ALS. NcD. Printed in G.S. Dunbar, "Henry Clay on Kentucky Bluegrass, 1838," *AH* (July, 1977), 51:522-23. 1. Allen, an agricultural writer and stockbreeder in N.Y. state, was sometime chairman of the Committee on Agriculture of the N.Y. state legislature. See *Franklin Farmer* (March 3, 1838), 1:205. 2. Or Kyloe, a breed of cattle found in the west highland region of Scotland. 3. Clay to Swartwout, August 10, 1838. 4. In the 1838 elections for the Indiana state senate, the Whigs won 38 seats to 17 for the Democrats. In the state house of representatives, the Whigs won 58 seats to 37 for the Democrats, 3 for the Conservatives and 1 with the party not given. *Niles' Register* (August 25, 1838), 54:401. 5. Clay to Swartwout, August 10, 1838. 6. *Ibid.*

To DAVID CROWELL Lexington, August 24, 1838

I have duly received your favor of the 2d. inst. I have to thank you for the compliment paid me by confering my name on the Coasting vessel which you have lately launched. If she should share the fortunes of her namesake, she will pass through many storms and troubles; but I hope, like him, she will survive them all, and finally reach a port of safety.

I have also to present to you my grateful acknowledgements for the friendly wishes and hopes which you are pleased to express about me. The prospects of a better state of public affairs are indeed highly encouraging, since, in every election which has occurred during the last year, those who have so much abused the powers of Government have been generally defeated; and, in the few instances where they have succeeded, they have prevailed by very diminished majorities. The late elections which have just taken place in the West[1] form no exception to that observation. . . .

ALS. NN. Crowell was a ship's carpenter in Perth Amboy, N.J. 1. Clay to Swartwout, August 10, 1838; Clay to Allen, August 21, 1838.

To HUGH L. WHITE Lexington, August 27, 1838

I am indebted to you, or to some other friend, for a copy of the speech which you delivered on the late occasion of a public dinner with which you and Mr. [John] Bell were complimented on your return from Washington.[1] I have attentively perused it, and with much satisfaction; and I cannot deny myself the pleasure of saying to you that it is candid, independent, and in perfect consistency with your own principles, character, and course. I might not be willing to admit the ambition which you ascribe to me; but I do not mean to insist upon that observation of yours as detracting from the general fairness of the speech. My chief object, however, in now addressing you, is to correct an error into which you have fallen, in respect to the last Presidential election.[2] You appear to be under the impression that Gen. Harrison was a candidate brought out by me, and brought out to avenge injuries which I had previously experienced from you. Now, I assure you, sir, that I had no more agency in presenting the General as a candidate than you had. It was done without any prompting of mine, and without any prior consultation with me, Nor did I, during the whole of the canvass, take any active part in it. I felt the difficulty of supporting the General, on account of the military basis of his pretensions:

and I felt the difficulty of supporting you, on account of the difference which existed between us on some leading points. But I never forgot that it was due to my own character to avoid becoming an active partisan. Towards the close of the canvass, in October of 1836, a great barbecue was gotten up in sight of my house, connected with the presidential election, and I was invited to it.[3] I could not decline going; and very much against my wishes, I was drawn out to say a few words on the subject of the approaching election. The main idea which I expressed was, that it was the duty of the people, in my opinion, to make the most determined opposition to Mr. Van Buren; and for one, I declared my hearty preference for either of the other candidates. I spoke of you in terms of high respect, and avowed my preference of you to Mr. Van Buren. Finally, I stated to the meeting that I should vote for Gen. Harrison, because I thought that he combined the greatest prospects of defeating Mr. Van Buren. Most certainly the General was not my first choice. I should have preferred Mr. Webster to him, and so stated.

The condition of the opposition to Mr. Van Buren at the last election, was unfortunate. No mode was devised, and none seemed practicable, to present a single candidate in opposition to him. The Southern, and Southwestern States would not unite in the election of Gen. Harrison or Mr. Webster, and their friends would not unite in your election. Under these circumstances it was thought to be the best that could be done, by those who took an active part in those matters, that all three of you should be run. On a review of the past, I think you must admit that the disappointment was greatest in those States which were supposed to be friendly to you. That may have been in consequence of the number of candidates in the field; but that cause did not prevent Gen. Harrison from obtaining quite as many votes as were ever expected. And I am sure you will regard it only as matter of history when I express the opinion that if the General had been out of the way, I do not think that you could have obtained the votes which he received. They would have gone to Mr. Webster, or, which is more probable, have been divided between him and Mr. Van Buren. In the course of a long conversation with Mr. Webster, months before the election, I expressed to him the opinion of the expediency of his retirement from the contest, but he did not retire.

If, as by this time I hope, you will believe that I had no agency in putting forward Gen. Harrison, and certainly no purpose of injuring you, you will do me no more than justice in believing the assurance that I now make; that I felt no injury from *you*, which required to be avenged. I certainly felt no obligation to the party of the late President to which you were once attached; but I had never understood that you had been distinguished by any peculiar enmity towards me. And at the period of the late election I regarded you with feelings far different from those of a political enemy or opponent.

I thought these explanations due. I hope they will be received in the same frank and friendly spirit in which they are made.

I hope you have recovered from the fatigue of our late exhausting session of Congress. Although I have not been five miles from home since my return, I feel the want of further repose. . . .

Copy. Printed in Nancy N. Scott (ed.), *A Memoir of Hugh Lawson White . . . With Selections from His Speeches and Correspondence* (Philadelphia, 1856), 366-68. 1. At Knoxville on August 1, 1838, White had made a speech, answering his critics and explaining why he preferred Clay over Van Buren for president in 1840, despite his disagreement with Clay on certain political issues. The speech is printed in Scott, *Memoir of Hugh Lawson White*, 356-66. 2. In the speech, White had said that Clay's "third candidate [Harrison] for the Presidency [in 1836] furnished the only argument which enabled the late Chief Magistrate [Jackson] to transfer the Southern States to his candidate [Van Buren]. For all this I care not. I had no claims on Mr. Clay." *Ibid.*, 365. See also 8:785. 3. At a festival on Oct. 5, 1836, in honor of Harrison, who was visiting Lexington, Clay had made a speech in which he endorsed Harrison. The local newspaper did not print the text of his remarks, because "justice could not be done them." Lexington *Observer & Kentucky Reporter*, Oct. 8, 1836.

To CORNELIUS C. BALDWIN Lexington, August 28, 1838

I received to day your[1] favor of the 15h. inst. and feel greatly obliged by the friendly sentiments towards me which prompted you to write it.

On every topic of your letter, respecting which you say information of my opinions is desired in Alabama, I expressed myself as fully and as explicitly as language can admit of, during the last Session of the Senate of the U.S. In regard to Slavery, and the powers of the General Government upon the subject of it, I offered a series of resolutions, embodying my opinions, most of the essential of which, with some amendments to which I assented, were adopted by the Senate.[2] And in respect to the Tariff and Internal Improvements, in my controversy with Mr. Calhoun, I explained my views fully and clearly.[3] To those resolutions, and to those Speeches, I beg leave to refer you. They were published in most of the papers of the day,[4] and I presume in some of those of Alabama.

As to Slavery I held

1st. That it was an institution over which the several States in which it exists have *exclusive* power.

2. That Congress has no power touching its existence.

3. That it has no power to prevent the removal of slaves from one Slave State to another Slave State.

And 4h. That Congress could not abolish it in the Dt. of Columbia or in the Territories, without a violation of good faith.[5]

In respect to the Tariff, I was willing to abide by the Compromise.[6]

In regard to Internal Improvements, I stated that so much had been recently done by the States themselves, and so much had been distributed by Congress among the States, and which they could apply to that object, that I thought the necessity for the exercise of the power by Congress was superseded; and that I desired nothing more to be done on that matter but to pass, at some suitable time, a bill to distribute among the States the proceeds of the public lands.[7]

With relation to a Bank of the U. States, I expressly declared that I had not made up any positive opinion as to the most proper place for its location; that N. Orleans, Charleston, Richmond, Balto. Philadelphia, N. York and Boston all deserved consideration; that its location was entirely a subordinate question; and that I went for the thing itself, for the benefits of the institution, and was indifferent as to the place of its location. These are my present sentiments.[8]

I have thus briefly given you an outline of the views presented by me at the last Session of the Senate, on the several subjects referred to in your letter, and which are to be found in propositions I made or in Speeches which I addressed to that body. But I cannot consent to the publication of this letter, nor to make any other public declaration about them. I should not address you, if I did not confide in your honor not to make a publication of this letter. My reasons are

1st. That I have in my public place fully explained myself.

2. That an authorized publication from me would imply a sensitiveness to public animadversion, and a solicitude for office, which I do not feel.

3. That if what I said in the Senate is not believed what I might now say would not be believed.

And 4. To appear in the public prints would only be to furnish a new occasion and fresh texts for commentary.

I have lived down the old Calumnies of which I was the object.[9] I mean, with the blessing of God, to live down the new ones.

It is remarkable that whilst the leading Abolition papers are attacking me as being ultra in my Slave notions, at the South I am assailed as being an Abolitionist! Intelligent men cannot misunderstand the object.

In this State the People have just passed upon the question submitted to them of a Convention, and decided against it by an overwhelming majority.[10] It was chiefly supported on the ground of Abolition. It was advocated in the Legislature, and among the People, principally by Van Buren men. I voted against it. In the County in which I reside, with 2500 voters, there were but thirty six for it.

I am no friend to Slavery. I think it an evil; but I believe it better that Slaves should remain Slaves than be set loose as free men among us. That is our true ground of defense. That was the ground of our Revolutionary Ancestors. That is a ground which is intelligible to the civilized world. But the modern ground assumed by the new school in South Carolina, that slavery is a *blessing* is indefensible, unintelligible, and brings reproach upon us. If slavery be a blessing the more of it the better; and it is immaterial, upon that hypothesis, whether the slaves be black or white.

I ought to add a few words on another altho' kindred subject. You have suggested that I might make some public declaration to apply the veto, in certain contingencies. You have justly supposed that I do not regard myself as a Candidate for the Presidency; but if I did; if the election had terminated successfully for me; and if I were installed in the office, I should deem it wrong to threaten, in advance, the application of the Veto, on any subject. Such a course would be, I think, indefensible on principle, and disrespectful to Congress.

I trust, Sir, that I shall continue to merit your good opinion of my frankness, when you peruse this letter. I shall be happy to deserve it in other respects. P.S. I could not more fully manifest my confidence in you than by sending this letter, in its rough state, without even retaining a Copy.

ALS. Courtesy of John C. Fix, Cincinnati, Ohio. 1. Probably Cornelius C. Baldwin, who published the Lexington (Va.) *Gazette* and the Buchanan (Va.) *Advocate and Commercial Gazette*. His brother, Joseph, lived for many years in Alabama and Mississippi.

VMHB, 9:131, 135; Lester J. Cappon, *Virginia Newspapers 1821-1935* (New York, 1936), 61, 113; J. Lewis Peyton, *History of Augusta County, Virginia* (Staunton, Va., 1882), 323. 2. Remark in Senate, Jan. 6, 1838; Speech in Senate, Jan. 9, 1838. 3. Speech in Senate, Feb. 19, 1838; Remark in Senate, June 28, 1838. 4. Clay to Gales and Seaton, April 25, 1838. 5. Comment in Senate, Dec. 18, 1837. 6. See 8:603, 621-22, 626-27. 7. See 8:494, 539-41, 609-10, 752, 812-13, 839, 846-47. 8. Comment in Senate, Sept. 26, 1837; Speech in Senate, May 21, 1838. 9. The "corrupt bargain" problem. See 7:660-61, 716-17, 719. 10. In Dec., 1837, the Kentucky general assembly had passed "An Act to take the sense of the good people of this Commonwealth as to the expediency and propriety of calling a Convention, to revise the Constitution of this State." Ky. Gen. Assy., *Acts . . . 1836-37*, pp. 20-21. On August 8, 1838, only 28,170 votes, out of 104,622 votes cast, favored a constitutional convention. In Fayette County only 1½% of the votes were in favor. Collins, *History of Kentucky*, 2:42-43. For the political implications of this movement, expecially concerning the issue of abolition, and the Whig opposition to such a convention, see Carl J. Fields, "Making Kentucky's Third Constitution 1830-50," Ph.D. dissertation, University of Kentucky, 1951, pp. 25-29.

To FRANCIS T. BROOKE — Lexington, August 28, 1838

I received your favor from the White Sulphur Springs, and was gratified to learn that the President had been so attentive to you. He is always courteous and civil in his manners.

Mr. [William C.] Rives' determination not to be a candidate for the Senate is wise.[1] Should he adhere to it, some embarrassment will be avoided at your next Legislature.

The elections of Kentucky[2] and Indiana[3] have eventuated successfully to the Whigs, without any diminution of their strength. I believe we have carried the election in Illinois,[4] but it is not yet certainly ascertained. The Locofocos have carried that in Missouri,[5] but by a greatly diminished majority.

I have remained at home since the adjournment of Congress, as quiet as I could be, which is not very quiet, for company is constantly with me. This is a very bustling week in consequence of the session at Lexington of the Board of Directors of the Charleston and Cincinnati Railroad Company.[6] They will get more soft words than hard money in Kentucky. . . .

Copy. Printed in Colton, *Clay Correspondence*, 4:428. 1. The election to fill the U.S. Senate seat then held by Conservative Democrat William C. Rives for the term beginning March 4, 1839, was set for Feb. 15, 1839. The Conservatives nominated Rives, the Whigs nominated former governor and U.S. Senator John Tyler, and the Democrats nominated John Y. Mason. The Whigs and Conservatives, who both opposed the Van Buren administration, held a majority in the Virginia legislature, but they divided their votes between Rives and Tyler. Thus, after numerous ballots, no candidate received a majority of votes. Chapman Johnson was then put forward as a compromise candidate, but he too failed to obtain a majority. On Feb. 23 the election was indefinitely postponed. In 1840 another attempt was made to elect a senator, but this also failed. Virginia was therefore represented by only one senator from March 4, 1839, until Jan. 18, 1841, when Rives was finally reelected. Simms, *The Rise of the Whigs in Virginia*, 131-42; Howard Braverman, "The Economic and Political Background of the Conservative Revolt in Virginia," *VMHB* (April, 1952) 60:283-87; Liston, "W.C. Rives: Diplomat and Politician," Ph.D dissertation, Ohio State University, 1972, pp. 274-78, 282-83, 286-87. See also Clay to Brooke, Dec. 20, 1838. 2. Clay to Swartwout, August 10, 1838. 3. Clay to Allen, August 21, 1838. 4. Clay to Swartwout, August 10, 1838. 5. *Ibid.* 6. The Louisville, Cincinnati & Charleston Railroad had been chartered in 1836 with Robert Y. Hayne as president and John C. Calhoun as one of its directors. Calhoun later resigned following a disagreement over the route of the railroad and because of Hayne's insistance that the railroad should also have a bank charter. Each of the states involved granted a charter to the railroad, but only in South Carolina did stock subscriptions meet expectations. The Panic of 1837 and the following depression eventually destroyed the company after only a few miles had been built. The last stockholder's meeting was held in Sept., 1839. Hayne died of a fever the following week, and the railroad was not completed for a generation.

Theodore D. Jervey, *Robert Y. Hayne and His Times* (New York, 1909), 385-429, 471-88, 505-14, *passim*; Wilson, *Papers of John C. Calhoun*, 14:53, 388, 450-51, 454-59, 465-68, 627-28, 630, 642; Hayne article in *DAB*.

To ALEXANDER HAMILTON Lexington, August 28, 1838

I recd., my dear Sir, your favor communicating a conjectural estimate of the vote of the several divisions of N. York, at the approaching Election.[1] I sincerely hope that it may be realized. I have feared the effect of the division of opinion, especially in the City, in regard to the Presidential question.[2] It will require much discretion to guard against it. It was, in view of that effect, that I thought the retirement of Mr. W[ebster]. from the contest would be salutary; but he seems resolved to persevere, and the Whigs must do the best they can. I hope a conciliatory course will be pursued.

We have beaten our opponents completely in Kentucky[3] and Indiana,[4] and I believe in Illinois,[5] altho' the latter is not ascertained certainly. We run them hard in Missouri.[6] In Alabama, the defection of the Nullifiers has enabled them to achieve a hard fought triumph.[7] North Carolina[8] more than counterbalances the loss. If we are successful in N. York, the States just mentd. will come in at the proper time.

The Board of Directors of the Charleston and Cincinnati R. Road is now in Session in Lexington.[9] Altho' we should be glad to see the work accomplished, and any other work of Int. Improvement, Kentucky is engaged on too many local objects to make a large pecuniary contribution.

ALS. NN. 1. Schermerhorn to Clay, Feb. 25, 1838. 2. *Ibid.* 3. Clay to Swartwout, August 10, 1838. 4. Clay to Allen, August 21, 1838. 5. Clay to Swartwout, August 10, 1838. 6. *Ibid.* 7. In the 1838 election in Alabama for the state house of representatives, the Whigs suffered a distinct defeat in that the Democrats won approximately 53 seats and Whigs 37; however, since party lines were not yet clear, in reality there were about 42 committed Democrats, 34 Whigs, and 14 swing votes. A third of the state senate was chosen each year; and although precise figures are not available, Democrats retained a decisive majority in that body. J. Mills Thornton III, *Politics and Power in a Slave Society, Alabama, 1800-1860* (Baton Rouge, 1978), 36. Information also supplied by Dr. Randall G. Lawrence, Birmingham, Ala. 8. Mangum to Clay, March 26, 1838. 9. Clay to Brooke, August 28, 1838.

To HARRISON G. OTIS Lexington, September 1, 1838

I hope that the Govt [*sic*, Govr] has taken his departure from your premises; and yet if he should prompt other such agreeable and sprightly letters as that which you addressed to me on the 27h. July,[1] I do not know if I ought not to desire his continuing with you a while longer. I postponed acknowledging the receipt of it until I should have something to communicate from this quarter. The story of our elections may be soon told. We have succeeded in Louisiana, Indiana and Kentucky, made a drawn battle in Illinois, and been defeated in Alabama and Missouri.[2] But the state of the vote authorizes the anticipation of success in all these States two years hence, if the Whig cause is maintained in the Eastern States, and if our divisions do not discomfit us.

I think Mr. Webster and his friends are decide[d]ly wrong in keeping him in the field. I feel perfectly confident that his retirement would be better for him and for the cause; but I defer to their superior judgment, and sincerely hope that neither he nor the cause may be injuriously affected by his perseverance. It will be, I think, almost a miracle if the collisions which are inevitable, I fear, between our respective friends, especially in the City of N. York, do not produce mischievous consequences.[3] And if it were possible for 15 millions of people to hold their breath, and suppress all expression of their wishes, until December 1839 when they shall be finally promulgated through the organ of a Nat. Convention,[4] the explosion, and the bitterness of disappointment, would then be only the greater.

I must reserve your kind congratulations on my escape from a supposed hazard, in descending the Ohio, for the occasion of a real disaster; for my friend [John J.] Crittenden and myself encountered none. We performed the voyage in safety, and had the satisfaction to relieve some Loco friends from the wreck of another Boat.[5]

We have just had a meeting of the President & Directors of the Charleston and Ohio Rail Road Co. at Lexington.[6] Our people gave them a great Barbecue and treated them otherwise with our accustomed hospitality. We have less objection to giving to the enterprize soft words than hard money.

ALS. MHi. 1. Reference obscure, letter not found. 2. For the results in Ind., Ky., Ill., Ala., and Mo., see Clay to Swartwout, August 10, 1838; Clay to Allen, August 21, 1838; Clay to Hamilton, August 28, 1838. In Louisiana the Whigs won 11 seats in the senate to 6 for the Democrats; they also carried the house 31 to 17 with 2 neutral. *Niles' Register* (July 21, 1838), 54:321. The Whig candidate for governor, Andre B. Roman, defeated the Democrat, David Prieur, by a vote of 7,588 to 6,776. *BDGUS*, 2:560. The Whigs also won all 3 congressional seats. *Guide to U.S. Elections*, 570. 3. Schermerhorn to Clay, Feb. 25, 1838; Clay to Porter, April 15, 1838. See also Clay to Letcher, May 5, 1837. 4. Porter to Clay, Nov. 14 and Dec. 30, 1837. 5. Clay to Swartwout, August 10, 1838. 6. Clay to Brooke, August 28, 1838.

From NICHOLAS BIDDLE Philadelphia, September 7, 1838

Your introduction of Mr [Albert T.] Burnley the Commissioner of Texas, makes it not unnatural to confer with you on the subject of the loan which he is endeavoring to negociate.[1]

The subject of Texas is one familiar to me since my connection in Paris thirty three years ago with the treaty of Louisiana the execution of a great portion of which fell under my own personal inspection.[2] On that subject I hold very decided opinions. But the question which now occupies my attention is this. The Minister from Texas just arrived in this City means to withdraw formally the proposal to enter the Union[3] So far the embarrassments & troubles which that measure threatened are for the present at least removed. The question is then becomes an open one, & it offers for consideration this point. Whether, if we are to consider the revolution there as complete, if this country will not permit Texas to be conquered by a new master, or reconquered by its old one, then is it not of great importance that her prosperity should be of our own creation, and that she should not be obliged to incur obligations to any other country? She now wants money to consolidate her power & fix her institutions. Is it not better far better that she should obtain it from us than from any other power? Now I am inclined to make the loan. At the same time I mean to do nothing rashly—nothing which shall not in my judgment be highly beneficial to our own country. But I do not wish to take any decisive step without the opinion of some friends on whose judgment I rely. Allow me then to ask what you think of the question? Do you think that Texas will maintain its independence, or that the United States would permit any power to deprive her of it? Do you think it would be wise to take the loan & not suffer her to owe her success to England?

If you feel any the slightest reluctance to say any thing about the matter—you will of course say nothing—But if you feel disposed to give any opinion, let it be such as hereafter if I should deem it useful to use your authority as confirming my own views I may quote & if necessary make public. I mention this in order that you may limit precisely the nature & extent of your communication.[4]

ALS. DLC-HC (DNA, M212, R5). 1. For Burnley, a native of Frankfort, Ky., who had emigrated to Texas in the early 1830s, see Wiltse, *Papers of Daniel Webster, Correspondence*, 4:385. Burnley had been commissioned in 1837 by the government of Texas to negotiate a loan in the United States. In 1839, in company with James Hamilton, he finally succeeded in obtaining a loan of $400,000 from Biddle's bank in exchange for 94,500 pounds sterling in Texas bonds bearing 10% interest. Joseph W. Schmitz, *Texan Statecraft 1836–1845* (San Antonio, 1941), 80-82, 84-85. 2. From 1804 to 1807 Biddle had served as unpaid secretary to John Armstrong, U.S. minister to France. One of his chief duties had been to certify and pay the claims of U.S. merchants against the French government. These claims had been assumed by the U.S. under the Louisiana treaty. Govan, *Nicholas Biddle*, 11, 13. 3. Texas formally withdrew its application for annexation to the U.S. on Oct. 12, 1838. Curtis, *The Fox at Bay*, 168. For Memucan Hunt, the Texas minister to the U.S. at this time, see *NCAB*, 10:388-89. 4. Endorsed on verso by Clay: "[Texas—answered approving the loan]". See Clay to Biddle, Sept. 14, 1838.

To NICHOLAS BIDDLE Lexington, September 12, 1838

It is possible that I may have occasion for the use in England of from five to ten thousand dollars. Can I get from your Bank a credit on Mr. [Samuel] Jaudon[1] for a sum not exceeding the latter limit, to be reimbursed in Philada. when and if the advance be made, at the rate of exchange then existing? And what shall I do to entitle myself to the credit? Must I give other guarrantys than my own name? And will it be requisite to offer one or more others?[2]

Should I have occasion to use the credit, it will be in the purchase of a stud horse—a fact which I hope you will consider in the nature of a Bank secret.

ALS. NjMoHP. 1. Samuel Jaudon, cashier of the U.S. Bank of Pennsylvania in Philadelphia, was at this time acting as the bank's agent in London. When Biddle chose Thomas Dunlap to be his successor as president of the bank, Jaudon was his second choice; but on the eve of the bank's failure in 1841, Biddle attempted to replace Dunlap with Jaudon. Govan, *Nicholas Biddle*, 119, 216, 265, 295-96, 305, 318, 336, 349, 356, 365, 378, 390, 398. 2. Biddle approved the loan. See Biddle to Clay, Sept. 20, 1838.

To PETER B. PORTER Lexington, September 12, 1838

So, you took French leave of me![1] I fully expected to have met you at the Barbacue given in Lexn. to the Rail Road Directors;[2] and anticipating that pleasure intended to ask you to dine with them the next day at Ashland. As I did not see you, I sent an invitation to you at the Hotel in Lexn; but I presume you did not receive it. You lost nothing, but *I lost* the satisfaction of seeing you.

I transmit the receipt which you wished for Bacon Hams and which had been prepared to deliver you in person. I think that the Hams would keep better if, in the Spring, before the fly appears, they were taken down from the Smoak house and packed away in hickory ashes, *or* sewed up in canvass and then immersed in lime water.

I shall not forget the Blue grass seed.[3]

Our latest accounts from the controverted election in Illinois are that Stewart [*sic*, John T. Stuart] is elected.[4] But, if our anticipated success is realized in the Empire States [*sic*, New York], these minor matters will lose their consequence.[5]

ALS. NBuHi. Addressed to Porter in Black Rock, N.Y. 1. Clay to Porter, August 15, 1838. 2. Clay to Brooke, August 28, 1838. 3. Clay to Allen, August 21, 1838. 4. John T. Stuart, a Whig, had defeated Stephen A. Douglas, a Democrat, by a vote of 18,248 to 18,213 for a seat in Congress from the third district in Illinois. *Guide to U.S. Elections*, 570. 5. Schermerhorn to Clay, Feb. 25, 1838.

To NICHOLAS BIDDLE Lexington, September 14, 1838

I received this morning your favor of the 7h instant communicating several inquiries, respecting Texas, on which you are desirous to obtain my opinion. This I have not the least objection to express; but without a strong necessity I should not wish it to be published. And my aversion to its publication arises solely out of the consideration that, at this time, I desire voluntarily to appear in the public prints as little as possible, lest I should be thought to be endeavoring to conciliate public support.

I am glad to learn from you that the Minister from Texas intends to with draw the application from Texas to be incorporated in our Union.[1] It is a wise step; for it is perfectly manifest that, whether it be expedient or not to annex it to the U States, the public mind in this Country is not in a temper to sanction such a measure, at this period. The longer agitation of the question can do no possible good to one party, whilst it has a positively injurious tendency upon the domestic interests and relations of the other. If the question were to be prolonged, and a foreign attack, other than from Mexico, should be made on Texas, I think that a majority of the American Congress could not be got to succor Texas in warding off such an attack Whereas, if the project of annexation be abandoned, and any European power were to attack the independence of the new Republic, I think it would be the inclination, as I am sure it would be the interest and the duty of the U S. to prevent the success of the attack.

Whether Texas will be able to maintain the Independence which she has declared, or not, I have no means of judging which you do not possess, perhaps not so many. I am inclined to believe that she will, if her Government is administered with reasonable ability. Texas [*sic*, Time(?)] is every thing to Texas, whilst delay is ruinous to the Mexican re conquest. The French Blockade operates most advantageously to Texas,[2] by rendering her secure against attack from the Gulph, which I have always thought her most vulnerable side. She ought to wish that this Blockade may be long continued In the mean time emigrants are pouring into Texas, and daily adding strength to her. I do not see how Mexico, torn as she is by factions, with her finances totally disordered, no efficient army nor commanders, and no good materials for an army to be sent on a distant conquest, can subjugate the revolted province. If, France were out of the way, and Mexico *had* and could *keep* the preponderance at Sea, Texas might be in danger.

If Texas is to be an independent power, it is the obvious interest of the U. S. to cultivate her friendship, as their nearest neighbour, in that quarter; and it is consequently their interest that Texas should feel that she has been well treated by them. Hitherto she has had no just cause to complain of the U. S. whatever they may have given to any other power. This feeling of friendship towards the U. S. on the part of Texas, for one, I should be happy to see strengthened, by all the good offices that can be rendered, consistently with our neutrality.[3] The loan, which she wishes to negociate, and which you are inclined to make, may unquestionably be effected, without any violation of any Neutral duty by which the people of this Country stand bound Of course, I give no opinion as to its terms, or the security which may be offered for its reimbursement. Assuming them to be satisfactory to the parties, I think it, in every aspect, highly desirable that Texas should contract an obligation for the loan in this Country, and not in any European State.[4]

I do not believe that the U. S. will or ought to interfere, so as to become a party to the contest, whilst it is confined to Mexico and Texas But if any European power, and especially if G. Britain or France, were to attempt the conquest of Texas, or to aid Mexico in re conquering it, in my opinion the U S. could not regard any such attempt with indifference.

I have thus, my dear Sir, frankly expressed my opinions. I shall be happy if you should be able to derive any assistance from them; but for the reason already stated, to which I should add that I send the first draft of my reply, without correction, and without retaining any copy, I do not wish publicity given to them without an urgent reason.

ALS. DLC-Nicholas Biddle Papers (DNA, M212, R20). 1. Biddle to Clay, Sept. 7, 1838. 2. Comment in Senate, June 30, 1838. 3. *Ibid.*; see also Biddle to Clay, Sept. 7, 1838. 4. *Ibid.*

From Harrison Gray Otis, Boston, September 14, 1838. Encloses an article clipped from the Boston *Atlas*, "the paper most devoted to Mr. Webster," which he has read with "great astonishment." Is not sure why the editor, Richard Haughton, "would thus blurt out so bold and unexpected a speculation without his [Webster's] privity and assent." Thinks, however, that Haughton, with or without Webster's "countenance," has raised a question "which cannot remain long without solution." ALS. DLC-HC (DNA, M212, R5). Letter marked "(Private)." See also Clay to Otis, September 24, 1838. For Haughton (1799-1841), see Frederick Hudson, *Journalism in the United States, 1690-1872* (New York, 1873; reprint ed., Ann Arbor, Mich., 1964), 321, 370, 391; *NEHGR*, 14:26; 44:405; 47:40, 42, 339; 89:397.

In the Boston *Atlas* article, which was reprinted in the Frankfort (Ky.) *Commonwealth* on October 3, 1838, Haughton blamed the Whig defeat in the Maine elections on the failure of the party "for some ten or twelve long years" to appeal to the masses. The lesson to be learned from the Maine defeat, he said, was the necessity "of selecting that man for our presidential candidate, who can bring into the contest the greatest capital in popularity, with the smallest drawback of popular dislike." Based on this criteria, he therefore rejected both Clay and Webster as presidential candidates in the 1840 election. He argued that although they were great statesmen, they had both been around too long and had made too many enemies. Clay's lack of popularity was shown in his inability to sustain John Q. Adams in power in 1828 and his own poor showing in the 1832 presidential election, while Webster's candidacy in 1836 leads to the conclusion "that Mr. Webster is not an *available candidate*." The fact that most of leading merchants, professional men, capitalists, and leading politicians prefer either Clay or Webster only increases the popular prejudice against them, he claimed. "There remains then," he concluded, "only General Harrison,—a man, who if his career has not been so brilliant as that of the two statesmen above named, has yet given evidence . . . of capacity, integrity, sound sense, and genuine patriotism; and who possesses above all, that essential requisite . . . to wit, the favor and good will of the mass of the people—in other words *popularity*."

An editorial in the Frankfort *Commonwealth* of the same day, October 3, called attention to the *Atlas* article, noting that when first published it had caused a sensation, because it was believed to express the views of Webster who was closely associated with the paper. It added, however, that the *Atlas* "has been forced to a hasty retreat from its position in relation to Mr. Webster, and comes forward with the confession that it has given an erroneous idea of his views of the approaching canvass." In fact, said the *Commonwealth*, it is now known that Webster disapproves the article "*in toto*."

To HARRY I. THORNTON Lexington, September 16, 1838

Although your obliging letter was not necessary to assure me of your continued friendship, I was glad on many accounts to receive it. The Whigs have done well in Alabama.[1] The defection which was to be anticipated from the extraordinary course of Mr. Calhoun[2] has produced less effect than I feared, although enough to defeat us for the present. Whether Alabama will be one of the four or five States which will remain to Mr. V. Buren depends upon herself. Great efforts, I am aware, have been made to retain her and to misrepresent and pervert my opinions; and I believe by no one more than my namesake [Clement C. Clay].

On Slavery, and the powers of the General Government touching it, wherever it exists; on the Tariff and the Compromise; and on Internal Improvements, I expressed myself so fully and explicitly in the Senate, at the last Session, that I have nothing to add, and wish to add nothing.[3] Indeed I have resisted all importunities to draw me into the public prints on those subjects and mean to continue to do so.

My opinion is that you have conducted the Campaign wisely in Alabama, as far as I have comprehended your plans. It is best openly to avow your policy and your preferences; and to attack—charge bayonet upon, your adversaries. A Bank of the U.S. you want and must have, and why not say so? And why not be equally explicit on other points?

My information from almost every State as to the Whig Cause is most cheering; and, as to myself, I could hardly desire any change in the existing state of things. Judging from all that I hear and see Mr. V. B. will not obtain the votes of more than N. Hampshire, So. Carolina, Alabama & Missouri, and possibly Michigan.[4] There are other States doubtless, which are nearly balanced, but the tide is running irresistibly against him.

Will you be represented in the Nat. Convention?[5] It is, I think, desirable that the representation should be as general as practicable to prevent any cavil about the composition of the Convention. You have seen accounts of the intention of the Loco foco's to concentrate on Genl. Harrison. I think the apple has been presented to him, but I have no reason to believe that he has accepted it. On the contrary he recently made public declarations directly adverse to his acceptance. If he should so far forget himself and his party (and I do not believe that he will) as to lend himself to such an object, it will be utterly unavailing. He would not get a vote equal to Mr. V.B; because he would lose more loco's than he would gain Whigs.

But enough of politics. We are in the midst of an extraordinary drought. It has lessened our Corn Crop, but I think we have a Sufficiency.

Mrs. [Lucy Crittenden] Thornton[6] has I dare say informed you that I had the satisfaction to pass some weeks in her company towards the close of the last Session of Congress and to travel with her to Kentucky. I hope she has reached Mobile in safety, altho' I have been so little from home, since my return, that I have not heard of her departure from K. I pray you to present my respectful regards to her. . . .

ALS. KyU. 1. Clay to Hamilton, August 28, 1838. 2. His switch from a states' rights-Whig (Anti-Jackson) orientation to Van Buren and the Democrats. Speech in Senate, Feb. 19, 1838. 3. Clay to Baldwin, August 28, 1838. 4. Of these states, Van Buren in 1840 carried all but Michigan. For the popular and electoral vote for president in 1840, see Thomas H. McKee, *The National . . . Popular and Electoral Vote*, 44-45. 5. Porter to Clay, Nov. 14 and Dec. 30, 1837. 6. Sister to John J. Crittenden. See 5:625.

From George & Robert Blackburn, Madeira, Portugal, September 17, 1838. Announce that they are shipping to Clay on board the brig *Cazmon* "one cased pipe [126 gals.] of . . . choice 'old reserve' Madeira Wine" via New York City and James Erwin in New Orleans and thence to Louisville and Lexington. Cost is $366.68, which includes casing and insurance. Freight charges not included. Assure Clay that "You will find this wine possessing every requisite which really superior Madeira should have—body & softness, combined with old, high, & fruity flavor;—we may indeed safely assert finer cannot be shipped from the Island, it being altogether the produce of the hot situations, and as we very much doubt if such is often exported from the Island, we hope you will reserve the pipe for your own use." ALS. DLC-TJC (DNA, M212, R14).

On September 18, 1838, March & Benson wrote from New York that they are also shipping to Clay via the packet *Saratoga* to New Orleans, and by steamboat up to Louisville, "A pipe superior" of Madeira and two boxes of Citron (1838). Costs: wine and Citron—$270.67; freight from Madeira—$7.00; duty paid in New York—$13.87; cartage—$1.50; insurance—(Atlantic Insurance Co.) N.O. to Louisville $9.00; total: $302.04. *Ibid.* (R10). On February 13, 1839, March & Benson wrote that the final bill for this shipment was $302.04. *Ibid.*

From Nicholas Biddle, Philadelphia, September 20, 1838. Reports receipt of Clay's request of September 12 for a loan of five to ten thousand dollars to facilitate "the visit of the illustrous stranger whom you propose to invite over." Approves loan and says there will be no need for a co-signer, since Clay "already possesses a good estate—with a very fair prospect of an addition to his income of $25000 a year." Concludes: "I shall keep your secret—not being a politician—and if at the coming election I should hear this taste for blood objected to you, I shall defend you—tho' perhaps you may not thank me for it, by declaring that you are a propagandist, only by proxy." ALS. DLC-HC (DNA, M212, R5). Copy in DLC-Nicholas Biddle Papers (DNA, M212, R20). For Clay's financial situation in Fall, 1838, see Clay to January, October 6, 1838. See also Clay to Biddle, September 12, 1838, and October 1, 1838.

To FREDERICK MARRYAT Lexington, September 22, 1838

I hasten to reply to your[1] favor of the 20h. inst. this moment received. I scarcely need say that it has excited both surprize and pain with me that the circumstance of your dining with me, which I am quite sure afforded mutual satisfaction, should have been made the occasion of the propogation of a report so unfounded as that to which you refer. Nothing could be remoter from the truth than that you contradicted or insulted me, or declined to drink a glass of wine with me. On the contrary, your whole conduct and deportment were perfectly gentlemanly. I derived much pleasure from your conversation and company; and you will recollect that, when we parted, I expressed a hope that I should again meet with you; and you made cordial acknowledgements for the very trifling attentions which I had been able to shew you.

It is even mortifying to me that you should find it at all necessary to resort to the testimony which I now cheerfully render.

My best wishes accompany you, with my anxious desire that, during the remainder of your abode in our Country, you may escape any further annoyance.

ALS. NcD. 1. Marryat (1792-1848) was a well-known British ship's captain who traveled in Canada and America in 1837-38 and subsequently (1839) published *Diary in America*. He was also author of *Mr. Midshipman Easy, Peter Simple*, and other stirring tales of the sea. See *DNB*.

To HARRISON G. OTIS Lexington, September 24, 1838

My astonishment was equal to your's on perusing the extraordinary article in the Atlas, which you did me the favor to transmit.[1] The time! just before the great battles which are to be fought in N. York[2] and Pennsa[3] pregnant with the fate of the Whig cause! The cause—my alleged want of popularity. As if that had any connection with our defeat in Maine![4] In Maine, where on every trial, my friends have shewn greater strength than those in favor of any other Whig candidate. Maine, which was shortly before rebuked by this same Atlas, for manifesting her preference for me!

There, the results so far of the campaign this year have been decidedly favorable to the Whig cause, the loss of Maine notwithstanding. Let us see: Mississippi,[5] Connecticut,[6] Kentucky,[7] Indiana,[8] Illinois,[9] North Carolina,[10] Rhode Island[11] & Vermont[12] have come out for us; whilst, on the other hand, Missouri,[13] N. Hampshire,[14] Alabama[15] & Maine have only appeared to be against us. I ought to have added the antient dominion [Virginia][16] to the former.

If Mr. Richard Haughton be the editor of the Atlas at this time, your astonishment at the article in question will be increased when you read the following extract from a letter which he addressed to me on the 7h. March last,[17] now before me:

"The public journals have conveyed to you 'ere this the resolutions which were adopted in our Legislative Whig Convention.[18] I may say to you confidentially that efforts were made by a few of our representatives at Washington to induce an expression of opinion favorable to Genl Harrison. They failed entirely. I do not believe there is a man in either branch of the Whig party in the Legislature who could have been influenced to that course. Indeed, were Mr. Webster withdrawn and Genl Harrison put in nomination by the Whig party, I could carry a ticket with the name of Henry Clay at the head of it against both the Harrison and V. Buren tickets, by an overwhelming majority."

So much for Mr. Haughtons then opinion of my want of popularity, and of Genl Harrison's possession of that commodity!

What State South of the Potomac has shewn any disposition to vote for the General? In what State South of the Potomac is there not a powerful party in my favor? Tennessee (with fair play and reasonable prospects) is just as certain for me as Kentucky. And Tennessee *once* was Jackson to the bone, and might be supposed to cherish those prejudices against me, which the Atlas dwells on at such length.

I am mortified—shocked—disgusted with the course of some men. I had hoped for better things of them.

I am most unwilling to believe that Mr. Webster has counselled or acquiesced in the course of the Atlas. And yet, putting all circumstances together, without an explicit disavowal from him, the conviction will be irresistible that his views and wishes have not been overlooked.

You are at liberty to shew this letter to Abbott Lawrence, to Col [Thomas H.] Perkins and to [Peleg] Sprague—all honorable men—but otherwise be pleased to regard it confidential.

ALS. MHi. 1. Otis to Clay, Sept. 14, 1838. 2. Schermerhorn to Clay, Feb. 25, 1838. 3. *Ibid.* 4. In the 1838 elections in Maine, John Fairfield (Democrat) defeated Edward Kent (Whig) for the governorship by a vote of 46,216 to 42,897. *BDGUS*, 2:602. There was no election for the state senate; however, the Democrats carried 107 seats in the lower house to 73 for the Whigs. *Nile's Register* (Oct. 6, 1838), 55:82. In the Maine congressional elections, Democrats won 7 seats to 1 for the Whigs. *Guide to U.S. Elections*, 570. 5. Clay to Porter, April 15, 1838. 6. Remark in Senate, May 31, 1838. 7. Clay to Swartwout, August 10, 1838. 8. Clay to Allen, August 21, 1838. 9. Clay to Swartwout, August 10, 1838. 10. Mangum to Clay, March 26, 1838. 11. Tappan to Clay, May 1, 1838. 12. In the 1838 elections in Vermont, Silas H. Jennison (Whig) was elected governor over William C. Bradley (Democrat) by a vote of 24,738 to 19,194. *BDGUS*, 4:1570. The Whigs also won control of the state senate by a margin of 20 seats to 10 and the lower house by 156 seats to 70, with 3 seats won by conservatives. *Niles' Register* (Oct. 6, 1838), 55:82. Three Whigs and two Democrats were elected to the U.S. House from Vermont. *Guide to U.S. Elections*, 571. 13. Clay to Swartwout, August 10, 1838. 14. Clay to Hale, Jan. 7, 1838. 15. Clay to Hamilton, August 28, 1838. 16. Clay to Porter, April 15, 1838. 17. Haughton to Clay, March 7, 1838. 18. Clay to Porter, March 4, 1838.

To MADISON C. JOHNSON *et al.*[1]

Lexington, September 27, 1838[2]

I am sorry that a bad Cold and a repugnance which I have to being out of my lodgings at night will prevent my attendance at the proposed meeting this evening of friends of Transylvania.[3] Concurring heartily in the object of infusing new vigor in that institution, I will, with pleasure, become one of the one hundred Subscribers proposed, and will agree to almost any measure that the meeting this evening may adopt to make Transylvania what its friends have always desired it should be.

ALS. KyLxT. 1. Also addressed to James C. Cross [3:136-38] and Robert Wickliffe, Jr. 2. Dated "Ashland Thursday evening"; endorsed in strange hand: "1839.—the meeting to organize Transa Institute." The editors, however, have determined the date to be Thursday, Sept. 27, 1838, the date known to be that on which the meeting to organize Transylvania Institute was held. 3. Robert Wickliffe, Jr., headed a movement to improve the financial stability of Morrison College of Transylvania University and "other Literary and Charitable institutions of Lexington" by persuading 100 men each to subscribe $100 per year for 5 years to an organization called the Transylvania Institute. The subscribers were to meet and complete their planning on Thursday evening, Sept. 27, 1838, at the Phoenix Hotel in Lexington. Although he did not attend the meeting, Clay became a subscriber and also president of the institute, with Wickliffe as his assistant. Their goal was to secure passage of a bill by the legislature incorporating the institute and providing for state funds to match those of the subscribers. Failing that, they desired a bill ceding Transylvania University to the city of Lexington, providing the city would match the subscriber's funds. In a law, approved on Feb. 20, 1839, the Kentucky legislature incorporated the Transylvania Institute, and provided for the election of Transylvania University trustees and for the appointment of overseers of the university by the governor. Lexington *Observer & Kentucky Reporter*, Sept. 22, 26, 1838; John D. Wright, Jr., *Transylvania: Tutor to the West* (Lexington, 1975), 152-54; Ky. Gen. Assy., *Acts* . . . 1838-1839, pp. 300-303. A copy of the constitution of Transylvania Institute with Clay's name affixed as a subscriber is in KyU.

To UNKNOWN RECIPIENT[1] Lexington, September 27, 1838

I received the first intelligence of the nomination made at the Whig Convention in Utica through your favor.[2] The proceedings of the Convention appear to me to have been marked by discretion and wisdom. And I trust that, at the election now near at hand, the Nomination will be triumphantly sustained.

I observe, with much gratification, that the [*Morning*] Courier [*and New-York Enquirer*] continues to be edited with great ability.[3] Its editorial articles cannot fail wherever they are read to produce good effect.

Was ever any thing more strange than the late movement in the [Boston] Atlas about the Presidency?[4] It does not deserve to be considered a Boston notion; for I am quite sure that all Boston disapproves it. The time! just before great elections. The *pretext* for it—the Maine election—as if my unfortunate and unpopular name had led to the defeat of our cause there![5] there, where a few weeks before this same Atlas rebuked expressions which burst out in my favor!

I have seen no satisfactory solution of the matter.

Respects to Col. [James Watson] Webb and congratulations on his safe return.

ALS. MHi. 1. The latter portion of the original letter has been cropped. The editors have concluded, however, that the recipient was probably John Osborne Sargent who had written political editorials for the Boston *Atlas* before moving to New York in 1838 to become associate editor of the *Morning Courier and New-York Enquirer*. See *DAB*. 2. The Whig convention which met in Utica, N.Y., in Sept., 1838, had nominated William Henry Seward for governor and Luther Bradish for lieutenant governor. Nevins, *Diary of Philip Hone*, 343. For the outcome of the election, see Schermerhorn to Clay, Feb. 25, 1838. 3. See footnote 2, above. 4. Otis to Clay, Sept. 14, 1838; Clay to Otis, Sept. 24, 1838. 5. *Ibid.*

To Nicholas Biddle, Philadelphia, October 1, 1838. Thanks him for the loan with which to purchase an English stallion [Clay to Biddle, September 12, 1838; Biddle to Clay, September 20, 1838], explaining that "I thought it expedient to open a new source of Revenue." Hopes his "secret" will not "get out." Concludes: "Reversing the appeal of the discomfited Richard [III] . . . I would not give my horse for a Kingdom." ALS. DLC-Nicholas Biddle Papers (DNA, M212, R20).

To COMMITTEE OF HENRY COUNTY TENNESSEE WHIGS Lexington, October 1, 1838

I am honored by the invitation, transmitted to me by you as the committee of the whigs of Henry county, in Tennessee, to a dinner proposed to be given to the hon. John Bell, on the 12th inst. I should be very happy to be able to attend on such an interesting occasion. It is a characteristic of that ferocious spirit of denunciation and persecution, of which I was long the chosen victim, to display its greatest venom against those who have last incurred its enmity. It has been the fate of a distinguished citizen in the eastern part of your state,[1] and of Mr. Bell, to be the latest objects selected for the vengeance of that spirit, and hence all the phials of wrath are poured out on their heads. I have been comparatively spared and forgotten. No state in the union has exhibited a nobler independence than Tennessee; and the people of it, in resolving to sustain those two citizens against unmerited attacks, have shown their sensibility to faithful and eminent services and a just abhorrence to gross injustice. I would gladly unite with the whigs of Henry, in the intended respect to Mr. Bell, but duties and engagements at home compel me reluctantly to decline the acceptance of your invitation.

Among other strange and dangerous principles of government which have been introduced within the last few years, none is more remarkable than the system of reward and punishments, which has been acted upon. Devotion to power is the highest, and often the only, recommendation to executive patronage whilst to question the fallibility of a leading administration is regarded as the greatest crime which a citizen can commit. Rejection by the people of a partizan of the executive, who is a candidate for office, is a sure passport to its favor. So that the most certain way to get an office is to lose one. Numerous examples might be given of this practice, but I will mention only two. A candidate for the governor of Pennsylvania, on the side of the administration, being rejected by the people, was soon after rewarded by a high executive office at Washington. And when he pouted and threatened in consequence of another rejected candidate for the same office, of less zealous faith, being appointed to a foreign mission he was quieted by being transferred to a lucrative office in Philadelphia.[2] The other instance is in your own state. A senator, who had lost the confidence of the people of Tennessee, has been recently compensated by a seat in the cabinet.[3]

Thus, gentlemen, you see with what contempt power treats the people. It has divorced itself from them. And it is the same spirit that, by means of the sub-treasury scheme,[4] it seeks to establish for itself one currency, leaving the people in the possession of another, and, as it alleges an inferior currency.

You will recollect that Mr. Adams' administration was bitterly denounced, because, in a single instance, it made an appointment of a postmaster at Nashville contrary to the recommendation of a majority of the Tennessee delegation.[5] The gentleman [John P. Erwin] appointed was of undoubted character, warmly recommended and eminently qualified for the office. He was afterwards if I mistake not, chosen by the people, mayor of that city. But there was one qualification for the office of postmaster of Nashville which he wanted—he was not in favor of the late election of the late president of the United States.

Judging from the events of the last year, another and better destiny awaits our union than [that] to which our rulers have been hurrying it.

I congratulate you on the auspicious prospect before us. When our deliverance is consummated, no state can look upon its accomplishment with prouder satisfaction than Tennessee. . . .

Copy. Printed in *Niles' Register* (Nov. 17, 1838), 55:186. 1. Hugh Lawson White. See Clay to White, August 27, 1838. 2. George Wolf was defeated for reelection as governor of Pennsylvania in 1835. President Jackson created a new post, comptroller of the U.S. treasury, and appointed Wolf to the job. In 1838 Van Buren made him collector of customs at Philadelphia. In Feb., 1838, Van Buren had appointed Henry A. Muhlenberg, who had also been defeated for governor of Pennsylvania in 1835, as minister to Austria. This was the appointment which apparently had upset Wolf. *BDGUS*, 3:1301-2; Mueller, *Whig Party in Pennsylvania*, 48. 3. Felix Grundy, who resigned his Senate seat on July 4, 1838, to accept appointment as attorney general of the U.S. He resigned the attorney generalship on Dec. 1, 1839, having been elected U.S. senator on Nov. 19, 1839, and died in the office on Dec. 19, 1840. See *BDAC*. 4. Speech in Senate, Sept. 25, 1837. 5. See 5:699.

To George W. Featherstonhaugh, Washington, October 1, 1838. Thanks him for his letter from Quebec. Regrets that Featherstonhaugh has resigned his position in the government. Had hoped, as "I expressed to you, at the dinner at Mr. Bodisco's," he might have remained even though "opposed to the existing state of things." As for his own future in politics, "the results of a few weeks will enable us to ascertain. If I were to judge alone from our cause, I could not doubt the issue; but a good cause does not always succeed, and we have a wary and powerful adversary, in the party to which we are opposed, and unfortunately are not free from difficulties among ourselves." ALS. DLC. The Count Alexandre de Bodisco was Russian minister to the United States from 1838 to 1854. Featherstonhaugh had resigned the position of U.S. geologist which he had held for some years. Washington *Daily National Intelligencer*, September 7, 1838.

To John S. Snead, Louisville, October 1, 1838. Announces his willingness to sell Snead two blooded calves and two heifers. Mentions that he has just sold another of his calves for $750 and a bull, Frederick, for $1,610. Adds: "If you make an importation, my opinion is that N[ew]. O[rleans]. is the best safest and cheapest route." ALS. MoU.

From Stephen Duncan, Natchez, Miss., October 4, 1838. Reports that all the cordage ordered from Clay has been received [Clay to T.H. Clay, May 11, 1838]. Declines "for the present" Clay's offer of his 1839 crop at 12½ cents. Says he can get rope in Louisville at 8 cents that is "of decidedly better quality than yours." Nevertheless, "this matters not, I am perfectly satisfied with my contract. I will not, however, contract again, unless the delivery can be made in June, and I would not at present be willing to contract at 12 cts." Warns, in this regard, that the Mississippi cotton crop "will be 100,000 bal[e]s short of last year," and cordage "will not I think maintain its present prices. . . . it is also believed that there will be a very large supply of Russia[n] cordage—or cordage manufactured in the North, from Russia[n] Hemp." Thinks Clay "too sanguine in regard to the success of the Whig cause in the approaching elections." Doubts that the Whigs can carry Ohio, New York [Schermerhorn to Clay, February 25, 1838], or Pennsylvania [Clay to Otis, September 24, 1838]. Believes, too, that had Van Buren's Sub-Treasury bill [Speech in Senate, September 25, 1837; Speech in Senate, February 19, 1838] "been permitted to pass," and the nation had had another year or more of "suffering from pecuniary embar[r]assments," the result might have led to a "radical" and "permanent change in the opinions of the people." Thinks Clay is decidedly wrong in demanding "publicity to Bank discounts." Has no wish to see his own name "figure on the list of discounters." Explains that "the publicity for which you contend, would inflict a severer blow on commercial confidence & credit,—than the far famed 'specie circular [8:861; Remark in Senate, January 6, 1837; Speech in Senate, January 11, 1837]' or the 'removal of the deposites [8:583-84, 681, 684-85, 728].' It would ruin thousands, where it would benefit hundreds. It would check enterprise—break up speculation—and paralise mercantile energy—Thousands are saved daily, by small discounts—who—would be deprived of them altogether if the amounts previously discounted for them, by other banks, were made public.—Mr. [Nicholas] Biddle once said, that he averted a complete commercial crisis—by the discount of 50,000$ at his branch in New York. Now, if this small sum, would save a whole city,—nay a whole country—a much smaller sum would save individuals—who if their previous discounts were known—could obtain no more.—you may rely upon it—you are deceived in regard to this matter. But I will not attempt to argue it with you." Also says he hopes Mississippi banks will resume specie payments [Comment in Senate, May 2, 1838; Remark in Senate May 26, 1838] on January 1, 1839. Notes that "There is, however, much opposition to it. and I fear some, even of our *River* banks, are not prepared for it. The Natches [*sic*] Banks, could resume tomorrow." ALS. DLC-TJC (DNA, M212, R14).

In the 1838 gubernatorial election in Ohio, Wilson Shannon, a Democrat, defeated incumbent Whig Governor Joseph Vance by a vote of 107,884 to 102,146. *BDGUS*, 3:1200-1201. In the Ohio congressional elections, 11 Democrats and 8 Whigs were chosen. Democrats won 13 seats in the state senate and 38 seats in the house, while Whigs won 6 senate seats and 34 house seats. *Niles' Register* (October 27, 1838), 55:129.

The Mississippi Union Bank was the last in the state to resume specie payment. It did so on January 1, 1839; all others had resumed in December, 1838. *Ibid.* (January 12, 1839), 55:305.

To ROBERT SWARTWOUT Lexington, October 5, 1838

I recd. today your obliging letter, and was greatly gratified by the account which it communicates of the fine spirit prevailing among the Whigs; and especially by your assurance that the differences, in regard to a Presidential Candidate will produce no prejudice. I have entertained serious apprehensions that it might have been otherwise in the City.[1]

The course of my friend C[harles] King surprizes me.[2] It is so contrary to our former relations, and to what I understood to be his intentions when I last saw him in the City of Washington, during the past Session. But I care not for this double fire to which I am exposed touching Slavery. It neutralizes itself. I have reason to believe that the charge of my being an abolitionist is dying away at the South West, as that of my being ultra, in my notions in favor of Slavery, will at the North.

We were subjected to momentary astonishment by the course of the [Boston] Atlas.[3] I am glad that Mr. Webster disavows any authority for it from him, *for his sake*. I hope that a regard to his character and to his *consistency* will keep him out of that trap.

The proceedings at Utica appeared to me to be characterized by much discretion.[4] Whilst I should have been most anxious for the success of any other of the Gentlemen, if any other had been nominated, I was delighted that the choice fell where it did.

ALS. NN. 1. Clay to Letcher, May 30, 1837; Clay to Davis, July 3, 1837; Clay to Otis, July 7, 1838; Clay to Swartwout, August 10, 1838; Clay to Sargent, August 11, 1838. 2. Reference obscure. 3. Otis to Clay, Sept. 14, 1838. 4. Clay to Unknown Recipient, Sept. 27, 1838.

To Thomas T. January, Morgan County, Ill., October 6, 1838. An agreement in which for $17,950 Clay sells his 300.4 acre farm in St. Louis County, Mo. [8:801], together with 370 adjoining acres, 100 additional acres lying five miles west, and 17 acres "on the Mississippi River." Total acres sold: 787.4. Payment schedule: March 1, 1839, $5,983; March 1, 1840, $5,983; March 1, 1841, $5,983. ADS, by Joseph Stettinius. DLC-TJC (DNA, M212, R17). In this transaction, James Brown Clay assisted his father as "attorney in fact."

On January 27, 1839, Clay wrote James advising him further on how to handle possible claims on and/or make alternate payment arrangements for part of the property. ALS. *Ibid.* (R14). Addressed to James at "Ashland near Lexn. K." For sale of his military bounty lands in Missouri in October, 1839, see Clay to Pindell, October 14, 1839, and Dunnica to Clay, November 19, 1840.

At this time, 1838-39, Clay was still paying Transylvania University $600 per annum interest on his $10,000 loan from the James Morrison estate. He was also paying $1,200 interest per annum on his $20,000 loan from John Jacob Astor [8:763]. Copy. MH-BA. See also Astor to Clay, November 18, 1840. ALS. DLC-TJC (DNA, M212, R14).

Clay paid $56.00 Lexington city tax for 1838 and for the same year a Fayette County revenue tax at 10¢ per $100 on $72,000, or $72.00. John Wirt to Clay, receipt, October 25, 1838. ADS. *Ibid.* (R18); R.S. Todd to Clay, receipt, October 31, 1838. D. *Ibid.* The tax records which are available indicate that in the city of Lexington, Clay owned property assessed at: $13,000 in 1837; $14,000 in 1838; $16,500 in 1839; and $500 in 1845. *Assessor's Book,* City of Lexington, 1837, 1838, 1839, 1845. The city tax rate for 1839 and 1840 was: 40¢ per $100 property; $1.50 poll tax; 5¢ on $100 property fire tax; 50¢ on each dog. *Lexington City Records,* 1840-43, no. 6. Available Fayette County tax records show Clay in 1841 with 672 acres of land, valued at $43,790, plus 48 slaves. *Fayette County Tax Assessor's Books,* 1841, microfilm, Ky. State Library and Archives. For Nicholas Biddle's assessment of Clay's financial situation in the fall of 1838, see Biddle to Clay, September 20, 1838.

From PETER B. PORTER Black Rock, N.Y., October 8, 1838

[Regrets he did not see Clay again before leaving Lexington. Says he is sending, via the Ohio Canal, about November 1, "a couple of pairs of pigs, one of China, and one of Berkshire." Thinks it best that Clay have a pair of each "so you may preserve them pure, or cross them as you please. I think the cross makes the best stock." Continues on a political note:]

Our political prospects yet remain exceedingly fair, although we shall have a tremendous contest at the November election,[1] and the Locofocos will move heaven and earth to carry the State. But the Whigs will not be idle, & from the best information I can get from every quarter, I cannot for a moment doubt but that we shall succeed triumphantly.

The Utica Convention of the 12th. which was a most respectable body of men, conducted their proceedings with great fairness, & the result was such as we wished.[2] *All* who voted for [William H.] Seward in the first instance were your political friends, while many of your friends voted both for [Francis] Granger and [Luther] Bradish on account of personal predilections. They closed with great unanimity and good feeling. Their address (drawn up by J[ohn]. C. Spencer) is I think, an able document, & will be read to advantage in other States as well as this.

Senator [Nathaniel P.] Tal[l]mage and lady spent a few hours at my house yesterday. He is in fine spirits, and desired me, if I should write to you, to say that he has recently made a tour, which he is now about completing, through almost every part of the State; has seen most of his political friends and taken great pains to canvas the votes of the different districts, and is *entirely satisfied* that we shall succeed at the coming Election. He is in constant correspondence with Mr. [William C.] Rives, & says that the report that has been recently circulated that a reconciliation had taken place between him and Mr. Van Buren, is wholly destitute of foundation; that Mr. Van Buren's late visit at his house, & their subsequent meeting at the Springs, were unsolicited & wholly unexpected on his part; and that in political feeling they are as wide apart as they were last winter. He says, moreover, that Mr. Rives is decidedly of opinion that the Whig ticket will succeed in Virginia at the next Presidential Election,[3] notwithstanding the unprincipled course and action of [Thomas] Ritchie. . . .[4]

Copy. OHi. 1. Schermerhorn to Clay, Feb. 25, 1838. 2. Clay to Unknown Recipient, Sept. 27, 1838. 3. Van Buren carried Virginia and its 23 electoral votes in 1840 by a margin of 43,893 to 42,501 over Harrison. McKee, *National . . . Popular and Electoral Vote*, 44-45. 4. Emissaries from Van Buren had persuaded Ritchie to switch his support for the 1838 elections from the Conservative Democrats to the administration Democrats. In exchange, the administration would cease its war against Ritchie's Richmond *Enquirer*. Charles H. Ambler, *Thomas Ritchie, A Study in Virginia Politics* (Richmond, Va., 1913), 200-207.

To FRANCIS T. BROOKE Lexington, October 9, 1838

I recd. your favor of the 27h. Ulto. but I can hardly say that I had very great pleasure from its perusal; for, upon my word, if you will excuse me for saying so, the paper and the writing are so bad that I do not know that I have guessed its contents.

As to the movement in the State of Massachusetts, you will have seen, that it is alleged to have been without authority and is retracted.[1] *If* we succeed in the elections of Pennsa.[2] and N. York,[3] I attach no importance to that or any similar movement, whether with or without authority. My impression is, that the Editor of the Atlas expressed sentiments which he supposed would be acceptable to Mr. W[ebster].

Your suggestion as to a Bank of the U. S. would do well, if it would conciliate support from those who are opposed to such an institution; but my impression is that it is to the thing, in any form, more than to a particular modification, that opposition exists. At present, however, it is useless to try to establish any Bank of the U. S. with any modification whatever. It should not be attempted until the People clearly call for it. This, I think, they will do; but if they do not; if they are opposed to it, I, for one, cheerfully acquiesce in their decision:

We have been, and yet are, terribly afflicted with drought. It has injuriously affected our Crops, but I presume not as much yours have been. . . .

ALS. ICN. Printed in Colton, *Clay Correspondence*, 4:428-29. 1. Otis to Clay, Sept. 14, 1838. 2. Schermerhorn to Clay, Feb. 25, 1838. 3. *Ibid.*

From Jacob Ridenour, Cincinnati, October 12, 1838. Thanks Clay for his hospitality while at "Ashland" buying cattle. Discusses the Alexander Duncan versus Nathanael G. Pendleton congressional election in the Cincinnati district, pointing out that the victory of Duncan, "the Republican," over Pendleton, the Whig, was in part because the latter was by "no means a Popular Man" in the city and "much less so in the Country, where he is only known [as] a Man of Wealth." Believes that the "unfavourable position our highly Reputed Governor, [Joseph Vance] has been made to hold by the Abolitionist[s] of this City and County, has been the cause of the triumph of the Administration party in this County." Reports that the Whig ticket carried Cincinnati by a 1,300 majority even though "there were at least 400 Whig votes not given in from the personal dislike of the candidate for sheriff [John Burgoyne] as well as the candidate for Congress." Considers Congressman-elect Duncan a man of unworthy character and attributes his victory to "the ignorance and depravity pervading the interior of our Country." Notes that in Preble, his home county, the Whig turnout in the Duncan-Pendleton race was 200 to 300 below its usual number, while the Democratic vote there remained stable. Concludes that "had all the Whigs voted, they would have gained the election," even though Pendleton "was not known in the greatest part of the district." Hopes that 1840 will be "a glorious year of a reformation throughout our Country" and that Clay will be elected president. ALS. DLC-HC (DNA, M212, R5).

In Hamilton County, Ohio's first congressional district, Alexander Duncan, a Democrat, defeated Nathanael G. Pendleton for the U.S. House in 1838 by 4,572 votes to 4,396. *Guide to U.S. Elections*, 571. In the 1838 sheriff's race in Hamilton County, Ohio, John C. Avery, a Democrat, defeated John Burgoyne, a Whig, by 4,668 votes to 4,365. Cincinnati *Daily Gazette*, October 13, 1838.

To Philip R. Fendall, October 24, 1838. Discusses what action the American Colonization Society should take in regard to "the case of Captain Ross's will in Mississippi." States that the executors "are willing to perform the trust" and the heirs, "whatever they may have threatened," have brought no suit to set aside the will. Given these facts, concludes "that the Society had better make a formal demand upon the Exors for all that it is entitled to under the will; and, if that be refused, measures of coercion can then be employed." ALS. DLC-Records of the American Colonization Society (DNA, M212, R20).

Capt. Isaac Ross had provided in his will that, after the death of his daughter, Margaret Ross Reid, his estate would provide funds to pay for the emigration of his 170 slaves to Liberia. His daughter, who died in September, 1838, left a will providing for the emigration of her 120 slaves to Liberia and leaving the remainder of her estate to the Mississippi Colonization Society. For the furor against freeing slaves by a will which resulted in Mississippi from this case, see Kane, *Natchez*, 207-18; D. Clayton James, *Antebellum Natchez* (Baton Rouge, 1968), 176.

To THOMAS H. PERKINS Lexington, October 24, 1838

I recd. your favor of the 10h. The sentiments which it expresses, in regard to a recent Editorial article of the Atlas,[1] are precisely such as I expected you would entertain. I never, for a moment, indulged the belief that the article would be approved by any gentleman of honor and probity in Massachusetts; and it has been very gratifying to learn, indirectly, through various channels, that it meets the unqualified condemnation of Mr. Webster.

The mischief is that such articles encourages our adversary, as you justly observe. And late events have shewn, God knows, that *we* ought not to have given him any encouragement. Should N. York[2] follow the unfortunate examples of Ohio[3] & Pennsa.[4] (which is now much to be apprehended) the only consolation which will be left to the Whigs will be that their condition this fall is not quite so bad, bad as it will be, as that of their opponents was last fall.

My son in law, Mr. James Erwin, was on the 10h. inst. in the City of N. York, his last letter to me bearing that date. He was then deliberating whether he should go to Europe, or return to Kentucky on his way to N. Orleans. I have not heard what his decision was. If he went to Europe, he is now probably on the ocean; and if he decided to return to K. he is now on his way hither. Mr. [Joseph D.] Beers'[5] (the Presidt. of some Bank in N.Y.) would be a proper person to transmit a letter for Mr. Erwin to, as they are, I believe, engaged in some important business together. . . .

ALS. MHi. 1. Otis to Clay, Sept. 14, 1838. 2. Schermerhorn to Clay, Feb. 25, 1838. 3. Duncan to Clay, Oct. 4, 1838. 4. Schermerhorn to Clay, Feb. 25, 1838. 5. For Beers, the president of the North American Trust and Banking Company, see Martha J. Lamb, *History of the City of New York*, 2 vols. (New York, 1877), 2:735.

To PETER B. PORTER Lexington, October 24, 1838

I recd. your favor of the 8h. and I am very thankful for the friendly intention of Mr. Allen and yourself to send me the Pigs. I shall consider them a most valuable present.

I sent for him and you, via Maysville, several weeks ago three bushels of Blue Grass Seed in chaff and put up in a barrel, to be forwarded through the Ohio Canal. I hope it will reach you in safety. We have found it a good way to sow the seed on the snow in the month of Feb. or March. The sod will not be thickly formed the first year, as it is very delicate when it first comes up, and requires time to spread its roots.

The issue of recent Elections has greatly surprized us, and that of Ohio[1] most of all. It is, I understand, attributed to the fact the Abolitionists in mass voted the Admon ticket. Our hopes now all rest upon N. York;[2] and yet it is almost too much to expect that she will be able to bear up against the adverse and discouraging causes which exist. If we are unfortunately beaten there, the Executive will acquire complete control, in all probability, at the next Congress,[3] and will be able to play what S[ub]. Treasury or other pranks it pleases.[4]

I shall be most happy to find myself able to accept your kind invitation to visit you at the Falls, and hope some day or other to surprize you there. . . .

ALS. NBuHi. 1. Duncan to Clay, Oct. 4, 1838. 2. Schermerhorn to Clay, Feb. 25, 1838. 3. Party strength in the 26th Congress (Dec. 2, 1839-March 3, 1841) showed, in the Senate: 28 Democrats, 22 Whigs, 2 others; House: 124 Democrats, 118 Whigs. Morris, *Encyclopedia of American History*, 406; Thomas B. Alexander counts in the House: 125 Democrats, 114 Whigs. Alexander, *Sectional Stress and Party Strength* (Nashville, 1967), 34. 4. The Independent or Sub-Treasury bill passed the Senate 24 to 18 on Jan. 23, 1840, and the House 127 to 107 on June 30, 1840. Van Buren signed it on July 4, 1840. Speech in Senate, Sept. 25, 1837, and Jan. 20, 1840; Clay to Porter, Dec. 27, 1838.

From Jesse Duncan Elliott, Carlisle, Pa., October 25, 1838. Encloses for Transylvania University a gift of coins he collected while commanding U.S. naval forces in the Mediterranean. Reports that some of the Arabian mares mentioned in a "previous note [not found]" are "now on their way West" to Boonville, Missouri, "on shares." Also encloses vegetable and flower seeds for "My old friend Mrs. [Lucretia Hart] Clay," noting that "The vegetables cannot but be acceptable as they are of a superior quality Their botanical names are in Spanish." ALS, incomplete. KyLxT.

To ALEXANDER HAMILTON Lexington, October 25, 1838

I recd. the letters with which you favored me from Philada. prior and subsequent to the Pennsa. Election.[1] Its issue, and that of other Elections excites surprize and regret. Should N. York catch the contagion,[2] and decide against the Whigs, it will furnish the occasion of deeper regret. If she determines otherwise, we shall find our cause yet safe. Let the worst come that may, the aspect of public affairs will be more favorable to us than it was to our opponents last fall. Still it would be discouraging. And I own that the corrupting influences of the Executive are very difficult to surmount. But why despair? despair of the Republic? You know, that we can do that when nothing else is left to us

The Ohio election most surprized me.[3] There, besides the exertions of the Admon put forth in an extraordinary degree, Abolition, and the case of a person surrend[er]ed by the Govr of Ohio [Joseph Vance] upon the demand of the Govr of Kentucky [James Clark], touching Slavery,[4] operated much against us. . . .

ALS. NN. 1. Schermerhorn to Clay, Feb. 25, 1838. 2. *Ibid.* 3. Duncan to Clay, Oct. 4, 1838. 4. John B. Mahan, a Methodist clergyman from Ohio, had been accused of assisting fifteen runaway slaves on their way from Kentucky to Canada. Gov. Clark of Kentucky demanded that Gov. Vance of Ohio deliver Mahan for trial in Kentucky, and Vance complied. In the trial, Mahan was acquitted because his deeds had been performed in Ohio, not Kentucky; therefore, Kentucky had no jurisdiction in the case. Weisenburger, *The Passing of the Frontier*, 3:349-50.

From Stephen Duncan, Natchez, Miss., October 30, 1838. Reports receipt of invoice showing shipment from Clay of 31,914 lbs. of bale rope @ 13 cents per pound [Clay to Henry Clay, Jr., September 8, 1837]. Has deposited to Clay's account in the Agricultural Bank of Natchez his note for $4,148.82 payable January 6, 1839. Remarks that "The manufacturers have not been as careful in the manufacture of your hemp this year, as last." Has heard the results of the elections in Pennsylvania and Ohio [Schermerhorn to Clay, February 25, 1838; Duncan to Clay, October 4, 1838]. Is convinced "it will be found, when too late,—that the Sub-Treasury bill [Speech in Senate, September 25, 1837] ought to have been permitted to pass." Thinks such passage would have put a desirable end to the issue politically. Says that personally he is sick of politics and that hereafter he "would be glad to see, all men of sense & integrity—leave the spoils, to the fools & knaves, to quarrel about." ALS. DLC-TJC (DNA, M212, R14).

To NATHANIEL P. TALLMADGE Lexington, October 31, 1838

I received your friendly message through Genl. Porter,[1] and have since had the pleasure to receive your letter of the 20h. instant. I am extremely sorry that the Whig Convention[2] did not nominate a Lieut. Governor from the Conservatives,[3] for the purpose of inspiring confidence among them. I have the pleasure of knowing Mr. G[ideon] Lee[4] very well, and indulged the hope that he would have been selected. But it was a matter in which I could only look on, without interfering. I presume that the Whig Convention had its own difficulties to reconcile jarring pretensions. It terminated, I understand, in great harmony and good feeling. I have perused, with much interest and satisfaction, the proceedings of the Syracuse Convention.[5] They breathe a firm and patriotic spirit. And if the Whig Cause should happily prevail in N. York, its success will be greatly indebted to those proceedings. But will it prevail? That important question will be decided by the time this letter reaches you. After the unexpected and disastrous issue of the Ohio Election,[6] I tremble for the result of yours.[7] I confess to you that I have strong suspicions that there has been foul play[.] The influence of Abolition, and the case of the delivery of the Methodist Clergyman, upon the demand of Govr. Clarke [*sic*, James Clark],[8] are not sufficient to account for the extraordinary change in Ohio, which nobody dreamt of three weeks before the Election. Up to September of this year, from September of last year, the current, deep and strong and increasing, was all running our way. Suddenly it turns What has occurred to direct it from its course? Amos Kendall was at Columbus the week before the election. For what purpose? How easy was it for him to issue orders to his deputies and to render them effectual by appropriate means, throughout the State?

If contrary to the fears which I entertain, New York should realize our hopes,[9] the Country will be yet saved, and the influence of the event upon your fortunes will be most salutary and happy.

Our friends in this quarter have been much dis spirited by the late events, most of all by that in Ohio, for which they were wholly unprepared. I tell them not to despair; that when nothing else is left to us, it will be time enough to yield to that sentiment.

I presume, with you, that the issue of the Elections will encourage the Administration to persevere in its financial policy; and that of consequence the Sub Treasury will be again proposed.[10] There are some who think that they had better be indulged with its passage. I confess I am not of that number; and that I continue to think that it is for the interest of the Country, and favorable to the ultimate expulsion of the party, that it should continue to be defeated. As to a Bank of the U. States there is no prospect of establishing one, and I trust that none will be proposed until it is loudly called for by the People. By the by, there are some circumstances which would indicate that the Executive intend[s] converting Mr. Biddles Bank into a Bank of the U.S. . . .[11]

ALS. WHi. 1. Porter to Clay, Oct. 8, 1838. 2. Clay to Unknown Recipient, Sept. 27, 1838. 3. Clay to Henry Clay, Jr., Jan. 28, 1837. 4. For Lee, a Conservative Democrat, see *BDAC* and Fox, *Decline of Aristocracy in New York Politics*, 383, 423. 5. A gathering of former New York Democrats, now calling themselves Conservatives, met at Syracuse on Oct. 3, 1838. Tallmadge was prominent among them. They endorsed the Whig gubernatorial ticket of William H. Seward and Luther Bradish. Hammond, *History of Political Parties in the State of New York*, 2:486. 6. Duncan to Clay, Oct. 4, 1838. 7. Schermerhorn to Clay, Feb. 25, 1838. 8. Clay to Hamilton, Oct. 25, 1838. 9. Schermerhorn to Clay, Feb. 25, 1838. 10. Clay to Porter, Oct. 24, 1838. 11. For the growing cooperation between Biddle's U.S. Bank of Pennsylvania and Van Buren's Treasury Department following the resumption of specie payments and the subsequent defeat of the Sub-Treasury bill in the House on June 25, 1838, see Govan, *Nicholas Biddle*, 335-37; Wilson, *Presidency of Martin Van Buren*, 116, 127-28. To cover emergency cash demands in mid-1838, the government sold to Biddle's bank two of the four bonds Biddle had issued it in 1836 in payment for U.S. shares in the expiring B.U.S. Secretary Woodbury also agreed to deposit the proceeds from the sale in Biddle's Philadelphia bank. He agreed further to withdraw these monies slowly, in the form of the bank's paper notes, and to spend these notes in the distant interior of the country. By Sept., 1838, Biddle was convinced that the administration was ready to designate his bank as "the general depository of government funds." See Clay to Brooke, Dec. 20, 1838; *Cong. Globe*, 25 Cong., 3 Sess., 46-47, 49; also see the resolutions of Sen. William C. Rives on Dec. 19, 1838, which questioned the treasury's sale of its bonds to Biddle and other particulars of the deal. For Rives's break with the Van Buren administration, see Clay to Porter, Dec. 27, 1838.

To JAMES G. BIRNEY Lexington, November 3, 1838

I recd. your letter of the 22d. Ulto. with "Emancipation in the W. Indies,"[1] and your correspondence with Mr. Ellmore [*sic*, Franklin H. Elmore][2] for which I am thankful. The latter I had seen in the public prints; and I will read the former as soon as I can find leisure, altho' I must say that its testimony, whatever it may be, would be far from being conclusive on the question of African slavery in the U.S. The insular condition of those islands; their dependence upon G. Britain; the force which she has applied and must continue to apply to preserve their peace; the liberal compensation which she made for the loss of property; & the total want of any voice of the W. India planters in the British Parliament, to say nothing of the inferiority of numbers compared to the Slaves in the U.S. make the question of abolition in those Colonies altogether different from the question of abolition in the U.S. Put two or three million of slaves in England, dispersed throughout the Kingdom, and let their proprietors be represented and representatives in Parliament, and you would have a case some what analogous to ours, with one important difference still existing, that whereas the Parliament would then have the power to emancipate the Slaves, whilst with us the power of emancipation is exclusively possessed by the Slave states.

You regret that K. has recently decided against a Convention and consequently against abolition.[3] Will you believe me, when I assure you that it is my clear conviction that the decision against a Convention was mainly produced by the agitation of the question of Abolition at the North? I will not say that, without that agitation, this State was ripe for gradual emancipation, but it was rapidly advancing to that point. We are thrown back fifty years. And here I must remark that you and others, no doubt unintentionally, have misconceived my opinions. I never, in my life, was in favor of the immediate emancipation of Slaves in K. At the epoch of 1798-9, I declare that I do not recollect a single individual, among all who espoused the cause of emancipation, that maintained that there ought to be abolition, according to the present import of that term.[4] We were for gradual emancipation, such as Pennsa. established, by which all born after a specified day were to be free at 28. I would be, in a State where the disproportion of the slaves to the whites was not too great, still in favor of such a cautious emancipation. I would oppose it in a State differently situated, where there might be danger of the Blacks acquiring the ascendancy. I have then changed no opinion. You will ask why I was opposed to the recent Convention proposed in K.? From the influence of the agitation of the question of Abolition, I saw evidence enough that there was not the remotest prospect of carrying any scheme of gradual emancipation; and I was unwilling to hazard all the good, in our excellent Constitution, in an experiment to effect an object, which I was confident was unattainable.

I feel grateful for the expression of your kind feelings and good will towards me. I do not complain of your opinion that the election of a Slave holder to the Presidency would be a public calamity, so far as it may be supposed to affect me. I have never yielded my consent to be a Candidate for that office, since the last election; and late events indicate a strong probability that, if I were a Candidate, your wishes are likely to be gratified. But

I think that your justice, on reconsideration, must lead you to question the propriety of a rule which would have deprived the Country of the services of Washington, Jefferson, Madison & Monroe in the highest executive office, and of [John] Marshall in the highest judicial office.

It is no part of my purpose to engage you in a correspondence for which perhaps neither of us may have inclination or leisure. Nor do I write now for any other purpose than to acknowledge the receipt of the publications with which you have favored me, and to correct an error under which you labor as to my opinions. Least of all do I write for the public press.

ALS. NHi. Printed in Joseph A. Boromé, "Henry Clay and James G. Birney: An Exchange of Views," *FCHQ* (April, 1961), 35:122-24. 1. J.A. Thome and J.H. Kimball, *Emancipation in the West Indies.* See Tappan to Clay, June 5, 1838. 2. Tappan to Clay, June 5, 1838. For S.C. Congressman Franklin H. Elmore, see *BDAC*. 3. Clay to Baldwin, August 28, 1838. 4. See 1:3-8.

To FRANCIS T. BROOKE Lexington, November 3, 1838

I received your favor of the 18th ultimo, and, as it informed me of your intention to go to Richmond, I address this letter to that city. You think I have too good an opinion of mankind. I confess that I have, throughout life, striven to think well of them, but the last thirteen years have shaken my faith very much. I yet, however, believe the mass to be honest, although very liable to deception.

You are certainly right as to one of the two gentlemen mentioned, perhaps as to both, being unwilling to see me elected Chief Magistrate. I was greatly surprised at the course of "The [Boston] Atlas;" and although Mr. Webster disavows its authority to speak for him, in that particular, there are intelligent persons near him who believe that "The Atlas" presumed upon his concurrence.[1] The issue of the elections, this fall, so far, have been very unfavorable to the Whig cause. From September of last year to September of this, the current ran deep and strong in our favor, and swept over every State, changing majorities against us, or, at least, diminishing them. All at once, and without any apparent cause, the current reverses its direction. What has produced it? To give you a proof that I am not too confiding, I can not forbear expressing my suspicion that a profuse and corrupt use has been made of the public money. It is almost impossible otherwise to account satisfactorily for what we have witnessed. Amos Kendall was at Columbus the week before the election. How easy was it for him to give orders throughout the State, from that central point of Ohio, to carry the election at any cost.[2] And how can he be brought to account, if he has given such orders?

Other circumstances will enable us to account for some of the results of these elections. In Ohio, the Abolitionists are alleged to have gone against us, almost to a man. Senator [Thomas] Morris, you know, is one of them, and that, put together with the unfortunate case of the Methodist preacher, delivered up by Governor [Joseph] Vance upon the demand of the Governor of Kentucky [James Clark], turned them against us.[3] Perhaps they were previously inclined toward Mr. Van Buren.

If New York goes against us, as is to be apprehended after what has occurred, our cause will look bad.[4] You will know the event by the time this letter reaches you. It is to be apprehended, because, whether changes have been produced in other States by voluntary impulse of the people, or by corrupt means, the same cause, whatever it may be, is likely to exert itself in New York.

The introduction of this new element of Abolition into our elections can not fail to excite, with all reflecting men, the deepest solicitude. It is, I believe, the first time it has been done. Although their numbers are not very great, they are sufficiently numerous, in several States, to turn the scale. I have now before me a letter from the Secretary [James G. Birney] of the American Anti-Slavery Society, in New York, in which he says: "I should consider (as in all candor I acknowledge I would) the election of any slaveholder to the Presidency a great calamity to the country."[5]

The danger is that the contagion may spread until it reaches all the free States; and if it ever comes to be acted on as a rule among them, to proscribe slaveholders, they have the numbers to enforce it. Union and concert with them will throw the whole Government into their hands, and when they have once possession, the principle by which they have acquired it will urge them on to other and further encroachments. They will begin by prohibiting the slave trade, as it is called, among the slave States, and by abolishing it in the District of Columbia, and the end will be———

My own position, touching slavery, at the present time, is singular enough. The Abolitionists are denouncing me as a slaveholder, and slaveholders as an Abolitionist, while they both unite on Mr. Van Buren.

I should be extremely happy to visit Richmond and see you and the many other friends I have there, but I can not do it while I remain a *quasi* candidate for the Presidency. A candidate in fact I can not say, and have not said to any human being I would be. I am strongly inclined to promulgate that I will not be, under any circumstances. How would it do? The principal objection which I perceive, is, that they would say that I saw the grapes were sour. But then, what need I care for any thing they may say?

Pray remember me affectionately to [Benjamin W.] Leigh. I rejoice to be able to infer, from a recent letter of his, addressed to another person and sent for my perusal, that his health was fully re-established. . . .

Copy. Printed in Colton, *Clay Correspondence*, 4:429-31. 1. Otis to Clay, Sept. 14, 1838. 2. Duncan to Clay, Oct. 4, 1838. 3. Clay to Hamilton, Oct. 25, 1838. 4. Schermerhorn to Clay, Feb. 25, 1838. 5. Clay to Birney, Nov. 3, 1838.

From Thomas Allen, Philadelphia, November 6, 1838. Reports that just before leaving Washington the other day, he heard on good authority that Clay was withdrawing his name from the presidential race. Asks if this be true. Says he has abstained from discussing the merits of the presidential candidates in his newspaper, the Washington *Madisonian*, but prefers Clay. Believes there are too many "strange & conflicting views of policy among the Whigs" and that unity is needed. Says he is "informed by several financiers here that the U.S. Bank has really gone over to Mr Van Buren body & soul [Clay to Tallmadge, October 31, 1838]. The interests of both parties may secure a permanent matrimonial alliance." Predicts a Whig victory in New York state; specifically, a Seward win by 5,000 to 7,000 votes in the gubernatorial race [Schermerhorn to Clay, February 25, 1838]. Adds: "The result of the first day in New York City (yesterday) is decidedly favorable to the Whigs." ALS. DLC-HC (DNA, M212, R5). For Allen, who founded the Washington *Madisonian* in 1837 and edited it in the political interests of the Conservative Democrat faction (William C. Rives, Nathaniel P. Tallmadge *et al.*), see Ames, *A History of the National Intelligencer*, 239-40; also *DAB*.

From Thomas F. Marshall, Versailles, Ky., November 12, 1838. Refers his conflict with Aaron K. Woolley to Clay and John J. Crittenden for mediation. ALS. DLC-John J. Crittenden Papers. Addressed to both Clay and Crittenden.

On November 21, 1838, Clay and Crittenden jointly issued their judgment on the dispute. They report that they have interviewed several gentlemen who had witnessed the confrontation that had occurred during the recent term of the Woodford Circuit Court. They find that Woolley was primarily at fault, that it was he who had first made a "threat of . . . violence" against Marshall accompanied by "insulting expressions." Recommend that "All other expressions of irritation, insult & ange[r] ought we think to be mutually withdrawn," but that Woolley should "make . . . atonement" for his threat of violence against Marshall. ADS, in Clay's hand. *Ibid.* For Woolley and Marshall, see Collins, *History of Kentucky*, 2:205, 767-68. The altercation had occurred when Woolley interrupted Marshall while he was speaking and threatened to strike him. Marshall waved his hand and replied: "Consider the blow struck, Mr. Woolley." Afterwards, Marshall challenged Woolley to a duel, but the intervention of friends brought about the mediation which settled the dispute amicably. Paul R. Shipman, *A Handful of Bitter Herbs . . .* (Lexington, 1953), 14.

To HARRISON G. OTIS Lexington, November 14, 1838

I duly received your obliging favor of the 5h. inst. as I did the preceding one, transmitting an article from a news paper which I read with attention and interest. It was very judicious, altho' it has not had the effect of restraining the indiscretions of the Atlas.[1]

The issue of the Elections in Maryland,[2] N. Jersey,[3] Pennsa.[4] and above all in Ohio[5] has been unexpected and discouraging. But I have not despaired. To that equable sentiment we can at last yield, when nothing else is left. Should N. York (from which I have not yet heard definitively)[6] follow the bad examples of her sisters, why the aspect of public affairs will not be good.

I have been provoked at the imputations to me of defeat in Ohio. Nothing can be more unfounded or absurd. Nothing can be more discredi[t]able. I have not been in the State for several years, and I have corresponded with it less this year than I have with you. It has been left entirely to Genl Harrison. He had traversed a large part of the State previous to the election. Both of the State Conventions have nominated him as a Candidate.[7] How could I then occasion its loss? According to my information, whatever County he visited has sustained a Whig loss! Ohio was the first, I believe, to propose a Nat. Convention.[8] It has not yet assembled. Have any of the Ohio Whigs, merely from the apprehension that their favorite may not obtain the nomination, slackened their exertions or gone over to the foe? If so, what must we think of their patriotism?

I do not myself suspect Genl Harrison, or any of his friends, of playing foul. He had too much at stake. We have lost the State by abolition, by the unfortunate surrender of the Methodist preacher,[9] by greater system and more strenuous exertions, perhaps also by the corrupt means, of our opponents.

I have sometimes been almost tempted, in some suitable public way, to declare that my name should not be used, under any circumstances, in connection with a high office. One can bear the taunts and reproaches and calumnies of open foes; but it is too much to be picked at by friends from Boston to Cincinnati. Some times the best service which can be rendered one's Country is not to serve it at all.

I am not surprized that in N. England you should display some sensibility to the wrongs which the South has some times done you. She has wronged you; but will you from feeling or passion be urged to wrong both her and yourselves? I hope not. Let us take care of the Country, and especially the Union, whatever may be the freaks or follies of parties. Every part of it is necessary to every other part. Our pursuits, our habits, our peculiarities all dove-tail admirably together, if we do not madly burst them asunder.

Our negro-slavery—what is that to you? Bad enough, some of us think it is for us, but it is our affair. Time, Providence will cure all—abolition nothing. It may ruin all; it can save none.

This is a gloomy Novr day, which will explain why I write thus to you. Ever since I have had the pleasure of knowing you, I have had great confidence in your patriotism; and I know that it is not necessary to press on you sentiments of attachment to the Country & the Union.[10]

We have differed—honestly differed; and who has been or may be right, time and events must disclose. You think that our public evils are traceable to the diffusion of the Elective franchise. I am not at all convinced of that. We do not find in States where it is more restricted less of error. The Cities are nearer right than the Country; but in the Country we should expect to find the most virtue.

I must conclude this desultory epistle—forced to do so by darkness, if not impelled, as I should be, by the desire to spare you from further infliction.

Should N.Y. go right, all *may be yet* right. It will depend upon ourselves. Individual ambition must be repressed; and if necessary I am ready to set the first example.

ALS. MHi. 1. Otis to Clay, Sept. 14, 1838. 2. The Democratic gubernatorial candidate in Maryland, William Grason, had defeated John Steele, the Whig candidate, by a vote of 27,722 to 27,402. *BDGUS*, 2:662-63. The Whigs, however, won 12 seats in the state senate and 40 in the house, while the Democrats won 9 senate seats and 36 house seats. In a special congressional election in the 4th district, the Whig candidate was victorious. *Niles' Register* (Oct. 6, 1838), 55:81. 3. In the New Jersey elections of 1838 the Whigs won a majority in both houses of the legislature. Also, Whig Governor William Pennington, Jr., was reelected by the legislature. Washington *Daily National Intelligencer*, Oct. 27, 29; Nov. 1, 8, 1838; *BDGUS*, 3:1017-18. Dispute over the congressional election produced the so-called "Broad Seal War" of 1838-39. Results seemed to indicate the election of 5 Democrats and 1 Whig; however, under the Great Seal of New Jersey, Gov. Pennington commissioned 6 Whigs as victors. This election became crucial in determining which party would organize the U.S. House when the 26th Congress convened in Dec., 1839. Eventually, the House seated 5 Democrats and 1 Whig from New Jersey. For further discussion, see Francis B. Lee, *New Jersey As a Colony and As a State* (New York, 1902), 3:329-33; Adams, *Memoirs of John Quincy Adams*, 142-67, 226, *passim*. 4. Schermerhorn to Clay, Feb. 25, 1838. 5. Duncan to Clay, Oct. 4, 1838.

6. Schermerhorn to Clay, Feb. 25, 1838. 7. The Ohio Whig conventions of 1837 and 1838. See Clay to Prentice, August 14, 1837; Clay to Porter, Jan. 5, 1838. 8. The Ohio Whigs had led the way in calling for a national convention at their 1837 state convention. Gunderson, *The Log-Cabin Campaign*, 50. 9. Clay to Hamilton, Oct. 25, 1838. 10. Otis, a delegate to the Hartford Convention of 1814-15 claimed the purpose of that meeting had been to air grievances, not to promote secession. Moreover, he had strongly opposed South Carolina nullification in 1832. Samuel E. Morison, *Harrison Gray Otis 1765-1848, The Urbane Federalist* (Boston, 1969), 353, 356-57, 376, 380-81, 451-52.

To ROBERT SWARTWOUT Lexington, November 15, 1838

Thanks, my dear General, cordial thanks, and a thousand of them, for the glad and glorious tidings contained in your letter of the 8h. I have been kept in my house two days by wet gloomy November weather; but the issue of your election[1] has made every thing bright and cheering around me. The patriotic service has been reserved for New York to save the Constitution, the Country and the cause of civil Liberty. Most nobly has she performed it! Immortal honors and immortal gratitude are her just due.

I have passed some painful moments, during the last four or five weeks. I did not despair. I never despair. Why should one? He can do that, when nothing else is left. But I saw that if N. York were lost, there would be occasion for long, strenuous and persevering exertions, possibly terminating in a Revolution, the last resource of an oppressed People. I had the greatest confidence in the Whigs of N. York; but when I reflected upon the boundless means of our opponents, their desperation, and their destitution of all principle, I trembled for you and my Country. I rejoice that our deliverance is at hand, and that the glory of the achievement belongs to N. York. At another epoch of our Country Virginia and Kentucky saved the State.[2] Kentucky will be proud of co-operating now with N. York in a similar good and glorious work.

I write without knowing the issue of the Governor's Election,[3] but with a conviction that, whatever it may be, there has been glory enough for these days.

ALS. NN. 1. Schermerhorn to Clay, Feb. 25, 1838. 2. Reference is to the famous Kentucky and Virginia Resolutions (1798-99) critical of the constitutionality of the Alien and Sedition Acts of 1798. 3. In the 1838 gubernatorial election in New York, William Henry Seward (Whig) defeated William L. Marcy (Dem.) by a vote of 192,882 to 182,461. Whig Albert H. Tracy defeated Democrat Luther Bradish for the lieutenant governorship. *BDGUS*, 3:1078.

To EDWARD GREENE Lexington, November 18, 1838

I seize a few moments, amidst busy preparations for my departure for Washington, to thank you[1] heartily for your several letters, respecting the glorious issue of the New York elections.[2] It has filled me with unspeakable joy; and opens new and brighter hopes for my Country and for mankind. . . .

ALS. KyU. 1. For Greene, a collector who resided at 153 Laurens in New York City, see Longworth, *American Almanac: New-York Register, and City Directory*. 2. Schermerhorn to Clay, Feb. 25, 1838.

To ELIAS W. LEAVENWORTH Lexington, November 18, 1838

I thank you[1] for your letter, communicating the issue of the Election in Onondaga, and details concerning it in other Counties of N. York.[2] Other letters which I have received leave no doubt of the triumph of the Whigs throughout the State. The Nation Posterity and Mankind owe the State a debt of eternal Gratitude.

ALS. NIC. 1. For Leavenworth (1803-87), a New York lawyer and later a congressman, see *BDAC*. 2. Schermerhorn to Clay, Feb. 25, 1838. Onondaga County went for Seward, the Whig gubernatorial candidate, but its district (23) elected two Democrats to Congress. Washington *Daily National Intelligencer*, Nov. 14, 15, 19, 1838; *Guide to U.S. Elections*, 571.

To ALEXANDER R. WYCKOFF Lexington, November 18, 1838

I duly received and thank you[1] for your obliging letter of the 8h. inst. That, and letters which I have received from other friends, communicate the glorious issue of your late elections,[2] which fills my heart, and ought to fill that of every patriot, with gladness and joy. Although I fervently hoped for the result, late events had inspired me with fears and apprehension. These, thank God, are now dissipated, and henceforth, we may I trust, look with confidence to the fulfillment of the high destinies of our Country. What a lesson does the part read us! To the patriot never to despair; to the ruler, who preaches liberty and practises despotism, beware!

I sincerely hope that your suspicions as to the fidelity of our friends, or professed friends, in certain quarters, may not prove to be well founded. And yet I must own that the coincidence of attack upon me by the Atlas at Boston[3] and at Cincinnati[4] surprized and grieved me. Why should I be held responsible for the issue of elections in States other than K. more than Messrs. W. & H?[5] I no more than they have been the acknowledged Candidate of the Whigs. I more than either of them have disclaimed being considered a Candidate. I have displayed less action than either of them. If manifestations have been made of public feeling in my favor they have been unprompted by me. Do they occasion regret any where? Is it my popularity, rather than the want of it, which forms an objection to me? If it be so, that is not my fault. What say the Whigs in N. York, has my name injured them? If so let it be withdrawn & forgotten.

But, my dear Sir, I hope that no step will be taken nothing done, which is not dictated by wisdom prudence & kindness, altho it may display firmness & decision. Union & concert harmony & victory are what we should go for.

ALS. KyU. 1. For Wyckoff (1803-49), who was associated with the Hudson River Railroad Co. and who lived in New York City, see Longworth, *American Almanac: New-York Register, and City Directory*, 686; New York *Evening Post*, July 16, 1849; Allan Nevins and Milton H. Thomas (eds.), *The Diary of George Templeton Strong, Young Man in New York 1835-1849* (New York, 1952), 357-58. 2. Schermerhorn to Clay, Feb. 25, 1838. 3. Otis to Clay, Sept. 14, 1838. 4. The Cincinnati *Republican* had charged that the Whig loss in Ohio would not have occurred if Harrison had been the only prominent Whig presidential candidate. Freeman Cleaves, *Old Tippecanoe: William Henry Harrison and His Time* (New York, 1939), 312. 5. Webster and Harrison.

To HENRY CLAY, JR. Wheeling, Va. (W.Va.), November 28, 1838

I reached this place this evening in safety. I have felt uneasy about the Election of a Senator from Fayette.[1] I could wish that some person could be selected as the Whig Candidate against whom so many personal objections and private enmities could not be brought to bear as Mr. [Robert N.] Wickliffe.[2] But if he be the Candidate, I hope that all our friends will vote for him. His defeat & the election of a Loco foco would be a great triumph to our opponents. They would blazon it forth as such on two accounts. 1st That it is in the County of my residence; and 2dly. that Mr. Wickliffe is a delegate from the State to the Nat. Convention,[3] which is to nominate Candidates for P. & V. President.

I should think that those who do not like Mr. Wickliffe, may nevertheless vote for him on the ground of public considerations, waiving their private feelings. . . .

ALS. Henry Clay Memorial Foundation, Lexington, Ky. 1. Wickliffe was defeated for Fayette County's state senate seat by Richard Hawes. Both men were Whigs. Lexington *Observer & Kentucky Reporter*, August 7, 1838. 2. Robert N. Wickliffe (1805-55), called "Greasy Bob" to distinguish him from other prominent Robert Wickliffes, was the son of innkeeper Charles Wickliffe. He was a lawyer, a noted orator, and editor of the Lexington *Observer & Kentucky Reporter* from 1833 to 1838. George W. Ranck, *History of Lexington Kentucky* (Cincinnati, 1872), 235-36; Collins, *History of Kentucky*, 2:180. Clay was mistaken in his assumption that Wickliffe was to be the delegate to the Harrisburg convention from the congressional district comprising Fayette County. William B. Kinkead was the delegate chosen from Clay's district, a selection not made until Oct., 1839. Lexington *Observer & Kentucky Reporter*, Nov. 13, 1839. 3. Porter to Clay, Nov. 14 and Dec. 30, 1837.

Remark in Senate, December 12, 1838. Protests that he was unaware that the administration's bill "to provide for the reduction and graduation of the price of the public lands" would be taken up today, and that he was "without any sort of preparation for its discussion." Asks for, and receives, postponement. *Cong. Globe*, 25 Cong., 3 Sess., 25. The bill, introduced by Sen. Clement C. Clay (Ala.) on December 5, was, according to Sen. Silas Wright (N.Y.), virtually identical to the bill "passed by such a large majority" by the Senate (27 to 16) in the previous session. *Ibid.*, 15, 24. For action on the price reduction and graduation bill in the 25th Congress, 2nd Session, see Remark in Senate, March 29 and April 9, 1838; and Speech in Senate, April 11, 1838. The measure passed the Senate, 27 to 22, on January 17, 1839, Clay voting nay. *Cong. Globe*, 25 Cong., 3 Sess., 122. On January 22, 1839, the House voted, 102 to 97, to table the bill; and on January 23 the House defeated, 99 to 98, a motion to reconsider the motion to table. *Ibid.*, 133, 135. So, by House action, the reduction and graduation bill died in the 25th Congress, 3rd Session.

To HARRISON G. OTIS Washington, December 13, 1838

Your favor addressed to me here has been recd. That directed to Ashland to which it refers has not reached me.

The affair on the Cumberland Road, altho' two such good friends as Mr. [John J.] Crittenden and I, to the surprize of those who knew us both, *fell out together*, inflicted no serious injury. My head, which I found was most injured, proved entirely sound.[1]

I transmit for your perusal the letter of the Editor [Richard Haughton] of the Atlas;[2] but, without his concurrence, I cannot consent to any public use being made of it. It is of no consequence to expose his treachery; and I should be unwilling to be liable to the charge of violating a private correspondence, altho' it relates to a public concern.

The arrangements between the friends of Genl Harrison and some of those of Mr Webster are in a progress of developement. It is now believed that the foundation of them was laid here during the last Session of Congress. The attack at Boston on me, for the loss of Maine, which appeared in the Atlas,[3] after that same Atlas had enjoined forbearance in the discussion of the pretensions of Presidential Candidates, was among the first evidences of that coalition. Another soon followed at Cincinnati,[4] by which *I* was assailed for losing Genl Harrison's *own State*. The Anti Masonic nomination at Philada. exposed still more unequivocally the plan of operations.[5] I learn that Mr. W[ebster]. was apprized beforehand and approved of that nomination. I presume you know that the Convention did not contain one member who had been elected at any primary meeting of Anti Masons; and, except from Pennsa, one member who held his seat in virtue of any election whatever.

The nomination has fallen still born. It will work directly in the opposite way from that which was intended. Prudence alone suppresses the public expression of the indignation which it has excited in the Whigs.

It is not to be disguised however that our cause is surrounded by embarrassments. These are chiefly to be traced to our divisions which constitute our weakness, as they do the hopes of our adversaries.

If matters remain just as they are, the public giving no expression of its wishes or preferences, there is reason to apprehend the defeat of the Candidates nominated by the National Convention, whoever they may be. There will be collisions as to the delegates to be sent to it; divisions in it; and disappointment and dissatisfaction afterwards. These will be followed by unfavorable predictions; and the prophet does not strive hard to defeat the fulfillment of his prophesy.

In my opinion, the best way to ensure success to our cause is by such a manifestation of the public choice as to leave no other duty to the Convention than to ratify & promulgate it The Convention ought to express not to make public sentiment; but to express it, it must know it; and it cannot know it unless the public demonstrate it.

If there should be a clear demonstration of the Whig choice, the consequence would be acquiescence, or at least acquiescence to an extent to ensure it success.

The course of some of the friends of Messrs. H. & W. [Harrison and Webster] absolves mine from all obligation to practice further silence & forbearance.

I need not say to you, that scarcely any where would action favorable to me tell with more effect than in your Legislature.[6] But all these matters I leave to the discretion of yourself & other friends.

The scenes at Harrisburg;[7] and the explosion of defaulters[8] leave us here no time hardly for thinking of any thing else—

We shall however soon get to work & see which way the Land lies.

ALS. MHi. Letter marked "(Confidential)." 1. Clay, Crittenden, and several members of the House of Representatives were riding in a stagecoach which overturned on the Cumberland Road injuring a number of the passengers, though none critically. Washington *Daily National Intelligencer*, Dec. 3, 4, 1838. 2. Richard Haughton. Not found, but see Otis to Clay, Sept. 14, 1838; see also Clay to Otis, Sept. 24, 1838, and Jan. 1, 1839. 3. *Ibid.* 4. Clay to Wyckoff, Nov. 18, 1838. 5. An Anti-Masonic national convention met in Philadelphia on Nov. 13, 1838, and nominated William Henry Harrison for president and Daniel Webster for vice president. No official account of the proceedings was kept and no roll call of delegates recorded; therefore, details of the convention are very sketchy. Specifically, no exact count of the names or numbers of delegates has survived. Mueller, *Whig Party in Pennsylvania*, 57; William P. Vaughn, *The Anti-Masonic Party in the United States 1826-1843* (Lexington, 1983), 180-81; Washington *Daily National Intelligencer*, Feb. 14, 1839. 6. The Massachusetts Whig convention, composed of the Whig members of the legislature plus delegates from towns which had no Whig representatives, met on Feb. 27, 1839, and passed a series of resolutions. One of these stated that "the Convention adhere to the opinion expressed last year that although retaining the peculiar preferences of Massachusetts . . . the Whigs of the State would yield to the decision of the Whig National Convention, and heartily support the candidate who may be selected by it." Washington *Daily National Intelligencer*, March 4, 1839. For the convention's action the previous year, see Clay to Porter, March 4, 1838. 7. The so-called "Buckshot War" was in progress at Harrisburg. This resulted from a dispute over the 1838 election returns of the Incorporated Northern Liberties section of Philadelphia County and led to the formation of two rival lower houses. One of these was based on the Democratic count, the other on the Whig/Anti-Masonic count when the legislature convened on Dec. 4, 1838. The conflict between the two became so intense that the governor finally called out the militia to restore order. For a history of the Buckshot War, see Mueller, *Whig Party in Pennsylvania*, 49-55; Charles McCarthy, "Anti-Masonic Party," in *American Historical Association Report, 1902*, 1:381, published in *House Docs.*, 57 Cong., 2 Sess., 1902-3, pp. 495-503. 8. For the renewed economic and banking crisis, stimulated in part by a second suspension of specie payment by Nicholas Biddle's U.S. Bank of Pennsylvania on Oct. 9, 1839, as well as for the depth and breadth of the national depression that followed (1839-42), see Wilson, *Presidency of Martin Van Buren*, 133-34; Govan, *Nicholas Biddle*, 365-75.

Remark in Senate, December 13, 1838. Presents three petitions, viz: from pin manufacturers asking for repeal or reduction of the duty on brass wire; from New York peace advocates asking Congress to promote the formation of a congress of nations; and from a group of people engaged in steam navigation on the Ohio and Mississippi rivers asking for modification of the recent act for the regulation of steamboats. *Cong. Globe*, 25 Cong., 3 Sess., 27. "An Act to provide for the better security of the lives of passengers on board of vessels propelled in whole or in part by steam" had been approved July 7, 1838. 5 *U.S. Stat.*, 304-6.

Later this day, Clay announces his intention to introduce a copyright bill [Comment in Senate, February 2, 1837] on December 17. *Cong. Globe*, 25 Cong., 3 Sess., 27.

Following this announcement, Clay rises to question the administration's bill, introduced by Sen. Silas Wright (N.Y.), to postpone again and indefinitely, the distribution to the states of the fourth installment of the treasury surplus under the act of June 23, 1836 [8:812, 846-47; Comment in Senate, September 15, 1837]. Moves to amend the bill so that the postponement period will end on January 1, 1840. Told by Wright that there is no "anticipation" by Secretary of the Treasury Levi Woodbury that there will be funds in the treasury with which to pay the fourth installment either before or after that date, Clay replies that no one can know what the condition of the treasury will be on January 1, 1840. Notes further that "after the defalcations of two public officers which had lately come to light, to the astonishment of this country—one for $1,000,000, and the amount of the other as yet unknown—no one could possibly tell. One thing they did know, and that was, if they could get back this money, or any part of it, the state of the Treasury would be very different from what it would be with the total loss of it. He knew nothing as to the amount of these defalcations, or as to the means of the Government to recover back the whole or any part of them, and therefore would not hazard any calculations as to their probable value. The gentleman from New York could not say that the Treasury would be in a condition to pay this money by the 1st of January, 1840; that was very true. Such was the nature of our financial concerns that no man could say with certainty, a year beforehand, what our receipts and expenditures would amount to." Asks for a vote on his motion to amend. Later in the debate, points out again "that the fourth installment was not paid; that the States had not the nine millions due them from the Government. He said the tariff was not the cause of the surplus, and the subsequent embarrassments of the country. It was the result of fatal 'experiments' of the executive branch of the Government. There was another measure—the land bill [8:539-41, 609-10, 753, 812-13, 846-47, 873-74]—that would have prevented a surplus. This bill, which had passed both branches of the Legislature, but which General Jackson retained in his possession—and which he had no doubt would have received the sanction of the constitutional majority of Congress, had it been returned—would have prevented a surplus. There would have been no distribution of a surplus, and no demoralization of public morals. The distribution act was necessary and proper, and should be called an act to save from wasteful and extravagant expenditure the amount of money so deposited with the States. He thought that the installment due to the States could be paid, and paid in the time proposed in his amendment. It could be paid by strict economy in expenditures. Bring down the annual expenditures to the $13,000,000 of Mr. [John Q.] Adams' administration, or even to the $15,000,000 proposed by the administration of General Jackson in 1831. Stop the leaks! Stop the leaks in the Treasury. Stop the flying sub-treasurers, and my life on it, you will have abundance of means to meet the installment." *Ibid.*, 27, 30.

The men guilty of defalcation were Samuel Swartwout, collector of the Port of New York, who from 1829 to 1838 had embezzled $1,225,705.69 from the customhouse, and William M. Price, New York district attorney, who had embezzled customhouse funds to his own benefit as well as having assisted in Swartwout's thefts. Both men had escaped to Europe in 1838. Leonard D. White, *The Jacksonians, A Study in Administrative History 1829-1861* (New York, 1954), 424-29; Mushkat, *Tammany*, 188.

Payment of the fourth installment of the surplus revenue to the states was postponed until January 1, 1839, but when that date arrived, there was no surplus. The fourth installment was therefore never paid. Years later, in 1883, the legislature of Virginia passed an act authorizing a claim to be made to the federal government for payment of the fourth installment. In the legal case which resulted, the Supreme Court ruled that the federal government was under no obligation to pay, since the installments were, in fact, temporary deposits only. Bourne, *History of the Surplus Revenue*, 39-43.

From Willis Hall, New York, N.Y., December 14, 1838. Rejoices that Clay was not injured in the coach accident which befell him during his trip from Lexington to Washington [Clay to Otis, December 13, 1838]. "I would urge you to take care of yourself. Your country never stood in so great need of you." As for the coming presidential contest, "The Atherton resolutions no longer leave any doubt as to the place of operations of the administration. The issue is to be made, if possible, on abolition and thus the South is to be won. This movement will secure your nomination—it is the only way that the Whigs of the North & of the south can avoid the issue. This, however, was certain before. The more embarrassing question is, how is it to effect your election? If three or four years were to elapse before the election I should feel no anxiety on this subject. On the contrary your course with reference to Slavery, independent of every thing else, would elect you by acclamation, but can the people be brought to understand this subject in the short time left to us? The ultra abolitionists in this state are violently opposed to you and say openly they prefer Van Buren because his course will Strengthen their cause. They act judiciously—they know your election could ruin them. But the great mass are moderate men and patriotic citizens & will sanction nothing which will infringe the rights of the other States or which will tend in any way to weaken the Union. These men are already disgusted with their leaders and since the election, declare boldly that they will abandon the societies if any farther attempt is made to make Abolition 'political'. All these men I am confident when they understand your views will be your warmest friends."

Asks whether the New York state Whig committee should publish the Atherton resolutions. Reports, further, that "It is thought here that our relations with England will effect materially the state of parties at the next Presidential canvass. You are probably aware of the secret 'patriotic societies' which exist from Maine to Wisconsin along the frontier. They embody a great many men—most of whom have hitherto been for the administration. But the late Message has given them mortal offence and your remarks last session [Comment in Senate, January 5, 1838] on the Maine boundary & on Canadian affairs has turned their attention to you. I am privately informed that [Louis J.] Papinau & [Wolfred] Nelson have gone to Washington with a view of having an interview with you. They will not it is said call upon the Presidt. &c—You have doubtless met with them & will know how to treat them The idea of a war with England would not be popular but the bold decided patriotic tone which you last winter assumed [Speech in Senate, January 9, 1838], towards that power will meet with a response in every part of the country."

Thinks it might be better to hold the Whig nominating convention [Porter to Clay, November 14 and December 30, 1837] in June, 1839, instead of December, since "The recent movements at Boston [Otis to Clay, September 14, 1838] & Philada. [Clay to Otis, December 3, 1838] have disgusted many of the friends of Webster & many of the friends of Harrison. The union is incongruous & unnatural and the design so thinly concealed as to deceive nobody." Notes in conclusion that "The monstrous defalcation of [Samuel] Swartwout & the absconding of [William M.] Price [Remark in Senate, December 13, 1838] coming upon the heels of the unexpected defeat have almost broken down '*the party*' in this city." Indeed, "the honest rank & file are yet rubbing their eyes in astonishment and evidently beginning to see." ALS. DLC-HC (DNA, M212, R5). Partially printed in Colton, *Clay Correspondence*, 4:431-32. Only the opening paragraph is printed; the slavery and abolition passages are omitted.

The five resolutions proposed by Rep. Charles G. Atherton (Dem.) of New Hampshire (*BDAC*) denied that Congress under the Constitution had the right to abolish slavery in the District of Columbia or the territories, prohibit the removal of slaves from state to state, or discriminate between the institutions of one portion of the Union and another. They further directed that all slavery petitions should on presentation "without any further action thereon, be laid upon the table, without being debated, printed, or referred." In short, the Atherton resolutions were, in part, a restatement and amplification of the gag rule [8:817-18]. All of the resolutions ultimately passed. See Frederick Jackson Turner, *The United States 1830-1850* (New York, 1935), 467-68; U.S. H. of Reps., *Journal*, 25 Cong., 3 Sess., 51-72.

In his Second Annual Message on December 3, 1838, Van Buren had sharply criticized U.S. citizens who had become involved in the Canadian rebellion [Porter to Clay, December 15, 1837; Comment in Senate, January 5, 1838]. He warned that anyone who violated the neutrality of the United States by interfering with the affairs of Canada would be liable to arrest and punishment. *MPP*, 3:481, 485-87. In the period 1838-39, five secret societies were formed in the United States to support the Canadian rebels and to foment war between the United States and Great Britain. The first of these, the Canadian Refugee Relief Association, was formed in Lockport, N.Y., on March 19, 1838. Joseph L. Papinau and Wolfred Nelson, both of whom had taken part in the Canadian rebellion, were in the United States attempting to persuade someone in Congress to bring forward an expression of sympathy for the rebels. See Clay to Featherstonhaugh, February 10, 1839. They also met with both John Quincy Adams and President Van Buren. Corey, *The Crisis . . . in Canadian-American Relations*, 70-81, 101; Adams, *Memoirs of John Quincy Adams*, 10:52-55. For Papinau and Nelson, see *DNB*.

For Willis Hall, a lawyer who at this time was attorney general for New York State, see *CAB*.

To AMBROSE SPENCER Washington, December 15, 1838

I received your letter of congratulations, in which I most cordially unite, on the occasion of your recent glorious triumph in N. York.[1] It has spread joy throughout this whole Country; and if a proper use is made of it, the corrupt and incompetent men at the head of our public affairs will no longer afflict the Nation. The power of N. York was before deservedly great, but this event must necessarily add vastly to her moral strength. Her voice now will command every where profound respect.

The re-election of Mr. Talmadge [*sic*, Nathaniel P. Tallmadge], which you state there is no doubt of,[2] will be regarded in every part of the Union as a just acknowledgement of the great & essential services which he has rendered.

In looking to the future, we discern no causes of apprehension but in our divisions, which are our weakness & the strength of our adversaries. I hope means may be found to diminish them. This can be no where more effectually done than at Albany.

What scenes have been exhibited at Harrisburg![3] What defalcations have been recently exposed![4] These subjects occupy a large share of our thoughts & conversation here.

ALS. PHi. 1. Schermerhorn to Clay, Feb. 25, 1838. 2. Tallmadge was renominated for the Senate by the Whig-dominated lower house of the New York legislature in Jan., 1839, but the state senate, controlled by the Democrats, refused to cooperate in his election. After the expiration of Tallmadge's term in March, 1839, the seat remained vacant until Jan., 1840, at which time the New York legislature reelected him. The election was effected because the Whigs had meanwhile gained control of the state senate as well as the house. *Niles' Register* (Feb. 9, 16, 1839), 55:369, 385; Alexander, *Political History of . . . New York*, 39; Hammond, *History of Political Parties in . . . New York*, 2:512-13, 523. 3. Clay to Otis, Dec. 13, 1838. 4. Remark in Senate, Dec. 13, 1838.

To JOHN W. WHITE[1] Washington, December 15, 1838

I regret extremely that my numerous engagements must limit me to a very brief reply to your favor, advising you to address the Revd. R[alph]. R. Gurley to supply any deficiencies in mine.

The [American] Colonization Society is moving on in its benevolent career, regardless of the proceedings of the Abolitionists. These, far from inducing relaxation, only furnish fresh motives to it for vigorous and prompt exertions. At the late meeting, held in this City, a fine attendance & a fine spirit prevailed. Better indeed, than at any former meeting for several years. The annual report, and an account of its proceedings, will soon be published.[2]

I think that whatever can be done ought to be done to stimulate the Auxiliary Societies, every where, to increased action. The object of the Society—the Colonization of the Free blacks—furnishes the most encouraging hope in the future. Amalgamation is impossible. The God of nature by the difference of color & of physical constitution, has decreed against it. Abolition is impossible, unless it be accompanied with Colonization. This then is the scheme which should bind and unite together all good men, of every persuasion.

Mr. Gurley is the Secy. of the Society, resides here, and is perfectly conversant with all its proceedings.

ALS. MH. 1. The Rev. John Whitney White (1812-86) was born in Maine but spent most of his life as a Methodist clergyman in Ohio. Information supplied by United Methodist Archives Center, Ohio Wesleyan University. See also the *DAB* for White's son, John Williams White. 2. *Annual Report of the American Colonization Society, With the Minutes of the Annual Meeting and of the Board of Directors.* Washington, 1839.

To ADONIRAM CHANDLER[1] Washington, December 17, 1838

My detention in reaching this place[2] prevented my receiving as early as I should have done your favor of the 23d. Ulto. and of expressing my hearty participation with you in the joy produced by your recent glorious triumph in N. York.[3] It has diffused that feeling throughout this entire Land, and will be long remembered with gratitude to the Whigs & Conservatives[4] of your State.

There is indeed, as you justly remark, cause of apprehension in the character of the divisions which unfortunately prevail in the opposition;[5] but we must hope for the best and honestly and diligently strive to produce it. My hopes greatly preponderate over my fears, and lead me to anticipate that a good cause must finally surmount all difficulties.

I regret that my numerous engagements do not allow me to say more. . . .

ALS. NcD. 1. For Chandler, a Whig member of the New York state assembly and a printer, see Harriet A. Weed (ed.), *Autobiography of Thurlow Weed*, 2 vols. (Boston, 1883), 1:408; William T. Bonner, *New York, The World's Metropolis 1623-4—1923-4* . . . (New York, 1924), 514. 2. Although the Senate convened on December 3, Clay did not take his seat until December 10. 3. Schermerhorn to Clay, Feb. 25, 1838. 4. Clay to Henry Clay, Jr., Jan. 28, 1837. 5. Opposition refers to those opposed to the Van Buren administration, i.e. a combination of Whigs, Anti-Masons, and Conservative Democrats.

To Thomas H. or James B. Clay, Lexington, December 17, 1838. Conveys instructions relating to the sale of three calves. ALS. NHi.

Remark in Senate, December 17, 1838. Withdraws petition of Dr. Coleman Rodgers presented during the previous session. Introduces a bill to amend the copyright laws of the nation [Comment in Senate, February 2, 1837]. *Cong. Globe,* 25 Cong., 3 Sess., 34.

To FRANCIS T. BROOKE Washington, December 20, 1838

I presume that this letter will find you quiet at St. Julien. I should have written to you before had I any thing interesting to communicate. To day, on a call for information as to the relations between the Bank of the U.S. and the Treasury Dept., Mr. [William C.] Rives came out in a Speech of remarkable vigor and decision, which shewed conclusively that he had cut loose forever from the Administration.[1] Of that I previously entertained no doubt, and now I think the public can entertain none. On the subject of his re-election to the Senate, it would be highly improper for me to interfere, and I do not mean to interfere; but I may to you say that those with whom I have conversed out of Virginia think that it would be attended with very good effect.[2]

In consequence of the Anti Masonic[3] and other movements, since the last Session of Congress, at the commencement of this, my friends were a little discouraged. They are recovering from it, think that things look much better, and entertain confidence that public opinion, in regard to the next Presidency, will remain unchanged, as it was at the last Session.

My own opinion is that, with a view to avert the unfortunate divisions which exist among us, to check the progress of intrigues, and to secure concentration, action at Richmond by the Whig portion of the Legislature (including if possible the Conservatives) is highly expedient.[4] Such a movement would probably be followed & seconded at Albany;[5] and in that case, I think the question would be settled, and our future difficulties would afterwards constantly decrease. In this opinion the most intelligent of our party, with whom I have conversed, fully concur.

It is highly important, if any thing is done, that the Conservatives should unite at Richmond; or if they cannot be prevailed on to do so, that there should be as little division as possible among the Whigs. The Northern Conservatives, including Mr. Talmadge [*sic*, Nathaniel P. Tallmadge], remain firm and decided. And my information from N. York generally is full of encouragement. The mock nomination of the Anti Masons has fallen still born,[6] and has produced no material effect even in the Anti Masonic portion of the State. It appears that in the pretended Convention, there was not a delegate elected by any *primary* meeting whatever of the Antimasons; that, except the delegates from Pennsa. (who were nominated at some p[r]evious Convention) not a member held his seat in virtue of *any* election whatever; and that some Rucker member from N. York assumed the power to cast the whole vote of that State! . . .

ALS. KyU. Printed in Colton, *Clay Correspondence*, 4:432-33, with minor changes in capitalization and punctuation and the omission of the derogatory adjective "rucker" from the penultimate line. 1. Rives spoke to the resolution he had introduced the previous day, Dec. 19, asking for information from the secretary of the treasury concerning government purchases of the bonds of Biddle's U.S. Bank of Pennsylvania. He also demanded more information about government withdrawals from and deposits in that bank. These financial actions, he charged, indicated that "an arrangement has been entered into by which it [the bank] has practically become the fiscal agent of the Government." He roundly attacked the Van Buren administration for its surreptitious policy of thus sustaining Nicholas Biddle's bank. *Cong. Globe*, 25 Cong., 3 Sess., 46-47, 49; see also Clay to Tallmadge, Oct. 31, 1838. 2. Clay to Brooke, August 28, 1838. For Clay's subsequent involvement in the Rives vs. John Tyler struggle for the Senate in Feb., 1839, an intervention which may or may not have included Clay's offer of the Whig vice-presidential nomination to Tyler if he would step aside for Rives, see Wise, *Seven Decades of the Union*, 157-61; Liston, "W.C. Rives: Diplomat and Politician," Ph.D. dissertation, Ohio State University, 1972, pp. 274-78, 282-83, 286-87; Oliver P. Chitwood, *John Tyler, Champion of the Old South* (New York, 1939), 157-63; Braverman, "The Economic and Political Background of the Conservative Revolt in Virginia," *VMHB*, 60:283-87. 3. Clay to Otis, Dec. 13, 1838. 4. On Sept. 25, 1839, the Virginia Whig state convention (not the Whigs in the legislature) met in Staunton and endorsed Clay for president and Nathaniel P. Tallmadge for vice president. Simms, *Rise of the Whigs in Virginia*, 140-41; Seager, *And Tyler Too*, 131. 5. Porter to Clay, Dec. 30, 1837. 6. Clay to Otis, Dec. 13, 1838.

To MATHEW CAREY Washington, December 22, 1838

I recd. your favor, and shall be glad to get your last work when the publication of it is completed.[1] The Copies of the extract from it I thank you for sending.

It was my wish, during my late short visit to Philada. to have had the pleasure of seeing you; but I had not the control of my time and movements, from engagements of Company and business. I saw your son,[2] enquired about you, and sent my respects by him to you.

I receive, with pleasure and gratitude, the renewed expression of your confidence & attachment. The Whig Cause is not free from difficulty and embarrassment; but I still hope and believe that it will finally triumph. I should rejoice if both of us should live to witness it.

AL, closing and signature missing. KyU. 1. Possibly Carey's *Philosophy of Common Sense: Containing Practical Rules for the Promotion of Domestic Happiness.* Philadelphia, 1838; or, more likely, *To Whom It May Concern, Report on Case of Industrious Females.* Philadelphia, 1839. 2. Henry Charles Carey.

From John D. Russ, New York, December 22, 1838. Submits a lengthy letter in which he suggests to Clay, as president of the American Colonization Society, how best to solve the slavery problem. Begins with the proposition that "all men of whatever colour, Sex or condition, have an inherent natural right to be Free—that this right is inalienable." Asserts that the emancipation of slaves was well underway in Tennessee, Kentucky, and Virginia when "a few misguided ze[a]lots, more anxious, perhaps, for notoriety than for the welfare of *the* Blacks; raised the senseless cry of 'immediate Abolition,' which, unless some compromise can be affected, will light a fire which perhaps can only be quenched by the dissolution of this Union." Points out that the "entire North and West, and even a portion of the South, are Abolitionists in principle, and only differ on the question of expediency." Adds that "sooner or later the day must come when whatever the colour he who treads on American soil must be Free—We may dismember the Union we may wade through seas of blood but it must come to this at last. The Negro as well as the White man will be Free. The cry is onward to the rescue—the response—we come—" Notes, however, that the abolitionists, "these Ultra Philanthropists content themselves with merely agitating without proposing a single plan to effect their purpose except the immediate unconditional surrender of the Slaves. One moments reflection we think must satisfy them that this can never be peaceably accomplished—" Argues that a peaceful solution to the problem must include compensated emancipation in some form. Estimates that the market value of all slaves totals some $750,000,000, a sum too large for the nation to handle. Suggests as an alternative: "*The purchase of every female slave arriving at the age of fourteen years would, we believe, in fifty years eradicate slavery from our land—would in twenty five years completely prevent the procreating of slaves and effect noiselessly and certainly without suffering or injustice, all and more than abolition will effect by the course it is persuing*—We see many objections to this plan but believe none of them insurmountable." Admits that the "institution of marriage presents another apparent difficulty in the operation of our plan—It would be unnatural and productive of vice and crime to prohibit marriage—yet if married at all most of the manumitted must be married to slaves—The Slaves owe their labour to their masters and it would be cruel and unjust to require the mother unassisted to provide for her own support and that of a rising family—This difficulty may be effectually overcome in three different ways—1st to make the emancipated slaves apprentices to their former masters until the age of forty and their children to the age of twenty one—& the 2d to allow no marriages between the slaves and the free negroes without the consent of the master and when such consent is given bind the master to support the children resulting from such marriage untill they are 14 or twenty one, the mother and the children in the mean time working for him as apprentices—The 3d to appropriate some portion of the time of the slave who may marry by consent of his master to the support of his family—" Presents arithmetical estimates of the U.S. slave population (2,400,000), the number of slave births annually (80,000), and the number of those born who die before reaching the age of 14 (16,000). Calculates that since half of the slaves born are female and the average price of a female slave at age 14 is $400, "we discover that the actual expense of purchasing all the female slaves that arrive at the age of 14 years would be a decreasing ratio, the maximum of which would be 12.800.000 and the minimum 511.111 the average of which for 25 years or the period of foccundity would be six million seven hundred thousand a year or the gross sum of 155.000.000 dollars. this is the extent of the mighty burden which would necessarily be incur[r]ed, and this too distributed over a period of 25 years. the whole of it only amounts to a yearly tax of 50 cents on every white inhabitant or a tax of \$$12\frac{50}{100}$ for the entire period. With the increase of our population and the *accumulating* resources of our country it is a mere bagatelle." Believes, further, that the Constitution permits such a purchase under Article I, Section 8 "which confers on Congress the power of paying the debts and providing for the common defence and *General welfare of the United States*"; but says that if this extension of power to the Congress seems inconclusive, "may we not appeal to precedent and ask if it is not as legitimate an exercise of the powers granted by that instrument as was the purchase of Louisiana?" Warns that the abolitionists intend "First to abolish slavery in the District of Columbia—next in the Ter[r]itories—then to prohibit the inter slave trade and finally to apply to European powers for discriminating duties in favour of *free* labour. By these means they hope without interfering with the Constitutional rights of the slave states to effect their object—" Argues that if the abolitionists force the South to dissolve the Union, the South cannot long survive as a rival republic to the North and still maintain slavery. Either the North would go immediately to war to preserve the Union, "a war which would arm every slave against his master," or the North would later "find cause for war," a conflict in which the South's slaves would surely support them. On the other hand, even if peace could be maintained between the two republics, the slave population in the South would grow so much more rapidly than the white population there that it would soon achieve an "overwhelming preponderance in physical strength," which the slaves would certainly "exert" against the whites. Concludes: "Under the most favourable circumstances therefore the ultimate emancipation of the slaves seems certain—the only question for the consideration of the South seems to be how this emancipation can be effected most safely advantageously and speedily. . . . It is in vain to cry peace—peace upon this subject—there will be no peace and presently no quarter—now is the hour for capitulation—" ALS. InU. For Russ (1801-81), a New York physician, founder of the New York Institution for the Blind, and reformer of prisons and asylums for juveniles, see *DAB*.

From Harrison G. Otis, Boston, December 24, 1838. Reports receipt of Clay's letter of December 13 and the Haughton to Clay letter [not found] enclosed therein. Remarks that the Boston *Atlas* has lately "been silent on a certain topic, but whether this be preliminary to a new outbreak a few days will determine [Otis to Clay, September 14, 1838]." Notes, with reference to Webster, that "A rumour has prevaild of his intention to decline a reelection, but of this I have no convincing evidence—I think there is a disposition among the Whigs here to speak plainly (and as you would approve) on a certain subject. But untill he unequivocally withdraws from the canvass you can easily see that they must feel under restraint—The most to be hoped prior to that event, is a declaration by the Legislature adhering to him, as their first choice & announcing yourself as the second [Clay to Porter, March 4, 1838; Clay to Otis, December 13, 1838]—Some pains will be taken to effect this—and I must at present think with success." States that the Massachusetts delegation to the Anti-Masonic convention in Philadelphia [Clay to Otis, December 13, 1838] was "an absolute burlesque." Believes that the real danger to the Whig cause is the possibility that they "will identify themselves at least in appearance with the abolitionists," an act which "will be folly & madness without excuse—So deeply impressed am I with an opinion of the extreme infatuation of this officiousness that I am reconciled to Athertens [*sic*, Atherton's] resolutions [Hall to Clay, December 14, 1838]." Says his friends are "horrified" at his "avowal" of these resolutions, but "they forgive me as an old gentle man whose vagaries do no harm." Adds: "By the by, I have been told that one of the 'Representatives' alluded to in H[aughto]ns letter is Mr [Caleb] C[ushin]g of this State now in Congress." Concludes with the observation that while at age 73, "I have little reason to calculate upon seeing you at the head of the nation the hope of it is not among the least of my septuagenarian comforts." ALS. DLC-HC (DNA, M212, R5). Printed in Colton, *Clay Correspondence*, 4:433-34.

To FRANCIS T. BROOKE Washington, December 26, 1838

I received your two favors of the 24th. What I may say on the subject of Mr. [William C.] Rives' re-election[1] must be regarded as expressed at your instance, and as presenting opinions which prevail exterior to Virginia, without any intention on my part to interfere in a local election in a State in which I am no resident.

Those out of your State are struck by the fact that a co-operation between the Whigs and Conservatives[2] will secure a majority against the Administration; and that without it the majority may be the other way.

The object, therefore, to be accomplished, if it be practicable, is to secure that majority co-operation; and to those at a distance Mr. Rives' re-election appears to be a probable means. If it be not; if a hearty co-operation can not be produced by it; if nothing is to be gained but Mr. Rives himself, quite a different view of the question would be entertained. Mr. Rives has himself no claim upon the Whigs but those which arise from his recent course; and confining the question to him alone, his expunging vote[3] and former course would more than neutralize his recent claims. But a more extended view should be taken of the matter. If he can be used as an instrument to acquire an accession of strength that would array Virginia against the Administration, the inquiry then would be, whether sound policy does not demand that we should sacrifice all feelings excited by a highly exceptionable vote, in consideration of a great object to be gained for the good of our country. I appreciate and feel sensibly all the difficulties in making such a sacrifice, but I think that I could submit to it, if I had a reasonable certainty of that object being secured.

It is manifest that, if we repel the advances of all the former members of the Jackson party to unite with us, under whatever name they may adopt, we must remain in a perpetual and hopeless minority.

Should we not extend to the repentant in politics the same forgiveness which the Christian religion promises to the contrite, even in the eleventh hour? The difference between Mr. Rives and some others now incorporated in our party, is, that their watches did not run together.

Already has some mischief been done in Ohio,[4] and in other places, by a refusal of all conciliation of the Conservatives. It was obvious that their position was temporary, and could not be maintained for any length of time. It was at a half-way house. They must therefore fall back into the ranks of their old associates, or be absorbed by us. And it seems to be a prevailing opinion here to be expedient to avail the country of the services of as many of them as we can get, either as allies or as a part of our consolidated force. I should add that it is feared, if he be not re-elected, the event will operate badly out of, as well as in Virginia.

This is the view which is taken by those out of Virginia. Its basis is the bringing about a co-operation in that State between the Whigs and Conservatives by his [Rives's] re-election. If that can not be effected (and of that those on the spot are the best judges), why, then, there will be another state of the question.

I transmit this hasty letter for your own eye only. I know how justly sensitive to all foreign intervention the people of Virginia are, and I should not have touched on this delicate topic but upon your invitation.

Copy. Printed in Colton, *Clay Correspondence*, 4:434-36. 1. Clay to Brooke, August 28 and Dec. 20, 1838. 2. Clay to Henry Clay, Jr., Jan. 28, 1837. 3. See 8:735. 4. Duncan to Clay, Oct. 4, 1838.

Remark in Senate, December 26, 1838. Notes the poor attendance in the chamber and asks that consideration of the public lands bill [Remark in Senate, December 12, 1838] be postponed until December 31. Agreed to. *Cong. Globe*, 25 Cong., 3 Sess., 60.

To PETER B. PORTER Washington, December 27, 1838

In passing through Maysville, on my way hither, I inquired about the Blue Grass seed,[1] and was informed that they had been forwarded to Portsmouth; and I hope therefore that they have safely reached their destination.

Upon my arrival here, I found that the proceedings of the mock Antimasonic Convention at Philada;[2] the attacks of the Boston Atlas[3] and at Cincinnati[4] upon me; and the stirring up of the Abolition feeling, produced some discouragement among my friends. They are gradually recovering from it. Still there is a portion of your delegation (Fillmore, Peck &c)[5] who, while they are free to avow their own preference for me, profess to be apprehensive about my election. Abolition is the cause of their fears. The state of the public feeling here is such as I have some times before witnessed in the public affairs. There is confidence that we have the elements of success, if they can be properly combined; but a repugnance to take any decided measure to lead to concentration. Now, I feel entirely satisfied that we are in great danger (I mean the whole Whig cause) without some decisive movement this winter. An expression of preference at Albany[6] & Richmond,[7] perhaps at either of them, couched in unoffensive language, and with reference to the Nat. Convention, would I think be conclusive. It would instantly form a rallying point, and again put in motion the current, which has been checked since the last Session of Congress by impediments thrown in by our own friends. Without it, we shall go on sowing the seeds of discontent among ourselves, until when the final contest comes we shall be exhausted in bickerings among our own party. With it, we should find all sinister attempts repressed, and the course of duty & policy clearly pointed out to all the members of the opposition.

I understand that at Richmond an attempt will be probably successfully made to get the Whig members of the Legislature, with or without the co-operation of the Conservatives, to signify the well known preference which they entertain. There is reason to anticipate the cooperation of the latter from the fact that Mr. [William C.] Rives has recently assumed unequivocal ground of opposition.[8]

Here, no doubt is entertained that no other Whig but myself can obtain the votes of the Southern & S. Western States, with the *possible* exception of Kentucky; and that there is a fair prospect of all of them being cast for me, except that of So. Carolina.[9]

Is there any prospect of action at Albany?[10] How is [Thurlow] Weed, [William H.] Seward &c? Do they stand unmoved, by any recent events? What is the prevailing feeling in the Western part of your State? I should be glad to receive your views & information.

The Subtreasury is to be again pressed; but I have heard as yet nothing to induce me to apprehend its passage.[11]

I saw Mr. John Breckenridge yesterday in good health. You are probably aware that he goes shortly to Texas.[12]

ALS. NBuHi. 1. Clay to Porter, Oct. 24, 1838. 2. Clay to Otis, Dec. 13, 1838. 3. Otis to Clay, Sept. 14, 1838. 4. Clay to Wyckoff, Nov. 18, 1838. 5. For Fillmore, see *BDAC*; for Peck, see Weed, *Autobiography of Thurlow Weed*, 1:95, 101, 161, 204, 207, 336; 2:20, 22, 195. Both men had been Weed's associates in the Anti-Masonic party. 6. Porter to Clay, Dec. 30, 1837, and Feb. 16, 1839. 7. Clay to Brooke, Dec. 20, 1838. 8. For Rives's open break with the Van Buren administration, see Comment in Senate, March 7, 1838; Clay to Brooke, Dec. 27, 1838; also *Cong. Globe*, 25 Cong., 3 Sess., 46-47, 49; Wilson, *Presidency of Martin Van Buren*, 113-14, 127-28, 138-39. 9. In 1840, Whig William Henry Harrison carried Conn., Del., Ga., Ind., Ky., La., Me., Md., Mass., Mich., Miss., N.J., N.Y., N.C., Ohio, Pa., R.I., Tenn., and Vt. Democrat Martin Van Buren carried Ala., Ark., Ill., Mo., N.H., S.C. [Electoral vote only], and Va. McKee, *National . . . Popular and Electoral Vote*, 44-45. 10. Porter to Clay, Dec. 30, 1837. 11. On Jan. 6, 1840, Sen. Silas Wright (N.Y.) introduced the Van Buren administration's third and final try at a Sub-Treasury (Divorce or Independent Treasury) bill. See Speech in Senate, Sept. 25, 1837, and Feb. 19, 1838; Comment in Senate, March 7, 1838. The Senate passed it 24 to 18 on Jan. 23, 1840, and the House followed suit 124 to 107 on June 30. It was a composite of features in the defeated 1837 and 1838 bills. Wilson, *Presidency of Martin Van Buren*, 123-46. 12. The Rev. John Breckinridge (or Breckenridge), formerly of Lexington, was at this time general agent for the Board of Foreign Missions of the Presbyterian Church. He became actively involved in 1839 in extending the mission work to the Republic of Texas. Alexander Brown, *The Cabells and Their Kin* (Boston, 1895), 497-98; Lexington *Observer & Kentucky Reporter*, March 27, 1839.

Remark in Senate, December 27, 1838. Presents petition "deprecating war, and praying Congress to adopt some measure for the formation of a congress of nations"; also a petition from starch manufacturers asking for a duty on imported starch. *Cong. Globe*, 25 Cong., 3 Sess., 64.

Remark in Senate, December 31, 1838. During debate on rescinding an earlier decision to print certain documents relating to the tariff on salt, raises a point of procedure on how to handle the withdrawal of a motion to rescind. Since such a motion requires a unanimous vote, he announces his opposition to the motion so as to force a formal division on the question. It was then approved. *Cong. Globe*, 25 Cong., 3 Sess., 81.

To HARRISON G. OTIS Washington, January 1, 1839

Allow me to offer you my cordial wishes for many happy returns of this day.

I duly received your favors, and the two first numbers of Constans.[1] They are characterized by good sense and sound discretion. I cannot be deceived in my conjecture as to their author.

With respect to the permission to use the letter of Mr. H[aughton].[2] by shewing it confidentially to one or two persons, I would observe that I have no solicitude about the matter but that I should not be justly chargeable with a breach of private confidence. Keeping that point in view, I leave it to your judgment. Altho' his course has been such as to absolve me from all obligations, I do not wish to do any thing inconsistent with the most scrupulous honor and good faith. Besides, he is not sufficiently important to make it an object to crush him.

What has occurred, since your General Court last met, is of sufficient consequence perhaps, to justify a renewed expression of its feelings and wishes, in respect to the P. election.[3] What was done on that subject last year was wisely done.[4] If Mr. W[ebster]. wou[l]d see fit to retire, our future difficulties would be small.

I think that the current, which was so strong last winter, in regard to the Presidency, but which had been somewhat checked by recent occurrences, is returning to its former channel. The discouragement which existed here at the commencement of the Session, among our friends, is gradually disappearing, and more hope and confidence are revived.

ALS. MHi. 1. A number of articles by "Constans" appeared in the Boston *Daily Advertiser* in Dec., 1838, and Jan., 1839. Constans argued against the attempts being made to persuade the Whigs in the Massachusetts legislature "to recant the declaration made by them last year, that Mr. Clay was their second choice [for president] after Mr. Webster." The proposition that the Whigs stand "for principles not men" was "irrelevant to the subject" of whom to nominate, he said, since Clay, Webster, and Harrison "are all agreed in their political principles." Furthermore, "When great and patiotic men have . . . been foremost in the struggle for principles, and have deserved and won the enthusiastic attachment and unbounded confidence of a party; the support of men in such instances becomes identified with the support of principles." He also denied that Harrison was a more popular candidate than Clay and urged the Massachusetts Whigs to stand firm on their earlier commitment. Boston *Daily Advertiser*, Dec. 31, 1838; Jan. 3, 10, 1839. 2. Otis to Clay, Sept. 14, 1838; Clay to Otis, Sept. 24 and Dec. 13, 1838. 3. The Massachusetts General Court had endorsed Webster for the presidency but promised to support Clay if he were nominated. See Clay to Porter, March 4, 1838. 4. Clay to Otis, Dec. 13, 1838.

Comment in Senate, January 2, 1839. Moves to refer the public lands reduction and graduation bill [Remark in Senate, December 12, 1838] back to the Committee on Public Lands with instructions that it be amended so as "to restrict its benefits to actual settlers." Points out that even though the Senate had passed a similar bill during the last session [Remark in Senate, March 29 and April 9, 1838; Speech in Senate, April 11, 1838], the body "was then constituted somewhat differently" from what it now is. Further, "Many members might have changed their opinions." Asks, therefore, for "thorough discussion" of the measure. Notes that the administration's bill as it now stands would reduce the price of public land from $1.25 to

75¢ per acre, would affect 71 million acres, and would cost the government $35 million in lost revenue. Mentions the government's present need for additional revenue. Asserts that he remains "radically opposed" to any change in the land system, and explains that his motion to restrict purchases to actual settlers was designed "to limit the waste of this public treasure" and "exclude speculation." Adds to his motion the proviso that the "actual settlers" also be limited to the purchase of 160 acres each.

Later in the debate, Clay responds to attacks on his motion by Sen. Robert J. Walker (Miss.) and Sen. Clement C. Clay (Ala.). Walker charged that Clay would not support the administration's bill even were his motion attached to it as an amendment, because the Kentuckian had "always opposed graduation in every form" and had often denounced the "limitation of the sales at the reduced prices to actual settlers" as being "odious, unjust, and unconstitutional." Walker also said he would support Clay's motion if Clay would in turn support the bill with his own motion amended into it. At the same time, Clay of Alabama accused Clay of attempting to stall consideration of the bill in order to kill it by inaction. Exclaimed that he had "heard his proposition with astonishment!" In addition, he criticized Clay for earlier having denounced the pioneer occupants of the public lands ("this worthy class of citizens," according to the Alabama lawmaker) as being little more than "lawless intruders, trespassers, and violators of the law." In reply, Clay suggests that Clay of Alabama, "in directing remarks against him personally, rather than to the subject before the Senate," might well be "actuated by some secret grief, some private animosity." Denies, as the Alabama senator claimed, that he is an enemy of the new states on issues relating to public land sales. Admits, however, that he is "opposed now," as in the past, "to the preemption law [Remark in Senate, January 23, 1838], not because he was opposed to the settlement and occupancy of the public domain, but because it was an appropriation to these individuals [preemptioners] of a public and general property." In reply to Senator Walker, asserts that he cannot pledge his support of the bill "in case the amendment I propose will be adopted." Wants to see the entire bill in its final form before committing himself. Affirms that he has "already disclaimed any intention of defeating the [administration's] bill by delay, and this ought to be deemed sufficient among men of honor." Fears, nonetheless, that once the process of price graduation downward from $1.25 per acre begins, the price of land will continue to descend—perhaps to as low as 12½¢ per acre, as it has on the lands in Mississippi acquired by treaty from the Chickasaw Indians. Concludes that "there is no doubt, if the bill before us—this entering wedge—is successful, that the public lands of the United States will be eventually reduced to the same price." *Cong. Globe*, 25 Cong., 3 Sess., 87; *ibid.*, Appendix, 44, 47-48. On January 17, 1839, Clay voted nay on the final version of the administration's graduation bill. *Cong. Globe*, 25 Cong., 3 Sess., 121. See also Remark in Senate, December 12, 1838, and January 3, 1839. For the Chickasaw treaty of May 24, 1834, see Parry, *Treaty Series*, 84:296-303 (espec. article 11, p. 300).

Also on this day, Clay presents a memorial of the New York Peace Society [Comment in Senate, April 30, 1838] asking Congress to arbitrate the French war in Mexico [Comment in Senate, June 30, 1838], and to promote the formation of a congress of nations that would formulate "an international code of laws." Also presents the petition of a New York woman for a pension for the services of her husband in the American Revolution. *Cong. Globe*, 25 Cong., 3 Sess., 86.

Remark in Senate, January 3, 1839. Continues participation in the debate of yesterday on the public lands price graduation bill [Remark in Senate, December 12, 1838], urging again his motion to recommit the legislation to committee. Speaks to various contrary points raised by Senators Robert J. Walker and Clement C. Clay.

Cites Van Buren's annual messages of December 5, 1837, and December 3, 1838, to demonstrate that "it was actual valuation, and not conjectural valuation, founded on the lapse of time, [that] was the principle on which the President recommended a reduction of the price of the public lands." Argues that the principle in this bill is "the one that the President decidedly condemned." Explains to his colleagues the law of supply and demand, "one of the established laws of political economy," specifically applying it to public land sales. Hopes Congress will delay legislating on this subject during the present session and until the 1840 census has been completed. The census will show "the amount of increase in the population and wealth of the new States," and whether a graduation act is "needed for their further advancement." Also states that delay is advisable because he does not believe that either of the two houses of Congress reflect "the genuine sentiment of the American people." Points out that recent elections have "very much changed the complexion of the two bodies" and that in one of the houses the changes that had taken place would "reverse the majority on the present question." *Cong. Globe*, 25 Cong., 3 Sess., Appendix, 49-50. Van Buren's statements on the price graduation question are in *MPP*, 3:384-89, 496. For party strength in the 25th Congress, see Morris, *Encyclopedia of American History*, 406; Clay to Brooke, March 7, 1837. For party strength in the 26th Congress, see Clay to Porter, October 24, 1838; see also Clay to Wilde, June 24, 1839. Clay apparently thought that the Whigs and pro-Whig Conservative Democrats would have a majority in the Senate in the 26th Congress. For voting on the price graduation bill in the 25th Congress, see Remark in Senate, March 29 and December 12, 1838.

Later this day, Clay of Alabama moves that Clay's motion to recommit the bill to committee with instructions to amend it [Comment in Senate, January 2, 1839] be divided into two motions—the first to recommit, the second to instruct. The motion to recommit passed 23 to 20. The motion to instruct was modified by "general consent" so that "the number of acres to be granted to each actual settler was left blank in the instructions." The instruction motion, as thus modified, passed 26 to 17. Clay voted yea on both motions. *Cong. Globe*, 25 Cong., 3 Sess., 89. The "bill providing for the reduction and graduation of the price of the public lands" was introduced in the 26th Congress, 1st Session by Clay of Alabama on December 24, 1839. It passed the Senate on April 24, 1840, by a vote of 28 to 8 [Remark in Senate, April 23, 1840]. The House received the bill on April 24 but took no action on it during the session. U.S. Sen., *Journal*, 26 Cong., 1 Sess., 41, 81, 333, 337; U.S. H. of Reps., *Journal*, 26 Cong., 1 Sess., 824. Clay of Alabama reintroduced the bill in the 26th Congress, 2nd Session on December 14, 1840. On December 28 it was postponed and was not taken up again during the session. U.S. Sen., *Journal*, 26 Cong., 2 Sess., 29, 47, 65. See also Hibbard, *History of the Public Land Policies*, 297-98.

Remark in Senate, January 4, 1839. Asks Sen. Robert J. Walker (Miss.), chairman of the Committee on Public Lands, to postpone until January 7 further consideration of the public lands price graduation and reduction bill [Remark in Senate, December 12, 1838] as amended yesterday and the day before yesterday. So ordered. *Cong. Globe*, 25 Cong., 3 Sess., 90-91.

To FRANCIS T. BROOKE Washington, January 7, 1839

I recd. your favors of the 29h. Ulto. & 5h. inst. I regret extremely the existence of so much division of opinion in Virginia, respecting the election of a Senator,[1] and sincerely hope that our friends may all become reconciled, and that what they may finally do may conduce to the success of our cause and the interest of our Country. I have no individual wishes separate from the common good. What is best to be done at Richmond those alone can determine who there have a view of all circumstances. It is not however to be disguised that what may be done will exercise an influence beyond the confines of the State.

I have been struggling to day & some previous days on the Land subject.[2] My friends are highly gratified with my exertions, and I hope & believe that they have had some effect. Whether it will be practicable much longer to save that great interest depends upon the future course of the old States. I can not much longer defeat the combined action of the Administration and the new States. . . .

ALS. KyU. Printed in Colton, *Clay Correspondence*, 4:436. 1. Clay to Brooke, August 28 and Dec. 20, 1838. 2. See his remarks on the Senate floor on the public land price reduction and graduation bill on Jan. 2, 3, 4, and 7, 1839. See also Remark in Senate, Dec. 12, 1838.

Remark in Senate, January 6 [*sic,* 7], 1839. Complains that the Committee on Public Lands has not conformed to its instructions from the Senate to limit to "actual settlers" the benefits of the proposed public lands price graduation and reduction bill [Remark in Senate, December 12, 1838]. Instead, it has added to the "actual settler" classification those people who only intend in good faith to become actual settlers; also those who already own and are actually cultivating adjoining lands. Attacks these changes in committee, pointing out that the effect of the clause pertaining to the owners and cultivators of contiguous land is such that "any farmer or planter in the new States will be enabled to purchase land at the reduced prices, while the citizens of the old States would be precluded from doing so." Calls this "invidious discrimination" against farmers from old states like Pennsylvania and Virginia. Asks again that action on this legislation be put over to the 26th Congress for the reasons he gave on the floor on January 3. *Cong. Globe*, 25 Cong., 3 Sess., Appendix, 53-54. Another version of these remarks, couched in the first person singular, and containing somewhat more statistical data, is printed in *ibid.*, 350.

Later in the course of this debate on January 7, Clay denies charges by Senator Walker that his complaint against the action of the public lands committee has been motivated by a desire (as Clay paraphrased Walker) "to array the old States against the new, and to contrast their population." Quite the contrary, Clay replies, such is the motive of Walker in his effort (as revealed in the fact of his contiguous land clause), to discriminate against the farmers of "the thirteen old States who established our independence." His "own object," Clay assures his colleagues, "has been to seek the good of the whole." Indeed, his initial effort [Comment in Senate, January 2, 1839] to limit coverage of the bill to "actual settlers" was designed to benefit "all the poor and indigent in all quarters of the Union." *Ibid.*, 54.

Remark in Senate, January 8, 1839. During the debate this day on the graduation bill, Sen. John J. Crittenden presents "an elaborate argument to prove that his colleague [Mr. CLAY] was not an enemy of the new States, and referred to the whole course of his life to contradict the assertion." Sen. Richard M. Young (Ill.) then rises to reply to Crittenden's charge that Clay had been "misrepresented, intentionally misrepresented; and that language has been attributed to him . . . which he never uttered." Young agrees that this "to some extent may be true. I have seen some newspaper reports of that debate which contained expressions which I do not remember to have heard in the terms supposed to have been employed; but the inferences drawn were, nevertheless, in most instances, correct logical deductions from the premises." States that "since I commenced these remarks . . . an extract" from the speech of Sen. John Tipton (Ind.) made on the preemption bill during the last session (January 27, 1838) "has been placed in my hands." Reads an extract from the pamphlet version of Tipton's speech quoting Clay as saying " 'the squatters on the public lands were a lawless rabble; that they might as well seize upon our forts, our arsenals, or on the public treasure, as to rush out and seize upon the public lands [Comment in Senate, January 26 and 27, 1838].' " Finds this statement in agreement with the notes he had personally made on the occasion and has repeated today. Adds that he read from "a portion" of these notes at the last session "and I did not understand him [Clay] as then denying them."

Clay asserts "it was untrue that any such paper had been shown to him" and that "he did not know that such a paper was in existence, until very recently" when he had learned that Young had used it against him "during the recess of Congress." Young replies that "he did not say that he had shown the paper" to Clay, but that "he had read from the same paper . . . at his table, when the Senator from Kentucky [Mr. CLAY] was in his seat, and must have heard him." Admits that he does not "undertake to say that the expressions attributed" to Clay "were used in connection, as I have them noted, and as I read them. They were used in the course of his remarks, and such only were taken down . . . as were deemed most exceptionable and offensive to the settlers on the public lands." Reasserts, however, that whether Clay "saw the paper or not, the statement it contains . . . is correct and true, and very nearly in his own language as I understood him." Says Missouri Sen. Lewis F. Linn in an audible voice: "It is true, every word of it."

Sen. Tipton then explains how he came to make any remarks on Clay's speech of January 26, 1838. Tipton, who had been briefly absent from his seat that day, returned to hear the conclusion of Clay's remarks and was told that "the Senator from Kentucky . . . had been saying hard things of his (Mr. T.'s) constituents." For that reason Tipton had replied the next day "defending the squatters on the public lands," and quoting "the words which he was informed" Clay had used. A few day's later, Clay had called Tipton's attention to this speech "as published in the newspapers, and stated that he did not use the words there attributed to him. He repeated words which he said he used on the occasion referred to. I adopted his own words, and they were published in the pamphlet copy of my speech. If these are the words now quoted by the Senator from Illinois—and I believe they are—they are the very words furnished by the member [Clay] from Kentucky. He surely has no just grounds to complain of these words being now repeated." *Cong. Globe*, 25 Cong., 3 Sess., Appendix, 55-56, 225-26. See also Comment in Senate, January 26 and 27, 1838; and Clay to Estes, June 1, 1839.

Remark in Senate, January 9, 1839. Presents a petition from line officers of the U.S. Army that their pay and that of staff officers be equalized. *Cong. Globe*, 25 Cong., 3 Sess., 102.

Later this day, Clay offers two amendments to the administration's bill to reduce and graduate the price of public lands [Remark in Senate, December 12, 1838] rather than offering a whole new bill. His amendments would authorize the purchase "by actual settlers" of lands unsold for 15 years at the following quantities and rates: 80 acres @50¢ ea.; 160 acres @75¢ ea.; 320 acres @1.00 ea.; and would add to the administration's bill the essence of the land bill he had sponsored in 1832 [8:539-41] which had been passed by Congress but pocket-vetoed by Andrew Jackson [8:609-10]. That legislation, he reminds his colleagues, would "divide the proceeds of the sales of the public lands among the States [after 1840]." *Ibid.*, 103.

Remark in Senate, January 10, 1839. Moves that Secretary of the Treasury Levi Woodbury be directed to report the amount each state would have received from public lands sales through January 1, 1839, had the public land sales distribution bill of 1832 [8:539-41] not been vetoed by Jackson [8:609-10]. Motion adopted. *Cong. Globe*, 25 Cong., 3 Sess., 105.

Later this day, Clay addressed (not recorded) the Senate in support of his January 9 amendments to the public lands price reduction and graduation bill, after which both amendments were defeated, 29 to 13. On the motion of Sen. Thomas H. Benton, however, the 80 acres-50¢ clause in Clay's first amendment [Remark in Senate, January 9, 1839] was passed 24 to 19, Clay voting yea. *Ibid.*

From Harrison G. Otis, Boston, January 11, 1839. Reports a conversation with a "very respectable and intelligent member of the Mass: Senate" who says he can find no one who approves the attack of the Boston *Atlas* on Clay [Otis to Clay, September 14, 1838]. Says the editor of the Boston *Courier* [Joseph T. Buckingham], and probably the editors of all the Whig papers in Boston, are "opposed to the doctrines" of the *Atlas* and of Richard Haughton, the "freak" who runs it. Notes that Webster "has again disclaimed his privity or approbation of the Atlas heresy and said he tho[ugh]t it unlucky." Thinks the analysis by Constans [Clay to Otis, January 1, 1839] on the state legislature's approach to the presidential question is not accepted by Webster. Has the impression that Webster thinks "you did him ill offices by favoring H[arrison] at his expense in 1836—and that you would still promote his H[arrison]'s interest next to your own." Adds that "it seems unimaginable that he [Webster] expects any important support." Assures Clay that his "opinions" on these matters are "well founded." Reports that the Massachusetts legislature will choose a U.S. senator on January 16. "Mr W[ebster] will be nominated *at his own request*—and will doubtless be chosen—Rumors were afloat of his intention to abdicate & the Govr. [Edward Everett] was preparing to cut in." Believes the Whigs might lose Massachusetts next election because of a local controversy created when "The last legislature passed an absurd act prohibitory of sell[in]g spirits in quantities less than 15 gallons—Now petitions are presented for a repeal." Thinks the whole thing "a monstrous abomination." Believes also that abolitionism will play a role in the presidential election in Massachusetts. "It is clear that the efforts of the Admin are d[i]rected to the identifying [of] whiggism and abolitionism—and the whig party has not sense enough to keep free from the coils of the black Snake." Assures Clay he has shown Richard Haughton's letter [Clay to Otis, December 13, 1838] to no one and perhaps will not; but will only state the substance of it "to 2 or 3 friends." ALS. DLC-HC (DNA, M212, R5). Printed in full in Colton, *Clay Correspondence*, 4:437-38.

Webster was reelected to the U.S. Senate on January 17, 1839, by a unanimous vote of the Massachusetts senate and in the house by a vote of 330 to 65 for Benjamin Hallett. Wiltse, *Papers of Daniel Webster, Correspondence*, 4:341.

The Boston Temperance Society was formed on February 21, 1838. It succeeded in getting a bill through the legislature on April 19, 1838, which limited the amount of liquor sold in Massachusetts to a minimum of fifteen gallons per sale. This unpopular act was repealed in 1840. Robert L. Hampel, *Temperance and Prohibition in Massachusetts 1813-1852* (Ann Arbor, Mich., 1982), 79-101.

Comment in Senate, January 14, 1839. Says he "heartily concurs" in resolutions of the North Carolina general assembly, passed in its last session, which, among other targets, sharply attacked the Expunging Resolution [8:735] as "an act of party servility, calculated to degrade the Senate." Both of North Carolina's U.S. senators, Bedford Brown and Robert Strange, had supported the controversial Expunging Resolution when it came to a vote on January 16, 1837, and was passed by a 24 to 19 margin. The points raised by Senator Brown on this day, when he rose to present the North Carolina resolutions to the Senate, were principally two: whether the language employed by the North Carolinians was disrespectful to the Senate (Clay thought not); and the larger question of whether the North Carolina resolutions, even though "they do not, on their face, profess to *instruct*," are to be "viewed by my honorable colleague [Robert Strange] and myself as instructions, or as the mere expressions of the opinions of the Legislature, leaving to us a discretionary power in exercising our judgments on the subjects to which they relate." Both senators declare now that had they received these instructional resolutions back in 1836-37, they would have obeyed them had they been mandatory in their language rather than seeming merely to express the opinion of the North Carolina general assembly on the expunging issue. While the expunging question was now essentially moot, Clay argues that the principle of the doctrine of instructions remains clear: "I hold to the doctrine as it stood in 1798; that, in general, on questions of expediency, the representative should conform to his instructions, and so gratify the wishes, and obey the will, of his constituents, though on questions of constitutionality his course might be different. . . . And what is the doctrine of instructions, as it is held by all? Is it not that we are to conform to the wishes of our constituents? Is it not that we are to act, not in our own, but in a delegated character? And will any who stand here, pretend, that whenever they know the wishes or will of those who sent them here, they are not bound to conform to that will entirely? Is it not the doctrine, that we are nothing more than the mirror to reflect the will of those who called us to our dignified office? That is the view which I take of the doctrine of instruction." As for the language in which instruction may be couched, "If the Legislature simply express their will, is that no equivalent to the word instruct?... Sir, I say to my man Charles, please to do so and so, and he does it instantly, and with much more pleasure, than if I was more peremptory. Suppose I should say, Charles, I instruct you; he would think it very curious language; but if I say, I would be obliged to you for my shoes or boots, he goes down and brings them as quick as possible." Adds that "on one subject, at least, these resolutions speak in decisive language... and that is the great subject of the public lands. . . . I am glad they have come in before the passage of the bill [Remark in Senate, December 12, 1838], and I hope, at least, on the subject of the public lands, we shall have the vote of the senators from North Carolina." This observation on the land bill, together with the fact that Clay had intervened in the question of the resolutions from the North Carolina legislature, "called forth a most violent philippic against him personally" from Brown. Clay responds that he "justified the remarks which he had now made, and especially by the apprehension which he felt, that the true doctrine of instructions, as stated in 1798, was now in danger of being subverted and destroyed." Copy. Printed in Colton, *Clay Correspondence*, 6:134-38. A much shorter version of Clay's participation in this debate (also in somewhat different language) appears in *Cong. Globe*, 25 Cong., 3 Sess., 111. No manuscript version has been found. The extensive remarks of Senators Brown and Strange on the North Carolina instructions and related matters are in *ibid.*, 109-12. When the public land price reduction and graduation bill came to a vote in the Senate on January 17, 1839, and was passed 27 to 22, both Brown and Strange joined Clay in voting nay. *Ibid.*, 122.

The North Carolina resolutions, passed in December, 1838, condemned the Expunging Resolution and stated that it should be rescinded, condemned the Sub-Treasury proposal, favored the distribution of the sale of public lands to the states according to the ratio of population, called for a decrease in the power and patronage of the federal government, and declared that their U.S. senators by voting to carry out these resolutions would represent a majority of people in the state. The resolutions were passed by the North Carolina house by a vote of 63 to 56 and by the senate 25 to 23. Washington *Daily National Intelligencer*, December 28, 31, 1838, and January 1, 1839. See also U.S. Sen., *Journal*, 25 Cong., 3 Sess., 120.

Later this day, Clay presented a pension petition on behalf of John S. Wilson. *Cong. Globe*, 25 Cong., 3 Sess., 113.

To JOHN O. SARGENT Washington, January 14, 1839

I was glad to find from your favor of the 10h. inst. and the Land article to which it refers in the [New York *Morning*] Courier [*& Enquirer*], that you were endeavoring to attract the public attention to the subject of the public lands.[1] I hope you may succeed in that object. I think that it has been too much neglected. It is my opinion that, if the public could have been awakened to its importance, and to the nefarious projects by which it has been attempted to squander it away and make it subservient to party views, the late Administration would have been overthrown and we should not have been afflicted with the present one. North Carolina has spoken out explicitly;[2] Virginia will, I understand, follow the good example,[3] and I hope that N. York will also let her views be publicly known.[4]

I am sorry that I have not by me a single Copy of any Report or Speech which I have made on the subject, except one that I delivered at the last Session on the graduation bill.[5] I transmit you a Copy of that. If you will turn to Niles's Register (1832-3), you will find the first Report I made,[6] which will put you in full possession of the general subject, and also a Speech which I delivered[7] that enters more into detail.

The Comee. to which the Copy-Right bill[8] was referred has not yet reported. I am apprehensive that there is no chance of its passage at the present Session. It does not contain any provision respecting the drama, but it is my intention to insert one during its progress, if we act upon it, to protect that interest. I will send you a Copy of the bill.

There seems to be at present, with the exception of the [Boston] Atlas,[9] but little said on the Presidential question. The danger to our cause lies in our divisions, which I sincerely hope means may be found to heal.

Pray, give my best respects to Col. [James Watson] Webb. . . . P.S. We are anticipating much pleasure from the representation of your late Dramatic piece.[10]

ALS. MHi. 1. Although the issue of the New York *Morning Courier & Enquirer* containing the article mentioned is not available, Sargent's editorial of Jan. 14, 1839, in that newspaper clearly presented his stand on the public land issue. In it, he accused some members of Congress of supporting the public land policy of the "present corrupt administration" in order to "purchase the votes and favor of the West." He praised Clay for his "noble disregard of personal consequence" in "contending with his accustomed fearlessness, ability and eloquence" against this scheme, and he also called upon New York to support Clay's position openly. 2. Comment in Senate, Jan. 14, 1839. 3. On Jan. 17, 1839, John Tyler introduced into the Va. house of delegates resolutions supporting the distribution of the proceeds of the sale of public lands among the states. He also complimented Clay during the course of debate. The resolutions passed the Whig-dominated house but were tabled in the Democratic senate. *Niles' Register* (Feb. 2, 1839), 55:356; Chitwood, *John Tyler*, 153. 4. There is no evidence that the New York legislature passed any resolutions concerning the public lands at this time. 5. Speech in Senate, April 11, 1838. 6. The report of Clay's Committee on Manufactures (April 16, 1832) was printed in *Niles' Register* (April 28, 1832), 42:163-68. See also 8:494. 7. Clay's speech of June 20, 1832, was printed in *Niles' Register* (Sept. 22, 1832), 43:57-64.

See also 8:539-41. 8. Comment in Senate, Feb. 2, 1837; Remark in Senate, Dec. 17, 1838. 9. Otis to Clay, Sept. 14, 1838. 10. It is unclear to which "late Dramatic piece" Clay refers, because many of Sargent's early works appeared under the name of his brother, Epes Sargent. It might be *Velasco; A Tragedy in Five Acts* which was published by Epes in New York in 1839. *DAB.*

Remark in Senate, January 16, 1839. Participates (not recorded) in debate on the public land bill [Remark in Senate, December 12, 1838] preliminary to a vote on its being engrossed for a third reading. The motion to engross passed 27 to 22, Clay voting nay. *Cong. Globe,* 25 Cong., 3 Sess., 121.

To FRANCIS T. BROOKE Washington, January 18, 1839

I received your two favors of the 16h. and 17h. instant. I am highly gratified with the prospect which exists at Richmond of general concurrence among the opposition as to the P. election, whatever divisions may unhappily exist on another question. It is of very great importance that there should be some expression of the preference which is entertained in Virginia;[1] and its influence elsewhere would be great, if not decisive.

I lament exceedingly the unfortunate divisions which prevail in respect to the Senatorial election.[2] Is it possible that there is any danger of the election of a friend of the Admon? Is it possible that any Whig can prefer such a friend to a Conservative?[3]

By the by Mr. [William C.] Rives, in conversation with me, expressed surprize at your opposition to his re-election.[4] He derived different impressions from his intercourse with you at the White Sulphur Springs. His surprize was not accompanied with any complaint, but on the contrary with declarations of high regard and personal esteem for you.

In answer to your enquiry, I have to say that Mr. R. has expressed, in the most explicit terms, his desire for my election, and has disclaimed entertaining any views towards the office of President himself.

ALS. KyU. Printed in Colton, *Clay Correspondence,* 4:439, with minor variations in punctuation and capitalization and with final paragraph omitted. Letter marked "(Confidential)." Written in "S[enate]. C[hamber]." 1. Clay to Brooke, Dec. 20, 1838. 2. Clay to Brooke, August 28 and Dec. 20, 1838. 3. See *ibid.*; also Howard Braverman, "The Economic and Political Background of the Conservative Revolt in Virginia," *VMHB* (April, 1952), 60:283-84, 286-87. 4. *Ibid.*

To HENRY CLAY, JR. Washington, January 18, 1839

I received your favor of the 6h. The measure adopted at Frankfort of sending Commrs. to Ohio will have good effect, whether it be attended with success or not.[1]

My friends are recovering from the discouragement which at the commencement of the Session they felt, in consequence of recent events which preceded it. In No. Carolina, it was ascertained, that the Whigs of the Legislature were unanimous in my favor.[2] Nearly the same unanimity is known to exist at Richmond;[3] and I have the strongest assurances, and every reason to believe, that N. York stands firm by her preference for me.[4] An effort is making to produce a prejudice against me as a Slaveholder in N. England, but I think it will be unavailing. I am inclined to believe that Mr. Webster has entered into the plan of electing Genl. Harrison.[5] If he has, he can not carry with him his own friends, & I believe that I shall be benefited at the South & finally not prejudiced at the North by that course should he pursue it.

The Antimasonic nomination has fallen stillborn.[6] It was a mere mockery; there not having been a single delegate in it elected by any primary meeting of Anti Masons, nor, except from Pennsa, a delegate from any other State. One man gave the whole vote of N. York and another that of Massachusetts.

I am not sure that any thing is necessary to be done at Frankfort. I think that if James T. Morehead could be substituted in place of Mr. [Robert N.] Wickliffe as a member to the Nat. Con. it would be a good change;[7] but Mr. W. ought to be treated with all proper delicacy.

My belief is that nothing but our divisions, can possibly save the present Admon. . . .

ALS. Henry Clay Memorial Foundation, Lexington, Ky. 1. On Jan. 5, 1839, the Kentucky legislature appointed James T. Morehead and John Speed Smith as delegates to the Ohio legislature to ask for a more effective law for the return of fugitive slaves than that provided in the federal act of 1793. Such an act was subsequently passed by Ohio though it was strongly opposed in the state senate. See Weisenburger, *The Passing of the Frontier*, 381-82; Collins, *History of Kentucky*, 1:43-44. 2. The Washington *Daily National Intelligencer* reported on Jan. 21, 1839, that the Raleigh *Register and North Carolina Gazette* had stated on Jan. 14 that a "free and unreserved interchange" with the members of the legislature justifies them in saying that "there is not a Whig in that body who does not warmly expouse the cause of Mr. Clay for the Presidency, in preference to any other candidate." Later, on Nov. 19, 1839, the North Carolina Whig convention endorsed Clay for president and Nathaniel P. Tallmadge for vice president. Lexington *Observer & Kentucky Reporter*, Nov. 27, 1839. 3. Clay to Brooke, Dec. 20, 1838. 4. Schermerhorn to Clay, Feb. 25, 1838. New York Whigs, however, did not endorse Clay. See Porter to Clay, Nov. 14 and Dec. 30, 1837. 5. Clay to Otis, Dec. 13, 1838. 6. *Ibid.* 7. Clay to Henry Clay, Jr., Nov. 28, 1838.

Remark in Senate, January 18, 1839. Supports motions related to controlling the financing of Cumberland Road construction in Ohio, Indiana, and Illinois in the total amount of $100,000; also moves to engross the bill for a third reading; and (on January 21) to pass it. Remarks not recorded. Engrossment motion carries 25 to 23; motion to pass carries 24 to 22. *Cong. Globe*, 25 Cong., 3 Sess., 125-26, 129.

From Peter B. Porter, Niagara Falls, N.Y., January 20, 1839. Says he wrote Sen. Nathaniel P. Tallmadge in Washington on December 30 giving him details of political developments of interest both to him and to you [Clay] and authorizing him "to show the letter to you, which I trust he has done." Reports: "An attempt, as you are aware, will be made by some of the leading Anti-Masons—how far it may be countenanced by the Eastern friends of Mr. Webster [Clay to Otis, December 13, 1838], you have better means of judging than myself—to bring Gen'l Harrison forward as the Presidential candidate of the Whigs, but I am satisfied that it will prove abortive, so far at least as this State is concerned." Says that the Anti-Masonic newspaper *Commercial Advertiser* ("one of the two principal daily Whig papers in Buffalo") has come out for Gen. Harrison. On the other hand, the influential Buffalo *Journal*, "organ of the old Democratic Whig party," will soon publicly endorse Clay. Is not sure yet whether the "present Legislature . . . will consent to make some public demonstration in your favour," but hopes so [Porter to Clay, November 14 and December 30, 1837, and February 16, 1839]. Notes that Tallmadge "stands high in this State and will doubtless be reelected to the Senate in February [Clay to Spencer, December 15, 1838], unless the LocoFocos of our Senate should prevent an election altogether, of which however I apprehend there is but little danger." Adds, further, that Clay's "bold, independent and magnanimous course . . . during the present session" of Congress has served to "increase the admiration" of "the intelligent and honest portions of the Whig party" toward him and "will add vigor to their efforts for your promotion." In response to an earlier question from Clay, reports that "Tillman [*sic*, Millard Fillmore], [Everard] Peck, &c, of whom you speak [Clay to Porter, December 27, 1838], are office-seeking Anti-Masons, and will go for Harrison, as long as there is any chance of his success. They are however pretty clever fellows, and it is desirable that you should be on good terms with them." Copy. OHi.

Remark in Senate, January 22, 1839. Participates in debate (not recorded) on bill for the relief of Pierre Menard and others. *Cong. Globe*, 25 Cong., 3 Sess., 132.

From William Turner & J. Turner Dodge, New York, January 22, 1839. Write on behalf of the Democratic Whig Association of the city's tenth ward. Praise his recent stance in the Senate on the public land price graduation and reduction issue [Remark in Senate, March 29, 1838; Speech in Senate, April 11, 1838; Remark in Senate, December 12, 1838], and lament the fact that his wise and popular 1832 land bill [8:539-41] was vetoed by Jackson [8:609-10]. Offer other ringing praises of his patriotism, eloquence, and political genius. Copy. Printed in *Niles' Register* (March 2, 1839), 56:5. See Clay to Turner & Dodge, February 9, 1839.

Remark in Senate, January 23, 1839. Opposes bill for the relief of Dr. John Campbell White of Baltimore. *Cong. Globe*, 25 Cong., 3 Sess., 134.

To HARRISON G. OTIS Washington, January 24, 1839

I duly recd. your obliging letter of the 11h. inst. I read all the pieces of Constans with very great satisfaction.[1] I saw the constraint under which he wrote, and appreciated fully the expediency of his submitting to the necessary control arising out of local circumstances, and the announced preference of the General Court.

So Mr. W[ebster]. is re-elected to the Senate,[2] and by his own request! He gives us but little of his presence or assistance. On the first day of his appearance in the Senate, he announced his approval of the *principle* of the graduation bill; but gave us the benefit of his vote.[3] I am happy however to inform you that that measure has fallen, as is believed, in the House.[4] My friends persuade me that by my strenuous and persevering opposition it received its mortal blow in one County, although it expired in another County.

I am very glad to learn that the Atlas & its clique stand alone on the Presidential subject; and that my friends in the Legislature remain firm in their attachment to me.[5] The only importance which belongs to a renewed expression of their attachment & confidence arises out of the facts of the course of the Atlas, Mr. Ws. presumed sanction of it, and his recent reelection to the Senate.

My friends have recovered from the discouragement which was felt when we assembled at the commencement of the Session; and now their hopes, on my subject, are nearly as confident as they were when we separated at the adjournment last Session. There is much reason for this change. And I think that this confidence will increase with the lapse of time.

The friends of Genl. Harrison from Ohio are stirring the question of bringing the period of the meeting of the Nat. Convention nearer to the present time than it was fixed at the last Session.[6] This, I understand, is in conformity with the expressed wishes of the Whig portion of the Ohio Legislature. My friends I believe are disposed to acquiesce in those wishes. Septr. is talked of.

[William C.] Rives's re-election is very uncertain, the probabilities are against it.[7] There is great division at Richmond on the Senatorial subject. On mine, scarcely any among the opposition.

I concur with you entirely as to the impolicy of your 15 gallon law.[8] It is, I think, wholly indefensible. The Temperance cause has done great good, and will continue to do so, as long as moral means are employed. But if it resort to legislation—to coercion—it will be resisted & ought to be resisted. No man likes to have, or ought to have, cold water or brandy, separately or in combination, put in or kept out of his throat upon any other will than his own.

ALS. MHi. Written in "S[enate]. Chamber." 1. Clay to Otis, Jan. 1, 1839. 2. Otis to Clay, Jan. 11, 1839. 3. Detained in Massachusetts, Webster did not take his place in the Senate until Jan. 14, 1839. His remarks that day on the public land price graduation and reduction bill [Remark in Senate, December 12, 1838] were not recorded; but, he joined Clay in support of a motion by Sen. William C. Rives (Va.) to postpone consideration of the bill indefinitely, a motion that lost 27 to 23. He did not, however, cast his vote on Jan. 16 on the motion to engross the bill for a third reading (it passed 27 to 22) or on the final vote on the measure on Jan. 17 (also passed 27 to 22). *Cong. Globe*, 25 Cong., 3 Sess., 109, 113, 121-22. 4. On Jan. 22, the House voted 102 to 97 to table the bill; and on the following day struck down, 99 to 98, a motion to reconsider the motion to table. *Ibid.*, 133, 135. See Remark in Senate, Dec. 12, 1838. 5. Otis to Clay, Sept. 14, 1838; Clay to Otis, Dec. 13, 1838. 6. Clay to Porter, Nov. 14, 1837. 7. Clay to Brooke, August 28 and Dec. 20, 1838. 8. Otis to Clay, Jan. 11, 1839.

Remark in Senate, January 25, 1839. Presents petition from citizens of Philadelphia asking Congress "to take measures for a congress of nations." *Cong. Globe*, 25 Cong., 3 Sess., 137.

To FRANCIS T. BROOKE Washington, January 28, 1839

I have received your several favors respecting the state of things at Richmond, in reference to your Senatorial election, and thank you for them.[1] I did not acknowledge them severally as they arrived, because they did not seem to call for any particular observation from me. The divisions and dissensions in the Legislature at Richmond, are deeply to be deplored, and I fervently hope that means may be found to heal and harmonize. At Annapolis, they have just elected, or re-elected, Mr. [William D.] Merrick, and concord, it is thought, will be again restored.[2]

The spirits of my friends are again revived, and they think that they see, in various quarters, indications of the final result which their partiality prompts them to desire. I believe myself, that the current in my favor, which for the moment appeared to be impeded, will again burst forward, with accumulated strength. The movement which you suppose will take place at Richmond, if made, would give great impulse to that current.[3]

Poor Mrs. Wickham, I see, is gone.[4] Those who are falling around us, should remind us that we, ere long, must follow them, and their departure diminishes the motives of our remaining here.

Copy. Printed in Colton, *Clay Correspondence*, 4:439-40. Written in Senate Chamber. 1. Clay to Brooke, August 28 and Dec. 20, 1838. 2. On Jan. 26, 1839, William D. Merrick, a Whig, was reelected to the U.S. Senate from Maryland, receiving 12 votes in the senate and 36 in the house for a total of 48, while 35 blank votes were cast. *Niles' Register* (Feb. 2, 1839), 55:353. 3. Clay to Brooke, Dec. 20, 1838. 4. Probably Elizabeth Selden McClurg (Mrs. John) Wickham, mother-in-law of Benjamin W. Leigh.

Remark in Senate, January 31, 1839. Presents the petition of Dr. Edward A. Theller asking for a definition of the rights of naturalized American citizens. Explains that Theller was born in Ireland and naturalized in the United States; that he had been captured and convicted of treason for having participated in the expedition that invaded Canada. At the time of his trial, the judge ruled his U.S. naturalization to be null and without effect and held that Theller's original citizenship still pertained. *Cong. Globe*, 25 Cong., 3 Sess., 150. Theller had commanded the schooner *Anne* against the fortress at Amherstville on the Detroit River during the recent Canadian rebellion [Porter to Clay, December 15, 1837; Comment in Senate, January 5, 1838]. For Theller, see *CAB* and Stevens, "The *Caroline* Affair," Ph.D. dissertation, Indiana University, 1982, p. 37.

Remark in Senate, February 1, 1839. Participates (not recorded) in the discussion of a bill to allow a drawback on foreign hemp manufactured into cordage and exported. *Cong. Globe*, 25 Cong., 3 Sess., 153.

Remark in Senate, February 4, 1839. Speaks to a petition from the North Carolina legislature complaining of shortages of specie small change in the state and asking that branch U.S. mints be authorized to coin silver change. Explains that the problem is caused by the Gold Coinage Act of June 28, 1834 [Speech in Senate, September 25, 1837], so that "when it became necessary to export specie, silver was exported in preference to gold, because the silver was more valuable in foreign countries." Hence its scarcity in North Carolina and elsewhere in the nation. Asserts that he had predicted this situation at the time the 1834 legislation changed the silver to gold ratio from 15:1 to 16:1. Defends himself from criticism by Sen. Robert Strange (N.C.) that he is improperly interfering in the internal politics of North Carolina [Comment in Senate, January 14, 1839]. Elaborates on his explanation of the flight of silver abroad. *Cong. Globe*, 25 Cong., 3 Sess., 157.

To PETER B. PORTER Washington, February 5, 1839

I have this moment recd. your favor of the 1st. as I had done that which you addressed to me prior to your departure from home. I am glad of your arrival at Albany[;] and we are all pleased with the harmony which characterizes the proceedings of the Whigs at Albany.[1]

Here, I do not know that there is any thing material to communicate. Several consultations have taken place among the Whigs here about fixing an earlier day for the meeting of the Convention, *at the instance of the friends of Genl Harrison*. It will be decided this week and probably decided favorably.[2] Septr. or some earlier month may be fixed on. My own opinion is in favor of it, especially as it will gratify Genl. Harrison's friends.

Mr. Webster has been here several weeks & wraps himself up, as far as I know, in perfect silence.

I am happy to tell you that my particular interests, are decidedly improved and fast improving here and everywhere else. A movement at Albany, favorable to me, would be conclusive.[3] Such an one is anticipated at Richmond.[4] I will write again if any thing interesting occurs. . . .

ALS. NBuHi. Written in "S[enate]. Chamber." 1. Clay to Spencer, Dec. 15, 1838. 2. Porter to Clay, Nov. 14 and Dec. 30, 1837. 3. *Ibid.*; also Porter to Clay, Feb. 16, 1839. 4. Clay to Brooke, Dec. 20, 1838.

From WINFIELD SCOTT Utica, N.Y., February 5, 1839

I have doubted, for twenty-four hours, whether I ought to trouble you with the perusal of the accompanying letter (copy) to the Secretary of War;[1] but having determined to risque the trespass on your time & friendship, I will take the liberty to add to the *voluntary* disclaimers made to the Secretary, others which I think due from me to you.

Having recently passed rapidly thro' many of the States (on public duty) I have been approached by persons, of more or less consideration, almost every where, who have tendered me assurances of eventual support for the office of President at the next election.[2] Those assurances have come from the friends of yourself, of General Harrison, Mr. Webster & Mr. Van Buren, respectively. In almost every case it was evident that the individual had some doubt of the success of his own favorite candidate, & only looked to me as his *second* choice. I made one general reply to all & each:—"that I was no *politician*, & could not claim the high distinction of being a *statesman*; that I was absolutely indifferent whether I ever reached the office of President; that I made no pretensions to it, whatever, & that there were already presidential candidates enough before the public without the addition of my name." To the *Whigs*, I made the further declaration—"that it ought not to be doubted that the convention, they were to hold, would reduce the number of their candidates to one—whom all would cordially support," & *to the supporters of Mr. Van Buren*, I further said—"that, in my bosom, I had had the misfortune to condemn almost every leading measure of the late & present administrations, & at least seven in every ten appointments which the two had made."

Being more strongly urged by some leading Whigs, than by the many alluded to above, & who seemed to think that the final battle would be fought the next year; I replied—"you ought not to despair of success with the one candidate who may be duly nominated by the convention;—should he, however, be defeated, I admit that your case will then become rather desperate; it will still be your duty to renew the contest, & should you then want a leader of the forlorn hope, & a better be not disclosed in time, you may reckon upon me for that service—with a possibility of success—upon the principle (the nation having been made rabid by one 'military chieftain') that the "hair of the dog is good for the bite." This may look like an argument in favour of my friend General Harrison, who, no doubt, & perhaps with good reason, thinks himself superior to me in general soldiership & in conflicts of the field, as he is as a politician & statesman; but, in quoting the adage, I was thinking of his being probably excluded from the next contest, by the intervening convention, &, of the fact, that when out, in the last, he was not accepted—which, perhaps, is a conclusive argument against any quack remedy. Be all this, as it may, you have in this, & the enclosed letter, "the head & front of my offending," or intermeddling in politics, & I shall continue to observe the same course in the singleness of sincerity.

I do not enclose the letter (copy) to the Secretary, as *information* against the Executive. *That* would be highly dishonourable in me, & therefore, I beg that it may not be made the ground of enquiry or comment in the Senate or elsewhere. *Au reste* I do not write in strict confidence—having no objection that you should show this communication to any discreet common friends—as Messrs. [John J.] Crittenden & [William C.] Preston, who may happen to be by you; but it is more probable that you will throw both papers into the fire, as of no value to you or any one else, except to myself.

The frontiers of Canada remaining quiet, I may have the pleasure of seeing you in two or three weeks. Indeed I am expecting an order to repair to Washington on that condition.

Copy. InHi. 1. Scott had written Joel R. Poinsett on Feb. 4, 1839, protesting that during his thirty-one years in the army he had not attended a party meeting, or gone to the polls. "I have never once committed the indecency of blending party feelings with public duty; but have ever given, to the utmost of my abilities, to the Executive, in *my military service*, an active and cordial support." Charles W. Elliott, *Winfield Scott, The Soldier and the Man* (New York, 1937), 369. 2. Scott, who had gained fame for fighting Indians and for helping to prevent hostilities over the Northeastern boundary [Clay to Hamilton, Feb. 24, 1839], was gaining support as a possible Whig presidential candidate in 1840. The Scott boom was especially strong in New York where William Henry Seward and Thurlow Weed were promoting him, at least partially in an attempt to head off Clay's nomination. For a discussion of Scott's candidacy, see *ibid.*, 367-82; Glyndon G. Van Deusen, *William Henry Seward* (New York, 1967), 61-62.

From Joshua R. Giddings, Washington, February 7, 1839. Reports that much is being said about "the remarks made by you in the Senate to day on the Subject of the abolition of Slavery in this district." Asks Clay to inform him "whether you believe that Congress has [the] power" to abolish slavery in the District of Columbia. ALS. OHi. Written in "House of Rep." For the particular interest of Giddings in this matter, see Van Deusen, *Life of Henry Clay*, 318.

Speech in Senate, February 7, 1839. Presents a petition from "several hundred" Washington and District of Columbia residents opposing the abolition of slavery in the district, "even if Congress possess the very questionable power of abolishing it" without the consent of those who would be most affected by it. Says he continues to believe that all petitions for abolition must be received and referred to committee, because the right of petition is a constitutionally guaranteed one [8:817-18, 833; Comment in Senate, December 18, 1837]. Thinks, however, that the misuse of this right by the abolitionists is "to agitate a subject fraught with the most direful consequences."

Points out that there are three classes of persons opposed to the continuation of slavery in the United States: (1) those, like the Society of Friends, who oppose the institution on humane and philanthropic grounds, but who also oppose the use of force in dealing with it; (2) the apparent abolitionists who, in upholding the right to petition, "cooperate with the Abolitionists for the sole purpose of asserting and vindicating that right"; (3) the "real ultra Abolitionists who are resolved to persevere in the pursuit of their object at all hazards, and without regard to any consequences, however calamitous they may be. With them the rights of property are nothing; the deficiency of the powers of the General Government is nothing; the acknowledged and incontestable powers of the States are nothing; civil war, a dissolution of the Union, and the overthrow of a Government in which are concentrated the fondest hopes of the civilized world, are nothing. A single idea has taken possession of their minds, and onward they pursue it, overlooking all barriers, reckless and regardless of all consequences. . . . they . . . promulgate to the world their purpose to be to manumit forthwith, and without compensation, and without moral preparation, three million negro slaves, under jurisdictions altogether separated from those under which they live. . . . in all their leading prints and publications, the alleged horrors of slavery are depicted in the most glowing and exaggerated colors, to excite the imaginations and stimulate the rage of the people in the free States against the people in the slave States. The slaveholder is held up and represented as the most atrocious of human beings. Advertisements of fugitive slaves [and of slaves] to be sold are carefully collected and blazoned forth, to infuse a spirit of detestation and hatred against one entire, and the largest, section of the Union. And like a notorious agitator upon another theater, they would hunt down and proscribe from the pale of civilized society the inhabitants of that entire section."

Argues that the ultra abolitionists have moved far beyond their initial professions of employing only persuasion to achieve their goals. Indeed, "To the agency of their powers of persuasion, they now propose to substitute the powers of the ballot-box; and he must be blind to what is passing before us, who does not perceive that the inevitable tendency of their proceedings is, if these should be found insufficient, to invoke, finally, the more potent powers of the bayonet."

Reviews U.S. history to show that there have been three epochs during which "the spirit of abolition displayed itself": (1) when the Constitution first went into operation and there emerged numerous newly-formed abolition societies, "comprising not merely the Society of Friends, but many other good men," which regularly petitioned Congress to abolish slavery; (2) during the debate on and the adoption of the Missouri Compromise in 1820-21; and (3) the present time. Believes the current agitation has been much stimulated by Britain's emancipation of the slaves in the British West Indies in 1833 [8:641]. Compares at length the British experience with slavery in their distant West Indian islands with that of the United States in its South, maintaining that the situations politically, geographically, and institutionally were quite different. Thinks the present excitement of the abolition issue is also related to the fact that it has become mixed into party and sectional politics. Notes that in the 1836 election even Van Buren was said to be an abolitionist. Asserts his belief that "it is not true, and I rejoice that it is not true, that either of the two great parties in this country has any designs or aims at abolition."

Addresses the question of the constitutional status of slavery in the District of Columbia, noting that the provision in the Constitution [I. 8. ¶16] which empowers Congress to legislate for the district, "preceded, in point of time, the actual cessions" of land which were made by the States of Maryland and Virginia to the new federal government for the purpose of creating the district. Explains: "In making the cession they supposed that it was to be applied, and applied solely, to the purposes of a seat of Government, for which it was asked. When it was made slavery existed in both those Commonwealths and in the ceded territory, as it now continues to exist in all of them. Neither Maryland nor Virginia could have anticipated that, whilst the institution remained within their respective limits, its abolition would be attempted by Congress without their consent. Neither of them would probably have made an unconditional cession if they could have anticipated such a result." Asserts, further, that slavery in the district "exists here in the mildest and most mitigated form" and that of a population of 39,834 (in the last census) only 6,119 were slaves. Also, "To abolish slavery within the District of Columbia, whilst it remains in Virginia and Maryland, situated as that District is, within the very heart of those States, would expose them to great practical inconvenience and annoyance. The District would become a place of refuge and escape for fugitive slaves from the two States, and a place from which a spirit of discontent, insubordination, and insurrection might be fostered and encouraged in the two States." Insists that the power granted by the Constitution to Congress to legislate for the district "ought to be interpreted and exercised solely to the end for which it was granted. . . . The language may possibly be sufficiently comprehensive to include the power of abolition; but it would not at all thence follow that the power could be rightfully exercised." Asks, in the final reckoning, "is the affair of the liberation of six thousand negro slaves in the District, disconnected with the three million slaves in the United States, of sufficient magnitude to agitate, distract, and embitter this great Confederacy?"

Contests the position of abolitionists who contend that the Constitution [IV. 3. ¶2] empowers Congress to legislate on the issue of slavery in the territories, specifically in the Territory of Florida. Points out that the existence and legality of slave property in Florida was built solidly into the 1819 treaty of cession with Spain and was reaffirmed by the 36° 30′ provision of the Missouri Compromise in 1820. Notes that "Florida is the only remaining Territory to be admitted into the Union with the institution of domestic slavery, while Wisconsin and Iowa are now nearly ripe for admission without it."

Denies, as well, the abolitionists' argument that Congress has the power to regulate the interstate slave trade under the commerce clause [I. 8. ¶2] of the Constitution. States that "The grant in the Constitution is of a power of *regulation*, and not prohibition. It is conservative, not destructive. Regulation *ex vi termini* implies the continued existence or prosecution of the thing regulated. Prohibition implies total discontinuance or annihilation. The regulation intended was designed to facilitate and accommodate, not to obstruct and incommode the commerce to be regulated."

Is convinced that all of these constitutional contentions by the "ultra Abolitionists are but so many masked batteries, concealing the real and ultimate point of attack. That point of attack is the institution of domestic slavery as it exists in these States. It is to liberate three million slaves held in bondage within them." Asserts catagorically that the general government has not the power to effect this since it is a "limited Government, comprising comparatively few powers, and leaving the residuary mass of political power in the possession of the several States [Amendment X]." Reminds his colleagues that the slavery question was one of the most difficult to resolve in the constitutional convention, but that it "was happily compromised and adjusted in a spirit of harmony and patriotism. According to that compromise, no power whatever was granted to the General Government in respect to domestic slavery, but that which relates to taxation and representation, and the power to restore fugitive slaves to their lawful owners. All other power in regard to the institution of slavery was retained exclusively by the States, to be exercised by them severally, according to their respective views of their own peculiar interest. The Constitution of the United States never could have been formed upon the principle of investing the General Government with authority to abolish the institution at its pleasure. It never can be continued for a single day if the exercise of such a power be assumed or usurped." Attacks the abolitionists for stirring up sectional strife on the slavery issue, for holding the South up to "scorn and contempt." Asks: "Why not leave it to us, as the common Constitution of our country has left it, to be dealt with, under the guidance of Providence, as best we may or can?"

Maintains that the real issue at stake is the fact that "The slaves are here; no practical scheme for their removal or separation from us has been yet devised or proposed; and the true inquiry is, what is best to be done with them? . . . I repeat, how are they to be best governed? What is best to be done for their happiness and our own? In the slave States the alternative is, that the white man must govern the black, or the black govern the white. In several of those States the number of the slaves is greater than that of the white population. An immediate abolition of slavery in them, as these ultra Abolitionists propose, would be followed by a desperate struggle for immediate ascendency of the black race over the white race, or rather it would be followed by instantaneous collisions between the two races, which would break out into a civil war that would end in the extermination or subjugation of the one race or the other. In such an alternative, who can hesitate? Is it not better for both parties that the existing state of things should be preserved, instead of exposing them to the horrible strifes and contests which would inevitably attend an immediate abolition? This is our true ground of defense for the continued existence of slavery in our country. It is that which our revolutionary ancestors assumed; it is that which, in my opinion, forms our justification in the eyes of all Christendom."

Sees another "impediment to immediate abolition" in the fact that about three million slaves, conservatively valued at $400 each, represent a total property value of 1.2 billion dollars. It is property "diffused throughout all classes and conditions of society. It is owned by widows and orphans, by the aged and infirm, as well as by the sound and vigorous. . . . And now it is rashly proposed, by a single fiat of legislation, to annihilate this immense amount of property! To annihilate it without indemnity and without compensation to its owners! Does any considerate man believe it to be possible to effect such an object without convulsion, revolution, and bloodshed?" Says he will not dwell long on the "visionary dogma which holds that negro slaves cannot be the subject of property. . . . That *is* property which the law declares *to be* property." Recalls that the British Parliament provided £120,000,000 to compensate their colonists for the loss of their property at the time of the emancipation of slaves throughout the empire. Asserts, therefore, that if "these ultra Abolitionists are seriously determined to pursue their scheme of immediate abolition, they should at once set about raising a fund of $1,200,000, 000, to indemnify the owners of slave property. And the taxes to raise that enormous amount can only be justly assessed upon themselves or upon the free States, if they can persuade them to assent to such an assessment; for it would be a mockery of all justice, and an outrage against all equity, to levy any portion of the tax upon the slave States to pay for their own unquestioned property."

Argues that abolitionist agitation has set back "for half a century" the prospect of voluntary emancipation, gradual or immediate, in any of the states. Cites as evidence for this statement the "large and respectable minority" sentiment that existed for the gradual emancipation of the relatively small slave population in Kentucky in 1798-99 [1:5-8, 12-14]; compares this with the decisive failure of a recent referendum in Kentucky to authorize a constitutional convention to discuss the question again [Clay to Baldwin, August 28, 1838]. Makes it clear, however, that even in Kentucky in 1798-99, "No one was rash enough to propose, to think, of immediate abolition. No one was rash enough to think of throwing loose upon the community, ignorant and unprepared, the untutored slaves of the State." Says he has not and cannot support emancipation in states where the proportion of slaves to the white population is considerable. Fears "the danger of an ultimate ascendency of the black race, or of a civil contest which might terminate in the extinction of one race or the other." Believes the vote for a constitutional convention in Kentucky last year, at which emancipation would have been discussed, would have been "much larger" than the 25% it commanded had "apprehension of the danger of abolition" not been a factor among the voters. Explains that because of abolitionist agitation in Kentucky, he himself was "constrained to take immediate, bold, and decided ground against" such a constitutional convention.

Contemplates "some of the consequences which would inevitably ensue" in the event of immediate abolition. Among them would be "the struggle which would instantaneously arise between the two races in most of the southern and southwestern States. And what a dreadful struggle would it not be! Embittered by all the recollections of the past, by the unconquerable prejudices which would prevail between the two races, and stimulated by all the hopes and fears of the future, it would be a contest in which the extermination of the blacks, or their ascendency over the whites, would be the sole alternative. Prior to the conclusion, or during the progress of such a contest, vast numbers, probably, of the black race would migrate into the free States; and what effect would such a migration have upon the laboring classes in those States? Now the distribution of labor in the United States is geographical; the free laborers occupying one side of the line, and the slave laborers the other; each class pursuing its own avocations almost altogether unmixed with the other. But, on the supposition of immediate abolition, the black class migrating into the free States, would enter into competition with the white class, diminishing the wages of their labor, and augmenting the hardships of their condition."

Criticizes the opposition of the abolitionists to the colonization of free Negroes in Africa, because they "strenously oppose all separation of the two races." Reminds them that colonization "disturbs no man's property" and that "the blessing of Providence" has "graciously smiled upon" the colonies already established. In opposing the separation of the races, do not the abolitionists, he asks, "perceive that in thus confounding all the distinctions which God himself has made, they arraign the wisdom and goodness of Providence itself? It has been His divine pleasure to make the black man black and white man white, and to distinguish them by other constitutional differences. It is not necessary for me to maintain, nor shall I endeavor to prove, that it was any part of His divine intention that the one race should be held in perpetual bondage by the other; but this I will say, that those whom he has created different, and has declared, by their physical structure and color, ought to be kept asunder, should not be brought together by any process whatever of unnatural amalgamation." Asserts that since the "Abolitionists oppose all colonization . . . it irresistibly follows, whatever they may protest or declare, that they are in favor of amalgamation. . . . Is it their purpose not only to create a pinching competition between black labor and white labor, but do they intend also to contaminate the industrious and laborious classes of society at the North by a revolting admixture of the black element?" Believes, however, that because the black population constitutes only one-fifth of the total U.S. population, and since the "European is constantly, though slowly, gaining upon the African portion," it is likely that some one hundred and fifty or two hundred years hence "but few vestiges of the black race will remain among our posterity." Says he has "ventured on a speculative theory" explaining the disappearance of the Negro "with which I will not trouble you, but which has been published to the world [2:670 and/or 6:88-92]."

Believes also that if the abolitionist movement succeeds in its present aim of "uniting the inhabitants of the free States as one man against the inhabitants of the slave States," the Union will surely dissolve in a bloody civil war, "a conquest of brother over brothers."

Makes it clear to his audience that he is "no friend of slavery" and that his heart "beats high and strong in the cause of civil liberty. Wherever it is safe and practicable, I desire to see every portion of the human family in the enjoyment of it. But I prefer the liberty of my own country to that of any other people, and the liberty of my own race to that of any other race. The liberty of the descendants of Africa in the United States is incompatible with the safety and liberty of the European descendants. There slavery forms an exception—an exception resulting from a stern and inexorable necessity—to the general liberty in the United States. We did not originate, nor are we responsible for, this necessity. Their liberty, if it were possible, could only be established by violating the incontestable powers of the States, and subverting the Union, and beneath the ruins of the Union would be buried, sooner or later, the liberty of both races."

Concludes: "I beseech the Abolitionists themselves solemnly to pause in their mad and fatal course. Amidst the infinite variety of objects of humanity and benevolence which invite the employment of their energies, let them select some one more harmless, that does not threaten to deluge our country in blood. I call upon that small portion of the clergy which has lent itself to these wild and ruinous schemes, not to forget the holy nature of the divine mission of the founder of our religion, and to profit by his peaceful examples." *Cong. Globe*, 25 Cong., 3 Sess., Appendix, 354-59. Printed in Colton, *Clay Correspondence*, 6:139-59. The speech was published under the title *Speech of Mr. Clay of Kentucky, on the Subject of Abolition Petitions. Delivered in the Senate of the United States, February 7, 1839*. Washington, 1839.

A sketchy summary of a few of the points made in this speech appears in the main section of the *Congressional Globe* for this date. It concludes with the observation: "Mr. C. illustrated and defended these and other positions in an able speech of nearly two hours in length, which will be presented to our readers after it is published." *Cong. Globe*, 25 Cong., 3 Sess., 167.

Among many replies to this speech was one immediately delivered by John C. Calhoun as soon as Clay took his seat. In this, he had high praise for Clay's shift of position on the true threat of the abolitionist movement, noting that when Clay had last addressed the issue in January, 1838 [Remark in Senate, January 6, 1838; Speech in Senate, January 9, 1838], when Calhoun's so-called "Six Resolutions" were being debated, he had "turned his eyes to State-rights, as the ark of our safety" in the face of the abolitionist menace. *Cong. Globe*, 25 Cong., 3 Sess., 167. Another reply, highly critical of Clay, one widely circulated among anti-slavery activists, was William E. Channing, "Remark on the Slavery Question In a Letter to Jonathan Phillips, Esq.," *The Works of William E. Channing*, 2:782-820. See also, below, Gerrit Smith to Clay, March 21, 1839.

According to contemporary reports, Clay read this speech to Sen. William C. Preston (S.C.) and others a few days before delivering it and asked Preston his opinion of it. There was at the time, said Preston in a speech in Philadelphia on March 11, 1839, "some conversation as to its probable effect upon the public mind; and it was remarked that it might be offensive to the ultras of both parties, in the great excitement which then existed. To this Mr. CLAY replied: 'I trust the sentiments and opinions are correct; I had rather be right than be President.' " Preston to Gales & Seaton, Washington, March 28, 1839, in Washington *Daily National Intelligencer*, March 30, 1839. For Preston's enthusiastic campaign speech for Clay in Philadelphia on March 11, 1839, see *Niles' Register* (March 23, 1839), 56:54-55, quoting the Philadelphia *United States Gazette*. In the *Niles* version, Preston quotes Clay as saying: "I did not send for you to ask what might be the effect of the proposed movement on my *prospects*, but whether it was *right*; *I had rather be right than be president*." *Niles' Register* (March 23, 1839), 56:55.

To JOSIAH RANDALL Washington, February 8, 1839

. . . . I regret not to have seen the exposition about the Anti Masonic Convention.[1] I think it could be done in one hour, that is all that is necessary. The main object is to shew that from no one of the States pretended to be represented were there any delegates chosen by the Anti Ms; that they were self made delegates; that one self made delegate from Massactts. cast the whole vote of that State; another from N. York did the same &c; and that Anti Masonry does not exist *in organization* in any State in the Union but Pennsa. & perhaps Vermont.

ALS. PHi. Addressed to Randall in Philadelphia. 1. Clay to Otis, Dec. 13, 1838.

Remark in Senate, February 8, 1839. Reports from the Committee on Foreign Relations the act for the relief of the legal representatives of William Tudor, Jr. [4:132]. *Cong. Globe,* 25 Cong., 3 Sess., 169.

To WILLIAM TURNER & J. TURNER DODGE Washington, February 9, 1839

[Thanks them for their letter of January 22, 1839. Continues:]

Faithfully administered, the public lands may be made powerfully instumental in the advancement of the prosperity of the present generation, and of their prosperity for a long succession of ages. But they have been in danger of being swept away by pre-emptions, Indian reservations, graduation bills, and finally cessions of the common property of all the states to the particular states in which it is situated. And most of these projects, urged under the plausible pretext of benefitting the poor settler, have stimulated speculation, and tended to aggrandize the speculator to the prejudice both of the honest emigrant and the people of the United States. I have felt it to be my duty to oppose these projects; and it is a deplorable evidence of the loose morality which prevails in respect to the public property, that I have been denounced and calumniated for my endeavor to protect and preserve it for the benefit of all the states and people of the union.

I share with you, gentlemen, in regret, on account of the failure of the bill to distribute the nett proceeds of the public lands, which passed both houses of congress. It was defeated by a high-handed and daring violation of the constitution.[1] If it had gone into operation, there would have been no extraordinary surplus in the treasury, no disturbance of the financial and business concerns of the country by a bungling removal of the deposits,[2] no temptation to those alarming and annual appropriations which have been recently made by the federal government, and I believe no suspensions of specie payments by the banks.[3] Now that the public attention is awakened to this great national resource, I trust that the projects to which I have adverted will be checked, and that it will be cherished and preserved for the common benefit of all the people of the United States and their posterity.

[Thanks them for sending him the resolutions of the Democratic Whig Association of the Tenth Ward.]

Copy. *Niles' Register* (March 2, 1839), 56:5. 1. See 8:552. 2. See 8:583-84, 681, 684-85, 728. 3. Speech in Senate, Jan. 11, 1837.

To George W. Featherstonhaugh, New York, February 10, 1839. Assures Featherstonhaugh that he has never said anything to Louis Joseph Papineau about British-Canadian relations that he has not said to British officials. States specifically that "So far from conveying the idea that the U. S. would, at a suitable time, interfere on the question of that relation, I took pains to inculcate that they would not interfere, on Canadian account, and never but as a collateral affair, when they might happen to be engaged, on their own proper account, in a contest with G. Britain." Assures him also that "No man in the U. S. is more anxious than I am to cultivate & preserve the most friendly relations with G. Britain. None more indisposed to take part in the contest between the parent Country & the Colony. All this is perfectly compatible with the sentiment, which I at the same time cherish, that all parts of this Continent may be liberated from Europenean [*sic*, European] dominion as fast as they are competent to self=government." ALS. ViU.

Remark in Senate, February 11, 1839. Speaks to a difference of opinion in February, 1833, between Sen. Thomas H. Benton (Mo.) and Sen. Mahlon Dickerson (N.J.) on the question of whether Sen. Daniel Webster (Mass.) was consulted on the compromise tariff bill of 1833 [8:603, 619-22, 626-27] before it was introduced. To this point, Dickerson, in a letter to Benton dated February 5, 1839, relates the following facts: that on the morning of February 12, 1833, the day Clay introduced the bill in the Senate, Webster told him [Dickerson] he was not aware that the bill was about to be introduced; also, that he [Dickerson] although chairman of the Committee on Manufactures at the time, did not see the bill until it was in print.

At this point in the discussion Webster confirms that, true, he was not consulted by Clay on the matter; but he recalls that while he differed with Clay on the wisdom of the 1833 tariff legislation, he then felt and now feels that there had been no lack of courtesy by Clay, when the bill was about to be introduced; also that he has "no complaint as to his not being consulted."

Clay recalls, on the other hand, that when he was in Philadelphia in December, 1832, where and when "the project of a compromise of this great and important question presented itself to his mind," Webster happened to pass through the city and that "the plan was communicated to him at that time." Says it is "true that the Senator expressed his disapprobation of it." Recalls, further, that after he returned to Washington, but prior to the introduction of the bill on February 12, 1833, he called a meeting of "eight or ten" of his "political friends" at his lodgings. There the pending bill was read and its provisions discussed. His "impression" now is that "the Senator from Massachusetts was there: certain he was that he was invited." Adds that the fact that he [Clay] "had such a measure in contemplation was notorious in both Houses of Congress." Finally, Clay notes that while he may have mentioned his compromise tariff bill to then Senator Dickerson as well, he has "no recollection of having done so." Webster concludes the exchange with the observation that while he might have been invited to Clay's rooms to discuss the pending tariff measure, he has "no recollection whatever of being present at any such consultation." *Cong. Globe*, 25 Cong., 3 Sess., 172-73.

To Thomas H. Clay, Lexington, February 12, 1839. Thanks him for his letter of February 4 [not found]; chides him for some unwise purchases made at public sales; and says that he too had anticipated the rise in the price of hemp because New York agents were expected to enter the hemp market. Indeed, "If it continue at the price to which they have carried it, you will have to limit the manufacture of Bale Rope, as it will not I fear be practicable to sell it, without loss. You must keep along as well as you can until I return." Reports that "I am highly gratified with the account of Henry's exhibition in the Legislature [Clay to Henry Clay, Jr., March 2, 1838], but I see he lost his cause. I send you a Copy of a Speech which I lately made that has produced much sensation [Speech in Senate, February 7, 1839]. . . . I hope to reach home by the 15h or 20h March." ALS. DLC-HC (DNA, M212, R5).

A great debate had taken place in the Kentucky legislature in January, 1839, concerning a bill to charter a bank of the Louisville, Cincinnati & Charleston Railroad Company [Clay to Brooke, August 28, 1838]. Henry Clay, Jr., spoke in reply to John Pope "in a manner highly creditable to himself, and satisfactory to the friends of the Bank"; however, the bill was defeated. This is probably the "cause" to which Clay refers. Lexington *Observer & Kentucky Reporter*, January 19, 30, 1839.

Remark in Senate, February 15, 1839. Presents memorial from New Orleans citizens "praying redress for injuries committed by the Mexican Government, and protesting against the convention lately agreed to for arbitrating the differences between the two Governments." *Cong. Globe,* 25 Cong., 3 Sess., 185.

A convention between the United States and Mexico, providing for a settlement of all claims by an arbitrator chosen by the King of Prussia, had been signed in Washington on September 11, 1838. Because of some misunderstanding, Mexico did not ratify the convention in the time agreed upon. A new convention for that purpose was thus signed on April 11, 1839. It created a board, composed of two commissioners on each side, and an umpire appointed by the King of Prussia. The arbitrators finally began their sessions in 1840. For the convention, see Parry, *Treaty Series,* 88:397-406. For the history of the claims convention, see Rives, *The United States and Mexico,* 417-44, espec. 431.

The petition Clay presented from citizens in New Orleans protested the submitting of claims against Mexico to the arbitration of an "European despot," opposed a renewal of the September, 1838 convention, and urged the United States to take prompt action to coerce Mexico into settling the claims. The petition is printed in *House Exec. Doc.* 197, 25 Cong., 3 Sess., pp. 1-2.

From PETER B. PORTER Albany, N.Y., February 16, 1839

I received your favour of the 6th[1] on my return from the Springs, four days ago, but thought best to defer answering it until the eve of my departure for home, that I might be able to give you what little political information I might collect during my short stay here, which I will now do, as I propose to leave here to-morrow morning.

And first in regard to your great abolition speech—[2] for it is indeed a great lucid, & constitutional explanation of that troublesome & exciting subject as well as a patriotic expostulation in regard to the dangers that surround it; and I think it will redound as much to your fame as any one you ever delivered. I rejoiced to see it myself, not only because I thought some great effort of this kind necessary to save the country from disunion & civil war into which the doctrines of those crazy men are leading us, but because I think it will on the whole add to your personal popularity. As regards the South & Southwest, it cannot fail to place you on high ground; and I am of opinion that it will not essentially injure your prospects in the North. I am glad to see that the whig papers in this State—& especially those in the city of New York, of which I entertained some fears, speak in high commendation of it, with the exception of the [New York] "American," which I believe has thus far been mute. Indeed I have heard but one single whig politician of any standing speak unfavorably of it—and his objections are not to its merits, but its expediency.

That you are the preferred candidate of a decided majority of the Whigs of this State, as well as of the members of the present Legislature, I am as fully satisfied as I ever have been—and yet that they should so long abstain from giving any public demonstration of this preference must appear strange to our friends abroad, who do not understand the complicated machinery, with which the politics of this State have been managed for some years past. It was the wish of the old uncontaminated, straight-going whigs, both of the last & of the present Legislature, to come forward openly & promptly & nominate you.[3] But they have been & still are deterred from doing so by the entreaties & remonstrances of the politicians, calling themselves Whigs, of a somewhat different complection, and who think that no political victory is worth achieving, if not gained by strategem.

A year ago, I thought that the Anti-Masons of this State would go, pretty much in a body, for Gen. Harrison, & that most of the friends of Mr. Webster, after finding their candidate impracticable would resort to your standard. The aspect of things is however now changed. I find that a good many of Mr. Webster's friends, associating themselves probably with the abolitionists and a portion of the Anti-Masons will make an effort for Gen. Harrison—while on the other hand many of the Anti-Masons will go with you.[4]

The Governor [William H. Seward] & Thurlow Weed (who at this moment is decidedly the most important man, politically speaking, in the State) are not only friendly to your election, but warmly & zealously so—but they deem it inexpedient to make public declarations of their preference at this time. From conversations which I & my friends have recently had with our new Secretary of State and Comptroller, Spencer & Cook,[5] both leading Anti-Masons, I have every reason to believe that they will also support you in preference to any other candidate. But all these gentlemen *want time*, and express a conviction that if an opportunity is afforded them to counsel & arrange with their respective friends, they can bring a much larger force into the field than if compelled to act at once. This consideration must account to you for the apparent inactivity among your old friends at this place.

I have had an interview with Mr. Weed this evening, and the following arrangement in respect to the presidential election, was proposed—and which, upon the supposition that we represented, as we think we did in the main, the view of our respective friends, will probably be carried into execution—it is this.

That at some proper time during the present session there shall be a caucus of the whig members of the Legislature, at which they shall resolve—1st. To recommend, or concur in the project of a national Convention to be held, as proposed, in December next; and to pledge themselves to the support of the candidate they may nominate. 2nd. To appoint two Senatorial delegates to the convention (say D.B. Ogden & myself). 3rd. To provide for the election of the remaining delegates by congressional districts.

The result will probably be that some half a dozen delegates will be chosen favourable to the election of Gen. Harrison, and the remaining thirty odd in favour of yourself.[6]

It would be very desirable to send to the convention the whole force of the State *undivided.* But there were difficulties attending this course which could not be well surmounted, As the result would have been to give the whole vote of the State to you, there might be difficulty in persuading the friends of Gen. H[arrison]. into the arrangement, or into a support of the nomination after it is made by the convention, and on the whole, I am inclined to think that course now proposed is the best.

I write this late at night & in haste, preparatory to starting for home in the morning, where I hope to hear from you soon. I must go to New York in April, & shall probably be here again before the Legislature adjourns. I shall certainly endeavour to be here if I think my presence can be of any public use.

I beg you to be cautious about shewing this letter, as if *some* of our members were to ascertain its contents they might, by writing to their friends here, blow Weed & myself up.

I spent an hour to-day with Judge [Ambrose] Spencer who is warmly your friend & will probably write to you soon. [Albert H.] Tracy, who was opposed to Mr. Talmage's [*sic*, Nathaniel P. Tallmadge] election,[7] in expectation that he would get the place himself, is now writing articles in the "Buffalo Commercial Advertizer" which are faithfully copied into the [Albany] "Argus" inviting & urging Mr. Talmage to decline the appointment in order that a whig may be appointed & the office not left vacant. Judge Spencer begged me to write to Mr. T. & request him to do no such thing. I will write if I have time; but surely it would be superfluous to caution him against embarrassing the movements of his Whig friends, by declining, or in any way interfering with an appointment which he has never solicited from them. *The Whigs do not wish him to decline.*

I am just informed that Charles King has come out against your speech, but I have not read his article,[8] nor do I believe that it will do you any injury.

Copy. InHi. Letter marked "(Confidential)." 1. Probably Clay to Porter, Feb. 5, 1839. 2. Speech in Senate, Feb. 7, 1839. 3. Porter to Clay, Nov. 14 and Dec. 30, 1837. 4. Clay to Otis, Dec. 13, 1838. 5. John C. Spencer and Bates Cook. 6. For the June, 1839, caucus of the Whigs in the New York legislature, the subsequent choice of delegates from that state to the Harrisburg convention, and the failure of the caucus to endorse a specific presidential candidate, see Porter to Clay, Nov. 14 and Dec. 30, 1837. Although not a delegate himself to the Whig national convention, Thurlow Weed attended and directed New York's delegates from the sidelines, attempting with the assistance of New York Governor William Henry Seward to secure the nomination for Winfield Scott. Of the New York delegates at Harrisburg, 20 were for Scott, 10 for Clay, and 2 for Harrison. When Weed concluded that Scott could not be nominated, he formed an alliance with Thaddeus Stevens of Pa. to nominate Harrison. Gunderson, *The Log-Cabin Campaign*, 58-62; Van Deusen, *William Henry Seward*, 61-62; Fawn M. Brodie, *Thaddeus Stevens, Scourge of the South* (New York, 1959), 82-83. 7. Clay to Spencer, Dec. 15, 1838. 8. In the New York *American*, which he owned and edited.

DRAFT OF SPEECH IN SENATE

Washington, *ca.* February 18, 1839

I have taken no part in the debate of which this bill has been the occasion,[1] and it is not now my purpose to trespass long upon the time of the Senate. I have prefered to listen to and profit by what has been so well said by other Senators, in opposition to this measure.[2] I think they have shewn that it is totally inefficient either for the settlement or reconquest of East Florida. You cannot get the men, whom it invites, to enter the Country which has been the seat of War; and, if you could, it would be at an enormous expence, unjustified by any object which they could possibly accomplish. The bill is another in that series of experiments, by which, in these late years, this Country has been so much afflicted; and if it passes its only operation will be to supply fresh aliment to speculation in the public domain.

This Florida War, Mr. President, is a subject on which no American Citizen can look but with feelings of surprize disappointment and mortification. It has been a War between a civilized nation of fifteen millions of people, on the one side, and some remnants of Savage tribes, not amounting to ten thousand, men, women and children, on the other. It has been carried on, in our behalf, under the direction of two Presidents of the U.S. two [*sic,* three] Secretaries of War, four Major Generals,[3] and, from first to last, not less, I believe, than fifty thousand troops of all descriptions. It has already cost about twenty five millions of dollars—a sum equal to the ascertained cost of the seven years Wars of Frederick the great, waged against all Europe and five times as much as was given for all Florida, when ceded by Spain to the U. States. The extent of the sacrifice of human life, in battle, or from disease, incident to a deleterious climate, is not certainly known; but it may be safely stated to be of a greater number than all the Indian warriors together with whom we have been contending. The War has lasted during the period of four years; and, instead of having expelled the Indians, which was its original object, we find our own people expelled and compelled to fly from the Country.

The Executive has been hitherto denied by Congress nothing which it has asked to prosecute the War with vigor and bring it to a successful termination. The treasure of the Nation has been poured out in copious streams, and its whole force has been at the command of the President. If there has been any neglect of duty on the part of Congress, it has been in its readiness to grant all the means asked for by the Executive, from time to time, with but little consideration, and without any investigation into the causes or conduct of this inglorious War.

It is impossible, Mr. President, to resist the conviction that there has been in the management of this War gross and culpable misconduct. When we consider the vast disparity in the power of the Belligerents, the immense force and means employed, the duration of the contest, and its actual results, we can arrive at no other conclusion. On whom the blame rests I do not undertake to say. That can be best ascertained by a careful & thorough investigation, too long delayed, which cannot be too soon made.

But, Sir, I should not have risen at all on this occasion, if I had not seen a statement in the public prints that an order had been sent to Cuba for the purchase of Blood hounds to be employed in this War.[4] This statement has some countenance from a dark & ambiguous intimation in the Report of the Secy. of War [Joel R. Poinsett] of the necessity of employing "other means than those hitherto tried." I hope there is no foundation. . . . [Remainder of the manuscript is missing.]

AD, draft fragment. DLC-TJC (DNA, M212, R10). The photocopy of this document is improperly placed with 1817-18 materials on Reel 10. While undated, the date assigned here by the editors is likely Feb. 18 or 19, 1839. See *Cong. Globe*, 25 Cong., 3 Sess., Appendix, 233, and *Cong. Globe*, 25 Cong., 3 Sess., 194. The first of these two citations (Sen. Thomas H. Benton's opening remark in his speech of Feb. 18, in reply to points on the Florida bill earlier made by Clay), suggests that Clay spoke against this bill on or before Feb. 18; the second suggests the possibility of a Feb. 19 date, since it was on that day that Clay is recorded in the *Cong. Globe* as participating in "an animated discussion" in which he "opposed" the armed occupation and settlement of Florida. The Florida bill passed 25 to 18 on Feb. 19, 1839, Clay voting nay. 1. For the legislative history of the bill providing for the armed occupation and settlement of Florida, see *Cong. Globe*, 25 Cong., 3 Sess., 89, 163, 171, 191, 194; *ibid.*, Appendix, 162-66, 233-34. The House did not act on it in the 25th Congress, 3rd Session. An armed occupation bill did not pass until 1842, by which time only slightly more than 300 Seminoles remained in Florida. See also Clay to Hale, Jan. 7, 1838, and Mahon, *Second Seminole War*, 308-15, 318, 326. 2. Senators Thomas H. Benton (Mo.) and Lewis F. Linn (Mo.). 3. Andrew Jackson,

Martin Van Buren, Secretaries Lewis Cass, Benjamin F. Butler, Joel R. Poinsett, and Major Generals Alexander Macomb, Winfield Scott, Richard K. Call, and Thomas S. Jesup. 4. The use of bloodhounds to track Indians in the swamps of Florida had been considered by General Jesup as early as 1837. In 1838 Sec. of War Poinsett authorized General Zachary Taylor to procure some dogs, but he did not do so. Subsequently, the Florida territorial government purchased three bloodhounds in Cuba, and on Jan. 27, 1840, Territorial Gov. Robert R. Reid offered the dogs to the army. Gen. Taylor accepted two of them on trial; but, when Florida billed him for $2,429.52, he declined to pay, saying the dogs had failed their tests. The importation of the hounds created a stir in Congress, especially among abolitionists who claimed they had been brought in to track down runaway slaves. Mahon, *Second Seminole War*, 265-67.

To HARRISON G. OTIS Washington, February 18, 1839

I received your favors of the 11h. and 12h. with their respective enclosures, for which I thank you. The [Boston] Atlas has taken another direction, I observe.[1] This I presume is the result of information from this place; and perhaps it will be wisest hereafter to take no further notice of its past aberrations. That which was handed to you by Mr. Armstrong (to whom I will thank you to present my best respects) was natural & appropriate.[2]

Have you seen the late analysis of the A. Masonic Convention, first published I believe in the U.S. Gazette? It strips that proceeding of all importance.[3]

I have not yet learnt that Mr. Webster, since his arrival here, has "defined his present position;" but I presume he will do this before the close of the Session.

From all quarters, the most gratifying intelligence is received as to my future prospects. I think now that the whole of the Southern & S.W. States will be represented in the Nat. Convention.[4]

I sent you a Copy of the Abolition Speech.[5] Its reception at the North, as far as I can judge, has exceeded my most sanguine anticipations. In other sections it will of course be well received, and I hope it will do good every where.

Excuse the brevity with which I am compelled to write....

ALS. MHi. 1. Otis to Clay, Sept. 14, 1838. 2. Reference obscure. 3. Clay to Otis, Dec. 13, 1838. 4. Arkansas, Georgia, South Carolina, and Tennessee did not send delegates to the Whig national nominating convention in Harrisburg, Pa., Dec. 4-7, 1839. McKee, *National . . . Popular and Electoral Vote*, 42-43. 5. Speech in Senate, Feb. 7, 1839.

Remark in Senate, February 18, 1839. Moves that the Senate adjourn in order to prevent the bill "more effectually to secure the public money in the hands of officers of and agents of the Government, and to punish defaulters," as amended, from being engrossed for a third reading. Motion defeated. *Cong. Globe*, 25 Cong., 3 Sess., 191.

On January 30, 1839, Sen. Silas Wright (N.Y.) had introduced this bill which was referred to the Committee on Finance and ordered to be printed. It was reported from the Finance Committee with amendments on February 8, 1839. On February 18, Sen. William C. Rives (Va.) proposed an amendment to it which struck out everything following the enacting clause and substituted ten new sections. These had to do with tightly regulating the collecting, securing, accounting for, and depositing of customhouse receipts; and for the general administration of customhouse funds and personnel [Remark in Senate, December 13, 1838; also *Cong. Globe*, 25 Cong., 3 Sess., 7]. The Rives amendment was defeated 15 to 27 with Clay voting in favor. Wright's version then passed the Senate 28 to 15 with

Clay voting nay [Remark in Senate, February 21, 1839]. It did not, however, pass the House. U.S. Sen., *Journal*, 25 Cong., 3 Sess., 175, 213, 233, 250, 261. For the wording of Rives's amendment, see *ibid.*, 246-50.

Remark in Senate, February 21, 1839. Moves to recommit to the Committee on Finance the administration's bill "more effectually to secure the public money" so that the substitute bill proposed by Sen. William C. Rives (Va.) can be amended into it [Remark in Senate, February 18, 1839]. Motion defeated, 25 to 16. The measure was then passed 28 to 15, Clay voting nay. *Cong. Globe*, 25 Cong., 3 Sess., 197.

To ALEXANDER HAMILTON Washington, February 24, 1839

I recd. your favor of the 22d. and hasten to say that with great confidence in your judgment, and entire conviction of the fidelity of your attachment, I nevertheless cannot consent to make the visit to your City and the tour you recommend. I could not do it without violating open and repeated pledges which I have made; and I must add, in all frankness, that I would not enter upon electioneering tours throughout the U. S. if I were perfectly sure that they would secure the prize of the Presidency. If, as you state, the cause of another is gaining, and rapidly gaining, be it so, I must acquiesce. I hope that my friends will not think of transmitting the invitation to which you refer, as I should be compelled to decline it.

My abolition Speech was made, after full deliberation.[1] I expected it would enrage the Ultra's more than ever against me, and I have not been disappointed. On the other hand, its reception at the North has far exceeded my most sanguine anticipations.

We are in a state of great anxiety about affairs in Maine. I hope that we shall not be precipitated into War unprepared and unexpected; but there is reason to apprehend it.[2] P.S. I wrote to Mr. Selden[3] expressing my regret that I could not visit the City

ALS. DLC-HC (DNA, M212, R21). 1. Speech in Senate, Feb. 7, 1839. 2. A civil posse, led by land agent Rufus McIntire, was sent out by the Maine government from Bangor to the Aroostook area during the first week in Feb., 1839. The mission of the expedition was to expel Canadian trespassers who were reportedly stealing timber. On Feb. 12 McIntire was captured by a group of "trespassers" and jailed at Fredericton. This action prompted the Maine government to send reinforcements to Aroostook. Meanwhile, the lieutenant-governor of New Brunswick issued a proclamation for volunteers for the provincial forces and denounced the posse's action as an invasion. The so-called "Aroostook War" that ensued greatly exacerbated tensions between the United States and Great Britain and increased the fear of war with Britain. In a message to Congress on Feb. 26 [*MPP*, 3:516-20], Van Buren admitted the rights of Maine but urged the state not to resort to arms. The following day the Senate Foreign Relations Committee proposed that both Maine and New Brunswick withdraw their troops. Sec. of State John Forsyth and British minister to the U.S., Henry S. Fox, agreed. Peace was restored in the region largely through the efforts of Gen. Winfield Scott whom Van Buren sent to Maine to pacify the belligerents. By the end of March, 1839, Scott had persuaded both the Maine and New Brunswick governments to withdraw their troops, and the Aroostook War was ended. See David Lowenthal, "The Maine Press and the Aroostook War," *CHR* (Dec., 1951), 32:315-36; Burrage, *Maine in the Northeastern Boundary Controversy*, 257-75; Elliott, *Winfield Scott*, 355-56. 3. Probably Dudley Selden.

To PETER B. PORTER Washington, February 24, 1839

I recd. your favor of the 16h. and was extremely glad to find that you entertained sentiments of such decided approbation of my Abolition Speech.[1] It has been gratifying to me to receive from the North, in every direction, corresponding testimonials, without exception other than among the Ultra-abolitionists. The reception of the Speech, judging from what I have seen and heard far exceeds in enthusiasm any anticipation I had made.

Your account of the state of things at Albany, and the contemplated arrangements, in regard to the Presidential election, is very satisfactory. The only disadvantage in the omission of the Legislature to signify its preference, is that misrepresentations are made as to the actual state of things existing there.[2] For example, Mr. Webster asserts that neither at the last nor in the present Assembly was or is there a majority of the Whigs for me, but on the contrary a very inconsiderable number. He has been endeavoring to make impressions to that effect. If an open expression of preference were made the truth would be known. This is however only a temporary disadvantage. The general current is again setting strongly in my favor, and, unless I am deceived, before autumn not a doubt will remain as to the choice of the Opposition.

David B. Ogden[3] has been evidently influenced by Mr. Webster in the Harrison direction, whether so strongly as to prevent his yielding to more true convictions I am not able to say. But I thought it right to apprize you of this, so that it might be considered whether it would not be expedient to appoint some other person.

We are in a state of great anxiety here about the Maine difficulties.[4] The apprehension is that we may be drawn into a War with G. Britain unprepared, and when no part of the Nation has anticipated the event. The President will send a message tomorrow or the next day on the subject to Congress.[5] Genl. [Winfield] Scott is here waiting instructions to proceed to the theatre of operations. I am afraid that this unfortunate state of things may lead to fresh Patriot incursions into Canada.

ALS. NBuHi. 1. Speech in Senate, Feb. 7, 1839. 2. Porter to Clay, Feb. 16, 1839; also Porter to Clay, Nov. 14 and Dec. 30, 1837. 3. Porter to Clay, Dec. 15, 1837 and Feb. 16, 1839. Ogden was appointed to serve as a N.Y. City delegate to the Whig national nominating convention in Harrisburg in Dec., 1839. 4. Clay to Hamilton, Feb. 24, 1839. 5. For Van Buren's message to Congress on the Maine boundary crisis, dated Feb. 26, 1839, see *Cong. Globe*, 25 Cong., 3 Sess., 209-10.

To AMBROSE SPENCER Washington, February 25, 1839

The approbation expressed in your friendly letter of the 18h. of the Speech on Abolitionism[1] could have come from no one, with more satisfaction and gratification to me. If I am to credit the favorable accounts which I receive from all quarters it will do good to the Country, and if it does I shall be happy.

The dissent from my opinion as to this District, which you express, does not surprize me nor detract from the pleasure I derived from the perusal of your letter. I do admit the power of Congress, to abolish Slavery here, but think that it ought not to be exercised whilst it remains in the two adjacent States, because it was not within the contemplation of the parties at the time of the cession, which was made for a specified and different purpose.[2]

After all, there is much exaggeration about the shocking spectacles of gangs of manacled slaves &c in this City. There may be such exhibitions but if there be they are of rare occurrence. After 32 years visiting this City, I do not recollect to have ever witnessed them.

We are all very anxious here about the North Eastern question[3] It will be deplorable if any indiscretion of one State shall be able to drag the other 25 into War not only without their consent but without preparation.

Judging from what I see at this distance, our friends at Albany are conducting the Legislative Campaign with sound judgment.[4] P.S. Do me the favor to present my respects to your son J[ohn]. C. Spencer Esq and say to him that I am glad to see him again in the public service.[5]

ALS. DLC-HC (DNA, M212, R5). Addressed to Spencer in Albany, N.Y. 1. Speech in Senate, Feb. 7, 1839 2. Ibid.; also Comment in Senate, Dec. 18, 1837. 3. Clay to Hamilton, Feb. 24, 1839. 4. Porter to Clay, Feb. 16, 1839; also *ibid.*, Nov. 14 and Dec. 30, 1837; Clay to Porter, Feb. 24, 1839. 5. John C. Spencer had recently become New York's secretary of state. *DAB*.

Comment in Senate, February 26, 1839. Notes that he has had "some official connection" with the Northeast boundary problem [7:666-67, 729-30] in the past and would like to make a "few observations" on it. Is gratified by the "pacific and moderate tone" of the president's message of this day and hopes war with Great Britain can be averted [Clay to Hamilton, February 24, 1839]. Points out, however, that Maine could not have a "clearer and more absolute right to the disputed territory than she already has," and asserts that he is "ready to resort to the military force of the country" if and when diplomacy proves incapable of securing to Maine and the United States "what rightfully belonged to them." On the other hand, he "could not consent, on such a solemn occasion as that of a war with a foreign Power, or on any other occasion, that the will of one of the twenty-six members of the Confederacy should control the entire Union, or that one should draw the entire Union, without their consent, into a war with a foreign Power." Believes, also, that the "present difficulties might possibly have been avoided" had Maine informed either President Van Buren or the government of New Brunswick of its decision to expel Canadian "intruders and trespassers" from the disputed territory and otherwise establish its jurisdiction there by force. Holds, further, that Britain has no claim whatever to jurisdiction over unoccupied portions of the disputed territory or over the occupied portions presently in dispute. Explains that under the pertinent clause of the Anglo-American treaty of 1783, the status of the occupied border territory was arranged so that, Clay asserts, "jurisdiction was to remain and be maintained as it was, both as regarded the holding of jurisdiction and the possession of property, and neither party was to make any advances to strengthen or increase their jurisdiction or possession." Criticizes the British for having recently marched a large military force through territory claimed by the United States and the lameness of their excuse for doing so. Argues that the British decision to give prior notice of this deployment to the United States, and the apology extended the U.S. for having to do it, reveals the weakness of their subsequent contention that they are entitled to exclusive jurisdiction in the disputed territory. At that time, Clay recalls, he "had insisted that this notice and apology by Great Britain was not sufficient, and that she ought first to have asked and obtained the direct and express consent of the United States before marching her troops over the disputed territory." Suggests that the United States take advantage of Britain's "late troubles in her American [Canadian] provinces [Porter to Clay, December 15, 1837]," noting that it is "evidently the true policy of the United States to press her at such a moment" for a "satisfactory explanation" of her aggressive behavior in disputed Northeastern borderlands. Urges a peaceful settlement of the question while reasserting his readiness "at whatever price, to secure the peace of the country, and maintain the rights of Maine to her jurisdiction and territory." *Cong. Globe*, 25 Cong., 3 Sess., Appendix, 212-13. For the "Aroostook War" of 1839 over Maine-New Brunswick boundary, see Clay to Hamilton, February 24, 1839.

U.S. Minister to Great Britain Andrew Stevenson noted on April 5, 1839, in a letter to Secretary of State John Forsyth that Lord Palmerston, British secretary of state for foreign affairs, had in December, 1837, admitted in "a conversation which he held with me" that the British "did not feel themselves at liberty to march Troops across the Territory from New Brunswick to Canada without a previous understanding with the United States' Government on the subject." However, there had been such troop movements on various occasions in 1838 and early 1839. It is not known to which one of these incidents Clay here refers. William R. Manning, *Diplomatic Correspondence of the United States, Canadian Relations, 1784-1860*, 4 vols. (Washington, 1940-45), 3:501; Washington *Daily National Intelligencer*, January 19, 1839; J. Mackay Hitsman, *Safeguarding Canada, 1763-1871* (Toronto, 1968), 134-35.

Comment in Senate, March 1, 1839. Announces his support of four resolutions on the Maine-New Brunswick boundary crisis [Clay to Hamilton, February 24, 1839; Comment in Senate, February 26, 1839] presented by the Committee on Foreign Relations on February 28 in response to President Van Buren's messages of February 26 and 27, 1839 [Clay to Porter, February 24, 1839]. Specifically, these resolutions (1) denied the existence of any past Anglo-American "explicit agreement" supporting British territorial claims of "exclusive jurisdiction" in the border area; (2) supported the action of Maine in having expelled from the disputed area "lawless trespassers" engaged in cutting timber there; (3) vowed retaliatory military operations if Britain moved troops into the disputed territory; and (4) resolved that should Britain refrain from the use of force and should Maine "determine to settle the controversy for herself by force, the adjustment of which is intrusted, under the Constitution, to the Federal Government, in such an event there will be no obligation imposed on that Government to sustain her by military aid." Says he particularly supports the committee's fourth resolution because he does not want Maine, in an act of recklessness, to plunge the other twenty-five states into a war. Repeats the opinion he expressed on February 26 that the U.S. government had missed an opportunity "to press this matter" with Britain "when the disturbances in Canada arose [Porter to Clay, December 15, 1837; Comment in Senate, January 5, 1838]." Explains that "the Executive Government seems to have been sleeping, instead of availing itself of the difficulties in the British provinces; and, worse than that, instead of our profiting by the Canada disturbances, or availing ourselves of any advantages from them whatever, the whole profit of them has been derived from Great Britain. And how is it that Great Britain has taken advantage of the insurrection in Canada? She has taken the opportunity to throw into her provinces a force of from fifteen to thirty thousand men; and under what pretext? That they were to suppress insurrection. But if there had been peace there, and the United States had seen regiment after regiment and corps after corps thus thrown into the provinces, would we not have increased our military means? But Great Britain, thus increasing her forces under cover of silencing Canada, is now ready for war, and may at once, with advantage, enter into hostilities with us, while our Government, instead of pressing the negotiation, has been asleep, and there has been no increase of the means on our part to meet the increased dangers of war." Asserts, further, that his "voice is for peace" if it can be maintained consistent with the honor and interests of the nation. Adds, however, that "It would be a sorry spectacle to see two kindred nations rushing into a state of war, without its duration being foreseen, for the sake of five or six millions of waste land, the whole of which would not be worth the expense of such a war for two or three months. Yet I must say that, holding the opinion that Great Britain has not the shadow of a claim to this territory, and that the clear right of Maine has been already too long withheld from her, if we now forbear sufficiently, and if at the termination of the negotiation we have no resource left but the final resort of nations, I repeat we shall be furnished with the contingency of a just war, which will be felt to be so by the people of the United States, and will be approved by Heaven; and in such a war I do not fear but that our country will come out of it gloriously and triumphantly, as it always has done in its contests with that power."

Rejoins the debate later in the day, arguing that there are two sides to the Maine-New Brunswick boundary controversy. Notes that "Great Britain has not invaded this territory"; whereas, "Maine has invaded it, with all the circumstance and pomp of war." Asks: "can a State make war? Yes she can, in fact; and I wish she may not be at war at this moment. Can we deny the fact that ten thousand militia, with arms in their hands, and sent by Maine upon Frederickton [*sic*, Fredericton], would be war upon New Brunswick? Who can deny it? It is not a constitutional, legitimate war; but it is war *ipso facto*, and it is against that that I wish the Legislature and the country to guard." Concludes, therefore, that he opposes the amendment of Sen. Richard M. Young's (Ill.) (supported vigorously by Sen. Webster) to the fourth resolution which would strike out the clause withholding military aid from Maine and substitute for it the following language: "And leave the ultimate adjustment of her [Maine's] grievances to the Government of the United States, to which it rightfully and constitutionally belongs." This amendment was adopted, 24 to 21, Clay voting nay. The first three resolutions, considered together, were then passed 44 to 1; resolution four, as amended, was adopted unanimously. *Cong. Globe*, 25 Cong., 3 Sess., 216; *ibid.*, Appendix, 309-10, 315-16. For Van Buren's messages of February 26 and 27, 1839, see *MPP*, 3:516-21.

To [JOSEPH] GALES & [WILLIAM W.] SEATON Washington, March 2, 1839

In the speech which I addressed to the Senate on the subject of abolition petitions [Speech in Senate, February 7, 1839], I ascribed to Dr. [Benjamin] Franklin the authorship of the law passed by the State of Pennsylvania in 1780 for the gradual emancipation of slaves. Such was the impression in my mind; but, from a communication which I have since received, I believe that the measure originated with another distinguished citizen of Pennsylvania, the late honorable George Bryan.[1]

I will thank you to make this correction, unimportant in respect to the use I made of the fact, but otherwise just and proper.

Copy. Printed in Washington *Daily National Intelligencer*, March 4, 1839. 1. For Bryan, Pennsylvania jurist and politician, see *DAB*.

From Joseph Richardson, Hingham, Mass., March 4, 1839. Reports that Clay's speech on the abolitionists [Speech in Senate, February 7, 1839] "gave great satisfaction" to his friends "in this part of our Union." Thinks the American Colonization Society should circulate "tens of thousands of that speech" in pamphlet form, since "Like antimasonry, abolitionism may have some effect on the next presidential election." Believes that the war in Florida against the Seminoles [Clay to Hale, January 7, 1838] and the Maine-New Brunswick boundary crisis [Clay to Hamilton, February 24, 1839; Comment in Senate, February 26, 1839], both of which are "embarrassments" to the Van Buren administration, will also affect the result of the coming presidential election in such manner as to "produce a political change." ALS. ViHi. Printed in *VMHB* (October, 1947), 55:315-16. Enclosed in Clay to Caldwell, March 18, 1839, below. For Richardson, see 7:67 and *BDAC*.

To JAMES CALDWELL Lexington, March 18, 1839

Your favor addressed to me at Washn. has been received by me here. I left that City under great confidence that we shall displace the present Administration; and entirely satisfied with the condition of my own personal interests. At the commencement there was some discouragement among some of my friends; but it was before the close of it entirely dissipated. The general conviction was that my cause was constantly gaining strength, and that I should certainly receive the nomination of the Nat. Convention.[1]

The propriety of the re-election of Mr. [William C.] Rives struck me as it did you.[2] Altho' it was an affair in which I could not interfere, I regretted extremely the state of things at Richmond. Your elections, now just at hand, will attract great attention.[3] Should they terminate favorably to Mr. Rives & the opposition, Mr. V. Buren will hardly be able to make a shew of fight.

I am happy to inform you that the reception, at the North of my Abolition Speech,[4] has been [received] with general approbation, to an extent far exceeding my most sanguine anticipations. At the South & S. West it will of course be acceptable.

I transmit enclosed one of many letters[5] that I have recd. from the North.... P.S. You may destroy the enclosed.

ALS. ViHi. Printed in *VMHB* (Oct., 1947), 55:314-15. Addressed to Caldwell at White Sulphur Springs, Va. (W.Va.). 1. Porter to Clay, Nov. 14 and Dec. 30, 1837. 2. Clay to Brooke, August 28 and Dec. 20, 1838. 3. In the 1839 state elections in Virginia, the Whigs won 12 seats in the state senate to 3 for the Conservative Democrats and 17 for the regular (Van Buren) Democrats. In the Virginia house, Whigs won 68 seats to 10 for the Conservatives and 56 for the Democrats. In elections for the U.S. House, the Democrats won 12 seats to 7 for the Whigs and 2 for the Conservatives. *Niles' Register* (June 15, 1839), 56:241. See also Clay to Brooke, April 2, 1839; and Braverman, "The Economic and Political Background of the Conservative Revolt in Virginia," *VMHB* (April, 1952), 60:285-86. The *Guide to U.S. Elections*, 572, groups the Virginia Conservatives with the Whigs. David Campbell, a Democrat, was reelected governor of Virginia in 1839. *BDGUS*, 4:1638-39. For the Virginia senatorial race, see Clay to Brooke, August 28 and Dec. 20, 1838. 4. Speech in Senate, Feb. 7, 1839. 5. Richardson to Clay, March 4, 1839.

From Gerrit Smith, Peterboro, N.Y., March 21, 1839. Writes in response to Clay's comments at the annual meeting of the American Colonization Society in Washington on December 15, 1835. On that occasion Clay focused on an anti-slavery speech Smith had delivered the previous autumn. In that speech, Smith recalls, "You distinctly take the ground, that slavery is a subject not open to general discussion." Charges specifically that "it is to this doctrine of non-discussion, which you and others put forth, that the North is indebted for her pro-slavery mobs, and the South for her pro-slavery Lynchings. The declarations of such men as Henry Clay and John C. Calhoun, that slavery is a question not to be discussed, are a license to mobs to burn up halls and break up abolition meetings, and destroy abolition presses, and murder abolition editors."

But it is Clay's "celebrated speech on the subject of slavery [Speech in Senate, February 7, 1839]" to which he wishes principally to respond in this letter. Assures the Kentucky senator at the outset that he writes "in accordance with . . . the truth of Jesus Christ," and apologizes to his colleagues in the American Anti-Slavery Society for "the great criminality of my long continuance in the [American] Colonization Society." Asserts that "Its avowed doctrine is, that, unless emancipation be accompanied by expatriation, perpetual slavery is to be preferred to it." Therefore, "not to oppose that Society, would be the greatest treachery to our holy religion, which requires immediate and unconditional repentance of sin. Not to oppose it, would be to uphold slavery. Not to oppose it, would be to abandon the [American] Anti-Slavery Society."

Proceeds to examine, attack, and refute, one by one, at considerable length, all of the anti-abolitionist points made by Clay in his February 7 speech in the Senate. Commences with the assertion that Clay's earlier support of the right of petition for the abolition of slavery has weakened; that he wrongly questions the power of Congress, under the commerce clause of the Constitution, to abolish both the international and interstate slave trade; and that he favors an increase in the number of slave states. Continues with the observation that Clay supports the proposition that Congress is powerless under the Constitution to prohibit slavery in new states entering the Union. Argues that Clay, in response to the anti-abolitionist attitudes of neighboring Virginia and Maryland, has retreated from his acceptance of the constitutional power of Congress to abolish slavery in the District of Columbia. Condemns his failure to see that the very existence of slavery in the United States is unconstitutional as well as his belief that slaves are private property and that such property is unassailable. Attacks Clay's view that both the high cost of compensated emancipation and the return of emancipated slaves to Africa render those alternatives impractical. Criticizes Clay's conviction that slavery is a sectional and states' rights issue in which the abolitionists have no more right to interfere than with the same issue in a foreign country. Notes, further, that Clay fails to see or chooses not to see that slavery is actually a cruel, tyrannical, immoral, inhuman, and, above all, sinful and unchristian institution, and criticizes his acceptance of the belief that black slaves are incapable of adapting their behavior to the moral and ethical standards of the civilized white man. Identifies as foolish Clay's confidence that the African colonization movement, designed to return free blacks to Africa, promises a solution to the racial problem. In addition, challenges Clay's beliefs that abolition and the abolitionists are confined entirely to the free states, that the abolitionists favor and seek the racial amalgamation of black emancipated slaves and white Northern workingmen, and that they conspire to reduce the wages of Northern white laborers by encouraging emancipated blacks to compete with them for jobs in the free states. Calls attention to Clay's mistaken view that there can be no question of emancipation because the federal government has no constitutional power to effect it and the South has no capability of absorbing into its social and economic structure some 3,000,000 former slaves.

Mainly, Smith attacks Clay for naively believing that the abolitionists are attempting to "stimulate the rage of the people of the free states against the people of the slave states" by publicizing "advertisements of fugitive slaves and slaves to be sold"; and for believing that abolitionists have no fear of civil war or dissolution of the Union if these acts become necessary to accomplish their aims. He also calls into question Clay's acceptance of the charge that the abolitionists have abandoned persuasion and appeal to reason as the means of accomplishing their goals and have turned instead to "the powers of the ballot box," the end result of which will bring them "to invoke finally the more potent powers of the bayonet." Takes particular exception to Clay's statement, made near the end of his February 7 speech, that "I [Clay] prefer the liberty of my own country to that of any other people, and the liberty of my own race to that of any other race."

Concludes with this advice to candidate Clay: That from the standpoint of his future political wealth, it is "Infinitely better, that you be honestly poor than dishonestly rich. Infinitely better to 'do justly' and be a Lazarus; than to become a Croesus, by clinging to and accumulating ill-gotten gains. Do you add to the fear of poverty, that of losing your honors—those which are anticipated, as well as those, which already deck your brow? Allow us to assure you, that it will be impossible for you to redeem 'Henry Clay, the statesman,' and 'Henry Clay, the orator,' or even 'Henry Clay, the President of the United States,' from the contempt of a slavery-loathing posterity, otherwise than by coupling with those designations the inexpressibly more honorable distinction of 'HENRY CLAY, THE EMANCIPATOR.' " Copy. Printed in pamphlet form as *Letter of Gerrit Smith to Hon. Henry Clay* (New York, 1839), 2-54. Smith had resigned from the American Colonization Society in 1835 and in so doing had paid off in a lump sum of $3,000 his earlier pledges to support various of its future activities. See Smith to Ralph R. Gurley, November 24, 1835, in *The African Repository and Colonial Journal* (January, 1836), 12:36-37. For Smith (1797-1874), New York abolitionist and later U.S. congressman, see *BDAC*. Smith's speech to which Clay referred in his comments to the American Colonization Society on December 15, 1835, was published under the title *The Crime of the Abolitionists. Speech in the Meeting of the New York Anti-Slavery Society, Held in Peterboro, October 22d, 1835.* N.p., 1835?

To HARRISON G. OTIS Lexington, March 22, 1839

Your obliging letter, transmitting a Copy of the Resolutions adopted at the late Legislative Convention of Massachusetts,[1] addressed to me at Washington, having reached that City after my departure from it, followed and was received by me here. I thank you for it. Although the resolution, respecting the Presidency, is susceptible of two interpretations, I think that since it repeats the expression of the *preferences* of the Convention, as announced the preceding year,[2] my friends ought to be satisfied with it. I am entirely so. Almost every day brings me fresh and strong evidence of the concentration of the opinions of the Whigs, throughout the Union, in a manner corresponding with the hopes and wishes of my friends. I am inclined to believe that, before the assembling of the Nation, there will be a degree of union upon this subject approximating to unanimity. I lamented to ascertain, prior to my departure from the City, more on his own than on my account, that Mr. Webster was endeavoring to turn the tide towards Genl Harrison.[3] He was not working very openly but very earnestly. I think he did not make the smallest advance towards his object. I understood that he spoke kindly but very despondingly of my pretensions. Indeed I was told that his tone was discouraging of the success of the Whig cause, under the banner either of Genl. Harrison or myself.

ALS. MHi. 1. Clay to Otis, Dec. 13, 1838. 2. Clay to Porter, March 4, 1838. 3. Clay to Otis, Dec. 13, 1838.

To FRANCIS T. BROOKE Lexington, April 2, 1839

I duly received your favor of the 13h. Ulto. and felt highly gratified with the favorable account of the state of public affairs in Virginia which it communicates. I must however retort upon you a charge that is often made against me, that I fear you are too sanguine. There seems to be making a prodigious effort on the side of the Administration, and I see no evidence of corresponding or counteracting exertions on the other side. Their late Convention will strengthen them,[1] because it is an organization of their party, and the members will return to their respective homes animated by the confidence and hopes inspired by their interchange of opinion and feeling. Where parties are nearly balanced, that which is disciplined and in a state of complete organization is almost sure to prevail over its adversary in the contest. I never was more perfectly convinced than I was in 1832 of the importance of a Convention, followed by a County & State Organization. In the autumn of that year, just before the Presidential election, the *young men* held a Convention in Lexington.[2] It was well attended, filled with the elite of the State. They made many stirring and eloquent Speeches, published an address to the State, put it into complete organization, by the appointment in all the Counties of large Committees of Vigilance & Correspondence, and returned home full of enthusiasm. The result was that Jackson was beaten by upwards of 7000 votes. If you could get a similar Conventicn of *young* men at Charlottesville or Staunton just before the election, I believe that it would be attended with a similar result.[3]

By the bye, is it possible that two of the Judges of the Court of Appeals attended and took part in the proceedings of the recent Convention, and that Judge Tucker presided? If it be true, I regard the fact as a strong mark of the degeneracy of the times.[4]

I have not enjoyed good health since my return home, from severe colds, but I am getting better and we have the prospect of an early and fine Spring. I found Mrs. Clay in her usual good health.

Is it possible that there will be no arrangement between Messrs Harvie and Botts, and that they will both persevere, with the certainty of both being defeated?[5] In such a state of things, the moral is with the declining party whichever it may be.

In Kentucky every thing looks fair. We may carry every Congressional district, and we may be defeated in three, I think not more.[6] From Tennessee[7] too, from Mississippi[8] & Louisiana,[9] I receive the most favorable accounts. . . .

ALS. DLC-HC (DNA, M212, R5). Printed in Colton, *Clay Correspondence*, 4:440-41. 1. The Virginia Democrats held a convention in Richmond on March 19-21, 1839. Henry St. George Tucker, president of the Virginia Court of Appeals, was chosen as its president. The purposes of the convention were to establish a campaign organization; to bring about a reconciliation of all Virginia Democrats, regular and Conservative; and to issue an address showing the merits of the policies of the Democrats over those of the Whigs. Richmond *Enquirer*, March 21, 23, 1839; Simms, *Rise of the Whigs in Virginia*, 135. 2. See 8:567-70. 3. Clay to Brooke, Dec. 20, 1838. 4. In addition to Tucker, Judges Richard E. Parker and Peter V. Daniel attended the Democratic convention in Richmond. Richmond *Enquirer*, March 21, April 6, 1839. 5. In the Richmond, Va., U.S. congressional district, John M. Botts and Gen. J.B. Harvie both sought the Whig nomination. Neither would agree to withdraw, but on April 10 the Richmond district Whigs met and nominated Botts by a majority of one vote over Harvie. Botts went on to win a seat in Congress, defeating the Democratic candidate by a vote of 1,459 to 1,251. Richmond *Enquirer*, March 14, April 11, 1839; *Guide to U.S. Elections*, 572. See also Clay to Caldwell, March 18, 1839. 6. Whigs won 10 U.S. House seats in the 1839 elections in Kentucky to 3 for the Democrats. *Guide to U.S. Elections*, 572. In the legislative elections of 1839, Whigs won 22 seats in the Kentucky senate to 16 for the Democrats. In the Kentucky state house of representatives, Whigs won approximately 62 seats to 38 for the Democrats. No gubernatorial election was held in 1839; however, on August 27 Gov. James Clark died, and Lt. Gov. Charles A. Wickliffe took the oath as governor, on Sept. 5. Frankfort *Commonwealth*, August 20, 27, 1839; Collins, *History of Kentucky*, 1:44. 7. Bell to Clay, May 21, 1839. 8. Clay evidently had been misinformed about the prospects of the Whig party in Mississippi. In the 1839 U.S. House elections in that state, Democrats won both seats; they also won an overwhelming majority in both houses of the state legislature. *Guide to U.S. Elections*, 572; Edwin A.

Miles, *Jacksonian Democracy in Mississippi* (Chapel Hill, 1960), 155. In the gubernatorial race in Mississippi, Alexander McNutt, a Democrat, defeated Edward Turner, a Whig, by a vote of 18,900 to 15,866. *BDGUS*, 2:807. 9. Possibly a reference to resolutions passed on March 19, 1839, by Whigs in the Louisiana legislature. These resolutions endorsed Clay for president. There were no state elections in Louisiana in 1839. Washington *Daily National Intelligencer*, March 30, 1839.

To J. GARLAND[1] Lexington, April 2, 1839

I have just received your letter of the 24h. Ulto. in which you request me to say, whether at any time you either intimated to me or to any of my friends, so far as came within my knowledge, that you would unite with the Whig party or support me for the Presidency, or that you were ever engaged in any negotiation or machination to unite or form a coalition between my friends and those of Mr. [William C.] Rives for the purpose of overthrowing the present administration.

If I were alone concerned in the imputations to which you refer, I certainly should take no notice whatever of them; but since, on your own account, you desire an answer from me to the above enquiries, in conformity with your request, I have no hesitation in saying, explicitly, that I never did learn from you, directly or indirectly, that you entertained any intention of uniting with the Whig party or of supporting me for the Presidency; that I never understood, and do not believe, that you ever communicated such a purpose to any of my friends; and that I have no knowledge, or belief, that you were ever engaged in any negotiation, or machination, to unite, or form a coalition, between my friends and those of Mr. Rives, for the purpose of overthrowing the present administration.

I have, on more than one occasion, heard some of my political friends express surprize and regret at the tenacity with which you generally adhered to the Administration.

ALS. DLC-HC (DNA, M212, R5). 1. Probably U.S. Rep. James Garland, Democrat, of Virginia. See *BDAC*.

To CHARLES HAMMOND Lexington, April 2, 1839

I perceive that the opinions and sentiments advanced by me in a Speech which I delivered to the Senate, on the subject of Abolition,[1] has not been so fortunate as to obtain your concurrence. I have seen only your remarks contained in one of your papers.[2] My copy of the [Cincinnati *Daily*] Gazette, which comes to this place, was not preserved by my family. As I can not doubt that your strictures are conceived in a spirit of fairness and liberality, I am very desirous to see the whole of them; and if you have and can furnish me with them in one collected form, or can send me the series in slips from your paper, you will very much oblige me.

ALS. InU. Letter marked "(Private)." 1. Speech in Senate, Feb. 7, 1839. 2. Hammond had written a series of editorials attacking Clay's speech, especially his argument that the Constitution granted Congress the power of "regulation, and not prohibition" of interstate commerce as applied to the slave trade. Just as Congress had already prohibited the external slave trade, it could also halt the interstate slave trade, Hammond asserted. He also criticized Clay's attack on the abolitionists in his Feb. 7 Senate speech. Nevertheless, Hammond praised Clay in an editorial on March 14 and endorsed him for president, saying that in pointing out the "grievious errors" in that speech, he had meant "no unkindness." Cincinnati *Daily Gazette*, March 7, 8, 11, 12, 14, 1839.

To George W. Morton, Lexington, April 9, 1839. Conveys to Morton a Lexington city lot jointly owned with his wife, Lucretia Hart Clay, fronting on High Street and Maxwell Street. Lists sale price at $5,000. Says the lot contains about five acres and was purchased by Clay on April 6, 1837, from James G. McKinney. ALS. KyU. Morton [2:96] at this time resided on the Winchester Road, five miles from Lexington. McKinney was mayor of Lexington and resided at "Pine Grove" on East High St. MacCabe, *Directory of the City of Lexington . . . 1838 & '39*, pp. 58, 130.

The 1837 transaction with McKinney is recorded in the Fayette County Court *Deed Book*, no. 13, p. 297. Clay had paid $3,000 for the property in 1837. For the indenture with McKinney and his wife Frances on April 6, 1837, see DS. DLC-TJC (DNA, M212, R18). See also, below, Clay to Erwin, April 10, 1839.

To NATHANIEL P. TALLMADGE Lexington, April 9, 1839

I transmit for your perusal the enclosed letter from Mr. [Robert P.] Letcher, whom you know, and who was the Speaker of our last [Kentucky] House of Representatives. You may destroy the letter. I send it to you for the purpose of your seeing what he states as to your standing in Kentucky. The Convention, at which he thinks you will be recommended, is to meet in Augt. and is to designate a Candidate for Govr.[,] Electors of P. and V.P. &c.[1] I have no doubt that the recommendation will be made.

If Mr. Letcher be right as to the present views of Mr. Calhoun, he is certainly the strangest fellow in the world. I heard, during the last Session, that he wanted to get back to the Whigs, but observed nothing in his public conduct that indicated such a wish. Of course, I presume, that nobody will attempt to make any bargain of any kind with him, if he wishes it.

Mr. [William C.] Rives's address to the People of Va. is marked with judgment and ability;[2] and I should hope would have great effect. His position now, in relation to Mr. V. Buren, can no longer be questioned.

I congratulate you on the pacific adjustment of affairs at the North East.[3]

We are looking out for the issue of the Connt. Election[4] and the Charter election in the City of N. York[5] with much interest

ALS. WHi. 1. The Kentucky Whig convention met at Harrodsburg on August 26, 1839. Thomas Metcalfe was chosen as its president. The Whigs nominated Robert P. Letcher and Manlius V. Thomson to run for governor and lieutenant governor, respectively, in August, 1840. The convention also chose electors for the 1840 presidential election but made no endorsement of any candidate for president or vice president [Clay to Tallmadge, Oct. 12, 1839]. In the 1840 gubernatorial race, Letcher defeated the Democratic candidate, Richard French, by a vote of 55,370 to 39,650. Thomson defeated Democrat John B. Helm for lieutenant governor by 52,952 votes to 36,199. Lexington *Observer & Kentucky Reporter*, August 31, 1839; Collins, *History of Kentucky*, 1:45. 2. In March, 1839, Rives had issued an address "in which he praised the intelligence and patriotism of the Whigs, declared that the Republican party deserted him, and denied that he had entered into any kind of combination relative to the election of 1840." Simms, *Rise of the Whigs in Virginia*, 136; Richmond *Enquirer*, March 30, 1839. 3. Clay to Hamilton, Feb. 24, 1839. 4. In the Connecticut elections in 1839, Whig Gov. William W. Ellsworth was reelected with 51.4% of the vote. *BDGUS*, 1:167. Whigs also won 15 seats in the state senate and nearly two-thirds of the Connecticut house seats. In the congressional election, Whigs won all 6 U.S. House seats. The Connecticut legislature also elected a Whig, Thaddeus Betts, to the U.S. Senate. Washington *Daily National Intelligencer*, April 5, 6, 1839; *Guide to U.S. Elections*, 459, 572. 5. In the New York City charter elections, held on April 9-11, 1839, Democrats won 24 seats to 10 for the Whigs. Also, Democrat Isaac Leggett Varian was elected mayor over Whig candidate Aaron Clark by a vote of 21,050 to 20,027. Mushkat, *Tammany*, 189; Holli & Jones, *Biographical Dictionary of American Mayors*, 375. There is some evidence that Thurlow Weed and his associates may have promoted a Democratic victory in New York City in an attempt to stop the nomination of Clay who drew much of his New York support from the city. Gunderson, *The Log-Cabin Campaign*, 52-56.

From John C. Crump *et al.*, Suffolk, Va., April 10, 1839. Inform Clay that at a recent meeting of Whigs in Suffolk, resolutions had been unanimously adopted praising "the gallant stand of the southern whig members of the late congress of the United States, and particularly the efforts of Messrs. Clay [Speech in Senate, February 7, 1839], of the senate, Stanley [*sic*, Edward Stanly] of North Carolina, [Sergeant S.] Prentiss of Mississippi, and [Henry A.] Wise, of our own state, of the house of representatives, to expose and check the fell demon of abolition." Also castigate the "flagitious misdeeds of our weak and vicious rulers," call President Jackson a man of "imbecility of intellect, and bellicose propensities and passions," and condemn Van Buren as a "wily little Dutchman, the Machiavel [*sic*, Machiavelli] of America," an unfit successor to an unfit predecessor. Praise Clay for his brilliance, patriotism, and statesmanship, and refer to him as "One, who, in all his actions 'had rather be right than be president [Speech in Senate, February 7, 1839];' and who throughout his life has endeavoured to unite his own glory with the welfare and happiness of his country." Copy. Printed in *Niles' Register* (August 17, 1839), 56:397. Signed also by John H. Cohoon [*sic*, John C. Cahoon] and Thomas C. P. [*sic*, H.P.] Godwin. See Clay to Crump, May 25, 1839, below, which is addressed to John C. Crump, John C. Cahoon, and Thomas H. B. Godwin. For Crump, previously from Surry County, Va., see *WMQ* (2) 3:272, 279. Godwin is probably Thomas Henry Pitt Godwin. See *VMHB*, 5:198-204. Cahoon or Cohoon has not been identified.

To JAMES ERWIN Lexington, April 10, 1839

We are all reasonably well here. Your children are in excellent health. The two little boys with us, especially Edward,[1] are as fat as seals.

Mr. [James] Shelby has made arrangements to distribute your Stock which were quite too numerous for the pastures of the Woodlands. I take several, and go over tomorrow to have fifteen of the Horse kind sent out to pasture. No orders have been recd. from you as to the horses to which your mares shall be sent. The General [James Shelby] and I think Zingaree the finest we saw in the exhibition of monday;[2] and if we do not hear from you to the contrary we shall order the best of them to be sent to him.

I have recd. two letters from you since my return home. I am sorry for the protest of the 1800$ draft. I understand however that Mr. Hunt (whose name induced me to take the bill) is good and prompt; and if you can hear from or see him I think he will take it up. Columbia (Arkansas) is his post office.[3] If it be not paid, I will thank you to bring or send one of the bills to me.

Dr. [Stephen] Duncan's has no doubt been paid;[4] and I hope 'ere this reaches you, the proceeds will have been remitted to me, deducting from them the amount you advanced for me for the Pipe of Wine (which I am obliged to you for paying) and the bill of the Mess Dicks.[5] I had forgotten that I had ordered such a pipe and really don't want it.

I should be very glad if the business of the Estate of Mr. [James] Brown could be brought to a close—the lot sold—the suit agt. [John] Humphries [*sic*, Humphreys] heard—and the controversy about the Washita Lands settled.[6] Do urge these matters.

I have been tempted to sell my lot in Lexn. on the Hill for $5000, being two more than I gave for it.[7]

James [Brown Clay] is doing very well. He has made an advantageous purchase of land near St. Louis, and has just left us for that City. He sold his stock for $4000, besides a Jack & Jenny[8]

We have just heard that the Whigs have elected in Connecticut all six of its members to the H. of R.[9] And the complexion of the political news is generally very good.

An amicable adjustment has been made of the possessory question about the N.E. disputed territory.[10] There is no danger therefore of present War.

Mr. [Nicholas] Biddle's resignation has given rise to much speculation.[11] My belief is that it has no connection in regard to any ulterior political arrangements, in respect to him.

I send this letter by Col. F[rancis]. Johnson,[12] to whom I would be glad that you would shew some kindness. P.S. Genl. Shelby had wisely altered all your bull Calves before Mr. Smith[13] knew of your wish to send one down.

ALS. NHi. Addressed to Erwin in New Orleans. 1. Andrew Eugene Erwin (b. 1829) and Charles Edward Erwin (b. 1835), sons of James and Anne Brown Clay Erwin (1807-35). 2. County Court Day had been held in Lexington on Monday, April 8, 1839, with unusually large numbers of blooded stock displayed. Lexington *Observer & Kentucky Reporter*, April 10, 1839. 3. Erwin had written Clay from New Orleans on March 21 reporting that "the draft for $1800 on Mr Hunt sent by you to Merchants Bank [New Orleans] had been protested, the parties all reside in Miss—all I can do is to write them." ALS. DLC-TJC (DNA, M212, R14). The Mr. Hunt referred to is probably Memucan Hunt from Mississippi who had emigrated to Texas. In 1837 he was appointed minister to the United States from Texas. He had returned to Mississippi and labored throughout the winter of 1837 in an attempt to secure annexation for Texas as well as a loan for the new republic from capitalists in Mississippi. He was in New Orleans in the summer of 1839. Stanley Siegel, *A Political History of the Texas Republic, 1836-1845* (Austin, 1956), 42, 84, 103, 138, 182. See also Biddle to Clay, Sept. 7, 1838. 4. Reference is to an expected payment to Clay (for hemp bagging and bale rope) from Dr. Stephen Duncan of Natchez, Miss. See Erwin to Clay, March 21, 1839, in DLC-TJC (DNA, M212, R14). On April 18, 1839, Duncan placed with Clay his annual order for bagging and bale rope. Duncan to Clay, April 18, 1839, in *ibid.* (R17). 5. N. & J. Dick & Co. of New Orleans, wine importers and forwarders. See Erwin to Clay, March 21, 1839, in *ibid.* (R14). In this instance Clay's wine was forwarded to Lexington via H. B. Hill & Co. in Louisville. 6. Clay to Ingersoll, Sept. 30, 1837. See also 8:739-40, 771-72. 7. Clay to Morton, April 9, 1839. 8. Clay to January, Oct. 6, 1838. 9. Clay to Tallmadge, April 9, 1839. 10. Clay to Hamilton, Feb. 24, 1839. 11. Biddle had resigned as president of the U.S. Bank of Pennsylvania on March 29, 1839, citing ill health as the reason for his retirement. Critics, however, charged that he had taken advantage of a temporary improvement in the bank's financial situation to exit before a new crisis developed. He was, in fact, in poor health, but it is also true that the bank was again forced to suspend specie payments only six months after his retirement. In 1841 it went into bankruptcy and closed its doors forever. Govan, *Nicholas Biddle*, 350; Hammond, *Banks and Politics in America*, 500-501. 12. See 3:42 and *BDAC*. 13. Possibly Thomas Smith.

To ALEXANDER HAMILTON Lexington, April 10, 1839

I thank you for the paper sent me, which afforded me a hearty laugh. The amicable adjustment of the question of exclusive possession of the disputed territory leaves us no longer any apprehension of an immediate War.[1] I have a strong conviction that England is even more disinclined to War than we are. It is more to be feared ultimately from the weakness of the British ministry than from any real difficulty in settling the controversy about the N. E. boundary. I hardly think that your conjecture of the offer of mediation, on the part of France, is, at least at present, well founded.

We are waiting, with anxiety, for the result of your Charter election.[2] The intelligence which we have so far recd. from Connt. is favorable.[3]

In all this Region of the U.S. the aspect of public affairs, in respect to the expulsion of the Administration, is encouraging.

ALS. DLC-HC (DNA, M212, R21). 1. Clay to Hamilton, Feb. 24, 1839. 2. Clay to Tallmadge, April 9, 1839 3. *Ibid.*

To NATHANIEL P. TALLMADGE Lexington, April 12, 1839

I received your favor transmitting a Copy of your Speech delivered at Masonic Hall in the City of N.Y.[1] I had previously perused it with much satisfaction, and I concur with you in most of the opinions and sentiments which it expresses. I agree with you, as to the three great systems of policy, Internal Improvements, the Tariff, and the U.S. Bank, which formerly divided parties, being now so disposed of that they no longer ought to agitate the Country or its Councils. I would avail myself of your friendly suggestion, on the subject of a B. of the U.S. to write a letter for publication, but that I think I expressed myself so fully and explicitly, when I last addressed the Senate of the U.S.[2] that I fear I should subject myself to the imputation of being over anxious to propitiate the opponents of a Bank. On that occasion you may probably remember that I said that I hoped no one would propose the establishment of such an institution, unless and until it was manifestly demanded by a clear majority of the People of the U. States.

With respect to the State institutions, I am disposed to make a full and fair experiment with them, so as to ascertain whether they can furnish a sound currency of uniform value, throughout the U. States, and perform the requisite financial offices for the General Government. It is certain, as you have stated, that the notes of the existing B.U.S. do circulate freely & maintain a uniform value in all sections of the Union.[3] This is probably partly owing to the long established habit of receiving and crediting those notes. But I think that the notes of the well established Banks of N. York, created under your new Banking law,[4] will also command general confidence and obtain free circulation in all parts of the Union. It was a happy provision in that system to secure Note holders in all contingencies. That feature of it will go far to stamp the notes as a general medium. Assuming that the local banks can supply a currency of unif[orm] value every where in the U.S. and can execute all the duties required of them, as a financial agent of the General Government, there will be no necessity to establish a Bank of the U.S. Whilst I most sincerely wish that this may prove to be the case, I must frankly own that I am not without contrary apprehensions. There are so many States in our Union, and so many Banks already existing, with a power and a freeness to create so many more, not one being under any legal responsibility to the General Government, that whilst it may be proper, in deference to public sentiment, to disavow any purpose of creating a Bank of the U.S., I think it would not be right to commit ourselves against the employment of such an Agency, if its establishment, in the public judgment, should become indispensable hereafter. I most sincerely hope that no such necessity will arise.

I tender to you cordial congratulations upon the issue of the election in Connecticut.[5] Our success there seems to have been complete; and if our majority is less than it was last year that fact may be fairly explained by the extraordinary and desperate exertions of our opponents. By another year, I trust that the Whigs & Conservatives[6] will act in hearty co=operation.

ALS. WHi. 1. Tallmadge's Masonic Hall speech of March 8, 1839, was published under the title *Speech on the Finances of the Government, Delivered at Masonic Hall, March 8, 1839. . . .* New York, 1839. 2. See Comment in Senate, Sept. 26, 1837; and espec. Speech in Senate, May 21, 1838. 3. Remark in Senate, April 17, 1838. 4. The New York Free Banking Act of 1838, sponsored by the Whigs, substituted a general law of incorporation for the old system of specific charter by act of the state legislature. It required new banks to have a minimum of $100,000 in capital stock. No maximum sum was fixed. It also required that sufficient capital stock in the form of state bonds and real-estate mortgages be placed in the keeping of the comptroller of the state for the purpose of securing the notes issued by a new bank. A small (12½%) specie reserve was also required to help sustain the integrity of the notes issued. Further, the legislation made no attempt to control the deposit liabilities of banks; each was left free to determine its own credit policies. By and large, the legislation relaxed regulatory restrictions imposed on N.Y. banks when the state's safety-fund banking system [8:90, 709] was launched in 1829, providing instead a free-trade atmosphere in which the state's banks could function. Bray Hammond, "Long and Short Term Credit in Early American Banking," *QJE* (Nov., 1934), 49:95-97; Robert E. Chaddock, *The Safety-Fund Banking System in New York, 1829-1866.* National Monetary Commission, *Sen. Docs.*, 61 Cong., 2 Sess., no. 581 (Washington, 1910), 259-309. For the structural and operational requirements, political implications, and historical importance of the 1838 legislation, see Wilson, *The Presidency of Martin Van Buren*, 117-21. 5. Clay to Tallmadge, April 9, 1839. 6. Clay to Henry Clay, Jr., Jan. 28, 1837.

To SAMUEL McKEAN Lexington, April 16, 1839

I was sorry to learn, from your favor of the 30h. Ulto. this day received, that you suffered in your journey home from indisposition. I can sympathise sincerely with you; for I too have suffered, from colds, since my return; but I am getting better and anxiously hope that you are. I thank you for the opportunity afforded me of reading the Revd. Mr. Burchs letter.[1] He belongs to a Religious community of which I have always thought very highly. I am gratified much, with *his* approval of the Speech[2] which he mentions, and of his placing it on the same high ground which a production of your's occupied.[3]

I receive favorable—very favorable accounts—in respect to the next Presidency. There must be an immense change in the tide of Mr. V. Buren's fortunes, or he will be beaten tremendously.

I am grateful for the renewal of your assurances of confidence and attachment towards me. I look back, with pleasure, upon our long acquaintance, unspotted by any instances of unkindness between us, even when we differed widely as to public men.

I continue to despair of Pennsa. All the good that I anticipate as being likely to be done for our cause or for me there is to complete the organization of the Whig party, and to effect a definitive but not unfriendly separation between that party & the Antimasons. I am firmly of opinion that the Whigs in Pa. ought to set up for themselves and act for themselves, in advancing the principles of their own cause. If the Anti

Masons choose to unite with them, be it so; but if not, let them, as they have a right to do, pursue their own course[.][4] My belief is that if such a separate organization is effected, and if, as I understand to be probable the Whig Convention in June should nominate me,[5] it will materially aid my friends every where beyond Pa. . . .

ALS. DLC—Manuscript Division. 1. James K. Burch was a Presbyterian minister who was pastor of a church in Georgetown, Ky., in 1839. At a Presbytery meeting in Danville, Ky., on Oct. 6, 1834, Burch had spoken in opposition to a resolution and declaration against slavery. Again, in Danville in July, 1835, he opposed an anti-slavery resolution, denying that the Presbyterian clergy was backing abolitionist James G. Birney as had been rumored. See *Minutes of the General Assembly of the Presbyterian Church . . . 1839* (Philadelphia, 1839), 246; Fladeland, *James Gillespie Birney*, 99, 116. 2. Probably a reference to his attack on abolition. Speech in Senate, Feb. 7, 1839. 3. Reference obscure. 4. Clay to Otis, Dec. 13, 1838; Mueller, *Whig Party in Pennsylvania*, 56-61; Vaughn, *Antimasonic Party*, 111-12. 5. The Pennsylvania Whig convention which met at Chambersburg in June, 1839, was under the control of Clay supporters. The delegates passed a resolution endorsing Clay for president but stating that they would support any candidate nominated by the national convention. A group of 17 Anti-Masons seceded from the Chambersburg convention and called for a "Union and Harmony Convention" to be held at Harrisburg on Sept. 4. This latter convention under the leadership of Charles B. Penrose, speaker of the Pennsylvania senate, and Thaddeus Stevens was dominated by Harrison supporters. Both Pennsylvania state conventions chose delegates to send to the national Whig convention at Harrisburg in Dec., 1839. Under the compromise worked out between the rival groups at the national convention, the Anti-Masons dominated the Pennsylvania delegation. Washington *Daily National Intelligencer*, June 19, 22, 1839; Gunderson, *The Log-Cabin Campaign*, 56; Mueller, *The Whig Party in Pennsylvania*, 58-60.

To JOHN P. KENNEDY Lexington, April 17, 1839

I very seldom read any Speech made in Congress—not even my own; but seeing one of your's in the [Washington *Daily National*] Intellr of the 11h. I was tempted to read it, and cannot refrain from expressing to you the high satisfaction which I have derived from its perusal. It sketches, with a masterly pencil, the character of Genl. Jackson, the dangerous principles of his Administration, the forlorn condition of Mr V Buren, and the weakness of the Cabinet by which he is surrounded. It is a document for the Historian to consult and follow, who shall undertake to record the transactions and events of the last ten years, in these States.[1]

In one respect I differ from you, and that is in the commendation which you bestow in the conduct of our foreign affairs, during Genl Jackson's administration. He had undoubtedly some success—the result of good fortune rather than diplomatic skill—in securing the payment of old claims upon Foreign powers.[2] But what else was achieved? It was a leading principle in his policy to propitiate G. Britain; and accordingly the Colonial carrying trade has been sacrificed,[3] the foreign tonnage greatly increased, and of consequence the American proportionately diminished, and the Protective policy crippled—its total destruction, which he no doubt meditated, only averted by the Compromise.[4] Witness too the bungling management of the question of the N.E. boundary![5] Then, how miserably have we been, and continue to be, represented abroad, every where?

I congratulate you on our success in Connecticut[6]—I hope I may add in the City of N. York also, altho the issue of that election, now known to you, has not yet reached me. . . .[7]

ALS. MdBP. 1. Kennedy had made the speech in the House of Representatives on Feb. 19, 1839, on a bill "making appropriations for the civil and diplomatic service for the year 1839." *Cong. Globe*, 25 Cong., 3 Sess., 194; Washington *Daily National Intelligencer*, April 11, 1839. 2. See 8:247-48, 448, 754-56, 818. 3. For the background of and subsequent results of the Anglo-American reciprocity treaty of 1830, as it applied to U.S. trade with the British West Indies, see 2:564-66; 3:729, note 21; 4:180; 5:632; 8:389, note 11; below, Clay to Clayton, May 27, 1843; F. Lee Benns, *The American Struggle for the British West India Carrying Trade, 1815-1830* (1923; reprinted ed., Clifton, N.J., 1972), 161-88. For arguments that the treaty was in some ways both advantageous and detrimental to U.S. trade with Britain and her colonies in the Western Hemisphere, see *ibid.*, 182-86; also see Munroe, *Louis McLane*, 272-79, 290-91. 4. Compromise Tariff of 1833. See 8: 604, 619-22, 626-27. 5. Clay to Hamilton, Feb. 24, 1839. For the complete background of the nagging Northeast boundary issue, see subject index entries in 7:666 (column 3), 729 (column 2). 6. Clay to Tallmadge, April 9, 1839. 7. *Ibid.*

From Wilkins Tannehill *et al.*, Louisville, April 18, 1839. Ask Clay to give the first talk in a proposed series of lectures scheduled to commence on November 11 next. "The sole object of these lectures is, to introduce into our Western cities a taste for social pleasures of an intellectual kind." Quote (inaccurately) a Latin phrase from Horace to show the importance of such intellectual activity. Add: "We think it especially important to furnish the mechanics and working men of our various cities an opportunity of thus enlarging and enriching their minds." ALS. ICU. Signed also by George Keats, Thomas H. Shreve, James Freeman Clarke, and Joshua B. Flint.

For Keats—brother of poet John Keats and a Louisville businessman who with Tannehill helped found the Kentucky Historical Society [Clay to Forsyth, May 24, 1838]—see Isabel M. McMeekin, *Louisville, The Gateway City* (New York, 1946), 82. For Shreve, a prolific Kentucky author, see Samuel M. Wilson, *History of Kentucky*, 2 vols. (Louisville, 1928), 2:485. For Clarke, a Unitarian minister and author in Louisville, see *NCAB*, 2:186. For Flint, who held the chair of clinical surgery at the University of Louisville, see Kentucky Writer's Project, *A Centennial History of the University of Louisville* (Louisville, 1939), 41, 49, 83.

On May 11, 1839, Clay informed Tannehill that while the lecture series was a "laudable" idea, his "public engagements are already so numerous, and the engrossment of my time so constant, that I cannot venture to add to them." ALS. MH.

To MATTHEW L. DAVIS Lexington, April 20, 1839

I received your favor of the 8h. and was highly gratified with the favorable aspect of political affairs which it presented. On one subject, your Charter election,[1] it appears, from the result, that the tricks and practices of our opponents surpassed the estimate you made of them, and that they have achieved a dear-bought victory. We must expect some reverses, especially where such means are brought into operation against us; but they should serve only to incite our friends to fresh and more vigorous exertions. I hope that the issue of this election will not have any discouraging effect on the State at large. Once get possession of the Legislature, and pass a Registry law,[2] and you will be thenceforward secure against the abuses by which the late election was lost.

I have a letter from the Honble [. . .][3] from your State full of the most interesting and encouraging details of information as to the state of public sentiment, in regard to myself, in the interior of N. York. He speaks with the most undoubting confidence, and coincides with Mr. Cook.[4]

In all this region, things look well. In Tennessee,[5] Illinois,[6] Indiana,[7] Mississippi,[8] Louisiana,[9] and Kentucky[10] our cause has been constantly gaining strength; and I think there is no doubt of any of them. In K. we have but three or four contested districts, and our friends feel confident of not losing more than one in the State. Manifee [*sic*, Menefee][11] has been obliged by his poverty to retire, and I am sorry for it; but his district is thought to be safe. There is an animated contest going on in Tennessee, but the issue of it is certain. . . .

ALS. KyLoF. 1. Clay to Tallmadge, April 9, 1839. 2. On March 30, 1840, the Whig-dominated legislature of New York passed a registry law for New York City. This law authorized the governor to appoint 3 commissioners to divide the city into districts of approximately 500 voters each; it also provided for election inspectors, registration of voters, challenging of doubtful votes, and punishment for false registration and/or illegal voting. Van Deusen, *William Henry Seward*, 72-73. 3. Name obliterated by hand in manuscript. 4. Probably Bates Cook of Niagara County, a Whig who had become comptroller of the state in 1839. Alexander, *Political History of . . . New York*, 2:36-37. 5. Bell to Clay, May 21, 1839. 6. There were no Illinois state elections in 1839 by which to judge the political sentiment there. However, on Oct. 7 the Illinois state Whig convention met in Springfield and expressed its "full confidence" in both Clay and Harrison, both "Harries of the West." The convention also appointed delegates to the Whig national convention, as well as presidential electors and members of the Whig state central committee. The Illinois Whigs promised to support any candidate nominated at the Whig convention at Harrisburg in Dec. Lexington *Observer & Kentucky Reporter*, Oct. 23, 1839. 7. Based on 1839 election results, Clay was too optimistic in regard to Whig prospects in some of these states. In Indiana, the Democrats carried the state house of representatives by 58 seats to 39 for the Whigs and the state senate by 10 seats to 9. Democrats also won 5 seats in the U.S. Congress to 2 for the Whigs; however, the legislature chose a Whig for the U.S. Senate. Riker and Thornbrough, *Indiana Election Returns*, 245-49; *Guide to U.S. Elections*, 462, 572. 8. Clay to Brooke, April 2, 1839. 9. *Ibid.* 10. *Ibid.* 11. Rep. Richard Hickman Menefee of Mt. Sterling, elected to the 25th Congress as a Whig, chose not to contest his seat in 1839 in order to practice law in Lexington. *BDAC*. The *Cong. Globe* variously spells his name Menefee and Menifee, usually the former. Collins, *History of Kentucky*, 2:602, spells it Menefee. In Menefee's district in 1839, Landaff W. Andrews, the Whig candidate, defeated his opponent by a majority of 735 out of 807 votes cast. Lexington *Observer & Kentucky Reporter*, August 17, 1839. For Andrews, see *BDAC*.

To RICHARD HENRY LEE Lexington, April 20, 1839

I have your favor of the 16h. Henry [Clay Duralde] reached home safely and without accident. We intend that he and his uncle John [Morrison Clay] shall leave here on Friday next to join your college,[1] and I am greatly obliged by your kind offer of accommodations for them in your house. I should greatly prefer their staying there to any other place; and they both seem pleased with the prospect of being your inmates.

Of John I must say to you *confidentially*, that whilst I am not aware of his having any bad habits, and with a decidedly good capacity, he has a prone[ne]ss to indolence, or rather, as he expressed to me once, he wants the will to study. You will place me under lasting obligations if you can encourage and incite him to exertion. He has a great aversion to Mathematical studies, and I am not surprized at it; but in most of the other usual branches of Education he has made good progress. He has high and irascible temper, but easily acted upon by kindness and persuasion.

I hope and believe that nothing will occur to prevent their arrival at Washington early in the week after next.

ALS. PWW. 1. Washington College, now Washington and Jefferson, in Washington, Pa. The college catalogue of the day lists John Morrison Clay as a part-time student in the class of 1840. This information provided by David W. Kraeuter, The Library, Washington and Jefferson College.

To Elisha Whittlesey, Canfield, Ohio, April 20, 1839. Says it has been a long time since he was in Europe, but feels he can provide Whittlesey with a letter of introduction to Baring Brothers & Co., financiers, in London. Regrets he now knows no one in Holland save King William I, "who I dare say cares no [more] for me than I do for his Majesty." As for former Speaker of the U.S. House Andrew Stevenson, now minister to the Court of St. James's, "My relations with [him] are such as to prevent any correspondence with him." ALS. OClWHi.

Clay wrote such a letter to Baring Brothers this same day, April 20, 1839. LS. *Ibid.* Rep. Whittlesey had resigned from Congress on July 9, 1838, having served there since 1823. *BDAC.*

To LEWIS F. ALLEN Lexington, April 23, 1839

I duly recd. your favor of the 12h. We are very well stocked with Durham Bulls in this neighbourhood, and I should think Ohio a better market for those you have to spare than K[entucky]. The avidity to acquire the Short horns with us is unabated. There are as many as four or five of my neighbours now in England or on their way home, who went to purchase that description of Cattle. We shall have in the course of next month or early in June a public sale of some ten or a dozen that will test their value. I have been making an experiment with a cross of the Durham bull on a Devon Cow and the produce is very promising.

The Lexington Intelligencer,[1] published in Lexn. will be a good paper for your brother to advertize in, if he should have occasion to use one.

I am thankful for your kind intentions in respect to the pigs which you propose sending to me. The Berkshire are rare with us and are most approved. I had a pair but have been unfortunate with them. We have never however made a fair experiment with the China. Those which I have seen are so prone to take on fat that they do not breed well; but I should suppose the cross between them & the Berkshire would be very fine. Messrs. [Andrew M.] January & [William] Huston at Maysville (K.) will receive and forward any that you may have the goodness & find it convenient to send to me. Maysville is not far below Portsmouth, the mouth of the Ohio Canal.

This Spring has been dry but otherwise fine. Our blue grass pastures look beautiful & afford now an excellent bite for our Live stock.

ALS. NcD. 1. The Lexington (Ky.) *Intelligencer*, a Whig newspaper, had been founded in 1833 with Julius Clarke & Co. as publisher and Edwin Bryant as editor. Robert Peter, *History of Fayette County* (Chicago, 1882), 370.

To John Holmes, [probably Alfred, Me.], April 26, 1839. Thanks him for sending a prospectus of his proposed book. Subscribes to it and believes it will be "very beneficial & acceptable to the public." ALS. Courtesy of J. Winston Coleman, Jr., Lexington, Ky. The book in question was probably *The Statesman, or Principles of Legislation and Law.* Augusta, 1840.

To W. B. Rose, April 26, 1839. Refuses to recommend Rose for a government job, noting that "I have recommended no person for any situation whatever, within the gift of the Fed. Executive, during the last nine years." ANS. KyLoF. Dated "[1839]" at bottom of document in a strange hand.

To SAMUEL WILKESON Lexington, April 26, 1839

I recd. your favor transmitting a letter for my brother,[1] which I have franked and forwarded to him, as I have n[ot] heard of his intentions to be here shortly.

I am happy to hear of your continued exertions in [the] good and glorious cause of Colonization, and sincerely hope that they will be crowned with the success which you and it richly deserv[e.] The great point of difficulty is the want of money, money, money. You know that we have no great surpluses of that powerful agent in this quarter; but we have good dispositions, and should a financial agent of the Society come hither, I hope he will pick up some thing.

ALS. DLC-HC (DNA, M212, R20). Addressed to Wilkeson at Franklin House, New York City. For Wilkeson, see 6:969. 1. Porter Clay.

To James Kent, New York City, April 29, 1839. Says that Aaron K. Woolley, professor of law at Transylvania University and judge "in one of our Superior Courts," will present this letter of introduction. Notes that "Everybody—but especially every member of the Profession of Law wishes to know you. Justly regarding you as its father, the feeling is quite natural." Assures Chancellor Kent that Woolley is a gentleman of "high respectability" as well as an "eminent" lawyer and judge. ALS. DLC-HC (DNA, M212, R21). Maj. Woolley (1800-1849) who attended the U.S. Military Academy (non-graduate of class of 1819), was later a prominent citizen and attorney in Port Gibson, Miss. He married Sally Howard Wickliffe, daughter of Robert Wickliffe, Sr., on October 9, 1827, and moved to Kentucky. He subsequently represented Fayette County in the state legislature (1834) and served as judge of the circuit court. Perrin, *History of Fayette County, Kentucky,* 343; USMA, *Register,* 175. See also 7:389 and 8:803.

To James K. Paulding, Washington, D.C., May 3, 1839. Raises with Secretary of the Navy Paulding the question of the poor health of his grandson, Midshipman Martin Duralde III, since he arrived in Norfolk to join the U.S.S. *Constitution.* Notes that "I have written to Norfolk still urging him to join the Constitution, if she has not sailed, unless the state of his health absolutely forbids it. If he should be prevented from accompanying her, I have to request that you will have the goodness to order him upon the West India or Mediterranean station, as may be most compatible with the public service." ALS. DNA, RG45, Misc. Letters Received, May/June 1839. Endorsed on cover by Paulding. AEI: "Write to Mr. Clay and express the regrets of the Dept. at the ill state of health of Mid. Duralde. His wish will be complied with in the event of Mr D_____ not being able to go out in the Constitution—Write to Com[modore] [Lewis] Warrington to apprise the Dept when Mid D_____ is capable of Service."

Also on May 3, Clay wrote to Commodore Lewis Warrington, commandant of the Norfolk navy yard, saying that Surgeon Thomas Williamson has informed him that the voyage of the *Constitution* to the Pacific would not likely promote the restoration of Midn. Duralde's health. Informs Warrington that Duralde "has no hereditary claims to Consumption, derived from either of his parents, & I cannot think there is any real danger in it." Adds: "You will oblige me to look a little into his condition[.] Consult with Dr. Williamson, and if you think the passage to the Pacific will not be injurious to him, to direct him to join the Constitution unless she shall have sailed. I am a little apprehensive that he has taken up an aversion to that service and has operated upon the kind feelings of Dr. W." ALS. KyU.

On May 24, Paulding responded to Clay's letter of May 3. He reported that

"Midn Durald[e]'s health was not such as to justify his rejoining the Constitution which sailed from New York three days since." He noted, however, that the U.S.F. *Brandywine* is fitting out in Norfolk for the Mediterranean station and that Duralde is being ordered to her in the hope that his health will permit him to join her. LS. DNA, RG45, Misc. Letters by Sect. of Navy, General Letterbook, 1798-1886, vol. 26, p. 114 (M209, R10).

On June 8, Clay thanked Paulding for his courtesy in the matter of Midn. Duralde, noted that the young man's health was restored, and urged the secretary to get the lad to sea in whatever naval vessel was scheduled to "take an early departure" from Norfolk. ALS. DNA, RG45, Misc. Letters Received, May/June 1839.

On or about November 1, 1839, in an endorsement on the envelope of a letter from Clay, dated October 25 asking that "an enclosed letter" to Duralde be forwarded, Paulding wrote: "Ackge. rec[e]ipt of this letter and say the Dept. will with pleasure forward the communication for Midn Duralde enclosed in it by the earliest opportunity to the Mediterranean and that the Brandywine went to sea on the_____[date not supplied]. An[swere]d 1 Nov 1839."

For Lewis Warrington (1782-1851), who had commanded the *Macedonian* before becoming a commissioner on the navy board and then served as commandant of the Norfolk navy yard, see *DAB*. For Thomas Williamson, a surgeon who was stationed at the Norfolk naval hospital in 1835 and presumably remained there in 1839, see *Biennial Register* 1835, p. 126; 1841, p. 152.

From Mackenzie Beverley, Spotsylvania Court House, Va., May 10, 1839. Asks Clay to assist him in the sale of a piece of land in Union County, Ky. Concludes: "It gives me great pleasure to inform you that the name of H Clay is bursting out in Va like the Damask rose and is as fragrant & new admirers are daily coming to support its growth I am as I have been for twenty years a devoted admirer of his Patriotism & great worth—" ALS. DLC-HC (DNA, M212, R5). For Beverley, son of Robert Beverley (of Essex County, Va.) and Maria Carter, see *VMHB*, 20:332-33; 21:305; 34:162.

From Mary Sophia Carroll [Mrs. Richard Henry] Bayard, Wilmington, Del., May 12, 1839. Thanks Clay for his sympathy note pertaining to the sudden death of her brother-in-law, Dr. Aaron Tucker. Says she has heard that Clay has "*again* been injured in the apparent security of *home*, after escaping the perils of a long-long journey [Clay to Otis, December 13, 1838]." Adds that "You are not very careful of a life on which may depend the happiness and welfare of thousands." Reports she has not yet made any summer vacation plans. Concludes with the observation that "I shall never regret the glimpse I have had of public life—and the little world of Washn. for though much of my enthusiasm is subdued, and many illusions have vanished forever, still there is left the remembrance of many happy hours—and the friendship and affection of the great and good—then I am wiser, & perhaps better for the little experience I have gained of the 'world and its ways', and no longer value brilliant follies of a fashionable life, for more than they are really worth—I ought not may be say this of myself, but you have given me the habit of telling you what I think & feel—"ALI. DLC-HC (DNA, M212, R6). Mrs. Bayard and her husband, U.S. Sen. Richard Henry Bayard (Del.) had departed Washington in March, 1839, when the senator resigned his seat to become chief justice of Delaware. For Bayard, who later returned to the Senate, see *DAB* and *BDAC*. Mrs. Bayard (1804-85) was a granddaughter of Charles Carroll of Carrollton, Signer of the Declaration of Independence. Her bereaved sister was Elizabeth Henrietta Carroll Tucker. Kate Mason Rowland, *The Life of Charles Carroll of Carrollton, 1737-1832. . . .* 2 vols. (New York, 1898), 2:438. The reference to Clay's injury at his "Ashland" home is obscure; neither Clay nor anyone in his family mentions it.

To JAMES ERWIN Lexington, May 14, 1839

I recd. your letter transmitting a check on account of the proceeds of the bill which had been accepted by Mr. Hunt & protested.[1] A box of Bacon Hams addressed to Wm. [C.C.] Claiborne [Jr.] left Louisville on the 7h. from Ashland. He is so much out of the way of the Steam Boats that I wish you would mention it to him. Hill & Co. who shipt it omitted to mention to me the name of the Boat.[2]

I have just recd. a letter from Mr. Bouligny[3] engaging for his friends three of my blooded Calves (Bull) and three heifers at fair prices. They are to be sent next fall, and you are to receive for me the amount.

I have sold my lot on the Hill in Lexn. at $5000.[4]

The boys and Lucretia have been with us near a fortnight, and are all in excellent health.[5] The boys went to town yesterday and Lucretia goes tomorrow. Mrs. Clay thinks, and I am inclined to believe, that the Bishop [Benjamin B. Smith] & his wife are too frequently absent from home.[6] When you come up (which we hope you will do as soon as you can) you can look into that matter. I have some thought of a Canadian trip, on which, if I go, I shall set out about the last of June. I expect James [Brown Clay] to accompany me.[7]

Our neighbourhood looks beautifully & every thing promises well. I believe Mr. Smith[8] has checked the intrusions at the Woodlands. I was sorry to observe there the other day that the Longleaf pines which you sent up were dead. They must have been badly put up at N.O. Is it too late (I fear it is) to have some brought up this Spring. P.S. Political affairs look well. My letters from N. York speak with the utmost confidence as to that State.[9] In regard to Virginia nous verrons.[10]

ALS. NHi. 1. Clay to Erwin, April 10, 1839. 2. Noted by Clay on the envelope: "The Box of Hams for Mr. Claiborne was shipped by the S[team] B[oa]t New Albany. 6th May." 3. Possibly Ursin Bouligny, Jr., the grandson of Dominique Bouligny, a friend of Clay. Grace King, *Creole Families of New Orleans* (New York, 1921), 299. 4. Clay to Morton, April 9, 1839. 5. The living children of James and Anne Brown Clay Erwin in 1839 were: Henry Clay Erwin (b. 1827), James Erwin, Jr. (b. 1828), Andrew Eugene Erwin (b. 1829), Lucretia Clay Erwin (b. 1830), Charles Edward Erwin (b. 1835). 6. Clay to Lucretia Hart Clay, May 21, 1838. 7. Clay to Porter, May 14, 1839. 8. Probably Thomas Smith. 9. Clay to Porter, April 15, 1838; Clay to Tallmadge, April 9, 1839. 10. Clay to Caldwell, March 18, 1839.

To PETER B. PORTER Lexington, May 14, 1839

I received your favor from Albany to day, and am very glad to learn from you a confirmation of the information which I had received from others of the favorable state of political affairs in N. York. Although our defeat in the Charter election of the City by a small majority against us produced some discouragement,[1] it was but momentary and has passed away.

I have recd. from Mr. [Nathaniel P.] Tallmadge a letter communicating similar views to those expressed in your letter as derived from him. I am glad to hear that the tone of Mr. Webster is changed,[2] and that he is now more friendly inclined. He owed it to his own character to make this change; but I yet doubt whether, as Mr. Tallmadge believes, he will say any thing to the public, prior to his voyage to Europe,[3] in respect to the Presidential question.

In respect to the matter of one term,[4] my opinion is, and has long been, that it would be a great improvement of our present Constitution, if the encumbent were limited to one term, even if it were extended to several years longer than the present. If I had the sole power of making a Constitutional arrangement on this subject, I would limit the office to one term, and fix that at six years. But whilst I entertain these opinions, I confess that I feel an insuperable difficulty, in *authorizing* any annunciation from me as to the course which I might pursue, in the event of my election. Such a publication would, I think, be undignified, and would display an eagerness to be elevated to the office, which I do not feel. If I were to determine upon that limitation, as to myself, a suitable time to announce it would be *after* & not *before* the Election.

It is my intention to leave home about the first of July on a visit to you and to Canada.[5] But it is my anxious desire to proceed on the excursion as quietly, and with as little noise and parade as possible. This is due to the public pledges which I have made, to my own feelings, and, I think, to every consideration of policy. If I believed that I could not be allowed to have my own way, in this matter, I would abandon the journey. I hope you will bear my wishes in mind, and assist me in executing them.

We have had a charming Spring, and our fine Country never looked more beautiful and interesting than it now does. I hope that you have been equally favored.

ALS. NBuHi. 1. Clay to Tallmadge, April 9, 1839. 2. Clay to Otis, Dec. 13, 1838. 3. Webster departed for London on the *Liverpool* May 18, 1839, and arrived back in New York City on Dec. 29, 1839. On June 12, 1839, Webster sent two letters, one to Edward Curtis and one to John P. Healy, in which he withdrew his name as a presidential candidate. Fuess, *Daniel Webster*, 2:74, 79; Wiltse, *Webster Papers*, 4:368-70. Webster's withdrawal appeared in the Washington *Daily National Intelligencer* on July 6, 1839. 4. Proposals for a constitutional amendment limiting the president to a single term of either four or six years have recurred frequently in American history. Jackson had called for such an amendment in several of his annual messages. Harrison urged the one-term limitation in several of his campaign speeches, and in his inaugural address on March 4, 1841, he renewed "the pledge heretofore given that under no circumstance will I consent to serve a second term." The concept was subsequently included in the second resolution of the Whig party platform in 1844. It was not, however, a dominant issue in the 1840 campaign. Arthur M. Schlesinger, Jr., *et al.* (eds.), *History of American Presidential Elections 1789-1968*, 4 vols. (New York, 1971), 1:678, 698; Edward Stanwood, *A History of the Presidency* (New York, 1898), 153-54, 221; *MPP*, 4:8-9. 5. For Clay's itinerary on this trip, see Clay to Giddings, July 13, 1839. His son, James Brown Clay, accompanied him. They departed Lexington early in July.

From Catherine L. Brooke, Philadelphia, May 16, 1839. As the teacher of a "seminary for Young Ladies in Philadelphia," and a Virginian "by birth and family," asks Clay his opinion on opening a seminary "in some part of the Western Country," preferably in Kentucky, which she and her three sisters would operate. "We are qualified, to teach, all, the branches; of an English education, together, with Music and French." Refers him to former Secretary of the Treasury William J. Duane and other prominent Philadelphians for testimony on "our standing in society." ALS. DLC-HC (DNA, M212, R5). In 1839 Brooke lived in a seminary located at 21 S. Schuylkill 7th. *A. M'Elroy's Philadelphia Directory for 1839* (Philadelphia, 1839), 28. Catherine was probably the daughter of Robert Brooke IV who married Philadelphian Ann Shee, the daughter of Gen. John Shee and Catherine Lawrence Shee. *VMHB*, 20:435 and information supplied by Mrs. George S. Southwell, Alderman Library, University of Virginia.

Clay responded to this letter on May 24, saying he knows little about female academies, or where a new one might best be located in the vastness that is the

West. But believes "a good female Academy" is "now wanting in Lexington." Suggests, however, that before moving to Lexington, she should consult Mr. and Mrs. McAlister [*sic*, Macalester], Lexington residents now visiting Mr. Macalester's brother [Charles], a banker in Philadelphia. ALS. KyU.

Female seminaries operating in Lexington in 1839 were: Saint Catherine's Female Seminary [Roman Catholic], Young Ladies' Seminary, Lexington Female Academy, and Select Class for Young Ladies. MacCabe, *Directory of the City of Lexington . . . 1838 & '39*, pp. 88-89. E. Macalester, merchant, partner in Brand & Macalester, did business at 62 N. Mulberry St. *Ibid.*, 58. For his brother, Charles Macalester, see *DAB*.

To JOHN P. KENNEDY Lexington, May 16, 1839

I duly received your favor of the 2d. inst. I fully share in all the forebodings which it expresses in respect to the politics of our Country. We have much to hope, but much too to fear. And it is a remarkable fact that in our Cities, where we had most to apprehend from political corruption, we have found most public virtue; whilst in the Country, where we had a right to expect most opposition to misrule, and wild and dangerous theories, they have received an alarming degree of countenance. This is especially the case in Pennsa. I suppose that it is to be ascribed to two causes, the greater degree of suffering and the greater extent of intelligence, on public affairs, in the Cities.

Such a work as you have described, well composed, and in a popular form, I think could not fail to produce a good effect; and I wish you would undertake it. It might be thrown into the form of a dialogue, or a work of imagination, or even a graver character, divided into suitable parts. There is no topic which, when well treated, is more likely to command the public attention and affect the public feelings than that of defaulters and peculations in the public revenue.[1] The vicious principle of Jackson's appointments, and the knowledge of the Heads of Departments and the President of delinquency, whilst it was in progress, have not yet, I think, been sufficiently exposed. And, if the Country could be made fully to comprehend the Agrarian aims which are directed against the foundations of all property and all good faith in the Community, I hope it would at last be aroused.

I consider the Abolition movements as belonging to the same loose and licentious spirit which characterizes Locofocoism. I should be the last person to defend Negro slavery, in the abstract, if the original question were now presented and it was to be decided whether it should be introduced and planted amongst us. But that is not the question; it is here already, and in spite of us, and the question is what is the best way to deal with it? If you have read Dr. [William E.] Channings recent pamphlet,[2] you must have been struck with its tone of arrogance and presumptuousness. All mankind have been hitherto wrong, and the Dr. and his school are the only infallibles. Negro slaves cannot become the subjects of property! We are asked to exchange the sober practical wisdom of Statesmen, Rulers and Legislators, in all ages, for the vague vain and visionary theories of Dr. Channing, Gerrit Smith[3] & Arthur Tappan The Dr. talks of natural property—of property existing independent of all Law. As if, in a state of nature, there were any property, except that resulting from occupancy, and during its continuance. As if all property were not the offspring of Convention, in other words of Law, which defines and protects it, authorizes its acquisition, and provides the mode of its transfer and succession.

If you have not read "Abolition is Sedition,"[4] and "Some thoughts on Domestic Slavery," let me recommend their perusal to you. They are remarkably well written, and the latter, I understand, is the production of Mr. [John L.] Carey of Carlisle College.[5]

[Richard H.] Menefee has declined offering for Congress, and removed from his late District and settled in Lexington.[6] We all regretted it very much, but his reasons were so strong—his poverty & the claims of a growing family—that we could not urge him to continue. He will probably be succeeded by a good Whig.

I had not supposed that there was any *immediate* danger of a general suspension of Specie payments, altho' that event, I take it, will certainly again happen. Judging from the state of Foreign Exchange, I had hoped it was not as nigh at hand as you seem to imagine it. If it is to happen, I fervently hope that it will not occur until our present rulers are dismissed.[7]

We shall now soon hear from Va.[8] If the results of her Elections should be conformable to our hopes, our future labors will be much lightened. If otherwise, we must go to work with redoubled energy and invigorated ardor. . . .

ALS. MdBP. 1. Probably Kennedy's satire on the Jackson administration, *Quodlibet, Some Annals Thereof, With an Authentic Account of the Origin and Growth of the Borough, and the Sayings and Doings of Sundry of the Townspeople; Interspersed With Sketches of the Most Remarkable and Distinguished Characters of That Place and Its Vicinity. By Solomon Second-thoughts, Schoolmaster*. Philadelphia, 1840. 2. Probably Channing's, *Remarks on the Slavery Question, in a Letter to Jonathan Phillips, Esq.*, published in Boston in 1839. The opening statement began: "On reading Mr. Clay's speech on Slavery, many thoughts were suggested to me. . . ." 3. Smith to Clay, March 21, 1839. 4. Calvin Colton, *Abolition a Sedition. By a Northern Man*. Philadelphia, 1839, first published in New York in 1838. For Colton (1789-1857), Episcopal clergyman, Whig political writer and later biographer of Clay, see *DAB*. 5. For Carey who was on the faculty of Dickinson College, see Charles Coleman Sellers, *Dickinson College, A History* (Middletown, Conn., 1973), 506, 509. Carey had published *Some Thoughts Concerning Domestic Slavery*. . . . in Baltimore in 1838. 6. Clay to Davis, April 20, 1839. 7. Clay to Otis, Dec. 13, 1838. 8. Clay to Caldwell, March 18, 1839.

From Addison Dougherty, New York City, [May 17], 1839. Sends Clay three questions drawn up by "the Young Men's Whig Committee of this City." Notes that they are also being circulated among "the Great Captains of the Whig party" as well as others in "various parts of the Country." The questions on the enclosed circular ask if it is (1) "expedient for the Whig Young Men of the Union to hold a Presidential Convention"; (2) if so, when and where should it be held; and (3) "what mode or ratio of representation should be adopted in choosing delegates." Solicits Clay's participation in the survey. ALS. DLC-HC (DNA, M212, R5). The circular of questions is dated May 7, 1839; Dougherty's letter, in which they were enclosed, is postmarked May 17, 1839. For Dougherty, who was one of the founders of the New York Life Insurance Co. (originally the Nautilus Insurance Co.), see Bonner, *New York, The World's Metropolis*, 440.

A national Whig Young Men's convention met in Baltimore on May 4, 1840, with delegates from every state, as well as the District of Columbia, in attendance. Both Clay [Speech in Baltimore, May 4, 1840] and Webster addressed the well-attended meeting.. The *Intelligencer* reported a throng of over 18,000 in Baltimore for these Whig political festivities. Washington *Daily National Intelligencer*, May 5-7, 1840.

From JOHN BELL Nashville, May 21, 1839

Your letter of the 22nd April came to hand without any unusual delay, but the canvass has been so active and animated in my district that I have had no leisure to reply to letters from any quarter. I have a respite of a day or two now, and I avail myself of it to notice and reply to your letter.

You furnished me with an excellent summary of the arguments which may be successfully urged against our opponents in this State, and we do not fail to urge them with spirit, and I trust with success. We are carrying the war into Africa in nearly every section of the State. We begin also to reap some of the fruits of our energy. Things look well for us, at present. Our Gov. [Newton Cannon] however is too sluggish and selfsufficient, or we might do better,—still if we can continue the excitement and activity which now prevail in our ranks, we shall beat [James K.] Polk 15000 votes at least[1]—secure a handsome majority in both branches of the Legislature[2] and elect ten out of the thirteen members to Congress.[3] I hope we shall do better than this in the Congressional districts, but feel no confidence that we shall do more. I do not count Jo. Williams as being with us on any close question.[4]

The real question now before the people of this state is will they take Henry Clay "to rule over them" and as the vote shall be in August next so will it be in 1840. What we have now in hand is to convince the people that you are the greatest man in America, & worthy of all trust; and you would be surprised to hear the variety of the cases which are every day conjured up for the abrupt change of opinion which is now rapidly developing itself upon that subject. Wilson county the most populous of my district and formerly the most devoted to Genl. Jackson, of any in the state, I have canvassed thoroughly since I came home. I have addressed twelve assemblies of the people, and generally in company with my competitor and the debate was always chiefly and directly upon the question of preference between you & Van Buren. Every old prejudice, of course, is sought to be removed—still I expect to get 2000 of the 3000 votes in that county,[5] and every one of the 2000 will be a Clay vote—Those who stand out upon their old prejudices will not vote for me—some will not vote at all who were for [Hugh Lawson] White at the last election. I need not say that any man besides yourself cannot and will not be thought for the present—nor do I think that any thing can be done afterwards for either of the other gentlemen.

This week the war commences in this county [Davidson], and I expect a more furious and bitter one, than we have ever seen *here before*, but I am confident of our success, but by a far less majority than in Wilson. If we get 300 of a majority here, it will do for Genl Jackson's county—It is also Mr. [Felix] Grundy's—indeed Mr. Grundy's connexions and influence are stronger in this county than the Genl. himself. I hope we shall have a majority of 300 nevertheless

I have no time to read newspapers now,—nor shall have until after August—therefore, if you have leisure, shall be glad to hear how things are going in other states—especially in Ohio[6] & Indiana.[7] I fear some mischief in Ohio especially. I give up Pennsylvania,[8] & do so without fear of consequences, if other states do their duty, but I have apprehensions of a serious season in Ohio. I have seen enough of [Charles] Hammond's course to satisfy me that *he* is bent upon mischief. I believe him to be an unprincipled man, and a hypocrite. His criticisms on your Anti-abolition speech[9] settled him with me. I can conceive of nothing more insidious and mischievous. He is a Malignant in his feelings, wherever the South or South West is concerned, or the men in those sections.[10]

The old hero [Andrew Jackson] is electioneering with all his usual zeal. He fills all the old men who visit him (& great pains are taken to get them to his house) with his malignant feelings against the leading men of our party. He is *trying* himself against me, but I shall foil him. He maddens at the idea that Ten[n]. can be got to go for you, and if this state shall give her vote to you, my opinion is he will not survive such a result. He will burst [a] blood vessel & expire. A few weeks ago, he attended a company muster where his neighbours say he had not been in 20 years.—He was careful to shake hands with, and say something civil to all. You may judge from this what an interest he takes. All his deputy orators over the country are full of cant about the cruelty of putting his old and inveterate enemy into power to triumph upon him in his old age—he is not yet dead they say—he soon will be—spare him until the grave closes over him—do not inflict this last insult upon the hero of N.O. and the Saviour of his country!—& much more of the same pathetic rant. It is truly a bitter pill & I often see his attached partizans gritting their teeth in rage and agony when the shouts of the people rise in approbation of some sentiment expressed in your favor.

I have not time to write more.—Mrs. [Jane Erwin Yeatman] Bell is not in very good health & sometimes talks of a visit to Lexington this summer but do not think she will make it. . . .

ALS. DLC-HC (DNA, M212, R5). 1. Polk, a Democrat, defeated incumbent Whig Governor Newton Cannon by a vote of 54,012 to 51,396. *BDGUS*, 4:1473. 2. Democrats won 14 seats in the Tennessee senate to 11 for the Whigs; they also carried the state house of representatives by a margin of 42 seats to 33 for the Whigs. Washington *Daily National Intelligencer*, August 23, 1839. 3. Of the 13 congressional seats in Tennessee, Whigs won 7 and the Democrats won 6. *Guide to U.S. Elections*, 572. 4. Joseph L. Williams, a Whig, won the seat in Tennessee's third congressional district. He was apparently unopposed. *Ibid.* 5. Bell's district was composed of Wilson and Davidson counties, which included the towns of Lebanon and Nashville respectively. Wilson Co. had a population composed of 19,528 whites and 5,944 slaves, while Davidson Co. had 16,460 whites and 11,662 slaves. Bell defeated Democrat Robert M. Burton for Congress by a vote of 3,895 to 2,665 votes. *Ibid.*; Stanley B. Parsons *et al.*, *United States Congressional Districts, 1788-1841* (Westport, Ct., 1978), 364. 6. In Ohio, Democrats won 25 state senate seats to 11 for the Whigs and 74 house seats to 23 for the Whigs. Lexington (Ky.) *Gazette*, Oct. 24, 1839. 7. Clay to Davis, April 20, 1839. 8. In the Pennsylvania legislative election in Oct., 1839, Democrats won 69 seats in the house of representatives to 31 for the Whigs, while Locofocos won 17 seats in the state senate to 15 for the Whigs. Harrisburg (Pa.) *Telegraph and Intelligencer*, Oct. 24, 1839; Mueller, *Whig Party in Pennsylvania*, 61. 9. Speech in Senate, Feb. 7, 1839. 10. Clay to Hammond, April 2, 1839.

To JAMES B. CLAY Lexington, May 22, 1839

I was sorry to learn from your letter of the 14h. inst. that your health was not good, and that your spirits were bad. Why should they be? You are young, with encouraging prospects before you. Don't let your imagination dwell on apprehensions of disease, and be regular in your habits. Above all avoid dissipation. I hope you will never play at any game. After much observation and some experience I can say, with perfect truth, that he who is addicted to play loses money, time, sleep, health and character.

The journey that we propose will I hope restore your health.[1] I think now that you ought to be here by the 25h. June, as I wish to leave home between that and the first of July.

I have made no purchase in Morgan, as recommended by your uncle Porter;[2] and shall make none until I see you. Indeed, I do not know that I can spare the funds to make one any where.

I have, sold my three Bull Calves, the white one, Nancy's and the Devon's for $500 each to Gentlemen in Louisiana, and three part blooded Heifers at $250 each. My Virginia mare has a colt by Medoc. [Mentions a land transaction in Lexington. Continues:]

Our Season has been fine up to this time, and the Crops promise well. . . .

ALS. DLC-TJC (DNA, M212, R10). Addressed to James at St. Louis, Mo. 1. Clay to Erwin and Clay to Porter, May 14, 1839. 2. Probably a reference to Morgan County, Ill., where his brother, Porter, had earlier recommended land purchases. See 8:658.

To JOHN C. CRUMP *et al.* Lexington, May 25, 1839

I duly received the letter which you did me the honor to address me,[1] transmitting a copy of a resolution adopted at a meeting of the whigs of Nansemond county [Va.], recently held.

Whilst I but too sensibly feel that they have placed an estimate entirely too high and flattering upon my capacity and upon the public services which I have been able to render, it affords me very great satisfaction to learn that I have been so fortunate as to obtain their approbation; and I request you to communicate to those whom you represent, my respectful and grateful acknowledgements for the sentiments of respect and esteem with an expression of which they have honored me.

At the session of congress prior to the last, I presented resolutions to the senate, touching the institution of domestic slavery,[2] embracing all the principles applicable to the subject, the maintenance of which appeared to me necessary to the security of property, the stability of our system of general government, and harmony among the states of the union. At the last session of congress, the ultra abolitionists had presented themselves under a new and alarming aspect. Instead of restricting their exertions to moral persuasion, addressed to the consciences of slave holders, keeping aloof from parties and politics, as they originally professed to be their intention, they had openly proclaimed their purpose to enter the political arena, and denouncing all who did not adopt their dogmas and agree with them, to force their principles and their men by the aid of the ballot box. It required but little foresight to discern the frightful consequences which would result from this change of their position, if they should succeed. The union would be first convulsed throughout, and finally broken into fragments. I thought therefore at the last session, that the time was suitable to warn the country of their designs and efforts; and hence the speech which has commended itself to the approbation of the whigs of Nansemond.[3] That speech is but an expansion of the argument embodied in the resolutions of the previous session. And I shall be most happy if it should contribute any thing towards arresting the mad career of these misguided men, and towards preserving that union which is the truest guarranty of all the high privileges which we enjoy.

In the constitution of that union there is not a solitary provision, fairly interpreted and fairly administered, which authorises any interference of congress with domestic slavery, as it exists in the United States. There is not one, relating to the subject, which does not recognise and treat slaves as lawful property, or look to the safety and security of that property. The clause which fixes the representation in the popular branch of congress, establishes a ratio founded upon the acknowledged existence of slavery; and in the appointment of direct taxes among the states, slaves are assumed to be lawful property. On the occasion of the imposition of a direct tax, to prosecute the last war with Great Britain, slaves were taxed by congress, *as slaves*, and their proprietors paid the tax accordingly. The provision which secures the surrender of fugitive slaves to their owners, of course, admits that they are legitimate property, and was intended to preserve peace and harmony among the states. I have seen, with inexpressible surprise and deep regret, that it has been contended not only that this conservative stipulation may be evaded, but that it is even meritorious to violate it. Meritorious to violate an express injunction of that constitution which many of us are solemnly sworn, and are all bound faithfully to support! If any citizens of the United States, who object to a particular part of the constitution, may elude and disregard it, other citizens, dissatisfied with other parts, have an equal right to violate them; and universal nullification of the sacred instrument would be the necessary consequence.

I agree with you, gentlemen, in most of what you say in regard to the present condition of our public affairs. In contemplating it there is much to depress, but I rejoice much also to animate and encourage the genuine patriot, and to stimulate his most energetic exertions. New and alarming principles, dangerous practices, great abuses and extensive corruption have been introduced into the general administration, during the few last years. I have witnessed their progress, with profound regret and deep mortification. But sentiments of despair are never to be indulged as to the fortunes or fate of the republic. An enlightened and virtuous people require only to be convinced of the evil to apply an efficacious remedy; and this conviction is forcing itself upon them, in spite of all the efforts which have been made, and are making, to deceive and betray them.

I thank you, gentlemen, cordially, for the friendly and flattering manner in which you have executed the commission assigned to you by the whigs of Nansemond. . . .

Copy. Printed in *Niles' Register* (August 17, 1839), 56:397-98. Addressed also to Thomas H.B. [*sic*, H.P.] Godwin and John C. Cahoon. 1. Crump to Clay, April 10, 1839. 2. Comment in Senate, Dec. 18, 1837; Remark in Senate, Jan. 6, 1838; Speech in Senate, Jan. 9, 1838. 3. Speech in Senate, Feb. 7, 1839.

To Francis Lieber, Philadelphia, May 26, 1839. Apologizes for such a belated response to Lieber's inquiry on a suitable person in Kentucky whom he might "address on subjects connected with Education." Suggests Madison C. Johnson, chairman of the board of trustees of Transylvania University, and the Rev. Mr. John C. Young [8:735], president of "the Danville College [Centre College]" in Danville, Ky. Hopes Lieber will visit Kentucky and "Ashland." ALS. KyU. For Lieber's writings on education during this period, see Freidel, *Francis Lieber*, 168, 173-74, 177, 181.

From Peter B. Porter, Niagara Falls, N.Y., May 26, 1839. Expresses delight that Clay will visit New York State and Canada, and promises that his trip north [Clay to Giddings, July 13, 1839] will be kept secret until his arrival in Buffalo. Understands, further, that he will accept no public dinner invitations, "*with one single exception however*, and that in favor of Buffalo." At that affair he will be expected to make a speech [Speech at Buffalo, July 17, 1839]. Realizes that Clay does not want to open himself "to the charge of making electioneering journeys." Outlines a specific route for him to take from Lexington: to Columbus, then to Cleveland or Sandusky on Lake Erie and thence by steamboat to Buffalo. Remarks that "one hour's ride from my house and three hours sail in a steam Boat will take you to Toronto, the Capitol of Upper Canada." Lists the interesting places Clay might want to visit in Canada. Thinks he should confine his travel in the interior of New York State to an area bounded by Niagara Falls, Lockport, Rochester, Canandaigua, Wadsworth's on the Genesee River, Avon, and Batavia. Explains: "The whole of this trip would be through the 'infected' or anti-Mason district and will embrace most of it. It is particularly desirable that you should visit this section of the State, where a large portion of the Anti-Masons and even Abolitionists, are already favorably disposed toward you and will support your election, and it is believed that the impulse occasioned by your presence (created by your appearance) would influence many more."

Reports his trip to New York City on May 19-20 where he failed to meet with Webster, as he had hoped he might. Was informed, however, by Nathaniel Tallmadge and David B. Ogden "that it was the general understanding among Webster's friends, that he would by some public act before his departure for Europe, withdraw his name, approve the national convention and recommend a hearty support of its nominee [Clay to Porter, May 14, 1839]. He (Ogden) agreed to see Mr. Webster, have a confidential conversation with him, urge upon him the expediency of withdrawing his name, and, in case of his doing so, assuring me that he and he believed most of Mr. W.'s other friends, would openly and cordially come forward in your support. He was to inform me of what should take place at the interview, but I have not yet heard from him."

Adds that "Our Whig Legislature, who were timid, inefficient and without tact, finally adjourned without doing anything on the presidential question, except approving the national convention [Porter to Clay, November 14 and December 30, 1837], agreeing to support its nomination, and leaving it to the Central Whig State Committee of the country of five members, all of them residing in Albany, to prescribe the time and manner of appointing the delegates to the convention. While at Albany on my return I saw Gorman [*sic,* Obadiah German] and [Thurlow] Weed on the subject; we got the committee together, 4 of whom are your decided friends, and the 5th balancing between the three candidates, but supposed to be somewhat more favorable to Harrison or Webster than to yourself. They agreed unanimously to convoke a State convention to be chosen in October and meet about the first of Nov'r, who are to appoint the whole 42 delegates to the national convention [Porter to Clay, December 30, 1837]. This plan was adopted, with a view to your interests, in preference to the election of delegates by congressional districts as the delegates will all be of the same cast, and give a powerful influence to the national convention." Copy. OHi.

There was no state-wide Whig convention in the fall to choose delegates to the national convention. There were, however, conventions of electors in the congressional districts as recommended by the State Whig Central Committee in the summer [Porter to Clay, November 14 and December 30, 1837; and February 16, 1839]; also a New York City Whig convention was held in November, 1839, and endorsed Clay. Members of the State Whig Central Committee (which numbered six rather than five) were: Lewis Benedict, John Townsend, Sanford Cobb, John Groesbeck, Robert Thompson, and Samuel Stevens. Washington *Daily National Intelligencer*, July 3, November 18, 22-23, 1839.

For Obadiah German, a friend of Weed's and a former Anti-Mason, see Alexander, *Political History of . . . New York*, 1:149, 170, 174, 190, 202, 258-59, 266; and *BDAC*.

From Schuyler Colfax, New Carlisle, Ind., May 29, 1839. Writes "As a Whig" to ask Clay's views on certain subjects. Believes "that a brief exposition of your views . . . would be of great advantage to the Whig party in this neighborhood and a disadvantage to the opposition." Requests an answer to the following "interrogatories": "Are you or are you not in favor of" (1) a Bank of the United States "with a right to establish Branches in every State of the Union"; (2) "having the Seat of Government moved to a western State and quiet in a measure the vexed Question of abolition in D.C."; (3) "having petitions of all kinds, which touch even on the border of slavery, abolitionism and colonisationism, laid on the table without reading"; (4) "having the Election of President and Vice President left entirely to the direct vote of the People"; (5) "having the election of United States Senator left to a direct vote of the People." Concludes with the hope "that you will soon be elevated to the highest office within the gift of the American Republic, and that I may live to see that glorious day." Copy. DLC-Schuyler Colfax Papers. For Colfax, see *DAB* and *BDAC*.

Colfax again wrote Clay on July 17, 1839, complaining that he had not received an answer to his letter of May 29. Notes that "I would fain suppose it had miscarried and you had not received it but when I think that almost every man in the Union has heard of you by name and reputation and that any letter would reach you even if only your name was endorsed on the outside I can not with any shadow of reason doubt but that it must long ere this have been placed in your hands." States that he desired answers to the questions so that he might "show it to my fellow citizens and thus . . . place before them a convincing proof of those great and important principles which the Whig party are now contending for." Specifically, he wants the answers "before the election for Congressmen in this state passed by" on August 5. Despite the fact that "it is now almost impossible for me to receive an answer . . . before that time," repeats the interrogatories.

States that "I cannot think that Henry Clay would be unwilling to declare his sentiments and I think that he will be willing to inform anyone who asks him . . . of his views in relation to National Question[s]." Adds that if this letter is not answered, "I might think a little less of Henry Clay as a man than I have formerly done—still as a statesman I would give him my cordial support and my humble aid in electing him to any office in which his friends would wish to place him. . . . it is my . . . wish to see the person to whom I am now writing placed in the Presidential Chair—" Copy. DLC-Schuyler Colfax Papers.

To ALSTON B. ESTES Lexington, June 1, 1839

The extracts from the [Washington] Globe[1] are entire perversions of what passed in the Senate on the occasions to which it refers—perversions which are habitual with that print whenever I am concerned.

I never used the expressions against pre-emptioners, which were attributed to me,[2] although I was opposed to the passage of pre-emption laws. At the last session of the Senate, an explanation was made of what I really *did say* at the previous session;[3] on which occasion a Senator from Illinois [Richard M. Young] acknowledged that he had *inferred* the exceptionable expressions from the tenor of my speech, and that *I had not used them.*[4] What passed was correctly published in the National Intelligencer,[5] but I regret that I have not a copy of it by me to transmit to you.

Copy, excerpt. Printed in *Kendall's Expositor* (April 15, 1844), 4:117. Estes published the Tennessee *Beacon* at Pulaski, Tenn. Walter T. Durham, "Charles Cassedy Early Nineteenth Century Tennessee Writer," *THQ* (Winter, 1977), 36:494. 1. See Washington *Globe*, Jan. 29 and 31, 1838. The full excerpt printed by Amos Kendall in the *Expositor* of April 15, 1844, in the form of a letter from Clay to an unknown recipient, dated Sept. 27, 1842, reads as follows: "My speeches on the pre-emption system were never regularly reported [Comment in Senate, Jan. 23 and 29, 1838; Remark in Senate, Dec. 12, 1838]. They were delivered, from time to time, in a sort of running debate, and I was shockingly caricatured in the Globe. When it was stated I think by Mr. [Richard M.] Young of Indiana [*sic*, Illinois], in the Senate, that I had applied degrading epithets to the Pre-emptioners [Comment in Senate, Jan. 26 and 27, 1838], I denied it positively, and my correction was published in the Intelligencer, but I regret that I have no copy by me. I was opposed to the pre-emption by itself. I thought it unequal to the public; was an irregular mode of acquiring the public lands, and led to disputes and controversies among the settlers. When public land was taken possession of, without the authority of law, I considered it a *trespass*, and characterised it as such. So did Mr. Van Buren, who used that identical word in one of his messages (in 1837 or 8) to Congress. On a general settlement of the land question, I was willing to allow pre-emptions properly guarded. Accordingly, you will find in the Senate Journal, 1840 and '41, pages 155 and 56, I voted for a resolution of Mr. [John J.] Crittenden, to allow pre-emptions to the poor settler, to the exclusion of the rich and the speculator [Remark in Senate, Jan. 19, 1841]. I voted at the Extra session of 1841, for the Distribution Bill [Clay to Ewing, April 30, 1841; Remark in Senate, June 9, 1841], in which a provision is incorporated for pre-emptions." 2. Washington *Globe*, Jan. 29, 31, 1838. 3. Reference to Clay's critical remarks about squatters on the public lands in the Senate on Jan. 26 and 27, 1838. See Comment in Senate, Jan. 26 and 27, 1838; also Washington *Globe*, Jan. 29, 31, 1838; and Remark in Senate, Jan. 8, 1839. 4. Remark in Senate, Jan. 8, 1839. 5. For the *Intelligencer*'s report of Clay's speech of Jan. 26, 1838, see Washington *Daily National Intelligencer*, Jan. 29, 1838. See *ibid.*, Jan. 28, 1839, for a defense of Clay against the charge that he had favored the old states over the new by voting for preemption in Tennessee and opposing it in the new states. The Washington *Globe*, Jan. 26, 1839, attacks Clay on this same issue. See also Remark in Senate, Jan. 8, 1839.

To KENNETH RAYNER Lexington, June 2, 1839

I have received your favor of the 20h. Ulto. stating that you are the Candidate for Congress in opposition to Mr. [Samuel T.] Sawyer,[1] and expressing a wish to obtain information from me, on certain points, relating to public affairs and to myself. One of these points is an alleged conversation which passed between Col. [William C.] Preston and me, of which Mr. Sawyer has endeavored to make a use disadvantageous to me.

I had before heard something of that alleged conversation, but without much particularity. I have no distinct recollection upon the subject of it. I remember to have met Col. Preston many years ago, at the Virginia mineral springs, and think it highly probable that I conversed with him on public affairs. It would be impossible for me now to detail the terms of any such conversation. I am, however, quite sure that I never advanced to Col. Preston, or to any other person, the idea that, in espousing the cause of the Tariff, I was influenced by the desire to bring Slave labor into competition with free labor, to diminish the value of the former, and thereby to create a necessity for its abandonment; because *no such motive* ever really actuated me. At the same time, if Col. Preston so represented the conversation, I have no doubt that he so understood it, because I think him incapable of a wil[l]ful misrepresentation. But if he did so represent it, I am sure that he misunderstood me. I have long entertained, in regard to our Slave population, this theory, that, in process of time, when the population of the U. States shall be greatly increased, and when free labor will be easily commanded, and cheaper than Slave labor, Slaves, becoming a burthen to their owners, slavery will be voluntarily abandoned. It is quite probable that this theory was alluded to by me, in the conversation with Col. Preston referred to, and that out of it may have grown the mistake, if a mistake were committed, in respect to what I really thought and said.

But, my dear Sir, it appears to me that the course of Mr. Sawyer, on this matter, as described by you; is undeserving of any serious attention, and I cannot consent to take any public notice of it. You say that he states, "He has in his possession a letter from a distinguished man (a member of Congress, you presume) stating that the writer was informed by Mr. Preston of So. C. that you said to him that one of your principal objects in supporting the Tariff was to bring the white labor of the North in competition with the Slave labor of the South, that the latter might be thus rendered less valuable, and the Southern slaveholders be thus compelled in process of time to emancipate their Slaves."

Well, now, all this is a very far fetched story. It relates professedly to a private conversation, perhaps general, loose and unguarded, of which no protocol was kept. When, how long ago, under what circumstances, is not stated. That the operation, which I am described as being desirous to bring about, was only to be consummated with distant posterity is clear. Can such a conversation, happening many years ago, furnish a safe rule to govern any man's opinions fairly of me? Can it be justly opposed to the facts, that I am a slaveholder myself, that I opposed the Missouri restriction,[2] and that I have again and again expressed myself adversely to Abolition?[3] What ought to be thought of that cause which seeks to sustain itself by a resort to private conversations, occurring among gentlemen many years ago, when neither of the parties ever dreamt that they were to become a topic of public animadversion?

As to a Bank of the U. States, my individual opinion is unchanged; and I do not believe that, as long as Banks exist, we can be sure of a sound and safe general currency, without the agency of such an institution.[4] But I do not claim for my opinion infallibility, and I am willing, for one, to make a fair experiment with the State Banks. What I have said and think is, that a Bank of the U. S. ought not to be established, unless and until it is called for by a majority of the People of the U. S. If, I have written any letter, inconsistent with what I now say, as I understand you to say Mr. Sawyer alleges, I challenge him to its production.

I do not write to you for publication, but for your own satisfaction. I cannot descend to answer in the public prints, in any form, all the misrepresentations to which I may be subjected.

ALS. ICN. For Rayner, a Hertford County, N.C., Whig who served in the U.S. House, 1839-45, see *BDAC*. 1. For incumbent Rep. Samuel Tredwell Sawyer, Edenton, N.C., Democrat who served in the U.S. House, 1837-39, see *BDAC*. In the Rayner v. Sawyer election, Rayner won by 2,635 to 2,009. Overall, in the N.C. congressional races, 4 Whigs and 9 Democrats were elected. *Guide to U.S. Elections*, 572. There were no state elections in 1839, because under North Carolina's new state constitution (adopted in 1835) all state elections were to be held biennially in even-numbered years. Marc W. Kruman, *Parties and Politics in North Carolina 1836-1865* (Baton Rouge, 1983), 13. 2. For Clay's stance in 1820 on the clause in the Missouri statehood bill which permitted slavery in Missouri while prohibiting it in the Louisiana Purchase territories north of 36° 30′, see 2:669-70, 740-48, 775-77, 785-86, 788. 3. See espec. Speech in Senate, Feb. 7, 1839. 4. Comment in Senate, Sept. 26, 1837; Speech in Senate, May 21, 1838.

To PETER B. PORTER Lexington, June 6, 1839

Your friendly letter of the 26h. Ulto. has been just received, and I thank you for your kind invitation to make your House my head quarters, and for the programme of excursions from it which you propose. But you almost frighten me from my purpose. If I submit to my friends at Buffalo, how can I resist them at Rochester and a hundred other towns in the West of your State? How can I reconcile an acceptance of their kindness with my repeated and constant declinings of similar testimonies of regard from other quarters? What I wanted was to pass along quietly, without noise, and without any personal public demonstrations; and what I feared was the difficulty of accomplishing that object amidst your dense population. Your letter augments my apprehensions, since it shews that even your philosophy is not a security for me. I am firmly convinced that both policy and principle unite in recommending one, situated as I am, to avoid, in appearance and in fact, all electioneering. I desire you and other friends to be fully impressed with this conviction, at least on my part, and to assist me in acting in conformity with it. Entertaining it, I must beg to be permitted to decline the despatch to Cleaveland [*sic*] or Sandusky of any Steam boat on my account, and to allow me to find my way to Buffalo as I can. My present intention is to leave home about the first of July and to pass through Ohio to Cleaveland, visiting some friends and viewing some land I own on the way. Mrs. [Lucretia Hart] Clay will not accompany me; but I expect to have along with me one, if not two of my sons.[1] The difficulty of fixing with precision, the day of my departure from Cleaveland for Buffalo, independent of other considerations, renders it inexpedient that I should accept the offer of a Steam Boat for my accommodation.[2]

I should have gone to your house, sans ceremonie, as I still intend doing, without your friendly invitation; for you know how much I have desired to see you under your own roof, and how much I esteem you. I think however and sincerely hope that your friendly efforts should be directed rather to repress than to stimulate public manifestations towards me.

I have mentioned that one or two of my sons would accompany me. James, now at St. Louis, where and in the neighbourhood he has been for a year or two, conducting himself in a manner highly satisfactory to me & advantageously for himself, writes me that he will be with me on the first of July to proceed on the journey. He is very young, and I wish him to accompany me for his gratification & improvement. I have invited Henry also to go with me but it is not certain that he can.

Our news from Va. is neither so good as we hoped nor as bad as we feared. We have gained in the H. of R. and in the State Senate, but lost in the lower house of their Legislature. The returns which have reached me are not complete, and it remains to be known which party has the majority on joint ballot.[3]

I will write you again prior to my departure from home. . . .

ALS. NBuHi. 1. James Brown Clay, at this time age 21, and Henry, Jr. Only James accompanied his father. 2. Clay to Giddings, July 13, 1839. 3. Clay to Caldwell, March 18, 1839.

To RICHARD HENRY LEE Lexington, June 9, 1839

I have to thank you for your favor of the 4h. and for your kind attentions to my two boys which it exhibits. I have a satisfactory letter from John [Morrison Clay] explaining his conduct towards Henry [Clay Duralde], of which the latter complained. I hope that hereafter there will be no difficulties and more harmony between them.

I transmit enclosed a check for $100 to be applied to their expenses.[1]

ALS. PWW. 1. Clay to Lee, April 20, 1839.

From James Henry & Co., Louisville, June 14, 1839. Report that they have already purchased "the principal part of our wool" in Ohio, payment six months hence, at "prices varying from 35 to 55 cts" per pound. Believing Clay's wool "to be of the best quality we will give you 55 cts p[er] lb for the lot: deducting one third from the weight of that part of it that is unwashed. You may draw on us at 6 Mos or we will send our note payable in Bank here for the amount." Add: "If you conclude to sell it please to send it to us soon; as we have to ship it to the factory near Steubenville, Ohio, and are afraid of low water." ALS. DLC-TJC (DNA, M212, R14). On June 16, Clay shipped 6 bales of wool to the Louisville wool merchants, variously weighing 126, 260, 95, 134, 55 and 142 lbs. per bale; or 812 lbs. gross. ADS. *Ibid.* (R18). James Henry & Co. was located on Main Street in Louisville.

To NATHANIEL P. TALLMADGE Lexington, June 18, 1839

Absence from home has delayed my acknowledgement of your friendly letter of the 3d. Ulto. I assure you, in all sincerity, that I receive[d] the suggestions and opinions which it contains in the same spirit of friendship and cordiality in which, I have not a doubt, they were conveyed.

In respect to the expediency of an amendment of the Constitution, limiting the office of President to a single term,[1] my opinion has been long deliberately formed. I think it would be an improvement of the Constitution. As it stands, it is incontestable that too many of the thoughts and exertions of the actual incumbent are directed to the object of securing a re-election, instead of being employed in devising measures for the advancement of the general weal. If I possessed myself the power of modifying the Constitution, as I think in this respect, it ought to be, I would restrict the office to one term, and make that term of the same duration with the Senatorial term. A shorter term than that would expose, I think, the Country to too frequent agitations. The termination would be the commencement of a Presidential Canvass; and there would not be time to carry out into full operation and perfect great measures which might be adopted by the President in office. But, so important do I regard the Cons[t]itution in [the] question that, if an amendment could not be obtained fixing the term at six years I would consent to one which should prescribe that of four years.

The question of the propriety of an amendment of the Constitution and that of what a President or a Candidate for the Presidency ought to do, under the Constitution, as it is, and the practice which has been adopted and is now firmly established, is not exactly the same. The case of an actual President and a Candidate is not exactly alike. A President in office, who has been elected without promises or pledges as to the length of time that he will remain there, would appear to act with forebearance if not magnanimity, by voluntarily limiting his continuance in office to a single term. But a Candidate who should declare beforehand that, if elected, he would only serve a single term, would inevitably expose his motives to suspicion and just animadversion. Such a declaration would be equivalent to saying to the People "Well you see I ask to be taken and tried only for a short time; you will soon get rid of me," and to aspirants for the office, "Give me your support for this brief term; I shall not be long in your way." I think such would be the construction placed upon a previous declaration.

Entertaining these views, I could not consent to authorize any annunciation of my purposes, in the event of my election. It would betray an anxiety to obtain the office, which I really do not feel, and which, if I did feel, I ought not to manifest. If I am elected, I must enter the office without previous pledges, and be left when there free to act according to my sense of what may then be right and proper. I concur with you in thinking that such an annunciation might possibly conciliate the support or neutralize the opposition of those who are themselves cherishing hopes of future elevation. But that very effect would be seen and be heard as an unworthy motive.

Whilst on the subject, I must say that I am inclined to think that a former communication which I made to you, in respect to Mr. Calhoun, was erroneous, although I have no doubt of the effect upon him if he could be sure that, in the event of my election, I would serve but one term. That communication was made upon information which I indirectly received, and nothing has since come to me to corroborate or confirm it

I have not seen any withdrawal of the name of Mr. Webster, as anticipated by you and by others; nor have I heard any thing further on the subject.[2]

Our election for delegates to a State Convention to nominate Candidates for Governor, Electors &c are now in progress in the several Counties In some instances there have been resolutions passed recommending you for the office of V. President; and I adhere to the opinion that some expression will be made by the Convention itself on your behalf.[3]

I congratulate you on the result of the Virginia elections.[4] If it be not all that we hoped and wished, under the extraordinary exertions of the Administration, and the unhappy divisions among the opposition, we ought to be satisfied with it. If New York can only maintain her ground the issue of the final contest will, I think, be certain. I hope that Mr [William C.] Rives will now be re-elected.[5]

I expect to leave home in about a fortnight on a trip to Canada via the Lakes, Niagara falls &c. and on my return may look into Saratoga, or some of the Sea Baths;[6] but I am almost afraid to [encounter?] the public demonstrations which the zeal of friends may prompt them to make. My wish is to move on quietly, without any parade; and if I was sure that I could not execute it, I would stay at home, altho' I have never seen the Lakes, the Falls, nor Canada.

ALS. WHi. Letter marked "(Confidential)." 1. Clay to Porter, May 14, 1839. 2. *Ibid.* 3. Clay to Tallmadge, April 9, 1839. 4. Clay to Caldwell, March 18, 1839. 5. The deadlock in the Virginia general assembly on filling the U.S. Senate seat to which both William C. Rives and John Tyler aspired was still unresolved as of this date. See Clay to Brooke, August 28 and Dec. 20, 1838. 6. Clay to Giddings, July 13, 1839.

To FRANCIS LIEBER Lexington, June 19, 1839

I have received your favor of the 6h. The alterations you suggest in the Copy right law are proper and just. The difficulties which have been encountered, and will continue to be encountered, in the passage of a liberal Copy Right law[1] proceed from *the trade*, especially the large book printers in the large Cities.[2] It is very active, and brings forward highly exaggerated statements both of the extent of Capital employed and the ruin that would be inflicted by the proposed provision for Foreign authors. These statements exercise great influence on members of Congress, many of whom will not enquire into the truth of them. These are the difficulties to be overcome; and they can only be subdued by enlightening public opinion, or causing it to flow in a correct channel. To this end, petitions numerously signed, the agency of the press and all other practicable demonstrations would be highly useful. And if a Committee of authors, well informed, sensible and judicious men could be got to attend Congress to answer and remove objections, before Committees of that body, I think it would be attended with the best effect.

I am glad to hear that the London papers speak of your P[olitical]. Ethics, in the terms of commendation which they well deserve. I was pleased and instructed with what I read of them.[3]

I expect to be absent from home during the months of July and August but to return to it early in Sept. and remain here during the autumn. I hope you will be able to visit us. You would have no difficulty in supplying yourself with a good K. saddle horse, nor in sending him to Columbia.

ALS. CSmH. Addressed to Lieber in Columbia, S.C. 1. Comment in Senate, Feb. 2, 1837. 2. See, for instance, "Cadmus" to Clay, Jan. 3, 1838. 3. Clay to Lieber, Sept. 16, 1837.

To JOSEPH R. INGERSOLL Lexington, June 24, 1839

Your obliging letter of the 17h. inst. brought me the first authenic intelligence of the transactions of the Chambersburg Convention,[1] and I thank you for it. I have not indeed yet seen in the papers any notice of its proceedings; but these I shall get by tomorrows mail.

The course of the Convention, aside from its nomination, of which it does not become me to speak, has been manly, independent, and I have no doubt will prove ultimately politic. The Anti Masons have it in their power to do much good, but not by dictation. Anti-Masonry, however right its votaries may be, can never become the basis of the politics of this whole Union. It is not sufficiently broad or comprehensive. You may be able to effect nothing, and I confess I have no hopes of any thing being effected, in

Pennsylvania for the good of the Whig Cause, in the approaching struggle, but you have laid the foundations for future success by the separate organization of the Whigs on which you have resolved.[2]

The pleasure of the acquaintance formed between Judge Wooley [*sic*, Aaron K. Woolley][3] and you was reciprocal. He spoke to me; on his return, in terms of high satisfaction with his reception in Philada.

I expect to leave home next week on an excursion to the Lakes, the Falls of Niagara and Canada, neither of which have I yet seen.[4] The only drawback upon the pleasure which I anticipate from the tour is the apprehension of parade or demonstrations on my account. These I shall avoid to the utmost of my power.

Pray remember me to your neighbours Messrs. [Horace] Binney & [John] Sergeant and do not forget Mr. [Josiah] Randall.

ALS. ViU. For Ingersoll, see *BDAC*. 1. Clay to McKean, April 16, 1839. 2. For the role of the Pennsylvania Anti-Masons in the campaign and election of 1840, especially the Anti-Mason and Whig political relationship in that state, see *ibid.*; also Vaughn, *The Antimasonic Party*, 108-12. 3. Aaron K. Woolley. See Marshall to Clay, Nov. 12, 1838. 4. Clay to Porter, May 14, 1839.

To RICHARD H. WILDE Lexington, June 24, 1839

Amidst preparations for a Summer excursion to the Lakes, the Falls of Niagara, and the Canadas, neither of which have I been able heretofore to visit, I have received, my dear Mr. Wilde, your interesting and agreeable letter of the 1st. May. Habitually brief in my correspondence, circumstances compel me now to more brevity than corresponds with the extent of pleasure I enjoyed in perusing your letter. I was happy to perceive in it that your buoyancy of spirits and your vein of humor were preserved, unabated, under the genial skyes and soft allurements of delightful Italy. It happened that, at the moment of the receipt of your letter, our friends Col. J[oseph]. M. White[1] & his Lady arrived in Lexington; and, but for your restriction, I should have gratified them with a perusal of your letter. They both look well and are on their way to the Eastern resorts of fashion and amusement.

Antonio, the bearer of the Bust which surprized you so much, ignorant as he is, is as wise as most of us, in regard to the person who will be the next President; and I am quite sure is as happy as that person will be. I am glad that Mr. Greenough[2] has succeeded so well in the likeness; which is the more creditable to his skill, because he was obliged, by illness, to quit the Model, before he had completed it.

And do you mean to bury yourself in those Libraries of which you give such glowing accounts? Why not come home and take part with us in the rough scenes of our Democratic strife? Many of us have regretted, sincerely regretted, your absence. I should think that the transition from Italy to Georgia would not be too great; and you would find, in the storm and the battle that are raging there, a reviving exchange for the poets, and the roses on which you have been reposing. And, then, you know that, notwithstanding your voluntary disfranchisement, if you could not be happy at home, we could again send you abroad, in certain contingencies.

You can make me no reproaches justly on account of the Library of the Count [Dmitrii Petrovich de] Bourtoulin. I did not say any thing in commendation of the proposed purchase,[3] and I must own did not feel very anxious about it; but the weight of your judgment and [William C.] Preston's earnest & eloquent endeavors forced me into a sort of acquiescence. I assure you, most truly, that the idea of any personal or particular interest of your's in the affair never entered my head, and was never heard of by me, until mentioned in your letter.

Congress has continued to deteriorate since you left it. Every new infusion of Jacksonism has been worse than that which preceded it; so that it has been constantly going down. The Senate exhibits distressing evidence of this disadvantageous change. If you were to see some of its late recruits you would wonder how they came there.

But I think, or rather should say, hope, that the worst times are passed, and that better and brighter days are opening upon our Country and its Councils. The next house of representatives will open with a majority of about thirty against Mr. V. Buren;[4] and against such a majority, if it be guided by ordinary discretion, he can not stand. The success of the Opposition to his re-election depends upon the harmony and concert among its elements. Judging from present appearances, the Whig Convention which in Decr. next is to nominate Candidates for the two highest offices,[5] will unite by a very large majority upon me. We have daily evidences of the concentration of the public opinion of the Whigs; and I believe—perhaps too sanguinely—that, after the nomination is made, there will be general & hearty co-operation. Every State, South & S. West of the Potomac, Alabama & Arkansas excepted, is against Mr. V. Buren, or doubtful. He will probably lose all the Western States, except Missouri; and amongst those in the Middle & in N. England, he can only count upon Pennsa. Maine & N. Hampshire. If we do not beat him, we deserve to be gibbetted.[6]

I should have been delighted, unobserved, to have looked on Mr. [George] McDuffie's[7] peregrinations through the Studios, Cabinets, Libraries & Saloons [*sic,* salons] of Florence, under your guidance. He is really a very honorable man but a very awkward one; a very able man but a very passionate one. I have no doubt that his sentiments towards me, in respect to the Compromise, are just and kind. Although I never had an interview with him in relation to it, he and Bob [Robert P.] Letcher could give a more faithful account of the negotiations which preceded it than any other two men.

I saw Bob a few days ago, and I was at his house. He is the same good natured fellow, with all the playfulness and humor which so remarkably distinguished him when you knew him. I shall hand or send him your letter, with which I am sure he will be highly gratified. Since he left Congress, he has been the Speaker of the popular branch of our G. Assembly, and has now a fair prospect of being the Governor of the State. . . .[8]

ALS. NHi. Wilde spent the years 1835-40 traveling in Europe. *BDAC*. 1. See 4:512 and *BDAC*. 2. For Horatio Greenough (1805-52), a sculptor who did much of his work in Florence, Italy, see *DAB*. The bust in question is likely that of President John Quincy Adams. Greenough later did a bust of Clay which Clay did not consider to be a good likeness. Clifford Amyx, "The Portraits of Henry Clay," 2 vols. Typed. Profusely Illustrated. Special Collections, University of Kentucky Library, 1980. 3. Sen. Preston had made the motion on Feb. 19, 1836, to purchase Bourtoulin's library. U.S. Sen., *Journal,* 24 Cong., 1 Sess., 177. See also 8:852. 4. Clay's count approximated that of

T.H. McKee who in 1906 counted 132 Whigs, 103 Democrats, 6 Independents, 1 vacancy. *National . . . Popular and Electoral Vote*, 39. On the other hand, R.B. Morris counts 124 Democrats and 118 Whigs. *Encyclopedia of American History*, 406; and T.B. Alexander, utilizing role call votes on various issues as guides, counts 125 Democrats, 114 Whigs. *Sectional Stress and Party Strength*, 34. See also Remark in Senate, Jan. 3, 1839. However, on the crucial first and second ballots for Speaker of the House on Dec. 14, 1839, during which party lines were reasonably intact, the results were: Dem. (John W. Jones—Va.) 113; Whig (John Bell—Tenn.) 102; scattered 20; and Dem. 113, Whig 99, scattered 22. *Cong. Globe*, 26 Cong., 1 Sess., 52-54. Following these indecisive ballots, local, sectional, factional, and personal considerations intervened to produce the election on Dec. 16 of Va. Dem. Robert M.T. Hunter on the eleventh ballot with 119 votes (necessary to elect—117). *Ibid.*, 55-56. 5. Porter to Clay, Nov. 14 and Dec. 30, 1837. 6. For the showing of the Whigs (Harrison and Tyler) in these and other states in 1840, see McKee, *National . . . Popular and Electoral Vote*, 44-45. 7. George McDuffie had traveled to Europe in 1838. Edwin L. Green, *George McDuffie* (Columbia, S.C., 1936), 178. 8. Clay to Tallmadge, April 9, 1839.

From Lambdin & Bennett, Natchez, June 27, 1839. Report receipt of Clay's shipment of bale rope and inform him that the current price for good rope is 12½ cents. Hopes Clay's will command 12½ to 13 cents, but warns him that "we may find some little difficulty in selling Rope without Bagging as the Stock of the latter article is very limited." ALS. KyLxT.

To Leslie Combs, Lexington, July 4, 1839. Writes from Maysville, Ky., that he has heard that the Austrian minister, H.E. Baron [Wenzell Philipp] de Marechal, has gone to Lexington and that he has provided him with letters of introduction. Adds: "Take him out to see Mrs. [Lucretia Hart] Clay, giving her some notice of his coming. And tell her to make up a little afternoon party for him, and give him some ice-creams, etc." Copy. Printed in Colton, *Clay Correspondence*, 4:441. For Marechal, see 5:507.

To JOSHUA R. GIDDINGS Niagara Falls, N.Y., July 13, 1839

I reached this place today; and having passed by and touched at y'r district, I wish to express to you my regret that I will not stop there long enough to have the pleasure of seeing you, and any of y'r Constituents that might have desired to see me. I have undertaken the journey w[hic]h. I am now pursuing mostly for the purpose of seeing the Lakes, this place, and Canada, neither of wh. had I ever visited.[1] As I am not making a political tour, I have thought it best to avoid all appearances wh. might tend to excite a belief that politics and not natural curiosities were the object of my excursion—I thought it especially proper that in Ohio I should not excite the suspicions of Gen'l Harrison or any of his friends. Hence I passed rapidly thro that State, stopping only a short time.

I hope that you will justly appreciate and approve the motives by which I have been actuated. Under other circumstances I should have been most happy to have seen you and my fellow Citizens of Astubula [*sic*, Ashtabula] and other parts of Ohio.

Copy. OHi. 1. Clay's trip, which became increasingly political as he moved through N.Y. State, took him from Niagara Falls to Buffalo (July 17), Lockport (July 20), Rochester (July 20-22), Canadaigua (*ca.* July 23-25), Oswego (*ca.* July 26-27), Montreal (late July), Quebec (early August), Saratoga (August 9-17), Troy (August 17), Albany (August 17-18), Poughkeepsie (evening August 19), Fishkill, Matteawan, Glenham, and Newburgh (August 20), New York City (August 21-24), Philadelphia (August 24-26), and Baltimore (August 26-27). See also Clay to Porter, May 14, 1839; Porter to Clay, May 26, 1839; Clay to Tallmadge, July 14, 1839; Van Deusen, *Life of Henry Clay*, 326-29.

To NATHANIEL P. TALLMADGE Niagara Falls, N.Y. July 14, 1839

I reached this place yesterday and have received here your obliging letter of the 10h. I must reserve for the occasion when I shall have the pleasure of meeting you what I have to say on the topics of which it treats, and on other topics.

I shall remain here and hereabouts some five or six days. I then purpose making an excursion to your Salt works,[1] which I am anxious to see, perhaps to Rochester &c. and on to Oswego, from which point I intend to descend to Montreal and Quebec. I expect to return by Lakes Champlain and George and to stop some six or seven days at Saratoga. I think that I shall arrive at Saratoga by or *before* the 10h. August; but from the sketch which I have given you of my route, you can judge as well as I can. I do not intend stopping at either Montreal or Quebec longer than two or three days.

They will, I understand, offer me a public dinner which I shall decline at Buffalo;[2] but I shall receive with pleasure all who are desirous of seeing me.

I will write you again from Quebec or Montreal.

ALS. WHi. Addressed to Tallmadge in Poughkeepsie, N.Y. 1. For early salt production in New York State, see Joshua V. H. Clark, *Onondaga Reminiscences of Earlier and Later Times. . . ,* 2 vols. (Syracuse, 1849), 2:7-44 and George Geddes (comp.), *Report on the Agriculture and Industry of the County of Onondaga State of New York* (Albany, N.Y., 1860), 50-70. 2. Speech in Buffalo, N.Y., July 17, 1839.

Speech in Buffalo, N.Y., July 17, 1839. Mentions the beauty of the western New York region and wishes that he might have passed through it "without display or parade." Thanks his audience for supporting the role he played during "the last war with Great Britain," and remarks that "Upon its causes, and upon its results, we may look back with entire satisfaction." Adds that while the U.S. border with Canada is now peaceful and far more secure militarily than it was in 1812, "the violation of our territorial jurisdiction, in the case of the *Caroline* [Comment in Senate, January 5, 1838], remains to be satisfactorily atoned for." Argues that the War of 1812 produced the economic conditions which brought him to concur "most heartily in the policy of protecting American manufactures, for a limited time, against foreign competition." Maintains that the protective tariff has produced a home market as well as a foreign market, and asserts that "it has placed this country at least half a century in advance of the position in which it would have been, without its adoption." Explains that "The compromise of the tariff [in 1833] was proposed to preserve our manufactures from impending ruin [8:604, 621-22, 626-27], menaced by the administration of General Jackson, and which would have been inflicted at the succeeding session, and to avert from the Union the threatened danger of civil war." Calls attention to the great improvements in roads, canals, riverine navigation, and harbors which followed the War of 1812. Initially encouraged and supported by federal funds, augmented by "the distribution of the large surplus recently made from the common treasury [8:812-13, 846-47, 873-74]," such improvements should now become the financial obligations of the states. Believes, however, that the government should complete the Cumberland Road and continue to improve the navigability of rivers. Insists that the "net products of the public domain should be equitably divided among all the States" before that domain is turned over to speculators by "loose and improvident legislation . . . under the plausible pretext of benefiting the poor [Clay to Estes, June 1, 1839]." Thinks the states could well use the income from public lands sales to pay for "great and costly" internal improvements. Concludes with the observation that this is not the occasion, nor himself the proper person, to speak "on the condition of our public affairs [Speech at Taylorsville, Va., June 27, 1840]." Will say only that "We believe that there is a radical maladministration of the government; that great interests of the country are trodden down; that new and dangerous principles and practices have been introduced and continued; that a fearful conjunction of the purse and the sword, in the same hands, already alarmingly strong, is perseveringly attempted; that the Constitution has been grossly violated; and that, by the vast accumulation of executive power, actual and meditated, our system is rapidly tending toward an elective monarchy. These are our convictions, honestly and sincerely entertained. They prescribe to us the duties which we have to perform toward our country. To correct past evils, and to avert impending dangers, we see no effectual remedy, but in a change of our rulers. The opposition constitutes the majority—unquestionably the majority of the nation. A great responsibility, therefore, attaches to it. If defeated, it will be defeated by its own divisions, and not by the merits of the principles of its opponents. These divisions are at the same time our weakness and his strength." States that if his candidacy "creates any obstacle to cordial union and harmony," he will retire from the contest. Asks in this regard: "What is a public man worth, who is not ever ready to sacrifice himself for the good of his country?" Copy. Printed in Colton, *Clay Correspondence*, 6:160-64. No manuscript version of this speech has been found.

On July 23, however, writing to editors Gales and Seaton from Canandaigua, N.Y., Clay enclosed a printed copy of the speech (not found) which had apparently appeared in a Buffalo newspaper, with instructions to correct a minor error therein if they reprinted the address in the Washington *Daily National Intelligencer*. ALS. NHi. The speech was published in the *Intelligencer* on July 26, 1839.

To FRANCIS GRANGER Niagara Falls, N.Y., July 19, 1839

I thank you for your friendly invitation. I go today to Lockport. Tomorrow to Rochester where I shall remain over the sabbath and leave it on monday morning. I wished to have seen Mr. Wadsworth's;[1] but as he is not at home (so his son whom I have seen here informs me) I hesitate. If I should abandon that excursion, I shall reach Canandaigua on monday next; otherwise on Wednesday. My wish is to see your Saltworks,[2] and after visiting them to pass to Oswego, and thence to Montreal & Quebec. My stoppage any where, during this detour, will be short.

Mr. Gregg [*sic*],[3] as well as yourself, has kindly asked me to his house. I will stay with one or the other of you, during my temporary sojourn, and will endeavor to apprize you more explicitly from Rochester. . . . P S. Do me the favor to make my best respects to Miss Granger[4] & to Mr. Gregg.

ALS. KyLoF. 1. Probably James Wadsworth of Genesco, N.Y., a prominent agriculturalist and a student of political economy. See *DAB*. 2. Clay to Tallmadge, July 14, 1839. 3. Probably John Greig of Canadaigua who later (27th Cong.) succeeded Granger in the U.S. Senate. See *BDAC*. 4. For Granger's daughter, Adele, who married first John E. Thayer and later Robert C. Winthrop, see Winthrop article in *DAB*.

To PETER B. PORTER Montreal, July 31, 1839

I arrived here last evening, worn down and prostrated by the incidents of the Journey. After you left me at Rochester, the same enthusiastic demonstrations which you witnessed there marked my progress. Quasi public dinners, suppers, vast concourses of people, Committees, & Speeches completely prostrated me. I escaped to the Provinces to find that freedom of which I found myself deprived in my own Country; but what do you think? I had scarcely got in sight of the nine mile point from this City when I beheld a Commee. from Burlington [Vermont] to invite me to that place!

Bronson[1] at Oswego and other friends made kind enquiries about you on my journey, and regretted that you did not come along. And our Rochester friends were unaffectedly sorry for an omission which occurred there.

I now expect to reach Saratoga on the 8h. proxa. which will be two days earlier than I expected.

Sir John Colborne[2] has sent his Aid[e] to wait on me, and I expect in an hour to pay him the respect due to his station. . . .

ALS. NBuHi. 1. Probably Rep. Isaac Hopkins Bronson, Democrat of Watertown, recently defeated for reelection to the 26th Congress. *BDAC*. 2. For Colborne, 1st Baron Seaton and governor general of Canada, see *DNB*.

From Committee of Whig Young Men of New York City, August 5, 1839. Write "to proffer to you the hospitalities of our city . . . during your present visit to the North." Note that "it would be more congenial to your tastes and feelings to be permitted to proceed on your route as a private citizen," but "you have already seen that this is impossible, and that wherever you go, the spontaneous acclamations that greet you on every side, will not be restrained." Add that the "simple announcement of your name is sufficient to draw forth the spontaneous homage of freemen to your genius and virtues." Express the desire to "participate in the free and unbought tribute to your character as one of the leading statesmen of our country," adding that "The Farmer and the Mechanic—the Merchant and the Manufacturer—acknowledge their indebtedness to your wise and fostering counsels for the past prosperity of their respective pursuits; while the plainness and simplicity of your life, uncontaminated by the refinements, luxury, and the atmosphere of courts, render you peculiarly dear to the most humble and hard-working of your countrymen in all situations." Thus, "we . . . tender to you, sir, the invitation to visit our city. And we trust that . . . you will afford our fellow-citizens an opportunity of taking you by the hand . . . and bidding you a cordial and unaffected welcome." Copy. Printed in New York *Morning Courier and Enquirer*, August 16, 1839.

On August 13, 1839, Clay answered, thanking them for "this new and distinguished proof" of their "esteem, and attachment" for him. States that since the "city of New York being directly in the route by which I shall return [home], I cannot deny myself the satisfaction of meeting such of my fellow citizens there as chose to favor me with an exchange of friendly salutations." Reports that he will arrive in the city on the 21st and will stay there two days. *Ibid.*

From Mark Hardin, Shelbyville, Ky., August 5, 1839. Writes on election day to assure Clay that regardless of how the current canvass turns out, Kentucky "is stronger against the administration than it has ever been [Clay to Brooke, April 2, 1839]." Believes that in races for the U.S. House in Kentucky, Linn Boyd will beat John L. Murray. Says he does "not know of any whigs who would like to see [Philip] Triplett beaten yet there are multitudes who would like to see him have a *very hard run*." Reports that Whig Representative Joseph R. Underwood "was under promise" to step aside in favor of Henry Grider but became a candidate without even consulting Grider. For this reason, "there are a good many whigs who would like to see him beaten—and all the aspirants may secretly or openly like to have him killed (politically) . . . as his family connection is now such as to make it probable he would like to be a life member." Considers Whig John L. Helm of Hardin County to be "the favorite" over Whig Willis Green of Boyle County for the seat surrendered by Whig John Calhoon, who was moving to Missouri. Describes the political impact of the news of the duel between Kentucky Whig Congressman William J. Graves and Jackson-Democrat Congressman Jonathan Cilley of Maine, in which the latter was killed [Clay to Speed, March 2, 1838], on "a collection of voters" gathered at "a sale in a strong Whig neighborhood of ours." Recalls that "the farmers 17 in number read the account" of the duel and when asked "who will vote for him (Graves) . . . not a voice was raised—He [Graves] was apprised a year since of the extreme repugnance of the community to have him as a candidate but declared he would be a candidate if he did not get one vote. There are many whigs who did not intend to vote will now vote against him." Expresses belief that former Democratic Congressman Patrick H. Pope of Louisville could have beaten Graves in the present election by "more than 1000 if not 2000 votes." Cites the opinion of the departing Rep. Calhoon that "Pope is tired of the party & would not run except as an opposition man, and therefore would not divide the party if this be true Graves will probably get his interest (personal) this year & next time Pope will receive Graves support; such an arrangement may elect Graves—I thus write you that you may be able to account for any seeming loss of strength in any part of the State." Copy, signed by Hardin. Courtesy of R.S. Sanders, Lexington, Ky.

Linn Boyd defeated John L. Murray for a seat in Congress from Kentucky's 1st district by a majority of 600-800 votes. Philip Triplett won the congressional election in the 2nd district. In the 3rd district Joseph R. Underwood defeated Elijah Hise, by 300-400 votes. Underwood had married Elizabeth Cox, daughter of Col. John Cox, mayor of Georgetown, D.C., on February 27, 1839. Willis Green defeated John L. Helm in the 6th congressional district. William J. Graves defeated [probably Elijah F.] Nuttal in the 8th district by a majority of 300 votes. Louisville *Public Advertiser*, August 9, 12, 1839; G. Glenn Clift, *Kentucky Marriages, 1797-1865* (Baltimore, 1966), 98.

From Peter B. Porter, Niagara Falls, N.Y., August 9, 1839. Thanks Clay for his letter of July 31 from Montreal. Warns him that he will be obliged to run the political gauntlet again when he travels back into New York from Canada. Believes his visit in New York State has impressed "many who were vacilating and undecided," and asserts that it has "drawn over to you from the Van Buren ranks in this quarter of the State a number of his most respectable and influential supporters." Reports on recent conversations "at my house" with Gen. Winfield Scott who "openly and on all occasions avows his determination not to become a candidate for the Presidency, but to give you his best support." Says he has recently had a letter from Gov. William H. Seward saying he hopes to meet with Clay at Auburn or Syracuse if his "official avocations" permit [Seward to Clay, August 17, 1839]. Urges Clay to make a political side trip from Saratoga to Utica. Copy. OHi.

To LUCRETIA HART CLAY Saratoga, N.Y., August 12, 1839

My reception has been most enthusiastic and gratifying. I leave here on saturday next for Albany & N. York. and I expect to leave N. York on the 24h. instant.[1] My hope is still that I shall be able to reach home at the time I intended when I left it. My fatigues have been great. James's [Brown Clay] horse fell with him yesterday and in recovering trod upon James's ancle and injured it a little. It is getting better.

The President [Van Buren] is here and has been very civil. He enquired, as he always does about you particularly. We lodge on the same floor and near together.

I have recd. Thomas's [Hart Clay] letter of the 26h. Ulto. which has relieved me from much anxiety.

There is a constant stream of Company pouring into my room, which has prevented me for the last two days from writing to you. At this moment there is a person in my room. I am compelled therefore to write briefly.

My love to all at home.

AL. Courtesy of M.W. Anderson, Lexington, Ky. 1. Clay to Giddings, July 13, 1839.

From William H. Seward, Auburn, N.Y., August 17, 1839. Regrets that his public duties and related travels have made it impossible for him earlier to meet with Clay. Suggests, however, that "inconvenient" though it would be, he could leave Auburn on the train for Albany on Saturday afternoon, August 24, and meet Clay in Albany on Sunday the 25th. That failing, "Our hurried interview on Lake Champlain must satisfy me. I hope it will be regarded on your part under the circumstances as a compliance with the ceremony of respect. I ask it to be no otherwise considered." Adds that "You will soon pass beyond the greetings of the hundred thousand friends you find in the state and will be able to judge then of the aspect of public affairs and of your personal position in regard to them." Comments on the warmth of Clay's reception by New York Whigs, especially at Saratoga. "Having passed through many points of your route I have had an opportunity also to learn the tone of the public mind after your departure." Reports that "among our friends in Essex, Clinton, St. Lawrence, Jefferson, Oswego and Cayuga, the spirit of the Whig party has been invigorated by your visit." Concludes: "I have no hesitation in saying to you that your election would to no man in the Union be more gratifying than to me and that it is desired with an earnestness second only to that which you yourself put always foremost[,] the defeat of the present unworthy incumbent." Draft, signed. NRU. Two drafts are in the Seward Papers; however, the letter was apparently never sent. The first draft, considerably more verbose, deals with the same points, but includes a harsher evaluation of Van Buren and more praise of Clay, especially Seward's anticipation of Clay's elevation to the presidency ("the wish of my heart"). *Ibid.*

For Seward's awkward chance meeting and conversation with Clay on Lake Champlain a few days earlier, at a time when the N.Y. governor was trying to avoid a meeting with Clay and was already supporting Winfield Scott for the Whig nomination, see Van Deusen, *William Henry Seward*, 61-62; Van Deusen, *Life of Henry Clay*, 327-29.

Speech in Troy, N.Y., August 17, 1839. The New York *Commercial Advertiser* of August 20, 1839, summarized Clay's remarks to a gathering of some 2,000 people as follows: "He touched in an appropriate manner upon his services in the congress of the nation, in the cabinet, and other public stations which have been assigned him by the government and the people, at different periods of his life, and asked if it was necessary for him to explain his position in regard to public measures, or if there was a man present who did not fully understand his own opinions upon all measures and questions of public concernment? To which a thundering 'no' burst from the dense mass of human beings before him, congregated for the purpose of listening to the accents of the champion of this country and the pride of the people. He exhorted the whigs to union, perseverance, and activity—to regard measures, not men—to concentrate their strength upon the candidates who have the greatest hold upon the affections of the people. He adverted to the manner in which his name had been used in connexion with the highest office in the gift of the people, and said, if it presented the slightest obstacle to that proper concentration of the whigs which he so heartily desired, he would implore them to blot it from the list of persons whose claims have been placed before the people for the station." Copy. Printed in New York *Commercial Advertiser*, August 20, 1839; reprinted in *Niles' Register* (August 31, 1839), 57:8.

SPEECH IN NEW YORK CITY

August 21, 1839

FELLOW CITIZENS: I thank you for the kindness with which I have this day been received in the city of New York, and on this occasion I can not but recur to the great civilities and attention which have been shown to me in every part of this state, while journeying from Buffalo to this place. When I survey the immense assembley which has here collected, however much I may feel personally gratified, I know, I feel conscious, that it is not for me, but for the cause which I have advocated, for the country and institutions which we all so much love, that I am greeted with so many evidences of kindness and respect.

My strength will not permit, and, were I in full vigor, it would be impossible that my voice should reach all, or any considerable portion of this vast multitude. I should rejoice at the opportunity of conferring with my fellow citizens upon the present condition of the country, and of laying before them my views of the grievances under which we labor, but the present is not the time nor the place for entering into such a discussion.

In returning my acknowledgments to my fellow citizens, let me, in an especial manner, thank them for the selection of the organ of their congratulations. For in him I recognize one who, on the floor of congress, dared to break from the shackles of party, and to abandon personal and political associations, in obedience to a sense of duty and the call of his country.

Before my recent arrival in this state, I supposed that I possessed a somewhat accurate knowledge of its resources; but when I reached Buffalo, that beautiful city in the west; when I surveyed those mighty lakes, bearing upon their waters the products of the western world; when I travelled along the line of your canals, the great outlet for those products; when I viewed Ontario and the St. Lawrence, and the hundreds of lakes and streams which beautify and enrich every section of this mighty state; when I viewed the thousand fields of agriculture, and the thousand busy sects of manufacturing industry springing upon all sides—I confess that I was struck with surprise and admiration, and thought within myself to what an extent, under good government, wealth and improvement might be carried, to what countless numbers the blessings of our institutions might be extended! I said, is it possible that a people enjoying the blessings of civil liberty can ever be induced or ever forced to surrender them, either to mad transports of partisan and factious zeal, or the encroachments of arbitrary power? Yet we cannot but observe that the recent tendencies of our government have been to transfer to the executive those powers which were delegated to the legislative and judicial departments, as the especial guardians of the rights and interests of the people.

Fellow-citizens, our difficulties are great and our dangers are threatening; yet, with you are the means of relief. As I recently passed over your illustrious battle fields, my mind was carried back to the times of the revolution. I recalled the series of disasters and defeats which followed the American arms in the early days of that eventful struggle. I recurred to that period when even hope had almost deserted our fathers. I directed my attention to events now passing before us, and I rejoiced when I said that, as in times past, so now, the country may be saved, and her liberties be secured on the same plains where they were originally won. From the moment that Burgoyne surrendered his arms and his army in New York, a new light dawned upon the fortunes of our country; and whatever may have been our temporary reverses or partial defeats in other sections, they were all lost in the victory won on the plains of Saratoga.

I feel most grateful for the cheering salutations with which the name of KENTUCKY has been received by this assembly; and although she may not compare with your own state in numbers, she will be ever found, with her, sustaining the principles upon which our government has been established. In discussing the great questions which now agitate the people, I assume the right which I trust every freeman will assume, of speaking my conscientious opinions, however they may differ from those of many whom I have the honor to address. While acting in the councils of my nation, I have deemed it my duty to resist many of the leading measures of the administration. I have sincerely believed that the tendency of those measures was to unsettle the constitutional relations of the various departments of the government; that those powers which were vested in the legislature were in the way of being surrendered; that the public money, in all free countries subject to the vigilance of the people's immediate representatives, had been illegally seized by the excutive; that the public domain, the rich inheritance of unborn generations, is exposed to waste in the struggle to retain political power; that the patronage of the government, instead of being the reward of merit, is employed in the purchase of mercenary partizanship; that the project of the sub-treasury, while it deranged the business of the country, was calculated, if not intended, to place in the hands of the president the means of corruption. On these grounds I have been found for years past in opposition to the executive. I have struggled with zeal, if not with success, to rouse the country to a true sense of its difficulties and perils; having the fullest confidence in the justice of my views, I shall continue that struggle while I retain a seat in our national councils, under every embarrassment, in opposition to every difficulty, with a perfect conviction that my fellow-citizens will ultimately understand and overcome those difficulties and perils. I may be charged with improper motives; with being actuated by ambition; I may be assailed by the public press; but while I have strength to raise my voice I will send forth the words of warning; and whether they, in their effect, produce a change in the management of our public affairs, or a change of our public men, in either case the interests of the country will be promoted.

Copy. Printed in New York *Morning Courier and Enquirer*, August 24, 1839; reprinted in *Niles' Register* (August 31, 1839), 57:8-9. "Our reporter occupied a position where he was enabled to catch nearly every word that fell from the speakers; and although the language is not literally accurate, the sentiment and spirit of the address we believe to be preserved throughout."

To Henry Helmuth *et al.*, Philadelphia, August 22, 1839. Responds negatively to an invitation of the Democratic Whig Young Men's General Committee of Philadelphia to meet and greet them as he passes through their city enroute from New York City to Kentucky. Pleads fatigue, hot weather, and the need to reach home by a fixed day. ALS. DLC-HC (unbound); also printed in *Niles' Register* (August 31, 1839), 57:9-10. Written in New York City. Addressed also to C.A. Repplier and John B. Kenney.

Speech in Baltimore, August 26, 1839. "His address, though not occupying more than half an hour, if so long, was characterised by much of the varied ability—the playfulness, the humor, the high patriotic feeling, and the florid eloquence, which combine to produce in him, one of the most splendid and efficient orators of his age. We [Baltimore *Patriot*, August 27, 1839] should vainly attempt to do justice to this address by any off-hand sketch, in our power, under the circumstances, and shall, therefore, make no such attempt. But we may give a summary of the points made, rather than the language used. . . .

"In glancing at the general aspect of the country, as affected by the '*reform*' administrations of the last ten years, Mr. Clay adverted forcibly to the moral revolution which had been wrought out or was at least in rapid progress, by that agency. In the good old times of Jeffersonian republicanism, it was the usage of the popular administrations of those days to follow PUBLIC OPINION instead of attempting to dictate to it. The practice of Jefferson, himself, the father of American democracy, was appealed to with effect, in support of this statement. . . . But lo the contrast! The Jeffersonian democracy counselled obedience to public opinion. The pretended democracy of those now in power, teaches that the administration is the fountain of wisdom, as it is unfortunately of official power; and that instead of being governed or swayed in its measures by the will of the people, public opinion, throughout the country must be regulated and governed by edicts from Washington. . . . Three times have the people and the people's representatives—he might (said Mr. Clay) almost say three times three—repudiated and condemned this specious scheme [Sub-Treasury] of the administration, to put money in the purses of its myriad of officers and agents. But does the administration desist from urging this scheme upon the country, in accordance with those unequivocal indications of the public will, in opposition? No! So far from acquiescing in the conclusions of the public mind, upon this exciting measure, the administration is but the more tenacious to its purpose, and intent upon forcing it upon the country, with all its attendant evils, utterly regardless of all the bearings of public opinion, and 'in spite of the lamentations here and elsewhere!' Nothing, indeed, could be plainer or more striking than the contrast thus put forth by the speaker, between Jefferson and Van Buren democracy. The much vaunted 'reforms' of the 'predecessor,' were also alluded to with effect, by the eloquent speaker [Clay]. The retrenchers and reformers were exceedingly lavish in their promises. Enlarging upon the abuses and extravagances of an administration under whose lavish rule, the expenditures of the government had almost reached thirteen millions a year, the reformers pledge themselves to the utmost economy in their expenditures, and to the most searching operations in laying bare the official abuses of the preceding administration. But lo, again, the result! The people, confiding partly in the accusations of past abuses, and partly in their promises of reform, which were dealt out so profusely, put the '*reform*' administration in power. And such has been their admirable handiwork in reducing expenditures—such their power and their will in reforming extravagances. that the public expenditures have grown under the hands of these 'retrenchers' from almost thirteen, to nearly thirty-nine millions of dollars per annum! O, wonderful retrenchment! . . . Under the administration of the *reformers*, the embezzlements, and defalcations of the government agents had amounted to a larger sum, in the aggregate, than all the moneys lost to the country, in a similar manner, for the previous forty years, or since the adoption of constitutional government! And why was this? Whence did it happen, that the '*reform*' peculations of the last ten years, exceeded the aggregate of the previous *forty* years? There was but one way to account for it. The conclusion was inevitable, that in the matter of plain every day honesty and integrity of character, the official corps were not a fair sample of the people at large. . . .

"The remarks of Mr. CLAY upon the policy of the *reform* administration in putting down the national bank, and thus giving full control of our monetary affairs to the bank of a foreign nation [Bank of England], were to the point, were heard with marked attention. The characteristic difference between the two money powers was striking. One, they had indeed called a 'monster;' but if it were a monster, it should always be recollected that we the people, had the control of its CAGE! It was bound in the iron meshes of a charter, granted by the national legislature, and therefore under the constant control of our laws, as well as subject, in its fiscal administration to be operated upon by the wants and wishes and sympathies of the American people. But how was it with the foreign 'monster' which by destroying the U.S. Bank has now got control of the money market of the world. . . . To further her interest, therefore, the Bank of England puts the screws upon the money market, and so reduces the prices of American staples [cotton and flour], utterly regardless of the adverse effect upon this side of the Atlantic! Such is evidently the operation and effects of one of the *reforms* brought about, by the reformers, namely, the reform which took the principal control of regulation of our monetary exchanges from a national institution of our own creation, and placed it in the hand of a foreign bank which cares not for us, and has no sympathies with our people." Copy. Printed in Baltimore *Patriot*, August 27, 1839; reprinted in *Niles' Register* (August 31, 1839), 57:10.

From Unknown Correspondent, Lee's Sulphur Springs, Va., August 28, 1839. Encloses (not found) a pamphlet he has recently written which illuminates doctrines of Henry Clay. Notes that "To serve our country (in whatever station it may please God to place us) is the duty of us all." Says he has worked for the Clay cause and supports Clay's presidential bid. Hopes his various services will be remembered "Should the pending struggle against corruption and misrule be successful." Copy. ViW. The name of Lee's Sulphur Springs near Warrenton, Va., was changed to Fauquier White Sulphur Springs in the mid-1840s. Perceval Reniers, *The Springs of Virginia, Life, Love and Death at the Waters* (Chapel Hill, 1900), 156.

From E. Southwick, Geneva, N.Y., September 9, 1839. Thanks Clay for his letter of August 9, noting that he is "much grattified to find one that stands so high in the estimation of a large proportion of the country should condesend to answer one of so simple & assinine an individual as I am." Raises the question of slavery in conjunction with Clay's presidential candidacy. "I must be plain with thee I think if Thou art not in favour of slavary thou sacrafised Principle to expendency when thou voted for Misouri to come into the union with the priveldge of keeping Slaves I think if the south would disolve the union rather than admit a new state into the union with out the privledg of keeping slaves it aught to be desolvd." Believes that Clay has it in his power "to make thyself popular at the North as well as with those in favour of abolition at the South & yet not loose thy friends that are in some sort in favour of Slavary [if] thou can state that thou has been at the North & from thy observation it is thy settle belief that hird labours is the cheepest & this I think Thou can do & speak the truth." Fears that slave insurrections and the running away of slaves to Canada "will be our worst enimies in case of a rupture with that government." Suggests that it would therefore be "good policy to have them gradually at liberty or any way that the state should think proper."

Asks Clay several questions about slavery, viz: Is farming in the North as well done with free labor as it is in the South with slave labor? Would slaves be emancipated sooner if the North stopped agitating the slavery issue? Should various Christian denominations discuss the abolitionist approach to slavery? Would Clay himself favor admitting another slave state into the Union? ("this I will keep to my self unless thee is willing to have it made public.) If thee can only say thee will never vote for another state to come into the union with the power to keep slaves I should not be much afraid to warrant thee to out run the little Dutchman [Van Buren]." Can a man in Kentucky free his slaves if he wishes and then employ them as free labor?

Warns that the abolitionist movement is growing in New York and that abolitionists there will not vote for Whig candidates unless they support the movement. Concludes: "I have written about enough but some how I want thee should come out a little more plain on the side of the slave," even though "I have not the least doubt" that many slaves are better off than they would be if free. ALS. DLC-HC (DNA, M212, R5).

To OLIVER H. SMITH Lexington, September 14, 1839

I am desirous to obtain as accurate information as may be practicable in respect to the probable course of your State, in the approaching Presidential contest,[1] and I know of no one who will be more likely to communicate it than yourself. I therefore take the liberty of applying directly to you,[2] and if you will indulge me, I will state the points on which I should be glad to be informed, in the shape of the following interrogation.

Was the result of your late elections[3] owing to the use of my name in connexion with the Presidential office?

Is it likely that it would have been otherwise, if my name had not been before the people as a candidate. In the event of a contest between Mr. Van Buren and me, for which will the vote of your State be probably cast. Is there any other name, and if so whose, that would more probably obtain the suffrage of your State than mine?

Is there any reason to believe that the issue of your late election was influenced in any degree by the use of public money?

Will your State be represented in the N. Convention which is to meet at Harrisburgh [*sic*, Harrisburg] in December next?[4]

The information which I seek is intended as well to guide my own course, as to enable me to form some reasonable conjecture, in respect to the final issue of the existing contest. I request therefore that you will communicate with me in the utmost frankness and sincerity. I can hear accounts unfavorable to myself, with as much composure, if not with as much pleasure, as those of an opposite character. I do not wish to limit you to a strict and formal response to the above interrogations. Whatever form you may choose to give to the information with which you may favor me, will be acceptable, and thankfully received; and if you should think proper to add any which is not called for by this letter, you will increase my obligations to you. . . .

Copy. Printed in Oliver H. Smith, *Early Indiana Trials: and Sketches, Reminiscences* (Cincinnati, 1858), 251. See Smith to Clay, Sept. 28, 1839, and Clay to Smith, Oct. 5, 1839. 1. Harrison carried Indiana by 65,302 to 51,695 for Van Buren. McKee, *National . . . Popular and Electoral Vote*, 44-45. 2. Clay wrote a similar letter of inquiry to Allen A. Hall in Tennessee on this same day. Hall to Clay, Sept. 23, 1839. 3. Clay to Davis, April 20, 1839. 4. Indiana was represented by D.J. McGuire, J.R. Mendenhall, A. Clarke, J. Perry, and E.M. Huntington. McKee, *National . . . Popular and Electoral Vote*, 42; Harrisburg *Telegraph and Intelligencer*, Dec. 5, 1839.

From JOHN TYLER Williamsburg, Va., September 18, 1839

In conversation with a friend of mine a few days ago in which you were chiefly spoken of he made his advocacy of you in the coming Presidential election to turn principally on the point of your opinion in relation to the power of removal from office—I inform[e]d him that I had over and over again heard your opinions expressed in debate upon that question, and that I had no hesitation in stating that you were decidedly against the power as an original question, and against its exercise as practic[e]d by the last and present administration and in proof of this refer[e]d him to the register of debates—[1] He said that he regarded it as a matter so intimately connected with the preservation of free government, that he could not and would not trust a reported speech, since that might have reciev[e]d the interpolations of the reporters and could not therefore be relied upon with accuracy—but went on to remark that if I would write you and recieve from you a clear but succinct exposition of your opinions on this question and it corresponded with my statement, he would not only support you but do all in his power to advance your election—He is a man of decided influence and is now the Delegate to the Legislature from this district—[2] Do I request of you too much in asking of you a few lines upon this subject: Your letter will only be used to satisfy the gentleman refer[e]d to, whose good opinion it is highly important to conciliate—I do not doubt his full and unconditional redemption of his pledge—There is another matter to which I desire to invite your attention as much for my own gratification as to enable me to satisfy others—I remember that in a day or two after the proclamation was issued,[3] I waited upon you, believing as I firmly did that you were the only man in the Union who at that perilous moment had influence enough to save the Union—The conversation turn[e]d on the Proclamation, and you unhesitatingly pronounced it *ultra-federal, black cockade* (I use your language) You afterwards expressed to me your dissatisfaction with the force Bill, and when afterwards you declar[e]d in the Senate, that had you been present you would have voted for it,[4] am I mistaken in the fact that in a conversation afterwards with me you ascribed that declaration to the circumstance that the Northern members requir[e]d you to make it as the condition of their support of the Compromise [tariff] Bill—I have frequently so stated it—I bear in distinct recollection your antipathy to the measure as is fully evidenc[e]d by the fact that your Compromise Bill[5] made it a dead letter—In short I have never heard you do other than declare that the govt was the creature of the States a compact among equals—and when we have differ[e]d it has been more in construing the constitution than on fundamental principle—Thus have I always regarded you as a republican of the old school or principle—who had indulg[e]d, where the public good seem[e]d to require it, somewhat too much in a broad interpretation to suit our Southern notions—

If any apology is necessary for this intrusion on your time ascribe it solely to the great solicitude I feel for your elevation to the Presidency—You are aware of my position in this part of Virginia where nine in ten are what are call[e]d State rights men—It is natural for me to desire to arm myself fully for the approaching conflict—while you may be assur[e]d that nothing that you may communicate will ever be us'd to your prejudice—

One word more—I have but just return[e]d from the North where I was sorry to find so many opposite opinions prevailing—I am however nothing daunted by what I see or hear—and cannot but conclude that you will recieve the nomination at Harrisburg,[6] and will not doubt but that our divisions will afterwards cease—I said to Mr. [John J.] Crittenden at Frankfort that I should regard your election as certain if in accepting the nomination you would emphatically declare your determination to serve but a single term—If you have liezure, will you read three numbers under the signature of *Civitas* publish[e]d in the Richmond Whig early in this month—[7]

I write you without reserve and in doing so furnish you the strongest evidence of my esteem and confidence . . . P.S. You can if you think proper, throw your answers, to the foregoing enquires into separate letters—

ALS. MH. 1. See 8:693, 699-700, 703. 2. James M. Gregory was the member of the Virginia house of delegates from the Williamsburg, James City, and York district. Richmond *Enquirer*, June 14, Nov. 22, 1839. 3. Jackson's "Proclamation to the People of South Carolina," Dec. 10, 1832. See 8:603, 626-27. 4. See 8:615, 625, 686, 797, 862. 5. See 8:604, 619-22, 626-27. 6. Porter to Clay, Nov. 14 and Dec. 30, 1837. 7. The three Civitas articles, advocating "the propriety of limiting the Presidency to a Single Term of Four Years," appeared in the Richmond *Whig and Public Advertiser* on Sept. 10 and 13, 1839.

From WILLIAM HENRY HARRISON North Bend, Ohio, September 20, 1839

The papers received from Cincinnati last evening announce your return to Ashland and I avail myself of the information to dispatch an answer to your kind letter written from Urbanna [*sic*, Urbana, Ohio] and which I received at Columbus two days after its date. I would have answered it before but the rapidity of your movements p[r]evented me from knowing where to take aim with a probability of my letters intercepting you.

No one who knows you would suspect you of poaching, but at any rate Ohio is a free Manor and you particularly ought to have as great privileges within her borders as any other person in the Union.

Whilst at Quebeck [*sic*, Quebec] you no doubt saw the defile in which the Gallant Montgomery fell,[1] and the hights of Abraham immortalised by the death of the rival commanders both distinguished and beloved in their respective countries.[2]

Knowing your great admiration of female beauty, you must have been highly gratified, by your reception at Saratoga.[3] That scoundrel Bennet [*sic*, James Gordon Bennett][4] however complains in his [New York] Herald of your dress. He says that "your friends should have bought you a hat and a pair of breeches." I hope that there was no unfortunate *breach* in the latter.

In relation to politics, I can only say that my present positio[n] as it regards[5] yourself is to me distressing and embarissing. How little can w[e] judge of our future destinies? A few years ago I could not have believed in the possibility of my being placed in a position of apparent rivalry to you. Particularly in relation to the Presidency. An office which I never dreamed of attaining and which I had ardently desired to see you occupy.

I confess that I did covet the *second*[6] but never the first office in the gift of my fellow citizens. Fate, as Bonaparte would say, has placed me where I am and I wait the result which time will determine with as little anxiety as any one ever felt, so situated. . . .[7]

Copy, with interlineations in Harrison's hand. DLC-HC (DNA, M212, R21); also a typed copy with minor differences in spelling and punctuation is in InU. 1. For the unsuccessful American attack on Quebec in Dec., 1775, led by Generals Benedict Arnold and Richard Montgomery, see Morris, *Encyclopedia of American History*, 88-89. 2. For the deaths of British General James Wolfe and French General Louis Joseph, Marquis de Montcalm, on the Plains of Abraham at Quebec in Sept., 1759, see *ibid.*, 68, 70. 3. Clay to Giddings, July 13, 1839; Clay to Lucretia Hart Clay, August 12, 1839. 4. For Bennett, editor of the New York *Herald*, see *DAB*. 5. Phrase "in relation to" struck out and "as it regards" substituted. 6. Harrison had hoped for the vice presidential nomination in 1828 on the John Q. Adams ticket. Dorothy B. Goebel, *William Henry Harrison: A Political Biography* (Indiana Historical Collections, Vol. 14, Indianapolis, 1926), 248-53. 7. The following day, Sept. 21, Harrison again wrote Clay (from Cincinnati) thanking him for his letter of Sept. 19. Says it has been "a long time" since he received a letter "more gratifying to my feelings as it at once relieved me from all apprehension of any existing coolness on your part toward me from the position which my destiny rather than my will has placed me." Mentions also that he had bought a Spanish jackass last Spring with the intention of going "largely into the mule business but the fellow if he ever had any has lost all his vigor in his voyage across the Atlantic." Asks if Clay has had the same experience with imported jacks and, if so, what remedy there is. As for his own vigor, "I enjoy as good as I ever did in my life." Copy. InU.

From Boyd McNairy *et al.*, Phoenix Hotel, Lexington, September 21, 1839. Report that the nine undersigned, "representing a large convention of your fellow citizens of Tennessee" which had assembled in Nashville on September 9, had arrived in Lexington "last evening" bringing with them a record of the Nashville proceedings. Affirm that these sentiments of political support are not limited to Nashville and its vicinity but pervade all Tennessee. Ask for an answer which they might take back to their constituents. Copy. Printed in *Niles' Register* (October 12, 1839), 57:102. Signed also by S.V.D. Stout, B.S. Weller, J.A. Battle, J.J. Hinton, W.H. Horn, J.P.W. Brown, W.F. Tannehill, and C.C. Norvell. They, along with McNairy, comprised a Committee of Invitation which had been appointed by a convention of "Whigs Mechanics and Young Men of Nashville" to travel to Lexington and invite Clay to visit Tennessee. Memphis *Enquirer*, September 20, 1839.

On September 23, Clay responds negatively to the Nashville convention's invitation to "visit Tennessee this fall." Pleads fatigue, poor health, pressing private affairs, and an early return to his duties in Washington. Says, however, that if his health improves and he is otherwise able to do so, he will "visit Tennessee prior to the approaching session of congress." If this proves impossible, he will attempt to visit the state after his return from Washington [Clay to McNairy, July 10, 1840]. Notes that "Nowhere, during a long public career, have I been more misunderstood or misrepresented than in your state." Therefore, sincerely thanks them for the "healing language" of their invitation. Copy. Printed in *Niles' Register* (October 12, 1839), 57:102.

From ALLEN A. HALL Nashville, September 23, 1839

Duly appreciating the motives which prompted your letter of the 14th inst., I proceed very frankly to reply to your interrogatories.[1] You ask, "Was the result of our late elections[2] owing to the use of your name in connection with the Presidential Office?"

The result was certainly affected by the use of your name in that connection, in consequence of the erroneous impressions under which a portion of the Whigs labored with regard to your public character and conduct. But these impressions *can* be removed by the diffusion of correct information, and I am unhesitatingly of the opinion, that the prejudices known to exist in the public mind against yourself constitute no valid objection, so far as this State is concerned, to your being the Whig candidate for the Presidency. Our opponents made the most of these prejudices at the late elections. They were long and actively engaged in exciting them in every county and neighborhood in the State, while the Whig candidates for the most part, either from timidity or want of the proper information, absolutely made no defence whatever. In this Congressional District they were met at the threshhold, and all of their charges against you refuted. The consequence is, that Mr [John] Bell's majority may be set down as your majority at the Presidential election, should you be the candidate. This was the case also in several other Congressional Districts; but in four or five of them, not one word was heard in your defence from the Whig candidates. All attempts to rouse many of your best friends in this quarter proved fruitless. In their over confidence, they folded their arms and would neither devote labor or money to the cause. Some four or five hundred dollars were all that could be raised in Nashville! Five thousand dollars laid out in the printing and distribution of the necessary documents would have given the Whigs the victory by a decided majority. I must be permitted to add, that the most efficient defence of your public character and conduct, was made by some of those who were opposed to your name being brought forward during the canvass. They apprehended that it would enable our opponents to make a more effective *use* of the prejudices existing against you; and of the erroneous impressions under which a portion of the Whigs labored in respect to your public course and your opinions concerning certain measures of national policy. Although the result, in some measure, justified these apprehensions, yet the very inconsiderable majority obtained by our opponents, under the peculiar and extraordinary circumstances I have mentioned, satisfies me and should satisfy every unprejudiced mind, that with even ordinary efforts on the part of the Whigs, they could have carried the State, notwithstanding the use which was made of your name in connection with the Presidential Office.

You ask: "In the event of a contest between yourself and Mr Van Buren, for which will the vote of our State be probably cast?"

I answer, for *you*. The Whigs have it in their power to cast the vote of Tennessee for you, if they will use reasonable exertions, and I believe they *will* use them. The counties are now organizing by the appointment of Committees; and when they are all thus organized, I shall consider the victory won.

"Is there any other name, and, if so, whose, that would more probably obtain the suffrage of our State than yours."

I answer decidedly, *no*! Most of our leading Whigs would support Genl. Harrison, should he be the candidate. I would myself, support him very cheerfully. But I doubt very much whether we could even get up a ticket for him. By no possibility, in my opinion, could he beat Mr Van Buren in Tennessee.[3]

These remarks will apply in some degree to the question, whether "it is likely that the result of our elections would have been otherwise, if your name had not been before the people as a candidate?" The result would have been infinitely more disastrous had Genl. Harrison's name been substituted for yours.

When I say, that no name would more probably obtain the suffrage of the State than yours, I, of course, except that of Judge [Hugh L.] White. I had reference, to the *other* individuals whose names have been mentioned in connection with the Presidency.

We have no *proof* that the issue of our late elections was influenced in any degree by the use of *public* money. It was undoubtedly influenced to a very great degree by the unprecedented circulation of printed documents which must have cost a large sum of money; but how the funds were raised or where obtained I am unable to say. If from private contribution, the liberality of our opponents is truly astonishing and incalculably surpasses that of the Whigs.

I do not think that our State will be represented in the National Convention to be holden in Harrisburg in December next.[4] Nothing less than a general and spontaneous rising up of the people and *their* appointment of delegates in their primary assemblies, could accomplish the object. Were the proposition to start with the *leaders* of the Whigs, it would infallibly ruin them. I doubt the propriety of any leading Whig advocating such a measure in Tennessee. The time is too short, I apprehend, for the great body of the Whigs to become as reconciled to the measure and so sensible of its propriety and importance, as to assemble in primary meetings and appoint delegates. If attempted, the project would probably fail, and we should reap all the odium, without any corresponding benefit.

Thus, My Dear Sir, have I, "in frankness and sincerity," as you requested; given you the best information in my possession touching the different points specified in your letter. Mr [John] Bell and Mr [Ephriam H.] Foster[5] concur generally in the view I have taken.

In case this should reach you before you have come to any determination concerning a visit to Tennessee, permit me to say, that I have recently heard from various parts of the State, and it appears to be the general desire of the Whigs that you should come,[6] if the sacrifice be not too great. There would be a greater concourse here, than was ever before congregated on *any* occasion, and I think the impression you would make, would be advantageous to the Whig cause.

ALS. DLC-HC (DNA, M212, R5). For Hall (d. 1867), prominent Nashville lawyer, journalist and diplomat, who was at this particular time proprietor of the Nashville *Republican Banner*, see *NCAB*, 7:535; also J. Wooldridge (ed.), *History of Nashville, Tenn.* (Nashville, 1890), 374. 1. See Clay to Smith, Sept. 14, 1839, for the questions asked. 2. On August 6, 1839. See Bell to Clay, May 21, 1839. 3. In Tennessee in 1840 Harrison defeated Van Buren by 60,391 to 48,289. McKee, *National . . . Popular and Electoral Vote*, 44. 4. Tennessee was not represented. *Ibid.*, 42. 5. See 6:12; also *BDAC*. 6. McNairy to Clay, Sept. 21, 1839.

To BENJAMIN W. LEIGH Lexington, September 25, 1839

Upon my arrival at home, I found here your favor of the 29h. June of which you spoke to me at the W. Sulphur Springs. The conversations which I had the pleasure of holding with you there render it unnecessary to dwell on the topics of that letter.

This I believe is the day of the assembling of the Staunton Convention;[1] and I sincerely hope that its proceedings may be characterized by the discretion and wisdom which we are authorized to anticipate from the eminence of its members.

I have received, since my return home, two letters from Genl Harrison,[2] both of which I transmit to you herewith as better indicating the spirit which animates him than any description of it which I might attempt. The last was written, in consequence of my addressing an enquiry to him, before I received the first, to ascertain if he had received my letter directed to him from Urbana, which I mentioned to you. I have heard nothing indirectly from him contrary to the dispositions which these letters manifest. You will observe that he does not say expressly that he will abide by the decision of the Harrisburg Convention; but I have no apprehensions that he will not. Indeed I learn that he counts confidently upon receiving the nomination.

It would be folly to conceal from ourselves the fact that the issue of the Elections of this year generally is not of a nature to inspire great confidence of final success. If, however, N. York should remain firm and unmoved[3] (and of that I should entertain no doubt but for our disappointment in other States) I think all will yet go well, especially if we secure the H. of R.[4] This now depends upon Maryland,[5] the result in which you will know about the time you receive this letter. I have heard but little from Ohio, since I got home. That little is encouraging; but I do not allow myself to indulge too strong hopes.[6]

A good spirit prevails in Tennessee;[7] and if our friends there act up to their present resolutions, the Whigs will redeem the State. They have sent a Comee. all the way to my residence to invite me this fall to visit Nashville.[8] I was obliged to decline the invitation at present. They have got so many agitating questions of a local nature (and especially that of Int. Improvements) in Indiana[9] that, until the smoak clears off, we can have no distinct view of their condition. Those new States have rushed prematurely and unwisely into vast and expensive systems of Int. Impts, relying upon effecting foreign loans to carry them on. The loans cannot be effected; and the works must stop. These systems were adopted chiefly whilst the Jackson party held sway in those States. And now that same party turns round & opposes them, and endeavors to lay the blame at the door of the Whigs! That party destroyed the Bank of the U. S.[10] under assurances that the State Banks would supply all its facilities. They arrested or rather modified the power of the General Govt to execute Internal Improvements, upon the plea that they had better be left to the States. And now edicts have gone forth from Washington to make vigorous war upon the Banks of the States, and upon the Internal Improvements of the States! Did any party ever exist which equals it in inconsistency? . . .

ALS. ViU. 1. Clay to Brooke, Dec. 20, 1838. 2. Harrison to Clay, Sept. 20, 1839. 3. Clay to Porter, April 15, 1838. 4. Clay to Wilde, June 24, 1839. 5. In the 1839

U.S. House elections in Maryland, 5 Democrats and 3 Whigs were chosen. In the election of the Maryland house of delegates on Oct. 2, 1839, 46 Democrats and 32 Whigs were selected, giving the Democrats a majority of 14 in the house of delegates and 11 on a joint house-senate ballot. No state senators were up for election in Maryland in 1839. Washington *Globe*, Oct. 4, 7, 1839; Washington *Daily National Intelligencer*, Oct. 7, 1839. 6. Bell to Clay, May 21, 1839. 7. *Ibid.* 8. McNairy to Clay, Sept. 21, 1839. 9. Clay to Davis, April 20, 1839. 10. See 8:552, 558, 583-85, 681, 728.

To WILLIAM H. SEWARD Lexington, September 26, 1839

I recd. your favor of the 18h. transmitting a communication from Genl. Smith of Florida,[1] which shall have due attention.

The same mail brought me a letter from a correspondent in the City of N. Y. informing me that reports have become general that I am about to withdraw from the Presidential contest. I know not whether the prevalence of these reports is likely to do good or harm. If it be worth while to contradict them (of which you will be pleased to judge) you are at liberty to say that they have no authority from me. The truth is that I have formed no determination, one way or the other, about the matter; and on this occasion, availing myself of Mr. V. Buren's habit of non commitalism, I mean to remain uncommitted, until the proper moment arrives for a decision. That moment has not, I think, yet arrived. And having formed no decision I could not announce any.

I hope that your anticipations will be realized in N. York.[2] I need not say how much depends on the event.

I will communicate to my son [James Brown Clay] your kind remembrances of him. At present he is absent.

ALS. CSmH. 1. Possibly Persifor F. Smith, adjutant general of Louisiana, who had served in Florida during the Seminole campaigns of 1836 and 1838. See *DAB*. 2. Probably a reference to Whig prospects in the Nov., 1839 state elections in New York. See Clay to Porter, April 15, 1838; Seward to Clay, August 17, 1839.

From Richard Henry Lee, Washington, Pa., September 27, 1839. Reports that Henry Clay Duralde will revisit "Ashland." Adds that Henry is a "youth of amiable temper and good principles—As a member of my family [Clay to Lee, April 20, 1839], he has uniformily behaved with correctness—We feel attached to him. As a Student, he has been punctual in all his College duties . . . always well prepared for his recitations, and is making great progress in his studies." Says young Duralde has told him he might attend Transylvania during the coming school year. If so, Lee would like to know by November 1, "as I am pressed to receive into my family, generally, more than I can accommodate." Remarks that Clay's friends in Washington, Pa., "have followed you through your recent journey [Clay to Giddings, July 13, 1839]" and have been delighted to see "the testimonies of feelings on the part of the people, alike just to you & honorable to their own heads & hearts." ALS. DLC-HC (DNA, M212, R5). Delivered "By Henry [Clay Duralde]." Endorsed on verso by Clay: "R.H. Lee. With a/cs. [accounts] to John [Morrison Clay] & Henry." See Clay to Lee, April 20 and June 9, 1839. For Lee, see 5:436 and 7:604; he was also the founder of Trinity Episcopal Church in Washington, Pa.

To PETER B. PORTER Lexington, September 27, 1839

At the moment of receiving your favor of the 18h. inst. I was thinking of writing to you, and telling of my safe arrival at last at home, and how much I was obliged and gratified by all your kind and friendly attentions.

There is no authority from me for the rumors, to which you refer, of my having with drawn from the Presidential contest. They have originated with others. I have reserved, and mean to reserve, to the last proper moment, the decision of that question. I have been some times provoked to break off, for ever, from public life; but on reflection I have thought that higher considerations than any which appertain to myself ought to restrain me, at present, from taking any such step. If I believed that the Whig Cause would not be destroyed, or seriously injured, by my retirement, and that any other could combine a larger amount of support than I can, I would retire, without regret and without a struggle. But I have feared (perhaps erroneously) that my retirement would be injurious to the Country and to the Whig Cause. I have resolved therefore to remain in my present position, unmoved by the wickedness of opponents or the indiscretion or folly of our friends. A short time will enable one to see the whole ground.

If your State remain firm;[1] and if we secure in the H. of R. of the U.S. a majority,[2] we may yet anticipate deliverance. Otherwise, the prospect will be gloomy. . . . P S. I have written to the Govr.[3] & to M[atthew]. L. Davis denying the truth of the above rumors.

ALS. NBuHi. 1. Clay to Porter, April 15, 1838. 2. Remark in Senate, Jan. 3, 1839; Clay to Wilde, June 24, 1839. 3. Clay to Seward, Sept. 26, 1839.

From OLIVER H. SMITH Indianapolis, September 28, 1839

Your letter of the 14th inst. which had arrived during my temporary absence, was received by me last evening, and I lose no time in answering its contents. I need scarcely promise that I shall with the utmost candor, and without concealment, give you my opinion on the subject of your communication. I am aware that you would be as incapable of asking, as I would of giving any other response. Still I am not unapprized of the delicacy of the task you impose upon me. Having long cherished for you the most friendly feelings, private and political, I have looked with an anxious eye, to the result of the late elections in this and other States, for the purpose of drawing conclusions from them, indicative of public opinion, relative to the approaching Presidential canvass, and the probable relative strength of the prominent Whig candidates, whose names will likely be presented to the NATIONAL CONVENTION. The late elections in this State are little understood abroad,[1] they did not turn mainly upon general politics. Our system of internal improvements, and the consequent high taxes, with which the Whig cause is unfortunately identified to a great extent, although both parties have been instrumental in bringing the system upon us, has had a controlling influence and it may continue for years. The name of neither of the candidates for the Presidency had much to do with the matter, either for or against the Whig cause, still, candor compels me to say, that I greatly fear that your name would not be sufficiently potent to stem the current that has set, and is still running against us. No name under heaven would be so well calculated as yours, to stimulate your original supporters of our party to a desperate contest. But on that class who joined us under the Harrison flag we can not rely, should you be the candidate. They have not forgotten the old contest when their idol Gen. Jackson and yourself were in the field. They still retain a deep-rooted prejudice against you, repeating the oft-refuted charge of bargain, intrigue and management, between you and Mr. Adams, and they are beyond the reach of reason or arguments. In a contest between you and Mr. Van Buren in this State, it will require desperate exertions to insure our success. The party opposed to us seem to be united and moved by one common impulse, while their watchword is Democracy, understood by few, but powerful with the masses, and however little the party is entitled to its name, it has it, and we have to meet the false issue made for us, with the additional and equally false cry of federalism ringing in our ears.

You ask me whether there is any other name that would be more likely than yours to obtain the suffrage of this State against Mr. Van Buren. I must answer this question in the affirmative. I have no doubt but that General Harrison could get a majority of this State against Mr. Van Buren. We contemplate sending delegates to the Harrisburgh [*sic*, Harrisburg] Convention in December next.[2] I have been named as a delegate, but have declined, thinking it impolitic to do so; besides, the Senate will be in session, and I have not thought it proper to leave my seat while the body is in session, when I could avoid it. Having briefly answered your interrogations, I might here close my remarks, and would most certainly do so, were it not for the indulgent request in the latter part of your letter, and the fact that I know you will fully appreciate the motives that prompt the few additional thoughts which I submit for your consideration. Your friends in this State, with whom I have conversed, and no man ever had more ardent ones, are looking with painful anxiety to the determination of the Whig National Convention, in the selection of the candidate. If they thought your success probable, they would not hesitate in warmly soliciting your name to be placed before them as their candidate; but, they can not bear the idea of seeing you placed in a doubtful and desperate contest at this time. Still if it must be so, they will do all in their power for you, though their own political fate may be involved in the question. The opinion of your friends, here, so far as I have been able to learn it, is that you and the party have much to gain and nothing to lose by your indicating in such terms as your own good sense may suggest, your willingness or desire that Gen. Harrison may be the nominee of the Convention, he standing pledged to a single term, and by your cordial support of the General, manifested in such manner as not to cool your friends, but increase their ardor, you could do more to identify yourself with his friends in another contest at the expiration of the term, than all the electioneering your friends could do for you; while your old supporters would rally again to the standard of their first choice, now and hereafter. We have seen the result of the late Pennsylvania Whig Convention,[3] but the sentiments above expressed were held by us before that convention was held, and are not prompted by it. If I have been more frank than the occasion required, I hope you will attribute it to an honest conviction of duty imposed upon me by your letter, connected with the portentous approaching crisis, and not to any abatement on my part, of the private and political friendship I have ever entertained for you. . . .

Copy. Printed in Smith, *Early Indiana Trials: and Sketches, Reminiscences*, 252-53. See Clay to Smith, Sept. 14 and Oct. 5, 1839. 1. Clay to Davis, April 20, 1839. 2. Porter to Clay, Nov. 14 and Dec. 30, 1837. 3. Clay to McKean, April 16, 1839.

From James F. Ruffin *et al.*, Somerville, Tenn., October 2, 1839. Convey a resolution of a meeting of Whigs of Fayette County on September 28 asking Clay to join them in a public dinner in Somerville at a time convenient to him. Note that "It cannot have escaped your attention that for some years past gross injustice has been done you in Tennessee. But we rejoice at being enabled to state that the obloquy with which your name has been attempted to be shrouded is yielding to truth and reason and that your devotion to the Cause of civil Liberty is being appreciated among us." LS, by Ruffin and 26 other men. DLC-HC (DNA, M212, R5).

To OLIVER H. SMITH Lexington, October 5, 1839

I duly received your favor of the 28th. ult.,[1] and cordially thank you for its interesting contents. The views which it presents will receive from me attention and deliberate consideration.

It has been the misfortune of the Whig party, that it has so long delayed the designation of its candidate for the Presidency: that has been my opinion. The danger, increased greatly by indiscretion, now is, that when it makes a nomination, no matter of whom, some of the friends of the persons not nominated will not go for the candidate designated. This is declared to be the case with some of the friends of Gen. Harrison, without their seeming to anticipate, that it may be also the case with some of the friends of other persons who have been spoken of. Another consequence of delay, is that our party has been broken off into fragments, for if its leaders will not act, the members of the party will act for themselves; when the officers will not steer the ship, the crew will assume the command; accordingly we perceive, that not content with one General in the field, our friends have brought out another,[2] and I assure you from all the information which I have, I am inclined to think that the last is the stronger of the two.

I hope these unfortunate divisions will be reconciled, and that we shall unite heart and hand in supporting the person nominated by the Convention, whoever he may be; that body bringing, as its members will do, information from all quarters of the Union, must be much better qualified, than any individuals, however patriotic and enlightened they may be, to make a judicious selection. As for myself, I have no wish to be the candidate, if there be any other Whig more acceptable to the greater number than myself, nor without a high degree of probability of success. It is proper to add, that the rumors which have been circulated of my intention to withdraw are unfounded. I have reserved to myself the decision of the question, whether I will consent to the use of my name as a candidate. I mean to avail myself of the lights I can in guiding my judgment, and when I have formed a determination it will at the proper time, and in some authentic form be publicly announced. I repeat the expression of my thanks for your frank and friendly communication. . . .

Copy. Printed in Smith, *Early Indiana Trials: and Sketches, Reminiscences*, 254. 1. See Clay to Smith, Sept. 14, 1839, and Smith to Clay, Sept. 28, 1839. 2. Scott to Clay, Feb. 5, 1839.

To NATHANIEL P. TALLMADGE Lexington, October 12, 1839

I have been intending to write to you ever since my return but have put it off from day to day. Our Harrodsburg Convention made no expression, as I had been assured they would to [*sic*, do], of their confidence in and preference for you.[1] There was at first a good deal of diversity of opinion among the members as to the Candidate for State Governor; and owing to that cause, I am informed that they deemed it best not to introduce any other subjects but such as were indispensably necessary. I understand however that as far as the sentiment of the members was elicited you were the decided favorite. They finally fixed upon Mr. [Robert P.] Letcher to run for Governor, and I think made the best nomination they could.[2]

But your name has been brought forward under much better auspices in Virginia, at the Staunton Convention,[3] than it would have been here. You will have seen the proceedings of that Convention and must have been highly gratified with the resolutions which were prepared by Mr. [Benjamin W.] Leigh.

The elections have this year gone most adversely to the cause of the Opposition; and if N. York should imitate the bad examples which have been set her,[4] political prospects will be gloomy enough. To what cause are we to attribute this painful state of things? Have the people changed and become enamoured of the Sub. Treasury? I think not. I have seen no evidences of any such change, unless it be furnished in the issue of Elections. What then is the cause? I fear it has been in the corrupt use of money, money! In every State, altho' the mass is sound, there is a sufficient number of corruptible voters which, if all thrown on one side, will turn the scale. The Admon, I confess, I apprehend, has been in the market and purchased up these votes. I can see no other explanation of what we have witnessed. And I think it not at all unlikely that, besides the levy of contributions made upon Officeholders, the public treasure has been freely used.

I should be very glad to have the pleasure of soon hearing from you. I observe that the Syracuse Convention was well attended and displayed a great deal of enthusiasm.[5] I trust that we are not destined to defeat in the Empire State.

The finest spirit prevails in Tennessee, and they are confident of a final triumph.[6] They are putting the State in a condition of the most effective organization.

ALS. WHi. 1. Clay to Tallmadge, April 9, 1839. 2. *Ibid.* 3. Clay to Brooke, Dec. 20, 1838. 4. Clay to Porter, April 15, 1838. 5. The Conservative Democrats had again [Clay to Tallmadge, Oct. 31, 1838] held a convention in Syracuse, N.Y., this one on Oct. 1, 1839. Nearly every county in the state was represented. Tallmadge was one of the principal speakers. Washington *Daily National Intelligencer*, Oct. 9, 1839; Lexington *Observer & Kentucky Reporter*, Oct. 16, 1839. 6. For the 1839 elections in Tennessee, see Bell to Clay, May 21, 1839. Harrison won all fifteen of Tennessee's electoral votes in the 1840 presidential election. McKee, *National . . . Popular and Electoral Vote*, 44-45.

To THOMAS WASHINGTON Lexington, October 12, 1839

I am greatly obliged by the friendly views and opinions contained in your letter of the 6h. inst. My own opinion, as to the most expedient time of visiting Nashville, is in accordance with your's, and was so expressed to the

Committee, who did me the honor to visit me.[1] But they were very urgent for an immediate visit; and it was not until after many conversations, and exhausting all my powers of argument and persuasion, that I could prevail on them to acquiesce in the contingent promise which I made. I still believe that it will not be in my power to go this fall; for altho' my general health is much better, the Rheumatism has not yet entirely left my arm, and I have still a great deal to do in my private affairs and in preparations for my journey to Washington. Your opinion will contribute to reconcile me to the necessity of postponing the period of seeing my Tennessee friends.

I agree also with you that vastly too much importance is attached to the circumstance of my visit. The zeal of kind friends misleads them. They imagine that, being pleased themselves with the presence of their favorite, all must be pleased; without reflecting that the source of their pleasure gives pain or bitterness to their opponents.

I should have been glad to have had your views of the late defeat of the Whigs in Tennessee[2]—a most disastrous event which, I fear, is likely to exercise great, if not fatal, influence far beyond the limits of Tennessee. What kept Mr. [Felix] Grundy so long in Tennessee? Can the expenditure of no money be traced to him to effect your Elections?

ALS. THi. For Washington, see 5:45, 1060; 6:30; 7:185. 1. McNairy to Clay, Sept. 21, 1839. 2. Bell to Clay, May 21, 1839.

To Richard Pindell, Lexington, October 14, 1839. Conveys to Pindell 2,560 acres in the Military Bounty Land in Howard County, Missouri, he (Clay) had received from James Morrison by deed dated November 13, 1819. Sale involves 14 quarter sections @ 160 acres each and a single half section of 320 acres. Total sale price is $5,000, payable by Pindell in three equal installments. However, the price was reduced to $3,333.34 on May 17, 1841, following a trip by Pindell to Missouri to examine his purchase, and upon his discovery there that "several of the tracts are sold for taxes [Dunnica to Clay, November 19, 1840]." D, part in Clay's hand, part in hand of Thomas H. Clay. DLC-TJC (DNA, M212, R18). See also Clay to January, October 6, 1838; Clay to James Brown Clay, October 30, 1840; and Dunnica to Clay, April 17, 1841. Pindell was the grandnephew of Esther Montgomery (Mrs. James) Morrison [3:538].

To NATHAN SARGENT Lexington, October 25, 1839

I received your favor communicating the results of the Election in the City and County of Philadelphia, and other information about it.[1] I thank you for the communication, altho' as you properly remark it is not encouraging. If bad political news were confined to Pennsa.[2] neither surprize nor disappointment would be excited, but unfortunately it is not so limited. The elections every where this year indicate unexpected success on the part of the Administration. And if in N. York[3] and Massachusetts,[4] as you seem to apprehend, the same degree of success should be achieved, political prospects will be sufficiently gloomy.

I have long since made up my mind to do my duty, and leave the issue to the People and to Providence. I shall, in that way, secure at least the approbation of my own conscience.

I am grieved to witness the divisions among the Whigs. Defeat and disaster do not, with them, seem to produce the usual effect of more concord and harmony. If these divisions unhappily continue, there will not even be hope left to us. And I see no other chance of reconciling them than through the agency of the Harrisburg Convention.[5] God knows with what alacrity I would consent to have my name withheld from the Convention, if it would have the effect of increasing our prospects of success.

I am greatly obliged by your friendly assurances of attachment &c. It has been a source of great satisfaction to me heretofore, as, in any event, it will be hereafter, to know that I enjoy the confidence of yourself and other estimable friends.

ALS. ViU. 1. In the 1839 Philadelphia city mayoral race, Whig John Swift won with 3,343 votes to 3,293 for Democrat John K. Kane and 2,670 for Whig John C. Montgomery. The Whigs also won all seats on the city assembly, select council, and common council; however, in Philadelphia County Democrats won all county offices, including all 8 seats in the county assembly. In the city of Philadelphia, Whig Henry S. Sparkman was chosen as state senator over Democrat Andrew Miller by a vote of 5,534 to 3,652. Philadelphia *Public Ledger*, Oct. 9, 10, 1839. 2. Bell to Clay, May 21, 1839. 3. Porter to Clay, April 15, 1838. 4. In the 1839 Massachusetts gubernatorial election, Democrat Marcus Morton defeated Whig Edward Everett by a vote of 51,034 to 50,725. The unpopular "15 gallon law [Otis to Clay, Jan. 11, 1839]" which Everett as governor had signed in early 1839 played a major role in his defeat. In addition, the issue of abolition entered the campaign when Everett was asked if he favored the immediate abolition of slavery in the District of Columbia and of the slave trade between the states; also if he opposed the admission of new slave states. When he replied to these questions in the affirmative, the abolitionist newspaper, *The Liberator*, endorsed his candidacy. For a discussion of these issues, see *BDGUS*, 2:701; Arthur B. Darling, *Political Changes in Massachusetts 1824-1848* (New Haven, 1925), 241-42; Hampel, *Temperance and Prohibition in Massachusetts*, 79-101. In elections for the Massachusetts state legislature, Democrats won 250 out of 542 general court seats and were also substantially outnumbered by the Whigs in the upper house. Darling, *Political Changes in Massachusetts*, 251; Hampel, *Temperance and Prohibition in Massachusetts*, 86. In a special congressional election in the first and second districts, Whigs won both seats. *Guide to U.S. Elections*, 572. 5. Porter to Clay, Nov. 14 and Dec. 30, 1837.

To Robert S. Chilton, New York City, October 29, 1839. In response to an inquiry from Chilton, "I state that I was born on the 12h. April 1777 in Hanover County in Virginia near the Court house and Black Tom Slashes." ALS. Courtesy of L. Burton Milward, Lexington, Ky. Chilton, who at this time resided at 263 Broadway, New York City, later married the niece of Daniel Brent [2:378]. During and after the Civil War he served as a clerk in the State Department. *VMHB*, 20:96; 72:427; *The Washington Directory, Showing the Name, Occupation, and Residence of Each Head of a Family & Person in Business. . . .* Washington, 1864.

To Whom It May Concern, November, 1839. Says he has examined "the School of Mr. H.B. Todd in my neighborhood," and proclaims himself "highly pleased with his method of instruction, with the good order . . . of the School, and with the progress of his pupils." Has determined that "at a suitable time" he will "place a youth under my charge, at Mr Todd's School." Copy. Printed in Lexington *Kentucky Gazette*, November 28, 1839.

Todd's Green-Hill Female Seminary was located about two miles from Lexington on Tate's Creek Road. MacCabe, *Directory of the City of Lexington . . . 1838 & '39*, 68.

To ROBERT SWARTWOUT Lexington, November 15, 1839

Your good news, my good friend, from the *State* of New York is very reviving.[1] I began to fear that we had at last met with a long lane that had no end. The result of your Election terminates the previous disastrous

Campaign[2] gloriously. It will reanimate the hopes, and, I trust, redouble the exertions of our friends every where.

If we can now banish all intrigues, quiet all divisions, and go to work like patriots, resolved to conquer or die, we shall save the Country, restore its prosperity, and preserve its liberties. And why should we not? We have referred the question, wisely I think, to the Harrisburg Convention[3] to designate our Candidates. Who can presume to have better information than that Convention? Will any individual venture to oppose his separate judgment to their united Councils?

The Convention will make the selection which it honestly believes is most likely to be successful; and whether it be [William Henry] Harrison, [Winfield] Scott, or any body else, let us all unite heartily and absolutely in its support.

ALS. NN. 1. Clay to Porter, April 15, 1838. 2. For N.Y. City elections for mayor and council in April, 1839, see Clay to Tallmadge, April 9, 1839. 3. Porter to Clay, Nov. 14 and Dec. 30, 1837.

To NICHOLAS DEAN[1] Lexington, November 18, 1839

I cannot deny myself the pleasure of acknowledging the receipt of your favor of the 11h. and your previous letter, announcing the issue of the late election in N. York.[2] It affords a just occasion for general and patriotic congratulation; and furnishes additional proof that, in a good cause, we should never despair.

I hope that the Whigs will profit by this great event; and preach, pray for, and practice in a spirit of Union until our Country is delivered from all the dangers which encompass it.

ALS. KyU. 1. For Nicholas Dean (1791-1855), a leading New York businessman, see *NEHGR*, 10:193; 15:94. 2. Clay to Porter, April 15, 1838; Clay to Sargent, Jan. 14, 1839.

To Ursin Bouligny, Jr., New Orleans, November 20, 1839. Reports he has hired Thomas Oates to take charge of the "valuable" calves "which you purchased from me for your friends" during their voyage downriver from Louisville to New Orleans. Will pay Oates $1.25 per day, plus expences, going and returning. Assures Bouligny that the man is a very experienced handler of cattle, having "come twice from Europe with imported Stock." Hopes Oates can leave today and that "our friends will be pleased with their purchase." ALS. DLC-HC (DNA, M212, R5). Oates was the son of William Oates of Muhlenberg County, Ky. The family was known there for its progressive farming and stock-raising practices. See *RKHS*, 30:377; Otto A. Rothert, *A History of Muhlenberg County* (Louisville, 1913), 92-93.

To Robert Gilmor, Baltimore, November 20, 1839. Agrees to search in his "great mass" of personal letters and papers when he returns from Washington for autographs of Gov. Isaac Shelby and Daniel Boone. Thinks that finding a Boone autograph is unlikely, since he was "a man of the woods and not of the Closet, a hunter, and not a scholar, or man of letters." Adds that "the issue of the N. York election [Clay to Porter, April 15, 1838] is very refreshing." ALS. PHi. For Gilmor and his family, see 5:163-64 and *NCAB*, 11:402.

From WILLIS HALL Albany, N.Y., November 20, 1839

You have ere this learned the gratifying result in this State.[1] We have a majority of 20 on joint ballot—8 in the Senate & 12 in the Assembly. The popular majority is about 4000. and one more county than we had last year. Striking the city of New York out of the question the case stands thus last year the country gave a majority of about 9000—this year of 6000. Of this difference more than one half is found in Erie County alone, two or three of our other strong whig counties will more than make up the balance. In these heavy undisputed counties it is not usual to bring out more than half our majorities on the Assembly & Senatorial ticket. The result proves that out of the city[2] we have gained strength since last fall. The city is governed by peculiar causes—the principal of which is the immense foreign vote—supposed from 8 to 10000.—which was this fall relinquished to the enemy without a struggle. One or two wholesome laws which we shall now have it in our power to make will if vigorously executed secure it to us by a large majority.[3]

The selection of candidates to the Harrisburgh [*sic*] convention[4] is now the subject of absorbing interest. Great efforts are making for Gen. [Winfield] Scott.[5] —A sort of panic has been got up—A great many of your staunchest friends have yielded to its influence. But I believe it has been thus far confined pretty much to the politicians At all events in the city, where I spent the last week, the masses are totally unaffected. In this place [Thurlow] Weed now declares openly for Scott as do all the heads of Departments. I hear the Govr. [William H. Seward] has declared himself in the same way but of this I have some doubt.

Gen. Harrison has a goodly number of staunch friends in Albany at the head of whom is Gen. S[olomon]. Van Rensselaer. They are exceedingly bitter against Gen Scott—so much so that many of them openly declare they will not vote for him under any circumstances. At the same time they profess (secretly) their readiness to give their cordial support to the ticket Clay for Presidt—Harrison for Vice Presidt. This state of things naturally leads to new combinations—The result of which may probably be that to prevent a Scott delegate being sent from this district of which there is considerable danger, we may probably unite with the friends of Harrison and send Gen. Van R[ensselaer]. Impressed as I am, that Harrison will not be thought of in the Convention for the Presidency I consider Gen V. R. the very best delegate whom we can send.[6]

I write these things to give you such information of matters here as may be interesting to you. I will venture to go a step further & express my opinion on the main question. With a controuling wish to place the strongest man in our ranks before the people, I have listened attentively to all that has been said by the friends of the prominent candidates. I have reflected long upon the arguments & objections and sincerely endeavored to weigh them impartially and I can conscientiously say my former opinion not only remains unshaken, but is confirmed. God forgive me if I am in error. I would not willingly deceive myself or deceive you in a matter of such vital importance to the country.

The result of the election satisfies me that we have a clear whig majority of at least 10 000 in the State. Consequently I believe that a strict party vote (which is conceded to you on all hands') will carry the state next fall.[7] The only serious question is about the Abolitionists. It must be borne in mind that they run a separate ticket last fall & also this fall & have done their utmost to defeat us.[8] The majority therefore on which I rely is not by their aid but in spite of them. There are three other important considerations connected with this topic. 1st. The clamor of the Abolitionists is got up with the avowed purpose of preventing your nomination and those who are loudest are the very ones who will vote for you if nominated. 2d. The answer which you will give to their interrogatories will (without retracting your ground) remove many false impressions & dissipate many unfounded slanders and thus produce a *favorable reaction*. 3d. The answer which Gen Scott *must* give will remove the general impression that he favors their views and thus produce an *unfavorable reaction*.

I confine my views to my own state & I will advert to but one other consideration which is an answer to the other great argument for the nomination of Scott, viz. that he will bring into the field a large body of new recruits—I answer—for every new man he will displace one or more of the old guard. I speak advisedly and after consultation with shrewd men, not interested in politicks but intimately conversant with the great commercial & moneyed interests of the country.

Many of this class are now waivering as to the Sub Treasury.[9] The nomination of Gen. Scott will drive them over in numbers to the support of that measure in dispair of getting any thing else. It will pass—give comparative relief in the present annihilation of domestic exchanges—produce a reaction—become suddenly popular & overwhelm its opponents.

All the great interests of the country are now suffering What hope of relief is held out to them by the election of Gen. Scott? Who knows what will be his policy?

Again—the bonds of party are loosed at once by the nomination of a man who has never been identified with us. This consideration is important as giving full scope to those before suggested—it leaves every body at liberty to try new measures from new party connexions and no where will its effects be more manifest than in this state especially if Van Buren's prospects should look successful this winter.

I beg pardon for commencing a new sheet but I have one or two things more to say.

There is not one feature of the American System which would not at this time command thousands of votes which it never commanded before.

The opinion is gaining ground rapidly that the Tariff must be renewed. Many are talking of it & the opinion is often heard that our present embarassments are owing in a great measure to its repeal.

The Public Lands are now a prominent familiar & favorite topic with the common people. The depreciation of State bonds, suspension of State internal improvements and the rapidly approaching alternative of State taxation or State bankruptcy will immediately turn the attention of this State to the Public lands with great intensity.

The same remarks are true of a National Bank[10] especially if you incorporate with it the right of the states to subscribe to the Stock & pay with their bonds for a certain portion.

I will not enter further into the reasons which influence my opinion but will only add the why I have volunteered it. I know you will receive from some of your friends opinions of a different character. It is not an uncommon thing to hear the friends of Mr Clay reproached with having deceived him. We are informed we ought to disabuse him of the opinion that this state is for him &c. I can now say I have given you my opinion & given it conscientiously as I would in the presence of my God.

You will probably by this mail receive the names of the Delegates from the city of N York. Wetmore Selden Smith & Hammond.[11] in all of whom you will recognize decided staunch friends.

Many I fear will be sent from the country as your friends who will go secretly pledged to support Scott.

I have just been conversing with a gentleman from Rensselaer who has been ploughed with, to run as a Clay man & finally go for Scott. But even these men when they meet in Convention & are undeceived as they will be will go right.

ALS. DLC-HC (DNA, M212, R5). 1. Clay to Porter, April 15, 1838. 2. Clay to Tallmadge, April 9, 1839. 3. Reference to a voter registration law. Clay to Davis, April 20, 1839. 4. Porter to Clay, Nov. 14 and Dec. 30, 1837. 5. Scott to Clay, Feb. 5, 1839; Porter to Clay, Feb. 16, 1839. 6. Solomon Van Rensselaer was a delegate to the Harrisburg convention. *NCAB*, 11:285. 7. Harrison carried New York State 225,817 to 212,519 for Van Buren with James G. Birney, Liberty party (abolitionist) candidate, getting 2,798. McKee, *National . . . Popular and Electoral Vote*, 44. The race for state offices in Nov., 1840 resulted in the Whigs winning 66 seats in the New York house to 62 for the Democrats, while in the state senate, Whigs won 21 seats to 11 for the Democrats. *Niles' Register* (Nov. 14, 1840), 59:164. In the New York elections for the U.S. House, Democrats won 21 seats to 19 for the Whigs. *Guide to U.S. Elections*, 573. Whig incumbent Gov. William Henry Seward was reelected over his opponent, Democrat William Bouck, by a vote of 222,011 to 216,808 with Liberty party candidate Gerrit Smith winning 2,662 votes. *BDGUS*, 3:1077-78. 8. The abolitionists had not actually fielded a separate ticket in 1838 or 1839; rather, they had devised a series of questions to present to various political candidates in order to determine which among them they should support. Based on candidates' answers to these questions in western New York in 1838, Gerrit Smith had a handbill, titled "Freeman's Ticket," printed and distributed throughout the state listing the names of those candidates he felt antislavery men could conscientiously support. This policy was soon recognized as a failure, and by late 1839 a movement developed to form a separate abolitionist party. This movement culminated in the formation of the Liberty party in 1840 which then proceeded to nominate Gerrit Smith for governor of New York and James G. Birney for president. Birney received a total of 7,059 votes in the 1840 presidential election. Fladeland, *James Gillespie Birney*, 177-89; Gerald Sorin, *Abolitionism, A New Perspective* (New York, 1972), 78-85. 9. Speech in Senate, Sept. 25, 1837, and Feb. 19, 1838. 10. Comment in Senate, Sept. 26, 1837; Speech in Senate, May 21, 1838. 11. Robert C. Wetmore, a merchant, had left the Democratic party because of Jackson's opposition to the Bank of the United States. Clay subsequently sponsored Wetmore's candidacy for appointment as collector for the Port of New York, a position he did not receive. Harrison did, however, appoint him navy agent in Brooklyn. Fox, *Decline of Aristocracy in the Politics of New York*, 364, 422; Gunderson, *Log-Cabin Campaign*, 145, 269; Seager, *And Tyler Too*, 587. For Dudley Selden, also a former Jacksonian, see 8:292, 687. For Robert Smith, a Whig mechanic who ran unsuccessfully for mayor of New York City, see Glyndon G. Van Deusen, *Horace Greeley, Nineteenth Century Crusader* (New York, 1953), 99-100. For Judah Hammond, a Conservative Democrat who had joined Nathaniel P. Tallmadge in sponsoring the 1838 Syracuse convention [Clay to Tallmadge, Oct. 31, 1838], see Fox, *Decline of Aristocracy in the Politics of New York*, 399-400; Mushkat, *Tammany*, 180, 182, 186.

To THOMAS METCALFE *et al.* Lexington, November 20, 1839

The public use which has been made of my name, in connexion with the office of President of the United States, furnishes the motive, as I trust it will form the apology, for this note. I address it to you, because our common residence in the same State appears to me to render you the most appropriate repository and organ of what I wish now to say.

The Convention at Harrisburg[1] to designate candidates of the Opposition to the present Federal Administration, for the offices of President and Vice-President of the United States, has been recommended, and the propriety of it has been generally concurred in by all who agree as to the necessity of a change in the General Administration. It appeared to me to be the best, if not the only practicable method of reconciling and uniting those who, coinciding in the general principle, entertained different views as to the most suitable candidates for those high offices, and I have accordingly frequently expressed, and now repeat the expression of my conviction of the expediency of an entire and cordial acquiescence in the recommendations of the Convention.

In the meantime, appeals directly and indirectly have been made to me by a highly respectable Convention holden in Pennsylvania,[2] and by private individuals, to decline giving my consent to the use of my name, upon the ground that a distinguished citizen of the State of Ohio [William Henry Harrison] is the first choice of the Opposition in Pennsylvania, and in the opinion of that Convention would be more likely to conciliate general support than I should. I have been also addressed by various respectable and intelligent citizens of New York, directly and indirectly, recommending me to decline the contest in behalf of another eminent citizen [Winfield Scott], who has been distinguished in both the military and civil service of the United States.

Whilst I have been thus urgently but respectfully approached, numerous private citizens and public meetings and conventions in various parts of the United States (one of these conventions, indeed, in Pennsylvania itself)[3] have done me the honor to express their confidence in me, and to intimate their wishes that I might be the candidate of the Opposition for the office of the Chief Magistrate.

It is perfectly manifest that I cannot comply with all these conflicting opinions and wishes, nor, I apprehend, with any one of them, without disobliging the others.

Under these embarrassing circumstances, I have thought it most advisable to leave to the Convention at Harrisburg the free selection of candidates as being the assembly to which, by common consent, that important duty has been referred. Representing, as it probably will, all parts of the United States, bringing together the feelings and views of all, and comparing and weighing the local information which it will derive from every portion, it will be most competent to make a nomination acceptable to the great majority of its constituents. That it will be faithful to the high trust confided to its judgment and patriotism, cannot be doubted; and having full view of the whole ground, it will be more likely to make a selection agreeable to the great body of the Opposition than any separate convention could do, however enlightened and patriotic it may be. If the Pennsylvania Convention, to which I have just alluded, be right in supposing that the distinguished citizen whom it prefers would be more likely to be successful than any other, he ought to be nominated, and undoubtedly, for that very reason, will be nominated by the Harrisburg Convention, should it entertain the same opinion.

With a just and proper sense of the high honor of being voluntarily called to the office of President of the United States by a great, free and enlightened people, and profoundly grateful to those of my fellow citizens who are desirous to see me placed in that exalted and responsible station, I must, nevertheless, say, in entire truth and sincerity, that if the deliberations of the Convention shall lead them to the choice of another as the candidate of the opposition, far from feeling any discontent, the nomination will have my best wishes, and receive my cordial support.

And, gentlemen, I hope that you, my friends and neighbors, will excuse the liberty I take in expressing to you my anxious desire that, discarding all attachment or partiality to me, and guided solely by the motive of rescuing our country from the dangers which now encompass it, you will heartily unite in the selection of that citizen although it should not be me, who may appear to be most likely, by his election, to bring about a salutary change in the administration of the General Government—a change without which we shall be mocked by the forms, and stript of the substantial benefits of free institutions.

From the tenor of this note, I scarcely need observe that you are at perfect liberty to make use of it as in your discretion may seem proper. . . .

Copy. Printed in Schlesinger, *History of U.S. Political Parties*, 1:407-9. Addressed also to Leslie Combs and the Kentucky delegation to the 1839 Whig national convention at Harrisburg. Combs presented the letter to the convention on Dec. 7, 1839, the final day of that conclave. 1. Porter to Clay, Nov. 14 and Dec. 30, 1837. 2. Clay to McKean, April 16, 1839. 3. *Ibid*.

To LESLIE COMBS Washington, December 1, 1839

I transmit you inclosed a letter.[1] I received that which you did me the favor to address to me from New York, and noted its contents.

All eyes are now turned toward your proceedings at Harrisburg,[2] which I hope may be such as to produce union, harmony, and success.

Copy. Printed in Colton, *Clay Correspondence*, 4:441. 1. Probably the letter from Clay to Metcalfe *et al.*, dated Nov. 20, 1839, which was presented to the Whig convention on Dec. 7. See Clay to Metcalfe, Nov. 20, 1839; also Combs to Clay, Dec. 6, 1839. 2. Porter to Clay, Nov. 14 and Dec. 30, 1837.

To LESLIE COMBS Washington, December 3, 1839

I have received and thank you for your several letters addressed to me from New York and Philadelphia.

You have found a most extraordinary state of things in respect to the Convention at Harrisburg[1] and General [Winfield] Scott.

I understand it to be conceded, by the Delegates and Members of Congress from New York, a majority of whom have waited on the General, that eight or nine tenths of the Whigs of that State prefer me. Nevertheless they prefer to make a nomination in conformity to the wishes of the one or two tenths.[2]

Now the question is, and it may be worked by the rule of three, whether it is easier to bring over eight or nine tenths to one or two tenths, or one or two tenths to eight or nine? whether the majority (and such a majority!)

can be easier drawn to the minority, or the minority, small as it is, to the majority?

What security is there that if a nomination is made, contrary to the wishes of a large majority, there is not danger of a loss, out of that majority, greater in extent than the one or two tenths who are only to be conciliated?

But I will not pursue this matter. The considerations must all be obvious to you.

Copy. Printed in Colton, *Clay Correspondence*, 4:442. 1. Porter to Clay, Nov. 14 and Dec. 30, 1837. 2. Porter to Clay, Feb. 16, 1839.

To HARRISON G. OTIS Washington, December 4, 1839

I was very glad to learn from your favor of the 29h. Ulto. of the improvement of your health, of which I had previously received unfavorable accounts. I sincerely hope that it may be fully restored and that you may be long spared.

Great events in the political world have transpired since I last had the pleasure of receiving a letter from you. I had been prepared like you for that in Massachusetts,[1] and like you I predicted it. Temperance is a very good cause unallied to power; but its destruction is inevitable whenever it ventures on the employment of co-ercion, or rather those are destroyed who authorize compulsion.[2] I hope that our friends will profit by their experience.

The results of the Elections of the year have been less favorable than we wished, but still there is enough left to authorize hope and encourage exertion. Indeed I believe that we shall succeed, if we observe honor and good faith among ourselves and become cordially united. Whether this union can be effected or not is the problem to be solved at Harrisburg, perhaps, this day. I most fervently pray for the best. To my very great surprize, on my arrival here, I found that the project, of which I had not been unaware, to run Genl. [Winfield] Scott had risen to an importance that I had never supposed it would reach;[3] and I am prepared to hear, without surprize, that he is nominated. Personally it will be a great relief to me. But as it is admitted that nine tenths of those who are to make a President, on our side, prefer another, it seems to me to be playing a rash game to stake these nine to one! You and I have both lived long enough to regard, with composure, whatever the bosom of time may unfold, altho' it was unexpected. That we may both yet live to see our Country once more under an administration of its Government honest capable & faithful I am sure is as sincerely desired by you as it is by [me].

ALS. MHi. 1. Clay to Sargent, Oct. 25, 1839. 2. Otis to Clay, Jan. 11, 1839. 3. Scott to Clay, Feb. 5, 1839.

To PETER B. PORTER Washington, December 4, 1839

Your letter of the 13h. Ulto. was received by me at Wheeling, on my way hither. The movement in behalf of Genl. [Winfield] S[cott].[1] which you so well understood and described is probably brought to a test by this time at Harrodsburg [*sic*, Harrisburg]. I should not be surprized if it turns out to be successful. A majority of your delegation to the Convention on their way to Harrodsburg was brought over at Albany and N. York; and the greater part of the members of the H. of R. have been also induced to concur in the project. Mitchell almost alone has stood firm.[2] To a man, I understand, both delegations express a preference for me,[3] and declare that nine tenths of their Constituents entertain the same preference. Yet they think that it is easier to carry nine to one than one to nine! The contingency ought to be very certain in which such odds as nine to one is staked.

I am informed that angry excitement was expected at Harrisburg between the friends of the two Generals [Harrison and Scott]. That and the firmness of my friends are the only security against the nomination of Genl. Scott.[4]

I addressed a letter to the delegation from K. with authority to submit it to the Convention, of which I anticipate your approval. It in effect left the matter to the decision of that body.[5]

Three days are passed and no Speaker, and no advance towards making one.[6] I write in great haste—

ALS. NBuHi. 1. Scott to Clay, Feb. 5, 1839; Porter to Clay, Feb. 16, 1839. 2. Reference is to two separate groups—(1) the New York delegation in the U.S. House of Representatives and (2) the New York delegation to the Harrisburg convention. Charles F. Mitchell was a New York congressman who was not a delegate to the Harrisburg convention. For Mitchell, see *BDAC*. 3. The New York delegation at the Harrisburg convention originally stood 20 for Scott, 2 for Harrison, and 10 for Clay. Under the unit rule adopted by the convention, however, all of the votes of one state went to the candidate supported by a majority of that state's delegation. Eventually, Thurlow Weed turned the New York delegation to Harrison after he became convinced that Scott could not win the nomination. Alexander, *Political History of . . . New York*, 2:39-40; Gunderson, *Log-Cabin Campaign*, 54-62. 4. Clay's large minority vote in the New York, Pennsylvania, and Ohio delegations was nullified by the unit rule. Gunderson, *Log-Cabin Campaign*, 58. 5. Clay to Metcalfe, Nov. 20, 1839. 6. Five of the six New Jersey seats in the House were in dispute [Clay to Otis, Nov. 14, 1838], and these would determine which party would organize the House and elect the Speaker. Eventually, it was decided that no one claiming the disputed New Jersey seats would be allowed to vote for Speaker. The 1st vote stood 113 for Democrat John W. Jones, 102 for Whig John Bell, 11 for William C. Dawson, 9 scattered. Finally, on Dec. 16, after numerous ballots, Independent/Democrat Robert M.T. Hunter of Virginia was chosen Speaker, with 119 votes (117 needed to elect). *Cong. Globe*, 26 Cong., 1 Sess., 56; Adams, *Memoirs of John Quincy Adams*, 10:142-65. For Hunter, see *BDAC*.

From Nathaniel Beverley Tucker, Williamsburg, Va., December 5, 1839. Asks Clay's opinion of whether his half-brother, John Randolph, was showing signs of insanity in 1821-22 when he drew up his will. Explains: "The will in question roundly charges my father [St. George Tucker] with an act of flagrant dishonesty and assigns that act as a reason for disinheriting all his descendants, and giving the estate to a stranger. I am prepared to disprove this charge, and to prove that my brother . . . knew it to be false. Thus in exculpating my father, I prove the man, whom next to him, I reverenced and loved, to be a slanderer and a knave. But he was neither. He was an unfortunate madman; and the drift of my whole course in managing the case will be to show that he was not himself, not only in 1832, when the will is said to have been cancelled, but in 1821.2, when it was made, and long before. . . . Without troubling you with more details, let me say that it is my aim to establish the occasional insanity of my brother, from the earliest time of which you could be expected to speak, and to show the progress of the disease tracing it down to his Russian mission. . . . Now you can see at a glance whether what you could say upon the subject would be favourable to my views or no. . . . You will see that there is no delicacy in your situation because the question is not whether your old antagonist was *ever* mad, but *when*." Recalls Clay's statement to him last August in which there was a "delicate intimation" of his doubt about Randolph's sanity, especially of "the distressing perplexity in which you were placed by an attack made on you in the Senate in 1825-6 [5:208-9, 211-12] [and] The apology which you then wished to have made for your assailant, but which you feared the public mind was not prepared to receive." Says he must now "make and establish" a similar point about Randolph's periodic insanity. ALS. DLC-HC (DNA, M212, R5).

For Randolph's will, which bequeathed his estate to William Leigh, William Meade, and Francis Scott Key, and for Tucker's subsequent failure to overturn it, see Hugh H. Garland, *The Life of John Randolph of Roanoke*, 2 vols. (New York, reprint, 1969), 2:149-51, 374-75; Peachy R. Grattan, *Reports of Cases Decided in the Supreme Court of Appeals of Virginia . . .* , 3rd ed. (Richmond, Va., 1897), 1:18-97. See also Robert J. Brugger, *Beverley Tucker: Heart Over Head in the Old South* (Baltimore, 1978), 90. Professor Brugger, a recent Tucker biographer, believes that Randolph likely suffered from Klinefelter's Syndrome, a disease that would help explain the erratic behavior of his young manhood and his feminine physical characteristics. Brugger to Seager, Charlottesville, Va., August 20, 1984. For Klinefelter's Syndrome, see Clayton L. Thomas (ed.), *Taber's Cyclopedic Medical Dictionary* (Philadelphia, 1979), p. K10.

To Luther Bradish, Albany, N.Y., December 6, 1839. Inquires about importing salt into Kentucky from New York, noting that while Kentucky has salt works, the inadequacy of their output is such that "we are obliged to resort to those of other states or Foreign Countries. The deficiency has been chiefly made up from Kanawha." Says he ordered a quantity of Syracuse salt for "Ashland" when he was in that town last summer and found that "all the varieties of it were excellent, and superior to any that I have been in the habit of getting." Thinks New York salt can compete successfully with that sold elsewhere along the Ohio River, "If you would take off the duty or allow a drawback, when it is sent beyond the limits of your state." ALS. NHi. For Bradish, see 5:698.

On December 7 and again on December 20, E.W. Leavenworth wrote Clay from Syracuse, N.Y. He reports in these letters that he is billing Clay for the salt he had purchased in Syracuse and asks him about "selling our Salt to advantage on the Ohio River." Says he will also write later "in detail in relation to the views & feelings of your friends here, in reference to the nomination at Harrisburg [Porter to Clay, November 14 and December 30, 1837]." ALS. DLC-TJC (DNA, M212, R14).

From LESLIE COMBS Harrisburg, Pa., December 6, 1839

You have been deceived betrayed & beaten by Northern abolition Antimasonry and the Dutch & the Dane—Last ballot Harrison 148. Clay 90—Scott 16—[1]

There has, in my opinion—been a deliberate conspiracy agt you by the friends of Mr [Daniel] Webster.—Mr [Alexander] Hamilton & Mr J[ohn]. A. King[2] of New York violated their instructions—I am told & were mainly instrumental in this catastrophe—to the Whig cause I may be mistaken—

Harrison did not get a *Slave State vote* on the last ballot—Nor *did you* get a *free State*—except glorious *Rhode Island.*[3] Illinois went for him & Connecticut for Scott—We have not yet determined what move now to take[4] —These votes were in committee & reported to the house—& then it adjourned—The bargain is no doubt to make Webster V.P. & thus carry out the Antimasonic nomination[5] which *they* have never declined—

There is a proposition to give them a rush tomorrow with Scott—but my opinion is, the course of dignity on the part of your friends is, to stand to their arms & let them carry out their operations as best they can.

Another is to leave & go home which also seems to me to be unwise—but I feel that the country & the *cause* have been so outraged that I shall not decide on my own course till tomorrow—

My opinion is that when the worst comes to the worst it is my duty to read your letter[6] as due to your fame [*&* to pos]terity [illeg. words]. . . . P.S. [Dudley] Selden has seen this & approves part—the last—& disapproves the first—but I believe it is true—every word of it—

AL. DLC-HC (DNA, M212, R6). Letter marked "*Confidential*"; written at 9:00 p.m. 1. This was the final ballot in the Committee of the Whole for the presidential nomination. For earlier ballots, see Gunderson, *Log-Cabin Campaign*, 59-62. 2. See 2:190; *NCAB*, 3:50; and *BDAC*. 3. In the margin of the letter at this point is written: "Glorious Rhode Island—Once, twice, & forever—" Clay had carried Rhode Island in the 1832 presidential election. 4. Porter to Clay, Nov. 14 and Dec. 30, 1837. 5. Clay to Otis, Dec. 13, 1838. 6. Clay to Metcalfe, Nov. 20, 1839.

SPEECH IN WASHINGTON, D.C. December 11, 1839

Mr Clay rose, and every person in the room rose with him, and gave as generous a welcome as ever a conqueror received just returning from the field of victory. In a moment all was breathlessly silent and attentive. Mr C. said that although he had accepted the invitation to participate in the festivities of the day, he expected to remain almost a silent spectator. But he could not remain silent—I am, said he, here to render honor to those, who, after performing a most arduous service in a National Convention, are about to return to their constituents. You, gentlemen, said he, have made a great and patriotic sacrifice,—you have travelled at an inclement season of the year, and some of you more than a thousand miles, to perform what may be considered as a high and important duty.—I am proud to honor those who have thus honored the country,—those who, at great sacrifices, have left their homes for the public good. Your body was composed of men of great weight of character and talent, and you are here after having travelled the length and breath of the land in this public service. There cannot be a single doubt as to the acquiescence of the Great Whig party of the Union at the result of your deliberations. It was your fortune or misfortune to meet with various opinions; but meeting and deliberating, as was designed, you have made a unanimous nomination. Surely, said Mr Clay, it becomes no member now to object to what was done. If the friends or favorites are disappointed, they are bound to forget their disappointment—they are bound by every consideration of patriotism—by their hopes of changing and destroying this corrupt Administration—by their desire to establish a purer and better Government, to acquiesce in the nomination which has been made.

"If,"—continued Mr Clay, with great earnestness of manner,—"if I have friends,—friends connected with me by the ties of blood, by my regard of common friendship,—if I have any one that loves me—I assure them that they cannot do me a better service than to follow my example, and vote heartily as I shall, for the nomination which has been made" (Immense applause.)—"Talk not of sacrifice," said Mr Clay.—What is a public man worth to the country,—in what does he show his patriotism if he is not always ready to sacrifice himself for his country. There has been no sacrifice.

We have not been contending for Henry Clay, for William Henry Harrison, for Daniel Webster, or for Winfield Scott,—No!—we have been contending for principles. Not men, but principles, are our rules of action. Look not then to Harrisburg but to the White House—not to the nomination, but to the mountain of corruption which it is designed to overthrow,—not to the man who has been nominated, but to the Goths and Vandals at the Capitol. William Henry Harrison and John Tyler are medicine which will cure us of the sacrifice, if sacrifices there be, but there is none. Go home then, gentlemen of the Convention, remember what you have seen here.

Tell your constituents of the nomination—of a bleeding Constitution—of the Executive power against which we are waging a war of extermination—of Executive machinery and Executive favor—of one President nominating his successor, and that successor his successor Tell them to put forth all the energies they possess to relieve the land from the curse which rests upon it; and if they can then be indifferent, from that moment, they cease to be patriotic.

Copy. Printed in Lexington *Observer & Kentucky Reporter*, January 1, 1840. Speech was delivered at Brown's Hotel at a dinner given to Whig delegates to the Harrisburg nominating convention.

To THOMAS HART CLAY Washington, December 12, 1839

I received today your letter of the 5h. the first I have recd. since I left home. I am glad to learn that the prospect of your getting Hemp is good. I have written to Mr. Embry[1] offering to let him have two Saxony Ewes at $25 each.

You will have learned that Genl. Harrison obtained the Harrisburg nomination. The event has created great and general surprize nevertheless, I have felt it to be my duty to express, as I have done on all occasions, my acquiescence in and submission to it; and I should be sorry that you or any of my friends or connexions should display any irritation or dissatisfaction about it.[2]

I hope to be able to go home early in the Spring.

I should be glad if you would write me frequently. . . .

ALS. PU. 1. Probably Jacob Embry who lived on Richmond Turnpike, 10 miles from Lexington. 2. Porter to Clay, Nov. 14 and Dec. 30, 1837. In 1872, in his book *Seven Decades of the Union*, pp. 171-72, Henry A. Wise, claimed he was eyewitness to Clay's emotional reaction to the news of Harrison's nomination at Harrisburg. "My friends are not worth the powder and shot it would take to kill them!" he is quoted as having said. "It is a diabolical intrigue, I know now, which has betrayed me. I am the most unfortunate man in the history of parties: always run by my friends when sure to be defeated, and now betrayed for a nomination when I, or anyone, would be sure of an election." It is doubtful that this quotation is genuine. Surely it does not comport with Clay's known reaction to events affecting his candidacy immediately before, during, and after the Harrisburg convention. Indeed, at all stages of the nominating process Clay was clearly willing to support whomever the convention chose—and he subsequently did so without hesitation or rancor. Most historians concerned with this problem, however, have chosen to cite Wise, the sole source on Clay's alleged outburst. See, *inter alios*, Seager, *And Tyler Too*, 145; Gunderson, *Log-Cabin Campaign*, 68; Schurz, *Life of Henry Clay*, 2:180-81; Chitwood, *John Tyler*, 174; Van Deusen, *Life of Henry Clay*, 334. A good quote, alas, takes on a life of its own.

Remark in Senate, December 12, 1839. Presents the credentials of John Henderson, newly elected senator from Mississippi. *Cong. Globe*, 26 Cong., 1 Sess., 46.

To ROBERT S. CHILTON Washington, December 14, 1839

In reply to your letter inquiring why a clause was not inserted in the Treaty of Ghent guarding against the future British impressment of American Seamen,[1] I have to say, that you will recollect that the peace of Europe was then established, and the U. States alone were at War with G. Britain. We were not in a condition to dictate the terms of peace. Impressment formed one of the topics of negotiation, but G. Britain was not prepared to renounce the practice of impressing as she said her own subjects. We did not think it necessary to continue the War to compel her to renounce it, if we could compel her, for various reasons. 1st. If there were a general peace, there would be no impressment, which only takes place in War, or in preparations for War. 2d. It was not necessary to have any Treaty stipulation to exempt us from the practice, our right to exemption depending upon higher ground than any treaty. And 3dly. If G.B. should renew the practice of impressment against our Citizens, we could renew the War; and we thought that we could prosecute a new War with more vigor and more ample means than we could continue the existing War, exhausted as we then were. In point of fact she has not renewed the practice of Impressment agt. us, and I think never will.

Copy. DCU. Printed in Lexington *Observer & Kentucky Reporter*, Oct. 3, 1857. 1. See 1:857-58, 867, 907-8, 936, 938-39, 941-44, 948, 953-54, 961-62, 991, 1000-1001; and, espec., 2:145-47.

To HENRY CLAY, JR. Washington, December 14, 1839

You will have heard of the event at Harrisburg.[1] It fell upon us all here with great Surprize. But, as by the common consent of the Whig party the question of the nomination of Candidates for President and V.P. had been referred to the Convention, and it had made the nomination, acquiesence was the only alternative. I have felt that it was the only course of honor good faith and duty. I have accordingly both publicly and privately expressed my determination to abide by and support the nomination. I shall be glad if you and my other connexions shall come to the same conclusion. What the issue of the contest will be it is impossible to say. So far the Whigs at the North & the Whig press appear to receive the nomination well. Be its fate what it may, does not change the path which I ought to tread.

The House will probably to day or to night elect a Speaker.[2] My opinion is that he will be of the Administration party.

Do you come here this winter? How are Julia [Prather Clay] and the children?[3] Give my love to them & let me hear from you.

ALS. Henry Clay Memorial Foundation, Lexington, Ky. 1. Porter to Clay, Nov. 14 and Dec. 30, 1837; Clay to Thomas Hart Clay, Dec. 12, 1839. 2. Clay to Porter, Dec. 4, 1839. 3. Henry III (age 6) and Anne (2).

From PETER B. PORTER Niagara Falls, N.Y., December 16, 1839

I have received your favor of the 14th, and should have written sooner, but that my hand has absolutely been paralysed by the surprise and mortification, not to say disgust with the institutions of my country created by the news from Harrisburg[1]

I knew that you had many active political enemies in this state, who would do what they could to defeat your nomination; and that, from the peculiar position they held and the mode adopted for choosing delegates, they would be able to effect the election of an undue proportion (compared with the known sentiments of the great body of the people) of such as would second their views[2] —But that they could secure anything approaching to a majority never occurred to me as possible. Indeed I still believe that a decided majority of our delegates left home for Harrisburg with a full determination to support you, in conformity with the known wishes of their constituents, but that they were artfully diverted from their purpose, as you suggest, after their arrival at Albany or New York, by being made to believe that your election was wholly impracticable, and moreover that your own private wish was, not to be nominated, although you could not with propriety withdraw.

You are aware that the power of the party in this State opposed to Jacksonism, has, for ten years past, been wielded by the anti-masons, among whom your personal opponents are to be principally if not wholly found, and that, of course, the machinery usually employed in the exercise of this power, has been, almost exclusively in their hands; the process of ascertaining public sentiment through local conventions, is carried on by a few artful individuals, and does not direct the real sentiments of one tenth part of the electors unless by chance, except in cases where extraordinary excitement can be produced, which rarely happens in those preliminary meetings

It was for these reasons that I have for the two winters past made strong personal efforts to produce an expression on the presidential question by the members of our Legislature, whose opinions—*being the honest representatives of the whole Whig party in the state*—could be relied on—Our friends however at Albany and I regretted to find it so, were from time to time put down by lectures on the necessity of harmony, and by whining deprecations of any measures that might effect the unity of the party.

The die however is now cast, and it is useless to say any more on the subject.

Gen. Harrison is nominated! And what is most extraordinary by a body of men three fourths of whom, as well as of their constituents if their own open declarations are to be credited are decidedly of the opinion that you ought to be the president of the U. States in preference to any other individual! This may be true and I fully believe it is so to a certain extent, being persuaded that if you had received the votes of those only who are honestly desirous of seeing you the president, you would have been nominated by a triumphant majority. But how sad a presage does even such a reflection afford, of the future destinies of this Republic

If I looked alone to your personal comfort, or I think I may add to your future fame, I should be glad, with all my heart, that Genl Harrison is nominated for we know that you have some bitter political enemies who would surely do all in their power to thwart you; and the scale of party is so nearly balanced, that a small diversion from our ranks would turn it, and if you were to be defeated you would be placed in a most unpleasant predicament—whereas now whatever may be the result you will by your magnanimous course, have secured the eternal admiration and gratitude of your country.

I have heard one argument—and I hope it may be verified—advanced by the friends of Gen Harrison and Scott respectively, which is, that in the event of the election of either of those gentlemen, *Mr. Clay* will be the actual president of the U. States, direct their counsels and prescribe their future policy. Although I am no friend to the policy of pursuing our objects by tortuous courses, *I still love my Country*; and therefore cannot but hail the success of any honest means calculated to promote its happiness and glory. I hope, at all events, that you will not think of abandoning public life *at present*. The times are greatly out of joint, and the country may have occasion to call, much sooner than it is now anticipated, on her patriotic citizens to rally for the preservation of her liberties; and in such an event, the continuation of your public and patriotic services might be invaluable.

We have received news of the proceedings of Congress up to the 10th day of its session, during which period the House of Representatives have done *absolutely nothing* This has created no serious uneasiness in my mind—for while the position taken by the Whigs is unquestionably correct, the course of the opposite party cannot but injure them in the public estimation and there appears to be no immediate danger of the controversy's resulting in any violent or revolutionary proceeding.

I hope you will do me the favor to let me hear from you occasionally during the winter.

ALS. NBuHi. Copy in OHi. 1. Porter to Clay, Nov. 14 and Dec. 30, 1837; Combs to Clay, Dec. 6, 1839. 2. Porter to Clay, Feb. 16, 1839.

From Nathaniel Beverley Tucker, Williamsburg, Va., December 16, 1839. Thanks Clay for information about John Randolph contained in his answer [not found] to Tucker's letter of December 5, 1839. Acknowledges his appreciation "of the delicacy of your situation" in the matter. Discusses at length the origins of Randolph's insanity and notes that had he died in 1806, "before the happening of those disasters which shook his mind, his fame would need no apologist." Understands Clay's awkward position at the time his duel with Randolph became necessary. "You felt the difficulty of *excusing* forbearance to the world by *alleging* that he was a madman." Still, no man knows better than Clay all Randolph's "strength and all his weakness, and none is more capable of establishing the fact that, even at those moments when his mind was all in ruins, it was capable of exhibitions of great method and power as well as brilliancy." Again asks for Clay's aid in breaking Randolph's will even while realizing "your natural reluctance to be called upon" and the "delicacy of your situation." Concludes with the political observation that "The doings at Harrisburg [Porter to Clay, November 14 and December 30, 1837; Combs to Clay, December 6, 1839] surprised and disgusted me. It is a mawkish dose, but I have made up my mind to swallow it, and to use my endeavour to persuade others to do so too. But I can only do this in conversation with individuals whose objection, like my own, is to the idea of elevating such a poor creature [William Henry Harrison] to the Presidency. But after all this may have as good effect. The throne is too high, and it may be well to place a man upon it who will degrade it by his imbecility. Had the necessity of curbing executive power been felt before Monroe's time, nothing would have been easier than to restrain it then. You must be sensible that, in that day, the Speaker's chair was the loftier seat." ALS. DLC-HC (DNA, M212, R5).

To HARRISON G. OTIS Washington, December 19, 1839

The surprize and dissatisfaction described in your letter of the 12h. as prevailing in Boston, with the Harrisburg nomination, are at first felt at many other places. It is a feeling that will give way to acquiescence, and, I trust, finally it will be followed by a resolution to render to the nomination cordial and active support. To the Convention having been assigned the duty of designating Candidates, and reconciling differences, now that it has performed that duty, I think honor and good faith require that the Opposition should sustain the nomination. There is no other path at least in which I can tread. I have, accordingly, publicly and privately, on all suitable occasions announced my purpose to abide by and support the nomination.

You are right in supposing that this event is a measure of relief to me. I feel, once more, a free man, at liberty to pursue my own inclinations, and unembarrassed by 10 or 12 months of turmoil.

I can offer no opinion of the result of the contest. It has my fervent wishes that our Candidates may succeed. The more immediate friends of the nomination (those I mean who had been at Harrisburg and were active in promoting it)[1] speak in a tone of great confidence of carrying N. York, Pennsa, Ohio & Indiana.[2] If they are right in their conjecture, I presume there will be support enough elsewhere to ensure it success.

The process of organizing the H. of R. is not yet completed. The Speaker [Robert M. T. Hunter] is the choice of neither party; but owes his election mainly to the Whigs.[3]

ALS. MHi. 1. Porter to Clay, Feb. 16, 1839. 2. The Harrison-Tyler Whig ticket carried all four of these states. 3. Clay to Porter, Dec. 4, 1839.

To Joshua Folsom, Zanesfield, Ohio, December 20, 1839. Reports that he has generally paid the taxes on his land in Logan County, Ohio, at Columbus, Ohio, and that Gen. Joseph Vance [3:259] usually handles the transaction for him. Asks Folsom to do it if Vance should forget. In answer to an inquiry from Folsom, recommends for the education of young ladies the "female department of the Catholic College at Bardstown" and "a very good female Catholic School at Lexn. (K.)." ALS. InU. For Folsom, a lawyer, farmer, and sawmill owner who had settled in Zanesfield in 1837 and died there on December 15, 1840—see O.L. Baskin, *History of Logan County and Ohio . . .* (Chicago, 1880), 181, 397-98, 411; and Robert P. Kennedy, *The Historical Review of Logan County, Ohio* (Chicago, 1903), 444, 449-50.

The Nazareth Academy in Bardstown, Ky., had been founded in 1812. By 1838 it had 115 boarders and was well-known throughout the South. In 1829 its name was changed to "The Nazareth Literary and Benevolent Institution." Sarah B. Smith, *Historic Nelson County* (Louisville, 1971), 85-87; also Matt Spalding, *Bardstown, A Town of Tradition* (Louisville, 1942), 40-41. The Catholic girls' school in Lexington at this time was Saint Catherine's Female Seminary run by the Sisters of Charity at 76 N. Mulberry Street. MacCabe, *Directory of the City of Lexington . . . 1838 & '39*, p. 88.

On January 6, 1840, Vance wrote Clay from Columbus, Ohio, enclosing "the certificate of the Sale of your Land for Taxes," and announcing that the total he had paid for back taxes, interest, and penalties for the four years 1836-39 had come to $106.83.8 mills. "I regret . . . the omission in the payment of these Taxes," he wrote, "but not having heard from you on the subject it entirely passed from my memory. All Taxes now have to be paid in the counties in which the Lands are situated." ALS. DLC-TJC (DNA, M212, R14).

To FRANCIS LIEBER Washington, December 28, 1839

I have, according to your request, franked & forwarded the letters transmitted in your favor of the 22d.

I have not yet received your letter on the reform of Penal law,[1] but presume it will come to me in safety. I shall seize the earliest opportunity to peruse it.

I am afraid that the prospect is bad of the passage of an International copy right law.[2] The two last Committees to which it was referred were adverse to it; and the activity of some of the large publishers has been such as to make strong impressions against it on the minds of many Senators.

ALS. CSmH. 1. *Letter to His Excellency Patrick Noble, Governor of South Carolina, on the Penitentiary System, by Francis Lieber*. 1839. 2. Comment in Senate, Feb. 2, 1837.

Comment in Senate, January 3, 1840. Speaks to Sen. John C. Calhoun's bill to cede public lands in Ala., Miss., La., Ark., Mo., Ill., Ind., Ohio, and Mich. to these "new states" in which they are located after June 30, 1842; this on the condition that 50% of the gross amount realized by subsequent sale of the ceded lands by these new states be paid to the United States, and with the understanding that the minimum price now fixed by law remain unchanged until June 30, 1842, after which the states would be authorized to graduate the price downward to as low as 25¢ per acre for land unsold for 25 years prior to June 30, 1842.

Clay asks that the Calhoun bill, which would donate "upwards of one hundred millions of acres of the common property of all the States of this Union to particular States," be referred to some committee other than Sen. Robert J. Walker's Committee on Public Lands, since four of the five senators serving on that committee represent the "new states" that would benefit most were the bill to become law. Asks also if the Van Buren administration supports Calhoun's proposal; and whether, as rumor has it, Calhoun's recent tense relations with the president "are entirely changed, and have, within a few days, been substituted by others of an intimate, friendly, and confidential nature," as possibly evidenced by his support of "this momentous measure." In response to Calhoun's insistence that his bill be referred to Walker's committee, and his testy refusal to discuss his personal relations with the president, Clay again points out the merits of removing the legislation from the initial jurisdiction of senators from the new states. Also, "He contended that his question, as to whether this was an Administration measure or not, was a proper one, as it was important for the public information. He again referred to the rumors of Mr. Calhoun's new relations with the President, and supposed from the declarations of the Senator, that these rumors were true; and that his support, if not pledged, was at least promised conditionally to the Administration. Was it of no importance to the public to learn that these pledges and compromises had been entered into?—that the distinguished Senator had made his bow in court, kissed the hand of the monarch, was taken into favor, and agreed henceforth to support his edicts?"

Calhoun responds angrily that Clay is much more experienced with "pledges, understandings, and political compromises, and sudden change of personal relations" than is he, and recalls that "the Senator had a great deal to do with such things, in connection with a distinguished citizen [John Quincy Adams], now of the other House." Adds that he has approved all of Van Buren's leading measures since he became president, "simply because they accord with the principles and policy on which I have long acted, and often openly avowed. The change, then, in our personal relations, [has] simply followed that of our political [relations]."

To this Clay replies with a defense of his actions in 1824-25, from which had derived the "corrupt bargain" charge [4:48, 53-54, 63, 84-85], pointing out that Calhoun had also supported Adams rather than Jackson at that time. As for his connection with "political compromises," he was proud of that connection, especially with the tariff compromise of 1833 [8:604], and he "thought no man ought to be more grateful for it than the Senator from South Carolina. But for that compromise, [he] was not at all confident that he would have now had the honor to meet that Senator face to face in this national Capitol." With reference to Calhoun's contention that his land bill was really an exercise in "State Rights," Clay retorts that it was, instead, "a bill to strip seventeen of the States of their rightful inheritance; to sell it all for a mess of pottage; to surrender it for a trifle—a mere nominal sum. The bill was, in effect, an attempt to strip and rob seventeen States of this Union of their property, and assign it over to some eight or nine of the States. If this was what the Senator called vindicating the rights of the States, [he] prayed God to deliver us from all such rights and all such advocates."

Following this observation, Clay delivers a lengthy defense of his motives and role in effecting the tariff compromise of 1833 [8:604, 619-22, 626-27], noting that in spite of Calhoun's obstructionism at the time, the compromise had "relieved him [Calhoun] from the difficulties in which he was involved" and had certainly saved the nation and "the gallant little State of South Carolina" from a bloody civil war. He is proud to say, further, that the compromise had saved the protective system from destruction "by the tremendous power of the individual [Andrew Jackson] who then filled the Executive chair." Says that the greatest service he could render protectionism was "to obtain for it 'a lease for a term of years,' to use an expression that had been heretofore applied to the compromise bill." Scoffs at Calhoun's threat "that in consequence of his [Clay's] remarks this very day, all obligations towards him on the part of himself [Calhoun], of the State of South Carolina, and the whole South, were cancelled." What right, Clay asks, "had the Senator to get up and assume to speak for the whole South, or even of South Carolina herself."

Concludes that he still wants to know if Calhoun's land cession bill is supported by the administration. It was not his intention, in asking this question, to wound the "feelings of the Senator from South Carolina. He said that new relations had arisen between that gentleman and the Administration, and therefore, he made the inquiry of him. Was it wrong in him to ask if this great measure had the support of his new friends? The Senator, instead of answering this plain inquiry, flew into a passion, and cancelled all obligations he was under towards him; but if he had only said, 'I know nothing of the views of the Administration; I introduce my own measure on my own responsibility,' there would have been no controversy between them. The Senator, therefore brought this controversy on himself." *Cong. Globe*, 26 Cong., 1 Sess., 96-98. Printed in Colton, *Clay Correspondence*, 6:165-68. See also Remark in Senate, February 17, 1840, and January 19, 1841; also, Speech in Senate, January 28-29, 1841. Calhoun's land cession bill is printed in full in *Cong. Globe*, 26 Cong., 1 Sess., 202. Senate action on the bill in the 26th Congress, 1st Session ended on May 13, 1840, with the submission of the report of the Committee on Public Lands, 20,000 extra copies of which were ordered printed. *Ibid.*, 391. For Calhoun's rapprochement with Van Buren, beginning in December, 1839, see Wiltse, *John C. Calhoun, Sectionalist*, 407-9.

Earlier this day, Clay gave notice of his intention to introduce a bill on international copyrights [Comment in Senate, February 2, 1837]. *Cong. Globe*, 26 Cong., 1 Sess., 96.

To JAMES B. SWAIN Washington, January 4, 1840

I received your letter transmitting a prospectus of a new magazine designed to promote the Whig Cause, which you purpose to commence in the City of N. York,[1] and requesting my support of it.

The want of such a periodical, ably conducted, to counteract the pernicious tendency of the Democratic Review,[2] is sensibly felt. To supply this want, you are aware, that a magazine has been published in Geo: town, during the last year; but it has languished and has not fulfilled the wishes of its projectors and patrons.[3] From what I hear, I apprehend it will go down. Its probable fate induces me to hesitate to encourage you in your undertaking; for I should regret extremely to be instrumental in your engaging in a losing concern. The D. Review has the patronage of the Executive [Martin Van Buren] to a great extent, without which I presume it could not be sustained.

It has been found in England, as you know, impracticable to keep up their leading Reviews without many contributors, and very liberal compensation for their contributions. And I apprehend that, in this Country, experience will indicate the necessity of employing the same means. I have a very favorable opinion of the capacity and diligence of Mr. [Horace] Greeley, whom you have engaged as Editor; and the question you have to consider is whether you can command the other requisite intellectual aid, and have a fair prospect of pecuniary remuneration? Your success will depend upon the *execution* of the work—that most important word in human language.

I have mentioned your intention to several members of Congress who seem to think well of it; but how far they will in fact contribute can only be tested by a direct appeal to them.

All that I can venture to promise, for myself, is that I will subscribe for the Magazine; and, if it should equal my hopes and expectations, that I will recommend it to my friends.

I am thankful for your kind wish to place a full length portrait of me in the first number of your Magazine. You enquire where one is to be had. Mr. Linen[4] of your City took such a portrait of me, of which good judges thought well. I believe it has been engraved, altho' I have not seen the engraving. Mr. Cook[5] also took a full length of me; but what he has done with it I do not know. I do not now recollect of any full lengths but these two. If both or either have been engraved, I presume it can be ascertained in N. York. . . .

ALS. KyU. 1. For Swain who founded *The Log Cabin* which ran from April, 1840 to Nov., 1841, see *DAB*. Horace Greeley edited *The Log Cabin* during its short run. 2. Clay to Payne, Oct. 12, 1837. 3. For the *National Whig Review*, which was started in Georgetown, D.C., in 1838 and apparently ran for only a little more than a year, see Henry Ridgely Evans, *Old Georgetown on the Potomac* (Washington, D.C., 1933), 44. 4. George Linen (1802-88). See Charles Henry Hart, "Life Portraits of Henry Clay," *McClure's Magazine* (Dec., 1897), 9:941-48; also Amyx, "The Portraits of Henry Clay." 5. Probably George Cooke (1793-1849). See Groce & Wallace, *Dictionary of Artists in America*, 145-46; and Clifford Amyx, "The Portraits of Henry Clay," Special Collections, King Library, University of Kentucky.

Remark in Senate, January 6, 1840. Presents petitions of a number of citizens asking for land grants in Oregon. Referred to Select Committee on the Oregon Territory. *Cong. Globe,* 26 Cong., 1 Sess., 103.

Later this day, Clay asks for and receives leave to introduce his bill relating to international copyrights [Comment in Senate, February 2, 1837]. Referred to Judiciary Committee. *Ibid.* The "Act to Amend the Several Acts Respecting Copyright" did not pass either house during the 26th Congress, 1st Session. On July 17, 1840, it was ordered to lie on the table in the Senate. It was not brought up in the 26th Congress, 2nd Session. U.S. Sen., *Journal,* 26 Cong., 1 Sess., 78, 87, 312, 522.

To John L. Carey, Baltimore, January 7, 1840. Thanks him for sending a copy of the second edition of his *Some Thoughts on Domestic Slavery* [Clay to Kennedy, May 16, 1839]. Is pleased that Carey has also sent copies to Mr. Franck Taylor, the Washington bookseller, since he has several friends in the capitol who want to buy it. ALS. ViU. Taylor's shop was located "On the avenue, this side of Gadsby's [Remark in Senate, February 13, 1840]."

Remark in Senate, January 9, 1840. Presents petitions from citizens in the coach-lace business in Philadelphia and in Bridgeport, Conn., asking for tariff protection on imported silk lace. *Cong. Globe,* 26 Cong., 1 Sess., 108.

To JAMES ERWIN Washington, January 10, 1840

I recd. your favor of the 28h. Ulto. I am thankful for the very satisfactory arrangement you made with Mr. [Ursin, Jr.] Bouligny about the Calves,[1] and I hope the amount will be paid on maturity of the draft. Perhaps the order you took on Mr. Anderson for $210 had better be forwarded to me, unless you have made some other disposal of it.

You will have seen the accounts of the extraordinary fraud of the Schuylkill Bank upon the Bank of K.[2] Whether this latter institution is responsible or not, in any and what degree, for the fraudulent certificates of Stock is not ascertained. I am not in the possession of facts to enable me to decide. It seems probable that the Commissioners of the K. Sinking fund have made investments to the amount of 2 or 3 hundred thousand dollars in the fraudulent Stock.[3]

From all that I can learn, I think that the suspension of the Banks of Pennsa. will be of indefinite & long continuance.[4]

Shelby is still here; but has yet completed nothing.[5] Jenifer[6] talks well about security; but has not yet given any. I think that all that can be done will be to get a mortgage on the Slaves upon the land. That I believe he will obtain. Mr Kent[7] has gone to Arkansas to try to sell the Land & Slaves, and gone, I understand, determined to sell the one or the other. Times are hard here & every where.

I wrote you requesting you to remit my funds in your hands at the end of the year, in March, to me by good drafts or checks on the Banks in Philadelphia, payable at two three or four months, upon the best terms you could. I still wish that done. But perhaps you may be able to get Specie checks or drafts on time on N. York upon terms that would be more favorable than the discount between N. York & Philada. On that point, I leave to your discretion the one or the other mode, as you may think best. My ultimate object will be to draw from Lexington on the fund thus created at Phila. or N. York.

I have received at last & filed the Record in the case of Brown & Keen [*sic*, Keene].[8]

The Harrison prospects continue favorable.[9] Judging from what I hear, if we had not been so often disappointed, I would say that he will beat Van tremendously. Things are working well for H. in Pennsa. & Ohio; and hard times & low prices if they continue must ensure his success.

I hope you will be able to make a satisfactory arrangement of the business of Mrs. Hitchcock[10] and prevail on her to go to the Woodlands.

All are well at home except Henry,[11] who has had an inflamed eye that has got better.

Give my love to the boys.

ALS. NHi. 1. Clay to Bouligny, Nov. 20, 1839. 2. In 1835 the Schuylkill Bank had become the agent for the transfer of stock in the Bank of Kentucky. When suspicion of fraudulent practices surfaced, an investigation began on Dec. 16, 1839. It was discovered that officials of the Schuylkill Bank, including cashier Hosea J. Levis, had overissued at least 12,997 shares of stock in the Bank of Kentucky and had used the proceeds to keep the Schuylkill Bank afloat. The Bank of Kentucky filed suit, and the court found that it was entitled to recover $1,184,738. The U.S. Supreme Court on appeal decided in 1849 that the Bank of Kentucky was entitled to the judgment of the lower court plus interest ($1,343,000); however total assets of the Schuylkill Bank amounted to only $430,000. Basil W. Duke, *History of The Bank of Kentucky 1792-1895* (Louisville, 1895), 64-90; Will D. Gilliam, Jr., "The Schuylkill Bank Fraud," *RKHS* (July, 1952), 50:249-55. See also Lexington *Observer & Kentucky Reporter*, Dec. 25, 28, 1839; Jan. 18, 1840. 3. Within a few years the Bank of Kentucky satisfied the claims of all the victims who had purchased the spurious stock; however, the Kentucky Sinking Fund, which received part of its funds from the dividends on state-owned stock in the banks, suffered a serious deficit in 1840 when the Bank of Kentucky did not pay its regular dividends because of the Schuylkill Bank Fraud. Will D. Gilliam, Jr., "Robert Perkins Letcher Whig Governor of Kentucky," *FCHQ* (Jan., 1950), 24:12. See also Duke, *The Bank of Kentucky*, 77; and Martin T. Gregory, "A History of the Kentucky State Treasury From 1792 to 1860," M.A. thesis, University of Kentucky, 1928, p. 39. 4. Clay to Otis, Dec. 13, 1838. 5. Reference obscure. 6. Probably Daniel Jenifer. This apparently refers to the conclusion, after four years, of the transaction discussed in Clay to Erwin, Feb. 22, 1836. See 8:829. 7. Gov. Joseph Kent had died in the interim, so the Mr. Kent in question is probably either his son Daniel or his son DeWitt. Dielman-Hayward File, MdHi. 8. Clay to Ingersoll, Sept. 30, 1837. 9. Clay to Porter, Dec. 27, 1838. 10. Reference obscure. 11. Henry Clay, Jr. See Clay to Henry Clay, Jr., Feb. 22, 1840.

To WILLIAM JONES, JR. Washington, January 10, 1840

I am very sorry that I have not a single Copy of the Speech made by me on the Land bill,[1] at any time, or I would take pleasure in transmitting that which you request. I believe they are all to be found in Niles's Register,[2] if you could get access to it.

You will have seen that I promptly avowed my determination to stand by and support the Harrisburg nomination. To that course I was urged by every consideration of duty of honor and of good faith; and I have been most happy to observe that my friends have followed my example. I sincerely hope that the nomination may be successful, and its prospects are certainly very encouraging.[3]

ALS. KyU. 1. Probably that of June 20, 1832, and/or that of Jan. 7, 1833. See 8:539-41, 609-10. 2. The speech of June 20, 1832, was printed in *Niles' Register* (Sept. 22, 1832), 43:57-64; that of Jan. 7, 1833, was printed in *ibid.* (March 23, 1833), 44:58-64. Also, Clay's comment of Feb. 9, 1837, on the public lands was printed in *ibid.* (May 6, 1837), 52:157. 3. Clay to Porter, Dec. 27, 1838.

Remark in Senate, January 14, 1840. Moves postponement of consideration of the administration's Independent Treasury bill until January 27. Participates (see following) in debate on his motion which was defeated 27 to 16. *Cong. Globe*, 26 Cong., 1 Sess., 120. For the legislative history of this bill in the 26th Congress, 1st Session, see citations in Speech in Senate, September 25, 1837; and in Clay to Porter, December 27, 1838.

Points out that so important a measure as the Independent Treasury bill should not be debated until five vacancies in the Senate have been filled by the state legislatures of New York, Pennsylvania, Delaware, Virginia, and Michigan. These men will soon arrive in the capital. To Sen. Silas Wright's contention that the filling of the vacancies would not change the comparative strength of partisans for or against the measure, Clay still counsels delay, noting also that in the past two years "there has been a reversal—a change—a very great change—and not an unimportant one, as it respects the origination of important measures" in Congress. Argues that bills of this sort, instead of originating in the "House of the people," as in the past, now frequently are introduced first in the Senate. Believes, therefore, that the Senate should delay action on this particular measure until the House begins work on it, especially since the first section of the bill clearly has an appropriations provision in it.

In response to Wright's charge that the problem of shifts in legislative origination during the past decade can be traced to Clay's act of introducing in the Senate during the 22nd Congress, 1st Session both his distribution of public land sale proceeds bill [8:539-41, 609-10] and his compromise tariff bill of 1833 [8:604, 619-22, 626-27], Clay explains he had no choice in either instance. "Some gentlemen," he recalls, "entertained the extraordinary notion that the sale of the public domain was a tax," rather than a revenue issue, and therefore successfully insisted that the Committee on Manufactures, over Clay's vigorous protest, proceed with fashioning the legislation. As for the compromise tariff bill, he reminds the Senate that civil war was threatening, and "The House of Representatives was at a stand, in a perfect balk, incapable of motion." Adds: "In that state of things I proposed the compromise bill. But was it a revenue bill? Was it to raise or augment the tariff? No; but to reduce, to cut it down. But I waive this point. A majority of the Senate decided it was not a revenue bill, such as must originate in the other House." *Cong. Globe*, 26 Cong., 1 Sess., Appendix, 106-7.

From WILLIAM HENRY HARRISON North Bend, Ohio, January 15, 1840

The generosity of your nature will not permit you to doubt that my feelings of gratitude towards you for the magnanimity of your conduct towards me in relation to the nomination for the Presidency are such as they ought to be altho I have so long delayed to express them directly to you.

I must beg you also to believe that if the claims derived from your superior talents & experience (so universally acknowledged by my supporters) had prevailed over those which accidental circumstances had confered upon me & enabled the Convention to name you as the Candidate, that you would have had no more zealous supporter in the Union than I should have been.

Our cause is prospering so well in this & the State west of us (within my own knowledge) & from information entitled to entire credit every where else as to create a general confidence in our success

Should our expectations in relation to this first victory be realized we must then prepare for renovating the political machine which has been so much impaired by the dishonesty rather than the ignorance of its present managers. Whether this will be an easy or Herculian labour will depend upon the disposition which the old able, & experienced hands may have to give themselves to the work

I must beg you to believe that I shall highly appreciate any advice or suggestions you may think proper to give me pending the canvass Indeed it is my sincere wish that our correspondence should be as free & unreserved as it once was. P.S. If you should meet with our friend John W. Allen of Ohio ask him to shew you a letter I have written to him on the subject of the movements of certain Members of yr. House. who are a disgrace to it & suggest either to him or to me directly your opinion of the course I should persue. I am extremely anxious to come out personally upon the Sandusky affair.[1] I pride myself upon my conduct in relation to that affair. It has been badly managed by all my Biographer[s]. excepting Hall[2] & he has omitted a most material fact—to wit—that of my having apprised the Secretary of War,[3] long before that I should do exactly as I did do. But whether right or wrong what was done was recommended by a Council of War (unanimously) of which McArthur Cass, Ball. Owen [*sic*] Paul [*sic*] & above all *Wood* were members[4]

ALS. PHi. In preparing this letter for his files, Clay indicated its importance by affixing it with a pointing-hand and finger symbol. 1. Harrison's "Sandusky affair" was a decision by himself and a council of his officers to pull his main army back from the vicinity of Frenchtown (River Raisin) following the disastrous American defeat there on Jan. 22, 1813. Goebel, *William Henry Harrison*, 154-61; Cleaves, *Old Tippecanoe*, 132-53. 2. James Hall's, *A Memoir of the Public Services of William Henry Harrison of Ohio* had been published in Philadelphia in 1836. For Hall, a Cincinnati lawyer, judge, author, and banker, see *CAB*. Other major biographies of Harrison through 1840 are: (1) Robert McAfee, *History of the Late War in the Western Country . . . From the Commencement of Hostilities at Tippecanoe, to the Termination . . . at New Orleans. . . .* Lexington, Ky., 1816; (2) Moses Dawson, *A Historical Narrative of the Civil and Military Services of Major General William Henry Harrison. . . .* Cincinnati, 1824; (3) Samuel J. Burr, *The Life and Times of William Henry Harrison.* New York, 1840; (4) Caleb Cushing, *Brief Sketch of the Life . . . of William Henry Harrison of Ohio.* Augusta, Me., 1840; (5) Richard Hildreth, *The Contrast: or William Henry Harrison Versus Martin Van Buren.* Boston, 1840; (6) William O. Niles, *The Tippecanoe Text-Book, Compiled From Niles' Register. . . .* Baltimore, 1840. 3. Probably William Eustis, but possibly James Monroe who became acting secretary of war in Dec., 1812, and served in that capacity until John Armstrong assumed the position in the spring of 1813. 4. Gen. Duncan McArthur, Brig. Gen. Lewis Cass, Maj. James V. Ball, Col. Thomas D. Owings, Col. George Paull, and Maj. Eleazer D. Wood. For Owings, see Francis B. Heitman, *Historical Register and Dictionary of the United States Army . . .* (Washington, 1903), 1:764 and Logan Esarey (ed.), *Governors Messages and Letters. Messages and Letters of William Henry Harrison*, 2 vols. (Indiana Historical Collections, vols. 7 and 9, Indianapolis, 1922), 2:530-31. For Paull, see Heitman, *Register . . . of the United States Army*, 1:776 and Esarey, *Messages and Letters of Harrison*, 2:530-31. For Woods, see *CAB*.

Remark in Senate, January 16, 1840. Presents a petition from a number of cigar manufacturers in Baltimore asking that the duty on imported cigars be raised. *Cong. Globe*, 26 Cong., 1 Sess., 123.

Later this day, submits a petition from the American Silk Society asking for government assistance in printing and distributing the society's journal [*Journal of the American Silk Society and Rural Economist*]. Adds, "while I am up," a vigorous statement endorsing the importance of increasing the domestic production of silk, pointing out that "we must make more at home, and bring less from abroad." Cites statistics showing recent increases in silk imports. Says that he is politically "powerless," but that "if my friends and myself had any power in the direction of this Government," he would impose a 20% duty ("the maximum which the [1833] act admits") on imported silk. "I would lay this duty on silk; and with a view, in part, to prevent a dangerous excess of revenue, I would distribute the annual proceeds of the sales of the public lands to the States as their own property, to which they are already entitled; and let this fund assist them to liquidate their debts, and to foster those great interests which are justly dear to them, so far as there is now freedom from debt."

Is asked by Calhoun whether he seeks to revive the "old, the tried, and condemned American system." Calhoun also warns Clay that "any measure that would, at this time, increase the credit of the States so as to enable them to sell more bonds in foreign markets," would be "positively injurious." Clay answers that he has no intention whatever of raising tariffs on any commodity above what the Compromise Tariff Act of 1833 allows. A tariff of 20% on a luxury item such as silk "is in no way incompatible with the compromise." As for state debts, "Sir, I should like to know by what right the subject of state debts is so frequently dragged into this Senate and the States are here chided and censured as if under our supervision." Maintains that the federal government has no authority over the contraction of debt by the various states. Asserts, however, that "honor and good faith" require the states to pay such debts. Makes it clear that he is not suggesting that the government assume these debts. "No, sir; no, sir." But believes that by distributing to the states the duties on luxury items, as well as the proceeds from public land sales, the states would derive income "sufficient to pay the interest on a debt of $100,000,000, and I believe the whole amount of the State debts is not much more than $100,000,000." Denies, in answer to a question by Calhoun, that the distribution of public land sales revenues to the states is, in effect, "an assumption of the State debts" by the federal government. Reminds Calhoun, in addition, that in 1816 it was he who was "the originator" of the American System; whereas, "I [Clay] was, then his humble follower on that subject and for years afterwards." *Ibid.*, 124.

Still later this day, Clay joins in the continuing debate on the Independent Treasury bill, triggered by Sen. Thomas Hart Benton's proposed amendment to sections 19 and 20 of the measure which would prohibit the use or acceptance of U.S. Treasury bills ("bills or paper issued under the authority of the United States") in the payment of government obligations after June 30, 1843. Clay participates intermittently in the discussion of the mechanics and other aspects of the bill, such as methods by which receivers of government funds would be able to move money by warrant from one sub-treasury location or custom house to another. Notes that if the Benton amendment is basically designed "to prevent the issue of all paper by Federal authority, and the establishment of a Government bank," it will accomplish little unless the bill also declares that "no future Congress shall authorize the issue or the receipt of paper money in the country." Adds: "Sir, I believe there is a Government bank lurking in this bill. Gentlemen say no; we do not mean to have a Government bank; we will have nothing but specie. So the Senator from Missouri [Mr. Benton] moved to strike out a certain clause inserted by his friend from South Carolina, [Mr. Calhoun] which admitted the receipt of paper of certain kinds. And I say the gentlemen will not accomplish their purpose by this alone, if they would have nothing but specie. The paper will be out." Predicts that before this coming June or July "you will find the Secretary of the Treasury [Levi Woodbury] asking for paper to meet the expenses of the Government. That will bring the mark as to what course these friends of specie will take on the subject. And what course will they take when such a proposition comes for Treasury notes? . . . If the Senator from South Carolina is for using the credit of the Government, and is opposed to notes and to Treasury notes, in what form would he use the credit of the Government?" *Cong. Globe*, 26 Cong., 1 Sess.,

Appendix, 123-25. Benton's amendment was carried 33 to 6, Clay voting with the majority. The bill as amended is printed in *Cong. Globe*, 26 Cong., 1 Sess., 139-40. For the language of Benton's amendments to sections 19 and 20, see *ibid.*, Appendix, 116.

Remark in Senate, January 17, 1840. Speaks to resolutions by Sen. Ruel Williams of Maine calling on the president to submit all correspondence, not already communicated, with the British government, its minister in Washington [Henry S. Fox], and the governor of Maine [John Fairfield] on Britain's "invasion of the State of Maine, and the exercise of jurisdiction in the disputed territory [Clay to Hamilton, February 24, 1839; Comment in Senate, February 26, 1839]"; speaks also to the additional resolution by Sen. John Ruggles of Maine asking what the president has accomplished militarily, if anything, since March, 1839, in the way of effecting "the removal or expulsion" of British troops from the disputed territory. To Sen. James Buchanan's observation that the Ruggles resolution "would seem to contain an implied censure upon the President," Clay says he sees no imputation of censure in the resolution; but he does inquire: "to what had we come, if the President was to be asked no question in regard to his official duties? . . . was there nothing to be allowed to a State whose rights had been so long withheld? Sir, . . . while we guard the President, let us not be insensible to the feelings and just rights of a member of this Confederacy. On this subject he saw no occasion to censure the President, but God knows he is sufficiently amenable to censure without going out of the way to find it." *Cong. Globe*, 26 Cong., 1 Sess., 126-27. The correspondence solicited by the resolutions of Sen. Williams is printed in *ibid.*, 134-38, 151-52.

To URSIN BOULIGNY, JR. Washington, January 19, 1840

I am obliged to you for the Copy of Govr. Roman's Message,[1] which I have perused with much satisfaction. It is clear condensed and able, and contrasts very advantageously with the long elaborate and never ending messages which this winter has produced. The Governor traces, with a pencil of light, the causes of the present intense distress and embarrassment. I wish there existed any hope of a remedy, emanating from here, but there is none—none at least until the 4h. Mar. 1841.

I am happy to hear that the Calves proved satisfactory to our friends;[2] and I hope they will survive the trials of next summer. In the mean time, the best use ought to be made of the young bulls. It was a mistake to send the third heifer, of which I was not aware until she had reached Louisville, when, on reperusing your letter, I observed that you had ordered but two. I am perfectly content with the arrangement you had the goodness to make with Mr. [James] Erwin for the extra[3] heifer.

If the nomination at Harrisburg[4] produced surprize, honor and good faith imposed upon me the duty of acquiescing in and supporting it; and I promptly & publicly avowed my purpose to do so. I am happy to tell you that accounts from all quarters are favorable beyond all anticipation and justify the hope of its triumphant success.

ALS. DLC-HC (DNA, M212, R5). 1. For Andre B. Roman, see 8:178. For Roman's message to the Louisiana legislature, see *Journal of the Louisiana House of Representatives*, 14th Legislature, 2nd Session, Jan. 7, 1840. 2. Clay to Bouligny, Nov. 20, 1839. 3. Word "capricious" struck through and word "extra" supplied. 4. Porter to Clay, Nov. 14 and Dec. 30, 1837.

Speech in Senate, January 20, 1840. Announces that although he has a "serious cold" he must make "one last although unavailing effort" to thwart the administration's Independent Treasury (or Sub-Treasury) bill [Speech in Senate, September 25, 1837, and February 19, 1838; Comment in Senate, March 7, 1838; Clay to Porter, December 27, 1838]. Points to five still unfilled seats in the Senate and calculates that the bill will pass by "less than a majority of the body." Explains that had the vacant seats been filled by the various state legislatures, and had the two Tennessee senators [Hugh L. White and Ephraim H. Foster] not resigned their seats but had remained in the Senate and obeyed the instructions of their legislature to oppose the measure, "there would be a clear majority against the passage of the bill."

Commences his attack on the Sub-Treasury bill with the observation that the federal and most of the state governments are in debt and that the nation is experiencing "universal and intense distress." Describes in detail the dimensions of the economic failure, noting that prices are falling, banks are in trouble, factories are closed or closing, and "We have no currency whatever possessing uniform value throughout the whole country." Says he will not go into the principal causes of the depression save to assert again his belief that the nation's "pecuniary distresses have mainly sprung from the refusal to recharter the late Bank of the United States [8:434, 443, 552, 558, 640-41], the removal of the public desposits from that institution [8:583-84, 681, 684-85, 728], the multiplication of State banks in consequence and the Treasury stimulus given to them to extend their operations, the bungling manner in which the law depositing the surplus treasure with the States was executed [8:813, 873-74], the Treasury circular [8:861; Speech in Senate, January 11, 1837; Remark in Senate, January 14, 1837], and although last, perhaps not least, the exercise of the power of the veto on the bill for distributing among the States the net proceeds of the sales of the public lands [8:610]." What is needed to restore prosperity is "A sound local currency, mixed with a currency possessing uniform value throughout the whole country; a reestablishment of regular exchanges between different part[s] of the Union; and a revival of general confidence. The people want, in short, good government at Washington; the abandonment of rash and ruinous experiments; the practice here of economy, and the pursuit of the safe lights of experience." Blames Van Buren for doing nothing to alleviate the suffering of the people and charges that his Independent Treasury bill will make matters worse, because "Its whole principle consists in an exaction from the people of specie, in the payment of all their duties and dues to Government, and the disbursement of specie by the Government in the payment of all salaries and of all the creditors of the Government. This is its simple and entire principle. . . . It does not touch, nor profess to touch, the actual currency of the country. It leaves the local banks where it found them, unreformed, uncontrolled, and unchecked in all their operations. It is a narrow, selfish, heartless measure. It turns away from the people, and abandons them to their hard and inexorable fate, leaving them exposed to all the pernicious consequences of an unsound currency, utterly irregular and disordered exchanges, and the greatest derangement in all business." Attacks the arguments used by the administration to support its hard-money approach to economic improvement, asserting that "in my opinion a currency purely metallic is neither desirable, in the present state of the commercial world, nor if it were, is it practicable, or possible to be attained in this country. And if it were possible it could not be brought about without the most frightful and disastrous consequences, creating convulsion if not revolution." Explains his thinking on this point. Adds that the reduction by half of the quantity of the nation's circulating medium that is inherent in the bill will adversely affect the classes most closely identified with the Democrats. Indeed, "if the effect of this hard-money policy upon the debtor class be injurious, it is still more disastrous, if possible, on the laboring classes. Enterprise will be checked or stopped, employment will become difficult, and the poorer classes will be subject to the greatest privations and distresses. Heretofore it has been one of the pretensions and boasts of the dominant party, that they sought to elevate the poor by depriving the rich of undue advantages. Now their policy is to reduce the wages of labor, and this is openly avowed; and it is argued by them that it is necessary to reduce the wages of American labor to the low standard of European labor, in order to enable the American manufacturer to enter into a successful competition with the European manufacturer in the sale of their respective fabrics." Expresses at length his deep concern for the well-being of the American workingman, and the importance of improving his wages by improving the general health of the economy in which he labors. Believes that the pro-specie argument does not take into account the dire situation that the workingman would face "during the transition from the paper to the specie medium," given the fact that the "adjustment of prices to the state of the currency is not so sudden as is imagined. Long after the specie standard should be established, the old prices of many articles would remain, and all foreign productions which enter into the consumption of the poor man would continue unaffected by our domestic currency. . . . The assumption that an exclusive hard-money circulation is best for the laborer, best for the manufacturer, best for the country, is against all the experience of the world." Discusses the success of British economy in this context, pointing out that "England is the greatest paper-money country that exists."

Argues that whether this bill passes or not, private banks chartered by the 26 states will continue to exist, continue to issue paper notes, continue to come into existence "in defiance of any policy which this Government may proclaim. . . . Banks, bank notes, a convertible paper money are therefore inevitable; there is no escape from them." Reminds his audience that he has never believed that the eight or nine hundred local banks scattered across the country, "were competent to supply such a general currency, of uniform value, as this people wants, or to perform those financial offices which are necessary to a successful administration of this Government. I pronounced them incompetent at the period of the removal of the deposits [8:583-84, 681, 684-85, 728]; and we foretold the unfortunate state of things that now exists. But the party in power, which now denounces them, proclaimed their entire ability not only to supply as good but a better currency than that which was furnished by the Bank of the United States, and to perform all the financial duties which that institution fulfilled. After that party had succeeded in putting down the Bank of the United States, and got their system into full operation, it continued, year after year, to announce to the public that all its expectations had been fully realized."

Remains convinced that "A Bank of the United States established by this Government would not only furnish it a currency in which it might safely confide, in all receipts and payments, and execute every financial office, but it would serve as a sentinel, a cement, and a regulator to the State banks." Explains that he does not have in mind something on the order of the present Bank of the United States of Pennsylvania, which is not the kind of national bank he envisages—even though its current difficulties stem from U.S. government hostility that has "tended to cripple its operations. And it is wholly without the deposits of the Government, which the former bank [Bank of the United States] possessed." Defends Nicholas Biddle's former management of that bank. As for launching a new Bank of the United States, he has "no wish to see it proposed . . . until it is demanded by a clear and undisputed majority of the people of the United States [Comment in Senate, September 26, 1837; Speech in Senate, May 21, 1838]." Continues: "Seeing that a Bank of the United States could not be established, two years ago I expressed my willingness to make an experiment with the State banks [Comment in

Senate, March 7, 1838] rather than resort to this perilous measure. And now, such are my deep convictions of the fatal tendency of this project of a sub-Treasury, that I would greatly prefer the employment of the agency of State banks. But while I should entertain hopes of their success, I confess that I should not be without strong apprehensions of their failure. My belief is that the State banks will be constantly exposed to disorder and derangement without the cooperation of a Bank of the United States, and that our banking system will only be safe and complete when we shall have both a Bank of the United States and State banks." Agrees, in part, with Van Buren's argument that the Bank of England exercises an important negative influence on the American economy, but holds that such influence grew out of Jackson's destruction of the old Bank of the United States. "You denounced this bank as a monster, and destroyed it, and you have thrown us into the jaws of a foreign monster which we can neither cage nor control. You tore from us our best shield against the Bank of England, and now profess to be surprised at the influence which it exercises upon our interests!" Blames the primary cause of U.S. dependence on England on "the unfavorable balance of our foreign trade. We import too much and export too little. We buy too much abroad, and make too little at home." On the other hand, the poor trade balance has nothing to do with "the character of the currency of the country." Notes that during the Colonial period, when "we had no currency but specie, and no bank," we were still "constantly and largely in debt to England," and our specie "was perpetually drained to obtain supplies" in Britain. Cites Benjamin Franklin on the economic effects of trade imbalances on the American colonies. Asserts that the remedy for our present dependence on Britain "is to increase our manufactures and purchase less of hers, and to augment our exports by all the means in our power, and to diminish our imports as much as possible. We must increase our productions, or economize much more than we have done."

Denies that the reintroduction of the Independent Treasury bill was demanded by a majority of the people in the November, 1839, state elections, even though the voters in a few states "were artfully led to believe that this bill would supply a corrective of the errors of the banking system." Reminds his hearers "That there were a vast majority of them opposed to it was demonstrated incontestably by previous elections." Condemns the Democrats for their long war on the Bank of the United States and points out that during "the progress of that war the State banks were the constant theme of praise, in speech and song." Charges that the Democrats then undermined those same private banks with their stand on hard money and the distribution of surplus issues, thus accelerating "the catastrophe of the suspension of the banks."

Announces that the main purpose of his speech today is to demonstrate that the administration's bill "lays the foundations deep and broad of a Government bank, a Treasury bank, under the sole management of the President." Develops this theme at length, emphasizing the inordinate power over the currency that this measure will place in the hands of the chief executive. Cites the proposed section 10 of the legislation to show that it invests the secretary of the treasury "with unlimited authority to transfer the public money from one depositary to another, and to concentrate it all, if he pleases, at a single point. But, without this provision, the city of New York necessarily must be the place at which the largest portion of the public money will be constantly on deposit. It collects alone about two thirds of the duties on imports, and is becoming, if it be not already, the money center of the United States." Notes also that section 10 of the bill provides that "for the purpose of payments on the public account, it shall be lawful for the Treasurer of the United States to draw upon any of the said depositaries as he may think most conducive to the public interests, or to the convenience of the public creditors, or both." Sees here "no restriction whatever as to the amount or form of the draft." Argues that "These [U.S. Treasury] drafts, to a considerable extent, will remain out, enter the general circulation, and compose a part of the common currency of the country, commanding at particular places, as notes of the Bank of the United States have done, and now do, a premium, but anywhere being certainly good for the amount on their face. All this is perfectly plain and inevitable." Fears, however, that "Sub-treasurers and receivers general may fly with the public money committed to their charge; may peculate or speculate as they please, and unlike the condition of banks, whose fraudulent officers squander the means of those institutions, the nation remains bound for the redemption of all paper issued under its authority." Insists that these treasury drafts will come to serve as the basic currency of the nation, since "They will be preferred to specie, because they will be more convenient and free from the hazards incident to the possession of specie." Thus, "more and more will the specie of the country accumulate in the custody of receivers general, until, after a few years, the greater part of the specie of the country will be found in the vaults of the depositaries, represented by an equal amount of Government paper in circulation." Some of this specie will flow out of the country because of the nation's unfavorable balance of trade with Europe; but much of it will remain and will flow into the vaults of the government in much larger amounts than the treasury paper in circulation that it supports. When this occurs, "what has been done before will be done again. Government, in a time of necessity, will be tempted to increase its paper issues upon the credit of this dormant specie capital. It will be tempted again and again to resort to this expedient, since it is easier to make emissions of paper than to lay the burden of taxation on the people." Believes also that in some instances the custodians of the public depositaries might even be "tempted to keep possession of the specie for the incidental advantages which it affords. Ah! sir, are we to overlook the possible uses to which, in corrupt days of the Republic, this dormant specie may be applied in the crisis of a political election or the crisis of the existence of a party in power."

Is confident that this bill, however it be regarded by friend or foe, will produce nothing less than a Government bank wholly run by the president and his secretary of the treasury. Asserts that "this Government bank will be the mere bank of the President of the United States. He will be its president, cashier, and teller [Remark in Senate, June 9, 1841]." This is simply too much power over the American economy to entrust to such hands, given the "power claimed by the Executive, and it is now daily enforced, of dismissing all officers of the Government, without any other cause than a mere difference of opinion." Condemns the patronage system run by Van Buren and his department heads, but sees, "thanks be to God! . . . a day of reckoning at hand." Trusts that on March 4, 1841, "the long account of the abuses and corruptions of this Administration, in which this measure will be a conspicuous item, will be finally and forever adjusted." Reviews the history of executive usurpation since 1830 and concludes that now "There scarcely remains any power in this Government but that of the President. He suggests, originates, controls, checks everything. The insatiable spirit of the Stuarts for power and prerogative was brought upon our American throne on the 4th of March, 1829. It came under all the usual false and hypocritical pretenses and disguises of love of the people, desire of reform, and diffidence of power. The Scotch dynasty still continues. We have had Charles I, and now have Charles II. But I again thank God that our deliverance is not distant, and that on the 4th of March, 1841, a great and glorious revolution, without blood and without convulsion, will be achieved." *Cong. Globe*, 26 Cong., 1 Sess., Appendix, 739-44. Printed in Colton, *Clay Correspondence*, 6:169-91. The Senate bill, in its final form, is printed in *Cong. Globe*, 26 Cong., 1 Sess., 139-41. It was passed by a vote of 24 to 18 on January 23, 1840, Clay voting nay. *Ibid.*, 141.

Earlier this day, Clay presented the petition of Mary Brush which was referred to the Committee on the District of Columbia. *Cong. Globe*, 26 Cong., 1 Sess., 129.

From Charles Hammond, Cincinnati, January 21, 1840. Congratulates Clay "that the burthen of being a candidate for the Presidency was not put upon you. In my view, the canvass was always full of degradation, and I think that nowadays its humiliation is greatly increased." Indeed, "A man has to give up his own self respect or every hour give offence to some pedagogue that stands over him with uplifted rod." No "upright independent man" can feel at ease in the presidency or permit himself, once there, to "make his own opinions the basis of his public acts." For example, "J Q Adams, in November last, wrote a strong letter on the Amistad case—How widely does it vary, in its positions of public law, from those urged upon the British Government by the Department of state, respecting slaves escaping to Canada [5:235, 472-73, 610; 6:235, 750], when Mr Adams was President of the united States!" Urges Clay to remain in the Senate, because "Every thing we see or hear or attempt to understand, points to approaching exigencies, in which the country must call you to the rescue." ALS. DLC-HC (DNA, M212, R5). Printed in Colton, *Clay Correspondence*, 4:443-44.

The *Amistad* case dealt with the question of whether or not slaves who had mutinied while being transported in a Spanish ship, seized the vessel, and were subsequently captured by a U.S. warship off Long Island, should be freed when they were brought on shore. The John Q. Adams letter was probably that which he wrote to the New York *Journal of Commerce* on November 19, 1839, calling for compassion for the *Amistad* slaves and criticizing the treatment given them by U.S. officials. Adams eventually argued their case before the U.S. Supreme Court which upheld the lower courts and freed the slaves. Christopher Martin, *The Amistad Affair* (New York, 1970), 153-54; Marie B. Hecht, *John Quincy Adams* (New York, 1972), 569-75, 577-80, 623-24.

Remark in Senate, January 21, 1840. Interrupts Sen. Robert J. Walker's speech in support of the administration's Independent Treasury bill at the point where Walker quotes from Clay's speech of March 30-31, 1824, in support of the protective tariff [3:684-85, 710], wherein Clay had discussed the collapse of the national economy, particularly the decline of the wages of workingmen. He had then blamed the situation, in part, on "the reluctant resort to the perilous use of paper money [Clay's words]." Walker reminds him that these economic problems had occurred "during the very climax of the power of the Bank of the United States." In Clay's speech of yesterday [January 20], Walker continues, while he was criticizing Jackson's assault on the bank, "all this seems to have been forgotten by him." Clay replies that "no such distress as the present had existed during the charter of the National Bank; but that never, during its existence had this distress been attributed, as it now was, to the power over us of the banks and currency of England." *Cong. Globe*, 26 Cong., 1 Sess., 138. Clay's speech of March 30-31, 1824, is printed in full in 3:683-730.

To DAVID LAMBERT Washington, January 22, 1840

I recd. your favor. The nomination at Harrisburg,[1] I think, ought to be supported, whether it be conformable to our wishes or not. It is the result of the full and general deliberations of the Whigs, in Convention. Honor and good faith required of me to support it, and I shall do so cordially.

I regret that I have not by me a single Copy of the Speech which you wish to possess. I have very seldom retained Copies of any Speech made by me.

The project of purchasing California, suggested by you, is a great one. I have been ever desirous to see our race, and our institutions, more and more diffused over this Continent. But is not that purchase premature? Whether so or not I have no idea that, in the present state of jealousy between the States, the Northern States would consent to it.

We have nothing here interesting. I apprehend that the Sub-Treasury will pass.[2]

Judging from all that I see & hear, I think the prospect is that Harrison will be elected with ease.[3]

ALS. MnHi. Enclosed in David Lambert to Henry H. Sibley, January 29, 1849. For Lambert, who worked for the Madison *Wisconsin Enquirer*, see *WMH*, 7:466. 1. Porter to Clay, Nov. 14 and Dec. 30, 1837. 2. Speech in Senate, Sept. 25, 1837, and Jan. 20, 1840. 3. Clay to Porter, Dec. 27, 1838.

Remark in Senate, January 22, 1840. Responds (not recorded) to a lengthy speech by Sen. James Buchanan (Pa.) in support of the Independent Treasury bill [Speech in Senate, January 20, 1840]. *Cong. Globe*, 26 Cong., 1 Sess., 133.

To LUCRETIA HART CLAY Washington, January 24, 1840

The winter here continues very severe. More snow than I have ever known. There fell, I have heard, three feet this week between Philada. & N. York. I am quite ill with a cold, but I go about and attend to my duties in the Senate. I made two Speeches this week, which my friends praised very much.[1] I had some personal altercation with little [Robert J.] Walker of Mississippi, whom I scornfully repelled.[2] My friends said that I annihilated him.

I have heard from N. Orleans about my Calves. They were all taken, the odd one and all, and probably are paid for by this time.[3] The gentlemen to whom they were sent were well pleased with them.

I received Thomas's [Hart Clay] letter of the 13h. He writes in high spirits about his business; but I regret to hear that Henry's [Clay, Jr.] health and spirits are not good. I wrote to him the other day, and mentioned to him that he might have Major.[4] So that if he wants him you may let him go to him.

I am uneasy about John [Morrison Clay]. Setting out from Missouri in the dead of winter, he must have a dreadful journey, if he gets home safely. I understand that he leaves Missouri entirely dissatisfied with it. That is what I expected.

Thomas does not write me any thing relative to your money affairs. and your milk business. I am afraid that you have had hard times; but this is the last winter that I shall be separated from you, whilst we both live.

Nobody has written me one word about Mrs. Morrison.[5] I should be glad to hear of her.

No intelligence is yet received here of the arrival of the Brandywine, in which Martin [Duralde III] sailed.[6] Henry [Clay Duralde], I see, has got back to Danville.[7]

Do my dear wife urge Thomas or John, if he has got home to write me fully about every thing at Ashland; and particularly how you get through the winter.

ALS. Courtesy of M.W. Anderson, Lexington, Ky. 1. Speech in Senate, Jan. 20, 1840; and probably the unrecorded Remark in Senate, Jan. 22, 1840. 2. Remark in Senate, Jan. 21, 1840. 3. Clay to Bouligny, Nov. 20, 1839. 4. A slave. 5. Esther Montgomery Morrison, widow of James Morrison, who was making changes in her will in 1839-40. See Fayette County Will Book P-1841, pp. 280-82. 6. Clay to Paulding, May 3, 1839. 7. Henry Clay Duralde apparently attended school briefly in Danville, Ky.

Remark in Senate, January 27, 1840. Presents a petition of citizens connected with the raising of silk. *Cong. Globe*, 26 Cong., 1 Sess., 148.

Later this day, Clay opposes (remarks not recorded) the adoption of a report from the Committee on Commerce which asserted that the present law on drawbacks was sufficient to provide relief to agents of steam packet companies engaged in the New York-Great Britain trade. These agents had petitioned that they be allowed a debenture on the coal used by their vessels on their return passages. *Ibid.*

From Peter B. Porter, Niagara Falls, N.Y., January 28, 1840. States that while he was "deeply mortified at the ingratitude displayed by your friends at Harrisburg in December [Porter to Clay, November 14 and December 30, 1837]," he is "now satisfied that it was sustained by many who entertained the kindest feelings towards you." Reports that some Whigs there would have brought Harrison forward as an opposing candidate had Clay been nominated, and "Although their number was small it might have been sufficient to turn the scale in a closely contested election." Thinks that Clay's commanding position in the Senate is better for him than being the party's candidate. Moreover, "should the Whig cause now succeed as we have reason to believe it will, the way will be open to you, & you may be placed if you choose it, by acclamation at the head of the Republic, which will have been regenerated by your personal exertions. . . . Your great measures, the public lands [8:539-41, 609-10, 873-74] and the Tariff [8:604, 619-22, 626-27] are gaining new favor with the people, & I am not without great hopes that you will yet be able to revive and carry them through triumphantly. . . ." Copy. OHi.

Remark in Senate, January 28, 1840. Participates (not recorded) in discussion of a motion to table a memorial from Joseph Smith, Jr., Sidney Rigdon, and Elias Higbee "in behalf of 'The Latter Day Saints,' commonly called Mormons," asking for a redress of grievances inflicted on them by the people of Missouri. Motion to table agreed upon viva voce. *Cong. Globe*, 26 Cong., 1 Sess., 149.

For Joseph Smith, Jr., founder of the Church of Jesus Christ of Latter Day Saints and Sidney Rigdon, one of his principle assistants, see *DAB*. For Elias Higbee, a judge and lawyer who also became a follower of Smith, see Joseph Smith, *History of the Church of Jesus Christ of Latter Day Saints*, 6 vols. (2nd rev. ed., Salt Lake City, 1948-51), 1:410. See also Smith to Clay, Nov. 4, 1843, and May 13, 1844.

Clay and Sen. John T. Stuart (Whig-Ill.) unsuccessfully attempted to win a hearing on the Senate floor for Mormon petitions protesting the persecutions that had driven them from Missouri and seeking compensation for loss of their property. The Senate Judiciary Committee, which considered the petition, submitted its report on March 4, 1840, stating that the Mormons would have to seek redress either in the courts of Missouri or the federal courts. For the petition, see Smith, *History of the Church*, 4:24-38; for the Judiciary Committee report, see *ibid.*, 90-92. See also Fawn M. Brodie, *No man Knows my history, The Life of Joseph Smith* (New York, 1971), 259-60.

Remark in Senate, January 31, 1840. Presents petitions from citizens in Philadelphia and in Maine asking for U.S. support for a "Congress of Nations." *Cong. Globe*, 26 Cong., 1 Sess., 158.

Remark in Senate, February 3, 1840. Presents a memorial from the Chamber of Commerce of Louisville complaining of the high tolls of the Louisville and Portland Canal and asking that the government buy up the privately-owned stock of the company [4:33]. Reports he has learned that for "the trifling sum of $150,000" the obstruction at the falls can be removed and the natural channel of the river made navigable. This would render the purchase of canal stock unnecessary. Denies the contention that the government, because it is a stockholder, cannot undertake to improve the natural channel of the river without depreciating the value of all the stock and thus violating an implied pledge to other stockholders. This, says Clay, is a "monstrous pretension, without the slightest foundation in law or equity."

Later this day, Clay presents a memorial asking for the establishment of a new executive department "devoted to the interests of Agriculture and Education." *Cong. Globe*, 26 Cong., 1 Sess., 158-59.

Remark in Senate, February 5, 1840. Presents petition from Fayette County, Pa., for a reduction of postage rates. *Cong. Globe*, 26 Cong., 1 Sess., 164.

To JAMES ERWIN Washington, February 6, 1840

I wrote you this morning expressing my surprize and mortification on account of a report which reached us last evening that you and Mr. Beall [*sic*, William H. Beal] had failed.[1] I have since received your letter of the 28h. Ulto. which relieves my apprehensions a good deal; but still the unexampled state of distress in N. O. and your responsibility for Mr. Beall create a solicitude from which I shall not be free, until you give me the most positive assurances that you are out of all danger.[2] I have not heard from James [Erwin, Jr.] for a long time, and wish you would urge him to write to me. And I beg you to keep me constantly and truly advised as to your situation.

ALS. NcD. 1. For Beal, a New Orleans commercial merchant, see Gibson, *Guide and Directory of . . . Louisiana.* 2. See Clay to Lucretia Hart Clay, March 6 and April 2, 1840.

To Theodatus Garlick, Washington, February 10, 1840. Testimonial statement that Garlick this day showed him a "likeness of me made in a composition resembling Parian marble; and I unhesitatingly pronounce it among the best, if not the very best, ever taken of me by any artist." ALS. OClWHi. For Garlick (1805-84), see *DAB*; and Amyx, "Portraits of Henry Clay," Special Collections, KyU.

To the testimonial about the accuracy of his plaster bas-relief of Clay, Garlick added the explanation that "I was this day introduced to the Hon. H. Clay, Senator from Kentucky [by] the Hon. J.R. Giddings, member of the House, from Ohio. I presented Mr. Clay with a copy of his likeness which I had executed in Bas Relief, of which this is a duplicate and he gave me the above testimonial of its correctness unsolicited–" ALS. OClWHi.

To LUCRETIA HART CLAY Washington, February 12, 1840

I send you by the Mail to day some Broccoli, Eggplant, and Early York Cabbage Seeds, which I hope will reach you in safety.

I was alarmed some days ago by intelligence from N. Orleans that Mr. [James] Erwin had failed.[1] I was relieved a few days after by a letter received from him in which he states that he is not broke nor can be broke, altho he is some what envolved by indorsements for Mr. Beall [*sic*, William H. Beal], which he thinks Mr. Beall will himself be able to pay.[2] This occurrence has made me more anxious to with draw my funds from his hands, and I hope to receive them next month.

Thomas [Hart Clay] informs me that you gave him the two checks which I left with you. As I have money in the Bank, I send you another, which I hope you will freely use. I wish you would say to Thomas that if Mr Suttons[3] Hemp and Bacon do not go too high that I think it well to purchase them.

I have changed my quarters, and now live with Mrs [E.S.] Arguelles where I was last winter.[4] I have a very good Mess consisting of Mr. [Leverett] Saltonstall & his family and Mr. [John] Henderson and his. I pay but fifteen dollars a week for Charles and myself.

I have received a letter from John [Morrison Clay] who I see has reached home.[5] I hope that he will conduct himself creditably and satisfactorily to you.

I have engaged to go to Richmond on the 22d. Feb.[6] When I consented to go, they promised me a quiet and unostentatious reception, but I find that they are making great preparations to receive me, and I fear that I shall be very much fatigued.

The suit between Mr. [James] Brown's Estate and Kean [*sic*, Richard R. Keene] was argued by Mr. [John J.] Crittenden & me the other day, but it is not yet decided. . . .[7]

ALS. Josephine Simpson Collection, Lexington, Ky. 1. Clay to Erwin, Feb. 6, 1840. 2. *Ibid.* 3. Probably either David Sutton who owned 500 acres on Henry's Mill Road or George W. Sutton who owned 800 acres on Georgetown Turnpike. MacCabe, *Directory of the City of Lexington . . . 1838 & '39*, p. 133. 4. During the 25th Congress, 3rd Session (Dec. 1838-March 1839), Clay had lived at Mrs. E.S. Arguelle's boarding house "nearly opposite Gadsby's" where his messmates had been Reps. Levi Lincoln (Mass.), William K. Bond (Ohio), and Edward Stanly (N.C.). At the beginning of the 26th Congress, 1st Session (Dec. 1839-July 1840) he and Charles, his body slave, boarded at Mrs. Denny's on Third Street, his messmates there being Reps. Rice Garland and Thomas W. Chinn, both of Louisiana. He joined Rep. Leverett Saltonstall (Mass.) and Sen. John Henderson (Miss.) at Mrs. Arguelle's in Feb., 1840. During the spring, the three men moved to Mrs. Cochran's on F Street [Clay to Saltonstall, May 31, 1840]. Clay resumed boarding at Mrs. Arguelle's during the 26th Congress, 2nd Session (Dec. 7, 1840-March 3, 1841) where his messmates were Delegate James D. Doty (Terr. of Wisc.), and Reps. Willis Green (Ky.), Edward Stanly (N.C.), John M. Botts (Va.), and George W. Crabb (Ala.). Goldman & Young, *U.S. Congressional Directories*, 342, 357, 370; see also E.S. Arguelle to Clay, April 18, 1840 (bill and receipt for room and board). ADS. DLC-TJC (DNA, M212, R18). For Rep. Saltonstall (Mass.), Sen. Henderson (Miss.), and other legislators mentioned in this note, see *BDAC*. 5. From Missouri. See Clay to Lucretia Clay, Jan. 24, 1840. 6. Clay departed Washington for Richmond on Feb. 22, returning to the capital on March 6. 7. Clay to Ingersoll, Sept. 30, 1837.

From Benjamin F. Farnsworth, District of Columbia, February 12, 1840. Refers to their recent conversation pertaining to the reorganization of Transylvania University, during which Clay had offered to nominate him for a professorship of Belles Lettres and Moral Philosophy at the school. Has "reflected on the subject with increasing interest," and asks Clay to proceed with the nomination. Says that his earlier connection with Georgetown College [Georgetown, Ky.] and his presidency of the Collegiate Institute of Louisville (since 1838) would not prevent his changing positions at an early date. Thinks he can help Transylvania secure "an extensive patronage and a permanency which it has heretofore been so unsuccessful in its attempts to sustain." Agrees entirely with Clay's "remark concerning the expediency of having the several religious denominations represented in the faculty." Is convinced that Clay's influence in the matter is "entirely sufficient to place my name on the list of the Faculty." ALS. KyLxT.

The Rev. Mr. Farnsworth, a Baptist minister who had served briefly as president and professor at Georgetown College (and who was not hired to teach at Transylvania) was visiting a friend of his in the District of Columbia when he wrote this letter. For the reorganization of Transylvania, see Robert Peter, *Transylvania University: Its Origin, Rise, Decline, and Fall.* Filson Club Publications, No. 11 (Louisville, 1896), 163-68; Wright, *Transylvania*, 152-53. For the reorganization of the Collegiate Institute of Louisville, about to become Louisville College, a reorganization that excluded Farnsworth, see Kentucky Writers' Project, *Centennial History of the University of Louisville*, 13-15. For more on Farnsworth, see *CAB* and Leland W. Meyer, *Georgetown College, Its Background and a Chapter in Its Early History* (Louisville, 1929), 52.

On this same day, February 12, Clay wrote Benjamin Gratz in Lexington, enclosing a letter from Farnsworth to the Transylvania trustees, and recommending Farnsworth for employment. ALS. KyLxT.

Remark in Senate, February 13, 1840. Presents the petition of the Kentucky State Agricultural Society requesting the endowment of an agricultural school or college in the state with funds from the Smithsonian legacy. *Cong. Globe*, 26 Cong., 1 Sess., 187. The Kentucky State Agricultural Society had been formed on February 3, 1838, to promote fairs, an agricultural school, and direct state aid for farmers. Collins, *History of Kentucky*, 1:42; Charles Kerr (ed.), *History of Kentucky*, 5 vols. (Chicago, 1922), 2:741. This request for a part of the legacy left to the United States government by James Smithson was only one of many made to Congress until it was finally decided in 1846 to use the bequest to found the Smithsonian Institution. See Webster P. True, *The First Hundred Years of the Smithsonian Institution 1846-1946* (Washington, D.C., 1946), 1-8, *passim*; and Paul H. Oehser, *Sons of Science, The Story of the Smithsonian . . .* (New York, 1949), 1-25, *passim.*

Later this day, in presenting a petition for the abolition of slavery, Clay defends the right of petition and hopes that "the crisis of this unfortunate agitation" has passed. Reports his having read, last summer, "some valuable works from Northern pens on the subject of Abolition," and considers them "the ablest defences of Southern institutions" he has seen. Identifies them as "The Review of Dr. Channing Reviewed," "Abolition a Sedition," and "Some Thoughts on Domestic Slavery [Clay to Kennedy, May 16, 1839]," and notes that all of them can be purchased at Mr. Franck Taylor's bookstore. Thinks the last of these titles particularly filled with "many profound philosophical truths," especially its development of the proposition "that two communities of distinct races cannot live together without the one becoming more or less in subjection to the other." Thinks this applies also to the French and British residents of Canada, as Lord [John George] Durham, the Canadian governor-general, pointed out in his *Report on the Affairs of British North America* in February, 1839. In response to John C. Calhoun's assertion that the right of petition was "among the least important of our political rights" since it has been superseded, in a great degree, by the far higher right of general suffrage," asks why then that right was "guarded with such sedulous care by the framers of our Constitution?" *Cong. Globe*, 26 Cong., 1 Sess., 187.

Still later this day, Clay reenters the debate on the mingling of races, abolition and related matters, pointing out that there has been "considerable difficulty in preserving peaceful relations" among the French and Anglo-Saxon races in Louisiana. Adds that "both the great parties had occasionally profited by Abolition, and instanced the recent election of a Democratic Governor in Massachusetts by their aid [Clay to Sargent, October 25, 1839]. He believed that, if put to the vote, there was not a single Senator who would not vote to maintain the rights of the South. Their institutions, whether right or wrong, were, from their nature, incurable. But he did not wish to mix it up with collateral questions." Asks, in conclusion, "why should we identify Abolition with rights guarantied by the Constitution. If we desire safety, let us stand upon the broad platform of the Constitution, and this would be the best guarantee of protection for the rights of the South." *Ibid.*, 191.

Remark in Senate, February 14, 1840. Presented with a number of documents from the Committee on Finance dealing with monopolistic and other nefarious practices in the manufacture and trade of salt, Clay identifies the printed documents as a "wasteful expenditure of public money," probably even less "valuable than the bundle of trash printed at the last session on the same subject." Denies Ohio Sen. William Allen's contention that monopoly conditions in the domestic salt industry may well produce the political despotism associated with national salt monopolies in Europe. Opposes the bill now under consideration "to effect a repeal of the duty on salt—a repeal of this miserable duty of six cents per bushel!"; and asks "how will that prevent the manufacturers from getting what every man has a right to get, the highest price for his productions?" Dismisses Allen's comments on the salt monopoly as "in conformity with that agrarian spirit . . . that leveling spirit . . . which first attacked the United States Bank, then the local banks and now is endeavoring to lay violent hands on the fishing bounties." *Cong. Globe*, 26 Cong., 1 Sess., 198; *ibid.*, Appendix, 177-78. For the history, up to 1840, of the "Act Laying a Duty on Imported Salt, Granting a Bounty on Pickled Fish Exported. . ." first passed on July 23, 1813, and subsequently amended many times, see *Sen. Docs.*, 26 Cong., 1 Sess., no. 368. On July 20, 1840, it was ordered that the Senate Committee on Finance be discharged from further consideration of the bill to repeal this act. Thus, the salt duty was not repealed by the 26th Congress. U.S. Sen., *Journal*, 26 Cong., 1 Sess., 546.

To HENRY CLAY, JR. Washington, February 22 [*sic, ca.* 17] 1840[1]

I recd. your letter of the 13h. inst. and was happy to hear that your eye was getting much better. Thomas [Hart Clay] had informed me of your affliction, which gave me great concern.

I am surprized and concerned at the rigorous course pursued towards you by the Northern Bank.[2] Considering that it does not pay its own debts, it should not be so decided in enforcing payment from others, especially where, as in this case, they have a perfect security. If you should be disappointed in negotitating the loan, which you were attempting, and the Bank will not continue the loan until my return, I see no alternative but for you to let it bring suit. When I get home, perhaps, we together may be able to devise some way of meeting it.

I wish you would pay some little attention to the Jacks being put in order. I have had an application for one or two of them, altho' I do not know that any thing will come out of it. I wish however to be prepared to take advantage of it. In the mean time if you can sell either do so.

Your mother has several times expressed a wish that I would let you have Major. He is old, slow, but I believe honest & faithful. If you can make any use of him, send for him. He may serve as a sort of Watch dog.

The Harrisburg nomination[3] takes better, far better, every where than

I anticipated. The first feelings of disappointment give way to acquiescence and a determination to support it. Here a strong conviction prevails among the Whigs that he will be elected; and some of the administration men begin to apprehend it. That party is getting in a bay [*sic*, bad] way both in Pennsa. & Ohio. It is cut up into divisions about the Banks.[4]

I have recd. a letter from Genl Harrison[5] in which he expresses lively gratitude to me, wishes a friendly correspondence, my advice &c.

Whatever are my impressions as to the intrigues among a few,[6] by which the nomination was brought about, depend upon it that the course I have taken has been the wisest.

I wish that you would write to me as often as you can. The minutest details about you & your family & about Ashland interest me.

I hope that [Albert] Florea may be able to assist you in breaking out your Hemp.

Give my love to Julia [Prather Clay] & your dear children.

ALS. Henry Clay Memorial Foundation, Lexington, Ky. 1. Editors have determined from internal evidence that Clay inexplicably misdated this letter, since it is apparent herein that he had not yet heard about the birth of Henry Clay, Jr.'s, son, Thomas Julian, nor the resultant death in childbirth of his wife Julia. Indeed, in a letter to Lucretia Hart Clay on Feb. 18, 1840, he sent congratulations to Henry, Jr., on the birth of a new son. Also, on Feb. 20, 1840, he wrote his son a letter of condolence on Julia's death; therefore, the most probable date of this letter would seem to be Feb. 17. 2. See Clay to Thomas Hart Clay, Feb. 21, 1840; Clay to Lucretia Hart Clay, March 6, 1840. 3. Porter to Clay, Nov. 14 and Dec. 30, 1837. 4. The administration's Sub-Treasury proposal. See Clay to Porter, Dec. 27, 1838; Speech in Senate, Jan. 20, 1840. 5. Harrison to Clay, Jan. 15, 1840. 6. Porter to Clay, Feb. 16, 1839.

Remark in Senate, February 17, 1840. Presents petitions variously asking for a congress of nations, additional duty on imported silk, and pension claims. *Cong. Globe*, 26 Cong., 1 Sess., 201.

Later this day, Clay again spoke in opposition to Calhoun's bill to cede the public lands to the states in which they were situated [Remark in Senate, January 3, 1840]. He noted that one argument advanced for it by Calhoun was that it was really "a plan to get rid of a thousand million of acres [so as] to diminish patronage." Charges that surely such a suggestion "could not command the serious approbation even of the Senator from South Carolina." This remark triggered an acrimonious personal exchange between Clay and Calhoun which turned on who had insulted whom in their past exchanges on public land issues. Calhoun's bill, Clay concluded, "was a clear grant of one moiety to the new States, which, in its inevitable consequence, would end in the absolute relinguishment of the whole; and the Senator chooses to construe that into an assault. . . . I repeat that I am as unwilling as any Senator to indulge in personalities, and as little in the habit of doing so. In that business I have been more sinned against than sinning. I have been far more an object of attack than the Senator from South Carolina—as well in the Senate as by the public press, and in private circles. I have sometimes treated it with contempt, sometimes with indignation, but have never been so peculiarly sensitive as the Senator." *Ibid.*, 202-3.

Still later this day, Clay offered no objection to having printed certain documents from the Committee on Finance on the salt tariff issue [Remark in Senate, February 14, 1840]. *Ibid.*, 204.

To LUCRETIA HART CLAY Washington, February 18, 1840

I received letters from Thomas [Hart Clay], Henry [Clay, Jr.] and John [Morrison Clay] yesterday and to day which give me very full details of information from home. I am truly concerned about Henry's continued indisposition.[1] Poor fellow! he has suffered a great deal. He informs me that we have another grand son,[2] and I congratulate [him] on the occasion....

[lines excised from manuscript]

I understand that [Albert] Florea has not been able to complete the clearing up of the Morton Woods. I wish you would tell him that I expect him to prepare and put in Hemp the part which he has cleared.

I sent you two other parcels of Seeds, after the first, all of which I hope will get to you safely.

I am most anxious to hear from N. Orleans more about Mr. [James] Erwins true situation.[3] I have not heard from him since the date of his letter mentioned in my last.

I shall go to Richmond [Va.] on friday of this week and expect to be gone about ten days....[4]

ALS. Josephine Simpson Collection, Lexington, Ky. Eight or nine lines excised from middle of manuscript. 1. Eye trouble. See Clay to Henry Clay, Jr., *ca.* Feb. 17, 1840. 2. Thomas Julian Clay who died, unmarried, on Oct. 12, 1863. 3. Clay to Lucretia Hart Clay, Feb. 12, 1840. 4. *Ibid.*

Remark in Senate, February 18, 1840. Interrupts the speech of Sen. Henry Hubbard (N.H.) on the Benton-Lumpkin resolutions, which opposed on constitutional grounds the federal assumption of state debts, to ask the names of the newspapers to which Hubbard referred in making the point that there was considerable press discussion of the assumption issue prior to the introduction of Sen. Thomas H. Benton's formal resolution on the subject. *Cong. Globe,* 26 Cong., 1 Sess., Appendix, 196.

Following Hubbard's speech, Clay moved adjournment. *Cong. Globe,* 26 Cong., 1 Sess., 208.

The issue of the assumption of state debts by the federal government was raised as a result of fears that several states were again on the verge of defaulting on their bonds. Benton's resolutions on the question, submitted on December 27, 1839, as subsequently revised and shortened by Sen. Wilson Lumpkin (Ga.) on January 7, 1840, denied the constitutional power of the federal government to assume debts contracted by states and localities for their own purposes. Both of these resolutions were referred to a Senate select committee. On the other hand, it was feared by some that the very act of publicly debating the Benton-Lumpkin resolutions would further weaken both domestic and foreign confidence in the integrity of state bonds. An amendment by Sen. John J. Crittenden (Ky.) on February 10, 1840, to support the financial structures of all the states (and by inference their bonded debt), by distributing to all twenty-six of them "in fair and reasonable proportions" the proceeds of the sales of public lands was attacked, amended, and counter-amended by administration spokesmen. Specifically, Crittenden's amendment, supported by Clay, was beaten 28 to 17 on March 6, 1840. Also on March 6, following votes on various other amendments and counter-amendments, the Senate finally passed a revised version of the Benton-Lumpkin resolution which held that assumption would not only be wholly unconstitutional, it would also be unjust, inexpedient, dangerous to the Union, and repugnant; and that while the several states had the constitutional right to contract debt, the federal government had no right to absorb such debts openly or directly, or under the guise of "giving security for their payment, or by creating surplus revenue." *Ibid.,* 82-83, 105, 158, 164, 178, 204-5, 209, 212, 244-45. The measure was not acted on by the House during this session.

The states of New York, Pennsylvania, Maryland, Indiana, Illinois, Michigan, and Arkansas temporarily defaulted on the interest on all or part of their indebtedness; however, within two years these defaults were made good. Mississippi and the territory of Florida repudiated outright the principal of two bond issues floated to provide capital for banks that had failed. In 1838 about $86,000,000 of English capital was invested in state bonds in the United States. This situation led many British banking houses to call for the federal government to assume the debts of the various states rather than allowing them to default. William J. Schultz & M.R. Caine, *Financial Development of the United States* (New York, 1937), 234-36; Joseph Dorfman, "A Note on the Interpretation of Anglo-American Finance, 1837-1841," *JEH* (Spring, 1951), 11:140-47; Benjamin U. Ratchford, *American State Debts* (Durham, N.C., 1941), 79-122.

Speech in Senate, February 19, 1840. Speaks "at length" on the report of the select committee on the assumption of state debts [Remark in Senate, February 18, 1840]. *Cong. Globe*, 26 Cong., 1 Sess., 209. Speech not recorded. No manuscript or printed version of it has been found. See Remark in Senate, February 20, 1840.

From Nathaniel Beverley Tucker, Williamsburg, Va., February 19, 1840. Compliments Clay on his Senate speech of January 20 [Speech in Senate, January 20, 1840] in opposition to the Independent Treasury bill. Reports that he will receive an invitation from a committee in Williamsburg to visit "our ancient city" on his way from Richmond to Norfolk and urges him to accept. Invites him to stay "under my roof." ALS. DLC-HC (DNA, M212, R5). Addressed to Clay in Richmond, Va. [Clay to Lucretia Hart Clay, February 12, 1840].

On February 24, writing from Richmond, Clay declines Tucker's kind invitation, citing as a reason the recent death of daughter-in-law Julia Prather Clay [Clay to Henry Clay, Jr., February 20, 1840], an event "which made me hesitate about coming here." ALS. ViW.

To HENRY CLAY, JR. Washington, February 20, 1840

I received last night your letter communicating the afflicting intelligence of the death of your dear wife my poor daughter Julia.[1] It was so sudden and appalling, and so unexpected to me that it overwhelmed me with sorrow and grief. I scarcely slept last night, and have risen hardly able yet to realize the loss which we have sustained. The manner of her death resembles so much that of my lamented Anne![2]

Yes, my dear Son, I do condole and sympathize with you, from the bottom of my soul. But I hope that you will not forget that she has left you tender & responsible duties to perform towards the children[3] of your mutual love and affection. These will require all your care, and I hope that you will command the fortitude requisite to the fulfillment of your duties to them.

How one after another are the objects which fastened me to the life passing away and leaving me with scarcely any wish but that I may soon follow them! Whatever might be my desire that must be my fate. During the short remnant of my life, I too shall need your kindness and affectionate attention. I beg therefore, on my account, as well as that of my dear Grand children you will take care of yourself.

Had you not better yet make your trip to N. O. and proceed from thence by the way of Augusta and Charleston to this place?

ALS. Henry Clay Memorial Foundation, Lexington, Ky. Addressed to his son in Louisville. 1. Apparently from complications attendant upon the birth of her baby, Thomas Julian Clay. Clay to Lucretia Hart Clay, Feb. 18, 1840. 2. Anne Brown Clay (Mrs. James) Erwin in Dec., 1835. See 8:808-9. 3. Living in 1840 were Henry III, Anne, and Thomas J.; Matilda and Martha had died in infancy in 1835 and 1838 respectively.

To LUCRETIA HART CLAY Washington, February 21 [*sic*, 20],[1] 1840

I passed a most distressing night last night and rose this morning unrefreshed by any Sleep. Just before I went to bed, I received a letter from Henry [Clay, Jr.] communicating the melancholy intelligence of the sudden death of poor Julia.[2] She appears to have gone off in a manner similar to that in which our lamented Anne [Brown Clay Erwin] left us.[3] Henry writes in terms of the greatest grief, and seems to be overwhelmed. Poor fellow; his life has not been long but he has had his full share of misfortunes. I have written to him communicating all the expressions of sympathy, soothing & condolence which I could employ. I have told him of his duties and responsibilities to the sweet little children that Julia has left him; and that during my short remnant of life I too shall want his care and kindness. I have advised him to prosecute his journey to N. Orleans and then come round by Augusta and Charleston to this place.

I have not failed, my dear wife, to think of the addition to your cares and responsibilities which this sad event may occasion; but I trust that the Prather family[4] will relieve you much from them. And we must submit to whatever Providence inflicts upon us.

I have no heart to make the excursion to Richmond[5] which I intended to do [to]morrow: but they have made such arrangements for my reception that I should create great disappointment if I did not go. And I have concluded that perhaps the journey, new scenes and other places may assuage, if they do not allow me, for a short time, to forget my sorrows.

I have this day received a letter from James [Brown Clay] at Natchez. He has been there some time, and I infer, from what he writes, that he is involved in some love affair. He does not mention the ladys name.

Give my love to John [Morrison Clay] & all of our children and grandchildren.

ALS. Henry Clay Memorial Foundation, Lexington, Ky. Written in "S[enate]. Chamber." 1. Incorrectly dated Feb. 21. Postmarked February 20. 2. Clay to Henry Clay, Jr., Feb. 20, 1840. 3. See 8:808-9. 4. Julia's widowed mother, Matilda Fontaine (Mrs. Thomas) Prather, brother William Prather, and sister Catharine—all of Louisville. 5. Clay to Lucretia Hart Clay, Feb. 12, 1840.

Remark in Senate, February 20, 1840. With reference to the assumption of state debts by the federal government [Remark in Senate, February 18, 1840], moves "to postpone the whole subject indefinitely." Defeated 15 to 27, Clay voting yea. *Cong. Globe*, 26 Cong., 1 Sess., 212.

To Thomas Hart Clay, Lexington, February 21, 1840. Urges his son not to draw on him for $1,250 or $1,500 unless "absolutely necessary." Explains that he cannot cover such a withdrawal until he has received remittances from James Erwin [Clay to Lucretia Hart Clay, February 12, 1840] in New Orleans. Adds: "If you draw, make it payable at the Bank of Commerce in N. York at ninety days, and you ought to get a large premium on it." Asks what is being done to meet his note due at the Northern Bank of Kentucky. ALS. DLC-HC (DNA, M212, R5). See also Clay to Lucretia Hart Clay, March 6, 1840.

From WILLIAM HENRY HARRISON North Bend, Ohio, February 25, 1840

You have probably seen that [Thomas] Ri[t]chie of the Richmond Enquirer attempted to sustain his charge of Federalism & Abolitionism against me by quotations from a Speech of mine delivered at Cheviot in this County [Hamilton] on the 4h. of July 1833.[1] When I first saw these charges I was confident that the extracts were garbled sentences from the speech, which when fai[rly] quoted would not only not sustain the conclusions of Richie but would exhibit sentiments of a precisely opposite Character. Having however no copy by me & not having seen the speech for several years I could not say in answer to the enquiries which were made of me by my friends at Richmond what were the particular words I had used in relation to the Abolition question & upon the subject of Mr Calhouns Nullification doctrines upon which last the charge of Federalism was attempted to be sustained Having however procured a Copy in pamphlet form[2] I sent it at the request of Dr. Rives of Cincinnati[3] to his brother Mr W[illiam]. [C.] Rives of Virginia. And a few days ago I received from the latter gentleman a letter containing his remarks upon it. They are highly flattering both as it regards the Composition & the Opinions it sustains on the political subjects of which it treats. With his letter he sent me a copy of his speech delivered in the Senate in Feby 1833[4] to shew the conformity of our sentiments with regard to each other & to the Virginia Resolutions of 1798. He (Mr Rives) also asserts that the speech taken together should be entirely Satisfactory to "The South" in relation to Abolitionism. The unreserved Commendation of this speech by so good a judge & a Southern politician induced me to apply to the Committee by whom it was published for some Copies. I received yesterday several one of which is herewith enclosed. I beg the favor of you to read it & give me your Opinion as to the propriety of Circulating them. There is no doubt of Richie having a Copy procured by Duncan[,][5] & Rives informs me that it will be published in the Yeoman a new Whig Weekly paper published in Richmond.[6] The only injury that I can see to arrise from its Circulation is the unqualified approbation it gives to "*the Proclamation*"[7] Altho my "sober second thoughts" would have modified the expressions I used in relation to it I entertained at the time the Speech was delivered so much abhorrence of the nullifing & those doctrines as to induce me to think that the decided opposition manifested to [the] Speech by Gen Jackson (a[l]tho personal hatred might have had much influence in producing it) merritted the eulogism I pronounced upon him.

It has been asserted in some of the southern papers that during the whole of the last canvas for the Presidency I remained perfectly silent on the subject of Slavery. By the last mail I sent to Mr W[illiam] C Preston evidence that this was not the fact & that my Vincennes Speech[8] was delivered many months after my nomination at many public meetings & after all the opposition papers in Indiana & many in Ohio had taken me up as the Whig Candidate. But so far from concealing my sentiments after this, being applied to by three Individuals of Vermont for my opinion upon the Abolition question I wrote an elaborate Argument in reply & it was not my fault that it was not published. I sent it to our friend John Chambers with a request that he would convince a few of my friends Abolitionists & Anti Abolitionists & determin[e] the propriety of surrendering it to them. I do not know who of the latter was selected by Chambers but [William] Slade was one of the former & I believe F[ranci]s Granger.[9] Slade protested against its being sent Observing that altho he would continue to support me it might be the means of my loosing Vermont & with all that the persons who had written to me were not entitled to an answer being enemies in disguise. Chambers informed me that the Southern men declared that they wished no fresh declarations of my sentiments. My votes on the Missouri & Arcansas [*sic,* Arkansas] bills[10] & my Vincennes Speech being sufficient to satisfy any reasonable Southern man. Chambers still has in his possession one of the duplicates of My letter. I have determined not to make the above circumstances public. I give them to you for the purpose of satisfying any individual friend to whom you may think it proper to communicate them.

Confidential—I received lately a letter from N. Y. (the City) containing a hint of a design in embryo which I wish to communicate to you but as it is not important that you should know it immediately I keep it for an other opportunity[11]

I use the freedom which I invite on your part towards me to say that I think that there are many & good reasons why you should be on an intimate footing with Mr Webster

ALS. DLC-HC (DNA, M212, R5). 1. Ritchie had charged in the Richmond *Enquirer* of Feb. 8, 1840, that Harrison, "if not an Abolitionist, is an Ultra Emancipationist." He further stated that Harrison "believes the General Government 'can aid' the cause of emancipation and that 'with the *sanction* of the States holding the slaves,' he can see no '*constitutional objection*' to the appropriation of the 'whole of its surplus revenue' to that object." 2. William Henry Harrison, *Address; Delivered on the 4th of July, 1833, at Cheviot, Ohio.* Cincinnati, 1833. 3. For Landon Cabell Rives, a physician who practiced and taught in Cincinnati, see Liston, "W.C. Rives: Diplomat and Politician," Ph.D. dissertation, Ohio State University, 1972, p. 3. 4. *Speech of Mr. Rives, of Virginia, on the Bill Further to Provide for the Collection of Duties on Imports.* Washington, 1833. Also in *Register of Debates,* 22 Cong., 2 Sess., 494-518. 5. Probably Alexander Duncan of Ohio. 6. The Richmond *Yeoman* was published from Jan. to Dec., 1840, by John S. Gallaher. It was essentially a campaign sheet for Harrison. Winifred Gregory (ed.), *American Newspapers, 1821-1936 . . .* (New York, 1937), 711. 7. Jackson's "Proclamation to the People of South Carolina," Dec. 10, 1832. 8. Harrison had said in a speech at Vincennes on May 25, 1835, that the "mischief" being perpetrated by the abolitionists was dangerous to the safety of the white population in the South. He also charged that the right of petition as used by the abolitionists was unjustifiable. Frankfort *Commonwealth,* June 30, 1835. 9. For Reps. John Chambers (Ky.), William Slade (Vt.), and Francis Granger (N.Y.), see *BDAC.* 10. In 1819 Harrison, then a member of the 15th Congress, voted against both a bill to admit Missouri as a state and a bill to organize the territory of Arkansas because they each included an amendment prohibiting slavery. Since public opinion in Ohio was predominantly in favor of the restriction against slavery, these votes became an issue in the next [1820] election in which Harrison was defeated. Cleaves, *Old Tippecanoe,* 248, 252-53; Glover Moore, *The Missouri Controversy 1819-1821* (Lexington, Ky., 1953), 205-6. 11. Reference obscure.

To LUCRETIA HART CLAY Washington, March 6, 1840

I returned this morning from Richmond,[1] not much recruited, as you may suppose, after the scenes through which I passed there. I should not have gone, after having heard of the melancholy loss of our poor Julia,[2] but that the most extensive arrangements had been made for my reception and I should have created a great disappointment. Nothing could have surpassed the enthusiasm and cordiality with which I was received and treated. And if our severe bereavement had not have forced its consideration upon me continually I should have enjoyed the trip very much. I went to Hanover to the place on which I was born, and which I had not seen for forty eight years. Every thing was changed, in so much that, if I had been put there without information I should not have been able to recognize it. The spot in which my father and maternal grand father and grand mother[3] were buried were marked by no stone or index, and a crop of wheat was growing over their remains. The row of May cherry trees, of which you have heard me speak, was in part standing but the remaining trees shewed the effects of age quite as much as I exhibited them myself. A hickory tree, which bore the finest fruit of that kind which I ever tasted was lying prostrate and in a state of decay. The old dwelling house was still standing but much altered, and the room in which I was born was pointed out to me and recognized by me. I met in Hanover one person only that I recognized as a relation—an old lady of eighty years old by the name of Perrin, a cousin of my mother.[4] She was evidently not long for this world. The Church at which I went two years to School was yet standing, but in a decayed condition which indicated that we should probably both tumble down about the same time.

I have received the letter from Julia's sister [Catharine Prather] which you directed to John [Morrison Clay] to send me; and I have received two letters from Henry [Clay, Jr.], since the occurrence of his heavy affliction. They were written in terms of deepest grief. I answered him, and endeavored to console him as much as I could;[5] but I entertain great apprehensions as to the effects upon him of this severe visitation. I need not say to you, my dear Wife, that if he comes to Ashland, I hope that you will do every thing in your power to console and soothe him.

I have received the deed for the lot which I sent you to execute.

Enclosed I send a check for $891:9 which I have endorsed to Thomas [Hart Clay]. I wish him to go to town, sell the check and deposite the proceeds to my credit with the Lexington Branch Bank. $500 of it will be applied towards the payment of a note I have in that bank. The check ought to bring a premium of two or three per cent.

I also enclose a note for $2500 to renew in part a note which I have in that Bank for $3000, and which is to be signed by Thomas. This business ought to be attended to immediately, and I wish for that purpose you would send directly for Thomas.[6]

We have had three or four weeks of delightful weather I have imagined you engaged in gardening and wished that I was with you. I still hope to be so in May.

I have several letters from Mr. [James] Erwin, which represent his situation to be better than I feared. He assures me that he is neither broken, nor in danger of being broken;[7] and that in no event need I fear for my funds in his hands. I have also a letter from his son Henry [Clay Erwin].

Give my love to Henry [Clay, Jr.], if he be with you, and to Thomas [Hart Clay], John [Morrison Clay], Mary [Mentelle Clay] and the children.[8]

ALS. Josephine Simpson Collection, Lexington, Ky. 1. Clay to Lucretia Hart Clay, Feb. 12, 1840. 2. Clay to Henry Clay, Jr., Feb. 20, 1840. 3. John Clay (d. 1782), George Hudson (d. *ca.* 1773), Elizabeth Jennings Hudson (d. 1781). 4. Elizabeth Hudson Clay who, having been widowed, married (1784) Henry Watkins. Her Perrin cousin was likely a kinsman of Henry and Samuel Perrin "of Hanover, near the Merry oaks [3:500]." 5. Clay to Henry Clay, Jr., Feb. 20, 1840. 6. For more on these financial manipulations involving the Lexington branch of the Northern Bank of Kentucky, see Clay to Thomas Hart Clay, Feb. 21, 1840. 7. Clay to Lucretia Hart Clay, Feb. 12, 1840. 8. At this time the children residing at "Ashland" and/or "Maplewood," Henry Clay, Jr.'s nearby farm, were probably those of Henry Clay, Jr., viz: Henry III (age 7), Anne (3), and Thomas Julian (infant) whose birth had brought about the recent death of Henry, Jr.'s wife, Julia Prather Clay; also the children of James Erwin and his deceased wife, Anne Brown Clay Erwin, viz: Henry Clay (13), James, Jr. (12), Andrew Eugene (11), Lucretia Hart (10), and Charles Edward (5). Various of the Erwin children occasionally joined their father in New Orleans for extended visits. See Clay to Hughes, June 18, 1837. The two Duralde grandsons, Martin III and Henry Clay, children of Martin and Susan Clay Duralde, who were taken in at "Ashland" and raised by Henry and Lucretia following the death of their mother in 1825, were no longer there; Martin III was a midshipman in the U.S. Navy in 1840 and Henry Clay Duralde was apparently in school in Danville, Ky. See Clay to Paulding, May 3, 1839; Clay to Lucretia Hart Clay, Jan. 24, 1840.

Remark in Senate, March 6, 1840. Participates in an "animated debate" (not recorded) on the issue of the assumption of state debts [Remark in Senate, February 18 and 19, 1840]. *Cong. Globe*, 26 Cong., 1 Sess., 244.

Later this day, Clay remarks that he has listened with amazement to the responses of James Buchanan (Pa.), William R. King (Ala.), and other administration spokesmen to his speech of January 20, 1840, in opposition to the Independent Treasury bill. Wonders if he is really in the U.S. Senate chamber, since "We now hear that there is no intention on the part of the friends of the Administration to injure banks, no desire to destroy the credit system of the country, no wish to reduce the wages of labor. Why, really, one is almost tempted to imagine that the present display has been the result of previous arrangement, to give an opportunity for a general recantation." Warns the nation not to trust the sincerity of these men. Challenged by King to cite any vote, sentiment, or other evidence that he (King) had recanted or otherwise changed his opinion on the Sub-Treasury question, Clay responds that he meant not to single out King but to call attention to "the former course of the party [Democrat] with which the Senator acted." *Ibid.*, Appendix, 338-39.

Remark in Senate, March 9, 1840. Presents petitions from stockholders of the Agricultural Bank of Natchez asking for an extension of time for payment of a sum due the government; also, petitions from those favoring the prevention of wars between nations. *Cong. Globe*, 26 Cong., 1 Sess., 250.

Later this day, speaking to a motion to set the day of adjournment on one of the Mondays in May, Clay says he is ready to vote for adjournment tomorrow, or even today, since "nothing was to be expected from the present session of the present Congress, either to advance the interests, or to relieve the embarrassments of the people. The sooner, then, that they went home and mixed with their constituents, the better. Let us go to the honest farmer, and take a chaw tobacco with him, and ask him 'how are his children—how the state of his crops, and what markets are afforded, in the present crippled state of the times, through the war made upon the banks and credit of the country;' and when we meet again . . . it will be under happier auspices; we shall then be likely to find a Congress better organized, and more disposed to regard the public weal."

Believes that Congress will probably have to stay in session long enough to vote on issuing eight to ten million dollars worth of treasury notes, the state of the government's finances being what it is. *Ibid.* The first session of the 26th Congress adjourned on July 21, 1840.

For Clay's earlier hostile views on the right and judgment of the government's issuance of treasury notes, see Comment in Senate, September 15, 1837; Speech in Senate, September 25, 1837. The Treasury note bill, introduced on February 9, 1840, passed the House on March 27 by a vote of 110 to 66. It passed the Senate on March 30 by a vote of 25 to 8, Clay voting nay. *Cong. Globe*, 26 Cong., 1 Sess., 211, 222, 225, 264, 294. The act extended the act of October 12, 1837, but provided that "the amount of notes outstanding at any one time" was not to exceed $5,000,000. It became law on March 31, 1840. 5 *U.S. Stat.*, 370. Ten million dollars in treasury notes had been issued under the act of October, 1837. A like sum was authorized in May, 1838. In all, $47,000,000 of such notes were issued from 1837 to 1844. Shultz, *Financial Development of the United States*, 233.

From Levi Woodbury, Treasury Department, Washington, March 9, 1840. Responds to Clay's complaint of this date about "two protested drafts" on the Citizens Bank. Thinks there might have been reluctance at the bank to pay the drafts "to a person whose name is spelt so differently." States that the bank's reputation has "always been considered fair and honorable," and assures Clay that he "will be happy to prevent any inconvenience" he might have suffered from the incident "by having the drafts made payable here or in New York if preferred." Copy. DNA, RG56, Letters to Individual Members of Congress (1838-41), 2:235-36. The bank referred to is probably the Citizens Bank of New Orleans, chartered with a capitalization of $12,000,000 in 1833 by the state of Louisiana. It was the only bank in New Orleans that continued to pay out specie in the panic of 1837. Fossier, *New Orleans*, 68-69, 72.

On March 12, 1840, Clay wrote James Erwin saying he "had recd. from the Treasury Dept. checks on N. York for the two drafts which you sent me." Also transmits "enclosed the letter which I received from the Secy. [Woodbury]." Adds: "The question is not yet decided what the Legislature of Pennsa. will do with the Bank; but I still think that it will not put them down." ALS. KyU. In the spring, 1840 session of the Pennsylvania legislature an attempt was made to force the state banks to resume specie payment immediately. This endeavor failed, however, and with the encouragement of Gov. David Porter a bill was passed requiring the resumption of specie on January 15, 1841. Govan, *Nicholas Biddle*, 373-75.

Remark in Senate, March 10, 1840. Presents petitions asking for a moderate duty on imported silks; also, various memorials remonstrating against the use of bloodhounds in the Florida war against the Seminoles [Speech in Senate, February 18, 1839]. *Cong. Globe*, 26 Cong., 1 Sess., 255.

To THOMAS HART CLAY Washington, March 12, 1840

I have not been able yet to conclude any contract with Mr. Chinn[1] as to Bagging and Rope. He is yet waiting for information from home, but tells me that he will engage his supply with me.

I think there is reason to fear that both those articles will not maintain this year the prices of the last. There is a tendency in every thing to go down, and I do not see that they can form an exception. Under these circumstances, it will be advisable for you to practise all the economy you can, manufacture the articles well & purchase hemp as low as you can get it. If the price keeps up at 6 dollars buy from time to time only enough to prevent your hands stopping. This I think will be your best course.

Since my return from Va.[2] I have had no letters from home. I do not know where poor Henry [Clay, Jr.] is, or what is the present state of his mind.[3] I hope all of you will exert yourselves to cheer & console him.

Give my love to Mary [Mentelle Clay] & kiss the little Lucretia[4] for me

ALS. DLC-HC (DNA, M212, R5). 1. Probably Richard Chinn of Lexington and New Orleans. 2. Clay to Lucretia Hart Clay, Feb. 12, 1840. 3. Clay to Henry Clay, Jr., Feb. 20, 1840. 4. Lucretia Hart Clay, daughter of Thomas H. and Mary Mentelle Clay, born in 1838.

From Charles A. Wickliffe, Frankfort, March 13, 1840. Asks Clay and John J. Crittenden, "As the more immediate representatives of the State of Kentucky, in the Congress," to attend to the matter of "a just demand on the General Government" for the value of the arms (and the interest thereon), given by Kentuckians to the federal government following the Battle of New Orleans. Assumes this matter will require some legislation. Copy. KyU.

On March 25, 1840, Clay and Crittenden wrote Secretary of War Joel R. Poinsett, inquiring whether "a quantity of arms" belonging to Kentucky which had been loaned to the federal government in 1814 can be replaced by authority of the president alone, or whether a special act of Congress would be required to effect the restitution [Remark in Senate, July 7, 1840]. ALS, by both Clay and Crittenden. ViU.

Poinsett replied on March 30 listing the additional data and documents that his office would need to proceed with the request of the Kentucky senators. He especially solicited the names and strengths of the affected Kentucky militia units and the names of the responsible officers thereof who had given over their arms to the commissary of ordnance when the Kentucky contingents were disbanded after the Battle of New Orleans. As to whether the president had the power to make good the claim without legislative action, Poinsett was not certain. Copy. DNA, RG107, Military Books, 22:81-82.

Clay and Crittenden answered on March 31. They regretted that the information they had already submitted was inadequate and said they would take the issue directly to Congress [Remark in Senate, July 7, 1840]. Requested that documents already transmitted to Poinsett be returned. ALS, by both Clay and Crittenden. Courtesy of Prof. Thomas D. Clark of Lexington, Ky.

On April 11, Poinsett returned the materials supplied him by Clay and Crittenden. Copy. DNA, RG107, Military Books, 22:111.

Governor Wickliffe again wrote Clay and Crittenden on July 2, 1840, enclosing "a claim against the United States for muskets taken from the Quarter Master of Kentucky after the battle of New Orleans." Requested a reply so that "I may leave on the record, evidence that I have in this respect complied with the expectations of the Legislature." Copy. Ky. See Remark in Senate, July 7, 1840.

To GEORGE ADLARD[1] Washington, March 17, 1840

I received your letter transmitting a sketch of alterations which the opponents of the Copy right bill[2] are desirous of effecting I do not think that which would limit the holding of the Copy right to American Citizens is just or liberal. Without the restriction, that would however probably be the practical operation of the measure. And, rather than do nothing, I would accede to these alterations.

ALS. MH. 1. For Adlard, a New York bookseller who in 1839 collected signatures for a petition supporting an international copyright law, see Barnes, *Authors, Publishers and Politicians*, 65, 74. 2. Comment in Senate, Feb. 2, 1837; Remark in Senate, Jan. 6, 1840.

To JOHN W. COCHRAN[1] Washington, March 18, 1840

Having witnessed some experiments in firing your Bomb Cannon in this city, I take pleasure in expressing the satisfaction which they afforded to me. Without pretending to much knowledge or skill on such matters, I was nevertheless struck with the value of your improvement in the greater safety in loading, the rapidity and efficiency in the discharges, and the diminished recoil. I should think that your Cannon ought to commend itself strongly to those who are charged with the care of the public defence.[2]

Copy. DNA, RG45, Naval Records Collection. Printed in Committee of the Thirteenth Annual Fair of the American Institute, "Report on Cochran's Bomb Cannon," [New York], n.d. [1840]. 1. For Cochran, an American inventor who lived in France and England from 1839 to 1847 before returning to the U.S. to manufacture and develop firearms, see *NCAB*, 11:269-70. 2. A brass six pounder featuring three distinct chambers that rotated into alignment with the barrel, the gun was tested on Oct. 20, 1840, by order of Congress [*Cong. Globe*, 26 Cong., 1 Sess., 358]. The test was conducted on board the U.S. Steamer *Fulton*, Capt. John T. Newton commanding. Although the piece fired five shots in sixteen seconds, Capt. Newton's report was mixed. He did not believe the multi-chamber concept could be applied to larger calibre guns.

Remark in Senate, March 19, 1840. Presents petitions from Jefferson and Belmont counties in Ohio asking for an increase in the duties on foreign silks. *Cong. Globe,* 26 Cong., 1 Sess., 278.

Remark in Senate, March 23, 1840. Presents the following petitions and memorials: from New York citizens asking for a general bankruptcy law; and from Stark County, Ohio, citizens asking for a tariff increase and the distribution of public lands. Also a memorial opposing the U.S. annexation of Texas, and another from Beaver and Mercer counties, Pa., asking for the recognition of the independence of the Republic of Hayti [Haiti] and the establishment of diplomatic and commercial relations with that country on a most-favored-nation commercial basis. Presents, finally, a resolution of the Kentucky legislature opposing "any measure which would cede the public lands to the States in which they lie [Comment in Senate, January 3, 1840]." *Cong. Globe*, 26 Cong., 1 Sess., 281.

Haiti had declared its independence from France in 1804 and formed an independent black state which by 1825 had achieved diplomatic recognition from all the major powers of Europe. In the United States the question of race was the major influence in the debate over recognition. When the abolitionists were silenced by the gag rule in the late 1830s, they responded by flooding Congress with petitions for the recognition of Haiti in an effort to keep the slavery question before the public. These petitions were regularly tabled. It was not until the 37th Congress, 2nd Session, after the South had seceded, that the United States recognized Haiti. The measure passed the Senate by a vote of 32 to 7 and the House by 86 to 37. President Lincoln signed it on June 5, 1862. Rayford W. Logan, *The Diplomatic Relations of the United States With Haiti 1776-1891* (Chapel Hill, 1941), 215-16, 221-36, 245, 266, 277-82, 296-303.

To A Committee for a Fort Meigs Celebration, March 26, 1840. Regretfully declines an invitation to make an address on June 11, 1840, "at a celebration of the raising of the siege of Fort Meigs." Notes that by the time of the festivities, "I shall have just reached my home, after an absence of six months." Copy. Printed in Colton, *Clay Correspondence*, 4:444. The celebration was to commemorate the success of Gen. William Henry Harrison and his troops in resisting the siege of

Ft. Meigs by a combined British and Indian force on May 1-9, 1813. Morris, *Encyclopedia of American History*, 145.

Remark in Senate, March 26, 1840. Speaks in opposition (not recorded) to Michigan Sen. John Norvell's amendment to the Cumberland Road bill which would appropriate funds to continue the improvement of all of the roads, rivers, and harbors commenced in the past by the federal government. *Cong. Globe*, 26 Cong., 1 Sess., Appendix, 297. For the Cumberland Road bill being considered, see *Cong. Globe*, 26 Cong., 1 Sess., 277. See also Remark in Senate, March 31, 1840.

Remark in Senate, March 31, 1840. Seeks (remarks not recorded) to modify the amendment of Sen. Clement C. Clay of Alabama to strike the two percent clause from the Cumberland Road bill [Remark in Senate, March 26, 1840]. *Cong. Globe*, 26 Cong., 1 Sess., 297; see also *ibid.*, Appendix, 319-23. For the two percent clause, see 8:764-65. The bill, which would appropriate $225,000 to continue the building of the road in Ohio, Indiana, and Illinois, was turned down on April 3, 1840, by a vote of 22 to 20, on a motion to engross it for a third reading. *Cong. Globe*, 26 Cong., 1 Sess., 302.

Later this day, Clay moved the adjournment of the Senate. *Cong. Globe*, 26 Cong., 1 Sess., Appendix, 323.

Remark in Senate, April 1, 1840. Presents a memorial from various citizens praying remuneration for errors in land surveys. *Cong. Globe*, 26 Cong., 1 Sess., 298.

Later this day, Clay addressed the Senate "at length" in support of the amendment of Sen. Clement C. Clay of Alabama to strike the two percent clause [8:764-65] from the Cumberland Road bill [Remark in Senate, March 31, 1840]. The C.C. Clay amendment was beaten 19 to 17. *Cong. Globe*, 26 Cong., 1 Sess., 298; and *ibid.*, Appendix, 366. No manuscript or printed version of Clay's lengthy address in support of C.C. Clay's amendment has been found.

To LUCRETIA HART CLAY Washington, April 2, 1840

Mr [James] Erwin has remitted to me $5500 on account of my funds in his hands,[1] which I have deposited with the [United States] Bank of Pennsa. to my credit. I have written to H.C. [Henry Clay] Hart offering to pay him my note, on certain terms, which I presume he will accept. If he does, I shall pay it out of that deposite. I have also lately through the B. of the U. States remitted to Miss [Eliza Jane] Weir a further sum of $500 with which she is to be charged in my account with her.[2] There are a few dollars standing to my credit in the B. of the U. States.

I mention all these things to you, as being proper to be known, in the event of any accident befalling me.

I learn by a letter from John [Morrison Clay] that James [Brown Clay] has returned home.[3] It has been a long time since I heard from him, but I suppose he will write to me soon. I learn also that Henry [Clay, Jr.] has gone to N. Orleans. I hope his health and spirits are better. I am glad that he has undertaken the journey which I advised him to make.[4]

It is very uncertain when Congress will adjourn.[5] There seems to be no disposition to fix a time for it. The possibility of a War with G. Britain has been added to the other motives which existed against fixing a time.[6] I hope and believe that there will be no War, but things look a little squally.

I am sincerely and unaffectedly tired of remaining here, and wish to God that I was with you at home. I am not well, but hope to regain my strength, when the weather, which has been bad, becomes better. A few days more and I shall reach my grand climacteric, which is always regarded as a critical period.[7] I should be glad to be spared a few years longer until I see the Country through its difficulties, and get over my own. But that depends upon the will and goodness of Providence. . . .

ALS. Josephine Simpson Collection, Lexington, Ky. 1. Clay to Lucretia H. Clay, Feb. 12, 1840. 2. Prenter to Clay, Jan. 16, 1837. 3. From a visit to Natchez. See Clay to Lucretia H. Clay, Feb. 20, 1840. 4. Clay to Henry Clay, Jr., Feb. 20, 1840. 5. Remark in Senate, March 9, 1840. 6. Clay to Hamilton, Feb. 24, 1839. 7. For the "grand climacteric," see "climacteric" in an unabridged dictionary. On April 12, 1840, Clay would reach his sixty-third birthday.

Remark in Senate, April 2, 1840. Contributes (not recorded) to several negative responses to Tennessee Sen. Hugh L. White's speech in support of the Cumberland Road bill and in opposition to Alabama Sen. Clement C. Clay's amendment thereto [Remark in Senate, March 31, 1840]. Announces his wish to address the Senate on the bill. *Cong. Globe*, 26 Cong., 1 Sess., 299; *ibid.*, Appendix, 329, 333.

Speech in Senate, April 3, 1840. States he will say only "a few, and very few, words" to explain his reasons for voting against the Cumberland Road bill [Remark in Senate, March 31, 1840]. Affirms that while he continues to believe that the federal government has the constitutional power to provide for internal improvements, he has "never thought it expedient to create a national debt in order to provide the ways and means to construct them." Would even be willing "to waive the exercise of the power in respect to canals and roads, especially if a law could be passed to distribute the net proceeds of the sales of public lands [8:539-41, 609-10, 812-13, 846-47, 873-74]." Funds from this source would be "abundantly sufficient for all desirable objects of internal improvement." Identifying the proposed Maysville-Lexington turnpike as "but a section of one arm of the Cumberland road," notes that since Jackson's veto of the Maysville Road bill in 1830 [8:214], "the operation of the Constitution of the United States as to the construction of artificial roads has been suspended in all parts of the United States, except in the three States of Indiana, Ohio, and Illinois. We have had, in effect, two Constitutions of the United States, one for these three States, and another for the rest of the Union." Asks why "our neighbors" north and west of the Ohio River have constitutionally appropriated funds to build the Cumberland Road in Ohio, Indiana, and Illinois while maintaining that it would be unconstitutional to build that road south of the river. Says he has voted "with great reluctance for appropriations for the continuance of the Cumberland road" since Jackson's veto. Also traces his reluctance in this regard to the fact that the three favored states have "constantly maintained the Administration which originated and inflicted this inequality. Nay, more; a majority of their delegations has been always opposed to a distribution of the proceeds of the sales of the public lands, by which other States, as well as themselves, might have acquired the requisite funds to construct their works." Points out that the secretary of the treasury has omitted the Cumberland Road from his budget estimates for the current year. Asks how an appropriation of $225,000 can be justified when "The Treasury is literally empty; and we are called upon to borrow money, as the issue of Treasury notes is called, to supply means for the current expenses of the Government." Calls for strict economy in government operations. Informs the Democrats that they have the votes in both houses to pass this bill if that is what they insist on doing. But wonders why it takes $13,000 to $14,000 to build a mile of road in Indiana, whereas Kentuckians, have lately built, "with our own means," some 400 to 500 miles of turnpike at an average cost not exceeding $6,000 per mile. Says he simply cannot vote for this bill given the "vast cost of this road" and the economic state of the government and the nation. Suggests, in conclusion, that the "whole subject" be left to "the administration of President Harrison" whose special interest in the welfare of Ohio, Indiana, and Illinois will secure for the Cumberland Road "a just and liberal patronage. Whether that patronage should be extended by a direct grant from the public Treasury, by a division among all the States of the proceeds of the sales of the public lands, or by other means, will then be fit subjects of inquiry." *Cong. Globe*, 26 Cong., 1 Sess., Appendix, 737-38. A much shorter version of this speech, a summary by clerks present in the chamber when Clay spoke, is found in the main body of the *Cong. Globe*, 26 Cong., 1 Sess., 302.

To ALEXANDER MILLER Washington, April 4, 1840

I should be most happy to assist you in effecting the loan which you desire to negotiate at the Eastward, but I am quite sure that from the severe pressure in the money market it would not be practicable at present to make it. There is a want of Capital and a want of confidence. I should be able to make the most satisfactory representations in relation to yourself and your friends; but there is a repugnance to lending money to distant borrowers that is inconquerable. I tried John J. Astor for a friend of undoubted ability some short time ago without success. If you should think proper to come or send in, I would take pleasure in supplying you or your agent, with suitable letters of recommendation; but I think it wholely useless to *write* from this place.

I am glad to be able to inform you that the most encouraging prospects exist of the election of Genl Harrison.

ALS. Courtesy of Mrs. Thomas T. Holloway, Dallas, Texas. For Dr. Miller, see 6:779-80.

Remark in Senate, April 9, 1840. Presents petitions dealing with preemption rights to an island in the Mississippi River and to military pensions. *Cong. Globe*, 26 Cong., 1 Sess., 310.

Later this day, Clay complains that he had not heard a single word by way of argument in favor of the bill granting to Michigan a "vast quantity of the public domain" to assist that state in constructing a canal around the Falls of St. Marie. Consideration of bill laid over. *Ibid.*, 310-11. It was passed by the Senate on April 29 by a vote of 20 to 16, Clay voting nay. *Ibid.*, 364. The federal government eventually provided a grant which enabled Michigan to build a canal which permitted ships to pass between Lakes Superior and Huron. The canal was completed in 1855. *World Book Encyclopedia* (Chicago, 1984), 18:483-84.

Still later this day, Clay participates (not recorded) in the discussion of a bill to revive the provisions of an act, passed on May 26, 1824, that permitted claimants of public lands in Missouri and Arkansas Territory to test legally the validity of their claims, and to extend those same rights to settlers in Louisiana and Mississippi. *Cong. Globe*, 26 Cong., 1 Sess., 311. The act of May 26, 1824, to enable "the claimants to lands within the limits of the state of Missouri and territory of Arkansas to institute proceedings to try the validiy of their claims" had been designed to allow validation of French and Spanish land claims in these areas made before March 10, 1804. 4 *U.S. Stat.*, 52-59. This act had been amended on May 24, 1828, and extended to 1830. *Ibid.*, 298. It was amended again on May 8, 1830, and extended to July 1, 1831. *Ibid.*, 400-401. The bill under consideration in 1840 to revive the 1824 act and to extend its provisions to the states of Louisiana and Mississippi passed the Senate on April 14, 1840. It was not reported from the House committee until the last day of the session and was not brought to a vote by the full House. U.S. Sen., *Journal*, 26 Cong., 1 Sess., 82, 133, 191, 230, 294, 304, 307; U.S. H. of Reps., *Journal*, 26 Cong., 1 Sess., 1346-47.

Remark in Senate, April 10, 1840. Again participates (not recorded) in the discussion of a bill to revive the act of May 26, 1824, as amended, dealing with the legal rights of certain public land claimants in Missouri, Arkansas Territory, Louisiana, and Mississippi [Remark in Senate, April 9, 1840]. *Cong. Globe*, 26 Cong., 1 Sess., 319.

TO GENTLEMEN IN WINCHESTER, VA. Washington, April 11, 1840

Sharing with you in entertaining a grateful sense of the important services rendered by the Hon. W.C. Rives, in opposing the ruinous financial and other measures of the present Federal Administration,[1] I should be most happy to be present and to assist at the public dinner proposed to be given to him, and to which you have done me the honor to invite me. But my public duties here will not allow me that satisfaction. I regret, therefore, that I cannot accept your obliging invitation.

I avail myself of the occasion to congratulate you on the conclusive evidences, which every day brings forth, of the signal rebuke that certainly awaits this Administration. A current is running against it as deep, as strong, as resistless as that of the Mississippi; and we hope that the Ancient Dominion will soon bring her noble and mighty tribute to swell the stream. The land of Washington, of Jefferson, of Madison, and of Henry cannot longer submit to the misgovernment which has spread ruin and bankruptcy throughout the whole extent of this devoted country. On the first day of January next we shall have a happy new year; for, by that day, a jury of twenty members of this Confederacy will have pronounced their verdict of condemnation against the greatest abuse of public authority that was ever perpetrated on any free country. . . .

Copy. Printed in Washington *Daily National Intelligencer*, April 20, 1840. 1. For the economic depression and Van Buren's proposal for an Independent Treasury, see espec. Speech in Senate, Jan. 11 and Sept. 25, 1837, and Feb. 19, 1838; Remark in Senate, Jan. 16, 1838; Clay to Biddle, May 30, 1838; Clay to Otis, Dec. 13, 1838. For Rives's opposition to the Van Buren administration, see espec. Clay to Henry Clay, Jr., Jan. 28, 1837; and Clay to Porter, Dec. 27, 1838.

To LUCRETIA HART CLAY Washington, April 12, 1840

I have received another remittance of $5000 from Mr. [James] Erwin, which I have sent to be deposited with the Bank of the U. States.[1] He writes me that his affairs rest on a stable footing.

Fears have been entertained here that we should have a War with G. Britain; but I think there will be no War.[2] On the arrival of the G. Western,[3] expected about three weeks hence, we shall be relieved from the uncertainty.

The Connecticut Election has gone entirely in favor of the Whigs by an increased majority.[4] All the information received here authorizes a confident expectation of Genl Harrisons Election.

Mr. Bodisco, the Russian Minister, was married the other day to a

Miss Williams of Geo. Town, a young lady of 16 years of age, he being upwards of 50.[5] There was a great wedding, six brides maids, and six attendants upon him. I was invited to the wedding, and asked by him to give him the bride. We met first at his house, and proceeded thence to the house of the bride, in eight or ten carriages. The streets were full, at both houses, of persons of all descriptions, drawn thither by the occasion. When the ceremony was performed the room was jammed as full as it could be, with the attendants relations of the parties and invited guests. After it was over, there was a profuse distribution of cakes creams and champagne. The wedding cake was three feet and a half in diameter at the base, surmounted with white flowers, and covered with a light airy drapery made of paper & loaf sugar. The marriage took place at ½ after 4 OClock; and a little before six we all returned to the Minister's and shortly after sat down to a splendid dinner of between 30 & 40 plates. After dinner a select party assembled and I left them dancing at 10 OClock. The marriage has been a subject of as much talk as the Maine War, and will be followed by numerous entertainments.

No time is yet fixed for an adjournment, nor will there be until we hear from G. Britain. I still hope that I shall be able to leave here in all the month of May.

We have lost one member of Congress.[6] There has been much sickness. The whole of Mr. Lawrences family, himself wife, daughter, servant have been all down for weeks.[7] Two of the K. members (Anderson & Williams) are now confined.[8] I have not been confined, altho' often ill.

This day completes my sixty third year.

I will thank you to give the enclosed letter to Thomas [Hart Clay] I wrote to him yesterday.

Give my love to James [Brown Clay] & John [Morrison Clay] & our grand children.[9]

ALS. Josephine Simpson Collection, Lexington, Ky. 1. United States Bank of Pennsylvania. 2. Clay to Hamilton, Feb. 24, 1839. 3. The *Great Western*, launched on July 19, 1837, was the first steamship especially designed for the Atlantic route between the United States and England. Earl Corlett, *The Iron Ship* (New York, 1975), 9-13, 139; David B. Tyler, *Steam Conquers the Atlantic* (New York, 1939), 48, 60, 110, 154, 166. 4. In the 1840 Connecticut elections, incumbent Whig Governor William Ellsworth was elected over his opponent, Democrat John M. Niles by a majority of approximately 4,000 votes. Whigs also won 19 out of 21 seats in the state senate and two-thirds of the seats in the state house of representatives. Hartford (Conn.) *Daily Courant*, April 14, 23, 24, 1840. 5. Count Alexandre de Bodisco, Russian minister to the U.S. (1838-54) aged 56, married 16-year-old Harriet Williams of Georgetown, D.C., on April 9, 1840. Washington *Daily National Intelligencer*, April 10, 1840. 6. Sen. Thaddeus Betts of Conn. See *Cong. Globe*, 26 Cong., 1 Sess., 309-10. 7. Rep. Abbot Lawrence of Mass. 8. Simeon H. Anderson and Sherrod Williams. 9. Clay to Lucretia Hart Clay, March 6, 1840.

Remark in Senate, April 13, 1840. Presents petition from citizens of Prince Georges County, Md., asking for a duty on foreign silk. *Cong. Globe*, 26 Cong., 1 Sess., 320.

Later this day, Clay participates (not recorded) in the debate to revive the act of May 26, 1824, pertaining to the legal rights of certain public land claimants in Missouri, Arkansas Territory, Louisiana, and Mississippi [Remark in Senate, April 9, 1840]. *Ibid.*, 320-21.

Comment in Senate, April 14, 1840. Enters the debate on the Northeastern boundary question [Clay to Hamilton, February 24, 1839] with Great Britain with the remark that he was "happy to hear the Senator from Maine [John Ruggles] say he was not for war" with Great Britain. Adds that "if there was any party in this country for war with Great Britain, it was a criminal party. There was no sufficient cause for war; and he took occasion to say, that so far as he was informed, the opinions both of the Administration party, and of the party with which he acted, were that war was to be avoided so long as it could be done without compromitting the rights and honor of the nation." Agrees with his colleagues that "the question of right" is with the United States and that Maine should obtain "a full and absolute possession of all the territory within her rightful limits." But insists that the president and the "councils of the whole country," not a single state, must decide between negotiation or war as the best means of obtaining this result. Indeed, "If Maine expects the Government of this country to secure her rights, she must confide to the Government of this country the whole agency in settling the controversy. If it is to be done by negotiation, it must be left to the Executive and his constitutional advisers. If it is to be by war, it should be left to that department of the Government to which the power of declaring war is confided by the Constitution." Does not believe, however, that a resort to war will be necessary. Feels instead that Britain, "enlightened" as she is, will eventually perceive that "right" lies with the United States and that "she has no claim." But even if she does not see it that way, a solution can be attained through joint commission action or by arbitration, as these are provided in Article 5 of the Treaty of Ghent [1:980, 1006]. Argues that such alternatives to war should not be discarded because earlier efforts to resolve the Maine boundary issue under the Anglo-American Convention of 1827 [5:447-48; 6:1059-60, 1100-1101; 8:552] were unsuccessful. The Convention of 1827, he contends, "remains in full force, binding the parties to refer this question, if unable to settle it amicably themselves, to an impartial tribunal." Urges Britain to choose the arbitration approach to the problem. Asserts that British military preparations in Canada gave him "no cause for alarm." Says England is the "weaker power" and is "preparing against invasion from us." Sees little likelihood of invasion from Canada because the United States is fully prepared for war, far better prepared than she was in 1812—a contest from which the nation emerged "with honor." Explains: "The construction of the great New York canal, our railroads, our population pressing up against the boundary line—all these are advantages which we did not possess in the last war. No preparation! Sir, we have the best preparations that ever a country boasted of: we have sixteen millions of freemen, with stout arms and bold hearts, who stand ready to vindicate the rights of their country." Believes that it is the "sincere desire of the Administration party to preserve the peace of the country, and it had been a matter of serious inquiry with him to ascertain their views. If there was a criminal party in this country, who, for their own sinister views, desired a war, he did not believe that the Administration party gave them the slightest countenance. This he must say as an act of justice." Supports the unanimous report and recommendation of the Committee on Foreign Relations to proceed slowly and prudently in the boundary matter, at the same time firmly asserting the territorial rights of Maine. *Cong. Globe*, 26 Cong., 1 Sess., 322-24.

Later this day, Clay opposed (not recorded) a bill, at the point of its third reading, to effect a land grant to Michigan to aid the state in constructing a canal around the falls of St. Marie [Remark in Senate, April 9, 1840]. *Ibid.*, 325.

For the negotiations and subsequent settlement of the Northeastern Boundary dispute by the Webster-Ashburton Treaty of 1842, see Samuel F. Bemis, *A Diplomatic History of the United States* (New York, 1936), 257-76; Chitwood, *John Tyler*, 308-16; Frederick and Lois B. Merk, *Fruits of Propaganda in the Tyler Administration* (Cambridge, Mass., 1971), 8-16, 39-92, *passim.*

Remark in Senate, April 15, 1840. Participates (not recorded) in discussion of a motion to recommit to the Committee on Public Lands the bill providing for grants of public lands to certain states for purposes of internal improvements. Bill tabled. *Cong. Globe*, 26 Cong., 1 Sess., 327. This bill would give to "other new States" grants of public land equal in quantity to lands earlier granted Ohio "for purposes of internal improvements within their respective limits." *Ibid.*, 12, 81, 120.

Later this day, Clay speaks to Calhoun's resolution of March 4 on the *Enterprise* case of 1835, as amended by the Committee on Foreign Relations. The resolution cited certain principles of international maritime law supporting Calhoun's insistence that the government compel the British to surrender to its American owners the brig *Enterprise* and its cargo. The vessel, engaged in U.S. coastal trade, carrying Negro slaves, had been blown by bad weather into Port Hamilton, Bermuda. The seizure and liberation of the Negroes on board by the local authorities, was Calhoun argues, "an act in violation of the laws of nations, and highly unjust to our own citizens to whom they belong." Clay asserts in reply that "not a man in the Senate or the country [is] more ready to defend our rights by all the means which God and nature had given us, in reference to that particular species of property which the Senator alluded to. He thought, however, that prudence and discretion should admonish us not too often to throw before the world questions in relation to it." Wonders, however, "what would the Senator propose but war for the redress of this injury, since all negotiation on the subject was at an end? Was that such an open, undisguised attack upon us as to justify such a measure? A vessel, pursuing her voyage from Norfolk to Charleston, is cast away on one of the Bahama islands, and the slaves on board, having been brought up before the authorities there on a *habeas corpus*, are liberated." Does not regard this as unnecessarily aggressive behavior on the part of the British. Repeats his view that the issue is moot anyway, since the British have flatly refused to negotiate the question or to compensate the slave owners. Says, nevertheless, that he will support Calhoun's resolution, "inasmuch as it contained truths," although he "regretted its introduction." *Ibid.*, 233, 327-28. For more on the *Enterprise* case, see Wiltse, *John C. Calhoun: Sectionalist*, 63; *Sen. Docs.*, 26 Cong., 1 Sess., no 119, *passim* (Calhoun's speech of March 13, 1840, on the issue).

Still later this day, Clay participates (not recorded) in a discussion of the bill for the reduction and graduation of the price of public lands [Remark in Senate, January 3, 1840]. *Cong. Globe*, 26 Cong., 1 Sess., 329.

Remark in Senate, April 17, 1840. Presents a petition asking for an increase of duties on imported woolen goods. *Cong. Globe*, 26 Cong., 1 Sess., 335.

Later this day, Clay participates (not recorded) in a discussion of the bill granting preemption rights to settlers on the public lands. On Clay's motion the bill was laid over until April 20. *Ibid.* This bill, designed to supplement the Preemption Act of June 22, 1838 [Remark in Senate, January 23, 1838; Comment in Senate, January 29, 1838], was passed 26 to 9 on April 21, following an attempt by Clay to recommit it to committee, an attempt which failed by 25 to 8. Clay "addressed the Senate at length in opposition to the bill" on April 21, a speech which was not recorded, but which was answered at considerable length by Sen. Clement C. Clay of Alabama. *Ibid.*, 17, 79, 342; and *ibid.*, Appendix, 381-84. The bill passed the House on May 26 by a vote of 121 to 64. U.S. H. of Reps., *Journal*, 26 Cong., 1 Sess., 1031.

Under the 1838 act, preemption rights had been limited to actual settlers who were defined as anyone "being the head of a family, or over twenty-one years of age, who was in possession . . . by personal residence thereon" at the time the act was passed and for the four months preceding. 5 *U.S. Stat.*, 251–52. The 1840 act extended the act of 1838 until June 22, 1842. It further provided that in cases where a settler resided in one quarter section and cultivated land in another section, "such settler may . . . enter either of said quarter sections, or legal subdivisions of each, so as not to exceed one quarter section in all." Also, it provided that any person who had made an improvement on the public land and then leased or rented it to another person would still retain preemption rights even though "he may have been out of possession of his improvement during said four months, or any part thereof." 5 *U.S. Stat.*, 382.

Still later this day, Clay urges the recommitment of the bill to supplement the act of March 3, 1835, which had established branches of the U.S. Mint at New Orleans, Charlotte, N.C., and Dahlonega, Ga. [8:763]. Attacks the provision of the bill that authorized the branches to coin small denomination silver change. Where, Clay asks, is the silver bullion to come from to keep these branch mints busy? Argues that the branches should be abolished since the mint in Philadelphia has the capability to coin all the bullion, gold or silver, in the nation. Is pleased to recollect that he had opposed the mint branching act in 1835. *Cong. Globe*, 26 Cong., 1 Sess., Appendix, 314-15. The motion to recommit was beaten 27 to 11, after which the bill passed. *Cong. Globe*, 26 Cong., 1 Sess., 335. It did not pass the House at this session.

To ALBERT T. BURNLEY Washington, April 18, 1840

I transmit to you enclosed the letter of introduction to the Duke of Broglie[1] which I promised you.

You depart from our Country,[2] leaving it in a state of great pecuniary distress, and in the midst of a political excitement and struggle surpassing any thing I have before witnessed.[3] I trust that, on your return, you will find us in a better condition both in our money and public affairs. Few men in the U. States possess an equal opportunity, with that which I have, to judge of the issue of the political contest. And I have no hesitation in saying that, unless there should be some great and unexpected change in the current, now running against Mr. Van Buren, he will be worse beaten than Mr. Adams was by Genl. Jackson.[4]

Wishing you a pleasant voyage, success in your mission, and a safe return,

ALS. KyU. 1. For the French Minister of Foreign Affairs, the Duc de Broglie (Achille Leon Victor), see M. Prevost (ed.), *Dictionnaire de Brographie Francaise* (Paris, 1956), 7:409-11. 2. Burnley went to Europe in 1840 with James Hamilton to attempt to negotiate a loan for the Republic of Texas and to negotiate treaties of recognition and/or commerce. They were unable to obtain a loan, but they did negotiate recognition of their independence from The Netherlands and Great Britain. Schmitz, *Texan Statecraft*, 140-49. 3. Clay to Otis, Dec. 13, 1838. 4. Harrison beat Van Buren in 1840 with 53% of the popular vote and 80% of the electoral vote; whereas, Jackson had defeated Adams in 1828 with 56% of the popular vote and 68% of the electoral vote. McKee, *National . . . Popular and Electoral Vote*, 25-26, 44-45.

From Steven S. L'Hommedieu, Cincinnati, April 20, 1840. As the executor of the estate of Charles Hammond [2:874], reports that shortly before Hammond's death (on April 3, 1840), he had stated that in the event of his demise his correspondence with Clay and others might be published "with a view to correct many misrepresentations made at the time by political opponents—and as properly forming a part of the history of the times. In doing this he thought justice might be done to all parties, particularly to yourself and W.H. Crawford." Asks for copies of Clay's letters from Hammond, promising that if it is decided to include them in a published work, such work would first be submitted to Clay for approval. ALS. DLC-HC (DNA, M212, R5). For L'Hommedieu, a partner with Richard L'Hommedieu and Charles Hammond in the ownership of the Cincinnati *Daily Gazette*, see Lewis A. Leonard (ed.), *Greater Cincinnati and Its People, a History*, 4 vols. (New York, 1927), 2:567; Charles T. Greve, *Centennial History of Cincinnati and Representative Citizens*, 2 vols. (Chicago, 1904), 1:418; and 7:929-30. There is no evidence that such a collection of Hammond's correspondence was ever published.

Remark in Senate, April 21, 1840. Speaks in opposition to the bill to grant to Michigan public land that would aid the state in building a canal around the St. Marie falls [Remark in Senate, April 9, 1840]. *Cong. Globe*, 26 Cong., 1 Sess., 342.

Later this day, Clay spoke at length (not recorded) against the bill to supplement the Preemption Act of June 22, 1838 [Remark in Senate, April 17, 1840], but failed in his attempt to send it back to committee. During Sen. Clement C. Clay's lengthy point by point reply to Clay's speech against preemption ("the Senator from Kentucky is entirely mistaken in regard to almost every material fact he has stated"), the Kentuckian interrupted the Alabama senator to inquire whether or not there had been "delay of the sales of land subject to private entry" under the Preemption Act of May 29, 1830 [Remark in Senate, January 23, 1838] as revived and extended for two years by the act of June 22, 1838. *Cong. Globe*, 26 Cong., 1 Sess., Appendix, 382. For Clay's hostility to and arguments against preemption in its several forms, see Remark in Senate, January 23, 1838; Comment in Senate, January 29, 1838; Clay to Estes, June 1, 1839; Remark in Senate, December 14, 1840, and January 6 and 15, 1841.

Remark in Senate, April 22, 1840. Compliments the Judiciary Committee for its handling of the General Bankruptcy bill, noting that "There were three distinct subjects which the committee mentioned as properly appertaining to a general system of bankruptcy. There were voluntary bankruptcy, where the debtor himself should apply for relief; involuntary bankruptcy, where the creditors should apply for a settlement of their debtor's affairs; and, lastly, the bankruptcy of corporations. Now these three subjects were certainly separate and distinct in their nature, and might be well considered in three separate and distinct bills. It must be concurred by the Senate that the voluntary class would embrace a vast majority of the cases, and that the bill on that branch of the subject would afford the greatest measure of relief to the country." *Cong. Globe*, 26 Cong., 1 Sess., 345; see *ibid.*, 441; *ibid.*, Appendix, 846-48; and Speech in Senate, June 4, 1840.

In his speech on June 4, Clay moved to strike out the so-called "compulsory" clauses which provided that all corporations, merchants, brokers, underwriters, insurers, or bankers could be declared bankrupt on petition of one or more of their creditors; also, that any single member of a partnership or any one of its creditors could force the partnership to declare bankruptcy. This motion failed 17 to 25. A motion to postpone consideration of the bill indefinitely was lost 16 to 28, Clay voting with the majority. On the motion of Sen. John J. Crittenden, it was then referred to a select committee of seven which reported it out on June 12. Clay voted yea when it was ordered (24 to 23) engrossed on June 24; but he was not recorded as voting when it passed the Senate on June 25 by a margin of 21 to 19. He had departed Washington for Hanover County, Va., to give a Whig campaign speech (see, below, Speech on the State of the Country Under Mr. Van Buren, June 27, 1840). The bill was tabled in the House on July 7, 1840, by a vote of 102 to 89. *Cong. Globe*, 26 Cong., 1 Sess., 444-46, 459, 483, 487, 512.

A bankruptcy bill was discussed but not passed by either house during the 26th Congress, 2nd Session.

During the 27th Congress, 1st Session, a bankruptcy bill, similar to the ones discussed in 1840 and containing the same "compulsory" clauses, was introduced in the Senate on June 10, 1841. It passed on July 24 by a vote of 26 to 23, Clay voting yea. It cleared the House, with amendments, on August 18, 1841, by a vote of 111 to 105, was concurred in as amended by the Senate on the same day without division, and was signed by the president on August 19. It was repealed on March 3, 1843. See U.S. Sen., *Journal*, 26 Cong., 1 Sess., 446, 455-56; *ibid.*, 26 Cong., 2 Sess., 68, 145, 156, 159, 160-61, 165, 168, 171, 176, 186, 191, 212; *ibid.*, 27 Cong., 1 Sess., 39, 63, 111-14, 174-75, 177; U.S. H. of Reps., *Journal*, 26 Cong., 1 Sess., 1153, 1160, 1229; *ibid.*, 27 Cong., 1 Sess., 377; *Cong. Globe*, 27 Cong., 1 Sess., 348-50; 5 *U.S. Stat.*, 440-49. The "compulsory" clauses are found in Sections 1 and 14 of the act. For more on early bankruptcy legislation, see Samuel W. Dunncomb, *Bankruptcy, A Study in Comparative Legislation*. New York, 1893; and Glenn G. Munn, *Encyclopedia of Banking and Finance* (5th ed., Cambridge, Mass., 1949), 58-59.

Remark in Senate, April 23, 1840. Presents a petition from Pennsylvania asking for a general bankruptcy law. *Cong. Globe*, 26 Cong., 1 Sess., 351. See Remark in Senate, April 22, 1840.

Later this day, Clay participated (not recorded) in "a highly animated and interesting discussion" of the bill to graduate and reduce the price of public lands [Remark in Senate, January 3, 1839], the upshot of which was the vote of 27 to 11 to engross the bill for a third reading. Clay voted nay. *Cong. Globe*, 26 Cong., 1 Sess., 352. On the following day, April 24, the bill was passed, 28 to 8, Clay not voting. *Ibid.*, 355. Sent to the House, it was tabled there on July 21, 1840, the final day of the session. *Ibid.*, 546.

To LUCRETIA HART CLAY Washington, April 25, 1840

Henry [Clay, Jr.] arrived here the evening before the last, in pretty good health, but still in very bad spirits.[1] He goes to Philada. for two or three days, and on his return he purposes to lodge a week or ten days with me.

I am going to day to Judge Brookes,[2] where I intend remaining two or three days. I feel great debility and I am in hopes that the excursion may do me good.

The news from Va. this morning is very favorable to the Whig cause. Five or six members of the Legislature are already understood to be gained, and amongst them one in my old native County.[3]

Tell John [Morrison Clay] that I received his last letter, and was very glad to hear from him. He gives me such a glowing account of Ashland that I long to be there. I still hope to leave here in all the month of May. . . .

AL, signature removed. Josephine Simpson Collection, Lexington, Ky. 1. Clay to Henry Clay, Jr., Feb. 20, 1840. 2. Francis T. Brooke's estate, "St. Julien," near Fredericksburg, Va. 3. Following the April, 1840 state elections in Virginia, Whigs controlled approximately 70 seats in the house of delegates to 60 for the Democrats with 2 delegates unspecified. Democrats controlled the state senate by 17 seats to 15 for the Whigs. Simms, *Rise of the Whigs in Virginia*, 189-92. Given the vagaries of party designations in Virginia at this time, Simms interprets these numbers to mean that the Whigs had a majority of 5 to 10 votes on joint ballots. *Ibid.*, 144. Charles Thompson, a Whig, was elected to the seat in the house of delegates from Clay's former home of Hanover County. *Ibid.*, 190. The state legislature elected Thomas W. Gilmer, a Whig, to the governorship. *BDGUS*, 4:1639. In a special election to the U.S. House, caused by the resignation of Charles F. Mercer, William M. McCarty, a Whig, was chosen over Cuthbert Powell, also a Whig, by a vote of 1,033 to 722. *Guide to U.S. Election*, 574; and *BDAC*.

Remark in Senate, April 29, 1840. Presents a petition from a number of hat makers asking for a duty on foreign articles used in the manufacture of hats. *Cong. Globe*, 26 Cong., 1 Sess., 363.

Speech in Baltimore, May 4, 1840. Predicts the election of Harrison because of the "ravages brought upon our country under the revolutionary administrations" of the "last ten years." Points as evidence to the national depression and the passage of the Expunging Resolution [8:735]. Believes, however, that the Democratic party is finished because of its destructive policies. Responding to the cheers of his audience, Clay continues: "We are . . . all whigs, we are all Harrison men. We are united. We must triumph." Assures them that "without a moment's hesitation, I gave my hearty concurrence" in Harrison's nomination at Harrisburg. Asserts that he is certain of Harrison's election. Indeed, "I feel sure, almost that there are twenty States who will give their votes for Harrison." But he warns the "more than twenty thousand freemen" who stand before him [Daugherty to Clay, May 17, 1839] not to become over-confident. Fears that if Van Buren is elected "the struggle of restoring the country to its former glory would be almost a hopeless one." Copy. Printed in Colton, *Clay Correspondence*, 6:192-94. Delivered to Whig National Convention of Young Men [Daugherty to Clay, May 17, 1839].

At this relatively early date Clay came very close to predicting the exact outcome of the presidential election held on November 3, 1840. Harrison carried 19 states with 234 electoral votes, rather than the 20 states Clay prophesied. Van Buren carried 7 states—Ala., Ark., Ill., Mo., N.H., S.C., and Va.—with 69 electoral votes. The popular vote was 1,275,017 to 1,128,702. Abolitionist candidate James G. Birney received 7,059 popular votes. McKee, *National . . . Popular and Electoral Vote*, 44-45.

From William Henry Harrison, Cincinnati, May 7, 1840. Apologizes for not having answered Clay's letters, explaining that he has had a "violent" cold that has put him behind in his correspondence, "altho I throw a full half of the letters I receive in the fire without replying to them." Says his campaign is "going ahead in all this North Western region & you may rely also on our getting Mississippi." Copy. InHi. Harrison carried Mississippi (4 electoral votes) by a 19,518 to 16,995 margin. In the "North Western region" comprising Ohio (21), Indiana (9), Illinois (5), and Michigan (3), he lost only the electoral votes of Illinois—by a popular vote of 47,476 to 45,537. McKee, *National . . . Popular and Electoral Vote*, 44-45.

Remark in Senate, May 7, 1840. Participates in "a very interesting and animated discussion" triggered by Sen. Thomas Hart Benton's motion to print 30,000 extra copies of Secretary of the Treasury Levi Woodbury's report, dated May 4, on the "aggregate amount of all expenditures or payments of every kind from the treasury in each year, from 1824 to 1839 inclusive," as ordered by Senate resolution of April 24. Clay's remarks on the printing issue were not recorded. *Cong. Globe*, 26 Cong., 1 Sess., 382. Benton's motion passed 22 to 14, Clay voting nay. Woodbury's report, presented as three tables of figures comparatively arranged, is printed in *ibid.*, 378-79.

In response, later this day, to remarks by Sen. John C. Calhoun, Clay expresses his pleasure in hearing the South Carolinian admit that the expenditures of the Van Buren administration have been extravagant. "Coming from him, it was an admission very important." Denies Calhoun's contention, however, that a protective tariff system had caused the surplus revenues of past years. Argues also that it does "not necessarily follow that a Government with a surplus would always be extravagant," although the "conclusion [is] . . . correct in regard to this Administration." Criticizes the increase in numbers of custom house officers to support his charge of fiscal waste by the Van Buren administration. Maintains that the accumulation of treasury surpluses could have been prevented by distribution of such surpluses to the states [8:539-41, 609-10, 812-13, 846-47, 873-74]. Pressed by

Calhoun on the relationship between tariffs and surpluses, Clay explains that while he opposes high tariffs, he favors some protection in the form of a system of countervailing or retaliatory duties. Asserts that he supports maintaining the Compromise Tariff Act of 1833 [8:604, 621-22, 626-27] and "affording protection within the limits to which it would reduce the duties." *Ibid.*, Appendix, 441-43.

To Thomas Hart Clay, Lexington, May 12, 1840. Assures him that "it is not my intention to exact from you more than a fair rate of interest upon the advances I make for you to buy hemp &c." Says he will assist Thomas in making the payment of all charges, including freight, up to the point of delivery, on the bagging rope for Stephen Duncan in Natchez. Explains how he wants to combine his own rope, which is stored with Lambdin & Bennett and with Mr. Ely in Natchez, with Thomas's in filling the Duncan order. Reports that Henry, Jr., will leave Washington toward the end of the week and that "He has improved, I think, in his spirits [Clay to Henry Clay, Jr., February 20, 1840]." ALS. NHi. Written in "S[enate]. Chamber." See January, Huston & Co. to Clay, May 13, 1840.

To JONES GREEN[1] Washington, May 12, 1840

I received your obliging letter, with Mr. Pendletons[2] P. S appended to it, communicating the friendly wish of our friends in Culpeper and some of the adjoining Counties to honor me with an old fashioned Virginia Barbacue, and inquiring at what time, during the ensuing summer, it would suit my convenience to attend it.

I need not say that their kind purpose is inexpressibly gratifying to my feelings, and I sincerely wish that I could accept the compliment intended me; but I regret to say that it will not be in my power. In the first place, after an absence from my family now of six months, it is my intention to return home, prior to the adjournment of Congress, unless some question as grave as one of Peace or War should be pending. Then, I have doubts of the policy and expediency, unless under very extraordinary circumstances, of my attending public political meetings out of the State in which I reside. But I must further say that, I feel that I have not the physical power (I hope that you will not disclose my secret, at least to any of the fair sex) to undergo the exciting scenes incident to large assemblages of my fellow Citizens, and, above all, that of addressing them, in the open air. It is a tremendous exertion of the lungs, and it is really wearing me away. I have not yet recovered from the effects of such an operation at Baltimore.[3]

To you I may add an auxiliary but subordinate motive which I am sure your good sense and friendship for me will justly appreciate. I owed it to the Country, and to my personal honor, to acquiesce in and approve of the nomination made at Harrisburg.[4] It was my duty that this approbation should be unequivocal, and publicly known. I have performed that duty. But, considering the attitude in which I have stood, and my character, I think self respect requires that I should not convert myself into an itinerant Lecturer or Stump orator to advance the cause of a successful competitor.

I know that your kind intentions and those of my friends in your quarter comprehended no such use of me. I know, on the contrary, that your sole aim was to render honor to me, and to testify your affectionate attachment, in a signal and impressive manner. But the movement would be viewed by others under a different aspect, and we are not at liberty to neglect appearances. And, so far as relates to my own heart, it is sufficient for that to know and gratefully to feel your friendly purposes.

Under these views, I shall be constrained to decline accepting the invitation, if it be sent, and should prefer that it be not transmitted.

I have been compelled, actuated by the above motives, to decline numerous invitations to public meetings recently. I have two engagements on my hands which embarrass me, and which I shall be obliged to execute, if I cannot negotiate myself out of them. One is to my native County, and the other to Nashville.[5] But there is no time yet fixed for either.

You may shew this letter to Mr. Pendleton. . . .

ALS. NjMoHP. Letter marked "(Confidential)." Addressed to Green at Greenoch, near Warrington Springs, Va. 1. For Green, see *VMHB* (July, 1900-June, 1901), 8:79; *TQHGM* (1922-24), 5:246-47; Philip Slaughter, *Genealogical and Historical Notes on Culpeper County, Virginia* (Culpeper, Va., 1900), 62, 66. 2. Possibly John S. Pendleton, a Whig from Culpeper Co., Va. See *BDAC*. 3. Speech at Baltimore, May 4, 1840. 4. Porter to Clay, Nov. 14 and Dec. 30, 1837. 5. McNairy to Clay, Sept. 21, 1839.

To HAMILTON C. JONES[1] Washington, May 12, 1840

I received your favor, stating that Mr. C. Fisher, the member of Congress from your district,[2] in a public address which he made to some of his constituents, asserted that I had opposed the appointment of Gen. Harrison, as Minister to Columbia [*sic*, Colombia],[3] because of his utter incapacity for the appointment; and inquiring of me as to the truth of the assertion.

I have no hesitation in saying that there is no foundation whatever for the assertion. The appointment of Gen. Harrison, as Minister Plenipotentiary and Envoy Extraordinary to the Republic of Columbia, had my entire concurrence; and, besides the usual credentials, I entrusted to his care a private letter to Gen. [Simon] Bolivar, the President of that Republic.

I know not on what authority Mr. Fisher had undertaken to make the assertion attributed to him; certainly none from me; and yet he has enjoyed abundant opportunities, during the present session of Congress, to ascertain from me personally whether the above assertion was true or not. But never have I had, at any time, any conversation whatever with him, in respect to Gen. Harrison's mission.

You are at liberty to show this letter to Mr. Fisher himself or make any use of it. . . .

Copy. Reprinted from Raleigh (N.C.) *Register* in Lexington *Observer & Kentucky Reporter*, June 10, 1840. 1. For Jones—a lawyer, humorist, and founder of the anti-nullification newspaper, the *Carolina Watchman*—see James S. Brawley, *The Rowan Story 1753-1953, A Narrative History of Rowan County, N.C.* (Salisbury, N.C., 1953), 113-14, 153, 178. 2. Charles Fisher of Salisbury, N.C. See *BDAC*. 3. See 7:308, 492-94.

From January, Huston & Co., Maysville, May 13, 1840. Report that they have received from Messrs. [Thomas Hart] Clay & Mentelle of Lexington a number of loads of bale rope and bagging during the past three or four weeks which they are directed to hold "subject to your order." Report they have on hand at present 270 pieces of bagging and 138 coils of rope. Suggest that he ship now to Natchez and New Orleans while the water level of the river is good, boats are in plentiful supply, and freight costs are low. Estimate freight cost of hemp at 40¢ per hundred-weight. ALS. Mary Clay Kenner Collection, Rogersville, Tenn. The Mentelle mentioned is Thomas H. Clay's brother-in-law, Waldemar Mentelle, who later became a partner in an iron foundry and machine shop in Lexington known as Lanckart, Mentelle & Co. C.S. Williams, *Lexington Directory, City Guide, and Business Mirror* (Lexington, 1859), 74, 82.

On May 18, 1840, Clay wrote Thomas Hart Clay instructing him to proceed with shipping the bagging and rope to Stephen Duncan at Natchez [Clay to Thomas H. Clay, May 12, 1840] and pledging to make good "any expenses, charges, etc." Says he is also instructing Lambdin, Bennett, & Mr. Ely in Natchez to release to Duncan the Clay & Mentelle-owned rope and twine in their warehouse. Is fearful that "some of it has been lost by the late Hurricane at Natchez." Reports that Henry Clay, Jr., left Washington this morning. ALS. Elsie Jackson Kelly Collection, Henry Clay Memorial Foundation, Lexington, Ky. For the destructive hurricane which struck Natchez in May, 1840, see Kane, *Natchez on the Mississippi*, 207. For earlier Clay-Duncan hemp transactions, see Clay to Henry Clay, Jr., September 8, 1837.

On May 19, 1840, Clay wrote Henry T. Duncan in Paris, Ky., thanking him for "arranging a contract between Thomas [Hart Clay] and Dr. [Stephen] Duncan for the supply of Bagging and Rope." Adds: "I have transmitted an order to the Dr. to receive such Rope as may be proportionate to the bagging from my stock at Natchez and Port Gibson. I shall esteem myself fortunate if the late terrible hurricane has not destroyed or injured what I had at Natchez. I should be glad if Thomas would supply all that Dr. Duncan wants; and if he cannot manufacture it in time perhaps you could assist him in effecting a loan from Mr. [Benjamin] Gratz. Advantage ought to be taken of the present favorable state of Navigation." ALS. Courtesy of Mrs. William Pettit, Lexington, Ky. Addressed to Henry T. Duncan, "Near Lexington," Ky. Dr. Stephen Duncan of Natchez and Henry T. Duncan of Paris, Ky., were second cousins. Julia S. Ardery, *The Duncans of Bourbon County* . . . (Lexington, 1943), 17-19; Edna T. Whitley, *Kentucky Antebellum Portraiture* (Paris, Ky., 1956), 139.

On August 10, 1840, Clay wrote Thomas Hart Clay from Louisville informing him that bagging is selling there at 27½ (cents per yard) on 90-days payment terms. Urges him to "Send out young [Waldemar] Mentelle" and not delay his (Clay's) purchases of hemp, the price of which "will rise." Adds: "Give six and a half [dollars per hundred-weight], if you cannot get it for less. I am afraid there will be a scarcity." ALS. DLC-HC (DNA, M212, R5). For the cost, packaging, and merchandising of hemp, see Hopkins, *History of the Hemp Industry in Kentucky*, 112-50.

Remark in Senate, May 15, 1840. Opposes a bill that would create an additional land office in Michigan in an area said to be virtually without white population. Pokes fun at the "usual argument for the increase of these offices," which was that "they were to accommodate the people, when no accommodation was yet needed. It must be done prospectively." Says this reminds him "of an anecdote, a proposition having been made to do something for posterity. It was asked, what has posterity done for us? What had these prospective people done for any body? They had not yet even got there, and when they had done so would be time enough." Notes the "vast increase" in the number of land offices since Jackson became president. Copy. Printed in *Niles' Register* (May 23, 1840), 58:187. The bill passed, 22 to 12, Clay voting nay. *Cong. Globe*, 26 Cong., 1 Sess., 398.

Remark in Senate, May 19, 1840. Presents the claims petition of Fielder R. Dorsett for an increase of his compensation, after which he participates (not recorded) in an "animated discussion" of the bill to satisfy the remaining claims to bounty land for services rendered during the War of 1812. *Cong. Globe*, 26 Cong., 1 Sess., 403. On June 29, further action on this bill was postponed to the next session. *Ibid.*, 490.

Remark in Senate, May 20, 1840. Opposes (not recorded) an adverse report from the Committee on Claims on a claim for restitution to William and James Crook, owners of a vessel seized (later sold) by U.S. authorities on Lake Ontario in June, 1812, for violation of embargo laws. Funds from the sale of the vessel had been deposited with the clerk of the U.S. district court. When a decree of restitution was later obtained, the proceeds of the sale were ordered to be paid over to the owners. Meanwhile, however, the clerk of the court had absconded with the funds. At this juncture, the matter had been introduced into diplomatic negotiations with the British. There it was paired with a similar long-pending case, "governed by the same principles," which the British had refused to adjust. For this reason, the committee now opposes restitution in this case "on the ground that the question remains as an unadjusted subject between the two Governments, and would give an undue advantage to the citizens of a foreign Government over those of our own." Following Clay's criticism and rejection of the committee's report, the issue was informally passed over. *Cong. Globe*, 26 Cong., 1 Sess., 405. See also Remark in Senate, May 21, 1840.

The *Lord Nelson*, owned by British merchants William and James Crook, had been illegally seized by a U.S. warship on June 5, 1812, just before the U.S. declaration of war against Britain. Manning, *Diplomatic Correspondence . . . Canadian Relations*, 3:115, 569-71.

To SAMUEL MOORE[1] Washington, May 21, 1840

I have read and return the Correspondence of Mr. [Christopher] Hughes which, by his request, you placed in my hands. It shews that he rendered essential service to Texas in bringing about an acknowledgement of her independence by France. I know not what judgement would be formed of his agency in that event, by the American Executive. He [Hughes] seems to desire that the Correspondence should be placed on file in the Department of State, and perhaps, therefore, it would be best to let it have the destination, which he has indicated.[2] I do not believe that he will receive any promotion from the present Chief Magistrate.[3] All the Foreign missions are filled; that to Russia has just been conferred on Mr. Cambreling [*sic*, Churchill C. Cambreleng].

ALS. MiU-C. 1. For Moore, a Baltimore merchant and brother-in-law of Christopher Hughes, see Chester G. Dunham, "The Diplomatic Career of Christopher Hughes," Ph. D. dissertation, Ohio State University, 1968, p. 171. 2. While visiting Paris in 1839 Hughes unofficially assisted James P. Henderson, representative of the Republic of Texas there, to arrange meetings with the French in order to attempt to win recognition of Texas independence and a treaty of commerce. Hughes reported his actions to Secretary of State John Forsyth hoping this unauthorized initiative would win him a promotion; however, President Van Buren and Forsyth decided that his report should not be placed in the government archives but should be sent back to him to keep with his private papers. *Ibid.*, 195-96. 3. Hughes remained as chargé d'affaires in Sweden through the Van Buren administration. On leave in the United States in 1842, he obtained a transfer by the Tyler administration from Sweden to The Hague as chargé, a position he held until his retirement in 1845. *Ibid.*, 196, 198, 211, 214, 225.

Remark in Senate, May 21, 1840. Participates (not recorded) in a discussion of the adverse report of the Committee on Claims on the petition of William and James Crook [Remark in Senate, May 20, 1840]. Clay supports said claim. Subject indefinitely postponed by a 25 to 14 vote, Clay voting nay. *Cong. Globe*, 26 Cong., 1 Sess., 407.

Later this day Clay participates (not recorded) in a discussion of the bankruptcy bill [Remark in Senate, April 22, 1840]. *Ibid.*

To SENECA WHITE[1] & JOHN KENNEDY Washington, May 22, 1840

I have duly received your communication, in behalf of the Seneca Nation, in respect to the late Treaty for the Sale of their land in the State of New York.[2] My opinion, in regard to that instrument, was expressed by my vote in the Senate of the U. States.[3] I regret exceedingly that the treaty is so unacceptable to the Seneca Nation. My opinion, founded in part upon personal observation, is that the interests of both races would be promoted by the Senecas acceding to the terms of the treaty, which are marked by great liberality. Nevertheless, I could not, in my conscience, vote for a treaty which did not appear to me to have the necessary sanctions.

Should Congress make the necessary appropriations to carry the Treaty into effect,[4] it seems to me that it would be most prudent in the Senecas to submit to what, in that contingency, it would probably be beyond their power to avoid. If Congress refuse to make the appropriations necessary, I suppose there would be an end of the treaty.

It is very doubtful whether the Supreme Court could entertain jurisdiction of the question, as to the validity of the Treaty,[5] supposing it to be recognized as valid by both the Executive and Legislative Departments of the Government.

I should be most happy to render any services that would be proper and in my power, to the Seneca Nation, towards which I cherish sentiments of sympathy and cordiality; but, I am so much withdrawn from professional pursuits, that I cannot venture to contract any positive engagement to act as one of their Counsel in the Supreme Court. All that I dare promise is that, if I should be here, and it should be convenient, I would take part in the Argument of the Cause, if, contrary to what I have undertaken to suggest, it should be brought up to the Supreme Court.

Copy. KyU. 1. For Seneca White (1794-1865), a congregationalist minister living at this time in Marshfield, Mass., see Daniel F. Secomb, *History of the Town of Amherst . . . New Hampshire* . . . (Concord, N.H., 1883), 927. Kennedy has not been identified. 2. Porter to Clay, Feb. 19, 1838. 3. The final vote on the Seneca Treaty took place on March 26, 1840. The tie vote of 19 to 19 (Clay voting nay) was broken by the vice president who voted in the affirmative. U.S. Sen., *Journal*, 26 Cong., 1 Sess., Appendix, 574. 4. On July 18, 1840, both the House and Senate passed a bill providing for the current expenses of the Indian Department and for "fulfilling treaty stipulations with the various Indian tribes." The president signed the bill on July 20. U.S. H. of Reps., *Journal*, 26 Cong., 1 Sess., 1313, 1341; U.S. Sen., *Journal*, 26 Cong., 1 Sess., 528. 5. The treaty did not go to the Supreme Court.

To SAMUEL STARKWEATHER Washington, May 23, 1840

I am extremely sorry not to be able to transmit to you[1] the copy of my Speech, requested in your favor of the 20h. inst. I seldom retain Copies of any Speeches which I deliver, and if any of them be worth preservation, I have to rely on the periodicals of the day, of which Niles's Register has been the best.

I am glad to receive your encouraging opinion as to the issue of the Presidential contest in N. York,[2] and sincerely hope that it may be realized. All around us the prospects are bright and cheering, and I have no doubt of the success of our Cause, if our friends will continue to make the exertions which so far they have employed. . . .

ALS. NHi. 1. For Starkweather (1786-1853), a prominent New York lawyer, see Carlton L. Starkweather, *A Brief Genealogical History of Robert Starkweather of Roxbury and Ipswich, Mass.* (Auburn, N.Y., 1904), 85, 129. 2. Harrison carried New York by 225,817 to 212,519. McKee, *National . . . Popular and Electoral Vote*, 44.

To JOHN M. CLAYTON Wilmington, May 29, 1840

You are not I find in all things a man of your word—Dover has more attractions for you than Wilmington, and I am disappointed in the interview here which you promised me.

I mentioned to you that I thought it expedient to present to the public some of the objects of a new administration, if one should come into power, and that, without committing any body, I entertained some intention of doing so, if a suitable occasion arose. These objects are stated in the enclosed paper,[1] which I send for your perusal in the first rough sketch of them. Do me the favor to examine them, tell me what you think of them, and whether any others occur to you. And favor me also with an expression of your opinion as to the propriety of promulgating any thing like a creed. The danger is of supplying fresh aliment for demagogues. On the other hand, I think, perhaps erroneously, that the Harrisburgh [*sic*, Harrisburg] Convention having omitted to publish any Address,[2] our cause suffers from the imputation of the other side that the Whigs have no principles which they dare openly avow. It is a safe general rule that it is best to remain silent and not act, unless you are fully convinced that what you mean to say or do is right; and in this instance I do not wish to depart from the rule. Unless therefore you and one or two other friends shall think the movement judicious I do not desire to make it.

I find among our friends here a strong wish that you should consent to run as the Candidate of the H. of R. What is your intention? If successful, you would have the merit of bringing the State back from the erroneous path into which it strayed two years ago.[3] If another wish which I entertain about you, and which I intimated at New Castle, could be gratified, I should feel that the Country would be much benefited. And in reference to that object your possessing a prominent position, as a member of one or the other house of Congress, at the moment of the formation of a new Administration, might have a favorable tendency to promote your appointment to a more distinguished place.[4] Whatever you may resolve upon as to a seat in either branch of Congress, it is of the highest importance that Delaware should be herself again, and return two Whigs to the Senate. With these, our hopes in other respects being realized, on the 4h. March next, the new Administration will open with a majority friendly to it.[5] Without them, there must be a majority against it.

I hope soon to hear from you at Washington, for which I expect to set out tomorrow.

ALS. DLC-John M. Clayton Papers (DNA, M212, R20). Letter marked "(Confidential)." 1. Not found. 2. That is a party platform. See Porter to Clay, Nov. 14 and Dec. 30, 1837. 3. Delaware had elected Democrat Thomas Robinson, Jr., to the U.S. House in 1838. He defeated Whig John J. Milligan by 4,451 votes to 4,399; however, the Whigs retained control of the state legislature by a majority of nearly 2 to 1. *Guide to U.S. Elections*, 570; Washington *Daily National Intelligencer*, Nov. 23, 1838. 4. Clayton, who had resigned his U.S. Senate seat in Dec., 1836, to become chief justice of Delaware, did not return to the Senate until March, 1845. 5. Morris reckons party strength in the 27th Congress in the Senate as: Whig 28, Dem. 22, other 2; McKee's count is the same. In the House in the 27th Congress, Morris counts Whig 133, Dem. 102, other 6; McKee lists Whig 132, Dem. 103, Indep. or other 6, vacancy 1; in the 27th Congress, 1st Session, Alexander reports Whig 135, Dem. 90, Indep. or other 17; in the 27th Congress, 2nd Session, he counts Whig 138, Dem. 101, Indep. or other 3. Morris, *Encyclopedia of American History*, 406; McKee, *National . . . Popular and Electoral Vote*, 46; Alexander, *Sectional Stress and Party Strength*, 39, 42-43, 46-47.

To ANNE SALTONSTALL Washington, May 31, 1840

Your acceptable present of Candy and I reached this City together last evening. I thank you for it and for your friendly recollection of me.

I found myself so quiet, and my cold so bad, at Wilmington that I protracted my sojourn there until yesterday morning. Nothing could exceed the kind and constant attentions of my good friends Mrs. Bayard and Miss Caroline;[1] and I profited by their ministrations. I have returned much better, and a few days more, aided by your present, will fully re-establish my health. F. street and Mrs. Cochrans,[2] upon my return, appear excessively dull and unanimated. You and your mother no more cheer the parlour! And Mrs. Henderson and Julia[3] too are gone! We are reduced to three bachelors, and feel something like our old father Adam must have done before his partner was created, with the exception that Mrs. Cochran's is any thing but a Paradise. Sir John Caldwell[4] passed the greater part of the week of my absence here, but he too had left it, and if he had remained he would not have diminished the regrets which we feel on account of those from whom we have been separated.

Your father[5] read to us at breakfast parts of your letter which he had just received; and, whilst I condole with you in the unexpected loss of your Aunt, I sympathize with you in the cheerful and inspiring scenes of green trees, birds, music and military parades with which you were surrounded.

I pray you to present my best respects to your excellent Mother,[6] and to say to your sister Lucy that I hope some future day to improve the acquaintance with her which, without her knowledge, I have already had the pleasure to make.

ALS. KyLoF. 1. Mary Sophia Carroll (Mrs. Richard H.) Bayard and daughter Caroline Bayard, later Mrs. Henry B. Powell. Thomas A. Glenn (ed.), *Some Colonial Mansions and Those Who Lived in Them . . .* (Philadelphia, 1897), 362. 2. Clay, along with Sen. John Henderson and Rep. Leverett Saltonstall had apparently moved from Mrs. Arguelle's since Feb., 1840. See Clay to Lucretia Hart Clay, Feb. 12, 1840. 3. Louisa Fourniquit Post (Mrs. John) Henderson and daughter, Julia Henderson. See John Henderson article in *DAB*. 4. For Sir John B. Caldwell (1775-1842), Canadian lawyer and formerly the receiver general of Canada, see *The Macmillan Dictionary of Canadian Biography*. 3rd ed., New York, 1963. 5. Rep. Leverett Saltonstall of Mass. 6. Mary Elizabeth Sanders (Mrs. Leverett) Saltonstall. See Leverett Saltonstall article in *DAB*.

Remark in Senate, June 1, 1840. Presents a petition from Ohio asking for an increase of duties on foreign silk. *Cong. Globe*, 26 Cong., 1 Sess., 430.

Remark in Senate, June 2, 1840. Presents petition of James C. Reynolds, former postmaster at Reynoldsburg, Ohio, asking for congressional action on his removal from that office without cause. Participates (not recorded) in a debate on this petition. Moves that it be tabled. *Cong. Globe*, 26 Cong., 1 Sess., 433, 439.

Later this day, Clay joins in the discussion that follows Alabama Sen. Clement C. Clay's motion to strike from the bankruptcy bill all references to banks and corporations. When that motion passes, 28 to 16, Clay voting yea, Sen. John J. Crittenden (Ky.) moves to refer the bill, as amended, to a select committee. Clay suggests that the "compulsory clause," section 18 [Remark in Senate, April 22,

1840], be stricken from the bill prior to such referral and moves to strike it. Senate adjourns prior to taking action on Clay's motion. *Ibid.*, 433-34. For Clay's defense of this motion to remove the compulsory clause, see Speech in Senate, June 4, 1840.

From George W. Featherstonhaugh, Foreign Office, London, England, June 3, 1840. Sends to Clay a copy of the "Report of Col. [Richard] Mudge and myself with its accompanying maps." Notes that Her Majesty's Government is sending this report to President Van Buren but has not yet submitted it to Parliament. Wants Clay to see it before it is made public. Since the report deals with the Northeastern boundary issue, believes "It will have to encounter a great deal of prejudice, the public mind in the United States having been so long prepossessed by other opinions; but I am not afraid to indulge a hope that when it has been read and well considered, a general opinion will grow up in the United States, that a moment has arrived, when we should all cease for awhile to say who is right and who is wrong, and turn all our Efforts to the quiet, prompt, and fair adjustment of this unprofitable dispute. Would that the disputed territory were at the bottom of the deepest part of the Ocean, rather than that the two Countries should get into a serious quarrel about a few acres, the total Annexation of which would be a serious injury to nobody but the Moose Deer. Continue my dear Sir to promote, as I perceive you have lately so efficiently done, the friendly, and Statesmanlike Settlement of this Question. It will be worthy of the public Career you have so nobly run." Mentions that while he faithfully supports the interests of Britain on the question, his efforts to settle it peacefully have brought "Sneers and the unfriendly assertion . . . in England, that I was too much of an American in my predilections to be entrusted with the Conduct of such a matter." Admits that he has "predilections for America"; that "I have been happy there"; and that he always aimed "to be useful to your country." Concludes that no matter how the dispute turns out, "my attachment to the old friends I left in America will continue." ALS. MnHi.

Featherstonhaugh and Mudge (see *DNB*) had been appointed by the British government to make a survey of the Northeastern boundary. They arrived in New York on July 28, 1839, to begin preparations for a trip to the boundary area. Their report added no information of any substantial value to either of the two contending governments. On June 27, 1840, Van Buren submitted to the Senate a copy of the communication from Henry S. Fox, British minister to the U.S., to Secretary of State Forsyth which contained the Mudge-Featherstonhaugh report. The president asked for an appropriation to continue the exploration and surveying of the boundary, and Congress responded in February, 1841, by providing $75,000 for that purpose. Burrage, *Maine in the Northeastern Boundary Controversy*, 252-56; *MPP*, 3:594-97.

Speech in Senate, June 4, 1840. Defends his motion [Remark in Senate, June 2, 1840] to strike out the 18th section, the compulsory clause [Remark in Senate, April 22, 1840], in the bill for the establishment of a general system of bankruptcy throughout the United States; also discusses other features of the proposed legislation.

Begins with an affirmation of the constitutionality of such legislation. Avoids attempting a precise definition of the phrases "bankruptcy" and "insolvency" even though they are generally used in the English vernacular in a synonymous sense. Instead, "I prefer to describe the properties or qualities" of each condition. Asserts that "The essential and characteristic difference between them is that the system of insolvency does not, or rather is supposed to be incompetent to grant, while the bankrupt system can confer an effectual discharge of the debtor from all pre-existing debts and obligations. That incompetency of the States to provide, in their systems of insolvency, for such a discharge, is supposed to result from that prohibition to the States, in the Constitution of the United States, against their passage of any law impairing the obligation of contracts."

Argues that the state ("I use that term in its broadest sense") has the "right" to assist "an honest and unfortunate debtor, borne down by a hopeless mass of debt, from beneath which he can never rise, is prostrated and paralyzed, and rendered utterly incapable of performing his duties to his family or his country. To say nothing of the dictates of humanity; nothing of the duties of a parental Government to lift up the depressed, to heal the wounds, and cheer and encourage the unhappy man who sees in the past, without his fault, nothing but ruin and embarrassment, and in the future nothing but gloom and despair, I maintain that the public rights of the State, in all the faculties of its members, moral and physical, is paramount to any supposed rights which appertain to a private creditor. This is the great principle which lies at the bottom of all bankrupt laws, and it is this which gives to the States the right to demand the passage and imposes upon Congress the duty of enacting a bankrupt system." Says that some authorities count 500,000 bankrupts in the United States today. Add to this number their families and friends and "the total number of all who are interested in the passage of a bankrupt system has been stated as large as two millions. I hope and believe that this is an exaggerated estimate. But the number is undoubtedly very great be it what it may."

Agrees that the states can, and most of them have, enacted legislation by which "all the property and credits of the debtor can be reached, surrendered, and distributed, and frauds and fraudulent transfers effectually guarded against." Thus he agrees that state governments are "competent to make full and adequate provision for all the interests of both creditors and debtors, except in the sole matter of granting an effectual discharge to the debtor." Also concedes that existing state laws protect creditors. But the problem that calls for federal legislation in the area of bankruptcy is that "the States cannot authorize, at least the general impression is that they cannot authorize, an effectual discharge of an honest debtor from all his existing debts after he shall have made a fair and full surrender of all his effects. Hence the necessity, and the exact extent of the necessity, of Federal legislation." Explains, further, that the "power vested in Congress being to pass uniform laws, and the insolvent laws of the States not possessing that requisite quality, it becomes necessary for Congress to establish a system, in detail, to operate alike throughout the United States. It is upon this, as well as other grounds, that I was opposed to including corporations in this bill, and voted to strike them out. Generally, their capital and their existence are identical; and after the seizure and distribution of their effects they would be defunct, and there would be no occasion for that discharge, which constitutes, it seems to me, the sole motive for Federal legislation in the case of individuals." Gives other reasons for excluding corporations, pointing out mainly that if banks are brought into a bankruptcy system "all incorporations, for any purpose whatever, which happened to suspend payment of their debts, would be brought within the operation of this system." Is fearful, therefore, of the possibility that an "immense mass of debts and effects" might thus be transferred from state to federal jurisdiction. "The imagination can hardly conceive the amount of property and debts which would be so transferred." Fears, for instance, what might happen were the federal government to become the receiver or assignee of the James River Company, the Chesapeake and Ohio Canal Company, and the Baltimore and Ohio Railroad Company as the result of corporate failures triggered by the collapse of banks holding their stocks as security for loans. This situation would constitute a greater step "toward consolidation than all other measures together which have been proposed or adopted since the origin of the Government. . . . I am not prepared to take such a frightful step; I shudder at the mere contemplation of it." Says he prefers to express no opinion, pro or con, as to whether the bankruptcy power in the Constitution includes corporations, but believes the states can better handle corporate bankruptcies than can the federal government.

Gives his reasons for striking out section 18 (the compulsory clause), which provides for "the case of compulsory or involuntary bankruptcies": It is a coercive approach "opposed to the habits and genius of the country." It adapts poorly to the business of merchants and traders in the interior who regularly extend large credits to farmers and planters who in turn, because of poor weather, are often delinquent in their payments. The latter should not be exposed to the possibility of bankruptcy proceedings. The last bankruptcy act, passed by Congress in 1800, "had but a short and unsatisfactory existence" and in renewing it we should simplify it. All the examples cited as evidence of bankruptcy in section 18 of this bill "are already provided for by the laws of some of the States, and are susceptible of provision by all the States." Finally, states that if a compulsory system is desirable it ought not to be included in this bill but should be introduced as a separate bill, "as was proposed by the Majority of the Judiciary Committee." Believes, therefore, that the voluntary and compulsory approaches should be placed in distinct bills. Denies that a bill incorporating only the voluntary class, which he favors, would be a "mere insolvent law. Not if I am right in supposing that the characteristic difference between a system of insolvency and a system of bankruptcy is the discharge of the debtor."

Concludes with the observation that "I have purposely abstained on this occasion from any inquiry into the causes which have produced or augmented the distress and bankruptcy which unhappily prevail, because I wished to excite no feelings and to make no reproaches which might have a tendency to endanger the bill. I have restricted myself to a consideration of the fact itself of the numerous bankruptcies existing in the country. Nor has my desire for the success of the bill been less, because there are only some eight or ten States of the Union in which it is most needed; for it has ever been with me a motive, regulating my public conduct, to concur in the adoption of any constitutional measure demanded by the wants or necessities of any part of the Union, although it might not be requisite to the prosperity of the State whose servant I am." Adds that the "wretched bankrupt" is deprived of the unalienable rights guaranteed him by the Declaration of Independence and that he should not be. *Cong. Globe*, 26 Cong., 1 Sess., 441; and *ibid.*, Appendix, 846-48. Clay's motion to strike section 18 failed by a vote of 25 to 17 on June 5. *Cong. Globe*, 26 Cong., 1 Sess., 444. See also Remark in Senate, April 22 and June 5, 1840.

Remark in Senate, June 5, 1840. Participates (not recorded) in discussion of Sen. Ambrose H. Sevier's motion to take up the question of the date of adjournment. Motion lost. *Cong. Globe*, 26 Cong., 1 Sess., 444.

Later this day, Clay, Webster, and Silas Wright (N.Y.) all made "further remarks" (not recorded) on the bankruptcy bill [Remark in Senate, April 22, 1840; Speech in Senate, June 4, 1840]; following these, Clay's motion to strike section 18 from the bill was defeated 25 to 17. As for suggestions to refer the bill to a select committee, or postpone indefinitely further discussion of the whole subject, Clay urges instead "taking a vote upon it now, to determine whether a majority of the Senate was in favor of a bill, in any form, on this subject." A motion to postpone consideration of the bill indefinitely was lost 28 to 16, Clay voting with the majority. On the motion of Sen. John J. Crittenden (Ky.), it was then referred to a select committee of seven. *Ibid.*, 444-46.

To Samuel Coffin *et al.*, June 6, 1840. Declines an invitation "to attend the general Convention of the People," to be held at Concord, N.H., on June 17. Notes that "it would afford me lasting pleasure if I could contribute to open the eyes of those who have been deceived by artful and designing men, given to Executive encroachments and usurpation," but explains that neither the press of his official duties nor his health will permit his attendance. Copy. Printed in Portsmouth (N.H.) *Journal of Literature and Politics*, June 27, 1840. Courtesy of Richard E. Winslow III.

To STEPHEN [*sic*, Steven] **WHITNEY**[1]

Washington,
June 8, 1840

The Whig members of Congress have deemed it expedient to engage the Honl. Rice Garland[2] to proceed to the Northern Capitals for the purpose of endeavoring to raise funds to defray the necessary expenses, in the conduct of the great contest in which we are engaged. The Whig members of Congress have, most of them largely & liberally contributed themselves, but you will readily conceive that their own resources require some auxiliary aid:

The brightest prospects of success exist; and nothing can defeat us but a failure to employ exertions proportionate to the magnitude of the great interests at stake. Our opponents are active, persevering and unscrupulous in the means they use—They must be met by all proper corresponding efforts—And the motive of this letter is to appeal to your patriotism and your liberality to assist Mr. Garland in accomplishing the object of his mission—I feel confidant that the appeal will not be unavailing, but that you will yourself, & engage your friends also, to contribute in that spirit of generosity which has ever marked your course—

LS. Written from "S[enate]. Chamber." 1. For Steven Whitney, wealthy New York City commission merchant and director of the Bank of America, see Philip S. Foner, *Business and Slavery, The New York Merchants and the Irrespressible Conflict* (Chapel Hill, 1941), 18, 25, 55, 89, 162; Bonner, *New York*, 408. 2. Rep. Rice Garland, Louisiana Whig, was at this time serving as chairman of the executive committee of the Whig national campaign organization. Gunderson, *Log-Cabin Campaign*, 148-49. For Garland, see *BDAC*.

Remark in Senate, June 10, 1840. Speaking to the question of printing 20,000 copies of the report of the Committee on the Militia, prefers not to push ahead with debate on the militia reorganization plan addressed in that report until relevant documents on the subject from Generals Henry Knox and William Henry Harrison are received by the Senate. Thinks it would not be fair to compare the committee's report, based substantially on the Knox and Harrison materials, with "the scheme" of Secretary of War Joel R. Poinsett until the missing documents are in hand. *Cong. Globe*, 26 Cong., 1 Sess., Appendix, 554. For Poinsett's militia reorganization plan (which called for a militia of 200,000 men—half on duty as a standing army, the other half serving as a reserve), the earlier militia plans of Knox and Harrison, and the failure of Poinsett's attempt to create a trained militia—a proposal killed dead in the political cross-fire of the 1840 presidential election—see J. Fred Rippy, *Joel R. Poinsett, Versatile American* (Durham, N.C., 1935), 175-77.

Remark in Senate, June 12, 1840. Speaks to the House bill that would change the method of computing mileage, for purposes of paying travel allowances between Washington and the places of residence of members of both houses. The new legislation would determine the mileage traveled by measuring it along a straight line rather than by way of the usual routes taken by travelers. Clay asks if it is true that the House really does not want to pass this legislation. Notes that the object of the bill is good, since it is an attempt to achieve a uniform way of calculating travel allowance payments. Asserts that he himself has always used the "long route," because "owing to the facilities of steamboats and railroads, that route was the cheapest and quickest." Favors sending the bill to a select committee. *Cong. Globe*, 26 Cong., 1 Sess., 460. This bill, amended to include a $20 allowance per member per session for stationery, rather than a free and unlimited issue of stationery to all members, was passed on July 11, 1840, by a 28 to 8 vote, Clay voting yea. *Ibid.*, 518-19, 522. The bill was reported back to the House with amendments on July 13, 1840, but did not pass; nor did such a bill pass in the 26th Congress, 2nd Session. U.S. Sen., *Journal*, 26 Cong., 1 Sess., 426-27, 478, 486, 493-94; U.S. H. of Reps., *Journal*, 26 Cong., 1 Sess., 1090, 1102-3, 1261.

Remark in Senate, June 15, 1840. Speaks to the fact that the charters of six banks located in the District of Columbia are due to expire on July 4, 1840. Argues that since Congress has been unable during this legislative session to "place the banking system on a stable and satisfactory footing," all that can be done now is "to continue the existing charters for one or two years"—this in the hope that in the intervening time "Congress could make a permanent arrangement." Criticizes the specie-payment feature of the bill now before the Senate that would "continue the corporate existence of the banks of the District for two years, with certain restrictions." Specifically, the bill would extend the charters of the six banks in the district to July 4, 1842, provided that none of these banks "shall issue and pay out the notes of any other bank, banker, or banking institution, or corporation, which is in a state of suspension or non-payment of its liabilities in specie." Clay observes, in criticism of certain features of this bill, that "the operation of such a prohibition will be upon the debtors of the banks, and not upon the banks themselves. Upon the debtors themselves it will operate severely. For if the banks are not allowed to pay out, they will be sure not to receive the notes of distant banks." He concurs, however, in Sen. James Buchanan's broader goal "of establishing a single bank for the District, to be placed in Washington, with branches in the other two cities [Georgetown and Alexandria]," adding that "those banking systems worked best in the several States, which consisted of two or three large and respectable banks, with branches conveniently located, instead of a multitude of small banks having no necessary connection with each other." *Cong. Globe*, 26 Cong., 1 Sess., 467-68.

For the legislation which extended the charter expiration dates of these banks, and the conditions attached to such extensions (mainly specie-payment requirements and the minimum denomination of bank notes that might be issued), see 5 *U.S. Stat.*, 232, 449-51. In spite of the specie-payment requirements, Clay supported charter-extension legislation as well as a proposal to establish a single District of Columbia Bank with branches in Georgetown and Alexandria, legislation which passed the Senate by 20 to 13 on June 16, but failed to clear the House. *Cong. Globe*, 26 Cong., 1 Sess., 310, 467-68, 503-7, 515. See also Remark in Senate, July 3, 1840.

Remark in Senate, June 16, 1840. Speaks to Sen. William C. Preston's motion to print 10,000 copies of Secretary Poinsett's report on a plan for a standing army of 100,000 militia [Remark in Senate, June 10, 1840]. Supports including with Poinsett's reports those of General William Henry Harrison on militia issues—reports which "breathed a spirit of liberty" and "deprecated a standing army." Stung by

Sen. Clement C. Clay's charge that he was ignorant of the contents of Harrison's militia reports, especially a proposal by Harrison to "give a military education to all the youth of the country," the Kentuckian remarks that the military education of youth was "desirable," and that Harrison had stated he would amend the Constitution to carry the plan into effect. Reminded by Clay of Alabama that Harrison had called for the constitutional amendment "six weeks after" his youth education proposal, Clay of Kentucky concedes that the general, "having found that some of his suggestions . . . were not in accordance with the constitution, promptly corrected the error into which he had fallen, and proposed that the constitution should be amended." *Niles' Register* (June 20, 1840), 58:252.

Remark in Senate, June 17, 1840. Rises to comment on Sen. Clement C. Clay's complaint that both the Washington *Daily National Intelligencer* and the Washington *Globe* had mishandled a passage in a speech of his on Secretary of War Joel R. Poinsett's project for a reorganization of the militia as a standing army [Remark in Senate, June 10, 1840]. Informs the Alabama senator that members of the body should not comment on newspaper articles relating to themselves. Asserts that he "had never done so, and he did not think it consistent with that dignity and elevation to which the Senate ought to aspire. And, if it were done in all cases, the Senate could do scarcely any thing else, for . . . he did not think he ever saw a single paragraph in the Globe in which he was correctly reported. For every one misrepresentation on his side, he believed there were ten on the other. Yet he had never commented on those reports in his place, but left his character to stand or fall by his acts. And suppose the Senate should appoint their own reporters [Remark in Senate, June 19, 1840], they would be appointed by a party majority, which would increase instead of correcting the evil." Says that the right of the press to express opinions, even if they are based on factual inaccuracies, "is one of the inestimable privileges of a free press, which, though liable to be abused, could not be interfered with without great danger." Points out that he too has the right to express his opinions on controversial matters before the Senate. He does, however, object to "members rising here, and consuming the time of the Senate in correcting the errors of a free press." As an example of the kind of semantic misrepresentation the Senate itself indulges in, points to the administration's [Calhoun's] reference to its land bill [Comment in Senate, January 3, 1840; Remark in Senate, April 23, 1840] as legislation to "cede" the public domain to the new states, whereas in reality such cession would constitute an "absolute donation." To this observation, C.C. Clay (Ala.) responds with a denial of Clay's interpretation of the land bill, a charge that Clay is attempting to confuse the issue, and an assertion that he will, as in the past, repel all personal assaults. He does not, however, "contend for the last word" on this question. Concludes Clay: "Well, you have got the last word." *Cong. Globe*, 26 Cong., 1 Sess., 470-71.

Remark in Senate, June 19, 1840. Participates (not recorded) in a discussion of Sen. Robert J. Walker's resolution of June 17 to consider the appointment of a select committee to study the "propriety of selecting Reporters for the Senate." *Cong. Globe*, 26 Cong., 1 Sess., 473. This resolution was passed on July 3 and a committee of five was promptly appointed. *Ibid.*, 503. No further action was taken on the idea during this session.

To James F. Babcock *et al.*, New Haven, Conn., June 21, 1840. Regrets that previous commitments make it impossible for him to attend the Whig celebration in New Haven on July 4; but, thanks Connecticut for "sustaining the cause of Liberty, the Constitution and the Country" during "the last Spring Election [Clay to

Lucretia Hart Clay, April 12, 1840]." ALS. NHi. For Babcock, a powerful Whig leader in Connecticut and for many years editor of the New Haven *Palladium*, see *CAB*.

From WILLIAM HENRY HARRISON North Bend, Ohio, June 21, 1840

Your letter of the 5th. of June I received upon my arrival at Cin[cinna]ti. the Evg before last on my return from Fort Meigs. I received at the same time the paper to which it refers. The necessity of adopting this is I immagine entirely superseeded by the publication of my letters to Mr Williams of Tennessee & Mr Lyons of Va. & The Louisville Committee.[1]

At Springfield in Clark County I met when surrounded by at least 15,000 people the account of the death of my son Benjamin.[2] I had no hopes of his living through the summer but I did not think when I left home that he was so soon to be taken off.

I will do as you recommend in relation to the publication of Specimens of the letters I receive

Nothing I assure you can be more ridiculous than the declaration of our opponents that they will get the vote of Ohio. There is not a township in the State in which there are not many changes open & avowed. In Crawford County for instance through which I passed in my late journey there is a township which has never given more than six Whig votes out of about 300. They have now a Tippecanoe Club of 65 enroled & at least 25 more have avowed their determination to support me. But this is not the worst feature in the present state of affairs for our friend Martin [Van Buren]. There is extensive treachery in his camp. My belief is, that there are many thousands in Ohio who will vote for me who yet appear to adhere to their old party. This is [Thomas] Ewings Opinion also whom you will probably see in a few days as he left me at Cleveland a Week ago on his way to New York

The state of feeling in my own Township affords a strong sign in our favor. We have always had a Whig majority here since Genl Jacksons late Election varying from 20 to 40. Last fall the average was 30. Out of the old voters (there are some Canal labourers) I am sure they cannot enumerate 20 that still adhere to them. I believe it will be generally admitted that neighbours who once take a stand aginst each other in politics are more difficult to reconcile than any others Without the least effort on my part to produce such a result Many of my former opponents have declared in my favor & there are many others who *now* declare they will not vote at all. This circumstance affords I should think the strongest evidence of the extent & deep rooted opposition to the Measures of the Administration by a large portion of its former friends.

I should be much gratified to see you on yr. way home. but the meeting must appear to be accidental. Can you arrange such a one?[3] [P.S.] I am in better health than you ever saw me

ALS. DLC-HC (DNA, M212, R5). 1. Democrats had charged that Harrison was an abolitionist and a Federalist, and that his words were being dictated by a "secret committee"—a reference to the Hamilton County (Ohio) Whig Correspondence Committee which was helping him answer his voluminous mail. Harrison wrote Rep. Joseph L. Williams of Tenn. refuting the allegation that he was subject to the dictation of any committee and saying that the Hamilton County group was simply assisting him and was expressing his own opinions. On June 1, 1840, Harrison wrote James Lyons, a Virginia lawyer and former Jacksonian who had become a Whig, denying that he was or had ever been either a Federalist or an abolitionist. On June 2, he wrote the Central Whig Committee for the Second District of Ky. (Louisville) saying that his earlier speeches and letters which had recently been republished still express his positions on political issues. The Louisville Committee then published a lengthy defense of Harrison against the abolitionist charge. Goebel, *William Henry Harrison*, 355-65; Lexington *Observer & Kentucky Reporter*, June 13, 17, 1840; Washington *Daily National Intelligencer*, June 11, 17, 1840. For Joseph L. Williams, see *BDAC*. For James Lyons, see Simms, *Rise of the Whigs in Virginia*, 49, 70, 80; Wise, *Seven Decades of the Union*, 178. 2. Harrison's 34-year-old son, who had been in poor health for some months, died at the family home on June 17, 1840. Cleaves, *Old Tippecanoe*, 324. 3. Clay and Harrison did not meet during Clay's trip home from Washington. See Harrison to Clay, August 6, 1840.

To JAMES D. ALLEN[1] Washington, June 22, 1840

I have received your favor, requesting an expression of a sentiment. I can only be very brief.

In my opinion, the most alarming fact which shakes the eye of an attentive observer, in surveying the face of our Country, is the corrupt and demoralizing practices to which the Administration party resorts, to maintain itself in power. Misrepresentation, falsehood, bribery, forgery, perjury, corruption of the Ballot boxes, have all been established upon members of that party. When one party employs such means, sooner or later, in self defense and from necessity, the other party will be tempted to appeal to the same arts. And the corruption of the whole mass will quickly follow. Then, farewell to Liberty. All my hopes rest upon November.

ALS. DLC-HC. 1. For Allen, a merchant in Menard Co., Ill., see Robert Don Leavey Miller, *Past and Present of Menard County, Illinois* (Chicago, 1905), 15.

To Samuel Greala [?], [Boston], June 23, 1840. Regrets that other engagements make it impossible for him to attend the July 4 celebration by Friends of Harrison and Reform in Boston Wards 9, 10, 11, and 12. Predicts, however, "a glorious victory" in November if Whigs make "the exertions demanded by the magnitude of the interests, involved in the contest." Offers a sentiment: "Whigs of the Union! Let your watchwords be Union, Vigor & Activity and a glorious triumph is inevitable." ALS. NcD. Written in Senate Chamber.

To J. P. CARVER Washington, June 24, 1840

Your favor is received. I should be delighted to be with you at Lyons[1] on the 4h. prox: and to listen to the ripe and experienced counsels of my venerable and patriotic friend A[mbrose]. Spencer Esq. But distance and duties deny me that pleasure.

I should be glad, if time permitted, to enter on a detail of the probabilities of the success of our cause in each State of the Union. My opportunities of information, from obvious causes, are not limited. But I am compelled, by my numerous engagements, and extensive correspondence, to be brief. And I will confine the communication to those parts of the Union most remote from you.

I believe that Govr. Harrison will receive the votes of Virginia, North Carolina, Georgia, Louisiana, Tennessee, Kentucky, Ohio, Indiana, and Illinois. A letter now before me, subscribed by a number of respectable gentlemen in Alabama, assures me that he will get the vote of that State. You may depend upon it, that our friends in Alabama, Mississipppi, Arkansas and Missouri will make a noble struggle, deserving success, if they do not achieve it, which is far from being improbable. That he will obtain the votes of Maryland & Delaware is beyond question.[2]

In short, I entertain not a doubt of a glorious triumph, if our friends, unaffected by false rumors & undismayed by idle boastings of our opponents, will pull off their Coats and go hard to work with the resolution of men who know that liberty like bread is only to be earned by the sweat of the brow.

My warm regards to Mr. Spencer.

ALS. OClWHi. 1. A Jonathan P. Carver appears in the 1840 census in Lyons, N.Y. Carver has not otherwise been identified. Information supplied by Marjory Allen Perez, Wayne County historian, Lyons, N.Y. Lyons, Wayne County, N.Y., was also the home of Ambrose Spencer from 1839 until his death in 1848. 2. See Speech in Baltimore, May 4, 1840. Of the 15 states Clay mentions here, Harrison carried all but Va., Ill., Ala., and Mo.

Speech on the State of the Country Under Van Buren, Taylorsville, Hanover County, Va., June 27, 1840. Asserts that it is his "fixed determination heartily to support" the election of Harrison even though there have been "misrepresentations" to the contrary. Expresses his joy in returning to the cherished scenes of his childhood.

Blames the sorry state of the national economy on a single factor—"the encroachments, and the usurpations of the executive branch of the government . . . during the last twelve years," which have produced in that office "an awful squinting toward monarchy." Condemns the fact that Jackson demanded total obedience to his commands by all government officers on pain of their dismissal from office; and that dismissals were (and are) effected without cause having been given. Gives examples of this abuse of executive power. Asks that given the concentration of such power, "who ever expects to see the day arrive when a President of the United States will be impeached; or, if impeached, when he cannot command more than one third of the Senate to defeat the impeachment?" Also criticizes Jackson's personal "supervising and attending to the execution of all the minute details of every one of the hosts of offices in the United States." Charges, further, that Jackson's seizure of the treasury in 1833 [8:681, 684-85] concentrated solely in the hands of the commander-in-chief of the Army and the Navy, the sword and purse of the nation. Notes that the employees of the executive branch and their dependents number some 100,000 people, and that "all of them, wherever they are situated, are bound implicitly to obey the orders of the president." Sees real possibilities of abuses of power in this situation and asserts that Van Buren has pledged to follow in Jackson's footsteps in these particulars. Already the "official corps" beholden to Van Buren has intervened in popular elections in the support of the "views and interests of the president and his party." Indeed, "the official corps is dispersed throughout the country, in every town, village, and city, mixing with the people, attending their meetings and conventions, becoming chairmen and members of committees, and urging and stimulating partisans to active and vigorous exertion. Acting in concert, and, throughout the whole Union, obeying orders issued from the center, their influence, aided by executive patronage, by the post-office department, and all the vast other means of the executive, is almost irresistible." Explains that Sen. John J. Crittenden introduced a bill "to restrain the subordinates of the executive from all interference with popular elections. . . . And how was this bill received in the Senate? Passed by those who profess . . . to pursue the principles of Mr. Jefferson? No such thing. It was denounced as a sedition bill."

Fears that the Army and the Navy are next, and "that the day was not distant when they, too, would be required to perform the partizan offices of the president. Accordingly, the process of converting them into executive instruments has commenced in a court-martial assembled at Baltimore. Two officers of the army of the United States have been there put upon their solemn trial, on the charge of prejudicing the democratic party, by making purchases for the supply of the army, from members of the whig party." Fears, too, that Secretary of War Poinsett's militia plan to create a "standing force of two hundred thousand men [Remark in Senate, June 10, 1840]" is "alarming and dangerous," and has "justly excited a burst of general indignation," because "no conceivable foreign exigency can ever make necessary" such a large force. Analyzes Poinsett's proposal in some detail.

Argues that neither the elective franchise nor the fact that the presidential term is of short duration can protect the liberty of the people. Believes that "if Mr. Van Buren should be re-elected, the power already acquired by the executive be retained, and that which is in progress be added to that department, it is my deliberate judgment that there will be no hope remaining for the continuance of the liberties of the country." Scoffs at the fact that the Democrats call him [Clay] a Federalist—"I, who had exerted the utmost of my humble abilities to arouse the nation to a vindication of its insulted honor, and its violated rights, and to the vigorous prosecution of the war against Great Britain, to which they were violently opposed, find myself, by a sort of magical influence, converted into a federalist!" As for differences between present-day parties, explains that the Democrats have "reduced the federal theory of a strong and energetic executive to practical operation. It has turned from the people, the natural ally of genuine democracy, to the executive, and, instead of vigilance, jealousy, and distrust, has given to that department all its confidence, and made to it a virtual surrender of all the powers of government. The recognized maxim of royal infallibility is transplanted from the British monarchy into modern American democracy, and the president can do no wrong! This new school adopts, modifies, changes, renounces, renews opinions at the pleasure of the executive. Is the bank of the United States a useful and valuable institution? Yes, unanimously pronounces the democratic Legislature of Pennsylvania. The president vetoes it as a pernicious and dangerous establishment. The democratic majority in the same Legislature pronounce it to be pernicious and dangerous. The democratic majority of the House of Representatives of the United States, declare the deposits of the public money in the bank of the United States to be safe. The president says they are unsafe, and removes them. The democracy say they are unsafe, and approve the removal. The president says that a scheme of a sub-treasury is revolutionary and disorganizing. The democracy say it is revolutionary and disorganizing. The president says it is wise and salutary. The democracy say it is wise and salutary. The whigs of 1840 stand where the republicans of 1798 stood, and where the whigs of the Revolution were, battling for liberty, for the people, for free institutions, against power, against corruption, against executive incroachments, against monarchy. . . . higher, nobler, more patriotic motives actuate the whig party. Their object is the restoration of the Constitution, the preservation of liberty, and rescue of the country. If they were governed by the sordid and selfish motives acted upon by their opponents, and unjustly imputed to them, to acquire office and emolument, they have only to change their names, and enter the presidential palace. The gate is always wide open, and the path is no narrow one which leads through it. The last comer, too, often fares best."

Sees William Henry Harrison's election as providing "assurance of the cessation of that long series of disastrous experiments which have so greatly afflicted the people." Indeed, public "Confidence will immediately revive, credit be restored, active business will return, prices of products will rise."

States that while he knows not what "grave and serious measures" will command the early attention of the Harrison administration, his own view of its priorities would include, first, "circumscribing the executive power." To this end, either by constitutional amendment or by remedial legislation, presidents should be restricted to one term of four years. Secondly, the president's veto power should be "subjected to further limitations and qualifications"; specifically, the pocket veto power should be abolished. Thirdly, "dismission from office" should be restricted and its exercise rendered more responsible by the device of requiring Senate concurrence in both the appointment and dismissal of "all important" officers. Fourthly, control over the U.S. Treasury "should be confided and confined exclusively to Congress"; specifically, the president should be deprived of "all authority" to dismiss a secretary of the treasury. Finally, congressmen should not be appointed by the president to office (to any but a "few specific offices") while actively serving in the Congress.

Believes, further, that the Harrison administration should do something to stabilize the value of the nation's currency, either by employing a system of "sound and safe State banks, carefully selected, and properly distributed, or by a new bank of the United States, with such limitations, conditions, and restrictions, as have been indicated by experience." Explains, however, that "Candor and truth require me to say, that, in my judgment, while banks continue to exist in the country, the services of a bank of the United States can not be safely dispensed with. I think that the power to establish such a bank is a settled question; settled by Washington and by Madison, by the people, by forty years' acquiescence, by the judiciary, and by both of the great parties which so long held sway in this country. I know and I respect the contrary opinion, which is entertained in this State. But, in my deliberate view of the matter, the power to establish such a bank being settled, and being a necessary and proper power, the only question is, as to the expediency of its exercise. And on questions of mere expediency, public opinion ought to have a controlling influence. Without banks, I believe we can not have a sufficient currency; without a bank of the United States, I fear we can not have a sound currency. But it is the end, that of a sound and sufficient currency, and a faithful execution of the fiscal duties of government, that should engage the dispassionate and candid consideration of the whole community. There is nothing in the name of the bank of the United States which has any magical charm, or to which any one need be wedded. It is to secure certain great objects, without which society can not prosper; and if, contrary to my apprehension, these objects can be accomplished by dispensing with the agency of a bank of the United States, and employing that of State banks, all ought to rejoice, and heartily acquiesce, and none would more than I should." Suggests, in addition, that the new Harrison administration should embrace a public land policy that treats the new states and territories and the old states on a basis of equality. Thinks his 1832 land bill, vetoed by Jackson [8:539-41, 609-10], would accomplish this. Calls attention to an unacceptable land bill recently passed by the Senate [Remark in Senate, January 3, 1839, and April 23, 1840] which is now pending in the House. "I have no hesitation in expressing my conviction, that the whole public domain is gone if Mr. Van Buren be re-elected." Assures his audience that the Compromise Tariff arrangement of 1833 [8:604, 619-22, 626-27] will be sustained by a Harrison administration; also, that Harrison will follow a policy of "strict and wise economy in the disbursement of the public money." Further, is confident that "the several States have made such great and gratifying progress in their respective systems of internal improvement, and have been so aided by the distribution under the deposit act [8:812-13; Speech in Senate, February 28, 1837], that, in future, the erection of new roads and canals should be left to them, with such further aid only from the general government, as they would derive from the payment of the last installment under that act [Comment in Senate, September 15, 1837; Remark in Senate,

December 13, 1838] from an absolute relinquishment of the right of Congress to call upon them to refund the previous installments, and from their equal and just quotas, to be received by a future distribution of the net proceeds from the sales of the public lands." Finally, states that "the right to slave property, being guarantied by the Constitution, and recognized as one of the compromises incorporated in that instrument by our ancestors, should be left where the Constitution has placed it, undisturbed and unagitated by Congress."

Concludes: "These, fellow-citizens, are views both of the structure of the government and of its administration, which appear to me worthy of commanding the grave attention of the public and its new servants. Although, I repeat, I have neither authority nor purpose to commit any body else, I believe most, if not all, of them are entertained by the political friends with whom I have acted. Whether the salutary reforms which they include will be effected or considered, depends upon the issue of that great struggle which is now going on throughout all this country." Copy. Printed in Colton, *Clay Correspondence*, 6:195-214. Printed also in James B. Swain (ed.), *The Life and Speeches of Henry Clay*, 2 vols. in 1 (New York, 1843), 2:420-442; misdated July 10, 1840. Only a single manuscript page of this speech has been found. ALS. NjMoHP. On this, in a strange hand, is explained: "Leaf from the Ms. of a speech made by Mr. Clay at Taylorsville, Hanover Co., Va. in 1840—Furnished by him to the columns of the "Political Arena" newspaper—Fredericksburg [Va.]."

For Clay's order of printed copies of this speech from Gales & Seaton, see Clay to Gales & Seaton, July 11, 1840. D. DLC-TJC (DNA, M212, R18). Clay remained in Hanover County for two days on this occasion. Clay to Lucretia Hart Clay, July 7, 1840. The speech was printed in pamphlet form under the title, *Speech of Mr. Clay, of Kentucky, Delivered June 27, 1840, On the Occasion of a Public Dinner, Given in Compliment to Him, at Taylorsville. . . .* N.p., 1840.

On December 21, 1838, Crittenden had introduced "A Bill to Prevent the Interference of Certain Federal Officers in Elections." The bill was brought up for debate on February 27, 1839, and, after the discussion of numerous amendments, it was defeated 28 to 5, Clay not voting. U.S. Sen., *Journal*, 25 Cong., 3 Sess., 67, 71, 178, 215, 223, 227, 230, 233, 237, 288-90.

Remark in Senate, June 30, 1840. In the course of debate on the bill "to provide for the better execution of the laws in the collection of duties on imports," Clay joins John C. Calhoun in stating that together they intend to support the principles of the Compromise Tariff Act of 1833 [8:619-22, 626-27] when the tariff comes up for revision in the next session. *Cong. Globe*, 26 Cong., 1 Sess., 493.

The "bill to insure the more faithful execution of the laws relating to the collection of duties on imports and tonnage" was reported first in the House on March 5, 1840, and passed on May 13, no vote count given. It was received in the Senate on May 13, and was amended and passed on July 8. Back in the House, it was referred to the Committee on Manufactures for consideration of the Senate amendments. It eventually died in committee. U.S. H. of Reps., *Journal*, 26 Cong., 1 Sess., 505, 1236-37, 1285, 1307; U.S. Sen., *Journal*, 26 Cong., 1 Sess., 368-69, 481.

To Unknown Recipient, n.p., n.d. [*ca.* June 30, 1840]. Reports that "I have looked into the Harrison Almanac and Log Cabin Anecdotes, and take pleasure in expressing the opinion that they are well adapted to promote the good cause which they have espoused, and merit general circulation & perusal." Copy. DLC-Caleb Cushing Papers (DNA, M212, R20). Also endorsing this campaign publication, on June 30, 1840, was the Executive Committee of the Opposition Members of Congress, specifically Reps. John C. Clark (N.Y.), Rice Garland (La.), John M.

Botts (Va.), and Truman Smith (Conn.); also Sen. Nathaniel P. Tallmadge (N.Y.). For the role of the *Harrison Almanac* and the *Log-Cabin Anecdotes* in the presidential campaign, see Gunderson, *Log-Cabin Campaign*, 128.

Remark in Senate, July 3, 1840. Notified that the corporate charters of six District of Columbia banks will expire at midnight tonight, Clay votes with the majority (23 to 11) to take up the District Bank bill [Remark in Senate, June 15, 1840] immediately. Suggests a way to suspend Senate rule 26, which requires a one day notice in such matters, so that the bill might receive its second and third reading today. At day's end, observes that the Senate had spent the day, "till six O'clock, in discussing a question of order; and yet a bill had been introduced, read a first, second and third time, and passed, and all this in the course of fifteen minutes." *Cong. Globe*, 26 Cong., 1 Sess., 503-4, 506-7. The House passed the bill, 115 to 75, this same day. *Ibid.*, 507-8. For Senate action on a similar House bill, see *ibid.*, 508, 510.

Remark in Senate, July 6, 1840. Participates in debate on two amendments to a House bill that would regulate the collection of tariff revenues in such ways as to eliminate various frauds currently being perpetrated on said revenues [Remark in Senate, June 30, 1840]. Specifically, Clay speaks (not recorded) to an amendment that "no mixed goods should be designated as silk, unless the value of the silk in the fabric should exceed all the other materials"; also to an amendment on whether the duties established in this legislation "ought to continue in force after June, 1842, when inconsistent with the act of 1833; and whether the compromise act would continue the duties at or below twenty per cent. on the value of the goods, after June, 1842, without further legislation by Congress." *Cong. Globe*, 26 Cong., 1 Sess., 510. For the language of the legislation as it made its way through the House, see *ibid.*, 297, 382-84, 386-87, 389-91, 540.

To LUCRETIA HART CLAY Washington, July 7, 1840

Congress has at last fixed a day of adjournment, the 20h. instant.[1] I shall leave here before it arrives. I intend to set out on sunday next.[2] I have not decided upon the route; but I hear unfavorable accounts of the river. If I should not get better, I shall return by the W. Sulphur Springs through Virginia. If the river be navigable I shall go by Wheeling. I am already packing up. Never was I so tired of the place; never so anxious to be with you.

We have heard from England, about the N. Eastern boundary, and there is no present danger of War.[3] As for any pending measures, I do not feel the necessity of my remaining here.

For several months I have been afflicted with constant colds and hoarseness. Two or three times have I put on and taken off my flannels. I have begun again to rub the surface of my body every morning with Spirits and Salt. I must find some relief, or I cannot survive.[4]

Each party appears to be confident of success in the P. Election, I think ours has most reason. My reception in Hanover was warm and enthusiastic. I staid there two days. My Speech will be published this week, and I will send you a Copy.[5]

Thomas [Hart Clay] writes me flattering accounts of the prospects of his Manufacturing. Tell him that we are passing a bill that will benefit the Bagging manufacturers by enforcing payment of the duty on the foreign article.[6]

I have heard such favorable accounts of a School near N. York that I am anxious Mr. [James] Erwin should send Henry [Clay Erwin] and James [Erwin, Jr.] to it. Mrs. Bell[7] has visited it & thinks it the best she ever saw. It is kept by Mr. [James] Such, an English Episcopalian Clergyman.[8]

As I hope soon to be with you, I add nothing more, but a request that you will give my love to all our Children & grand children.

ALS. Courtesy of M.W. Anderson, Lexington, Ky. 1. Congress adjourned on Tuesday, July 21. 2. He departed Washington on Sunday, July 12. 3. Clay to Hamilton, Feb. 24, 1839; Comment in Senate, April 14, 1840. 4. On July 10, Clay settled his medical bill with Dr. William Thomas in the amount of $15. Other bills and receipts with Washington druggists C.H. James and R.S. Patterson, dated Dec. 1, 1839, to July 9, 1840, indicate that Clay regularly purchased such palliatives as salts (Epsom and other), camp pills, Verbena Cream, various liniments, ointments, and lozenges, and Gum Arabic. These were prescribed, variously, to relieve the sore throat, raspy cough, irritated mucous membranes, and aching muscles associated with severe common colds. This information courtesy of Prof. John Scarborough, Univ. of Wisconsin, Madison. Clay to Patterson, July 8, 1840. ADS. DLC-TJC (DNA, M212, R18); Clay to James, July 9, 1840. *Ibid.*; Clay to Thomas, July 10, 1840. *Ibid.* 5. Speech . . . in Taylorsville, Hanover County, Va., June 27, 1840. 6. Remark in Senate, June 30, 1840. 7. Jane Erwin Yeatman (Mrs. Jchn) Bell. 8. James Such, who died on March 26, 1859, in his 58th year, had made a deposition in 1839 declaring his intention to become a U.S. resident. See Kenneth Scott & Rosanne Conway, *New York Alien Residents, 1825-1848* (Baltimore, 1978), 108. Although identified here as an Anglican clergyman, there is no evidence that he permanently filled an Episcopal church pulpit in New York. He is listed only as a pewholder at Grace Episcopal Church, Jamaica, and as a "teacher" in Henry Onderdonk, Jr., *Antiquities of the Parish Church, Jamaica . . . History of Grace Church . . .* (Jamaica, N.Y., 1880), 117. Gertrude A. Barber, comp., "Deaths Taken From the New York Evening Post, From January 24, 1859 to February 21, 1860." Typescript (New York: New York Genealogical and Biographical Society, 1941), 36:20. See also Gratz to Clay, Oct. 28, 1840.

Remark in Senate, July 7, 1840. Asks permission to take up, out of order, the joint resolution directing the United States to return to Kentucky the 195 stands of arms turned over to the government by Kentucky militia units after the Battle of New Orleans in 1815. After Clay "explained the merits of the case," an explanation not recorded, the resolution was ordered to be engrossed. *Cong. Globe*, 26 Cong., 1 Sess., 512. It had been introduced by Sen. William C. Preston (S.C.) on May 18, 1840. *Ibid.*, 402. The Senate passed the resolution on July 8, 1840, without further discussion. *Ibid.*, 514. See also Clay to Poinsett, March 25, 1840.

Remark in Senate, July 9, 1840. Participates in the discussion of a bill to publish a seven-volume edition of the laws and treaties of the United States. Asserts his intention first to vote for an amendment by Sen. Wilson Lumpkin (Ga.) to strike out language which would distribute a free set, of the work to each member of Congress; and then to vote against the bill as amended. The Lumpkin amendment passed 31 to 6, Clay voting yea; the motion to engross the bill was defeated 23 to 17, Clay voting against it. *Cong. Globe*, 26 Cong., 1 Sess., 515-16.

Later this day, Clay's motion to table a proposed amendment to the Constitution to limit the tenure of office of all federal judges, in order to take up instead the mileage-allowances bill [Remark in Senate, June 12, 1840], fails 22 to 21. He explains that the mileage bill has been scheduled for today's calendar, and notes also that while the measure came from the House "three or four weeks ago" nothing has yet been done about it in the Senate. Following the passage, 21 to 19, of his motion to table the joint resolution on the judicial tenure of office amendment, he promises a "few remarks" on the mileage-allowances bill "tomorrow morning." *Ibid.*, 516.

Comment in Senate, July 10, 1840. Speaks in favor of the bill, received from the House, having to do with computing mileage allowances for members [Remark in Senate, June 12, 1840] traveling to and from their homes. Points out that the House had passed a similar bill some ten years ago and had passed this bill by a "nearly unanimous vote." States that since the time of his "retreat from public life" is "not very distant," he can be candid about abuses by members. Believes, specifically, that there are and have been misstatements in claims for mileage costs by members, especially when traveling by railroad or steamboat. Asserts also that there are "abuses in every way" in the franking privilege. Calls attention to sharply rising costs of the expenses of Congress for stationery, printing, fuel, etc. Votes for an amendment to limit members to twenty dollars worth of stationery. Votes also against a motion to postpone this legislation. Questions whether basing members' travel mileage on the known distances of the most usual mail routes would be workable, since it is difficult to determine which mail route is the "most usual." Opposes, without explanation, an amendment to the bill that would remove the franking privilege from all packages and from all letters of greater weight than one ounce. *Cong. Globe*, 26 Cong., 1 Sess., 518-19. The bill, as amended, was ordered to be engrossed by a 31 to 9 vote.

To Boyd McNairy *et al.*, Nashville, July 10, 1840. Thanks them for their invitation to visit Nashville on August 17 next [McNairy to Clay, September 21, 1839], but pleads that he is "worn down by the fatigues of an exhausting Session of Congress" and cannot come so soon. Suggests late September or October instead. ALS. ViU.

Remark in Senate, July 11, 1840. To the observation by Sen. Benjamin Tappan (Ohio) that there is "no great urgency" in taking up ahead of the Naval Appropriation bill the District Bank bill [Remark in Senate, June 15, 1840], Clay states that there is "urgency in a case where the entire business of the whole District was at a stand, persons driven out of employ, and industry paralyzed." *Cong. Globe*, 26 Cong., 1 Sess., 521.

Later this day, Clay opposes an amendment to the members' mileage allowance bill [Remark in Senate, June 12, 1840; Comment in Senate, July 10, 1840] that would recommit it to the Judiciary Committee. Wants this bill to pass, now that he has learned, with "shock," the abuses in the use of stationery and other behavior engaged in by members. Does not want to undo the "good work done yesterday" in amending the House bill to limit members to twenty dollars worth of stationery per session. *Ibid.*, 522. The amendment to recommit failed by 23 to 9. The motion to pass carried 35 to 8, Clay voting aye. *Ibid.*

From Moore, Morton & Co., Illinois Land Agency, Quincy, Ill., July 20, 1840. Ask him to remit $50 to cover taxes, fees, and "a Moderate Compensation for our trouble" on his Illinois lands for 1840. ALS. DLC-TJC (DNA, M212, R14).

On August 6, 1840, Clay wrote to Thomas C. Patrick at "Clay's Prairie" in Edgar County, Ill., instructing him to pay his 1840 taxes, to "see that all the land is paid for," and, in future, "to pay the taxes every year." ALS. Courtesy of J. Winston Coleman, Jr., Lexington, Ky.

For the year 1843, Clay paid state and county taxes of $29.56 on approximately 1521.31 acres, assessed at $7,606, in Edgar County, Ill. This sum was calculated at 20 cents on $100 of assessed value for the state tax ($15.21), and 16⅔ cents on $100 of assessed value for the county tax ($12.68), plus 6% ($1.67) fee for the Assessor. Clay to R. Bloomfield (Collector), n.p., n.d. [1843]. ADS. DLC-TJC (DNA, M212, R10). See 8:132 for more on Clay's land in Illinois.

To [THOMAS S.] GHOLSON[1] *et al.* Lexington, July 21, 1840

You will perceive, from the place at which my letter is dated, the impracticability of my accepting your kind invitation to "an old-fashioned South Side [Virginia][2] barbecue," which was received at the moment of my departure from Washington, under circumstances which prevented my transmitting an answer.

Accustomed to such entertainments in Kentucky, where we keep up the good old customs derived from our Virginia ancestors, I should have been most happy to be present at that on the 31st inst. near Boydton [Va.]. I regret exceedingly that I can not be there. I should have been glad of an opportunity to have publicly but respectfully expressed my convictions that many of my fellow-citizens in Mechlenburg [*sic*, Mecklenburg] are greatly deceived by the men in power; that while they are decrying a bank of the United States they are secretly, but surely, establishing a far more pernicious and dangerous bank of the Government; that at the instant of their denouncing internal improvements they are prosecuting them with increased vigor and at augmented expense; that they have finally accomplished their object of uniting the purse and the sword[3] and now only want more money and more men to place the liberties of the country completely at their mercy; that they have, without the smallest pretense of right to the denomination, erroneously assumed the name of Democrats, and that, under color of that name, they have made rapid and fearful progress in consolidating an elective monarchy.

And I should have seized with pleasure to occasion to make a solem[n] appeal to the honest and patriotic, but deceived and misguided portion of our fellow-citizens, and to have seriously asked them, will they allow ancient and obsolete points of controversy to induce them to [o]verlook present, practical and alarming dangers? Artfully stimulated in their prejudices against former measures of policy, will they shut their eyes to the immediate perils which surround them? Will they permit themselves to be drawn into disputes about interpretations of the Constitution which have no longer practical bearing, until there remains no Constitution to dispute about? Are they content to have an elective monarch reigning over them, provided they can enjoy the privilege of calling themselves Democrats and their differing fellow-citizens Federalists? Do they honestly believe that the Federal Government has been warily and justly administered by Mr. Van Buren? Are they satisfied with the present state of the country, its business, its general interests? Do not they feel that there is something wrong in our condition at this time? If there be, who is responsible for it—they who had power or those who had it not? Finally, I would respectfully but earnestly ask them, whilst yet they may, and before it is too late, seriously to reflect upon what is due to their ancestors, to themselves, and to their posterity. It is my deliberate opinion that the inevitable consequences of Mr. Van Buren's re-election, should that event unfortunately happen, will be such as to present for grave consideration at no distant day the single alternative of submission to slavery or resistance by force to the tyranny which must ensue.

But, gentlemen, I can not be with you on the 31st, and I congratulate you that no such alternative as I have stated will arise. Mr. Van Buren will meet with an overwhelming defeat. During my journey hither, as prior to my departure from Washington, the intelligence that I received and the demonstrations which I witnessed gave me the strongest assurance of that approaching event. Kentucky, ever among the most forward in battle, and behind no State in peace or war in defense of civil liberty, will, the week after next, exhibit her firm and fixed purpose to drive from power those who have abused it, and from their places those who have dishonored them. . . .[4]

Copy. Printed in New York *Sun*, Dec. 14, 1883. 1. For Gholson, a Petersburg lawyer and later a circuit judge, see *DAB*. 2. "South Side," Virginia is generally considered to be the area south of Petersburg, lying between South Boston and Suffolk, and bounded on the south by the North Carolina line. 3. Remark in Senate, June 10, 1840. 4. Kentucky voted 58,489 to 32,616 for Harrison. For a county breakdown of the presidential vote in Kentucky see, Jasper B. Shannon and Ruth McQuown, *Presidential Politics in Kentucky, 1824-1948: A Compilation of Election Statistics and an Analysis of Political Behavior* (Lexington, Ky., 1950), 13-15. See also Clay to Worthington, July 25, 1840.

To A Committee of Gentlemen, Erie, Pa., July 23, 1840. Regrets that he cannot attend the celebration on September 10 next commemorating the U.S. naval victory on Lake Erie on that day in 1813. In response to political observations in their letter of invitation, Clay assures them that "No man living . . . can be more penetrated with the absolute necessity of a change of our rulers than I am, nor more desirous of it. I have hitherto done all in my power to effect it, and am willing to continue my exertions to the final moment." Explains also how much pressure he is under to attend various political and patriotic functions throughout the nation. "I yesterday sent off seven answers to such invitations, and have several others yet to answer. If I could divide myself into twenty parts, I should find full employment for each." Wishes he could go to "every state, county, city, village of the Union and stimulate my fellow citizens to the most vigorous exertions. For, in my conscience, I do believe that everything dear to free men is now at issue and will be determined in November." Copy. Extract printed in catalogue of The Rendells, Inc., *The American Frontier . . . Exploration and Settlement to the Mississippi River* [Newton, Mass., 1982]. Vol. I, Item 348, p. 284.

To JACOB SMOCK, JR.,[1] *et al.* Lexington, July 24, 1840

In reply to your letter, I take pleasure in expressing the opinion that Genl Harrisons election is certain, if proper exertions are made. My belief, founded upon extensive information, is that he will obtain the votes of at least twenty States,[2] unless there should be culpable neglect. Of the importance of his election to the welfare of the Union and to the preservation of our free institutions I have so often expressed my sincere opinion that it is not necessary now to repeat it.

ALS. InHi. 1. For Jacob Smock, Jr., of Mercer County, Ky., who served as a private in the War of 1812, see G. Glenn Clift (ed.), *Kentucky Soldiers of the War of 1812* (Baltimore, 1969), 304. 2. See Speech in Baltimore, May 4, 1840.

To S.D. Morgan *et al.*, Nashville, July 25, 1840. Thanks them for their invitation to attend the Whig convention in Nashville on August 17. Notes that prior to his departure from Washington he had turned down "a similar invitation" from another committee at Nashville [Clay to McNairy, July 10, 1840] for reasons of personal fatigue, distance, and summer heat. Regrets that he must decline this invitation as well. Concludes: "I concur with you fully, Gentlemen, in all the sentiments you have expressed. The alternatives, in the contest in which we are engaged, are honesty, fidelity and ability, in the Administration of public affairs, or corruption, treachery and incompetency, Liberty or Slavery, an elective Monarch or a Constitutional President. In such alternatives, Republican Tennessee, cannot hesitate. Her neighbour and Sister Kentucky will, the week after next, announce her firm determination in thundering tones, not to be mistaken." ALS. KyU. See Speech in Nashville, August 17, 1840.

To William C. Worthington, July 25, 1840. Says he cannot accept the invitation to speak in Jefferson County, Ky. Explains he had left Washington a few days before adjournment because of "fatigues incident to arduous service" and returned to Lexington. Assures him that the Whig cause has great prospects in the West. Reports news of a decisive victory in state elections in Louisiana and believes Kentucky will achieve a "victory not less decisive." ALS. KyU. Worthington was most likely the William Worthington who was nephew to Gov. Thomas Worthington of Ohio. It is known that Gov. Worthington's daughters were friends of Mrs. Henry Clay and that his nephew, William, had resided in Kentucky as early as 1812. Alfred B. Sears, *Thomas Worthington, Father of Ohio Statehood* (Columbus, Ohio, 1958), 150, 178.

In the 1840 elections in Louisiana, Whigs won 27 seats in the state house of representatives to 23 for the Democrats, while the latter carried the state senate by 9 seats to 8. There was no gubernatorial election in 1840. In the contest for the U.S. House, 2 Whigs and 1 Democrat were elected. New Orleans *Daily Picayune,* July 26, 1840; *Guide to U.S. Elections,* 573. In addition, the legislature chose Alexander Barrow, a Whig, for the U.S. Senate. *Guide to U.S. Elections,* 465.

In the 1840 elections in Kentucky, Whig Robert P. Letcher defeated Democrat Richard French for governor by a vote of 54,999 to 39,158. *BDGUS,* 2:518. Whigs won 23 seats in the state senate and 76 seats in the state house of representatives to 14 in the senate and 24 in the house for the Democrats. *Niles' Register* (September 5, 1840), 59:2-3. James T. Morehead, a Whig, was elected to the U.S. Senate by the Kentucky legislature. *Guide to U.S. Elections,* 464. See also Shannon and McQuown, *Presidential Politics in Kentucky,* 13-15.

To JOHN SLOANE Lexington, July 27, 1840

I received here your letter addressed to me at Washington. The place at which my letter is dated indicates my return home. I could not accept the invitation to Steubenville. Having been absent more than Eight months from home, and being much worn down by arduous service, I could not think of prolonging my separation from my family and encountering new fatigues. You can have no conception of the number of pressing invitations I receive to attend Conventions and other public meetings of the People. I have been at home about a week, and I have answered more than twenty; and before I left Washington, for weeks a day never elapsed without my receiving more or less invitations to all parts of the Union. If I could divide myself into a hundred parts, I could find full employment for each.

In one aspect, these movements of the people are full of interest. They shew that a spirit is abroad which will expel from power the miserable faction which has got possession of the Government. And I congratulate you, who, with me fifteen years ago, endeavored to avert what has since befallen our Country, upon the encouraging prospect of a better and sounder state of things.

ALS. NjP.

To FRANCIS T. BROOKE Lexington, July 28, 1840

My anxiety to get home speedily induced me to take the route by Wheeling. If I could have had a week to spare, I should have passed by that of the W. Sulphur Springs.

Without troubling you with details, the aspect of political affairs in the West, is very good. We shall next week give a larger Whig majority in K.[1] than we have done for many years; and from what I have heard I entertain no doubt of Ohio[2] or Indiana.[3]

You shewed me at your house the original letter of Mr. Madison, declining in 1828 to be an Electoral Candidate of the Adams ticket.[4] It was characterized by all the delicacy and propriety which distinguished the conduct and writings of that eminent man. You have seen the late letter of Jackson possessing directly opposite characteristics.[5] It has occurred to me that the publication of these two letters, in juxtaposition, would be attended with good effect; and if you concur in this suggestion, I hope you will have it done in the [Richmond] Whig.

I shall remain at home during the summer. I am very much pressed to attend Conventions and other public meetings of the people. Scarcely a day elapses that I do not receive four or five invitations. If I could divide myself into a hundred parts, I should find full employment for each. . . .

ALS. NcD. 1. Clay to Tallmadge, April 9, 1839; Clay to Worthington, July 25, 1840. 2. In the 1840 elections in Ohio, the Whig candidate for governor, Thomas Corwin, won with 145,442 votes to 129,312 for the Democratic candidate, Wilson Shannon. *BDGUS*, 3:1202. Whigs won 51 seats in the state house of representatives to 21 for the Democrats. Of the 18 seats up for election in the state senate, the Whigs and Democrats each won 9, giving the Democrats a total of 22 seats and the Whigs 14. *Niles' Register* (Oct. 31, 1840), 59:119, 134. Whigs also won 13 of Ohio's U.S. House seats and the Democrats won 6. *Guide to U.S. Elections*, 573-74. 3. In the 1840 state elections in Indiana, Whigs won 15 seats in the state senate and the Democrats won 2, giving the Whigs a majority of 31 seats to 15. The Whigs won 78 seats in the state house of representatives, while the Democrats won 22. *Niles' Register* (Sept. 12, 1840), 59:21. A Whig won the special election for a U.S. House seat from the 7th congressional district. Also, Whig Samuel Bigger was elected governor over Democrat Tilghman A. Howard by a vote of 62,932 to 54,274. *BDGUS*, 1:400. 4. See 6:1356; 7:124. 5. On Feb. 22, 1828, James Madison had written to Francis T. Brooke declining to be a candidate for presidential elector and saying, in effect, that ex-presidents should not participate in partisan politics. *Letters And Other Writings of James Madison . . .*, 4 vols. (Philadelphia, 1865), 3:622-23. The Jackson letter to which Clay refers is probably that of June 23, 1840, to the editor of the Nashville *Union* in which he participated directly in the 1840 election by criticizing Harrison's abilities as both statesman and military leader and by openly endorsing Van Buren's reelection. Nashville *Union*, June 25, 1840.

To M. SHAW Lexington, July 29, 1840

[Regrets to hear of Shaw's poor health. Continues:]

Contrary to your apprehensions, I sincerely hope that you may not only live to witness the overthrow of our present faithless rulers, but much longer, to experience the benefit and the blessing of the wise administration, which I trust will ensue. It has been long an ardent desire with me to be spared so long as to see the Government of our Country once more in honest and competent hands; and I am thankful to Providence for his goodness in prolonging my life to a period at which we may, I think, with great confidence anticipate a better and brighter state of public affairs. For I consider the election of Genl. Harrison as certain as any future human event can be. Every day brings some fresh intelligence, or some new event, to strengthen this opinion. I shall be greatly disappointed if Mr. V. Buren should receive the vote of more than six States.[1]

I request your acceptance of my thanks for the honor done me in bestowing my name on one of your sons. May he realize the fondest wishes of your heart, be an ornament to his Country and a blessing to his connections! I add an expression of my fervent wishes for the complete restoration of your health.

ALS. Courtesy of Mr. and Mrs. George Schaust, Minneapolis, Minn. 1. He carried seven; Harrison carried the other 19. See Speech in Baltimore, May 4, 1840.

To JAMES COLLIER Lexington, July 30, 1840

I received your favor, transmitting evidences of the expressed opinions of Mr. Senator [Benjamin] Tappan, in respect to the effect of the Sub treasury[1] in the reduction of wages and prices; and I concur with you in the expediency of an extensive circulation of these evidences. It would be especially advantageous to diffuse them in Pennsa. and in N. England.

It is perfectly true that similar opinions were expressed at the last Session of the Senate by Messrs. [James] Buchanan, [Robert J.] Walker and [John C.] Calhoun. I hope before the Senate meets again we will have laid the foundation, at intermediate election, of getting rid of the Sub treasury, its authors, and all their pernicious measures.

ALS. KyU. For Collier, see 5:813. 1. Clay to Porter, Dec. 27, 1838; Speech in Senate, Sept. 25, 1837, and Jan. 20, 1840.

To WILLIAM BROWNE Lexington, July 31, 1840

At the moment of my departure from Washn. I received your obliging letter of the 9h. instant. The sentiments of personal attachment towards me, which it contains, and the causes which you assign for that attachment, are highly gratifying to my feelings; and I beg you to be assured that they will be held in grateful remembrance.

That the condition of our Country may not be all that we could desire, in either contingency of the contest now going on, can not be denied. In the most successful & desirable result of the contest, we cannot be free from all apprehension as to the future. Genl Harrison, if elected, may not fulfill all our hopes. Artful men may avail themselves of weaknesses and passions, from which he is no more exempt than other men. And I lament the necessity, real or imaginary, which has been supposed to exist, of appealing to the feelings and passions of our Country men, rather than to their reasons and their judgments, to secure his election. The best, and only, justification of this course is to be found, in the practice, which was resorted to, in the instance of the election of Genl Jackson. But that does not prevent my regret that either party should have ever been induced to employ such means.

If, however, my dear sir, in the event of the election of Genl Harrison, we shall not be without our fears and free from all danger, I must say that, in the contrary event, I shall have lost all hopes of the Country. In my conscience, I do believe, that, if Mr. V. Buren be re elected, the Government will be ruined. Corruption, Demagoguism, and Humbuggery will receive an accelerated movement, and the only alternative remaining will be to submit quietly to that horrible state of things, or to make open & decided resistance by force. In short, according to my opinion, the difference in the election of the one or the other of the two Candidates is, that with Harrison there is hope, much hope, with V. Buren there is no hope whatever.

Such was the view of the matter which brought my mind to the conclusion of supporting the election of Genl Harrison, notwithstanding any objections which might have existed as to the means which were employed to bring about his nomination at Harrisburg.[1] With all these means, I am perfectly acquainted; but they did not occasion me to hesitate one moment. And I must add that subsequent reflection and observation have fully confirmed me in the correctness of my decision.

It is pleasing to our private feelings of attachment & friendship to see the person elevated to the highest office whom our partiality prefers. I know that I have many inestimable friends who have looked towards me with that fond anticipation. I am grateful for their preference. If their wishes had been realized, I should have exerted my utmost ability to fulfill their hopes and to justify their confidence; but circumstances beyond their control have ordered it otherwise, and as good Citizens and good men we ought to submit to what is inevitable, and which, contrary to our apprehensions, may turn out to be best. Above all we should ever recollect that our private friendships should be held in strict subordination to our public duties. These in my opinion clearly & emphatically demand the election of Genl Harrison; and I shall be most happy, my dear sir, if, concurring in these sentiments, you will enter the contest with all the zeal and influence which you can exert.

ALS. NcD. 1. Porter to Clay, Nov. 14 and Dec. 30, 1837, and Feb. 16, 1839.

To Robert C. Winthrop *et al.*, Boston, August 5, 1840. Regretfully turns down their invitation to speak at the Massachusetts Whig convention to be held at Bunker Hill on September 10th. Reports that the Kentucky general election [Clay to Tallmadge, April 9, 1839; Clay to Worthington, July 25, 1840] is in its third and final day and that "Judging from the partial returns which have reached me, there will be a greater Whig majority than was ever given in this State." ALS. InHi.

From William Henry Harrison, North Bend, Ohio, August 6, 1840. Reports that Van Buren is due for a "sad disappointment" in the Indiana and Ohio state elections [Clay to Brooke, July 28, 1840], since returns from but ten counties in Indiana have gone "by decided Majorities in our favor." Thinks Democratic strategy in Ohio has unwisely centered on the Locofoco campaign of "representing me as . . . entirely decrepid & imbecile." Concludes that "As the best means of obviating the effects of this story I accepted the invitation to Fort Meigs & lately to Greeneville [*sic*, Greenville]. In going & returning from each place I met at the intermediate towns large bodies of the people & at their request addressed them. On this day week I travelled 30 Miles & made three speeches two of them occupied (each) two hours. I am fortunate in having no failure in the strength of my voice & made myself heard to the outer edge of the Multitudes I addressed when others could not. Providence indeed seems to counteract the calumnies against me in every way. My bodily health being at present actually better than it has been for ten years." ALS. DLC-HC (DNA, M212, R5).

To LUCRETIA HART CLAY Nashville, August 16, 1840

We arrived here yesterday afternoon. We travelled slow and leisurely, and I bore the fatigues of the journey better than I anticipated. We were met at Tyrees Springs (21 miles from this place) by some of the Comee. who attended us to town. About 2 miles from the City we met a prodigious escort, military and Civil, on horseback, in carriages and on foot, with music bands &c. It was one of the largest and longest processions I ever witnessed. Two of the Commee, Mrs. Smith and I rode in an open Barouche, and passing through the principal Streets, we were received with the greatest enthusiasm, amidst the roar of Cannon, the ringing of the Bells and Martial music.[1]

We met Mr. Erwin and the boys here.[2] I have not yet seen Mrs. Hitchcock, who I believe is with them. John[3] and I stay at Dr. [Boyd] McNairys. Mr. Erwin has taken possession of Mr. [John] Bells house,[4] and Mr. & Mrs. Smith, Mrs. Combs[5] and Miss Scott,[6] Col. Farrow[?] and Mr. Duncan[7] stay with him (Mr Erwin) Nothing could exceed the cordiality of my reception.

I am very hoarse yet. It was increased by Mr. [John J.] Crittenden and myself being compelled to speak at various points on the Road. Mr. Crittenden left me at Bells to go by Gallatin, where there was to be yesterday a great Assemblage which he was to address.[8] I could not encounter the service, as I wished to reserve myself for tomorrow. How I shall be able to acquit myself I do not know.

Mr Brenan arrived yesterday and brought Johns new Coat.

They desire to detain me here some time, but it is my intention to leave here towards the last of next week.

Henry and James Erwin have grown a good deal. Mr Erwin thinks of leaving here in a few days.

ALS. DLC-TJC (DNA, M212, R10). 1. For the most complete account of Clay's trip to Nashville for the Whig convention which was attended by delegates from various states, see Nashville *Whig*, August 17, 24, 1840. 2. Son-in-law James Erwin and grandsons Henry Clay Erwin and James Erwin, Jr. 3. Probably John Morrison Clay. 4. Because of financial difficulties John Bell had sold his Nashville home to his brother-in-law, James Erwin, in 1837 for the sum of $24,000, but the Bells had apparently continued to live in the house for some time thereafter. Parks, *John Bell*, 117, 163, 174. 5. Probably Mrs. Leslie Combs of Ky. 6. Possibly a relative of Dr. D.T. Scott, one of the marshals of the Nashville Whig convention. Nashville *Banner*, August 6, 1840. 7. Probably Garnet Duncan of Ky. who was one of the vice presidents of the convention. Jonesborough (Tenn.) *The Whig*, August 26, 1840. 8. Crittenden's speech in Gallatin, Tenn., has not been found.

Speech in Nashville, August 17, 1840. Defends his vote in 1825 for John Quincy Adams, pointing out that he had merely obeyed the wishes of his constituents in the matter. Explains: "It was true that the Legislature of Kentucky at the time, made a request that [I] should give a different vote; but that body, in making the request, went beyond its province; it had no right to interfere in the matter; the right belonged exclusively to [my] constituents, in the counties of Fayette, Woodford, and Jessamine. Each of these counties sustained, approved, and ratified [my] conduct at the time, and neither of them has ever, to this day, revoked or annulled that approbation." As for his motives in this matter, he would say nothing at this time. They were, however, "known to, and would be adjudged by, [my] God." Assures his audience that he possesses "no unkind feelings" toward

Andrew Jackson, "the illustrious captain in this neighborhood [Tennessee]." What shall I talk about today, he asks this "assembly of so many thousands." Shall I "dwell upon a ruined currency, upon the prostration of business, the stagnation of trade, and the destruction of commerce? Or shall I speak of the wasteful extravagance of the present powers that be?" Contrasts the modest expenditures of the John Quincy Adams administration with those of the wasteful Van Buren administration. Decides to mention the "very extraordinary doctrines now advanced by those who profess to entertain the greatest veneration and regard for the State rights doctrines," especially those who supported "the ridiculous manoeuver, in the United States Senate, at the late session, on the subject of the debts of the several States [Remark in Senate, February 18, 1840]. A long report was made, that the general government would not assume the payment of those debts—a thing that nobody ever dreamed of!" Links Sen. Felix Grundy (Tenn.) to this proposal and ridicules him for his stance. Upon learning that lawyer Grundy was away from Nashville and was in East Tennessee stumping for the Van Buren administration, Clay remarks: "Ah! . . . at his old occupation, defending criminals!"

Attacks Van Buren's effort in 1837 to get a "bankrupt law bearing exclusively upon State banks as evidence of his regard for State rights," as well as his Sub-Treasury bill [Speech in Senate, September 25, 1837; Comment in Senate, March 7, 1838], as examples of the president's actual hostility to states' rights. Asserts that members of the party in power wrongly profess to be "democrats *par excellence*!"; whereas, he [Clay] was a "true democrat" who had "learned his democracy in the school of '98 and '99," at the time of the Virginia and Kentucky Resolutions against the Sedition Act. Criticizes the "new democracy" as one designed only to deliver votes and pay for them "with inducements and bribes, which Jefferson's democracy did not." Points to several instances of defalcations by employees in the public land offices. Also mentions the fact that Edward Livingston was appointed secretary of state by Jackson in 1831, at a time when the president knew him to be in a state of default [Clay to The Public, August 20, 1840]. Asks the Democrats in his audience: "Have all your hopes been realized, in regard to the administration of the government? Have the pledges that were made you been fulfilled? Take, for example, the one term for the presidency. Did not the great captain promise you that one term was enough for a president to serve? Was it carried out? How was the promise, not to appoint members of Congress to office, carried out? How was the promise, to reduce the extravagant expenditures fulfilled? What principle was carried out? what promise kept? what pledge redeemed? Is there an administration man in this vast assemblage that will answer. . . .[?]" Urges Tennesseeans to march with Kentuckians against the "boisterous office-holders, the praetorian band, the palace slaves" of Van Buren. Notes that earlier in history "They stood side by side; their sons fought side by side at New Orleans. Kentuckians and Tennesseeans now fight another and a different kind of battle. But they are fighting now, as then, a band of mercenaries, the cohorts of power. They are fighting a band of office-holders, who call General Harrison a coward, an imbecile, an old woman! Yes, General Harrison is a coward! but he fought more battles than any other general during the last war, and never sustained a defeat! He is no statesman! and yet he has filled more civil offices of trust and importance than almost any other man in the Union! [A man in the crowd here cried out, "Tell us of Van Buren's battles!"] Ah! . . . I will have to use my colleague's language, and tell you of Mr. Van Buren's three great battles! He says that he fought general commerce, and conquered him; that he fought general currency, and conquered him; and that, with his Cuba allies, he fought the Seminoles, and got conquered!" Copy. Printed in Colton, *Clay Correspondence*, 6:215-19. No manuscript version of this address has been found. For Andrew Jackson's response to two of the charges made by Clay herein, see Clay's Address to the Public, August 20, 1840. For Van Buren's 1837 plan to exercise direct federal control over state banks in matters dealing with the suspension of and resumption of specie payments, and the issuance of paper money, see Wilson, *The Presidency of Martin Van Buren*, 73, 77, 81, 83, 137, 143; also Speech in Senate, September 25, 1837; Comment in Senate, March 7, 1838; Remark in Senate, February 18, 1840.

To THE PUBLIC Nashville, August 20, 1840

Your surprize, I am quite sure, will be as great as mine was, on the perusal of a note, signed Andrew Jackson, addressed to the Editor of the Nashville Union, and bearing date on the 18h. inst.[1]

The circumstances of my present visit to Nashville are well known here. I declined repeated invitations to attend the Convention holden on the 17h. inst,[2] and finally yielded to an unusual appeal, with which I was honored, and which it would be difficult for any man to resist.

I was called upon to address the [Whig] Convention.[3] In what terms of respect and, for his military services, of praise I spoke of the distinguished individual who is the occasion of this note all who heard me can testify. Among the subjects which I discussed, was that of the degeneracy in public virtue, and especially the delinquency and infidelity in public officers, of which within the last few years we have had such lamentable proof. In assigning the causes for this deplorable state of things, I stated, as among them, the subversion of the rule laid down by Mr. Jefferson of honesty, capacity & fidelity to the Constitution, and the substitution to it of one founded on devotion and subserviency not to the Country but to the chief of a party. That persons appointed to office too often considered themselves as being only put in possession of their legitimate share of the spoils of victory instead of feeling bound by the obligations of a sacred trust confided for the benefit of the people. In respect to defaulters, I referred to the case of Mr. [Edward] Livingston., of whose attainments as a jurist, not more consistent with truth than my feelings, I spoke in the highest terms. He was one of the earliest & one of the greatest defaulters.[4] His case occurred under Mr. Jefferson's administration. The records both of the Executive & Judicial departments established his default. He remained a defaulter about a quarter of a century if not more. How he finally liquidated the bal. against him, and when, I do not certainly know but I believe it was by property & under the first term of Genl Jackson. But whenever and however it was, a tardy payment or composition of the debt could not and did not expunge the fact of his original default.

In arguing from cause to effect, I contended that the appointment of Mr. Livingston was a pernicious precedent. That it was a virtual proclamation to all who were or might be defaulters that their infidelity, in a public trust, constituted no insuperable barrier to a promotion to one of the highest offices in Govt. I did not attribute to Genl. Jackson a knowledge of the default. I went even so far as to say that he might not have reflected upon the consequences of the appointment of an individual so situated. I must now say that, until Genl Jackson otherwise asserts, I am constrained to believe that he could not have been ignorant of a fact, so conspicuous in the annals of our Country, as that of the default of Edward Livingston Esq. as Attorney of the U. States, in the district of N. York, during the administration of Mr. Jefferson, to the amt of about $100,000

It was in the train of the same thought & argument, that I adduced the example of the appointment of Mr. S[amuel]. Swartwout to the Office of Collector of the most important port in the U. States, as one of most unfortunate & injurious example. His participation in the schemes of Col. [Aaron] Burr was a fact of such universal notority[5] that I supposed, and yet suppose, no man, the least conversant with the history of the Country, could be ignorant of it. But it was not upon Genl Jackson's knowledge of that fact, it was upon the *fact itself* that I dwelt.

It is now said that the appointment of Mr. Swartwout was recommended by Citizens of N. York. I know nothing of these recommendations. Whether they were cause or effect—whether they were gotten up—to produce or to give color & cover to the appointment previously determined to be made—their secret history only could disclose. The appointment occasioned general surprize among the friends & foes of the administration, at the time, and the sequel demonstrates how unwise it was.[6]

These topics of my address to the Convention on monday last have been selected by Genl Jackson for comment and animadversion. He was not present on the occasion. He has made no application to me for a correct account of what I actually said, but has been contented to rely upon "being informed," by whom, with what motives, and with what objects, I have no means of conjecturing. Whether his informer may not be some friend of Mr. V Buren who, in the present desperate state of his political fortunes, wishes to bring the General into the field and to turn the tide of just indignation on the part of the People from the Generals protegé, the exhibition of his name only would enable the public to decide.

With regard to the insinuations,[7] and gross epithets contained in Genl. Jackson's note, alike impotent malevolent, and derogatory from the dignity[8] of a man who has filled the highest office in the Universe,[9] respect for the public and for myself allow me only to say that, like other similar missiles, they have fallen harmless at my feet, exciting no other sensation than that of scorn and contempt.

ALS. THi. Reprinted in the *Virginia Free Press*, Charles Town, (Jefferson County), Va. (W.Va.), Sept. 10, 1840, from the Nashville *Union* of August 19, as reprinted by the Nashville *Whig* of August 21, 1840. 1. Reprinted from the Nashville *Union* in the Nashville *Whig* of August 21. In this letter Jackson castigated Clay for the charge made in his Nashville speech of August 17, that he (Jackson) had appointed Edward Livingston to the office of secretary of state knowing him to be a defaulter. "I am justified in declaring the charge to be false." Speaks also to Clay's charge in that speech that he had appointed Samuel Swartwout to be collector of the Port of New York, knowing him to have been an associate of Aaron Burr. States: "To this charge it is proper to say that I knew of Mr. Swartwout's connection with Aaron Burr, precisely as I did that of Mr. Clay *himself* [1:253, 256-59, 272-75], who if the history of the times did not do him great injustice, was far from avoiding an association with Burr when he was at the town of Lexington in Kentucky. Yet Mr. Clay was appointed Secretary of State, and I may say confidently with recommendations for character and fitness not more favorable than those produced to me by the citizens of New York in behalf of Mr. Swartwout. Mr. Clay too at the time of his own appointment to that high office, it will be recollected, was directly charged throughout the Union with having bargained for it [4:45-48, 143-66; 5:655-58], and by none was this charge more earnestly made than by his present associates in Tennessee, Messrs. [John] Bell and [Ephraim H.] Foster. Under such circumstances how contemptible does this demagogue appear, when he descends from his high place in the Senate and roams over the country, retailing slanders against the living and the dead." [The printed version of Clay's speech of August 17 in Nashville includes no direct reference to Samuel Swartwout.] 2. Following this word, the phrase "with which I was honored" is struck through. 3. Speech in Nashville, August 17, 1840. 4. For criminal acts (the theft of $44,000) in the collection and handling of federal taxes by a Treasury Department clerk assigned to the office of the U.S. attorney for the district of New York, at a time (1803) when Livingston was serving as the U.S. attorney there and was legally responsible for the agent's defalcation, see William B. Hatcher, *Edward Livingston, Jeffersonian Republican and Jacksonian Democrat* (Baton Rouge, 1940), 93-99. In Feb. 1830, he finally paid off a court judgment (handed down in 1803) against himself in the amount of $100,000. *Ibid.*, 174-89. 5. See 1:272-75, 280-81. 6. For Swartwout's defalcations while collector of the Port of New York, see Remark in Senate, Dec. 13, 1838; Wilson, *The Presidency of Martin Van Buren*, 125-29. 7. Following the word "insinuations" is the word "innuendos," struck through. 8. The word "character" is struck through and replaced with "dignity." 9. Following the word "universe," the phrase, "and they are derogatory from the character of any respect for the public and for myself [word illeg.] constrain me to hurl them back upon their author with [word illeg.] scorn and contempt" is struck through.

To ROBERT C. WINTHROP Lexington, September 1, 1840

Upon my return home from the Convention at Nashville, 210 miles S.W. of this place,[1] I found here your obliging letter of the 10h. Ulto.[2] urging my attendance upon the Bunker Hill Convention on the 10h. instant. I had previously replied to an invitation, and expressed my regrets that I could not accept it. During the last nine months I have been with my family only about three weeks! I am quite persuaded that you will regard that single Circumstance, independent of all others, (and there are several others) as forming a sufficient excuse for my non attendance. I know how much I lose by my absence—I know the cordiality, hospitality and friendly consideration with which I should be received and entertained at Boston. For I shall never forget the pleasure which I enjoyed when I was last there, nor your kind agency in producing it.

We have much cause of felicitation on the bright prospects of the success of the Whig Cause. I adhere, with strengthened confidence, to the opinion I expressed in May, that Mr. V. Buren will not obtain more than the votes of six States.[3] I believe that the majority in Tennessee will not be far behind that of Kentucky.[4]

ALS. MHi. 1. Speech in Nashville, August 17, 1840. 2. Not found; but see Winthrop *et al.* to Clay, August 5, 1840. 3. Speech in Baltimore, May 4, 1840. 4. The Harrison majority was 25,873 (he received 64.2% of the vote) in Kentucky and 12,102 (55.6%) in Tennessee. McKee, *National . . . Popular and Electoral Vote*, 44.

To William Goodrich, Knoxville, Tenn., September 3, 1840. Regrets that "Indispensable engagements" make it impossible for him to attend the Knox County (Tenn.) Whig convention at Cumberland Gap, Tenn., on September 10. ALS. Courtesy of Thomas D. Clark, Lexington, Ky. Goodrich was a Knoxville businessman who, in 1852 along with Joseph L. King, founded the Miners and Manufacturers Bank in Knoxville. Information supplied by Special Collections Dept., University of Tennessee Library, Knoxville, Tenn. For the Cumberland Gap convention, see Frankfort *Commonwealth*, September 8, 15, 22, 1840.

On September 7, Clay also sent his regrets to Messrs. Bradley, Whitesides *et al.* for their invitation to the Cumberland Gap convention. Copy. Printed in Knoxville *Register*, September 23, 1840.

On September 7, Clay wrote Oliver H. Smith in Connersville, Indiana, that "no old plough or coal-horse ever wanted rest more than I do," and for that reason he could not attend the celebration of the Battle of the Thames in Indianapolis on October 5. Copy. Printed in Smith, *Early Indiana Trials*, 255.

On September 26, Clay wrote Philip W. Engs in New York City, declining an invitation to a celebration of the Battle of the Thames in New York on October 5. Adds a political observation: "I rejoice in all the popular movements, by which the current year is so much distinguished, demonstrating a fixed determination of the People to dismiss faithless and incompetent rulers. And I rejoice with you in the bright & glorious prospects of their speedy and ignominious dismission. Maine was one of the six States which, in a spirit of great liberality, I assigned to Mr. Van Buren; but she scorns the association. I never doubted her patriotism, but I feared the Custom house influence which encircles almost all her borders." Copy. Printed in The Rendells, *The American Frontier*, 1:286. For Engs, a wine merchant whose business was located at 112 Front, New York City, see Longworth, *American Almanac: New-York Register, and City Directory*, 1838-41 ed. In the 1840 elections in Maine, Whigs and Democrats each won 4 seats in the U.S. House. *Guide to U.S. Elections*, 573. Also, Whigs won 14 seats in the state senate to 7 for the Democrats as well as carrying the state house of representatives by a margin of 94 seats to 66. *Niles' Register* (September 26, 1840), 59:51. In the gubernatorial election, Whig Edward Kent won a plurality of 67 votes over Democrat John Fairfield; but, because no candidate received a majority of the popular vote, the election was thrown into the Whig-dominated state legislature which chose Kent. *BDGUS*, 2:601.

To HENRY HENSON Lexington, September 5, 1840

I have received your letter, written at the instance of the Tippecanoe Club of Rushville, requesting a communication of my opinion of the probable issue of the existing Presidental contest. I take pleasure in replying to it, but I am compelled to do so briefly.

As far back as May of the present year, I expressed publicly the opinion that Mr. V. Buren would not obtain the votes of more than six of the twenty six states composing the Union.[1] That opinion was not lightly expressed. It was the result of a deliberate consideration of extensive information derived from all parts of the Country. I now not only adhere to it, but it has been strengthened and confirmed by additional information, and by the events of important elections which have taken place since it was first announced. I do not mean to say, that Genl Harrison is absolutely certain to obtain the votes of twenty States; but my intention is, to express my conviction, that he is certain to receive the votes of most of that number, and that there is much greater probability that he will receive the votes of the residue of the twenty, than that Mr. V. Buren will.

Since I expressed that opinion, Louisiana,[2] Kentucky,[3] North Carolina,[4] Indiana,[5] Alabama,[6] Illinois,[7] Missouri[8] and Rhode Island[9] have, respectively, held their elections. The Harrison majority in Louisiana, Kentucky, North Carolina, Indiana, and Rhode Island has exceeded my most sanguine expectations. I have been disappointed only in Illinois, and the disappointment there is neutralized by the unexpected Whig success in Alabama. The result in Illinois is attributable to local questions of policy, and to the illegal admission of unnaturalized foreigners to vote. I firmly believe that her vote will be cast in Novr. for W. H. Harrison.[10] Nor shall I be surprized if a similar result should take place in Alabama.[11]

It was therefore in a spirit of liberal calculation that I supposed Mr. V.

Buren might obtain the votes of six States, and the six I alluded to are Maine, N. Hampshire, South Carolina, Alabama, Arkansas and Missouri.[12] In most of those States our Whig friends are making strenuous and patriotic exertions, and in some of them they may possibly succeed, but I have anticipated a different event.

Judging from all the information which I collected, at the late great Convention at Nashville,[13] and previously, I believe that Genl Harrison will receive the votes of every Southern & S. Western State except So. Carolina Alabama and Arkansas. A finer or more patriotic spirit never existed than now prevails in Tennessee.[14] Her proud and independent sons scorn all dictation but that which proceeds from their own unbiased bosoms.

But cheering and bright as the prospects of success are, it might be fatal to the salvation of the Constitution and the Country, to relax in honorable exertions. Every Whig throughtout the whole Union should act upon the conviction that, upon his sole efforts, the liberty and the prosperity of the Nation may depend. You, in New York, and they, in other States, should recollect that we, in the West, are battling in confidence that you and they will do your whole duty. The Whig, therefore, who in this, perhaps, the last struggle for pure uncorrupted self government and Civil liberty, neglects to preform his duty, is guilty of a double treachery—a treachery to his Country and a treachery to his Whig brethren in other parts of the Union, who are exerting all their energies to ensure success to our glorious Cause

ALS. KyBgW—Ellis Hartford Collection. Addressed in strange hand to Henson at Rushville, Gates [*sic*, Yates] County, N.Y. 1. Speech in Baltimore, May 4, 1840. 2. Clay to Worthington, July 25, 1840. 3. Clay to Tallmadge, April 9, 1837; Clay to Gholson, July 21, 1840; Clay to Worthington, July 25, 1840. 4. In North Carolina John M. Morehead, a Whig, was elected governor in 1840 with 44,484 votes to 35,903 for R.M. Saunders, the Democratic candidate. *BDGUS*, 3:1130. Whigs also won control of the legislature by a margin of 6 seats in the senate and 32 seats in the house. Raleigh *Register and North Carolina Gazette*, August 28, 1840. 5. Clay to Brooke, July 28, 1840. 6. The 1840 state legislative elections in Alabama resulted in the Democrats controlling approximately 21 seats in the senate to 12 for the Whigs; in the house the Democrats controlled about 53 seats to 47 for the Whigs. This was a significant increase for the Whigs in the lower house. *Niles' Register* (Oct. 10, 1840), 59:88; Mills, *Politics and Power*, 93. 7. Elections to the Illinois state legislature in 1840 resulted in the Democrats winning 25 senate seats to 15 for the Whigs and 49 house seats to 42 to the Whigs. *Niles' Register* (Sept. 12, 1840), 59:21. 8. Two Democrats were elected in the 1840 congressional elections in Missouri. *Guide to U.S. Elections*, 573. The Democrats also won the governorship when Thomas Reynolds was elected with 29,656 votes over Whig John B. Clark with 22,265 votes. *BDGUS*, 2:841. In the state legislature the Democrats held a majority of 13 on joint ballot. *Niles' Register* (Sept. 12, 1840), 59:21. 9. In the 1840 Rhode Island elections Whig candidate, Samuel W. King, won the governorship with 4,797 votes to 3,418 for Thomas F. Carpenter, the Democratic candidate. *BDGUS*, 4:1341. Whigs won all 11 seats in the state senate and 49 seats in the house while the Democrats won 23 house seats. *Niles' Register* (Sept. 19, 1840), 59:38. 10. Van Buren carried Illinois and its 5 electoral votes by 47,476 to 45,537. 11. Van Buren carried Alabama and its 7 electoral votes by 33,991 to 28,471. 12. See Speech in Baltimore, May 4, 1840. 13. See Speech in Nashville, August 17, 1840. 14. Clay to Winthrop, Sept. 1, 1840.

To ROBERT P. LETCHER Lexington, September 7, 1840

I received your letter with a paper exhibiting the financial condition of the State, which is certainly not very unfavorable. Still I think you ought not to encourage too strong a hope of the practicability of effecting a Loan for some months.[1] To the previous difficulties, in the way, is now to be added the fact that the Banks of Philada. have resolved to resume specie payments on the 15h. Jan.[2] All other sound suspended Banks will follow the example. Capitalists, always timid, will be cautious until the effect of resumption is developed.

It will aid the negotiation of a Loan if you would in your message make a strong flourish about the honor and good faith of the State, and your determination to uphold its credit and to contribute all in your power to maintain inviolably all its obligations; accompanied by a strong recommendation to make full and adequate provision for any deficiencies in existing sources of Revenue.[3] It would add still more if the Genl. Assembly would lay some taxes specifically pledged to the payment of interest on State Bonds.[4] I indicated some of these taxes, such as an Auction tax, a tax on successions, on Carriages, on Licenses to sell spirituous Liquors, on Lawyers &c.

I will immediately open a correspondence with some of the Eastern Capitalists and ascertain what can be done.

I believe I suggested the expediency of a recommendation to the Legislature of provision for the Election of members of the H. of R. in the contingency of an extra Session of Congress.[5]

Have you seen the correspondence between Biddle & Webster?[6] Biddle's letter contains some fine thoughts & expressions about State credit, honor, faith &c.

ALS. NcD. 1. In his first annual message, Dec. 8, 1840, Letcher projected a deficit in state revenue of $17,000 for the coming year. On Feb. 18, 1841, the legislature passed an act empowering him to sell state bonds and assign the proceeds to the Board of Internal Improvement. Although no new contracts for public works were authorized during Letcher's administration, the sum of $420,000 was appropriated in 1842 to finish obligatory contracts and to prevent damage to unfinished public works. To raise this sum, the governor was empowered to sell 30-year bonds, at 6% interest. In his last annual message, Dec. 30, 1843, Letcher reported an improved financial situation for the state with a surplus for the year of $64,600.10. Will D. Gilliam, Jr., "Robert Perkins Letcher, Whig Governor of Kentucky," *FCHQ* (Jan., 1950), 24:6-27. 2. The United States Bank of Pennsylvania resumed specie payment on Jan. 15, 1841, but was forced to suspend such payments on Feb. 4, 1841. At this point the bank essentially closed its doors, although attempts were made throughout the spring and summer of 1841 to resume business. See Clay to Porter, Feb. 7, 1841. On Feb. 5, 1841, a run began on other Philadelphia banks which were also attempting to resume paying specie. Banks in the South and West originally planned to resume at the same time as the United States Bank of Pennsylvania but decided it was not expedient to do so. Hammond, *Banks and Politics in America*, 500-501, 511-12; Govan, *Nicholas Biddle*, 329. 3. Letcher included all of these recommendations in his message to the legislature on Dec. 8, 1840. He especially emphasized that the state should incur no new debts and should take decisive action so that it could pay the interest and ultimately the principal on its loans. Frankfort *Commonwealth*, Dec. 8, 1840; Gilliam, "Robert Perkins Letcher," 9. 4. The legislature passed a bill raising the property tax rate from ten cents per $100 taxable property to fifteen cents per hundred. The extra five cents was to go to the Sinking Fund to pay off the internal improvement bonds. The bill was approved Feb. 17, 1841. Ky. Gen. Assy., *Acts . . .* 1840-41, pp. 59-60. 5. In the special election, held April 28, 1841, to choose Kentucky's representatives in the U.S. House, the Democrats won 2 seats and the Whigs 12. *Guide to U.S. Elections*, 575. The "extra session" (officially the first session) of the 27th Congress convened on May 31, 1841, and adjourned on Sept. 13, 1841. 6. In his letter to Webster on August 7, 1840, Biddle argued that the United States could be proud that it had always paid off its foreign debts, while foreign countries now critical of the United States had not always done so. He pointed out that Pennsylvania had agreed to make up to foreign creditors the difference between specie and the state's domestic currency. *Niles' Register* (Sept. 12, 1840), 59:24-25.

From James Buchanan, Pittsburgh, September 17, 1840. Has learned "with great astonishment" that it is being said in Pittsburgh that he "had used some harsh language in relation to yourself" in a speech in Erie, Pa. Assures Clay that "I never speak of you publicly or privately except in terms of respect." ALS. DLC-HC (DNA, M212, R5).

Clay responded from Lexington on September 26, noting that such a rumor had not reached him. "I should have been slow in believing it, if it had, without your contradiction. With it, I should of course regard it as altogether unfounded." ALS. PHi. Addressed to Buchanan in Lancaster, Pa.

To The North Carolina Convention, September 21, 1840. Declines an invitation to attend a convention in Raleigh on October 5, citing his long absence from home; indeed, for "more than eight out of the last ten months." Describes the current presidential election as a contest "between the President and the People. It is a contest between Arbitrary Power and Constitutional Liberty. It is the old battle which our Revolutionary Fathers fought, except that they contended against a foreign monarch, whilst their descendants are struggling against the erection of a domestic throne; and that they fought with bayonets, whilst we are yet allowed to use more peaceful instruments." Fears that "if the Whigs of the present day should unhappily be less fortunate than their Whig sires of 1776 were, and if, as I sincerely believe, an elective monarchy should be the consequence, in which the President will designate his successor . . . when shall we be able to get rid of our American monarchy? Never, never! unless by a dissolution of the Union and civil war." Believes, however, that there are "bright and cheering prospects which assure us that our soil is not to be polluted by royalty under any form. Among these prospects, none has given more joy to patriots everywhere than the glorious issue of your recent election [Clay to Henson, September 5, 1840]." Predicts also that the "coming contest in Kentucky" will prove favorable for the Whigs [Clay to Gholson, July 21, 1840; Clay to Worthington, July 25, 1840]. Copy. Printed in Frankfort *Commonwealth,* November 3, 1840.

To SAMUEL STARKWEATHER Lexington, September 23,1840

I have received your favor of the 16h. inst. and I am greatly obliged by the information which it communicates.

I adhere still to the opinion expressed by me several months ago that Mr. V. Buren will not obtain the votes of more than six States in the Union.[1] Every thing that has since occurred—every election that has since taken place tends to strengthen & confirm it. Of those six States, Maine and Alabama are two,[2] and he can no longer count with confidence upon either of them in November.

Our information, derived from the Southern part of Ohio, coincides with yours from the Northern, that Genl Harrison will obtain its vote by an overwhelming majority.[3]

We rely upon the vote of N. York,[4] notwithstanding we are prepared to hear of the Administration carrying the City.[5]

ALS. NHi. 1. See Speech in Baltimore, May 4, 1840. 2. Clay to Goodrich, Sept. 3, 1840; Clay to Henson, Sept. 5, 1840. 3. Clay to Brooke, July 28, 1840. 4. For the outcome of the presidential and state elections in New York State, see Hall to Clay, Nov. 20, 1839. 5. Van Buren carried New York City over Harrison by 21,936 votes to 20,961 with James G. Birney receiving 170; 223 votes were scattered. New York *Herald,* Nov. 12, 17, 1840.

To JOSEPH GALES, JR. Lexington, September 27, 1840

I thank you for your obliging attention to my request in the case of Mr. [Edward] Livingston.[1] I have received the papers which you were good enough to send me, and think with you that they fully sustain all that I said about him.

The news from Maine is truly glorious.[2] My calculation, according to which I allowed Mr. V. Buren six States, will not be found wide of the truth.[3]

My information from Ohio is very satisfactory. Bets have been offered upon a majority of 10.000, and declined by the other party.[4]

ALS. InU. 1. Speech in Nashville, August 17, 1840; Clay to the Public, August 20, 1840. 2. Clay to Goodrich, Sept. 3, 1840. 3. See Speech in Baltimore, May 4, 1840. 4. Clay to Brooke, July 28, 1840. Harrison carried Ohio by 23,375 votes. McKee, *National . . . Popular and Electoral Vote*, 45.

To The Ladies of Cincinnati, September 28, 1840. States that although he had previously declined an invitation from a committee of Cincinnati gentlemen to attend a convention in Cincinnati on October 1, "upon learning your wishes that I should attend it, I resolved to make a new effort to rid myself of the professional engagement which constituted the impediment to my leaving home." Has, however, failed to get the court trial in which he is involved "postponed, or my professional services dispensed with." Continues: "You are right, ladies, in feeling and manifesting a lively interest in the issue of the great political struggle, of which our country is the present theatre. I hope the day will never come when American ladies will be indifferent to the fate and fortunes of our common country, nor fail, on rare and critical occasions, to demonstrate their patriotic solicitude, in a manner suitable to the delicacy and dignity of their sex. You are right, also in my humble but deliberate opinion, in the anxious desire which you entertain for the election of your neighbor and friend, Gen. Harrison. In that event, I sincerely believe, is comprehended the preservation of the morals, the purity, the prosperity, and the liberty of the nation. And who will say that, when all these great interests are involved, the female portion of the community should look on, without emotion and without sympathy, careless whether their husbands, their brothers, and their sons were corrupt and impoverished slaves, or pure and independent freemen." Copy. Printed in Frankfort *Commonwealth*, September 28, 1840.

To JOHN HOGAN[1] Lexington, October 8, 1840

I received your favor dated the last of Aug. and post marked the 3d. of Oct. and was glad to hear that our friends in Illinois stood firm, and not discouraged by the issue of your late election.[2] They have every reason to animate their spirits and stimulate their exertions.

I am afraid that I may not find any private conveyance by which I could send you any copies of the Blue Book.[3] In lieu of it, and as the best temporary substitute for it, I transmit herewith a late number of the [Washington *Daily*] Nat. Intellr. which contains some of the most valuable matter, for your purpose, which could be extracted from the Blue book.

Wishing you great success, and that, when I have the pleasure of meeting you again, we may be authorized to exchange mutual congratulations on the political state of our Country. . . .

ALS. MoSHi. 1. For Hogan, a Methodist clergyman, businessman, and later an Illinois congressman, see *DAB* and *BDAC*. 2. Clay to Henson, Sept. 5, 1840. See also Charles M. Thompson, *The Illinois Whigs Before 1846* (Urbana, 1915), 87-88. Thompson describes 1840 as the "high water mark in the history of the Illinois Whigs," and notes that "extending over a period of almost a year to the November election of 1840, they displayed an enthusiasm unequalled during any other period of their history." Nonetheless, Van Buren carried the state in 1840 by 47,476 to Harrison's 45,537. 3. Or *Bienniel Register*.

To Thomas Ewing, New Lancaster, Ohio, October 23, 1840. Congratulates him on the outcome of the state elections in Ohio [Clay to Brooke, July 28, 1840]. Thinks there are now "bright prospects of the Success, at last, of the Whig cause." Has strong hopes of carrying Pennsylvania. ALS. DLC-Ewing Family Papers (Supp. Roll 2).

In the October, 1840 state elections in Pennsylvania, Whigs won a slim 2-seat majority in the house, unless one professed conservative member was counted with the Democrats, in which event the house was evenly divided. Of the 11 seats up for election in the state senate, the Whigs won 7 and the Democrats 4, giving the Whigs a majority in the senate of 20 to 13. In the U.S. House elections, the Democrats won 16 seats to 14 for the Whigs. *Niles' Register* (October 24 and November 14, 1840), 59:117, 165-66; *Guide to U.S. Elections*, 574. Harrison carried Pennsylvania over Van Buren by a popular vote of 144,021 to 143,676. McKee, *National . . . Popular and Electoral Vote*, 44.

To Samuel L. Southard, Trenton, N.J., October 23, 1840. Thanks him for his letter containing news of the "triumph" in New Jersey. Calls attention to "the glorious news all around us." ALS. NjP.

In the 1840 state elections in New Jersey, the Whigs won 13 seats in the senate to 5 for the Democrats and also carried the house 41 to 12. The legislature reelected Whig William Pennington, Jr., as governor. In the U.S. House elections, Whigs won all 6 seats. Frankfort *Commonwealth*, November 24, 1840; *BDGUS*, 3:1017; *Guide to U.S. Elections*, 573. Harrison carried New Jersey by a popular vote of 33,351 to 31,034. McKee, *National . . . Popular and Electoral Vote*, 44.

From Benjamin Gratz, Philadelphia, October 28, 1840. Reports that Clay's grandsons, James Erwin, Henry Clay Erwin, and Henry Clay Duralde, have arrived safely in New York. Encloses a statement of the latter's travel and incidental expences in the amount of $65. Adds: "I consider the presidential contest doubtful in this state." ALS. DLC-TJC (DNA, M212, R14). Harrison beat Van Buren in Pennsylvania 144,021 to 143,676. McKee, *National . . . Popular and Electoral Vote*, 44. Clay's grandsons, James Erwin, Jr. (1824-48), Henry Clay Erwin (1827-59), and Henry Clay Duralde (b. 1824), were enroute to a private school in Jamaica, Long Island, near New York City, run by the Rev. James Such, an Anglican clergyman. See Clay to Lucretia Hart Clay, July 7, 1840; Clay to Such, November 14, 1840; also Porter to Clay, December 20, 1840; and Such to Clay, March 11, 1841.

To ROBERT P. LETCHER Lexington, October 28, 1840

I am sorry that I cannot go to Frankfort this week. I wished to have gone to day, but the weather has disappointed me, and other circumstances will interfere during the residue of the week.

I have prepared two papers, which I send you under another cover, one relating to the Sinking fund, and the other an exposé of the condition, credit & resources of the State.[1] I wish you would read them & return them, and say if they meet your approbation.

The first point will be to ascertain if the facts and figures are entirely accurate; and the next whether they will be likely to have good effect.

In the latter case, it might be well to have some copies printed or made by a copyist, to be sent to the Bankers &c. and ultimately to get them inserted in some leading prints, such as the [Philadelphia] Nat. Gazette, [Washington *Daily National*] Intellr., [New York] Courier & Enquirer &c. However, in this I am perhaps displaying, what I really do not feel, some pride of authorship. Let me hear soon from you, as the time for action is now nigh at hand.

ALS. NcD. 1. Although these two documents have not been found, Letcher addressed these issues in his first annual message, Dec. 8, 1840. See Frankfort *Commonwealth*, Dec. 8, 1840, and Clay to Letcher, Sept. 7, 1840.

To JAMES B. CLAY Lexington, October 30, 1840

I received your letter dated at Louisville. Enclosed is a letter to Mr. [William F.] Dunnica which I wish you would deliver or send to him. And I wish that you would ascertain if the taxes are paid on all my Missouri lands, and Col [James] Morrisons.[1] I feel uneasy about them. I believe I have none remaining in my own right but the 680 tract in the forks of the Missouri & Mississippi, the tract in Lincoln, and 40 Acres at the mouth of I believe Grand river, the quarter of a quarter section.[2]

I wish you to sell the Lincoln tract for what you can get for it,[3] taking care that the paymt be made secure. I suppose you can get at least five dollars per acre.

We are well, but the weather has been very bad ever since you left us.
P.S. Read & seal & direct the letter to Mr. Dunnica

ALS. DLC-TJC (DNA, M212, R10). Addressed to son James at Columbia, Boone County, Mo. 1. For Clay's purchase and sale of military bounty lands in Missouri, acquired in partnership with Col. James Morrison, see 2:578; 3:346, 627-28; 8:339, 649, 662-63; also Clay to Pindell, Oct. 14, 1839. For the purchase and sale of a farm in St. Louis County, to be operated by his son, James B. Clay, see 8:801 and Clay to January, Oct. 6, 1838. 2. For his 680 acres in the "forks of the Missouri and Mississippi," across the river from Alton, Ill., see Clay to James B. Clay, Dec. 18, 1837 and Davis to Clay, March 18, 1843. His 40-acre property at the juncture of the Grand and Missouri rivers was located near Brunswick, Carroll County, Mo. See Samuel to Clay, April 12, 1838. 3. The Lincoln County tract measured 232.42 acres. Hiram H. Baber to Clay, Auditor's Office, Jefferson City, Mo., Dec. 22, 1840. D, partially printed. DLC-TJC (DNA, M212, R18). At this point in his life, Clay's financial obligations included: A renewed loan of $10,000 from the trustees of Transylvania University at 6%, the money coming from the James Morrison Estate legacy to the institution. Receipt. Madison C. Johnson to Clay, Oct. 1, 1840. ADS. *Ibid.*; Order, Clay to Johnson, Oct. 5, 1840. *Ibid.* Also a loan of $20,000 at 6% from John J. Astor [8:763, 802]. In addition, on Oct. 18, 1840, James Blythe [2:596] entered suit against Clay for payment of a $10,000 loan, contracted by Benjamin W. Dudley, David A. Sayre, Benjamin Gratz, and Clay on Oct. 21, 1835. Clay was therefore summoned to appear in Fayette County Circuit Court on Nov. 1, 1840. See *James Blythe* v. *Henry Clay*, Box 111, Drawer 985, Fayette County Circuit Court Cases. For Astor's loans, loan renewals, and loan extensions to Clay, see Van Deusen, *Life of Henry Clay*, 273, 380; also 2:686, 863, 884-85; 3:83-84; 4:38.

From William Henry Harrison, Cincinnati, November 2, 1840. Reports full returns from 16 Ohio counties and partial returns from 7 others in the presidential election. These show a Whig majority of 8,731. Notes, however, that in Hamilton, his own county, his majority was but 26, that of Thomas Corwin, Whig candidate for governor, was only 20, while that of Nathaniel G. Pendleton, Whig candidate for the U.S. House, was 165. Explains that "The difference between P[endleton's]. & my vote is oweing in part to the vote of the Abolitionists 47. to Berney [*sic*, James G. Birney]. & a number of others who did not vote who had supported Pendleton." Mentions that he will depart for Louisville, enroute to Frankfort on November 5 or 6 to consult with Charles A. Wickliffe about land in Kentucky he had acquired from his brother Benjamin in 1793 in exchange for $5,000 and some land in Virginia. "I will write you from one of this [these] places so that we can meet at the latter." ALS. DLC-HC (DNA, M212, R5). Postmarked at Covington, Ky. As it turned out, Harrison did not leave his home at North Bend for Louisville until November 16. See Harrison to Clay, November 15, 1840; and Clay to Saltonstall, November 22, 1840. Wickliffe was interested in the possibility of purchasing Harrison's land claims in Kentucky for $11,000. Cleaves, *Old Tippecanoe*, 14, 329. For the political significance of Harrison's searching out of Charles A. Wickliffe at this particular time, see Van Deusen, *Life of Henry Clay*, 337.

In official returns for Hamilton County, Ohio, Harrison received 5,873 votes to 5,835 for Van Buren. W. Dean Burnham, *Presidential Ballots 1836-1892* (Baltimore, 1955), 684. Whig Nathaniel G. Pendleton defeated Democrat Alexander Duncan for the U.S. House by 6,119 votes to 5,959. *Guide to U.S. Elections*, 573. Also, in the gubernatorial race Whig Thomas Corwin received 6,081 votes in Hamilton County to 6,060 for Democrat Wilson Shannon. Cincinnati *Daily Gazette*, November 17, 1840.

To ROBERT P. LETCHER Lexington, November 4, 1840

I received your favor of yesterday. I should be very ungrateful if, after your puff of the Expose,[1] I did not recollect and attend to your wishes as to the currency and public lands.[2] But as you will perceive I may possibly see you before the 16h or 17h.

[3]Confidential. I have a letter from Genl Harrison dated the day before yesterday in which he says: "I have a long account to settle with C. Wickliffe and about thursday or friday next will set out via Louisville for Frankfort. I will write you from one of these places so that we can meet at the latter."[4]

I suppose therefore that he will be at Frankfort next Saturday or Sunday; and when I hear of the time I shall go down to meet him. I wish you to be at home, as you ought to be, to meet the President elect. Mention the matter to [John J.] Crittenden and to no one else.

The account with Mr. [Charles A.] Wickliffe is some old Land Companys affairs.

ALS. NcD. 1. Clay to Letcher, Sept. 7 and Oct. 28, 1840. 2. Clay to Letcher, Sept. 7, 1840. 3. At this point Clay inserted a pointing hand symbol. 4. Harrison to Clay, Nov. 2, 1840.

From Peter Dudley, Frankfort, November 11, 1840. Announces that Clay is entitled to purchase 20 shares of Frankfort Bridge Company stock. In reply, Clay submits $124, "For call of $5=per share on 20 Shares of Stock formerly owned by Tran[sylvania]. University. . . . $100"; and "For interest on same from 1st. Oct. 1836 to 1st. Octr. 1840. 4 years. . . . $124." ADS. DLC-TJC (DNA, M212, R18). See 8:40-41.

On April 1, 1843, Clay thanked Dudley for transmitting a check for $230, "being the dividend upon my Bridge Stock, declared the first of January." ALS. Courtesy of Edgar Hume, Frankfort, Ky. Copy in KyHi.

To PETER B. PORTER Lexington, November 13, 1840

I recd. your favor from Buffalo communicating the glorious results of the P. Election in Western N. York. Your anticipations as to the issue of the contest in the State appear to be realized.[1] And now no doubt remains of the election of Genl Harrison, whatever may be the votes of Virginia[2] and other States yet unascertained.

I will not now speculate on this great & gratifying event, but confine my self to the expression of hearty and cordial congratulations.

ALS. NBuHi. 1. Harrison took New York from Van Buren by 225,817 to 212,519, with Birney's Liberty party receiving 2,798. McKee, *National . . . Popular and Electoral Vote*, 44-45. 2. Van Buren carried Virginia by 43,893 to 42,501. *Ibid.*

To JAMES SUCH Lexington, November 14, 1840

I duly received your favor, transmitting receipts &c. We shall preserve your letter respecting the State of the education of the boys[1] at the time they come under your care.

I have written to Duralde that he must prosecute his study of the Greek, as well as his other studies.

During the winter Mr. [James] Erwins residence, and consequently his address, is N. Orleans.

I am obliged by the offer of the hospitality of your house. Should I make my contemplated visit about Xmas, I may accept of it for one night. P. S. I remitted a few days ago a Check to you for $250.

ALS. British Library, London, England. Copy in InHi. 1. Grandsons Henry Clay Duralde, Henry Clay Erwin, and James Erwin, Jr. See Gratz to Clay, Oct. 28, 1840.

From WILLIAM HENRY HARRISON North Bend, Indiana, November 15,1840

I shall set out for Louisville in the Mail boat Tomorrow. I have written to Mr C[harles A.] Wickliffe with whom I have the business which takes me to Kentucky to meet me in Frankfort (having understood that he has removed to Bardstown.)[1]

Since my [November 2] letter to you I have thought that our personal meeting might give rise to speculations & even jealousies which it might be well to avoid for altho I have made up my mind to disregard things of that sort when they are unavoidable yet as all the objects to be answrd by our seeing each other might be accomplished through a Mutual friend or friends I submit to you whether it would not be better to adopt this mode of Communication. If you think so, I request you to name to me the friend at Frankfort to whom I may Communicate my Views upon a certain important action of mine & receive yours in return. Upon the subject to which I allude I assure you I have had no sort of Communication with any one unless it be impertinent suggestions by unknown[2] individuals. I inclose this to Mr [John J.] Crittenden. I shall stay but one day in Louisville if I can get away.

ALS. DLC-HC (DNA, M212, R5). Printed in Colton, *Clay Correspondence*, 4:446. 1. Harrison to Clay, Nov. 2, 1840. 2. Adds at this point, in the form of a footnote, called out in the text by an asterisk, the phrase: "With but one exception I refer to two letters written by a man whom I know suggesting a general principle."

To ROBERT P. LETCHER Lexington, *ca.* mid-November, 1840

I recd. your favor of yesterday, and will send for the Roller tomorrow, which I have no doubt will be satisfactory.

Genl. Mercer came on *his* Special mission, and went from me satisfied that none to England was necessary.[1]

I want much to see you and [John J.] Crittenden; but I cannot go to Frankfort until monday evening next. When there, I mean to remain two or three days. In the mean time give my respects to the Atto. General.

ALS. NcD. 1. Gen. Charles F. Mercer, former Virginia congressman, and a life-long promoter of the American Colonization Society, was at this time cashier of a bank in Tallahassee, Fla. On Nov. 22, 1840, while on his way to England, he took breakfast with John Quincy Adams in Philadelphia. At this meeting Adams received the impression that Mercer was going to London "to raise the wind" for the Tallahassee bank; however, while in Britain in 1841 and 42, he attempted (in vain) to convince Lord Palmerston, British foreign secretary, to extend diplomatic recognition to the Republic of Liberia. Adams, *Memoirs of John Quincy Adams*, 10:360-61; Betty Fladeland, *Men and Brothers, Anglo-American Antislavery Cooperation* (Chicago, 1972), 278-79.

From William F. Dunnica, Glasgow, Mo., November 19, 1840. Reports that Richard Pindell has been to Missouri, has examined the status of the military bounty land [Clay to Pindell, October 14, 1839] he said he purchased from you "only conditionally," and has discovered that James Morrison's deed for this land has some legal difficulties inherent in it. Further, "I find notwithstanding all the pains I have taken to keep your lands free from embarrassment some are claimed by residents under tax title." Asks Clay for a list of all his Missouri lands. Wants to know, too, for which tract he has a tax receipt and the date of that receipt "so that I may compare them with the Auditors & see their true situation." Says he will pay any tax due on these tracts as well as on those still owned by the Morrison estate. Doubts that the person who bought Clay's 1,020-acre tract in Pike County "for the taxes" will accept "any reasonable amount for its releasement." Concludes with an apology for the fact that Van Buren carried Missouri in the recent presidential election and that the state is therefore still "clinging to the skirts of one who has degraded and disgraced us, and still *keeps* a masterly grasp upon us." ALS. DLC-TJC (DNA, M212, R14). Van Buren carried Missouri by 29,760 to 22,972. McKee, *National . . . Popular and Electoral Vote*, 44-45.

To Lunatic Asylum of Kentucky, Lexington, November 20, 1840. Pays $104 for board at the local asylum for the year 1840 for son Theodore Wythe Clay. Receipt signed on November 20 by John W. Hunt, chairman of the hospital board and John B. Baxter, clerk of the institution. ADS. DLC-TJC (DNA, M212, R18). Founded in 1824 as an institution for the treatment of mentally ill paupers, Eastern State Lunatic Asylum admitted an occasional inmate whose family was willing and able to pay the cost of treatment. See Ronald F. White, "A Dialogue on Madness: Eastern State Lunatic Asylum and Mental Health Policy in Kentucky, 1824-1883," Ph. D. dissertation, University of Kentucky, 1984, *passim.*

To THOMAS SPEED Lexington, November 21, 1840

I reciprocate your kind congratulations on the glorious issue of the P. election, and add an expression of my thanks for your friendly feelings manifested towards me.

On the two points of your letter I say, without any hesitation, 1st. That it is expedient for the Genl Assembly to make an early, strong & decided expression of its opinion in favor of establishing a Bank of the U. S. Whether that can be done at the next, or must be postponed to some subsequent Session, must depend on the circumstances we find at Washn; but that does not affect the question of the propriety of a Legislative expression.

2dly. I think there ought to be a permanent provision by law for the emergency of an Extra Session of Congress, by investing the Govn. with power to direct it by proclamation.

Events may render an Extra Session[1] after the 4h. of March next indispensible; and I am induced to believe that in any event it will be necessary. . . .

ALS. NhD. 1. The so-called "Extra Session," called by Harrison on March 17, 1841, is officially designated by the *BDAC* as the 1st Session (of three) of the 27th Congress. It convened on May 13, 1841, and adjourned on Sept. 13, 1841. Clay's arguments for convening such a session are in Notes for Newspaper Editorial, Feb. 4, 1841. The 1st Session was followed by a 2nd (Dec. 6, 1841-August 31, 1842) and 3rd (Dec. 5, 1842-March 3, 1843) Session. A Special Session of the Senate of the 27th Congress convened on March 4, 1841, to consider presidential appointments, especially to deal with the issue of dismissing Francis P. Blair and John C. Rives as printers to the Senate [Remark in Senate, Feb. 19, 1841]. It adjourned on March 15.

From Gustavus A. Henry, Clarksville, Tenn., November 22, 1840. States that Tennessee Whigs expect John Bell to be offered a place in Harrison's Cabinet because he is talented and because he deserves it as Tennessee's "most distinguished whig." Asks: "The whigs of Tennessee, are anxious to vote for you four years hence, I should like to know amongst other things, if it is *your* opinion we shall have that pleasure or not." ALS. DNA, RG59, A. and R. (M531, R4).

To LEVERETT SALTONSTALL Lexington, November 22, 1840

I have received your favor of the 11h. & reciprocate all your congratulations on the glorious issue of the P. Election. I am also highly gratified to hear of your re-election[1] in a manner so flattering and honorable to you.

I parted with Genl Harrison yesterday but expect him to dine with me on Wednesday.[2] I think the strength of his mind is unabated, but his body is a good deal shattered. He appears to be animated by the most patriotic dispositions; and if he adheres to them, the Country will not be disappointed in his administration.

I leave home on the 26h. for Washn. I have made, and until my arrival there shall probably make, no arrangements for my quarters this Session. . . .

ALS. KyU. Addressed to Saltonstall in Salem, Mass. 1. Saltonstall, a Whig, had defeated Democrat Robert Rantoul for a seat in the U.S. House from Massachusetts's 2nd district by a vote of 6,153 to 4,276. *Guide to U.S. Elections*, 573. 2. For Clay's meeting with Harrison in Frankfort on Nov. 21 and the dinner at "Ashland" at 2:30 p.m. on Nov. 25 in Harrison's honor, see Cleaves, *Old Tippecanoe*, 330; Van Deusen, *Life of Henry Clay*, 338. For the fact that Clay declined the post of secretary of state, before Harrison formally offered it, recommending Webster for the job instead, see *ibid.*; also Fuess, *Daniel Webster*, 2:89. Among the guests invited to "Ashland" for the Harrison dinner was W.P. Browning, local dealer in blacksmith, farm equipment, and other hardware supplies. Clay to Browning, Nov. 23, 1840. Copy. InHi.

From John Sloane, Wooster, Ohio, November 24, 1840. Congratulates Clay on "the almost entire extirmenation of the Jackson-Van Buren party." Had feared that history "would never do justice to the demerits of Jackson & his despotic rule," since there seemed to be "such an infatuation in the public mind in regard to him" and "so little did the body of the people know of his real character." Thinks now, however, that events have shown him to be the "outrageous imposter" he is. Reports his vigorous stump-speaking activities for Harrison in Ohio, and notes that the favorable outcome of the election there "fully confirms" the use of that political tactic. Admits, however, that he has no idea how Harrison will actually perform in office. Sees "an awful responsibility resting upon our party" and its president-elect. Would like to talk personally with Clay "on the prospect before us." Has made up his mind on one point: that the entire "official corps" of the Jackson-Van Buren administrations must be removed if the "generous principles" of the Constitution are to be preserved. Unlike the situation in the John Quincy Adams administration, when officers were mostly "selected by preceeding Administrations" without reference to politics, and at a time when "The doctrine of executive Unity was not then thought of," there had been "no combination: no organization; no unity of political action: whereas the present officers of government constitute a corps, as distinct from the proper as were the Janizares [*sic*, Janissaries] of Turkey, or the Swiss guards of Louis the 14. This corps must be disbanded, or all our late efforts go for nothing–" ALS. MH.

From William L. May, Springfield, Ill., November 27, 1840. Explains why he is $27,000 in debt and asks for a federal job even though Harrison lost Illinois to Van Buren. Attributes the loss to the "brute force of locofocoism." Says he worked assiduously for Harrison throughout the congressional district he formerly represented in Washington, noting that the Whigs carried it by over 3,000 votes. "That locofocoism has . . . received its final death blow even in this state I do not entertain a doubt." Is certain that the present incumbent [James Whitcomb] of the General Land Office will be removed. Hopes he might be considered for that post. ALS. DNA, RG56, Entry 209, Box 19. For May, see *BDAC*. Van Buren beat Harrison in Illinois by a 47,476 to 45,537 margin. McKee, *National . . . Popular and Electoral Vote*, 44-45. President John Tyler replaced Whitcomb as commissioner of the General Land Office with Elisha M. Huntington. U.S. Sen., *Executive Journal*, 5:388.

From Peter B. Porter, Saratoga Springs, N.Y., November 29, 1840. Reports that Harrison's majority of 15,300 over Van Buren was "about what we anticipated," while William H. Seward polled "some six or eight thousand less" in his victory over Democrat William Bouck for the governorship [Hall to Clay, November 20, 1839]. Explains this discrepancy with the observation that Seward's "dishonest course in regard to the Harrisburg nomination [Porter to Clay, February 16, 1839] lost him many friends; and it would have been an easy matter to have prevented his renomination, and many were disposed to do so. But this would probably have lost the State to the Whig party on the Presidential question, and it was thought most advisable to retain him, but with a hope which it seems has been realized, that he would be rebuked by a diminished number of votes." Hopes that Clay will not take a position in Harrison's Cabinet. Suggests instead that he "be minister to Great Britain where you would be detached from the political squabbles of the next four years, and preserve unimpaired your political reputation which could scarcely stand fairer than it does at present." Asks Clay to use his influence in favor of the appointment of William A. Bird of Black Rock, N.Y., to the job of postmaster at Buffalo or collector of customs there. Explains Bird's background and virtues at length. Copy. OHi. Bird (1797-1878) was Porter's nephew and had worked as his secretary when his uncle served on a commission to settle the Northeastern boundary controversy [7:176-79, 186, 300]. In addition, Bird served in the New York legislature and as president of the Erie County Savings Bank of Buffalo. Henry P. Andrews, *The Descendants of John Porter of Windsor, Connecticut . . .* (Saratoga Springs, N.Y., 1882), 33. See also Clay to Porter, December 8, 1840. The Northeastern boundary issue is indexed in 7:666, col. 3, and 667, col. 1.

From Abraham R. Lawrence, New York, November 30, 1840. Considers Harrison's great victory "a proud result" for Clay since "your example of self-devotion has in this instance secured the salvation of the Country." Feels certain that the new president will sweep "from the principal Offices within his nomination the Mercenaries who have been so long in the service of the adverse party." Recommends his brother, John L. Lawrence, for the office of collector of the Port of New York and hopes Clay will support his candidacy. Lists his brother's superior virtues and qualifications, discusses his background and genealogy, and mentions his "thirty years of consistant republicanism." Notes that his brother needs the job because he is the father of ten young children. ALS. DNA, RG56, Entry 247, Box 145. In addition to having served as secretary in the U.S. legation in Sweden in 1814, John L. Lawrence had sat in the N.Y. state legislature, participated in the state's constitutional convention of 1821, and at this moment [November, 1840] was a N.Y. presidential elector for Harrison. Both he and his brother Abraham had been removed from public office by Jackson in 1828. His wife was the daughter of former U.S. Sen. John Smith of New York.

President Harrison appointed Edward Curtis as collector of the Port of New York on March 18, 1841, after Congress had adjourned on March 15; thus, he was not confirmed before Harrison's death. On June 16 President Tyler also appointed Curtis and he was subsequently confirmed by the Senate on September 10, Clay voting nay. See Curtis in *BDAC*; U.S. Sen., *Executive Journal*, 5:384, 393, 434-35. For Clay's opposition to Curtis's appointment and the controversy surrounding it, see George R. Poage, *Henry Clay and the Whig Party* (Gloucester, Mass., 1965), 31-32; Van Deusen, *Life of Henry Clay*, 339-43.

From Edward M. Samuel, Liberty, Mo., November 31 [*sic*, 30], 1840. Congratulates Clay on the outcome of the presidential election. "We now breathe the pure air of liberty; despotism no longer is smelt in the breeze, thanks to yourself and the noble hearts who have so manfully breasted the storm. To you Sir, let me say, the Whig party owes its elevation. When all were desponding you stood up; 'undismayed by power', you Kept right on and prevented our party from disbanding—I say to you belongs the Victory." Recommends that Col. James H. Birch of Missouri be appointed commissioner of the General Land office. He is the choice of "all the Whigs in Mo. for that station, and his appointment thereto, will, in my opinion, in one year, break down the Great *Ball Roller*, Col [Thomas Hart] Benton—" Elaborates on the many virtues of Birch, including his early support of Jackson, and his later hostility to Jackson and Benton. Emphasizes the point that Birch's support of Clay's land bill [8:539-41, 609-10, 812-13, 846-47, 873-74] had triggered the breach with Benton and Jackson. ALS. DNA, RG56, Entry 209, Box 3. Other recommendations of Birch came from Missourians Nathaniel W. Watkins (dated December 20, 1840), *ibid.*; and Thomas M. Allen (December 21, 1840), *ibid.*

For the appointment of commissioner of the General Land Office, see May to Clay, November 27, 1840. For Birch, a newspaper editor who later served as register of the land office in Plattsburg, see Floyd C. Shoemaker, *Missouri & Missourians*, 5 vols. (Chicago, 1943), 3:255-56.

From David Campbell, Abingdon, Va., December 1, 1840. Refers to an open letter to Daniel Webster, reprinted from the Louisville *Journal*, in which the unknown author defends the "power and patronage" now in the hands of the president of the United States. Regrets that it comes "from a writer living in the republican State of Kentucky [Clay to Campbell, December 11, 1840]." Asserts that since Clay "upon two memorable occasions" had saved the nation from civil war, he must now step forward again and lead the movement to reduce "this dangerous and uncontrollable executive power that threatens the nation." This must be done during the first session of Congress after Harrison takes office. Suggests, specifically, that the president be deprived of control over the Treasury and Post Office departments and that the heads of these agencies be elected annually or biennially by joint vote of both houses of Congress; also, the president should be denied the power of removal of federal employees from office without Senate assent, save his Cabinet officers (excluding the postmaster general and secretary of the treasury) and members of the diplomatic corps. Cites the British example to support his contention that it is not "a generally received opinion that the energy of a government is in the Executive Department." Instead, the energy of the British government rests "in the people and their representatives in parliament." Congratulates Clay for the great victory the Whigs have achieved "in the election of Genl Harrison, over a most corrupt administration of the Federal Government, supported and defended by the whole band of office holders and all the impudent and unprinciple[d] demagogues in the country." ALS, draft. NcD. For Campbell, see 3:385.

From Anthony B. Shelby, Houston, Texas, December 5, 1840. Asserts he was "compelled to abandon my native country for a foreign land—owing to the maladministration of the Government by Gen. Jackson and his satilites," but would now like to return to the United States. Wants to be appointed marshal of the southern district of Mississippi. Asks Clay's assistance in securing this post. Reminds him of their connection in Lexington in 1805-8 when he was a student at Transylvania and when "Susan & Nancy Shelby lived at your house and went to School to Mrs. Beck."

Shelby, a resident of Mississippi in 1830-38, migrated to Texas in 1838 to escape "the effects of the political proscription and pecuniary oppression" of the Jacksonians. Says he is now a judge of the 1st judicial district of the Republic of Texas and, *ex officio*, one of the judges of the new nation's supreme court. Unfortunately, "such is the impoverished condition of our Country she cannot pay her Office[rs]." ALS. DNA, RG59, A. and R. (M531, R4).

For Mrs. George Beck's day and boarding school, see Charles R. Staples, *The History of Pioneer Lexington, 1779-1806* (Lexington, Ky., 1939), 263-64, 303; Wilson, *History of Kentucky*, 2:502-3. For more on Shelby, see Howard S. Galloway, *The Shelby Family Ancestry and Descendants* . . . (Mobile, Ala., 1964), 74-75, 95-98.

From Mortimer M. Jackson, Mineral Point, Wisconsin Territory, December 6, 1840. Reminds Clay that they met in New York City "a few years since" when Jackson, a friend of Matthew L. Davis, was serving on a committee of Whig young men that welcomed Clay to the city. Reports that "Loco-foco-ism" in Wisconsin has exerted "a *most baleful influence*" there and for several years "has had, indeed, an *entire monopoly* of all the offices in the Territory." Asserts that Whigs are a majority in the territory and that they seek and support, in Washington, as well as in Wisconsin, "a pretty general system of removal—a pretty thorough cleaning of the 'Augean stable.' " Is convinced that the present U.S. attorney for the territory will be removed. Says he is a candidate for that job and asks for Clay's support. Informs him also that "the *protection* of *American industry*—with which *your* name is so honorably and so gloriously identified, is that system alone which can sustain our great *mining* interest." ALS. DNA, RG59, A. and R. (M531, R4). For Jackson, a lawyer in New York City and later in Wisconsin Territory where he became attorney general in 1841 and later a judge, see *DAB*.

To FRANCIS T. BROOKE Washington, December 8, 1840

I arrived here safely the day before yesterday. Prior to my departure from home I received your favor addressed to me there as I now have that of the 6h. addressed to me here. I deeply regretted the loss of the Virginia vote; but presumed it was the result of fraud and other causes.[1] We are looking with great interest to the course of your Legislature. The want of a quorum in the Senate has prevented the reception of the Presidents Message.[2] We shall get it to day or tomorrow

I left Genl. Harrison at Lexington, and I have seen and conversed a good deal with him. He is much broke[n]; but his mind retains all its strength and vigor. He appears to be animated by the best dispositions; and if he acts in conformity with them our hopes will be all realized. I communicated to him that, during the short time I expected to remain in public life, I had no desire to change my position in the Senate. He professed, and I have no doubt now entertains, sentiments of warm regard and attachment to me. I do not believe that he had then made up his mind as to the members of his Cabinet. I think it probable, although he did not say so, that he will invite [John J.] Crittenden and [Thomas] Ewing to take places in it. Beyond that I will not venture even a conjecture.[3] I thought it right to explain frankly to him my feelings and relations towards Mr. Webster, and I stated to him that, although my confidence in that gentleman had been some what shaken, during the last eight years, I did not see how any Whig President could overlook him; that if I had been elected, I should have felt my self constrained to offer him some distinguished station; and that if he [Harrison] chose to appoint him to office, it would not diminish the interest I felt in the success of his administration, nor my zeal in its support, if it were conducted on the principles that I hoped it would be. I added an expression of my opinion that he was not suited to the office of Secy of the Treasury, which I had understood some of his friends wished him to fill.[4]

The Genl. is to be here in a few weeks, to go to Virginia and to return about the 4h. of March.

ALS. KyU. Printed in Colton, *Clay Correspondence*, 4:446-47. Letter marked "(Confidential)." 1. Van Buren defeated Harrison in Virginia by a vote of 43,893 to 42,501. McKee, *National . . . Popular and Electoral Vote*, 44. For the April, 1840 state elections in Virginia, see Clay to Lucretia H. Clay, April 25, 1840. 2. For Van Buren's message of Dec. 5, 1840, see *MPP*, 3:602-20. 3. Clay to Porter, Dec. 8, 1840. 4. *Ibid.*

To CHARLES F. MAYER[1] Washington, December 8, 1840

I received your letter on the subject of the wishes of our friend D. Hoffman Esq.[2] I am well acquainted with his merits and services; and should be glad to see any thing done for him that can be consistently with the public interests. As I have no expectation of being otherwise connected with the new administration than as a member of the Senate, I do not know that I shall have any means of aiding him; but whatever may be my situation I would take pleasure in testifying to his merits.

I think if he should make any application to the new President, he had better postpone it until the 4h. of March, as I happen to know that he regards all previous applications as premature.

ALS. ViU. 1. For Mayer, see 2:907. 2. For David Hoffman, see 6:143 and *DAB*.

To PETER B. PORTER Washington, December 8, 1840

I received here yesterday your favor of the 29h. Ulto. and reciprocate cordially your congratulations on the great event which has rescued the Government of our Country from the hands of those who were degrading & ruining it.

I left Genl Harrison on the 26h. Ulto. at Lexington. He had dined with me and I saw and conversed with him a great deal. His body is much weather beaten, but I perceived no abatement in the vigor of his mind. He appears to be animated by the best and most patriotic dispositions; and if he adhere to them he will fulfill the hopes which brought him into the high office which he is to fill.

My main desire, in a long interview with him, was to ascertain his views as to public measures; and I was happy to find him coinciding with those which I entertained.

During the interview with him, I stated that I had no desire, during the short time that I hoped to remain in public life, to change my position in the Senate. He did not appear surprized at my resolution, nor was I pressed to change it. Mr. Webster's name having been incidentally mentioned, I remarked that, altho' during the last eight years, my confidence in that Gentleman had been somewhat diminished, I did not see how he could be overlooked by any Whig President; that if I had been elected President, notwithstanding the opinion I entertained of him, in deference to public opinion, his services & his standing, I should have felt bound to offer him some distinguished place; and that, if he chose to appoint him Secy of State or Minister to England,[1] it would not lessen the interest which I took in the success of his administration, nor cool the zeal with which I should support it, if it were conducted on the principles which I believed would govern it. I stated that I had heard that his friends wished him to go into the Treasury Department; and I expressed the opinion that he had not the requisite qualifications for that office.

The Genl. appeared gratified with these sentiments expressed by me; but did not intimate any purpose in respect to Mr. W. Nor did he communicate the name of any individual that he had made up his mind to invite into his Cabinet. I *infer* however that Messrs. [John J.] Crittenden & [Thomas] Ewing will be offered places in it, altho' he did not say so to me. I think Ewing will be appointed P.M. General. I judged that he had not yet satisfied himself as to the persons whom he may finally call around him.

He intends visiting Washn. some weeks before the 4h. of March, going from here to see his connections in Virginia and returning to the inauguration.

His expressions and professions of friendship towards me were strong, and all that I could possibly desire.

I observe what you say in regard to your nephew Mr. [William A.] Bird,[2] of whom I entertain a lively & friendly recollection. It will afford me very great pleasure if I should have it in my power to render him any assistance in the accomplishment of his wishes, altho' it is not very probable I shall. I would advise no application to the new President prior to his qualification, as I happen to know from himself that he regards all such applications as premature and not very favorably.

I should be delighted if you would extend your visit to this place. Why not? I want to visit about Xmas my grandsons at Jamaica,[3] in which case I may have the pleasure of seeing you, en passant, in N. York.

ALS. NBuHi. Letter marked "(Confidential)." 1. Webster was appointed secretary of state, Harrison having offered him on Dec. 1 a choice of either the State or Treasury departments. Fuess, *Daniel Webster*, 2:89; Harold D. Moser (ed.), *The Papers of Daniel Webster, Correspondence, 1840-1843* (Hanover, N.H., 1982), 5:346. Other of Harrison's

Cabinet appointments were Thomas Ewing (Ohio), Treasury; John J. Crittenden (Ky.), attorney general; John Bell (Tenn.), War; George E. Badger (N.C.), Navy; and Francis Granger (N.Y.), postmaster general. 2. Porter to Clay, Nov. 29, 1840. 3. Gratz to Clay, Oct. 28, 1840.

To JESSE M. CHRISTOPHER Washington, December 9, 1840

I have duly received and attentively read your letter of the 3d. inst. It would be premature to apply to Genl Harrison for any office before the 4h. of March next. This I know is his feeling. The appointments to which your letter refers will pass through the new Secy. of the Treasury, and to him, when appointed, your application should be addressed.

As I do not expect to change my present position in the Senate, during the short time that I hope to remain in public life, it is not probable that I shall be in a situation to render you any service.

I cannot conclude without an expression of my thanks for the honor done me in bestowing my name upon two of your sons. I hope the Survivor of them will prove a blessing to you.

In writing to you, I depart from a general rule which the great number of letters I receive, soliciting appointments, has forced upon me. But I could not refrain from testifying my respects to you. . . .

ALS. NRU.

To JAMES T. AUSTIN Washington, December 10, 1840

I received your two favors,[1] and shall be most happy to see you here, when I can converse with you much more fully & freely than I can venture to write. For the present, I will say that I shall make no change in my position but remain in the Senate as long as I continue in public life. On that point my mind has been long & unalterably fixed.

I saw a fortnight ago Genl Harrison & had a great deal of conversation with him.[2] He is animated by the best dispositions. The name of no one person was stated to me to be called into his Cabinet. I learnt from others (not from him) that he intended to invite Mr. [John J.] Crittenden to a seat in the Cabinet, and *probably* to the office of Atto. General. I believe however that his mind was not definitively settled as to other members, if it were as to Mr. Crittenden, whose name, by the by, was not mentd. during the interview[3]

He is to be here in a few weeks, remain some days, visit his relations in Virginia & return about the 4h. March.

I write briefly because of the anticipated pleasure of seeing you soon. . . .

ALS. MHi. Letter marked "(Confidential)." For Austin, a Boston, Mass., lawyer, writer, and politician, see *DAB*. 1. On Dec. 4, 1840, Austin wrote Clay seeking the appointment of his son, Elbridge Gerry Austin, as federal district attorney. ALS. DNA, RG59, A. and R. (M531, R4). 2. Clay to Saltonstall, Nov. 22, 1840. 3. Clay to Porter, Dec. 8, 1840.

Remark in Senate, December 10, 1840. Moves that when the Senate adjourns it next meet on December 14. *Cong. Globe*, 26 Cong., 2 Sess., 13.

To DAVID CAMPBELL Washington, December 11, 1840

The political essays, to one of which you allude in your favor of the 2d.

[*sic*, 1st],[1] in respect to the mode of electing a President, I understand to be the productions of Mr. Nicholas, a gentleman of ability, altho' of great peculiarity.[2] I have not read them but looked enough into some of them to perceive that they are tinctured with his excentricity. They ought not to be taken as any evidence of public opinion in K.

I am persuaded that your friendly feelings towards me have prompted you to overstate what I have done or am capable of effecting. It is however my purpose to remain in the Senate where, during my continuance in public life, which I expect not to be long, I think I can render more useful service than in any other place.

The new Administration will have grave duties and great responsibilities. The first attention should be directed to the current administration of public affairs, the Sub. Treasury, the Revenue, the Currency, the Public Lands &c.

These matters disposed of, a consideration will then follow, in due order, of the structure of the Government itself, the shocks it has received, and the repairs that are needed.

Attention will be pretty much concentrated on the Executive branch. I adhere to the opinions I expressed at Hanover.[3]

Your suggestion of detaching the P. Office Department from the influence of the Executive is worthy of serious consideration.

We must take care nevertheless not to let reaction against the Executive function be pushed too far.

If I am spared, it is my intention to move in these matters, or some of them, in due Season, if no one else does.

What I am most anxious about, in the great and blessed change which has taken place, is that the new Administration, in power, will fulfill all the promises and redeem all the pledges which our party made, when it was out of power. That would be a glorious example which History has scarcely ever been authorized to record.

As already intimated, I remain in statu quo. Mr. Webster and Mr. [John J.] Crittenden probably will go into the new Cabinet; and Mr. [Thomas] Ewing of Ohio will be P.M.G. if he please.[4] Beyond this all is conjecture.

ALS. NcD. 1. Campbell to Clay, Dec. 1, 1840. 2. Samuel Smith Nicholas (1769-1869) was a lawyer, state legislator, and judge who was considered by some to be one of Louisville's most able writers. He was the son of George Nicholas and was married to Matilda Prather (d. 1844), sister of Julia Prather Clay. The essays in question were probably those published under the title, *Letters on the Presidency, by a Kentucky Democrat*. . . . Louisville, 1840. See H. Levin (ed.), *Lawyers and Lawmakers of Kentucky* (Chicago, 1897), 216-18. 3. Speech at Taylorsville, Hanover Co., Va., June 27, 1840. 4. Clay to Porter, Dec. 8, 1840.

From Andrew Erwin, Nashville, December 11, 1840. Asks Clay to support "an old personal friend who has labored zealously in the cause of Reform (Mr. G. Sublett)" who is currently an applicant for the office of marshal of Middle Tennessee. ALS. DNA, RG59, A. and R. (M531, R4). Andrew Erwin was the father of James, husband of Clay's deceased daughter, Anne Brown Clay.

On December 19 William Prather, brother of Julia, deceased wife of Henry Clay, Jr., writes from Louisville to ask Clay to support William S. Vernon of New York for the consulship in Harve. *Ibid.*

To Nathaniel Beverley Tucker, Williamsburg, Va., December 11, 1840. Reports that he has decided to remain in the Senate rather than serve in the Harrison Cabinet and that "This resolution I have communicated to Genl. Harrison, whom I saw prior to my departure from home [Clay to Saltonstall, November 22, 1840]. He appears to be animated by the best dispositions, and if he acts in conformity with them, I think all the hopes which we have entertained as to his Administration will be realized." Adds that "The routed party, from such indications as have yet been given, seem unconscious of their loss of power. But I hope we shall be able to prevent any mischief, if we should prove incompetent to effect any good, during this Session." Promises that "I shall strive to induce the successful party to fulfill in power, honestly and faithfully, all the promises, and to redeem all the pledges, which it made when out of power." ALS. ViW.

To Henry A.S. Dearborn, Boston, December 12, 1840. States that "a great wrong was done" when Jackson replaced Dearborn as collector of customs at Boston in 1829 [4:670–71], but points out that he will fill no position in the new administration and cannot therefore effect "your restoration" to that post. Suggests that he not approach Harrison on the appointment until after the inauguration. ALS. PHC. President Tyler appointed Levi Lincoln as collector of the port at Boston. U.S. Sen., *Executive Journal*, 27 Cong., 1 Sess., 5:384, 393.

To ROBERT P. LETCHER Washington, December 13, 1840

I received your favor, and other letters recd. here (one by [John J.] Crittenden) confirm the offer made by Genl H. to Mr. W[ebster]. with some little variation.[1]

You know that I am prepared for any thing; and I shall not be greatly disappointed if H. falls into sinister hands. But nous verrons. His letter to Crittenden evinces great confidence in him.

The temper here with the defeated party is, I think, to do nothing good. And if they can stick together (which I doubt) an Extra Session will be indispensible.

I send you a pamphlet relating to the controversy between the State & the Trust Co. which you ought to read.[2] It is accompanied by a letter from Jack Downing.[3] The pretensions of the Bank are sustained, you will see, by strong opinions. Would it not be well to get an authority from the Genl Assembly to submit the point to arbitration?

ALS. NcD. 1. Clay to Porter, Dec. 8, 1840. 2. Probably the Schuylkill bank fraud. See Clay to Erwin, Jan. 10, 1840. 3. Pseudonym used by numerous political writers of the day.

From Peter B. Porter, Carleton House, New York, December 14, 1840. Replies to Clay's letter of December 8. Reports that "There is a strong and almost universal sentiment of indignation expressed by the members of the Whig party in this State, at the unworthy stratagem, which is now fully understood, played upon the Harrisburg Convention [Porter to Clay, November 14 and December 30, 1837]. The issue of that Convention is not likely to satisfy the expectations of the clique in this State by whom it was brought about. The magnanimous course pursued by yourself which has secured to you the admiration and applause even of your enemies, and the recent manifestations by Gen. Harrison that he will pursue an honest course and not be the instrument of their intrigue, has disappointed and mortified them excessively. They now profess to be your greatest admirers, and will have no other man for their next President. Perhaps they may act up to this declaration, but if so it will be from policy alone. They dislike you, and the more so because they have abused you, and would play the same game again, if they could anticipate Success. But I trust we shall not be again thus deceived."

Agrees with Clay's decision to turn down Harrison's offer of a Cabinet post [Clay to Porter, December 8, 1840]. Approves the prospect that Webster might become secretary of state and that Thomas Ewing might be named postmaster general. Hopes John J. Crittenden will be offered the treasury because "he is equal to any place in the Government" and because "it wields more political power than any other office in the Government, save the Presidency." Mentions that among the "dozen candidates" for collector of customs in New York are Charles King and Edward Curtis. Thinks that the appointment of either would be unpopular or inexpedient. Remarks that Curtis is also the son-in-law of John Cramer, a Locofoco who is "as intriguing and unprincipled a politician as we have in the State." Recommends John L. Lawrence [A.R. Lawrence to Clay, November 30, 1840] for the collectorship.

Looks forward to seeing Clay in New York at Christmas time, pointing out that he has a son at the same school in Jamaica, Long Island, which Clay's grandsons attend [Gratz to Clay, October 28, 1840]. Copy. OHi. For Charles King, see 2:21 and *NCAB*, 5:419. For John Cramer, see *DAB* and *BDAC*.

Remark in Senate, December 14, 1840. Presents a petition from the New York Peace Society. *Cong. Globe*, 26 Cong., 2 Sess., 14.

Later this day, Clay presented a resolution requiring the secretary of the treasury [Levi Woodbury], pursuant to the Senate resolution of April 25, 1828, to submit answers to these questions: How much public land, having been offered at the minimum price, remained unsold as of June 30, 1828; what proportion of this unsold land was "first rate land," how much was "unfit for cultivation," and what was its average value per acre; what amount of the land unsold as of June 30, 1828, has since been sold and at what prices at various district land offices? The secretary shall also provide a chart "exhibiting in one connected view the quantity of land unsold on the day aforesaid [June 30, 1828] in each district, the amount since sold, the value as assessed or estimated by the said officers [registers and receivers of the land offices], and the prices at which the lands have since actually sold; and the aggregate value of the land as assessed, and the aggregate amount of the sales made since the 30th June, 1828, in each land district." *Ibid.* For the resolution, see also *Sen. Docs.*, 26 Cong., 2 Sess., no. 10.

On this same day, Sen. Thomas Hart Benton (Mo.) introduced his bill "to establish a permanent prospective pre-emption system, in favor of settlers on the public lands, who shall inhabit and cultivate the same, and raise a log cabin thereon." The bill entitled future settlers on the public land and those who had settled on such land since June 30, 1840, and who agreed to raise or who had already raised a log cabin on the property, and otherwise intended to improve or had already improved said property "to a pre-emption in the purchase of one quarter section, to be paid for at the minimum price of such land at the time of paying for same." Other provisions were designed to assist settlers or would-be settlers in purchasing adjacent or contiguous parcels so that a full quarter section (160 acres) could more easily be put together, thus qualifying the settler for the benefits of the proposed legislation. In this regard it provided, further, that when 160 acres could not be put together from contiguous lands, "entries may be made in tracts of eighty acres, or forty acres, or in fractions." No termination date of this legislation was included in the bill. See *Cong. Globe*, 26 Cong., 2 Sess., 14-15, for the complete language of the bill. For Clay's speeches in the 26th Congress, 2nd Session in opposition to various aspects of this bill, see Remark in Senate, January 4, 1841; Speech in Senate, January 6 and 28-29, 1841; Comment in Senate, January 20, 1841. For John J. Crittenden's proposed amendment to this bill, and John C. Calhoun's substitute bill, see Remark in Senate, January 19, 1841.

The "bill to establish a permanent prospective pre-emption system" passed the Senate on February 2, 1841, and went to the House the following day. It was defeated in the House on March 3 by a vote of 116 to 23. U.S. Sen., *Journal*, 26 Cong., 2 Sess., 30, 43, 47, 77, 156; U.S. H. of Reps., *Journal*, 26 Cong., 2 Sess., 226, 376.

Still later this day, Clay presented a resolution asking for the repeal of the "Act to provide for the collection, safe-keeping, transfer, and disbursement of the public revenue [the Sub-Treasury or Independent Treasury Act of July 4, 1840]," and to instruct the Committee on Finance to report such a bill. *Cong. Globe*, 26 Cong., 2 Sess., 14. For Clay's participation in the controversial Sub-Treasury issue debate in previous sessions, see Speech in Senate, September 25, 1837; Remark in Senate, January 16, 1838; Speech in Senate, February 19, 1838; Comment in Senate, March 7, 1838; and Clay to Porter, December 27, 1838. His main speech in opposition to this legislation during the 26th Congress, 1st Session, was delivered on January 20, 1840; for the fate of Clay's unsuccessful effort to repeal the Independent Treasury Act during the 26th Congress, 2nd Session, see Speech in Senate, December 15, 1840.

Speech in Senate, December 15, 1840. States that in offering his resolution yesterday [Remark in Senate, December 14, 1840] to repeal the Independent Treasury Act of July 4, 1840, he was not trying to start an argument for the sake of argument. Knows he is not going to convince supporters of the act that "this Sub-Treasury measure ought to be abandoned." He has therefore introduced the repeal resolution because it is "his duty so to do." Notes that the Sub-Treasury issue has been argued for a period of three years and three months and that further discussion would seem unnecessary. Declares, however, that "the nation decrees the repeal of the measure," and that nineteen states have sent their representatives to Washington with instructions to repeal it. Argues that "whatever else" the recent presidential election might have decided, it certainly "decided against this Sub-Treasury measure." Asserts that so sweeping was the Whig majority in the election that there is no need even to refer the repeal resolution to committee. "What Senator would stand there in his place and say he opposed himself to the will of the nation?" Wishes that Van Buren in his annual message [*Cong. Globe*, 26 Cong., 2 Sess., 2-6] had magnanimously renounced the Sub-Treasury arrangement. As it is, the incoming Congress and new president will have to do that for him. Denies Van Buren's contention in his message that the operation of the Sub-Treasury system has been "very successful" and Secretary Woodbury's statements in support of that evaluation [*ibid.*, 6-11]. Demands specific evidence of its successful operation rather than mere affirmations thereof. Says there is "not the slightest difference" in banking procedures prevailing now from those in operation prior to the advent of the Sub-Treasury Act in July, 1840. Indeed, he understands now, as then, that the notes of all the specie-paying banks are accepted as cash (specie) by the receivers at the Sub-Treasury depositories in such ways as to conceal the fact that the notes are paper rather than specie. Explains in detail how the merchants and receivers cooperate in clouding the real nature of these currency transactions. Argues, therefore, that the operation of the Sub-Treasury system has been "exceedingly limited" and if the act is repealed, the U.S. Treasury will simply return to "the same state of things" which existed prior to July 4, 1840, "without interfering with the financial affairs of the Government." Adds that the Senate has little choice but to effect repeal as demanded by public opinion and by the nineteen state legislatures that have instructed their senators on this matter.

Responds to taunts and questions from Sen. Silas Wright (N.Y.) who wonders what principles the Whigs stand for, what next they plan to do after destroying the Sub-Treasury, and whether they might attempt to reestablish the Bank of the United States. Clay says that it is enough that the Whigs handle only the Sub-Treasury issue at this time. "Let them remove that out of the way, and then those coming into power would bring forward their measures." Notes that Wright has said that "the party coming in were coming without principles, and they would be at liberty to adopt any measure they pleased. But did not the gentleman know that the party coming in were opposed to the Sub-Treasury? Did he not know that they were in favor of a sound and safe regulation of the currency, as far as it can be done consistently with the Constitution of the United States? Did he not know they were for economy, and against the extravagance of the downfallen Administration? Did he not know they were for retrenchment, and that they were opposed to the extent and alarming magnitude, and fearful usurpation and abuse of Executive power? And therefore, the gentleman could not reprove them for a want of principle." *Cong. Globe*, 26 Cong., 2 Sess., 19-21. Printed in Colton, *Clay Correspondence*, 6:220-24. No final Senate action was taken on Clay's motion to repeal the Sub-Treasury Act of 1840 during the 26th Congress, 2nd Session. It was tabled on February 20, 1841. See Remark in Senate, February 20, 1841. On January 29, 1841, a motion by Whig Rep. Calvary Morris (Ohio) in the House to suspend the rules so that a bill to repeal the Sub-Treasury Act might be taken up was beaten 87 to 79. *Cong. Globe*, 26 Cong., 2 Sess., 132. That ended the repeal effort in the 26th Congress. For Morris, see *BDAC*.

From Harrison Gray Otis, December 16, 1840. Describes the Whig party as "a coalition of persons, brought together from the four ends of our earth, led by instinctive impulse, not merely by compact of leaders, & united, (so far as the evidence goes,) as yet in only one defined object—a change of men. The other object, a change of measures, is far enough from being *defined*." Believes it would be wise "in Genl. Harrison to throw upon the shoulders of yourself and a few leaders and representatives of the great subdivisions of party, the responsibility of forming his cabinet. . . . Such measures only should be attempted as all are agreed in, & this should be pushed with vigor and carried." Predicts that in this way "a broad foundation could be laid for the formation of a great 'Country party,' on primary principles and mutual concession, extending in every direction & embracing all the great interests of the Country. Such a party has not yet existed among us; Events seem to indicate the practicability of forming it." Warns that "Unless it be done, the cossacks will be upon you in one or two years." Copy, extract. Printed in Samuel E. Morison, *The Life and Letters of Harrison Gray Otis, Federalist, 1765-1848*, 2 vols. (Boston, 1913), 2:299.

To JOHN M. CLAYTON Washington, December 17, 1840

Your letter of the 13h. has anticipated me. I have intended ever since I came here to write you, but had put it off, you know how.

The message[1] is justly characterized by you. Its financial statements were exposed yesterday by Webster,[2] and other parts of it will, in due season be commented on.

I have kept the Compromise in view; and before the Senate adjourns, I mean to submit a resolution calling upon the Secy of the Treasury to prepare and report a plan for home valuation &c.[3]

Now for other matters. I saw a good deal of Harrison about three weeks ago. He dined with me at Ashland, and I had a long confidential conversation with him.[4] He is animated by the best dispositions, and if he adheres to them, the Country will not be disappointed in his Admon. I told him that I desired no change in my official position, but prefered remaining in the Senate, during the short time I hoped to continue in public life. To put him at his ease about Webster I told him that whatever might be my opinion of him, I did not see how he could overlook him; and that, if I had been elected President I should have felt myself bound to offer him some distinguished place &c. He did not mention to me the name of one person that he had resolved to invite into his Cabinet;[5] but we were interrupted at the point, when I supposed he was going to speak freely on that subject, and no opportunity afterwards occurred to resume the conversation.

He has offered the Dept. of State to Webster, and I believe he has accepted it. [John J.] Crittenden is to be Atto. General, and [Thomas] Ewing P. M. G. if he please.[6] Beyond this all is speculation. [William C.] Preston has no wish to enter the Cabinet. Nor [Nathaniel P.] Tallmadge.

As to the three Depts. of the Treasury, War, and Navy, there is much conversation in the circles. Some of us (Preston among others) are very desirous to see you Secy of the Treasury or of the Navy.[7] Whether our wishes will be gratified or not remains to be seen. I must observe that, notwithstanding professions of the most ardent attachment to me by Harrison, circumstances have transpired which confirm an opinion I have long since formed, that he is apprehensive that the new Administration may not be regarded as *his* but mine. Artful men for sinister purposes will endeavor to foster this jealousy. And to preserve my utility, I must avoid giving it any countenance.

He is to be here in a few weeks, to go hence to Va. after remaining here some eight or ten days, and then to return to the inauguration.

[John] Sergeant is among the persons spoken of for the Treasury, and will be pressed. The course you took about the Compromise of the Tariff commends you strongly to Southern men; and I indulge the hope that you may be selected for one of the two places mentioned. Whatever may be the issue, I pray you to be assured of my warm and ardent friendship.

I am going to see three Grandsons of mine at N. York,[8] and perhaps may start tomorrow. On my return I wish to take my Xmas dinner with [Richard Henry] Bayard, and perhaps may stop there a day or two. Can't you meet me there? I have many things to converse with you about not fit nor convenient to write. By the by (since you do me the favor to ask my wishes) I should be very glad to see Bayard returned to the Senate.[9]

ALS. DLC-Clayton Papers (DNA, M212, R20). 1. Van Buren's Fourth Annual Message of Dec. 5, 1840. *MPP*, 3:602-20. 2. *Cong. Globe*, 26 Cong., 2 Sess., 26-28. 3. Compromise Tariff of 1833. The resolution was submitted on Jan. 16. 1841. See *Cong. Globe*, 26 Cong., 2 Sess., 105. 4. Clay to Saltonstall, Nov. 22, 1840. 5. Clay to Porter, Dec. 8, 1840. 6. *Ibid.* 7. *Ibid.* See Clay to Clayton, Feb. 12, 1841. 8. Gratz to Clay, Oct. 28, 1840. 9. Richard Henry Bayard, chief justice of Delaware (1839-41), returned to the U.S. Senate on Jan. 12, 1841, and served there until March 3, 1845. See *BDAC*.

From Peter B. Porter, New York, December 20, 1840. Asks that he be guest of honor at a "great body of the oldest and most respectable Republicans" in New York City for a public dinner when he comes to the area to visit his three grandsons at the Rev. Mr. Such's school in Jamaica, Long Island [Gratz to Clay, October 28, 1840] during the Christmas holiday. Mentions that Mr. Daniel Jackson and Mr.

Reuben Withers, both of whose sons are also at the Such school, would like to entertain Clay and his grandsons in their homes while they are visiting in the city. Copy, summary. OHi.

Withers was cashier of the State Bank of New York. See Moses Y. Beach (ed.), *The Wealth and Biography of the Wealthy Citizens of the City of New York* (New York, 1846), 31. Jackson has not been identified. Mr. Such, a Cambridge University graduate, and his wife, "both accomplished as scholars & teachers," established the boarding school in Jamaica "where they had accomodations for ten boys." Copy, summary attached to Porter to Clay, December 20, 1840. Peter B. Porter's youngest son was also a student at the Such school.

While visiting the Rev. and Mrs. Such in Jamaica in December, 1840, Clay provided the English clergyman with a letter of introduction to Josiah Quincy. Clay to Quincy, Jamaica, N.Y., December 21, 1840. ALS. MHi. For Quincy, see *DAB* and *BDAC*.

From MAHLON DAY[1] Washington, December 22, 1840

Joseph John Gurney[2] who addressed to thee his "Familiar Letters describing a winter in the West Indies"[3] gave it in Charge of myself—his Companion—early to forward thee a Copy of the work, which I attempted to do by mail, through the franking privilege of the Secretary of the Senate. I was very sorry recently to hear, incidentally, that thou never received the book. I am now in Washington for the purpose of handing thee a Copy. I regret very much thy absence, as I wish to explain to thee personally, the reason of the apparent neglect. Please to accept this Copy of the work and the assurance of the respect of J.J. Gurney and [myself] . . . .

ALS. DLC-HC (DNA, M212, R5). 1. For Day, a Quaker abolitionist and bookseller in New York City who devoted the last fifteen years of his life to charitable and educational activities, see *CAB*. 2. For Gurney, a Quaker philanthropist and religious writer from England and also an abolitionist, see *DNB* and Fladeland, *Men and Brothers*, 235, 251-54. 3. For several months in 1839-40, Gurney and Day had traveled in the British West Indies investigating the results of emancipation there [8:641] and preaching to the former slaves. On returning to the United States, Gurney lectured on the success of abolition in the British West Indies and spoke on that subject with many of the nation's political leaders. He felt that he "was listened to with great attention, and by no individual more so than by Henry Clay, of Kentucky." He believed that Clay's "mind is not steeled against a lively feeling of interest in the cause of emancipation," and he hoped that Clay could be persuaded to embrace the cause of abolition in the United States. To that end, he wrote a report of his experiences in the British West Indies in the form of public letters addressed to Clay. The book was first published in the newspaper press in the United States and then in book form. By early 1841 it had sold out three English editions and one American edition. In these letters—dated June 1, 2, 3, 4, 5, 6, 8, 10, 12, 24, 26, 29, July 1, 3, 1840—Gurney contended that the positive results of emancipation which he had observed on the trip were: a rise in property values, an increase in production (in most areas), a decrease in crime, an increase in trade, the growth of schools and churches, and an improved moral tenor as evidenced by an increase in the number of marriages. He pointed out the ill effects of slavery which he had observed in the United States, as well as the involvement of Americans in the illegal slave trade in the West Indies, and called on Clay in his declining years to use his influence against slavery. Joseph John Gurney, *A Winter in the West Indies Described in Familiar Letters to Henry Clay, of Kentucky* (London, 1841), xi, xii, *passim*. See also Fladeland, *Men and Brothers*, 251-54 and James A. Rawley, "Joseph John Gurney's Mission to America, 1837-1840," *MVHR* (March, 1963), 49:653-74.

To HARRISON G. OTIS Wilmington, Del., December 28, 1840

I received here your two obliging letters addressed to me, one at Washn. and the other at N. York, and both after Xmas, which you had kindly invited me to pass with you. I should have been most happy to have been able to accept your hospitality; but it would not have been in my power. It would have been gratifying to me to have conversed historically with you on the past, and speculated on the future.

I think that the defeated party is annihilated, unless it shall be revived by want of discretion or wisdom on the part of the new Administration. Harrison (of whom I saw a great deal lately)[1] is animated by patriotic dispositions, and if he can adhere to them the hopes of the Country will be realized. He will appoint Mr. Webster Secy of State, [John J.] Crittenden Atto. General & [Thomas] Ewing of Ohio P.M.G. Beyond that, I believe all is undecided, or unknown.[2]

The Currency and the Tariff are the subjects which will give to the new Admon the most embarrassment. If a new Bank of the U.S. can be established, and the principles of the Compromise can be adhered to, my belief is that all will go well. Without a Bank, the new vessel of State will be thrown on the same Rock which was fatal to the old one. If the Compromise is departed from, there will be no security, no stability, but constant fluctuation. What our Manufacturers want is steadiness, revival of confidence, sound currency & regular exchanges.

I agree with you that a system of measures should be settled early; and I hope that there is already a general good understanding on that point. In the interviews which I recently had with Genl Harrison, I was happy to find that my opinions in the main coincided with his. You know him. His strong points are honesty, patriotism, a good education, some experience in public affairs, and a lively sensibility to the good opinion of the virtuous and intelligent. His weak are, vanity & egotism. And the problem to be solved is whether the former can afford protection against the sinister influences to which the latter expose him. Nous verrons.

I am glad to perceive that your sprightliness & cheerfulness continue, from which I infer your health. May it long continue.

ALS. MHi 1. Clay to Saltonstall, Nov. 22, 1840. 2. Clay to Porter, Dec. 8, 1840.

To JOHN M. CLAYTON Wilmington, December 29, 1840

I have been quite ill, my dear Clayton, since my arrival here, with a severe cold which confined me forty hours to the bed, and almost the whole time to my room. I am better now, and leave this place tomorrow for Washington. Before my departure, I must acknowledge the receipt of your favor by [Richard H.] Bayard and say a few words more. I should have been glad to have seen you, as one can say many things in person which he would not care to put on paper; but perhaps it was most expedient that you should not meet me here.

I am pleased to be in possession of your views, which could not be more inviolably safe in your own bosom than they will be in mine.

In Philada. I found your name, as at Washington, spoken of in conjunction with that of Mr. [John] Sergeant, in connection with the Dept. of the Treasury, and to my surprize, the preference was expressed for you.[1] I say surprize, because I had supposed that *there* local considerations would have outweighed all others.

Upon my return to Washn. I presume I shall find greater maturity in the opinions of our political friends than prevailed when I left that City. Genl Harrison is expected there about the middle of January.

Whatever can be done with propriety, I shall do to avail the public of your services in his Cabinet. You may rest assured that I shall do nothing inconsistent with the delicacy or honor of your character. I presume he will consult me; and if he does I shall urge the offer of a place to you in the strongest terms. The whole South and West would hail your appointment with pleasure, and the North would, I am sure, see it with satisfaction. If he does not consult me, I will nevertheless take care that my opinions shall reach him.

I find that our friend Bayard has his return to the Senate more at heart than I was aware of before I saw him, and more than he expresses generally. He thinks that he was a victim to the unfortunate distractions which prevailed among our friends in Sussex two years ago, and that he is entitled to the amende honorable. It strikes me that there is weight in that consideration. Then, since you will not yourself go to the Senate, is not there more good service, more outcome in him, than in any others whose names have been mentioned? During the greater part of the time that I have been in Congress, Delaware was one of the best represented States in the Union; but at this time, I regret, that it is not so. In the House, she has in fact no representative but in name. From what I have heard of her representative [Thomas Robinson, Jr.], her honor & character are best promoted, perhaps, by his habitual absence from his seat. In the Senate, instead of two Senators for two years our worthy friend, your namesake and relative [Thomas Clayton], has stood, solitary and alone.[2]

You ought then to have your representation in both houses full, and well filled. Delaware should, in all respects, be herself again. She confided to Bayard the noble duty of moving to expunge the infamous expunging resolution.[3] And I should rejoice, as I am sure many others would, to see him again sent to the Senate to complete what he so worthily begun.

I will write you from Washington as soon as I have any thing worth communicating. . . .

ALS. DLC-Clayton Papers (DNA, M212, R20). 1. Clay to Porter, Dec. 8, 1840. 2. Richard H. Bayard had resigned his Senate seat on Sept. 9, 1839, to become chief justice of Delaware. His seat remained vacant until he himself occupied it again on Jan. 11, 1841. The other Delaware senator at this time was Thomas Clayton, cousin of John M. Clayton. Robinson was Delaware's lone representative in the 26th Congress. A Democrat, he was at this juncture serving his only term in the House. *Ibid.* For all three men, see *BDAC*. 3. See 8:735.

From Isaac Montgomery, Indianapolis, December 29, 1840. Reports that Indiana is "head over ears in debt" because of heavy expenditures for internal improvements. Recommends that the proceeds from public lands sales be distributed among the states [Speech in Senate, January 28-29, 1841]. Thinks this would help western states such as Indiana pay off their debts [Remark in Senate, February 18, 1840]. Supports Clay's efforts to repeal the Sub-Treasury act [Remark in Senate, December 14, 1840; Speech in Senate, December 15, 1840], and asserts that all the Whigs in the Indiana legislature support such repeal, as well as the establishment of a new Bank of the United States. Hopes also that Clay will someday be president. Says he has always been for Clay and is an uncompromising Whig who was born in Virginia in 1776 to a mother who was a Crockett and a father who was a

Montgomery. Asks Clay to support the appointment of either of two people for the job of U.S. district attorney for Indiana. ALS. DNA, RG59, A. and R. (M531, R4). For Montgomery, who served numerous terms in the Indiana Senate and was an Adams presidential elector in 1828, see *IMH*, 19:41; 20:388; 26:122; 36:257.

From William W. Worsley, Louisville, December 31, 1840. Reports information from New Orleans that for baling their cotton, planters there are buying foreign cloth, free of duty, that enters the country as "gunny bags," "gunnybag cloth," "India floor cloth," or "Jupe." Quotes a New Orleans informant to the point that "most of the orders from planters are for gunny bags or India, *perem[p]torily*." Explains also that such cloth is thought to be cheaper than Kentucky bagging and that it is also favored "by prejudice and exasperation against the Kentucky article, on account of the high rate asked for it here during the summer." Warns that Kentucky manufacturers of hemp products will feel the effects of resistance to the cost of their output "next year" in the New Orleans market. Notes that Missouri bagging is selling for 10¢ per yard and good Missouri rope at 7¢ per lb.; whereas, Kentucky bagging is selling at 20¢ or 21¢. Adds that Kentucky manufacturers have to pay $7 per hundredweight for hemp [Clay to Henry Clay, Jr., September 8, 1837]. Believes that "hundreds of planters would use gunny bags in preference to Ky. bagging at 15 cents," and that "Ky. bagging will come down to 18 cents." States, further, that Kentucky bagging will not fetch "higher than 20 during the whole of the approaching season, and that it will not be safe for manufacturers to give more than $4 or $4.50 for Hemp." Concludes: "If it is impossible to prevent the frauds on the revenue, in introducing articles under fictitious names, which are used for baling cotton, I am fearful that the heretofore very profitable business of raising hemp and manufacturing cotton bagging, will in a great measure be lost to Kentucky." ALS. DNA, RG59, A. and R. (M531, R4).

To AMBROSE SPENCER Washington, January 1, 1841

With the compliments of the Season, I have the pleasure to acknowledge the receipt of your favor, which arrived here during my temporary absence, and to reciprocate cordially your congratulations upon the glorious termination, I hope, of all our political troubles. Genl Harrison will enter on the arduous duties of his high office, under the best auspices. His character affords many securities for the realization of all our hopes as to the prosperity & happiness of our Country. And I feel myself authorized to add, from a recent intercourse with him, that he appears to be animated by patriotic dispositions.

It is understood here, and I believe, that Mr. Webster will be Secy of State, Mr. [John J.] Crittenden Atto. Genl. and Mr. [Thomas] Ewing P.M.G. Beyond these arrangements, all is conjecture and speculation.[1] I remain in Statu-quo. whilst I continue in public life.

If, as I hope, some good system of administration can be deliberately settled, I think we shall have nothing to apprehend in the future. There are many points of coincidence among the elements of our party, and but few of disagreement. These latter I trust may be reconciled. Such at least is my hope & shall be my effort.

ALS. PHi. 1. Clay to Porter, Dec. 8, 1840.

To Benjamin F. Thompson, Hempstead, Long Island, January 3, 1841. Compliments him on the usefulness of his *History of Long Island*. Reports that he was much impressed with what he saw of Long Island during his recent visit there [Clay to Gratz, October 28, 1840]. Also reciprocates Thompson's "congratulations on the signal & glorious triumph of the Whigs." ALS. NN. Written from Washington following his trip to New York City and nearby Jamaica, L.I., to visit his grandsons there during the 1840 Christmas holidays.

For Thompson (1784-1849), a lawyer and historian, see Charles J. Werner, "Biography of Benjamin F. Thompson," in Benjamin F. Thompson, *History of Long Island*, 2 vols. (New York, 1918), 1:xxv-l. Thompson's *History of Long Island* was first published in 1839; a second edition came out in 1843.

From Peter B. Porter, New York, January 4, 1841. Regrets that he did not see Clay on the day of his departure from the city. Reports that all of the students in the school of the Reverend James Such [Clay to Gratz, October 28, 1840] in Jamaica came into New York City on December 24-28, during which time "I gave them all a couple of night's entertainment at the circus and the Bowery with which they appeared to be much gratified."

Believes Clay's own visit to the city "went off exceedingly well," and notes that his political friends there had expressed the "confident hope & belief that you are yet to perform an important part in the affairs of our country." Says that it is "a source of much satisfaction to the great body of the Whig party of this State to know that Gen. Harrison enjoys *your* confidence, and that you predict for him . . . a happy and successful career." Expounds at some length on the proposition that the "misfortune of our day is that politics have become a trade"; and specifically, that "cliques, or political joint stock companies, are already forming among the different branches of the Whig party." Each is hoping "to relieve the President of a portion of his executive duties, & most especially of that of making appointments to office." Cites the Anti-Masons as "One of the most dangerous of these cliques." Argues that from a political standpoint New York is and will continue for some time to be "the most powerful State in the Union," and that New York City, "generally speaking," determines the "political character" of the entire State. Explains: "The elections of the city will continue to be, as they now are, controlled by the federal office holders, and I consider the Collector of the Customs of the City of New York, from his immense patronage in the appointment of subordinate officers, as possessing more political power than any other man in the Government with the exception of the President himself. A great effort is now making, as you well know, to give this office to Mr. [Edward] Curtis, who is an Anti Mason, a shrewd and managing man, and who, if successful will do everything in his power to establish the ascendancy of that clique, and I hope, my dear Sir, that you will do whatever may be fairly within your power to prevent his appointment."

Concludes with the observation that the "revival of the miserable affair" of the *Caroline* [Comment in Senate, January 5, 1838] by Congress and by the diplomats of both governments has produced "a pretty theme for the liberty-loving demagogues of Congress to descant upon, but it may be followed by deep and disastrous consequences." Condemns the American crew of the *Caroline* as "a miserable set of loafers and pirates, who have given us so much trouble." Copy. OHi. For the war scare that accompanied the revival of the *Caroline* issue with Great Britain, and in Congress, which was occasioned by the arrest (in November, 1840), imprisonment, and trial of Alexander McLeod (a Canadian) by New York authorities for his complicity in the destruction of the *Caroline* as well as for the controversial behavior of Henry S. Fox, British minister to the U.S., during the British government's attempt to secure McLeod's release without trial, see Corey, *The Crisis . . . in Canadian-American Relations*, 37, 130-45.

Remark in Senate, January 4, 1841. Presents two petitions in favor of "abolishing the spirit portion of the navy ration, and the substitution of healthful beverages therefor." *Cong. Globe*, 26 Cong., 2 Sess., 77. For the movement to abolish the spirit ration in the U.S. Navy, a dimension of the larger national prohibition reform effort, see Harold D. Langley, *Social Reform in the United States Navy, 1798-1862* (Urbana, Ill., 1967), 242-69. The grog ration in the Navy was finally abolished in September, 1862. Clay played no role of consequence in the national prohibition crusade. Indeed, on January 2 and February 23, Clay purchased from Edward Simms, Washington grocer, a total of three dozen bottles of champagne, two dozen of sherry, and one dozen of Madeira, total cost was $46.50. DS, signed by R.E. Simms for Edward Simms. DLC-TJC (DNA, M212, R19).

Also on this day, Clay participated in the debate on the permanent preemption system bill [Remark in Senate, December 14, 1840; Speech in Senate, January 6, 1841]. He moved the vote on an amendment that would limit the right of preemption to whites, an amendment which was adopted 37 to 1, Clay voting yea. He also spoke to the question of whether aliens could preempt public lands and to an amendment that would exclude them from this privilege. Informed that individual states determined and regulated alien acquisition of public lands within the state, Clay responds that be that as it may, he is "opposed on principle to the proposition that aliens should be invited from every portion of the habitable globe, to take possession of the public lands on terms so peculiarly favorable as were proposed in this bill." Objects to the government's extending "an invitation to aliens to come and purchase our lands; and yet such would be the effect of this bill." The amendment to deny aliens the right to preempt public land failed 30 to 12, Clay voting for denial. *Cong. Globe*, 26 Cong., 2 Sess., Appendix, 22-23. For earlier Clay involvement in the continuing preemption debate, see Remark in Senate, January 12, 1837, and January 23, 1838; Comment in Senate, January 29, 1838.

Remark in Senate, January 5, 1841. Speaks to a bill that would compensate New Hampshire for the services of state militia on the Canadian border in 1835-36. These militiamen had been sent into northwestern Coos County to protect the state's interests in a disputed border area in which civil jurisdiction was being contested with the British. It was argued by Sen. Franklin Pierce (N.H.) that British-Canadian authorities had triggered an incident by first employing a small body of "armed men" against Americans residing in the region. Clay asks several questions about all this: "whether there had been an actual invasion of this territory by a foreign power . . . and if not, was there a threatened invasion, or imminent danger of an invasion? And . . . supposing there was a threatened invasion, was there time to apply to the General Government to repel this threatened invasion? for to the General Government belonged the decision whether there should be peace or war." As answers to his own questions, Clay was directed by Sen. Henry Hubbard (N.H.) to "an elaborate report upon the subject" made to the House by Rep. Benjamin C. Howard (Md.), chairman of its Committee on Foreign Affairs in January, 1839. Clay agreed to "examine" this report. The bill was read a third time and passed *viva voce. Cong. Globe*, 26 Cong., 2 Sess., 83.

For the Howard report, see *Reports of Committees*, 25 Cong., 3 Sess., no. 176. The bill, entitled "an act for the settlement of the claims of New Hampshire against the United States," was introduced by Hubbard in the Senate on December 15, 1840, and passed on January 19 (no vote count given). It did not pass the House. U.S. Sen., *Journal*, 26 Cong., 2 Sess., 34, 112, 115; U.S. H. of Reps., *Journal*, 26 Cong., 2 Sess., 196.

To DANIEL ULLMANN[1] Washington, January 5, 1841

I received your favor. Should a suitable occasion occur, without my seeming to make it, I will embrace it to testify, as far as I can with truth, to the good qualities of our German population.

I should be most willing to hear any thing which Mr. [Josiah Ogden, Jr.] Hoffman[2] might choose to say to me, in regard to the Harrisburg Convention.[3] On that subject both he and Mr. [Samuel L.] Southard have preserved a silence, which I did not think I ought to break

AL, signature removed. NN. Addressed to Ullmann in New York City. Endorsed by Ullmann: "(Signature given away for an autograph)." 1. For Ullmann, who at this time was master in the court of chancery in New York and later a candidate for governor, see Johnson, *Twentieth Century Biographical Dictionary*. 2. For Hoffman, a New York Whig congressman, see *DAB* and *BDAC*. 3. Porter to Clay, Nov. 14 and Dec. 30, 1837.

To FRANCIS T. BROOKE Washington, January 7, 1841

I received your favor of the 5th. I should have written to you before but I really had nothing to write. I am sorry that mere rumors about the composition of the Cabinet[1] should fill any Virginia Whig with apprehension of the Spring elections.[2] I venture to say that Gen. Harrison will have a better Cabinet, and less of federalism in it than even Jackson or Van Buren had. What more is wanted? Are not some of our friends too nervous? Mr. Webster, I suppose, will be a member of it; but among all the rest talked of I know of no Federalist. "The Enquirer"[3] calls Mr. [John J.] Crittenden most untruly a Federalist. So it does me. But I hope that Virginia will no longer be affected by the slang of "The Enquirer."

The exact time is not known when General Harrison will be here. It is conjectured that it will be from the 15th to the 25th instant.

Copy. Printed in Colton, *Clay Correspondence*, 4:447-48. 1. Clay to Porter, Dec. 8, 1840. 2. In the April, 1841 state elections in Virginia, Whigs won 17 seats in the state senate while the Democrats won 15. The Whigs also carried the lower house by a margin of 55 to 54 seats. Richmond *Enquirer*, April 30, 1841. In Virginia's congressional elections, Democrats won 9 seats to 10 for the Whigs. In addition, in district 9 Robert M.T. Hunter—an Independent/Democrat—was elected with 263 votes over Whig Corbin with 209 votes and Democrat Braxton with 79 votes. *Ibid.*, April 27, 1841. Corbin was probably Robert B. Corbin, a Whig who had served in the state house of delegates from Caroline County, while Braxton was probably Dr. Corbin Braxton, a Democrat who had served in the state senate from the same district. Simms, *Rise of the Whigs in Virginia*, 181, 189. In congressional district 13 two Democrats—William Smith and Linn Banks—claimed victory and both served from March 4, 1841, to Dec. 6, 1841, when Smith was finally given the seat. *Guide to U.S. Elections*, 576; and *BDAC*. Conservative William C. Rives was elected to the U.S. Senate from Virginia on Jan. 18, 1841, and served until March 3, 1845. *Guide to U.S. Elections*, 479. In March John Rutherford, a Democrat, was chosen governor. *BDGUS*, 4:1640. See also Tayloe to Clay, April 21, 1841. 3. Richmond *Enquirer*, edited by Thomas Ritchie.

To PETER B. PORTER Washington, January 8, 1841

I received your favor of the 5h. [*sic*, 4th] inst. I am greatly obliged by your kind attentions to my little grand sons.[1] I have no doubt that they enjoyed very much their visit to the City.[2]

There is no material change in the state of our information as to the composition of the new Cabinet,[3] since I had the pleasure of seeing you. Webster, Crittenden and [Thomas] Ewing are to go into it. Beyond this nothing certain is known. [John] Sergeant, [John M.] Clayton, [John] Bell, & [Francis] Granger are all much talked of for the other three vacant seats. Granger is more prominent than any other Citizen of N. York. Is there any Anti Mason that would do better than him in the Cabinet? We shall know the final arrangements of the Cabinet only after the arrival of Genl Harrison, now looked for in a fortnight.

I concur with you in your opinions as to the Collector of N. York, and the unfitness of Mr. [Edward] Curtis.[4] My efforts will be directed to prevent an unworthy appointment, and to have the office well filled by a competent man of high character, rather than to promote the success of any *particular* individual.

I perceive that your nephew P. B. Porter [Jr.] is elected Speaker.[5] I am rejoiced at it. Do me the favor to present him my respects and my congratulations.

The affair of the Caroline will not I think lead to any serious consequences.[6] It is to be remembered that Mr. [Henry S.] Fox in his recent demand of the surrender of [Alexander] McLeod acted without instructions.

ALS. NBuHi. 1. Gratz to Clay, Oct. 28, 1840. 2. Porter to Clay, Jan. 4, 1841. 3. Clay to Porter, Dec. 8, 1840. 4. Porter to Clay, Dec. 14, 1840. 5. For Peter B. Porter, Jr. (1806-71), son of Augustus Porter and his second wife Jane Howell, see Andrews, *The Descendants of John Porter*, 20. Porter had been elected speaker of the New York assembly on Jan. 4, 1841, by a vote of 46 to 19 over John M. Holley. New York *Morning Courier & Enquirer*, Jan. 7, 1841. 6. Comment in Senate, Jan. 5, 1838; Porter to Clay, Jan. 4, 1841.

Remark in Senate, January 8, 1841. Opposes a resolution by Sen. Robert J. Walker (Miss.) to procure and print copies of the debates in the British Parliament prior to 1820 on the Northeastern boundary issue [Clay to Hamilton, February 24, 1839]. Points out that the diplomats are working on the problem and already have easy access to the debates if needed. Believes that since 1815 "the Executive action of the Government on this question [has] been much impaired by extraneous action." Cites, on this point, the fact that the recent report by Richard Z. Mudge and George W. Featherstonhaugh [Featherstonhaugh to Clay, June 3, 1840] had not been adopted by the British government; also that it had been "ably answered" by Albert Gallatin, "whose information on this subject" is "unsurpassed, if equalled, by any one on this continent."

As for the *Caroline* incident, a case of "much delicacy," assures the Senate that the British minister to the United States, Henry S. Fox, had acted without instructions when he asked for the release of Alexander McLeod [Porter to Clay, January 4, 1841]. Asks that this issue be "left in the hands of the Executive," where the Constitution places it. Says that if "collision should unfortunately ensue," he will "not be hindmost in the defence of American rights," but feels that "the probability of such rupture with Great Britain" is entirely unlikely. *Cong. Globe*, 26 Cong., 2 Sess., 92. The extensive background of the nagging Northeastern boundary dispute and Clay's role in it, is indexed in 7:666, col. 3; 667, col. 1; 729, col. 2; 730, col. 1.

Gallatin's 40,000-word essay, accompanied by a 37,000-word appendix plus maps, was published under the title, *The Right of the United States to the North-eastern Boundary Claimed by Them. . . .* New York, 1840. For a discussion of this matter, see Raymond Walters, Jr., *Albert Gallatin, Jeffersonian Financier and Diplomat* (New York, 1957), 342-43, 373-75.

From Peter S. Smith, St. Augustine, Florida, January 8, 1841. Reports "the proceedings of a meeting of inhabitants of East Florida to protest agst a 'Treaty'—*now*—at this time of day—to suffer the Indians to remain in Florida. It would at once drive every white Inhabitant from East Florida." Says East Florida does not want to be joined with Middle and West Florida when the territory becomes a state, but would rather be a separate state "whenever our population & property shall justify the measure." Explains at length his qualifications for appointment as collector of the port of St. Augustine. Asks Clay to assist East Florida to separate from West Florida. Mentions that he has in his office a bust of Clay "purchased last Spring by me of Fowler your phrenologist in Ph[iladelphi]a. a truly capital likeness & readily recognized by all that have ever seen you." ALS. DNA, RG56, Entry 247, Collectors of Customs, Box 43.

Peter S. Smith, brother of abolitionist Gerritt Smith, had been defeated for a seat in Congress from the Oneida (N.Y.) district in 1832. He subsequently moved to Florida and in 1839 was a member of a committee to draft resolutions asking Congress to make East Florida a separate state whenever the Florida Territory achieved statehood. Charles M. Snyder, *Oswego From Buckskin to Bustles* (Port Washington, N.Y., 1968), 122; Dorthy Dodd, *Florida Becomes a State* (Tallahassee, 1945), 122, 337-38, 451; and *DAB*.

It had been rumored that the commanding general of the army operating in Florida had been authorized to conclude a treaty with the Seminoles which would cede a large section of East Florida to the Indians. A public meeting was held in St. Augustine on January 2 and 5, 1841, and Smith was appointed to the committee to draw up resolutions protesting the proposed treaty. No such treaty was ever negotiated. St. Augustine *Florida Herald and Southern Democrat*, January 8, 1841.

For Orson S. Fowler (1809-87), a phrenologist and author of such books as *Amativeness: or, Evils and Remedies of Excessive and Perverted Sexuality, including Warning and Advice to the Married and Single*, see *DAB*.

From Robert Slaughter & Rice C. Ballard, New Orleans, January 9, 1841. Promise to pay Clay "the sum of five thousand dollars, as follows to Wit Rice C. Ballard paying four thousand four Hundred dollars part thereof, and Robert Slaughter paying one thousand dollars the balance thereof in addition to his fee already stipulated and agreed upon, in the case of Moses Groves vs Robert Slaughter Now in the Supreme Court of the United States, Provided that the decision of the said Court in the said Case settles fully the question, as to the Validity of all contracts, for the sales of Slaves in the State of Mississippi since the year 1833 or between the year 1833 and the time, when the Mississippi legislature passes the act fixing the penalty for the introduction of Slaves, say about May or June 1837—Otherwise the above Obligations to be void—" ADS, by R.C. Ballard. Promissory note. DLC-TJC (DNA, M212, R14).

In an enclosed note, also dated January 9 and marked "purely confidential," Slaughter and Ballard explain that "In the case of [Robert] Slaughter vs [Moses] Groves Now in the supreme Court of the United States, we are satisfied that we are represented by able counsel who will use their best efforts in our behalf for the price already stipulated, But relying on your ability and best exertions more particularly, We feel justified in enclosing you, the above obligation, believing that thereby, we do no injustice to those associated with you in the case." *Ibid.* Associated with Clay in the case were Charles L. Jones and Daniel Webster.

The case, *Moses Groves and James Graham* v. *Robert Slaughter*; and *John W. Brown, Moses Groves, R.M. Roberts, and James Graham* v. *Robert Slaughter*, was argued in the U.S. Supreme Court in the January term, 1841. The issue turned on the validity of a promissory note given by John W. Brown of Louisiana to Robert Slaughter. Slaughter, a non-resident of Mississippi in 1836, had sold to Brown slaves he had imported into Mississippi in 1835-36 as merchandise for resale. Brown's promissory notes were endorsed by Moses Groves and James Graham. When the notes came due, the endorsers refused payment on the ground that the contract of sale violated the Mississippi state constitution. Specifically, Groves and Graham claimed in the U.S. circuit court for the eastern district of Louisiana that the note was invalid and void, since Slaughter had violated the Mississippi state constitution of October 26, 1832, which prohibited such slave importations for sale as merchandise after May 1, 1833. They also maintained, and the circuit court agreed, that the Mississippi constitutional clause dealing with slave importations had not been carried into law by specific legislative enactment until May 13, 1837, or after the sale. In reversing the circuit court decision so as to benefit Slaughter, the U.S. Supreme Court argued, in part, that "The construction of the provision in the constitution of Mississippi, relative to the introduction of slaves for sale, into that state, has not been so fixed and settled by the Courts of Mississippi, as to preclude the Supreme Court of the United States from regarding it as an open question." The court declared, further, that to hold "all contracts made for the purchase of slaves, introduced as merchandise, or for sale, from the first of May, 1833, until the passage of the law of 1837, illegal and void; when there was such an unsettled state of opinion and course of policy pursued by the legislature; would be a severe and rigid construction of the constitution; and one that ought not to be adopted, unless called for by the most plain and unequivocal language." The court also asked "What would become of the slaves thus introduced, if the construction is such as to give the provision [1837 law] immediate operation? Will they become free immediately, on introduction, or do they become forfeited to the state? These are questions not easily answered; and although these difficulties may be removed by subsequent legislation, yet they are proper circumstances to be taken into consideration, when inquiring into the intention of the convention, in forming the [state] constitution." For *Groves* v. *Slaughter* in the Supreme Court, see 40 Peters, 449-517; and for subsequent debate on the principle involved, see Helen T. Catterall (ed.), *Judicial Cases Concerning American Slavery and the Negro*. Vol. III, *Cases from the Courts of Georgia, Florida, Alabama, Mississippi, and Louisiana* (Washington, 1932), 278-79, 533-37.

The notes used by Clay in his oral argument of the case before the Supreme Court include such lines as: "The slaves did not become free by the introduction [of the 1837 law]"; "After the introduction, the rights of property continued unimpaired"; "The Slaves did not become free. They were not forfeited by the legislature & cannot be by the Courts"; "Slaves sustain two characters, one as person, the other property"; "Slavery exists exclusively in virtue of the municipal law of a state"; "Congress has neither the power to disturb the existing institution or to establish it within a State"; the power of regulation of slavery in the U.S. Constitution "implies continued existence–Life not death–Preservation not annihilation [–] The unobstructed flow of the stream, not to check or dry up its waters"; "Congress cannot therefore do what the Abolitionists seek." AD. MH. Endorsed in strange hand on cover: "Mr Clays notes in the Mississippi Case."

In the December, 1844, term of the U.S. Supreme Court, Clay successfully sued Rice C. Ballard for $4,000 plus interest and court costs claimed due him under the agreement spelled out in the promissory note of January 9, 1841. Catterall, *Judicial Cases Concerning American Slavery. . . . Louisiana*, 563-64.

From Arthur F. Hopkins, Tuscaloosa, Alabama, January 11, 1841. Recommends friends for various federal appointments. Reports that "The friends of Genl. Harrison in this State are very desirous that he would say something in his inaugural address, which shall put down forever the unjust suspicion that he is favorable to the views of the Abolitionists or feels his dependence upon them too much to do anything that would displease them. The leaders of his Southern opponents affect to entertain the suspicions & with [this have] alarmed many of the ignorant & credulous." Concludes with the news that "The Legislature of this State adjo[ur]ned on the 9th. instant without adopting the recommendation of our Gove[r]nor [Arthur P. Bagby] to call a Convention of the slaveholding States." ALS. DNA, RG59, A. and R., Series 331, Box 39. For Hopkins, former judge of the Alabama supreme court, see 5:18 and *NCAB*, 4:356.

Harrison's inaugural address contained no specific reference to abolition. *MPP*, 4:5-20. In his message to the Alabama legislature in November, 1840, Gov. Bagby stated that it was "a matter of imperious necessity" that the slaveholding states meet in convention in order to consult "with those whose rights stand upon the same footing with our own, to adopt the most effective measures for our mutual happiness and safety." No action was taken on the proposal at that time. Washington *Daily National Intelligencer*, November 26, 1840. For Bagby, see *BDGUS*, 1:11.

Remark in Senate, January 11, 1841. Presents certification from Kentucky that John J. Crittenden has been reelected to the Senate. *Cong. Globe*, 26 Cong., 2 Sess., 94.

From Aaron Clark, New York City, January 12, 1841. Expresses his "high & unfeigned satisfaction" with Clay's (and Crittenden's) stance withholding the right of preemption of public lands by foreigners [Speech in Senate, January 6, 1841]. Explains: "The public lands should be the heritage & home of our native citizenry as much as possible & surely in *preference* to aliens. I am most unhappy when I reflect that our *real* enemies, and the *secret* enemies of our institutions are taking peaceable & unresisted possession of our rich vallies, our cities, ballot boxes & patronage. I hope & trust you will nobly persevere in your advocacy so well proclaimed."

Asks Clay to support his interest in appointment as collector of the port of New York for "one Term—no more." Wonders if there is "a move to have N.P. Talmadge [*sic*, Nathaniel P. Tallmadge] leave the Senate & to place Govr. [William H.] Seward there? Is so for what purpose? Is it the work of [Winfield] Scott & his praetorian Guard? One thing—it cannot mean any good for our honl. friend Mr. Clay, I fear." ALS. DNA, RG56, Entry 247, Collectors . . . Box 143.

For Aaron Clark, an exchange broker and former mayor of New York City, see Holli and Jones, *Biographical Dictionary of American Mayors*, 66-67.

Remark in Senate, January 12, 1841. Reminds the Senate that Calhoun's amendment to Crittenden's motion to recommit the preemption bill [Remark in Senate, December 14, 1840] to the Public Lands Committee contains a blank which should be filled before a vote is taken. *Cong. Globe*, 26 Cong., 2 Sess., Appendix, 61. Crittenden's motion to recommit also instructed the committee to report back a bill that would distribute the proceeds of public lands sales among all the states. Calhoun's amendment to Crittenden's motion was in the form of a complete substitute bill that would cede the public lands to the states in which they were situated. *Ibid.*, 52.

To THOMAS HART CLAY — Washington, January 13, 1841

I received your letters of the 5h & 6h instant. I regret that you cannot negotiate your acceptances in N. Orleans. I apprehend the difficulty at

N. York to negotiate them would be at present as great as at Lexington; but I think exchange will be less unfavorable there in a few weeks.

You are hereby authorised to draw upon me for $2500 at ninety days after date of the bill, payable at the Bank of Commerce in N. York, at the Bank of Penna. in Philada. or at some Bank in Balto. as you can best negotiate the bill at one or the other of those places.[1]

You may send me one of the acceptances or all of them if you please; but if you do, send difft. numbers by different mails.

ALS. DLC-HC (DNA, M212 R5). Written in "S. Chamber." 1. Clay to Lucretia Hart Clay, March 6, 1840.

To THOMAS C. GRATTAN Washington, January 14, 1841

I received your[1] favor with the article from the N[orth]. A[merican]. Review.[2] I have been able only to glance into it (amidst my multiplied & multiplying avocations, that is all I can now do) reserving the pleasure of a more deliberate perusal for a season of more leisure. Your conversations had confirmed my partiality for your Countrymen. Your article in the Review (for I presume it to be your's) almost makes me regret that I was not born an Irishman.

I shall be most happy to see you here at the inauguration, and to cultivate and extend an acquaintance which has left nothing but the most agreeable recollections. . . .

ALS. KyLoF. 1. For Grattan, an Irish writer who had been appointed British consul in Massachusetts in 1839, see *DNB*. 2. "The Irish in America," *NAR* (Jan., 1841), 52: 191-234.

Remark in Senate, January 14, 1841. Presents memorials favoring the passage of a general bankruptcy law [Remark in Senate, April 22, 1840]. Also presents one asking that a special joint committee of Congress be appointed "to report on the various memorials from peace societies presented at the last and present sessions of Congress." While he "must concur" in the object of the American Peace Society memorial, he says, he also sees practical "difficulty" with the request because of the other business of the session. Mentions, however, that he will "cheerfully" vote for a motion for a joint committee if someone else makes it. No one did. *Cong. Globe*, 26 Cong., 2 Sess., 99.

To Miss Sidney Edmiston, Lexington, Ky., January 15, 1841. Reports that when he was recently in Philadelphia he ordered the firm of Ogle & Watson [7:386-87] to make a carriage "for your aunt." It will be finished and sent to Kentucky in April. Discusses interior and exterior colors decided upon. ALS. CtY. Miss Edmiston's aunt was Esther Montgomery (Mrs. James) Morrison. Leavy, *A Memoir of Lexington*, 255.

On May 6, 1841, on behalf of her aunt, Sidney Edmiston gave Clay a receipt for the $1,000 he had paid for a "half year's annunity" due to Mrs. Morrison under her husband's will. AD, in Clay's hand, signed by Sidney Edmiston for Esther Morrison. DLC-TJC (DNA, M212, R19).

Remark in Senate, January 15, 1841. Twice interrupts Alabama Sen. Clement C. Clay's lengthy speech on the preemption bill [Remark in Senate, December 14, 1840; Speech in Senate, January 6, 1841]: first to restate his view that the preemption laws passed since 1830 have generally served to reduce the value of all public lands; and, second, to challenge figures and other facts cited by the Alabamian (among them some used by President Van Buren in his annual message in December, 1837) to demonstrate that public land prices have remained more or less stable since the Land Act of 1820—or have, in some instances, actually gained a few cents of value per acre. *Cong. Globe*, 26 Cong., 2 Sess., Appendix, 83. For the Land Act of 1820, see Hibbard, *History of the Public Land Policies*, 97-103.

During Clement C. Clay's speech this day on the preemption bill, he also criticized that feature in the Kentucky senator's failed land bills of 1832 and 1833 [8:540-41, 609-10, 812-13] which would distribute the income from public land sales among the states in such manner as to give "12½ per cent. more [than] the amount proposed to be given to the new States above an equal dividend with the old States." In reply, Clay explained that since distribution amounts would generally have been determined by state population levels in his 1833 bill, his reason for proposing the 12½ percent differential was to compensate the new states for the great growth in population they were certain to record in the 1840 census. He felt, in sum, that "a great injustice therefore would be done if they were to receive [distribution] by the census of 1830. That was the main motive." *Cong. Globe*, 26 Cong., 2 Sess., Appendix, 87.

Remark in Senate, January 16, 1841. Submits two resolutions: (1) requiring the secretary of the treasury to inform the Senate of his plan for "a permanent change in the tariff," which he had mentioned in his annual report of December 7, 1840, whenever either house of Congress should ask for it; and (2) requiring the secretary of the treasury to report "as soon as practicable, a plan of assessing the value of goods, wares, and merchandise in the ports of the United States instead of foreign countries." *Cong. Globe*, 26 Cong., 2 Sess., 105. The Annual Report of the Secretary of the Treasury, dated December 7, 1840, is in *ibid.*, 6-11. In it Woodbury noted that commencing on December 1, 1841, the rate of reduction of tariff schedules, as provided in the Compromise Tariff Act of 1833, would reduce federal tariff income by $2.5 million right away and by another $2.5 million commencing July 1, 1842. He suggested several ways that this approaching deficiency of $5 million might be handled and promised to submit a specific recommendation to that end whenever either house requested it. *Ibid.*, 9. On January 19, Van Buren submitted to the Senate Woodbury's recommendations on tariff policy which anticipated the substantial reductions in tariff schedules in December, 1841 and again in July, 1842 as provided by the Compromise Tariff Act of 1833. See *ibid.*, 109-12. In his report of January 19 Woodbury recommended revising the tariff by placing a rate of 15 to 20% on free-list items, specifically on luxury items and those in direct competition with U.S. products. He estimated that these levies would make up the anticipated $5 million decline in 1842 and noted that if, indeed, surplus revenue was produced, tariffs might then be lowered on necessary items. He emphasized also that any tariff revision must accord with the principles of the Compromise Tariff Act of 1833 in that after 1842 no item should be taxed at more than 20% and that, in principle, U.S. tariffs should be for revenue only. He did not set forth in the report a plan for home valuation of goods. *Sen. Docs.*, 26 Cong., 2 Sess., no. 93. No new tariff was passed during this session.

To JOHN M. CLAYTON Washington, January 17, 1841

I recd. your two favors, in respect to the election of our friend [Richard H.] Bayard.[1] It has afforded me much satisfaction, and I am sure that to your friendly exertions the event is to be ascribed.

I yesterday got the Senate to accept his resolutions, calling upon the Secy. of the Treasury, one for his plan of a permanent change in the Tariff, and the other for a plan of home valuations.[2] I should have presented the first earlier but for some diversity of opinion among our friends as to the expediency of a call. I concluded however that there could be no hazard in making the Secy. shew his hand.

The conversation among the members continues as to the formation of the new Cabinet. Mr. [John] Sergeant and yourself are yet talked of as Secy. of the Treasury.[3] I think that opinions are strengthening and uniting in your favor. [Henry A.] Wise has been a good deal out of humor because S[ergeant]. was not offered the Dept. of State. Yesterday he told me that he wanted the Treasury offered to him but that, with his consent, he shd. not accept it; that he never would serve in any Cabinet with [Daniel] Webster &c. I threw out the idea of the mission to England, and I thought that, from his manner, it was not ill received. I really wish that some thing clever may be done for Sergeant. The South supports you with zeal. So does Talmadge [*sic*, Nathaniel P. Tallmadge]. It is perfectly manifest that your appointment will give more general satisfaction than that of any other person. But every thing of course depends upon Harrison who is now shortly expected.

ALS. DLC-John M. Clayton Papers (DNA, M212, R20). Letter marked "(Confidential)."
1. Clay to Clayton, Dec. 17, 1840. 2. Remark in Senate, Jan. 16, 1841. 3. Clay to Porter, Dec. 8, 1840.

Remark in Senate, January 18, 1841. In response to Clay's resolution of December 14, 1840, Secretary of the Treasury Woodbury submits this day a report from the commissioner of the General Land Office dealing with sales of the public lands. Clay moves that one thousand additional copies of the report be printed and speaks (not recorded) to his motion, which was passed. *Cong. Globe*, 26 Cong., 2 Sess., 107.

Later this day, Clay introduces a resolution calling on Woodbury to submit additional information "showing in tabular form the lands, the titles for which were closed under the relief laws of 31st March, 1830, and 25th February, 1831, giving the numbers of acres in each district which were sold at and under $5 per acre; from $5 to $10 per acre; from $10 to $15; from $15 to $20; from $20 to $30; from $30 to $40; from $40 to $50; from $50 to $60; from $60 to $70; from $70 to $80; from $80 to $90; from $90 to $100; and $100 and upwards per acre; the amounts paid on such sales respectively and forfeited; the rates at which such sales were closed per acre; also, the gross amount of lands patented under each of these two laws in each district; the amounts in gross for which they were originally sold, the gross amounts paid on them and forfeited; and the gross amounts finally received for them." *Ibid.*

The "Act for the relief of the purchasers of public lands" of March 31, 1830, allowed land-office debtors, who were paying off their earlier purchases of public land by virtue of various credit-extension arrangements, a preemption (until July 4, 1831) at $1.25 per acre above what they had previously paid, the total sum not to exceed $3.50 per acre. Cash payments were accepted at 62½% of balances due. Failure to comply with the act would result in forfeiture and resale of the land. 4 *U.S. Stat.*, 390-92; Hibbard, *History of the Public Land Policies*, 96. The act of February 25, 1831, entitled, "An Act supplemental to" the act of 1830 extended the provisions of the earlier act to more people. 4 *U.S. Stat.*, 445-46.

To JAMES B. CLAY Washington, January 19, 1841

I sent to Mr. Downing Monarch's Advertisement,[1] of which I send you a

Copy, to guard against its miscarriage. I wish it printed in the paper and at the office of the [Lexington] Intellr

Col. [Wade] Hampton[2] has offered me one half of Sovereign & Monarch for $12500 payable on the 1st of Novr. next, and he throwing in this season of Monarch.

I have no thought of accepting it, without some three or four others would join me. Pe[r]haps Dr. [Benjamin W.] Dudley, Henry [Clay, Jr.] and Mr. [James K.] Duke[3] might think it worth while to make the purchase with me. Will you consult them?

Tell Henry that I have recd. a partial remittance from N. Orleans, and will send him one as soon as I get a check from Philada.

Give my love to your Mama & brothers.

ALS. DLC-TJC (DNA, M212, R10). Envelope addressed to Mr. James B. Clay at "Ashland" carries instruction: "(in his absense, Mr. J. M. Clay)." 1. Josiah Downing to whom Clay gave a check for $500 on April 7, 1841. ADS. *Ibid.* (R19). Also, on July 12, 1841, Josiah Downing, acting as agent for Clay, entered into an agreement with Peter Gatewood to breed four mares to Monarch, the produce to be divided equally between Clay and Gatewood when the animals reached the age of one year. ADS, by Downing, signed also by Gatewood. Josephine Simpson Collection, Lexington, Ky. For Monarch, an imported bay horse by Priam, out of Delphine by Whisker, see J. S. Skinner, *The Gentlemen's New Pocket Farrier . . . . and Stud Book* (Philadelphia, 1853), 96. 2. For Wade Hampton (1791-1858), owner of "Millwood" plantation near Columbia, S.C., see *DAB*. 3. For Duke, a noted thoroughbred breeder and turfman, see Perrin, *History of Fayette County*, 142, 144.

From James Love, New Orleans, January 19, 1841. Relates the background of the emigration to the Republic of Texas of John J. Crittenden's nephew, Alexander Parker Crittenden, together with his wife and two small children, soon after his graduation from the U.S. Military Academy in 1836; also mentions Alexander's study of law in Texas and the difficult time financially he is now experiencing as a lawyer there. Asks Clay to procure Crittenden's appointment as secretary of the U.S. legation in Austin. This failing, "I will support him for a year." Congratulates Clay "on *your* triumph. *You* have redeemed the country from the bad hands of a bad party." ALS. DNA, RG59, A. and R. (M531, R4). For A.P. Crittenden (1815-70), who resigned from the Army in 1836, was later a successful lawyer in California, and was murdered near San Francisco in 1870, see Albert D. Kirwan, *John J. Crittenden: The Struggle for the Union* (Lexington, Ky., 1962), 273; USMA, *Register*, class of 1836. For Love, see *BDAC*.

Remark in Senate, January 19, 1841. Interrupts the lengthy speech of Sen. Albert S. White (Ind.) on the preemption bill [Remark in Senate, December 14, 1840; Speech in Senate, January 28, 1841] to inquire whether Indiana has resorted to new loans with which to pay the interest on her state debt. *Cong. Globe*, 26 Cong., 2 Sess., Appendix, 78.

White had argued, in part, that either the Crittenden amendment to the administration's preemption bill or the Calhoun substitute for that bill would seriously worsen Indiana's financial situation. His state, he pointed out, is now "largely a debtor State." He admitted, upon resuming his speech, that "some domestic funds" had been appropriated for the purpose of managing the state debt. *Ibid.*, 78-79.

White identified Sen. John J. Crittenden's amendment to the preemption bill as "a renewal of a measure offered nine years ago by another distinguished Senator [Clay] from the same State [8:539-41, 609-10]." He argued thusly because Crittenden's proposal would return the administration's bill to the Public Lands Committee with instructions to report out a bill that would distribute public land sales receipts among all the states; and would also limit the size of a preemption to 320 acres at $1.25 per acre and require that the prospective preemptors be bonafide settlers whose personal estates did not exceed $1,000 in value. For Crittenden's amendment of January 11, 1841, and his speech the following day explaining and defending it, see *ibid.*, 47-48, 56-57.

Calhoun's substitute bill was introduced on December 22, 1840. *Cong. Globe*, 26 Cong., 2 Sess., 45. It required the government to cede to the several states the federal lands lying within their boundaries and turn over to those states the management (preemption and price-graduation laws) of the land ceded. In return, the states would pay to the central government 65 percent of the proceeds of their subsequent public lands sales. For Calhoun's explanation and defence of his proposal on January 12, 1841, see *ibid.*, Appendix, 52-56.

Calhoun's substitute bill was defeated on January 19, by a vote of 18 to 22, Clay voting nay. *Cong. Globe*, 26 Cong., 2 Sess., 112. Crittenden's proposal was defeated 22 to 29, on February 2, Clay voting yea. Immediately following this vote, the question was taken on the administration's original preemption bill. It passed 31 to 19, Clay and Crittenden voting nay, and was sent to the House for concurrence. *Ibid.*, 138. See Remark in Senate, December 14, 1840.

Comment in Senate, January 20, 1841. Argues that since a general preemption bill had been passed in 1840, to continue for two years [Remark in Senate, April 17, 1840], there is "no pressing necessity at all" for legislation dealing with preemption during this session [Remark in Senate, December 14, 1840]. Sees new abuses by land speculators under the provisions of the administration's current preemption proposals, viz: "A company of speculators would employ a number of men to go on this fresh and rich land, put up a log building by a spring, and thus obtain pre-emption rights to each man. The company will immediately purchase from them for a trifle, and, distributing their rights on the adjacent land, would thus possess themselves of a choice tract of the best land at Government price. . . . Suppose a hundred men should be employed to settle, and it should be found that they could not get their hundred quarter-sections on land immediately adjoining that on which they set themselves down, would they not spread themselves through the township, or over into a contiguous township? for the provision in the law must be interpreted so as, if possible, to satisfy the right of the party claiming under it; and if they could not lay their pre-emption on lands immediately contiguous, they must do the next best thing to comply with the law, and take their lands somewhere in the neighborhood." Complains, also, that the current preemption bill has in it no clause limiting its continuance to two years, that it opens to preemption lands not yet surveyed, and that the bill, in effect, is "a virtual repeal of the auction system, for when all the good land should be taken up, what would there be left for the auction to operate on?" Notes, too, that the practical effect of this bill is to eliminate the provision in the 1840 legislation that "the sixteenth section in every township shall be reserved for purposes of education." This, Clay explains later in this day's debate in reply to a question from Sen. Clement C. Clay (Ala.), is because such a section "is not reserved by the words of the bill." Asks rhetorically, what effect the bill will have from "a financial point of view? The Government is now aground. The cry for Treasury notes! Treasury notes! is the only remedy sounded forth from the head of the Treasury Department. The denouncers of banks, and bank paper, and the credit system, now cry in our ears for more, and more, and yet more *paper money*." Answers that "The Administration who are about to surrender the public Departments to the possession of those whom the people have chosen to be their successors, are leaving every thing topsy turvy, and in a state of the utmost confusion, dilapidation and decay. The financial effect of this bill will be to diminish the current expenses of the year by every pre-emption that shall be sold; and . . . I predict that the greatest amount derived next year from the public lands will be from sales to pre-emptioners; and, as they have a year's credit, the money will not come into the Treasury till the year following."

Responds sharply to Sen. James Buchanan's eulogy to General Jackson during the course of the Pennsylvanian's remarks supporting the administration's pre-emption bill. States that Buchanan's great loyalty to Jackson stemmed from his appointment by Jackson as U.S. minister to Russia and was not "prompted by his heart," as Buchanan claimed. Also chides Buchanan for his belief that "poor Mr. Van Buren came into power under very disadvantageous circumstances. It may be so; and, what is still more unfortunate, these disadvantageous circumstances have been aggravated during every year since by an excess of $8,000,000 a year in our expenditures over the receipts at the Treasury. But this was only the poor gentleman's *misfortune*." Further, Clay challenges Buchanan's assertion that he (Buchanan) is really "a great friend to our old and well-tried land system; that he will not disturb it; but is, it no alteration of that system to sustain a bill which goes to supersede some of its most important provisions? He tells us that Gen. Harrison is a pre-emptioner, and that he is advocating the doctrines of Gen. Harrison against his friends here. But where, I ask, is the evidence of his friendship for our land system and his unwillingness to disturb it, when he opposes such a just and reasonable restriction as is now proposed, and leaves the bill almost boundless in its application and interminable in point of time?" Denies Sen. Clement C. Clay's charge that he (Henry Clay) has been and remains dedicated to the proposition of distributing public land sales receipts in such manner as to discriminate against the new states. Specifically defends the approach he used in his land bills of 1832-33 [8:539-41, 609-10, 812-13, 873-74] which in principle distributed those receipts equally (by population) among all states because of expected population changes between 1830 and 1840, but added 12½ percent to the share to be given the rapidly growing new states [Remark in Senate, January 15, 1841]. Concludes: "From a view of the whole subject, I am opposed to the bill, as impairing the amount of revenue to come into the Treasury during the present year, thereby augmenting a deficit for which provision ought long since to have been made, and as fraught with evils passing all imagination, from the disputes and contests for title among that flood of settlers which is invited from all the quarters of the known world to rush in a mass upon our public domain. I have made, and shall continue to make opposition, as heretofore, with this difference, that, whereas formerly I opposed pre-emption bills, though only retrospective in their operation, and confined to a particular district, I oppose this the more as being prospective, interminable, and reaching to the entire extent of the public domain. And, most marvelous of all, it is yet said that all this involves no interference whatever with our admirable, our venerable, and long-tried land system." *Cong. Globe*, 26 Cong., 2 Sess., Appendix, 194, 198, 200-202.

To JOHN C. WRIGHT Washington, January 22, 1841

I received your friendly letter, and thank you for the sentiments towards me which it kindly conveys.

We must thwart and defeat our Opponents by the wisdom of the measures of the new Administration and the revival of general prosperity. In regard to the successor of Genl Harrison's, I think it would be entirely premature to be making any particular arrangements about that matter[.]

Should I consent to the use of my name (a point which I reserve for consideration) when the proper time comes, I will notify you, and will treat you, as I always have regarded you, as a sincere friend.

You ask if we are to have an Extra Session? I think it indispensable.[1] Rendered so by the course of our Opponents. But it rests exclusively with Genl Harrison.

The President in office [Van Buren] has convoked the Senate for the 4h. Mar.[2]

I am compelled to write briefly. . . .

ALS. ViU. Original on deposit there, courtesy of Hamilton M. Hutton, Falls Church, Va. Addressed to Wright [2:874] in Cincinnati where at this time he was the publisher (1835-48) of the Cincinnati *Gazette*. 1. Clay to Speed, Nov. 21, 1840. As early as January 25-30, 1841, John J. Crittenden wrote Kentucky Gov. Robert P. Letcher from Washington informing him that the "almost unanimous" opinion of Whig senators there was that an extra session of Congress was "absolutely necessary." Mrs. Chapman Coleman, *The Life of John J. Crittenden*, 2 vols. (Philadelphia, 1871), 1:139-41. 2. Proclamation, dated Jan. 6, 1841. *MPP*, 3:640.

From A. C. Baine, Grenada, Miss., January 25, 1841. Asks Clay to support a friend of his, Thomas Hardeman, for appointment as marshal of the northern district of Mississippi. In making this request, identifies himself as a "genuine Nullifier," and warns Clay against bringing forward a protective tariff. Explains that while a retaliatory tariff would be popular in the South, he senses that "a new feeling is now being engendered among the *people*, themselves" in favor of such a tariff, but not one that is essentially protective. "I beg you . . . not to attempt a protective tariff." ALS. DNA, RG59, A. and R. (M531, R4). For Thomas Hardeman, who later emigrated to Texas, see Samuel C. Williams, *Beginnings of West Tennessee . . . 1541-1841* (Johnson City, Tenn., 1930), 147-48. He received no federal appointment at this time.

To ROBERT P. LETCHER Washington, January 25, 1841

We had an informal meeting of the Whig members of the Senate on Saturday evening, and it was their unanimous opinion that an Extra Session is *indispensible*. Two, first doubted but finally concurred with the others who were positive. This expression of opinion (and it is the general opinion here) will be communicated to Genl H[arrison]. who alone can decide.

I think we shall have a Called Session, and that it will be in May.[1]

It is therefore important that the [Kentucky] General Assembly should provide for the contingency. P.S. You may shew this letter to any of our discreet friends.

ALS. NjMD. Written in "S[enate]. Chamber." Letter marked "(Confidential)." Addressed to Gov. Letcher in Frankfort. 1. Clay to Speed, Nov. 21, 1840.

Remark in Senate, January 25, 1841. Presents resolutions of the Kentucky state legislature that ask for the reestablishment of a Bank of the United States [8:434, 443, 552, 558, 640-41; Comment in Senate, September 26, 1837; Speech in Senate, May 21, 1838], oppose the cession of public lands to the states in which they lie [Comment in Senate, January 3, 1840; Remark in Senate, December 14, 1840 and January 19, 1841], and seek the distribution of the proceeds of public lands sales to all the states, according to population [Remark in Senate, January 15, 1841; Comment in Senate, January 20, 1841]. Reports that these resolutions had passed both houses of the Kentucky legislature with a total of but four dissenting votes and that they reflect the "sentiments of nine-tenths of the people of the State." *Cong. Globe*, 26 Cong., 2 Sess., 124.

Later this day, Clay also presents a Chamber of Commerce memorial remonstrating against the passage of any bankruptcy law [Remark in Senate, April 22, 1840] that "acted retrospectively," a feature, Clay notes wryly, that is "the principal merit of a bankrupt law." *Ibid.*

From Peter B. Porter, Saratoga Springs, N.Y., January 27, 1841. Reports that James Watson Webb aspires to appointment to the office of postmaster of the City of New York and asks Clay to support his candidacy. Sees as Webb's greatest qualification for the post the fact that "As a political man, Col. Webb has always been a uniform, consistent & ardent Republican of the old school, and, I believe, kept himself aloof from those combinations & cliques, so common at the present day, whose object is to advance the interests of particular Individuals, rather than to sustain the great principles of our Government: and I have no doubt that, whether successfull in his present application or not, he will give a cordial & efficient support to Gen. Harrison's administration." ALS. CtY. For Webb's attempts to achieve a public appointment, see James L. Crouthamel, *James Watson Webb, A Biography* (Middletown, Conn., 1969), 96.

From Peter B. Porter, Saratoga Springs, N.Y., January 28, 1841. Believes that the "political atmosphere at Albany is becoming somewhat more pure" because "Our Whig 'Regency' are alarmed at the effects of their late attempts at exclusive domination, and shew a disposition to consult and harmonize with the other portions of the party—still however their aim evidently is to make such a distribution of offices as to keep the balance of power in their own hands."

Reports that when he arrived at Albany about a week ago he received from Thurlow Weed, through the agency of his nephew (Peter B. Porter, Jr.), speaker of the New York assembly [Clay to Porter, January 8, 1841], a "confidential communication" in which Weed requested a personal conference with Porter. During this conference, Weed urged the appointment of Edward Curtis as collector of the port of New York, a job which Gov. William H. Seward "considers as second only, in influence, to that of [U.S.] Post Master General." Weed mentioned the belief of Seward and "his friends" that the politically skillful Curtis "could, on all important occasions, command the vote of the City of New York, & par consequence, of the State"; and that "he is the intimate friend of Mr. Webster, and possesses such influence over him as to be able to direct all his important political movements." Weed cited as an example of the influence of Curtis his personal role in "withdrawing Mr Webster's name from the list of presidential Candidates without his knowledge or consultation with him, because he was fully satisfied that Mr W. could not then, as he now is that he *never* can, be elected to that office." Porter was also given to understand by Weed that Curtis has "great respect for your [Clay's] political character, and opposed your nomination only because he was convinced that if you had been nominated, you could not have been elected; that, your position being altered, you are now the only prominent candidate of the Whig party for the next term, and cannot fail of success, unless some most unexpected event should interpose to prevent it—" In sum, according to Weed, Curtis wants Clay's "good wishes" on the collectorship appointment even though "he thinks nothing can defeat it."

Porter mentions, further, that he explained to Weed that while he had no knowledge of Harrison's views on patronage appointments, he did feel that "you [Clay] were extremely anxious to retire from the turmoil of politics" and patronage problems, and that "I thought it would be presuming too much to expect you to interfere in behalf of Mr. Curtis, with a full knowledge, which you must be presumed to possess, of the industry & zeal he had displayed in defeating your nomination, and that too in total disregard of the known wishes of a large majority of the whigs of this State." Believes, however, that Weed's analysis of the political influence and skill of Curtis is correct; that is, Curtis can very likely prevent Webster from running for the presidency again in 1844 and that it probably is "his present wish & intention (especially if you shall favour his views) to support you." But says he prefers not to express an opinion to Clay on the collectorship matter. Clay must decide this for himself.

Concludes that Harrison "is to have a most unpleasant & embarrassing duty to perform in the selection of his officers, from among the phalanx of applicants who are rushing to Washington, backed by the importunities of their respective friends; and that your personal regard for him, and your anxiety for the success of his administration, will involve you, more or less, in his troubles." Is certain, therefore, that in New York City "I know that you & Genl. Harrison will feel disposed to make some provision, for several of our old & worthy republican friends, who have seen better days, so far as it can be done consistently with a due regard to the public interests." Mentions, specifically, Thomas Morris [2:138] who deserves a "snug place . . . in the Custom House"; Gen. Robert Swartwout [5:28], "one of natures noblest men"; Judge Ogden Edwards [3:487] who wants "the place of *Naval Officer*"; and, finally, "I should not forget our friend [Jeremiah N.] Reynolds, the Explorer, who is looking, I believe, for some diplomatic agency." ALS. InU. Printed in Colton, *Clay Correspondence*, 4:448-50, but lacking first paragraph. Copy, with substantial differences in DLC-Robert Todd Lincoln Papers (DNA, M212, R21).

Thomas Morris was the son of Robert Morris (Pa.), signer of the Declaration of Independence and the Constitution of the United States. Ellis Paxson Oberholtzer, *Robert Morris: Patriot and Financier* (New York, 1903), 263-65, 303-7, 347. For Reynolds—a scientist, writer, and South Seas explorer—see W. Patrick Strauss, *Americans in Polynesia, 1783-1842* (East Lansing, Mich., 1963), 108-12, 114, 116-18, 120, 160; and Daniel Henderson, *The Hidden Coasts: A Biography of Admiral Charles Wilkes* (New York, 1953; reprint, Westport, Conn., 1971), 30-31, 35, 109. None of these men recommended by Porter received appointments in the Harrison administration.

Remark in Senate, January 28, 1841. In response to Sen. William C. Preston's introduction of a copyright bill, says he would have again presented such a measure [Comment in Senate, February 2, 1837] "but from the apprehension there was little prospect of its passage at the present session." Promises to press the matter in the next session, if he is still a member of the Senate. *Cong. Globe*, 26 Cong., 2 Sess., 129.

Later this day, Clay began his lengthy speech on public land preemption and distribution. See below.

Speech in Senate, January 28 and 29, 1841. The *Congressional Globe* notes that at 2:00 p.m. Clay began speaking on Sen. John J. Crittenden's motion to return to committee the Van Buren administration's bill to establish a permanent prospective preemption system with instructions to report out a new bill that would distribute the proceeds of public land sales among the states [Remark in Senate, December 14, 1840, and January 19, 1841]; and that at 3:30 p.m., having not completed his remarks, Clay gave way to a motion to adjourn. *Cong. Globe*, 26 Cong., 2 Sess., 129, 131.

The administration's graduation bill (as distinct from its preemption bill which was introduced by Sen. Benton on December 14, 1840) was introduced in the Senate by Clement C. Clay (Ala.), also on December 14, 1840, and was referred to the Committee on Finance. Silas Wright (N.Y.) reported it from committee with amendments on December 21, moving that it be made the order of the day on January 4, 1841; however, it was never taken up by the Senate. U.S. Sen., *Journal*, 26 Cong., 2 Sess., 29, 47, 65; *Cong. Globe*, 26 Cong., 2 Sess., 14-15. The concepts embodied in both bills were roundly attacked by Clay in his lengthy speech of January 28-29, 1841. While the administration's graduation bill [Remark in Senate, January 3, 1839] made no headway in the 26th Congress, 2nd Session, its preemption bill passed the Senate on February 2, 1841, by a 31 to 19 margin only to be beaten in the House on March 3 by a vote of 116 to 23. *Cong. Globe*, 26 Cong., 2 Sess., 138; U.S. Sen., *Journal*, 26 Cong., 2 Sess., 30, 43, 47, 77, 156; U.S. H. of Reps., *Journal*, 26 Cong., 2 Sess., 226, 376.

Clay begins his lengthy remarks on January 28 with the observation that his name has been associated with the distribution of public land sales receipts to all the states for eight or ten years, a prospect "I conscientiously believe to be one of the most important and beneficial measures ever submitted to the consideration of an American Congress." Notes that the Democrats have always opposed his version of a distribution bill; and even though they have brought the financial affairs of the nation to its present "wretched condition," they still refuse to regard the distribution of the income from public land sales as an important source of both state and national revenue. Had hoped that a proper bill could be passed before the new administration took office on March 4, but now despairs of that possibility. Criticizes the defect in the Constitution that permits a defeated administration to hang doggedly onto power, "refusing to use it, or to permit others to use it, for the benefit of the people." Believes that the administration's introduction of its so-called "permanent prospective preemption system" bill in this session is motivated by politics, by a desire to prevent more important issues from being discussed fully, and to give to its spokesmen, "who have themselves contributed to bring the country to the brink of ruin," an opportunity to decry "beforehand those measures of the coming administration which are indispensable, and which they must know to be indispensable, to restore the public happiness and prosperity." Attacks the various projects of the Democrats "to squander the public domain" by means of legislation effecting price graduation and reduction [Remark in Senate, January 3, 1839, January 3, 1840, and April 23, 1840], the cession of lands to the states in which they lie [Comment in Senate, January 3, 1840, and Remark in Senate, January 12 and 19, 1841], and the right of preemption [Remark in Senate, January 23, 1838, April 17, 1840, and December 14, 1840].

As for the level of tariffs in the months ahead, states flatly that "It is absolutely necessary to increase the public revenue." Adds that the only way to increase public revenue when the Tariff Act of 1833 expires is to impose duties on protected articles, and/or on free articles, including luxury items. Chides opposition senators for identifying any tariff levied on silks and wines as evidence of Whig dedication to a high-tariff philosophy. [The manuscript version of the speech adds here: "the greater part of the wine which is consumed in this country is from other countries than France: to be sure there is a good deal of Champaign drunk of late among us, & a considerable amount of Bordeaux wine such as Chateau Margot (here Mr Clay ran, with great seeming familiarity, over a long list, smacking his lips as he proceeded), the rest are from Madeira or from Portugal. I say, therefore, that a tax on wines & Silks is not a tax on the trade of France."] As for the level of consumption of wine in America, and the fact that the South invariably denounces tariffs on wine, Clay says: "I venture to assert that there is more champagne wine consumed in the Astor House, in the city of New York, in one year, than any State south of the Potomac consumes in a year [A laugh]." Calls attention to the highly unfavorable balance of trade with France annually ($17,000,000) and asks that steps be taken to correct it.

Estimates that tariff revenues will decrease by $5,000,000 between December 31, 1841, and June 30, 1842, thanks to provisions in the 1833 tariff legislation. Asserts that Congress must face up to the fact of this additional deficiency in the public revenue during this session and do something about it. Invites Democrat James Buchanan to "unite with us in the imposition of duties sufficient to produce an adequate revenue," even though he and his Democrat "friends denounce, in advance, the idea of imposing duties on articles of luxury! They denounce distribution! They denounce an extra session, after creating an absolute necessity for it! They denounce all measures to give us a sound currency, but the sub-treasury, denounced by the people! They denounce the administration of President Harrison before it has commenced!" Asks for the cooperation of the opposition party in restoring the prosperity of the nation. Indeed, if the opposition "gentlemen are for peace and harmony, we are prepared to meet them in a spirit of peace and harmony, to unite with them in healing the wounds and building up the prosperity of the country. But if they are for war, as it seems they are, I say, 'Lay on, Macduff.' (Sensation and a general murmuring sound throughout the chamber and galleries.)" [The manuscript version reads: ". . . but if you are for war—as it seems you are—I say 'Come on McDuff!' "]

Disputes Sen. Silas Wright's contention ("I deny the position, utterly deny it") that there is nothing in the Constitution "which allows you to lay duties on imports for the purpose of making up a deficiency produced by distributing the proceeds of the public lands." Finds this specific power in the territorial clause [Art. 4, section 3, paragraph 2] which gives to Congress the power "to dispose of . . . Property belonging to the United States." Such property, he argues, includes public lands and the proceeds from the sale of such land. Further, the general welfare clause permits and authorizes the distribution of those proceeds among the several states. In addition, "Has it not been shown that the taxing power, by a specification of the objects for which it is to be exercised, excludes an idea of raising money for the purpose of distribution? And that the land power places distribution on a totally different footing?" Contends, at length, that "by adopting the distribution principle, you do not exercise or affect the taxing power"; and that "you will be setting no dangerous precedent, as is alleged." Notes that "In the opposition to distribution, we find associated together the friends of preemption, the friends of graduation, and the friends of the cession of the whole of the public lands to a few of the States." Announces his intention to "unmask these gentlemen" who are willing to talk about distribution for the purpose of raising revenue only when a "bill to distribute the proceeds equally among all the States is pending." [Manuscript version reads: "But I want to unmask our opponents on this revenue subject I promised to show that the purpose of raising revenue from the public domain is not *bona fide* their purpose, but that we the friends of Distribution wish this money for paying the debts of the Union and that the others are opposed to any revenue from the public Lands."] As soon as the bill "is got rid of" these "gentlemen relapse into their old projects of throwing away the public lands."

Traces the history of opposition to distribution based on the argument that it is unconstitutional as a revenue-raising device. Recalls the attempt of the Jacksonian opposition to embarrass him politically in 1832 by referring his public land (distribution) bill [8:494, 539-41, 609-10] to the Committee on Manufactures rather than to the Committee on Public Lands because he was a member of the former and had also at that time been prominently mentioned for the presidency. Their strategy was to make sure "that no measure, for permanently settling the question of the public lands, could emanate from me that would not affect injuriously my popularity, either with the new or the old States, or with both." Says he is still proud of the bill he finally devised in 1832-33 which distributed the land sales proceeds to all the states and which was eventually passed by both houses of Congress only to be pocket-vetoed by President Jackson [8:609-10, 671]. Because he feared that Congress would override a regular constitutional veto, the president chose an "arbitrary . . . irregular and unprecedented proceeding" in that he "resolved not to return the bill, and did not return it to Congress, but pocketed it!"

Reviews the legislative history of his 1832-33 land bill, citing quotations by Jackson in his annual message in December, 1832 to show that while the then president supported the constitutional power of Congress to dispose of the public lands in such manner as to advance the general interest of the American people, he also believed that these lands should "cease, as soon as practicable, to be a source of revenue." Recalls that in April, 1832, as soon as the Committee on Manufactures reported a public land bill that would have distributed the land sales revenue to all the states, the Jackson party, rather than act upon it, referred it to the Committee on Public Lands—a "curious parliamentary anomaly of referring the report of one standing committee to another standing committee." On May 18, 1832, the Public Lands Committee issued its own report which, in essence, abandoned the proposition that public land sales were an important source of public revenue. Instead, "Give away the public land was the doctrine of that report," Clay asserts. Quotes from Jackson's belated veto message of December 4, 1833, which killed Clay's 1832-33 land bill. This was, he recalls, the "memorable veto message—one of the most singular omnibusses that was ever beheld—a strange vehicle, that seemed to challenge wonder and admiration, on account of the multitude of hands evidently employed in its construction, the impress of some of them smeared and soiled, as if they were fresh from the kitchen." (Manuscript version reads: ". . . the impress of some of them much smeared and dirtied as tho recently from the kitchen, very visibly impressed on many parts of it.") The Veto message demonstrates Jackson's belief that the public land should be sold off as soon as possible by graduating and reducing the price of unsold land; and that, as the president phrased it, "the refuse, remaining unsold, shall be abandoned to the States, and the machinery of our land system entirely withdrawn." This has been the unfortunate philosophy and policy of the Jacksonians on public land issues for the past twelve years, Clay notes. It is a policy, he charges, of "reduction of the price, by graduation, by pre-emptions, and by ultimate cessions, to get rid of them as soon as practicable." Quotes other Democrats who support such a policy. Denies that the "old" states [the original thirteen, plus Vt., Ky., Tenn., Ohio and La.] and the "new" states [Ind., Miss., Ill., Ala., Mo., Ark., and Mich.] should be treated differently and less generously in terms of the distribution levels provided in federal cession policy. Attacks the opposition's perennial "graduation" bill, again introduced by the Democrats in the current session, and scheduled to go into operation in April, 1842, as simply another poorly disguised device to give away fifty million dollars worth of the public land. Chides Sen. Silas Wright of N.Y. for bringing such a bill to the Senate floor from the Committee on Finance, which he chairs, with no report other than a verbal recommendation "that the bill do pass [A general laugh]."

Argues, further, that if one applies the principle in Sen. John C. Calhoun's bill [Comment in Senate, January 3, 1840; Remark in Senate, January 19, 1841] that would cede the public lands lying in the nine "land states" now in the Union to those states [La., Ohio, Ind., Miss., Ill., Ala., Mo., Ark., and Mich.] then one must extend the same principle "to other new States . . . [later] admitted into the Union, until the whole public land is exhausted." Wonders where Calhoun "derives the power" to limit the cessions of public land to but nine states and to determine that 35 percent of the income realized from the sale of those ceded lands be distributed solely to those states; and where does he get the power to discriminate against "the revolutionary States, by whose valor a large part of it [public domain] was achieved." How is the 65 percent of the state income from the sale of public land that is to be paid to the central government to be collected, especially if the state has allowed squatters on the government's portion? Quotes at length from the report of his Committee on Manufactures, dated April, 1832, which dealt in part with various schemes then considered for dividing land to be ceded to the new states or to the United States. Calls attention to the report's conclusion that "Upon full and thorough consideration . . . it is inexpedient either to reduce the price of the public lands, or to cede them to the new States," and its statement that once the public debt is liquidated the income from public land sales might "be beneficially appropriated to some other objects for a limited time."

Presents statistics and arguments to show how badly Ohio, for example, would fare in the future if Calhoun's nine-state cession plan were adopted; and how well Ohio would fare if his proposal for the distribution of public land receipts to all the states were embraced instead. Maintains that Ohio is being asked by Calhoun to accept 35 percent of the proceeds of the sale of the remaining 800,000 acres of public land lying in that state; whereas, "For this trifling consideration she is to surrender her interest [one-tenth interest based on her population] in one hundred and sixty millions of acres" presently available and in what "eventually [will be] . . . a billion" acres comprising the remainder of the "whole public domain." Notes: "A capital bargain this, to which I supposed the two senators [Benjamin Tappan and William Allen] had assented, by which, in behalf of their State, they exchanged one hundred millions of acres of land against eight hundred thousand. [A laugh.]" [Manuscript version reads: ". . . for the sake of these 800,000 acres they have voted away the interest of Ohio in 160 millions of acres—which would have been exactly *Sixteen Millions*. But if the whole billion of acres is to be distributed, then Ohio will get 100 millions. So the two Sen[ato]rs from Ohio have voted away 100 millions, & got in exchange 800,000. (A laugh)."] Adds: "Go home, Messieurs Senators from Ohio, and tell your constituents of your votes. Tell them of your preference of a cession of all their interest in the public lands, with the exception of that inconsiderable portion remaining in Ohio, to the reception of Ohio's fair distributive share of the proceeds of all the public lands of the United States, now and hereafter." [Manuscript version reads: "That is their bargain for Ohio. Yes—go home Messrs Senators from Ohio, go—tell your constituents the votes you have given—give them an account of your preferences for Cession over Distribution."]

Notes particularly that Calhoun's "plan of cession among the nine new States" is such that "The States with the smallest population get the most land. Thus, Arkansas, with only about one fifteenth part of the population of Ohio, will receive upward of twenty-eight times as much land as Ohio. The scheme proceeds upon the idea of reversing the maxim of the greatest good to the greatest number, and of substituting the greatest good to the smallest number." Complains that "all kinds of distribution of the public lands or their proceeds may be made—to particular States, to pre-emptioners, to charities, to objects of education or internal improvement, to foreigners, to Indians, to black, red, white, and gray, to every body, but among all the States of the Union. There is an old adage, according to which, charity should begin at home; but, according to the doctrine of the opponents of distribution, it neither begins nor ends at home."

"[Here Mr. Clay gave way to an adjournment.]"

Speech in Senate, January 29, 1841 (continued). Says he will not "inflict upon the Senate even a recapitulation of the heads of argument" made in yesterday's address. Does, however, add several facts about the tariff that relate to his discussion yesterday of the nation's unfavorable balance of trade with France.

Proceeds then to discuss the history of that portion of the public domain acquired by the War of the Revolution to show that one important motive of the states which held and subsequently ceded their crown lands to the government established by the Articles of Confederation was to create a fund from which to extinguish the war debt. Also argues, on the basis of this fact, that "from the moment of the adoption of the federal Constitution, the proceeds of the public lands ought to have been divided among the States." Recalls in this connection that the seven revolutionary states which magnanimously ceded their "waste lands" first to the Confederation government, then to the new national government, in order to create interstate harmony, did so for the benefit of all the states, even for those six which had no such land to cede. Asks: "Now what is the measure of the senator [Calhoun] from South Carolina? It is in effect to restore the discordant and menacing state of things which existed in 1783, prior to any cession from the States. It is worse than that. For it proposes that seventeen States shall give up immediately or eventually all their interest in the public lands, lying in nine States, to those nine States. Now if the seven States had refused to cede at all, they could at least have asserted that they fought Great Britain for these lands, as hard as the six. They would have had, therefore, the apparent right of conquest, although it was a common conquest. But the senator's proposition is, to cede these public lands from the States which fought for them in the revolutionary war, to States that neither fought for them nor had existence during that war." Adds the observation that "To me, it appears clear, that, either from the epoch of the establishment of the present Constitution, or certainly from that of the payment of the revolutionary debt, the proceeds of the public lands being no longer applied by the general government, according to that rule, they ought to have been transferred to the States upon some equitable principle of division, conforming as nearly as possible to the spirit of the cessions." Points out that his and Sen. Crittenden's plan of the distribution of land sale income [Remark in Senate, January 19, 1841] is based fairly on population statistics, that is, "on federal numbers, which are made up of all the inhabitants of the United States other than the slaves, and three fifths of them. The South, surely, should be the last section to object to a distribution founded on that rule. And yet, if I rightly understood one of the dark allusions of the senator from South Carolina (Mr. Calhoun), he has attempted to excite the jealousy of the North on that very ground."

Insists that while the public domain is the common property of all the states, its use and enjoyment was designed to benefit the individual members of the alliance of states. In support of this view, calls attention to his report of May 2, 1834 [8:723], in response to Jackson's veto of the 1832-33 land bill [8:609-10, 671], in which he had cited Virginia's deed of cession of its crown lands to the Confederation in 1784 to sustain his contention that "the language of the deed seems to contemplate a separate use and enjoyment of the fund by the States individually, rather than a preservation of it for common expenditure. The fund itself is to be a common fund for the use and benefit of such of the United States as have become, or shall become, members of the confederation or federal alliance, Virginia inclusive. The grant is not for the benefit of the confederation, but for that of the several States which compose the confederation. The fund is to be under the management of the confederation collectively, and is so far a common fund; but it is to be managed for the use and benefit of the States individually, and is so far a separate fund under a joint management." Believes, therefore, that "Distribution and only distribution, of the proceeds of the public lands, among the States, upon the principles proposed, will conform to the spirit, and execute the trust, created in the deeds of cession."

Charges Silas Wright with juggling numbers in his effort to demonstrate that the public domain has cost more over the years to maintain and administer than the $120,000,000 from land sales it has brought in. Challenges specific debits mentioned by the New York senator, such as the $80,000,000 cost of conducting the nation's relations with the Indians, especially the expense of removing them to the west side of the Mississippi. Thinks this expenditure cannot reasonably be charged to the cost of maintaining the public domain. Regrets that a foreigner, listening to Sen. Wright's views on the distribution controversy, might conclude "that we were not one united people, but that there were two separate and distinct nations; one acted upon by the general government, and the other by the State governments. But is that a fair representation of the case? Are we not one and the same people, acted upon, it is true, by two systems of government, two sets of public agents; the one established for general, and the other for local purposes?"

Refers at length to the problem of state debts (much of it contracted to pay for internal improvements), to defaults on state bonds, and to the suggestion that the central government should assume such debts and guarantee such bonds [Remark in Senate, February 18, 1840]. The concept of assumption he characterizes as "a wicked, malignant, Danton-like proposition" that further undermines the confidence of European creditors in the ability and good faith of the debtor states to make good their debts. Sees distribution as a way for these debtor states to solve their financial problems. Suggests that the Whig approach to these state financial problems is based on the conviction that "this government has the power, and, as I think, is under a duty, to distribute the proceeds of the public lands; and that it has the power, which the States have not, to lay duties on foreign luxuries; we propose to make that distribution, pay our debt to the States, and save the States, to that extent at least, from the necessity of resorting to direct taxation, the most onerous of all modes of levying money upon the people. We propose to supply the deficiency produced from the withdrawal of the land fund by duties on luxuries, which the wealthy only will pay, and so far save the States from the necessity of burdening the poor. We propose, that, by a just exercise of incontestable powers possessed by this government, we shall go to the succor of all the States, and by a fair distribution of the proceeds of the public lands among them, avert, as far as that may avert, the ruin and dishonor with which some of them are menaced. We propose, in short, such an administration of the powers of this government as shall protect and relieve our common constituents from the embarrassments to which they may be exposed from the defects in the powers or in the administration of the State governments."

Assures his Senate colleagues that it is the Whigs who have at heart the distress of the poor, not the Democrats who claim to champion them. Explains: "At this session, a tax, which would be borne exclusively by the rich, encounters their opposition. And now we have proposed another mode of benefiting the poor, by distribution of the land proceeds, to prevent their being borne down and oppressed by direct taxation; and this, too, is opposed from the same quarter! These gentlemen will not consent to lay a tax on the luxuries of the affluent, and, by their votes, insist upon leaving the States under the necessity of imposing direct taxes on the farmer, the laboring man, the poor, and all the while set up to be the exclusive friends of the poor! [A general laugh.] Really, sir, the best friends appear to be the worst enemies of the poor, and their greatest enemies their best friends."

Charges that the Democratic party has not the "slightest pretension" to the word democratic. Says he was raised as a true democrat. Indeed, "In the school of 1798, in which I was taught, and to which I have ever faithfully adhered, we were instructed to be watchful and jealous of executive power, enjoined to practice economy in the public disbursements, and urged to rally around the people, and not attach ourselves to the presidential car. This was Jefferson's democracy. But the modern democrats, who have assumed the name, have reversed all these wholesome maxims, and have given to democracy a totally different version. They have run it down, as they have run down, or at least endangered, State rights, the right of instruction—admirable in their proper sphere—and all other rights, by perversion and extravagance. But, thank God, true democracy and true democrats have not been run down."

Summarizes, in conclusion, the two basic plans submitted to Congress from time to time to dispose of the vast public domain. One of them accepts the proposition that land sales revenue should not be regarded as a source of revenue for either the central or state governments and contends that "the general government, being, unfit, or less competent than the State governments, to manage the public lands, it ought to hasten to get rid of them, either by reduction of the price, by donation, by pre-emption, or by cessions to certain States, or by all these methods together." The second, or "rival plan," the one supported by Clay, is "for the general government to retain the public domain, and make distribution of the proceeds, in time of peace, among the several States, upon equal and just principles, according to the rule of federal numbers, and, in time of war, to resume the proceeds for its vigorous prosecution. We think that the administration of the public lands had better remain with the common government, to be regulated by uniform principles, than confided to the States, to be administered according to various, and, perhaps, conflicting views. As to that important part of them which was ceded by certain States to the United States, for the common benefit of all the States, a trust was thereby created, which has been voluntarily accepted by the United States, and which they are not at liberty now to decide or transfer."

Asserts that the "measure which I have the honor to propose settles this great and agitating question forever." Thinks his approach to the problem, in that it will benefit all the states, will "tend to the perpetuity of our glorious Union!" It will also be of especial benefit to future states, perhaps "thirty or forty more new States," because "this measure would cement them all fast together." Mentions the efforts of Sen. Lewis F. Linn (Mo.) to extend American settlement and influence into Oregon. Visualizes new states soon coming into existence on the Pacific coast. Asks rhetorically if those states, "Proud of the commission they bear, and happy to find themselves here in council with friends, and brothers, and countrymen, enjoying the incalculable benefits of this great confederacy, and, among them, their annual distributive share of the issues of a nation's inheritance, would even they, the remote people of the Pacific, ever desire to separate themselves from such a high and glorious destiny?" Copy. Printed in Colton, *Clay Correspondence*, 6:225-70. Not printed in *Cong. Globe*, 26 Cong., 2 Sess., or its appendix. The *Globe* mentions only that Clay spoke on January 28 and concluded his remarks on January 29, 1841. *Ibid.*, 129, 131. An undated manuscript of this speech, in a strange hand, probably that of a Senate clerk, has been found. D. DLC-HC (DNA, M212, R5). It covers only that segment of the speech delivered on January 28. Apparently, it is the manuscript on which Colton's printed version was based—a corrected manuscript that includes numerous editorial changes by Clay and possibly by Colton himself. Among these are deletions, additions, interlineations, and even the softening of especially bombastic language. Comparisons of the manuscript, corrected manuscript, and Colton's printed version reveal, however, no essential variations in order or substance. Excerpts from Clay's remarks on January 29, identical to the wording found in Colton, *Clay Correspondence*, 6:264-65, 269-70, were reprinted in the 1844 campaign volume titled, *The Ashland Text Book, Being a Compendium of Mr. Clay's Speeches, on Various Public Measures, Etc. Etc.* (Philadelphia, 1844), 66-70.

On January 30, 1841, Calhoun replied to Clay's speech of January 28-29 and to one by Webster on the same subject. *Cong. Globe*, 26 Cong., 2 Sess., Appendix, 135-40. At the conclusion of Calhoun's remarks a vote was taken on his substitute [Comment in Senate, January 3, 1840; Remark in Senate, January 19, 1841] for the administration's preemption bill [Remark in Senate, December 14, 1840; Comment in Senate, January 20, 1841]. It was defeated 20 to 31, Clay and Crittenden voting nay. Fourteen of the 18 senators from the nine "new" states voted yea. Only four from those states voted nay. *Cong. Globe*, 26 Cong., 2 Sess., Appendix, 140.

As soon as Clay took his seat on January 29 he was the recipient of sharp criticism from Sen. Benjamin Tappan of Ohio for "the extraordinary attack" made personally on him and his colleague, Sen. William Allen, during the speech on the distribution of public land receipts just concluded. Tappan vigorously denied Clay's charge, ("not founded in truth") that he and Allen had voted for a proposal that would, in effect, trade Ohio's share of the income from the sale of 160,000,000 acres of western public land for 35 percent of the income from the sale of the 800,000 acres of public land remaining in Ohio; and rejected his order "to us to go home and account to our constituents for this gross sacrifice of the interests of Ohio." So bitter, personal, and wide-ranging was Tappan's reaction to Clay's "matchless insolence" that Clay finally called him to order and was sustained in this by Vice President Richard M. Johnson. Clay then rose to explain that he "had not the remotest intention of insulting the Senators from Ohio" and was simply advising them to take up the distribution question with their constituents when they got home. *Cong. Globe*, 26 Cong., 2 Sess., 130.

From John Stearns, New York, January 29, 1841. Seeks the office of U.S. marshal for the southern district of New York. Believes the job will give him "a few hours each day that I may exclusively devote to my favourite Theory." Explains that "You have probably read an essay on the mind founded on principles entirely new & original which I recently published & which I fully believe to be founded on the basis of truth. I have submitted this theory to the critical inspection of professors and Lecturers on Mental Philosophy While some have yielded their entire approbation, no one has advanced any solid objections. My desire is to carry out this theory in all its minute details and in a manner that shall produce conviction that it constitutes the only true basis of mental philosophy. But the incessant pressure of professional calls entirely deprives me of the leisure necessary to carry this object into effect, without which I must abandon my purpose in despair." ALS. DNA, RG59, A. and R. (M531, R4). For Stearns (1770-1848), a physician and former member of the New York state senate, see *NCAB*, 6:538. The essay mentioned was published under the title *Philosophy of Mind, Developing New Sources of Ideas, Designating Their Distinctive Classes, and Simplifying the Faculties and Operations of the Whole Mind*. New York, 1840.

From Benjamin Reeder, Shinnston, Harrison County, Va. (W.Va.), January 30, 1841. Recommends, at length, Gideon Draper Camden for district attorney in the western district of Virginia.

Agrees with the reported opinion of Daniel Webster that all departments of the outgoing administration should be thoroughly investigated for evidence of "extravagance, folly and Corruption" when the new administration takes office. Thinks $50,000 would be well spent in this enterprise. Believes also that the Whigs can elect members of Congress from the three northwest Virginia districts if "all the Materials" are "properly employed." Is certain that in the district of Andrew Beirne of Union (Monroe County) "harmony exists and a Whig will be elected." But in the districts of Joseph Johnson of Bridgeport (Harrison County) and Lewis Steenrod of Wheeling "there are Schisms, that I fear cannot be healed, and if not we must lose. . . . in Steenrods district they may settle down to a Single Candidate but under disadvantages that very probably will produce defeat." ALS. DNA, RG59, A. and R. (M531, R4). For Reeder, see 5:167.

Beirne did not run for reelection in Virginia's 19th congressional district. In it, George W. Summers, a Whig, was elected over two opponents. Johnson did not seek reelection from the 20th district. There Samuel L. Hayes, a Democrat, defeated Whig candidate, Augustine J. Smith. Lewis Steenrod, a Democrat, was reelected without opposition in the 21st district. For all of Virginia's 1841 elections, see Clay to Brooke, January 7, 1841.

Remark in Senate, February 1, 1841. Presents a memorial from Logan County, Ohio, asking for U.S. recognition of and the establishment of diplomatic relations with Haiti [Remark in Senate, March 23, 1840]. Notes, however, that nothing can be done with this issue this session "if indeed any thing ought to be done at all," with it. Moves successfully to table the memorial. *Cong. Globe*, 26 Cong., 2 Sess., 135.

To JAMES WATSON WEBB Washington, February 3, 1841

I received your two favors, with the enclosure contained in one of them.[1] I have never doubted your persevering friendship. As to repelling advances from a certain quarter, I am unaware of the fact of any such advances being made, and consequently I cannot knowingly have repelled them. If it be meant, that I should co-operate with those who are desirous to place Mr. [Edward] Curtis in the office of Collr. of N. York,[2] I must say, and say explicitly and irrevocably, that I can afford no such cooperation, because I believe that gentleman has neither the requisite qualifications, nor the requisite confidence of the community. At the same time, it is well known, that I shall have no power to withhold or grant the office. And, in regard to official appointments, the rule, which I have adopted, is that of noninterference, with the sole limitation of endeavoring to prevent, on rare and important occasions, an improper appointment.

There is a meeting of the members of the H. of R. to night to consult as to the propriety of an Extra Session[3] &c.

ALS. KyU. 1. Reference obscure; but see Porter to Clay, Jan. 27, 1841. 2. Lawrence to Clay, Nov. 30, 1840; Porter to Clay, Dec. 14, 1840. 3. Clay to Speed, Nov. 21, 1840. See also Notes for Newspaper Editorial, Feb. 4, 1841.

NOTES FOR NEWSPAPER EDITORIAL Washington, *ca.* February 4, 1841

The question of an Extra Session[1] begins to be much discussed in the circles of the Metropolis. We think that question was decided by the People in Novr last when they decided that there should be a change of the C Magistrate of the U.S. They decided that there should be a change of administration—a change of policy—a change in the measures of govt. They determined that Mr. V. B.s admon. should cease on the 4h March next; and that Genl. Harrison's Admon should begin on that day. If it were practicable, [the?] change of measures, Legislative as well as Executive, ought to commence on that day, but since it cannot, as far as the Legislative action is necessary, the Legislature ought to be convened at the earliest convenient & practicable day.

Those who are opposed to an Extra Session are, in effect, in favor of the continuation of Mr V. B'[s] Admon 12 or 18 months after its constitutional termination; for it would take that time to mature in Congress any important measure. The continuation of Mr. V. Buren's Admon, Subtreasury[2] and all! An exaction of Specie payments, and a still greater exaction on the 1st. of July next at a moment when the Banks are struggling to resume & maintain resumption of Specie payments. The people want *new* measures, which shall provide for their welfare, and which shall look both to the Govt. and from the Govt. to them. Those who oppose an Extra Session, virtually maintain, that these measures are all to be postponed some 15 or 18 months—that is to say put off until a large part of the term of the Admon, which was to mature and adopt them, has passed away!

If the view of the question of an Extra Session were restricted to the condition of the Govt alone, without regard to the wants & the good of the people, an affirmative decision would be inevitable—There is now, incontestibly, a deficient Revenue. During the next ordinary Session, five millions more of this deficient revenue will be abstracted by the operation of the Compromise act.[3] On the 31st Decr. of this year, one half of that sum goes off. Suppose Congress not to meet until the first Monday of that month, how is it possible to provide in season for this additional deficiency? How, and give reasonable notice to the Merchants to regulate their importations?

But if the People had not decided in favr of an Extra Session, our opponents have resolved by their course during the present Session, to render it inevitable. They seem determined to leave every thing in the state of the greatest disorder & confusion. They have made, and refuse to make, any provision for the deficit in the Treasury. Their financial ability does not rise above the issue of due bills, or Treasury notes[4] to supply present necessities. These, they think, will relieve them, altho' they know that the charge which they will make upon the two last quarters of the year must greatly embarrass the new administration. In one branch of Congress, scarcely any thing has been done, whilst in the other four weeks have been spent of the most precious time of the Session in duplicating preemption laws[5]

We feel fortified in the strong conviction which we entertain of the indispensable necessity of an Extra Session, by the repugnance with which our good friends of the present admon regard it. They appear to be greatly grieved & shocked by the idea of it. Without it, they know that their measures, their implements, their instruments will continue to operate. With it, they see the prospect of the establishment of those Salutary Measures of relief, of reform and of economy, which the wants of the People demand and the will of the People has decreed.

Some superficial thinkers fear that as Mr. V. B. had an abortive Extra Session, an Extra Session may prove injurious to Genl. H[arriso]n. But what was his called for? To relieve the People? No such thing. That purpose was expressly repudiated. It was called to propose that last most disastrous link in the chain of rash experiments—the Sub Treasury. It was called not for the People but for the Office holders. Genl Harrisons Extra Session (if he summon one) will be convened for the benefit & for the interest both of the People & of the Govt.

We have thought the occasion prompted the expression of our opinion. We speak of Course for ourselves only, as the conductors of an Independent paper.[6] If we have expressed ourselves in strong language, it has been because we feel strong convictions.

AD. KyLoF. 1. Clay to Speed, Nov. 21, 1840. 2. Speech in Senate, Sept. 25, 1837, Feb. 19, 1838, Jan. 20, 1840, and Dec. 15, 1840. See also Remark in Senate, Jan. 16, 1838, and Dec. 14, 1840; Comment in Senate, March 7, 1838; and Clay to Porter, Dec. 27, 1838.

3. Compromise Tariff Act of 1833. See 8:604, 619-22, 626-27; also Remark in Senate, Jan. 16, 1841. 4. Comment in Senate, Sept. 15 and 25, 1837; Remark in Senate, March 9, 1840; Speech in Senate, April 3, 1840. 5. Remark in Senate, Dec. 14, 1840; Speech in Senate, Jan. 6 and 28-29, 1841; Comment in Senate, Jan. 20, 1841. 6. This draft was published with substantial changes in phrasing and punctuation in the Washington *Daily National Intelligencer*, Feb. 5, 1841.

Remark in Senate, February 4, 1841. Presents a memorial from Camden, S.C., asking for a general bankruptcy law [Remark in Senate, April 22, 1840]. *Cong. Globe*, 26 Cong., 2 Sess., 142.

Later this day, in response to the observation that there was not time enough remaining in the session for the House to act on the bankruptcy bill, and to a motion that the bill be tabled, Clay urges the Senate to get on with the bill "without reference to the other branch of Congress." *Ibid.*, 144.

To Francis T. Brooke, February 5, 1841. With reference to an appeal from Brooke to assist him in arranging a patronage appointment, states: "During the twelve last years I have recommended no person for any place whatever, to the appointing power of the Federal Government." Adds: "I have been constrained, after a full consideration, and on a deliberate survey of the whole ground, to adopt the principle of non-interference with the new Administration, as to official appointments. Without it, if the day had a duration of forty-eight hours instead of twenty-four, I should be unable to attend to the applications I receive." Copy. Printed in Colton, *Clay Correspondence*, 4:451.

Remark in Senate, February 5, 1841. Participates (not recorded) in the debate on a joint resolution that would transfer to the state of Maryland stock in the Chesapeake and Ohio Canal [8:734, 742, 828] held by the United States. *Cong. Globe*, 26 Cong., 2 Sess., 147. This resolution was debated briefly on January 14 and was passed *viva voce* by the Senate on February 8. It was not acted upon in the House during this session. *Ibid.*, 100, 152.

The proposal had first been made in 1839 to transfer the federal government's $2,500,000 worth of stock in the canal company to the state of Maryland which, if this transfer occurred, would guarantee the completion of the eastern section of the canal. In 1843 another attempt to transfer the U.S. government's stock to Maryland failed. Work on the canal continued intermittently amid much political controversy until the eastern section was finally completed in the fall of 1850. Walter S. Sanderlin, *The Great National Project, A History of the Chesapeake and Ohio Canal* in *John Hopkins University Studies in Historical and Political Science*, vol. 64 (Baltimore, 1946), 141-61, *passim.*

To PETER B. PORTER Washington, February 7, 1841

I received your favor from Saratoga.[1] It exhibits the conduct of Mr. [Edward] Curtis in a light so base and perfidious towards Mr. Webster, that I want you to leave it at my discretion to shew your letter to this Gentleman. How can such a man as C. be trusted? My determination not to co-operate in his appointment is irrevocable.

I have been constrained, after full deliberation, to adopt the rule of non interference in official appointments further than, on rare and important occasions, to endeavor to prevent very bad ones. There are so many and such weighty considerations for this rule that I am sure, if I had time to state them all, that I should secure your approbation of it.

I shall be unable therefore to aid the friends whom you have named,[2] except that, if the appointing power should apply to me, I would with pleasure render testimony favorable to them.

The suspension again of the Philada. Banks[3] must have the effect, I think, of aiding the establishment of a new Bank of the U.S.

The President elect has arrived at Balto. and is expected here tomorrow.

We shall probably have an Extra Session.[4] In my opinion it is perfectly indispensible.

ALS. NBuHi. 1. Porter to Clay, Jan. 28, 1841. 2. *Ibid.* 3. On Feb. 8, 1841, Clay wrote Joseph Trotter that before his bank's suspension of specie payments on Feb. 4 he drew a check on it for $2000, which he sent to Kentucky, specifying that it be paid in specie or lawful currency. "I should regret that it should be protested, when presented." ALS. ViU. For the third suspension of specie payments by Nicholas Biddle's United States Bank of Pennsylvania on Feb. 4, 1841, and soon after by other Philadelphia banks, see Govan, *Nicholas Biddle*, 388-400; also Clay to Otis, Dec. 13, 1838, and Clay to Letcher, Sept. 7, 1840. Trotter was president of the Bank of Pennsylvania which suspended specie payments on Feb. 5, 1841. See Elva Tooker, *Nathan Trotter, Philadelphia Merchant 1787-1853* (Cambridge, Mass., 1955), 9-11, 46-47, 51-55, 60-62, 168-70; and Washington *Daily National Intelligencer*, Feb. 8, 1841. 4. Clay to Speed, Nov. 21, 1840; Notes for Newspaper Editorial, *ca.* Feb. 4, 1841.

From Benjamin Gratz, Lexington, February 8, 1841. Recommends his brother, Jacob, for appointment as naval officer in the Philadelphia customhouse, noting that he has served for three successive years in the Pennsylvania state legislature and for several years was president of the Union Canal Company. Concludes with the observation that "The Hemp manufacturers have gloomy prospects before us, the introduction of the Gunny Bags is 'playing hob' with us, notwithstanding your efforts I fear we are doomed to suffer." ALS. DNA, RG56, A. and R. Gunny bags were coarse, heavy sacks made of jute or hemp. At this time many of these bags were being imported from Scotland and East India for use in wrapping cotton bales. Hopkins, *Hemp Industry in Kentucky*, 145.

For Jacob Gratz (1788-1856), a Philadelphia merchant who had served in both houses of the Pennsylvania legislature, see William V. Byars, *B. and M. Gratz, Merchants in Philadelphia, 1754-1798* (Jefferson City, Mo., 1916), 278.

From John Henderson, Washington, February 10, 1841. Reports on sherry wines that Duncan Robertson can supply, quoting from a letter from Robertson to himself as follows: "1st. Two quarter casks very old *Amontillado* or extra pale sherry $4.50 per gallon. This wine can be no where else found in our country. I am most desirous that Mr Clay should possess it. 2nd. Three quarter casks old pale lightly flavoured Sherry—dry—$3¼. per gallon. 3rd. One quarter cask similar to that I sent you at $3. per gallon. (This wine we all concur in pronouncing excellent. J.H.). 4th. Eighteen qrs. Casks very pale & delicate, a wine of known worth, & particularly esteemed during Summer months & my favourite $3/. pr gall." Assures Clay that Robertson's "word & judgment may be relied on." ALS. DLC-TJC (DNA, M212, R19).

On March 29, 1841, Duncan Robertson wrote Clay from Norfolk, Va., thanking him for his March 12 order of a quarter cask of "Extra Pale Amontillado Sherry wine," which measured 30 gallons @4.50 per gal. ($135.), together with $8. worth of bottles and $9. worth of boxes, corks, lathing, and packing—a total order of $152. Order was sent to Lexington. *Ibid.* (R14). Letter endorsed by Clay: "Pale Sherry—paid for by a check on the Bank of Pennsa. 23 Apl. 1841."

To Margaret Smith Hughes, Baltimore, February 10, 1841. Transmits a letter from "my valued friend," her father, Christopher Hughes, resident in Stockholm. Reports that her father informed him "of your fortunate deliverence from the imminent danger to which your life was exposed by the disaster which last May befel the Poland." Congratulates her that it has "pleased God to preserve one so dear to your bereaved father and sole surviving parent." ALS. MiU-C. Addressed to Miss Hughes at Col. Samuel Moore's residence on St. Paul Street, Baltimore. For Moore, see 2:232 and Clay to Moore, May 21, 1840. Laura Sophia Smith (Mrs. Christopher) Hughes had died in Sweden on August 7, 1832, of pulmonary tuberculosis. Dunham, "Diplomatic Career of Christopher Hughes," Ph.D. dissertation, Ohio State University, 1968, p. 167.

Margaret Hughes had been on board the *Poland* when it was struck by lightning and set on fire in the Atlantic on May 16, 1840. Passengers and crew fled to lifeboats from which they were picked up by the *Clifton* from Liverpool on May 18. Washington *Daily National Intelligencer,* May 28, 1840.

To JOHN M. CLAYTON — Washington, February 12, 1841

I have omitted to write to you, for some days past, amidst the intrigues, workings and arrangements connected with the formation of the new Cabinet,[1] because I was not able to communicate any thing positive or definitive. Your friends have not been unmindful of their feelings or duties towards you, altho' the final result has not corresponded with my anxious wishes. I discovered some time ago a movement to put Mr. [Thomas] Ewing in the Treasury instead of the P. Office. That movement had a Northern origin, and among other objects had in view the appt. of some one from the interior of Penna. as P. M. G. I did not approve the movement and so told Mr. Ewing. I said to him, "the people every where have pointed to you as P. M. G. and you had better conform to that indication." But the movement has nevertheless been crowned with success, and Mr. [Francis] Granger is to be P. M. G. Genl. Harrison informed the Southern members of Congress that, if they could agree upon any man from the South as Secy. of the Navy, his name would be favorably considered. They had various meetings and made several attempts to agree upon a man, but they could not unite. The N. Carolina delegation went for Mr. [George E.] Badger,[2] others for Mr. [William C.] Preston &c &c. In this state of things I had an interview with him last night, and urged your appointment as Secy. of the Navy.[3] He expressed himself, as he had before done, in the strongest terms of your abilities, services and merits; but did not give me much hope of my desire being realized. And since I commenced this letter I learn that Mr Badger of N. Carolina is designated for the Navy Dept. If it be so, as I presume it to be the Cabinet is complete, and will be composed of Webster, Ewing, [John] Bell, Badger, [John J.] Crittenden, Granger.

It is useless for me to dwell on my disappointment in respect to yourself. You know my heart, and can appreciate my feelings. It is of some consolation to me to anticipate that your disappointment will be far less than my own.

We must support this Administration, or rather, I should say, we must not fall out with it because precisely the friends we could wish have not in every instance been called to the Cabinet. I have strong fears & strong hopes. And some times the one & sometimes the other predominate. But we must under all circumstances do our duty to our Country. I shall strive to perform mine.

ALS. DLC-John M. Clayton Papers (DNA, M212, R20). Written in Senate Chamber. 1. Clay to Porter, Dec. 8, 1840. 2. For Badger, see *BDAC*. 3. It may have been at this interview, during which Clay pressed the president to appoint Clayton, that Harrison allegedly exclaimed: "Mr. Clay, you forget that I am the President!" This quotation however, dates from an August 31, 1880, recollection. Tyler, *Letters and Times of the Tylers*, 2:10; Poage, *Henry Clay*, 20.

From Manuel Eyre, Philadelphia, February 12, 1841. Asks Clay to support the candidacy of his son-in-law, R.C. Griffiths, former law professor at the University of Virginia, for a consulship in Marseilles. Points out that ill health makes it necessary for Griffiths to reside in a warm climate. Adds: "I have had for the last two years a most unpleasant task as Director of the Bank U States [U.S. Bank of Pennsylvania] in endeavouring to develope the Delinquencies and hidden transactions of that Bank by the former & Present Presidents & Cashiers. The Committee of Stockholders are now examining [and] will report [on] 1t Monday in April to the adjourned meeti[n]g of the Stockholders and I am afraid more moral depravity will be brought to light than we have ever witnessed in Philada." ALS. DNA, RG59, A. and R. (M531, R4).

For Eyre, Philadelphia businessman, director of the United States Bank of Pennsylvania, and major stockholder in the Schuylkill Navigation Co., see 2:283 and *PMHB*, 25:587; 49:183; 62:177, 188. Eyre was apparently the leader of a group seeking to discredit Nicholas Biddle and his management of the bank by proving that some directors and officers had been permitted by the exchange committee to borrow large amounts from the bank for private speculations and that their losses endangered the bank. The stockholders' investigating committee reported on April 5, 1841, that Biddle and other bank officers were guilty of "gross mismanagement," and a "most wanton disregard of the interests of the stockholders," as well as "culpable breaches of trust." Govan, *Nicholas Biddle*, 376-87, 391-97.

From George C. Sibley, Lindenwood, near St. Charles, Mo., February 13, 1841. Reports, at great length, his views on the nation's hostile policy toward the Indian tribes these past ten or twelve years. Hopes Harrison and Clay will not overlook "the many objects to be revised and corrected." These include "the rights of humanity, and the National honour, as well as the peace and safety of our border settlements." Points to the recent mismanagement of Indian affairs that has produced a "brooding storm" on the frontier which could lead to Indian attacks on white settlements there. Calls for "Justice and humanity to the Indian." Reviews the history of the white man's degredation of the Indian, his seizure of Indian land, the unequal treaties by which he has ousted the Indians from their rightful lands and transported them beyond the Mississippi, etc. Admits that his pro-Indian sentiments began in 1805 when President Jefferson, who harbored "well known benevolent views toward the Aborigines," sent him to reside among the Missouri Indians. Agrees that while "there is much to disgust and to deplore in the Indian Character," he still believes that Indians have many noble human traits and that the use of "proper means" can bring "the blessings of Civilization and Christianity" to them.

Calls for complete government control of Indian trade "*under the immediate Supervision and watchful inspection of their own responsible Agents.* Controul their Trade, and you infallibly controul the Indians." Develops this point in detail. Argues also that the Indians should be settled "on their *own* lands individually." Quotes at length from a letter on "the progress of Indian Civilization" which he wrote in October, 1820 [*sic*, April 15, 1822] to the "Indian Department," a letter that was printed in part in *Niles' Register* on May 25, 1822. It was misquoted in Congress by Rep. Thomas Metcalfe of Kentucky on May 4, 1822, in such manner as to imply that Sibley despaired of the possibility of civilizing the Indian. Denies that Metcalfe represented his views accurately. "I was not aware of the unfair use of my letter 'till within the last five or Six years." Explains that an extract "has been quoted in the Register and by Mr. Metcalfe, as Some evidence against any further effort to Civilize the Indian—" Insists, however, that "*The Whole* purport and evident intention of my letter (which Mr. Metcalfe, I am Sure, could not have known) goes to Show that Civilization *is* entirely practicable, but must not be expected to result Suddenly, or very Soon, from *any* plan of operations, It can only be accomplished by degrees; generation after generation, and is undoubtedly what *must* be accomplished, before the destruction and extinction of the native Tribes can be arrested and effectually prevented—" Also suggests administrative changes in the Indian Bureau and the relocation of certain Indian Bureau regional offices.

Concludes with a summation of his suggestions for improvements and calls for legislative action. Offers his services to the new administration in whatever capacity President Harrison might wish to employ him. Says he is not, however, seeking office but reminds Clay of his twenty years of service in the Indian Bureau. ALS. CSmH.

This letter was enclosed in Sibley to Clay, Lindenwood, February 17, 1841, a routine letter of transmittal, which Clay endorsed as follows: "G.C. Sibley [Communication on the subject of the Indians and wishes an Indian Agency]." *Ibid.* For Sibley, see 5:372. For Metcalfe's speech, see *Annals of Congress*, 17 Cong., 1 Sess., 1792-1801.

From John M. Clayton, Dover, Delaware, February 14, 1841. Thanks Clay for his letter of February 12 and his "friendly offices in my behalf." Says he is not upset at having failed to receive a Cabinet appointment since he had not sought one. "I am now content. I agree with you as to the course we ought to pursue. Let us stand by the country. I shall satisfy my friends with what is done though just at this moment they are chagrined and vexed." As for himself, "I take the maxim of Jacob Faithful for my own—'better luck next time.' " Thinks he will soon leave Delaware for some city or large town where he can find more legal business. "At the age of 44 I do not wish to *rust out*." ALS. DLC-HC (DNA, M212, R5).

Jacob Faithful was a novel by Frederick Marryat, published in 1834. Jacob's three maxims were: "What's done can't be helped"; "Better luck next time"; and "Take it coolly." Oliver Warner, *Captain Marryat, a Rediscovery* (London, 1953), 162.

From Preston W. Farrar, New Orleans, February 19, 1841. Introduces the bearer, John Gibson [7:364], editor of the New Orleans *True American*, who has gone to Washington for his health and to witness Harrison's inauguration. Mentions that Gibson and his paper have "done battle in the Cause for the last fifteen years." Points out that while Gibson has not gone to Washington as a "mendicant for office. . . . it would be gratifying to the 'Ancient party' here, to see something thrown into the hands of an old & willing servant." ALS. DNA, RG59, A. and R. (M531, R4).

For Farrar, who was later speaker of the Louisiana house, see Alcée Fortier, *A History of Louisiana*, 4 vols. (New York, 1904), 3:247-48, 250.

Remark in Senate, February 19, 1841. Opposes the attempt by an "expiring Administration" to proceed with the election of printers to the Senate who would serve during the 27th Congress, "Especially when it was known that the individuals [Francis P. Blair and John C. Rives] to be appointed were so utterly odious to those who were in a few days to succeed to the possession of the Government, that, if they were going to act like men and fearlessly discharge their duty, it was impossible they could allow such persons to remain in office for one single moment. I will now say . . . that so far as I know the sentiments of my friends, there is not one of us who is not firmly and irrevocably determined, if the election is rescindable, to rescind it." Reminded by Sen. Ambrose H. Sevier (Ark.) that Joseph Gales and William W. Seaton had been reappointed printers to the House by the partisans of the outgoing John Quincy Adams administration (and remained in the post during the first two years of the Jackson administration), and that President John Adams had made important appointments "in the very last hour of his term," Clay explains that his conception of government service is that "every man who is not faithful, capable, and honest, and who has not abstained from using the power he derives from the possession of office to interfere with the freedom of elections, ought to be expelled from the office he has abused: I never said that all ought to be turned out who had displeased the Whigs." Notes that while the appointment of the "midnight judges" by the expiring administration of John Adams was entirely constitutional because "Those appointments were made to fill existing vacancies," the act had nonetheless "produced one universal burst of indignation throughout the country." Argues, however, that late appointments to unfilled offices by outgoing administrations are acceptable, whereas last minute appointments to offices which are already filled by the Senate are unacceptable. Believes the attempt by the Democrats to reappoint Blair and Rives to the job they presently hold is being undertaken "simply because they have the naked power to do it, to force upon the succeeding administration an individual known to be abhorrent to all the feelings of their hearts, insomuch that nothing can be conceived more unacceptable to them than his occupation of that office." Vows that "my friends" will turn them out "the first moment we possess the power." *Cong. Globe*, 26 Cong., 2 Sess., 192-93, 195. The debate on the printers was followed by a vote on a motion by Sen. Jabez W. Huntington (Conn.) to postpone the appointment of printers until March 4. It was defeated 19 to 26, Clay voting yea. On the following day, February 20, the Senate cast 26 votes for Blair and Rives for printers, and one vote for F.P. Blair alone. Opposition senators present did not vote. Senators Alfred O.P. Nicholson (Dem., Tenn.) and Isaac C. Bates (Whig/Fed., Mass.) were absent. *Ibid.*, 197. This decision was reversed by the Senate on March 11, 1841, during the 27th Congress, Special Session of the Senate. Sen. Willie P. Mangum, speaking for the new Whig majority, introduced a resolution to dismiss Blair and Rives on March 5 and carried it by a 26 to 18 vote six days later. For the lengthy debate on this issue, see *Cong. Globe*, 27 Cong., Special Session of Senate (printed in *Cong. Globe*, volume 9, covering 26 Cong., 2 Sess.), 236-56. See also Remark in Senate, March 5, 1841.

Later on February 19, Clay moved to take up his resolution to repeal the Independent Treasury (Sub-Treasury) bill [Remark in Senate, December 14, 1840; Speech in Senate, December 15, 1840]. Motion passed 23 to 22, Clay voting aye. After the vote Clay announced that he "had no intention of pressing a vote on the resolution tonight, and would therefore move an adjournment." Motion to adjourn carried 22 to 12. *Cong. Globe*, 26 Cong., 2 Sess., 195.

From Peter B. Porter, Niagara Falls, February 20, 1841. Has received Clay's letter of February 7 and agrees that the behavior of Edward Curtis toward Daniel Webster [Porter to Clay, January 28, 1841] should be made known to the Massachusetts senator. Refuses, however, to have such a communication made through himself "—for various reasons, one of which, and that decisive, is that the matters mentioned in my letter were imparted to me in strict confidence, and under such injunctions of secrecy, as would forbid their going abroad, most especially in that particular direction. Another reason is, that although I had a conversation with Mr [Thurlow] Weed predicated entirely on the facts communicated by him through my nephew [Peter B. Porter, Jr.], I cannot now be positive whether the *whole* of these facts were distinctly stated by both, or by one & which of them only [Porter to Clay, January 28, 1841]." Further elaborates on his nephew's communication with Weed in which "Mr Curtis was made to say—That Mr Webster was a great and ambitious man; that his affections had been long set upon the presidency; that he had recently been quite unfortunate in his private pecuniary speculations, and repeated disappointments in these had already given a dispeptic or hypochondriacal hue to his mind & feelings; and that his friends were afraid that he might fall into the indulgence of habits which such a state of dispondency is too liable to produce, & would prove ruinous to him: That it was therefore incumbent on them to treat him with great delicacy, and rather to encourage than to thwart him in his ambitious aspirations. And that it was under such views of Mr W's situation that Mr C. thought it inexpedient to disclose to him, *at present*, his real opinion in regard to Mr W's future prospects for the presidency." [End of Colton's version of this letter.]

Remarks that another of his nephews, William A. Bird of Black Rock, N.Y., seeks a government job and that he (Porter) is "extremely anxious" that Bird be appointed collector of customs of the ports of Buffalo and Black Rock "for reasons which operate very strongly with me." Mentions that Bird was the leading candidate last year for the office of canal commissioner for western New York but was "maneuvered out of it by our Governor [William H. Seward], for the benefit of one of his antimasonic friends of very equivocal pretensions." Explains the recent patronage history of the collectorship of Buffalo-Black Rock, a post currently held by George Clinton, son of DeWitt, and son-in-law of John C. Spencer, New York's secretary of state. Reports that Spencer wants young Clinton, a tippler, to give up the job and return to his law practice "in the hope that it may reform his habits."

Hopes that an extra session [Clay to Speed, November 21, 1840] will be called so that the Whigs can sooner unite on a "fair, wise & honourable course of measures" rather than having to wait a year, during which time "an opportunity will have been afforded for the formation of local or party cliques," and members will have "imbibed personal & sectional views that will render them intracticable, or as the french say, *opiniatie*, on particular subjects.

Refers to a letter [not found] he wrote Clay from Albany "a few days since on the subject of a national Bank, to be owned by the several states in their corporate capacities—The capital to be raised on a pledge by each state, of its interest, or the proceeds of it, in the national domain, guaranteed by the credit of the General government, which would at once ensure the realisation of any desired amount—The power of organising and directing the operations of the Institution, to be divided between & exercised by the General Government & the several states upon the great principle of seperate and yet combined & harmonious powers now exercised in relation to other great interests. It seems to me that, between this and the first of June next, if Congress shall then meet, you may . . . form a system of finance, and of future wealth & revenue, that will add to your already exalted fame."

Adds, in a postscript, that one of his Buffalo friends sees difficulties for the new administration on patronage policy unless Harrison "should adopt it as a general rule to dismiss *the whole* of the present incumbents, and especially where they happen to be, as in most cases they are, the mere *retainers* of the party now in power; and to appoint occasionally in their stead, a loco foco, where one can be found, worthy, in other respects, of his favourable notice." ALS. InU. Partially printed in Colton, *Clay Correspondence*, 4:450.

Remark in Senate, February 20, 1841. Speaks (not recorded) in support of his resolution to repeal the Independent Treasury (Sub-Treasury) Act [Remark in Senate, December 14, 1840; Speech in Senate, December 15, 1840] as amended by Sen. William Allen (Ohio). Replies to an explanation by Allen of the "motion he was about to make," which would table the whole subject; but withdraws this motion at Clay's request. *Cong. Globe*, 26 Cong., 2 Sess., 197. Another motion (not by Allen) to table the Independent Treasury repeal bill passed later this day by a 27 to 25 margin, Clay voting nay. *Ibid.*, 198.

To THOMAS HART CLAY Washington, February 21, 1841

I transmit the enclosed for your decision. I have written to Dr. D.[1] that I did not think you could contract for less than 22 & 10,[2] and that you had contracted on those terms with Col [Wade] Hampton.[3] But you know best & must decide.

I am still overwhelmed with business correspondence and Company. My love to Mary [Mentelle Clay].

ALS. DLC-HC (DNA, M212, R5). 1. Stephen Duncan, in Natchez, Miss. 2. Twenty-two cents per yard for hemp bagging and 10¢ per pound for hemp bale rope. See Clay to Henry Clay, Jr., Sept. 8, 1837; January & Huston to Clay, May 13, 1840. 3. For Hampton, see Clay to James B. Clay, Jan. 19, 1841.

Remark in Senate, February 22, 1841. Presents a memorial from East Tennessee seeking a duty on foreign silks. *Cong. Globe*, 26 Cong., 2 Sess., 199.

Later this day an "animated debate" followed the reading of Secretary of State-designate Daniel Webster's letter resigning his Senate seat and a comment by Sen. Alfred Cuthbert (Ga.) that he wished Webster were present so that before he departed the body he might explain or retract "certain opinions," earlier held, "on a subject of vital interest" to the South. Clay interrupts to express his "deep regret" that Cuthbert had raised this point while Webster was "absent from these halls." Eulogizes Webster, pointing out that he had been in his seat this afternoon "till near three O'clock" and that Cuthbert's "interrogatories to be put had no connection with any subject now before the Senate." Explains that Webster "had on all occasions declared it as his sentiment, that the Constitution of the United States conferred upon Congress no power, directly or indirectly, to touch the subject to which he presumed the Senator alluded [the transportation of slaves for sale from one state to another], certainly not beyond the limits of the District of Columbia; and although he might be of the opinion that such congressional power did exist in the abstract, within the District, he believed just as strongly that it would be inexpedient to exercise it. On what subject, then, did the South want guarantees as to his course in a higher and more extended sphere of action?" To Cuthbert's counter-charge that Clay's sentiments about Webster lacked sincerity, Clay said: "I call that Senator to order; he cannot be permitted to use such language in application to me." *Ibid.*, Appendix, 328-29. For the Cuthbert-Webster confrontation on the power of Congress to regulate the interstate slave trade, see *ibid.*, 329-32; also Moser, *Papers of Daniel Webster, Correspondence*, 5:100-101. For the continuation (on March 1, 1841) of Cuthbert's attack on Webster and Clay's defense of him, see Remark in Senate, March 1, 1841.

To JAMES WATSON WEBB Washington, February 22, 1841

I received your favor,[1] with the accompanying testimonials. They are very strong. But I regret to be obliged to say that the attack upon you referred to cannot change my resolution of non-interference. It might excite my sympathy, or provoke my indignation, if it deserved either; but it can confer no authority or [*sic*] upon me nor change my public duties.

ALS. KyU. 1. Not found. Reference obscure; but see Porter to Clay, Jan. 27, 1841.

To JOHN M. CLAYTON Washington, February 23, 1841

I received your two last favors. There is certainly, as you have stated, a difference between them in tone & feeling. Of the tenor of the first[1] I had spoken to several friends in high terms of commendation. There is much—a great deal—of ground for several of your observations in the last.[2] You ought to have been in the Cabinet of the new Administration. I thought so, and was most anxious for it. The Country, I believe, wished it. In my opinion the appointment of no one would have given more general satisfaction. But, after saying so much, I must with equal frankness and friendship, express the opinion that *you* are the last person in the Union that ought to manifest any disappointment or dissatisfaction with what has been done. I shall shew your last letter to no one. I shall burn it.

Nothing now would give me more delight than to see you in the Senate.[3] I should be most happy to co-operate with you in the establishment of those great principles and measures for which we have both contended.

Prior to the receipt of your letter, I had heard Mr. Tho. Clayton casually remark that he wou[l]d accept no office under the Government. But after your letter was received, I resolved to ascertain more distinctly his views and inclinations. Yesterday, in a conversation with him, in the course of which I expressed my regret that you were not a member of the new Cabinet, and how much I should be pleased to see a state of things, agreeable to all parties, which would admit of your again being on this theatre, I asked him, if there were any place at Washn. which he [Thomas Clayton] would accept? I stated that this inquiry originated with myself. His answer was, in conformity to what I had before heard him say, that there was no place under the Government that he would accept. But he added that his health, always bad, was getting worse, and that he should not long remain in the Senate.

Now I must correct some misconceptions of fact under which you labor, in respect to Mr. [George E.] Badger. I understand that he has been a member of no Legislative body since the year 1818; that altho' a Jackson man, he ceased to be so upon or shortly after the formation of his first Cabinet; that he has been a warm & decided opponent ever since of the Admon of Jackson & V. Buren; and that he is the most eminent Lawyer in No. Carolina. I believe his designation to have been the result of perhaps rather an imp[r]udent rule adopted by Genl Harrison, in respect to the geographical distribution of the members of his Cabinet.

The accounts which reach us here import the general satisfaction of the community with the Cabinet.

Come, my dear friend, to the Senate, if you possibly can. I think your namesake [Thomas Clayton] may be induced to vacate his seat; but you know him better than I do.

ALS. DLC-John M. Clayton Papers (DNA, M212, R20). Written in Senate Chamber and marked "(Confidential)." 1. Probably Clayton to Clay, Feb. 14, 1841. 2. Not found, burned. See Clay to Clayton, March 3, 1841. 3. Clayton was reelected to the Senate on Jan. 14, 1845, and served there from March 4, 1845, until Feb. 23, 1849, when he resigned to become secretary of state. He joined his cousin, Thomas Clayton, in the Senate in 1845. The two Claytons, both residents of New Castle, Del., served together there until March 3, 1847, when Thomas retired from public life. *BDAC*.

From Samuel J. Donaldson, Baltimore, February 23, 1841. Announces that "I wish it to be Understood that I fully Concur in & approve of the Sentiments Expressed in the Senate by you a few days since [Remark in Senate, February 19, 1841] relating to the removal of Officers. Those who are honest & Capable, & who have not abused their office, for party purposes, I should be Sorry to See disturbed." Proceeds to recommend a Baltimore friend for any job the new administration might be able to provide. ALS. DNA, RG59, A. and R. (M531, R4). For Donaldson (1784-1865), a prominent Baltimore lawyer, see Baltimore *Sun*, November 27, 1865.

To State of South Carolina, Charleston District, In Chancery, February 23, 1841. In his capacity as president of the American Colonization Society, points out that he represents the society in a legal challenge to the will of Alexander Watson of South Carolina by Samuel Cordes and Dunbar Paul, executors of the will. Notes that their challenge is aimed at that section of the will which bequeathed "the children of the servant Lizzy" to "John Fenton Mercer of Virginia, and his successor and successors in office as President of the Colonization Society of the United States." Explains that the executor's technical point is that "there is not and never has been any said person as John Fenton Mercer, President of the Colonization Society aforesaid." Clay argues herein that while there is or was no *John* Fenton Mercer, president of the Colonization Society, there is a *Charles* Fenton Mercer who "is or has been a vice-president thereof, and that this defendant [Clay] is now the president of the said society" and is thus qualified to act as successor to Mercer within the context of the intent of the framer of the will. LS. Sc. "Answer of Henry Clay," Charleston Equity Bills, Number 134.

On February 23, 1841, Clay appeared before U.S. Supreme Court Associate Justice James M. Wayne in Washington and submitted a statement swearing that the facts in this document were correct. ALS. *Ibid.*, appended to above document. This statement was filed on March 2, 1841.

In a report, dated November 6 and filed on November 8, 1841, J.W. Gray, "Master in Equity," in the case of *The Executors of Alexander Watson* v. *Henry Clay*, in Chancery, Charleston District, it was recommended that a fee of $1,000 be paid to the counsel of Watson's children, Hugh S. Legare, from that part of the estate awarded the children. ADS. *Ibid.*

Alexander Watson had chosen the means set forth in his will as a device to circumvent South Carolina's stringent laws on manumission and thereby to free his five children by his slave Lizzy. Clay successfully argued that the error concerning Mercer's name was immaterial and that the wording of the clause in the will constituted "a plain and sufficient designation [of] . . . the president for the time being of the Society." Thus, on June 23, 1841, the children were delivered to Clay according to the terms of the will and were made wards of the Orphan's Court of Washington County, District of Columbia (Lizzy having predeceased Watson). The Rev. William McLain was named as their guardian, in charge of their share of Watson's estate which amounted to $59,274.18. Paul Begley *et al.*, "Serendipity, Henry Clay and the Santee Delta," *SCHM* (July, 1982), 83:249-52.

In a "Master's Special Report," dated June 20, 1842, J.W. Gray notified the Orphan's Court that the sureties given by William McLain on his $45,000 bond to the court "are good & approved." ADS. Sc.

From John M. Austin, Uniontown, Pa., February 26, 1841. Adds a postscript to a letter recommending a patronage appointment: "PS When you get to England tell them we back-woods-boys dont want to fight-for *roostock* [Aroostook County, Maine] lands; That all of it is not worth as much money as Henry Clay township on the top of our mountains; But If they will fight, we are ready for them at moments notice, from Laurel Hill [Pa.] to the rocky Mountains." ALS. DNA, RG59, A. and R. (M531, R4). For Anglo-American tension on the Maine-New Brunswick border, and the "Aroostook War," see Clay to Hamilton, February 24, 1839. For Austin, a prominent Uniontown lawyer, see *PMHB*, 7:182.

Henry Clay Township is located in Fayette County in southwestern Pennsylvania. Rand McNally's *1982 Commercial Atlas and Marketing Guide*, 113th ed. (New York, 1982), 189.

Remark in Senate, February 27, 1841. Moves to table the bill to declare the rights of children of United States citizens born abroad. *Cong. Globe*, 26 Cong., 2 Sess., 216. On February 17, 1841, the bill had been reported from the Judiciary Committee and was read and passed to a second reading. On February 27 it was taken up by the Senate acting as Committee of the Whole. It was engrossed, read a third time, and tabled. It was not taken up again during the session. U.S. Sen., *Journal*, 26 Cong., 2 Sess., 188, 214.

From HENRY CLAY, JR. N.p. [probably Lexington], *ca.* late February or early March, 1841

On my arrival here from Louisville a fews days since I ascertained that a letter from you had been sent to that place in quest of me. I have at length received it and find that it is your letter of 11th inst. containing Mr [John J.] Crittenden's communication. It is needless to assure you that I regret the delay which has taken place.

Be good enough to present Mr Crittenden my grateful acknowledgements for his friendly interest in my welfare. In regard to the post at St Petersburg I mean the chargéship I consider it highly honorable to me and above my desert, but if the arrangement is satisfactory to the Administration I pledge to the service of the Country my most zealous and faithful attention. As to the Secretaryship of Legation I consider it a drawback to which I am willing to submit with the perfect understanding that that appointment is not long to endure. In all frankness the only objection whatever to an arrangement which presents many advantages some of which you have sketched is its indefiniteness. As I seek employment and only in such grade as I may be deemed worthy to fill a permanent arrangement would be highly satisfactory. But as I presume from your letter that something of the Kind is intended, if Mr Webster still retains the same views upon the reception of this letter I can be ready to go out upon a notice of a few days.[1]

I trust I have made my meaning clear. The only point on which I must insist is that I be not retained long a Secretary of Legation. I beg that upon the first occasion you will represent to Mr Webster the sense I entertain of his Kind consideration.

As this is Sunday all the family now in Ky are here They are all well and join me in affectionate regards to you John [M. Clay] & [Henry Clay] Duralde

ALS. Henry Clay Memorial Foundation, Lexington, Ky. 1. Henry Clay, Jr., did not receive a diplomatic post during Daniel Webster's tenure as secretary of state.

Remark in Senate, March 1, 1841. Following a report on U.S. relations with Great Britain submitted by the Committee on Foreign Relations, Clay refers specifically to the adjustment of the Northeast boundary crisis [Clay to Hamilton, February 24, 1839] and to the *Caroline* and McLeod cases [Comment in Senate, January 5, 1838]. Supports negotiating an Anglo-American convention that would submit the boundary question to arbitration, laments that there has been delay on the part of the British in addressing elements of the *Caroline* problem, and expresses the hope that Alexander McLeod "be brought to a place where he can have a fair and impartial trial; and whatever should be the result of that trial, that his personal safety should be put beyond all question." Hopes McLeod will be acquitted. As for British efforts to end the slave trade, especially their policy of stopping, searching, and seizing suspected slavers on the African coast that were flying the American flag, Clay makes it clear that "the Government of Great Britain should understand that this country will not submit to the right of search, which was the cause of the last war." Notes that while he had "not begun to think of the possibility of any immediate war with Great Britain," he nonetheless "looked upon the condition of our navy and the want of steam batteries, and the absence of all those floating means of defence, as matters of just and deep concernment; and he did hope they would have a very early and constant attention, that the country might be prepared for any possible emergency." *Cong. Globe*, 26 Cong., 2 Sess., 218.

Following this statement, Sen. Alfred Cuthbert (Ga.) rises to announce that he has "proofs in relation to the sentiments of Mr. WEBSTER in regard to the constitutional power of the Government over the transportation of slaves from one State to another [Remark in Senate, February 22, 1841]." Points out also how inconsistent it is for Clay to defend Webster on this important constitutional question, given the fact that he has differed with him on so many other issues over the years.

As he had on February 22, Clay again took the floor to defend the absent secretary of state-designate. Interrupted by Cuthbert, in this endeavour, Clay snapped, "with some warmth," that "I will not, I cannot, be interrupted. I will not permit an interruption. The practice is much too common; it is not parliamentary; it is too much tolerated in another place in this Capitol, and I trust it will not be continued here." Goes on to explain the background of the constitutional provision giving Congress the power to regulate interstate commerce. Notes, insofar as this power might be applied to the interstate slave trade, "that the power to regulate did not imply prohibition, but the removal of obstacles." Asks rhetorically, if Webster differs with him on this interpretation of the Constitution, "was he to be judged by a single error of opinion?" No, Clay asserts, no more so than Cuthbert's earlier opposition to nullification should be judged by his friend Calhoun's support of it. Admits that he has in the past differed with Webster on some issues, such as the wisdom of declaring war on Britain in 1812 and on the Compromise Tariff of 1833 [8:604, 619-22, 626-27]; but recalls that Webster had joined with him in standing against the tyranny of Andrew Jackson—a stance for the "liberties of the people" that had not been supported by Cuthbert. As for the question of abolition, he was certain "that the opinions of the Senator from Massachusetts were just as much adverse to Abolition as the opinions of the Senator from Georgia himself were adverse to Abolition." Believes that the "greatest danger which threatened this country. . . . was in ultraism. It was in the ultraism of the South on the one hand—of a small portion of the South on the one hand, and ultraism of Abolition on the other The course of safety lay in a moderate, firm, resolute determination to maintain the rights of the South, in their fullest extent, against all attacks, not being led off into an extreme by attacks on the one hand, or frightened into extremes on the other." Further, reminds Cuthbert that on the tariff issue of 1824, Webster had supported Cuthbert and the Southern position, not the arguments then expressed by Clay [3:535-39, 642-44, 647-51, 657-60, 683-730].

Cuthbert responds to Clay's statement in language "inaudible at the Reporter's desk," but understood to characterize something as being "audacious." This brought Clay to his feet with a demand "to know if the Senator applies to me? If he does, I will call him to order." Cuthbert replies that "the Senator from Kentucky was himself in the habit of using very provoking language to others. . . . when the Senator from Kentucky learned proper courtesies towards his opponents, he should meet with nothing but courtesy from him [Cuthbert] and not till then." *Ibid.*, Appendix, 331-32. Printed in Colton, *Clay Correspondence*, 6:271-73.

From William O. Brown *et al.*, Lockport, N.Y., March 2, 1841. Recall that back in July, 1840, they had informed Clay "on the general subject of the Whig Party in western New York being composed by the amalgamation of the old National Republican & Anti-Mason Parties—and of the cause which a few of the old leaders of the Anties give the Nationals for dissatisfaction by their clanning together to monopolize the Public Offices." Suggest the name of a local Whig for the office of collector either of the district of Niagara or of Genesee and explain his qualifications. ALS. DNA, RG56, Entry 247, Collectors of Customs, Box 150.

Remark in Senate, Evening Session, March 2, 1841. Seconds, with "peculiar satisfaction," the resolution of Sen. Willie P. Mangum (N.C.) praising Vice President Richard M. Johnson (Ky.) for the dignity and impartiality with which he has presided over the Senate. Resolution passed unanimously. *Cong. Globe*, 26 Cong., 2 Sess., 224.

From Scofield Cassion & Co. *et al.*, Walden, N.Y., March 3, [1841]. As "friends of Home Manufactures" who seek "fair payments of the duties on foreign fabrics," nominate Jacob T. Walden of New York City as one of the appraisers of customs in that port city, to serve independent of the collector of customs there. Call attention to the "notorious frauds" in the New York customhouse. Argue that the "Manufacturing interests should have at least one *known friend* among the appraisers to guard their Interests in some degree." Say they turn to Clay on this matter because he is a "fast friend of Home Manufactures." ALS. DNA, RG56, Entry 910, Appraisers of Customs, Box 41.

To JOHN M. CLAYTON Washington, March 3, 1841

I have received your favor of the 27h. Ulto. I believe the information to be entirely correct, which I communicated to you as to Mr. [George E.] Badger. It was derived from an authentic source. I knew him personally better than I did his history, as he boarded here several weeks with me two winters ago.[1] Still as he has had but little experience, in the political career, his success is a matter of experiment and of course uncertainty. I believe you are right as to the motives of some who desired his appointment, but they will be deceived, or I shall be greatly so.

I spoke to Harrison, on his return, in terms of high commendation as to the manly and magnanimous spirit evinced in your first letter.[2] He seemed highly pleased, and renewed an expression of his regret that circumstances had not been such as to admit of an invitation to you to form a part of his Cabinet.

Things generally look well. If there be breakers ahead they have not yet been discernible.

I hope to see you at the Extra Session,[3] which I think may be regarded as definitively settled. I have a perfect Bank in my head. I should like to converse with you about it. Now, I can only write you briefly. . . . P.S. I burnt your second letter.[4]

ALS. DLC-John M. Clayton Papers (DNA, M212, R20). 1. At the boarding house of Mrs. Arguelles, nearly opposite Gadsby's. Goldman and Young, *U.S. Congressional Directories*, 342. See also Clay to Clayton, Feb. 12, 1841. 2. Clayton to Clay, Feb. 14, 1841. 3. Clay to Speed, Nov. 21, 1840; Notes for Newspaper Editorial, Feb. 4, 1841. 4. Marginal amendation. See Clayton to Clay, Feb. 23, 1841.

From John Jacob Astor, New York, March 4, 1841. Endorses the candidacy of Robert Stuart, treasurer of the state of Michigan, for the office of commissioner of Indian Affairs. Identifies Stuart as "one of the party I sent out to Columbia River in the Autumn of 1810 in the unfortunate 'Tonquin'—He returned overland to this City in 1813, and was connected with me in the Indian Trade until 1834, when I gave up the business, he having resided at Mackinac 15 years as the Agent of the American Fur Company." LS. NN.

Robert Stuart was a nephew of David Stuart, one of the original shareholders in Astor's Pacific Fur Company. Eventually he acquired two of his uncle's five shares. He had sailed with the *Tonquin*, the first vessel sent out by the company as a coastal trader, in 1810. In June, 1811, the ship was wrecked and twenty-seven crew members massacred by west coast Indians. Kenneth W. Porter, *John Jacob Astor, Business Man*, 2 vols. (Cambridge, Mass., 1931), 1:180-94; John U. Terrell, *Furs by Astor* (New York, 1963), 176-86. On June 18, 1841, John Bell recommended Stuart as agent for the Ottawa and Chippewa Indians. President Tyler nominated him for the job on June 23 and the Senate confirmed him on September 13. U.S. Sen., *Executive Journal*, 5:391, 393, 440.

Remark in Senate, March 4, 1841. Presents credentials of James T. Morehead, newly elected senator from Kentucky. *Cong. Globe*, 27 Cong., Special Session of Senate (printed in *Cong. Globe*, volume 9, covering 26 Cong., 2 Sess.), 232. For Morehead, called "James P. Moorehead" here by the *Globe*, see *BDAC*. The special session of the Senate in the 27th Congress convened on March 4 and adjourned on March 15.

Remark in Senate, March 5, 1841. Speaks to the resolution by Sen. Willie P. Mangum to dismiss Francis P. Blair and John C. Rives as printers to the Senate [Remark in Senate, February 19, 1841]. To the point of order as to whether the Senate, presently acting in its executive capacity, has the power to dismiss employees earlier elected by the Senate, acting in its legislative capacity, Clay argues that "Separate from the House," the Senate "might do any thing which it was competent to do"—and this includes the election or dismissal of its employees. Asserts that the bond initially issued to Blair and Rives to do the duties of the printer's office was no legal hindrance to their dismissal at this time, since "if the Printers went out the bond [is] vacated by the fact." Also contends that the Constitution gives the Senate the "power, exclusively of the House, or the President, or any other authority, to elect its own officers," and notes that the printers are Senate officers in the sense that they perform the duties of Senate clerks "using types instead of pens." Cites the Senate vote on a resolution by Thomas H. Benton in an executive session of that body on March 9, 1829, which dealt with the purchase of the *Register of Debates*, then owned by Joseph Gales and William W. Seaton. Sees this as earlier Senate recognition of its power "to transact the business of the Senate" while in executive session, and its competence, therefore, "to proceed to elect" new printers during such sessions. *Cong. Globe*, 27 Cong., Special Session of Senate (printed in *Cong. Globe*, volume 9, covering 26 Cong., 2 Sess), 236-37. See also Remark in Senate, February 19, 1841.

Remark in Senate, March 8, 1841. Resists an attempt by Democrat James Buchanan (Pa.) to abolish the presently vacant office of sergeant-at-arms. Says the office will need to be filled if President Harrison calls an extra session [Clay to Speed, November 21, 1840; Notes for Newspaper Editorial, February 4, 1841] as now seems likely. Thinks the annual salary involved ($1,500 plus $250 for the extra session) is not a significant problem, even though the Democrats had promised a year's salary to the widow and family of the recently deceased occupant of the office. Accepts the opposition's charitable motives in the matter, but not to the point of abolishing a necessary office on grounds of economy. *Cong. Globe*, 27 Cong., Special Session of Senate (printed in *Cong. Globe*, volume 9, covering 26 Cong., 2 Sess.), Appendix, 317. Sen. Benton's motion to postpone consideration of the resolution was defeated 20 to 26, Clay voting nay. Maryland Sen. William D. Merrick's resolution to fill the post was passed 26 to 19, Clay voting aye. Edward Dyer of Washington was then elected sergeant-at-arms with 26 out of the whole number of 46 possible votes. *Ibid.*, 319.

Later this day, Clay resumes his participation in the debate on the motion [Remark in Senate, March 5, 1841] to dismiss Blair and Rives as printers to the Senate [Remark in Senate, February 19, 1841]. Claims that the election of Blair and Rives as printers to the 27th Congress by Senate Democrats on February 20, 1841, was viewed by the Whigs as "one of the most extraordinary instances of the exercise of high-handed power they had witnessed" during the 26th Congress, 2nd Session. It was "an act of power—of pure, naked, unqualified power," one which the Whigs were determined to reverse "at the earliest possible period." Reviews the history of how the Senate has gone about electing its printers since 1819 to demonstrate that the Senate's election of Blair and Rives on February 20 cannot be considered a binding contract for future years. Instead, it binds only and is subject only "to the will of the appointing power." Asks if the Democrats really believe that the new "party in power were going to consummate the triumph of proscription by retaining" Blair? Indeed, "if there was no other ground for his dismissal" it could be accomplished "on the ground of infamy of character of the print [Washington *Globe*] and the Printer [Remark in Senate, March 9, 1841]." Adds: If senators "regarded the character of the country at home or abroad, he [Blair] ought to be dismissed. . . . on the ground of the character and reputation of the man and of the paper [*Globe*], they owed it to Christendom—they owed it to themselves—they owed it to the purity of the national character, to disconnect themselves at once and forever from these men [Blair and Rives]. On the ground of the notoriously bad character of the print and the Printer, he should urge the Senate to displace them, and give them no longer the sanction of an official character." In addition, both Blair and Rives knew perfectly well that they would be dismissed by the new Whig majority in the Senate on March 4. "They were notified of it." Their bond should be returned to them. *Cong. Globe*, 27 Cong., Special Session of Senate (printed in *Cong. Globe*, volume 9, covering 26 Cong., 2 Sess.), 242-43.

Remark in Senate, March 9, 1841. Listens to a question by Sen. Perry Smith (Conn.), viz: In characterizing Francis P. Blair yesterday as an "infamous" person [Remark in Senate, March 8, 1841] was Clay not also labeling as infamous those senators who supported Blair's reelection as printer to the Senate [Remark in Senate, February 19, 1841]?

Also hears criticism by Sen. William R. King (Ala.) that he (Clay) could not grasp the fact that the Senate had made a legal contract with Blair and Rives on February 20 to continue them as printers and that such a contract could not and should not be broken by Clay and the Whigs for political and patronage reasons. King calls attention to Clay's close personal friendship with Blair in Kentucky in the mid-1820s ("Was he infamous then?"), and asserts that in terms of Blair's "kindness of heart, humanity, and exemplary deportment as a private citizen, he could proudly compare with the Senator from Kentucky." As for all the Whig talk about the evils of proscription as practiced by the Democrats, notes that in proscribing Blair the Whigs have also assaulted his character. Indeed, Whig senators have put him on trial before the nation while denying him the right to be heard in his own defense. Asks: Is "this the promised reform?" Is "this the high, the liberal, the manly spirit which was to actuate the Whig party?"

Clay responds to Kings's comments and questions with the observation that his own position in the Senate and before the nation was such that he was, "as heretofore, to be the object of attack, or concerted attack. He stood now, as he had stood heretofore, firm and erect, and ready to repel assaults, when worthy of his notice, from whatever quarter they came." Further, his statement yesterday that he "believed the Globe to be an infamous paper, and its chief editor [Blair] an infamous man" was not to suggest that senators who support Blair on the printer-reappointment issue are themselves infamous. Such would be an "unlawful inference and illogical deduction." Attacks Smith, "the Senator who sits in the corner yonder," for making such an inference, and asks the Senate "to excuse him if he considered him [Smith] unworthy of his notice." Adds that he has "scarcely ever looked at a paper, edited by this man [Blair] in which his [Clay's] name appeared, which was not filled with untruths and misrepresentations." Recalls attacks earlier made by Blair on "John Catiline Calhoun," specifically Blair's charge that it was "impossible for him [Calhoun] to speak the truth." Says that King's comparison of his (Clay's) character with Blair's is "false, untrue, and cowardly." This language brought King to his feet: "Mr. President, I have no reply to make—none whatever." When Smith rejoined that it seemed he (Smith) was "not worthy" of Clay's notice, Clay snapped: "Not at all." *Cong. Globe*, 27 Cong., Special Session of Senate (printed in *Cong. Globe*, volume 9, covering 26 Cong., 2 Sess.), 245, 247-49. On this same day, a motion by King to the effect that the Senate was not competent to annul the election of Blair and Rives and should uphold the contract made with them was beaten 18 to 25, Clay voting nay. *Ibid.*, 245-46.

So tense was the Clay-King confrontation on the Senate floor this day that on the following day, March 10, Clay and Willis Green appeared before two justices of the peace for Washington County and posted peace bonds of $5,000 each promising, in the words of the bond, to "keep the peace of the United States towards all persons, and particularly towards WILLIAM R. KING." Copy. Printed in *Kendall's Expositor* (April 15, 1844), 4:124; from a file owned by Cassius M. Clay. For Henry Clay's apology to King, see Comment in Senate, March 15, 1841.

To JOHN M. CLAYTON Washington, March 11, 1841

Your favor is recd. There is enough in the stipulation in the Compromise act,[1] to raise a Revenue from imports, to found an argument upon in favor of the passage of the Land bill.[2] As to the levying of a direct tax, there are not ten men in either house that would vote for it.

There will be probably an Extra Session, at which will be considered 1st. A bank of the U. S. 2. The repeal of the S. Treasury.[3] 3. The imposition of duties on the free articles & 4h. the Land bill. The question of protection, upon the principles of the Compromise, or without regard to them, will not I think come up until the ordinary Session.

I do most fervently hope that you will be able to return to the Senate.[4]

We shall adjourn today or tomorrow. There will be no removals until after the adjournment.

ALS. KyLoF. 1. Of 1833. See 8:604, 619-22, 626-27. 2. His version of a land bill which would distribute the income from public land sales to all the states rather than restrict distribution to the seven so-called "new states [Ind., Miss., Ill., Ala., Mo., Ark., Mich.]." See Speech in Senate, Jan. 28-29, 1841; Clay to Ewing, April 30, 1841. See also 8:539-41, 609-10, 812-13, 846-47, 873-74. For the legislative history of Clay's land sales distribution and preemption bill in the 27th Congress, 1st Session, see Remark in Senate, June 9, 1841; also Chitwood, *John Tyler*, 294-95. 3. Clay to Speed, Nov. 21, 1840; Notes for Newspaper Editorial, Feb. 4, 1841. For the Whig legislative agenda in this session, see Comment in Senate, June 7, 1841. 4. Clay to Clayton, Feb. 23, 1841.

Remark in Senate, March 11, 1841. Since so many members are absent, "being necessarily occupied in preparation for their departure for their homes," moves that those present go into executive session. But soon noticing that most senators are now in their seats, Clay waives his motion so that the final vote on the dismissal of Blair and Rives as printers to the Senate [Remark in Senate, February 19, 1841] can be taken. Following the 26 to 18 vote to dismiss Blair and Rives, Clay voting aye, the Kentuckian moves that the performance bond earlier posted by the two men to execute the printing of the Senate be returned to them. The vote on this motion was "precisely similar" to that on dismissal—26 to 18. *Cong. Globe*, 27 Cong., Special Session of Senate (printed in *Cong. Globe*, volume 9, covering 26 Cong., 2 Sess.), 256.

From James Such, Jamaica, N.Y., March 11, 1841. Explains why he felt he had no authorization to take Clay's three grandsons [Gratz to Clay, October 28, 1840] and two other of his students to Washington for the inauguration and why he was unwilling to trust the boys to go alone. Hopes "this Explanation will restore me to that place in your estimation which I am most solicitous." Reports that the summer holidays will be in August and September, that the boys [Henry Clay Erwin, James Erwin, Henry Clay Duralde] are "in excellent health & always have been so," that young Duralde "has turned over a new leaf & is pains taking & *industrious*," and that he has received Clay's check for $250. ALS. DLC-TJC (DNA, M212, R14).

To FRANCIS T. BROOKE Washington, March 12, 1841

You complain of my arrearage in our mutual correspondence, and with, at least, apparent cause; but I have never passed a winter of so much pressure as the one which has just terminated, if indeed it can be said to have terminated. The painful alternative was presented to me of a neglect of my private correspondence, or of my public duties. I could not hesitate which branch of it to adopt. I have not been able to transmit an answer to one out of every hundred letters that I have received.[1]

Moreover, I have had but little of interest to communicate of which the papers did not inform you.

The new Senate has opened with a decided, practical, and available majority of twenty-nine to twenty-two,[2] there being one vacancy from Tennessee.[3] That majority, I think, may be relied on in almost all of the measures of the new Administration.

The Senate will adjourn on Monday. The appointments made are, almost exclusively, to fill existing vacancies. General Payton [*sic*, Bernard Peyton][4] has received that of Post-master at Richmond. . . .

Copy. Printed in Colton, *Clay Correspondence*, 4:451-52. 1. On Sept. 14, 1841, Clay wrote a card which was published in the Washington *Daily National Intelligencer* of Sept. 16, explaining that during "the last winter session of Congress . . . which has just expired, I received vast numbers of letters, the receipt of which I did not acknowledge. The alternative was presented of my omitting to answer them, or a total neglect of my public duties." Apologizes and hopes his correspondents understand "that my apparent neglect did not proceed from any insensibility to the value or importance of their communication." 2. Clay to Clayton, May 29, 1840. 3. Democrat Alexander O. Anderson had served out the Senate term of Hugh L. White (deceased in April, 1840), which expired on March 4, 1841, leaving a vacancy. Gov. James K. Polk, apparently fearing charges of extravagance in his administration and uncertain of the ability of the Democratic party in the Tennessee state legislature to control the election of a U.S. senator, refused to call a special session of the legislature to fill the seat. Thus, Democrat Alfred O.P. Nicholson, who was serving out the unexpired term of Democrat Felix Grundy (deceased in Dec., 1840), was Tennessee's sole senator during this session. Nicholson served until Feb. 7, 1842. From that date through the session ending March 3, 1843, thanks to inaction in the state legislature, Tennessee had no senators in Washington. Whig Ephraim H. Foster was finally elected to Grundy's old seat on Oct. 17, 1843, and took it on Dec. 4, 1843. The former White seat, filled by Anderson until March 4, 1841, was vacant from that date until Oct. 17, 1843, when the legislature elected Whig Spencer Jarnagin to it. Jarnagin took it on Dec. 4, 1843. See *BDAC*, 28th Cong., Tennessee; and Parks, *John Bell*, 194-95. 4. For Peyton, a well-known merchant who had once served as adjutant general of Virginia and was postmaster at Richmond from 1838 to 1844, see Horace E. Hayden, *Virginia Genealogies* (reprint ed., Washington, 1931), 515, 547. He had been reappointed to the postmastership by Harrison on March 9. U.S. Sen., *Executive Journal*, 5:372-73.

From WILLIAM HENRY HARRISON

Washington, March 13, 1841

You use the priviledge of a friend to lecture me[1] & I will take the same liberty with you—You are too impetuous. Much as I would rely upon your judgement there are others whom I must consult & in many cases to determine adversely to your suggestions. In the matter to which your communication of this morning refers there is no difference of Opinion as to the measure & there would be none as to the time but for the situation of Tennessee[2] to whom we owe so much. Her feelings & interest must not be sacrificed if it can be avoided. The question will be finalled [*sic*, finally] settled on Monday having been adjourned over from a discussion which took place this morning.

I preferred for many reasons this mode of answering yr. note to a conversation in the presence of others. Yours with great haste. . . .

ALS. DLC-HC (DNA, M212, R5). Salutation reads: "My dear friend." 1. It is not clear that Harrison's anger was triggered entirely by Clay's letter of this date urging an extra session of Congress. It has been suggested that Clay's stance on patronage issues in general, and the pending appointment of Edward Curtis as collector of the port of New

York [Porter to Clay, Dec. 14, 1840] in particular, fueled Harrison's ire; there is also the suggestion that he and Webster were concerned that an extra session might be dominated by Clay. Cf. Cleaves, *Old Tippecanoe*, 339-41; Van Deusen, *Life of Henry Clay*, 340-41; Poage, *Henry Clay*, 27-31. The assertion that Clay, on receipt of this letter, flew into a tantrum sometime during the evening of Monday, March 13, the same evening he also attended a stag dinner at the White House, is attributed only to a statement made in 1875 by newspaper correspondent Nathan Sargent who alone witnessed the scene. Nathan Sargent, *Public Men and Events*, 2 vols. (Philadelphia, 1875), 2:115-16. The editors have found no additional evidence to corroborate Sargent's recollection. 2. The terms of the Tennessee representatives in the U.S. House expired on March 4 and new ones would not be elected until the regular state elections in August. This situation would leave Tennessee unrepresented in the House during the proposed early, special ("extra") session unless Democratic Gov. James K. Polk called for special congressional elections. More critical from the Whig point of view was the fact that at the next meeting of the Tennessee legislature two U.S. senators were to be chosen. The Democrats narrowly controlled the Tennessee legislature, but the Whigs had high hopes of electing a majority in August and then of choosing two Whig senators. Thus, some Whigs feared that a special summer session of Congress would cause Polk to call a special session of the state legislature in order to elect the senators while the Democrats still controlled that body. Poage, *Henry Clay*, 28. In the August elections in Tennessee, Whig James C. Jones defeated Polk, the incumbent, for governor by a vote of 53,586 to 50,343. *BDGUS*, 4:1474. The Democrats won control of the state senate by a margin of 13 seats to 12 for the Whigs, while the Whigs controlled the lower house by a majority of 3 seats. Jonesboro *Tennessee Whig*, August 18, 1841; Parks, *John Bell*, 195. Sen. Alfred O.P. Nicholson, appointed to fill the vacancy caused by the death of Felix Grundy, took his seat on Jan. 11, 1841, and served until Feb. 7, 1842, when his appointment expired. The state legislature failed to fill the two vacancies until the 28th Congress met.

To WILLIAM HENRY HARRISON

Washington, March 13, 1841

Will you excuse me for suggesting the propriety of a definitive decision about an Extra Session,[1] and of announcing the fact? There is much speculation and uncertainty about it, in circles and among the members of Congress. Time is rapidly passing away, and members of your Cabinet have, it is alleged, added to the uncertainty.

After all that has occurred; after what you have said at Richmond and elsewhere, if the purpose of calling one should be abandoned, there is danger of the imputation of vascillating counsels.

I have never doubted for a moment about it since Novr. In my deliberate opinion, the good of the Country and the honor and the interests of the party demand it.

By way of stating the grounds for the convocation, I have sketched the rough draft of a proclamation[2] which I respectfully submit to your perusal, as best indicating what strikes me as expedient.

I think *your* election should occupy the front & most prominent ground. The financial difficulties of the Govt. alone form too narrow a basis to put the call upon; but the draft now enclosed covers that and all other grounds.

Altho' not well, I shall have the honor of dining with you today,[3] when I should be most happy to learn your final decision.

ALS. DLC-HC (DNA, M212, R5). Letter marked "(Confidential)." 1. Clay to Speed, Nov. 21, 1840. 2. The enclosed, proposed proclamation, undated [March 13, 1841], reads: "Whereas the just expectations of the people of the U. States, in regard to measures adapted to their prosperity, as evinced by a recent political event; the great and general embarrassments in the Commerce, Currency, and Business of the Country; and the financial condition of the Government of the U. States form an extraordinary occasion for convening Congress at a period earlier than that which is fixed by the Constitution: I do therefore, by these presents, appoint the ________ day of ________ next for their meet-

ing at the Capitol in the City of Washington, and require the respective Senators and Representatives then and there to assemble in Congress, in order to receive such communications as may be made to them, and to deliberate and determine on such measures as, in their wisdom, may be deemed meet and proper. In testimony whereof I have caused the seal of the U. States to be affixed hereunto, and signed this proclamation with my own hand. Done at the City of Washington the ________ day of March in the year of our Lord 1841, and of the Independence of the U. States the Sixty fifth." AD. DLC-HC (DNA, M212, R5). For the wording of Harrison's proclamation of March 17 calling for an early ("extra") meeting of the 27th Congress, 1st Session, see *MPP*, 4:21; Poage, *Henry Clay*, 32.
3. Clay kept this dinner appointment. See Adams, *Memoirs of John Quincy Adams*, 10:444.

Comment in Senate, March 14, 1841. Apologizes to Sen. William R. King (Ala.) for his hostile reaction to King's speech of March 9 which had equated the character of Francis P. Blair with that of Clay [Remark in Senate, March 9, 1841]. Admits that his characterization of King's comparison as "false, untrue, and cowardly was unfair." Says he misunderstood King's intention in making the comparison and is thus pleased to withdraw "every epithet in the least derogatory to him, to his honor, or to his character." Agrees that members may choose to attack the persons, personalities, and characters of non-members of the Senate as they see fit; but notes that they must never attack other members personally. Explains that he was mistakenly carried away in the heat of his criticism of Blair on March 8 [Remark in Senate, March 8, 1841] and should probably have remained silent that day, "Notwithstanding ten years of the most unparalleled abuse and wanton and unscrupulous attacks" on himself by the editor of the Washington *Globe*. Explains that to hear King compare the infamous Blair's character with his own character on the following day struck him as a premeditated personal assault. Regrets the entire incident. *Cong. Globe*, 27 Cong., Special Session of Senate (printed in *Cong. Globe*, volume 9, covering 26 Cong., 2 Sess.), 256-57.

Following Clay's remarks, King also apologized for his role in the affair. *Ibid.*, 257.

To WILLIAM HENRY HARRISON Washington, March 15, 1841

Your incessant engagements preclude the probability of my having any opportunity of a private conversation with you, prior to my departure from this City.[1] I therefore adopt this mode of saying a few words to you before I go.

I was mortified by the suggestion you made to me on saturday,[2] that I had been represented as dictating to you[3] or to the new administration—mortified, because it is unfounded in fact, and because there is danger of the fears, that I intimated to you at Frankfort,[4] of my enemies poisoning your mind towards me.

In what, with truth, can they allege a dictation or even interference on my part? In the formation of your Cabinet? You can contradict them In the administration of the public patronage? The whole Cabinet as well as yourself can deny that. I have recommended nobody for any office. I have sought none for myself, or my friends. I desire none. A thousand times have my feelings been wounded, by communicating to those who have applied to me, that I am obliged to abstain inflexibly from all interference in official appointments.[5]

I learnt to day, with infinite surprize, that I had been represented as saying, that Mr. [Edward] Curtis *should not* be appointed Collector of N. York. It is utterly unfounded. I never uttered such expressions in relation to that or any other office, of the humblest grade, within your gift. I have never gone beyond expressing the opinion that he is faithless and perfidious and in my judgment unworthy of the place. It is one of the artifices by which he expects to succee[d]

If to express freely my opinion, as a Citizen and as a Senator, in regard to public measures be dictation, then I have dictated, and not otherwise. There is but one alternative, which I could embrace, to prevent the exercise of this common right of freedom of opinion, and that is retirement to private life. That I am most desirous of, and if I do not, promptly indulge the feeling, it is because I entertain the hope—perhaps vain hope, that by remaining a little longer in the Senate I may possibly render some service to a Country, to whose interests my life has been dedicated.

I do not wish to trouble you with answering this note.[6] I could not reconcile it to my feelings to abstain from writing it. Your heart, in which I have the greatest confidence, will justly appreciate the motives of, whatever others may say or insinuate, Your true & faithful frien[d] . . . .

ALS. DLC-HC (DNA, M212, R5). Letter marked "(Private and Confidential)." Endorsed by Clay on verso: "Letters from H. Clay to Genl Harrison Returned to me June 1841 by his [Harrison's] grand nephew [Henry Harrison]." Printed in Colton, *Clay Correspondence*, 4:452-53. 1. Clay probably departed Washington on Wednesday, March 17. See bill and receipt, dated March 17, 1841, for five day's board at $15.00 per week. DS., by E.T. Arguelles. DLC-TJC (DNA, M212, R19). 2. Harrison to Clay, March 13, 1841. 3. Cleaves, *Old Tippecanoe*, 340. 4. Clay to Saltonstall, Nov. 22, 1840. 5. In an undated [*ca.* mid-March, 1841] letter to William Ogden Niles, son of the deceased (d. April 2, 1839) Hezekiah Niles, Clay wrote: "I recd. your favor, and I should be most happy to serve you, if I could, both on your own account, and that of your lamented father. I should be glad that you would get the vacant Clerkship which you desire. But self respect will not allow me to make any recommendation to any quarter, where I have reason to suppose that it might not be well received. And such I am constrained to believe would be the fate of any I might give." ALS. KyU. Letter marked "(Private)." 6. This was Clay's last known communication with Harrison, who died on April 4. The editors have found no evidence to sustain Edward Curtis's story, told to Thurlow Weed in a letter dated March 28, 1841, that Clay spent Tuesday evening, March 16, the day before he left Washington, laughing, joking, and drinking with him (Curtis) and others; and that he called on Harrison the next morning again to protest the Curtis appointment; and that he wrote the president from Baltimore, in an effort once again to stop Curtis's appointment. Van Deusen, *Life of Henry Clay*, 342. G.R. Poage asserts that Clay did not see Harrison again after their dinner meeting on the evening of March 13 [Clay to Harrison, March 13, 1841]. Poage, *Henry Clay*, 31.

To UNKNOWN RECIPIENT Washington, March 15, 1841

I have received the box containing the Shirts and Stocks, which you had the goodness to send me, and for which I request you and Mrs. P[ ]er[1] to accept my grateful thanks. The shirts are very tastefully made, and fit me remarkably well. As soon as I have an opportunity of seeing Genl Harrison I shall deliver your message; and I would send him one of the shirts but that I know it will not fit him.

Present my regards to your little daughter, and tell her that I am obliged to her for the share she had in making up the shirts.

I expect to leave here in a few days (perhaps tomorrow) for my residence.[2]

When I again visit N. York, I shall call and deliver my respects and thanks to Mrs. P. in person. . . .

ALS. ViU. Name of recipient removed. 1. Two letters missing. 2. He left Washington on March 17 and returned to the capital on May 27 or 28.

From Daniel Webster, Department of State, Washington, March 15, 1841. Believes the U.S. consulate in Paris should continue to be filled but that the $2,000 per annum salary for the post should be discontinued. Says he will discontinue the salary, beginning with next year's budget, "for the reasons which have been suggested by you." LS. DLC-HC (DNA, M212, R5).

To JAMES F. CONOVER Lexington, April 9, 1841

I received your favor of the 8h. The distressing intelligence of the death of Genl. Harrison had reached me.[1] It is greatly to be deplored, although it does not surprize me much, from what I observed of his habits and excitement.

Waiving other considerations of weight, the short interval between now and the meeting of Congress, and the yet feeble state of my strength,[2] would prevent my undertaking the office, which you kindly propose to me, of pronouncing an Eulogy upon our departed President.

I am sorry that you were unsuccessful in your endeavor to procure a suitable appointment at Washington. You have my best wishes, and I am sorry that I cannot do more. The best and most amicable relations exist between the Vice President and myself; but what his course will be I can only conjecture. I hope and believe that he will contribute to carrying out the principles and policy of the Whigs. But as to the administration of the public patronage, I see no reason to change the rule of non-interference which I had deliberately adopted. I am sure, if I departed from it, that I should be exposed to continual vexations and my friends to frequent disappointments. I trust that they will reflect that I have no power, not the bestowal of a single office; and, if I am to judge from what has already happened, I believe that my influence is greatly overrated.

V.P.[3] Tyler will, I presume, not confine the patronage of the Govt. exclusively to any particular class of the Whigs.

ALS. ViU. 1. Harrison died at 12:30 a.m. on Sunday, April 4, 1841. For his last days, see Cleaves, *Old Tippecanoe,* 341-43. 2. Leaving Washington on March 17, Clay went to Baltimore where he became seriously ill. 3. For the question of what title a vice president, suddenly elevated to the presidency should carry, and how the relevant constitutional provision (Article II, Section 1, paragraph 6) defines the office or the powers and duties of the office devolving on a vice president becoming president, see Seager, *And Tyler Too,* 148-49; Chitwood, *John Tyler,* 205-6.

To David Lambert, April 11, 1841. Notes that he has previously expressed his "sincere wish that you should obtain some suitable appointment," and "I could & can do no more." Adds that he has adopted the policy "of non interference in official appointments" after "much consideration. . . . It occasioned me panic because I feared that some friends might imagine that I was indifferent to the success of their applications for office—They wrong me if they suppose so." Copy, extract. Printed in Henry T. Shanks (ed.), *The Papers of Willie Person Mangum,* 5 vols. (Raleigh, N.C., 1950-56), 3:153. Extract of letter is quoted in David Lambert to Willie P. Mangum, May 7, 1841, in *ibid.,* 3:152-54. During the Tyler administration, Lambert went to Wisconsin to establish a Tyler newspaper; subsequently he was appointed to a position in the New York customs office. *Ibid.,* 3:109.

To JOHN L. LAWRENCE Lexington, April 13, 1841

I recd. your favor of the 7h. and I share with you in surprize and regret on account of the unexpected death of the President.[1] I cannot say that it was altogether unexpected to me; for, altho' I did not anticipate it quite so early, I told some of his Cabinet that, unless he changed his habits, he could not live long.

I have known long and intimately the V. President. He has ability quite equal to his predecessor, is amiable, and I think honest and patriotic. His defect is want of moral firmness. I believe—I should rather say, hope that he will interpose no obstacle to the success of the Whig measures, including a Bank of the U.S.[2]

My opinion coincides with your's that the Cabinet ought to have tendered their resignations. That may have been prevented by Mr Tyler's invitation to them to continue in their respective stations.[3]

I thank you for the papers sent me containing the late foreign news

ALS. ViU. 1. Clay to Conover, April 9, 1841. 2. Clay to Clayton, March 11, 1841. 3. On the pros and cons of Tyler's decision to retain the Cabinet selected by the deceased Harrison, see Seager, *And Tyler Too*, 149.

To SAMUEL STARKWEATHER Lexington, April 15, 1841

I have recd. your favor of the 4h. Your apprehensions have been realized as to the death of Genl Harrison.[1] It is to be greatly lamented. But I cannot help thinking that his successor will enterpose no obstacles to the success of the Whig measures

I regret the state of political apathy which prevails in your City. I hope it will not continue until the Mayor's election.[2] They appear to have given you a good example in Connecticut.[3]

I have no intention of visiting Washn. until shortly before the Extra Session.

Give my respects to Mr. Low and tell him that I have no connection in Arkansas, nor am I able to recommend a suitable person to him as an Agent.

I was extremely sorry to hear of the criminal conduct of Mitchell.[4] We all thought well of him. But there is a most lamentable state of demoralization too generally prevailing. Witness the recent disclosures in the administration of the B. of the U. States.[5]

ALS. NHi. 1. Clay to Conover, April 9, 1841. 2. In the April, 1841 mayoral election in New York City, Democrat Robert H. Morris defeated Whig J. Phillips Phoenix by a vote of 18,606 to 18,200. The Democrats also carried 10 of the city's 17 wards, giving them control of 20 of the 34 seats in the bicameral common council. A number of factors figured in the Whig defeat. Morris had been removed from the office of recorder for maladministration by Gov. William H. Seward and the Whig-dominated state senate, allowing the Democrats to depict him (Morris) as a martyr of partisan politics. Also, snowstorms during the days of the election kept the "silk-stockings of the Whig party" at home. However, a recent historian has concluded that the "fundamental reason for the Whigs' apparent indifference [to the election] . . . was their exhaustion from the presidential contest of November 1840." The Whigs apparently "had not tried very hard to get out the vote," and Morris "was elected mayor on the straight party vote." Nevins, *Diary of Philip Hone*, 540; Ira M. Leonard, "New York City Politics, 1841-1844: Nativism and Reform," Ph.D. dissertation, New York University, 1965, pp. 40-41, 66-67, 72-73. 3. Whig William W. Ellsworth was reelected governor of Connecticut with 56% of the votes. *BDGUS*, 1:167. Whigs also won all 6 seats for the U.S. Congress. *Guide to U.S. Elections*, 575. 4. Charles F. Mitchell, a former member of Congress from New York, and friend of Thurlow Weed and James Watson Webb, had been convicted of committing forgeries estimated as amounting to $10,000-$20,000. New York *Herald*, April 3, 5, 1841. See also *BDAC*. 5. Eyre to Clay, Feb. 12, 1841.

To NATHANIEL BEVERLEY TUCKER Lexington, April 15, 1841

I received to-day your favor of the 3d. I observe from the P.S. that intelligence of the death of General Harrison has reached you.[1] We are in a painful state of uncertainty as to the effect upon the policy of the government. I can hardly suppose that V.P. Tyler will interpose any obstacle to the adoption of measures on which the Whigs are generally united. Still, his administration will be in the nature of a regency, and regencies are very apt to engender faction, intrigue, etc.

[Here followed the rejection of the Tucker plan, a long argument in favor of a national bank, and finally the programme resolutions moved at the extra session.][2]

I have not had time to dwell on other features of the Bank. *The objection to its constitutionality is now confined to Virginia. Ought not our friends there yield to Mr. Madison's view of that question!*[3]

Copy, excerpt. Printed in L.G. Tyler, *Letters and Times of the Tylers*, 2:30. 1. Clay to Conover, April 9, 1841. 2. This bracketed insertion by Lyon Gardiner Tyler, son of the president, on N.B. Tucker's proposal for a new national bank and Clay's negative reaction to it (in a now-lost letter to Tucker) is discussed in L.G. Tyler, *Letters and Times of the Tylers*, 2:29-31; see also Chitwood, *John Tyler*, 215. 3. See 3:626; also Irving Brant, *The Fourth President, A Life of James Madison* (New York, 1970), 558, 596-97 and Gaillard Hunt (ed.), *The Writings of James Madison*, 9 vols. (New York, 1910), 9:442-43.

To Henry B. Bascom, Augusta, Ky., April 17, 1841. Regrets he cannot assist Bascom with a patronage request for a friend. Says he is "constrained to adopt the rule of non-interference in official appointments" and that the "lamented death" of Harrison "will not occasion any departure from the rule under the administration of his successor." Believes that the Tyler administration "is in the nature of a Regency and a Regency is often weak, factious and intriguing. Mr. Tyler's disposition, I cannot doubt, will be to cooperate in adopting the measures of the Whigs. He has indeed just said as much. He will want however the popularity, real or apparent, of Genl Harrison, to give moral weight to his recommendations." Copy. KyHi. For Bascom, see 4:312. See Tyler's Inaugural Address of April 9, 1841, for sentiments Clay considered as evidence of his "adopting the measures of the Whigs." *MPP*, 4:36-39.

From William F. Dunnica, Glasgow, Mo., April 17, 1841. Reports Richard Pindell's belief that his purchase of land in Missouri from Clay has been a "bad bargain" and his hope that "you would be willing to cancel the contract [Clay to Pindell, October 14, 1839; Dunnica to Clay, November 19, 1840]." Some of the land covered by the contract, Pindell complains, was sold for taxes as long ago as 1830. Given this confusion, Dunnica asks Clay "to make out a list and set opposite each tract the years you have tax receipts for and forward it to me." Says Clay's descriptions of his lands in Lincoln and St. Charles counties are so vague that the local auditor cannot identify them. Has discovered further, that the St. Charles tract was sold off for taxes in 1831, 1833, and 1835. Notes also that Clay's deeds to his land in the New Madrid area are improperly drawn. Encloses tax receipts for Clay's Lincoln County tract for 1838 and 1840. ALS. DLC-TJC (DNA, M212, R14). For Clay's earlier difficulties with his Missouri lands, especially his efforts to sell some or all of it, see Clay to January, October 6, 1838, and Clay to James B. Clay, October 30, 1840. See also 8:801 and relevant index headings under Clay, James Brown (son).

To JOHN M. BERRIEN Lexington, April 20, 1841

I received only to day your favor of the 7h. inst. We shared with you here in regret on account of the death of the late President,[1] and in solicitude as to what might be the course of his successor. On the latter point we are a good deal releived by the address of Mr. Tyler to the people of the U. States, the fair interpretation of which is, that he will concur in the leading measures of the Whigs.[2] That address has made its appearance since the date of your letter. Indeed, after his acceptance of the nomination for the V. Presidency; and after his assumption of the duties of President, devolved upon him by the death of Genl. H.,[3] I think an obligation is fairly to be implied upon the V. President to stand by, and carry out the measures of the Whigs. I am glad you have written to him. I too addressed him before I saw his official publication.[4] We shall probably each obtain from him some satisfactory confirmation of the principles which, I hope he entertains in common with you & I.

Should the elections to take place before the Extra Session not be very disastrous, I shall repair to Washn. with all the confident hopes of the success of our measures, which I expressed to your [*sic*, you] before our late separation at Washn. So far Connecticut has done very well.[5] The City of N. York not so ill as I feared,[6] but not so well as it would have done if there had not been some bad appointments for that City made at Washn. We shall do well in Kentucky.[7] I do not think that we shall lose, and probably may gain, a Whig vote in the H. of Representatives.

My health, respecting which you have done me the favor to enquire, is better, but my strength is not yet restored. I must await the coming of the warm weather for that. I should be extremely happy to embrace your friendly prescription of a journey by N. Orleans & the South to Washington, but the vacation is too short to admit of my enjoying such a treat.

ALS. NcU. 1. Clay to Conover, April, 9, 1841. 2. For Tyler's Inaugural Address of April 9, see *MPP*, 4:36-39; also Clay to Bascom, April 17, 1841. 3. Clay to Conover, April 9, 1841. 4. Probably on April 15. See Tyler to Clay, April 30, 1841. 5. Clay to Starkweather, April 15, 1841. 6. *Ibid.* 7. Clay to Letcher, Sept. 7, 1840.

From Benjamin Ogle Tayloe, Washington, April 21, 1841. Reports that his brother Henry, in Marengo County, Alabama, is prepared to order from Clay 3,750 yards of hemp bagging @25 cents per yard and 2,652 lbs. of hemp bale rope @10 cents per pound, both to be delivered at Mobile as soon as practicable, "free of expence to us." Payment to be made in New York City on March 1, 1842. Will Clay accept this proposition? Mentions his deep concern about Clay's illness in Baltimore enroute home to Kentucky from Washington. Says that the city of Washington mourns Harrison's death, but derives "consolation from the expectation that President Tyler will supply his place in consonance with your own views." Predicts a "signal victory" at the polls by the Whigs in Virginia tomorrow. Adds: "We are encouraged to hope that at least twelve Whigs will be elected to Congress, and that [Robert B.] Corbin will beat [Robert M.T.] Hunter, and [Corbin] Braxton, the loco foco candidate." ALS. KyLxT.

Tayloe (1796-1868) was the grandson of Benjamin O. Tayloe, Virginia's tenth governor, and brother of Edward Thornton Tayloe [4:937]. See *TQHGM* (October, 1920), 2:80. For Virginia's 1841 elections, including Hunter's election to the U.S. House over Corbin and Braxton, see Clay to Brooke, January 7, 1841.

To WADDY THOMPSON, JR. Lexington, April 23, 1841

I recd. today your favor of the 12h. and, according to your request, I have directed my manager, Mr. Downing,[1] to obtain your bay mare from Mr. Toddhunter [*sic*][2] to be served by Monarch. You do not state the price of the moiety or the whole of the Stock mentd. by you. I do not want it, but if I knew the terms possibly I might aid the sale of it.

I learn in the most satisfactory manner that Tyler will support all the Whig measures, including a Bank. I have not yet seen [John J.] Crittenden, who is at Frankfort, but understand that his language is that of entire confidence. Independent of the future, and looking entirely to the past, honor & good faith impose on him (Mr. Tyler) that obligation; but if he has further hopes; if, as is quite probable, he may cherish the hope of being elected hereafter to the Presidency, would he not endeavor to retain the confidence of those political friends through whose selection for the second, he has been enabled to reach the first office, in the Nation?

The affair of the Mexican mission[3] I was assured, prior to my departure from Washn, was definitively settled. If there should any difficulty arise about it, I hope you will let me know it.

If we are to credit the Boston Atlas, the Speakers Chair will be sought by Mr. [Caleb] Cushing, contrary to Mr. D's expectations. I was not aware that Mr. [William C.] Dawson had put his heart upon it. The idea which I entertained in common with others was that he was looking to the office of Govr of Georgia.

I had no hand in bringing out Mr. [John] White, altho' he is a warm friend & one whom I highly esteem. I was not aware that he was spoken of for the office until shortly before I left Washn, and then I was informed that he was urged by others to run as a Candidate. Our friend [William] Cost Johnson is also spoken of, and his pretensions are very respectable. The matter ought to be settled in a Caucus.[4]

I hope [William C.] Preston does not suffer himself to be annoyed by any thing that the Calhoun party can do or say to his prejudice.[5]

ALS. MH. 1. Probably Josiah Downing. 2. Probably Parker E. Todhunter. See 6: 1296. 3. On Feb. 5, 1842, President Tyler nominated Thompson as minister to Mexico, a position he held until 1844. U.S. Sen., *Executive Journal*, 6:25 and Thompson article in *DAB*. 4. Neither Caleb Cushing (Mass.), William C. Dawson (Ga.), nor William Cost Johnson (Md.) was elected Speaker of the House. Rep. John White of Kentucky was elected on the first ballot on May 31, 1841. He defeated John W. Jones (Dem., Va.) 121 to 84, with 16 votes scattered. *Cong. Globe*, 27 Cong., 1 Sess., 2. Apparently White had been chosen by the Whig caucus which had met on May 29. Adams, *Memoirs of John Quincy Adams*, 10:470. Although White was known as a Clay Whig, after his election as Speaker, Clay again denied he had played any role in the selection. See Clay to Letcher, June 11, 1841; Van Deusen, *Life of Henry Clay*, 345. For White, see *BDAC* and *NCAB*, 13:60. 5. Preston was being repeatedly attacked in the press for his support of the Whig position on such matters as the national bank, the tariff, and distribution to the states of the proceeds of the sale of public lands. For example, see Washington *Daily National Intelligencer*, May 11, 12, 22, 28, 1841; Washington *Globe*, May 5, 1841; Washington *The Madisonian*, May 21, 1841; also, Shanks, *The Papers of Willie Person Mangum*, 3:157.

To PETER B. PORTER Lexington, April 24, 1841

I was not aware that I was so much in arrear to you before I recd. your favor to day. You must not attribute my delinquincy to any want of high appreciation of your friendly correspondence.

The death of Harrison is not likely to produce as much effect upon public measures as was at first feared; for I hear through a variety of channels that Tyler will concur in all the Whig measures, including a B. of the U. States. The scheme, which you suggested, of a Bank based upon the public lands, did not strike me as favorably as it did you; perhaps because I have had a distribution of their proceeds so long and so much at heart. I think that such a distribution is indispensible to some of the States. I must say also that I think in constituting a new Bank we had better go as much as possible by the light of experience, avoiding all mere experiments, and adopting such improvements in the Charter as have been indicated to be necessary by passing observation.

Briefly, I think we ought to have a Bank with a Capital say of about Fifty millions.

With a power of branching.

No bonus; but in lieu of bonus a limitation of the dividends to six or seven per Cent, and the excess to be paid into the Treasury.

The greatest publicity to the proceedings of the Bank.

No parent director to have accommodation in any form; but in lieu of it a per diem for every days attendance on the Board.

Out of the excess of dividends beyond the prescribed limit, an appropriation to be made to make the dividends come up to the limit when in any year they are below it; and perhaps also to make up the Capital, if there be any deficiency at the end of the Charter.

The effect of all which would be a fixed Bank interest of six or seven per Cent. and a sure Capital.

The Govt to take one fifth, and to have the appointmt of one fifth of the directors.

For the Govts. fifth its bonds bearing five per Cent to be issued, and not redeemable until the end of the Charter; with authority to sell these bonds immediately abroad. &c &c[1] I believe that such a Bank may be put in operation by the first of October.

I have undiminished confidence in the preservation of Peace with G.B. So has our Cabinet. I agree with you as to the case of [Alexander] McLeod. G.B. has made herself responsible for the Capture of the Caroline;[2] and justice & national dignity both prompt us to look to her for reparation, and not to consider the individual amenable to our Courts. In pressing for that reparation we cannot shut our eyes to the nature of the service in which she was engaged at the time of the capture. This view of the case was not at first taken by Mr. Webster, but I presume he has now adopted it.

I intend if I can to go to Washn. a few days before the commencement of the Extra Session. Where will you be this summer? I have a thought of trying for the first time in my life a Sea Bath after the session. What say you to meeting me in Long Island where we could see our boys?[3]

ALS. NBuHi. 1. For an 1838 assessment by Clay of the features required by a new Bank of the United States, see Speech in Senate, May 21, 1838. 2. For the *Caroline* incident and McLeod case, see Comment in Senate, Jan. 5, 1838; Speech in Senate, Jan. 9, 1838; Porter to Clay, Jan. 4, 1841. 3. Clay to Lucretia Hart Clay, July 7, 1840; Porter to Clay, Dec. 20, 1840, and Jan. 4, 1841.

To JOHN Q. ADAMS Lexington, April 29, 1841

I received your favor from Washington. I was extremely sorry to learn from it, as I had through other channels, that considerable dissatisfaction with some recent Federal appointments prevailed in N. York, and in such degree as to have affected injuriously the late election of Mayor.[1] I apprehended that such would be the effect; and I left Washington with a positive assurance from the late President that one of those appointments should not be made.[2] I hope that our friends in N. York and every where will not allow any unacceptable appointments to induce them to relax their exertions, until the great measures which we have in view are all accomplished.

I have confident hopes of President Tyler. I think he will not fail to look impartially towards all who contributed to the late Revolution. And I trust that he will appreciate justly the merits and services of our friend Mr. Talmadge [*sic*], who, I think, has had some just cause of complaint.[3]

As the Extra Session approaches, my solicitude increases for the success of those measures which the condition of the Country and the Government both demand. With that view, I am waiting with great anxiety to hear the results of recent elections. Ours are just over, and probably have terminated as in the last Congress. . . .[4]

AL, signature removed. KyU. 1. Clay supporters in New York City felt that the influence of anti-Clay men had been "supreme in procuring appointments" from Harrison and that Webster's friends had received all the offices. Goebel, *William Henry Harrison*, 375. However, other factors seem to have been more important in bringing about the Democratic victory in the mayoral race. See Clay to Starkweather, April 15, 1841. 2. Reference obscure. 3. Nathaniel P. Tallmadge had apparently hoped to be the Whig vice presidential candidate in 1840. Failing that, he had also been passed over for any major appointment in the Harrison administration. Clay to Tallmadge, April 9, June 18, Oct. 12, 1839; Clay to Clayton, Dec. 17, 1840. Tyler appointed him governor of Wisconsin Territory, a post he held from June 17, 1844, to May 13, 1845. *BDAC*. 4. Clay to Berrien, April 20, 1841.

From Thomas C. Patrick, Clays Prairie, Ill., April 29, 1841. Encloses receipts for taxes paid on Clay's land [8:131-32, 655-56, 658]. Notes the sale of one of the horses on Clay's farm; also reports a poor corn crop in 1840 and an "extraordinary wet" spring this year. ALS. DLC-TJC (DNA, M212, R14). See also Moore, Morton & Co. to Clay, July 20, 1840.

To THOMAS EWING Lexington, April 30, 1841

Mr. [John J.] Crittenden, from whom I parted yesterday at Frankfort, communicated to me your wish that I would write to you on the subjects of the Bank of the U. S. and the new duties. I do not know that I can add any thing to what passed between us, in several conversations, prior to my departure from Washn. As to the Bank, I hope you will have prepared a bill by the meeting of Congress.[1] I observed a piece in the Intellr of the 22d. which contained some of those features about which we talked and others worthy of consideration. Either the board of control or a restriction against any discounts by the parent bank, and limiting it simply to issues for the branches and to deposites (similiar to the Indiana bank)[2] may be very proper. If it has the faculty of discounting, then there ought to be a prohibition agt. any accomodation whatever to any director of the parent bank. If all the paper be issued at the parent bank, and it be subjected to the restriction above mentioned, I see no objection to making all the notes payable at the place where the parent bank is located, but that it might occasion too great concentration of specie at a single point. I adhere to the idea of a limitation upon the profits (I think six per Cent) and, in lieu of bonus, the paymt into the Treasury of the excess, with a stipulation in the Charter that out of that excess there should be, from time to time, an appropriation to make the dividends six per Cent whenever they fall below it; and *perhaps* a further stipulation to make the Capital good at the end of the Charter out of that excess, if any remain. With such a provision, I see no necessity for the reservation of a contingent fund, or rather that itself is a contingent fund. I go for the greatest publicity in the proceedings of the Bank, not excepting the accounts of individuals. At least all accounts, without exception, should be open to the inspection of the Secy of the Treasury, and to Congress, through appropriate agencies.

I think we ought most sedulously to avoid agitating the policy of protection at the Extra Session. It will be time enough next winter, when the question of home valuation comes up. I would, therefore, make the proposal of new duties consistent with the Compromise. And they ought to be of such an amount as will supply an abundant revenue, and enable the Treasury to dispense with the proceeds of the P. lands after the 1st. of January next, at which time, if not before, I hope the system of distribution will commence. It seems to me that, upon all free articles (except those which by the act of Compromise, are always to remain free) and upon all articles now paying an ad valorem duty of less than 20 per Cent. a duty of 20 per Cent may be proposed and levied.[3] According to a very able late report, made to the H. of Commons by a Comee. of which Mr. [Joseph] Hume was chairman, it would be wise to levy duties only upon the productive articles, allowing those which would produce very little to be entered free of duty.[4] That suggestion has the recommendation of simplicity. You will be the best judge, after suitable calculations and estimates, as to the extent on which that idea can be acted. That same report seems to favor an uniform rate of duty, and that an ad valorem duty, for all articles whatever. There are some obvious advantages in such a fixed rule. Extensive frauds would be avoided, and we should no longer see a constant endeavor to get a dutiable article thrown into the free class or placed in a class paying a lower rate of duty. If there were one fixed rate of duty, much of the machinery now employed in the collection of the Revenue might be dispensed with.

It was apprehended, when the Compromise act passed, that it would be extremely difficult to make the biennial reductions on articles paying specific duties. It was asked how will you reduce a Specific duty to an ad valorem duty, which you must do, to ascertain what is the excess of duty beyond 20 per Cent? I believe the difficulty apprehended has not been realized in practice. Specific duties are most simple but least just, because articles of different values pay the same duty. The Coffee of Morea or Java pays the same duty and no more than the inferior Coffee of Cuba &c. Ad valorem duties have the recommendation of being more just, since, according to the theory of them, at least, every article pays a duty in proportion to its exact value. They would be perfect, but for the diversity of opinion, and other difficulties in arriving at *precise value*.

Without intending positively to express the opinion that there should be only one rate of duty for all imports, I think the fewer the classes the better; and I confess that I am strongly inclined to a single rate, and that an ad valorem one.

I know not whether the President and his Cabinet can all unite in adhering to the Compromise. My opinion, you know, is that, considering that measure to have received the sanction of all parts of & all interests in the Union; that it has a well defined & fixed rule; that it affords reasonable, although moderate protection; and that, if not departed from, it will supp[l]y the desideratum of stability, so much desired by our Manufacturers, it is most desirable that we should not again open the whole subject of the Protective policy.

If by general consent that measure could be adhered to, what troubles should we not avoid! But if it is to be disregarded, there is no necessity of producing, at the Extra Session, the agitation which the overthrow of the Compromise must inevitably excite.

The imposition of duties on the free articles will benefit the manufacturing interest as well as other interests. Its tendency will be to prevent that unfavorable balance against us in the Foreign trade, and to lessen the export of the precious metals.

I see no reason to doubt the success of the Whig measures at the Extra Session. The death of Genl Harrison[5] deprives us of the advantage of the popularity of his name; but all the causes which led to his election remain in full force. The condition of the Country &c &c still requires the adoption of certain great measures. I am happy to see the new President entering upon the duties of his high office with such good dispositions. Let us have hearty & faithful co-operation between the President & his Cabinet, and their friends in Congress, and we cannot fail to redeem all our pledges and fulfill the just expectations of the Country.

ALS. DLC-Ewing Family Papers (Supp. Roll 2). 1. For Ewing's so-called "Fiscal Bank of the United States" plan, which came before the Senate on June 12, see Van Deusen, *Life of Henry Clay*, 345-46; Chitwood, *John Tyler*, 219-20; *Cong. Globe*, 27 Cong., 1 Sess., 18-21, 48-49. 2. The board of directors of the State Bank of Indiana could "Limit and control the discounts of a branch bank after they should reach one and one-fourth times the paid-in capital." William F. Harding, "The State Bank of Indiana," *JPE* (Dec., 1895), 4:4. 3. Two bills were passed during the 27th Congress, 1st Session ("Extra Session") that interlocked the distribution and tariff issues: (1) the "Act to Appropriate the Proceeds of the Sales of the Public Lands and to Grant Pre-Emption Rights" (signed by President Tyler on Sept. 4, 1841) provided for the distribution of public land sales proceeds to all the states on the basis of population; but also authorized an additional payment of 10% to nine states of the proceeds of the land sold within their boundaries, viz: Ohio, Ind., Ill., Ala., Mo., Miss., La., Ark., and Mich. Such distribution would be suspended, however, whenever tariff duties exceeded the 20% level set by the Compromise Tariff Act of 1833. See 5 *U.S. Stat.*, 453-58; (2) the "Act Relating to Duties and Drawbacks" (signed by the president on Sept. 11, 1841) sought to increase government revenue by imposing a 20% *ad valorem* duty on articles previously on the free list. See 5 *U.S. Stat.*, 463-65. See also Chitwood, *John Tyler*, 295-96; Clay to Clayton, March 11, 1841; Remark in Senate, June 9, 1841. 4. On May 5, 1840, Hume had successfully moved for appointment of a select committee "To enquire into the several duties levied on imports into the United Kingdom: how far those duties are for protection . . . or whether the duties are for the purpose of revenue alone." Lucy M. Brown, *The Board of Trade and the Free Trade Movement 1830-1842* (Oxford, England, 1958), 71-72. For Hume, see *DNB*. 5. Clay to Conover, April 9, 1841.

From Ralph Randolph Gurley, London, England, April 30, 1841. Addresses Clay as president of the American Colonization Society and Sir Thomas F. Buxton as president of the African Civilization Society, saying that they represent "in an eminent manner, the more sober general views . . . in regard to the measures demanded for the relief and elevation of the African race." Notes that he can now be more objective because he is no longer officially connected with the American Colonization Society. Surveys the dispersion of Africans around the globe, noting "that the whole number of Africans in exile in all parts of the world is small compared with that of those still residing on the soil of Africa." Believes "the greatest physical evils endured by the African race result from the slave-trade." This evil is "so terrible, so enormous, [that] it becomes all humane and Christian men immediately, solemnly, and with their might, to exert themselves . . . [and] to unite in measures the most efficient for the relief of such inexpressible miseries and the redress of such atrocious wrongs as are involved in the slave-trade." Thinks, however, that all measures will prove futile unless they include "the civilization and elevation of the African race."

Discusses at great length the requirements of Christian duty in aiding the Africans. Concludes that colonization is the best means of achieving this goal. Summarizes the history of Liberia. Thinks also "that the colonial system of England, though not on the whole an evil, is very imperfectly adapted to develope the power and exalt the character of the native population of the countries over which it extends."

Points out that "friends of the coloured race in England and America" are divided between those who direct their efforts "mainly, if not solely, to the emancipation of all slaves in Christian countries" immediately and those who favor colonization. Contends that the latter "avoids those collisions and angry controversies inevitably connected with the scheme of abolition. Regards much of the writing and proceedings of abolitionists "as unjust to the people of the United States, particularly to the slaveholders."

Expresses the hope that the American Colonization Society and the African Civilization Society may work together so that "liberty to the whole African race may follow in their footsteps." Copy. Printed in Ralph R. Gurley, *Letter to the Hon. Henry Clay, President of the American Colonization Society . . . On the Colonization and Civilization of Africa . . .* (London, 1841), 1-30. For Buxton (1786-1845), a philanthropist and former member of parliament, see *DNB*.

On June 20, 1840, Clay had written "To Whom It May Concern" a letter of introduction for Gurley who was then embarking on a trip to Britain. Gurley, *Letter to the Hon. Henry Clay*, iii.

Gurley had secured money in 1840 from New York colonizationists to go to England to collaborate with the British African Civilization Society and to survey the British government's intentions in west Africa. During his prolonged absence, the directors of the colonization society deposed him as its secretary, although he was later reappointed to the post. P.J. Staudenraus, *The African Colonization Movement, 1816-1865* (New York, 1961), 238-39.

From JOHN TYLER Washington, April 30, 1841

Your letter of the 15h—[1] was received some days ago and its acknowledgement at an earlier day has been prevented by pressing engagements—At its date you had not probably seen my address to the people of the U. States[2] which was designed as an exponent of the principles on which I should administer the govt. Considering the brief time allowed me and the extreme pressure on my time, it will not be expected that I shall come before Congress with matured plans of public policy connected with deeply interesting and intricate subjects—There are some points so simple in them selves as to require but brief consideration—The repeal of the subtreasury,[3] and if necessary additional burthens for the relief of the Treasury—The wants of the Treasury will be made manifest and the state of our military defences requires immediate attention—There is not a Seaport town that does not hold its existence at the will of a great Naval power—Altho' I am not apprehensive of a war,[4] yet I cannot but feel solicitude as to the ability of the Country to repel invasion—If these shall be the only matters attended to at the Extra session, great good will have been done—The pressing wants of the Treasury will have been reliev[e]d—the war on the currency will have ceas'd, and the Banks be plac[e]d in a condition to afford partial relief—Should legislation stop here, the public monies would be restored to the custody provided for them by the act of 1789—[5] which law has been abrogated by the course of Jackson and his sucessor—To these objects the late President's proclamation convening Congress,[6] seems exclusively to have look[e]d—It will however be for Congress to decide whether other measures shall claim its attention—The Citizens of this District should undoubtedly not be forgotten—

My opinions on the subject of a distribution of the proceeds of the sales of the public lands were promulg[ate]d some three winters ago in a report submitted to the H. of Delegates of Virginia—[7] I made the basis of that distribution an abandonment of that course which has for some time prevail[e]d, of annual appropriations to harbours and rivers—a course wholly indifensable in any view in which I can regard it—thereby substituting a wholesome, sound and equal action in place of one unequal and therefore unjust, not to say any thing of its want of constitutionality—and without which substitution the loudest and most violent complaints will be urg[e]d against the Distribution at this time—

As to a Bank I design to be perfectly frank with you—I would not have it urg[e]d prematurely—The public mind is still in a state of great disquietude in regard to it—The late exposures at Philadelphia have not been calculated to put it to rest—The misnomer given to that Bank by the injudicious policy pursued by those who obtain[e]d its charter, and the late disclosures,[8] have furnished the Demagouges with new weapons to assail those who advocate a Bank Charter—Whilst the close division of votes by which, if at all, it will pass through Congress, will encourage the *Ultraists* in efforts to destroy it before it can go into operation—I apprehend a strong protest from the minority, and an avow[e]d purpose to cancel it—the charter at a future day—[9] Should this be done, are you sure that Capitalists will adventure thier capital in it—The fact is before the world that Jackson tore the charter of the old Bank into tatters—[10] and his followers will go forth as agitators and the result of thier agitations may prove dissastrous—If however you see nothing in this of force, then I desire you to consider whether you cannot so frame a Bank as to avoid all constitutional objections—which of itself would attach to it a vast host of our own party to be found all over the Union—I make these suggestions for your consideration—and make them in that spirit of frankness which will always characterize my course towards you—I have no intention to submit any thing to Congress on this subject to be acted on—but shall leave it to its own action—and in the end shall resolve my doubts, by the character of the measure propos'd, should any be entertain[e]d by me—

My attention is turned to the removals from office after the manner that you suggest—and I hope that to the recent appointments you have nothing to object. The P. office at Lexington shall be attended to—[11]

I deriv[e]d very great pleasure in affixing my signature to the Commission of Mr. Duralde for the appointment of Naval Officer at New Orleans—[12]

ALS. ViU. 1. See Clay to Berrien, April 20, 1841. 2. *MPP*, 4:36-39 (April 9, 1841); Clay to Bascom, April 17, 1841. 3. The Independent (or Sub-Treasury) Treasury Act of 1840 [Speech in Senate, Sept. 25, 1837] was repealed by the Senate on June 9, 1841, by a vote of 29 to 18 and by the House on August 9 by a vote of 134 to 87. *Cong. Globe*, 27 Cong., 1 Sess., 36, 312-13. See 5 *U.S. Stat.*, 439-40. 4. For the Northeast boundary, *Caroline*, and McLeod crises with Great Britain, see Comment in Senate, Jan. 5, 1838; Speech in Senate, Jan. 9, 1838; Clay to Hamilton, Feb. 24, 1839; Comment in Senate, April 14, 1840. 5. Under section 4 of the act of Sept. 2, 1789, "to establish the Treasury Department," it was "the duty of the Treasurer to receive and keep the monies of the United States, and to disburse the same upon warrants drawn by the Secretary of the Treasury, countersigned by the Comptroller, recorded by the Register." 1 *U.S. Stat.*, 65-67, espec. 66. 6. Harrison's proclamation of March 17, 1841, calling Congress into session on May 31, 1841. *MPP*, 4:21. 7. While serving as chairman of the select committee on public lands in the Virginia house of delegates, Tyler submitted a detailed report to that body on Jan. 17, 1839, arguing in favor of distribution. He linked it, however, to an abandonment of appropriations for river and harbor internal improvements, not to tariff adjustments upward, as Clay proposed in 1841. As president, Tyler resisted the linkage of tariffs to distribution, as he had earlier in his career. Chitwood, *John Tyler*, 153. 8. Eyre to Clay, Feb. 12, 1841. 9. For Tyler's vetoes of the two bank bills the Whigs sent to him—the first veto on August 16, 1841, the second on Sept. 9, 1841—and the explosion in Whig ranks occasioned by these vetoes, see Van Deusen, *Life of Henry Clay*, 344-55; Chitwood, *John Tyler*, 219-48; Seager, *And Tyler Too*, 150-61. The first bank bill, the so-called "Fiscal Bank of the United States" bill [Clay to Ewing, June 2, 1841; Comment in Senate, June 21, 1841], was passed by the Senate on July 28 by a vote of 26 to 23 and by the House on August 6 by a margin of 128 to 97. *Cong. Globe*, 27 Cong., 1 Sess., 260, 303. The second, or "Fiscal Corporation" bill, was passed by the House, 125 to 94, on August 23. By a vote of 27 to 22 the bill was passed in the Senate on Sept. 3. *Ibid.*, 372, 423. Tyler's veto messages are dated respectively, August 16 and Sept. 9, 1841. *MPP*, 4:63-68, 68-72. For a comparison of the contents of the two vetoed bank bills, see Remark in Senate, August 24, 1841; and for the Tyler-Clay conflict in a broader political context, see David W. Krueger, "The Clay-Tyler Feud, 1841-1842," *FCHQ* (April, 1968), 42:162-77. 10. See 8:434, 443, 552, 558, 640-41. 11. Joseph Ficklin [3:183; 6:915-16] was removed from the Lexington postmastership in July, 1841. He was reappointed to the post by Tyler in March, 1843. In the interim, Thomas S. Redd was Lexington's postmaster. For Redd, said to be "a great friend" of Clay, see Thomas L. Walker (comp.), *History of the Lexington Post Office From 1794 to 1901* (Lexington, 1901), 25-26. 12. Martin Duralde, Jr., Clay's son-in-law. His salary was $3,000. The civilian office of Naval Officer in the Department of the Treasury, was concerned with customs functions.

To Benjamin Ogle Tayloe, Washington, D.C., May 1, 1841. Thanks him for his letter of April 21 and the offer therein to purchase hemp. Explains that while the prices quoted are exactly those prevailing in Louisville, his son, Thomas Hart Clay, and son's partner, Waldemar Mentelle, have decided to accept the offer. They have also agreed to absorb the shipping costs from Louisville to Mobile for two reasons: "1st. That they will receive specie funds or their equivalent in N. York; but more particularly 2dly. because they hope to contract with your brother for his supplies next year and succeeding years. They would be willing now to fix the rates at the same prices for another year." Closes with the political hope and confidence "that the course of President Tyler will be such as to lessen the injury which the public would have otherwise sustained in the death of Genl Harrison." ALS. NN. Written from Lexington.

To JANE ERWIN YEATMAN BELL Lexington, May 6, 1841

I am afraid that you have forgotten my good friend Captn. Meany,[1] your protege. He writes to me, from time to time, not in any spirit of complaint (for he is the best natured man in the world) sending numerous Copies of recommendations & testimonials in his favor from City Councils, Commodores and I know not how many other dignitaries. I cannot see how it is possible for Mr. [John] Bell to resist the weight of these evidences, and I sincerely hope that he will give him that place at Frankfort [*sic*, Frankford], near Philada. for which I am quite sure he was expressly made by nature.[2] I shall hold you responsible for his getting it.

They are all well at the Woodlands[3] as we are here.

ALS. DLC-Misc. Manuscripts Collection (St. James School folder). Jane Bell was the wife of John Bell [4:848; Clay to Lucretia Hart Clay, August 16, 1840], newly appointed secretary of war. 1. Possibly Capt. John Meany. See 5:1034. 2. Meany did not get a position at the U.S. Arsenal in Frankford, Pa. 3. Lexington estate owned by James Erwin, Mrs. Bell's brother.

From THOMAS EWING Washington, May 8, 1841

I received your favor of the 30th. Ult. & with it, what I very much desired, an abstract of your views on the two important subjects, a Bank & Tariff, in a shape that I can refer to them in the progress of my preparation for the special session—

As to the Bank—All that I supposd. will be due from me to the public at the opening of the session will be to state the objections to the present Fiscal agent and the wants of the Treasury in that respect—leaving Congress, if they choose, to call on me for the project of a Bank and my special reasons in favor of it—[1] We have attacked the past administration for dictation to the Legislative branches of the Government—Any just imputation of this kind I would wish to avoid & at the same time I am willing to assume any responsibility which properly devolves on me—The President cannot without manifest inconsistency recommend a Bank in his Message—He would wish if possible to avoid the question at the special session. That, as a matter of course, I presume Congress will not permit—[2]and when the question shall be presented to him, sanctioned by the representatives of the States & the people, I have no doubt that he will acquiesce in what they may will—In one thing however our friends in the several states have been remiss—They might have embodied the public opinion of almost the whole mass of the people, in the Northern & Western States & in many of the Southern also, in favor of a Bank & against the infliction of further torture on the business community by experiments on the currency—

So to the Tariff[3] we shall have no difficulty from the President or in the Cabinet—Your views are, as far as I know, ours on that subject—There may be dissent but not opposition in the Cabinet—No man can be better disposed than the President—His former opinions, some of them unfortunately of record will trouble *him* but *not*, I think, *the country*—He speaks of you with the utmost kindness, & you may rely upon it his friendship is strong & unabated—

I had a letter from [John M.] Clayton yesterday—He is in fine spirits & is coming to see us in a day or two—

ALS. DLC-HC (DNA, M212, R5). 1. For Secretary of the Treasury Ewing's report to Congress, dated June 2, 1841, see *Cong. Globe*, 27 Cong., 1 Sess., 18-21. In it he attacked the Independent Treasury Act of July 4, 1840, called for its repeal, and proposed the reestablishment of a "fiscal agent" similar to the government-chartered Second Bank of the

United States. Specifically, he called for a new bank "so conceived in principle and guarded in its details as to remove all scruples touching the question of constitutional power." See also Tyler to Clay, April 30, 1841; Clay to Ewing, June 2, 1841. 2. In that part of his message to Congress, dated June 1, 1841, dealing with finances, Tyler argued that the anti-B.U.S. policies of Jackson [8:434, 443, 552, 558, 640-41], and Van Buren had been supported by most of the people and noted that while the presidential election of 1840 had resulted in a popular renunciation of Van Buren's Independent Treasury idea [Speech in Senate, Sept. 25, 1837, and Feb. 19, 1838], "no other scheme of finance seemed to have been concurred in." He thus placed the controversial bank issue in the hands of Congress, "reserving to myself the ultimate power of rejecting any measure which may, in my view of it, conflict with the Constitution or otherwise jeopardize the prosperity of the country." *Cong. Globe*, 27 Cong., 1 Sess., 5-8; *MPP*, 4:45-47. 3. Clay to Ewing, April 30, 1841.

To FRANCIS GRANGER Lexington, May 8, 1841

I received to-day your favor of the first. It ought to have reached me the day before yesterday or, certainly, yesterday. But the delinquency is not so great with letters as with news papers. Since my return home, these have come to me with the most provoking irregularity. To day; I have recd. an [Washington] Intellr. of the 24h. April! I suspect too, from what I hear, that the letters of some gentlemen (your's among others, for example) are transmitted with more regularity than they are generally.

I am sorry that Mr. Bryant[1] is disappointed, as I understood he was strongly recommended to you by some of our delegation, as he deserved to be, and was named by me to you orally before I left the City. I do not know Mr. Smith,[2] but, from your statement of him, I presume he is quite competent.

Mr. [Joseph] Ficklin, the P.M. at Lexington, ought not to be retained.[3] He was originally palmed upon our community not very fairly, and has been in office some eighteen or twenty years. He was a most thorough going & active partizan, of the two late Administrations, not boisterous at the polls, but plausible, cunning, efficient & untiring. He formed a sort of rallying point for the party in Kentucky and in the West, and his office a place of rendezvous, for his political friends. I have often witnessed this with my own eyes, when calling for my mail. We have had reason to believe that he would put forward or keep back the latest intelligence, to subserve his party. In short, if Mr. Ficklin be not removed, there are very few if any that ought to be removed from political considerations. I have not supposed that the propriety of his removal ever admitted of any doubt; and whatever delay that has occurred I imagined to be the result of a want of information as to a suitable successor.

I had thought of Mr. Smith, who married a connexion of Mrs. Clays, as a person that would discharge the duties of the office well;[4] but he declines accepting it. If you determine (as I presume and hope you may) to remove him, I recommend Mr. Thomas S. Redd,[5] a native of Lexington, a deputy sheriff of the County of Fayette, and a highly respectable and efficient person of business. I have no connection with him, have not mentioned to him this recommendation, nor has he solicited the office.

I have made enquiries respecting the objections urged to the appointment of Col. F. Johnson as P.M. at Louisville.[6] I believe them to proceed chiefly from other gentlemen desiring that office or their friends. I adhere to the opinion as to the suitableness of his appointment, and so do the

Govr. my Colleague, and Mr. [John J.] Crittenden, whom you will see soon. Expecting also to have that pleasure in a few weeks of meeting you....

ALS. NHi. 1. Possibly Edwin Bryant who was appointed as a post office "special agent" for southwest New York. *Biennial Register*, 1841, p. 2. 2. Reference obscure since several Smiths received postmasterships. 3. Tyler to Clay, April 30, 1841. 4. Probably Thomas Smith who was married to Mrs. Clay's niece, Nannette Price Smith. 5. Tyler to Clay, April 30, 1841. 6. Probably Francis Johnson. See 3:42 and *BDAC*. George L. Douglass, who had been appointed postmaster at Louisville by Van Buren in 1840, was reappointed. *Biennial Register*, 1841, p. 227; U.S. Sen., *Executive Journal*, 5:253, 256.

To HENRY B. BASCOM Lexington, May 10, 1841

I have this day to acknowledge the receipt of your friendly letter of the 1st. I shall take pleasure in mentioning to some of the faculty and trustees of Transylvania Dr. Reese[1] favorably.

I am greatly obliged by your communication of the complaints which have reached you against me of neglect in my correspondence, and to personal applications. It is the office of a true friend to apprise his friend of any thing said to his prejudice, and I receive any such communication with gratitude and composure.

It was impossible for me to answer the letters I received at Washington. I could not have replied to one in a hundred. If the days had 48 instead of 24 hours their duration would have been too short for me to answer all. I did not pretend therefore to reply to letters, generally, soliciting office. I do not think that I treated any personal applications with disrespect.

The rule of noninterference in official appointments, which I adopted after much consideration, I explained verbally and by letter to many friends. I do not recollect an instance in which it was not approved. I am more and more satisfied of its propriety.

I have a long letter from President Tyler[2] on public affairs and other information as to his views &c. I have strong hopes, not, however, unmixed with fears, as to the success of our Whig measures and his co-operation in their support.

ALS. ViU. Addressed to the Reverend Mr. Bascom at Park Lodge, near Augusta, Ky. 1. Possibly John James Reese (1818-92) who had graduated from the medical school of the University of Pennsylvania in 1839 and was at this time practicing in Philadelphia. He did not obtain an appointment at Transylvania University, but he later taught at Pennsylvania College and the University of Pennsylvania. See *DAB*. 2. Tyler to Clay, April 30, 1841.

To WILLIAM EDWARDS Lexington, May 11, 1841

Your[1] favor comes to me amidst preparations for my journey to attend the Extra Session of Congress, and I must therefore be brief.

My opinion is, that nothing ought to be brought forward at the Extra Session but measures which suggested the necessity of convening it. I do not think that the Copy Right bill[2] will be brought forward until the regular Session.

The inventors of useful machines or instruments are entitled to the most friendly & favorable consideration; and, if the laws are defective or wanting in liberality, I should be happy to concur in any proper amendment of them.

ALS. CtY. 1. For Edwards, a farmer and inventor, see *DAB*. 2. Comment in Senate, Feb. 2, 1837.

To CHARLES L. PEYTON[1] Lexington, May 11, 1841

I recd. your favor communicating some suggestions in respect to a plan of a U. S. Bank. I will give to them fair consideration. Considering the past, I must, however, frankly own to you, for one, that I think we ought to avoid as much as we can all mere experiments, and govern ourselves by the light of actual experience.

I believe there is a majority in favor of the establishment of a Bank of the U.S. in every State in the Union except three or at the most four, and I place Virginia among those four, with some doubt & hesitation.[2]

ALS. DLC-HC (DNA, M212, R5). Addressed to Peyton, near Lewisburg, Greenbrier County, Va. (W.Va.) with instruction on envelope: "Via Washn. City." 1. For Peyton, a physician and great-nephew of Thomas Jefferson, see Hayden, *Virginia Genealogies*, 556. 2. Virginia's delegation in the U.S. House voted 10 in favor of repealing the Independent Treasury Act, 11 were opposed, and 1 did not vote. Both Virginia senators voted for repeal. The Virginia congressmen voted 8 in favor and 14 opposed to both the first and second bills to institute a new Bank of the United States. Both Virginia senators voted against the first bank bill. Although the roll call vote is not given for the final passage of the second bank bill, on the vote to pass it to a third reading one senator (William C. Rives) voted against and one (William S. Archer) voted in favor. U.S. H. of Reps., *Journal*, 27 Cong., 1 Sess., 324-26, 344-45, 409-10; U.S. Sen., *Journal*, 27 Cong., 1 Sess., 37, 125, 234-35. See also Tyler to Clay, April 30, 1841.

To JOHN TYLER Lexington, May 12, 1841

I have made the case of Mr. P. R. Fendall an exception to my general rule of non-interference in official appointments. He was with me in the Dept. of State, was dismissed about the time I left it, is a person of excellent attainments and of great worth, and has borne towards me the most intimate relations of confidence and friendship. He is poor, but honest, capable and faithful.

When I left Washn. I supposed it was settled that he was to be appointed Atto. of the District.[1] From not having seen his appointment announced, and presuming that there could not exist the smallest hesitation about dismissing the present incumbent, I have feared that some difficulty may have arisen; and hence I take the liberty with you, which I exercised with President Harrison, of bearing strong and decided testimony to the great merits of Mr. Fendall.

ALS. NcD. Hand copy made by Clay for Philip Ricard Fendall [3:360]. 1. Fendall was appointed district attorney in the District of Columbia and served in that capacity in 1841-45 and 1849-53.

From Jacob Barker, New Orleans, May 13, 1841. States that the "nation look to you for the adoption of both" a national bank [Tyler to Clay, April 30, 1841; Clay to Ewing, June 2, 1841; Speech in Senate, June 21, 1841; Porter to Clay, mid-July, 1841] and a national bankruptcy law [Remark in Senate, April 22, 1840, and December 28, 1841]." Predicts that if these do not pass at the extra session of Congress, "the great object of the political change which has taken place will be lost, as new feelings, new men, with new objects, will spring up before the annual session, which will not be likely to pass either law." Hopes Clay will "exert yourself in favor of prompt action."

Advises that "It will not make any difference where you place the 'mother bank;' " discounting should be left to the branch banks; but "to get rid of the Constitutional objections as far as possible, which will probably be the most formidable the friends of the measure will have to contend with, it will be best to establish the mother bank at Washington, with power to establish branches wherever the State legislature may authorize it." Warns that if the Sub-Treasury [Speech in Senate, December 15, 1840] and Specie Circular [8:861; Speech in Senate, January 11, 1837] are repealed "in any other way than by substituting a national bank therefor . . . a national bank will not be created," because "the local banks are too powerful." Copy. Printed in *Incidents in the Life of Jacob Barker, of New Orleans, Louisiana* . . . (Washington, 1855), 126-27. For Barker—a merchant, financier, and lawyer—see *DAB*.

To FRANCIS T. BROOKE Lexington, May 14, 1841

I have received your favor of the 6th. instant. My health, or perhaps I should rather say, my strength is not fully re-established, nor do I expect it until warm weather, if that should ever again come.

I leave home for Washington on the 20h. inst.[1] I expect to go by Wheeling, and without Mrs. Clay.

I repair to my post in the Senate with strong hopes, not however unmixed with fears. If the Executive will cordially co-operate in carrying out the Whig measures, all will be well, otherwise every thing is at hazard. The Western elections, as far as I have yet heard, have terminated favorably. . . .

ALS. KyU. Printed in Colton, *Clay Correspondence*, 4:453-54. 1. Clay departed at about this time and arrived in Washington on May 27 or 28. DS, per Samuel Hiernecke. DLC-TJC (DNA, M212, R19).

To John O. Sargent, Boston, May 16, 1841. Says he would like to see Sargent's brother, Epes, appointed consul at Tangier, "but I am not sure that I shall have it in my power to aid him." Adds: "Many of the considerations, which seemed to me to enjoin non interference on my part, in official appointments, remain; some have ceased, but others have sprung up in their place. Until I reach Washn. and have a survey of the whole ground, I cannot decide upon the propriety of my interposing in any case. I shall be most happy to find there a state of things admitting of my furthering your brothers views." ALS. MHi. Written from Lexington. Epes Sargent did not get the consulship at Tangier.

Remark in Senate, May 31, 1841. Suggests that a joint committee to wait upon the president cannot be formed until the House of Representatives is organized. Moves adjournment until tomorrow. Carried. *Cong. Globe*, 27 Cong., 1 Sess., 1.

Remark in Senate, June 1, 1841. Thinks that for reasons of economy the printing of 5,000, rather than 10,000, copies of the president's message to Congress will be sufficient. Moves that the election of standing committees take place tomorrow; states that tomorrow he will also move to elect a select committee [Select Committee on the Currency] to consider that part of the president's speech "as relates to the currency and finances, with a view of suggesting such remedy as should be deemed advisable." Asked by an unidentified senator the "nature of the remedy" he had in mind, Clay replies: "a National Bank." *Cong. Globe*, 27 Cong., 1 Sess., 8. See Remark in Senate, June 2, 1841.

To THOMAS EWING Washington, June 2, 1841

I have made several ineffectual attempts to see you, and one this afternoon.

Our official hours being the same, I should be glad to make some arrangement by which I could occasionally *certainly* see you at some other hours.

I wished now to know whether you have made any, and, if any, what progress in the draft of a Bank Charter? A movement was made on that subject to day [Wednesday] in the Senate; and, if possible, I should be glad that a bill could be reported on monday next.[1]

Col. [Thomas H.] Benton to day proposed a number of resolutions, calling for information.[2] They may be called up tomorrow. You will see them, I suppose, in the morning papers. Will you inform me, by a note or otherwise, after you have seen them, whether there be an objection to any of them? and whether they will occasion much trouble at the Department?

Have you had any conference with [John J.] Crittenden as to the parts of the Sub Treasury bill to be retained?[3]

ALS. DLC-Thomas Ewing Papers (DNA, M212, R21). Letter marked "(Private)" and dated "Wednesday afternoon." 1. Ewing's treasury report was submitted on June 2. In a letter, dated only "Saturday Afternoon" and probably written on June 5, 1841, Clay wrote Ewing asking for "another Copy of your report [of June 2] and bill." ALS. DLC-Thomas Ewing Papers (DNA, M212, R21). On Monday, June 7, Clay moved that the administration submit a plan for the incorporation of a national bank. Not until Saturday, June 12, however, did Ewing's plan for a bank bill reach the Senate. See *Cong. Globe*, 27 Cong., 1 Sess., 22, 48-49. Ewing's proposal empowered the bank, located in the District of Columbia, to establish branches in the several states only with the assent of those states—a concession to states' rights opposed by Clay. For Clay's variations in the proposed Ewing plan, see his Speech in Senate, June 21, 1841. See also Clay to Letcher, June 11, 1841. 2. See Remark in Senate, this date. 3. Tyler to Clay, April 30, 1841.

Remark in Senate, June 2, 1841. Moves to print Sen. Benton's package of seven related resolutions requesting the president to submit a broad range of information of specific operations of the U.S. Treasury since March 4. Moves also to proceed to elect chairmen of the standing committees of the Senate. *Cong. Globe*, 27 Cong., 1 Sess., 11-12. Benton's seven resolutions are printed in *ibid.*, 10-11; they were variously amended, combined, and passed *viva voce* on June 8. *Ibid.*, 29. Cf. *ibid.*, 10-11 and U.S. Sen., *Journal*, 27 Cong., 1 Sess., 17-18, 27-28. Omitted from this surgery, however, was the original resolution 4 on Benton's list of June 2, requesting the president to "lay before the Senate a schedule of payments made from the Treasury during the months of March, April, and May, of the present year." On June 16, Clay accepted Benton's fourth resolution and an amendment to it by Sen. Levi Woodbury which added the request that the president also supply estimates of treasury expenditures in various categories from June 1 to December 31, 1841, especially the administration's estimate of any appropriation designed to purchase "stock for capital to be invested in a National Bank." *Cong. Globe*, 27 Cong., 1 Sess., 56. See Clay to Ewing, June 16, 1841.

Later this day, Clay moves the selection of a special committee of nine members, soon referred to as the "Select Committee on the Currency," to deal with the problem of providing "a uniform currency, and a suitable fiscal agent." *Cong. Globe*, 27 Cong., 1 Sess., 11. On the following day, June 3, the committee was chosen. It consisted of Clay (chairman), Rufus Choate (Whig, Mass.), Nathaniel P. Tallmadge (Conservative Dem., N.Y.), John M. Berrien (Whig, Ga.), Richard A. Bayard (Whig, Del.), William A. Graham (Whig, N.C.), Jabez W. Huntington (Whig, Conn.), William R. de V. King (Dem., Ala.), Silas Wright (Dem., N.Y.).

Ibid., 12. Its report, submitted by Clay on June 21, 1841, is printed in *Sen. Docs.*, 27 Cong., 1 Sess., no. 32, pp. 7-20. See also Speech in Senate, June 21, 1841.

To JOHN O. SARGENT Washington, June 2, 1841

I duly recd. your favor of the 26h. Ulto. As Mr. [Philip R.] Fendall, a confidential friend of mine had, some time ago, a connection with an enterprize similar to that which has engaged your attention,[1] I placed your letter in his hands, and you will receive with this some communications from him. I sent yesterday to you by mail a Copy of the former publication of my speeches.[2]

I think the plan you have adopted a good one.[3] I like particularly the sketch you propose of the subject to which the Speech relates,[4] and the fate of it in Congress &c. I believe the Lithographic likeness of me, mentioned by Mr. F., is deemed the most faithful.[5]

If it be not lost (and I will write home to ascertain the fact) I had a pretty good sketch of Ashland,[6] the dwelling house, lawns, grounds &c. Another can be obtained, if it be deemed material, should that be lost.

I have some reason to hope that your brother [Epes] will succeed in his application.[7]

ALS. MHi. 1. See 8:252-53. 2. *Ibid.* 3. In 1842 under the name of John O. Sargent's brother, Epes Sargent, *The Life and Public Services of Henry Clay* was published in New York. A new, revised, and enlarged edition was published in New York in 1844. 4. Probably Clay's speech of Feb. 19, 1838, on the Sub-Treasury which received major attention in the Sargent biography. *Ibid.*, (1844 ed.), 38-39, 67-68, *passim*. 5. Probably the lithograph by Francis D'Avignon which served as the frontispiece of Sargent's 1844 edition. 6. No engraving of "Ashland" appeared in the Sargent biography; however, reference may be to the engraving which appeared as the frontispiece in vol. 2 of the 1843 and 1844 editions of Daniel Mallory's *The Life and Speeches of the Hon. Henry Clay*. The picture was drawn by W. Lewis and engraved by A.L. Dick. 7. Clay to Sargent, May 16, 1841.

Remark in Senate, June 3, 1841. Benton accepts Clay's request that his (Benton's) resolutions of the previous day [Remark in Senate, June 2, 1841] lie over until the report of Secretary of the Treasury Thomas Ewing on the nation's finances is received. Dated June 2, 1841, Ewing's report reached the Senate later this day. *Cong. Globe*, 27 Cong., 1 Sess., 13. It is printed in *ibid.*, 18-21. It called specifically for an end to Van Buren's Independent (or Sub) Treasury scheme and the reestablishment of the Bank of the United States in such form as to "remove all scruples touching the question of constitutional power [Tyler to Clay, April 30, 1841; Ewing to Clay, May 8, 1841; Clay to Ewing, June 2, 1841]."

On June 8, Clay moved that 1,500 additional copies of Ewing's report of June 2 be printed. U.S. Sen., *Journal*, 27 Cong., 1 Sess., 27. See also Remark in Senate, June 8, 1841. Clay's motion to print Ewing's report triggered a broad attack by Democrats—principally Senators Calhoun, Wright, and Woodbury—on the operations of the U.S. Treasury, and the effect of such operations on the national economy since the Whigs took power on March 4, 1841. Implicit and explicit in these attacks (Clay regarded them as delaying tactics) was the pending national bank issue [Tyler to Clay, April 30, 1841]. See *Cong. Globe*, 27 Cong., 1 Sess., 64-65, 70-72, 81-82. The motion to print was finally passed on June 21. *Ibid.*, 83.

Following his request to Benton on this day, Clay offers a resolution to repeal the Independent Treasury Act of July 4, 1840 [Speech in Senate, September 25, 1837, and February 19, 1838], and instruct the Committee on Finance to report a bill to that effect. Notes that this resolution is the "same in substance" as the one he had introduced in the previous session [Remark in Senate, December 14,

1840; Speech in Senate, December 15, 1840; Tyler to Clay, April 30, 1841]. Says he wants "a speedy repeal of the Sub-Treasury system," and asserts he will not enter into discussion of the resolution; indeed, he "hoped and presumed that no discussion would be necessary in any quarter." Urges the Finance Committee to report a repeal bill "at once." Adds the observation that insofar as changing the views of the Democrats on the Independent Treasury issue, he "would as soon address an argument on that measure as attempt to convince a convicted criminal with the rope round his neck that his conviction has been just and right." Is distressed that the papers have "represented him as having compared the gentlemen of the Senate who differed from him in opinion with regard to that measure as a company of convicts with halters round their necks." Protests "to Heaven that nothing could be further from his mind than any such a thought." Is willing, therefore, to accept Sen. Silas Wright's amendment to his resolution to include the right of the committee to examine the "expediency" of repealing the Independent Treasury law. Says he believes that there were "some portions of the law which it might be expedient to retain." Rejects Calhoun's contention that the special Select Committee on the Currency, called into existence just yesterday, might well handle the related repeal issue, rather than sending it singly to the Finance Committee, since the repeal of the Independent Treasury implies the substitution of something else for it. Clay asserts, however, that he wants the repeal of the Independent Treasury even if nothing is put in its place. What he and his friends seek, frankly, is a "Bank of the United States"; but before addressing that need the Senate should have before it "a clean and fair sheet of paper . . . to inscribe upon it" whatever fiscal institution might be most expedient for the public good. Considers Calhoun's point that because the repeal of the Independent Treasury would reinstate Jackson's pet bank system, and since a new Bank of the United States would supersede the pet banks, the two issues should be linked legislatively. Clay remarks that he "most heartily concurred with the sentiment expressed by the Senator from South Carolina, that the only alternative before the nation was the Sub-Treasury or a Bank of the United States. Undoubtedly; there was no other alternative. The Senator [Calhoun] with great manliness, had admitted this; so had the other Senator [Silas Wright] on a former occasion." This being the case, "and the people of the United States having most decidedly and unequivocally condemned and repudiated the Sub-Treasury, it only remained that Congress should provide in due season a Bank of the United States. But this was not a session for talking; it was preeminently the season for action." Adds, "with great emphasis and animation," that "The day of judgment is come . . . the day of judgment, I hope, is come—at least to our political world." Opposes a proposal that would require the Finance Committee to study and report a substitute for the Independent Treasury, because that effort would nullify the work of the special select committee appointed to deal with the currency and fiscal agent issues. Participates in turning back two Calhoun amendments (both by 27 to 19 margins), designed to refer both the treasury repeal resolution and the currency and fiscal agent resolution to the Finance Committee, and to require that committee to report a substitute institution for the repealed Independent Treasury. Clay's counter-resolution, finally agreed to, read: "That the Committee on Finance be directed to inquire into the expediency of repealing the act entitled 'An act to provide for the collection, safe-keeping, transfer, and disbursement of the public revenue.' " *Cong. Globe*, 27 Cong., 1 Sess., 13-14.

Remark in Senate, June 4, 1841. Announces that the Committee on Finance is prepared to report a bill to "repeal . . . the act commonly called the Sub-Treasury law [Tyler to Clay, April 30, 1841]." Bill read, ordered printed, and made the order of the day for Monday, June 7. *Cong. Globe*, 27 Cong., 1 Sess., 21.

Later this day, Clay attempts to postpone to the next session the presentation of routine petitions. Fears that such "customary business" might well convert this "extra session" into an "ordinary session" and thus protract it "beyond all reasonable calculation." To the suggestion by Sen. Lewis F. Linn (Mo.) that some limits on subject matter might well be imposed, Clay promises to consider that idea "with a view of making up a sort of protocol of the subjects" which ought to be taken up during this session [Comment in Senate, June 7, 1841]. *Ibid.*, 22.

From James Gordon Bennett, New York, June 5, 1841. Writes that "at an expense of nearly two hundred dollars per week," he has employed "a *corps* of reporters, to give daily reports of the debates in both Houses of Congress" for the New York *Herald.* Notes that "In the House there is no difficulty, but in the Senate there is a rule . . . excluding from the reporters' seats all not connected with the Washington press." Complains that this rule is "illiberal and injurious both to private enterprise and public advantage." Requests Clay "as one of the most liberal and enlightened members of your body" to make a motion "for the repeal of the rule in question." Copy. Printed in Don C. Seitz, *The James Gordon Bennetts . . .* (Indianapolis, 1928), 91.

Bennett's Washington bureau was so effective that Samuel L. Southard, president *pro tem* of the Senate, invoked an old rule that the privilege of the floor was limited to two men from each Washington paper. Bennett charged that this action shielded the Washington papers from competition and aided them in "robbing the public treasury." Bennett promised that his reporters would provide "better and more comprehensive" reports of debates at no charge to the government. James E. Pollard, *The Presidents and the Press* (New York, 1973), 217. The question of official and reliable reporting of the debates was considered during the 1st Session of the 27th Congress, with Clay appealing for reform of the system. For a discussion of this matter, see Elizabeth G. McPherson, "The History of Reporting The Debates and Proceedings of Congress," Ph.D. dissertation, University of North Carolina-Chapel Hill, 1940, pp. 128-31.

To James Harlan, Frankfort, Ky., June 5, 1841. Reports that "we shall carry all our measures"; also notes that the "finest spirit generally prevails in the Senate— it is not quite so good in the House, but there the majority is great [Clay to Brooke, March 12, 1841; Clay to Clayton, May 29, 1841]." ALS. Courtesy of Dr. Alan Westin, Yale University. For Harlan, see 5:295.

To LUCRETIA HART CLAY Washington, June 6, 1841

Genl. [James] Shelby arrived here last night & brought me intelligence that all were well at home.

I think the health of John [Morrison Clay] is improving. He is of that opinion, and so is his physician. Duralde[1] has been with us a week. He and John lodge near us in another house and eat with us. He is grown very much. He is fitting himself out very well with Cloathes at the expense of my pocket, and will soon sail again for the Mediterranean.

Observing a large Sale of plants and flowers, I put your list into the hands of the public gardner,[2] and he has procured all of them but one. He insists upon presenting them to you, and will not receive from me their price. He is to pack them in a box the day after tomorrow, and he says they will live some few weeks. The difficulty is in getting them out to you, if the river should be low at Wheeling. I shall however do the best I can.

I have heard lately from Mr. [James] Erwin.

They have thrown on me a great weight of business and responsibility. I shall get through it as well as I can. I rise now between 4 & 5 O' Clock, take a ride of 6 or 8 miles, and get to hard work immediately after breakfast.

Tell Thomas [Hart Clay] & James [Brown Clay] that Mr. Erwin thinks that Bagging & Rope will be high, and that *I* must not be in a hurry to contract for any. I have heard of the safe arrival at Charleston of that destined for Genl. [Wade] Hampton; and I believe I sent them word that Mr. Barrow got his.[3]

Tell them also that they must write to me, without regarding whether I write or not. I suppose James now believes Banjo Bill to be a first rate horse

ALS. Josephine Simpson Collection, Lexington, Ky. 1. Midn. Martin Duralde III, USN. See Clay to Paulding, May 3, 1839. 2. James Maher. *Biennial Register*, 1841, p. 179. 3. Probably U.S. Senator Alexander Barrow of Baton Rouge, La. See *BDAC*.

From Francis O.J. Smith, Washington, June 6, 1841. Complains that his loss of the election for the post of clerk of the House of Representatives on May 31 revealed "the injustice and treachery practised towards a large portion of the Whig party in the House . . . as well as towards myself personally . . . and which no doubt had specially in view *the breaking up* of the obviously grow[ing] political affinities between the north, middle and weste[rn] states." Because of this, he has been urged to run for secretary of the Senate but will not do so without Clay's clear support. Castigates the present secretary [Hugh A. Garland] as being "notoriously a pet and protegé of the Van Buren party," administratively incompetent, and responsible for extravagant expenditures of the Senate's contingency fund. Asserts that without Garland's removal, the Whig party cannot regard itself as a reform party. ALS. MeHi. For Smith's unsuccessful race for the House clerkship, won by Matthew St. Clair Clarke, see *Cong. Globe*, 27 Cong., 1 Sess., 3. He was not a candidate for secretary of the Senate. Asbury Dickins was elected to that post. *Ibid.*, 22. For charges linking Hugh A. Garland with administrative irregularities, see *ibid.*, 26 Cong., 1 Sess., 282-83, 335-36.

For Francis O.J. Smith, a former Maine congressman, see *BDAC* and Merk, *Fruits of Propaganda*, 59-62. For Hugh A. Garland, a Mecklenburg County, Va., lawyer and former professor of Greek, see *CAB*.

Comment in Senate, June 7, 1841. Presents a petition from certain citizens of Dahlonega, Ga., asking that the U.S. branch mint there be closed. *Cong. Globe*, 27 Cong., 1 Sess., 22.

Also presents a list of subjects to which the Senate should limit its deliberations during the present session [Remark in Senate, June 4, 1841], viz: "1. The repeal of the Sub-Treasury; 2. The incorporation of a bank adapted to the wants of the people, and of the Government; 3. The provision of an adequate revenue for the Government by the imposition of duties, and including an authority to contract a temporary loan to cover the public debt created by the last Administration; 4. The prospective distribution of the proceeds of the public lands; 5. The passage of necessary appropriation bills; and 6. Some modification of the banking system of the District of Columbia for the benefit of the people of the District." Concludes with the resolution "That it is expedient to distribute the business proper to be done at this session, between the Senate and House of Representatives, so as to avoid both Houses acting on the same subject at the same time." *Ibid.* See also Brown, *Politics and Statesmanship*, 132-33.

Later this day, calls attention to the fact that Secretary of the Treasury Ewing, in his June 2 report to Congress on the state of public finances, had included "an explicit expression of the Secretary's opinion in favor of a United States Bank [Tyler to Clay, April 30, 1841; Ewing to Clay, May 8, 1841; Clay to Ewing, June 2, 1841]." Moves, therefore, that Ewing communicate to the Senate, as soon as practicable, "a plan of such a bank . . . as, in his opinion, is best adapted to the public service." Defends this resolution on the ground that the act of Congress of 1789 requires the secretary of the treasury, on demand, to provide such information. Accepts an amendment to his resolution which strikes the phrase "plan of such a bank," substituting for it the phrase "plan of such a Bank or fiscal agent . . . free of constitutional objections." *Cong. Globe*, 27 Cong., 1 Sess., 22-23. For Ewing's completed bank plan, dated June 12, 1841, see *ibid.*, 48-49. For the Treasury Act of 1789, see 1 *U.S. Stat.*, 65-67.

Still later this day, explains and defends the bill reported by the Committee on Finance repealing the Independent Treasury Act [Tyler to Clay, April 30, 1841]. Points out that upon repeal of this act, the finances of the nation would temporarily be governed by the 1789 law establishing the Treasury Department, by the resolutions of 1816 on the medium receivable in payment of public dues [Remark in Senate, March 14, 1838], and by the deposit law of June 23, 1836, which established "what was familiarly called the pet bank system [8:583-84, 684-85, 813]." This last Clay proposes "by amendment to repeal." Notes that the treasury repeal bill in its second section, re-enacts, strengthens and clarifies the embezzlement section of the Independent Treasury Act. Anticipates that Congress will repeal the 1836 deposit act soon after repealing the Independent Treasury Act and will speedily follow that action with "another bill providing for a Bank of the United States, or for some competent fiscal agent" that will ensure "a sound and uniform currency." In the event, however, of an interval of a month or six weeks between the repeal of the Independent Treasury Act and the completion of a new bank bill, or the passage of neither, he now proposes to amend a third section to the Finance Committee bill that repeals the 1836 deposit act. Announces he has no intention in all this to debate again the Independent Treasury system, "a question . . . already sufficiently argued." Points out that if the repeal of the 1836 law is achieved and the bank bill is somehow delayed, the U.S. Treasury would operate under the law of 1789 "til a new law should be enacted."

To the question of executive power over the nation's finances during a transition period, recalls the "wholly arbitrary and tyrannical" power Gen. Jackson had claimed and exercised in 1836 over the national treasure, Treasury Department, and secretary of the treasury. Says he wants to experience no more of that situation. Assures Calhoun and others that he has "considered the law of 1789 as always in force; the union of the purse and the sword was in the face of that law. . . . If opposite principles, indeed, prevailed at this day, as they had in 1836, if there were now any danger of the removal of the deposites by the Executive mandate, and of the repetition of the Specie Circular [8:861], then it might be dangerous to repeal this law of 1836: but such was not the case; and if the law of 1836 were repealed, the law of 1789 would immediately revive, and in union with the resolutions of 1816 would prescribe the duties of Government in relation to the public moneys." To those senators who would prefer living under the 1836 deposit act rather than the Independent Treasury scheme, because the 1836 legislation better diffused a president's control over the financial operations of the government, Clay lists and discusses at length the various financial problems the nation would suffer if the 1836 act were to be continued in force. In sum, he says he has heard no sound arguments against his amendment to repeal the 1836 legislation.

To his claim that four-fifths of the banks operating under the 1836 law were non-specie paying, an argument Calhoun challenges with reference to South Carolina and other banks in the South, Clay replies: "O, well, there may be exceptions, I admit. What I mean is the general prostration of the State banks." *Cong. Globe*, 27 Cong., 1 Sess., 23-26.

From Thomas Ewing, Washington, D.C., June 7, 1841. Writes to Clay as chairman of the Senate Finance Committee, stating that the sum of $7,695.28 has been paid into the U.S. Treasury by the British government "for Slaves carried into Nassau . . . and liberated by the local authorities there." States that Congress must now make appropriation "for the payment of the claims of the owners of those Slaves." Copy. DNA, RG56, Series "E": Letters in Answer to Inquiries & Resolutions of Congress, 1838-1857, pp. 77.

On February 18, 1843, an act to reimburse the owners of the slaves in the amount of $7,965.28 became law. See 5 *U.S. Stat.*, 601. Whether $7,965.28 or Ewing's figure of $7,695.28 was correct, or whether a numerical transposition has occurred, has not been determined.

Remark in Senate, June 8, 1841. Participates in the debate on the bill to repeal the Independent Treasury Act of 1840 [Tyler to Clay, April 30, 1841] and on changes that are required in the Deposit Act of 1836 were it to be revived as the result of a delay between the repeal of the Independent Treasury and the advent of a new Bank of the United States [Tyler to Clay, April 30, 1841; Clay to Ewing, June 2, 1841]. Argues that amendments and amendments to amendments of the Deposit Act by Sen. Calhoun and himself have basically left the Independent Treasury repeal bill, in Clay's words, "in the form in which it had been reported. If it should in this form pass both Houses of Congress, and become law, the State bank system, as regulated in 1836, would be revived and continue in force until a substitute should be adopted by Congress." He takes it for granted that "a substitute of some description would pass; but if, unfortunately, Congress should be unable to agree upon any substitute, whether in the form of a bank or other fiscal agent, then . . . Congress would set about discharging the duty of rendering the State bank system as efficient and perfect as possible." He also considers it proper for him to state that "he would vote for that system under no circumstances—none whatever—none." Noting that he has consistently opposed the pet bank plan, he confesses that he "would not have given his vote for the law of 1836, on any other ground than that that law contained the principle of a distribution of the surplus fund among the States." At the same time, he makes it clear that he wants a new Bank of the United States. To this end, he "never doubted that the law of 1836 would revive; but, when he had introduced his bill to repeal the Sub-Treasury, he had given notice that that was the first in a series, and had avowed, openly, his preference for a Bank of the United States. If, then, the law of 1836 did revive in its present form, he hoped it would be but for a very short time. But, if otherwise, it must undergo a complete revision." Meanwhile, he announces his support for an amendment that would strengthen the anti-embezzlement element in the 1836 Deposit Act. On the other hand, he opposes an amendment by Sen. Benton that the Pennsylvania Bank of the United States never again be permitted to collect, keep, transfer, or disburse public money. Clay admits he has "no hesitation in declaring, after all the disclosures that had recently been made [Tyler to Clay, April 30, 1841], that he should deprecate as much as any gentleman could do the employment of that bank by the Government as a depository of the public funds." Thinks, however, that mentioning a single bank by name in this regard, when there are others that might also be named, is unwise. *Cong. Globe*, 27 Cong., 1 Sess., 32-34.

Earlier this day, several of Benton's resolutions [Remark in Senate, June 2, 1841] requesting the president to submit information on recent Treasury Department operations, were adopted *viva voce* with "unimportant amendments." *Ibid.*, 29.

On this day, Clay also moved that 1,500 additional copies of Secretary Ewing's report of June 2 [Remark in Senate, June 3, 1841] on the nation's finances be printed. U.S. Sen., *Journal*, 27 Cong., 1 Sess., 27.

Remark in Senate, June 9, 1841. Announces that tomorrow he will introduce a bill for "the appropriation for a limited time of the proceeds of the public lands [Speech in Senate, January 28-29, 1841]." *Cong. Globe*, 27 Cong., 1 Sess., 35.

For the background of Clay's 1841 distribution-preemption-internal improvements bill, see Clay to Ewing, April 30, 1841. This bill, initially passed 116 to 108 by the House on July 6, 1841, was debated, amended, and passed by the Senate, 28 to 23, on August 26. In its final form (see 5 *U.S. Stat.*, 453-58) the legislation provided for the distribution of the proceeds of public lands sales to all the states in amounts determined by the size of each state's representation in Congress—except that Ohio, Ind., Ill., Ala., Mo., Miss., La., Ark., and Mich. would receive, in addition, "ten per centum upon the nett proceeds of the sales of the public lands . . . made within the limits of each of the said States respectively." There was also a proviso (the Berrien amendment) that distribution would cease if and when the tariff on any imported item became inconsistent with the Tariff Act of 1833; that is, if it exceeded the 20 percent *ad valorem* level. Further, the legislation granted 500,000 acres of public land to Ohio, Ind., Ill., Ala., Mo., Miss., La., Ark., and Mich., the nine so-called "land states" (or the "new states" plus La. and Ohio) "for purposes of internal improvement." It also included a preemption section which allowed settlers, actual and potential, to purchase (at the minimum price) up to 160 acres of public land on which they resided and on which each "has or shall erect a dwelling." An attempt on August 11 by Senate Democrats to add a price-graduation element to the preemption section failed 18 to 27. *Cong. Globe*, 27 Cong., 1 Sess., 156-57 (printed copy of original House bill); 162, 320, 322 (graduation amendment attempt); 364 (Sen. John M. Berrien's amendment to link distribution to the 1833 tariff [Clay to Ewing, April 30, 1841]; 368-70 (Berrien amendment passed, 24 to 18); 388 (amended Senate bill passed and returned to House), and 405-6.

Later this day, in an effort to speed up debate on the repeal of the Independent Treasury Act [Tyler to Clay, April 30, 1841], Clay offers a resolution, which he requests be tabled, to the effect that if the Senate adjourns on a given day during the present session of Congress while in the midst of consideration of a given subject, the discussion of that same subject would be resumed at the Senate's next meeting "without waiting for the usual hour of one o'clock." *Ibid.*, 36. See Remark in Senate, June 12, 1841.

Still later this day, during debate on repeal of the Independent Treasury Act, Clay's voice is heard to say (above Sen. Levi Woodbury's argument that not a single dollar has been lost or squandered by the Independent Treasury) that "the accounts have not been yet settled." Later interrupts Woodbury's lengthy attack on the repeal bill—during which the New Hampshire senator quotes the Clay of January, 1840 [Speech in Senate, January 20, 1840], to the Clay of today—on the Kentuckian's earlier point that the proposed Independent Treasury was essentially a government bank of which the president of the United States would be president, cashier, and teller. At this juncture, Clay asks Woodbury whether he "rightly understood him as now admitting that the Sub-Treasury was a bank." Woodbury answers no. He also denies Clay's January 20, 1840, contention that the secretary of the treasury had the power under the Independent Treasury scheme to divide his drafts into small sums and use them as bank notes. "Well, and could he not do it?" Clay asks. "He did not do it," Woodbury replies, admitting, however, that Clay's "argument itself is a fair one." *Cong. Globe*, 27 Cong., 1 Sess., Appendix, 19, 21.

Also later this day, in response to an amendment by Sen. Samuel McRoberts (Ill.) to the bill to repeal the Independent Treasury Act, an amendment that would provide guards to protect the deposits when they were physically moved from the state banks to new depositories, Clay states that there is "no earthly necessity for any such provision." The McRoberts motion was rejected 18 to 28, Clay voting nay. *Ibid.*, 29.

Remark in Senate, June 10, 1841. Introduces a bill to distribute the proceeds of public lands sales [Remark in Senate, June 9, 1841], and asks that it be read twice and referred to the Committee on Public Lands. To a motion that the bill immediately be printed, Clay suggests that that would be unnecessary "as it was identically the same bill as had heretofore passed the Senate [and] was familiar to all [8:539-41, 609-10]." On reflection, waives his objection to having it printed at this time. *Cong. Globe*, 27 Cong., 1 Sess., 38.

To HENRY C. CAREY Washington, June 11, 1841

I have received your favor, with the paper enclosed,[1] for which I thank you. I receive a multitude of plans, communications and suggestions about Banks. I have scarcely time to read, none to discuss them.

I am tired of experiments. My opinion is that if we make a new Bank, as I think we ought to do, we had better conform substantially to the models of those we have tried, introducing such amendments as experience has shewn to be necessary.[2] Among these, I think there should be a limitation on the dividends; requiring the Bank to pay the excess into the Treasury &c.

As the dividends arise from the employment of the Capital, the circulation, and the deposites, the tendency of the above limitation would be to check the use of the deposites.

Should you make the Table you propose, as to the B. of the U.S. I should be glad to get a Copy of it, altho' I cannot think of troubling you to construct it on my account.

ALS. PHi. 1. For Henry C. Carey, the son of Mathew Carey, see 3:829 and *DAB*. In 1840 H.C. Carey had published in Philadelphia a pamphlet, *Answers to the questions: What constitutes currency? What are the causes of unsteadiness of the currency? and what is the remedy?* 2. Tyler to Clay, April 30, 1841. For Clay's thoughts on what provisions a new bank bill might properly include, see Clay to Porter, April 24, 1841, and Clay to Ewing, April 30, 1841.

To ROBERT P. LETCHER Washington, June 11, 1841

I have received several of your favors, and stand in arrear to you.

[John] White was elected Speaker.[1] He does not come up yet quite to my hopes; but I trust he will improve. I took no part in his election.

We are in a crisis, as a party. There is reason to fear that Tyler will throw himself upon Calhoun, Duff Green, &c &c and detach himself from the great body of the Whig party.[2] A few days will disclose. If he should take that course, it will be on the Bank.[3] It is understood that he wants a Bank located in the District, and having no power to branch without the consent of the State where the branch is located. What a Bank would that be!

The complexion of the Senate is even better than I anticipated.[4] And although Mr. [John Quincy] Adams has created some disturbance in the house[5] there is a fine spirit generally prevailing there.

ALS. NcD. Save for first paragraph, printed in Coleman, *Life of John J. Crittenden*, 1: 156-57. 1. Clay to Thompson, April 23, 1841. 2. Comment in Senate, August 19, 1841; David W. Krueger, "The Clay—Tyler Feud, 1841-1842," *FCHQ* (April, 1968), 42:162-77. 3. Tyler to Clay, April 30, 1841. 4. Clay to Clayton, May 29, 1840; Clay to Brooke, March 12, 1841. 5. For Adams's continuing fight against the "gag rule," see Adams, *Memoirs of John Quincy Adams*, 10:470-81.

Remark in Senate, June 11, 1841. Defends the constitutional power of the president as commander-in-chief, to transfer Gen. Mathew (or Matthew) Arbuckle from Fort Gibson (near present-day Muskogee, Okla.) to Baton Rouge. Notes that Congress has no authority over the army or navy and no right to question the commander-in-chief's disposition of men, equipment and war vessels in time either of peace or war. Fears, otherwise, that "in a crisis when all depended upon secrecy and celerity in military operations, the plans of the commander might be thwarted by the interference of the legislative branch of the Government." *Cong. Globe*, 27 Cong., 1 Sess., 42. For Arbuckle, see Heitman, *HRDUSA*. The Senate considered and laid on the table a resolution calling on the president to explain why Gen. Arbuckle had "been removed from his command at Fort Gibson, west of Arkansas, to Baton Rouge . . . where there are no United States troops." U.S. Sen., *Journal*, 27 Cong., 1 Sess., 22, 39.

To CHRISTOPHER MORGAN Washington, June 12, 1841

I took pleasure in presenting to the Senate to day the petition which you transmitted for a general bankrupt law.[1] It was referred, on my motion, to the Comtee. on the Judiciary, which is charged with the subject.

ALS. NHi. Written from the Senate Chamber. For Morgan, see *BDAC*. 1. The petition, from New York City, requested passage of a bankruptcy law [Remark in Senate, April 22, 1840]. *Cong. Globe*, 27 Cong., 1 Sess., 44. See also Remark in Senate, June 12, 1841.

Remark in Senate, June 12, 1841. Requests Sen. Ambrose H. Sevier (Ark.) to table for today his resolution directing the secretary of war to provide information bearing on fraudulent arrangements (bribery) between army contractors in the Southwest and those charged with disbursing large amounts of money for the emigration and subsistence of Indians. *Cong. Globe*, 27 Cong., 1 Sess., 44. Printing of resolution approved. Secretary of War John Bell had sent Lt. Col. Ethan Allen Hitchcock to the West to investigate rumors of profiteering in contracts for Indian rations. Hitchcock returned to Washington in mid-April, 1842 with a "bushel of documents" implicating government agents and other citizens in frauds against the Indians. President Tyler claimed the findings could not be verified and invoked executive privilege in refusing to make a full disclosure of the report. He finally bowed to congressional pressure, however, and submitted Hitchcock's report to the House on January 31, 1843, after being threatened with impeachment on this and other grounds. Ronald N. Satz, *American Indian Policy in the Jacksonian Era* (Lincoln, Nebr., 1974), 192-94; *Sen. Docs.*, 27 Cong., 1 Sess., no. 18; *House Reports*, 27 Cong., 3 Sess., no. 271.

Presents petitions from New York City and Washington City asking for a bankruptcy law [Remark in Senate, April 22, 1840] and praying that district banks be allowed to issue notes smaller than $5.00 that would be payable in specie [Remark in Senate, June 15, 1840]. *Cong. Globe*, 27 Cong., 1 Sess., 44.

Later this day, Clay takes up his resolution of June 9 which provided that during the present session of Congress any discussion of a given subject interrupted by an adjournment of Congress would be resumed at the next meeting of the Senate prior to 1:00 p.m. [Remark in Senate, June 9, 1841]. Challenged by Sen. Thomas H. Benton on his political motives in proposing such a change in Senate rules, Clay argues that the proposed change would be for "the present extra session alone," and would result in a more efficient use of Senate time. Points out the quantity of important business lying ahead of the Senate–bank, preemption, distribution–and asserts he has "no idea of exhausting the time of the Senate by collateral discussions having no connection whatever with the business for which Congress had been called together." Hopes that no one present wants this session "protracted beyond the month of July." Pleads: "Let us meet at 10 o'clock, if necessary. Let us meet early and sit late; let us finish the work that is expected of us, and then go home." Defends at length the need for the time change he has suggested. Defends also the speed with which the Senate had repealed (on June 8) the Independent Treasury Act [Tyler to Clay, April 30, 1841]. Asks if "gentlemen really expect, after the expression of public opinion which had taken place from one end of this land to the other, that they were to stand here five or six days on a stretch discussing that which the people had already decided? To what good end? Would it change the opinion of a single man? Would it do any thing but consume the public time?" Chides Sen. Silas Wright for his three-hour speech on June 8 in opposition to the reestablishment of a national bank, which was not even the subject being discussed that day. Suggests this was a waste of the Senate's time. Notes that the British Parliament handles its debates far more expeditiously than does the U.S. Senate. *Ibid.*, 45-46. For Wright's speech, delivered on June 8 but dated June 9 in the appendix of the *Congressional Globe*, see *ibid.*, Appendix, 21-27.

As debate on the proposed rule change broadened, with Democrats charging that Clay's resolution sought to control the pattern of debate on banking legislation sought by the Whigs, Clay was successful in turning aside amendments that would have tabled his resolution or undermined its intent. "Did the gentlemen really imagine," he wonders, "that because as a minority they possessed certain rights, they had the right of controlling the business of Congress?" Hopes that his colleagues will "not insist on going, at this called session, into general unrestricted legislation." He agrees, however, after further debate, to modify his resolution so as to allow one hour each day, after the Senate first meets, for the discussion of subjects other than the one interrupted by adjournment the previous day. "If the Clerk will follow me, I will dictate a modification, though I do not like to be a dictator in any sense," Clay remarks while working out this compromise. "You do it so well, you ought to like it," Buchanan notes. "That's fair," Sen. Silas Wright adds. "That's fair," other voices in the chamber repeat. Asked by Sen. Ambrose H. Sevier if the resolution, as modified, was not virtually a word for word restatement of the existing rule of the Senate, Clay replies: "Very well; if it is there is less harm done." And so, without formal vote, Clay's resolution, as modified, was adopted. *Cong. Globe*, 27 Cong., 1 Sess., 47-48. Rule 15 of the Senate's rules read: "The unfinished business in which the Senate was engaged at the last preceding adjournment, shall have the preference in the orders of the day, and no motion on any other business shall be received, without special leave of the Senate, until the former is disposed of." *Sen. Docs.*, 16 Cong., 1 Sess., no. 5, p. 2.

On this same day, June 12, Secretary Thomas Ewing submitted his "PLAN OF A FISCAL BANK OF THE UNITED STATES" and an accompanying bill [Clay to Ewing, June 2, 1841], both of which were referred on motion by Clay to the Select Committee on the Currency [Remark in Senate, June 1, 1841]. He moved also that 1,500 additional copies of the plan be printed. *Cong. Globe*, 27 Cong., 1 Sess., 49. Ewing's report is printed in *ibid.*, 48-49.

To THOMAS EWING Washington, June 14, 1841

I received your note this morning. The Comee.[1] met at 10 O'Clock and we read over your Bank bill, but took no question. The Whigs of the Senate will meet in Caucus tomorrow at 10 O'Clock to decide, or at least to consider, the features of your Bill.[2] If you can come to my lodgings at any time between 6 OClock & Eight this evening, I shall be glad to see you, and we will not be interrupted in my bed chamber.

ALS. DLC-Thomas Ewing Papers (DNA, M212, R21). Written in Senate Chamber. 1. Select Committee on the Currency, chaired by Clay. See Remark in Senate, June 2, 1841. 2. Clay to Ewing, June 2, 1841. In a brief, confidential note to Ewing, undated, but probably *ca.* June 8-11, Clay wrote: "I have called the Senates Currency Comee. tomorrow [Remark in Senate, June 2, 1841]. If you have matured the branching section [Porter to Clay, mid-July, 1841] suppose you send me a Copy of it [Speech in Senate, June 21, 1841] either this evening or early tomorrow morning?" ALS. DLC-Thomas Ewing Papers (DNA, M212, R21). Letter marked "(Confidential)."

Remark in Senate, June 14, 1841. Successfully opposes the printing of a citizen's "plan of a national currency" for the reason that "We have fifty projects of the kind which have as much right to be printed as this." Proceeds next to carry (by 22 to 19) his motion to table the Benton-Woodbury resolution [Remark in Senate, June 2, 1841] asking the administration to submit an accounting of money spent in March, April, and May of 1841, as well as treasury estimates of funds likely to be spent from June 1 to December 31, 1841. Calls attention to his motion of June 8 to print 1,500 additional copies of Secretary Thomas Ewing's report of June 2 [Ewing to Clay, May 8, 1841; Remark in Senate, June 3, 1841], on the nation's economic condition, but agrees to let it lie over. *Cong. Globe*, 27 Cong., 1 Sess., 50.

To William E. Robinson, June 14, 1841. Regrets he cannot "contract the engagement to deliver an address on the 17th of August next, as proposed in your letter just received." Believes he may be detained in Washington at that time, but, if not, "I shall be too much jaded and worn down to think of further public speaking." Accepts the honorary membership "you have had the goodness to tender me in behalf of the society of 'Brothers in Unity.'" Is sorry he does not have "a copy of my land speech" to send. Copy. Printed in Louisville *Courier Journal*, June 24, 1889.

The "land speech" to which Clay here refers is probably that of January 28-29, 1841; but see also Speech in Senate, January 6, 1841. For Robinson a Yale student, at this time who later became a lawyer, journalist, and politician, see *DAB*. The Brothers in Unity was a literary society formed at Yale University in 1786. See Franklin B. Dexter, *Sketch of the History of Yale University* (New York, 1887), 39-40.

Remark in Senate, June 15, 1841. Insists that 26 votes for Thomas Allen for printer to the Senate constituted Allen's election since but 51 senators had been elected to the 27th Congress; hence a quorum was present. Bows to observations that the constitutional number of senators was presently 52 and that 27 votes were thus necessary to elect. The chair (president *pro tempore* Samuel L. Southard) then directed that there be a second ballot. This too resulted in but 26 votes for Allen. At this point, Clay observes that some senator had voted for "Mr. Allen" rather than for Thomas Allen and urges use of the "Christian name" on the next ballot. On the third ballot "Thomas Allen" received 25 votes while "Mr. Allen" received 2 votes. Allen thus secured a majority of the constitutional number of senators. *Cong. Globe*, 27 Cong., 1 Sess., 52. For Whig strength in the Senate, see

Clay to Clayton, May 29, 1840; Clay to Brooke, March 12, 1841. Sen. Southard had been chosen president of the Senate, on March 11, 1841, by a vote of 26 over William R. King who received 15 votes, with 2 votes scattered. *Niles' Register* (March 20, 1841), 60:47; see also Shanks, *The Papers of Willie Person Mangum*, 3:155-56.

Later this day, Clay informs the Senate that he will not today call up his resolution of June 8 to have printed an additional 1,500 copies of Secretary Ewing's report of June 2 [Remark in Senate, June 3 and June 8, 1841]. *Cong. Globe*, 27 Cong., 1 Sess., 52.

Still later this day, Clay spoke to the motion by Sen. William C. Rives (Va.) on June 3 asking that that portion of the president's message of June 1 relating to foreign affairs be referred to the Committee on Foreign Affairs. *Ibid.*, 14, 30, 36, 38, 52. Clay's remarks were not recorded.

The delay in taking up Rives's motion was occasioned in part by the continuing McLeod case [Porter to Clay, January 4, 1841], specifically by Sen. James Buchanan's request that recent correspondence between British Minister Henry Fox and Secretary of State Daniel Webster be reviewed prior to a vote on the Rives motion. *Ibid.*, 52; *MPP*, 4:41. For the referenced Fox-Webster correspondence of April, 1841 on the McLeod issue, see Corey, *The Crisis . . . in Canadian-American Relations*, 133-45.

To THOMAS EWING — Washington, June 16,1841

H. Clays respects to Mr. Ewing, with a request that he will direct his attention to the accompanying [Benton] resolution and [Woodbury] amendment,[1] and say whether there is any objection which ought to prevent their passage. If there be none, that is serious, they had better be allowed to pass. Mr. Ewing is requested to reply this evening or early tomorrow morning.

AN. DLC-Thomas Ewing Papers (DNA, M212, R21). Written in Senate Chamber.
1. The Benton-Woodbury resolution. See Remark in Senate, June 2, 1841.

Remark in Senate, June 16, 1841. Presents petitions from New York asking for bankruptcy legislation [Remark in Senate, April 22, 1840] and from hatters in Connecticut and New York favoring a duty on hats.

Opposes taking from the table the Benton-Woodbury resolution on treasury expenditures, recent and estimated [Remark in Senate, June 2, 1841]. His stance on this point produced a vigorous protest from Sen. Calhoun who asserted his right to have such information. So insistent was Calhoun's demand in this regard that Clay informed him that "It is not worth while getting into a passion" about and informed him that "The majority also have rights." Indeed, Clay regarded time spent on the Benton-Woodbury resolution as "delaying the business" of the Senate—which was to take action on his motion of June 8 to print additional copies of Secretary Ewing's June 2 report on the nations's banking and general economic situation [Remark in Senate, June 3 and June 8, 1841]. Nevertheless, he agreed to take up the Benton-Woodbury resolution tomorrow. Following this agreement, debate on his June 8 motion resumed. *Cong. Globe*, 27 Cong., 1 Sess., 56.

Remark in Senate, June 18, 1841. Presents a petition from citizens of St. Louis asking for a national bank. *Cong. Globe*, 27 Cong., 1 Sess., 70.

Soon after Clay presented this petition and participated briefly in talk of an early adjournment today, debate resumed on his motion of June 8 to print additional copies of Secretary Ewing's report of June 2 on the state of the nation's finances [Ewing to Clay, May 8, 1841; Remark in Senate, June 3, 1841]. Finally, at 5:00 p.m., it also being Friday, there were cries in the chamber of "Adjourn-adjourn." Calhoun therefore moved adjournment on condition that he be granted an hour's time on Monday, June 21, to discuss further the Kentuckian's motion on Ewing's report. Clay, however, opposes Calhoun's motion to adjourn, pointing out that a "mere motion to print" would not be worth an hour of the Senate's time on Monday when such important issues as the bill to renew the charters of District of Columbia banks [Remark in Senate, June 15, 1840] and the anticipated report of the Select Committee on the Currency on a fiscal agency [Tyler to Clay, April 30, 1841; Clay to Ewing, June 2, 1841; Speech in Senate, June 21, 1841] would be before the members. Calhoun's motion to adjourn was passed, nonetheless, 16 to 11. *Ibid.*, 70, 72.

The bill to renew for two years the charters of three banks in Washington City and three in other parts of the District of Columbia (Georgetown and Alexandria) passed the Senate on August 5, 1841, by 29 to 15, Clay voting yea; and passed the House on August 18, 1841, by 108 to 58. President Tyler signed it on August 25, 1841. *Ibid.*, 297, 351; U.S. Sen., *Journal*, 27 Cong., 1 Sess., 140; U.S. H. of Reps., *Journal*, 27 Cong., 1 Sess., 381 (which reports 107 aye votes); 5 *U.S. Stat.*, 449-51.

To THOMAS EWING Washington, "Saturday morning" [June 19, 1841]

I return the clause,[1] with another[2] which seems to me more explicitly to assert the power.[3]

After all, it is to be feared that, if the project contemplated could succeed, it would not conciliate foes but might alienate many friends.

ALI. DLC-Ewing Family Papers (Supp. Roll 2). Dated only "Saturday morning."
1. Note in Clay's hand on a slip of paper separate from the letter which reads: "The said Corporation shall establish at least one office of Dt. [Discount] & Dt. [Deposit] whenever Congress shall by law require the same in any State or Territory; and shall also establish one in any State or territory (in which two thousand shares shall have been subscribed & may be held) whenever upon the application of the Legislature of such State or Territory the Corporation may think fit so to do. When established the said Offices shall only be withdrawn or removed by the said Corporation, with the consent of Congress." The first sentence of this statement appears almost verbatim as the first sentence of Section 11, fundamental article 16 of the final draft of the Fiscal Bank bill submitted to the Senate on June 21. See Clay to Ewing, June 2 and June 14, 1841; Speech in Senate, June 21, 1841; *Sen. Docs.*, 27 Cong., 1 Sess., no. 32, p. 32. See also Chitwood, *John Tyler*, 219-36, espec. 219-21. 2. Note in Ewing's hand on a slip of paper separate from the letter which reads: "Offices of Discount & Deposite in any such places as might be necessary & proper for the collection, safe keeping & disbursement of the public revenue without any reference to the assent of the States." This statement was either copied by Ewing from another source, or represents a shift from his position on the branching power of the proposed bank as expressed by him in his reports to Congress on June 2 and June 12. *Cong. Globe*, 27 Cong., 1 Sess., 21, 48. See also Clay to Ewing, April 30, 1841; Ewing to Clay, May 8, 1841; Clay to Ewing, June 2 and June 14, 1841; Speech in Senate, June 21, 1841; Chitwood, *John Tyler*, 219-21. 3. Of the power of the proposed bank to establish branch offices in the several states. For the debate and eventual compromise on this point, see Speech in Senate, June 21, 1841, and, most particularly, Porter to Clay, mid-July, 1841.

Speech in Senate, June 21, 1841. Reads a report "principally in his handwriting" from the Select Committee on the Currency [Remark in Senate, June 2, 1841] on its bill to incorporate the subscribers to the Fiscal Bank of the United States. Moves the introduction of the bill and its printing in the number of 1,500 extra copies for Senate use. The bill as introduced on June 21, 1841, is printed in *Sen. Docs.*, 27 Cong., 1 Sess., no. 32, pp. 7-20. The House version, introduced on June 24, is in *House Docs.*, 27 Cong., 1 Sess., no. 22, pp. 1-14.

Begins with the observation that the committee agreed with the opinion of Secretary of the Treasury Ewing [Ewing to Clay, May 8, 1841; Clay to Ewing, June 2, 1841; Remark in Senate, June 3, 1841], expressed in his report of June 2, that a new Bank of the United States should be established with as little delay as practicable. Says he will spend no time on the question of whether Congress has the constitutional power to establish a national bank, that question having long ago been settled. Nor did the committee devote time to a discussion of the expediency of establishing a bank. "On this there was even less contrariety of opinion than on the former question." The primary question his committee addressed, therefore, was the "particular form, powers, and faculties with which it may be expedient to invest such an institution." Believes that the structure of the successful second Bank of the United States, chartered in 1816, should be the basis of a new bank, "engrafting upon it such restrictions, guarantees, amendments, and conditions, as have been found necessary by actual experience." Notes that the committee relied heavily on the 1816 bank charter, much of which Secretary Ewing had also incorporated in his own bank proposal of June 12 [Remark in Senate, June 12, 1841].

Outlines his (and the committee's) specific proposals, viz: The principal (parent) bank is to be located in Washington, D.C.; the parent bank is to have no power to make discounts or loans except to the government as authorized by law; the parent bank's directors shall number nine, paid by the corporation, and denied other compensation "in the usual form of bank accommodations"; the capital of the bank is to be $30,000,000 as suggested by Ewing, but Congress would have the power to augment this by $20,000,000 if necessary; dividends on bank stock are to be limited to 7% and maintained at that level with treasury surpluses; debts due the bank cannot exceed the amount of capital stock actually purchased plus 75% of that sum, "which is a greater restriction than usual"; the total amount of debt authorized, over and above deposits, is not to exceed $25,000,000, "which is also a greater restriction than was placed upon the late Bank of the United States"; all books and transactions of the bank, including private accounts, are to be public information; no renewals of loans are to be permitted; no further discounts or loans are to be allowed whenever the bank's notes in circulation exceed three times the amount of specie in its vaults; no paid officer of the bank is to be permitted to borrow therefrom, or serve as a proxy for stockholders; no proxy can give more than 300 votes; the bank cannot deal in stocks or engage in commerce; public denunciation and punishment (as a felony) of bank employees involved in embezzlement will occur.

Admits, in continuing, that he and the committee regrettably could not accept Secretary Ewing's states' rights strictures on the branching power of the parent bank—that is, its "power to establish branches or offices of discount or deposite in the several States, with the assent of the States [Clay to Ewing, June 2, 1841]." States flatly that "A derivation of power to the General Government from the consent of particular States would be unsound in principle, and the committee apprehend dangerous in practice. Admit such consent to be a legitimate source of power, the Government would not operate equally in all the States, and the Constitution, losing its uniform character, would exhibit an irregular and incongruous action. Entertaining these deliberate views, the committee are decidedly of opinion that no bill for the establishment of a Bank in the District of Columbia will be effectual which does not contain a clear recognition of the constitutional power of Congress to establish branches wherever, in the United States, the public wants, in its judgment, require them. They cannot consent that a Bank, emanating from the will of the nation, and imperatively demanded by the necessities of the Government and of the nation, shall be wholly dependent for its useful operation upon the will of each and every State, distinctly expressed. Accordingly, in the draught of a bill now reported, the right is asserted to exercise the branching power of the Bank independent of the assent of the States."

Discusses at length the advantages that will accrue to the nation's domestic economy and foreign trade (especially with England) if and when a new national bank is established. Argues, specifically, that "If it be true that money is power, its concentration under the direction of one will, sole or collective, must augment the power. A nation, without such a concentration of power, maintaining extensive commercial intercourse with another nation possessing it, must conduct that intercourse on a condition of inequality and disadvantage. National Banks, in other countries, beget the necessity, therefore, of a National Bank in this country, in like manner as National Governments in foreign nations must be met by a National Government in ours."

Clay concludes his speech with motions to print the bill and discharge the Select Committee on the Currency. Both carried. *Cong. Globe*, 27 Cong., 1 Sess., 79-81. The manuscript of this speech has not been found. For earlier Clay thoughts on what a third national bank charter should contain, see Comment in Senate, September 26, 1837; Speech in Senate, May 21, 1838; Clay to Porter, April 24, 1841; Clay to Ewing, April 30, 1841. For analyses of the critical branching question—whether the B.U.S. should or could establish branch banks in the various states, with or without their consent, specific or implied—the issue which more than any other single factor produced Tyler's veto of both Whig bank bills in summer, 1841 [Tyler to Clay, April 30, 1841], see Tyler, *Letters and Times of the Tylers*, 2:39-106; Seager, *And Tyler Too*, 150-60; Chitwood, *John Tyler*, 219-36; Van Deusen, *Life of Henry Clay*, 344-54; *MPP*, 4:63-72; *Cong. Globe*, 27 Cong., 1 Sess., 18-21, 48-49, 132, 152, 256, 260, 303. See also Porter to Clay, mid-July, 1841.

Following his speech on the bank, Clay presents two petitions from New York asking for bankruptcy legislation [Remark in Senate, April 22, 1841]; also a resolution to the effect that commencing tomorrow, June 22, the Senate's hour of meeting should be 10:00 a.m., rather than noon [Remark in Senate, June 12, 1841]. *Cong. Globe*, 27 Cong., 1 Sess., 81.

Later this day, following a long speech by Calhoun on the general state of the nation's finances, a speech ostensibly related to Clay's June 8 motion to print 1,500 additional copies of Ewing's June 2 report on the nation's economy [Ewing to Clay, May 8, 1841; Remark in Senate, June 3, 1841], Clay complains that Senators Calhoun, Levi Woodbury, and Silas Wright have all employed "a mere motion to print" as a device to delay for several days the important work of the Senate. Indeed, "So many speeches [have] been hung upon this slender peg, that it [can] evidently bear no more." Sen. Woodbury in response chides Clay for attempting to stifle broad discussion of various measures recommended by Secretary Ewing in his June 2 report, especially since Clay himself, just this morning, had abandoned Ewing's insistence on state assent to branching, "leaving him to be whistled down the wind." Clay retorts that "the Senator from New Hampshire should have waited until the measures alluded to by the Secretary had been brought before the body for its action. By so doing, he would have saved a little of his wind, which, from his large size, he supposed was a commodity exceedingly useful to him." *Ibid.*, 83. For other lengthy speeches by Democrats on Clay's "mere motion to print," see *ibid.*, Appendix, 55, 61-64.

Soon after the Clay—Woodbury exchange, Clay's motion to print additional copies of Ewing's June 2 report was finally accepted *viva voce*. *Cong. Globe*, 27 Cong., 1 Sess., 83.

Remark in Senate, June 22, 1841. Responds to Ohio Sen. William Allen's report of a recent Democratic party meeting in Cincinnati at which a remonstration against the bank charter [Speech in Senate, June 21, 1841] had taken place. Allen moves it be accepted and asserts he will begin to work to repeal the new bank bill the moment it becomes law. Clay replies that if Allen thinks he (Clay) and his friends "were to be driven from their purpose by threats of civil war and rebellion, he was mistaken." Moves to table the motion to print. Refuses to withdraw this motion upon Allen's request, a refusal prompting Allen to threaten that he would "embrace another opportunity" some day when Clay "would not have an opportunity to gag him with his motions." Replies Clay: "Any time: any place." Motion to print was tabled, 27 to 18. *Cong. Globe*, 27 Cong., 1 Sess., 86. "Democrats against a national bank" had held a meeting in Cincinnati on June 5, 1841, and had adopted twelve resolutions against a national bank and for the Independent Treasury system. There had been no disorder at the rally. For the details of this meeting, see Cincinnati *Enquirer*, June 7, 1841.

Later this day, Clay's motion of June 21 to change the meeting hour of the Senate [Speech in Senate, June 21, 1841] from noon to 10:00 a.m. was taken off the table and adopted. Also passed was his bill reported from the Committee on Finance, authorizing appropriations to pay for the first session ("extra session") of the 27th Congress. *Cong. Globe*, 27 Cong., 1 Sess., 86-87.

Remark in Senate, June 23, 1841. Responds to Sen. Benjamin Tappan's resolution of inquiry on comparative costs of Senate and House printing in such manner as to cause Tappan not to press his resolution. *Cong. Globe*, 27 Cong., 1 Sess., 94.

Later this day, Clay voted with the majority to recommit without instruction the District Bank recharter bill [Remark in Senate, June 18, 1841] to the Committee on the District of Columbia. Following this, he moved to consider the bank bill [Tyler to Clay, April 30, 1841; Speech in Senate, June 21, 1841] "section by section." In response to Sen. Silas Wright's request for more time to study the printed version of the bill, which had been placed on senators' tables only this morning, Clay moved to proceed into Executive session. *Ibid.*, 97.

Remark in Senate, June 24, 1841. Listens to Buchanan's chiding accusation that the Whigs, who were now removing Democrats from federal office, had long been hostile to the doctrine of proscription. Recalls that Clay himself had repeatedly denied the constitutional power of the president to remove public employees from office. Replies Clay: "I have said that power does not belong to the President, though it has grown into use. It has been a subject of legislation, and as such it is not questioned." To this, Buchanan countered with the observation that Clay and the Whigs had conveniently shifted their view of proscription from constitutional to legislative grounds. Had Clay not, he asked, "over and over again, denounced the late Administration on the ground of proscription?" Replies Clay "(from his seat, in a jocular way,) I did sir; but our practice now grows out of the necessity of our case. We cannot allow your friends to remain in our confidence." *Cong. Globe*, 27 Cong., 1 Sess., 102. This exchange proceeded from Buchanan's motion of June 17 calling on the president to furnish the names of persons removed from public office since March 4. *Ibid.*, 63-64. See also *ibid.*, Appendix, 99, for a similar exchange this day between Clay and Sen. Samuel McRoberts (Dem., Ill.). During this, McRoberts quoted Clay statements made in March, 1834 and February, 1835 condemning the constitutionality of Jackson's proscriptions. Clay interrupted him to assert that "I have not changed my opinion since I . . . made the remarks, which have been read by the Senator from Illinois." *Ibid.*

Later this day, Clay addressed the Senate [speech not found] "at length" on the various provisions of his bank bill [Speech in Senate, June 21, 1841], pointing out, in conclusion, that support for the bank went "far beyond" the Whig party. Indeed, a "large number of the opposition party were openly in favor of a Bank, and a still greater portion privately entertained the same opinion." A "large portion" of the American people were also in favor of the bank, he asserted. Having concluded his speech, he rose several times in angry opposition to Calhoun's motion that further consideration of the bank bill be postponed until tomorrow. *Cong. Globe*, 27 Cong., 1 Sess., 103-4. The motion to postpone prevailed by 35 to 13.

Still later this day, during a lengthy debate on a bill to appropriate $25,000 for relief of the widow [Anna Symmes Harrison] of William Henry Harrison, Clay informed his colleagues that the general's estate had "large outstanding debts" against it and when these were paid, "there would be very little, if any thing remaining for his widow or family." Clay then moved the third reading of the bill, a motion which required unanimous consent; there was, however, an objection. *Ibid.*, 110-11. The bill granting $25,000 to Mrs. Harrison was passed 28 to 16 on June 25; and the legislation extending the franking privilege to her was passed on September 3. *Ibid.*, 116-21, 423. The House passed the Harrison relief bill on June 18 and the franking bill on September 3. *Ibid.*, 73-77, 312, 423.

To Thomas Ewing, Washington, June 25, 1841. Transmits copy of a resolution "just submitted" by Sen. Levi Woodbury. Asks if there is "any and what objection to its passage"; and whether Ewing has "any observations to offer about it?" ALS. DLC-Ewing Family Papers (Supp. Roll 2). Written in Senate Chamber.

Woodbury's resolution sought information on whether Secretary Ewing had been authorized by the President since March 3 to disburse funds newly appropriated during the 26th Congress, 2nd Session; also the total amount of disbursements from the treasury since March 3, and by what authority, if any, these were made. *Cong. Globe*, 27 Cong., 1 Sess., 115. This resolution was amended and passed on July 16, 1841. See *ibid.*, 207-8; also U.S. Sen., *Journal*, 27 Cong., 1 Sess., 62, 94.

Remark in Senate, June 25, 1841. Introduces a memorial from New York favoring a bankruptcy law [Remark in Senate, April 22, 1840]. *Cong. Globe*, 27 Cong., 1 Sess., 115.

During debate on the bank bill, calls Calhoun to order for attempting to raise the question of whether support for the bank in the United States was stronger than was the Whig party, as Clay had asserted yesterday [Remark in Senate, June 24, 1841]. "I really do not see that this is the time to discuss that point," Clay insists. "I rise to a question of order, sir." Withdraws the point of order at the request of Sen. William A. Graham (Whig, N.C.). *Ibid.*

Later this day, when debate on the bank bill was again joined, Clay acquiesced in reading the bill section by section [Speech in Senate, June 21, 1841], during which amendments to various provisions were debated. Rose to speak to section 11, paragraph 18, which would forbid the issuance of notes in denominations of less than $10. Clay held that if the "public convenience" would be advantaged by $5 notes, he would "not object" to them. An amendment to this effect was lost 21 to 26, Clay voting yea. *Ibid.*, 121; *Sen. Docs.*, 27 Cong., 1 Sess., no. 32, pp. 7-20.

Remark in Senate, June 28, 1841. Moves that the Senate concur in a House resolution to attend the funeral of Major General Alexander Macomb. *Cong. Globe*, 27 Cong., 1 Sess., 124. For Macomb, see *DAB*.

Remark in Senate, June 29, 1841. Presents memorials from New York City and State for and against a bankruptcy law [Remark in Senate, April 22, 1840]. *Cong. Globe*, 27 Cong., 1 Sess., 124.

During debate on the bank bill, Clay moves to make the stock of the bank transferable to the buyer on payment of the second installment instead of the third. Carried 26 to 21. Moves to amend the bill to permit the bank to extend the debt it might contract from $25,000,000 to $30,000,000. Defeated 22 to 25. Moves to amend section 11, paragraph 14, to give the secretary of the treasury more flexibility in paying out surplus funds. Carried 25 to 23. Moves an amendment to remove the restriction on bank loans when the value of the bank's notes exceeded three times the amount of its specie. Carried *viva voce*. Moves an amendment authorizing the presidents and cashiers of the branches of the bank to sign the notes made payable at their particular offices. Carried 28 to 21. *Ibid.*, 124-25. See Speech in Senate, June 21, 1841; *Sen. Docs.*, 27 Cong., 1 Sess., no. 32, pp. 7-20.

To PETER B. PORTER Washington, June 30, 1841

I have this moment received your favor. You will have seen that I have made a Bank report, presenting a scheme essentially variant from Mr. Ewings plan.[1] Its fate is however uncertain in Congress, and at the *White House*. We have difficulties from this latter quarter, which I hope may be surmounted, but which may be fatal.[2]

I hope that you will come here. I want much to see you.

The Opposition are determined, if possible, to defeat *all* our measures; and unfortunately there are a few of our own party that are not indisposed to co-operate with them.

I retain my wish to visit one of the Sea baths. But whether I can indulge that desire or not depends upon the duration of the present Session.[3]

ALS. NBuHi. Copy in OHi. Written from Senate Chamber. 1. For changes made by Clay in the bank plan submitted by Secretary Thomas Ewing on June 12 [Clay to Ewing, June 2, 1841], see Comment in Senate, June 21, 1841. See also *Cong. Globe*, 27 Cong., 1 Sess., 79-80. For Clay's earlier thoughts on some of the features a new national bank should have, see Clay to Porter, April 24, 1841; Clay to Ewing, April 30, 1841. 2. Tyler to Clay, April 30, 1841. 3. See Clay to Henry Clay, Jr., Sept. 13, 1841.

Remark in Senate, June 30, 1841. Reacts to a Board of Trade petition, 250 feet long, from New York City, signed by fifteen to twenty thousand citizens, asking for a national bank [Speech in Senate, June 21, 1841]. Unrolled, it "reached from the Secretary's table to Mr. CLAY'S desk" and beyond. Clay notes that in one precinct "five Loco Focos" had failed in their attempts to create a public disturbance designed to prevent the signing ceremony there; instead, four of them signed the petition after being converted to the bank cause by "a good Whig" who was present. Suggests that this Whig and his four Locofoco converts come to Washington and talk to Democrats opposing the bank bill. He "was sure, if they could but have an opportunity of setting down in one of the committee rooms together, and take a chew of tobacco and a glass of grog sociably, while discussing the subject, they [the Democrats] would stand some chance of being converted by their New York brother Loco Focos, and would be saved the necessity of making speeches for no other purpose but to keep alive their old Jackson prejudices." *Cong. Globe*, 27 Cong., 1 Sess., 129. Explains to Sen. James Buchanan, who challenged this story, that if the Democrats would just lay aside "their Jackson notions of yellow-boy currency," they would "very soon become converts, too." *Ibid.*

On this day, the Senate voted 33 to 16 to restrict to U.S. citizens the right to purchase stock in the proposed Fiscal Bank of the United States, Clay voting yea. U.S. Sen., *Journal*, 27 Cong., 1 Sess., 51, 68, 178-93.

While silent on the bank stock purchase issue, Clay participated (not recorded) in a "long and very animated debate" on another amendment by Sen. John Henderson (Whig, Miss.) to the bank bill that would permit one or more of the bank's stockholders "to examine and inspect all private and individual accounts, dealings, and accommodations at any of the offices of discount and deposite." *Cong. Globe*, 27 Cong., 1 Sess., 130. The amendment was lost 22 to 26, Clay voting nay. See also Remark in Senate, July 8, 1841.

Comment in Senate, July 1, 1841. Speaks at length to a protracted defense by Sen. William C. Rives of his amendment to section 11, paragraph 16 of the bank bill [Speech in Senate, June 21, 1841]. Rives's amendment would permit the proposed fiscal corporation to "establish a competent office of discount and deposite in any State, by the assent of the Legislature of such State, whenever the directors may think fit so to do; and when established, the office shall not be withdrawn without the assent of Congress." Rives's wording would replace the language of section 11, paragraph 16, of Clay's bill which read, in part: "And the said directors may also establish competent offices of discount and deposite in any State, Territory, or district of the United States." See *Sen. Docs.*, 27 Cong., 1 Sess., no. 32, p. 15; also, Speech in Senate, July 27, 1841.

Regrets that Rives felt constrained to submit such an amendment, because "No good—nothing, I fear, but unmixed mischief—can come out of it, although I am quite sure that is far from the intention of the Senator. The people want at our hands a Bank—a real old-fashioned Bank; such an one as they and their fathers have tried, and experienced the benefits of. Now the institution, the proper organization of which we are considering, is to be a National Bank or a local Bank. If it is to be a National Bank, we have the power to make it, or we have not. If we have the power, if the States have already consented, in the Constitution, to the establishment of a National Bank, no further or other consent from them is necessary. . . . If we have no power to make an undisguised National Bank, we ought not to attempt it. We ought not to seek to accomplish indirectly what we are not authorized or forbidden to do directly." Argues that Rives's conception of a national bank chartered in the district and possessing no power to branch throughout the nation as needed is no more than "a mere local bank of the District of Columbia"; it could amount to nothing other than "a rickety, imbecile, incompetent local bank." Wonders if we must ask "the previous consent of the States in every instance of the exercise of the powers granted in the Constitution to the Federal Government?" Must we, for instance, have previous consent to establish a post office in a state? Believes that the "voluntary forbearance to exercise a given [constitutional] power amounts to a virtual surrender of that power," and warns that if the triumphant Whigs refuse to exercise their constitutional power to establish a national bank, that refusal will "be hereafter construed as a virtual or implied relinquishment of the power." Wants no more banking experiments such as Rives's approach would provide. The Rives amendment also proceeds from the "erroneous assumption that the branch is introduced for the sole benefit of the particular State. But that is not the case. It is put there for the benefit of the Union, including the particular State." Asks, with reference to Rives's clause requiring the assent of Congress to withdraw a branch, "Now, if your power be incompetent to plant an office of discount and deposite within the limits of a State, without the consent of the State, how, after it is put there, can you hold and maintain it there in spite of and against the will of the State?" [Rives interrupts to insist that the power of withdrawal would be part of the compact between the bank and the sovereign state]. Clay proceeds with the observation that a branch, located in a state by the consent of that state, "to all intents and purposes would be a local institution, governed by the local laws." Develops this point, asking what degree of legal protection would the branches enjoy in those states which might admit them? Commends Rives for his support of that section of the bill which compels the parent bank to exercise its power of discounting in its offices outside the district, but feels that if the bank be regarded as a "mere District bank," as Rives apparently does, such power "would be certainly a most anomalous, if not ridiculous feature."

Thanks Rives for his spirit of concession, compromise, and conciliation in these deliberations, but maintains that a principle is involved which cannot be compromised: "The question is, a National Bank or no National Bank, constitutionality or unconstitutionality, power or no power. How are these opposite properties or qualities to be reconciled or compromised? There is no mean or middle term." Rives's amendment, however, "calls upon us to make . . . a concession of every thing on our side, and nothing on his—a compromise in which he gets all and gives nothing!" [Rives interrupts to point out that his amendment had also been proposed by Secretary of the Treasury Thomas Ewing (Clay to Ewing, June 2, 1841) on June 12]. Clay replies that that is true, and Senator Rives "is entitled to all the benefit he can derive from that fact"; but he is "quite sure . . . that the Secretary does not entertain a different opinion of the constitutional power of Congress from ours."

Reviews the history of the "bank power," beginning with President Madison. Has heard it said, however, that unless the Rives amendment is added to the present bank bill, President Tyler will not accept it. Explains: "Whatever inferences gentlemen may have felt themselves at liberty to draw, I am perfectly confident that the President has given authority to no one to say how, in a given contingency, he would act. Such gratuitous intimation, in advance, on a question of such delicacy and difficulty, I think I am not mistaken when I say his sense of official propriety would restrain him from making." Believes that the long-debated bank issue can only be agitated further if the Rives amendment is adopted. But "Pass an old-fashioned Bank . . . such a Bank as the people want and demand; such as the committee have reported, and I believe, in less than six months, that we shall have on this subject tranquility and acquiescence." Anticipates no disagreement between Congress and the president on this issue of a Bank of the United States; but if there is disagreement, "I hope we may differ in a season of profound peace, in respect to the proper constitution of such an institution, without the infliction of any irremediable evil upon our country." *Cong. Globe*, 27 Cong., 1 Sess., Appendix, 354-55. Rives's speech of July 1 in support of his branching amendment is in *ibid.*, 351-54. The amendment is printed in *Cong. Globe*, 27 Cong., 1 Sess., 133. Rives's motion to substitute his amendment for section 11, paragraph 16 of the Clay-Select Committee bill was defeated 10 to 38 on July 6. *Ibid.*, 152. See also Van Deusen, *Life of Henry Clay*, 347-48; Porter to Clay, mid-July, 1841.

From James Such, Jamaica, Long Island, N.Y., July 1, 1841. Sends account of Henry Clay Duralde's expenses showing a balance due of $586.25. Adds that he hopes "you wod. be pleased to make this house yours during your continuance in the neighbourhood of Sea-bathing." Mentions also that Clay's grandsons [Clay to Lucretia Hart Clay, July 7, 1840] may spend the summer holidays at the school for the sum of "$240 for the three boys for the two months board & tuition"; but that if they do not stay, he must go into New York City to work for the two months, because "I cannot afford to be idle." ALS. DLC-TJC (DNA, M212, R14). Letter endorsed by Clay: "Mr. Such a/c &c rect.—Sent the bal in a check drawn by the Secy of the Sena[te] on a B. in Washn."

From William D. Lewis, Philadelphia, July 2, 1841. Sends receipt for $500 paid for a bill of 100 pounds sterling to be sent by Clay to his ward, Eliza Jane Weir in

Dromore, Ireland, and encloses "a check for the $62.50 being the balance of your remittance [Prenter to Clay, January 16, 1837]."

Thanks Clay for "sending me the Bank Bills [Tyler to Clay, April 30, 1841; Speech in Senate, June 21, 1841]," noting that the secretary of the treasury of Texas [John G. Chalmers] has "requested a friend of mine to send him various Bank charters." Continues: "I perceive that the opposition, thoroughly organized, and aided occasionally by a Stray whig or two, are battling the Bank Bill at every step, and indications appear to warrant the apprehension that it may be so emasculated as to render it if passed, of no value to the Country.— The Whigs are poor troops for a pitched battle. However, we must hope for the best." Adds that "if upon any point you may think my experience can be made serviceable to you in its progress, it will afford me great pleasure to furnish you with any facts or opinions in my possession." ALS. KyLxT.

Remark in Senate, July 2, 1841. Responds to Sen. Rufus Choate's (Whig, Mass.) statement in support of the Rives amendment to the bank bill [Comment in Senate, July 1, 1841], in which Choate asserted that he "had no doubt, indeed he would say that he knew, if this amendment were not agreed to, no bank bill would pass into a law during the present session." Clay demands to know how Choate "*knows*" this, and to explain the "grounds on which he makes this broad assertion." Choate replies that it would be a "breach of privilege" or violation of a parliamentary rule were he to answer Clay's question; but he repeats the main point made: "I tell the Senator again there will be no Bank this session unless this [Rives] amendment prevails." Sen. William S. Archer (Dem., Va.) suggests that the Rives amendment is simply "the scheme of the Executive." Clay interrupts Archer to make clear his view that the fact stated by Choate does not necessarily depend "on the determination of the Executive." Suggests that perhaps Choate had polled one or both houses of Congress and "found that the thing now presented was the only measure that could be carried." Choate responds that he had not used the name or authority of the president in making his initial statement, but had derived it "from many facts and deductions." Clay insists on knowing where Choate got his information. Choate replies only that he had "stated my own conviction" in the matter. Clay presses him: Will the Senator repeat his earlier assertion that he cannot "disclose the source of his convictions without a breach of privilege and violation of parliamentary rule?" Demands a direct answer to this question, which he puts a second and third time. Sen. William C. Preston rises to call both Choate and Clay to order. *Cong. Globe*, 27 Cong., 1 Sess., 140. Both Choate and Preston voted for the Rives amendment on July 6. *Ibid.*, 152.

Remark in Senate, July 3, 1841. Listens to complaints that newspaper reporters admitted on the floor of the Senate were no longer fairly, accurately, or fully reporting the proceedings of the body; and to recommendations that Congress must employ its own reporters if it wants the public to have correct accounts of its activities. Indeed, just yesterday [Remark in Senate, July 2, 1841], Clay asserts, a Washington newspaper had printed "in a sort of running analysis . . . a misrepresentation, calculated to wound the feelings of an honorable Senator [Rufus Choate], and to present himself (Mr. CLAY) in the erroneous attitude of endeavoring to fasten on that Senator a denial of an assertion or contradiction, which would reflect upon his character for veracity." Denies that he had "the slightest intention to place that honorable Senator in any such position." Reviews at length the previous day's exchanges with Choate and William S. Archer to demonstrate that his "sole purpose" was to obtain the source of Choate's information about the Rives amendment [Comment in Senate, July 1, 1841] to the bank bill.

He had no thought whatever "of placing his friend, the Senator from Massachusetts, in a questionable position." Adds that he was pleased to learn this morning, on entering the chamber, "that the difference of opinion which yesterday threatened to interrupt the harmonious relations between his friends, the Senators from Virginia [Archer and Rives], had been mutually explained, so as not to leave a trace of unpleasant misunderstanding between them." *Cong. Globe*, 27 Cong., 1 Sess., 145.

To FRANCIS T. BROOKE Washington, July 4, 1841

I thank you for your kind suggestions as to the best mode of preserving my health. The attack last March in Balto. was more severe than I was aware of at the time; but, thank God, my health now, notwithstanding all my labors, is better than it was when I came here. This I attribute to the exercise which I take every morning, and to the perfectly regular life that I lead.

It is very uncertain when Congress will adjourn. I begin now to fear that it will not be until September.[1] I shall probably return by the route of the White Sulphur,[2] but of that there is no certainty.

Mr. Tyler's opinions about a Bank are giving us great trouble.[3] Indeed, they not only threaten our defeat on that measure, but endanger the permanency, and the ascendancy of the Whig cause. Is it not deplorable that such a cause should be put in jeopardy in such a way! He conciliates no body by his particular notions. The Loco's are more opposed to the scheme than to an old fashioned bank, and ninety nine out of a hundred of the Whigs are decidedly adverse to it.

ALS. KyU. Printed in Colton, *Clay Correspondence*, 4:454. 1. Congress did not adjourn until Sept. 13, 1841. 2. Clay to Henry Clay, Jr., Sept. 13, 1841. 3. Tyler to Clay, April 30, 1841.

To Ann Maury, July 4, 1841. Thanks her for "the testimony she has communicated . . . in respect to Mr. Madison's opinions as to a Nat. bank [Clay to Tucker, April 15, 1841]," but notes that what had caught her eye, in Mr. [William C.] Rives's statement on those opinions, pertained to Mr. Jefferson, not Mr. Madison. AL. ViU.

For Maury (1803-76), daughter of James Maury, U.S. consul in Liverpool, see Sue Crabtree West, *The Maury Family Tree, Descendants of Mary Anne Fontaine (1690-1755) and Matthew Maury (1686-1752) And Others* (Birmingham, Ala., 1971), 117-18.

In a speech on July 1, 1841, William C. Rives had mentioned Jefferson's 1813 suggestion that the states should, individually rather than by constitutional amendment, cede to Congress the power to establish banks. See *Cong. Globe*, 27 Cong., 1 Sess., Appendix, 351-54, *espec.* 352.

Remark in Senate, July 6, 1841. Opposes a resolution to change the Senate's temporary daily hour of meeting from 10:00 a.m. to 11:00 a.m. Complains that Congress has been in session for five weeks and has passed no important bill. Points out that ten days have already been spent in the Senate on the bank bill with probably ten more to go before passage [Tyler to Clay, April 30, 1841; Speech in Senate, June 21, 1841]. Pleads for speed. Says he would rather begin work at 8:00 or 9:00 a.m. Explains and urges emulation of his daily early-morning schedule. Says he "rose seldom later than 5 o'clock. . . . then took exercise, principally on horseback, for an hour, or an hour and a half. . . . then made his toilette, took his breakfast, read the newspapers, and was ready to go to work." Adds, in connection with this, that he "always retired to bed at 10 o'clock—seldom later. If his friends would pursue this course, he would not only insure their health, but would engage to pay their physician's bill." *Cong. Globe*, 27 Cong., 1 Sess., 151-52. The resolution was defeated 13 to 31.

From THOMAS EWING Washington, July 7, 1841

Would it not be well to lay your Bank Bill[1] on the table & have it printed with its amendments, & take up the Land Bill[2] just passed by the House? It is wise to do *something* while it is in our power—And no one can tell where we will be two weeks hence—Besides you have one feature in the Bill (denying to foreigners a right to hold stock) which in my opinion is perfectly fatal to it—You might perhaps, by a little effort get that out—[3]

ALS. DLC-Ewing Family Papers (Supp. Roll 2). 1. Clay to Ewing, April 30 and June 2, 1841; Tyler to Clay, April 30, 1841; Ewing to Clay, May 8, 1841; Speech in Senate, June 21, 1841. 2. Also referred to as the Distribution bill. See Clay to Clayton, March 11, 1841; Clay to Ewing, April 30, 1841; Remark in Senate, June 9, 1841. 3. This feature, limiting stock ownership to institutions, states, or individual citizens of the United States, remained in both the House and Senate versions of the bill. U.S. H. of Reps., *Journal*, 27 Cong., 1 Sess., 498; U.S. Sen., *Journal*, 27 Cong., 1 Sess., 178, 185. For Clay's support of this principle, see U.S. Sen., *Journal*, 27 Cong., 1 Sess., 68-69 and Remark in Senate, June 30, 1841.

To THOMAS EWING Washington, July 7, 1841

I have received your friendly suggestion.[1] There will be some five or six days *perhaps* taken by the Opposition in debating the Bank bill[2] and proposing amendments. After that, I intend to propose to have all the amendments printed. Whether we can put aside the bank bill, and take up the Land bill,[3] will then be decided by circumstances. But I am sorry to tell you that there is no certainty of the passage of the Distribution bill in the Senate.

ALS. DLC-Ewing Family Papers (Supp. Roll 2). Letter marked "(Confidential)" and written from the Senate Chamber. 1. Ewing to Clay, July 7, 1841. 2. Tyler to Clay, April 30, 1841; Ewing to Clay, May 8, 1841; Clay to Ewing, June 2, 1841; Speech in Senate, June 21, 1841. 3. Also called the Distribution bill. See Clay to Clayton, March 11, 1841; Clay to Ewing, April 30, 1841; Remark in Senate, June 9, 1841.

Remark in Senate, July 7, 1841. Upon Sen. James Buchanan's motion to strike from section 1 of Clay's bank bill [Speech in Senate, June 21, 1841] the phrase "District of Columbia" (designated as the locus of the parent bank), Clay notes that since opponents of the bill had refrained from interfering with proceedings while its proponents were presenting their amendments, the latter are now returning that courtesy. "We are . . . perfectly willing to let honorable Senators have the argument, if they will let us have the Bank." *Cong. Globe*, 27 Cong., 1 Sess., 158. The motion to strike out was defeated 20 to 29. *Ibid.*, 159.

During Buchanan's lengthy speech, he complained that Clay's proposed bank, unlike the Second Bank of the United States, would pay into the treasury no "bonus"—or payment for the privilege of holding an exclusive 20-year charter. He asserted that Clay's no-bonus stance was based on his belief that if the government borrows money at 5% to pay for its allotted shares of bank stock, and the stock pays 7% dividend interest, the 2% differential is bonus enough. Not so, Clay interrupts. "I never said that the difference between the five and seven per cent. was to be the bonus; but I urged this to prove that it was no bad bargain on the part of the Government." *Ibid.*, Appendix, 165. Buchanan's speech of July 7 is in *ibid.*, 161-69.

Later in Buchanan's address, Clay challenges Buchanan's contention that the Second Bank of the United States [1816-36] never paid much over 5¼% on its stock and that at best the first bank [1791-1811] paid but a small fraction over 7¼%. "Eight per cent.," Clay interrupts. *Ibid.*, 166.

Remark in Senate, July 8, 1841. Opposes an amendment to the bank bill [Speech in Senate, June 21, 1841] by Sen. Robert J. Walker (Dem., Miss.) that would require all cashiers of the proposed parent bank and its branches to submit annually to the presiding officer of both houses of Congress a detailed report of all notes discounted, all bills of exchange bought and sold, together with the names of all drawers, endorsers, and acceptors of these instruments. Clay remarks that he is "friendly to publicity, reasonable publicity" and cautions that "No man in the early stages of banking thought it expedient or necessary to exhibit the affairs of the institution even to a committee. Then probably there was more mystery than was necessary." However, he believes there are adequate provisions in the existing bill to insure proper public scrutiny of the new bank. Discusses these. *Cong. Globe*, 27 Cong., 1 Sess., 162-63. Amendment defeated 23 to 25, Clay voting nay. *Ibid.*, 163.

Later this day opposes ("No, sir, I will not consent to it") a somewhat similar amendment by Walker that would permit a group of ten or more bank stockholders to examine the "accounts, &c. of private individuals." *Ibid.* Amendment carried, 24 to 23, Clay voting nay. See also Remark in Senate, June 30, 1841.

Still later this day, Clay opposes as "wholly unnecessary" another Walker amendment to the bank bill that would require the bank and its branches to keep a written record of all discounts, these records to be open to scrutiny by directors of the parent bank. How could this effectively be done in a place like New York City where there might be 400 to 500 notes discounted daily? Clay asks. *Ibid.* Amendment modified by Sen. Richard H. Bayard (Whig, Del.) and passed *viva voce*.

Near the close of this day's debate, Clay opposes an amendment to the bank bill by Sen. Thomas H. Benton (Dem., Mo.) that would prevent the bank from paying out bullion as well as its own notes and gold or silver coin. Benton presumes that permitting such bullion transactions was probably written into Clay's bill inadvertently. Not so, replies Clay. "The bank [has] as much right to deal in bullion as to deal in stocks, in houses, in lands, &c." *Ibid.*, 164; also *ibid.*, Appendix, 144. Benton's amendment to strike the word "bullion" passes 26 to 21, Clay voting nay.

Remark in Senate, July 9, 1841. Opposes an amendment to the bank bill [Speech in Senate, June 21, 1841] by Sen. Robert J. Walker that would prohibit loans to directors and officers of the proposed bank; also loans to members of Congress. If the privilege of borrowing is denied to bank directors and to members of Congress, Clay argues, "you would get the worst kind of men, while men of business would be left out. Were gentlemen on the other side prepared for such a state of things as this? Why was a member of Congress to be proscribed, the whole class denounced, and a *Cain*-like mark to be set on them? Why say, while all may borrow, a member of Congress shall not? Could gentlemen vote as though they were afraid to trust them? If so, he did not envy them their feelings; though there might have been bad members of Congress, and doubtless there might be some still so, as a class, he believed them to be as high-souled and as patriotic a set of men as ever existed." *Cong. Globe*, 27 Cong., 1 Sess., 172. The Walker amendment, further amended by Walker to permit loans to bank officers and directors up to

$10,000, passed 25 to 21, Clay voting nay. A parallel amendment, prohibiting the bank "from granting accommodations to members of Congress," was passed 23 to 22, Clay voting nay. *Ibid.*, 173.

Remark in Senate, July 10, 1841. Following his presentation of a Barbour County, Ala., petition for a national bank, Clay argues that an amendment to the bank bill [Speech in Senate, June 21, 1841] by Sen. Levi Woodbury that would prohibit the proposed bank's directors or stockholders from making any donations from bank funds "went a little too far." Sees possible "beneficial" uses of such donations, particularly for humanitarian purposes. Suggests, instead, an amendment to Woodbury's amendment that would prohibit the making of donations to any officers of the bank. Amendment passes 26 to 21. Clay then moves that the word "stockholders" be stricken from Woodbury's amendment as amended, "thus leaving them [stockholders] the power to act" on decisions to make donations. Challenges Woodbury's charge that this would give foreign stockholders control over the funds of the bank. Does Woodbury, Clay asks, "not know that by solemn vote of the Senate [Remark in Senate, June 30, 1841] foreigners were not only prohibited from voting, but owning any stock?" In response to Woodbury's counter-charge that in a speech in [February] 1811 Clay had made "a strong argument" against foreign ownership of the stock of the Bank of the United States on national security grounds [1:538-39], Clay admits he had made such a speech; he admits also that he changed his position on the bank issue between 1811 and 1816 [2:200-205, 216-19], and explains that his shift from an anti-bank to a pro-bank stance had been caused by the War of 1812. "But what was the difference between 1811 and 1816? At the latter period came the war debt, with a ruined Treasury; that war could not be carried on without the aid of banks." He had, therefore, publicly "changed his opinion in favor of a Bank," even though as Speaker of the House he "need not have disclosed his opinions." Suggests that Woodbury read his June, 1816 speech which, he assures the New Hampshire senator, had indeed been published [2:205]. Following his exchange with Woodbury, Clay's amendment to strike "stockholders" from Woodbury's amendment was carried 28 to 21. *Cong. Globe*, 27 Cong., 1 Sess., 176-77.

Later this day, Clay again engages Woodbury in debate on the bank bill, opposing Woodbury's amendment to eliminate the $30,000,000 capitalization feature, a change which would render the proposed bank "a mere Bank of deposite." Clay wonders if such opposition amendments were "merely intended to procrastinate debate." *Ibid.*, 178-79. Woodbury's amendment was defeated 22 to 26, Clay voting nay.

Remark in Senate, July 12, 1841. Participates in opposition to Sen. Silas Wright's amendment to the bank bill to strike out the clause in section 1 requiring the government to subscribe to 100,000 shares of bank stock. The purpose of his amendment, Wright admits, is "to separate the United States from the corporation." Clay again rises to the defense of his bank bill [Speech in Senate, June 21, 1841], pointing out that the "object of the bill was to furnish a sound national currency." At the same time, however, the proposed national bank would also generate more income for the government, provide more security for deposits, and be less costly to operate than either Van Buren's Independent Treasury or Jackson's "pet bank system." Experiences "ineffable astonishment" to hear Wright deny this, given "all the Swartwoutings [Remark in Senate, December 13, 1838], peculations, and defalcations which had taken place under the late Administration." Explains at length the relationship between the interest to be paid for the money subscribed and the dividends to be paid on the bank's stock [Remark in Senate, July 7, 1841] to demonstrate his contention that the proposed institution will also be more profitable an investment for the government (the people) and more economical to administer than were both the first and second Bank[s] of the United States. So obvious was all this to Clay that he "could not help regarding the opposition to this bill as one eminently calculated to delay the public business" at a time "when the whole country is crying out in an agony of distress for measures of relief." Complains that this is the third week of discussion of this bill, and that the "extra session" seems likely to continue to the last of autumn. States, on challenge by Sen. Calhoun, that he attributes no "motives" to the opposition on the matter of the consumption of time; he speaks only of the "effect" of their amendments on the wasting of the time of the session. In sum, he does "not attribute to the Senators any motives for delay. . . . only . . . of the matter of fact." He was, however, "ready for the adoption of a rule which would place the business of the Senate under the control of a majority of the Senate." *Cong. Globe*, 27 Cong., 1 Sess., 183-84.

Later this day, Clay rejoins the debate on Wright's amendment prohibiting the government from purchasing stock in the proposed bank. Reviews again the reasons for creating a new national bank. Is dismayed to hear threats of repeal of the bank bill in the chamber even before it is passed. Warns the opposition, Sen. James Buchanan in particular, not to defer the bank bill until the next session or inject it into the fall elections. "Let them make this question, and my life on it, they will receive a more overwhelming defeat than even that of November last." *Ibid.*, 186-87. Wright's amendment was defeated 22 to 28, Clay voting nay.

Still later this day, Clay opposes an amendment to the bank bill by Alabama's Clement C. Clay that would permit the president to regulate the purchase of government stock and the appointment of the government's directors in such manner as to avoid having a period during which the government might initially hold two-thirds of the stock sold and control but one-third of the bank's management. Remarks Clay: "One of the strongest objections on the side of the opponents of this measure [is] that it was a Government Bank; and now a proposition is made which will make it out and out a Government Bank." *Ibid.*, 187. C.C. Clay's amendment was defeated 17 to 27, Henry Clay voting nay.

To THOMAS EWING Washington, July 13, 1841

We shall have the Loan bill[1] from the House this day. I presume the condition of the Treasury to be such as to require its prompt passage. What is the amount of the receipts from the customs the first half of the present year?[2] If the general returns are not received, what is the amt. at the port of N. York?[3]

I will call & see you this afternoon at or before Six O'Clock. Shall I call at your house or at your Office?

ALS. DLC-Ewing Family Papers (Supp. Roll 2). Letter marked "(Confidential)." 1. The Loan Act of 1841 [5 *U.S. Stat.*, 438] authorized the government to borrow up to $12,000,000 by the device of selling U.S. Treasury "certificates of stock," at a rate of interest not exceeding 6% per annum. It also authorized the use of these borrowed funds to redeem the Van Buren administration's U.S. Treasury "notes" [Comment in Senate, Sept. 15, 1837; Remark in Senate, March 9, 1840] as they fell due. The loan would be reimbursable either at the will of the secretary of state, upon giving six months notice, or at any time after Jan. 1, 1845. The House passed the loan bill by 124 to 93 on July 12; the Senate passed it 23 to 20 on July 19, Clay voting nay. It was signed into law by President Tyler on July 21. *Cong. Globe*, 27 Cong., 1 Sess., 111, 191, 226. 2. Customs receipts for the first quarter of the year—Jan. 1 to March 4, 1841—had been announced in the Treasury Report of June 3, 1841, as amounting to $1,974,836.46. *House Exec. Doc.* 2, 27 Cong., 2 Sess., p. 2. The Treasury Report of Dec. 20, 1841, gave the customs receipts for the first three quarters of 1841 as $10,847,557.44 and estimated that the fourth quarter would provide an additional $4,000,000. *Sen. Docs.*, 27 Cong., 2 Sess., no. 17, pp. 1-2. On July 16, 1841, Clay estimated U.S. customs receipts for the first half of the year as $5,703,000, a figure probably supplied him by Ewing in response to this inquiry. See Remark in Senate, July 16, 1841. In a Comment in Senate, Sept. 4, 1841, he stated that customs receipts for the first half of 1841 had, in fact, been $6,113,410.51. 3. On March 14, 1842, Edward Curtis reported to the secretary of the treasury that revenue collected at the port of New York for the year 1841 had amounted to $10,802,119.94. *House Exec. Doc.* 212, 27 Cong., 2 Sess., p. 337.

Remark in Senate, July 14, 1841. Presents a petition from New York citizens asking for a bankruptcy law [Remark in Senate, April 22, 1840]. Following this, Clay reports from the Senate Finance Committee the House bill authorizing a loan of $12,000,000 [Clay to Ewing, July 13, 1841]. Given "the condition of the Treasury," asks that this legislation "be passed with as little delay as possible," preferably "this week." *Cong. Globe,* 27 Cong., 1 Sess., 197.

Returning to the debate on the bank bill [Tyler to Clay, April 30, 1841], Clay supports, with one reservation, an amendment by Clement C. Clay (Dem., Ala.) which provides that if the parent bank or any of its branches suspend specie payments, its notes would not be received in any debt or other payment owed the government. Clay moves to amend C.C. Clay's amendment so as to confine the length of the prohibition on the receipt of notes specifically "to the time during which the Bank remained in a state of suspension." Clay's amendment to C.C. Clay's amendment carries 25 to 21, after which Clay blocks an attempt by C.C. Clay to withdraw his original amendment altogether. Now regards C.C. Clay's amendment, as amended by himself, as "a very good provision"; perhaps because, in the hostile view of Benton and Calhoun, it would legalize specie suspension in advance, recognize the legality of suspension, and be applicable to the waiver of related criminal penalties involved in suspension. In Calhoun's words, the vote on the C.C. Clay amendment as amended by H. Clay is "the most ominous vote yet given by gentlemen on the opposite side as to the character of this institution." Responds Clay: "Everything is ominous or a crisis, with the Senator." Replies Calhoun: "When the Senator is an actor." Adds: "I told the Senator [Clay] in '37 that he would ride the Bank to death, as he had the American system, and every other hobby which he had ever mounted." Says Clay in reply: "Well, I will have a good horse and a pleasant ride." Following Benton's amendment of Clay's amendment of C.C. Clay's amendment—an adjustment which added to H. Clay's language the provision that suspension of specie payments would be held to be "a cause of a forfeiture of the charter" of the bank—the C.C. Clay amendment as twice amended passed 41 to 0. *Ibid.,* 197-99.

C.C. Clay, "encouraged from the good success of his last effort," now offers another amendment to the bank bill—this one to the effect that if or when any bank used as a public depository of funds suspends specie payment, that bank shall receive no further government deposits. Since this concept, as C.C. Clay admits, came directly from the Deposit Act of June 23, 1836 [8:813], legislation which also empowered the president to remove government deposits from offending non-specie paying banks and relocate them in banks of his own choice, H. Clay immediately challenges it. Indeed, "it put the power over the public money into the hands of the Executive, and this he never would consent to with the remembrance of the former gross abuse of that power in the removal of the deposites [8:583-84, 684-85, 813]. Congress alone should have the power over the public money." Asked why, then, he had voted for the 1836 bill, he replies that it also "contained the provisions to distribute the surplus revenue among the several States." Asked, further, what would happen if the new national bank did actually suspend specie payments, Clay remarks that "the Government would share the fate of the private depositors." Objects to the emphasis by opposition senators on "mere possibilities" of what might or might not happen to the proposed bank. Wants to speed up debate on this bill. Makes it clear, however, that "For his own part, sooner than countenance the system of Executive interference with the Treasury, he would prefer to lose the entire amount of the public money in the vaults of the Bank." Adds, however, that the administration should be given the temporary power to deposit treasury funds as it sees fit were the national bank required to suspend specie payments during a period when Congress was in recess. *Ibid.*, 199. C.C. Clay's amendment was defeated 19 to 25, H. Clay voting nay.

To THOMAS EWING Washington, July 15, 1841

I call your attention to the second sect. of the Loan bill.[1] It provides, "cause to be prepared Certificates of Stock, signed by the Secy, and countersigned by the *Register* of the Treasury." The bill had been reported to the Senate before I recd. your note. If the amendmt suggested be made, it must be done in the Senate. But I submit whether the Secys. signature is likely to be required so frequently as to make it important? If you think it does, I will propose the amendment; but in that case some other officer must be proposed in lieu of the Register; who shall it be?[2]

ALS. DLC-Ewing Family Papers (Supp. Roll 2). Written from Senate Chamber. 1. Clay to Ewing, July 13, 1841. 2. The final version of the Loan bill, signed into law by President Tyler on July 21, required that the register of the treasury countersign the stock certificates. 5 *U.S. Stat.*, 438.

Remark in Senate, July 15, 1841. Urges his colleagues to take up the loan bill [Clay to Ewing, July 13, 1841] immediately, even at the expense of postponing debate on the bank bill [Tyler to Clay, April 30, 1841; Speech in Senate, June 21, 1841], because "the pressing necessity of the Treasury required prompt and speedy action on it—there was no time to be lost." Notes that the treasury has on hand but $900,000, "not more than enough to cover the expenditures of a fortnight." States that the House has proceeded much more quickly than has the Senate on important bills, having already passed the land (distribution) bill [Clay to Ewing, April 30, 1841; Remark in Senate, June 9, 1841] and the loan bill [Clay to Ewing, July 13, 1841]. Attributes this to the fact that "the minority here control the action of the Senate." Is scornful ("could he really be serious?") of Calhoun's suggestion that the administration raise money through a temporary issue of treasury notes. Given Whig hostility to treasury note issues in the past, Calhoun might as well ask him "to go for a Sub-Treasury, and forego the Bank." No, Clay continues, he wants "the real old fashioned way of borrowing money by a regular loan bill, and not . . . shifting expedients." Emphasizes again the need for a Senate rule, like that in the House, that would limit lengthy speeches and thus "give the majority a control of the business of the Senate." Believes that there is no subject on which any man, regardless of his genius, can speak "sensibly or usefully . . . for more than a quarter of an hour." Notes that the House, with its 240 members, could never permit speeches lasting an hour or more. "When would a session terminate?" Challenged to end discussion on the bank bill by calling for a vote on it, Clay explains that a "fair test" of it, either now or in a day or two, cannot be made because of the absence of some senators. Recalls past instances when the Whigs, then a minority party, permitted the business of the Senate to go forward; requests the same courtesy. With reference to debate on the loan bill, Sen. Lewis F. Linn (Dem., Mo.) accuses Clay of attempting to impose a "gag law" on the minority party in the Senate for reasons entirely political. *Cong. Globe*, 27 Cong., 1 Sess., 203-5.

The 28th rule of the House of Representatives was amended by a vote of 111 to 75 on July 7, 1841, to provide that "no member shall be allowed to speak more than one hour to any question under debate." U.S. H. of Reps., *Journal*,

27 Cong., 1 Sess., 218, 226-27. For Clay's unsuccessful attempt to adopt a similar rule in the Senate, see George H. Haynes, *The Senate of the United States; Its History and Practice* (Cambridge, 1938), 394-96.

From "Union Jack," Council Bluff [near Memphis, Tenn.], July 15, 1841. Addresses Clay "not as a politician, whig, or party man . . . but as an American statesman" who has "ever stood forth as the great champion of Southern and Western interests at home." Wants to call attention "to the monopoly, which has hitherto been enjoyed by a few Atlantic States, of all the local advantages to be derived from the Navy," such as the establishment of dockyards. Points out that the only navy yard "South of Mason & Dixon's line" is that at Gosport, Va., which Virginia "established at her own expense . . . and in 1800 ceded to the United States, on condition that the General Government should maintain there a Navy-yard forever." Advocates locating naval establishments on the Mississippi River and recommends Memphis, Tenn., as "the most suitable place." Details the benefits to be derived from such action and concludes that it would be an act of "justice to the West." Copy. Printed in *Southern Literary Messenger* (October, 1841), 7:724-25. In 1841 Congress appointed commissioners to locate a navy yard somewhere in the Mississippi Valley. The site chosen was at the mouth of the Wolf River at Memphis. This yard was completed in 1846. Young, *History of Memphis*, 82; U.S. H. of Reps., *Journal*, 27 Cong., 1 Sess., 282.

In letter "No. II" written on the same day, July 15, "Union Jack" calls also for founding a naval academy in Memphis. Discusses the need for such an institution, saying "I should . . . hail with delight, the establishment of a school any where for the Navy—even on the top of the Rocky Mountains." Believes this would allow for the development of a reserve corps of naval officers and that a school for engineers for naval apprentices could be included in the plan. Also proposes that the government appropriate money to pay one-fifth of the cost of ocean-steamers which would serve as private merchant packets in peacetime but, "when required for war, the vessels to be turned over to the United States at par valuation." Presents statistics to demonstrate the cost-effectiveness of such a practice, and concludes: "I have just seen the report of Mr. [Thomas B.] King [Ga.] from the Committee on Naval Affairs, and shall press this subject no further." Copy. Printed in the *Southern Literary Messenger* (October, 1841), 7:725-27. The House Committee on Naval Affairs had submitted a report on July 7, 1841, which called on the secretary of the navy "to inquire into the expediency of aiding individuals or companies in the establishment of lines of armed steamers." *House Exec. Doc.* 3, 27 Cong., 1 Sess., p. 6.

On July 17, 1841, "Union Jack" wrote from Council Bluff proposing a national foundry to be located "on the waters of the Mississippi, *above* Memphis—at an intermediate point between the Gulf and the Lakes." This would be "*essential* for the purpose of furnishing ordnance to the vessels built and equipped" at a navy yard in the West. Also says "as an act of justice to the West, and for the security and prosperity of the Union," the Great Lakes should be linked to the Mississippi River by a national canal. Adds that "You were the Hercules of the National Road," and argues that "the same powerful arguments which you used for proving the importance, the national character, and the constitutionality of that undertaking, might be repeated with like, nay, with more force of eloquence and reason for a National Canal." Copy. Printed in *Southern Literary Messenger* (October, 1841), 7:728.

"Union Jack" wrote again on July 20, 1841, comparing naval defenses above and below "Mason & Dixon's line" and pointing out that hitherto the South and the West have not complained about "this partial protection, and unequal distribution of the national bounty." Notes that presently "it would take twenty or thirty days for a Naval force, from the nearest port of the North, to carry relief to the property of our citizens in the Gulf of Mexico," thus making "most of the European powers, with their steam ships-of-war . . . actually nearer to our commerce in the Gulf of Mexico, than we ourselves." Asks: "Is protection less due to the South, than to the North?" Ascribes "the defenceless condition of the South and the West" to the apathy of those regions as well as "to their numerical weakness" in Congress, adding that "It rests with you to rouse them up." Believes Key West "is the Gibraltar" for the Gulf of Mexico and that the South and West will never be secure, "nor their defences complete, until this be made a strong hold." In addition, thinks a "Naval establishment at Pensacola" would have "many advantages." *Ibid.*, 728-29.

From PETER B. PORTER Washington, *ca.* mid-July 1841

Listen, I entreat you, with patience to the following suggestions:

It is my clear and decided opinion that your Bank Bill,[1] with the pending amendment[2] (introduced by yourself as a measure of conciliation, & sustained in the manner in which you alone are capable of doing such a thing) would be much better calculated to promote, in its practical operations,[3] the best interests of the country, and of the party, and at the same time advance your personal fame, than would be the naked bill without the amendment if forced through (as it must be if passed at all) the several branches of the Legislature.

Should the latter Bill succeed it would be considered as in defiance of the constitutional scruples of Virginia & some other States, such as South Carolina, Pa. & Missouri, who would probably resent the affront by the passage of resolutions by the Legislatures of these respective States, to forbid the establishment of branches within their local jurisdictions.[4] Whereas by the concessions made to them by this amendment they would be much more likely to appreciate the courtesey, & abstain from the exercise of the right thus conceded to them of repudiating an institution, of which it will be found they all stand in need.

It would besides be the means of securing the continued coöperation & support of several valuable Whig friends whose minds would doubtless be more or less estranged & embittered by pursuing the opposite course. And moreover the constitutional question would in the course of a single year by the voluntary consent of all, be established upon a basis, which could not afterwards be assailed with any hopes of success. Should you approve of this course of proceeding, I think I may safely pledge myself that Mr. [William C.] Preston will before any further measures are taken, agree to support the amendment & sustain the Bill throughout.[5]

Amend Mr. Clay's Bill by adding the following proviso at the close of the 16th Section.

Provided, nevertheless, that if the people of any particular State, shall, either because they consider such an institution as derogating from their State rights, or its operations as interfering with, or unfriendly to their habits of business, or for any other reason, deem the existence of an office of discount and deposit within their territorial limits to be inexpedient; and if they shall by an act or declaration of their Legislature to be passed according to their ordinary forms of legislation at the first session it shall hold after the passage of this act, signifying their dissent to the existence of any office of discount and deposit in such State, it shall then be the duty of the President & directors of the Bank hereby created to forbear the establishment of any office within such State; or, in case one shall have been already established, immediately to withdraw it. But in case of their omission to make such declaration their assent to the propriety of such establishment shall be thereafter presumed.[6]

Copy. OHi. 1. Tyler to Clay, April 30, 1841; Ewing to Clay, May 8, 1841; Clay to Ewing, June 2, 1841; Speech in Senate, June 21, 1841. In the original bill, the language of the branching clause in section 11, paragraph 16 read, in part: "And the said directors may also establish competent offices of discount and deposite in any State, Territory, or district of the United States." *Sen. Docs.*, 27 Cong., 1 Sess., no. 32, p. 16. 2. See below. 3. Word "results" struck through, replaced by "operations." 4. To encourage such anti-branching behavior at the state level was the intent of the Rives amendment to section 11, paragraph 16 which was introduced on July 1, 1841, and defeated 10 to 38 on July 6. See *Cong. Globe*, 27 Cong., 2 Sess. (July 1, 1841), 133; *ibid.* (July 6, 1841), 152. Compare Ewing's approach to the question of automatic versus state-approved branching [*ibid.* (June 12, 1841), 48-49; Clay to Ewing, June 2, 1841] with that of Rives and that of Porter (below). 5. Preston had spoken for and voted for the Rives amendment. See *Cong. Globe*, 27 Cong., 1 Sess. (July 1, 1841), Appendix, 355; *Cong. Globe*, 27 Cong., 1 Sess. (July 6, 1841), 152. But he also contributed to and voted for the final version of the bill as amended by Clay on the advice of Porter. *Ibid.* (July 27 and 28, 1841), 256, 260; Porter to Clay, July 24, 1841. 6. The comparable wording used by Clay in his amendment of July 27 was: "Provided, in respect to any State which shall not, at the first session of the Legislature thereof held after the passage of this act, by resolution or other usual legislative proceeding, unconditionally assent or dissent to the establishment of such office or offices within it, such assent of the said State shall be thereafter presumed." *Cong. Globe*, 27 Cong., 1 Sess., 254; U.S. Sen., *Journal*, 27 Cong., 1 Sess., 123-24. See also Speech in Senate, July 27, 1841, in *Cong. Globe*, 27 Cong., 1 Sess., 254, 256; and *ibid.*, Appendix, 362. The primary conceptual difference between the Porter and Clay versions of the branching power statement was the addition of the following words to the amendment by Clay: "That, whenever it shall become necessary and proper, for carrying into execution any of the powers granted by the Constitution, to establish an office or offices in any of the States whatever, and the establishment thereof shall be directed by law, it shall be the duty of said [bank] directors to establish such office or offices accordingly." *Ibid.* See also Speech in Senate, August 19, 1841. For Porter's role in persuading Clay to amend the branching clause, see Van Deusen, *Life of Henry Clay*, 348-49. The origin of the compromise branching amendment has also been attributed to Rep. John Minor Botts (Whig, Va.). Chitwood, *John Tyler*, 222-23.

Remark in Senate, July 16, 1841. Pleads with his colleagues to take up the loan bill [Clay to Ewing, July 13, 1841]. Assures them that if it is "not passed on at once, there would be no telling what the consequences might be." If the bill is delayed further "the wheels of Government must stop. I tell you [Calhoun], sir, we must pass this bill, and that this week." Denies that the loan bill is in any way connected with the distribution bill [Clay to Ewing, April 30, 1841; Remark in Senate, June 9, 1841], as Sen. Silas Wright has suggested. The "design of this [loan] bill was not to provide [funds] for the distribution of the proceeds of the lands. If the land bill was passed, it would not take effect till next year, and with the money derived from the lands, this bill was still necessary. It was the [tariff] duty bill [Clay to Ewing, April 30, 1841] which Senators could oppose on this ground, and not the loan bill." *Cong. Globe*, 27 Cong., 1 Sess., 208-9.

The tariff bill was reported in the House on July 14, 1841, by the Committee of Ways and Means and passed the House on July 31 by a vote of 116 to 101. On August 2 it was read in the Senate and referred to Clay's Committee on Finance. It was reported with amendments and ordered printed on August 5. The bill was then tabled on September 1 by a vote of 34 to 14 but was taken up and considered again on September 4. It passed the Senate on September 8 by a vote of 33 to 11. It next went to a conference committee (of which Clay was a member) to work out differences in the amendments of the two houses. On September 11, after the concurrence of both houses, the bill was presented to the president who signed it that day. U.S. H. of Reps., *Journal*, 27 Cong., 1 Sess., 241, 302; U.S. Sen., *Journal*, 27 Cong., 1 Sess., 131, 139, 227, 237, 247, 252, 254-56; 5 *U.S. Stat.*, 463-65. See also Clay to Ewing, April 30, 1841.

Later this day, Clay engages in a controversy with Senators William R. King and John C. Calhoun over the real differences, if any, between Whig "loan" bills and Democrat "Treasury note" bills; and over the rumor (heard by Calhoun) that he (Clay) had entered into an agreement with King to trade the taking up of the loan bill in return for restricting the size of the loan to the "immediate exigencies of the Treasury." Clay denies that he has agreed to reduce the amount of the proposed loan by half (to $6,000,000); whereupon King announces that his agreement with Clay is "to take up the bill and amend it so as to limit the amount to the exigencies only of the Treasury." As for the differences between treasury loans and treasury notes, Clay explains that "The loan bill would, in fact, be less objectionable than the Treasury note system, because the power of raising money by loan was express in the Constitution; but objections were entertained by some as to the constitutionality of Treasury notes. The difficulty is avoided—the end is the same—the only difference is as to the shape of the loan. When allowed to explain the bill, he would show the exigency for a twelve million loan."

It having been agreed finally to discuss the loan bill, Clay explains the dire condition of the treasury; specifically, he cites estimates from Secretary Ewing showing a probable deficit of about $9,500,000 from an income of $20,730,395 and expenditures of $30,260,313. To this last, however, must be added $10,000,000 in treasury notes that "will probably fall due this year," thus bringing the possible deficit to $19,500,000. Even if $2,500,000 is not spent on fortifications, as Ewing proposes, or $2,000,000 is not set aside in a reserve fund, as he suggests, the total need still adds up to about $14,500,000; or to $2,500,000 over the proposed loan. Adds: "As for the plan of the bill, it was not a loan to be taken up immediately for the whole twelve millions. The language of the bill was precisely like that of the Treasury Note bill—authorizing the President to borrow not beyond the amount required by the exigencies of the Government." Discusses at length the necessity of incurring public debt at critical times in the nation's history—such as during the War of 1812 and at the present. Opposes Sen. Wright's amendment prohibiting the early retirement of treasury notes not yet due or for any purpose other than the payment of current expenses with funds raised by the loan. Clay asks instead that the secretary of the treasury be given more latitude in handling the total government deficit. Asked what was the amount of customs receipts for the first half of 1841, Clay replies that it was "less than the lowest estimate, being $5,703,000 [Clay to Ewing, July 13, 1841]." Also states that given the expected decline of tariff income when the 1833 schedules finally expire, "the twelve million loan would be far short." Disagrees with Calhoun on how much income would be produced by raising duties to 20% on articles carrying less duty, and by imposing a 20% duty on various articles on the free list [Clay to Ewing, April 30, 1841]. Thinks such duties will bring in twenty-two or twenty-three million dollars rather than $25,000,000.

Also challenges Calhoun's statement that the "staple States" pay more than their "due share of the imports; that tariffs, debts and taxes, fall heavily upon them, and that they receive but very little remuneration in the shape of disbursements"; and that the government has become "the agent to delude and plunder the people under the mystification of general terms—banks, stocks, loans, and the like." Clay responds with the observation that Kentucky pays more tax per capita than does South Carolina, and ventures also to say that "the people of the free Atlantic States pay more than the white inhabitants of South Carolina." Doubts that Calhoun's constituents pay much in the way of taxes given the state's "300,000 niggers and a moiety of whites!" As for government disbursements, Clay points out that "this is not all the complaint. The expenditures are not in his [Calhoun's] section of the country; they are in another place. Well, this unequal disbursement of the public money resulted from the nature of things, and if the Creator had made the tides to rise higher at Boston and New York than on the Gulf, it was no fault of this Government. We could not reverse the laws of nature for the sake of spending precisely as much money in South Carolina as was necessary to be expended in the same space in other parts of the Union, and of the world. And if this be a fixed and unchangeable law, what is the case made out by the Senator but an argument for the dissolution of the Union, though he would not attribute that purpose to him? The taxes of this Government were paid by the consumers, and there was more consumption by the free whites than by the slaves, and there was consequently more paid by the free States than the slave States." At this juncture in the debate Clay renews his motion to strike out the clause in the loan bill that would prohibit the redemption of treasury notes not yet due. This amendment to Wright's amendment carries 27 to 21. *Cong. Globe*, 27 Cong., 1 Sess., 210-11.

Following this vote, Wright insists that it be made quite clear in the language of the loan bill that funds raised by the legislation would not be used, as he put it, "to facilitate the purposes of the distribution bill." Clay opposes the inclusion of such a statement in the bill on the ground that he was "not willing to preclude Government in advance," a view upheld in a 23 to 26 vote (Clay voting nay) against Wright's position. *Ibid.*, 211-12.

Remark in Senate, July 17, 1841. Speaks to Calhoun's complaint that an editorial in this morning's Washington *Daily National Intelligencer* has called for limitation of debate in the Senate, citing Calhoun's attempt to prevent discussion of the declaration of war bill on June 4, 1812. Not so, Calhoun insists, explaining what had actually happened that day. The larger question on that day and this, Clay notes, is "the question of consideration—that is, a measure being introduced, the question was taken, if demanded, Shall it be considered?" It was a question he had faced as Speaker of the House on June 1, 1812, in a confrontation with John Randolph [1:660-63] on the war issue. The continuing problem, therefore, from a parliamentary standpoint, is how "to give to the majority the control of action on the business of Congress." When Calhoun flatly denies the accuracy of Clay's account of parliamentary procedure in the Randolph case, Clay retorts: "No, sir, no." Insists Calhoun: "Yes, sir." *Cong. Globe*, 27 Cong., 1 Sess., 215-16. See also Charles M. Wiltse, *John C. Calhoun: Nationalist 1782-1828* (Indianapolis, 1944), 64-66.

When next the loan bill [Clay to Ewing, July 13, 1841] was taken up, Clay repeats the figures on the deficit he had cited yesterday [Remark in Senate, July 16, 1841]—$14,500,000 excluding $2,500,000 for fortifications and $2,000,000 for a reserve fund. Opposes an amendment by William Allen (Dem., Ohio) that the loan should be used mainly for the liquidation of outstanding debts, with the residue going entirely to national defense. Allen's amendment was beaten 19 to 24, Clay voting nay. *Cong. Globe*, 27 Cong., 1 Sess., 216.

Later this day, Clay's deficit figures and loan bill requirements were roundly attacked by opposition senators Levi Woodbury, John C. Calhoun (who sneeringly referred to Clay as "the Chancellor of the Exchequer"), Silas Wright, and other Democrats. Amendments suggesting various numbers lower than twelve million were proposed. For example, Woodbury's amendment to reduce Clay's borrowing limit from twelve million to six million was beaten 21 to 26, Clay voting nay; similarly, an amendment by William R. King (Dem., Ala.) to substitute nine million for Clay's twelve million was defeated 22 to 26, Clay voting against. There were others, all of which were defeated by four or five votes. *Ibid.*, 216-22.

Clay opposes all of these amendments, insists that $12,000,000 is less than the sum likely to be needed, urges prompt action on the bill, and blocks motions to adjourn. To Sen. James Buchanan's (Dem., Pa.) insistence on Sen Ambrose H. Sevier's (Dem., Ark.) amendment to prohibit the secretary of the treasury from reissuing "any Treasury notes that may hereafter be redeemed," Clay, his patience apparently wearing thin, informs the Pennsylvanian that he opposes the Sevier amendment because it implies "a want of honor and bad faith" on the part of the president and Secretary Ewing. Explains that "At last it comes to this: confidence or no confidence. We have confidence in the Administration; the Senators on the other side have none. Then let them make their propositions, and let us vote them down."

"Mr. BUCHANAN was sorry that the Chancellor of the Exchequer manifested so much excitability.

"Mr. CLAY of Kentucky. Not at all; not at all. I wish I had a more lady-like manner of expressing myself.

"Mr. BUCHANAN. I am afraid the Senator will lose the proper intonation of his voice if he pitches it on so high a key.

"Mr. CLAY. Not unlikely, as you put my voice so often in requisition. . . . [I will] modulate [my] voice to suit the delicate ear of the Senator from Pennsylvania."

Following this tense exchange, Sevier's amendment, as amended further by Wright, was beaten 19 to 25, Clay voting nay. *Ibid.*, 222-23. It being after 5:00 p.m., a motion to adjourn until July 19, was passed "by a large majority" in spite of Clay's effort to get a vote on the third reading of the loan bill prior to such adjournment. *Ibid.*, 224.

To PETER B. PORTER Washington, July 18, 1841

I send you the modified draft.[1] Perhaps it will be best not to let the copy in my hand writing pass out of your hands.

ALS. NBuHi. Letter marked "(Confidential)." Addressed to Porter "at Mr. Gadsby's," Washington, D.C. 1. The Fiscal Bank bill. See Clay to Porter, April 24, 1841; Clay to Ewing, April 30 and June 2, 1841; Tyler to Clay, April 30, 1841; Ewing to Clay, May 8, 1841; Speech in Senate, June 21, 1841; Porter to Clay, *ca.* mid-July, 1841.

To A. T. KEELER Washington, July 19, 1841

I received your favor, transmitting a Memorial in behalf of the passage of a general bankrupt law,[1] which I took great pleasure in presenting to the Senate. My impression is that, in the Senate, the prospects of the passage of such a law are better than they were at the commencement of the Session; but on a question, the decision of which depends in one house upon the opinions of upwards of 240 members, and in this upon the opinions of fifty one, it is impossible to anticipate, with any confidence, the final result.

ALS. ViU. Letter written from Senate Chamber. 1. Remark in Senate, April 22, 1840. See also Speech in Senate, June 4, 1840.

Remark in Senate, July 19, 1841. Interrupts debate on the loan bill [Clay to Ewing, July 13, 1841] to express his understanding at the conclusion of Saturday's session [July 17] that there was to be but one speech more on the bill and already today there have been three (by Calhoun, A.O.P. Nicholson of Tenn., and Woodbury); "and how many more, nous verrons." Corrects Nicholson's arithmetic, noting that the bill should properly ask for fourteen instead of twelve million, because the last administration had left a debt of $10,000,000 in treasury notes. "We propose," says Clay, "to pay this debt . . . in the good old fashioned form—by bond." It was either pay it this way or by issuing more treasury notes. Explains that he prefers the use of treasury bonds. Is deeply concerned that the Democrats oppose "paying the debts of their own contracting. What had astonished him more than any thing else was, the principle openly avowed by a leader, if not leaders of the party, that they would stop the supplies of Government! Now, let us look what would be the results from the adoption of such a system. The credit of the country destroyed, her honor blighted, her fame tarnished, the Government itself dissolved! All these evils would occur to arrest this Republic in its onward and glorious march to pre-eminence. And by whom was this to be effected? By the very creators of this debt! I call . . . on the Senate and the country to witness that this principle has been avowed without a blush by the representatives of the honor and interests of this Republic—sentiments which I have never listened to since that fierce opposition during the last war [of 1812], when not only did they vote against the raising of men, but of supplies." Flatly rejects the opposition charge that the debt had been created by the Congress rather than the Van Buren administration. "Oh no!" Clay insists with sarcasm, "It was Congress, forsooth. It was Congress that excited all this extravagance—Congress, that did not choose to surrender itself to the Executive branch, but made its appropriations under its own sense of what was right, and therefore the Executive was not to blame for the extravagance. . . . Why, you ought to be ashamed of yourselves! This Administration will never offer so mean and skulking a defence. If these appropriations had been so loosely and vaguely made, had the President not the veto power! Why did you not rally and arrest this extravagance?" *Cong. Globe*, 27 Cong., 1 Sess., Appendix, 128.

At the end of this day, following a lengthy speech against the loan bill by Sen. Benton, the Senate finally passed the bill 23 to 20, Clay voting yea. *Cong. Globe*, 27 Cong., 1 Sess., 226. The House having passed the measure on July 12; President Tyler signed the bill into law on July 21. See 5 *U.S. Stat.*, 438.

Remark in Senate, July 20, 1841. Opposes Sen. A.O.P. Nicholson's (Dem., Tenn.) amendment to the bank bill [Tyler to Clay, April 30, 1841; Clay to Ewing, June 2, 1841; Comment in Senate, June 21, 1841] permitting to any state the right to tax the real and personal property of the proposed bank. Says such a provision would "place the bank in the power of the State." Notes that "The States already had the power to tax the property of the bank and the stockholders, but they had no right to tax the corporation itself." The amendment was beaten 21 to 27, Clay voting nay. Also beaten (16 to 23) was an amendment to adjourn, Clay again voting nay. To Sen. Robert J. Walker's (Dem., Ala.) observation that there was "a fixed majority of five here for a Bank, and also a majority in the other House [Clay to Clayton, May 29, 1840; Clay to Brooke, March 12, 1841]," Clay remarks that "it was rather more than he . . . had calculated." Dismisses as "an experiment" Walker's amendment to employ the whole capital of the proposed bank to create a limited bank of exchange, rather than a bank authorized to discount notes. This was defeated 9 to 28, Clay voting nay. *Cong. Globe*, 27 Cong., 1 Sess., 230-31.

To PETER B. PORTER Washington, July 21, 1841

I will try to see you this morning on my way to the Capitol. Far from being wounded by any thing you have said or done, during your sojourn here, the patriotic purposes, which you have manifested, have added fresh claims to my esteem. I saw [William C.] Preston after I parted from you. He almost consented to my clause,[1] and I to his, or rather your's.[2] But a fresh difficulty has sprung up, rendering it doubtful whether, even if we could agree, it would be of any avail elsewhere.[3]

ALS. NBuHi. Addressed to Porter "at Mr. Gadsby's," in Washington. 1. Clay's bank-branching clause. See Porter to Clay, mid-July, 1841. 2. *Ibid.* 3. Many of the bank's proponents were fearful either that the Whigs would fail to agree and the bill would thus be defeated in the Senate or that, if it passed, the president would veto it (as, indeed, he did). See, for example, Wayne Cutler (ed.), *Correspondence of James K. Polk* (Nashville, 1979), 5:711-13, 720-21; Adams, *Memoirs of John Quincy Adams*, 10:498; Kirwan, *John J. Crittenden*, 150; Tyler, *Letters and Times of the Tylers*, 2:53.

Remark in Senate, July 21, 1841. Throughout this day Clay rose frequently to his feet to oppose a series of proffered amendments to the bank bill [Tyler to Clay, April 30, 1841; Speech in Senate, June 21, 1841] by Democrats. Opposes an amendment by William Allen (Ohio) forbidding corporations from buying stock in the bank. Corporations, Clay points out, are of "various natures" and it would be desirable if "corporations for the education of youth" were permitted to invest their funds at 7% interest in the bank. Also, savings banks operated for the "laboring portion of the community" should be encouraged to invest in the stock of the bank. Notes that states can by law prevent their own corporations from buying the stock of the proposed bank. Amendment defeated, 21 to 25. *Cong. Globe*, 27 Cong., 1 Sess., 234.

Opposes an amendment by Robert J. Walker (Miss.) preventing the bank or its branches from making loans to corporations. This, Clay observes, would make it impossible for the bank to assist various incorporated banks that were in financial distress. Amendment defeated, 20 to 26. *Ibid.*

Opposes an amendment by Calhoun that would strike from the bill a clause permitting the secretary of the treasury to sell, without the consent of Congress, whatever part of the stock allotted to the United States (one-third of the total) that remains unsubscribed. Points out that this prohibition "deprived the Government of an immense advantage. If the stock rose, it ought to be in the power of the Government to sell it." Hopes unsubscribed government stock can be sold in Europe where it will command a higher price and "add so much to the existing specie means of the country." Amendment fails, 21 to 26. *Ibid.*, 235. U.S. Sen., *Journal*, 27 Cong., 1 Sess., 105.

Opposes another amendment by Calhoun insisting that the bank pay semi-annual dividends on its stock, not exceeding 3½%; and requiring that profits over this disbursement level would be paid into a surplus fund in the treasury that would be used to maintain the 3½% dividend rate in future years. Clay notes that such a restriction on the actual operation of the bank would be unwise, and asks "why should the Government, owning only one-third [of the stock], take all this profit?" Urges the distribution of all profit to the stockholders, except enough to maintain an emergency surplus fund. Thinks, however, that a surplus fund of $2,000,000 is too large in that it would tie up too much potentially productive capital. Amendment beaten, 22 to 26. *Cong. Globe*, 27 Cong., 1 Sess., 236.

Opposes an amendment by James Buchanan (Pa.) that the bank would not discount its notes or issue additional notes when those of its notes in circulation, or in the "*private deposites*" (Buchanan would add this phrase), exceeded three times the amount of specie in its vaults. Clay points out that such a regulation would be impossible technically to administer. How could Congress "regulate the circulation by this daily and hourly fluctuation of deposites? How could it be known, when a note was to be issued, how much deposites were in branches? He hoped the amendment would not be adopted, and that Senators would cease shingling the bill with amendments." Amendment defeated, 22 to 26. *Ibid.*

A motion by C.C. Clay (Ala.) to distribute the capital of the bank among its branches in proportion to the domestic exports of the state in which each branch was located, and to adjust these proportions every five years, was dismissed by Clay of Kentucky as "wrong in principle and utterly impracticable." It was beaten, 14 to 27. *Ibid.*

Opposes an amendment by A.O.P. Nicholson (Tenn.) providing that if the directors of any branch convert public money to their own use, in any way whatever, or lend public money, with or without interest, such acts will constitute violations of the bank charter. Defeated, 19 to 26. *Ibid.*

Opposes (statement not recorded) an amendment by Reuel Williams (Dem., Me.) providing that the notes of the bank shall be redeemable at the branches where paid out. Rejected *viva voce.* Opposes an amendment by Thomas H. Benton to strike out the clause that fixes the value of gold coins to be received by the bank. Rejected 22 to 25, Clay voting nay. A similar motion by Benton to strike out the clause authorizing the bank to deal in coin was defeated 22 to 26, Clay also voting nay. *Ibid.*, 236-37.

Supports a motion by John M. Berrien (Whig, Ga.), the effect of which, Clay explains, is to advance by one month the commencement of the Bank's operations. Passed, 27 to 22. Following this action, the amendment process having been completed, Clay moves that the bill be tabled and printed. Passed *viva voce. Ibid.*, 237. For the voting on amendments to the bank bill this day, see also U.S. Sen., *Journal*, 27 Cong., 1 Sess., 103-10.

From PETER B. PORTER New York, July 23, 1841

Mr. Webster as you will perceive in the [New York] Commercial Advertiser of this city, is out on the Bank question,[1] and is endeavoring to make an issue between you & himself; or rather between you and the President, of whom he confesses himself to have been an adviser on this occasion. He says many plausible things in favor of harmony & concession, & wd. therefore advise the Whigs to take Mr. [Thomas] Ewing's Bill,[2] or your Bill with Mr. [William C.] Rives' amendment.[3]

Mr. Webster is evidently very apprehensive of an explosion of the Whig party, and, if one is to take place I feel immensely anxious that you should have the vantage ground, & be unmoved by it.

Between the Cabinet bill,[4] or yours with Mr. Rives' amendment, & the latter with Mr. [William C.] Preston's last & short amendment,[5] the difference in principle as well as in practical operation, is immense; and my reason for wishing you to adopt, without being forced to it, this last amendment is, that you will thereby deprive Mr. Webster's argument of the whole of its force. I have conversed with many of our principal Whigs in the city since my return, and I run no hazard in saying that they would be exceedingly gratified to see you make this small & really innoxious concession for the sake of harmony, & to preserve the integrity of the party; provided always that your friends in Congress will (as it can hardly be doubted they will) go with you.

Copy. OHi. 1. The New York *Commercial Advertiser* on July 20, 1841, printed a letter from Webster to Hiram Ketchum, dated July 16, 1841, in which Webster urged the Whigs to unite and pass Ewing's bank plan. See Wiltse, *Papers of Daniel Webster, Correspondence*, 5:137-38. 2. Clay to Ewing, June 2, 1841; *Cong. Globe*, 27 Cong., 1 Sess., 48-49. 3. Porter to Clay, mid-July, 1841; Comment in Senate, July 1, 1841. 4. Apparently a reference to Secretary of the Treasury Ewing's message to Congress of June 2 and/or his "Fiscal Bank of the United States" plan of June 12 as either or both related to the branching function of the proposed new bank. *Cong. Globe*, 27 Cong., 1 Sess., 20-21, 48-49. See also Clay to Ewing, June 2, 1841. 5. Porter to Clay, mid-July, 1841; Clay to Porter, July 21, 1841.

Remark in Senate, July 23, 1841. Toward the end of a long debate on the bankruptcy bill [Remark in Senate, April 22, 1840], Sen. Benton explains that he and many of his friends are not ready to vote on the legislation; he therefore moves suddenly to table the bill, a motion that passed, 20 to 17, *viva voce*. "What!" exclaims Clay, "The motion prevails? Then I give notice that to-morrow morning I will take up the Bank bill [Tyler to Clay, April 30, 1841; Speech in Senate, June 21, 1841]." On Clay's motion, the Senate reversed itself and voted, 27 to 22, to take up again and continue discussion of the bankruptcy bill. Several amendments to the bill were proposed by Democrats and struck down by Whigs. At day's end, by a vote of 26 to 22, Clay voting yea, the Senate ordered the bill to a third reading. *Cong. Globe*, 27 Cong., 1 Sess., 243-44. It passed, 26 to 23, the following day (July 24), Clay voting yea. *Ibid.*, 246. The House passed it, 110 to 106, on August 18, and Tyler signed it on August 19. *Ibid.*, 350; 5 *U.S. Stat.*, 440-49.

From Peter B. Porter, New York City, July 24, 1841. States that during his visit here, he has "seen many of the most prominent men of the different sections of the whig party in this city," among them John W. Lawrence of one faction and Charles King of the other faction. Reports having had long conversations with them concerning the national bank issue, and says he showed them "the short amendment, which we called [William C.] Prestons [Speech in Senate, June 21, 1841; Porter to Clay, mid-July, 1841]." Says he intimated that Clay would "prepare something of this kind in case everything else should fail." Adds that this "was not only uniformly & warmly approved, but an undivided opinion was expressed that the sooner this course should be adopted, the better would it be for the harmony & integrity of the party." ALS. NBuHi. See Porter to Clay, mid-July, 1841.

John W. Lawrence was at this time a Democratic member of the New York State assembly and was later elected to Congress. See *BDAC*. It is possible Porter actually was referring to John L. Lawrence who was a New York Whig.

Remark in Senate, July 24, 1841. Opposes an amendment to the bank bill [Tyler to Clay, April 30, 1841; Speech in Senate, June 21, 1841] that would prohibit the assignment or transfer of stock to other than citizens or corporations of the United States; the penalty for doing this would be forfeiture of the stock which would accrue to the surplus fund of the bank. Says this proposal adds another restriction on the stockholder, thereby impairing "the value of his property." Thinks other provisions in the bill prohibiting foreign ownership are sufficient. Amendment passes, 26 to 24, Clay voting nay. *Cong. Globe*, 27 Cong., 1 Sess., 246.

Strongly opposes an amendment to the bank bill which would extend to groups of ten or more stockholders the privilege to examine all private and individual accounts, dealings, and accommodations in and by the bank and its branches. "Such a clause," exclaims Clay, "would place the institution completely at the disposal of its enemies. Persons, from whim, caprice, or malice, could derange or interrupt its functions." Moves, instead, that any group of potential examiners must have possessed collectively, for at least three months, no fewer that 500 shares of bank stock. To the accusation by Robert J. Walker that Clay's amendment to the amendment meant the opening of the examination of bank affairs only to the few and the rich, rather than to the poor, Clay exclaims: "The poor! the poor! were to be abridged of their rights! How so? Was it to be supposed that any ten stockholders who might get hold of a single share for the purpose of prying into private accounts of individuals, or of destroying the institution, would be permitted to do so? What merchant, what business man, would keep his accounts or make his deposites in such an institution, under such circumstances? . . . The principle of his amendment came from the other House—the popular, the democratic branch. . . . The Senator from Mississippi was mistaken in supposing that each one of the stockholders should hold five hundred shares; it was that amount in their aggregate capacity." Clay's amendment was defeated by the tie vote of 25 to 25; so too was an amendment by Augustus S. Porter (Whig, Mich.) that would require each member of a not fewer than ten-man investigating group to own at least five shares of bank stock. Porter's amendment was beaten 24 to 26, Clay voting nay. *Ibid.*

To WILLIAM P. GRINNELL Washington, July 25,1841

I received and thank you for your friendly letter. I am glad to have it in my power to inform you that we yesterday passed through the Senate a bankrupt bill.[1] If we can carry all our other leading measures (and I entertain now hopes that we may) I believe the House will pass the Bankrupt bill.

I am sorry that there should be complaints among the Whigs as to the administration of the patronage of the Government. If there be cause for them, I regret it, but have no power to apply any remedy.

ALS. Courtesy of Dr. Thomas D. Clark, Lexington, Ky. 1. Remark in Senate, April 22, 1840.

Remark in Senate, July 26, 1841. Presents a petition to recharter the banks in the District of Columbia for a limited time [Remark in Senate, June 15, 1840 and June 18, 1841]. *Cong. Globe*, 27 Cong., 1 Sess., 248.

Offers a change in the language of the amendment to the bank bill [Tyler to Clay, April 30, 1841; Speech in Senate, June 21, 1841] that prohibits the bank from increasing its debt when its notes in circulation exceed three times the amount of specie in its vaults [see Buchanan amendment, Remark in Senate, July 21, 1841]. Wants it to read that the bank would not "knowingly" issue additional notes under such conditions and would take measures to restore the 3:1 proportion as soon as it learned that a disproportionate condition existed. Suggested change in wording accepted without division. *Ibid.*

Participates in the discussion of two amendments to the bank bill proposed while the Senate sat as a Committee of the Whole. The first of these would strike from the bill a provision, the effect of which would limit to $10,000 the amount any director of a branch bank could borrow from the bank. Clay opposes this limitation on the ground that it "would deter many practical business men from becoming directors of the branches, as the directors receive no salary, and by this amendment it was proposed to cut off all loans to them." He contends, instead, that "the entire prohibition of loans to the salaried directors of the [parent] Bank was a sufficient restriction" on the activities of the branch directors. The amendment was defeated 23 to 25, Clay voting nay. *Ibid.*; U.S. Sen., *Journal*, 27 Cong., 1 Sess., 116.

A second amendment offered by the Committee of the Whole had to do with prohibiting members of Congress from becoming borrowers of the bank. Clay opposes this as an "unreasonable interdiction" of congressmen as a group. He denies that loans to congressmen would automatically produce a corrupt connection between bank and legislature. He says, however, that he is willing to accept, though not necessarily vote for, an amendment to this amendment by Robert J.

Walker which stated, less sweepingly, "That no note or bill shall be discounted for any member of either House of the United States." After considerable debate, and after Walker's amendment to the committee's amendment was, by "general consent," substituted for the latter, it was passed, 27 to 24, Clay voting nay. U.S. Sen., *Journal*, 27 Cong., 1 Sess., 116-17; *Cong. Globe*, 27 Cong., 1 Sess., 249.

Following this, Clay opposes, without significant comment, a series of some 15 amendments and amendments to amendments by opposition senators designed to change various elements of the structure and function of the proposed bank in ways that would better reflect the anti-bank sentiments of the Democrats. At the end of a long day of parliamentary maneuver, Clay rose to announce that he would take the question on the bank bill at noon tomorrow "without debate." Sen. William R. King (Dem., Ala.) promptly accused him of having delayed a final vote on the bill until all senators known to favor the legislation were in town and were ready and able to vote. U.S. Sen., *Journal*, 27 Cong., 1 Sess., 117-21; *Cong. Globe*, 27 Cong., 1 Sess., 250-52.

Speech in Senate, July 27, 1841. Clay rises early in this day's session to announce that "it was known to the Senate, and known pretty generally to the country, that the [bank] bill, in its present shape [Porter to Clay, mid-July, 1841], could not pass the Senate, and were the vote taken, it would probably stand 25 for the bill and 26 against it. Under these circumstances, for the purpose of reconciling the conflicting opinions in the Whig ranks, a friendly consultation had been had, and the result was a compromise, in which he hoped the friends of the measure would unite." He therefore moves to strike out the branching-power section of the bill (section 11, paragraph 16) and insert instead the following:

"And the said directors may also establish one or more competent officers of discount and deposite in any Territory or District of the United States, and in any State, with the consent of such State. And when established, the said office or offices shall be only withdrawn or removed by the said directors prior to the expiration of this charter, with the previous assent of Congress: *Provided,* in respect to any State which shall not, at the first session of the Legislature thereof, held after the passage of this act, by resolution or other usual legislative proceeding, unconditionally assent or dissent to the establishment of such office or offices within it, such assent of the said State shall be thereafter presumed; and provided, nevertheless, that whenever it shall become necessary and proper for carrying into execution any of the powers granted by the Constitution to establish an office or offices in any of the States whatever, and the establishment thereof shall be directed by law, it shall be the duty of the said directors to establish such office or offices accordingly [see Porter to Clay, mid-July, 1841]."

Explains that since it is clear that there is a "decided majority" in the Senate in favor of a national bank, and since only a national bank can satisfy the "just expectations of a suffering people," it is better to compromise on the branching issue in a "spirit of conciliation and concession" than "return home without fulfilling the hopes of those who sent us here" to establish a bank. Points out that he "does not know, does not wish, and has not sought to know" the opinion of the president on the amendment he is submitting to the 16th paragraph ("fundamental rule") of section 11 of the bill [Tyler to Clay, April 30, 1841], not because of lack of respect for that "exalted person," but because the deliberations of the legislative branch should not be influenced by the "opinions, real or imaginary, of the Executive head." Points out that "Two opposite opinions prevail as to the branching power. According to one, the previous assent of the States is necessary; according to the other, it is not. The difficulty has been to reconcile these conflicting opinions. That is the object of this amendment." Notes that a state opposing the establishment of a branch is being asked only to exercise its dissent "within a reasonable time." Believes that the time specified in his amendment is adequate, and that it would not be unusual "to infer assent from silence" if a state legislature chooses not to act one way or another on the question. Discusses in detail the fairness of his proposed amendment and its practical application in the several states. Assures his colleagues that even if half a dozen states "expressly dissent, that fact will not at all impair the utility of this national institution. For if in the large commercial capitals of the Atlantic States, and if at Cincinnati and Louisville, or Lexington, in the interior, branches be established, all the national purposes of the institution may be fully accomplished." If the bank be not established during this session of the Senate it will be at the next. Asserts that he and his friends "have made a great sacrifice of our own wishes and preferences in consenting to the proposed modification of the branching power. But it has been made for our country and our friends. And he ardently hoped that there would be a just appreciation of the concession, and the spirit of the concession, now proposed; that it would be met here and elsewhere by a corresponding friendly spirit; and that the whole nation might rejoice in having once more restored to it the inestimable benefits of a sound currency, regulated exchanges, revived business, and restored prosperity." *Cong. Globe*, 27 Cong., 1 Sess., 254; *ibid.*, Appendix, 362.

To Clay's appeal, Sen. William C. Rives (Va.) responds that the Kentuckian's compromise branching amendment tricks the Senate in two ways: "While it kept the promise to the ear, it broke it to the sense. It said to the States, we will establish these branches with your assent; if you do not dissent in a specified time, we will establish them; and even if you do dissent, we will by decreeing them necessary and proper [to execute the Constitution], force them on you." Upon hearing this, Clay expresses surprise at Rives's intimation that he will vote against the amendment. Asks: "Did that not come nearer to his views [Comment in Senate, July 1, 1841; Porter to Clay, mid-July, 1841] than the original bill; and if so, could not he have voted for the amendment, even if he had voted against the bill afterwards?" To this, Rives replies that the basic principle in Clay's amendment is simply unconstitutional. *Cong. Globe*, 27 Cong., 1 Sess., 256.

Rives's response was followed by the votes on Clay's amendment and on engrossing for a third reading the bill as amended. On both votes Clay's position prevailed by a 25 to 24 margin. *Ibid.* On the following day, July 28, without further comment from Clay, the bill (as amended by Clay) passed 26 to 23. *Ibid.*, 260. See Tyler to Clay, April 30, 1841.

To SAMUEL JAUDON Washington, July 29, 1841

I send you a Copy of the Bank bill as ordered to be printed, after most of the amendments were made.[1] It has not yet been printed, with a few other amendments, as it passed the Senate.

We have not given a sufficient length of time either to the 12 million[2] or the Bank loan.[3] The shortness of the periods of both is to be ascribed to the d[is]inclination to create a Nat. debt of any long duration.

ALS. NN. Written from Senate Chamber. Addressed to Jaudon [Clay to Biddle, September 12, 1838] in Philadelphia. 1. Tyler to Clay, April 30, 1841; Speech in Senate, June 21 and July 27, 1841; Porter to Clay, mid-July, 1841. 2. Clay to Ewing, July 13, 1841. 3. *Ibid.* For subsequent extensions of the Loan Act of July 21, 1841, see Remark in Senate, August 18, 1841.

Remark in Senate, July 30, 1841. Participates in debate on a House bill appropriating $789,310 to maintain a home squadron in the U.S. Navy consisting of

2 frigates, 2 sloops, 2 small vessels, and 2 armed steamers. Speaks to Thomas H. Benton's amendment to supply the vessels, in part, and as an experiment, with canvass and cordage manufactured from American water-rotted hemp so as fully to test such hemp; and to Sen. Lewis F. Linn's (Dem., Mo.) suggestion that Benton's amendment "specify Missouri hemp," since the "hemp of that State brought twenty dollars more per ton than the Kentucky hemp, and . . . if water rotted . . . was superior, and greatly superior to any other hemp, either domestic or foreign." Clay says the proposed amendment is unnecessary, asserting that American water-rotted hemp is "equal to any in the world" and requires no further testing or experimentation. If, on the other hand, Benton "would embody his amendment in a resolution directing the Secretary of War to make proposals for the purchase of American water-rotted hemp, he would vote for it." Benton withdrew his amendment. *Cong. Globe*, 27 Cong., 1 Sess., 270. The House bill on the home squadron, which was passed 184 to 8 on July 21, was also passed this day by the Senate *viva voce*. *Ibid.*, 200, 240, 270.

To HENRY C. CORBIT Washington, August 2, 1841

I have a moment only briefly to acknowledge the receipt of your[1] letter, and to say that the Revenue bill[2] has passed the House and been received in the Senate. I think it ought to pass, and that it probably will pass the Senate. But of course I can only speak as to probabilities.

ALS. RPB. Written from Senate Chamber. 1. For Corbit, a Philadelphia merchant whose business was located at S.E. Second and High Streets, see *M'Elroy's Philadelphia Directory for 1840.* 2. Clay to Ewing, April 30, 1841. The act is in 5 *U.S. Stat.*, 463-65. See also, Chitwood, *John Tyler*, 295.

Remark in Senate, August 2, 1841. Presents petition of glass manufacturers stating that if a duty is placed on those free articles used to make glass it would injure their interests as manufacturers. *Cong. Globe*, 27 Cong., 1 Sess., 276.

Later this day, during debate on the fortifications bill (one of a number of separate appropriations bills) Clay opposes as an "enormous" expenditure an appropriation of $75,000 to purchase a site for a "Western armory" being sought by Sen. Thomas H. Benton (Dem., Mo.). Thinks that because of this item he might vote against the entire bill. *Ibid.*, 281. For the legislative history of the much amended, counter-amended, and counter-counter amended fortifications bill, particularly amendments to the Benton amendment for a western armory, as well as the subsequent activities of the joint House-Senate conference committee which reduced the $75,000 cost of Benton's proposal to $5,000 for the more limited purpose of selecting a national armory site somewhere "on the Western waters," see *ibid.*, 233, 292-94, 297, 353-54, 363, 407, 411-13, 429. The joint committee's version of the bill was approved September 4, ending a controversy which began with House passage on July 20 and Senate passage on August 5. On September 9, 1841, President Tyler signed the legislation, the cost of all "fortifications" for 1841-42 being about $2,468,000. See 5 *U.S. Stat.*, 458-60; also *Cong. Globe*, 27 Cong., 1 Sess., 453-54.

On February 9, 1843, President Tyler submitted to Congress the report of the commissioners he had appointed to select a site for an armory on the western waters. The report was referred to the Committee on Military Affairs. No new national armory was established until the Civil War, when a new government weapons factory was opened at Rock Island, Ill. Russell F. Weigley, *History of the United States Army* (New York, 1967), 191-92, 202, 364; U.S. H. of Reps., *Journal*, 27 Cong., 3 Sess., 342.

Remark in Senate, August 3, 1841. States that this is not the time or circumstance to consider the resolution of Sen. William Allen (Ohio) to hold open-door Executive sessions of the Senate except when treaties are being discussed. More important business is before the chamber. Moves to table the resolution. Motion carried, 26 to 20. *Cong. Globe,* 27 Cong., 1 Sess., 283-84.

Later this day, during discussion of the Fortification bill [Remark in Senate, August 2, 1841], announces he will vote against Sen. Benton's amendment to provide $75,000 for a "Western armory." Thinks it "inexpedient in the present condition of the public Treasury." *Ibid.,* 288.

Remark in Senate, August 4, 1841. Continues yesterday's criticism of Benton's amendment to the Fortification bill to provide a $75,000 armory for the West. Believes the proposal is too costly, and asserts that the existing armories at Springfield, Mass., and Harper's Ferry, Va., can provide the nation's arms needs. Might vote for a third armory at another time—he already had, he announces, "six or seven propositions for its location in Kentucky"—but not in the present condition of the treasury. *Cong. Globe,* 27 Cong., 1 Sess., 292. Benton's amendment, as amended to authorize the purchase for $75,000 of an armory site in the west, southwest, or northwest, the site to be selected by the president of the United States, was passed on this day 28 to 11, Clay voting nay. U.S. Sen., *Journal,* 27 Cong., 1 Sess., 136; *Cong. Globe,* 27 Cong., 1 Sess., 292. See Remark in Senate, August 28, 1841.

Remark in Senate, August 5, 1841. Opposes a motion by Thomas Hart Benton to print a memorial from a public meeting in Fauquier County, Va., remonstrating that the extra session of Congress is "not called for or justified on any of the pretexts on which it was convened." Specifically, in support of their remonstrance, the meeting had submitted to Benton a series of resolutions to be presented to the Senate. These resolutions bitterly attacked a national bank, distribution of the proceeds of public land sales, tariff increases, and the creation of a national debt; also included was a pledge to work unceasingly for repeal of the bank bill should it become law. Clay listens to Benton's motion that the Fauquier proceedings and resolutions lie on the table and be printed. "Why should a paper be printed which contains such gross charges against a majority of this body?" He moves to table that part of Benton's motion having to do with printing. Calls the question on his motion "without further delay," noting that "It is not debatable." Says Benton: "Then I shall move to take it up the moment it is laid down." Clay retorts, "Very well; get a majority to sustain you if you can." The vote to table Benton's motion to print was passed 21 to 20.

At this point, Benton moves that the Senate take up his motion to consider the Fauquier proceedings and resolves and commences to speak to the subject of the remonstrance and supporting documents or "papers." Clay calls him to order. "The point of order is, that on a proposition to take up, or lay on the table, it is not in order to discuss the merits of the subject." Sen. Lewis F. Linn (Dem., Mo.) disagrees, suggesting that while the motion to print had been tabled, "the papers now remained before them, open to discussion." Benton sharpens this distinction with the observation that "The decision against the motion to print, was not to lay the memorial on the table." Asked for a ruling on the question, the chair, Sen. Samuel L. Southard (Whig, N.J.), president *pro tempore* of the Senate, states that "the motion to print which had been laid on the table . . . carried with it the paper also."

This ruling produced angry dissents from Democrats Calhoun, Walker, Cuthbert, and King; and from Southard the statement that "if the decision was erroneous, it remained for the Senate to decide." At this juncture, Benton formally appeals the decision of the chair. Clay then moves to table the appeal, noting that it was not debatable. Calhoun interrupts to insist that an appeal, being a privileged question, cannot be tabled. Clay calls him to order; the chair, however, rules that Calhoun was in order. The morning hour having ended, the subject was passed over as the Senate turned to other business. U.S. Sen., *Journal*, 27 Cong., 1 Sess., 139; *Cong. Globe*, 27 Cong., 1 Sess., 295-97. For further debate, discussion, and decision on the controversial point as to whether or not a vote to lay a motion to print on the table carried with it the subject matter, as Southard had ruled, see Remark in Senate, August 6, 7, and 10, 1841.

Remark in Senate, August 6, 1841. Participates briefly and occasionally in a summation and continuation of yesterday's debate [Remark in Senate, August 5, 1841] on Southard's ruling on Benton's motions relating to printing and tabling the Fauquier remonstrance and its accompanying proceedings and resolutions (or "paper"); also on Benton's appeal from Southard's ruling and Clay's motion to table Benton's appeal. The issue, in Calhoun's view, is "whether it was in order to move to lay an appeal from the decision of the Chair on a point of order, on the table." Indeed, whether Clay's motion to table Benton's appeal of Southard's ruling is in order. Southard asserts that it is in order. During this debate, the chair (Southard) explained that he "regarded the decision on the appeal to lay on the table, as a mode of deciding the question of order on which the motion to lay on the table was made." U.S. Sen., *Journal*, 27 Cong., 1 Sess., 142; *Cong. Globe*, 27 Cong., 1 Sess., 300-301.

Remark in Senate, August 7, 1841. Expresses the hope that certain bleaching powders will be added to the exempted list in the tariff bill [Clay to Ewing, April 30, 1841; Remark in Senate, July 17, 1841]. *Cong. Globe*, 27 Cong., 1 Sess., 304.

Resumes participation in the debate on Southard's ruling of August 5 [Remark in Senate, August 5 and 6, 1841] as to whether Benton was in or out of order in his handling of his motions on printing, tabling, and discussing the Fauquier remonstrance and its accompanying "paper." Further, in the words of Sen. George Evans (Me.), "can an appeal from the decision of the Chair on a question of order be laid on the table?" Clay speaks at length in defense of Southard's decision in the matter, calling on precedent from the House of Representatives to sustain his argument. Speaks to Sen. Cuthbert's criticism of his "excessive warmth" while debating this question on August 5. Accepts the Georgian's reprimand that he (Clay) "was at times a little too warm" in debate.

Following a lengthy lecture from Calhoun on the parliamentary history of motions debatable and undebatable in the House of Commons, Clay defends the practice of the U.S. House of Representatives on the limitation of debate and the admissibility of motions, citing also the authority of Thomas Jefferson's *A Manual of Parliamentary Practice* in these matters. Insists that "To say, then, that the decisions of the House of Representatives are not to be looked into in preference to the decisions of the House of Commons in England, was a doctrine which he hoped the Senate was too patriotic not to repudiate. He really thought there had been enough of this contest, and that, for the sake of getting on with the business of the country so anxiously looked for, the whole subject ought to be laid on the table." Explains that the documents ("paper") Benton submitted on August 5 from Fauquier County, Va., "relate to measures before the other House, condemning in gross and offensive language, this extra session of Congress, and characterising the proceedings of the present Administration in the most insulting terms. It could not be expected that such papers would be permitted to be printed. He (Clay), in duty to his friends, moved to lay the whole subject on the table." Clay's technical point here is that when he later called Benton to order on August 5, he was not arguing that the Fauquier remonstrance, proceedings, and resolutions just tabled, could not be called up. They could be; but the merits of the issues they raised could not be debated until the Senate specifically voted to take them up. Given the fact that such a vote was not taken on August 5, and considering the offensive political language of the Fauquier resolutions, he assures Benton that "No, sir: I never will, for one consent to print such papers. The Senate may, if it pleases." *Ibid.*, Appendix, 187-88, 193-94; U.S. Sen., *Journal*, 27 Cong., 1 Sess., 144.

The vote to sustain Southard's August 5 ruling was defeated 9 to 30, Clay voting aye. Specifically, the language of the defeated motion dealt with "the appeal, by Mr. Calhoun, from the decision of the President pro tempore, Viz. 'that the motion by Mr. Clay, of Kentucky, *that the appeal*, made by Mr. Benton, *lie on the table*, was in order.'" Thus decisively overturned was Southard's ruling that Clay's motion to table Benton's appeal was in order. U.S. Sen., *Journal*, 27 Cong., 1 Sess., 144.

This brought the point-of-order question back to Benton's appeal of Southard's ruling that "The motion to print, ordered to lie on the table, carried with it the paper itself." But Benton withdrew his motion when Southard explained that his decision was "not intended as a general parliamentary rule, but was founded on the peculiar state of the question, supposing that the paper had actually been laid on the table, by the practice of the Senate, as a matter of course." The question thus reverted to Clay's point of order of August 5 "That the motion to take up the subject ordered to lie on the table, should be decided without debate." This motion passed, 25 to 18, Clay voting yea, following which Southard announced that "the question of order made by the Senator from Kentucky was well taken." *Cong. Globe*, 27 Cong., 1 Sess., 304; U.S. Sen., *Journal*, 27 Cong., 1 Sess., 144-45. Thomas Jefferson's *A Manual of Parliamentary Practice . . .* (Washington, 1801) is reprinted in Joseph B. Burleigh (ed.), *The Legislative Guide . . .*, 4th ed. (Philadelphia, 1853), 146-94. The rules of the Senate, as they existed in 1841, are in *Sen. Docs.*, 16 Cong., 1 Sess., no. 5, pp. 1-6.

To THOMAS EWING Washington, August 9, 1841

I should be glad to be furnished informally with statements

1st. of the receipts, exclusive of Treasury notes and the proceeds of the Loan, and of the expenditures, with the same exclusion, of the year 1841.

2. Of the receipts of 1842, supposing the Revenue bill[1] pending before the Senate to pass, and also supposing the Home valuation and Cash duties to be enforced from the 1st. of July 1842.[2]

Do the articles proposed to be admitted free, according to the paper E annexed to your report on the Finances, include Specie?[3]

Have you not estimated the *moiety* of the excess of duties beyond 20 per Cent, which remains after the 31st. Decr. next and until the 1st. of July following, at too large an amt. in supposing it will be 2 & a half millions? Should it not be half that sum?[4]

In estimating the drawbacks at three millions did you intend to say that, after the passage of the Revenue bill, that sum would be sufficient to include the drawbacks arising under that bill as well as under previous laws?[5]

What are the articles (exclusive of refined sugar & spirits distilled from molasses) on which the privilege of drawback is usually claimed? In other words, would that privilege be likely to be asserted on many of the articles upon which the Revenue bill imposes a duty?[6]

If the error as to the amt. of drawback on refined sugar &c. be corrected, as is proposed in the Revenue bill, what will be the saving annually made?

Will not there be a considerable increase of Revenue (and how much) secured by the prevention of those frauds and evasions of which Mr. [Levi] Woodbury & you both have complained? And will not the pending revenue bill correct or lessen them?[7]

ALS. DLC-Ewing Family Papers (Supp. Roll 2). Letter marked "(Inofficial)." 1. Clay to Ewing, April 30, 1841. 2. At this point, in pencilled notation in strange hand, probably an employee in the Department of the Treasury, is written "19.358,000." 3. At this point is pencilled "Answer No." 4. This paragraph is bracketed with the notation in the margin "2.785.589.96." 5. This paragraph is bracketed with the notation in the margin "3.500.000." 6. At this point is pencilled "Answer Yes." 7. This letter is accompanied by a document labelled "Comptrollers letter to Secy of the Treasury," dated Feb. 1, 1841, and written in the same hand as the pencilled notations on the letter. It provides statistics showing that the average duties for the six years ending 1839 were "23.176.000"; the average drawback on foreign merchandise exported was "2.256.000." D. DLC-Ewing Family Papers (Supp. Roll 2). For Ewing's estimates on public revenue and expenditures, submitted in his treasury report of June 2, 1841, see *Sen. Docs.*, 27 Cong., 1 Sess., no. 10, pp. 1-23.

To PETER B. PORTER Washington, August 9, 1841

I received your various letters, addressed to me after you left this City, including that of the 4h. at the [Niagara] Falls.

The bank bill[1] passed the House, without any amendment, by a most decisive vote; and is now before the President. What he will do is unknown to me or to his Cabinet. There is a most agonizing state of uncertainty in the public mind. It is impossible to foresee the tremendous consequences of a Veto.[2] If the bill should be approved, we shall probably carry all our great measures; if rejected, we may lose most of them. The Land bill,[3] the Bankrupt bill,[4] The repeal of the Subtreasury[5] & the Revenue bill[6] have all passed one House, and are pending before the other.

ALS. NBuHi. 1. Tyler to Clay, April 30, 1841. 2. *Ibid.* 3. Clay to Ewing, April 30, 1841; Remark in Senate, June 9, 1841. 4. Remark in Senate, April 22, 1840. 5. Speech in Senate, Dec. 15, 1840; Tyler to Clay, April 30, 1841. 6. Clay to Ewing, April 30, 1841; Remark in Senate, July 16, 1841.

Remark in Senate, August 10, 1841. Benton moves to take up the document he had presented on August 5 [Remark in Senate, August 5, 1841] "containing the proceedings of the meeting at Fauquier county, which had created the debate on the point of order and appeals from the decision of the Chair [Remark in Senate, August 5, 6, and 7, 1841]." Motion agreed to. Benton then moves that the document be printed, and Clay calls for the yeas and nays. Motion to print defeated, 22 to 23, Clay voting nay. *Cong. Globe*, 27 Cong., 1 Sess., 313; U.S. Sen., *Journal*, 27 Cong., 1 Sess., 149.

Following this vote, Clay moves that the House bill to repeal the Independent Treasury Act [Tyler to Clay, April 30, 1841], as amended, be referred to the Committee on Finance. *Cong. Globe*, 27 Cong., 1 Sess., 313.

Participates in the discussion of an amendment to the Land bill [Clay to Clayton, March 11, 1841; Clay to Ewing, April 30, 1841; Remark in Senate, June 9, 1841] by Clement C. Clay (Dem., Ala.) that would prohibit the distribution of public land sales proceeds until the public debt has been paid. In this connection,

Clay challenges the contentions of Calhoun that Whig administration expenditures are estimated to be about $27,000,000 annually, that the annual deficit will be about $9,000,000, and that to close the deficit gap tariffs will have to be raised at least 27%, or well above the 20% ceiling demanded by the Compromise Tariff Act of 1833 [8:604, 619-22, 626-27]. Calhoun sees a violation of the compromise tariff as highly likely unless the Whigs abandon their plans to distribute to the states public land sales receipts. No, Clay replies. The twenty-seven million figure is the Van Buren average for four years, whereas he (Clay) favors an annual expenditure of twenty-two million; or even one as low as twenty million. Says he stands firm for the 1833 compromise tariff and announces that the current tariff bill [Clay to Ewing, April 30, 1841; Remark in Senate, July 16, 1841] will yield a revenue of twenty-eight to twenty-nine million. Explains that this will occur "by the slight increase of duties, and taking the home valuation, which was done by adding twenty per cent. to the foreign valuation. The compromise bill was passed with the understanding that the revenues of the Government were to be derived from the customs alone." Dismisses Calhoun's insistence that home valuation is unconstitutional. "It is easy to make these flippant assertions of unconstitutionality." Asserts that the tariff bill of 1833 contained "a positive stipulation to resign the lands as revenue, and raise it all from customs." He did "not care a fig what was the understanding; there was the law, and he held them to the bond." *Ibid.*, 314.

Remark in Senate, August 11, 1841. Calhoun presents the memorial, proceedings, and resolutions of a number of citizens of Isle of Wight County, Va., attacking, primarily on states' rights grounds, the power of Congress to establish a national bank, the plan to distribute the proceeds of public lands sales, federal assumption of the debts of the states [Remark in Senate, February 18, 1840], the protective tariff; and the bill granting $25,000 to the widow of William Henry Harrison [Remark in Senate, June 24, 1841]. He moves that these documents be printed and requests that the secretary of the Senate read the memorial and resolutions into the record. Following this, Calhoun renews his motion to print. Motion defeated, 19 to 20, Clay voting nay. Calling this outcome part of "a general gag system," Calhoun moves to lay the Isle of Wight papers on the table, but withdraws this motion to permit Sen. Benton to discuss and defend the political substance of the Fauquier County proceedings and resolutions [Remark in Senate, August 5, 6, 7, and 10, 1841]. At the end of Benton's exposition, Clay points out that Calhoun had withdrawn his motion to table so that Benton could speak, therefore the Isle of Wight papers are "not laid on the table yet." The chair (Southard), however, takes the position that Calhoun had only "suspended" his motion to permit Benton to speak. Clay argues that since the Isle of Wight papers have been read to the Senate, and have been printed "in a Virginia paper this morning," there is no need to print them. He therefore moves to lay the Isle of Wight proceedings and resolutions on the table, a motion that fails, 21 to 21, Clay voting yea. Calhoun attacks Clay's stance on printing, claiming that his attempt to "gag the people—to stifle their voice. . . . afforded another proof of the reckless violence that marks the conduct of that Senator." Calhoun then moves to lay the Isle of Wight proceedings and resolutions on the table; and it was done. U.S. Sen., *Journal*, 27 Cong., 1 Sess., 152; *Cong. Globe*, 27 Cong., 1 Sess., 318-19.

Later this day, Clay reports from the Committee on Finance the bill to repeal the Independent Treasury Act [Tyler to Clay, April 30, 1841] as amended by the House. Urges that the bill, as amended, be taken up and passed "now." Notes that it is "well known that the President had before him another important matter [Fiscal Bank bill] immediately connected with this subject, and it would be well that both matters should be before him at the same time." Moves to disturb the order of business to the extent of postponing the scheduled discussion of the land (distribution) bill [Clay to Clayton, March 11, 1841; Clay to Ewing, April 30, 1841; Remark in Senate, June 9, 1841] and taking up instead the two House amendments to the bill to repeal the Independent Treasury. Clears the way by moving to table the distribution bill. This passes, 23 to 22. Moves to take up the repeal bill. After considerable discussion, this motion passes, 26 to 21. Supports endorsement of the House amendments, the first of which would also repeal the Deposit Act of 1836 except its 13th and 14th sections, thus ending "what was familiarly called the pet bank system [8:583-84, 684-85, 813]"; the second would repeal the 1836 law which prohibited the government from making its payments with specie-supported notes smaller than twenty dollars in denomination, a prohibition made irrelevant by the current bank bill which provides for the use of notes as small as five dollars. Explains to a critical Calhoun the desirability of Tyler's having the bank bill and the Independent Treasury repeal bill "before him at once. . . . it would enable him to act more understandingly on them." *Ibid.*, 319-20; U.S. Sen., *Journal*, 27 Cong., 1 Sess., 153-54. The pension act establishing a twenty dollar denominational minimum on specie-backed notes used by the government, dated April 14, 1836, is in 5 *U.S. Stat.*, 9. The House amendment to the Senate bill repealing the Independent Treasury Act which would also repeal the Deposit Act of 1836 [5 *U.S. Stat.*, 52-57], save its 13th and 14th sections, was passed 25 to 23, Clay voting yea. The House amendment dealing with denominations of bank notes was passed 26 to 23, Clay voting yea. So it was resolved that the Senate concur in the House amendments to the bill, following which the Distribution bill was again taken up. U.S. Sen., *Journal*, 27 Cong., 1 Sess., 155; *Cong. Globe*, 27 Cong., 1 Sess., 321-22.

To BENJAMIN O. TAYLOE Washington, August 11, 1841

I transmit you a memo. of the amt. of bagging and rope supplied your Alabama Estate, and a bill drawn by my Son & his partner[1] on you and your brother [Edward T. Tayloe] payable in N. York, on the first of March next, which I believe was the time (was it not?) agreed on for paymt.

Be pleased to accept the bill & return it to me, specifying in your acceptance the Bank or House in N. York at which it will be paid.

We are in painful uncertainty as to the fate of the Bank bill.[2]

ALS. NN. Addressed to Tayloe "at Mrs. Dickinsons, Troy, N. York." 1. Thomas Hart Clay and Waldemar Mentelle. 2. Tyler to Clay, April 30, 1841.

Remark in Senate, August 12, 1841. Presents a memorial from Philadelphia asking for a 20% duty on bleaching materials and a duty-free status for indigo. *Cong. Globe*, 27 Cong., 1 Sess., 324.

Later this day, Clay entreats the senators from Pennsylvania (James Buchanan and Daniel Sturgeon), to follow the instructions of their state legislature and support the bill [Clay to Ewing, April 30, 1841; Remark in Senate, June 9, 1841] providing for the distribution of public land sales receipts, not hobble the bill with amendments that in effect weaken it. He is, he said, "afraid the bill would be lost without their votes; whereas, with them, it might be passed." In the exchange that followed, Buchanan sharply rebuked Clay for once again bringing the issue of the instructions of state legislatures to U.S. senators into a Senate debate, stating, in addition, that while he was willing to be a friend of Clay's "upon terms of perfect equality," he would certainly not want him as a master, since he was clearly "a severe master." Retorts Clay: "Ask Charles if I am not a kind master." To this remark Buchanan replies that Clay had brought Charles's name so often before the Senate that he was "now almost as notorious as his master." Advises Clay to stop talking about Charles "if he wished to spare himself and his political friends from the shafts of ridicule which were aimed at him and them in the public journals all over the country." If so, he should "never, hereafter, on this floor, mention the name of that well known individual." *Ibid.*, 328-29. Charles Dupuy, Clay's body servant, was emancipated in 1844. See Richard L. Troutman, "The Emancipation of Slaves by Henry Clay," *JNH* (April, 1955), 179-81. For the legislative history and content of the 1841 Land (Distribution) bill [5 *U.S. Stat.*, 453-58], see Clay to Ewing, April 30, 1841; Remark in Senate, June 9, 1841.

Remark in Senate, August 14, 1841. Responds to Sen. Clement C. Clay's resolution asking why information relating to the issuance of military land script, asked of the secretary of the treasury last session, has still not been received by the Senate. Demands such information "without delay." Clay sees no reason "why the imputations of blameable delay should be in the resolution." Does not believe the administration or Congress should be burdened with such matters during the extra session. *Cong. Globe*, 27 Cong., 1 Sess., 335-36.

To JOHN R. THOMPSON[1] Washington, August 14, 1841

In answer to your enquiry about the word "locate," I have to say that whether it be an English word or not, I think it a very good American one.[2]

ALS. ViU. 1. For Thompson (1823-73), at this time a student at the University of Virginia and later a lawyer, editor, and author, see *DAB*. 2. In both U.S. and English usage, to "locate" means to place or establish in a place; in U.S. colloquial usage it also means to find or to take up residence in. Margaret Nicholson, *A Dictionary of American-English Usage* (New York, 1957), 322-23.

To THOMAS HART CLAY Washington, August 15, 1841

I recd. your favor of the 8h. I have not been able to write to you and the other members of my family as often as I could wish this Session. You know the cause.

Mr. [Alexander] Barrow has accepted the bill, and I have sent to Col. [Wade] Hampton and Mr. [Benjamin O.] Tayloe those addressed to them for their acceptances.[1]

Mr Pettigru [*sic*, Ebenezer Pettigrew] of No. Carolina, who wrote about mules, is now here, and I shall see him & ascertain in a day or two whether he will take your's or not.[2] If he does not, as I wish Mr. [Josiah] Downing to start with Monarch[3] about the 1st. Septr, would it not be well to send on the Mules (I mean yours, and mine, if in order) and after Mr. Downing delivers Monarch let him take the care of them & sell them? I believe I shall not take Sovereign;[4] the expences are so great & success so uncertain. I will write to you in a day or two again after I see Mr. Pettigru.

Henry [Clay, Jr.] has been here with improved health, & has gone to N. York with an intention to return in a few days.

The greater excitement & the most painful suspense prevail here in regard to the decision of the President on the Bank bill.[5] It is now believed that he will veto it. In that event the most important consequences are anticipated, one of which is the separation of the President from the Whigs. We shall know this determination by the 19h. as, if he does not return the bill by that day, it will become a law.

Our adjournment, I think, cannot be protracted beyond the 30h. & it may take place earlier.[6]

My love to Mary [Mentelle Clay] & the children.[7]

ALS. DLC-HC (DNA, M212, R5). 1. Clay to Tayloe, August 11, 1841. 2. Clay to James B. Clay, August 16, 1841. 3. Clay to James B. Clay, Jan. 19, 1841. 4. Sovereign was an imported bay horse by Emilius, dam Fleur de Lis by Bourbon. Skinner, *The Gentleman's New Pocket Farrier*, 99. 5. Tyler to Clay, April 30, 1841. 6. Congress adjourned on Sept. 13, 1841. 7. Lucretia Hart Clay and Henry Boyle Clay.

To JAMES B. CLAY[1] Washington, August 16, 1841

I have this day engaged to deliver to Mr. Pettigru [*sic,* Ebenezer Pettigrew] of North Carolina[2] 24 mules of my lot of 2 years old put at $90 each. I wish 24 of the best picked out, wei[g]hed, & sent to him. I hope they are in good order; but I wished them well fed until they start and during the journey. For the purpose of having them delivered, in good order, I wish some careful hand engaged to accompany Mr. [Josiah] Downing on his return with Monarch,[3] so that after Monarch is delivered, if necessary, Mr. Downing may go & attend to the delivery of the Mules. Mr. Pettigru was formerly a member of Congress from North Carolina & lives about 150 miles below Raleigh, which is the point to be made for. The person having charge of the Mules will having [*sic,* have] nothing to do but the delivery of them, as Mr. P. is to pay me for them by a bill on Balto. John's [M. Clay] horse, and any other of my young horses may be taken along with the mules & sold. Do attend to this affair for me. I will write you again in a few days I shall decline taking Sovereign. Tell Thomas that I tried to sell his Mules to Mr. Pettigru; but he preferred two years old.

The President sent a Veto of the Bank to day.[4] P.S. I must ask you, if necessary to advance the money to pay the expences of the Mules.

ALS. DLC-TJC (DNA, M212, R10). 1. Addressed to James B. Clay or "(in his absence Mr. Tho. H. Clay)." 2. For Pettigrew, see *BDAC.* 3. Clay to James B. Clay, Jan. 19, 1841. 4. Tyler to Clay, April 30, 1841.

From JOHN J. CRITTENDEN Washington, August 16, 1841

It is understood that the President concedes the power of establishing agencies or branches, with authority to deal in the purchase & sale of Bills of exchange & to do all other usual banking business except to discount promissory notes, or obligations–And that with the Assent of a State branches may be established with authority to discount *notes,* & to do all other usual bank business–[1]

Upon this basis it does seem to me that a bank may be constructed, with a larger recognition of Federal authority, and of more efficiency, than the one which the President has refused to Sanction.

It should be done by conferring on the Bank and its branches *all* the usual Banking powers, & then by *restrictions* & *exceptions, limiting* them to the basis before stated. There is less danger of error & embarrassment in this form of legislation, than in the attempt to limit the powers of the institution by specific description & enumeration of them.

I pray you to consider this well, with all the great consequences that attend it, & do whatever your known liberal spirit of *compromise* & your *patriotism* may direct. Mr. Clay can lose nothing by a course of conciliation—His *opinions* are known to all—And to whatever extent he may forbear to act or insist upon them, it will be regarded only as another & further sacrafice made to his country.

Do not beleive that the least *selfishness* influences me in any thing I have here suggested. P.S. Consider if it would not be better to drop every thing about the *assent* of States—And making the branching power a mere emination of Congressional Authority, exclude it from the discounting of promissory notes—The monied transactions of men will be put into the shape of bills of exchange, and the Bank thus formed, may be easily amended by future legislation if the power of discounting notes should be found useful or desireable.[2] The *political effect* of set[t]ling this matter now, & by *your means*, will be great

ALS. DLC-John J. Crittenden Papers (DNA, M212, R20). 1. For the president's veto of the national bank bill and the controversy over the branching issue, see Tyler to Clay, April 30, 1841; Speech in Senate, June 21, 1841; Porter to Clay, mid-July, 1841. 2. See Remark in Senate, August 24, 1841.

Remark in Senate, August 16, 1841. Presents the proceedings and resolutions of a meeting of citizens of Buckingham County, Va., supporting a national bank, repeal of the Independent Treasury, a distribution bill, and a bankruptcy law. Moves that the proceedings be tabled and printed. Done. *Cong. Globe*, 27 Cong., 1 Sess., 336.

Later this day, Tyler's message vetoing the bill to incorporate the Fiscal Bank of the United States [Tyler to Clay, April 30, 1841] was received and read, discussion of the land distribution bill being "passed over informally" to permit its presentation. During and at the conclusion of the reading it was said that there were hisses in the gallery. "I heard them, sir," claims Senator Benton, "and I feel indignant that the American President shall be insulted." Recalls that he himself had been "insulted by the hisses of ruffians in the gallery, when opposing the old Bank of the United States." Demands that those who hissed be pointed out to the sergeant-at-arms and be "turned out of the galleries." Following much discussion on hissing and hissers, Clay expresses the hope that there will be no discussion of the veto until the veto message is printed and time for "deliberate consideration" of its contents has been afforded. Makes it clear, however, that he will lead an attempt in the Senate to override the veto, beginning at noon tomorrow. *Ibid.*, 339-40. Tyler's veto message is printed in *ibid.*, 337-38, and in *MPP*, 4:63-68.

The burden of Tyler's argument was that for 25 years he had held the view that Congress had no constitutional power "to create a national bank to operate *per se* over the Union." He stated that "With a full knowledge of the opinions thus entertained and never concealed, I was elected by the people Vice-President of the United States." And as president he had taken an oath to "preserve, protect, and defend the Constitution of the United States." He also objected to the compromise branching clause (section 11, paragraph 16) in the bill [Porter to Clay, mid-July, 1841] as a potential infringement on states' rights. As he interpreted the compromise branching power amended into paragraph 16, section 11 of the bill, the states had little real control over whether or not a branch of the bank could be located within their borders. Specifically, their "assent or dissent is to be expressed *unconditionally at the first session of the legislature, by some formal legislative act*; and if not so expressed its assent is to be *implied*, and the directors are thereupon invested with power, at such time thereafter as they may please, to establish branches, which cannot afterwards be withdrawn except by resolve of

Congress. . . . This iron rule is to give way to no circumstances; it is unbending and inflexible. It is the language of the master to the vassal." Because of this, he could not accept, as he understood the situation, the power of Congress "to establish offices of discount in a state not only without its assent, but against its dissent." Further, he objected to the provision giving the bank the power to loan promissory notes within the states, a power designed to exercise some control over the lending policies and practices of state-chartered private banks. See also Chitwood, *John Tyler*, 226-28. On August 19, 1841, following a lengthy speech of condemnation by Clay [Speech in Senate, August 19, 1841], the Senate voted 25 to 24 to pass the bill—far short of the necessary two-thirds majority needed to override a presidential veto. It was not therefore sent to the House. *Cong. Globe*, 27 Cong., 1 Sess., 352.

Remark in Senate, August 18, 1841. Presents a memorial from manufacturers of chemicals and dye stuffs asking that cremor tartar be admitted free of duty. *Cong. Globe*, 27 Cong., 1 Sess., 345.

Later this day, Clay voted yea on a motion to postpone debate on the president's veto of the bank bill [Remark in Senate, August 16, 1841] until tomorrow noon, Thursday, August 19. Motion passed 29 to 21. Following this decision, Clay pleaded with his colleagues to conclude debate on the distribution bill [Clay to Ewing, April 30, 1841; Remark in Senate, June 9, 1841] so as to get immediately to "some other loan bills" designed to keep the Government solvent past mid-December, 1841. *Ibid.*, 347. The Congress passed no additional legislation that authorized the borrowing of money during the 1st Session. During the 2nd Session, however, another issuance of treasury notes [Comment in Senate, September 15, 1837; Speech in Senate, September 25, 1837], for a period of one year and in an amount of up to $5,000,000, was authorized and became law on January 31, 1842 [5 *U.S. Stat.*, 469]. On April 15, 1842, the Loan Act of July 21, 1841 [5 *U.S. Stat.*, 438] was extended for a year and the borrowing of an additional sum of $5,000,000 was authorized [5 *U.S. Stat.*, 473-75].

Speech in Senate, August 19, 1841. In a speech of one and a half hours, attacks Tyler's veto of the bank bill [Remark in Senate, August 16, 1841] point by point, charging at the outset that the president "has not reciprocated the friendly spirit of concession and compromise which animated Congress in the provisions of this bill, and especially in the modification of the sixteenth fundamental article [section 11, paragraph 16] of the legislation [Porter to Clay, mid-July, 1841]." Says the language of the veto message is "harsh, if not reproachful." Claims that in Tyler's "emphatically . . . Whig address [Clay to Bascom, April 17, 1841] (his Inaugural Address of April 9) the president had promised to support a national bank bill if it were constitutional. As to what is or is not constitutional, Tyler had said he would "resort to the fathers of the great Republican school for advice and instruction." Clay maintains that he and most Americans have interpreted that statement to mean that "the President intended to occupy the [James] Madison ground, and to regard the question of the power to establish a National Bank as immovably settled." Continues: "Entertaining this opinion of the Address, I came to Washington, at the commencement of the session, with the most confident and buoyant hopes that the Whigs would be able to carry all their prominent measures, and especially a Bank of the United States, by far that one of the greatest immediate importance. I anticipated nothing but cordial co-operation between the two departments of Government; and I reflected with pleasure that I should find at the head of the Executive branch, a personal and political friend, whom I had long and intimately known, and highly esteemed. It will not be my fault if our amicable relations should unhappily cease, in consequence of any difference of opinion between us on this occasion. The President has been always perfectly familiar with my opinion on this Bank question." Discusses his growing realization that he and Tyler were talking about different kinds of banks, even though he [Clay], in drafting the legislation, had made a number of compromises and concessions to the president's views, especially on the branching provision.

Attacks in detail the arguments and observations made by Tyler in his veto message. Traces the history of the first and second Banks of the United States, noting that Presidents Washington and Madison supported the institution in 1791 and 1816 respectively. Asserts that President Jackson "testified to the utility of a Bank of the United States" even though he vetoed the recharter of the second bank in 1832. As for the constitutional power of Congress to establish such a bank, the Supreme Court under the "illustrious" John Marshall had "unanimously decided that Congress possessed this bank power." Reports that "an unanimous Cabinet were all united in favor of the bill." Wonders, therefore, whether Tyler "viewed with too lively sensibility the personal consequences to himself of his approval of the bill." Wonders, too, "How is it with that numerous class of public men in this country, and with the two great parties that have divided it, who, at different periods, have maintained and acted on opposite opinions in respect to this very Bank question?" Indeed, how does one explain Madison's opposition in 1791 to the first bank and his approval in 1816 of the second?

Suggests that one honorable option open to Tyler was to allow the bill to become law without his signature. "If the President had retained it three days longer, it would have been a law, without his sanction and without his signature. In such a contingency, the President would have remained passive, and would not have been liable to any accusation of having himself violated the Constitution. All that could have been justly said would be, that he did not choose to throw himself in the way as an obstacle to the passage of a measure indispensable to the prosperity of the nation, in the judgment of the party which brought him into power, of the Whig Congress which he first met, and, if public fame speaks true, of the Cabinet which the lamented Harrison called around him, and which he voluntarily continued." As for Tyler himself, "long my personal friend," it cannot be forgotten "that he came into his present office under peculiar circumstances. The people did not foresee the contingency which has happened. They voted for him as Vice President. They did not, therefore, scrutinize his opinions with the care which they probably ought to have done, and would have done, if they could have looked into futurity. If the present state of the fact could have been anticipated—if at Harrisburg, or at the polls, it had been foreseen that General Harrison would die in one short month after the commencement of his administration; that Vice President Tyler would be elevated to the Presidential chair; that a bill, passed by decisive majorities of the first Whig Congress, chartering a National Bank, would be presented for his sanction; and that he would veto the bill, do I hazard any thing when I express the conviction that he would not have received a solitary vote in the nominating Convention, nor one solitary electoral vote in any State in the Union?" Believes that since five Congresses, four presidents, and the Supreme Court had supported the establishment of a national bank, Tyler "might have suppressed the promptings of all personal pride of private opinion, if any arose in his bosom, and yielded to the wishes and wants of his country." Recalls Tyler's courage in resigning his U.S. Senate seat in February, 1836 rather than obey an instruction from the Virginia general assembly to vote for the expunging resolution [8:735, 820]. Observes: "This he did because he could not conform, and did not think it right to go counter, to the wishes of those who had placed him in the Senate. If, when the people of Virginia, or the General Assembly of Virginia, were his only constituency, he would not set up his own particular opinion in opposition to theirs, what ought to be the rule of his conduct when the people of twenty-six States—a whole nation—compose his constituency? Is the will of the constituency of one State to be respected, and that of twenty-six to be wholly disregarded?" States that he is "firmly convinced, and it is my deliberate judgment, that an immense majority, not less than two-thirds of the nation," desire a national bank.

Discusses the political issues involved in the branching clause of the bank bill. Believes Tyler should know that every one of the 26 senators and 131 representatives who voted for the bill, "if left to his own separate wishes, would have preferred the branching power to have been conferred unconditionally"—as it had been in the charters of the two previous national banks. Yet when Congress consented "to the restrictions upon the exercise of that [branching] power, he [Tyler] must have been perfectly aware that they were actuated by a friendly spirit of compromise and concession. Yet nowhere in his message does he reciprocate or return this spirit." Criticizes Tyler's assertion in the veto message that the branching clause "is the language of the master to the vassal" because that clause denies state legislators the "high privilege" of submitting the branching question to their constituents. Sees no merit in Tyler's further claim that the lower house ("popular branch") of a state legislature could express opposition to a branch bank "by a unanimous vote, and its resolution may be defeated by a tie vote in the Senate"; or that "both branches of the Legislature may concur in a resolution of decided dissent, and yet the Governor may exert the veto power conferred on him by the State constitution, and their legislative action be defeated. . . . To inferences so violent, and as they seem to me irrational, I cannot yield my consent." Clay explains that the language of the compromise branching clause protects the states which want no branch. Clay admits that the Congress "did not, it is true, concede every thing; they did not absolutely renounce the power to establish branches without the authority of the States during the whole period of the existence of the charter; but they did agree that reasonable time should be allowed to the several States to determine whether they would or would not give their assent to the establishment of branches within their respective limits." Estimates that the various states, as they saw fit, would have four to nine months to reject a branch bank. Charges that Tyler has relied on "extreme cases" to attack the branching power in his veto message. Says that Tyler misinterprets the last proviso of the compromise branching section [Porter to Clay, mid-July, 1841, note 6] which, in Clays words "was intended to reserve a power to Congress to compel the Bank to establish branches, if the establishment of them should be necessary to the great purposes of this Government, notwithstanding the dissent of a State. If, for example, a State had once unconditionally dissented to the establishment of a branch, and afterwards assented, the Bank could not have been compelled, without this reservation of power, to establish the branch, however urgent the wants of the Treasury might be." Chides the President for regarding "as objectionable that provision in the clause which declares that, a branch being once established, it should not afterwards be withdrawn or removed without the previous consent of Congress. That provision was intended to operate both upon the Bank and the States. And, considering the changes and fluctuations in public sentiment in some of the States within the last few years, was the security against them to be found in that provision unreasonable?"

Asks just what kind of a bank, if any, Tyler does favor, since he has vetoed this proposal, and "I think it is fairly to be inferred that the plan of the Secretary of the Treasury [Clay to Ewing, June 2, 1841] could not have received his sanction." Has heard that Tyler might be willing to "concur in the establishment of a Bank whose operations should be limited to dealing in bills of exchange, to deposites, and to the supply of a circulation, excluding the power of discounting promissory notes. And I understand that some of our friends are now considering the practicability of arranging and passing a bill in conformity with the views of President Tyler [Tyler to Clay, April 30, 1841]. Whilst I regret that I can take no active part in such an experiment, and must reserve to myself the right of determining whether I can or cannot vote for such a bill after I see it in its matured form, I assure my friends that they shall find no obstacle or impediment in me. On the contrary, I say to them, go on: God speed you in any measure which will serve the country, and preserve or restore harmony and concert between the Departments of Government. An Executive veto of a Bank of the United States after the sad experience of late years, is an event which was not anticipated by the political friends of the President; certainly not by me. But it has come upon us with tremendous weight, and amidst the greatest excitement within and without the metropolis. The question now is, what shall be done?"

Concludes with the rhetorical question: "Shall we adjourn, and go home in disgust? No! No! No! A higher, nobler, and more patriotic career lies before us. Let us here, at the east end of Pennsylvania avenue, do our duty, our whole duty, and nothing short of our duty, towards our common country. We have repealed the Sub-Treasury [Tyler to Clay, April 30, 1841]—we have passed a Bankrupt law [Remark in Senate, April 22, 1840], a beneficent measure of substantial and extensive relief. Let us now pass the bill for the distribution of the proceeds of the public lands [Clay to Ewing, April 30, 1841; Remark in Senate, June 9, 1841], the Revenue bill [Clay to Ewing, April 30, 1841], and the bill for the benefit of the oppressed people of this District. Let us do all—let us do every thing we can for the public good. If we are finally to be disappointed in our hopes of giving to the country a Bank which will once more supply it with a sound currency, still let us go home and tell our constituents that we did all that we could under actual circumstances; and that if we did not carry every measure for their relief, it was only because to do so was impossible." *Cong. Globe*, 27 Cong., 1 Sess., Appendix, 364-66. Printed in Colton, *Clay Correspondence*, 6:274-91. A briefer, summary version of this speech, prepared by *Congressional Globe* reporters, with a rejoinder by Sen. William C. Rives (Dem., Va.), and a counter-rejoinder by Clay, is printed in *Cong. Globe*, 27 Cong., 1 Sess., Appendix, 222-24. See also Krueger, "The Clay-Tyler Feud, 1841-1842," *FCHQ* (April, 1968), 42:162-77. The manuscript version of the speech has not been found.

At this point, Sen. William C. Rives (Dem., Va.) rose to defend Tyler's veto, his character, his behavior as a U.S. senator during the expunging issue of the mid-1830s, his view of the Constitution, his role in the 1840 presidential campaign, specifically, his treatment of the issues in the 1840 election, and his long-standing hostility to a national bank. He presented a detailed refutation of Clay's charges, reminded his audience of Clay's own anti-bank arguments in 1811, and questioned Clay's version of how the Fiscal Bank bill had originated and what it could do for the nation. Clay interrupted Rives seven times with protests and clarifications during his presentation. *Cong. Globe*, 27 Cong., 1 Sess., Appendix, 366-68.

In response to Rives's speech ("I have no desire to prolong this unpleasant discussion"), Clay again takes the floor. He attacks Rives for his lack of party identity and consistent political principles—"there he still stands, solitary and alone, shivering and pelted by the pitiless storm. . . . and now, when there is as complete and perfect a reunion of the purse and the sword in the hands of the Executive as ever there was under General Jackson or Mr. Van Buren, the Senator is for doing nothing!" At a time when "a vast majority of the people of the entire country [are] crying out to us for a Bank—with the people throughout the whole valley of the Mississippi rising in their majesty, and demanding it as indispensble to their well being, and pointing to their losses, their sacrifices, and their sufferings for the want of such an institution—in such a state of things, we are gravely and coldly told by the honorable Senator from Virginia that we had best go home, leaving the purse and the sword in the uncontrolled possession of the President, and above all things, never to make a party Bank!"

Hopes that Rives is not a member of a rumored cabal, "a new sort of kitchen Cabinet—whose object is the dissolution of the regular Cabinet—the dissolution of the Whig party—the dispersion of Congress, without accomplishing any of the great purposes of the extra session—and a total change, in fact, in the whole face of our political affairs." Proceeds to attack Rives's defense of Tyler, pointing out that throughout his [Clay's] criticism of the president's veto message, "I was constantly expressing, over and over, my personal respect and regard for President Tyler, for whom I have cherished an intimate personal friendship of twenty years' standing, and . . . I expressly said that if that friendship should now be interrupted, it should not be my fault. Why, sir, what possible, what conceivable motive can I have to quarrel with the President, or to break up the Whig party? What earthly motive can impel me to wish for any other result than that that party shall remain in perfect harmony, undivided, and shall move undismayed, boldly, and unitedly forward?" That there may be some who are trying "to place me in inimical relations with the President, and to represent me as personally opposed to him, I can well imagine—individuals who are beating up for recruits, and endeavoring to form a third party, with materials so scanty as to be wholly insufficient to compose a decent corporal's guard. I fear there are such individuals, though I do not charge the Senator as being himself one of them."

Points to the "spectacle" that is the activity of the political enemies of Tyler who have suddenly become "his exclusive and genuine friends" because of his bank veto. As for himself, "I have . . . known the President too long, and cherished toward him too sincere a friendship, to allow my feelings to be affected or alienated by any thing which has passed here to-day. If the President chooses—which I am sure he cannot, unless falsehood has been whispered into his ears or poison poured into his heart—to detach himself from me, I shall deeply regret it, for the sake of our common friendship and our common country." Assures Rives that he is wrong in declaring that the bank question was not an issue in the 1840 election. Perhaps it was not an issue in Virginia, but "wherever I was—in the great valley of the Mississippi, in Kentucky, in Tennessee, in Maryland—in all the circles in which I moved, every where, 'Bank or no Bank' was the great, the leading, the vital question. At Hanover, in Virginia, during the last summer [Speech in Taylorsville, Hanover County, Va., June 27, 1840], at one of the most remarkable and respectable and gratifying assemblages that I ever attended, I distinctly announced my conviction that a Bank of the United States was indispensable." Also denies Rives's contention that he [Clay] had called for Tyler's resignation. Explains: "I intimated no personal wish or desire that he should resign. I referred to the fact of a memorable resignation in his public life. And what I did say was, that there were other alternatives before him besides vetoing the bill; and that it was worthy of his consideration whether consistency did not require that the example which he had set when he had a constituency of one State [Virginia], should not be followed, when he had a constituency commensurate with the whole Union. Another alternative was to suffer the bill, without his signature, to pass into a law under the provisions of the Constitution. . . . I referred to the majorities in the two Houses of Congress as further and strong evidence of the opinion of the people of the United States in favor of the establishment of a Bank of the United States. And I contended that according to the doctrine of instruction which prevailed in Virginia, and of which the President is a disciple, and in pursuance of the example already cited, he ought not to have rejected the bill." As for Tyler's veto of the bank bill, "It did not enter into my imagination to conceive that one who had shown so much deference and respect to the presumed sentiments of a single State, should display less towards the sentiments of the whole nation." Concludes with a reaffirmation of his "personal regard and esteem" for President Tyler. *Ibid.*, 368-69.

Rives responded with a second speech in defense of Tyler in answer to Clay's second speech in opposition to Tyler's veto. *Ibid.*, 369-70. Colton prints Clay's second speech in *Clay Correspondence*, 6:291-96. These speeches were published in pamphlet form under the title, *Speeches Delivered by H. Clay, of Kentucky, in the Senate of the United States, on the 19th of August, 1841, on the Message of President Tyler . . . and in Reply to Mr. Rives. . . .* Washington, 1841. Clay later complained that his anti-veto speech was "published without my revisal" and hoped to be able to "correct and revise it before it is published in any durable collection [Clay to Swain, July 18, 1842; Clay to Sargent, August 20, 1842]." For the membership of the "new sort of kitchen cabinet" said by Clay to surround Tyler, most of whom (in Clay's opinion) also comprised the president's "Corporal's Guard," see Chitwood, *John Tyler*, 270-71.

From Wade Hampton, near Columbia, S.C., August 20, 1841. Hopes Clay will decide to purchase Sovereign [Clay to Thomas H. Clay, August 15, 1841], "a horse, in very high form," which "will I think suit your countrymen, better than Monarch, being much more showy."

Regarding politics, states that "We are anxiously expecting to hear the fate of the Bank bill [Tyler to Clay, April 30, 1841; Clay to Ewing, June 2, 1841; Speech in Senate, June 21, 1841]." Adds: "Should the President return it with his veto, I for one, shall dispair for the Republic; if our friends betray us, what can we expect from our opponents." ALS. DLC-TJC (DNA, M212, R10). Printed in Colton, *Clay Correspondence*, 4:454-55.

From Peter B. Porter, Buffalo, August 20, 1841. Reports that he arrived "here about an hour ago, and met the Veto of the President on the Bank Bill [Tyler to Clay, April 30, 1841; Clay to Ewing, June 2, 1841; Speech in Senate, June 21, 1841]." States that "This extraordinary step of the President, although long threatened, was never realized nor believed until this moment, and has excited universal dissatisfaction and even disgust among the members of the Whig party. The Locofocos are of course, in an extacy of pleasure." Believes that a general meeting of the Whig party will soon be held in Buffalo "for the purpose of Expressing, mildly, but yet decidedly, our disapprobation of the President's course." Copy. OHi. The Whigs held a meeting in Buffalo on August 30 to disapprove Tyler's bank veto. New Yord *Herald*, September 3, 1841.

Remark in Senate, August 20, 1841. During debate on the land (distribution) bill [Clay to Ewing, April 30, 1841; Remark in Senate, June 9, 1841], Clay asks William S. Archer (Va.) not to persist in his amendment to set aside 500,000 acres to satisfy existing Virginia military claims. Assures Archer he will later, as a separate measure, see to it that those claims are justly dealt with. *Cong. Globe*, 27 Cong., 1 Sess., 357. The Archer amendment was voted down *viva voce*.

During this same debate Calhoun observes that an amendment by Levi Woodbury (Dem., N.H.) to the distribution bill, which would halt distribution whenever the government had to borrow money or raise import duties above 20% to meet public expenditures, was an opportunity for "Southern members to test the sincerity of the gentlemen on the other side, with regard to the Compromise [tariff] act" of 1833 [8:604, 619-22, 626-27]. To this Clay remarks that "they would be able to prove their sincerity when the tariff bill [Clay to Ewing, April 30, 1841; Remark in Senate, July 16, 1841] came up." When Calhoun insists that the time to adopt the 20% tariff limit is now, Clay asks that he be patient "till the tariff bill came up," and promises him that the new administration will also undertake "all necessary retrenchment and economy" of government. Asked by Calhoun if he would care to talk about other Whig "virtues," such as the administration's proscription policy, Clay, from his seat, responds: "We will talk about that in cooler weather." *Ibid.*, 358. Woodbury's amendment was beaten, 15 to 26, Clay voting nay.

Remark in Senate, August 23, 1841. Urges his colleagues to proceed with the land (distribution) bill [Clay to Ewing, April 30, 1841; Remark in Senate, June 9, 1841] until it is disposed of so that the important revenue (duties and drawbacks) bill [Remark in Senate, July 16, 1841] can be taken up. During debate this day on the distribution bill, Woodbury introduces an amendment that would halt distribution whenever the government had to borrow money [Remark in Senate, August 20, 1841] and resume it only when the national debt was extinguished. Clay responds that the Democrats had created such a large debt which the present administration now has to pay off "it might be necessary to effect a further loan [Clay to Ewing, July 13, 1841] in December to meet the wants of the Treasury." Adds that a loan of five or six million might have to be made in September, in anticipation of income from the tariff bill, if that legislation is passed. Hopes that under the proposed new tariff legislation the debts of the Van Buren administration can be paid off in four years; also, the expenses of the government under decreasing revenue can still be met. Asserts that Woodbury's amendment will "destroy" the distribution bill. *Cong. Globe*, 27 Cong., 1 Sess., 369-70. The Woodbury amendment was defeated, 21 to 26, Clay voting nay.

Remark in Senate, August 24, 1841. Seconds the motion that a second bank bill [Tyler to Clay, April 30, 1841], styled "the Fiscal Corporation of the United States," received from the House this day, and twice read, be referred to a select committee. Asks that he not be placed on the select committee. Adds that whether he supports this bill or not will depend on whether his "friends on the committee" can present "some practicable and useful scheme of a Bank of the United States." *Cong. Globe*, 27 Cong., 1 Sess., 372. The Senate's Select Committee on the Fiscal Corporation, appointed on this day by president of the Senate, *pro tempore*, Samuel L. Southard (Whig, N.J.), consisted of John M. Berrien (Whig, Ga.), George Evans (Whig, Me.), William S. Archer (Whig, Va.), James T. Morehead (Whig, Ky.), and Jabez W. Huntington (Whig, Conn.). U.S. Sen., *Journal*, 27 Cong., 1 Sess., 213.

For the legislative history of the Fiscal Corporation bill in the House, which passed the measure 125 to 94 on August 23, after but two and a half days of debate, see *Cong. Globe*, 27 Cong., 1 Sess., 363-64, 366-68, 370-72. The bill is printed in U.S. H. of Reps., *Journal*, 27 Cong., 1 Sess., 497-509. Compare its provisions with the language of its predecessor, the Fiscal Bank [*Sen. Docs.*, 27 Cong., 1 Sess., no. 32, pp. 7-20] bill. Note that the corporation's capitalization was $21 million rather than the bank's $30 million. Its debt limit was $17.5 million rather than $25 million. Its branches were called "agencies" rather than "offices of discount and deposit" and could be established at any time in any state or territory. Like its predecessor, the corporation's agencies could receive, disburse, and transmit public monies; they could also deal in foreign and/or interstate bills of exchange. The principal difference, however, between the corporation and the bank (a result of criticisms in Tyler's veto of the latter) was that the agencies, unlike the offices of discount and deposit, could not make local discounts on commercial paper such as promissory notes [Crittenden to Clay, August 16, 1841]. On the other hand, the Fiscal Corporation bill did not address Tyler's constitutional concern that Congress, acting as the national legislature rather than the legislature of the District of Columbia, was creating a corporation with power to operate (in the words of his veto) "*per se* over the Union." He feared, too, that the corporation and its agencies might enter the local discount business under the guise of dealing in bills of exchange. See Chitwood, *John Tyler* 242-46; Van Deusen, *Life of Henry Clay*, 351-54; Speech to Whig Senatorial Caucus, September 13, 1841.

Later this day, Clay opposes a motion to go into executive session, hoping instead that the land (distribution) bill [Clay to Ewing, April 30, 1841; Remark in Senate, June 9, 1841] would be passed today and returned to the House. Motion withdrawn. The debate on the land bill continues, but without coming to a final vote. *Cong. Globe*, 27 Cong., 1 Sess., 372. The land (distribution) bill was passed 28 to 23 on August 26.

Remark in Senate, August 25, 1841. During Sen. Levi Woodbury's lengthy speech attacking the administration's public land (distribution) bill [Clay to Ewing, April 30, 1841; Remark in Senate, June 9, 1841], at the point he was explaining that the projected distribution amounts were so low that they would have little or no real effect on the massive debt levels of most of the states, Clay interrupts to ask: "What will you do with North Carolina who owes nothing?" Woodbury asks for Clay's patience, promising an answer in a moment. *Cong. Globe*, 27 Cong., 1 Sess., Appendix, 250.

Remark in Senate, August 27, 1841. States that he did not expect the tariff (duties and drawbacks) bill [Clay to Ewing, April 30, 1841; Remark in Senate, July 16, 1841] to come up today. Explains, however, why the Committee on Finance recommends an amendment to the House bill that would raise the duty on certain gold and silver items (watches, jewelry) from 12½% to 20%. Since these were clearly luxury items, there were both political and economical reasons for passing the amendment, even though the smuggling of these articles might increase. Asks for a vote on the amendment in spite of Calhoun's complaint that the Senate required prior notice that the tariff issue would be brought up. Says Clay: "I give you notice now. Start! Start!" Following passage of the amendment, 41 to 5, further discussion of the bill was postponed when Clay agreed that the Senate go into executive session. *Cong. Globe*, 27 Cong., 1 Sess., 390-91.

To AMBROSE SPENCER Washington, August 27, 1841

The death of our friend Mr. G. Lee, for which your favor of the 5h. prepared me, is announced.[1] I lament it extremely. He was a good man; and his loss will be felt extensively.

The papers will inform you of the extraordinary state of things here. The Whigs present the image of a Body with its head cut off. Yet that body is powerful, united & indivisible. We have lost a few, but very few, by desertion; the residue are stronger from that fact. In what all this state of things will end, it is difficult to conjecture. The President, I apprehend, will leave us; it is more doubtful where he will go.[2] We have made some sacrifices, may make more, to retain him; but the seeds of mutual distrust are, I fear, so extensively sown that it will be difficult to reunite and harmonize us all again.

We have now passed in Congress all our great measures, and one more (the Bankrupt bill)[3] than I thought was practicable at this Extra Session. If the President had been cordially with us what a glorious summer this of 1841 would be!

ALS. InHi. Letter marked "(Confidential)." 1. For Gideon Lee, see *BDAC*. He died on August 21. 2. Tyler to Clay, April 30, 1841; Speech in Senate, August 19, 1841. 3. Remark in Senate, April 22, 1840.

From AARON CLARK New York, August 28, 1841

I learn that the Commissioners to enquire into matters Connected with our Custom House left our City yesterday for Washington City.[1] I have never troubled you with a note relative to our situation & prospects as a party occasioned by the appointment of a Collector for us. I was in March a candidate for it, and Genl. Harrison behaved towards me so insanely, & so much like a drunken Barbaric chieftain, that I was disgusted & silent. Now, tho' I would Cheerfully take the Office I am not contending for it[.] We have many Whigs competent & worthy, but to say how they are to obtain a nomination—that's the wonder!

Well—the Commissioners are gone—will report & we hope strict & exact justice will be done. Believing as I do statements semi official made to me, I do not see how Mr. Curtiss [*sic,* Edward Curtis] can be Confirmed.[2] Of these you will judge on examination of the report. And here let me say that Govr. [George] Poindexter has Conducted himself while here in a manner to command the esteem & high Consideration of all the people.[3] As an Officer, a man & a gentleman he has won many golden Opinions in addition to those which constituted his acknowledged fame before. *He* has properly regarded the responsibilities of his appointment. Should there be a change of Cabinet I should rejoice to see him in the War Dept—He would win laurels there.

But let us suppose that there were no charges whatever against Mr. Curtiss, the fact of two young men, *both members of Congress* returning to this City with the two best Offices of our nation in their own pockets is enough to ruin any party & especially a high minded & honorable one.[4] I believe I speak advisedly & correctly when I declare that so long as Mr. Curtiss remains Collector there is no hope of carrying this City for the *Whigs*—Of this I am perfectly confident. We spent our time & money to put Mr. Curtiss into Congress for four years—when he was *honored* by our Suffrages—In the mean time we have been laboring for the Whig ascendancy presuming that should we triumph our members of Congress would advise & aid us as to office. But no—nothing got me but the cold Shoulder—No Countenance—but on applying found our members claimed that they made Genl Harrison President by defeating the nomination of Mr. Clay & they successfully insisted upon the best places for themselves—they got them—And now having overwhelmed the Prest. by their Congressional pipe laying, & nearly broken down our party by their sinister policy, they will exhort us to Union—to vigorous action—to magnanimity—& cry out that the Constitution is in danger. But Sir we shall not & wi[ll] not be led by Mr. Curtiss—no mistake.

Pardon my frank mention of another matter. We know the *monstrous* extent of Mr. Curtiss' labors to defeat the nomination of Mr. Clay previous to the last Convention: that by various givings out he thrust Mr. Clay from a nomination—Immolated him—Mr. Curtiss *knows* that for this Mr. Clay must & does most deeply detest & despise him.[5] He will forever war on Mr. Clay. Already many of the former friends of Mr. Clay now placed under Mr. Curtiss in the Custom House declare that Mr. [Winfield] Scott will & must be the next President. But the most of those whom he retains & whom he appoints are known to be those who always go against Mr. Clay. I am not speaking at random. Once more let me say that Mr. Curtiss cannot carry our party with him—no[r] do us any harm if relieved of his power in the Custom House. I send you a newspaper containing a touch of his ingenuity, & respectfully Solicit you to ask Gov. Poindexter if it be *true*?[6] I understood him very differently. We are grieved to observe the general aspect—of affairs at Washington. But Comment from me would be unavailing. I forbear—& wait the issue. Another grief we have is that a purse-proud locofoco holds our Post Office—[7]

Rely upon it D[ea]r. Sir, that while Mr. Clay, like many others is addressed by some hypocrits & jesuits he has had many thousands of warm friends—thousands will [words illeg.] honor him who has so often "dared be hone[s]t in the worst of times—" yes they will ch[e]rish affectionately the fame of him.

"Who stands like Mount Atlas when Storms & tempests thunder on its brow. And Oceans break their billows at its feet"—

ALS, manuscript torn. DLC-Willie P. Mangum Papers (DNA, M212, R22). 1. Allegations of corruption in the New York customhouse led to the appointment on May 10, 1841, of George Poindexter, Alfred Kelley (later replaced by William A. Bradley), and William M. Stuart as a commission to investigate the situation. Poindexter's report is published in *House Reports*, 27 Cong., 2 Sess., no. 669 and the report of the entire commission (which failed to agree on the allegations) is in *House Exec. Doc.* 6, 27 Cong., 2 Sess. When Tyler submitted the report to Congress on April 30, 1842, he recommended legislation to prevent fraud in the future collection of revenues. *MPP*, 4:152-54. 2. Lawrence to Clay, Nov. 30, 1840. 3. See footnote 1, above. 4. Edward Curtis and Francis Granger, appointed collector of customs in New York and postmaster general, respectively. 5. Porter to Clay, Feb. 16, 1839; Lawrence to Clay, Nov. 30, 1840; Porter to Clay, Jan. 28, 1841. 6. Reference obscure. 7. J.I. Coddington had been appointed as New York City postmaster by Van Buren and held the office until John L. Graham was confirmed for the post on March 12, 1842. U.S. Sen. *Executive Journal*, 6:36, 38, 40.

Remark in Senate, August 28, 1841. Urges the Senate to proceed with the fortification bill [Remark in Senate, August 2, 1841] and concurring or not in the House amendments to it. Opposes the Senate amendment which would appropriate $75,000 for purchase of an armory site in the West, Southwest, or Northwest. Points out that if the selection of the site is left to the president (as proposed in the amendment), he would leave it to a Cabinet secretary who would in turn leave it to a bureau head. For such an "enormous price" as $75,000 "Congress should retain control." Notes that in the House all but two Whig representatives from the West had voted against the western armory proposal. Notes particularly that placing it in Pittsburgh would not be a good idea, since "in case of a certain horrible event [war with Britain]" the new armory would be located in "an eastern city at the head of a river which . . . [is] dried up all summer and frozen up all winter." *Cong. Globe*, 27 Cong., 1 Sess., 396-97. The amendment was again passed, this time by 24 to 19 margin, Clay again voting nay. For earlier Senate action on the western armory concept, see Remark in Senate, August 2, 1841.

Later this day, during debate on the tariff bill [Clay to Ewing, April 30, 1841; Remark in Senate, July 16, 1841], Clay notes that the amendment (which passed) putting palm leaf on the free list was really of small consequence, since the item was of "little value" and was "used by the girls of the nation to make bonnets and hats." *Cong. Globe*, 27 Cong., 1 Sess., 399.

Also favors an amendment putting foreign-grown sumach on the free list, since it was often cheaper than the domestic product. Informs Calhoun, who cheers this presumed evidence of Clay's sudden dedication to free trade, that his stance on the sumach amendment should not be interpreted to mean that he was a convert to free trade. Accuses Calhoun of trying "to reduce everything to his system of abstractions," and notes that he bases those "abstractions on the theories of books—on English authorities, and on the arguments used in favor of free trade by a certain party in the British Parliament." Reminds Calhoun that a recent general election in England removed from power the [Melbourne], Ministry dedicated to the free trade principles of "that astute and ingenious Scotchman, Mr. [Joseph] Hume" whose "own constituents repudiated him and his principles. On that very question he lost his election." Asserts that on the tariff issue the English are increasingly adopting the actual "practice of nations"; they are renouncing "men, theories, and abstractions" and have, instead, decided that "the first duty of their Ministry is to protect the British nation, and British interests, in preference to running wildly into abstract principles." Denies Calhoun's contention that the principles and policies of the British Tory party and the American Whig party are identical, especially on such issues as corporate monopolies, high tariffs, and a national bank; also on such laws as the protective corn laws, which are oppressive to most of the people, and on sympathy for the Negroes of the West Indies [8:641]. Points out that the issue now before the Senate is "whether *sumach* was or was not to be admitted free of duty," not a continued analysis of the parties and party politics of the British. Amendment passed *viva voce. Ibid.*, 399-400. Lord Melbourne's government, which in the spring of 1841 was twice defeated on a tariff measure in Commons, appealed to the country and was defeated. He finally resigned on August 28 following a vote of censure and was succeeded by Sir Robert Peel. William L. Langer (ed.), *An Encyclopedia of World History*, 4th. ed. (Boston, 1968), 659. For Hume's report, see Clay to Ewing, April 30, 1841. Hume lost his seat in Commons from the Leeds district in the 1841 elections. *DNB*.

Moves that bleaching powder and cream of tartar be added to the free list. Amendment laid over. Supports next an amendment by James Buchanan (Dem., Pa.) that would repeal the laws which admit iron for railroads free of duty. Notes that a duty on iron would encourage American railroad growth, protect the domestic iron-manufacturing industry, and "add very considerably to the revenue." Amendment laid over. *Cong. Globe*, 27 Cong., 1 Sess., 400.

From James Ogden, New York, August 30, 1841. Writes to urge that the Senate not give up on passing a second national bank bill. Notes that "It now appears . . . that after securing the passage of nearly every measure, (*save one*) . . . the key stone of the arch, is to be defeated by the ignorance and treachery combined, of an accidental President [Tyler to Clay, April 30, 1841]." Believes "the only remaining question" is: "*Shall the present bank bill be permitted to sleep on the table of the Senate*?" Asks: "Is it President Tyler who wishes this course to be pursued, in order to spair him the *pain* or the consequence of another veto? What possible consideration does he deserve at the hands of a cabinet whom he has deceived and insulted—of a party whom he has not only slighted but betrayed—" Continues: "What certainty exists that the Ho[use] of Repre. which has so nobly performed its duty, this Session, will condescend, at the next, to submit another bank bill to John Tyler? Can any reasonable hope be entertained that John Tyler, of the next Session, will be a different man from John Tyler of the present? Can any reliance be placed on his promises? Did he not ask the advice of his cabinet, and then without informing them of any change of mind, send in his veto without deigning to submit it to their consideration? Did he not give assurances that he would sign the first bill? Did not his constitutional advisers believe, untill almost the last day, that he might or would sign that bill? while at the same time the ennemies of the measure, and the Opponents of his administration, knew, with certainty, its approaching fate?" Asks if the second bank bill has not been prepared in conformity with "the opinions contained in the veto message." Believes, nevertheless, that "this bill, too, after passing Congress, must, when it reaches the President, share the fate of its predecessor."

Doubts that Clay is particularily "aware of the degree of *lukewarmness* that exists in some quarters—among some interests, and among certain men who lead public opinion in their own districts, on the subject of a real efficient national bank." Argues for "the absolute necessity" of passing the second bank bill and thus "requiring of John Tyler either to sign or to veto," because "if the bill be not presented to him, inferences will be drawn far less unfavorable to him than to them who shall have prevented its passage in the Senate. . . . True policy therefore demands that the President should be required to sign or to veto the bill of his own adoption, if not creation. a bill of which even our new England brethren would not disapprove—a fiscal agent which loco focoism itself could not condemn, an act which State rights *abstractionists* must admit to be within the power of Congress to pass. Compel the President to veto this bill and you put him in a position he richly deserves, and gain over him all the advantage which our present unfortunate position, arising from his conduct, enables us to secure." Thinks that if the Whigs give up on the bank bill now, they "would surrender the cardinel point of their policy, and without which all their other measures lose more than half their value." ALS, manuscript torn. DLC-Willie P. Mangum Papers (DNA, M212, R22).

For Ogden (*ca.* 1790-1870), a New York merchant, see *NCAB*, 1:499. For Tyler's own bank plan proposal, his so-called "Board of Exchequer," see Clay to James Brown Clay, December 10, 1841.

Remark in Senate, August 30, 1841. Presents a memorial from manufacturers of chloride of lime (bleaching powders) asking for a duty on the imported article. Tabled. *Cong. Globe*, 27 Cong., 1 Sess., 402.

Later this day, complains that three hours have already been spent today debating Buchanan's amendment of August 28 to put a duty on railroad iron [Remark in Senate, August 28, 1841]. Urges his colleagues to move more expeditiously on this legislation if they hope to adjourn soon. Points out that when iron was placed on the free list in 1832, "the Treasury was overflowing," which is not the case now. Also notes that at the present time the United States and Europe have "nearly an equal capacity to produce iron" and that in less than five years, if Buchanan's amendment is adopted, the price of foreign iron will drop because there will be "an American rival in the trade." To Calhoun's suggestion that if Clay really wants to terminate this session of the Senate soon, he need only withdraw his [second] bank bill [Tyler to Clay, April 30, 1841; Remark in Senate, August 24, 1841] and his tariff bill [Clay to Ewing, April 30, 1841; Remark in Senate, July 16, 1841], Clay responds: "Never, never! No, not if we stay here till Christmas." Informs Sen. Robert J. Walker (Ala.) that while his mind is "thoroughly made up" on the second bank bill, he will not now announce how he will vote on it. *Ibid.*, 404. Buchanan amendment tabled.

Still later this day, during debate on the Senate amendments to H.R. 4, the House distribution and preemption bill [Clay to Ewing, April 30, 1841; Remark in Senate, June 9, 1841], Clay asks that the Senate support the motion of Sen. Oliver H. Smith (Whig, Ind.) to recede from those three of its 23 amendments to the bill not accepted by the House—amendments 2, 3, and 6—which "provide that the distribution shall be made to the States according to their respective Federal representation in the two Houses of Congress." Points out that "the opposition to the motion was made solely with a view of defeating the bill," and urges "friends of the measure to rally in its support and prevent that object." *Ibid.*, 405-6; U.S. Sen., *Journal*, 27 Cong., 1 Sess., 221-22. The Smith motion to recede from amendments 2, 3, and 6 was passed 25 to 18, Clay voting yea.

To HENRY CLAY, JR. Washington, August 31, 1841

I have not heard from you since I transmitted some letters to you, at your request. From home my last accounts were very favorable.

All here is uncertainty as to the course and designs of the President. The general belief is that he will veto the new bank bill,[1] if it be sent to him. We are to take it up tomorrow in the Senate. The present state of painful suspense is worse than any conceivable condition, and I sincerely hope that the President will soon define his actual position. I shall vote for the new bank bill upon the same grounds which all our friends will occupy—not because it is what we would have it, but because it has been framed to suit the Presidents views, as I understand they were communicated.

When will you join us? I hope the Session will not be prolonged beyond next week. . . .[2]

ALS. Henry Clay Memorial Foundation, Lexington, Ky. Addressed to Henry Clay, Jr., in New York City. 1. Tyler to Clay, April 30, 1841. 2. The session ended on Sept. 13, 1841.

Remark in Senate, August 31, 1841. On the question of whether the appropriation for the Post Office should include an amendment to hire 13 additional clerks at a cost of $13,000, Clay supports a modification of the amendment which would limit to no more than one year the service of such clerks. Amendment carried 29 to 18, Clay voting yea. *Cong. Globe*, 27 Cong., 1 Sess., 408.

Later this day, Clay complains that the business of the Senate is proceeding too slowly and reports that the "other House . . . was now ready to adjourn at any moment." Asks that such problems as the franking privilege and the mileage payment to members be put over to the "regular session" in December. Points out that only two bills remain to be disposed of—the bank bill and the tariff bill. Says it is a "matter of very little consequence how they were disposed of, although he confessed he had a wish upon that point." Hopes, however, that the Senate will either pass or reject them "at once." Objects to allusions by the Democrats that he has established "gag laws" in the Senate. Thinks this charge is ridiculous and expresses again his "conviction of the necessity of insuring to the majority in the Senate the same control of the business which the majority in the other House had secured to itself." *Ibid.*, 410-11.

Remark in Senate, September 1, 1841. Says that it is his understanding that the bank bill [Remark in Senate, August 24, 1841] was to be taken up today, rather than the tariff (revenue) bill [Clay to Ewing, April 30, 1841; Remark in Senate, July 16, 1841]. If so, explains that the bank ("Fiscal Corporation") bill "came to the Senate from the Committee on Finance precisely in the form in which it had been sent from the House of Representatives; it was a bill to establish a Bank of Exchange; it was just the half of that whole, which, as he understood, the Senator from Virginia [William C. Rives] had been prepared to advocate; though but half the loaf, it still was better than no bread; and, although it was for a Bank not exactly such as [he] could desire, he was nevertheless prepared to vote for it. It was not without reluctance that he had brought up his mind to that point; but, having done so, he had now come to the Senate to give that vote." Motion to take up the Fiscal Corporation bill, setting aside the tariff bill, passes 34 to 14, Clay voting yea. *Cong. Globe*, 27 Cong., 1 Sess., 417-18.

Later in this same debate, Clay reports that while the Fiscal Corporation bill falls "short—far short" of providing the kind of bank the nation needs and expects, it nonetheless "proposed the establishment of a bank which would accomplish two of the great objects, which any bank could effect; the one was the regulation of the exchanges of the country, and the other, the supply of a currency possessing an uniform value throughout the Union." He would therefore vote for the bill "because, although it did not all the good which might be effected from an institution of this kind, it did much—a great deal." Concludes his remarks on this day with the presentation of a petition from Erie, Pa., asking for the establishment of a "United States Bank." Requests that it be tabled. *Ibid.*, 418.

Comment in Senate, September 2, 1841. Joins the "long and animated debate" on the Fiscal Corporation bill, pointing out that there "are two great faculties which ordinarily belong to banks: one is to deal in that sort of commercial paper which is called promissory notes; the other to deal in bills of exchange, also an ordinary commercial instrument. By the present bill, the Bank which is to be created is deprived of one of these faculties, while the other is left to it [Remark in Senate, August 24, 1841]: and there is no more danger of abuse in the exercise of the retained faculty by this corporation than in the ordinary banks of the country." Condemns Tyler's veto of the Fiscal Bank bill [Tyler to Clay, April 30, 1841; Remark in Senate, August 16, 1841], and asserts that the Whigs "are willing to go before the people" in opposition to the belief of the Democrats in "Executive Supremacy" and "the arbitrary principle that the will of one man shall prevail against the will of the whole country," which is "an odious and detestable doctrine." Regrets that on the night of Tyler's veto (August 16) there were disturbances on the White House grounds. Says that he has heard "that about eight or nine o'clock on that same night of the famous 16th of August, there was an irruption on the President's House of the whole Loco Foco party in Congress. . . . I understand that the whole party were there. No spectacle, I am sure, could have been more supremely amusing and ridiculous. If I could have been in a position in which, without being seen, I could have witnessed that most extraordinary reunion, I should have had an enjoyment which no dramatic performance could possibly communicate. I think that I can now see the principal *dramatis personae* who figured in the scene. There stood the grave and distinguished Senator from South Carolina [Mr. CALHOUN here instantly rose, and earnestly insisted on explaining; but Mr. CLAY refused to be interrupted or to yield the floor.]

"[Clay continues:] There, I say, I can imagine stood the Senator from South Carolina—tall, care-worn, with furrowed brow, haggard, and intensely gazing, looking as if he were dissecting the last and newest abstraction which sprung from metaphysician's brain, and muttering to himself, in half-uttered sounds, 'This is indeed a real crisis!' [Loud laughter.] Then there was the Senator from Alabama, [William R. King] standing upright and gracefully, as if he were ready to settle in the most authoritative manner any question of order or of etiquette that might possibly arise between the high assembled parties on that new and unprecedented occasion. Not far off stood the honorable Senators from Arkansas and from Missouri [Ambrose H. Sevier and Thomas H. Benton], the latter looking at the Senator from South Carolina, with an indignant curl on his lip and scorn in his eye, and pointing his finger with contempt towards that Senator [Calhoun], whilst he said, or rather seemed to say, 'He calls himself a statesman! why, he has never even produced a decent humbug!' [Shouts of laughter.]

"[Mr. BENTON. The Senator from Missouri was not there.]

"[Clay continues:] I stand corrected; I was only imagining what you would have said if you had been there. [Renewed laughter.] Then there stood the Senator from Georgia [Alfred Cuthbert], conning over in his mind on what point he should make his next attack upon the Senator from Kentucky. [Laughter.] On yonder ottoman reclined the other Senator from Missouri on my left [Lewis F. Linn], indulging, with smiles on his face, in pleasing meditations on the rise, growth, and future power of his new colony of Oregon. The honorable Senator from Pennsylvania [James Buchanan], I presume, stood forward as spokesman for his whole party; and, although I cannot pretend to imitate his well-known eloquence, I beg leave to make an humble essay towards what I presume to have been the kind of speech delivered by him on that august occasion: 'May it please your Excellency: A number of your present political opponents, in company with myself, have come to deposite at your Excellency's feet the evidences of our loyalty and devotion. . . . We are here more particularly to present to your Excellency our grateful and most cordial congratulations on your rescue of the country from a flagrant and alarming violation of the Constitution, by the creation of a Bank of the United States; and also our profound acknowledgments for the veto, by which you have illustrated the wisdom of your Administration, and so greatly honored yourself. . . . We had been, ourselves, struggling for days and weeks to arrest the passage of the bill, and to prevent the creation of the monster to which it gives birth. . . . And we have now come most hardily to thank your Excellency that you have accomplished for us that against your friends which we with our most strenous exertions were unable to achieve.' [Roars of laughter.]"

In a less facetious vein, Clay wonders if it is possible that "a President of the United States, elected by the Whig party to a different station, and having arrived at the Presidency under circumstances calculated to call forth his most profound gratitude, should abandon the party which elevated him; should commit an act worse than treason, and join that party of which the Senator [Buchanan] is a distinguished member, but to which the President has been diametrically opposed?" Explains that "I do not pretend to know what may be his [Tyler's] feelings, but sure I am that were I in his situation, and the possibility of such an act of treachery were affirmed of me, the reproach would fill my heart to its inmost recesses with horror and loathing." Points out past differences between Tyler's stances on various political issues and that of "the Loco Foco party." Cannot believe that Tyler can now make an accommodation with the Democrats, because "The soil of Virginia is too pure to produce traitors. Small, indeed, is the number of those who have proved false to their principles and to their party. I knew the father of the President, Judge [John] Tyler, of the General Court in Virginia, and a purer patriot or more honest man never breathed the breath of life; and I am one of those who hold to the safety which flows from honest ancestors and the purity of blood."

Concludes with the observation that Democrats "are exulting over an event which never can and never will happen. No, gentlemen, the President never will disgrace himself, disgrace his blood, disgrace his State, disgrace his country, disgrace his children, by abandoning his party, and joining with you. Never, never. If it were among the possibilities of human turpitude to perpetrate an act like that, I cannot conceive on what principle or for what reason the President could rush upon a deed so atrocious, and deliver himself over to infamy so indelible. . . . what does history tell us the fate has been of every traitor? And what ought that fate to be? If there is any thing like agreement between John Tyler and the Loco Foco party, it is simply and exclusively on this question of a Bank. On that one point I admit that there is a great and unhappy difference of opinion between him and his political friends; but how can he by possibility go over to the other party, from whom he has always differed on every other point? On all other points—the distribution of the proceeds of the public lands, the bankrupt law, public economy and reform—he agrees with us. Gentlemen chuckle in the confidence that he is going to veto this bill [Tyler to Clay, April 30, 1841]. I do not myself think he will. But, even if he does; still I say it is a moral impossibility that there ever can exist so infamous, so unnatural a union, as that between a President who has betrayed one party, and the other party directly opposed to him, who must have too much regard to their character and the opinion of mankind to receive and embrace him, if it were possible that he could prove false and faithless to his friends." *Cong. Globe*, 27 Cong., 1 Sess., Appendix, 344-45. For an account of the anti-Tyler demonstration on the White House lawn during the night of August 16-17, and the burning of Tyler in effigy the following evening, see Chitwood, *John Tyler*, 228-30.

Later in this day's debate on the Fiscal Corporation bill, Sen. William C. Rives (Va.) expressed his indignation at the "impropriety and unparliamentary character of the debate." Criticizes the "strong terms of denunciation hypothetically employed" by Clay—a denunciation conditioned by the possibility of Tyler's veto of the bill. Not so, Clay responds. Asserts that his remarks "were conditioned on the President foresaking his party, and going over to the Loco Focos." *Cong. Globe*, 27 Cong., 1 Sess., Appendix, 346.

Remark in Senate, September 3, 1841. Following the passage this day of the Fiscal Corporation bill [Tyler to Clay, April 30, 1841; Remark in Senate, August 24, 1841] and further debate on the amendment to the fortification bill reducing from $75,000 to $5,000 the appropriation for a western armory site survey [Remark in Senate, August 2, 1841], Clay remarks that "the sessions had been so long and exhausting of late, that he did not feel disposed to go on with the revenue bill [Clay to Ewing, April 30, 1841; Remark in Senate, July 16, 1841] this evening." Asks that it be taken up tomorrow and promises that his remarks thereon will take but 30 to 45 minutes [Comment in Senate, September 4, 1841]. *Cong. Globe*, 27 Cong., 1 Sess., 423.

Comment in Senate, September 4, 1841. With reference to the pending revenue (tariff) bill [Clay to Ewing, April 30, 1841; Remark in Senate, July 16, 1841], and with the assumption that it will not pass, Clay submits Treasury Department figures to show that the actual federal revenue from customs, public land sales, and various miscellaneous items for the first half of 1841 totalled $7,642,075.76, while expenditures for the same period totalled $14,431,512.75—thus there is already this year a known deficit of $6,789,437.00. Predicts that government income for the second half of 1841 will likely be $7,005,026.29 and expenditures $16,116,560.47, or a probable deficit of $9,111,534.18. The total deficit for 1841 will therefore be $15,900,971.18. Notes that the whole of the $12,000,000 loan [Clay to Ewing, July 13, 1841], as well as the $4,500,000 appropriated by the Extra Session (first Session), will be wholly absorbed by this projected deficit and that "at the end of this year, there would not be a single dollar in the Treasury." Predicts that in 1842 "there would be only four millions of clear revenue, after paying off the incumbrances left by this year's expenditure, to meet the expenditures of 1842, under the present tariff." Believes the tariff bill [Clay to Ewing, April 30, 1841; Remark in Senate, July 16, 1841] now before Congress will add $8,500,000, and perhaps as much as $10,000,000, to federal income in 1842. This sum, together with the expected $4,000,000 of "ordinary revenue," would total $14,000,000 for 1842; "and if no part of the twelve million loan is paid, it will amount to eighteen million." Reports that the Treasury Department predicts an average annual income of $25,000,000 "for a series of years to come," and notes that while this year's expenditures will approach about $28,000,000, he hopes that this sum can be reduced to an annual average of $22,000,000 during Tyler's presidential term. If so, the Treasury might pay off "in four years the twelve million loan recently authorized." Given these numbers, announces that he will "vote for the tax on tea and coffee. It was necessary, under his calculations; and, as he feared he was to be deserted by a portion of his friends, he trusted that some of those opposed to him would vote for this tax. If they did not, the result would inevitably be, that at the next session the tax would be certainly imposed, or a higher duty than is authorized by the [1833] compromise act [8:604, 619-22, 626-27] levied on other articles. He looked upon a new loan in December next, which a few days since he had spoken of as not improbable, now as likely to be almost indispensable." *Cong. Globe*, 27 Cong., 1 Sess., 424. Tea and coffee were exempt from duty in the revenue (tariff or duties and drawbacks) act of September 11, 1841, although it was anticipated that $2,000,000 annually might be raised by a tariff on these commodities. The vote for exemption of these commodities, later this day, was 39 to 10, Clay voting nay. *Ibid.*, 428; see also 5 *U.S. Stat.*, 463. The "new loan" predicted by Clay was an act of January 31, 1842, authorizing the issue, during a one year period, of $5,000,000 in treasury notes [Remark in Senate, January 21, 1842]. This was followed on April 15, 1842, by a one-year extension of the Loan Act of July 21, 1841, and an addition to it of $5,000,000. *Ibid.*, 469, 473-75.

Later in the debate this day on the revenue bill, and in response to John C. Calhoun's suggestion that there be a postponement of discussion of the bill until Monday, September 6, so that Clay's facts and figures might be more closely examined, Clay explains that while he had not spoken from a written text, he would supply the South Carolinian with his "tables and calculations." Argues against postponement because the House has finished its business and "it would be difficult to keep that body together longer than next Wednesday [September 8]." Speaks (not recorded) against the amendment to place tea and coffee on the free list prior to the final vote on it. *Cong. Globe*, 27 Cong., 1 Sess., 427-28.

Remark in Senate, September 6, 1841. Addresses the question posed by Sen. Thomas H. Benton as to whether the president is aware that 8,500,000 acres of public land have been prepared for sale but have not yet been offered for sale; and opposes Benton's motion to the effect that since the treasury is in such a distressed condition, the president should know of this untapped source of revenue and act now to secure it. Clay notes that Tyler is already aware of this situation. Explains, further, that these lands have mainly been withheld from market "to favor those very pre emptions of which gentlemen on the other side had talked so much. They were afraid that if the lands were put up the speculators would buy up their improvements. Now, although he had never said so much in favor of the pre-emptive principle, still he had ever been from first to last against the speculators." *Cong. Globe*, 27 Cong., 1 Sess., 429. Benton's motion was tabled.

Later this day, Clay opposes an amendment by William Allen (Dem., Ohio) to the revenue (tariff) bill [Clay to Ewing, April 30, 1841; Remark in Senate, July 16, 1841] that would place salt on the free list. He particularly objects to opposition party arguments that the amendment would benefit the poor, stating that "the very circumstance of the universality of its [salt] use was a reason it should come in for its share of taxation. He never talked about the poor, but he believed he felt as much, and probably more, than those who did. Who were the poor? Why we were all poor; and any attempt to select certain classes for taxation was absurd, as before the collector came round they might be poor. He expressed the hope that the tax might not be interfered with. . . . He could tell them, if they desired to preserve the compromise [tariff of 1833], they must leave the salt tax alone." *Ibid.*, 430. The Allen amendment was defeated 21 to 23, Clay voting nay. The Tariff Act of September 11, 1841, which went into effect on September 30, 1841, did not place salt on the free list. 5 *U.S. Stat.*, 463.

Still later this day, Clay "differed *in toto*" with Sen. John C. Calhoun's interpretation of the Compromise Tariff Act of 1833 [8:604, 619-22, 626-27]; also with Calhoun's amendment to the present revenue bill reflecting that interpretation—an interpretation based on his contention that "no article now duty free, could be taxed till the 30th June, 1842," and certainly not as early as September 1, 1841, the date it was proposed this tariff legislation would take effect. In Clay's view, "the [1833] compromise related entirely to the protected articles—it did not relate to wines, silks &c. Suppose under an economical Administration, revenue sufficient could not be collected, then he [Clay] would go for a duty beyond twenty per cent. The spirit of the compromise was, that they should not go beyond 20 per cent. duty, if possible, in the exercise of an economical administration. The compromise only applied to dutiable articles and not to those free of duty. If this amendment prevailed the bill would not produce more than a half million dollars. He hoped the Senator [Calhoun] would perceive this literal interpretation of the act was beyond all practical purposes, and would reduce the revenue by this bill from ten million dollars to half a million." *Cong. Globe,* 27 Cong., 1 Sess., 430. Calhoun's amendment was defeated 11 to 30, Clay voting nay.

To John O. Sargent, September 6, 1841. Announces that Gales and Seaton are publishing in pamphlet form his speech [Speech in Senate, August 19, 1841] on President Tyler's veto [Tyler to Clay, April 30, 1841] of the first (Fiscal Bank of the U.S.) bank bill and that he will send Sargent a copy. ALS. MHi. This publication was titled *Speeches Delivered by H. Clay of Kentucky in the Senate of the United States, on the 19th of August, 1841, on the Message of President Tyler, Returning the Bank Bill, With His Veto, and in Reply to Mr. Rives, Defending the Message.* Washington, 1841.

From Benjamin O. Tayloe, Troy, N.Y., September 6, 1841. Regrets that he has delayed so long in acknowledging the bill for the bagging and rope [Clay to Tayloe, August 11, 1841], but explains that he has been absent "from Troy, on a tour."

Turns to politics, remarking: "In this quarter we are in painful uncertainty as to the views of the President in regard to the Second Bank Bill, as we have been led to apprehend a second veto, with other pernicious consequences [Tyler to Clay, April 30, 1841]. Your own views meet universal applause from the Whigs I have met." Notes that a friend in Connecticut, "when speaking of you," recently said "that 'no public man ever stood as high in the esteem of New England'; and he wished you to know with what affection your name is cherished." Mentions also that "I have this morning received letters from Alabama and Virginia expressing the general sentiment of their neighbourhoods ardently approving your course," and adds that "Amid the clouds and breakers that have threatened our ship of State, my own faith has been reposed in you as the Pilot to weather the storm; and I trust confidently in not being disappointed."

States that the idea that Edward Everett's nomination may be rejected "on the ground of [his] being charged with Abolitionism" is creating a sensation in the North. Believes Everett's position reflects "the prevailing sentiment in New England." Adds that he is about to write Philip R. Fendall "to furnish him my testimony that it was the intention of Gen Harrison to appoint him District Attorney [Clay to Tyler, May 12, 1841]; he having so informed my Mother about ten days before his death." ALS. DLC-HC (DNA, M212, R5).

The appointment of Edward Everett as minister to Great Britain was confirmed by the Senate on September 13, 1841. U.S. Sen., *Executive Journal,* 5:438.

Remark in Senate, September 7, 1841. Presents a resolution from citizens of Pike, Hocking, and Jackson counties in Ohio, supporting the performance of the Whigs during the present session and condemning the veto power. Observes that "more intelligent and patriotic men did not exist than those in the valley of Scioto." Motion tabled. *Cong. Globe,* 27 Cong., 1 Sess., 433.

During debate on the revenue (tariff) bill [Clay to Ewing, April 30, 1841; Remark in Senate, July 16, 1841] this day, Clay opposes an amendment adding tallow to the free list. Motion to do so defeated. Opposes Calhoun's amendment that any change in the pending revenue act which by provision of the Compromise Tariff Act of 1833 [8:604, 619-22, 626-27] could not take effect prior to July 1, 1842, be postponed until that date [Remark in Senate, September 6, 1841]. Points out that "The object of the bill was to raise money. Suppose there was revenue wanted and could only be obtained by going beyond the compromise, they would have to do it. He was desirous to preserve the compromise act inviolate, and his hope and belief was that they might by economy be able to do so; but, with all they were doing with this bill, there would still be a deficit of some ten or twelve millions of dollars, if the loan [Clay to Ewing, July 13, 1841] was to be met." Explains, further, that "next year there would be a deficit of eight millions. Well, the land bill [Clay to Ewing, April 30, 1841; Remark in Senate, June 9, 1841] under the most prosperous state of things would be only three millions; which, deducted from the eight millions, would still leave a deficit of five to be provided for. The vote of the Senator and his friends in exempting tea and coffee, had helped to swell the deficiency. He thought tea and coffee the most desirable articles on which to raise revenue, for reasons which he had given on another occasion [Comment in Senate, September 4, 1841]." Calhoun's amendment was defeated 11 to 24, Clay voting nay. Also opposes Sen. Thomas H. Benton's amendment to put Indian blankets not costing over 75 cents on the free list because such blankets were "used generally by poor people." Such a decision, responds Clay, would "destroy the manufacture in this country of blankets for the Indian trade, and throw it altogether into the hands of the British manufacturer." Amendment defeated 20 to 25, Clay voting nay. *Ibid.*

Later this day, during the continuing debate on the revenue (tariff) bill, Clay moves that the legislation take effect after September 30, 1841, rather than September 1. Argues that this later date would benefit the planning of merchants involved in foreign trade. Speaks at length to Sen. Silas Wright's review of the legislative history of the extra session, particularly to Wright's statement that his votes against passage of the revenue bill and the loan bill [Clay to Ewing, July 13, 1841] stem from his conviction that such legislation has been designed by the Whigs to provide funds for their distribution bill [Clay to Ewing, April 30, 1841]. Clay denies this and scolds Wright for not mentioning other important Whig economic legislation that the present session has passed, legislation which has nothing to do with distribution. Among these acts are the "Sub-Treasury law [Tyler to Clay, April 30, 1841], the idol measure of the Senator, had been repealed, and the Bankrupt bill [Remark in Senate, April 22, 1840] had passed, a measure which the constituents of the Senator, more than those of any Senator from any other State in the Union, desired and demanded, and yet for that he had not voted. . . . [Therefore] let the Senator go home and meet, if he can, those constituents, after having voted against that great measure, and now against granting supplies to carry on the Government." *Ibid.*, 437. At the end of this day's work, the revenue (tariff) bill of 1841 was passed 33 to 11, Clay voting yea. *Ibid.*, 438.

Remark in Senate, September 8, 1841. Speaks to the proposed amendment of a law of July 7, 1838, which in part required that the funds and the interest thereon from the bequest of the late James Smithson of London be invested in state stocks paying not less than 5% interest until the Smithsonian Institution was launched. The amendment asked that funds held in trust by the United States, and the interest earned on it be invested in federal government stocks paying not less than 5% interest. Clay supports this amendment on the ground that such financial relations "between the Government and the States, of the latter being debtors to the former, ought always to be avoided; for what means could be used to coerce the States if they refused to pay?" Further, he regards the "Smithsonian fund as a sacred trust which the Government would be bound to restore if it should ever be lost; and that being the case—the Government being responsible for them, it would be better that they should remain in the Treasury, under our charge." *Cong. Globe*, 27 Cong., 1 Sess., 441; see also 5 *U.S. Stat.*, 267. Amendment passed *viva voce*.

Later this day, Clay successfully urges Sen. Willie P. Mangum (N.C.) to withdraw his amendment to the naval ordnance and stores appropriation bill that would increase the Marine Corps by a number not exceeding 500 men. Thinks the amendment will be voted down and fears that such action will "prejudice its success in future, when it should be acted on." *Cong. Globe*, 27 Cong., 1 Sess., 442.

Remark in Senate, September 9, 1841. Clay moves that the House amendment to the revenue (tariff) bill [Clay to Ewing, April 30, 1841] providing that "no duty that may be laid or collected by virtue of the second section shall exceed 20 per cent ad valorem" be rejected. Motion passed and a Senate Committee of Conference ordered. *Cong. Globe*, 27 Cong., 1 Sess., 443. Section 2 of the bill as it stood at this point read that "no duty higher than twenty per centum ad valorem . . . shall be levied and paid on any unmanufactured article." 5 *U.S. Stat.*, 464. It was further amended the following day. See Remark in Senate, September 10, 1841.

Remark in Senate, September 10, 1841. Asks Sen. Benjamin Tappan (Ohio) to withdraw his motion fixing a day for the adjournment of Congress until the revenue (tariff) bill [Remark in Senate, September 9, 1841], "now pending between the two Houses" is disposed of. Later this day a message from the House reports that a joint resolution fixing the adjournment date at noon on September 13 has been passed. Tappan moves concurrence by the Senate. Motion tabled. *Cong. Globe*, 27 Cong., 1 Sess., 445-46.

Reporting from the Committee of Conference on the disagreement between the two houses on section 2 of the revenue bill [Remark in Senate, September 9, 1841], Clay announces a compromise which reads: "if . . . any duty exceeding the rate of 20 percentum ad valorem shall be levied prior to the 30th of June, 1842, the same shall not, in any wise, affect the disposition of the proceeds of the public lands as provided for by an act [Clay to Ewing, April 30, 1841; Remark in Senate, June 9, 1841] passed at the present session of Congress; *and provided further*, that no duty higher than 20 per cent. ad valorem shall be levied and paid on any unmanufactured article." Compromise concurred in by Senate. *Ibid.*, 446; 5 *U.S. Stat.*, 464.

To THOMAS H. CLAY Washington, September 11, 1841

Insprs. [Wade] Hampton, [Alexander] Barrow and [Benjamin O.] Tayloe have now all accepted the bills you sent to me.[1]

I have this day agreed with Mr. Barrow that you shall supply him next year with the same quantity of Bagging & Rope that you did this year, and on *the same terms*. You had better keep this letter as a memo.

I hope to leave here on Tuesday or Wednesday next.[2] P.S. Henry's [Clay, Jr.] health has greatly improved. Don't be alarmed—I shall make no other contracts than the above.

ALS. DLC-HC (DNA, M212, R5). 1. Clay to Tayloe, August 11, 1841. 2. Clay to Henry Clay, Jr., Sept. 13, 1841.

Remark in Senate, September 11, 1841. Supports a joint resolution that would equalize printing costs paid by the executive departments and by both houses; calls it a "desirable retrenchment of expenditure," opposes postponing consideration of it, and calls for the yeas and nays on it. Motion to postpone indefinitely passes without division, Clay having withdrawn his objection upon learning of an existing law requiring that printing contracts be awarded to the lowest bidder. *Cong. Globe*, 27 Cong., 1 Sess., 449.

Offers no objection to a House joint resolution that Congress adjourn on September 13 [Remark in Senate, September 10, 1841] now that the revenue and other bills [Clay to Ewing, April 30, 1841; Remark in Senate, July 16, 1841] have passed both houses. Notes, however, that "Whether certain events, and measures growing out of them, may or may not require some delay of the Senate past that time in Executive session, he could not say; but all knew from rumor to what he alluded. It was not for the Senate now to consider that; it was in the hands of another department of the Government." Suggests that the hour of adjournment on the 13th remain flexible. *Ibid.*, 449-50.

Speaks to Sen. William C. Preston's motion that adjournment be postponed for "a few days" so that a temporary measure "modelled on the deposite act of 1836 [8:813, 873-74]" can be devised "to place the public Treasury under the control of law." Agrees with the South Carolinian that "the purse and the sword should not be in the hands of the President of the United States. The President has signed the bill repealing the Sub-Treasury and the pet bank system [Tyler to Clay, April 30, 1841; Comment in Senate, June 7, 1841]; and at the same time says he will not sign a bill to charter a National Bank; and there being no other system that any one ever dreamed of in this country for receiving, safekeeping, and disbursing the public money," Clay wonders "what system he can propose, that will not be any of these three, and they are all out of the question, that is, a Bank of the United States, Sub Treasury, or pet bank system? What sort of system does he [Preston] expect will meet the approval of the President?" Says he "would be very glad if he knew what it was, to stay here and bring it to maturity." Believes, however, "that the wit of man—and he thought he had some, but not enough for the purpose—could not devise a plan that would meet the views of the President. No doubt members were going home, leaving the purse and the sword entirely in the hands of the President . . . [who] says he will prepare some plan to recommend to Congress on the opening of next session—some institution to act as a Fiscal Agency [Clay to J.B. Clay, December 10, 1841], free from all constitutional objections." Reminds his colleagues of "the mere historical fact" that the president had before him bills to repeal the Independent Treasury system and to establish in its place a Fiscal Bank, both of which measures he had "recommended" in his message of June 1, 1841. Argues that the latter recommendation "could not be understood to mean any thing but a United States bank." Given this situation, Tyler had "signed the one and rejected the other." *Ibid.*, 450.

Following Preston's withdrawal of his motion to postpone adjournment, Clay moves to strike from the House motion to adjourn on Monday, September 13, the words "eleven o'clock" so that Congress "should have the whole day for business if necessary." *Ibid.* The Senate in executive session, did not adjourn finally until late in the evening of September 13. See *ibid.*, 452.

To Henry Clay, Jr., Astor House, New York, September 13, 1841. Announces that he will start for home "the day after tomorrow." Wishes his son were traveling with him, but "as you could not come, I have other Company." Says his route will be "via Wheeling and through Ohio." Adds that the newspapers "will inform you of the extraordinary events which have occurred here." ALS. Courtesy of

J. Winston Coleman, Jr., Lexington, Ky. Written in Senate Chamber. Clay reached Lexington on September 22. See Clay to Pettigrew, September 24, 1841; also Clay to Thomas H. Clay, September 11, 1841.

To THE WHIG CAUCUS Washington, September 13, 1841

Mr. Chairman [Sen. Nathan F. Dixon, Whig, R.I.],[1] this is a dark night. There is no moon, and the little stars are slumbering in their beds, behind the dark canopy that is spread over the heavens. This is not the first time that the heavenly lights have been obscured, and the world kept in temporary darkness. Is this emblematic of our party? It may be so; but not of our principles. We, Senators, will soon pass away, but our principles will live while our glorious Union shall exist. Let our hearts be cheerful. Let our minds look through the temporary clouds that overspread the heavens, and see the sun there, as in mid-day, shining upon our principles, fixed above like planets in the firmament. They may be obscured for a time by the cry of the demagogue, by the political treason of those we have cherished in our bosoms—but they must and will prevail in the end. The American people will always be divided between political parties; and leaders may direct the masses, for a time, to measures opposed to their true interest, but in the end the truth of experience will prevail, and justice will be done to the memory of those who have stood firm, as the friends of the people. My friends, we have done our duty. We have maintained the true policy of the Government. Our policy has been arrested by an Executive that we brought into power. [Benedict] Arnold escaped to England, after his treason was detected. [John] Andre was executed. Tyler is on his way to the Democratic camp.[2] They may give him lodgings in some outhouse, but they never will trust him. He will stand here, like Arnold in England, a monument of his own perfidy and disgrace.

We are soon to separate. We go to our constituents to tell them the story of their wrongs. Let us part with light and not desponding hearts. The sun sets at night under the western horizon, he is obscured by the revolution of the earth, but in the morn he rises in all his majesty in the east; so with our principles. I repeat, they may seem to have set, but like the sun they will rise again, warm, and fructify the United States. We must have for America, an American policy—our people are entitled to the protection and benefits of the Government under which they live. The policy of Europe is not suited to our people; the doctrines of free-trade preached, but never practiced, by other nations, may do for demagogues to talk about, but their effects are to break down our manufactures, paralyze the industry of the people, and drain our country of the precious metals. The currency question is of the highest importance to every industrial interest; without a sound currency there can be no safe, just reward to the industry of the country. I was at one time opposed to the Bank of the United States [2:200-205, 210, 216-19; 3:620], it was afterward chartered, I saw and experienced the benefits of its operations,—such an institution alone, can give a safe circulating paper medium, of uniform value in every part of the nation. If we use a paper currency at all, that is the kind of paper that we want, the local banks may give a local paper circulation, but they can not furnish a currency of extended uniformity of value. My conviction is confirmed by long observation and experience, that our principles, are right for the best interest for the American people and should prevail.

Mr. Chairman [Dixon], before parting, I wish to say a word gratulatory to yourself, as to the presiding officer of the Whig caucus. You took the chair with evident distrust of your ability to discharge its high and important duties. Night after night we have looked upon your good-natured, gentlemanly countenance; we have seen with high gratification, the very able and impartial manner in which you have discharged your duty, and especially the manner in which you have, by a single look, kept order at our meetings; the most excited, the most boisterous, has been quieted at once, and brought into lamb-like docility. Your remarkable qualifications for the chair, the astonishing manner in which you have exercised them, has been a theme of universal commendation by every member of the caucus, and could you have been seen while presiding, by the whole civilized world, Europe, Asia, Africa and Oceanica would have raised a united voice in your praise.[3] Gentlemen, one and all, permit me to bid you an affectionate farewell! . . .

Copy. Printed in Oliver H. Smith, *Early Indiana Trials: and Sketches, Reminiscences* (Cincinnati, 1858), 594-96. 1. In his book Smith, a Whig senator from Indiana, remarks that "Mr. Dixon, as a presiding officer [of the caucus], at once adopted the idea, that each Senator was bound to keep himself in order, and if he did not, the dignity of the chair would not permit him to interfere. The debates, therefore, at times assumed a personal character not very becoming in brethren of the same political party. Some of the finest speeches I have ever heard from Mr. Clay, Mr. [William C.] Rives [Whig, Va.], Mr. [Samuel L.] Southard [Whig, N.J.], Mr. [John J.] Crittenden [Whig, Ky., U.S. Attorney General], Mr. [Garrett] Davis [Whig, Ky., U.S. Rep.], Mr. [Rufus] Choate [Whig, Mass.], Mr. [William C.] Preston [States' Rights, S.C.], Mr. [James F.] Simmons [Whig, R.I.], I have heard in the Whig caucus." *Ibid.*, 593. For all of the above-mentioned men, see *BDAC*. 2. Tyler had vetoed [Tyler to Clay, April 30, 1841] the Whig's second bank bill, the so-called "Fiscal Corporation of the United States" bill on Sept. 9. *MPP*, 4:68-72. See Chitwood, *John Tyler*, 237-48; Shanks, *Papers of Willie Person Mangum*, 3: 230. For the unsuccessful (103 to 80) attempt in the House on Sept. 10 to override the veto by a two-thirds majority, and the main speeches attacking (Rep. John M. Botts, Whig, Va.) and defending (Rep. George H. Proffit, Whig, Ind.) Tyler, see *Cong. Globe*, 27 Cong., 1 Sess., 447-49, and *ibid.*, Appendix, 385-89 (Botts), 389-91 (Proffit); see also speeches by Reps. Samson Mason (Whig, Ohio) and Henry S. Lane (Whig, Ind.) in *ibid.*, 391-94. For Botts, Proffit, Mason, and Lane, see *BDAC*. For the resignation of Tyler's entire Cabinet, save Secretary of State Webster, on Sept. 11, see Chitwood, *John Tyler*, 272-74. 3. To Clay's tongue-in-cheek praise of Dixon, the Rhode Island senator facetiously responded: "Gentlemen, I have heard with infinite delight the remarks of the Senator from Kentucky, and more especially those he has been pleased to address directly to myself, so just and so true. I have been fully aware for some time, that I never had but one equal as a presiding officer, and he was the Senator from Kentucky himself, when he presided over the House of Representatives; others might make the Senator an exception, but to be entirely candid, I can not; I believe I am greatly his superior, especially in keeping order. You will all bear me witness, with what promptness, judgment, and energy, I have at all times interfered to keep order among the most disorderly body that was ever assembled. The Senator from Kentucky at one time during his address, looked as if he was not in full earnest; but when you are all as well acquainted with the Senator as I am, you will give him full credit for sincerity, for any remarks he may make before ten o'clock at night, after that there may be some doubts."

To Robert Gilmor *et al.*, Baltimore, September 14, 1841. Regrets he cannot accept an invitation to visit Baltimore where "signal public demonstrations" have been planned for him. Now that the session has ended, feels he must travel home "without delay." Continues: "If . . . all has not been accomplished at the late Session of Congress. . . . If we have been greatly disappointed in the failure of repeated attempts to establish a sound currency, regulate exchanges, and separate the Purse from the sword [Tyler to Clay, April 30, 1841], what American Citizen, what Whig will, on that account, surrender himself to the sentiments of an ignoble despair? Who will not say that we will persevere, with redoubled courage, until every remaining object of the glorious revolution of November last shall be completely consummated? Shall we be discouraged because one man presumes to set up his individual will against the will of the nation? On the contrary, let us superadd to the previous duties which we lay under to our Country, that of plucking from the Constitution this sign of arbitrary power, this odious but obsolete vestige of Royal prerogative. Let us, by a suitable amendment to that instrument, declare that the Veto—that parent & fruitful source of all our public ills [Speech in Senate, January 24, 1842]—shall itself be overruled by majorities in the two Houses of Congress." Argues that the nation is "as much injured by the arrest of the enactment of good laws as by the promulgation of bad ones!" Believes that, "notwithstanding the astounding developments recently made here," the Whig cause is "stronger than ever it was." ALS. PHi.

For Gilmor, see 5:164 and *NCAB*, 11:402.

To Ebenezer Pettigrew, September 24, 1841. Reports that "the Mules had started on their journey to your residence on the 15h. instant." Adds that "My son [Either James B. or Thomas H. Clay] informs me that they were in good order but not so fat as he wished." Believes, in fact, "they were among the best lots of two year old mules which ever left this State." ALS. NcU. See also Clay to Thomas H. Clay, August 15, 1841, and Clay to James B. Clay, August 16, 1841.

From Elisha Warfield *et al.*, Lexington, September 24, 1841. As a committee of invitation appointed by the citizens of Lexington and Fayette County, they welcome Clay home from Congress where he has performed "arduous and important duties." Send a copy of resolutions passed at a public meeting which set October 7 as the date of a public dinner in Clay's honor. Note that while he has "studiously avoided compliments of this kind . . . we feel that *we* have claims upon you, not common to our whole country, which should . . . lead you to make this an exception to your general rule." Conclude: "You have been our neighbor and friend for 40 years; we are a portion, too, of a constituency that have never faultered in your support, during your whole public career." Copy. Printed in Frankfort *Commonwealth*, October 5, 1841.

On September 25, 1841, Clay replied offering "my cordial thanks, and assurances of my lasting gratitude." Acknowledges "your superior claims upon me," but adds that "the very ground on which you justly place them, encourages the hope that you will kindly receive the reasons which compel me, with regret, to decline accepting your obliging invitation." Adds: "An arduous session of Congress has been followed by a long and fatiguing journey; and both make me intensely feel the want of repose. A barbecue, with public speaking in the open air . . . would greatly add to my present exhaustion, if it did not produce more serious effects." Hopes that "in lieu of a Public Festival," they will "substitute that private, informal and friendly intercourse, so much more congenial with my feelings, and compatible with my health." *Ibid.*

From David Evans, Philadelphia, September 30, 1841. States that the "Cooler which I had in the Rotunda was $35.—the size which I sent you was larger than that, and the price $40." Explains further that it "is precisely the same size and price as one which I sold [Henry] T. Duncan, of Lexington, and others." Denies that he ever agreed to deliver the cooler to Clay, as "I never undertook to deliver one in my life." ALS. DLC-TJC (DNA, M212, R14). Endorsed by Clay: "Paid in check on the B. of Pennsa."

For Duncan, to whom Clay in his will left "my ring containing a piece of the Coffin of General Washington," see 6:1055-56; and Clay's Last Will and Testament, July 10, 1851. D.S. Fayette County Will Book T, pp. 474-78; also, Ardery, *The Duncans of Bourbon County*, 19. Evans, is listed as a lumber merchant in the 1840 and 1841 editions of *M'Elroy's Philadelphia Directory*.

From A.T., September 30, 1841. Expresses disappointment on "the course of President Tyler on the Fiscal agency bill [Tyler to Clay, April 30, 1841; Speech in Senate, August 19, 1841]," and says if Harrison ("that good old man") had lived, "we most assurredly would have had a Bank in successful operation by the time Congress met again." Believes the bank "is an adjunct to our plans for the emancipation of the colored race so unjustly kept in bondage by their unfeeling taskmasters." Suggests that at the next session of Congress "a large number of Southern votes can be obtained" for a national bank by providing "a moderate discount." Explains that "such is the needy situation of many slaveholders in Congress, and the extravagance, and gambling propensities of others . . . they may make a few states rights flourishes, for the sake of appearances, but with ruin to themselves . . . staring them in the face . . . they will either dodge the question, or come over to us bound hand and foot." Continues: "If we should be again disappointed it will only be an incentive to more strenuous exertions in favour of your elevation to the 'White house', and we hope you will continue to deserve our support which you have richly merited ever since the delivery of your speech in the Senate contending that our petitions ought to be respectfully received and refered [8:817-18, 833, 853]. That is what we call the half way house, and when a man utters those sentiments we consider him as good as one of ourselves." Mentions that "We expect soon to see the day when our efforts will be crowned with success, and those odious prejudices against the colour of the skin removed. Then our Colored fellow men will be taken by the hand by the whites, and elevated to that rank in the human family their virtues and long suffering entitle them to hold." Adds that when he was in Santo Domingo, "I was astonished to find how soon my early prejudices against the color of the skin vanished."

Predicts that at the next session of Congress an "unusual effort will be made . . . in favor of our good cause, and we confidently look to you for support." Promises that "as one good turn deserves another our well known abilities shall be exerted in your favour, to place you where you richly deserve to be, at the end of Tyler's term, whose days are numbered, in spite of the efforts of the miserable Cabal who are struggling to sustain him."

Explains why he is signing only his initials: "The nature of this communication make it improper to trust my name through the post office . . . but you know me—that is enough—it is not names that are wanted, but mutual aid, with yours for our cause and ours for yours, *success is certain!*" Copy. Adams Papers, Letters Recd., 519. This letter was postmarked "Washington Railroad, Oct. 1" and addressed to John Quincy Adams who forwarded it to Clay on October 6. A.T. has not been identified.

From Frederick G. Gilmer, Auburn, Lincoln County, Mo., October 6, 1841. Offers to buy Clay's "land in this vicinity" for $5.00 per acre, "one fourth to be paid on the first day of June next and the remaining three fourths in one two and three years thereafter with interest from the date." Will consider himself "bound for sixty days from this day by the above proposition." Hopes to pay the first payment with proceeds from the sale of some property near Russellville, Ky. Notes, however, that as yet he has been unable to sell the property, which includes "a young negro man who I was unwilling to part from his wife," at a fair price. ALS. DLC-TJC (DNA, M212, R10). Gilmer is listed in the 1840 and 1850 censuses as a physician and a resident of Lincoln Co., Mo. See Weston Arthur Goodspeed, *History of Lincoln County, Missouri* . . . (Chicago, 1888), 315, 320-21, 328.

James Finley wrote Clay from Lincoln County, Mo., on October 26, 1841, saying that Major Alexander Martin had offered to pay "six Dollars fifty cents per acre in hand for your land in this County." ALS. DLC-TJC (DNA, M212, R14). Letter postmarked "Clay Village Ky" on November 5. The now extinct post office of Clay Village was named for Henry Clay and was located five miles east of Shelbyville. Robert M. Rennick, *Kentucky Place Names* (Lexington, Ky., 1984), 60. James Finley of Lincoln Co., Mo., was a farmer who served in the state senate in 1840 and the state house of representatives for 1844-46. Goodspeed, *History of Lincoln County*, 331-32, 339. Alexander Martin, also of Lincoln Co., served as circuit court clerk from 1854-69. *Ibid.*, 332-33.

On November 7, 1841, Clay wrote Col. William H. Russell in Fulton, Calloway County, Mo., telling him "to desist from selling" to Gilmer unless he had already done so, because "I have recd. a letter from Mr. James Finley of Lincoln, stating that he has been offered $6:50 Cash in hand for my Lincoln land." ALS. NcU. For Clay's dealing in this and other Missouri lands, see Clay to January, October 6, 1838; Clay to James B. Clay, October 30, 1840; Clay to Pindell, October 14, 1839; and Dunnica to Clay, April 17, 1841.

To JOHN M. BERRIEN Lexington, October 7, 1841

I intended, my dear Sir, prior to my departure from Washington, to have had the pleasure of calling to see you; but the bustle of preparation for my journey, and the eagerness of my Compagnons de Voyage to start prevented me. I wished to have expressed to you how much, during the Extra Session, you had inspired me with sentiments of regard & esteem.

What wonderful but mortifying & humiliating disclosures are made of the President by [Thomas] Ewing, [John] Bell & [George] Badger![1] But one link, in the chain of testimony, remains to be disclosed; and that you, Mr. [John] Sergeant and Mr. [William C.] Dawson could supply.[2] Whether it be necessary or not, you and they are most competent to decide.

The next will be a most anomalous Session of Congress. Which of the parties will support & be responsible for public measures? Will those recommended by the President and the Heads of Dept. be Whig or Locofoco, or partly one & partly the other, or neither?

I am considering whether I shall return or not to the next Session, with a strong inclination to stay at home.[3]

Do tell me soon what the result of your Election is, and give me good tidings. . . .[4]

ALS. NcU. Endorsed on verso: "answd 19th Oct '41." 1. Ewing, Bell, and Badger had published their reasons for resigning from the Cabinet. See Washington *Daily National Intelligencer*, Sept. 13, 1841. See also Speech to Whig Caucus, Sept. 13, 1841. 2. These men had conferred with Tyler on the second bank bill in an effort to formulate a plan of which Tyler would approve. They apparently had believed that the second bank bill met all of Tyler's requirements. Maurice G. Baxter, *One and Inseparable, Daniel Webster and the Union* (Cambridge, Mass., 1984), 306-7; Chitwood, *John Tyler*, 240-42. 3. Clay returned to Washington for the next session but did not complete it. In a letter to the general assembly of Kentucky, dated Feb. 16, 1842, he resigned from the Senate, effective March 31. 4. In the Georgia gubernatorial election of 1841, Democrat Charles J. McDonald defeated Whig William C. Dawson by a vote of 37,487 to 33,703. *BDGUS*, 1:293. The Democrats also won control of the state legislature with a majority of more than 50 seats on joint ballot. Milledgeville (Ga.) *Recorder*, Oct. 19, 1841.

GREAT SALE

OF

BLOODED CATTLE,

HORSES,

ASSES, MULES, &c.

On Saturday, 16th of October, 1841,

WILL BE SOLD AT ASHLAND, NEAR LEXINGTON, KENTUCKY,

Between 30 and 40 Head of Cattle, male and female; but chiefly 2 and 3 year old Heifers.[1]

Among them are all the varieties of Improved Short-horn Durhams—Hereford Reds—Devons—Ayreshire—Kyloes, &c. Several of the Cows are IMPORTED COWS.

Also—Several head of young Blooded Horses; among them a beautiful 2 year old Medoc colt.

Also—Several Jackass Colts, and about 30 head of Mules, yearlings and two years old.

The TERMS OF SALE will be Cash for all sums below $20, and twelve months credit for all sums above $20; the purchaser giving his note, negotiable at the Northern Bank of Kentucky, with good security.

H. CLAY.

ASHLAND, SEPTEMBER, 1841.

LEXINGTON INTELLIGENCER PRINT.

D, printed. WvU. 1. A complete printed list of the animals offered for sale, with marginal notes in Clay's hand, is in DLC-HC (DNA, M212, R5).

From Thomas Speed, Nelson County, Ky., October 18, 1841. Calls to Clay's attention "an article in the Cultivator (a paper you doubtless read) on the subject of a National Agricultural Society, in the No. for Octr." Warns that "However honestly the friends of that project may desire to promote the interests of Agriculture," it may, in fact, be designed to subvert "the cause of democracy." Fears "such an institution might be made a most powerful engine of influence," and solicits Clay's opinion of the matter.

Asks "What is to be the effect of the late scisms in our Whig ranks?" Wonders if there is any chance that Tyler "may yet relent & sanction a Bank [Tyler to Clay, April 30, 1841; Clay to J.B. Clay, December 10, 1841]" or, "if not, that, the inevitable consequences—increased depreciation of paper, & consequent fluctuation in prices of property, will produce so much injury & distress in the settlement of debts, as will unite the people *in favor* of those who have forseen, & endeavored to guard against those evils, & *against* those whose policy has brought them on."

Mentions that "I was surprised, & indeed mortified that the Representative who I had supported should propose The plan of a Bank so objectionable as that of Mr [John] Pope—a plan directly subversive of distribution of the proceeds of the public lands—Known by him to be one of the objects of policy of the whig party." Believes that Pope's bank plan not only would "thwart the plan of distribution," but would "be expensive—insecure for the public funds," and "would result in giving the control of accommodations to the Executive."

Remarks that "As to our standing here—I think the whig strength decided[ly] preponderates." Notes that "[Benjamin] Hardin professes to be anxious to keep the party united," but thinks "it quite likely that his present position [is] as much or more the result of his greater dislike to his rival & relation the P.M. General [Charles A. Wickliffe], than to yourself . . . [or] to his whig principles." ALS. NhD.

The Cultivator, established by Jesse Buel in Albany, N.Y., in 1834, was at this time operated by Willis Gaylord and Luther Tucker. It was one of the leading agricultural newspapers in the country until its demise in 1865. See Albert L. Demaree, *The American Agricultural Press, 1819-1860* (New York, 1941). 340-41. Solon Robinson, a well-known agriculturist, had proposed a national agricultural society in 1838, but the idea lay dormant until 1841 when a meeting was held in Washington in September to form the National Society of Agriculture. This organization was short-lived; however, it did "set forces in motion" which culminated in the establishment of the U.S. Department of Agriculture in 1862. See Herbert A. Kellar (ed.), *Solon Robinson, Pioneer and Agriculturist*, 2 vols. (Chicago, 1936), 1:87, 265-72.

On February 15, 1842, Rep. John Pope proposed the creation of a national bank with a capital stock ($60 to $80 million) to be subscribed by the U.S., the states, and private American citizens. The parent bank would be located in Washington with branches in the states which had given their assent. Included in his proposal was a plan for setting aside the proceeds of public land sales to support a government stock issue of $100,000,000 which was to be distributed to the states to pay for new internal improvements and to pay off debts incurred for past improvements. Also, additional government stock would be issued to purchase rights of ways for state roads in order to facilitate the movement of public mails, stores, troops, etc. A percentage of the Post Office Department's proceeds would be used to support the stock and interest thereon. Finally, he proposed an amendment to the Constitution limiting the amount of debt a state could contract during peacetime. *Cong. Globe*, 27 Cong., 2 Sess., 240. Apparently Pope had suggested this plan while at home during the recess preceding the meeting of the 27th Congress, 2nd Session.

After the resignation of the entire Cabinet (with the exception of Secretary of State Daniel Webster) [Speech to Whig Caucus, September 13, 1841], Tyler appointed Walter Forward as secretary of the treasury, John C. Spencer as secretary of war, Hugh S. Legare as attorney general, Charles A. Wickliffe as postmaster general, and Abel P. Upshur as secretary of the navy. U.S. Sen., *Executive Journal*, 5:443. Charles A. Wickliffe was a cousin of Benjamin Hardin. Hardin held no official office at this time.

To JOHN SLOANE Lexington, October 23, 1841

Before I acknowledge the receipt of your favor of the 18h. instant, I must request you to excuse my omission to answer one which you addressed to me during the Extra Session of Congress, and which proceeded entirely from the extent of my labors, and the extent of my correspondence. (You would do me great wrong if you supposed there had been any abatement in my feelings of regard and esteem towards you.)

I share in all the feelings of regret and disappointment, on account of the present state of public affairs, which you express.[1] It is inexpressibly mortifying that, after a struggle of such bitterness and duration, terminated last year by a result so glorious and so full of hope,[2] we should find our Country in such a condition as it now is. It is painful in the extreme to reflect upon it. Consolation is only to be found, if found at all, by enquiring what our duty is, in the present most extraordinary posture of public affairs, and performing that duty faithfully to the last, without regard to consequences.

In considering that question we must remember that the Whigs have majorities in both branches of Congress.[3] The power of these majorities may be greatly obstructed or even circumvented by the President, as it might be greatly assisted by the existence of union and harmony between him & them. But those majorities draw after them a certain responsibility, in respect to public measures. Suppose the Whigs do nothing or attempt nothing, will they not be reproached, and justly reproached, for their non action? They have made certain promises and pledges to the Country; ought they not in good faith to endeavor to redeem them? Will their silence or inactivity avail them against the known fact of their majority in Congress?

Taking this view of the matter, I confess that it seems to me that the Whigs ought to proceed in all their plans of reform & economy, and in all their measures of security, against the increase and abuses of the Executive, just as if they had the hearty co-operation of the President. If they succeed, they will have fulfilled their engagements; if they fail, they will be without fault, and the causes of their failure will be seen and judged.

In regard to plans or measures emanating from the Presidt., I see no better ground than that occupied by the Whigs in their address at the close of the Session,[4] which was to concur in supporting them when right, and opposing them when wrong.

I agree with you in thinking that the strong tendency of the current of the future is to Union between the President and the other party. He may possibly struggle a little while longer to construct his third party,[5] and that failing, as fail it must, he will go over to our Adversaries. They will not take him up as their candidate. They will be greatly embarrassed to know what to do with him, when the time arrives for designating their Candidate, but they will not adopt him. That may lead to other divisions and bickerings which, in the end, may more than neutralize any prejudice which the Presidents course may have inflicted upon us.

The Whig party, by announcing that the President has impaired their confidence in him, and by exposing themselves to the consequent loss of his patronage, has demonstrated its adherences to principle, and its devotion to the Country. Such noble disinterestedness ought to commend it to the confidence and support of all good men.

The line of conduct which I have suggested, does not run in fact as much in opposition to that which you have delieneated for the Whigs as it appears to do. You propose that the field should be abandoned to Mr. Tyler & his Cabal. You are right *in his sphere*. But in Congress the majority cannot abandon the field, and it must therefore act in its sphere—not to control the Executive, nor to propose measures for him, but to redeem pledges made during the Canvass of last year.

I am considering whether I should return to the Senate, with a strong disinclination to go. I shall not decide, until the time, not now far off, arrives, when I must decide.

ALS. MH. 1. Tyler to Clay, April 30, 1841; Speech to Whig Caucus, Sept. 13, 1841. 2. Clay to Porter, Dec. 27, 1838. 3. Clay to Clayton, May 29, 1840; Clay to Brooke, March 12, 1841. 4. At the suggestion of Sen. Willie P. Mangum (Whig, N.C.) at a Whig caucus on Sept. 11, a committee was appointed to explain to the nation why Whig measures had not passed at the current session. The paper, drawn up by John P. Kennedy, blamed Tyler for vetoing the most important of the Whig measures. It also promised a future effort to curb executive power and patronage excesses, to regulate the currency and encourage industry, and to reform the administration of the nation's finances. Shanks, *Papers of Willie P. Mangum*, 3:230. 5. For Tyler's third party movement in 1843-44, as distinct from his efforts to secure the Democratic nomination, see Seager, *And Tyler Too*, 219-29; Chitwood, *John Tyler*, 369-78; Robert J. Morgan, *A Whig Embattled, The Presidency of John Tyler* (reprint ed., Hamden, Conn., 1974), 147-77.

To PETER B. PORTER Lexington, October 24, 1841

I have received your favor of the 11h. It is true that I am considering whether I shall return to Washn., with a strong inclination to resign my seat in the Senate. I shall decide in a few weeks, with the advantage of having your opinion, to which I shall give great weight. I am not however sure that my retirement from public life will lessen the resentment of my opponents, or disarm the envy and jealousy of my rivals. That is a work which death only can accomplish or the total loss of public confidence. Whether in the public Councils or at my quiet home, I should be regarded not less in their way. Would they not even make the fact of my resignation, at this time, the ground of new attack? Charging me with abandoning friends, and leaving a sinking Ship? &c &c. &c.

If I should determine to go once more to the Senate, it will be only to remain a part of the Session, and to close some matters, chiefly of a private nature &c.[1]

The issue of the Elections this fall demonstrates the fatal effects of Veto's.[2] Altho' I should have been glad if our friends had attended the polls and made exertions worthy of them and of the goodness of their cause, what has happened is perfectly natural and ought to excite no surprize. Men who have been betrayed will not fight, unless they see a distinct, & satisfactory object. They would fight against their betrayers. I shall not be much disappointed if we lose your State at the approaching election.[3] Shall we be able to rally hereafter & recover the ground which the Veto's have lost?

I read, with interest, and generally with approbation, the Declaration of the Syracuse Convention.[4] I am very thankful and grateful for the friendly notice which it takes of me, in which I think they went quite far enough.

That is a curious Cabinet which Mr. Tyler has made.[5] If they work well together, it will be against all the laws of union and harmony; for a more incongruous collection of gentlemen could hardly have been got together.

You will hear with regret that Dr. Satterwhite[6] was killed yesterday in Lexington by a fall from his horse. His death is much lamented.

We have had so far a most disagreeable October—Rain, rain, almost incessant rain. P.S. We have heard of [Alexander] McLeods acquitall, with pleasure.[7] I hope that nothing else will occur to menace the Peace of the Country.

ALS. NBuHi. 1. Clay to Berrien, Oct. 7, 1841. 2. Tyler to Clay, April 30, 1841; Speech to Whig Caucus, Sept. 13, 1841. 3. In the 1841 elections to the New York legislature, the Democrats won 8 seats in the senate to 2 for the Whigs, giving the Democrats a 17 to 15 predominance. In the lower house, Democrats won 15 seats to 5 for the Whigs, giving them a majority over the Whigs of 95 seats to 33. *Niles' Register* (Nov. 13, 1841), 61:165. 4. The New York Whigs had held a convention at Syracuse on Oct. 7, 1841, in which they commended the Cabinet for resigning, expressed disapproval of Tyler's policies, and thanked Henry Clay. Chitwood, *John Tyler*, 251. 5. Speed to Clay, Oct. 18, 1841. 6. Dr. Thomas P. Satterwhite. See 3:814. 7. Porter to Clay, Jan. 4, 1841.

To FRANCIS T. BROOKE Lexington, October 28, 1841

I received your favor of the 21st today, from which I infer your good health, as I think I recognize in its tone, your buoyant spirits. Without ever having laid up, I have not been always well since my return from Washn. I have worked too hard, and want rest. This feeling has given rise to a serious question which I have now under consideration, and that is, whether I shall not resign my seat in the Senate.[1] If I should return, it will be with the hope of getting away before the close of the Session, and with a resolution to take a less active part in public business.

You enquire what will be done with the Va Land warrants. I believe I have expressed my opinion to you heretofore fully about them; but, without being able to specify the time when they shall be passed on by Congress, I should not be surprized if they are ultimately provided for.[2]

So Mr. G.[3] says we are to have no fiscal agent! That is what I have expected. Having rejected a Nat. Bank, the State Banks, and the S. Treasury, I could not conceive what other project of an Agent even Mr. Tylers ingenuity could present.[4]

The issue of the Elections this fall, however much to be regretted, perhaps ought not to surprize us. An army which believes itself betrayed by its Commander in Chief, will never fight well under him or whilst he remains in authority. Our defeats have not been produced by any accession of strength to our adversaries, but simply because our friends would not go to the polls. I think they were wrong, but their conduct was natural.

ALS. KyU. Printed in Colton, *Clay Correspondence*, 4:455. 1. Speed to Clay, Oct. 18, 1841. 2. A bill to extend the time for locating Virginia military land warrants and returning surveys thereon to the General Land Office was passed by the House on August 12, 1841, and by the Senate on August 14. It was signed by the president on August 19. U.S. H. of Reps., *Journal*, 27 Cong., 1 Sess., 296, 350, 385; U. S. Sen., *Journal*, 27 Cong., 1 Sess., 158, 163. 5 *U.S. Stat.*, 449. In the next session of Congress an act was passed on July 27, 1842, providing "for satisfying claims for bounty lands, for military services in the late war with Great Britain [1812], and for other purposes." It extended the act of Jan. 27, 1835, and provided that cases not finally disposed of within that time would be "for ever barred." 5 *U.S. Stat.*, 497. For Clay's views on the Virginia military bounty lands, see 8:765. 3. "Mr. G." unknown; but for Tyler's plan for an Exchequer, see Clay to J.B. Clay, Dec. 10, 1841. 4. Tyler to Clay, April 30, 1841; Speech to Whig Caucus, Sept. 13, 1841.

To JOHN W. ALLEN Lexington, October 29, 1841

I have received and perused, in the friendly spirit in which it was written, your favor of the 26h. inst. Without reference to the future object, to which you and other friends are looking, I am unaffectedly desirous of retirement from public life; and I am now considering the question of my return to Washn. Whatever may be my final decision, I shall not remain long in the Senate.[1] I am not sure however that I shall be secure, in private life, against those attacks to which you refer. I am, on the contrary inclined to believe, that the violence and malevolence of some of my political enemies are unappeasable. Nothing but my death or my being put hors du combat will satisfy them.

The result of the State Elections this fall, altho' proceeding from the cause you assign, is greatly to be regretted. Why, for example, should the misconduct of Mr. Tyler,[2] induce any of our friends in Ohio[3] to absent themselves from the polls, and allow the vast powers of the State Government to pass into the hands of their opponents? Are the delinquents sure that when they wish to make an exertion, our opponents will not in the mean time have been so encouraged that all efforts will be ineffectual?

ALS. NHi. 1. Clay to Berrien, Oct. 7, 1841. 2. Tyler to Clay, April 30, 1841; Speech in Senate, August 19, 1841. 3. In the Oct. 12, 1841 elections for the Ohio legislature, Democrats won control of the House by a majority of 37 seats to 35 for the Whigs and of the Senate by a majority of 10 to 8. *Niles' Register* (Nov. 13, 1841), 61:167-68.

To Arius Nye, Tarlton, Ohio, October 29, 1841. Regrets not being able to stop longer when he passed through Tarlton on his way home [Clay to Henry Clay, Jr., September 13, 1841]. Continues: "I share with you in regrets on account of the course of our President [Tyler to Clay, April 30, 1841; Speech in Senate, August 19, 1841]. After the great exertions which were so long made, it is a sad disappointment; but we must bear up under the misfortune, and remember that we have a fine Country, to which we ought to perform our duty to the last[.]" ALS. Courtesy of Lorenzo P. Baker, Jr., Baker Art Gallery, Columbus, Ohio. For Nye (1792-1865), a lawyer and oft-time member of the Ohio state legislature, see George I. Reed (ed.), *Bench and Bar of Ohio . . .*, 2 vols. (Chicago, 1897), 1:210-12.

From William B. Astor, New York, October 30, 1841. Acknowledges receipt of $450, "being the balance of interest due . . . on your bond to my father [John Jacob Astor]." Thanks Clay for sending "a copy of your speeches on the Veto Message, and in reply to Mr. [William C.] Rives [Speech in Senate, August 19, 1841; Clay to Sargent, September 6, 1841]." Thinks "They are truly excellent . . . and . . . equal to your happiest efforts—" ALS. DLC-TJC (DNA, M212, R10).

To NATHANIEL P. TALLMADGE

Lexington,
October 30, 1841

I received your obliging letter from Tioga Co. and am thankful for the account which it communicates of the proceedings of the Syracuse Convention.[1] Their declaration is characterized by vigor, ability and discretion; and from the harmony which presided in their deliberations I hope we may look forward to favorable effects. Considering our defeats elsewhere in the State elections, I confess, however that I am apprehensive of the issue of your November election.[2] These defeats shew the operation of a general cause, and there can be no doubt that Mr. Tyler's Vetos' are that cause.[3]

I am greatly obliged by your friendly advice as to my retirement from the Senate.[4] I have that question now under consideration. If we had maintained our ground this fall, I should have less difficulty in deciding upon my course; but I own that I feel some repugnance in resigning at a moment of such general disaster. My feelings prompt me not even to seem to desert my friends, but to meet them once more and to cheer console and consult with them. If, therefore, you should meet me at Washington it will be from the predominance of that feeling. But beyond this Session, under no circumstances, have I a thought of remaining in the Senate. Indeed, if I should go back, I hope to be able to quit before the close of the Session.

My latest advices from Washington represent Mr. Tyler as still entertaining a purpose of proposing some Fiscal Agent, without having fixed, in his own mind, the form which it ought to assume. I am most curious to see to what conclusion he will come; for, having rejected a Nat. Bank, the Sub Treasury, and the State Banks, I am unable to conceive any other rational plan.[5]

I congratulate you on the acquittal of [Alexander] M[c]Leod,[6] and the disappearance of all cause at least of immediate hostilities with G. Britain. From what I have heard, I believe the event of a War, if not desired was expected by the Executive.

What ought our friends to do at the next Session? Should they fold their arms and say that, because Mr. Tyler has applied his Veto to the Bank, they will do nothing? I think not. They constitute the majorities in both houses,[7] and are under the responsibility which that fact imposes.

I think, therefore, that they should proceed to fulfill all the promises and pledges made to the People, during the last year, as far as depends upon them, just as if Genl Harrison had lived or as if Mr. Tyler had proved faithful. They ought to reduce the Nat. Expenditure, abolish unnecessary offices, introduce more economy, & curtail the Executive power by legislation, where it can be applied, and by proposing amendments to the Constitution,[8] where Legislation is incompetent. In no other way does it appear to me can we stand acquitted to our consciences and to our Country.

There are those who think that the field ought to be abandoned to Mr. Tyler and to his little Cabal. Within his sphere that may be right enough, or rather it will take place. But within the Constitutional sphere of Congress, I think the majority ought to perform, in good faith, its whole duty. Can the infidelity of Mr. Tyler authorize or justify infidelity to the People, on the part of Congress?

I make these suggestions for your consideration, being quite sure that you will give them such friendly attention as they deserve.

ALS. KyLoF. 1. Clay to Porter, Oct. 24, 1841. 2. *Ibid.* 3. Tyler to Clay, April 30, 1841; Speech in Senate, August 19, 1841. 4. Clay to Berrien, Oct. 7, 1841. 5. Clay to J.B. Clay, Dec. 10, 1841. 6. Porter to Clay, Jan. 4, 1841. 7. Clay to Clayton, May 29, 1840; Clay to Brooke, March 12, 1841. 8. See Speech in Senate, Jan. 24, 1842.

To JOHN M. CLAYTON Lexington, November 1, 1841

I received your favor of the 25h. Ulto. with the letters inclosed, which I now return, according to your request.

I do not believe that you and I differ in opinion about Mr. Webster. I do however doubt whether he exercises the influence you suppose with Mr. Tyler, altho' I may be mistaken. One thing is certain that those who are known to possess the confidence of Mr. Tyler, in an eminent degree, are in the habit of speaking most contemptuously of Mr. Webster. Su[c]h is the case with Mr. [Henry A.] Wise, and, I understand, Mr. [Abel P.] Upsher also.

Mr. Webster's continuance in the Cabinet, after the resignation of his Colleagues,[1] and notwithstanding he was the organ of the President in communicating to members of Congress his readiness to approve the second Bank Charter, must injure him to an extent that he will find it difficult ever to repair.

I do not think that you ought to entertain any regret on account of Mr. Tyler's failure, from whatever cause, to offer you a place in his Cabinet, as recommended by Mr. [Elisha] Whittlesey. After all that has occurred, could you have accepted it with honor? Considering who your Colleagues[2] would have been, could you have accepted it with personal ease and comfort?

I wish I could share with you in the good opinion you still entertain of Mr. Tyler. I do not see how it is possible to entertain such an opinion after understanding his notorious course on the Bank question.[3] That the second Charter was prepared according to his wishes; and that he stood pledged to approve it cannot be now controverted. How is he to be justified for his breach of good faith?

There are too many circumstances to allow one to doubt that his aim has been the formation of a third party, with a view to his own aggrandizement. And the man that, as I believe, has exerted much more pernicious influence with him than even Mr. Webster, is Mr. Wise, who has plyed him with flattery, and held out to him vain hopes of another Election.

He must soon see the error of his course, if he be not blind to madness. The Locofoco's, inflated by their recent successes in the State Elections (produced by the two Veto's)[4] will throw off the mask, bring out their own Candidate, and continue to use Mr. Tyler not for his advancement but for their own purposes. In the meantime he will have completely alienated the great body of the Whigs.

The next Session of Congress must be a most extraordinary one—more so if possible than that which recently terminated. It will present probably the spectacle of an administration without a party. Who will support Mr. Tyler's measures? The Loco's or the Whigs? How will he redeem his pledge to propose a fiscal agent?[5] What sort of a one *can he* propose?

I am greatly obliged by your friendly caution as to the place of my boarding next winter. I shall be relieved of any difficulty on that score if I remain at home;[6] and I have now under consideration the question whether I shall return or not. Whether I go or stay, or wherever I may be, I pray you to be assured of the warm sentiments of regard. . . .

ALS. DLC-John M. Clayton Papers (DNA, M212, R20). 1. Speech to Whig Caucus, Sept. 13, 1841. 2. Speed to Clay, Oct. 18, 1841. 3. Tyler to Clay, April 30, 1841. 4. For instance, see Clay to Porter, Oct. 24, 1841, and Clay to Allen, Oct. 29, 1841, for Whig losses in New York and Ohio state elections in Oct. and Nov., 1841. 5. See Clay to J.B. Clay, Dec. 10, 1841. 6. Clay to Berrien, Oct. 7, 1841.

To JOHN SLOANE Lexington, November 6, 1841

I am glad to perceive from your favor of the 1st. inst. that the difference in opinion between us, as to the duty of Congress, under actual circumstances, is more apparent than real. I think with you that the President should be left to his own course & counsels; whilst the Whigs in Congress ought to strive to do all the good in their power.

I have determined upon the *principle* of resigning my seat in the Senate; the only question is, as to the time, whether it shall be at the commencement, during the progress, or at the end of the approaching Session.[1] That question I shall give full consideration to.

I am not surprized at the mortification which the Governor [Thomas Corwin], Mr. [Thomas] Ewing and yourself feel, on account of the result of your recent Election.[2] I sincerely sympathise with all of you. I know not what is to become of your Banking system.

ALS. MH. 1. Clay to Berrien, Oct. 7, 1841. 2. Clay to Allen, Oct. 29, 1841.

To SAMUEL STARKWEATHER Lexington, November 7, 1841

I received your friendly letter of the 1st. inst. and thank you for the information which it communicates.

I shall give full consideration to your suggestions about my resignation of my seat in the Senate.[1] The unfavorable results of the State Elections this fall interpose a difficulty.[2] I could not bear to act so as to give even color to the reproach of desertion or infidelity towards friends, especially at a period of defeat and disappointment.

ALS. NHi. 1. Clay to Berrien, Oct. 7, 1841. 2. Clay to Clayton, Nov. 1, 1841.

To CITIZENS OF DAYTON, OHIO Lexington, November 9, 1841

[Thanks them for the plough which they sent him. Continues:]

I am, gentlemen, inexpressibly thankful and grateful for the confidence you have so kindly conveyed in my public career. It is perfectly true that it has been one full of difficulties; resulting sometimes from political opponents, and recently from both professed friends and open foes. Whether proceeding, however, from one or the other, or from both, my rule of conduct has been, and, during the short time I expect to remain in the public councils, will be, to discharge my duty fully, firmly, and faithfully, regardless of all personal consequences. Your testimony is highly gratifying, coming as it does from a respectable portion of Ohio, to which I have been always under the greatest obligations. I tender a heartfelt acknowledgment of these to you and to those whom on this occasion you represent.

Copy. Printed in *Kendall's Expositor* (Dec. 16, 1841), vol. 1, no. 26, p. 410; reprinted from Washington *Daily National Intelligencer.*

To EBENEZER PETTIGREW Lexington, November 10, 1841

I received your favor of the 19h. Ulto. A few days before its arrival, Mr. Weimar reached home and informed me of the safe delivery of Twenty three of the mules, one having died on the way. I am extremely happy to learn, both from your letter and through Mr. Weimar, that you are pleased with them. As you had purchased without previously seeing them, I felt very solicitous on that point. If you will have them worked lightly and fed well the approaching winter, I think that you will afterwards find that they will work better and wear longer than any lot of Mules you have ever had. The black mules are chiefly the get of a Poitou Jack that I imported from France; the two light bays mentioned in your letter were, I believe, the get of a Jack, owned also by me, that was produced by a Maltese Jack and a Jennette descended from the Knight of Malta, the property of Genl. Washington.

I cannot think of availing myself of your liberal offer to bear one half or the entire loss of the Mule that died. My stipulation was to deliver the Mules to you, and the loss must therefore be mine. The Twenty three Mules at $90 each produce $2070 from which deduct $50, advanced by you to Mr. Weimar, and there remains a balance of $2020. Under the authority contained in your letter, I have this day drawn a check for $2020 on the Farmers and Planters Bank of Baltimore. P. S. I transmitted a letter under cover to Mr. Stanley[1] for you, and one by Mail. Of course they will now require no Answer.

ALS. Nc-Ar. 1. Probably Congressman Edward Stanly of North Carolina. See *BDAC*.

To CHRISTOPHER HUGHES Lexington, November 15, 1841

It is exactly one week since the date of your letter, the receipt of which I now acknowledge. I had seen in the papers, which generally announce the arrival & movements of the great, that you had returned to the U.S. and intended to welcome you, but did not know precisely when you would get to Balto.

And why did you not come forthwith to Ashland? I should have given you a most hearty and cordial reception, and among other things, in a plain way, some Hughes's pale Sherry, if you had not joined the Temperance Society.

My carnal and careless observations are remembered by others with much more tenacity than by myself; for I have no recollection of any that I made about you to your brother,[1] altho' I do not deny nor admit the report to you of what I may have remarked. Of one thing I am sure that, whatever criticisms may have fallen from me, I never said or thought any thing of you in other than a spirit of the most perfect friendship.

I am considering whether I shall return to Washington,[2] which has ceased or is ceasing to have any charms for me. If I go, I shall have the pleasure of seeing you at Balto. or at the Metropolis; and will then say more than I could now conveniently write about Naples, Sweden, and our old Secretary of the Ghent Mission.[3] If I do not go, I will write you again....

ALS. MiU. 1. George Augustus Hughes. 2. Clay to Berrien, Oct. 7, 1841. 3. Christopher Hughes himself.

From James G. King, New York, November 15, 1841. States that "some months ago—tempted by the price—my house bought for themselves—and a friend some *twenty thousand dollars,* Bonds of the State of Kentucky." Notes that they are redeemable in five or six years and bear six percent interest, payable at Frankfort. Says they did not realize at the time of purchase that the bonds had to be presented "at the State Treasury, in order that the payment of interest may be endorsed upon them." Reports that in order to avoid transmitting these bonds through the mail twice a year, "we applied thru' our friend G. Winker Esqr . . . to the Treasurer [James Davidson]—to permit us to send him a national certificate . . .

that upon receipt and filing at the Office of the Treasurer—of such national certificate—that he would pay our draft for the same amount." Notes that the treasurer declined this arrangement; asks, therefore, if Clay will lay this letter before the treasurer or the governor [Robert P. Letcher]. Points out that it is "of the highest importance in raising and sustaining the credit of the Stock" that "everything should be done, to obviate inconvenience or loss to the creditor." ALS. Ky. Clay evidently gave this letter to the governor, because it is presently located in Letcher's papers.

For James G. King, see 6:358-59 and *DAB*.

To Unknown Recipient, near Richmond, Va., *ca.* December, 1841. In a printed extract of a letter, gives advice on raising hogs. Prefers the Berkshire breed, and recommends that they be bred the first week in December so that the pigs will be born in early April. Adds that "about the 10th of May, when they [the pigs] can crack corn, have the sows all spayed and the boars altered. They will form the best part of your pen of killing hogs the ensuing fall. Select your boars and sows from the April pigs to produce another year—keep them apart until the first week in December." Admonishes "that no one of the domestic animals should ever suffer for food. . . . Starving never succeeds with man or beast." Copy, extract. Printed in *The Southern Planter*, Richmond, Va., (December, 1841), 2:249.

To JAMES B. CLAY Washington, December 10, 1841

I arrived here on sunday evening with a very bad cold, which detained me at my lodgings two days, and from which I am now recovering.

When I left home, [Josiah] Downing had not returned, altho' he was daily looked for.[1] Thomas's [Hart Clay] principal reliance to cover the bill in the hands of K. S. & Co. depended upon his return with funds.

I am very anxious to hear from you, and to hear frequently from you, as to your prospects in N. Orleans. The last account I saw represented that there was a little more activity in your articles in the market. I hope it may prove true, altho' a letter I have received from Dr. [Stephen] Duncan presents a very unfavorable prospect. He thinks Bagging will come down to 16½ & Rope to 7—or 7½.

There is no developement of opinion here among the members of Congress generally as to Mr. Tylers plan for supplying a paper medium.[2] I do not think that it meets with great favor in either party; but it is too soon to form any positive judgment.

Give my respects to Mr. [James] Erwin & to Mr & Mrs. [Thomas] Smith.

ALS. DLC-TJC (DNA, M212, R10). 1. Clay to Thomas Hart Clay, Dec. 19, 1841. 2. For the origin, fate, and thrust of Tyler's so-called "Board of Exchequer" bank plan, a plan similar to one outlined by President Jackson in his Annual Message of Dec. 6, 1830 [*MPP*, 2:529], see Chitwood, *John Tyler*, 291-93 and Harold D. Moser, "Subtreasury Politics and the Virginia Conservative Democrats, 1835-1844," Ph.D. dissertation, University of Wisconsin-Madison, 1977, pp. 242-45. This plan is explained in *MPP*, 4:82-87 and *Cong. Globe*, 27 Cong., 2 Sess., 6-7, 34-40, 238-49. The report, submitted by Secretary of the Treasury Walter Forward, is in *House Exec. Doc.* 20, 27 Cong., 2 Sess.

To EDITOR OF THE NORTH AMERICAN[1] Washington, December 10, 1841

Finding it necessary to lessen the number of newspapers, for which I am a subscriber, I have to request that you will discontinue my subscription to the North American, & send me my account. At the same time I think it right to assure you that I have no complaint whatever against the N. A. with which I have been generally well pleased.

ALS. MH. 1. The Philadelphia *North American* was edited in 1841 by Walter Colton, C.G. Childs, and Atwill. Information supplied by The Historical Society of Pennsylvania.

Remark in Senate, December 16, 1841. Asks if the Committee on Printing has yet been appointed. Informed by the president *pro tem* (Samuel L. Southard of N.J.) that he would make these appointments today, Clay suggests that the annual report of the secretary of the Senate (Asbury Dickins of N.C.) not be ordered printed until there was a committee to which to refer it. Motion to print withdrawn. *Cong. Globe*, 27 Cong., 2 Sess., 22.

To THOMAS HART CLAY Washington, December 19, 1841

I received your letter of the 10h. I suppose that by this time you have seen Mr. [Josiah] Downing and adjusted with him your Mule account.[1] I shall be glad to hear how it turns out.

This letter will reach you by the time of the hiring which annually takes place of negroes. I adhere to the opinion which I expressed to you. I would not be tempted to give those high prices for hands. If the business succeed another year, it can only be by the greatest economy & retrenchment in every branch of it. I see Bagging & Rope quoted at Maysville at 15 & 7![2]

I have been very ill, since I came here, with colds. I am now confined to the House.

I do not believe that Mr. Tylers Currency plan will succeed.[3]

Give my love to Mary [Mentelle Clay] & the children.[4]

ALS. NHi. 1. Clay to Pettigrew, Sept. 24 and Nov. 10, 1841. 2. That is, fifteen cents per yard for bagging, seven cents per pound for bale rope. 3. Clay to James B. Clay, Dec. 10, 1841. 4. Lucretia Hart and Henry Boyle Clay.

To JAMES B. CLAY Washington, December 24, 1841

I have been confined a week with a swelled face, the effect of a bad cold, and during my confinement I have received your letter of the 10h. inst. I am getting better but feel weak from debility.

Your letter represents the state of things as to the business of Thomas [Hart Clay] and yourself worse than I had anticipated. I suppose the arrangement you have made with Messrs. Kelly & Conyngham[1] the best you could do. It prevents an immediate sacrifice of your articles, and gives you the chance of their use in the Spring. But will their advance enable you to meet all your engagements on & about the 1st. Jan.? And how are you to meet those subsequently coming round, including the $5000 which I went into Bank for?

It is very likely that you are right in withdrawing from the business another year. Situated as Thomas was I thought it best that he should continue it on a reduced scale, provided he can hire hands at reasonable prices. I fear that he may be tempted to give more than he ought.

I am sorry that you did not deliver to Mr. Peyton,[2] my letter immediately upon your arrival; for I have yesterday received from him a letter dated the 7h inst. expressing his regret that he will not be able to pay his note at maturity. This will be a great disappointment to me; and I know not how I shall be able to get along without the money. When I lent it to Col. Peyton, it was under full confidence that it would be paid at the maturity of his note. Besides the letter I have written to him by you, I wrote to him from this place, and shall again write to him, expressing my regret and disappointment. If you cannot get the money, I do not wish you to protest the note or to sue upon it.

I shall be very sorry to lose that Wine that was sent by the Creole. As that vessel is again in the port of N. Orleans, can you not ascertain what was done with it?

I have heard from Thomas but once since I left home. [Josiah] Downing had at last arrived, and, without particulars, Thomas writes me in the general that he did well.[3]

I have nothing new to write you from this City. No discussion has taken place on Mr. Tyler's currency plan.[4] My opinion is that it will not pass, in the form proposed, but will be rejected by the great body of both parties. And I think that it is not probable that it can even be amended so as to secure a majority.

Give my love to Mr. [James] Erwin & to Mr & Mrs. [Thomas] Smith.

ALS. DLC-TJC (DNA, M212, R10). 1. The firm of Kelly & Conyngham, commission merchants, was located at 61 Camp Street, New Orleans. It was owned by Alexander D. Kelly (*ca.* 1806-70) and David Conyngham (d. 1853). Information supplied by Collin B. Hamer, Jr., City of New Orleans Public Library. 2. For Balie Peyton, a lawyer and former Tennessee congressman who had moved to New Orleans in 1841, see *BDAC*. For more on the debts owed by Peyton to Clay and John J. Crittenden, see Kirwan, *John J. Crittenden*, 158. 3. Clay to Thomas Hart Clay, Dec. 19, 1841. 4. Clay to James B. Clay, Dec. 10, 1841.

To HENRY CLAY, JR. Washington, December 26, 1841

I recd. to day your favor of the 18h. the only letter I have got from home since I left it but a short one from Thomas [Hart Clay]. I am obliged to you for it.

I have been ill & confined to my lodging for a week by a swelling in my upper lip & nose, which gave me intense pain. It proceeded from a cold, and I have now got better. I hope to be able to attend the Senate tomorrow.

The Currency plan of Mr. Tyler[1] does not stand the least chance of being adopted, in the form proposed. The great body of both parties are opposed to it. All feel (at least among the Whigs) the necessity of doing something to remedy the disorder of the Currency and of Exchanges; but most of them apprehend that nothing can be made of Mr. Tylers plan. My belief is that nothing will be done.

The Treasury is empty, with very little prospect of being speedily filled. Indeed, I have never witnessed such a state of affairs as exists here—an administration, disclaimed by both parties, and drawing from neither any considerable support. In what all this is to end, I cannot see. Yet Mr. Tyler affects to believe that the People are with him, and the Politicians alone against him. Poor deluded man!

Among the Whigs, it is not to be denied, that there is some depression of spirits. This is the result of the treachery of the Head of the party. On the other hand, the other party has its troubles, its dissentions, its difficulties. It is far from being comfortable, and the very relations which exists between it & Mr. Tyler adds to its embarrassments.

I hope you found all your children[2] in good health. Give my love to all of them. . . .

ALS. Henry Clay Memorial Foundation, Lexington, Ky. Addressed to Henry Clay, Jr., in Louisville, Ky. 1. Clay to James B. Clay, Dec. 10, 1841. 2. Henry III, Anne, and Thomas J. Clay.

Remark in Senate, December 28, 1841. Opposes printing additional copies of the report of Secretary of the Treasury Walter Forward, enclosing the report of the General Land Office, because the maps included were "very expensive and useless." If treasury needs them, let treasury pay for the "extraordinary charges" involved. *Cong. Globe,* 27 Cong., 2 Sess., 62.

Later this day, announces that tomorrow he will introduce three joint resolutions [Remark in Senate, December 29, 1841] proposing three amendments to the Constitution that would (1) restrict the president's veto power; (2) vest the power to appoint the secretary of the treasury in the Congress rather than in the executive; (3) prohibit members of Congress from accepting offices from the president during the term of office for which they were elected. Adds that he will also support a pending resolution for an amendment to limit the duration of the president's term. *Ibid.* For Clay's main speech on these proposals, see Speech in Senate, January 24, 1842.

Still later this day, Clay speaks to Sen. Thomas H. Benton's bill to postpone until July, 1842, the operation of the Bankruptcy Act of August 19, 1841 [Remark in Senate, April 22, 1840], scheduled to take effect on February 1, 1842. Benton asks that the delay be granted so that the act might be amended, especially with regard to extending its provisions to banking corporations. Clay agrees that some amendments to the legislation may be necessary to satisfy public demand for modifications. Concludes that "if he could be satisfied, beyond all controversy, that the public were opposed to the law, or the retention of it upon their statute-books, he would have no objections to suspend its operation or favor its repeal." *Cong. Globe,* 27 Cong., 2 Sess., 63. For the 1841 Bankruptcy Act, see *Cong. Globe,* 27 Cong., 1 Sess., 348-50; also 5 *U.S. Stat.,* 440-49, and Remark in Senate, April 22, 1840. For Clay's main speech against amending, postponing, or repealing this act, see Speech in Senate, January 28, 1842.

Sen. Thomas Hart Benton had introduced the "bill to postpone the operation of the bankrupt law" (Senate bill 98) on December 27, 1841. This bill to *postpone* was rejected by the Senate on February 15, 1842, by a vote of 18 to 23. A "bill to repeal the act establishing a uniform system of bankruptcy" (House bill 72) was introduced in the House on December 15, 1841, and passed on January 17, 1842, by a vote of 126 to 94. This bill to *repeal* was read in the Senate for the first time on January 18 and was defeated in the Senate on January 28 by a vote of 22 to 23, Clay voting nay. U.S. Sen., *Journal,* 27 Cong., 2 Sess., 53, 97, 130, 166; U.S. H. of Reps., *Journal,* 27 Cong., 2 Sess., 81, 213. Benton introduced on December 8, 1842, a "bill to repeal the bankrupt act" (Senate bill 1). This bill was postponed indefinitely on February 24, 1843; however, an almost identical bill to repeal (House bill 614) was introduced in the House on December 13, 1842, and passed on January 17, 1843, by a vote of 140 to 72. It also passed the Senate on February 25, 1843, by a vote of 32 to 13 and was signed into law on March 3, 1843. U.S. Sen., *Journal,* 27 Cong., 3 Sess., 20, 30, 146, 216, 229; U.S. H. of Reps., *Journal,* 27 Cong., 3 Sess., 50, 215; 5 *U.S. Stat.,* 614.

Remark in Senate, December 29, 1841. Introduces the three joint resolutions mentioned yesterday [Remark in Senate, December 28, 1841], proposing to amend the Constitution in such a way as to produce "the curtailment of Executive power."

Says they need not be referred to committee, and asks that they be made the order of business for January 12, 1842. Explains that "the party to which he belonged came into power pledged to carry out that principle; and whether they were prepared to carry it out or not, so far as he was individually concerned he intended to redeem that pledge as far as practicable." *Cong. Globe*, 27 Cong., 2 Sess., 69.

From Benjamin Bosworth Smith, "Kalorama," near Louisville, Ky., January 3, 1842. Is concerned, "As the period approaches when my term of office expires as Superintendent of Public Instruction for this Commonwealth," that he will not be reappointed by Gov. Robert P. Letcher. Notes: "It is whispered that I shall not be, in view of rotation in office. If that be the principle, farewell to all hope of the success of this noble, and much needed enterprize. If my claims for the first appointment were good, experience has render[ed] me doubly fit for the office." Adds that "It is whispered that I must be made the scape goat, for bringing to light educational statistics, injurious to the fame of Kentucky. It seems to me the only question should be, are they true? Another years travel, especially in the mountainous counties enables me, more than to substantiate my former statements. God forbid that I should take pleasure in exposing the nakedness of the land. But I thought, and still think, that the extent of the malady must be known before we can be aroused to apply the remedy." Says he was "most abused for stating that 15 Grand-jurors were found in Judge [Wiley P.] Fowlers District (I never stated publicly where) not one of whom could read or write," but that he has discovered this was also true in at least two other districts. Concludes: "If this be the ground of my removal, so be it, I cheerfully submit. My sacred office long since taught me, that the surest way of making an enemy, is to tell him the truth."

Is particularly upset that "It is whispered (and with great confidence) that as I was first in, by a Wickliffe Executive, I shall be sure to be turned out by a Clay Executive. *That would* indeed be hard, since, as far as I understand matters and things, in all points where those interests differ, I am, as I have ever been a Clay man." Asks, therefore, if Clay will "address a letter to Governor Letcher in my behalf: Not by any means if you feel any doubt as to my competency or efficiency, for the cause itself is too dear to me to wish to have it hindered for my private benefit." Mentions also that the office "is specially desirable to me, for private reasons" because he has gone into debt by purchasing a house to retire to in his old age and is spending additional sums to render it "commodious for twenty young Lady Boarding Scholars." Notes that he and his wife "*may* be able to work through without my official salary," but "it would be much easier & more certain with it." Nevertheless, wants his application considered "only upon general and public reasons."

Believes that the office of superintendent of public instruction ought to be continued and that his background, "growing out of my New England training, & residence in Philadelphia & Virginia," provides him with "some special points of fitness for it." Contends that the "labours, researches, and reflections of two years in this Department *fully* satisfy me of its substantial adaptation & practicability, here in Kentucky, as much as in New York, especially if your grand scheme of the threefold division of the proceeds of the sale of Public Lands [8:812-13] could take effect." ALS. Ky.

Smith had been appointed superintendent of public instruction in February, 1840 and served until the term expired in February, 1842. He was not reappointed. Ky. Sen., *Journal* . . . 1839-1840, pp. 47, 71; *ibid.*, 1841-1842, pp. 41-42. Smith and his wife continued for many years to operate the school for young ladies at their residence "Kalorama" near the Bardstown Road in the east end of Louisville. *RKHS* (July, 1951), 49:187.

Wiley P. Fowler of Salem, Ky., was circuit court judge in the 16th district. David H. Williams (ed.), *The American Almanac and Repository of Useful Knowledge for the Year 1841* (Boston, 1841), 229.

To ROBERT P. LETCHER Washington, January 6, 1842

I have this moment received your Message[1] which has some good reading in it, which I like very much.

The Senate has now been engaged more than a week in the discussion of the President's Curr[enc]y. plan.[2] In the form in which he has presented it, it meets with no favor from any quarter, and stands no chance of passing. So far from any Senator coming out in its favor, almost every Senator has declared himself against it.

I should regret the passage of any instruction, by our General Assembly, on the subject of the Bankrupt law, not on my own but on public account.[3] The truth is that the Bankrupt law was a part of a system of measures of relief. The Distribution bill[4] could not have been carried without the Bankrupt bill; and if the latter be repealed, there is *much reason to fear* that the Distribution bill may also be repealed. And if we thus retrace our steps, amidst our other difficulties, how will it be possible for the Whigs to maintain their ascendancy?

ALS. KyU. Written from "S. Chamber." 1. In his annual message of Dec. 31, 1841, Letcher had argued strongly for a national bank and for distribution of the proceeds of public land sales to the states. Ky. H. of Reps., *Journal* . . . 1841-1842, pp. 11-19. 2. Clay to James B. Clay, Dec. 10, 1841. 3. On Dec. 31, 1841, the Kentucky house passed a resolution instructing "our Senators in Congress . . . to use their exertions to have the Bankrupt Law . . . repealed." The Kentucky senate passed the house resolution on Jan. 27, 1842. Ky. H. of Reps., *Journal* . . . 1841-1842, p. 11; Ky. Sen., *Journal* . . . 1841-1842, p. 179. 4. For the Distribution Act of 1841, see Clay to Ewing, April 30, 1841. This act provided that when tariff duties rose above 20%, the operation of distribution would be suspended. On Feb. 15, 1842, Clay introduced a resolution declaring that the 20% proviso should be repealed and the tariff raised above 20% in order to supply the government with needed revenue. In a special message on March 25, 1842 [*MPP*, 4:108-10], President Tyler declared that he would sign no tariff bill that repealed the 20% proviso. Thus, the proposed tariff bills in 1842 were linked with the issue of the distribution of public land sales receipts. On June 3, Rep. Millard Fillmore introduced the so-called "Little (or provisional) tariff" bill in the House. It passed that body on June 15 by a vote of 116-103 and the Senate on June 24 by a vote of 24-19. On June 25 the House concurred in a Senate amendment to the bill which postponed from July 1, 1842, to August 1, 1842, both the reduction in tariff rates due under the Compromise Tariff of 1833 [8:604, 619-22, 626-27] and the distribution of public land sales revenues. Because this bill retained the distribution principle, Tyler vetoed it on June 29 [*MPP*, 4:180-83]. *Cong. Globe*, 27 Cong., 2 Sess., 637; U.S. Sen., *Journal*, 27 Cong., 2 Sess., 428. A "Great (or permanent) tariff" bill was introduced in the House by Fillmore on June 9. This bill, which also contained the distribution feature, passed the House by 116-112 votes on July 19 and the Senate on August 5 by 25-23. Tyler vetoed it on August 9 [*MPP*, 4:183-89]. *Cong. Globe*, 27 Cong., 2 Sess., 717, 762, 852. On July 23, Daniel D. Barnard (Whig, N.Y.) reported in the House an amended version of the "Little tariff" which omitted the distribution clause. This bill passed the House on August 22 by 104-103 votes and the Senate on August 27, no vote count given. The president signed this bill into law on August 30 [5 *U.S. Stat.*, 548-67]. U.S. H. of Reps., *Journal*, 27 Cong., 2 Sess., 1151, 1385; U.S. Sen., *Journal*, 27 Cong., 2 Sess., 629. A separate bill repealing the 20% proviso of the Distribution Act of 1841 was introduced in the House on August 25, 1842, and passed that body on August 26 by a vote of 104-86. It passed the Senate on August 29 by 23-19 votes. The president disposed of it by pocket veto. U.S. H. of Reps., *Journal*, 27 Cong., 2 Sess., 1409-11, 1423, 1444; U.S. Sen., *Journal*, 27 Cong., 2 Sess., 631. See also George M. Stephenson, *The Political History of the Public Lands From 1840 to 1862* (Boston, 1917), 64-65, 74-87, and Remark in Senate, Feb. 3, 1842.

Remark in Senate, January 6, 1842. Introduces a bill amending the several acts relating to copyrights. *Cong. Globe,* 27 Cong., 2 Sess., 96. The bill died in committee.

Also presents a petition of New York citizens remonstrating against the repeal or postponement of the Bankruptcy Act of 1841 [Remark in Senate, April 22, 1840, and December 28, 1841]. U.S. Sen., *Journal,* 27 Cong., 2 Sess., 72.

To ROBERT C. WINTHROP Washington, January 8, 1842

H. Clay's compliments to Mr. Winthrop, with his thanks for the opportunity afforded him of perusing the observations of Mr. Lawrence[1] on the plan of the Exchequer.[2] The objections to it are so numerous so weighty & so decisive that there is more difficulty in selecting than in perceiving them. Mr. Lawrence has struck upon some of the strongest.

ALS. MHi. 1. Probably Abbott Lawrence. 2. Clay to James B. Clay, Dec. 10, 1841.

Remark in Senate, January 10, 1842. Presents a petition from Ohio and Mississippi river pilots asking for legislation that would keep untrained and incompetent pilots off those waterways and thereby reduce "the disasters on those rivers." Clay supports the need for such safety legislation. *Cong. Globe,* 27 Cong., 2 Sess., 109.

To CHRISTOPHER HUGHES Washington, January 11, 1842

I received your kind invitation, and should be most happy to accept it, if I could; but waiving other objections, the state of my health, which is not good, and my engagements, public and professional, which are now pressing and numerous, will not allow me. And yet I want much to see you, not merely to give you a cordial shake by the hand, but to correct a most erroneous impression on your mind, that I have failed to perform any office of friendship towards you. You seem to think that all the world, and I among the rest, had neglected to obtain your diplomatic promotion. You forget that when I had some little power, among its last acts, was your nomination to Holland,[1] and that from that day to this I have been as powerless as the Chargé des Affaires to Sweden,[2] if not more so.

When do you mean to come here?

Wishing that your daughter's[3] party may realize all the pleasure anticipated from it . . .

ALS. MiU-C. Addressed to Hughes in Baltimore, Md. 1. Hughes had been appointed chargé d'affaires to The Netherlands by the John Q. Adams administration in 1825. See 4:85-86. 2. Hughes himself. 3. Margaret Smith Hughes.

Remark in Senate, January 11, 1842. Speaks to an amendment of Sen. Augustus S. Porter (Whig, Mich.) to a resolution by Sen. John C. Calhoun calling on the president for information about the slave uprising on the brig *Creole,* including the murder of a passenger and the wounding of four crewmen, about events on board the vessel after it reached Nassau in the British Bahamas, and what steps have been taken by the president to punish the guilty slaves and redress British insults to the American flag. Porter's amendment would strike out the word "slaves" and substitute the word "persons," because the Constitution did not use the former. Clay hopes that the nation can remain unified on this issue and that it will not become a "party question." Informs Porter, however, that he has read the protest submitted by the passengers and officers of the *Creole* when they finally reached

New Orleans and that "With regard to the occurrences on board of the vessel, there could be no earthly doubt that the murder was committed by slaves. He would here mention a circumstance which was highly creditable, and it was, that, of the thirty-eight slaves, only nineteen took a part in the murder; the rest, if for no other reason, looked on with dread, or took part with their masters; and this was especially the case with the female slaves. There could be no earthly doubt that the murder was committed by slaves on board of the vessel." Adds that he has "learned the subsequent proceedings at Nassau with infinite regret, because it added greatly to our difficulties with the British Government, which claimed that slaves, thrown into the Bahama Islands by the act of God, were entitled to their liberty, and the vessel was thrown into its port by an act of mutiny and murder. It remained to be seen whether this course was to be persisted in; if so, they would be virtually denied the benefit of the coasting trade around their own country; and a vessel could not proceed from one port to another with safety to the property which might be on board." Informs Porter that the word "slaves" had been frequently used in Anglo-American relations, specifically, that it appears in the first article of the Treaty of Ghent with reference to indemnity payments for those slaves removed from the United States by the British at the end of the War of 1812. Asks Porter not to press his amendment. *Cong. Globe*, 27 Cong., 2 Sess., 116. Porter withdrew his amendment and Calhoun's resolution was adopted unanimously. For Porter, nephew of Peter B. Porter, see *BDAC*. Following the uprising of 19 of the 135 slaves on board the *Creole* on November 7, 1841, the mutineers took the vessel to Nassau where the British authorities eventually tried and hanged the actual murderers, detained the others, and freed the nonparticipants by virtue of their having reached British soil. U.S. property claims growing out of these British emancipations were not settled until 1853. See Howard Jones, "The Peculiar Institution and the National Honor: The Case of the *Creole* Slave Revolt," *CWH* (March, 1975), 21:29-33, 36; *Sen. Docs.*, 27 Cong., 2 Sess., no. 51, pp. 1-51; Baxter, *One and Inseparable*, 327-28.

Remark in Senate, January 12, 1842. Presents memorials from five New York mercantile firms, and one from Harrisburg, Pa., asking that there be no interference with the Bankruptcy Act [Remark in Senate, April 22, 1840, and December 28, 1841] "as it now exists." Asked to say "something favorable" on the subject, says that the time for discussion [Comment in Senate, January 17, 1842] is not ripe and that he regrets the existence of the movement for repeal or postponement. *Cong. Globe*, 27 Cong., 2 Sess., 120; U.S. Sen., *Journal*, 27 Cong., 2 Sess., 82.

To CORNELIUS MATHEWS Washington, January 13, 1842

I recd. your letter on the subject of the Copy right bill.[1] I have introduced the same bill [precisely?] that I formerly presented. It was referred to the Comee. on the Judiciary, which has not yet reported. It is impossible to say at what time it will be taken up in the Senate.

The opposition to its passage has hitherto been prompted by some of the large Book printing establishments. They have contrived to enlist with them the paper makers, book binders, and other classes of the community. In this way quite a formidable array has been made. They will probably repeat this operation. If any thing can be done to counteract it, undoubtedly, it would facilitate the passage of the law.

I am thankful for your kind offer of Arcturus;[2] but receiving now more periodicals & news papers than I can read, I would not wish to put you to the trouble of sending it to me.

ALS. DLC. 1. Comment in Senate, Feb. 2, 1837. 2. Mathews, a lawyer and writer in New York City, was at this time editor of *Arcturus*, a monthly journal of books and opinions. For Mathews, see *DAB*.

To Charles B. Penrose, solicitor of the treasury, Washington, January 13, 1842. Transmits letter from Dr. Stephen Duncan of Natchez, Miss., concerning the debt due to the United States by the Agricultural Bank of Natchez. Asks: "If nothing else can be done . . . could you not agree to give them another year from the 31st. March next, when I understand the present suspension of execution expires, upon the condition of their paying on that day . . . one third of the debt?" Believes this "would afford some relief" from "the present intense distress that prevails there." ALS. DLC-DNA, RG206, Bank Cases 1836-48 (R14).

On January 15, 1842, Penrose replied to Clay, enclosing a letter to Dr. Duncan "open for your perusal." Notes "You will observe that I have adopted your suggestion by agreeing to give a suspension of execution for one year." Copy. DLC-DNA, RG206, Letters on Duty Bonds, vol. 6, pp. 272-73. For Penrose, a Pennsylvania lawyer, see *DAB*.

Remark in Senate, January 13, 1842. Presents a memorial from New York citizens remonstrating against the amendment, postpontment, or repeal of the Bankruptcy Act of 1841 [Remark in Senate, April 22, 1840, and December 28, 1841]. *Cong. Globe*, 27 Cong., 2 Sess., 124; U.S. Sen., *Journal*, 27 Cong., 2 Sess., 85.

To ROBERT SWARTWOUT Washington, January 14, 1842

I think as gloomily as you do of the present posture of our public affairs. I am distressed at finding myself utterly unable to realize the hopes, with which you say so many of our fellow Citizens turn towards me. What can I do? In former epochs, the object to be accomplished was to reconcile conflicting opinions *in Congress*. If that were now the case, I should not be without hope. But it is far different. Now the object is to reconcile conflicting opinions between Congress, and the President; between a faithful Congress and a faithless President. That President is moreover jealous, envious, embittered towards me. He has power; I have none. What can I do to reconcile *his* opinions & action with those of Congress?

As to the project of a Convention, with a view to a change of measures, and a redress of grievances, if expedient, it ought to originate with the people & be their work.[1] As to its expediency, that will depend upon whether it is gotten up generally & with spirit, and upon the wisdom of its proceedings.

ALS. NN. 1. Probably a reference to a convention which would endorse a Whig presidential candidate. In fact, the New York Whig state convention which met in Syracuse on Sept. 7, 1842, passed resolutions supporting Clay for president in the 1844 election. Also, a Convention of Whig Young Men of New York met at Auburn on Sept. 21 and added its support for Clay. Washington *Daily National Intelligencer*, Sept. 13, 26, 1842.

To PETER B. PORTER Washington, January 16, 1842

I received your two favors dated at Albany and Saratoga. I should have written to you before, if I had any thing to communicate, of which the papers did not inform you. The plan of an Exchequer[1] meets with but little favor from either party. I did not take any part in the debate to which it gave rise in the Senate; but my opinion is decidedly against it. Nor do

I think that any thing can be made out of it. The House will pass a bill to repeal the Bankrupt law; and its fate in the Senate is doubtful.[2] Kentucky is against it, and I shall probably be instructed to vote for its repeal![3] I shall, as at present advised, not do so; and yet if I were to yield to the feelings of natural resentment I might; for a base & groundless insinuation has been made at the North that I was at the bottom of the movement for its repeal. Instead of being credited for the firmness & independence with which I stand alone from my State, I am charged with sinister motives because I cannot control the judgment of my State & its whole delegation. Was there ever such injustice! Was ever man before treated as I have been & am now!

All is confusion, chaos & disorder here. No system! No concert of action! No prospect of union and harmony! I have been a looker on at Verona. And I shall continue so generally whilst I remain here.

This discouraging state of things I believe attributable to the President, who yet shews no disposition to change his fatal course. To what it will all lead God only knows. Our bleeding Country is the sufferer. I some times think that an awful crisis is nigh at hand. Most certainly the existing state of things any where but in the U. States would lead to civil commotion.

Can't you join us here? Perhaps your presence and your Counsels might help us. I should be most happy to see [you]. . . . [P.S.] 17h. The bill to repeal the Bankrupt law has just passed the House 126 to 94.

ALS. NBuHi. 1. Clay to James B. Clay, Dec. 10, 1842. 2. Remark in Senate, April 22, 1840, and Dec. 28, 1841. 3. Clay to Letcher, Jan. 6, 1842.

Comment in Senate, January 17, 1842. Presents a number of memorials—from N.Y., Md., Pa., N.J., Mass., and Ky.—signed by hundreds of citizens (one from Frankfort, Ky., was signed by 400 persons) remonstrating against interference with the Bankruptcy Act of 1841 [Remark in Senate, April 22, 1840, and December 28, 1841]. Points out the error in an earlier opinion of a prominent businessman in New York that were the bankruptcy bill to become law, it would operate to throw $100,000,000 worth of property "into the market to be sacrificed." This was mere conjecture, Clay maintains, and it is not likely to occur. Says that the law passed on August 19, 1841, "came recommended to Congress, not only by all considerations of justice, of humanity, and benevolence, but recommended no less by the appalling condition of the country. If, among all the other distresses, discontents, and disorders, which everywhere prevailed to so alarming an extent, this Legislature should now slam the door in the faces of those unfortunate men who had at length hoped to be liberated from irretrievable embarrassment, by the beneficent operations of this law, it would produce such a state of excitement, distress, disorder, and despair, from one end of the land to the other, that no man could foresee, or even conjecture, the consequences." Characterizes as "base and dishonorable" charges circulating in the House that he had initiated the movement in that chamber to repeal the bankruptcy law. Notes that when the bankruptcy bill came up for a final vote in the House last August, every member but one of the Kentucky delegation in that body had voted against it. Even so, there are those who now hold him responsible for the behavior of the Kentucky delegation. Asserts that those who imagine "that Kentuckians were made of so supple, servile stuff, as to take their public course in legislation, from the dictation of any man, had yet to learn their true character." Repeats his complaint that the accusation linking him to the repeal of the bankruptcy law is "base and despicable"; assures both friends and foes that "whatever might have been the errors of his head, he had, at least, sought to live, as he hoped to die, an HONEST MAN—honest in his public, as in his private life." *Cong. Globe*, 27 Cong., 2 Sess., 136. Printed in Colton, *Clay Correspondence*, 6:297-300.

Remark in Senate, January 18, 1842. Moves that the petition of Richard Higgins, Jr., on the files of the Senate, be referred to the Committee on Public Lands. U.S. Sen., *Journal*, 27 Cong., 2 Sess., 96. "An Act for the relief of Richard Higgins," allowing him to prove his preemption right to certain land lying in Crittenden County, Ark., was signed into law on August 11, 1842. See 6 *U.S. Stat.*, 853.

Remark in Senate, January 19, 1842. Presents citizens' memorials, four from New York and one from Philadelphia, protesting the postponement or repeal of the Bankruptcy Act of 1841 [Remark in Senate, April 22, 1840, and December 28, 1841]. *Cong. Globe*, 27 Cong., 2 Sess., 145; U.S. Sen., *Journal*, 27 Cong., 2 Sess., 99.

From Robert S. Oakley, New York, January 20, 1842. Mentions a rumor recently circulating about Clay (that he will support repeal of the bankruptcy law), disclaims any belief in it, and attributes it to "the bitter state of feeling produced by the alarming prospect of being disappointed in the cherished hopes resulting from the anticipated action of the Bankrupt law [Remark in Senate, April 22, 1840, and December 28, 1841]." Notes that "It needed not the formal denial of the charge [Comment in Senate, January 17, 1842], for Mr. Clay's friends would soon have been assured by their own observation of the fallacy of the rumour; at the same time his vindication of himself from the Charge can do him no injury." Views Clay's conduct in differing from "the wisdom of the people of his own State [Clay to Letcher, January 6, 1842; Porter to Clay, January 20, 1842], as another Evidence of that nobleness of soul, which will Ever sacrifice personal considerations to the welfare of the majority—the idea of *instructing* the *Nation's representatives is absurd."*

Does not know "how high a valuation Mr. Clay places upon the Presidency of these United States, but taking it for granted that he will feel it due to his friends and party, to lend himself as their Candidate in 1844, I feel assured that New York will vindicate herself from the discredit that the machinations of a few fastened upon her at the Harrisburgh [*sic*, Harrisburg] Convention [Porter to Clay, November 14, 1837, December 30, 1837, and February 16, 1839], and give her voice En masse for him, when the time comes. But he who gets her vote must show himself the friend of the Bankrupt law." Thinks that "There are those who think Mr. Clay occupies a higher station where he now is, than were he to fill the presidential chair, after its recent incumbents." ALS. DLC-HC (DNA, M212, R5). No Robert S. Oakley appears in the New York State or New York City Census for 1840.

From Peter B. Porter, Niagara Falls, N.Y., January [20], 1842. Reports "an immense excitement in every part of this State, and I believe throughout the Northern States, on the question of the repeal of the Bankrupt Law [Remark in Senate, April 22, 1840]." Realizes that this "places you in a situation of peculiar difficulty and delicacy, exposing you to a cross fire, from a decided majority of the people of the United States on one side, and the people and Legislature of Kentucky on the other [Clay to Letcher, January 6, 1842]." Notes that "the obvious and safe course of ordinary men would be to follow the opinions and instructions of his own State. But if you go in opposition to them, and oppose the repeal as I hope and infer from some observations which have lately dropped from you in the Senate [Remark in Senate, December 28, 1841], you will in my humble opinion add new strength and eclat to your reputation. You have a political capital which will enable you to do that from choice from which ordinary men would shrink and which would destroy them." Mentions that the "remarks of your colleague, Mr. [James T.] Morehead, in which he so happily contrasts his position with yours, will give a fair opening and lead to the course which we understand you intend to pursue."

Reports also that he has talked recently with political friends at Albany and Niagara Falls and that "Our present project is . . . to draw up a private & confidential paper, or declaration, to be circulated and signed during the winter as extensively as possible among our principal political friends in every part of the State, by which the signers shall pledge themselves to support you for the next Presidency." Wants to know Clay's opinion of this plan. Copy. OHi.

James T. Morehead, Clay's colleague from Kentucky in the Senate, had announced on January 18 that he would vote for repeal of the Bankruptcy Act of 1841. He had contrasted his position to Clay's by indicating that his own stance in the Senate could not be regarded "in any light other than connecting him with the State which he represented. But his colleague occupied higher ground; . . . Proud as Kentucky was of the public service of his colleague, she was not so selfish as to appropriate him exclusively to herself. The poorest citizen of the Union, without regard to State, might recognize him as a representative, and he, that poor citizen as a constituent." *Cong. Globe*, 27 Cong., 2 Sess., 141.

Remark in Senate, January 20, 1842. Presents memorials from manufacturers, merchants, and other citizens in Philadelphia asking for amendment or repeal of the Bankruptcy Act [Remark in Senate, December 28, 1841]. Says he does not concur in reasons given by the petitioners for repeal, but thinks some of their proposed amendments "worthy of consideration." Also presents memorials from citizens in Erie County, Pa., and Summit County, Ohio, protesting the postponement or repeal of the Bankruptcy law. *Cong. Globe*, 27 Cong., 2 Sess., 148; U.S. Sen., *Journal*, 27 Cong., 2 Sess., 102.

Remark in Senate, January 21, 1842. Presents two memorials from New York citizens protesting the amendment, postponement, or repeal of the Bankruptcy Act [Remark in Senate, April 22, 1840, and December 28, 1841]. U.S. Sen., *Journal*, 27 Cong., 2 Sess., 104.

Later this day, Clay responds to information that the Alabama legislature has rejected "with indignation and scorn" the payment to which it was entitled under the distribution law of September 4, 1841 [Clay to Ewing, April 30, 1841; Remark in Senate, June 9, 1841]. Submits a resolution, to lie over until tomorrow, asking for study of a possible law that "whenever any State or States shall refuse their proportions of the proceeds of the public lands, such proportion shall be distributed among the residue of the assenting States." Following this, moves to table a resolution by Sen. William C. Rives (Va.) to require the secretary of the treasury to submit a detailed plan of how he proposes to balance government income and expenditure and to estimate what retrenchments may be necessary to do so. Argues that "in view of the pressing necessity of action on the Treasury Note bill," the Rives motion, although an important one, should be tabled and printed. Clay's motion to table passed 27 to 19, he voting yea. *Cong. Globe*, 27 Cong., 2 Sess., 153. The Treasury note bill was passed by the Senate on January 22, 1842, by a 21 to 20 vote, Clay not voting. *Ibid.*, 160. The House concurred on January 29, 1842, with a vote of 101 to 100, Speaker John White (Whig, Ky.) voting yea to break the initial tie. *Ibid.*, 196. Signed into law by Tyler on January 31, the legislation authorized the issue of $5,000,000 in treasury notes under the provisions of the Treasury Note Act of October 12, 1837 [Comment in Senate, September 15, 1837; 5 *U.S. Stat.*, 201-4], save that the issuing authority would expire in one year. See 5 *U.S. Stat.*, 469.

Still later this day, Clay replies to Sen. Levi Woodbury's explanation and defense of his amendment to the Treasury note bill that would pledge the proceeds from public lands sales to the redemption of the notes, rather than distributing them to the states, and, to accomplish this, repeal the first nine sections [the distribution sections] of the Distribution and Preemption Act of September 4, 1841 [Clay to Ewing, April 30, 1841; Remark in Senate, June 9, 1841; 5 *U.S. Stat.*, 453-55]. Since Woodbury emphasizes in presenting his amendment the various problems having to do with the depreciation of existing treasury note values, increasing national budget deficits, a decrease in public confidence in the government's credit, and the need for the nation to return to the "good old fashioned mode of providing for a loan. . . . which [is] to pledge something tangible for the redemption of the debt about to be incurred," Clay chides him with rhetorical questions: "What did the honorable Senator do, when at the head of the Treasury Department? His policy [seems] to have changed"; and "whence this new born zeal in regard to taxation?" If he is now so concerned about deficit and credit problems, "Where was he . . . when we had the tax [revenue] bill [Clay to Ewing, April 30, 1841; Remark in Senate, July 16, 1841; 5 *U.S. Stat.*, 463-65] before us? Did he not rather choose to sip his tea and coffee a little longer, and to withhold the tax from those luxuries?" Points out that when Woodbury was secretary of the treasury, he had twice recommended the issuing of treasury notes, but now he says he is "opposed to the whole system of issuing Treasury notes and that he could not vote for this bill, unless his vote was necessary to save it." As for the public lands, "The Senator talks . . . as though they were thrown away. Did not the people have the benefit of them? But why . . . this covert attack upon the Land [distribution] bill when another bill is under consideration?" In response to Woodbury's reply to his attack, Clay "contrasted the Senator's precepts now, with his example at the head of the Treasury Department." *Cong. Globe*, 27 Cong., 2 Sess., 156. Woodbury's amendment was defeated 19 to 26, Clay voting nay. Woodbury voted against the Treasury note bill the following day (January 22). *Ibid.*, 157, 160. A bill to repeal sections 1-6 (providing for the distribution of land sales proceeds to the states) of the Distribution and Preemption Act of September 4, 1841, and to use that income instead for "the common defense of the Union," had been introduced by Sen. Louis F. Linn (Dem., Mo.) on December 21, 1841. The bill failed to command a majority vote as to which committee it should be referred. On December 28, 1841, the measure was placed on the Senate calendar, "subject to be disposed of at any time." That time never came. *Ibid.*, 64.

From James Watson Webb, New York, January 21, 1842. In reference to repeal of the Bankruptcy Act [Remark in Senate, April 22, 1840, and December 28, 1841], states: "All our acc[ou]nts agree that the repeal cannot pass the Senate; & that if it should, *John Tyler* will veto it. *This must not be.* If the Bill should be rejected, the House will probably pass a bill postponing the time for the Law to go into effect. This we think would pass the Senate; & this too, would be promptly *vetoed*. Now, it appears to me that the true policy, is to keep the repeal bill before the Senate for sixty days. The Law in the mean time goes into effect. Then reject it, & it will be too late to attempt to pass a Bill postponing its operations. This to me, appears the only safe ground of proceeding."

Emphasizes the importance "that *you* should be identified with the promotion of the Law as it is. . . . 'Save the Bankrupt Law & return to Ashland.' *You* will have then have done all that *you* should do, & the *people* will perform their duty."

Describes himself as "a disinterested Supporter" who will "never again be a candidate *for any office*," and whose motto is " 'Harry of the West or a Loco Foco.' " ALS. DLC-HC (DNA, M212, R5).

To PETER B. PORTER Washington, January 22, 1842

I recd your favor of the 20h. which not mentioning a letter I addressed to you at the City, I suppose it had not reached me [*sic*, you]. The fate of the Bankrupt law is uncertain[1] I think that I shall give no just occasion for dissatisfaction to our N.Y. friends, whatever may be the case with those in Kentucky.[2]

My own opinion is that it is now premature to agitate the question of the next President. Still it will be difficult much longer to suppress public manifestations. They are to have a State Convention in N. Carolina on the 4h Apl next, and I understand that I shall be then nominated.[3] The Whig portion of the Delegation has unanimously recommended it.

With respect to the plan proposed by our friends in N. York, I see no objection to it.[4] The contemplated declaration should be prepared as if it would meet, as I presume it will meet the public eye.

I adhere to my purpose to resign my Seat in the Senate to take effect towards the last of March.[5]

ALS. NBuHi. 1. Remark in Senate, April 22, 1840, and December 28, 1841. 2. Clay to Letcher, Jan. 6, 1842. 3. The North Carolina Whigs, meeting in Raleigh on April 4, 1842, did, in fact, nominate Clay for president. *Niles' Register* (April 16, 1842), 62:112. 4. Porter to Clay, Jan. 20, 1842. 5. Clay to Berrien, Oct. 7, 1841.

Remark in Senate, January 22, 1842. Presents petitions remonstrating against modification, amendment, or repeal of the Bankruptcy Act [Remark in Senate, April 22, 1840, and December 28, 1841]; also a petition from New York City praying for tariff revisions that would provide for ample revenue as well as insure the partial protection and security of domestic labor. *Cong. Globe*, 27 Cong., 2 Sess., 159. For the tariff bills of 1842, see Clay to Letcher, January 6, 1842.

Speech in Senate, January 24, 1842. Speaks at length on the three constitutional amendments he had proposed as joint resolutions in late December [Remark in Senate, December 28 and 29, 1841], viz: no presidential appointments of members of Congress to any federal civil office during their elected terms of office; restrict the president's veto power by authorizing the overriding of a veto by simple majority vote rather than by two-thirds majority vote, and by limiting the pocket veto power of the president so that bills not acted upon by him during the final ten days of a session shall become law if not acted upon during the first three days of the succeeding session; vest the power of appointing annually, by joint vote of both houses, the secretary of the treasury and the treasurer of the United States, and the power to remove these officers by separate, concurrent votes of the two houses, it being understood that neither of these officers can be removed by the president.

Says the subject of limiting the president's veto power has long been on his mind and has not been prompted by "any recent exercise of the power," although "recent events [Tyler to Clay, April 30, 1841] had certainly not tended to weaken . . . his impressions on the general subject." States that he had helped draft such legislation as long as seven years ago and that in June, 1840 he had urged restraints on the veto power, and the general "circumscribing of the Executive power," in a campaign speech at Taylorsville, in Hanover County, Va. [Speech on the State of the Country Under Van Buren, June 27, 1840]. Quotes at length from this speech. Restraining the veto power was to "redeem the pledges and fulfil the promises it [Whig party] made when out of power." On all proposals limiting executive power made by the Whigs during the recent presidential campaign, "in a word, on every great question of national policy to which the party to which he considered himself as belonging were pledged to the people and to the world, they would find him, on all occasions, during the short time in which he expected to remain a member of the body, heartily ready to co-operate in carrying out into practice all they had avowed in principle." Discusses the history of the veto power, beginning in ancient Rome, continuing through British and French practice in the eighteenth century, and into the American and French revolutions. Asserts that "At the head of all the grievances stated in that paper [Declaration of Independence], as reasons for our separation from Great Britain, was placed the exercise of this very power of the Royal Veto." Traces this sentiment into the constitutional convention of 1787 where, unfortunately, the veto power was grafted into our Constitution. "No doubt the idea of engrafting this power upon our own Constitution was adopted by the Convention from having always found it as a power recognised in European Governments, just as it had been before derived by them from the practice and history of Rome. At all events, the power was inserted as one feature, not only in the general Constitution of the Federal Government, but also in the Constitutions of a portion of the States." Believes, however, that the time has come, fifty years later, to review that decision and to recognize "that one great and radical error which possessed the minds of the wise men who drew up that instrument was an apprehension that the Executive department of the then proposed Government would be too feeble to contend successfully in a struggle with the power of the Legislature." These fears have not been borne out. True, much has "been said about the encroachments of the Federal Government on the Governments of the States-rights party and its opposite; but an examination of the facts of the case would demonstrate that no solitary instance had yet occurred of any such encroachment by the General Government . . . on the contrary . . . there [has] been an abandonment by that Government of the exercise of its own just powers in relation to the States, and this to such an extent that the existing state of the country presented very much the same aspect as the old Confederation had once done, with all its weakness and imbecility. . . . But while there had been no such thing in practice as an encroachment by the Federal upon the State Governments, there [has], within the Federal Government itself, been a constant encroachment by the Executive upon the Legislative Department." Gives detailed examples of such encroachments, viz: attacks on the Senate's treaty-making power; dismissals from office of persons appointed by and with consent of the Senate [8:703]; seizure of the power of the purse as seen in Jackson's removal of the public deposits from the Bank of the United States [8:583-84, 684-85, 813], and his dismissal of three secretaries of the treasury who would not assist him in this action; the raising of armies by executive mandate, as in the instance of the Florida volunteers after Congress had specifically refused to sanction such a force. Explains the growth of executive power in that while Congress meets only periodically ("the moment it adjourned its power disappeared"), the "Executive branch of the Government was eternally in action; it was ever awake; it never slept; its action was continuous and unceasing like the tides of some mighty river which continued flowing and flowing on, swelling and deepening and widening in its onward progress, till it swept away every impediment and broke down and removed every frail obstacle which might be set up to impede its course. Let gentlemen look at all history, and they would find that it had been ever so."

Believes that the members of the constitutional convention conferred the veto power on the president because they mistakenly felt that he might need protection from the legislature, and that it was prudent "to guard the country against the injurious effects of crude and hasty legislation." Argues that neither of these concerns was realistic given the role of the judiciary in the constitutional system and the fact that both executive and legislature had a direct appeal to the people if either encroached upon the other. Reports the results of his study of the veto power in the twenty-six state constitutions, some of them older than the national Constitution: "Nine of them gave to the Executive the veto power unless controlled by two-thirds of the Legislature. Eight other States conferred the veto, but controlled it by a second vote of a majority, as was proposed in the amendment now under consideration. While the nine remaining States had not inserted the veto at all; and at the head of these stood one which had been called the mother of States—Virginia." Suggests that "If there had been this very great danger of Executive encroachment and of hasty legislation, one would suppose it would have been heard of in these nine States. Had any instance yet occurred to show that such a danger did exist?" The answer is none. Wishes the Democrats would undertake to prove that "if such dangers both of encroachment and rashness as were pretended as a pretext for the veto did actually exist, how it happened that in the nine States he had named, during so long a period as had elapsed since their constitutions were formed, no instances had occurred either of encroachment by the Legislature on the powers of the Executive, or of such rash and hasty legislation as called for the restraint and safeguard of a single sovereign will?" Explains at length how difficult the overriding of a veto actually is in a Senate of 52 members in which a two-thirds majority is 36, and in the House of 242 members where the two-thirds number is 162. The majority vote numbers (27 and 122) are much to be preferred, he argues. States that the veto power, as it currently stands, is "neither more nor less than an absolute power. . . . Not a solitary instance had yet occurred in which the veto once exerted had ever been overruled, nor was such a case likely to happen." Another weakness inherent in the veto power is that its effect was to "consummate legislation" in that the "officer of Government in whose hands the Constitution placed a power so formidable, was supposed in theory to remain profoundly silent as to the passage of great measures of public policy, until they were presented to him in a finished form for his approbation and sanction. This was the theory; but . . . in practice this veto power drew after it the power of initiating laws, and in its effect must ultimately amount to conferring on the Executive the entire legislative power of the Government. With the power to initiate and the power to consummate legislation—to give vitality and vigor to every law, or to strike it dead at his pleasure—the President must ultimately become the ruler of the nation."

Assures his audience that his criticisms of the veto power are not to be construed as an attack on President Tyler. Still, the expectation in Congress that the president would veto the recent bank bills certainly influenced the vote on the "famous 16h section [Porter to Clay, mid-July, 1841]" of the first of those two bills [Tyler to Clay, April 30, 1841]. Indeed, Clay declares "he did not know a solitary man among those who voted for the bill who would have voted for that section but as a measure of conciliation, and in the hope that, so modified, the bill would receive the sanction of the President. True, that expectation was not realized, the sacrifice was vainly made, but it had been made with a view to that end, and that alone. And so in regard to the second of those bills [Tyler to Clay, April 30, 1841; Remark in Senate, August 24, 1841]. That bill, as he was informed, came to Congress precisely as it had left the President's hand. So anxious had Congress been to secure the approbation of the President that, although almost every thing in the bill would either have been omitted or amended by a majority they took it as it came from the Presidential hand, and passed it, letter for letter, as they received it. Without going further, did not this fact prove that the possession of the veto power drew after it the power of initiating laws?" With reference to Tyler's Exchequer bank plan [Clay to J.B. Clay, December 10, 1841] in the current session, there is not one man in Congress who would have proposed such a scheme; but the feeling now is, "Must we go home without doing something? . . . [must we] take what the Executive offers, or get nothing?" Fears that soon in the nation's history "the whole legislation of this country would come to be prepared at the White House." Adds: "the veto power must be modified and restrained."

Notes that lately there has also been talk "that some curb was necessary upon the power of majorities, and that without this the safety of the country must be in danger." Defends the principle of majority rule, observing that "this doctrine that minorities must govern, whether with or without the veto, was advanced by gentlemen who professed and called themselves members of the Jeffersonian school." Denies this contention, quoting Jefferson on the point that absolute acquiescence in majority rule was necessary in a free, republican government. Also questions the belief that the South "would be more safe under the continuance of the veto power than without it." Perhaps so, but what security will the South possess if "Sooner or later the President would be in a majority himself." Points out, further, that "if a majority of Congress should put itself in opposition to the interest of the South, neither Presidents nor vetoes would avail to protect it." The South had best rely for its security on "the sacred provisions of the Constitution, and then they had the character of our Government as a Confederacy—the existence of these interests long before the adoption of the Constitution, and the rights and duties of the Government in regard [to] them recognised and laid down by that sacred instrument. That was the security of the South." There is no security in the "miserable despotic veto power of the President of the United States." Admits that amending the Constitution to limit the veto power is not likely; the process is too difficult. Indeed, it is "extremely doubtful whether any gentleman here present would ever live to see the Constitution amended; but still it was the duty of every friend of his country to use proper efforts to have it improved." Believes that his resolution to amend into the Constitution the power of Congress to appoint and dismiss the secretary of the treasury might be put aside if his friend, Sen. William S. Archer (Va.), can succeed, as an alternate approach, in establishing what Clay had years ago [1834] attempted, without success, to demonstrate [8:693, 699-700, 703]—"that Congress did possess the constitutional power to define the tenure of office, and to defend it against the power of dismission." Claims that public opinion is in favor of limiting the executive power, a power increasingly viewed with apprehension by the people. Says it is "very true that the personal popularity of the incumbent might add much to his power, but the power itself was official, not personal, and its danger arose from its tendency and ability to accumulate." Warns: "Let not gentlemen deceive themselves by names. The unpretending name President of the United States was no security against the extent or the abuse of power. The power assigned to a public individual did not depend on the title he might bear; the danger arose not from his name, but from the quantum of power at his command. Whether he were called Emperor, Dictator, King, Liberator, Protector, Sultan, or President of the United States, was of no consequence at all. Look at his power: that was what we had to guard against." Sees the possibility that an American president, surrounded by "a cordon of favorites, flatterers, and fawns," isolated from the nation in the fastness of the District of Columbia, could lose touch with "the real sufferings, wants, and wishes of his countrymen" to a much greater extent than the 242 representatives and 52 senators, and in so doing come to exercise "a power not merely to annul the national will, as lawfully uttered by its own chosen Representatives, but the power to initiate legislation itself, and to substitute for the will of the nation an alien will, neither of the nation nor of its Representatives."

Amidst calls for adjournment, says he will speak another time on his amendment to allow Congress to appoint and dismiss the secretary of the treasury and the treasurer of the United States; and the amendment forbidding the appointment of members of Congress to executive posts during their elected terms.

Explains, in conclusion, that while he favors abolishing the veto power altogether, he deems it prudent first to experiment with the substitution of a majority vote for the present two-thirds vote in overriding a veto. Cites in support of this substitution the experience of the states where such a provision is found in their constitutions. *Cong. Globe*, 27 Cong., 2 Sess., 164-66. Printed in Colton, *Clay Correspondence*, 6:301-19.

Clay's remark concerning the raising of troops by executive mandate in the instance of the Florida volunteers probably refers to Jackson's sanction in December, 1835, without a congressional appropriation, of a payment of $3,000 for the expenses incurred by 500 militiamen taken into federal service at the beginning of the Second Seminole War. Mahon, *Second Seminole War*, 101.

Clay's constitutional amendment resolutions were introduced on December 29, 1841. They were last debated on March 4, 1842, but never came to a vote. U.S. Sen., *Journal*, 27 Cong., 2 Sess., 58, 119, 136, 153, 166, 187, 191, 203.

Remark in Senate, January 25, 1842. Presents memorials from Pittsburgh, Pa., and Newark, N.J., for the amendment or repeal of the Bankruptcy Act of 1841 [Remark in Senate, April 22, 1840, and December 28, 1841]; the Newark petitioners maintaining that the law was "a prelude to the general distribution of property." Also presents memorials from Erie, Pa., Albany, N.Y., and Medina, Huron, Clark, and Hamilton counties, Ohio, and Chillicothe, Ohio., opposing amendment, postponement, or repeal of the Bankruptcy Act. *Cong. Globe*, 27 Cong., 2 Sess., 168; U.S. Sen., *Journal*, 27 Cong., 2 Sess., 119-20.

Remark in Senate, January 26, 1842. Presents resolutions of the Kentucky general assembly, unanimously passed in both houses on January 14, condemning repudiations of state debts [Remark in Senate, February 18, 1840] on grounds that "such conduct would be . . . shocking to the sense of Christendom, a lasting reproach to republican government, and a stain on the American name." Clay notes that these sentiments are "entirely coincident with his own." Resolutions tabled and ordered printed. Also presents a petition remonstrating against amending, postponing, or repealing the Bankruptcy Act [Remark in Senate, April 22, 1840, and December 28, 1841]. *Cong. Globe*, 27 Cong., 2 Sess., 172; U.S. Sen., *Journal*, 27 Cong., 2 Sess., 123-24.

To JAMES WATSON WEBB Washington, *ca.* January 26, 1842

I thank you for your friendly suggestions,[1] to which I shall give deliberate consideration.

It has not been found practicable to delay acting on the repeal of the Bankrupt law[2] to a period beyond the commencement of its operation; and the Senate is now engaged on it. Its fate is uncertain. If the repeal can be defeated it will be most likely by a tye vote; but the accidental absence of members from sickness (two are now so unwell that they cannot attend)[3] from non attendance during this Session (Mr. Cuthbert)[4] or from resignation (Mr Mouton)[5] may affect the ultimate decision, one way or the other.[6]

ALS. ViU. 1. This undated letter, probably written from Washington, is apparently an answer to Webb to Clay, Jan. 21, 1842. 2. Remark in Senate, April 22, 1840, and

Dec. 28, 1841. 3. Sen. Nathan F. Dixon (R.I.) died on Jan. 29, 1842. *BDAC*. 4. Sen. Alfred Cuthbert (Ga.). *BDAC*. 5. It was known that Sen. Alexander Mouton had been elected governor of Louisiana. He resigned from the Senate on March 1, 1842, to assume his new post. *BDAC*. 6. The Senate vote on Jan. 28 to repeal the Bankruptcy Act was 22 for, 23 against, Clay voting nay. Neither Mouton nor Cuthbert were recorded as having voted. *Cong. Globe*, 27 Cong., 2 Sess., 186. See also Remark in Senate, Dec. 28, 1841.

To FRANCIS T. BROOKE Washington, January 27, 1842

I have my old apology for not writing to you, which I have to submit to your kindness, to which I must add that I have not been very well, and really nothing of interest to write.

I was glad to learn that you had it in your power to accept the office of President of the C[our]t. of Ap[peals]. and think you were right to decline it.[1] As we advance in years, our labors ought to be lighter. With the view to lessen mine, and in contemplation of the unhappy and distracted state of our public councils, arising out of the course of Mr. Tyler, I mean to resign my seat in the Senate, during this Session.[2] I want rest and my private affairs want attention. Nevertheless, I would make any personal sacrifices, if by remaining here I could do any good; but my belief is that I can effect nothing, and perhaps my absence may remove an obstacle to something being done by others. I shall therefore go home in the Spring.

The papers will inform you of the afflicting scenes passing in the H. of R.[3] They must fill every patriot bosom with deep distress.

ALS. NjMoHP. Printed in Colton, *Clay Correspondence*, 4:456. 1. Brooke had previously been president of the Virginia court of appeals from 1824-31. He remained on the court until his death in 1851. See also 8:206, 335-36. 2. Clay to Berrien, Oct. 7, 1841. 3. Probably a reference to the bitter controversy in the House concerning the so-called "gag rule" and the related debate on a proposed censure of John Q. Adams. *Cong. Globe*, 27 Cong., 2 Sess., 157-59, 160-64, 167-80; Adams, *Memoirs of John Quincy Adams*, 11:59-80.

Remark in Senate, January 27, 1842. Presents petitions from Erie, Pa.; Washington County, Pa.; Cincinnati, Ohio; Wayne, Lorain, and Stark counties in Ohio; and from New York, all opposing the amendment, postponement, or repeal of the Bankruptcy Act of 1841 [Remark in Senate, April 22, 1840, and December 28, 1841]. U.S. Sen., *Journal*, 27 Cong., 2 Sess., 126; *Cong. Globe*, 27 Cong., 2 Sess., 177.

Later this day, informs Sen. Willie P. Mangum, that his petition for payment of a pension arrearage, a petition that had earlier been adversely reported upon by the Committee on Pensions, could not be acted upon because of the Senate rule prohibiting further action on such petitions. *Cong. Globe*, 27 Cong., 2 Sess., 178.

Speech in Senate, January 28, 1842. Having presented memorials from Pennsylvania, Ohio, and New York opposing the amendment, postponement, or repeal of the Bankruptcy Act of August 19, 1841 [Remark in Senate, April 22, 1840, and December 28, 1841], Clay speaks at length on why he opposes repeal of this act.

Notes at the outset that the law is constitutional because its applicability is uniform; that is, creditors and debtors in each state are placed in the "same condition" in regard to bankruptcy. Argues also "that the power vested in Congress fully authorizes the retrospective operation of the law. All bankrupt laws that ever existed, all insolvent laws, all laws, ancient and modern, which have operated like bankrupt laws, from the Jubilee of old to the present day, have this retroactive character." Believes that bankruptcy legislation should not be viewed as a states' rights issue, with each state passing its own version of such laws. Instead, "We are a family of States; and, like any other family, if we are to preserve peace and satisfaction, union, and harmony, we must sympathize with each other, and make mutual concessions." Recalls that "some twenty years ago [*sic*, in 1818]" he had supported a uniform bankruptcy bill in the House [2:440-41]. Two years ago he had supported Sen. John J. Crittenden's bankruptcy bill in the Senate [Remark in Senate, April 22, 1840; Speech in Senate, June 4, 1840]. Points out that in 1840 there was little interest one way or the other in such a law in Kentucky, whereas "recently there has been an exhibition of a strong feeling in opposition to it." But asserts that Kentucky, because of her patriotism, will stand by a law which is of "vital importance to other States in the Union." Kentuckians will not "quarrel about a measure of relief demanded by unparalleled sufferings and misfortunes in other States, from which their happier condition in a great degree exempts them. A measure alike just to the creditor and humane to the debtor! A measure which, excluding the fraudulent from its benefits, is intended only for the honest and unfortunate debtor, after he shall have made a full and fair surrender of all his property and effects. A measure which will lift up the depressed, cheer the desponding, and bring back to life to hope a large, active, and enterprising class, who have been plunged into ruin partly by the erroneous policy of Government itself. Surely, surely, it could only be a merciless creditor that, with lynx eyed vigilance, would watch the future earnings of his debtor, after a fair surrender of all he had—the future earnings of his wife, his child, snatch the bread from their mouths, and appropriate those earnings to a pre-existing debt."

Explains that the Whigs, during the previous session, had attempted to address the nation's economic crisis with a "large, liberal, and comprehensive system of measures of relief." This system included two bank bills [Tyler to Clay, April 30, 1841] designed to "re-establish a sound currency and provide for the reduction of the enormous rates of exchange. . . . Their unfortunate fate is too well known. . . . [even though] Either of those bills, if it had been approved, I have no doubt, would have been sensibly felt, in its beneficial effects, by every interest and in every section of the country." The Whig relief plan also included a distribution measure [Clay to Ewing, April 30, 1841; Remark in Senate, June 9, 1841] which by distributing among all the states the proceeds of public land sales would obviate "the necessity of levying an amount equal to the distributive fund upon their respective inhabitants, in the most onerous from of all taxation—that of a direct tax." Then came tariff legislation [Clay to Ewing, April 30, 1841; Remark in Senate, July 16, 1841] "to relieve the General Government itself, by replenishing its empty coffers. For this purpose a duty was laid upon free articles, which will produce some seven or eight millions of dollars, and which, if certain articles had not, I think, been improperly omitted, would have yielded three millions more." Following this was the Bankruptcy Act [Remark in Senate, April 22, 1840] and the act rechartering the District of Columbia banks [Remark in Senate, June 15 and June 18, 1841]. Nevertheless, "To this whole system of measures of relief, and to each of its parts, our opponents made the most strenuous resistance, upon grounds which they no doubt considered satisfactory, although we could not concur with them. They would now gladly accomplish the subversion of that system which they could not then defeat. To assail the whole system, they are perfectly aware would be unavailing, and they have hope of success but by attacking it in detail. Accordingly, we find them all, with but few exceptions, arraying themselves against the Bankrupt law, as the entering wedge to the destruction of the entire system. Let them carry the repeal, and we shall hear the shouts of triumph and witness the charge of bayonets upon every other part of the system." Already Sen. Linn of Missouri has moved to repeal the distribution act and seems only to be "waiting the repeal of the Bankrupt law to press on his measure with invigorated strength and undoubting confidence." For this reason the repeal of the Bankruptcy Act must be prevented.

Further, the economic conditions that stimulated the need for these relief measures have not changed. "Alas! sir, not only have all these causes, which derange the business of the country, continued, but they have been greatly increased and aggravated since we met here in the summer. And I lament to say that, in looking forward as far as we can catch any glimpses of the future, prone as I am to gaze on the happier side of the picture, I see nothing bright and cheering nigh at hand; but, on the contrary, still greater distress and suffering in every department of industry, further depression in the value of property and in the products of agriculture, and individual ruin and distress more widely spread and more intensely felt. If ever there existed a period of general calamity [it] is now present and that period now exists." Let us not, therefore, "subvert the whole system of beneficient measures adopted at the extra session, by beginning with the repeal of the bankrupt law and ending with that of the law for the distribution of the proceeds of the public lands."

Concludes: And let us not "deprive creditors of the great benefits which are secured to them, to let loose the rigors of the law upon honest debtors, and to replunge them in hopeless despair. Their condition resembles that of innocent and unfortunate men long and unjustly incarcerated within the dark walls of a jail. Its door is half open; they are rushing towards it, pale, emaciated, and exhausted; the light of heaven has once more beamed upon their haggard faces, and once more they begin to breathe the cool and pure air of an uncontaminated atmosphere. At this instant of time, the Senate is called upon to drive them back to their gloomy and loathsome cells, and to fling back that door upon its grating hinges. And I am invited to unite in this work of inhumanity and cruelty! I have not the heart to do it! I have not the hand to do it! I cannot, I will not do it!" *Cong. Globe*, 27 Cong., 2 Sess., Appendix, 98-99. A summary of this speech by Blair and Rives, clerk-reporters, is in *Cong. Globe*, 27 Cong., 2 Sess., 185-86. At the end of this day's debate a motion to repeal the Bankruptcy Act was defeated 22 to 23, Clay voting nay. *Ibid.*, 186.

To THOMAS HART CLAY Washington, January 30, 1842

I recd. to day your letter transmitting the two first numbers of bills of Exchange for $4500 & I have written to N. York to ascertain if they can be negotiated.

To meet the bill which I authorized you to draw on me for $2500, I expect funds from Mr. [James] Erwin who has promised to remit them early in April.[1] I am a little apprehensive that they may not arrive in time to meet a Sixty day bill from the 15h. Feb. But you may make it payable at Seventy days from that date, which I hope will accommodate Mr. Craig.[2]

ALS. DLC-HC (DNA, M212, R5). 1. For Thomas's financial problems, see also Clay to James B. Clay, Dec. 24, 1841. 2. Possibly Elijah Craig.

To JAMES WATSON WEBB Washington, January 30, 1842

You or C[harles]. King Esq.[1] can render me an act of justice, which I am quite sure either of you will be willing to perform.

You will have remarked that Mr. [Henry A.] Wise has dragged my name into the unfortunate affair of poor [Jonathan] Cilley.[2] And he has totally misrepresented any agency of mine in it;[3] but I do not intend, at least in the present aspect of it, if ever, to take any notice of it myself.

It so happened that, on the day of the duel, Mr. King came to me, as your friend, to consult as to the practicability of arresting it. I advised the calling out of the Police, and recommended him to go, for that purpose, to C[harles]. F. Mercer & F[rancis]. [Scott] Key. I understood he did do so, that the police were called out, but unfortunately mistook the Road, on which the parties left the City. Now, this is the fact which I wish to be brought out by one or both of you; and in such suitable manner as may be deemed most proper.[4]

ALS. ViU. Letter marked "(Confidential)." 1. Charles King wrote a statement, dated Feb. 4, 1842, giving his recollections of the Graves-Cilley duel [Clay to Speed, March 2, 1838] and Clay's involvement in it. He said that on Feb. 23, 1838, he had met William J. Graves in the parlor at Gadsby's. When he asked Graves where Henry A. Wise was, Graves "informed me that a challenge had passed between himself & Mr [Jonathan] Cilley, that it had been accepted, [and] that Mr Wise was arranging the preliminaries." King was "greatly shocked" at this information, for "although I had heard rumors that, at the request of Mr. [James Watson] Webb . . . Mr. Graves had called on Mr. Cilley for explanation of language used by that gentleman in allusion to Mr. Webb, I had also heard and certainly believed the matter was adjusted." On informing Webb of the proposed duel, "Mr. Webb . . . at once said the meeting must be prevented. He beckoned to Mr. Reverdy Johnson . . . and the matter having been explained to him, it was agreed that Mr. Johnson and myself should immediately call on Mr Clay, and ask his assistance to arrest the hostile proceeding. We immediately went to Mr Clay's lodgings & there found Mr Graves seated with him." When they explained the object of their visit, Graves left "saying . . . that he could permit no interference with any thing that touched his honor." When they then appealed to Clay, he replied that he "ought not . . . to have been Consulted, but having been, the honor of his friend who was the challenger, might be compromised, by any advance on his (Mr Clay's) part to arrest the progress of the affair." He also "showed to or explained to us the correspondence of the challenge & acceptance" from which they assumed that since Graves had no rifle [the weapon of choice], "the meeting could not take place the next day." King and Johnson then sought Wise, but failed to find him at his lodging. Early the next morning King was roused from bed by Webb who said that Graves and Cilley had gone out. King then roused Johnson and together they went to Clay's lodgings. "When informed that the parties had gone out," Clay "declared it impossible, and sent his servant instantly for Mr Graves. The answer was that Mr Graves had gone by the early train to Baltimore," as had John J. Crittenden and Richard Menefee. "Mr Clay seemed greatly distressed and perplexed, and after some consultation as to the best mode of yet preventing the duel, if possible—for which he seemed as earnest as we were—he suggested that Gen. [Charles F.] Mercer or Mr. [Francis Scott] Key, or both, should be seen without delay." King found Gen. Mercer and they were joined by Waddy Thompson, Jr., in an attempt to discover "the route taken by the parties." However, "All effort was unavailing, and the result is known." ADS. ViU. Also printed in *Kendall's Expositor* (March 5, 1844), 4:73, no. 5. On Feb. 7, 1842, Reverdy Johnson, at the suggestion of Charles King, also wrote a statement of his recollection of events leading to the duel which, he said, "with a few immaterial particulars . . . are precisely such as are detailed by Mr. King." Johnson explained that he and King had not seen the challenge and acceptance "but had them explained to us only by Mr. Clay." Also, he had not been aroused from bed by King but had already been awakened by delivery of a note from Wise alluding to the proposed duel, from which he inferred "that the meeting was to take place that day." When sent for by King, Johnson hurried out, and "As soon as we met, we went at once to Mr. Clay's lodgings, & what took place there is . . . set forth by Mr. K with perfect accuracy. Mr. Clay's surprise at discovering that the duel was to occur that day was evidently as great as ours had been, & his desire to arrest it manifestly as sincere & ardent as ours. To say nothing of his manner throughout the interview, this was most abundantly proved by the means he advised us to pursue." ADS. ViU. 2. Wise had been unable to escape opprobrium in acting as Graves's second since he himself bore personal animosity against Cilley and had allowed the parties to fire three times rather than terminating the duel earlier. See Craig M. Simpson, *A Good Southerner, The Life of Henry A. Wise of Virginia* (Chapel Hill, 1985), 37-44; Crouthamel, *James Watson Webb*, 73-74. See also Clay to Speed, March 2, 1838; Graves to Clay, Feb. 16, 1842; Wise to Clay, Feb. 25, 1842; Clay to Wise, Feb. 28, 1842. 3. A confrontation took place in the House between John Q. Adams and Henry A. Wise beginning on Jan. 21 when Adams, attempting to provoke a debate which would result in a discussion of slavery, introduced a petition from Georgia calling for his own removal as chairman of the House Foreign Relations Committee. In defending himself, Adams read from a letter Wise had written to his constituents in Accomac County, Va., opposing diplomatic recognition of Haiti. On Jan. 24 Adams presented a petition from citizens of Haverhill, Mass., calling for dissolution of the Union. During the exchanges which followed, Wise accused Adams of being an English agent working to break up the Union. Adams, referring to Wise's involvement in the Graves-Cilley duel, retorted that Wise was "a man with his hands and face dripping with the blood of murder," a man more guilty than the one who "happened to draw the trigger." Wise on Jan. 28, declaring that he was now going to vindicate himself, appealed indirectly to Clay and John J. Crittenden who were present in the House to be witnesses to the fact "that his advice was not the advice relied on or followed in the preliminaries of that duel—it was the advice of another, higher, better, and more distinguished man." This statement was generally viewed as an accusation against Clay. *Cong. Globe*, 27 Cong., 2 Sess., 158-62, 168, 170-77, 179-84, 186-94, espec. 176, 194. 4. An editorial on Feb. 12, 1842, in Webb's New York *Weekly Courier and Enquirer* criticized certain newspapers for endeavoring to injure Clay by inculcating as truth Wise's claim that Clay was the "instigator and adviser" in the Graves-Cilley duel. Not only was this a great injustice, the editorial charged, but also if Clay had not been deceived by Wise and his associates as to the time and place of the confrontation, the civil authorities at Clay's instigation would have intervened and prevented the duel. Webb referred to the statements of Charles King and Reverdy Johnson [see note 1 above], as proof of the latter statement. In another editorial on March 19, 1842, Webb exonerated Wise from John Q. Adams's accusation that Wise was the instigator of the duel. Rather, he had simply meant in the Feb. 12 article that in not choosing Bladensburgh, Md., the usual duelling ground, Wise had prevented the interference of the civil authorities. He reiterated his statement that if Clay had known the time and place of the duel, it would have been prevented.

To WILLIAM H. PEARSON Washington, February 2, 1842

I am glad to find that you coincide in opinion with me respecting the Veto.[1] My Speech on that subject was published from the notes of the Reporter, without the correction of a word by me;[2] and I regret that I have not a single Copy of it by me. If I can find the time, it is my purpose to correct it. . . .

ALS. NcD. 1. Speech in Senate, Jan. 24, 1842. 2. The speech was published in the Washington *Daily National Intelligencer* on Jan. 25, 1842.

Remark in Senate, February 2, 1842. Presents seven memorials—four from Ohio and three from New York—opposing the amendment, postponement, or repeal of the Bankruptcy Act [Remark in Senate, April 20, 1840, and December 28, 1841]. U.S. Sen., *Journal*, 27 Cong., 2 Sess., 132.

In response to Sen. William C. Preston's (S.C.) opposition to funding the completion of the harbor at St. Joseph, Indiana, on Lake Michigan, and his remark that the Congress has no constitutional power to build harbors, Clay calls attention to government-funded harbor improvements and lighthouses in Charleston harbor and asks: "Let us alone, was the wish of the Senator. Had South Carolina withdrawn from the Union? Had she seceded from it? Had she separated from the other States of the Union, that she wished to be let alone? He would ask, too, what have you a navy for, but to protect your commerce, but to enlarge it, and extend it to every sea? Have we in the West no commerce to look after no commercial interests? What are the lakes themselves but great inland seas? and are not harbors to be made for them?" Agrees that the state of the nation's finances is such that it might not be "politic or proper" to fund harbors just now, but if "the let-alone policy . . . advocated by the Senator, was to prevail, nothing could be done; and I deny that there is no common bond of union in these objects . . . or that they are not legitimately the proper objects of our legislation. The principles of the Senator from South Carolina, carried out, would throw us back into the Confederation, and I am afraid we are going back to that point of our colonial history." As for the Constitution, "what right has he [Preston] to get up here and say *ex cathedra* what is and what is not constitutional—that this was right and that was wrong. It was well known that there were opposite theories in regard to this Constitution of ours: one denying all powers, and the other the reverse of this. The former tells us their interpretation of the Constitution, and it is seen that they strip the General Government of all power. The others take another extreme. The safe position was the middle ground between those two opinions. I am not . . . for going back to the Confederacy." Maintains that the Constitution sustains the right of Congress to fund harbor improvements under the power of the Congress to regulate commerce. Further, that the commerce clause of the Constitution applies just as much to permitting such improvements on the Great Lakes as on the Atlantic seaboard; and also that the role and duty of the Navy in protecting U.S. commerce is similar on both the inland lakes and the oceans. Asks that Preston not make a constitutional distinction between lakes and oceans and the need for harbor facilities on both. Concludes: "The Senator admits that the navy is to protect our commerce, and that it has a right to this protection. Does he not remember that we have commerce on the lakes, and that there is a foreign power there too? Would he make this Constitution a one-sided paralytic Constitution, with one side of it dead, and the other vigorous, young, and healthy?" He hopes not. Apologizes for saying "so much" on this subject since he had planned to make only "a single incidental remark in reply to the Senator." *Cong. Globe*, 27 Cong., 2 Sess., 199.

Remark in Senate, February 3, 1842. Asks that his colleagues discuss the question of authorizing the Committee on Manufactures to employ a clerk rather than "run off into the whole subject of the tariff." Counters Sen. John C. Calhoun's argument that for the government to maintain expenditures at the $25,000,000 level the tariff must be 26%, or well above the 20% maximum allowed by the Compromise Tariff of 1833 [8:604, 619-22, 626-27]. Contends that a tariff of 20% or "even thirty per cent" was not "extravagant" if required to "supply the wants of the Treasury." Asks Calhoun to reconsider his view that "Free trade . . . was at one time the greatest of all blessings, and it was relied upon to give to South Carolina a share of benefits. But she had had a moiety of free trade for eight or ten years; and where did she stand? Her great staple [cotton] was at a lower price than it had been since the late war with Great Britain; and this was the result of the policy of the Senator." As for the possibility of economy and retrenchment, there could be no progress on that subject unless and until the Democrats "by wooing and courting" Tyler could "get hold of his practical aid." Claims he "heard it said the other day by a Loco Foco friend, 'We hold you (the Whigs) responsible for taking the President by the jaws; he vetoed your Bank bills, and we like him for that; and, whenever he does any thing to please us, we flatter him for the act.' [Laughter.]" Reports, however, that he has drawn up resolutions to reduce the expenses of all members of Congress, that he contemplates a reduction and regulation of mileage allowances for them [Remark in Senate, February 15, 1842], and that this is the first of a series of economy measures he intends to submit. *Cong. Globe*, 27 Cong., 2 Sess., 204.

For the Tariff Act of August 30, 1842, see 5 *U.S. Stat.*, 548-67. Tyler's willingness to sign a protectionist tariff measure that returned the general level of duties to 1832 levels is discussed in Chitwood, *John Tyler*, 295-304, as are his vetoes (on June 29 and August 9) of two earlier (June 25 and August 5, 1842) tariff measures, both of which contained sections providing for the distribution to the states of public land sales receipts. For the two veto messages, see *MPP*, 4:180-87. For the voting on all three tariff measures in the 27th Congress, 2nd Session, including failures to override Tyler's vetoes, see *Cong. Globe*, 688, 717-18, 762, 852, 912, 923-26, 960, 973. For tariff-level comparisons, 1816-42, see Davis R. Dewey, *Fi-*

nancial History of the United States (New York, 1912), 238-39. See also Clay to Letcher, January 6, 1842.

To J.T. Leath, Memphis, February 4, 1842. Clay and William C. Preston acknowledge receipt of a letter "transmitting the resolutions and proceedings of a public meeting of a portion of the citizens of Memphis, at which you presided as chairman." Note that "in consequence of the failure of the Legislature of Tennessee to appoint Senators of the United States [Clay to Brooke, March 12, 1841], the meeting has done us the honor to adopt us as the Senators of that State, as fully as the meeting has the power to do, and to request us to watch over, protect, and defend the peculiar interests of the State of Tennessee." Deplore the failure of the Tennessee legislature to appoint senators, because "it deprives the Senate of the benefit of their counsels . . . and because it is a dangerous precedent, which, if followed by a sufficient number of States, might lead to a subversion of the Government, and a consequent dissolution of the Union." Say they feel "highly honored" by this request from the citizens of Memphis and promise that "we shall, during our continuance in the Senate of the United States, perform that duty with . . . pleasure and satisfaction." Copy. Printed in Washington *Daily National Intelligencer*, March 5, 1842. For Leath, see Cutler, *Correspondence of James K. Polk*, 6:297.

When the Tennessee legislature convened in October, 1841, two U.S. Senate seats were to be filled. The Whigs controlled the lower house of the legislature, while the Democrats controlled the state senate by one vote. Traditionally, the Tennessee legislature had chosen U.S. senators by joint ballot of both houses, but in this instance the Democrats, attempting to prevent the election of two Whigs, insisted that each house vote separately. A stalemate resulted and the legislature eventually adjourned without electing any U.S. senators. Tennessee's seats in the U.S. Senate, then, remained vacant until the election of Ephraim H. Foster and Spencer Jarnagan (both Whigs) in October, 1843. Parks, *John Bell*, 194-202.

To PETER B. PORTER Washington, February 7, 1842

I recd. your favor of the 31st. Ulto. from N. York. Nothing very material has occurred here since my last. Their convention in N. Carolina will take place on the 4h. of April.[1] I shall resign my Seat on the 31st. March;[2] so that the nomination, which will be made, I understand certainly, at that Convention, will be after my retirement. Of the effect of those popular movements in N.Y., in connection with that event, to which you refer, my friends are better judges than I am.[3]

It is certain that Genl. [Winfield] Scott is so sanguine as to be entirely confident of his Election. He told a common friend the other day that he would get a majority of 25.000 West of the Cayuga Bridge. Genl. W[addy]. Thompson is here & told me that he had lately been travelling very much in Alabama; Louisiana, Georgia & the Carolinas, and that he never met with one solitary Whig who was not for me. Genl. Scott must, therefore, count upon a nomination, if there be a Convention; & his nomination could only be procured as that of Genl Harrison was made.[4]

Consultations are now in progress, among the Senators, to ascertain if we can defeat nominations of Loco focos made by the President; for he continues to make them. We shall know what we can do in a few days. Judging from present appearances there does not exist the remotest prospect of any reconciliation between Mr. Tyler & the Whigs. . . .

ALS. NBuHi. 1. Clay to Porter, Jan. 22, 1842. 2. Clay to Berrien, Oct. 7, 1841; Clay to General Assembly of Ky., Feb. 16, 1842. 3. Porter to Clay, Jan. 20, 1842. 4. Porter to Clay, Nov. 14 and Dec. 30, 1837.

Remark in Senate, February 7, 1842. Objects to Sen. William R. King's (Dem., Ala.) assertion that his (Clay's) resolution of January 21, 1842, ("whenever any State or States shall refuse their proportions of the proceeds of public lands, such proportion shall be distributed among the residue of the assenting States") could not have been seriously intended [Remark in Senate, January 21, 1842]. "Surprised" by this comment, Clay says he "never moved in a proposition without reflection, and without an intention of prosecuting action upon it." Speaks (not recorded) further in defense of his distribution resolution, but accepts an amendment to it by Sen. Willie P. Mangum which reads: "Or in what manner these proportions ought to be disposed of, or whether any disposition of them ought to be made." A motion by Sen. King to strike from the resolution the words "such proportions shall be distributed among the residue of the assenting States" was blocked by Sen. Mangum's motion to adjourn. *Cong. Globe*, 27 Cong., 2 Sess., 213-14.

To JAMES WATSON WEBB Washington, February 7, 1842

I am greatly obliged by the prompt attention of yourself and C[harles]. King Esq. to my request[1] respecting the affair of Messrs. Graves and Cilly.[2]

In regard to the course of Mr. [Thomas F.] Marshall towards yourself,[3] I can only express my regrets. He is a very peculiar person, who, with considerable genius, mingles some other qualities of not the most amiable kind. I never in my life had much intercourse with him, and less at this Session than ever. Our relations, altho' not hostile, are far from being intimate. He never seeks advice of me, and I never tender it when unsought—at least with persons of his temperament. I beg you to consider me as irresponsible for any thing he says or does.

The political darkness, in which we have been enwrapped, continues here undiminished. I believe that there is not the remotest prospect of any reconciliation between the Whigs and Mr. Tyler.

ALS. KyU. 1. Clay to Webb, Jan. 30, 1842. 2. *Ibid.*; Clay to Speed, March 2, 1838. 3. Webb in the pages of the New York *Courier and Enquirer* and Congressman Marshall of Ky. from the floor of the House had been sniping at each other for months over repeal of the Bankruptcy Act [Remark in Senate, April 22, 1840, and Dec. 28, 1841; Speech in Senate, Jan. 28, 1842] which Marshall supported and Webb opposed. This situation led to a duel in which Webb was slightly wounded on June 25, 1842. Crouthamel, *James Watson Webb*, 74-75.

From Carter Beverley, Urbana, Middlesex County, Va., February 8, 1842. Proclaims that "Although the time is quite far gone, since I became very innocently instrumental in circulating throughout the country, a very great attack upon your character and virtue as a gentleman, and certainly a very heavy one, as a public man, I feel exceedingly desirous to relieve you, as far as I can, from the slander." Also seeks to relieve himself "from the severe compunction that is within me, of having been, though neither directly nor indirectly, your personal accuser." Denies "any design to do you injustice," stating: "I did not solicit the account, that gave the gross abominable scandal of you; but merely asked, if it was, or could possibly be true? I had long heard of it. . . . The reason of my having mentioned it . . . was, that I thought it an infinite scandal upon the country, if true; and if not true, it would give you a fair opportunity of exculpating yourself." Emphasizes that "I most assuredly and most certainly never entertained the smallest prejudice or unfavorable idea of you until the affair of the Fayetteville letter [6:448-49, 718-19, 728-30] that appeared under my signature, upon which was founded . . . the charge which galloped through the Union against you." Asserts that "This letter is intended to show you" that he became convinced "long ago" that "the very greatest injustice was done you in the charge made."

Mentions that he has recently gone through a file of old newspapers, "containing the whole affair," and has "never seen any evidence to substantiate at all the charge." Indeed, "Mr. [James] Buchanan, who was represented to be your accuser, exhibited no proof whatever against you; and he even denied having ever made the charge upon you [6:819-20, 839-41, 886-88, 1009, 1030-31]."

Concludes by saying he believes "that you are to be the whig candidate for the next election of president of the United States" and that "The greatest objection that has been yet stated against you for that high post, I am concerned to say, hinges upon the old affair." Hopes this letter will remove "as far as I have any influence, the representation I made against you." Thinks the matter "can surely now no longer be [a] matter of doubt . . . for he who was generally believed to be the circulator of the egregious slander against you, hereby revokes his belief in it, and unequivocally declares that it is unproved, and stands utterly unsupported to this time—a period of fifteen or sixteen years." Anticipates that in a spirit of "malevolence, it will be still said by some" that this letter is the product of "an understanding between us, and that it is all designed for political effect," but affirms that "You and I can most readily meet the charge," because "I have had no intercourse, or interview . . . with you, for at least ten or eleven years." Copy. Printed in Colton, *Clay Correspondence*, 1:395-97.

For other entries on the "corrupt bargain" charge, see 6:763-79, 1204-5, 1394-96, and the extensive entry in the subject index under the heading: Election of 1828—Corrupt Bargain issue and related campaign literature, 7:719, col. 1. See also Van Deusen, *Life of Henry Clay*, 218-26; and Robert V. Remini, *Andrew Jackson and the Course of American Freedom, 1822-1832* (New York, 1981), 94-95, 105, 128, 146.

Remark in Senate, February 8, 1842. During debate on repeal of the Bankruptcy Act [Remark in Senate, April 22, 1840, and December 28, 1841], rises to a point of order. When Sen. Thomas H. Benton (Dem., Mo.) shouts at him from a seated position, Clay bridles: "The Senator shall not address *me* in his seat; and if he does, it shall be followed by language corresponding to such conduct." Explains that when Benton, seated, had yelled "False, false" at a statement by Sen. Nathaniel P. Tallmadge (N.Y.) opposing repeal of the Bankruptcy Act, he was clearly out of order because Tallmadge legally held the floor. Indeed, Clay notes that Tallmadge also had said that Benton was "an habitual disturber" and agitator on the bankruptcy issue and was partly responsible for the national depression that rendered bankruptcy legislation necessary. This sparks additional shouts of "False, sir; false, sir; false, sir," from Benton. Clay asserts on inquiry from Sen. Louis F. Linn (Mo.) that this instance of disorder by Benton was unique, quite unlike the confrontation he (Clay) had had with Sen. William R. King (Dem., Ala.) in March, 1841 [Remark in Senate, March 9, 1841]. It was different, Clay asserts, in that "what had been said on either side on that occasion had been uttered when the persons speaking were in lawful possession, and on their feet addressing the Senate. But here, while a member was speaking to the Senate on a great and momentous national subject, a Senator throwing himself back in his chair, exclaimed 'False, false,' and, when called to order, continued to repeat the language." Says that while a resolution dealing with such disorder is "directly in order," he is not certain how it should be framed. *Cong. Globe*, 27 Cong., 2 Sess., 216-17.

Later this day, Clay slightly amends his resolution to distribute the public land sales receipts due those states which have refused to accept them to those states which agree to receive them [Remark in Senate, January 21, 1842], this in an effort to attract additional support for it. Following further unsuccessful efforts to table or amend Clay's resolution, it passes 25 to 19, Clay voting yea. *Ibid.*, 217.

Remark in Senate, February 9, 1842. Expresses the opinion that a Senate resolution to adjourn Congress on May 30 should properly come from the House, "with whom the great burden of business would originate." Thinks the resolution premature and moves to table it. Withdraws motion. *Cong. Globe*, 27 Cong., 2 Sess., 221.

Later this day, during debate on Clay's three resolutions for amendments to the Constitution to restrict the president's power [Speech in Senate, January 24, 1842], Clay informs Sen. William S. Archer (Va.) that he intends "to press the resolutions to final action," but that he will give careful attention to Archer's promised amendment to the effect that (in the Virginian's words) "a bill vetoed shall not be decided on till the session succeeding the one at which it was vetoed, and that a majority of both Houses shall then be competent to pass it into law." *Ibid.*

Remark in Senate, February 10, 1842. Supports the January 25 resolution of Sen. Franklin Pierce (Dem., N.H.) calling on the secretary of the treasury for information gathered during the late investigation by the Poindexter Commission into the operations of the customhouse in New York [Clark to Clay, August 28, 1841]. Points out that "on a revenue of less than eight millions of dollars collected at New York, there had been an extravagance in the collection amounting to nearly eight per cent. which was larger, by three or four times, than the expense incurred when the revenue collected at that port was sixteen millions, the collection was made with less than one-third of the number of persons now employed." Blames this "frightful increase" in the number of collectors on Sen. Levi Woodbury's tenure as secretary of the treasury, and hopes that customhouse "extravagance" will be "probed to the bottom." Challenged by Woodbury on the accuracy of his numbers, Clay admits that the increase in collectors "perhaps . . . occurred under the administration of the Senator's immediate predecessor [Roger B. Taney]." Pierce resolution tabled. *Cong. Globe*, 27 Cong., 2 Sess., 224.

Later this day, during the voting on a bill dealing with Louisiana land claims, states he would not vote on the issue because "a relative of his had an interest in the claim." *Ibid.*

Remark in Senate, February 11, 1842. Presents memorials from citizens in Alabama, Ohio, and New York opposing repeal or amendment of the Bankruptcy Act of 1841 [Remark in Senate, April 22, 1840, and December 28, 1841]; also presents a petition of a U.S. Navy widow asking for a pension. U.S. Sen., *Journal*, 27 Cong., 2 Sess., 157; *Cong. Globe*, 27 Cong., 2 Sess., 227.

To THOMAS HART CLAY Washington, February 12, 1842

I have received your letters & Mr [Elijah] Craigs[1] transmitting the bills of Exchange. I have made some unsuccessful efforts to negotiate them. It is probable that, as the time which they have to run diminishes, I may be able to negotiate one or more of them.

If Mr [James] Erwin does not disappoint me in remitting funds I may be able to meet the bills you have drawn on me in favor of Mr. Craig. But times are very hard in the Eastern Cities.

Balie Peytons protested bill,[2] drawn by Mr [John J.] Crittenden & I, must wait until my return home I wish you or James [B. Clay] would call at the N[orthern]. Bank [of Kentucky] & say so, & say that we are perfectly safe by a deed of Trust on Land & Slaves. . . .

ALS. Courtesy of Dr. Thomas D. Clark, Lexington, Ky. 1. Clay to Thomas H. Clay, Jan. 30, 1842. 2. Clay to James B. Clay, Dec. 24, 1841; Clay to Lucretia H. Clay, Feb. 13, 1842.

From JOHN TYLER Washington, February 12, 1842

I have received this morning through the Post office under the accompanying envelope, the enclosed letter from Gen. [George] Poindexter to yourself;[1] and presuming that it has been either lost by you, or surreptitiously obtained from you, I lose not a moment in restoring it to your possession. The envelope is sent along with the letter in order that you may compare it with the hand writing of the letter itself, or refer to any other test you may think proper. Nothing else accompanied the letter.

You will not fail to appreciate *the sole motive* by which I am actuated.

Copy, typescript. InHi. 1. Enclosure not found.

To JAMES WATSON WEBB Washington, February 12, 1842

I received your favor of the 8h. inst. and its enclosures. I sent that addressed to the Edit: of the [Washington *Daily National*] Intellr. and it appears in their paper this morning.[1] For your friendly & purposes towards me, disinterested & liberal as they are, I pray your acceptance of my grateful thanks. I handed some of your prospectuses to a member of the H. of R. and requested his attention to your wish to obtain names, which he promised me to give. I am afraid that in the form of direct pecuniary aid but little is to be expected from members of Congress, so much & so often are appeals made to them. There are two new papers published here (the Independent[2] & True Whig)[3] both of which are laboring under pecuniary difficulties, and are soliciting aid. Indeed I fear that they will not be sustained.

In regard to the next Presidency, I have not made up my mind to consent to the use of my name. I shall shortly go into retirement,[4] and shall be content to bid a lasting farewell to public life. I have seen enough of it; and, although my career has been attended with its gratifications, I have also experienced serious drawbacks, among which is that my private condition is far less comfortable than it would have been if I had devoted more of my time to its improvement.

There is but one contingency in which I would agree to the use of my name for the office of Chief Magistrate, and that is a clear manifestation that my services were desired by a majority of my Country men. If there is to be any scramble for the office; if there be great divisions among the People as to a suitable person, demonstrating a doubtful issue, I prefer to be left alone in the enjoyment of that repose of which I am in so much need.

These are my unaffected feelings, and my sincere opinions.

With regard to the proper time for an exhibition of popular opinion & preferences, I confess that I have been inclined to think that it is yet premature to make it. At all events, I am desirous that no just imputation shall lie against me or my friends for a premature agitation of the public *mind*, on this exciting subject.

I am glad to inform you that an excellent spirit now prevails in the Senate—much better than at any former period, since the commencement of the Extra Session. If I am to judge, by professions & declarations, there is not one Senator, in the Whig Ranks, who is not well disposed towards the Whig party, and who is not exempt from all tincture of Tylerism. Proof of this was given yesterday, in the rejection of Barker as Comptroller[5] by a vote of 23 (all whigs) against 17 (all Loco's) I think this vote will be followed up by the exercise of a salutary Constitutional participation & control of the Senate, in the appointing power.

ALS. ViU. Letter marked "(Confidential)." 1. Editors of the *Intelligencer* were William W. Seaton and Joseph Gales. The article which appeared in the *Intelligencer* on Feb. 12 gave a prospectus for the weekly and semi-weekly issues of the New York *Courier and Enquirer*. 2. The Washington *Independent*, edited by Edward N. Johnston, Joseph Segar, and John H. Pleasants, was a pro-Clay paper started in Dec., 1841. Hudson, *Journalism in the United States*, 240. 3. Calvin Colton edited the Washington *True Whig*, also a pro-Clay paper, beginning on Dec. 14, 1841. See Colton article in *DAB* and Washington *Daily National Intelligencer*, Dec. 15, 1841. 4. Clay to Berrien, Oct. 7, 1841. 5. Tyler had appointed James N. Barker as first comptroller of the treasury. U.S. Sen., *Journal*, 27 Cong., 2 Sess., Appendix, 677.

To LUCRETIA HART CLAY Washington, February 13, 1842

I was taken with a pain in the small of the back, which was so severe, on friday evening that I should have fallen to the floor on rising from my seat, if I had not been caught. I am now better, and think the Lumbago, as it is called, will pass away.

I suppose James [B. Clay] has by this time reached home, as he was to leave N. O. on the 1st.[1] Tell him to write to me.

Thomas [H. Clay] probably told you that a bill drawn by Mr. [John J.] Crittenden & me on Balie Peyton was returned dishonored.[2] Mr. Peyton has deceived me; but we are in no danger of ultimately suffering, as we have a deed of trust on Land & negroes, worth twice as much as our responsibilities are for him. But when one is so often deceived as I have been it is very discouraging in rendering acts of kindness. Hereafter, I shall confine them to my own family.

Henry [Clay, Jr.] informs me that there are $700 in Bank for me. I shall want here all the money I can get to meet some drafts of Thomas. I send you a Check therefore for the $700, out of which I wish you to retain any money you may want, and desire Henry to convert the residue into a Check on N. York or Balto. & send it to me by mail.

I am very much urged to remain throughout this Session. They pretend to say that they cannot do without me, and that the Whig party will be destroyed if I go away. But I adhere to my purpose of resigning to take effect on the 31st. March.[3]

The winter has been so mild here, that they have no ice. I am afraid that you have not been able to fill our Houses. If there should fall a snow, I would advise the Houses to be filled with that, & have it well ramed in. . . .

ALS. DLC-TJC (DNA, M212, R10). 1. Clay to James B. Clay, Dec. 10 and Dec. 24, 1841. 2. Clay to James B. Clay, Dec. 24, 1841. 3. Clay to Berrien, Oct. 7, 1841; Clay to General Assembly of Ky., Feb. 16, 1842.

Comment in Senate, February 14, 1842. Following presentation of a petition from Alabama opposing repeal or amendment of the Bankruptcy Act [Remark in Senate, April 22, 1840, and December 28, 1841], Clay joins the debate on Sen. Franklin Pierce's resolution calling on the secretary of the treasury to submit to the Senate the findings of the Poindexter Commission's investigation of the customhouse in the port of New York [Clark to Clay, August 28, 1841]. Criticizes Tyler's appointment of the Poindexter commissioners without the authority of Congress, and challenges the president's contention that the phrase in Article II, Section 3 of the Constitution enjoining him to "take care that the laws be faithfully executed" was sufficient authority for those appointments. Indeed, Clay asserts, "If this practice should be persisted in, hosts of officers might be appointed for any other purpose, and the powers of Congress thereby be in a great degree superseded by the act of the Executive. They had too much of this kind of construction of the Constitution." At the same time he is convinced that there has been much abuse of the public trust during the past twelve years, especially in the New York customhouse. Has been told by one of the commissioners that 250 pages of the commission's report had been written; and while it is still not completed, it would be in a few days and then would be sent to Congress. Asks: "But why this impatience to call for the report at this time? Had gentlemen lost all confidence in the President and his two vetoes [Tyler to Clay, April 30, 1841]? If they had, he hoped that they would hereafter refrain from expressing their sentiments of gratitude and adoration to the Executive for his services to the country in resisting two of the measures of the extra session. Gentlemen would have the report in a few days, and then they would hear of more abuses than they had stomachs to bear." Reviews the defalcation of Samuel Swartwout [Remark in Senate, December 13, 1838; Clay to the Public, August 20, 1840], pointing out, in addition, that during the collectorship of Jonathan Thompson [4:548] the cost of collecting the customs in New York had risen 1.43 percent; under Swartwout it had risen 2.67 percent; and under Jesse Hoyt it had increased 5.17 percent. Similarly, the number of employees in the New York customhouse had climbed from 163 to 470 during the collectorships there of these three Democrats. Clashes with Sen. James Buchanan on whether or not Samuel Swartwout had ever been a candidate for or been nominated for the vice presidency of the United States; Clay says he had not been while Buchanan maintains that the collector of customs had been "on the same Presidential ticket with a distinguished gentleman now in the cabinet [Webster]" and instructs Clay to read the newspapers more carefully. Clay argues that the Whigs have not yet been long enough in office to ferret out and "correct all the abuses of the Government which had existed for so many years"; and asserts that when the Whigs came to power "They found, as an inheritance, an empty Treasury, a bankrupt Government, embarrassment everywhere. They were compelled to supply these deficiences, and how had they been aided as much as themselves in the preservation of the honor of the country? Gentlemen had opposed them in all their efforts to relieve the Government in most of the measures of the extra session." To Sen. James Buchanan's promise that at a future occasion he would review the conduct of the two political parties since March, 1841 to show that Whig extravagance during the 27th Congress, 1st Session [the "Extra Session"] had cost $5,000,000, Clay retorts: "Very well, sir. Come on Macduff." *Cong. Globe*, 27 Cong., 2 Sess., 231-32. For Jesse Hoyt, see Donald B. Cole, *Martin Van Buren and the American Political System* (Princeton, N.J., 1984), 89, 192, 248, 298, 337-38, 351, 375-76, 421.

No evidence has been found supporting Buchanan's contention that Samuel Swartwout had been a vice presidential candidate or nominee. It is possible, however, that he had been touted for that office by some local group in New York City.

From Richard Rush, Sydenham, near Philadelphia, February 14, 1842. Has heard Clay is going to retire from the Senate [Clay to Berrien, October 7, 1841], "and if so, I am unable any longer to stand out against an impulse that puts the pen into my hand, making me say how amidst all the mutations of the last ten years—I have under all circumstances done justice to your patriotism, in alliance with all the other qualities to mark you out as the true head of the party whose principles you have so preeminently espoused." Adds that "Such a testimony can be of no value to you, but it gratifies me to give it utterance . . . founded as it is on convictions derived whilst associated with you in the public service; and although not able to side with that party in its public measures, I continue to think that it will do great injustice to itself if it does not regard you as its natural candidate for the highest honor it can bestow." Says he also expressed this opinion at a 4th of July celebration in Boston in 1840. ALS. DLC-HC (DNA, M212, R5). Printed in Colton, *Clay Correspondence*, 4:456-57.

Rush wrote again the following day, February 15, 1842, saying that in 1833 "I threw out a volume founded on my mission to England in the course of which . . . I alluded to your early exertions in behalf of Spanish American emancipation." Says he is "contemplating some continuation of the work" and may comment more fully on the English claim that George Canning was the "first [who] called that part of our continent into independent existence [5:1050-51]." Asserts: "This is not true, though he had great merit in that question—more I think than any statesman of England, or Europe, of that day." Asks if Clay will "drop me a few lines . . . giving me the date of your first movement in the H.R. on this subject; I mean the one which distinctly looked to our recognition of the new states?" ALS. DLC-HC (DNA, M212, R5). Printed in Colton, *Clay Correspondence*, 4:457-58. For early expressions of Clay's interest in the independence of the new Latin American nations, and U.S. recognition of them, see 1:624; also 2:135-36, 155-56, 291, and espec. 541-62.

In 1833 Rush had published in Philadelphia a book called *Memoranda of a Residence at the Court of London* which covered events from 1817 to January, 1819. His second work by the same title was published in Philadelphia in 1845 and covered the period from 1819 to 1825.

Remark in Senate, February 15, 1842. Says he has decided to proceed with the presentation of eleven resolutions on the economy since his friends, having been consulted, seem generally to concur in all but two or three of them. Lists them: (1) While the government has a duty to provide for adequate revenue, to do so through loans or the issue of treasury notes [Remark in Senate, January 21, 1842; Clay to Ewing, July 13, 1841] is a pernicious expedient; (2) an adequate revenue cannot be obtained save by tariff duties above 20 percent, as provided in the Compromise Tariff Act of 1833 [8:604, 619-22, 626-27]; (3) therefore, the 20 percent rate should be raised sufficiently to produce a net revenue of $26 million, viz: $22 millions for ordinary expenses, $2 millions for payment of the existing debt, $2 millions as a reserve fund for contingencies; (4) the principles of the Compromise Act should, however, be adhered to and a new maximum *ad valorem* rate of duties should be established "from which there ought to be as little departure as possible"; (5) the provision of the act passed by the Extra Session (27 Cong., 1 Sess.) that would suspend distribution of public land sales receipts if the tariff level went above 20 percent [Clay to Ewing, April 30, 1841; Remark in Senate, June 9, 1841] ought to be repealed; (6) it is the duty of the government during this period of "general embarrassment and pecuniary distress" to abolish all useless institutions and offices, curtail all unnecessary expenses, and to practise rigid economy"; (7) the contingent expenses of both houses of Congress should be "greatly reduced," especially the mileage allowances of members which should be regulated and more clearly defined; (8) the expenses of the federal judiciary should be lowered; (9) the diplomatic relations of the United States with foreign powers, "unnecessarily extended" during the past twelve years, should be reduced; (10) the franking privilege should be further restricted, postage rates should be reduced on letters and raised on books, pamphlets, and packages according to their weights; (11) the secretaries of state, treasury, war, and navy, and the postmaster general, should report on which offices in their charges can be abolished and what other retrenchments in costs might be made. Suggests that these resolutions be placed on the calendar for February 22. Assures John C. Calhoun that he has no objection to these resolutions being considered by the Senate constituted as a committee of the whole; nor does he believe, as does Calhoun, that the Compromise Tariff Act is "to be violated in its spirit." *Cong. Globe*, 27 Cong., 2 Sess., 235-36. Clay defended these resolutions in a lengthy Speech in Senate, March 1, 1842.

Later this day, during debate on a resolution designating May 30 as the date of adjournment, Clay argues that setting such a date three months in advance is premature, especially since "very little had been done in either House of Congress." Favors as short a session as possible. Moves to table the resolution. Motion to table carries 21 to 16. *Ibid.*, 236.

Still later this day, Clay also moves to table, for further consideration, a resolution favoring adoption of a joint rule that no amendment involving an appropriation not required by pre-existing law should be made in either house to appropriations bills. Following this, he agrees to vote "at once" on the bill to postpone until July 1, 1842, the operation of the August 19, 1841, Bankruptcy Act [Remark in Senate, April 22, 1840, and December 28, 1841]. The vote on the motion to engross the postponement bill for a third reading fails 18 to 23, Clay voting nay. He then moves to take up his three proposed constitutional amendments to restrict executive power [Speech in Senate, January 24, 1842]. *Ibid.*, 237.

From William Faulkner, Norwich, Conn., February 16, 1842. Sends "one of my papers containing the closing part of your eloquent speech in favor of the unfortunate bankrupt [bill]" [Remark in Senate, April 22, 1840, and December 28, 1841], and says this "is the only mode by which I can, at present, express to you my gratitude." Confesses that for "Thirteen years have I been deceived by Thomas H. Benton & Co:—and have worked faithfully in the Loco-foco cause—supposing that the party with which I have acted, was the *democratic* party." Reports that from 1828 to 1834 he published a Democratic newspaper containing "articles to the prejudice of Henry Clay—truly supposing that I was thus doing God service—But your *acts* during the past two years have opened my eyes—what Henry Clay *was*, Henry Clay *is*—the liberal, the consistent, the warmhearted democrat and friend of the poor and the oppressed."

States that after Jackson's second election he sold his paper, "The 'Norwich Republican,' " and during the past seven years has "engaged in Mercantile business." Nevertheless, he has "not been an inactive partisan in the cause of Locofoco-ism—excepting the past year—during which time I have grown more and more *sick*. . . . With thousands, I have been prostrated in business—I have paid to my creditors the last red cent which I possessed. . . . The party which I have *opposed* and *abused*, say go *free* and *unfettered*; while those with whom I have acted say '*no*!'—'you must be *punished* for your *misfortunes*—you must be imprisoned for life! . . .' is this the democracy which I have labored so hard to build up? God forgive me—"

Mentions that he is still engaged in the mercantile business as an agent and has started another newspaper—a "neutral" one which is designed "to break down the ultra spirit of Locofoco-ism—in this district—[and] bring back . . . the genuine democrats." ALS. DLC-HC (DNA, M212, R5). Endorsed on verso by Clay "Mr. Wm. Faulkner [Recantation]." From 1843 to 1848 Faulkner published a paper called The Norwich *News*. For Faulkner, see Frances M. Caulkins, *History of Norwich, Connecticut* . . . (Chester, Ct., 1976), 582-83; *Vital Records of Norwich 1659-1848*, Part II (Hartford, 1913), 12.

To THE GENERAL ASSEMBLY OF KENTUCKY Washington, February 16, 1842

When I last had the honor of an appointment as one of the United States senators from Kentucky,[1] I intimated, in my letter of acceptance, the probability of my not serving out the whole term of six years. In consequence of there having been two extra sessions of Congress, I have already attended, since that appointment, as many sessions of Congress as ordinarily happen during a senatorial term, without estimating my services at the present session.

I have for several years desired to retire to private life, but have been hitherto prevented from executing my wish from considerations of public duty. I should have resigned my seat in the senate at the commencement of the present session, but for several reasons, one of which was, that the general assembly did not meet until near a month after Congress, during which time the state would not have been fully represented, or my successor would have had only the uncertain title of an executive appointment.

The time has now arrived, when I think that, without any just reproach, I may quit the public service, and bestow some attention on my private affairs, which have suffered much by the occupation of the largest portion of my life in the public councils. If the Roman veteran had title to discharge after thirty years' service, I, who have served a much longer period, may justly claim mine.

I beg leave, therefore, to tender to the general assembly, and do now hereby tender, my resignation of the office which I hold, of senator in the senate of the United States, from the state of Kentucky, to take effect on the 31st of March, 1842; and I request that the general assembly will appoint my successor to take his seat on that day.[2] I have fixed that day to allow me an opportunity of assisting in the completion of some measures, which have been originated by me.

I embrace this opportunity to offer to the general assembly my most profound and grateful acknowledgments for the numerous and distinguished proofs, by which I have been honored, of its warm attachment and generous confidence during a long series of years. . . .

Copy. Printed in Colton, *Clay Correspondence*, 2:404-5. 1. Clay to General Assembly of Ky., Jan. 16, 1837. 2. The Ky. legislature appointed John J. Crittenden, and he took the seat on March 31.

From WILLIAM J. GRAVES Louisville, February 16, 1842

I hasten to respond to your favour of the 10th Inst, which reached me by the mail of this morning. I have been extremely pained, and most deeply mortified, at the manner in which the Boston Morning Post,[1] and other political papers, have wantonly connected your name with the unfortunate affair between the late Mr Cilly [*sic*, Jonathan Cilley] and myself.[2]

Painful, however, as it is, for me to allude to this melloncholly event, or the circumstances connected with it; and Certain as I am, that should this meet the public Eye, the relentless spirit of party will tear open afresh, wounds but partially healed by time, Yet it would be much less afflicting to me than to see you suffer unjustly, on account of your involuntary connection with that affair. I therefore forward you my statement, as nearly as my recollection serves me, after the lapse of four years, with the privilege of using it, as circumstances, in your opinion require.

From the commencement of the difficulty, between Mr Cilly and myself, up to the time I wrote him the challenge I do not recollect that I mentioned it to you, or any other collegue or friend, except Mr Thompson[3] & Mr [Henry A.] Wise. I know it was my purpose, to communicate on the subject, with such persons only, as I had determined to select as my friends, should the matter not terminate amicably Hence my friend & collegue Mr [William W.] Southgate,[4] who sat by my side at the same table, when I wrote the correspondence knew not a word of the affair, from me, untill it was over. I hoped from the first, that it would be amicably adjusted, and felt a strong solicitude that it should be known to as few persons as possible.

I do not recollect nameing the subject to you, untill the morning before the meeting, when I called at your room, I think in company with Mr Wise, and exhibited to you the correspondence, and perhaps detailed to you the circumstances of the affair. I remember, that you suggested to me some modification in the praseology of the challenge, which I had written but had not sent by which milder language was empoleyed & the door was not so completely closed against adjustment. I recollect well at the time you suggested the modifications, which, I believe, was perhaps written by yourself, on another piece of paper. You stated that you thought the matter ought, & would be amicably adjusted & in this I remember Mr Wise concured with you in opinion. I recollect this the better, from a connection resting on my mind at the time that, there were influences, which I thought I saw more fully, than any of my friends, that militated against this view of the subject:—Some of which I think I mentioned to you in reply to your suggestion that you thought the matter would be adjusted without a hostile meeting:

I think I adopted your form, with but little if any modification, and I suppose destroyed it, & that drawn originally by myself. I do not think I alluded to this subject in your presence again untill about nine Oclock of the night preceeding the meeting when I had but a moments conversation with you, in which I made known to you my want of skill in the use of the we[a]pon selected by my adversary.

It is utterly untrue that you ever exhibited to me any wish that the meeting should take place. I believe I had no fr[i]end in Washington who more regreted it. I recollect after the affair, when we met at our boarding house, you seemed to sympathise more deeply with me in my misfortune.— You wept, and was unable to utter a word.

It is also charged in this Boston paper, that Mr [John J.] Crittenden, was responsible for, and was one of the main actors, in the preliminaries that brought on this melloncholly affair.

Now, although you, Mr Crittenden Mr [Richard] Menefee & myself were boarding together Mr Crittenden knew not a word of the dif[f]iculty untill about ten or eleven Oclock of the night before the meeting. When Mr Menefee & myself, & I think Mr Wise went after him at Mr Joseph Gales's, where he & his family were spending the evening. Mr Crittenden was very reluctant to be one of the two friends, who under the preliminaries upon which Genl [George] Jones & Mr Wise had agreed,[5] were to accompany each second, and it was not untill I made the request in person, for reasons that I think I gave him for my solicitude, that he should be present, that he finally consented I was the more anxious that he should be on the ground, because in Ky & wherever else he was well known, no man was more distinguished for his mildness, and humanity. I believed his presence would be the best evidence I could offer at home, that I did not intend to act rashly or go beyond the requirement of those laws under which I went to the field.

As soon as there had been a refusal to rec[e]ive the note of Col [James Watson] Webb. I called to my aid the advice of Mr Menefee & Mr Wise, & from that time I do not recollect that any thing whatever was done either by them or myself, that did not meet the most entire approbation of all. They acted as my friends, & represented me in the affair, & I only am responsible for what they did. They could have had no motive to do any thing more than to protect my life & my honour

It would be much less painful to me, if those who feel themselves called on, to renew the discussion of this most disagreeable subject would spair my friends, and let their Censure and denunciations fall exclusively on my head

Just before leaving the City for the ground, I informed the friends who accompanied me, that I had but one suggestion to make, & that was in order to avoid any inadvertance, growing out of the haste & excitement, incident to the adjustment of such affairs on the ground, that they should confer together, and agree among themselves upon the basis of an adjustment, And, after doing so, not to be driven from it by any considerations connected with my safety. In persuance of this suggestion they did as, I afterwards learned, reduce to writing, their views as to the grounds, upon which an adjustment of the affair, if made, ought to rest you may not find it necessary to place this letter before the public; but if you think it necessary in your vindication I repeat again it is at your service. . . .

ALS. ViU. 1. On Feb. 4, 1842, the Boston *Morning Post* printed a letter to the editor, dated Jan. 31, 1842, and signed "Algernon Sidney Hampden." The letter charged that Clay and Crittenden were the "main actors in the preliminaries" which led to the Graves-Cilley duel in 1838. The motive which caused Clay to promote the duel, the writer said, was that James Watson Webb "was involved in a difficulty" with Cilley. Clay, therefore, hoping to win for himself the support of Webb's newspaper, which then espoused the interests of Daniel Webster, persuaded Graves to take up Webb's cause with Cilley. Thus, "Jonathan Cilley was murdered to propitiate the fortunes and ambition of Henry Clay." 2. Clay to Speed, March 2, 1838; Clay to Webb, Jan. 30, 1842. 3. Probably Whig Congressman Waddy Thompson, Jr., of S.C. 4. For Ky. Whig Congressman William W. Southgate, see *BDAC*. 5. Gen. George Wallace Jones of Wisconsin was Cilley's second while Henry A. Wise of Virginia served as Graves's second. See *BDAC* and Stevens, *Pistols at Ten Paces*, 223. The latter erroneously identifies Cilley's second as George W. Jones of Tenn. who was not in Congress until 1843.

Remark in Senate, February 16, 1842. Speaks to Sen. Robert J. Walker's resolution asking the president to submit to the Senate all papers in the possession of the executive departments from U.S. citizens pertaining to their claims against Mexico;

also communications from the mixed commission authorized by the convention between the United States and Mexico to adjudicate such claims; and (as an amendment to Walker's resolution by Sen. Silas Wright) the names of all citizens whose claims have been acted upon and the disposition of each of these cases. Clay asks that the Committee on Foreign Relations take up this issue. Wonders "What purpose was to be answered by this call? Why, they might get up a hostile spirit against Mexico, and by an exposure of this transaction by the public press, their negotiations with that power might be materially injured." Recalls that public anger had been stirred up unnecessarily by prematurely releasing information relating to the *Creole* case [Remark in Senate, January 11, 1842], and hopes this error will not be repeated. Defends his citation of the *Creole* case as an example of poor foreign policy management in answer to criticism by Calhoun. Pushed further by Calhoun, gives another instance of the negative effect of the premature release of information from his personal experience as U.S. commissioner at Ghent in 1814 [1:852-53]. After further debate, Walker's resolution was postponed. Adopted unanimously, however, was Sen. Louis F. Linn's resolution of February 8 that the president submit information on recent outrages against the U.S. consul in Santa Fe [Manuel Alvarez] and against other American citizens there and throughout the northern Mexican provinces. At day's end, Clay reminds the Senate that his three joint resolutions to amend the Constitution [Speech in Senate, January 24, 1842] are still scheduled to come up on February 22. *Cong. Globe*, 27 Cong., 2 Sess., 241. For Mexican "outrages" against U.S. citizens in the Santa Fe region, see Manning, *Diplomatic Correspondence . . . Inter-American Affairs*, 8:100-108; Rives, *United States and Mexico*, 1:480-84, 503-13.

To CARTER BEVERLEY Washington, February 17, 1842

I have received your favor of the 8th inst. The subject to which it relates—the attack of General Jackson on me, of which you were the organ of publication—has been of late very rarely thought of by me,[1] insomuch that I found it necessary to resort to your Fayetteville letter[2] to revive my recollection of the particulars of your agency in it. Nevertheless, I am thankful for the justice your letter has done me, which is creditable to your heart. Resting always under a perfect consciousness of my own rectitude, the letter was not necessary to the tranquility of my own bosom; but, as there may be others not convinced of the calumny of which I have been the object, I shall avail myself of your authority, and publish your letter. . . .

Copy. Printed in Frankfort *Commonwealth*, April 19, 1842. 1. Beverley to Clay, Feb. 8, 1842. 2. See 6:448-49, 718-19,728-30.

From Peter B. Porter, New York City, February 17, 1842. Reports having seen "with much regret the late violent and accrimonious attacks on Mr. Webster by papers in Louisville and Washington which are understood to be the special organs of your views & wishes." While agreeing that "he deserves all that is charged against him, and even more," believes "he is sinking and has already sunk deeply in public estimation, but his fall would . . . be retarded rather than accellerated by the harsh treatment of those who have been his friends."

States that the "only news of this city is that a son of the Secretary of War [John C. Spencer] was yesterday arrested and is now in prison on a charge of forgery," because he "signed his father's name to two or more drafts for money." Has heard that this is not his first offense, but that "his former forgeries were concealed by the payment of money by his friends." Copy. OHi.

A report in the Louisville *Daily Journal* had charged Webster with assaulting the wife of one of the clerks in the State Department when she applied for a position as transcriber. Webster denied the allegation and the *Daily Journal* subsequently retracted the story. Louisville *Daily Journal*, January 8, 11, 19, 25 and February 14, 1842; Moser, *Papers of Daniel Webster, Correspondence*, 5:190.

Ambrose Spencer, son of the secretary of war, had been arrested in Albany for forging his father's name on checks amounting to $500. New York *Evening Post*, February 26, 1842.

Remark in Senate, February 18, 1842. Denies the contention of Pennsylvania memorialists that the Compromise Tariff Act of 1833 [8:604, 619-22, 626-27] had caused the financial embarrassments under which the nation is now suffering. Explains his motives in sponsoring that legislation: "Two motives had operated upon his mind, and he believed on the minds of others, to induce them to concur in the passage of the law. The first was to avert the calamity of civil war, the fire of which, having been lighted up in South Carolina, threatened to extend its flames over the whole Union; the second was to preserve from utter destruction, the system of protection which Pennsylvania favored when the law was passed. . . . if the Compromise act had not been adopted, the whole system of protection would have been swept by the board by the preponderating influence of the illustrious man then at the head of the Government (Gen. Jackson). . . . it was a great mistake to say that any portion of the embarrassments of the country had resulted from it. Other causes had contributed to this result, and it was to be attributed to the experiments which had been made upon the currency. The embarrassments were also attributed to the action of the States, which, by plunging into schemes of internal improvement, had contracted debts abroad, and thereby given a false and fictitious appearance to the prosperity of the country; and, when their bonds depreciated, the evils under which they now suffered, as a consequence, ensued." Asserts that he still stands by the "original principles" of the compromise tariff, and hopes that "providing for an adequate revenue" and affording "incidental protection" can both be accomplished in pending tariff legislation. Points out to critic John C. Calhoun that the Congress could have repealed the Compromise Tariff Act at any time it chose, and that it was Jackson's removal of government deposits from the Bank of the United States [8:583-84, 684-85, 728, 813], not high revenues from the Tariff Act of 1828, that had caused the currency expansion which in turn had caused the speculation of the mid-1830s. In answer to James Buchanan's defense of Jackson's course of action on the relationship between the compromise tariff and South Carolina's nullification of the tariff legislation of 1828 and 1832 [8:388-89, 473, 598, 603, 615], Clay assures his audience that he could "prove . . . that General Jackson was opposed to the compromise act, and signed it with the greatest reluctance"; but whether he liked the compromise legislation or not, the fact was that "he signed the bill." *Cong. Globe*, 27 Cong., 2 Sess., 249-50. Partially printed in Colton, *Clay Correspondence*, 6:320-21. For the various tariff bills in 1842, see Clay to Letcher, January 6, 1842.

Remark in Senate, February 21, 1842. On a motion by Sen. Robert J. Walker, amended by John C. Calhoun, that information from the president on the *Creole* case [Remark in Senate, January 11, 1842] be received, printed, and referred to the Committee on Foreign Relations; and that one thousand additional copies be printed, Clay holds that there is no need for the additional copies and is sustained in this view. *Cong. Globe*, 27 Cong., 2 Sess., 256.

Remark in Senate, February 24, 1842. Delivers an eulogy to the late Rep. Lewis Williams of North Carolina, with whom he has maintained a friendship since his return from Europe in fall, 1815. Lauds Williams, known as "Father of the House," for his work as chairman of the House Committee on Claims and especially for his handling so well the difficult claims cases growing out of the War of 1812. *Cong. Globe*, 27 Cong., 2 Sess., 263. For Williams, who died on February 23, see *BDAC*.

From HENRY A. WISE Washington, February 25, 1842

I enclose to you an editorial from the "Weekly Courier and New York Enquirer," edited by James Watson Webb, of the 12th inst.[1]

In response, I presume, to the call upon you contained in this piece to "give publicity to the testimony" therein referred to, you have, in this morning's Intelligencer, published a letter from W. J. Graves, Esq.,[2] accompanied by statements of Charles King and Reverdy Johnson.[3]

Now, sir, I most respectfully inquire of you, 1st. Whether by your publication in the Intelligencer of these statements, in connexion with the editorial referred to, you mean to give countenance to the imputation contained in this editorial, that *I ever deceived you, either as to the time or place of meeting* between Messrs. Graves and [Jonathan] Cilley? 2d. Whether you were so deceived by me or my associates, as therein charged? And, if by them, who of them? 3d. Were you not fully informed the day beforehand of all the terms prescribed by Mr. Cilley for that meeting, and did you not advise their adoption? 4th. Did you not draw the form of the challenge which I bore for Mr. Graves to Mr. Cilley on the morning of Friday, the 23d day of February, 1838? 5th. Had you, before that day, the 23d, been advised with by Mr. Graves and his friends as to his correspondence and his course preliminary to the challenge, and was your advice not followed?

I trust you will fully perceive the propriety, and necessity even, of these inquiries, and that your own sense of honor will appreciate the justice to me of candid and full answers to them. . . .[4]

Copy. Printed in *Kendall's Expositor* (March 5, 1844), 4:73-74, no. 5. 1. The *Courier and Enquirer* on Feb. 12, 1842, accused anti-Clay newspapers of attempting to injure Clay by presenting as truth Wise's charge that Clay was the "instigator and adviser" in the Graves-Cilley duel [Clay to Speed, March 2, 1838]. No greater injustice was ever done a public man, the editorial intoned, adding that if Clay had not been deceived by Wise and his associates as to the time and place of the duel, civil authorities would have intervened and prevented it. Evidently referring to statements by Charles King and Reverdy Johnson [Clay to Webb, Jan. 30, 1842], the editorial called upon Clay to publish the evidence he had obtained from two "unimpeachable" sources proving this point. 2. Graves to Clay, Feb. 16, 1842. 3. Clay to Webb, Jan. 30, 1842. 4. See below Clay's response to Wise on Feb. 28, 1842.

From William H. Russell, St. Louis, Mo., February 26, 1842. Deed of sale for a tract of land consisting of 680.55 acres in St. Charles County, Mo., for the sum of $1.00 "in hand paid by the said Clay." States that Russell "hath heretofore purchased the tract of land hereinafter mentioned and described for Taxes, in the name of Anthony Saugrain or in some other name," and that he "will warrant and defend the right and title of the tract of land . . . against all persons claiming under the said Russell, but against no other person whatsoever." AD. DLC-TJC (DNA, M212, R19). See also Clay to January, October 6, 1838; Clay to Erwin, April 10, 1839; Clay to Pindell, October 14, 1839; Clay to James B. Clay, October 30, 1840; and Dunnica to Clay, April 17, 1841.

To HENRY A. WISE Washington, February 28, 1842

The Honble Mr. [Lewis F.] Linn of the Senate, on Saturday night last, delivered to me an open letter from you, under date the 25h. instant, propounding certain enquiries to me, relative to the unhappy affair between Messrs. [William J.] Graves and [Jonathan] Cilly [*sic*, Cilley].[1]

Before I proceed to return a more specific answer to your note, I must recall to your recollection certain circumstances which have occurred, during the present Session of Congress.

Some weeks ago, and prior to any allusion to the unfortunate duel, made in the H. of Representatives by Mr. [John Q.] Adams and yourself,[2] I was informed that a letter written from this City had appeared in the N. York Herald,[3] charging me with having instigated and caused the duel, and with having prepared the challenge which led to it. Prior also to that allusion, it was currently whispered about in this City that I occasioned the duel and prepared the challenge. The naked fact of my having prepared the challenge, suppressing the attending circumstances, and especially the motive of an amicable adjustment, which induced me to propose the modification, was thus brought before the public. Now, you[,] Mr. Graves and I were only present when I proposed that modification. Not for a moment could I believe that he furnished the fact of the challenge to the writer of the letter to the N. York Herald. I did not; and my conclusion was not unreasonable that you did.

When the subject was adverted to by Mr. Adams and you in the H. of R. and you stated that the *preliminaries* had been arranged by another, without mentioning my name, the previous circumstances were such as to fix attention on me, and you were as distinctly understood to refer to me as if my name had been expressly designated.

Afterwards a long and elaborate exposition, professing to give all the circumstances of the affair, appeared in the Madisonian,[4] which was believed to have been your production, or to have been prepared with your assistance or sanction. In that exposition, the design is clearly manifested to transfer the responsibility of the duel to me, the terms of the challenge are recited, and by a call of the public attention to what is denominated its "ear marks" an insinuation is made of my being its author. A design as unfounded in respect to me, as it is unjust towards Mr. Graves! As if I, without an earthly motive, should force him into a duel contrary to his own deliberate judgment!

During all these proceedings, without any appeal to you, I remained passive and silent, suffering under conscious injustice, but abiding in undoubting confidence that, in this, as in other instances, truth would ultimately triumph.

I applied to Charles King Esq.[5] for a statement of what had occurred in two interviews in my room between him, Reverdy Johnson Esq[6] and myself. Mr. King came to me, as the friend of Col. [James Watson] Webb; and althoug[h], being the friend of Mr. Graves, I cou[l]d not invoke the authority of the police to prevent the duel, I informed him that I thought no such obstacle applied to him, and that he might with entire propriety cause the parties to be arrested. I, therefore, recommended the police to be called out, and for that purpose advised him to confer with Genl. [Charles F.]

Mercer & F[rancis]. [Scott] Key, gentlemen that I knew would promptly lend their aid to prevent the duel. Mr. King accordingly made a statement, forwarded it to R[everdy]. Johnson Esq who added his own, without my solicitation, and transmitted both to me.

I enclosed to Mr. Graves[7] a most false and malignant attack upon me, in regard to the affair, which appeared, I think, in the Boston post; and he, in consequence, addressed to me the letter bearing date the 16h. instant.[8]

Those two statements and his letter I handed to the Editors of the [Washington *Daily*] N[ational]. Intellr. for publication[9] not, as you suppose, in *response* to any call made by Col. Webb upon me (for altho' he might have known of the two statements, he could not at N. York on the 12h. of Feb. have known of a letter of Mr. Graves bearing date the 16h. of that month at Louisville in K.) but in response to and in refutation of an attack upon me, which I had reason to believe had either its origin with you or had been made upon information supplied by you.

Such are the circumstances under which your appeal is now made to me to furnish you with testimony, in answer to prepared interrogatories, for the purpose either of your own vindication or to implicate me. I can recognise no right on your part to make such an appeal, until all agency of yours' in the transactions to which I have herein referred for the purpose of my inculpation, is disavowed or satisfactorily explained. Nevertheless, animated by a sense of right and fairness which would prompt me to do justice even to an enemy, and feeling an entire consciousness of my being beyond any reproach, on account of the deplorable event which forms the subject of our correspondence, I will now reply particularly to such parts of your letter as appear to me to require an answer.

I never thought or said that I was *deceived* by you or by any other person as to the time and place of the meeting of Messrs. Graves and Cilly. I positively aver that I had no knowledge of the day nor the hour nor the place of their hostile meeting. And, when on the day of its actual occurrence, Messrs. King and Johnson called at my room, in the manner related by them,[10] and informed me that it was to take place on that day, I felt all the surprize which is described in their statements. I immediately sent my servant to the respective rooms of Messrs. Graves, [John J.] Crittenden and Menifee [*sic*, Richard Menefee], and finding that they had, without my knowledge, left them early in the morning, for the first time I apprehended that the meeting was to take place that day. I did not suppose that it would occur on that day, because, having understood that Mr. Graves had met with difficulty in getting a rifle, I did not know that he had obtained one. I had no right to know the time and place of the meeting of the parties. I only regretted my ignorance of it, because, if I had known it, I could have advised where the police might have been directed to arrest the parties & prevent the duel.

My belief is that I never saw the terms according to which the combat was to be conducted, prior to the duel, although I think they were stated and explained to me, probably by you[.] Mr. King thinks they were shewn or read by me to him. Mr. Johnson, who was present, does not agree with him in that particular, and my memory coincides with Mr. Johnsons. But I do not regard it as of the least consequence. I had no hand in their preparation. That was the work of one or both of the seconds.[11]

When, on the day preceding the duel, Mr. Graves, in company with you; came to my room, I was informed that he had determined to challenge Mr. Cilly, and he shewed me the challenge which he had drawn. Upon reading it, I thought it closed the door to all accommodation, stated that objection, & sketched a draft in my own hand writing, which would admit of an amicable adjustment. For, from my first knowledge of the affair to the hour of its fatal termination, believing that the difference ought to be settled, I clung to the hope of a friendly adjustment of it. What became of the sketch I drew I do not know. I did not see the challenge which was actually transmitted. I refer to the statement in Mr. Graves's letter, on this branch of the subject, in which I entirely agree with him.

I did not know that Mr. Graves bore a note from Col. Webb to Mr. Cilly, until after the delivery of the note, and after Mr. Graves received from him a verbal answer. In that stage of the transaction, for the first time, Mr. Graves communicated the matter to me, and I congratulated him on the fact of that answer being perfectly satisfactory, and such as to absolve him from all obligation to pursue the affair further. This has probably escaped Mr. Graves's recollection, but I add it, as being within my own. On conversing together, we both agreed that, to guard against future misunderstanding & misrepresentation, it was desirable that Mr. Cilly should put in writing what he had verbally answered. That Mr. Graves said he had no doubt would be readily done. But an unfortunate misunderstanding arose between the parties, as to the terms or nature of the verbal answer, which terminated in the challenge.

I have no recollection of having seen their correspondence between the verbal answer and the challenge. It was not conducted under my advice. If any person asserts that I saw it, I should be unwilling to contradict him, so uncertain is my memory about it. I have no doubt that, if I did not see it, I was informed of its purport, at the time I suggested a modification of the challenge.

Any communication which was made to me, concerning the affair, was received by me with regret. I was sorry that it was broached to me at all; but Mr. Graves was my friend, my colleague in Congress, and my messmate, and I could not decline receiving from him any communication, touching his honor and interests, which he might think proper to make. And I admit, without any reservation whatever, that on all the points of the controversy respecting which he asked my opinion, I gave it to him freely, according to the best of my judgment.

And now, having made such answer to your note as I think becomes me, I will add a few observations more.

In consequence of a slight indisposition, I did not leave my house during the day of the duel. I never saw the arms with which the parties fought. Not having been on the ground of combat, I cannot be held responsible for any of the occurrances there.

I have never joined in any censure of you for the part you bore in the conflict or for your conduct previous to it or on the ground. On the contrary, I was glad that the honor and life of my friend were under the care of one that I regarded so competent to guard both. I never hesitated to believe that you served him with zeal & fidelity, without any departure from the line of honor towards his lamented antagonist.

In the investigation in the H. of R. which ensued after the fatal catastrophe,[12] no attempt was made to implicate me. None was made in the subsequent publications under your signature, to which it gave rise. During all that time, and until recently, you stood in amicable relations to me. You, have, without any cause known to me, thought proper to establish different and inimical relations between us. Since this change, and during this Session of Congress, in the manner to which I have already adverted, for the first time, within my knowledge, the attempt has been made to fix the blame and responsibility of the duel upon me. Whether you have originated or been accessory to this attempt, your heart can best tell, and the public can best judge. . . .[13]

ALS. ViHi. Endorsed: "The following memorandum was made by Dr [Lewis F.] Linn—Received from Mr Clay in the morning March *1st 1842 and* handed to Mr Wise on the 2nd of March." Also printed with minor variations in *Kendall's Expositor* (March 5, 1844), 4:73-74, no. 5. 1. Clay to Speed, March 2, 1838; Clay to Webb, Jan. 30, 1842. 2. Clay to Webb, Jan. 30, 1842. 3. On Jan. 17, 1842, an article appeared in the New York *Herald* which charged that there was a concerted plan to prejudice the public against Wise by blaming him for the Graves-Cilley duel. In fact, the *Herald* asserted, "It was Mr. Clay, and not Mr. Wise, who governed all the preliminary proceedings in the Cilley duel. . . . The only error of Mr. Wise consisted in . . . risking every thing to guard the life of a friend [Graves], who was constrained to fight by the interference of Mr. Clay." Again on Jan. 31, 1842, the *Herald* accused Clay of pushing the matter to its extremity and also of trying to provoke a duel between Wise and Thomas F. Marshall of Ky. 4. *The Madisonian* on Feb. 16, 1842, reprinted Webb's editorial which appeared in the New York *Courier and Enquirer* of Feb. 12 [Clay to Webb, Jan. 30, 1842] and refuted it in great detail, charging that Webb was the true cause of the duel and denying that Wise had ever said that Clay "instigated" the duel. However, the article asserted that "all who were concerned with the duel know . . . and have known from the date of the duel to this day, that Mr. Clay's advice was the advice relied on by Mr. Graves." It also denied that Wise had deceived Clay as to the time and place of the confrontation. 5. Clay to Webb, Jan. 30, 1842. 6. *Ibid.* 7. Not found, but see Graves to Clay, Feb. 16, 1842. 8. Graves to Clay, Feb. 16, 1842. 9. Graves's letter to Clay of Feb. 16, along with the statements of Charles King and Reverdy Johnson, were published in the Washington *Daily National Intelligencer* on Feb. 25, 1842. 10. Clay to Webb, Jan. 30, 1842. 11. Wise as second for Graves and George W. Jones for Cilley. 12. The report of the Select Committee appointed to investigate the duel was published in *House Reports*, 25 Cong., 2 Sess., no. 825. 13. Wise's defense "To the Public," written on March 4, 1842, was published with an appendix of documents in the Washington *Daily National Intelligencer* on March 7, 1842.

Speech in Senate, March 1, 1842. Speaks for some two hours and a half on the eleven resolutions he introduced on February 15 [Remark in Senate, February 15, 1842], which, taken together, he says, constitute a "system of policy which, in my opinion, lies at the bottom of any restoration of the prosperity of the country." Says, too, that it is not his wish or intent "to revive any subjects of a party character." Rejects the notion that he should have offered these resolutions as separate bills. Thinks it "perfectly legitimate" for the Senate to discuss general problems of expenditure and retrenchment even though, under the Constitution, bills for raising revenue must originate in the House.

First resolution: That while it is the duty of the general government to raise "an adequate revenue," to do so by a loan or the issuance of treasury notes [Clay to Ewing, July 13, 1841; Remark in Senate, January 21, 1842] "must lead to pernicious consequences." Believes that for the past five years an adequate revenue has not been raised, and that the treasury-note expedient was adopted instead of imposing tariffs on "the free articles, according to the provisions of the [1833] compromise act [8:604, 619-22, 626-27]." The Van Buren administration should have made up annual deficiencies with tariff income, not treasury notes, Clay argues.

Second, third, and fourth resolutions: Says he will consider these together since "all relate to the same general subjects"; restates them, viz: The tariff rate must be raised above 20 percent, as permitted in the compromise legislation of 1833, the principles of which, however, "generally should be adhered to"; the new rate must be high enough to produce a net annual revenue of $26,000,000—$22 million for ordinary expenses; $2 million for debt payment; $2 million reserve for contingencies; a new maximum rate should be established "from which there ought to be as little departure as possible." Defends the $26 million figure as an approximate amount that the government needs to derive from tariff income and challenges the assertion of Senators John C. Calhoun, Louis F. Linn, and other Democrats that the Whig party, when out of power, had maintained that it could run the government for not more than $13,000,000 annually. Asserts there is no proof for this charge, denies it flatly, and explains that the $13 million figure grew out of the fact and observation that "During the four years of the administration of Mr. [John Q.] Adams, the average amount of the public expenditure was but thirteen millions; and you [Democrats] charged that administration with outrageous extravagance, and came yourselves into power on promises to reduce the annual expenditure; but, having obtained power, instead of reducing the public expenses, you carried them up to the astonishing amount of near forty millions." The Whigs, on the other hand, promised retrenchment, but gave no base annual expenditure figure. "I repeat that the exact amount is difficult to be ascertained. I have stated it in the resolution I now offer at *twenty-two millions*; and I shall soon show how I have arrived at that amount." Reviews annual expenditures of the four Van Buren years, claiming an aggregate sum of $142,561,945, or an average per year of $35,640,486. Sees his own figure of $22 million as a reduction of $13.6 million, or "a sum greater than the whole average expenditure of the extravagant and profligate administration of Mr. Adams, which they told us was so enormous that it must be reduced by a great 'retrenchment and reform.' " Admits that every administration encounters "many items of extra expenditure which may never occur again." Points out, for example, that since Van Buren spent less than was required on national defense—the navy and coastal fortifications—the Whigs must now spend more for "putting our navy and our fortifications in a better state to defend the honor and protect the rights of the nation." Believes, however, that even if one makes "all the allowances which its warmest friends can ask for the expenses of the inglorious war in Florida [Clay to Hale, January 7, 1838]—a contest which has profusely wasted not only the resources of the treasury, but the best blood of the nation—making the amplest allowance for this, and for all other extras whatever, the sum expended by the last administration still remains to be far, far beyond what is proposed in these resolutions as sufficient for the present and for years to come. It must, in candor, be conceded that this [$22 million figure] is a very great diminution of the national expenditure; and such, if nothing else were done, would redeem the pledge of the whig party." Argues that a national expenditure of $13,000,000 annually in 1825, compared with the $22 million he is now anticipating, represents an increase of expenses that "will be found not to go beyond the proportional increase of our population within the same period. That increase is found to be about four per cent. annually; and the increase of government expenditures, at the rate above stated, will not exceed that. This is independent of any augmentation of the army or navy, of the addition of new States and Territories, or the enlargement of the numbers in Congress." Thinks his $22 million figure is thus both reasonable and defensible, and notes that it "does not preclude further reductions." Explains why the Whigs could not effect economies at the beginning of and during the 1st [Extra] Session of the 27th Congress. Any new administration "cannot, at once, look back at the past abuses; it is not practicable to do so; it must have time to look into the pigeon-holes of the various bureaus, to find out what has been done, and what is doing. Its first great duty is to keep the machine of government in regular motion. It could not, therefore, be expected that Congress would go into a thorough process of reform at the extra session. Its peculiar object then was to adopt measures of immediate and indispensable relief to the people and to the government [Clay to Clayton, March 11, 1841]. Besides which, the subsequent misfortunes of the whig party were well known. President Harrison occupied the chair of state but for a single month; and the members of his cabinet left it under circumstances which, let me here say, do them the highest honor [Clay to Lawrence, April 13, 1841]."

Discusses in detail the arithmetic of how he reached his $22 million estimate, and how that sum might best be procured. Using the value of exports, rather than imports, as a basis, explains "why it is I have taken the exports as the ground of my calculations, adding thereto 15 per cent, for profits. The exports are one means of making foreign purchases. Their value is ascertained at the ports of exportation, under the act of 1820, and the returns generally present the same value. The price of cotton, as an example, at home, is always regulated by the price in the Liverpool market. It follows, therefore, that, by taking the value of any commodity at the place of its export, you reach its true value; for, if the price realized abroad be sometimes above and sometimes below that amount, the excess and deficiency will probably neutralize each other. This is the fairest mode for another reason: If, in any one year, more foreign goods shall be purchased than the exports of that year would pay for, a credit is created abroad, which must be extinguished by the exports of some succeeding year." Calculates the annual value of exports since 1836 at an average of about $109 million—after adding profit and deducting the interest and principal on the American debt abroad. Since $109 million in exports is also roughly the same sum in imports, asks: "Of this amount of importation, how much is now free from duty? The free goods, including tea and coffee, amount to 30 millions; from which amount I deduct for tea and coffee, assuming that they will be subjected to moderate duties, 12 millions; leaving the amount of free articles at 18 millions: deduct this from 109 millions, the amount of exports, and it will leave a balance of 91 millions, which may be assumed as the amount of dutiable articles for some years to come." Asks rhetorically how the government can raise $26 million out of $91 million worth of dutiable goods, and what must be the percentage rate of the tariff to accomplish this? Answers that if tariffs are calculated on the basis of home valuation of dutiable items (which he strongly favors), rather than valuation by foreigners at the foreign port of export, and if customhouse fraud in U.S. ports involving valuation can be eliminated, the new tariff rate should scale between twenty to twenty-five percent, or only about five percent over the rate set in the Compromise Tariff Act of 1833. If, however, the practice of foreign valuation continues, as he assumes it will, a duty level of 30% will be required to produce nearly $26 million. Anticipating complaints that this level would violate the principles of the 1833 legislation, Clay insists that the six main principles of the Compromise Tariff Act of 1833 be clearly understood. Reviews those principles, viz: (1) there should be a fixed rate of *ad valorem* duty, and flexible discrimination below it; (2) duties above 20% should gradually be scaled down so that by June 30, 1842, they would be 20%; (3) after June 30, 1842, the government is authorized to lay "*such duties* . . . for the purpose of raising *such* revenue as might be necessary for an economical administration of the government . . . excluding all resort to internal taxation, or to the proceeds of the public lands"; (4) after June 30, 1842, all duties must be paid in cash, not credit; (5) after the same date, "the assessment of the value of all imports should be made at home and not abroad"; (6) after June 30, 1842, "a list of articles specified and enumerated in the act should be admitted free of duty, for the benefit of the manufacturing interest." Explains that "These are the principles, and all the principles, of the compromise act. An impression has been taken up, most erroneously, that the rate of duty was never to exceed twenty per cent. There is no such limitation in the act. I admit that, at the time of the passage of the act, a hope was entertained that a rate of duty not exceeding twenty per cent. would supply an adequate revenue to an economical administration of the government. Then we were threatened with that overflow of revenue with which the treasury was subsequently inundated; and the difficulty was to find articles which should be liberated from duty and thrown into the free class. Hence wines, silks, and other luxuries were rendered free. But the act, and no part of the act, when fairly interpreted, limits Congress to the iron rule of adhering forever, and under all circumstances, to a fixed and unalterable rate of twenty per cent. duty." Quotes at length from sections 1 and 3 of the act to demonstrate this interpretation, concluding: "I contend, therefore, with entire confidence, that it is perfectly consistent with the provisions of the compromise act to impose duties to any amount whatever—thirty, forty, or more per cent.—subject to the single condition of an economical administration of the government." Explains, further, how the framer of the act [Clay himself] intended it to work. Asserts that whether the tariff be *ad valorem* or specific, "I would observe that the actual measure of protection does not depend upon the *form*, but on the *amount*, of the duty which is levied upon the foreign rival article."

Fifth resolution: That the act passed in the last session suspending distribution of public land sales receipts if the tariff level went above 20 percent [Clay to Ewing, April 30, 1841; Remark in Senate, June 9, 1841] should be repealed. Believes that even if such repeal occurred, "it will not dispense with the necessity of a great increase in the existing rate of taxation," especially since he has shown that "a duty of 30 per cent. will not be too much to furnish the requisite amount of revenue for a just and economical administration of the government." Further, in terms of income from public land sales, which last year was $1.5 million, the same amount realized this year would only permit the lowering of a 30% tariff level to 28.5%; in sum, this would be "a trifling difference."

Sixth and seventh resolutions: Retrenchment that would abolish all unnecessary institutions and offices and reduce mileage and other expenses paid members of Congress should "begin in an especial manner, here, with ourselves, in Congress itself, where is found one of the most extravagant of all the branches of the government. We should begin at home." Points out that the contingent expenses of the two Houses has climbed from $86,000 in 1824 to $384,333 in 1840. Also suggests substantial reductions in the amount of stationery furnished members.

Eighth resolution: This would lower the costs of running the federal judicial system. Notes that this expense has risen from $209,000 in 1824 to $471,000 in 1840. Charges abuses in expenditures in some judicial districts. Laments this development.

Ninth resolution: This would reduce the cost of diplomatic relations with foreign powers. Deplores sharp increases in the number of ministers and chargés since 1828, suggests abolishing unreciprocated U.S. Missions in Constantinople, Vienna, and Naples, as well as cutting mileage allowances for diplomats. "Why, we have ministers abroad who are seeking for the governments to which they are accredited, and the governments are not to be found!"

Tenth resolution: This would restrict the franking privilege and determine the postage on books and packages on the basis of their weights. Gives examples of abuses and corruption in the use of the frank and criticizes the unrealistically low cost of sending packages as compared with the relatively high cost of letters.

Eleventh resolution: The secretaries of state, treasury, war, navy, and the postmaster general shall report what offices under their jurisdictions can be abolished and what retrenchments within their power might be made in the interest of economy. Asks for cooperation on this, especially from the secretaries of war and navy who "come to us asking for appropriations far beyond any that have heretofore been demanded in time of peace, and that with a full knowledge of the fact of an empty treasury." Asks, too, that "several useless mints which only operate to waste the public money" be closed, especially the one in New Orleans, and that all coinage be handled by the Philadelphia mint.

Believes these eleven resolutions, if enacted into law, will secure to the government "an adequate amount of revenue, without being obliged to depend on temporary and disreputable expedients, and thus preserve the public credit unsullied—which I deem a great advantage of the plan." Adds that it will preserve the national credit by reducing the annual public expenditure and will check the flow of precious metals to foreign countries which is a main cause of the nation's depression. Explains at length how the bullion drain abroad undermines the specie basis of paper money issued by American banks because "the withdrawal of it not only obliges the banks to withhold discounts and accommodations, but to draw in what is due from their debtors, at the precise time when they, sharing in the general stricture, are least able to meet the calls. Property is then thrown into market, to raise means to comply with those demands; depression ensues; and, as is invariably the case when there is a downward tendency in its value, it falls below its real worth." This would occur even if the circulating medium consisted of nothing but precious metals. Is willing, however, "to make one concession to the gentlemen on the other side. I admit that, if the circulation were in coin alone, the thermometer of our monetary fluctuations would not rise as high or fall as low as when the circulation is of a mixed character, consisting partly of coin and partly of paper." Argues that to check the foreign specie drain, "We have tried free trade. We have had the principles of free trade operating on more than half the total amount of our imports for the greater part of nine years past. That will not do it, we see." Develops this contention, observing, in passing, that in spite of Sen. Robert Y. Hayne's claim in 1832 [8:446] that abolition of tariff protection would return prosperity to his native South Carolina, that state has not materially benefitted from nine years of the increasingly freer trade provided by the 1833 compromise tariff. "Nine years (from 1824 to 1833) we had the protective policy of a high tariff; and nine years (from 1833 to 1842) we have had the full operation of free trade on more than a moiety of the whole amount of our imports, and a descending tariff on the residue. And what is the condition of South Carolina at this day? Has she regained her lost prosperity? Has she recovered from the desolation and ruin so confidently imputed to the existence of a high tariff?" No. Points out that cotton is currently selling at the lowest levels since 1815. "These are the facts: let casuists and theorists, and the advocates of a one-sided paralytic free trade, in which we turn our sound side to the world, and our blighted and paralyzed and dead side toward our own people, make of them what they can. At the very moment that England is pushing the resources of Asia, cultivating the fields of India, and even contemplating the subsidizing of Africa, for the supply of her factories with cotton; and when the importations from India have swelled from 200,000 bales to 580,000, we are told that there are to be no restrictions on free trade." Asserts, again, that only a tariff "giving to the country a revenue which may provide for the economical wants of the government, and at the same time give an incidental protection to our home industry" can check the flow of specie abroad. Admits that a few items—shoes, hats, ready-made clothing, sugar, iron, and paper—"may not derive the protection which they need from the plan I propose"; but this problem can be handled by supplemental legislation that would raise the proposed maximum rate on specific commodities.

Advises those states having an economic stake in protecting a given commodity to send to Congress delegations ("without regard to political denominations or distinctions") prepared to work and vote solidly for specific protective tariffs. "They must look into the matter, and, if they take it up and bring forward their propositions, and make out a clear case of exception to the general rule, I shall be an humble follower of their lead, but I will not myself take the lead in any such case. . . . I am ready to follow, but I will not lead." Indeed, "I say that with me it [protectionism] always was a question of expediency only. If the nation does not want protection, I certainly never would vote to force it upon the nation; but, viewing it as a question of expediency wholly, I have not hesitated heretofore, on the broad and comprehensive ground of expediency, to give my assent to all suitable measures proposed with a view to that end." Concludes with an appeal for unity and patriotism "to devise the best mode of relieving the public distress. It is in this spirit that I have brought forward my proposed plan: and I trust in God—invoking as I humbly do the aid and blessing of his Providence—that the Senators, on all sides of the Chamber, will lay aside all party feelings, and more especially that habitual suspicion to which we are all more or less prone, (and from which I profess not to be exempted more than other men,) that impels us to reject without examination, and to distrust, whatever proceeds from a quarter we have been in the habit of opposing. Let us lay aside prejudice: let us look at the distresses of our country, and these alone." *Cong. Globe*, 27 Cong., 2 Sess., Appendix, 192-98. A summary version of this speech appears in the regular columns of the *Cong. Globe* for March 1, 1842, pp. 269-70. Clay worked from notes when delivering this lengthy discourse and a portion of these notes, covering his conclusions, is found in DLC-HC (DNA, M212, R5). Printed (the Appendix version) also in Colton, *Clay Correspondence*, 6:322-51. This speech was published under the title *Speech of Mr. Clay, of Kentucky, Upon His Resolutions Concerning the Tariff, and Other Great Objects of Public Policy, Delivered in the Senate of the United States, March 1, 1842*. Washington, 1842.

Resolutions 1 and 6 were agreed to in the Senate on March 30, 1842. The other resolutions were referred to committee where they died. U.S. Sen., *Journal*, 27 Cong., 2 Sess., 164, 191, 194, 198, 202-3, 215, 217, 219, 223, 226, 228, 230, 232, 236, 243, 245, 255-56, 258. See also Clay to Letcher, January 6, 1842.

From C.P. Green *et al.*, Warrenton, N.C., March 2, 1842. Announce that the Whigs of Warren County "have with pleasure seen the invitation [Clay to Hines, March 21, 1842] tendered by the Whigs of Wake [County]" for Clay to attend the convention at Raleigh on April 4 [Clay to Porter, January 22, 1842]. They second the invitation and praise Clay for his "long and brilliant political career," adding that "thousands anxiously wish to greet your arrival" in North Carolina. Copy. Printed in Raleigh *Register and North-Carolina Gazette*, April 5, 1842.

Clay replied on March 21, 1842, thanking them for the invitation but expressing regret that he is unable to come at this time. Promises, however, that the visit "is not abandoned, but . . . only postponed." Adds: "I eagerly desire to shake hands, on their own soil, with those patriotic sons, whose noble sires, at Mecklenburg, were the first to announce the Independence of the thirteen Colonies [8:774-75]." *Ibid.*

Remark in Senate, March 2, 1842. Asks Sen. Silas Wright not to use the appropriation and expenditure estimates of the Tyler administration in evaluating the numbers in his (Clay's) speech yesterday [Speech in Senate, March 1, 1842]. Requests that his figures and their figures be considered "separate and distinct." Invokes the one-hour rule. *Cong. Globe*, 27 Cong., 2 Sess., 273-74. The one-hour rule required scheduled business to be dealt with no later than one hour after commencement of the daily session.

Remark in Senate, March 3, 1842. During the course of this day's session, Clay presents petitions favoring a specific duty on foreign window glass and complaining of the abuse of the congressional franking privilege. Also asks postponement of debate on his retrenchment and reform resolutions [Speech in Senate, March 1, 1842] so that Sen. John M. Berrien (Ga.), absent today because of an indisposition, could speak on the subject. Also moves to refer to committee the House joint resolution delaying for the present the appropriation for payment of the printing of the Compendium of the Sixth Census. *Cong. Globe*, 27 Cong., 2 Sess., 276-77.

To HENRY COLEMAN Washington, March 4, 1842

My engagements of a public nature here are such that I cannot answer one letter in 20 that I receive, and[1] I must reply very briefly to your's[2] as to the mode of cultivating Hemp. I once wrote an essay on the subject, of which I regret that I have no copy by me to send you. It was published in some Agricultural periodical published at Cincinnati.[3]

The best soil is a rich vegetable mould, with a Clay substratum, either fresh, or which has been long in pasture. Any stable or ordinary manure is good, if it be necessary to use any, which depends upon the degree of the fertility of the soil. Hemp exhausts very little, and I have known it cultivated for successive years in the same field without any diminution of the Crop.

The ground should be prepared exactly as you would make the best preparation for wheat. A bushel & a peck of seed, or, if the land is uncommonly rich, a bushel & a half, to the acre should be sowed, broad cast, from the first to the 20h. of May. All the plants, male and female, are gathered, by pulling or cutting close to the ground by a cutting knife resembling a Reap hook, but shorter. The plants intended to produce seed are sowed by themselves in drills, and cultivated with the plough and hoe, so as to keep them clean.

The Crop Hemp is pulled or cut (for there is not much difference between the two methods, although I prefer cutting) about the 20h. or 25h. August; and the proper time is indicated by the Hemp leaves turning a little yellow, and the ferina escaping when the stalks are agitated. When cut or pulled, the stalks are suffered to remain on the ground a few days, until they are cured, and if a rain falls on them so much the better as it will render the separation of the leaves from the stalk easier. After being cured, the hemp is tyed up with a hemp stalk in small bundles, convenient to handle, and shocked in the field. The best farmers, in a week or two afterwards, stack them on the field, throwing the tops inside and the roots outside.

Late in November or in December the stacks are broken, and the Hemp spread down on the field, or on sod, to ret. The length of time it should remain depends upon whether the season is wet or dry, but it will not be less than seven or eight weeks, and may be longer. It is spread as you would spread flax regularly, and avoiding its being tangled. You cannot judge whether it is sufficiently retted or not but by taking up a handful and ascertaining if the lint will separate easily. When sufficiently thus retted it is taken up, and again shocked, and broken out, in the months of Feby., March, April &c. as convenient, by a large hand brake. I task my hands 80 lb. per day, and allow them a Cent per pound, for every pound beyond that. I have known, in some instances, as much as 250 lb. per day broken out. As each handful is broken out, the shoes, that is the little particles of the stalk which adhere to the lint, are carefully beaten off, so as to make it clean, and the hemp is laid away, and at night tyed up in a bale or bales and carried to the Hemp house. All attempts to substitute Hor[s]e, Water or Steam power to the Hand brake, and there have been many, have hitherto failed.

The above method is what we call Dew retting. I have never tried water retting. That is effected by immersing the Hemp Stalks in bundles, in water, and keeping them under with weights. September is the best period, and standing better than running water. The length of time may be a few days or more, according to the temperature of the water. You judge, as in the other mode, when it is sufficiently retted.

The Hemp intended to produce seed is suffered to remain in the ground until the first light frost, is then cut, and after a few days the seed are thrashed out. . . .

ALS. DLC-Stone Autograph Collection. 1. Lines struck through to this point. 2. For Coleman (1785-1849), an agricultural writer and Unitarian minister, see *DAB*. 3. See 8:272-78.

Remark in Senate, March 4, 1842. Opposes distribution of 300 copies of the land laws and opinions printed under the Senate resolution of February 28, 1837, and 1,400 copies of the five-volume state papers on the public lands to the nine states and three territories containing public lands. Says all states, whether they once had public lands or not, should share in the distribution. *Cong. Globe*, 27 Cong., 2 Sess., 282. For the Senate resolution of February 28, 1837, see U.S. Sen., *Journal*, 24 Cong., 2 Sess., 298. The book in question concerning the land laws was Matthew St. Clair Clarke's *Laws of the United States . . . and other Documents Respecting the Public Lands*, first published by Gales & Seaton in Washington in 1828. The 5 volumes of the state papers referred to is the *American State Papers, Documents . . . in Relation to Public Land*, edited by Walter Lowrie (Washington, n.d.) and published by Duff Green. See Lawrence Schmeckebier, *Government Publications and Their Use* (2nd ed., Washington, 1969), 189, 205.

Later this day, defends and further explains the background of his resolutions for a constitutional amendment to restrict the president's veto power [Speech in Senate, January 24, 1842]. Asks that further debate on the veto resolution be scheduled for March 11. *Cong. Globe*, 27 Cong., 2 Sess., 282-83.

To JAMES B. CLAY Washington, March 7, 1842

I received your letter of the 28h. and am glad to find that you have confidence in the arrangements to take up my note on the 17h inst. I am most anxious that it should be taken up, as I assured the Bank it should be done. Mr. [James] Erwin is a very bad correspondent, as I have not heard from him for two months. He has always assured me that he would remit my money in his hands towards the last of this month. You perhaps know something of his intentions. I shall be greatly disappointed, if he does not remit it. If you know that he will, and if you be disappointed in raising funds to take up my note, I authorize you to draw on me, for that purpose, for any sum not exceeding $2000 at 60 days after date, payable at the Bank of Commerce in N. York. It will be a specie draft & you ought to get a premium accordingly.

I have been hitherto unable to negotiate any of the bills which Thomas [H. Clay] sent me,[1] and fear that I cannot do it. But before my return I may go to N. York and Philada. and make another trial Whil[s]t Exchange is so much agt. N. Orleans in N. York I fear you will have difficulty in negotiating bills with the Lexington Banks. You ought to get your Creditors to wait awhile, as the Exchange on N. Orleans will improve.

Except the Wickliffe mare and my imported mare, all the rest may be put to Royal. I will stop one year breeding blooded animals. I suppose the imported would be given a Season, by any of the horses gratis. If not let Mr. Toddhunter [*sic,* Parker E. Todhunter] have her put to Post boy on the shares.

I am glad that you find pleasure & occupation in the Study of the Law. You are young enough, and have talent enough, to distinguish yourself at the Bar, if you will be industrious & diligent, very industrious and diligent.

I sent by the last mail to your Mama the seeds which she had requested through John [Morrison Clay].

My love to her & to him.

ALS. DLC-TJC (DNA, M212, R10).   1. Clay to Lucretia Hart Clay, Dec. 9, 1842; Clay to Silsbee, March 18, 1843.

Comment in Senate, March 7, 1842. Presents a memorial "from a number of ladies of Rahway, New Jersey, who . . . judging from their autographs, were very beautiful indeed," asking for a higher duty on ready-made clothing. Since these seamstresses had "no other means by which to support themselves," their livelihood, they pleaded, was endangered by foreign competition. Clay agrees with them and hopes that the "chivalry of South Carolina" in the person of John C. Calhoun, will "rush forward and protect their fair country women from foreign competition."

Following the rise of Calhoun to this facetious bait, Clay presents a Pennsylvania petition asking for protection of the "iron interest"; also one from northern Alabama, signed by both Democrats and Whigs, lamenting postponement of action on or repeal of the Bankruptcy Act [Remark in Senate, April 22, 1840, and December 28, 1841; Speech in Senate, January 28, 1842]. Chided as "unkind" by Sen. James Buchanan (Dem., Pa.) for having "presented the petition from so many fair ladies," leaving him (Buchanan) to present those of the iron manufacturers, and for having appropriated "all those fair ladies to protection, such as he [Clay] could give them," Clay responds that the reason he had not let Buchanan present the petition of the Rahway ladies was because "the Senator had lived for thirty-five years and upwards, without having taken any lady under his protection." As for the petition on bankruptcy, it "showed that his Democratic friends, especially his Democratic friends of '98 [1:36; 2:464] and the war [of 1812], and all along that time, had come out from their party associations in support of this law, notwithstanding they approved of the vetoes and some other measures equally obnoxious." *Cong. Globe,* 27 Cong., 2 Sess., 287-88.

During the course of this day's session, Clay participates in the debate on his resolution of January 21, 1842, which provided for the redistribution of public land sales revenues due those states not wishing to participate in the federal distribution program; Clay would transfer such revenue to those states which elected to participate in distribution. Assures Sen. William R. King (Dem., Ala.) that his resolution is a serious one because there would be some state legislatures voting not to receive such federal funds during the next few years. In reply to Sen. King, asks what if Alabama "refused to receive it [distribution share], what then? Why this disobedience of a law of Congress is worse than nullification. . . . Now, if Alabama or South Carolina refused to receive her portion, let it be given to others. . . . Gentlemen had called the distribution policy one of robbery and plunder. How robbery? How plunder? If he was disposed to retort, he might show that the robbery rested not with the receiving States. Nothing was to be gained by this language. Who were the robbers? Congress was the agent of this robbery, and the States the receivers of the stolen goods. Congress, after ten years laboring to effect the object, had passed this bill, and the people of the States receiving their proportions would have the benefits of it. And this was called robbery. What was to be gained by such crimination?" Asserts that distribution "is merely a change from direct to indirect taxation; for every man who votes for the distribution, votes for relieving his lands and his houses, his horses, his cattle, and his property of every taxable denomination, from so much State taxation as his share of the distribution would cover." Responds to Sen. William Allen's (Dem., Ohio) contention that federal distribution, conceived of as relief from state taxation, is unconstitutional and must lead to, in Allen's words, "civil convulsions terminating in violence and revolution" because "it will put the whole property of the people in the hands of those administering the Government, to be offered in distribution as a reward to the vicious for their support." Clay hopes that "civil war would be averted, and would be found to exist only in the vivid imagination of the honorable Senator from Ohio. It was a very common thing for the gentlemen opposite to talk of civil war, and think to alarm the majority in Congress from doing its duty by that epithet. But it had grown too stale to alarm even the old women of the country. Civil war! For what? For taking what the largest portion of the people of the United States think is their right? And there is going to be a civil war, because Congress is giving them what they demand!" Asserts that he has always been "opposed to the power of raising taxes for mere purposes of distribution." Congress has no power to effect this kind of distribution. Distributions of public land sales receipts are not distributions of income from taxes, "they are debts due to the States." States can accept or reject the receipt of such debt payments. Those accepting these payments merely save themselves from "so much State taxation; or refuse it, and go on paying so much in direct taxes." South Carolina can do what it wants to do on this question. [Calhoun interrupts to say that "the tendency of the act of distribution is to dissolve the Union."] "Well," Clay resumes, "let it be the *tendency*." Demonstrates that quite the opposite is true, that distribution will tend to hold the states together. Explains: "what is the effect of this law if undistributed? Is it not that during that three, four, or five hundred years, every State would be in the receipt of her portion, provided she continues in the confederation? but the moment she would separate herself from her sister States, she would, by her own act, lose her portion. If a State rose in rebellion, it would forfeit all claim to its distributive share. It is perfectly plain, then, that, so far from the tendency of the measure being towards disunion, it is directly the reverse. Its tendency is one of union and fraternity." The main issue now is whether to distribute anew the rejected portions.

Answers at length various technical objections to his distribution resolution, specifically one from Sen. William S. Archer (Va.) as to how he (Clay) can "consistently take what belongs to one State and give it to another?" Also, do undistributed land sales funds still belong to states voting not to receive them and should they remain in the treasury untouched? Should they be held in trust and loaned out at interest? Can rejecting states also reject the interest earned? Has Congress the power to distribute these funds without the consent of the rejecting states? Clay's position is that funds returned voluntarily to the treasury become part of the total funds of the general government and can be spent as are all other funds in its keeping regardless of source. In answer to the question must every state obey the distribution law, if passed, whether it wants to receive distributed funds or not, Clay remarks: "does the Senator [Archer] mean to say that a State may, if it chooses, resist the law? If it is not ready and willing to co-operate in carrying the law into effect, what is the next step but resistance? Is the Senator prepared to see the doctrine of nullification carried out, and in this sneaking and cowardly form of refusing to carry out a law of Congress instead of the bold and daring mode assumed by South Carolina on a former occasion, when she put her hand upon her sword to nullify the laws of the land? The time is not far distant, if the forebodings of the opposite side have any foundation, when the strength of unanimity will be the security of the country." *Cong. Globe*, 27 Cong., 2 Sess., Appendix, 141, 143, 145. At the end of this day's debate, Clay's resolution was adopted 25 to 19. *Ibid.*, 146. See also Clay to Letcher, January 6, 1842; Remark in Senate, January 21, 1842.

From James Watson Webb, New York City, March 7, 1842. Writes that "Few men have been more grossly deceived by treacherous friends than yourself, and considering the character of others who have heretofore wormed themselves into your confidence from this quarter, it is only [a] matter of surprise that you have not suffered in the estimation of the people. But the truth is you understand the people, & they appear to have an intuitive appreciation of your character which nothing can shake." Warns Clay against J. N. Reynolds, Robert Wetmore, and some other New York Whigs saying, "They all pretended friendship for me, but I knew that if they were my friends it was because they feared me." States that "It is their treachery that prompted some of your best friends to ask me to write you & let you know the true character of Reynolds and his associates." Encloses a short article from "Saturday's paper" which was written in an effort "to check an intrigue to place Reynolds at the head of the 'Clay Clubs' which would have disgusted them in our ranks."

Describes Reynolds's "treachery" on the Thursday evening preceding the meeting of the Harrisburg convention [Porter to Clay, November 14 and December 30, 1837] when a group of delegates from western New York had attempted to convince Webb and Reynolds "that our only hope of success was in the nomination of Genl. [Winfield] *Scott* [Scott to Clay, February 5, 1839; Porter to Clay, February 16, 1839]." Continues: "Mr. Reynolds said he was thoroughly convinced of the truth of their position, and was ready to give up you his first choice, from that time forward. I said that . . . inasmuch as I looked on the whole Scott movement as the work of [Thurlow] Weed, N[athaniel]. P. Tal[l]madge, [Edward] Curtis, & [a] few other leaders, with which the people had nothing to do, and as it could only succeed by treachery to you, I should adhere to your cause & through my columns urge more strenuously than ever the necessity of the Convention nominating you! Our little Caucus then adjourned; & I afterwards learned that *Reynolds* was acting only as a Stool Pidgeon to catch me & that he had been with them & of them for weeks preceeding, & that at that very time *Curtis* had raised for hire at his request, the necessary means for paying his expenses to Harrisburgh [*sic*, Harrisburg, Pa.] to electioneer for Scott. . . . Such is Mr. Reynolds; & I have since told him that when he again attempted to obtain a position in our ranks, I would expose him." Adds that "if he should visit Washington, it is my desire that you exhibit him this letter; or if you please, that you write to him & let him know its contents."

Reiterates also that Nathaniel P. Tallmadge "was the Master Spirit of the Scott movement, although *Curtis* the more active person. He will desert us as soon as you go home, & with *John C. Spencer* pretend to be for *Tyler* until that *poor devil* discovers he has no party, & then carry the whole administration for *Scott.* This I am quite sure, is their game." Concludes, however, that "If I mistake not, we will have three fourths of the Whig Party in this State pledged in unity before three months are past; & then we shall hear no more of expediency." ALS. DLC-HC (DNA, M212, R5).

In an article in the New York *Weekly Courier and Enquirer* on Saturday, March 5, 1842, Webb had charged Reynolds with being false to the Whig cause in 1839 by his support of Gen. Winfield Scott for the party's presidential nomination. He argued that those who "never pretended to be in favor of Henry Clay in 1839, but openly and manfully opposed him, and are now disposed to do him justice" should not be placed at the head of a Clay Club, although they should be treated kindly.

Remark in Senate, March 8, 1842. Explains that he came to the Senate this morning even though he was ill, because of his "indignation" at a newspaper paragraph, brought to his attention, that was "so shocking, so atrocious" that he could not do other than correct it. Recalls that yesterday, during his exchange with Sen. James Buchanan on the petition of the Rahway ladies [Comment in Senate, March 7, 1842], he had remarked that while Buchanan had "lived a certain number of years, had never taken any lady under his protection! But a newspaper reporter had represented him as having assigned to the Senator from Pennsylvania the extraordinary age of fifty-five!! He called upon every grave Senator and upon every lady in the gallery who heard him, to testify whether he made any such remark. He believed that he said thirty-six years and upwards. [Laughter.]" *Cong. Globe*, 27 Cong., 2 Sess., 292. Buchanan, who was 47 days from his 51st birthday, responded with feigned outrage and equal facetiousness. *Ibid.*

Remark in Senate, March 9, 1842. Moves that the Senate take up and order engrossed the bill from the House, amended yesterday, authorizing the banks in the District of Columbia "to receive and pay out depreciated bank paper for one year, or until the banks in Baltimore or Richmond resume specie payments." *Cong. Globe*, 27 Cong., 2 Sess., 300. Bill passed 21 to 18, Clay voting yea.

House bill 112 to suspend for a limited time the operation of section 5 of "An act to revive and extend the charters of certain banks in the District of Columbia [5 *U.S. Stat.*, 449-51]" was introduced in the House on February 9, 1842, and passed on February 15 by a vote of 97 to 83. It was amended and passed by the Senate on March 9. It then went back to the House for concurrence with the amendment where on June 1 it was ordered to lie on the table. U.S. H. of Reps., *Journal*, 27 Cong., 2 Sess., 339, 402-3, 406, 514, 888, 893; U.S. Sen., *Journal*, 27 Cong., 2 Sess., 215. See also Remark in Senate, June 15, 1840, and June 18, 1841.

Later this day, Clay moves successfully to table an amendment to the public land distribution and preemption act of September 4, 1841 [Clay to Ewing, April 30, 1841; Remark in Senate, June 9, 1841] so that the special order of the day—discussion of his first resolution (of eleven) of February 15 [Remark in Senate, February 15, 1842; Speech in Senate, March 1, 1842], dealing with improving the state of the nation's economy—could be obeyed. Yields, however, to Calhoun's request to put discussion over until tomorrow so that he (Calhoun) could speak to the resolution. *Cong. Globe*, 27 Cong., 2 Sess., 300-301.

To WILLIAM C. RIVES Washington, March 9, 1842

The unexpected course of business in the Senate is such that I am inclined to think that it will be best, when we take up the Tariff resolutions,[1] to go through with them, without the intervention of any other business. This will most probably throw the Veto resolution[2] over to next week. I hope to get up the Tariff resolutions to day, and I suppose they may absorb this week. I mention this arrangement, hoping that it may meet your approbation. It will allow you further time for regaining your strength & for preparation.

ALS. DLC-William C. Rives Papers (DNA, M212, R22). Written from Senate Chamber.
1. The 2nd, 3rd, and 4th of Clay's eleven resolutions of Feb. 15, 1842. See Remark in Senate, Feb. 15, 1842, and Speech in Senate, March 1, 1842. 2. Speech in Senate, Jan. 24, 1842.

Remark in Senate, March 11, 1842. During debate on his resolution of February 15 [Remark in Senate, February 15, 1842; Speech in Senate, March 1, 1842] advocating the raising of the tariff above the 20% level, answers Calhoun's criticism of home valuation of imported items (for the purpose of establishing *ad valorem* tariff charges) by reminding him that he (Calhoun) had voted for the home valuation provision in the Compromise Tariff Act of 1833; and that he had so voted even while protesting the concept and in the expectation that it would not be carried into effect. Recalls that Calhoun's stance on the home valuation issue influenced the decision of Sen. William C. Rives (Va.) to support the compromise bill. Asserts his firm conviction that "the bill never could have been passed without the insertion of the clause in question." Claims it is the only alternative to "false and fraudulent reports." The value of imported articles on which tariff levels are assessed "should be done by our own [customs] officers, and under supervision of our own laws." Points out to Rives some disadvantages of foreign valuation. *Cong. Globe*, 27 Cong., 2 Sess., 310-11.

To LUCRETIA HART CLAY Washington, March 13, 1842

In less than three weeks my service in the Senate will terminate. Although my health has not been good the past winter, and is not now good, the prospect of my deliverance from the cares and responsibilities of public life cheers and consoles me. I may be detained here, and in the Northern Cities, a fortnight after I leave the Senate, I hope to reach Ashland somewhere about the 20th of April.[1]

March, until within the last day or two, has been as mild & warm as the month of May. The grass has put up, the trees are in bud & blossom, and the whole of the fields & the forests exhibit the appearance of a premature Spring. The cold of yesterday and today will check vegetation somewhat. If you have had equally fine weather at Ashland, the gardens & the lawns must look very beautiful. I hope the roots I sent you in a box & the seeds I sent in the mail have reached you in safety.

I have not received, nor heard from you about the remittance I requested of what money I had in the Lex. B[ranch]. Bank that you did not want. If it has not been made before this letter reaches you, it need not be made. I have at last received a letter from Mr. James Erwin. He writes me that, amidst the general crash around him, he will stand up safe & unhurt; and he promises to remit my funds in his hands.

I am sorry that Henry [Clay, Jr.] was disappointed in selling his place.[2] The times are really gloomy enough; but we must all try to preserve our spirits, and not sink beneath their pressure.

The gentleman who purchased my Alton land for taxes has conveyed his title to me.[3]

Tell John that I am glad to hear that he has got his license.[4] When I reach home, we will consult about the best place to establish himself.

My love to all the boys.[5]

ALS. DLC-TJC (DNA, M212, R10). 1. Clay left Washington on April 21, 1842, and arrived in Lexington on May 2. Washington *Daily National Intelligencer*, April 22, 1842; Frankfort *Commonwealth*, May 10, 1842. 2. Either his property in Louisville or his estate "Maplewood" in Lexington. It is known that in July, 1841 he had appointed an attorney to sell land in Louisville to the Methodist Episcopal Church. William J.B. Burger, *Historical Americana . . . Catalogue*, 1985. 3. Probably a reference to land purchased from William Russell by deed of Feb. 26, 1842. See Russell to Clay, Feb. 26, 1842. 4. Reference obscure. 5. James Brown Clay, John Morrison Clay, Henry Clay Duralde.

To MARGARET (Mrs. Harman) BLENNERHASSETT Washington, March 14, 1842

I received only two or three days ago your letter, and that of Mr. Emmet,[1] accompanying your petition for reparation of the wrongs inflicted upon your island in the Ohio river.[2] I took great pleasure in presenting it to the Senate today,[3] adding such observations in support of it, as I thought best calculated to procure you justice.

I regret that my early retirement from the Senate[4] will probably deprive me of an opportunity of rendering you further assistance; but I sincerely hope that you may obtain full, although it will be, tardy redress[5]

ALS. DLC-Harman Blennerhassett Papers (DNA, M212, R20). 1. For Robert Emmett, a New York lawyer who became a justice of the state superior court, see *CAB*. Emmett wrote Clay that "Mrs. Blennerhassett is now in this (New York) city, residing in very humble circumstances, bestowing her cares on a son, who, by long poverty and sickness, is reduced to utter imbecility, both of body and mind; unable to assist her, or provide for his own wants. In her present destitute situation, the smallest amount of relief would be thankfully received by her. Her condition is one of *absolute want*, and she has but a short time left to enjoy any better fortune in this world." Emmett to Clay, n.d. [*ca.* Early March, 1842]. Copy, excerpt. Printed in William H. Safford, *The Life of Harman Blennerhasset . . .* (Chillicothe, Ohio, 1850), 207-8. 2. Petition not found, but see Remark in Senate, March 14, 1842; Blennerhassett to Clay, mid-March, 1842. 3. Remark in Senate, March 14, 1842. 4. Clay to Berrien, Oct. 7, 1841; Clay to General Assembly of Ky., Feb. 16, 1842. 5. Mrs. Blennerhassett had returned to the United States from England in 1842 in order to seek relief from the government for the despoiling of their property in 1806-7. Her petition was reported from committee in the Senate on August 5, 1842, and ordered to lie on the table on August 17, Mrs. Blennerhassett having died on June 29, 1842. U.S. Sen., *Journal*, 27 Cong., 2 Sess., 219, 542, 581; Safford, *Life of Blennerhassett*, 209; Alysonia R. Todd, "Burr and Blennerhassett at Chaumiere," *RKHS* (Jan., 1916), 14:45-46; Columbus *Weekly Ohio State Journal*, June 29, 1842.

From Mark Hardin, Shelby County, Ky., March 14, 1842. An exhortation, replete with numerous Biblical citations thought to be appropriate, arguing that the movement and distribution of the U.S. mail on Sunday is an abomination in the sight of God and a violation of scripture. Assures Clay that "if there is a peculiarly favored people of God on earth you will agree with me that we are that people." But warns that Sabbath mail delivery is but one reason underlying "God's intention to punish us." In addition, he notes that weak rulers have taken over the American government, citing as his authority the lamentation in Ecclesiastes 10:16. "I Hold then that a negative character at the head of our government must be disastrous[,] for God has said so—We must retrace our steps we must have at the helm a practical man & one who understands government as a Science—then men will have time to contemplate God and His dealings with nations.... We must reserve the Sabbath day." ALS, draft. Courtesy of R. S. Sanders, Lexington, Ky. Hardin quoted only the first sentence of Ecclesiastes 10:16 ("Woe to thee, O land, when thy king is a child")—which meant, he explained, "when the head of the Government, be he young or old, is in the arms of nurses." He did not, however, quote or cite the first sentence of the following verse which reads: "Blessed art thou, O land, when thy king is the son of nobles. . . ."

Despite petitions against the Sunday mail which dated back more than a decade, Congress in 1825, passed a law which required that post offices at which mail arrived on Sunday be kept open all day. Opposition to this legislation gained national attention after the formation in New York in 1828 of a general union for the observance of the Sabbath. An attempt to persuade Congress to outlaw Sunday mail distribution failed in 1829-30; however, many religious groups continued to agitate for such a measure. For instance, in 1844 a National Sabbath Convention was held in Baltimore with John Q. Adams presiding. Anson P. Stokes, *Church and State in the United States*, 3 vols. (New York, 1950), 2:12-20; 3:153-58.

Remark in Senate, March 14, 1842. Presents a petition from western Pennsylvania charging that Congress had adopted no measures since convening in early December to advance the welfare of the nation; and since continuance of the body "is attended with great expense to the people," it should adjourn. Clay notes that "there was some foundation for the complaint." Clay presents a memorial from Orleans County, N.Y., condemning "the long debates and disgraceful scenes of disorder in Congress, and the consequent neglect of the public business" and recommending "thorough reform." *Cong. Globe*, 27 Cong., 2 Sess., 315.

Presents, explains, and advocates action on a petition from Margaret Blennerhassett, widow of Harman Blennerhassett [1:290-91, 300-301] who was "supposed to be in some way connected with the famous enterprise of Colonel [Aaron] Burr [1:256-59, 272, 332-33, 337-42]." Points out that considerable property damage was done by some 150 Virginia militiamen on Blennerhassett Island in 1806-7 after she and her husband had been expelled therefrom. Asserts that Harman Blennerhassett was "wholly unfit for any such purpose as the world supposed him to be connected with Burr to accomplish." Recalls a personal visit to the island in the spring of 1837 when there were still "to be seen the remains of its former beautiful condition." Asks that the widow Blennerhassett's appeal for restitution be honored, since she is "now in extreme indigence"; also, her claim is based on "the most conclusive evidence" and is additionally supported by facts known by Clay personally to be correct. Asks for speedy action on the claim and pleads that "ample justice" be given "this greatly injured and meritorious lady." *Ibid.* See also Clay to Margaret Blennerhassett, March 14, 1842; Margaret Blennerhassett to Clay, n.d. [*ca.* mid-March, 1842].

Remark in Senate, March 15, 1842. States he has no objection to a discussion of Sen. William Allen's resolution asking the secretary of the treasury for a report on how the proposed plan to suspend the distribution of public land sales receipts will work if the tariff level exceeds 20% [Clay to Letcher, January 6, 1842; Remark in Senate, January 21, 1842]; specifically, how distribution would affect the national economy, assuming that it would not interfere with his (Clay's) "retrenchment and tariff resolutions [Remark in Senate, February 15, 1842; Speech in Senate, March 1, 1842]." *Cong. Globe*, 27 Cong., 2 Sess., 318.

To JAMES WATSON WEBB Washington, March 15, 1842

I received your favor, with the English news paper and Genl. [Lewis] Cass's letter, now returned, for the opportunity of perusing both of which I thank you.[1] The debate in the H. of Lords, on the case of the Creole,[2] almost entirely overlooks the property aspect of the question. If their law does not admit of the surrender of property, coming into their possession, under such circumstances, the law ought to be changed. But, whilst we feel that the conduct of the British, is unfriendly and unjustifiable, no considerate man would think of making the case of the Creole a sole or substantial cause of War. In such a War we should be without the sympathies of the world, and without those of many of our own Country men, exclusive of abolitionists. We must put the case of the Creole on that list of wrongs which some day or other must be redressed by War.

It is far from my intention to interfere in any organization of our friends in N.Y. But I do hope that conciliation & mutual forbearance will be practised as far as possible, sometimes throwing a veil on the past for the sake of the future.

ALS. KyLoF. 1. See Webb to Clay, March 7, 1842; Lewis Cass's letter not found. 2. Remark in Senate, Jan. 11, 1842.

From Margaret (Mrs. Harman) Blennerhassett, *ca.* mid-March, 1842. States that "Having formerly had the pleasure of knowing you and Mrs [Lucretia H.] Clay, I feel the less hesitation in applying to you now for aid in your influential public station, to assist me in recovering (if possible) some remuneration for losses that I sustained during a period of public excitement which at that time would have rendered all appeals to National justice quite hopeless.—I will not enter into particulars further than to state that in estimating our losses I have not taken into the account the sufferings which I then endured, when in the absence of my Husband my House was converted into a Prison for me and my Children, my very Servants taken from me!!" Adds that but for the presence "of the late Mr Morgan Livell . . . , Mr. Wm Robinson and several other Gentlemen from Pittsburg[h], all *my fellow Prisoners* in my own House, I should have been quite unprotected." Believes that her petition for redress will be "greatly strengthened" by Clay's support. Expresses her gratitude for the "very handsome manner in which you have introduced my Petition in the Senate [Remark in Senate, March 14, 1842]." Feels "that your eloquent eulogy goes far beyond the merit of only a *common* place Subject she who alas, has only gained a 'sad celebrity.' " ALS, draft. MoSHi. See Clay to Blennerhassett, March 14, 1842; Remark in Senate, March 14, 1842.

To MARTIN VAN BUREN Washington, March 17, 1842

Your cutting us in passing by Washington, prevented my saying in person what I will now communicate in writing, that is, that I anxiously hope during your present tour, that you will visit us in Kentucky.[1] Do me the favor to come directly to Ashland and make it your Head quarters. We shall be glad to see you, and will give you a hearty welcome every where. Both Mrs. Clay and I will be happy to receive and entertain you as our guest specially. And I shall not think it kind if you disappoint us.

ALS. MHi. 1. Van Buren, writing from the "Hills of Santee," Sumter County, S.C., on March 26, 1842, explained that he might not "stay long enough in Kentucky to pay Mrs. Clay and yourself a visit, but if it should be so you may rest assured, that I shall not deny myself that gratification." Adds that it will be at least the beginning of May before his arrival. ALS. DLC-HC (DNA, M212, R5). Printed in Colton, *Clay Correspondence*, 4: 458. It was, in fact, May 20 when Van Buren, accompanied by James K. Paulding, arrived at Ashland where he stayed for several days. It was during this visit that some historians believe Clay and Van Buren reached an agreement to exclude the issue of the annexation of Texas from the 1844 presidential campaign; others, however, doubt that any such agreement was made. See Van Deusen, *Life of Henry Clay*, 359; Cole, *Martin Van Buren*, 384-85, 393-94; Poage, *Henry Clay*, 115. For Clay's description of the Van Buren visit, see Clay to Sargent, May 31, 1842, and Clay to Crittenden, June 3, 1842.

Remark in Senate, March 18, 1842. Presents a petition from New York glass cutters lamenting the depression in the glass industry and asking for "a specific duty, if not an ad valorem duty," to protect them against foreign cut glass. Remarks that these people must make out a case to support their petition. *Cong. Globe*, 27 Cong., 2 Sess., 334.

To Richard Hines *et al.*, Wake County, N.C., March 21, 1842. Regrets he cannot accept the invitation of Wake County Whigs to attend the party convention which will be held in Raleigh on April 4. Rejoices to hear of the "fine spirit which prevails" in the North Carolina Whig party.

Deplores the sad condition of the country, saying: "Instead of mutual confidence between the acting President and Congress, there is mutual distrust. Instead of him throwing himself upon the principles and the party that elevated him, he makes war upon both. Instead of harmony and cooperation, there is discord and opposition. A President without a party, and parties without a President! A President denouncing his friends and courting his political opponents, who, in their turn, without entertaining for him the least respect or confidence, give him flattery and praise enough just to deceive and delude him. A President who, affecting to soar in an atmosphere above that of all parties, and to place himself upon the broad and patriotic foundation of the whole nation, is vainly seeking, by a culpable administration of the patronage of the Government, to create a third party! This, gentlemen, is a faithful picture of the present posture of our national councils."

Realizes some will "think that it would be more prudent not to exhibit" this situation to the world, but personally believes "that public virtue and the public interests are always better subserved by promulgating rather than concealing the truth." Thinks that the "Whig party, by a faithful adherence to its principles at the hazard of being proscribed by those whom it advanced to high power, and the members of the late Cabinet, by a voluntary surrender of exhalted stations, which they believed they could no longer hold without dishonor and disgrace, have demonstrated to the whole world that with them the love of country is paramount to the love of office." Concludes: "I go into retirement, but I shall not be there an idle or indifferent spectator, without sympathy or interest in the welfare of the Union." Copy. Printed in Washington *Daily National Intelligencer*, March 21, 1842.

On February 28, 1842, Hines *et al.* had written Clay from Raleigh asking him, on behalf of the Whigs of Wake County, to attend their convention on April 4. Copy. Printed in Raleigh *Register and North-Carolina Gazette*, March 29, 1842.

Remark in Senate, March 21, 1842. Objects to consideration of a resolution that would refund to General Andrew Jackson, with interest, a fine imposed upon him in January, 1815 by a federal judge in New Orleans for events stemming from his having declared martial law there. Resolution tabled. *Cong. Globe*, 27 Cong., 2 Sess., 340. For this incident and its legal aftermath, see Marquis James, *The Life of Andrew Jackson*, 2 vols. in 1 (New York, 1938), 262-65, 748, 760; also Clay to Crittenden, January 14, 1843.

Following this, Clay says he is pleased to present a petition from a group of young boys in York County, Pa., asking for a "high duty on all importations, to encourage American industry." They fear there will be no jobs for them when they grow up if the national depression continues. *Cong. Globe*, 27 Cong., 2 Sess., 340.

Later this day, during debate on his various tariff, distribution, and retrenchment and reform resolutions [Remark in Senate, February 15, 1842; Speech in Senate, March 1, 1842], he expresses the view that debate on these resolutions should soon be brought to a close, noting, however, that he plans to say a "few words" on them at the conclusion of said debate. Hopes a final vote can be taken on them on "Tuesday next [March 22]," at which time three presently absent senators might be able to vote, and a fourth, who has to be absent on Tuesday, will have arranged a pairing off. *Ibid.*, 341.

To John Smith *et al.*, Fayetteville, N.C., March 21, 1842. Regrets that he cannot accept the invitation "of a portion of the Citizens of Fayetteville and Cumberland County to me, to visit them, after my retirement from the Senate," because "the preparations for my departure and the necessity of my presence at Ashland . . . deprive me of that satisfaction at this time." Promises that his visit is "not abandoned, but only postponed." ALS. NcD.

Remark in Senate, March 22, 1842. When the orders of the day were announced, which called for debate on Clay's resolutions on the tariff, distribution, retrenchment, and reform [Remark in Senate, February 15, 1842; Speech in Senate, March 1, 1842], Clay, who was expected to take the floor, rose to report that he was "too indisposed to address the Senate" and to request that his speech be postponed until tomorrow. Agreed. *Cong. Globe*, 27 Cong., 2 Sess., 343-44. For Clay's second major speech on his eleven resolutions, his first being on March 1, 1842, see his Speech in Senate, March 23, 1842.

Speech in Senate, March 23, 1842. Although still not feeling well, speaks for nearly three hours, in somewhat disjointed fashion, on his eleven resolutions to increase the tariff above 20%, to repeal the act suspending the distribution of public land sales receipts if and when the tariff level exceeds 20%, and to retrench and economize government expenditures [Remark in Senate, February 15, 1842; Speech in Senate, March 1, 1842]. Thanks Sen. George Evans (Whig, Me.), chairman of the Finance Committee, for his "very able arguments" in support of the eleven resolutions. Denies Calhoun's charge that these resolutions are designed to violate the Compromise Tariff Act of 1833 [8:604, 619-22, 626-27]. Makes it clear, however, "that he had himself never attributed to the compromise act such an absolute and sacred inviolability as would forbid the least interference with its enactments, under any circumstances, however urgent or extreme." Further, instead of abandoning the principle of protection, which would have brought about the defeat of the measure in Congress, "the act did modify the protective policy; but in that modified form, it recognized, proclaimed, and perpetuated that policy." Specifically, Clay attacks, at length, the South Carolinian's three contentions that (1) the resolutions were designed to increase the tariff by enlarging the free list; (2) that the land fund [Clay to Ewing, April 30, 1841; Remark in Senate, June 9, 1841] had not been restored, nor if it were restored, that a need for more revenue than 20% for the operation of the government had been shown; and (3) that expenditures, instead of being retrenched, were being maintained by appropriations creating a necessity for "transcending the limit of 20 per cent. which . . . cannot be exceeded without a violation of the compromise." The original compromise, Clay rebuts, "left the whole question open to the discretion of Congress, merely enjoining the principle of laying no higher duty than necessary to raise an adequate revenue for the support of the Government." Analyzes in detail the language of the third and fifth sections of the compromise act, noting that while the fifth section does indeed state that as of June 30, 1842, no tariff shall exceed 20%, section three modifies that prohibition by maintaining that after that date Congress may raise duties necessary to provide for the administration of the government. And in view of section three, "the true key to the whole act," Clay asserts that "there is not only nothing in the act to prevent Congress from imposing duties beyond twenty per cent., but directly the contrary, after the 30th, June next, if necessary." Develops this point. Adds that "the great difficulty, when we passed the act, was to get rid of the large amount of surplus revenue which then pressed as an incubus on the Treasury, and threatened such dangerous consequences to the public prosperity."

As for Calhoun's concern about the distribution of public land sales receipts if the tariff does exceed twenty percent [Remark in Senate, January 21 and February 15, 1842; Speech in Senate, March 1, 1842], Clay claims that "the avails of the public lands were never intended to enter into the exchequer as a part of the ordinary revenue of the Government." Quotes from section 3 of the Compromise Tariff Act to demonstrate that after June 30, 1842, only tariff revenue was to be used to sustain the government, not funds from public land sales. Reminds his colleagues that he had personally fashioned both the compromise tariff bill and the distribution bill in 1833 and had specifically limited expenditure of the income from the public lands to internal improvements, education, and the colonization of free blacks in Africa.

Continues with criticism of Calhoun's charge that the failure of Congress to reduce government spending was designed to permit the twenty percent limit in the Compromise Tariff Act to be breached. Points out that it was Calhoun's new-found friends in the opposition party in 1837 who so significantly and irresponsibly increased the cost of government operations after that date. And what has the nation to show for this "vast and profligate" expenditure? "It has been sunk in the morasses of Florida, or worse than wasted by the transfer of Indian tribes from one side of a river to the other, and by locating them in the immediate vicinity of our frontier settlements, creating the cause for new expenditures for the defence of our citizens thus endangered. Where, I ask again, are the monuments of all this expenditure? What has the nation got to show for its money?" Asks why it is that Senators Levi Woodbury (N.H.) and Silas Wright (N.Y.), both Democrats, both now professing "such patriotic solicitude" over excess annual expenditures, did nothing whatever about retrenchment when Woodbury was secretary of the treasury and Wright was chairman of the Senate Committee on Finance? Suggests political hypocrisy related to the outcome of the election of 1840 as an answer. Presents figures showing excessive expenditures by the Van Buren administration, subsequent Whig efforts to cope with the deficits they thus inherited in March, 1841, and the ways in which they are now dealing prudently with the problem. Argues that to put the Democrats back in power would mean that expenditures would soon again be out of control.

Turns to United States relations with Great Britain, noting at the outset that Whig reductions in domestic expenditures have in large measure been applied to "the defense of the country at a time when, in the opinion of many, there exists imminent danger of a foreign war." Laments attacks made by some Americans on Lord Ashburton, "the distinguished individual who comes to our shores bearing the olive branch of peace [Ashburton to Clay, April 11, 1842]." Thinks highly of the British envoy, reporting that Ashburton has had no personal connection with the "banking house [Baring Brothers] with which his name and some of his family have been associated for near twenty years past." Believes Ashburton will be able to compromise the Maine boundary dispute or arrange for its arbitration [Comment in Senate, April 14, 1840]. Hopes too that Ashburton will successfully settle the *Caroline* case [Comment in Senate, January 5, 1838; Speech in Senate, January 9, 1838; Porter to Clay, January 4, 1841] which, while "not absolutely without any provocation," was "a direct violation of our territorial jurisdiction" which demands a "full explanation and indemnity." Also believes that Ashburton will fairly negotiate the *Creole* case [Remark in Senate, January 11, 1842] in which Britain is "in the wrong, and stands bound to make full indemnity for the value of the slaves"; explains, however, that "in the absence of all stipulations by treaty, one nation is not bound, in strict right, to surrender offenders and fugitives from justice who take refuge within its dominions, she has no right to afford facilities to escape, by liberating and discharging persons under a foreign flag. But this is a matter for negotiation; and negotiation has hardly yet begun." On the question of America's maritime neutral rights, Clay makes a distinction between Britain's "right of visitation" of ships fraudulently flying the American flag—so as to verify their true nationality with a view toward suppressing the African slave trade—with her assertion of a "right of search" in "respect to impressment." To resume the latter "would be the signal of immediate and inevitable war." Is certain that "*in principle*" both sides accept this distinction. Asks: "seeing that the suppression of the abominable African slave-trade is an object of humanity which both countries have at heart, may not some convention be agreed upon for a mutual right of search, under suitable restrictions as to seas, and proper regulations as to practice?" Discusses past efforts in this regard. Asserts that "it is not every cause of complaint that should lead to war. On so grave and solemn a question there ought always to be some just proportion between the magnitude of the wrong or injury and the terrible consequences of war. Nations should remonstrate, and negotiate, and protest earnestly and long, before they resort to actual hostilities. Honest difference of opinion may exist between nations as well as between individuals; and there may be at last a class of injuries, not rising to the importance of justifying an appeal to arms, which should be put aside on a catalogue, to be redressed when the dreadful day of war comes, as sooner or later (the later the better) it must come. With respect to the differences between the two countries, I would make one concluding observation. Whatever complaints there are, menacing the peace of the two nations, they are complaints on our side against Great Britain. She has none against us, of a nature threatening a rupture. If war be necessary, and the only remaining alternative, it must be proclaimed by us, not by her." Notes, however, that "I perceive no cause of apprehension of immediate war."

Returns to consideration of the tariff and the cost of running the general government. Criticizes the Van Buren administration for raising expenditures each year in 1837-40 while duties from the Compromise Tariff of 1833 "diminished more and more." Estimates that the deficit was about $8,000,000 "during every one of the years of his administration." Recalls that he (Clay) warned of government overspending at that time.

Discusses possible war with Mexico. Hopes there is no more chance of it than with Britain, but notes the "insolent language recently employed by an upstart tyrant and usurper [Santa Anna]" toward Western Americans. Remarks that "Our navy, justly a favorite with all, and which every one seems to vie with his neighbor in nursing and preserving, is now fallen into a state of comparative dilapidation. All our fortifications, which were neglected, and even abandoned, by the late Administration, have now to be repaired. All these additional expenditures have devolved on our hands."

Shifts to the subject of free trade with the observation that he would favor world-wide free trade if it could ever be accomplished; but it has never existed and never will so long as each individual nation presses "its own individual interest, regardless, in comparison, of the interests of all the rest of the world." Scorns the usefulness of tariff figures presented by Sen. John C. Calhoun and others proporting to show some of the advantages of free-trade with Great Britain. Shows instead the actual British tariff on American tobacco, beef, pork, hams, lard, lead, candles, and soap. British duties on these items range from 1900% on manufactured tobacco and 933% on unmanufactured tobacco to 112% on beef, 100% on pork, 200% on lead, and 166% on sperm candles. "This is the freedom of trade on which the Senator dwells with such enthusiastic delight that he likens it to the divine right of kings; it came, he tells us, from heaven itself—a divine ordinance!" Compares Britain's so-called free trade with America's "protective system, as modified by the [1833] compromise," to the latter's distinct advantage. Defends the protective system adopted in 1824, pointing out that "in every single instance in which sufficient protection was afforded, the price, instead of being augmented, was actually reduced. I do not recollect a single exception." Explains how this has happened: "it has been asked, if an increase of duty produces a diminution of price, why do the manufacturers ask for an increase of duties? I will answer the question. The augmented duty is thrown on the foreign producer. By increasing the duty, you compel him to submit to a reduction of price equal, or nearly equal, to the duty; but to such a reduction they cannot submit but from necessity. A diminished importation ensues; and a vacuum being thus created in the market, it is filled by the rival fabrics of the American manufacturer, who, in his turn, finds his compensation for the reduced price in his quiet possession of a greater portion of the American market, and in the steadiness of that market. There is the whole theory of the matter. There is no mystery, no inconsistency: The case is perfectly clear: and facts prove it to be just as we told you in 1824 that it would be. I know no wiser course for a statesman than to recur to history, and thence to draw his lessons as to future policy."

Discusses Britain's current trade problems, pointing out that her products are gradually being excluded from continental ports, that her trade with Brazil is threatened, and that "of all that remains of her former trade, that with the Brazils and with this country is the most profitable to her." Cites and recommends "Dr. [Archibald] Alison's invaluable work on population" as it relates to Britain's present trade policy, noting that it is filled with "many weighty facts" and that Alison is "strongly in favor of the corn laws, (and so are the present [Robert Peel] ministry of Great Britain,) and equally opposed to all treaties of reciprocity." Argues that Britain's presumed interest in free trade is a sham because if things go badly for her international trade, she can still fall back "on the resources of her own immense empire. She will cherish foreign commerce as long as she can deceive you into notions of free trade." Predicts that "Our immense and young Confederacy . . . exhibiting a compact, consolidated, continous, unbroken territory . . . inhabited by one race of men . . . speaking the same common language . . . enjoying the inestimable blessings of civil liberties and freely worshipping at the pure altar of the only true God," will endure long after the British empire "Detached and dispersed in broken fragments, insular and continental, inhabited by different and discordant races of men, speaking various and unknown tongues, obeying an infinite diversity of laws, originating in every stage of human society, from the highest state of civilization to the lowest depth of barbarism, and worshipping the Christian and Heathen gods," has vanished. Nor will her great naval power, "the cement of these heterogenous and incongruous elements" be able to hold the empire together. Thanks God for "his gracious bounty" to the United States.

Shifts back to his attack on Calhoun's free trade doctrines, pointing out that as the compromise of 1833 moved the nation closer to free trade, the prosperity of South Carolina has declined. Notes particularly that the average price of slaves there has declined from $500 each to $200-$300 each, and that in Charleston five weeks ago there were 800 unsold slaves; also, at a public sale there of four plantations, including slaves, the total price realized was "less than one of them had cost." Still, Calhoun "clings to his free-trade doctrine, though it has proved so ruinous to his own State, and to Southern interests as well as Northern; to that free trade which has depressed the price of cotton to a point below what it has ever brought since the close of the last war. In spite of all the teachings of experience, as well in his own as in all other nations, still he deafens us with the cry of free trade! free trade! Really the case of the honorable gentleman is without any parallel that I know or ever heard of." Repeats, however, that he is "not espousing the cause of any high protective tariff of duties. I am for such a scheme of duties as will preserve all the essential principles of the compromise act, as I understand them." Says he has "ever believed that *stability*, with a moderate amount of protection, better than a very high tariff without it." Attacks the Democrats for their hostility to protection and to the entire "American system." Laments that while the "great Ajaxes of the tariff policy" once came from Pennsylvania, all are now silent. Not one Pennsylvania Democrat in either house champions the encouragement of home industry in the state. All have repudiated the American System and call now for free trade. In this they are joined by Whig legislators from the South and Southwest, and although they differ on other national issues, their alliance comprises "so large a majority as to render it impossible, were it desirable, (which I think it is not,) to pass a *high* protective tariff." Urges both parties to unite on a tariff high enough to sustain the general government in its hour of need. Specifically, "I hope that the honorable Senator from Pennsylvania (Mr. Buchanan) will go as far as a general duty, it may become necessary, as far as thirty-three and a third per cent. I trust there will be no diversity of opinion, but that we shall all be found ready to go for that rate of duty which may be requisite to meet the reasonable wants of the Government."

Discusses next the land question. Recalls that he has earlier "argued that question so elaborately... particularly... at the last winter's session [Speech in Senate, January 28-29, 1841]," that he will here and now state only his "leading motives" in advocating passage of the land bill. Reviews the history of land bills back to the Jackson administration, details various and conflicting differences of approach as to what best to do with land sales revenues, and recalls that he had proposed the distribution of these revenues to the states for two reasons: (1) Congress had the constitutional power to authorize such distribution; (2) it was expedient to do so. Reviews at great length the constitutional dimension of the issue, especially the nature of the deeds of cessions of state lands to the Confederation government in the 1780s. Asserts that the distribution of land sales revenues to the states, which is constitutional, is not the same thing as the distribution of tariff revenues to the states. Distribution of the latter sort would be unconstitutional, since such revenue is constitutionally designated as income for the purpose of sustaining the general government. Public land sale revenue, therefore, is not the same as tax or tariff revenue. Indeed, "The public lands stand on special and separate ground—a ground fixed by the deeds of cession and the terms of the Constitution relating to them. The power granted in the Constitution begins and ends with the public lands." Distribution is also a fair and orderly way to dispose of the public domain, saving it from "various wild and squandering projects" as "an invaluable resource for the present generation, and a precious inheritance for posterity." Asserts that income from the sales should be distributed to "*all the states*"; it should not flow into the national treasury, even though among some senators "Suddenly there has sprung up... a new zeal for the revenue derivable from the public lands."

Concludes with a final plea for his eleven resolutions. Asks all senators "to unite, by adopting these resolutions, or by some other practical plan, in supplying the indispensable financial wants of the Government. The vaults of the Treasury are empty, its credit dishonored, the public engagements violated. Who brought the Republic into this deplorable state? The Senators on the opposite side and their party when in power—by their large scale of national expenditure; by their disbursement of every available means—stock in the late Bank of the United States and all—which they could command; by the debt which they devolved on their successors; and by their total neglect to provide a revenue within the year to meet the current expenses of the year. Are the Senators on the other side not bound, as men of honor, to come forward and unite with us in retrieving the errors of past administration, and in lifting the Government out of its present degraded condition? But if no compunctions visiting of conscience, no personal considerations, will prompt them to co-operate with us, let me adjure them, as countrymen, as brethren, as patriots, at least to unite on this occasion, and for this purpose, heart and hand, with us." *Cong. Globe*, 27 Cong., 2 Sess., Appendix, 322-29. A summary of this speech appears in the regular pages of the *Globe* for this date. See *Cong. Globe*, 27 Cong., 2 Sess., 347-48.

For Archibald Alison (1792-1867)—historian, lawyer, and sheriff of Lanarkshire—see *DNB*. Alison's anti-Malthusian work on population, which included a chapter supporting the Corn Laws, was written in 1808 and published in 1840 under the title *The Principles of Population and Their Connection with Human Happiness*, 2 vols., London, 1840.

Remark in Senate, March 24, 1842. Laments that his eleven resolutions of February 15 [Speech in Senate, March 1, 1842] have become "so overshadowed by amendments" that he will "hardly be able to find them." Points out to Sen. William C. Rives, (Va.), who wants public land sales income included in the general funds of the treasury, that "The restoration [to the U.S. Treasury] of the land fund, therefore, would not restore the credit of the Government in the money market. That credit was affected by other circumstances quite independent of the abstraction from the Treasury of the uncertain proceeds of the public lands. It is the pressure on the domestic capital of the country that has injured the credit of the Government—an injury, in a great measure, occasioned by the depreciation of State stocks, aggravated by dangerous and pernicious doctrines [Remark in Senate, February 18, 1840] promulgated from certain quarters. The only efficient way of raising the credit of the Government from its present depreciation, was, to inspire confidence by an energetic and efficient course of policy—by laying on a tariff sufficient to supply the Treasury with adequate means." Argues that Rives's tariff-raising proposals would provide only twenty-one of the twenty-seven millions the government needs. Urges that the first and last (eleventh) of his resolutions [Remark in Senate, February 15, 1842] be brought to a vote today, and that the others be held over until March 29 "because he perceived there were six Senators absent on his side of the question." Acquiesces in a motion to bring only the final resolution—requiring a report from the secretaries of war, navy, and the postmaster general on what offices might be abolished in the interests of economy—to a vote now, a motion adopted unanimously. Hopes the other resolutions can be voted upon on March 28 or 29. *Cong. Globe*, 27 Cong., 2 Sess., 353.

To JAMES F. SIMMONS[1] Washington, March 24, 1842

For God's sake come back to us and bring Mr. [William] Sprague[2] as soon as possible. Six Whig Senators are now absent, and on some Land questions we are in the minority.

I finished the debate yesterday on my resolutions,[3] taking three hours in the reply. I shall try today to get them laid over until Monday or Tuesday.

ALS. DLC-James F. Simmons Papers. 1. For Simmons, a Rhode Island Whig senator, see *BDAC*. 2. For Sprague, who had been elected as a Whig to the U.S. Senate in 1842 to finish the term of Nathan F. Dixon, deceased, see *BDAC*. 3. Speech in Senate, March 23, 1842. See also Remark in Senate, Feb. 15, 1842, and Speech in Senate, March 1, 1842.

To LUCRETIA HART CLAY Washington, March 27, 1842

I have written to you less of late because I expect soon to have the happiness of being with you.[1] For the last three days I have been confined by an excrutiating stricture in my left breast, produced by rheumatism or cold. On wednesday last, I made a Speech of three hours duration in the Senate,[2] and the next day I was attacked. I suffered great pain & was cupped and purged. The pain has left me, but I am much debilitated.

I have not recieved from Mr. [James] Erwin the remittances I expect from him, and I apprehend I shall be detained two or three weeks after the 31st March to recieve them. As I have come under acceptances for the boys, I cannot leave the Eastern Cities until I meet them. I recieved to day from Henry [Clay, Jr.] the duplicate draft for $648, the first it appears having miscarried

They are going to give me a Public dinner on the 9h.[3] and a Ball on my birth day.[4] My friends never appeared more warmly or ardently attracted to me. With the President I have no intercourse, and very little with his Cabinet.

I owe to the University [Transylvania] $300 due on the 1st. April I would send a check for it, if I could get one, but I cannot. I wish you would ask Thomas [Hart Clay] to pay it to the Treasurer for me, and if he cannot, I will send a Check in a few days.

Majr. Reilly [*sic*] and Ellen[5] called to see me to day. I had before seen them several times. He is going to return to Texas to take part in the War, and he will leave Ellen at Lexington.

I have heard of your box of Roots &c arriving safe at Wheeling, and being sent to the Januarys[6] at Maysville. I hope it has got safe to Ashland.

Give my love to our Sons & to H.C.D. [Henry Clay Duralde]

ALS. DLC-TJC (DNA, M212, R10). 1. Clay to Berrien, Oct. 7, 1841. 2. Speech in Senate, March 23, 1842. 3. On March 23, 1842, Willie P. Mangum and a number of other "friends and associates in the National Councils" wrote Clay, expressing their desire to show "their respect for your virtues" and their "admiration of your talents" by providing a public dinner "at the close of a career which you have rendered pre-eminently distinguished . . . by the force of your genius, the splendor of your eloquence, and the fervor and purity of your patriotism." Copy. Printed in Washington *Daily National Intelligencer*, April 11, 1842. In a letter dated March 24, 1842, Clay accepted the invitation to the dinner which would be given on April 9 in his honor. ALS. Lincoln National Life Foundation, Ft. Wayne, Indiana. The letter was addressed to Willie P. Mangum, George Evans, William C. Preston, Alexander Barrow, R. W. Thompson, John M. Botts, Millard Fillmore, John P. Kennedy, and M. P. Gentry. For an account of the evening, see Washington *Daily National Intelligencer*, April 11, 1842. 4. The ball, given on Clay's birthday (April 12), was "numerously and handsomely attended." See Washington *Daily National Intelligencer*, April 14, 1842. 5. On March 28, 1842, Clay wrote Major Charles Nourse asking him to negotiate a bill of exchange of $1,200 on James Erwin for "My friend & near connexion Majr. Reilly Chargé des Affaires of Texas." ALS. PHi. For James Reily 1811-63), Texan chargé to the United States, see Johnson, *Twentieth Century Biographical Dictionary*. 6. January & Huston.

Remark in Senate, March 29, 1842. Presents petitions asking, variously, that the duty on imported iron be restored to the 1839 level, that the Bankruptcy Act [Remark in Senate, December 28, 1841; Speech in Senate, January 28, 1842] be repealed, and that legislation be passed repudiating the British doctrine of perpetual allegiance to the Crown (this from the New Haven Hibernian Society). Clay notes that the New Haven Irish petitioners are fearful that in a war with England they might be captured and subjected to punishment for treason if the perpetual allegiance law is not struck down. They ask for protection. Says Clay: "The only protection that we could give them against such doctrines [is] . . . with the cannon of the country." Doubts, however, that Britain would actually apply the doctrine in event of war. Explains the origin of the doctrine. *Cong. Globe*, 27 Cong., 2 Sess., 365.

Later this day, participates in the continuing debate on amendments to his eleven resolutions on the national economy [Remark in Senate, February 15, 1842; Speech in Senate, March 1, 1842]. Agrees to a minor change of wording in his first resolution and it was passed. Asks that the remainder of his resolutions be taken up in succession and voted on. Comments briefly on a point having to do with the suspension of land sales proceeds as this in the past had been linked to the parallel suspension of land grants to old and new states. *Ibid.*, 366.

Remark in Senate, March 30, 1842. Presents petitions protesting repeal of the Bankruptcy Act [Remark in Senate, December 28, 1841; Speech in Senate, January 28, 1842] and asking for an international copyright law [Comment in Senate, February 2, 1837]. Notes that the name of Washington Irving, U.S. minister to Spain, is prominent among the distinguished literary names on the latter petition. Recalls his own past efforts for such legislation [Comment in Senate, February 2, 1837; Remark in Senate, January 6, 1840]. Wishes this issue had been settled earlier since his retirement from the Senate will take place tomorrow [Clay to Berrien, October 7, 1841]. Explains the issues involved in an international copyright law, noting that opposition to it "arose chiefly from two great book establishments, one in New York [Harper & Brothers] one in Philadelphia [Carey & Lea]," and charging that these firms "treat with . . . indifference the production of American authors" because it is cheaper for them to pirate the works of foreign authors. Suggests that the principle in the current U.S. patent law, which extends patents to foreigners, "might with equal propriety be extended to literary works of genius." *Cong. Globe*, 27 Cong., 2 Sess., 370.

Later this day, during continuing debate on various amendments to his resolutions on the national economy [Remark in Senate, February 15, 1842; Speech in Senate, March 1, 1842], Clay regrets that the question of revoking the distribution to the states of public land sales receipts has been raised, as well as the problem of whether incorporating the land fund into the general revenue is or is not consistent with the Compromise Tariff Act of 1833 [8:604, 619-22, 626-27]. The main issue, he argues, is raising or not raising the tariff. Reviews the background of land distribution to the old and new states and explains the cession of lands to the Confederation government by the old states. Argues anew that "the possession of the lands [by the general government] was only in trust for the States," and denies that "the grant to the new States of five hundred thousand acres of land each, was independent of the measure of distribution." Thinks there is collusion ("a very remarkable coincidence") between the movements against distribution by Sen. William C. Rives of Virginia and by others in the House, "both corresponding with the movement made by the Executive himself in his message a few days back [March 25] to Congress." Following an exchange with Rives on the charge of collusion, Clay challenges the Virginian's assertion that in 1833 the estimated income from public lands sales was three million dollars. He maintains that the question is "could the land fund now be relied on for more than one million. He then adverted to the charges made against him of a proposition to break in upon two compromises—one the [1833] compromise [tariff] act, and the other the compromise clause [section 6] in the distribution act [Clay to Ewing, April 30, 1841; Remark in Senate, June 9, 1841]. He denied that the construction he had given to the compromise act, in relation to its being contrary to the principles of that act to consider that the Government was to be supplied with a revenue from any other source than customs, was any other than the express construction. He defended this construction at considerable length, and then adverted to the compromise clause in the distribution act with a view of showing that it ought to be repealed, and that there was an understanding to that effect."

Urges that a vote on his resolutions be taken now since he will be giving up his seat tomorrow. His motion to refer to the Committee on Finance his second, third, fourth, and fifth resolutions, as amended by Sen. Silas Wright (Dem., N.Y.), is carried without division. After this, he asks the Senate to reject the proposition to commit the others to committee and to vote upon them now. In this he is unsuccessful. The remaining motions, save for the first and sixth, were amended, combined, and variously referred to the Committees on Retrenchment, Judiciary, Foreign Affairs, and Post Office. Clay's remaining resolutions, the first and sixth, were then agreed to without division. *Ibid.*, 371-73. His reference to collusion between Sen. Rives and President Tyler on the related tariff and distribution questions was based on Tyler's message to Congress on March 25. In this, the president linked his support of tariffs above the 20% level with the suspension of distribution, as required by section 6 of the Distribution and Preemption Act of September 4, 1841. See U.S. Sen., *Journal*, 27 Cong., 2 Sess., 249-53, or *Cong. Globe*, 27 Cong., 2 Sess., 358-59. Clay's resolution number five (of the original eleven) sought to repeal this section.

From Luther Bradish *et al.*, Albany, N.Y., March 31, 1842. As "members of the Senate and Assembly of the State of New York," write of the "deep concern" they feel upon hearing "that you have resolved to retire on this day from the councils of the nation." Note that "From the year 1806 . . . you have, with one or two short intervals, been constantly engaged in the service of your country." Continue: "The course of your policy has in all things been eminently American. In peace and war, as a Senator, an Ambassador, the head of the Department of State, you have secured for your country abroad the respect of her sister nations, while at home you have protected our seamen and our ships, and extended our commerce, fostered our home industry, and sustained domestic manufactures, and completed our emancipation from colonial dependence. True to your principles, true to your friends, and, above all, true to your country, it has been your rare felicity to be a cherished leader among your political friends, and the foremost champion of their principles, and at the same time to enjoy the respect and possess the generous confidence of all your fellow-citizens of every political denomination." Add that "there is one great measure which more than any other has occupied your ears . . . THE PROTECTION OF HOME INDUSTRY," and assert that "the deficiency in the existing laws on the subject are attributable to no fault or remission on your part."

Thank Clay "for these great national services" and "acknowledge the vast debt of gratitude which we owe you." Furthermore, "we declare our solemn conviction that through your whole political life, you have been governed by the loftiest patriotism and the most unsullied integrity." State that although "We speak in our own names, . . . we believe we speak the sentiments of those whom . . . we have the honor to represent." Hope that he will enjoy in retirement "the proud consciousness of having been *the benefactor of your beloved country*." Copy. Printed in Washington *Daily National Intelligencer*, April 26, 1842. For Clay's answer, see Clay to Bradish *et al.*, April 15, 1842.

SPEECH IN SENATE Washington, March 31, 1842

Mr. Clay rose and said, before offering the motion which it was his intention to submit to the Senate, he desired to make a single observation with regard to a subject which he was about to leave unfinished—he meant the resolutions which he had submitted, proposing certain amendments to the Constitution of the United States.[1] It had been his wish, prior to his retirement, to have obtained a vote upon these resolutions, and also to have replied to the arguments which had been advanced by their opponents; but owing to the feeble state of his health, he had been unable to enter upon a reply, and owing to the absence of several of his friends, he had come to the conclusion that it would be better to commit the subject into the hands of the Senate, to be disposed of according to their judgment and discretion whenever it might come up; and he would dismiss this subject with a simple remark in reference to the conviction which he entertained of the propriety of the different amendments which he had suggested; those convictions he still deliberately entertained, notwithstanding all that he had heard upon the subject.

And now . . . allow me to announce, formally and officially, my retirement from the Senate of the United States, and to present the last motion which I shall ever make within this body; but, before making that motion, I trust I shall be pardoned for availing myself of this occasion to make a few observations. At the time of my entry into this body, which took place in December, 1806, I regarded it, and still regard it, as a body which may be compared, without disadvantage, to any of a similar character which has existed in ancient or modern times; whether we look at it in reference to its dignity, its powers, or the mode of its constitution; and I will also add, whether it be regarded in reference to the amount of ability which I shall leave behind me when I retire from this chamber. In instituting a comparison between the Senate of the United States and similar political institutions, of other countries, of France and England for example, . . . the comparison might be made without disadvantage to the American Senate. In respect to the constitution of these bodies: in England, with only the exception of the peers from Ireland and Scotland, and in France with no exception, the component parts, the members of these bodies, hold their places by virtue of no delegated authority, but derive their powers from the crown, either by ancient creation of nobility transmitted by force of hereditary descent, or by new patents as occasion required an increase of their numbers. But here . . . we have the proud title of being the representatives of sovereign States or Commonwealths. If we look at the powers of these bodies in France and England, and the powers of this Senate, we shall find that the latter are far greater than the former. In both those countries they have the legislative power, in both the judicial with some modifications, and in both perhaps a more extensive judicial power than is possessed by this Senate; but then the vast and undefined and undefinable power, the treaty making power, or at least a participation in the conclusions of treaties with foreign powers, is possessed by this Senate, and is possessed by neither of the others. Another power, too, and one of infinite magnitude, that of distributing the patronage of a great nation, which is shared by this Senate with the Executive magistrate. In both these respects we stand upon ground different from that occupied by the Houses of Peers of England and of France. And I repeat that with respect to the dignity which ordinarily prevails in this body, and with respect to the ability of its members during the long period of my acquaintance with it, without arrogance or presumption, we may say, in proportion to its numbers, the comparison would not be disadvantageous to us compared with any Senate either of ancient or modern times. Full of attraction as public service in the Senate of the United States is[2]—a service which might fill the aspirations of the most ambitious heart—I have nevertheless long desired to seek that repose which is only to be found in the bosom of one's family—in private life—in one's home. It was my purpose to have terminated my Senatorial career in November, 1840, after the conclusion of the political struggle which characterized that year. But I learned very soon, what my own reflections indeed prompted me to suppose would take place, that there would be an extra session;[3] and being desirous, prior to my retirement, to co-operate with my friends in the Senate in restoring, by the adoption of measures best calculated to accomplish that purpose, that degree of prosperity to the country, which had been, for a time, destroyed, I determined upon attending the extra session, which was called, as was well known, by the lamented Harrison. His death,[4] and the succession which took place in consequence of it, produced a new aspect in the affairs of the country. Had he lived, I do not entertain a particle of doubt that those measures which, it was hoped, might be accomplished at that session, would have been consummated by a candid co-operation between the Executive branch of the Government and Congress; and . . . allow me to say, (and it is only with respect to the extra session), that I believe if there be any one free from party feelings, and free from bias and from prejudice, who will look at its transactions in a spirit of candor and of justice, but must come to the conclusion to which, I think, the country generally will come, that if there be any thing to complain of in connection with that session, it is not as to what was done and concluded, but as to that which was left unfinished and unaccomplished. After the termination of that session, had Harrison lived, and had the measures which it appeared to me it was desirable to have accomplished, been carried, it was my intention to have retired; but I reconsidered that determination, with the vain hope that, at the regular [2nd] session of Congress, what had been unaccomplished at the extra session, might then be effected, either upon the terms proposed or in some manner which would be equivalent. But events were announced after the extra session—events which seemed to throw upon our friends everywhere present defeat—this hope, and the occurrence of these events, induced me to attend the regular session, and whether in adversity or in prosperity, to share in the fortunes of my friends. But I came here with the purpose, which I am now about to effectuate, of retiring as soon as I thought I could retire with propriety and decency, from the public councils.

From the year 1806, the period of my entering upon this noble theatre of my public service, with but short intervals, down to the present time, I have been engaged in the service of my country. Of the nature and value of those services which I may have rendered during my long career of public life, it does not become be [*sic,* me] to speak. History, if she deigns to notice me, and posterity—if a recollection of any humble service which I may have rendered shall be transmitted to posterity—will be the best, truest, and most impartial judges; and to them I defer for a decision upon their value.

But, upon one subject, I may be allowed to speak. As to my public acts and public conduct, they are subjects for the judgment of my fellow-citizens; but my private motives of action—that which prompted me to take the part which I may have done, upon great measures during their progress in the national councils, can be known only to the Great Searcher of the human heart and myself; and I trust I shall be pardoned for repeating again a declaration which I made thirty years ago; that whatever error I may have committed—and doubtless I have committed many during my public service—I may appeal to the Divine Searcher of hearts for the truth of the declaration which I now make, with pride and confidence, that I have been actuated by no personal motives—that I have sought no personal aggrandizement—no promotion from the advocacy of those various measures on which I have been called to act—that I have had an eye, a single eye, a heart, a single heart, ever devoted to what appeared to be the best interests of the country.[5] Yet . . . during this long period, I have not escaped the fate of other public men, in this and other countries, I have been often . . . the object of bitter and unmeasured detraction and calumny. I have borne it, waiting in unshaken and undoubting confidence, that the triumphs of truth and justice would ultimately prevail; and that time would settle all things as they ought to be settled. I have borne them under the conviction, of which no injustice, no wrong, no injury could deprive me, that I did not deserve them, and that He to whom we are all to be finally and ultimately responsible, would acquit me, whatever injustice I might experience at the hands of my fellow men.

But I have not been unsustained during this long course of public service. Every where on this widespread continent have I enjoyed the benefit of possessing warm-hearted, and enthusiastic, and devoted friends—friends who knew me, and appreciated justly the motives by which I have been actuated. To them, if I had language to make suitable acknowledgments, I would now take leave to present them, as being all the offering that I can make for their long continued, persevering and devoted friendship. But . . . if I have a difficulty in giving utterance to an expression of the feelings of gratitude which fill my heart towards my friends, dispersed throughout this continent, what shall I say—what can I say—at all commensurate with my feelings of gratitude towards that State whose humble servitor I am?[6] I migrated to the State of Kentucky nearly forty five years ago. I went there as an orphan, who had not yet attained his majority—who had never recognised a father's smile—poor penniless, without the favor of the great—with an imperfect and inadequate education, limited to the means applicable to such a boy; but scarcely had I set foot upon that generous soil, before I was caressed with parental fondness—patronized with bountiful munificence—and I may add to this, that her choicest honors, often unsolicited, have been freely showered upon me; and when I stood, as it were, in the darkest moments of human existence—abandoned by the world, calumniated by a large portion of my own countrymen,[7] she threw around me her impenetrable shield, and bore me aloft, and repelled the attacks of malignity and calumny, by which I was assailed. . . . It is to me an unspeakable pleasure that I am shortly to return to her friendly limits; and that I shall finally deposite (and it will not be long before that day arrives) my last remains under her generous soil, with the remains of her gallant and patriotic sons who have preceded me.

. . . a recent epithet, (I do not know whether for the purpose of honor or of degradation,) has been applied to me; and I have been held up to the country as a dictator! Dictator! The idea of dictatorship is drawn from Roman institutions; and there, when it was created, the person who was invested with this tremendous authority, concentrated in his own person the whole power of the State. He exercised unlimited control over the property and lives of the citizens of the Commonwealth. He had the power of raising armies, and of raising revenue by taxing the people. If I have been a dictator, what have been the powers with which I have been clothed? Have I possessed an army, a navy, revenue? Have I had the distribution of the patronage of the Government? Have I, in short, possessed any power whatever? Sir, if I have been a dictator, I think those who apply the epithet to me must at least admit two things: In the first place, that my dictatorship has been distinguished by no cruel executions, stained by no deeds of blood, soiled by no act of dishonor. And they must no less acknowledge, in the second place, (though I do not know when its commencement bears date, but I suppose, however, that it is intended to be averted, from the commencement of the extra session,) that if I have been invested with, or have usurped the dictatorship, I have at least voluntarily surrendered the power within a shorter period than was assigned by the Roman laws for its continuance.

. . . if to have sought, at the extra session and at this, by cooperation with my friends, to carry out those great measures which the majority of 1840 desired to see adopted and executed—if to have desired to see the currency and exchanges of this country once more regulated[8]—if to have desired to replenish the empty coffers of the Treasury, by an imposition of suitable duties—[9]if to have desired to extend relief to the unfortunate bankrupts of the country,[10] ruined, in a great measure, by the operation of the previous policy of the Government—if to have desired, by co-operation with my friends, to limit and restrain and regulate the Executive action,[11] because it had become dangerous towards the other departments of the Government in my opinion, and in the opinion of the majority of 1840—if to have desired to preserve the honor and credit of the country untarnished by adequate and suitable provisions for revenue,[12] sufficient for fulfilling all the public engagements—if the faithful purpose of executing all these measures—if an ardent desire to carry out and redeem every pledge which was fairly made by my friends when struggling for the acquisition of power—if I say these efforts and this co-operation constitute my dictatorship, then I suppose I must bear the odium or the honor of the epithet whichever it may be considered.

. . . that my nature is warm, my temper ardent, my disposition in the public service enthusiastic, I am ready to own. But those who suppose they may have seen any proof of dictation in my conduct, have only mistaken that ardor for what I at least supposed to be patriotic exertions for fulfilling the wishes and expectations by which I hold this seat; they have only mistaken the one for the other.

. . . during my long and arduous services in the public councils, and especially during the last eleven years, in the Senate, the same ardor of temperament has characterized my actions, and has no doubt led me, in the heat of debate, in endeavoring to maintain my opinions in reference to the best course to be pursued in the conduct of public affairs, to use language offensive and susceptible of ungracious interpretation towards my brother Senators.

If there be any who entertain a feeling of dissatisfaction resulting from any circumstance of this kind, I beg to assure them that I now make the amplest apology. And, on the other hand, I assure the Senate, one and all, without exception and without reserve, that I leave the Senate Chamber without carrying with me to my retirement a single feeling of dissatisfaction towards the Senate itself or any one of its members. I go from it under the hope that we shall mutually consign to perpetual oblivion whatever of personal animosities or jealousies may have arisen between us during the repeated collisions of mind with mind.

And now, allow me to submit the motion which is the object that induced me to arise upon this occasion. It is to present the credentials of my friend and successor, who is present to take my place. If . . . any void could be created by my withdrawal from the Senate of the United States, it will be filled to overflowing by my worthy successor [John J. Crittenden], whose urbanity, gallant bearing, steady adherence to principle, rare and uncommon powers of debate, are well known already in advance to the whole Senate. I move that the credentials be received, and at the proper moment that the oath required be administered.[13] And now, in retiring as I am about to do from the Senate, I beg leave to deposite with it my fervent wishes, that all the great and patriotic objects for which it was instituted, may be accomplished—that the destiny designed for it by the framers of the Constitution may be fulfilled—that the deliberations now and hereafter, in which it may engage for the good of our common country, may eventuate in the restoration of its prosperity, and in the preservation and maintenance of her honor abroad, and her best interests at home. I retire from you . . . I know, at a period of infinite distress and embarrassment. I wish I could have taken leave of the public councils under more favorable auspices: but without meaning to say at this time, upon whom reproaches should fall on account of that unfortunate condition, I think I may appeal to the Senate and to the country for the truth of what I say, when I declare that at least no blame on account of these embarrassments and distresses can justly rest at my door. May the blessings of Heaven rest upon the heads of the whole Senate, and every member of it; and may every member of it advance still more in fame, and when they shall retire to the bosoms of their respective constituencies, may they all meet there that most joyous and grateful of all human rewards, the exclamation of their countrymen, "well done thou good and faithful servants." Mr. President, and Messieurs Senators, I bid you, one and all, a long, a last, a friendly farewell.

Copy. Printed in *Cong. Globe*, 27 Cong., 2 Sess., 376-77 and in Colton, *Clay Correspondence*, 6:352-58, with various semantic flourishes, recastings, and emendations not found in the *Globe* version. Also printed in pamphlet form under the title, *Speech of Henry Clay, Delivered at Lexington, Kentucky, June 9, 1842. With the Address of Chief Justice Robertson, also Mr. Clay's Farewell Speech in the Senate of the United States.* New York, 1842. 1. Remark in Senate, Jan. 24, 1842. 2. The editors follow Colton's rendition on this particular phrase. 3. 27th Cong., 1st Sess. 4. Clay to Conover, April 9, 1841. 5. For similar, almost identical, statements of his purity of motives, see 2:581; 3:359, 364-65, 464, 506-7, 641, 777, 870-71; 5:655; 7:100. The same sentiment appears on Clay's sarcophagus in Lexington Cemetery, Lexington, Ky. 6. In Colton's version is inserted: "[Here Mr. Clay's feelings overpowered him, and he proceeded with deep sensibility and difficult utterance.]" 7. See 7:660-61, 716-17, 719. 8. See Clay to Porter, April 24, 1841; Clay to Ewing, April 30, 1841. 9. Remark in Senate, Feb. 15, 1842; Speech in Senate, March 1, 1842. 10. Remark in Senate, April 22, 1840, and Dec. 28, 1841; Speech in Senate, Jan. 28, 1842. 11. Speech in Senate, Jan. 24, 1842. 12. Remark in Senate, Feb. 15, 1842; Speech in Senate, March 1, 1842. 13. The seating of Mr. Crittenden was duly effected at the end of Clay's speech.

To Francis L. Smith *et al.*, Alexandria, Va., April 1, 1842. Acknowledges receipt of their note "inviting me to visit" Alexandria and "partake [of] the hospitality which they are good enough to tender, prior to my departure from this City [Washington]." Regrets, however, being unable to accept the invitation.

Thanks "the Whigs of Alexandria . . . for the approbation which they have been pleased to express of my public service." Regrets "the present unfortunate state of our public affairs," and says he would remain "in the public Councils . . . if I believed" it "would have been attended with any public benefit." Continues: "But the existing relations, between the Legislative and Executive Departments, are without any example in this or any other Country, in this or any other age. Never did any Legislative body assemble with a majority more disposed to perform its whole duty towards the Country than the present Congress; but it has been thwarted and circumvented, when it should have met with nothing but cordial co-operation and support. And it so happens that of all the members composing the body, no one was honored with a larger share of Executive enmity than I have been; for no other reason than that I professed to endeavor to carry out the just wishes of the people rather than conform to the caprices of a weak, vaccillating, and faithless Chief Magistrate. Under such circumstances, I perceived no adequate motive to restrain me from executing my long cherished wish to retire into private life." Adds the hope "that my absence from the public Councils may remove one obstruction with the Executive in concurring in measures of public relief, which may be devised by the wisdom of Congress." ALS. NcD. For Francis L. Smith, a prominent lawyer in Alexandria, Va., see Mary H. Powell, *The History of Alexandria, Virginia* (Richmond, 1928), 321-22.

From Carter Beverley, Fredericksburg, Va., April 2, 1842. Is glad "to find that the communication I . . . made to you [Beverley to Clay, February 8, 1842], was well recd. & kindly acknowledg'd." Feels a "high satisfaction . . . that I discharg'd the obligation which feeling & duty dictated in doing the justice I design'd of effacing the indignity cast upon you by the unfortunate, & to me unhappy Fayett-Vill [*sic*, Fayetteville, N.C.] letter that was, and has been so much the subject of injury to you in the public mind." Concludes: "It is now I trust put entirely to rest in the minds of all honorable & candid men of whatever political persuasion; for, surely none can, or will hence forward presume to countenance the miserable slander that went forth in that communication to the public against you. The entire revocation of it given by me, ought to overwhelm the author of it, w[it]h. utter shame & mortification." ALS. DLC-HC (DNA, M212, R5). Printed in Colton, *Clay Correspondence*, 4:459. See also 6:448-49.

From Lord Ashburton [Alexander Baring], Washington, April 11, 1842. Thanks Clay for his "very agreeable proposal" and looks forward to "a little conversation with you & to renew our acquaintance" before Clay departs Washington. Says that "Tomorrow I am at your service as soon as you please after ten o'clock." Expresses the hope that their two countries can "live on more friendly terms and . . . end bickerings," because they "have in truth a sincere respect and affection for each other." Adds: "Your good wishes for the success of this attempt is most acceptable to me." ALS. DLC-HC (DNA, M212, R5). Printed in Colton, *Clay Correspondence*, 4:460. For the Webster-Ashburton Treaty, signed on August 9, 1842, and ratified on August 20, dealing with the Northeast boundary, suppression of the African slave trade, and the extradition of fugitive criminals, see Parry, *Treaty Series*, 93:415-25. For Alexander Baring, Lord Ashburton, see *DNB*. For the Webster-Ashburton negotiations, on which Ashburton was at this time embarking, see Baxter, *Daniel Webster*, 338-52; Merk, *Fruits of Propaganda in the Tyler Administration*, 62-92; also Fuess, *Daniel Webster*, 2:106-15; Curtis, *Life of Daniel Webster*, 2:94-107, 111-24. The treaty ratification process is handled in Burrage, *Maine in the Northeastern Boundary Controversy*, 341, 343-51 and in U.S. Sen., *Executive Journal*, 6:118-32.

To Anne C. Saltonstall, Washington, April 12, 1842. Thanks her for the watch she has given him "on this day of my birth." Adds that it "will not more truly mark the revolving time, than my memory will recall the agreeable hours I have passed with you and your good father [Leverett Saltonstall] and mother, and your fun-loving, laughing, accomplished Sisters." ALS. Courtesy of J. Winston Coleman, Jr., Lexington, Ky.

To GILBERT H. SAYRES Washington, April 12, 1842

I received, and perused with great interest and attention, the letter which you[1] did me the favor to address to me. I cordially thank you for the sentiments of esteem and confidence an expression of which you have so kindly communicated. And I request your acceptance of my grateful acknowledgements for the lively interest you are pleased to take in my spiritual welfare. I hope that I shall profit by it. My mind has been often seriously impressed by grave considerations of preparation for a future state; but, like the crowd in the active bustle of life and its varied occupations, I have perhaps too much neglected so weighty a matter. My retirement will afford me leisure for a more serious, and I hope more practical contemplation of it.

Do me the favor to accept a copy of a little farewell speech I recently made in the Senate[2] accompanying this letter under another envelope, the interest of which, if it have any, is to be found in attending circumstances

Copy. DLC-TJC (DNA, M212, R10). Printed in Colton, *Clay Correspondence*, 4:459-60.
1. For the Rev. Gilbert H. Sayres, an 1808 graduate of Columbia University and an 1814 graduate of Union Theological Seminary, see *Officers and Graduates of Columbia University*, 110. 2. Speech in Senate, March 31, 1842. This speech was published under the title *Speech of Henry Clay, Delivered at Lexington, Kentucky, June 9, 1842. With the Address of Chief Justice Robertson, also Mr. Clay's Farewell Speech in the Senate of the United States.* New York, 1842.

From G.P. Walker, Clayton, N.Y., April 13, 1842. Is writing after "reading your Farewell Address to the Senate [Speech in Senate, March 31, 1842]; which drew tears from my eyes, and so kindly touches the heart." States that "Your allusion to Kentucky we can not read without the deepest emotion; and when you speak of your early orphanage; (it having been my own condition;) you touch a sympathetic chord." Hopes "that one more honor" will "yet be conferred, by a large majority of all the States." Adds: "I have never had the honor of a personal acquaintance with you, but Still I love you. Strange as it may seem:—I have communed with your mind, and the name Henry Clay is endeared by 10,000 recollections." ALS. DLC-HC (DNA, M212, R5).

From Stephen Duncan, Natchez, Miss., April 14, 1842. Reports he has uncovered "some special deposites made by me—in 1840" in the Commercial Bank of Natchez and has found one for $2,291.50 "to your order." Says he is having the notes endorsed "so as to entitle you to the 8 per ct. Inst." This will be done "today" and placed "as *a special deposite in the Comml Bk of Natchez* subject to your order—" ALS. DLC-TJC (DNA, M212, R14).

On May 24, 1842, Duncan wrote Clay from "Washington House," Philadelphia, saying that the deposit mentioned in his letter of April 14 "was *special* & subject to *your* order. I took for granted, you would attend to it—& therefor[e] lost sight of it altogether—until it was discovered by accident; otherwise, I would have fe[l]t culpable for not having attended to it at an earlier period." Believes "that you will *ultimately*—receive payt. of both principal & Int. in full," but notes that the "paper of this bank, is at present, much depreciated." *Ibid.*

To LUTHER BRADISH *et al.* Washington, April 15, 1842

I have received by the hands of the Hon. N.P. TALLMADGE the communication which you did me the honor to transmit to him for me on the 31st ultimo,[1] and I have perused it with lively and grateful sensibility. Such a testimony, proceeding from a source highly distinguished and respected, presented at the close of my public life, will be cherished by me in my retirement with the highest satisfaction, and will add great strength to the consciousness I feel that, in all the public stations to which I have been called, I have honestly labored faithfully to perform my whole duty to the public.

In the brief but flattering review which you have taken of my public career you have justly conceived the motives of my conduct. With respect to the measures themselves, to the adoption of which I may have contributed, I will not undertake to pronounce any decisive judgment. Of their influence upon the interests, the honor, and the character of the nation, the present generation, and posterity, if a recollection of my agency in maturing them shall survive me, are and will be the most competent and impartial judges of them and of me. But you have truly attributed to me a genuine American spirit in whatever concern I have had in public affairs, and especially in reference to a great system of National policy.

Divided as mankind are, ever have been, and will continue to be, into distinct nations, it is the solemn duty of each, whilst it deals justly and liberally towards others, constantly and sedulously to advance, protect, and maintain its own separate interests. To attempt to legislate for them, or to expect or permit them to legislate for us, would be alike vain and improper.

It was a view of this condition of the world, and instructed by lessons of experience drawn from its history, and the practice of other nations, that early led me to a conclusion in favor of the protection of the domestic industry of our own country. My convictions have acquired additional strength from every reflection I could give the subject, and from both past and present experience in the United States. Free trade is a beautiful vision, existing only in the imagination of philosophers and theorists, and practically repudiated by all nations. An indispensable condition to the adoption of it by any one nation is its adoption by all. But, instead of regulating their trade according to that theory, we everywhere behold restrictions, burdens, and prohibitions; and those nations which make the nearest approximation to it are in the least prosperous state. During the last nine years, about one-half of our imports have been admitted free of duty; and, as to the other moiety, a descending scale of duties has been in progress, which is now rapidly bringing them down. If there were any reality in the boastful promises of the partisans of free trade, our country ought at this moment to be in the enjoyment of an enviable prosperity. But directly the reverse is its melancholy condition. Never were the products of agriculture selling at more discouraging prices; and the great Southern staple of cotton, which was to have been so highly benefited by a reduction of duties, is now sold at a price less than it has commanded at any time since the last war with Great Britain.

Nothing can be more erroneous than to suppose the existence of any real incompatibility between the interests of agriculture, commerce, and manufactures. A conflict between them would be just as unnatural and absurd as between the members of the human body. Each prospers most when all of them flourish. Agriculture requires but little protection, because its position secures it against much foreign competition; or, rather, protection to commerce and manufactures is the best form of affording protection to agriculture.

Without a diversity in the occupations of society, if all are engaged in one common pursuit, there can be no subjects produced for mutual domestic exchanges, and consequently no home market, by far the best, most steady, in war and peace, and most valuable of all markets.

We shall not, I fear, rise from our embarrassed condition until we produce, within our own country, more of the supplies necessary to consumption, and depend less upon foreign countries. Until that object is accomplished, we shall be constantly exposed to an exhausting drain of the precious metals, and to sudden alternations of delusive prosperity and real adversity. One of the obvious modes of accomplishing that object is the regulation of our foreign trade by means of a properly adjusted tariff, stimulating production at home and diminishing importations from abroad. And all experience has shown that, on whatever object our manufacturing industry has been successfully employed, its price to the consumer has been almost invariably reduced. This is the necessary effect of the law of competition.

The question is sometimes asked, how the manufacturer can be benefited by an increase of duties if the effect be to reduce prices? The answer is, that he is benefited by obtaining possession of a greater extent of home market, and by the greater steadiness which prevails in it; whilst the foreign producer, in order to share any part of that market, is obliged first to submit to a reduction in the price of his commodity equivalent to the duty, and his commodity is finally excluded from the market by the operation of the principle of domestic competition.

Fortunately for the harmony of the different parts of the Union, and without the danger of reviving topics which formerly agitated and exasperated parties, the actual wants of the Treasury now require a tariff which, while it supplies a necessary revenue, may be so arranged as to afford incidental protection to manufactures without any material departure from the principles of the compromise act. The opponents of the protective policy have never controverted the right of Government to give such incidental protection; and the friends of that policy, looking to the substance rather than the name of things, I should think, ought to be content if their object is attained, whether it be made in the form of a revenue tariff or a protective tariff. . . .

Copy. Printed in Washington *Daily National Intelligencer*, April 26, 1842. 1. Bradish to Clay, March 31, 1842.

From Hamilton Jackson, Brooklyn, N.Y., April 16, 1842. Believes Clay's "retirement will not be of long duration—but that like Cincinnatus and Washington you will be summoned from the plough, by the acclamations of a grateful people, to preside over their destinies." Mentions that he is "the representative of an old family in . . . this part of the country" and that he wants to do something toward improving his native city. To that end, he wants "to found a Mechanics Institute to which I hope that I shall have it in my power to bequeath a good library, and a gallery of pa[i]ntings" including "portraits of our eminent men," especially "the portrait of the 'Hercules of the Country', who has for nearly forty years formed an integral part of our history." Concludes: "Although not personally known to you I have taken the liberty to send to Washington an artist [De França] of great merit, and a friend of mine, for the purpose of painting your portrait.—I shall be much gratified if the numerous avocations which necessarily occupy your valuable time will permit the indulgence of my request." LS. DLC-HC (DNA, M212, R5). For Jackson, said to own properties valued at $200,000, see Beach, *The Wealth and Biography of the Wealthy Citizens of The City of New York*, 16.

At the instance of Jackson [Clay to Jackson, April 20, 1842], Manuel Joachim De França, a Portuguese painter did a portrait of Clay which is used as a frontispiece in volume 1 of *The Papers of Henry Clay*. See also Amyx, "Portraits of Henry Clay," typescript, University of Kentucky, vol. A.

From Lord Morpeth [George Howard], New Orleans, April 16, 1842. Reports that he will "ascend the Mississippi by the 'Henry Clay,' " to Louisville at the end of April. Hopes to visit Clay in Lexington provided he has reached home from Washington by that time. Asks if "you will . . . address a line to me at Post Office Louisville." Concludes: "I should be quite ready already to tender you my vote, if I only had one, for the next Presidential Election." ALS. DLC-HC (DNA, M212, R5). Printed in Colton, *Clay Correspondence*, 4:471, but misdated as October 16, 1842. For George Howard, sixth Earl of Carlisle, Lord Morpeth, see *DNB*. He visited Clay at "Ashland" for a few days, arriving there on May 4, 1842. See Washington *Daily National Intelligencer*, May 14, 1842.

To SAMUEL C. MORTON[1] Washington, April 18, 1842

I duly received your friendly letter, transmitting the Resolutions and proceedings of my friends and fellow citizens in Dock Ward,[2] expressive of their sentiments and views upon various important subjects of public concern. For the confidence, attachment and friendly consideration which they entertain for me, I request you to offer to them assurances of my grateful acknowledgments. Especially I thank them for their kind wishes for my health and happiness in retirement. Long as has been the period of my public service, and great as have been my private sacrifices, incident to it, I should not have hesitated to have increased them, if I had seen that my exertions, by remaining in the public Councils, would have been attended with any certain public benefit; but there is a painful state of relations between the Legislative and Executive Departments of the Government, unprecedented as it is unfortunate, from the existence of which I have cherished the hope that our Country may derive some advantage by my withdrawal from the Senate.[3] At former threatening epochs, in our history, the difficulty arose out of discordant opinions in Congress, and the object was to adjust it, by reconciling them. But now there is a large and united majority in Congress, animated by the most patriotic views, from which the Executive branch of the Government differs on radical points of policy. Between that majority and the President, if a reconciliation of opinion on those points be practicable, I am quite sure that it cannot be brought about through my agency; nor I fear without a surrender of the independence of the Legislature, which I presume it is not prepared to make, but to which, at all events, I could not consent. My opinions are so well known, on the various subjects of public policy, specified in one of the Resolutions of the meeting in Dock Ward, that it is not necessary to repeat an expression of them here. I will add a few words only on one of the topics of the resolutions.

The meeting has resolved to organize itself, and to establish a Club, to which they propose to do me the honor of giving my name, in reference to the next election of President of the U. States. That election is the affair of the People, to whose exclusive direction and judgment it should be left, without any sort of interference on the part of any person who may be thought of for the office. Whether I shall ever consent or not to the use of my name, in connection with that exalted station, is a question demanding the most deliberate consideration, and on which I do not wish, at this time, to express any opinion. When, in my judgment, the proper time shall arrive for a decision I will embrace some suitable mode of announcing it. At present I think it would be premature. In the mean time, and whatever may be my final determination, I beg leave to tender to my friends and fellow citizens of Dock Ward my cordial and respectful thanks for the distinguished proof they have given of their good opinion of me and of their partiality towards me.

ALS. KyLoF. 1. For Morton, a commission merchant in Philadelphia, see Shanks, *Papers of Willie Person Mangum*, 3:392. 2. The Dock Ward was located in central Philadelphia and was bounded by the Delaware River and by Seventh, Walnut, and Spruce streets. See H.N. Borroughs's "Map of Philadelphia, 1846." Courtesy of Gwen Curtis, Map Dept., University of Kentucky Libraries. 3. Clay to Berrien, Oct. 7, 1841.

To HAMILTON JACKSON Washington, April 20, 1842

I have received by your nephew[1] your obliging letter, and request your acceptance of my cordial thanks for the friendly sentiments which you have done me the honor to convey in it. Your nephew also delivered me the cane which you have done me the favor to present. Its length exactly suits me, and for so beautiful and acceptable a testimonial of your regard and esteem, I tender my grateful acknowledgements.

The noble enterprize of founding a Mechanics Institute,[2] which you have in view, is worthy of your name, and honorable to your patriotism and opulence. I offer my best wishes for its success and usefulness.

Mr. Franconia [*sic*, Manuel Joachim De França], at the instance of your liberality, has made a portrait of me, which, as far as I can judge, is a good likeness.[3] He has succeeded in some features, in respect to which most of the artists have failed. . . .

ALS. Henry Clay Memorial Foundation, Lexington, Ky. 1. Reference obscure. 2. Jackson to Clay, April 16, 1842. 3. *Ibid.*

To Harry I. Bodley *et al.*, Lexington, May 6, 1842. Has received the invitation to a public entertainment extended by "a meeting of the citizens of Lexington and Fayette county, convened for the purpose of making arrangements connected with my return home," and accepts with "cordial thanks."

Also thanks them for their "testimonials of approbation, confidence and affection," which coming as they do "from my neighbors . . . the eye witnesses of my conduct both in private and public life, . . . fill me with the most agreeable and touching emotions." Is pleased to learn "that my quitting the public councils of our country, at this time [Clay to Berrien, October 7, 1841], is not disapproved." Adds that he deeply regrets "the state of general embarrassment and distress which exists" and that he would have stayed in public office to seek to restore prosperity had he not concluded that there is "no prospect of accomplishing any good."

Discusses the possibility of seeking public office, saying "I trust that I shall be always allowed, at proper times, to decide whether I ought to give my consent or not to the use of my name in any connection which may be proposed for it with any public office, whatever it may be." Promises that "When a suitable time arrives for decision," he will be governed by "the probable wishes of those who have the power to bestow the office." Copy. Printed in Frankfort *Commonwealth*, May 17, 1842.

To MARTIN VAN BUREN Frankfort, May 12, 1842

I have been looking some time anxiously for your arrival at my residence. Under the expectation that you would pass through Louisville, I addressed a letter to you at that City the object of which was to engage you to bring Mr. [James K.] Paulding[1] with you to Ashland, and any other person in your company. I was not aware, when I wrote to you at Col. [Richard] Singleton's[2] that Mr. Paulding accompanied you. I hope he will consider this an apology for my omission to comprehend him in my invitation, and that he will do me the favor to come with you to Ashland. Hoping soon to have the pleasure of seeing you both. . . .[3]

ALS. KyU. Addressed to Van Buren in Harrodsburg, Ky. Written on envelope: "The P.M. is requested to deliver this letter, as Mr. V.B. passes through Harrodsburg." 1. For Paulding, see 8:632-33. See also Clay to Van Buren, March 17, 1842. 2. For

Richard Singleton, South Carolina planter, whose daughter Angelica was married to Van Buren's eldest son, Abraham, see Cole, *Martin Van Buren*, 346, 385; Niven, *Martin Van Buren*, 493. 3. Clay to Van Buren, March 17, 1842.

To Committee of Cincinnati Whigs, May 16, 1842. Thanks them for their resolution expressing "their approbation of my public service, and their regrets on account of my retirement from it." Adds that such "testimonials from one of the most intelligent communities, and from the largest and most beautiful city in the Western States, are received by me with great and grateful sensibility." Explains that his retirement "was necessary to my health and to my private affairs," and that, due to the "posture of affairs at Washington," he had concluded that he might best serve the country "by not serving it at all." Regrets that he is "compelled" to decline their invitation to a public dinner in his honor and "to seek the tranquility of my own home" instead. Copy. Printed in Columbus *Weekly Ohio State Journal*, June 1, 1842.

From John Scott, Ste. Genevieve, Mo., May 26, 1842. Expresses gratification to Clay "for your kind indulgence" in waiting "long and very patiently [Clay's words]" for him to pay his debt. Notes that when he "was . . . driven from my unfortunate position . . . I found on examination that I was some twenty thousand dollars worse than insolvent." Says he has "Laboured without Stint to Sustain my family and pay up all Ballances," and he is "now within about five thousand dollars of the desired end." Pleads: "You must ther[e]fore Still let me rest for a while." Also implores Clay not to sue him, because "what can be done shall be done without this," although "I cannot Say any particular time." ALS. DLC-TJC (DNA, M212, R14). Clay had written Scott on May 16 [letter not found] asking him for payment. For Scott and the background of his ancient debt to the estate of James Morrison, of which Clay was executor, see 2:578-79 and 6:843-45.

To THOMAS M.T. McKENNAN Lexington, May 31, 1842

I take very great pleasure in offering you my cordial congratulations on your recent election to the H. of R. by a majority so decided for Washington County.[1] Much of that result I am sure was owing to your personal popularity, but I hope that it was in part also the result of a better and more encouraged tone among the Whigs.

I am glad to see the H. of R. cutting down the appropriations for the Navy and the Army,[2] founded, as I think, upon estimates, without regard to the state of the Treasury or of the Country, and proceeding rather too much from a desire of the new heads of those Departments to produce a brilliant effect. We ought to carefully preserve the general esteem, in which the Navy is justly held, by avoiding all extravagance.

Shall we have a good Tariff?[3] Or will divisions defeat the measure? You appear to approach it tardily if not reluctantly.

ALS. KyLoF. 1. For Rep. McKennan of Washington, Pa., and his election to the 27th Congress to fill the vacancy caused by the death of Joseph Lawrence, see 4:381-82 and *BDAC*. 2. For the debates within and between the House and Senate on the particulars of the 1842 Army and Navy appropriations bills, see U.S. H. of Reps., *Journal*, 27 Cong., 2 Sess., 356, 919-27, 1043, 1160-61, 1393; 5 *U.S. Stat.*, 500-502, 508-10. The upshot of the argument was an appropriation in 1842 for the Navy of $6,553,733.12, to which was added $250,000 authorized earlier and a carry-over of $742,000 unexpended from the 1841 appropriation. The appropriation in 1841 was $5,927,337. The effective funding for the Navy in 1842 was thus $7,545,7333.92, the largest amount to date in peacetime in its history. Even so, this was a great deal less than the amount Secretary of the Navy Abel P. Upshur had asked for. The appropriation for the Army in 1842 was $5,908,660.16, down

$601,258.84 from its 1841 funding level. See 5 *U.S. Stat.*, 508-10; also Claude Hall, *Abel Parker Upshur* (Madison, Wisc., 1963), 137-45, in which the figure $6,588,894 for the 1842 appropriation is given. 3. Clay to Letcher, Jan. 6, 1842; 5 *U.S. Stat.*, 548-67.

To NATHAN SARGENT Lexington, May 31, 1842

Mrs. [Lucretia H.] Clay was very much obliged, and desires me to thank you, for your present of a Copy of my Valedictory so handsomely printed on Satin,[1] and for your friendly letter which accompanied it.

Is there any improvement in *the* Captain[2] since I left you? Any better state of relation between him and the Whigs, or the Loco's? What are the prospects of the Tariff,[3] which I observe is much delayed?

I am curious to know what was threatened, and what is finally resolved upon, in respect to removals at the Custom House in Philada? And how my old friend [Jonathan] Roberts has deported himself on this trying occasion.[4] I forbear to write to him, from considerations of delicacy.

I am glad that the affair between our friend [Edward] Stanly and Mr. [Henry A.] Wise has been accommodated;[5] for I take it for granted that it has been done honorably.

Mr. Van Buren left me a few days ago,[6] after remaining here four or five. His health is apparently good. Without much conversation on party politics, we had a great deal on other subjects, and I found him interesting often & some times amusing. Mr. [James K.] Paulding seemed heartily tired of crowds, committees &c. They gave the little magician (who by the by tells me that he weighs 172 lb.) a very good procession & reception in Lexn.[7] of which I was very glad. I doubt whether he has had one so imposing any where since he left home.

ALS. ViU. 1. Clay's speech of March 31, 1842, printed on satin, is located in KyU. 2. A reference to President Tyler who had served briefly as a Virginia militia captain in the War of 1812. See Seager, *And Tyler Too*, 58-60. 3. Clay to Letcher, Jan. 6, 1842. 4. Tyler had appointed Jonathan Roberts, a Clay supporter, as collector of customs in Philadelphia. In mid-July 1842, however, he ordered Roberts to remove 31 employees there and replace them with pro-Tyler employees. When Roberts refused, Tyler sacked him in Sept., 1842. Chitwood, *Tyler*, 370-71. Tyler then nominated Thomas S. Smith to replace Roberts on Dec. 20, 1842, but the Senate rejected him on March 3, 1843. Tyler immediately nominated Calvin Blythe for the post, and he was confirmed the same day, March 3. For a discussion of Tyler's record on appointments to and removals from office, see his son, Lyon Gardiner Tyler, *Parties and Patronage in the United States* (New York, 1891), 68-78; and Seager, *And Tyler Too*, 588-89. See also U.S. Sen., *Executive Journal*, 6:155-57, 164, 167, 169, 182, 185. 5. Stanly and Wise were frequent verbal combatants on the floor of the House. In an encounter on May 7 when leaving the race track, Stanly rode by Wise, brushing his horse and splashing him with mud. Wise caught up to Stanly and broke his whalebone cane over Stanly's head. An argument ensued which almost led to a duel; however, negotiations headed off such a confrontation. Shanks, *Papers of Willie Person Mangum*, 3:331, 337, 339-44; Adams, *Memoirs of John Quincy Adams*, 11:10-11, 148, 160; Washington *Daily National Intelligencer*, May 14, 16, 18, 1842. 6. Clay to Van Buren, March 17, 1842. 7. For an account of the reception for Van Buren, held on May 20, the day of his arrival in Lexington, see Lexington *Kentucky Gazette*, May 28, 1842.

To EBENEZER PETTIGREW Lexington, June 1, 1842

I postponed acknowledging the receipt of your friendly letter of March until my return home, that I might make enquiry as to the state of the fact in respect to two of the mules in the lot which Mr. Weimar[1] delivered to you for me. I have accordingly made enquiry of my servant who accompanied him, and you are right in your conjecture. The servant says that two of the mules gave out on the journey from lameness, and not standing the journey well, and Mr. Weimar swapped them for the two which you got. I suspect some fraud in the exchange, but if there were I have not been able to get it out of the servant, and I have not seen Weimar, of whom, by the by, I know very little. He was engaged by my son [James B. or Thomas H. Clay], in my absence, to take charge of the Mules. I hope the two obtained in the exchange may turn out well, as I feel quite sure the others will; but I shall regret extremely if you should be disappointed with any of them.[2]

I thank you, my good friend, for your kind wishes for my happiness and prosperity in my retirement. I should have been very happy if it could have been under more auspicious circumstances. But the state of things at Washington, produced by the death of Genl Harrison, and the accession of Mr. Tyler is most deplorable, and such as to leave me no personal regret in quitting Washington.

I agree with you in thinking that the moral, political and pecuniary condition of the Country is very discouraging. And what adds to our discouragement is that we cannot distinctly see any termination to the embarrassment which so generally prevails. I thought that North Carolina and Kentucky were probably suffering less than most of the other States, but on my return home, I find that I was mistaken as to this State. Here, all men in active business, other than Agriculture; all manufacturers of Hemp, all traders to the South, and all who are largely in debt, experience the greatest distress.[3]

It has taken twelve years to bring about this unhappy state of things, by a great maladministration of the General Government. I hope it will not require as long a term to restore to the Country its lost prosperity; but I am fully persuaded it will be a considerable time before we recover from the errors of our rulers. In the mean time, we should not despair. If the good portion of the Community, yielding to sentiments of despondency, abandon all care of the Government, and of popular elections, the bad will take undisturbed possession and continue to rule. In all situations and conditions in life, there is one line of conduct to which we ought constantly to adhere, and that is, to do our whole duty, honestly and faithfully. Having done that, if things turn out ill, we have nothing to reproach ourselves with. Where as, if we neglect the discharge of our duty, we shall be tortured by the reflection that we might possibly have prevented the evils which have arisen.

I should be very glad to see you under my roof. Do you never think of visiting Kentucky? If instead of going to the North, you would direct your course towards the West, I am persuaded that your health would be benefited, and that you never would have occasion to regret the journey. I hope that we shall meet again. . . . P.S. I have a lot of Mules about the same size and description as that which I sent you. If any of your neighbours[4] should want such a lot, I should like to supply them.

ALS. NcU. 1. Mr. Weimar has not been identified. 2. For the mule deal with Pettigrew, see Clay to James B. Clay, August 16, 1841; Clay to Pettigrew, Sept. 24 and Nov. 10, 1841. 3. Clay to Lucretia Hart Clay, Dec. 9, 1842. 4. In Tyrrell County, N.C. For Pettigrew, see *BDAC*.

To JOHN J. CRITTENDEN Lexington, June 3, 1842

I received your favor of the 27h. Ulto with its enclosure. I was glad to perceive that you had taken ground in favor of a numerous H. of R.[1] I have long entertained that opinion, and I believe the larger house will have always a greater effect in checking Executive power, as well as being a better representation of the people.

I am very sorry that you think so little good is to come out of Captain [John] Tyler. I hoped that my absence from Washn. might have contributed to his improvement; but if it has had no such effect he must be incorrigible. Is it true that he has threatened and means to turn out the Collector of Philada.? Because he would not dismiss some thirty or forty Whigs from office?[2]

There is very great embarrassment and distress prevailing in K[entucky]., much more than I imagined before I came home. Every description of property, without exception, is greatly depressed, and still declining in value. And, what aggravates the distress, no one can see when or how it is to terminate. Most of our Hempen manufacturers are ruined, or menaced with ruin. Bagging and Rope were never known at any time heretofore to be so low as they now are. This is owing to the introduction of India and other foreign stuffs used as bagging. Our people say that they cannot do with a less protection than five Cents the square yard upon bagging. By the application of machinery to the spinning and weaving of the article, the cost of it is much reduced; and there is no danger of the planter being obliged to give an unreasonable price for it. He is secure against that from the domestic competition. When the Tariff gets to the Senate (will it ever get there?) You and your Colleague [James T. Morehead] are expected to take care of this single Kentucky manufacture.[3]

I am glad that our friends in Congress bear up so cheerfully under recent adverse results of State elections.[4] Seeing however that the Captain [Tyler] claims the victory, whether it be won by Democrats or Whigs, with rather more pleasure when achieved by the former, I hope that our friends will recover from their apathy and disgust, and treat him with some Whig victories.[5]

Will you not concur in the Senate in the reduction made by the House of the enormous appropriations asked by the Departments of War & Navy?[6] It seems to me that the state of the Country, the state of the Treasury, and the interest of the Whig party all unite in favor of that reduction. The senseless cry of the defences of the Country, the augmentation of the Navy &c &c ought to be wholly disregarded. Had the estimates been double what they are, and a proposition had been made to bring them down to their present amount, the same cry would have been raised.

Mr. Van Buren spent four or five days with me,[7] accompanied by Mr. [James K.] Paulding. We had a great deal of agreeable conversation, but not much on politics. Both the gentlemen appeared to be pleased with their visit. The public reception was quite imposing in Lexn; much better than he has probably received any where during his journey.

Present my warm regards to Mrs. Crittenden, and to your Messmates Genl. [Willis] Green[8] & lady. P.S. I received your letter of Atto. to take up [Balie] Peyton's bill,[9] which I have postponed until I hear from him.

ALS. DLC-John J. Crittenden Papers (DNA, M212, R20). 1. Reference is to the number of representatives to be set for the House under "An Act for the Apportionment of Representatives Among the Several States According to the Sixth Census." The previous apportionment act of May 22, 1832 [4 *U.S. Stat.*, 516], had provided for a ratio of 1 congressman for every 47,700 persons computed according to the rules prescribed by the Constitution, or 242 representatives in all. Debate on the new apportionment bill centered on the ratio in light of the 1840 census. The bill, reported on Jan. 22, 1842, was amended and passed by the House on May 3, providing for a ratio of 50,179 persons for each representative. It then went to the Senate which passed it on June 13 after amending it by changing the ratio to 70,680 to 1. On June 13 the House rejected the Senate amendments by a vote of 114 to 95. After the Senate voted on June 15 to *insist* on their amendments, the House voted 110 to 102 on June 17 to concur in the Senate changes which set the ratio at 70,680 to 1, or 223 representatives. The president approved the bill on June 25. This act provided for the first time that congressmen be elected by specific geographical districts "composed of contiguous territory equal in number to the number of Representatives . . . to which said State may be entitled, no one district electing more than one Representative." U.S.H. of Reps., *Journal*, 27 Cong., 2 Sess., 33, 36, 40, 86, 107, 113, 127, 263-64, 774-77, 781, 960-66, 970, 991-94, 1003, 1025; U.S. Sen., *Journal*, 27 Cong., 2 Sess., 327, 340, 359-62, 370, 372-78, 385-93; 5 *U.S. Stat.*, 491. See also Clay to Adams, July 24, 1842; and Adams to Clay, Sept. 20, 1842. 2. Clay to Sargent, May 31, 1842. 3. Clay to Lucretia Hart Clay, Dec. 9, 1842. The tariff of 1842 raised the duties on imported bagging made of cotton, hemp, flax, or "of any other material, or imported under the designation of gunny cloth" to five cents per square yard. 5 *U.S. Stat.*, 550; Hopkins, *Hemp Industry in Kentucky*, 145. 4. In the 1842 elections up to this time, June 3, Rhode Island, Connecticut, New Hampshire, and Virginia had held their elections of state officials. In Connecticut, Democrats won control of the state legislature, and, as a result, the legislature reelected by a vote of 139 to 68 Democratic incumbent Gov. Chauncey F. Cleveland over Whig William W. Ellsworth, even though Cleveland had not received a majority of the popular vote. *BDGUS*, 1:168; *Niles' Register* (April 9, 1842), 62:96. In New Hampshire, Democrats carried a majority of the state legislature; also, Democrat Henry Hubbard defeated Whig Enos Stevens for the governorship by a vote of 26,831 to 12,234. *BDGUS*, 3:955; *Niles' Register* (March 19, 1842), 62:48. In April the Virginia elections for the state legislature went to the Democrats by a large majority, with some Tidewater counties voting Democratic for the first time. Washington *Daily National Intelligencer*, May 5, 1842; Ambler, *Thomas Ritchie*, 226. In addition, numerous local elections such as city elections in Baltimore (Md.), Albany (N.Y.), Brooklyn (N.Y.), Portland (Me.), and New Orleans (La.) had been won by the Democrats. *Niles' Register* (April 2, 16, 1842), 62:80, 112. For the confused situation in Rhode Island resulting from the Dorr Rebellion, see Speech in Lexington, June 9, 1842. 5. As a result of the 1842 mid-term elections, the Whigs still controlled the U.S. Senate by a majority estimated at 3 to 6 seats. However, in a major reversal, the Democrats won control of the House for the 28th Congress. According to Morris, Democrats held 142 seats in the newly apportioned 223-seat House to 79 seats for the Whigs and 1 other; McKee lists 142 Democrats and 81 Whigs. Morris, *Encyclopedia of American History*, 406; McKee, *National . . . Popular and Electoral Vote*, 46. Tyler called the 1842 House elections "the greatest political victory ever won within my recollection, and was achieved entirely upon the vetoes of the Bank bills." L.G. Tyler, *Letters and Times of the Tylers*, 2:341. Some historians, however, have attributed the loss to the lack of a Whig program after Tyler's vetoes of the party's economic program, and to Whig party factionalism. Harold von Holst, *The Constitutional and Political History of the United States*, 8 vols. (Chicago, 1881-92), 2:437-40, 465-67; John W. Burgess, *The Middle Period, 1817-1858* (New York, 1910), 286-88; Ambler, *Thomas Ritchie*, 226. 6. Clay to McKennan, May 31, 1842. 7. Clay to Van Buren, March 17, 1842. 8. For Willis Green, a Whig congressman from Kentucky who served from the 26th to the 28th Congresses, see *BDAC* and Collins, *History of Kentucky*, 2:312. Note, however, that the *BDAC* mistakenly combines Willis Green, father and son, under one entry. 9. Clay to J.B. Clay, Dec. 24, 1841.

To WILLIE P. MANGUM Lexington, June 7, 1842

I congratulate you on your appointment to the honble station of President of the Senate pro. temp. I perceive that some division existed among our friends, and that a portion of them united with the Loco's, and concentrated on Mr. Bayard.[1] I am curious to know who they were that thus separated themselves from the body of their associates. Your appointment must have given particular satisfaction at the White House.

I should have been in the minority on the question of the ratio. I have been long and firmly convinced that the H. of R. ought to be large.[2] It would increase the dignity & moral influence of the House, awe Executive power, and ensure greater responsibility of the individual members to their Constituents. The argument in favor of a small house assumes that the house is a bad thing and that the less you have of it the better. I think that the experience of the Extra Session demonstrated that, with suitable rules, a large house can get along as well as a small one. Indeed the House proceeded at that Session with more dispatch than the Senate. It is a mistake therefore to suppose that the proper transaction of business depends upon the size of the body; it depends on its rules.

What will you do with the tariff? What with the restriction in the distribution bill?[3]

I am afraid that my apprehension that Southard would die in six months will be realized. His vital organs, I fear, are irrecoverably prostrated. His father [Henry Southard], I see, has gone.[4]

I am very quiet here now, since Mess. Van Buren and [James K.] Paulding left me. We gave them a distinguished reception.[5] The day after tomorrow will however give me some excitement, at the Barbecue. . . .[6]

ALS. NcD. 1. Mangum to Clay, June 15, 1842. 2. Clay to Crittenden, June 3, 1842. 3. For the tariff bills of 1842, their relationships to the Distribution Act of 1841 [Clay to Ewing, April 30, 1842], and their treatment by President Tyler, see Clay to Letcher, Jan. 6 and June 24, 1842. 4. His father died a few days before Samuel L. Southard resigned on May 31, 1842, as president *pro tem* of the Senate. Southard himself died on June 26, 1842. Birkner, *Samuel L. Southard*, 198, 245. 5. Van Buren to Clay, March 26, 1842; Clay to Sargent, May 31, 1842. 6. For Clay's so-called "Barbecue Speech" in Lexington on June 9, 1842, see below.

To LEVERETT SALTONSTALL — Lexington, June 7, 1842

Some delay having arisen in the arrival of my books from Washington, I have not transmitted the work on the British Customs as early as I wished, according to my promise.[1] I send it by this day's Mail, under cover to the Speaker [John White], to whom you will be pleased to apply for it. It will reach you time enough, I preceive, for the Debate on the Tariff. What will be the fate of that measure?[2] Seeing that it is impracticable to get a bill through by the 30h. instant, would it not be well for the Comee. of Ways and Means to propose a temporary continuation of the existing law until a Tariff is passed?[3]

I am glad to see a spirit of economy demonstrated in the House. Such a spirit is in sympathy with the intense embarrassment of the times, of which I had no just conception until my return home. It moreover is in conformity with a pledge given by the Whigs when out of power. . . .

AL, signature removed. KyU. 1. Reference obscure. 2. Clay to Letcher, Jan. 6, 1842. 3. *Ibid.*

SPEECH IN LEXINGTON — June 9, 1842

Begins with thanks to God for the "copious and genial" rain with which Lexington has just been blessed—"a refreshment of which it stood in much need." Then, in humorous vein, notes that he was not offered a glass of wine during the "sumptuous repast from which we have just risen" and complains (to "great laughter") that "you offered me nothing to drink but cold water." Says, however, that this does not mean he is opposed to the temperance movement. "On the contrary, I think it an admirable cause that has done great good and will continue to do good as long as legal coercion is not employed and it rests exclusively upon persuasion and its own extrinsic merits." Says, jokingly, that so great a crowd did not gather merely to hear him speak, but because a "fat whole virgin Durham Heifer . . . that cost $600" had been served.

Extends his "heartfelt thanks" to all the people of Kentucky for the high political offices they have conferred upon him over the years and for "the scornful indignation with which they repelled an infamous calumny [4:48, 53-54, 73-74, 80-85, 113-14, 144-50, 157-59] directed against my name and fame at a momentous period of my public career." Defends himself once again against the charge of having entered into a corrupt bargain with John Q. Adams in February, 1825.

Expresses his pleasure that so many women are in attendance today. Asserts that "If the delicacy and refinement of their sex will not allow them to mix in the rougher scenes of human life, we may be sure that wherever by their presence, their smiles and approbation are bestowed, it is no ordinary occurrence. That presence is always an absolute guaranty of order, decorum and respect. I take the greatest pleasure in bearing testimony to their value and their virtue. I have ever found in them, true and steadfast friends, generously sympathising in distress, and, by their courageous fortitude in bearing it themselves, encouraging us to immitate their example. And we all know and remember how, as in 1840, they can powerfully aid a great and good cause, without any departure from the propriety and dignity of their sex."

Harks back to his boyhood, the death of his father in 1781, when he was but four, his legal education under Virginia Attorney General Robert Brooke and Chancellor George Wythe, and his arrival in Lexington in 1797 "without patrons, without the favor or countenance of the great or opulent, without the means of paying my weekly board, and in the midst of a Bar uncommonly distinguished by eminent members. I remember how comfortable I thought I should be if I could make £100. Virginia money, per year, and with what delight I received my first fifteen shilling fee. My hopes were more than realized. I immediately rushed into a large and lucrative practice." Mentions his early career in the Kentucky state legislature, the U.S. Senate, and the U.S. House, noting that at every stage of his public life he had had "bitter, implacable, reckless enemies." Through all this, however, "I never but once changed my opinion on any great measure of national policy, or on any great principle of construction of our national Constitution. I adopted the principle of interpreting the Federal Constitution which had been so ably developed and enforced by Mr Madison in his memorable report[1] to the Virginia Legislature, and to them as I understood them, I have constantly adhered." States that his single shift of opinion was in 1816 when he endorsed the national bank; explains why he changed to this view [2:200-205, 210, 216-19].

Confesses, however, "that I am and have been long satisfied that it would have been wiser and more politic in me to have declined accepting the office of Sec'y of State in 1825. Not that my motives were not as pure and as patriotic as ever carried any man into public office. Not that the Calumny which was applied to the fact was not as gross and unfounded as any that was ever prop[a]gated." [At this point someone in the crowd shouted out that Mr. Carter Beverley, who had reported and spread Andrew Jackson's charge in 1827 [6:448-49] that there had been a bargain and intrigue between Clay and Adams, had recently renounced that charge [Beverley to Clay, February 8, 1842] as being unfounded. True, replies Clay, repeatedly touching his heart "with great earnestness and emphasis . . . amid tremendous cheers," while asserting that Beverley's testimony is not as important to him as is the proof of his innocence that lies "here—here—here . . . here is the best of all witnesses to my innocence." Goes on to defend the John Quincy Adams administration as high in "economy, purity, prudence and wisdom," and to state that although Adams and his administration were "annoyed, assailed and assaulted . . . no man could have shown a more devoted adherence to the Union."

Admits that he has "been accused of ambition; often accused of ambition," but defies his enemies "to point out any act or instance of my life in which I have sought the attainment of office by dishonorable or unworthy means." Cites his lack of ambition in the fact of having turned down President James Madison's offer of the posts of minister to Russia and secretary of war [2:88-89, 226] and President Monroe's offer of the positions of secretary of war or the mission to England [2:88-89, 226, 233, 391; 4:56]. Also, on the subject of his ambition, notes that while it was "the general impression" that he would get the Whig presidential nomination at Harrisburg in December, 1839 [Porter to Clay, November 14 and December 30, 1837], he cheerfully acquiesced in Harrison's nomination and campaigned for him. Asks, further, "Was it evidence of unchastened ambition in me to resign, as I recently did, my seat in the Senate,—to resign the Dictatorship with which my enemies had so kindly invested me, and come home to the quiet walks of private life?" Denies being ambitious "because some of my countrymen have seen fit to associate my name with the succession for the Presidential office." Argues that popular movements favoring his candidacy "are entirely spontaneous and not only without concert with me, but most generally without any previous knowledge on my part. . . . I have been and I mean to remain a passive spectator." Adds that at this moment he has not decided whether he would answer a summons from "the majority of the People of the Country," although he would feel "highly honored" by such a call. At the same time, "it is hardly necessary to remark that it is no part of my purpose to condemn, or express any opinion whatever upon those popular movements which have been made or may be contemplated with respect to the next election of a President of the U.S." Cites his many services to the nation, such as providing a protective tariff, curbing executive power, and working to end the nation's economic distress. Notes that "if these services, exertions and endeavors justify the accusation of ambition, I must plead guilty to the charge."

Turns to consideration of "the present actual condition of the Country," hoping that in so doing he will not offend the many Democrats present here today. Points, first, to the "appalling picture" of economic distress and embarrassment across the nation, comparing and contrasting it with the widespread prosperity that prevailed ten years ago. Quotes at length from his Senate speech of February 2, 1832, defending the American System against an attack upon it by South Carolina's Robert Y. Hayne [8:455-56]. States that in that speech he had called attention to the existence of national prosperity, especially during the years 1825 to 1832, and had linked that prosperity to the protective tariff legislation of 1824. What then, has caused the present disaster? It is not because of "speculating and over-trading" as some have suggested. It can be traced directly to three unfortunate events: "The first was the veto of the recharter of the Bank of the U.S. [8:434, 443, 552, 558, 640-41]. The second was the removal of the deposits of the U. States from that Bank to local Banks [8:583-84, 684-85, 728, 813]. The third was the refusal of the President of the U. States by an arbitrary stretch of power, to sanction the passage of the Land Bill [8:609-10]. These events all occurred in quick succession in 1832, 33, and each of them deserves particular consideration." Discusses each of these factors at considerable length, citing supportive statistics. Blames the wild inflation and speculation that began in 1837 on the demise of the Bank of the United States and the resultant proliferation of poorly capitalized state banks, as well as on the circular of the Treasury Department [8:583-84; Speech in Senate, January 11, 1837; Remark in Senate, January 14, 1837] which entrusted to "pet State banks" the custody of the Federal revenue. Reviews the means and methods used by the opposition to destroy the Bank, viz: "The Bank was denounced as a Monster, aiming as was declared, to rob the People of their liberties and to subvert the Government of the Country." Condemns Jackson's veto [July 10, 1832] of the bank recharter legislation, claiming that he did so in order to force pro-recharter Pennsylvania Democrats to the support of his administration on party-loyalty grounds. Explains, further, that Jackson's decision to remove government deposits [September 26, 1833] from the Bank of the United States prior to the expiration [March 1, 1836] of its existing charter, and to disperse those funds among various irresponsibly administered local banks, had stimulated inflation and speculation, especially in the buying and selling of public lands. Indeed, had Jackson not pocket-vetoed Clay's 1833 land bill, which would have distributed among the states the proceeds of public land sales, instead of allowing tens of millions of dollars of those proceeds to be deposited in the shaky private banks then being used by the government, where they simply fueled inflation, all would have been well. In Clay's words: "The [land] bill passed in 1833; and in a short time after, the sales of public land were made to an unprecedented extent . . . so much that in one year they amounted to about 25 millions of dollars and in a few years to an aggregate of about fifty millions. It was manifest that if the fund so rapidly accumulating remained in the custody of the local banks, in conformity to the Treasury circular, and with their interests, it would be made the basis of new loans, new accommodations, fresh bank facilities. It was manifest that the same identical sum of money might, as it in fact did, purchase many tracts of land by making the circuit from the land offices to the Banks and from the Banks to the land offices, besides stimulating speculation in other forms. Under the operation of the measure of distribution, that great fund would have been semi-annually returned to the States, and would have been applied under the direction of their respective legislatures, to various domestic and useful purposes. It would have fallen on the land like the rains of heaven, in gentle, genial and general showers, passing through a thousand rills, and fert[i]lizing and beautifying the country. Instead of being applied to purposes of speculation, it would have been applied to the common benefit of the whole people. Finally when the fund was accumulating and had accumulated to an alarming degree, it was distributed among the States by the [1836] Deposit act [8:813], but so suddenly distributed and in a manner so totally in violation of all the laws and rules of finance, that the crisis of suspension [Speech in Senate, January 11, 1837] in 1837 was greatly accelerated. It would have been postponed if not altogether avoided, if the land bill of 1833, had been approved and executed." Concludes from this analysis that "If the bank had been rechartered, the public deposits suffered to remain undisturbed where the law required them to be made, and the land bill had gone into operation, it is my firm conviction that we should have had no more individual distress and ruin than is common, in ordinary & regular times, to a trading community." But also blames the nation's present and continuing economic difficulties on the "hard money theorists," particularly on the Democrats who had foolishly inflicted [July 11, 1836] the Specie Circular on the country [8:861; Speech in Senate, January 11, 1837; Remark in Senate, January 14, 1837].

To cure the nation's economic ills, Clay advocates strict economy and frugality in both public and private affairs. Argues, too, that the nation must have "a sound currency of equal value throughout the Union . . . redeemable in specie upon the demand of the holder," and insists that to insure this the country must create some sort of a national bank, "safe and certain and free from the influence of government, and especially not under control of the Executive department." Notes that Congress twice passed legislation during the "Extra Session" in summer, 1841 [27th Congress, 1st Session] that would have provided such a bank only to have "acting President" Tyler veto both on the branching issue [Clay to Ewing, April 30, 1841; Tyler to Clay, April 30, 1841; Speech in Senate, June 21, 1841; Porter to Clay, mid-July, 1841; Speech in Senate, August 19, 1841; Remark in Senate, August 24, 1841]. Attacks Tyler's "dishonor and bad faith" on the bank issue and his hostile patronage policy toward members of "the great body of the Whig party." Asserts that the Whigs now bear no responsibility for the conduct of Tyler; and charges that Tyler "was bound in honor and good faith" to decline the Whig vice presidential nomination at Harrisburg in December, 1839, rather than accept it knowing his principles were not Whig. States that "the sound currency such as I have described is unattainable under the administration of Mr. Tyler. It will be if it can only be attained through the instrumentality of a Bank of the U. States, unless he changes his opinion as he has done in regard to the land bill."[2] Regrets that, unlike the practice in the English parliamentary system, the president does not have to resign and stand for election when he has lost the support of the people. Believes that another remedy for the ailing American economy and its unsound currency would be the adoption of a tariff level that would "ensure an adequate revenue and reasonable protection" but, at the same time, would not stimulate sectional tensions. "Union is our greatest interest. No one can look beyond its dissolution without horror and dismay. Harmony is essential to the preservation of the Union. It was a leading although not the only motive in preparing the compromise act [8:604, 619-22, 626-27], to preserve that harmony. The power of protecting the interests of our own country can never be abandoned to foreign nations without a culpable dereliction of duty. Of this truth all parts of the nation are becoming every day more and more sensible." Adds his conviction that distribution to the states of public land sales receipts [Clay to Ewing, April 30, 1841; Remark in Senate, June 9, 1841; Remark in Senate, January 21, 1842] would also help improve the national economy, but says he will not discuss that matter today, save to note that "Independently of all other considerations, the fluctuation in the receipts from sales of the public lands, is so great and constant, that it is not a resource on which the government ought to rely for revenue." Better to rely on the tariff.

Calls attention to the fact that there are differences of opinion on the relief measures he has suggested because of the unfortunate existence of "the two leading parties into which our people are unhappily divided." Hopes that men can patriotically rise above party in solving the nation's economic problems. Does believe, however, that there are other issues and instances "in which, I think, our political opponents have exhibited a [spirit] and bearing disorganizing and dangerous to the permanency and stability of our institutions." Enumerates nine of these dangerous Democratic party actions and attitudes, viz:

1. The irregularities attending upon the recent admission of territories into the Union. Specifically, "without any previous sanction or authority from Congress, several Territories have proceeded of themselves to call conventions, form constitutions and demand admission into the Union; and they were admitted. I do not deny that their population and condition entitled them to admission; but I insist that it should have been done in the established and regular mode. In the case of Michigan, aliens were admitted to vote, as aliens have been allowed to become preemptors in the public lands, and a majority in Congress sanctioned the proceeding." Such sanction should not have been given to aliens "who have just landed on our shores, who have not yet renounced their allegiance to Foreign potentates."

2. The New Jersey election in which irregularities were tolerated "and a majority thus secured to the Democratic party."[3]

3. The doctrine of nullification [8:388-89, 473, 598, 603, 615] which Clay defines as "an assumption by one State to abrogate within its limits a Law passed by 26 States in Congress assembled."

4. "A late revolutionary attempt in Maryland to subvert the existing government and set up a new one, without any authority of law."[4]

5. The action of the minority [Democrats] members of the Whig-dominated Tennessee state legislature in preventing the appointment of two U.S. senators [Harrison to Clay, March 13, 1841; Clay to Brooke, March 12, 1841]—this by the device of blocking the attendance of at least two-thirds of the members required by the state constitution. This policy of contrived absences from roll-calls was also, according to Clay, a violation

of the U.S. Constitution which requires states to appoint U.S. senators. Explains: "In principle, that refusal was equivalent to announcing the willingness of that minority to dissolve the Union. For if thirteen or fourteen of the 26 States were to refuse altogether to elect Senators, a dissolution of the Union would be the consequence. That minority for weeks together and time after time, deliberately refused to enter upon the election, and if the Union is not in fact dissolved, it is not because the principle involved would not lead to its dissolution, but because 12 or 13 other States have not, like themselves, refused to perform a high Constitutional duty."

6. The "foul stain upon the American character, cast chiefly by the Democrats of Mississippi," which was the repudiation of that state's debt.[5]

7. Democratic party "support given to Executive usurpations and the expunging of the records [8:735] of the Senate of the U. States."

8. The recent refusal of state legislatures "to pass laws to carry into effect the [1841] act of Distribution. An act of Congress passed according to all the forms of the Constitution, after ample discussion and deliberate consideration, and after the lapse of ten years from the period when it was first proposed: It is the duty of all to submit to the laws, regularly passed. They may attempt to get them repealed. They have a right to test their validity before the Judiciary, but whilst the laws remain in force unrepealed, and without any decision against their Constitutional validity, submission to them is not merely a Constitutional and legal but a moral duty." Adds: "If a minority may refuse compliance with one law, what is to prevent minorities from disregarding all laws? What right have the servants of the People (the legislative bodies,) to withhold from their masters their assigned quotas of a great public fund? Is this any thing but a modification of nullification?"

9. The "last though not the least instance of the spirit of disorganization which I shall notice, is the recent convention in Rhode Island." Discusses at length the background and progress of the so-called Dorr Rebellion in Rhode Island which sought, by means legal and illegal, to abolish state constitutional limitations on the right to vote. Condemns the activities of the followers of Thomas Dorr who, in opposing incumbent Governor Samuel W. King and his conservative Charter party, wrote a new constitution which expanded the franchise, established a rival legislature, elected Dorr as a rival governor and then, with two separate governments in operation, "proceeded to collect, to drill, to marshal a military force and pointed their cannon against the arsenal of the State." Lauds President Tyler for having authorized the use of federal troops to assist the state militia, under the command of Governor King, in maintaining order. "I have as much pleasure in expressing my opinion that he [Tyler] faithfully performed his duty in responding to that call, as it gave me pain to be obliged to animadvert upon other parts of his conduct."[6]

Complains, however, that the "leading presses of the Democratic party at Washington, Albany, New York and Richmond and elsewhere, came out in support of the Dorr party, encouraging them in their work of Rebellion & Treason. And when matters had got to a crisis and the two parties were preparing for Civil War, and every hour it was expected to blaze out, a great Tammany meeting was held in the city of N. York,[7] headed by the leading men of the party, the Cambreling's [*sic*, Churchill C. Cambreleng], the Vanderpools [*sic*, Aaron Vanderpoel] and [Stephen] Allens[8] &c, and with a perfect knowledge that the military force of the union was to be employed if necessary to suppress the insurrection, and notwithstanding, they passed resolutions tending to awe the President and to countenance and cheer the Treason." Notes that "fortunately" the Dorr movement collapsed [following an unsuccessful attempt by the Dorrites to seize the state arsenal on May 18, 1842] and that the charter government, "unaided by the actual force of the Federal authority" was able to maintain law and order in Rhode Island. Doubts that all Democrats either supported Dorr or Tammany's support of Dorr's rebellion, but charges that "Under their sway, we have seen not only individuals, but whole communities abandon their long cherished interests and turn round and oppose them with violence." Asks: "Did not the Rebellion in Rhode Island find for its support a precedent established by the majority in Congress, in the irregular admission of Territories as States into the Union, to which I have heretofore alluded? Is there not reason to fear that the example which Congress had previously presented, encouraged the Rhode Island rebellion?" Explains at some length that the Dorr Rebellion cannot be defended with the doctrines of the Declaration of Independence, citing particularly Jefferson's belief that "Prudence indeed will dictate that governments long established shall not be changed for light and transient causes." Does not believe that whenever a society gets itself into difficulty the "major part of it may establish another and another new government in endless succession." Explains that "this would overturn all social organization, make Revolution,—the extreme and last resort of an oppressed people—the constant occurrence of human life, and the standing order of the day. How such a principle would operate in a certain section of this union, with a peculiar [black] population, you will readily conceive. No community could endure such an intolerable state of things anywhere, and all would, sooner or later, take refuge from such ceaseless agitation and convulsion, in the calm repose of absolute despotism."

Points out that in all nine of these "examples of a dangerous spirit of disorganization and disregard of law," he has discussed, "the Democratic party as it calls itself, (a denomination to which I respectfully think that it has not the least just pretension) or large portions of that party, extending to whole States, united with apparent cordiality. To all of them the Whig party was constantly and firmly opposed. And now let me ask you, in all candor, in all sincerity, to say truly and impartially, to which of these two parties, can the interests, the happiness and the destinies of this great people be most safely confided?"

Concludes: "Whigs, arouse from the ignoble supineness which encompasses you. Awake from the lethargy in which you lie bound,—cast from you that unworthy apathy which seems to make you indifferent to the fate of your country—Arouse, awake, shake off the dew drops that glitter on your garments, and once more march to Battle and to Victory. You have been disappointed, deceived and betrayed—shamefully deceived and betrayed. But will *you* therefore prove fickle and faithless to your Country, or obey the impulses of a just and patriotic indignation? As for Captain

Tyler, he is a mere snap—a flash in the pan—pick your Whig flints and try your Rifles again."

DS. ICU. Printed in Colton, *Clay Correspondence*, 6:359-84, with minor variations in punctuation and paragraphing; also in *Niles' Register* (July 9, 1842), 62:290-94. At the end of this speech appears this statement, possibly written by Clay himself: "The conclusion of the speech was followed with general and tremendous cheering; and the largest and one of the most respectable multitudes ever assembled in Kentucky, dispersed, without a solitary instance of disorder or indecorum occurring. H. Clay." Although this lengthy speech has here been summarized, the editors have presented it in the form of a primary document because of its intrinsic importance in the campaign of 1844. Shortly after this speech Robert P. Letcher wrote John J. Crittenden that "The old Prince [Clay] is taking a pretty considerable rise everywhere, I can tell you. I guess he now begins to see the good of leaving the Senate,—of *getting off* awhile merely to *get on* better. He must hereafter remain a little quiet and *hold his jaw*. In fact, he must be *caged*,—that's the point, *cage him!* He swears by all the gods, he will keep cool and stay at home. I rather think he will be prudent, though I have some occasional fears that he may write too many letters; still, he is quite a handy man with the pen, and his letters have *some good* reading in them." Letcher to Crittenden, June 21, 1842, in Coleman, *Life of John J. Crittenden*, 1:182-83. 1. Reference is to Madison's Virginia Resolutions of 1798 and his subsequent report to the Virginia legislature in opposition to the Alien and Sedition Acts. See *The Virginia Report of 1799-1800, Touching the Alien and Sedition Laws; Together With the Virginia Resolutions of December 21, 1798*. . . . Richmond, 1850; Irving Brandt, *James Madison*, 6 vols. (Indianapolis, 1940-61), 4:12. 2. Tyler had signed the Distribution Act of Sept. 4, 1841. See Clay to Ewing, April 30, 1841; Remark in Senate, June 9, 1841; 5 *U.S. Stat.*, 453-58. For Tyler's actions on distribution in 1842, see Clay to Letcher, June 24, 1842. 3. Clay to Otis, Nov. 14, 1838. 4. Probably a reference to the attempt in 1836 by a group of Maryland Democrats to thwart the election of members of the state senate in an effort to bring about constitutional reform. J. Thomas Scharf, *History of Maryland*. . . , 3 vols. (Baltimore, 1879), 3:190-95. 5. In his message of Jan. 5, 1841, Mississippi Democratic Gov. Alexander McNutt recommended that the state repudiate the bonds it had sold to meet and pay for its subscription of stock in the Union Bank of Mississippi. The legislature did not concur that year; however, the repudiators were successful in electing their entire state ticket and a majority in both houses at the next legislative canvass, and they ultimately repudiated the bonds. The Whigs, in general, strongly favored honoring the debt. Robert Lowry and William H. McCardle, *A History of Mississippi* . . . (Jackson, Miss., 1891), 280-93. 6. In the April elections in Rhode Island, Thomas Dorr had polled some 6,604 votes for governor in an unauthorized election held under the so-called "People's Constitution." In the legal election under the old charter, Whig incumbent Gov. Samuel W. King defeated ex-Gov. Thomas F. Carpenter by 4,864 votes to 2,211. *BDGUS*, 4:1341. For more on the Dorr Rebellion, see Chitwood, *John Tyler*, 326-30; George M. Dennison, *The Dorr War: Republicanism on Trial, 1831-1861*. Lexington, 1976; Marvin E. Gettleman, *The Dorr Rebellion: A Study in American Radicalism, 1833-1849*. New York, 1973. 7. The Tammany Hall meeting in support of the Dorr Rebellion was held on April 27, 1842. See Nevins, *Diary of Philip Hone*, 598. 8. For Allen (1767-1852), see *NCAB*, 4:256.

To WADDY THOMPSON, JR. Lexington, June 11, 1842

The enclosed letters sufficiently explain their object of obtaining the liberation of James M. Alexander, supposed to be confined at Pueblo.[1] I am sure they will excite your sympathies and engage your friendly offices, without any enforcement from me. I had supposed, from the address of Santa Anna to Mr. [Powhatan] Ellis,[2] that all the Citizens of the U. States were released; but the friends of young Alexander think that he is not.

I can add nothing to the information which the News papers will communicate. There is no improvement at Washn. in the relations between the Executive and Congress. They are probably worse than when you left.

Great pecuniary embarrassment continues in the Country. No one escapes it.

Wishing you great success in your mission. . . .

ALS. ScU. Addressed to Thompson, U.S. minister to Mexico, c/o Luis C. Hargous, Mexican consul in New York City. 1. A large number of American traders, as well as volunteers who were to protect them on their way to Santa Fé, had been captured by the Mexicans in the fall of 1841. Most were released in Feb., 1842, and the remainder on June 16, 1842. Presumably, Alexander, who has not been identified, was among these. Rives, *The United States and Mexico*, 1:480-84, 508-13. 2. In his reply to Ellis's farewell address, Gen. Antonio L. de Santa Anna said on April 21, 1842, that Ellis could take home with him "the six citizens of the United States, who have not yet obtained the benefit of liberty." *Niles' Register* (June 4, 1842), 62:210. No account of Alexander's release has been found.

From WILLIE P. MANGUM Washington, June 15, 1842

I have received your obliging favor[1] and am glad to hear that you are well. You must keep yourself so; for everything interesting to thorough Whigs depends (to an extent that I regret to see) upon your Continued life and health. I regret it because such a cause & the principles involved in it ought to be able to succeed in many hands. Such I think, is obviously not the Case.

As far as I can judge, I think, the cause is constantly brightening. All eyes are turned in a single direction. The indecision, vacillation & the manifest want of good faith—not to say, common honesty on the part of those who administer the government, have fixed the public eye upon the admitted head of the Whig party, with an intensity of interest, that I am very sure, has never happened before in my time.

If this session of Congress could close auspiciously, I think, there would be but little ground for apprehensions as to the future. I fear, it may not close well—Every thing is now at sea. The Country most imperatively demands a good Tariff, and I am happy to see that your Views on that subject have been most cordially received in almost every quarter,[2] & especially at those points, where the most powerful interests would seek to array opinion against them. The admn. seem resolved to get rid of the Land distribution law. It is given out in all forms, that a veto will meet any Tariff measure, if it shall be accompanied with a removal of the restriction on the distribution law. I doubt, whether Tyler would dare to Veto, yet the extremest rashness often accompanies the highest degree of feebleness & imbecility.[3] What I most fear is, that Congress through both seduction & intimidation may fail in its duty. If the failure shall happen on the part of Congress, it is obvious that the Whig party must suffer deeply. There is great doubt as to *both Houses*. I am glad to find the Northern & Eastern men generally, holding on tenaciously, to the Land Law,[4] even Choate & Bates.[5] It is so, in both houses. Great pains have been taken to convince them that their true interest is to stand by all the Measures. That Southern Whigs will go very far to gratify them in a Tariff, if they shall stand by the Land Law, & that the surrender of the Land Law, or any faltering on the subject, puts an end to all hopes for the present, of passing any Tariff Law at all.

Every effort will be made to bring Congress up to the point of its duties. If it shall succeed, & the responsibility shall be placed on the Executive, we must abide the result, and may do it with a feeling of security.

Mr. [Samuel L.] Southard is at Fredericsburg [*sic*, Fredericksburg], Va. & the last advices leave scarcely hope for his recovery.[6]

I am in his place in the Senate,[7] & how I got there I scarcely know. [John J.] Crittenden takes the right view of it, perhaps, "Through a Senate that may well be denounced as factious by Mr Tyler's, J[ohn B.] Jones[8] for having elected not only the most *odious*, but the most unqualified man in the Senate." Your old friend [Richard H.] Bayard was the Executive favorite, judging from indications here, as well as in the penny press & N.Y. Herald. The hope was to elect him by a Combination of our Windshaker Whigs & the Loco's. It was accordingly proposed that the Whigs in Caucus, should simply engage to elect a Whig, without the designation of a Candidate. The policy was so shallow & obvious, that all saw the design, & of course, repealed it.

In Caucus, I got the nomination by a majority, Bayard having 4 Votes. [Nathaniel P.] Tallmadge, who desired it, yet behaved quite well, got 3.

We resolved to press perseveringly to the end, a Clay Whig. & some of us would have taken My Lord *Bullion* [Thomas Hart Benton], rather than one of the Conquered Tylerish *Clique*. It was Clear, that no one could succeed except Crittenden or myself. Crittenden promptly declined for many & conclusive reasons. It was important to carry [William C.] Preston, & it was in my mind, very doubtful whether after me, he would not go, next for Bayard.

To elect Bayard was to Consummate a Tyler triump[h]. To elect Tallmadge, (who alone had any prospect of success) might have been regarded as a Clay defeat—his Exchequer notions[9]—to say nothing, of other matters—yet it is due to him to say, that he is as much a Clay man (in his way) as any of us.

The question of slave holding & non-slave holding states was attempted to be moved—it was no go. All the Whigs present (excluding myself who did not vote) 25 in number, voted for me except Bayard & [Albert S.] White[10]—White declining solely on the sectional ground—His Whiggism being entirely sound in other matters. The Calhoun Loco's & all that gang, holding themselves ready for Coalition. But my excellent friend My Lord Bullion (Benton) [was] in no wise disposed to play that game. I learned this from [William S.] Archer. At a third ballot Benton & his troops would have come in to battle on the Whig side. I am glad, it did not go to the third ballot, as I very *much* desired, if elected at all, to be elected by Whig Votes, exculsively.

The Wailing & gnashing of teeth at the White house were as ridiculous, as weak & excessive. It was an "insult, personal insult" &c. &c. &c. The Madisonion every sunny Morning, for a week, paid me especial respect.

It seems to be the general opinion, that for a few days Mr Tyler felt every bone & muscle in him acheing with pain—doubting wheth[er] he could live to hold on to his place.[11]

It has been the subject of much merriment here in Whig circles.

I shall expect in a day or two to hear from Geo[rgia]. where every thing is expected to go well[12]—Calhoun has gone to Geo. to see Gold mines ostensibly[13]—If he can, he will prevent a nomination there

His friends could not get a nomination for him in No. Ca[rolina]. lately,[14] though all the papers were "Cut & dried" here. Poor Man[agemen]t.

ALS. DLC-HC (DNA, M212, R5). Dashes placed after periods, some 40 in number, have been removed by the editors. 1. Clay to Mangum, June 7, 1842. 2. Clay to Letcher,

Jan. 6, 1842; Remark in Senate, Feb. 3, 1842. 3. Clay to Letcher, Jan. 6, 1842; Remark in Senate, Jan. 21, 1842; Clay to Letcher, June 24, 1842. 4. Distribution Act of 1841. See 5 *U.S. Stat.*, 453-58. 5. Senators Rufus Choate and Isaac C. Bates of Mass. See *BDAC*. 6. Clay to Mangum, June 7, 1842. 7. Mangum had been elected president *pro tem* of the Senate on May 31, 1842, following Southard's resignation. On the second ballot Mangum achieved the 23 votes needed to win. Richard H. Bayard followed with 13 votes, William King had 7, Nathaniel P. Tallmadge 1, and Robert Walker 1. No roll call vote is available. *Cong. Globe*, 27 Cong., 2 Sess., 554. 8. For Jones, editor of *The Madisonian*, see *DAB*. 9. On Feb. 21, 1842, Tallmadge had reported from a Senate Select Committee the bill to create a Board of Exchequer [Clay to J.B. Clay, Dec. 10, 1841]. *Cong. Globe*, 27 Cong., 2 Sess., 256. 10. For White (Ind.), see *BDAC*. 11. Mangum's election as president *pro tem* was taken as another Whig thrust at the president, for, if Tyler were impeached, Mangum would then succeed him. Oscar D. Lambert, *Presidential Politics in the United States 1841-1844* (Durham, N.C., 1936), 54. 12. The Georgia States' Rights Whig convention met in Milledgeville on June 13, 1842, and nominated Clay for president. *Niles' Register* (June 25, 1842), 62:259. 13. Calhoun had purchased the O'Bar mine in Dahlonega, Ga., in 1833. A gold strike was made there in May, 1842. See Wiltse, *John C. Calhoun: Sectionalist*, 126-29. 14. For the North Carolina Democratic convention of May 20-21, 1842, at which a letter from Calhoun was read but no presidential nomination was made, see *Niles' Register* (June 18, 1842), 62:242-43.

From Joseph H. Bush, June 21, 1842. Recalls "an act of disinterested friendship you once accorded to a friendless boy" over 25 years ago, and remarks that he has "never for one moment forgotten it." Reports that while he could have made some payment on the debt over the years, he has delayed doing this in the hope that someday he would be able "to accompany the principal with the interest (which would now be considerable), but in this I have been doomed to disappointment" because of the "unexpected failure of the Commercial Bank of Natchez" in which all his "humble means" were invested. Nevertheless, enclosed a check on the Bank of Louisville for the "original sum of $450" for fear that if he waits much longer "we may both die of old age." Closes with profuse thanks for Clay's earlier kindness to "a friendless boy." Copy. InHi. For Bush, see 2:230.

To ROBERT P. LETCHER — Lexington, June 24, 1842

The 1st. of July is near at hand, and it has occurred to me to suggest for your consideration the propriety of taking immediate measures for demanding at Washn. the State's quota of the Land fund. It is clear that the instalment then due ought to be paid, as no bill can possibly now pass to deprive the State of that, whatever may be the ultimate fate of the reduction.[1]

ALS. InU. 1. The Distribution Act of Sept. 4, 1841, provided that after Dec. 31, 1841, the proceeds of the sales of public lands would be distributed to the states, but that such distribution would be suspended "if . . . there shall be an imposition of duties on imports inconsistent with the provisions of the act of March second one thousand eight hundred and thirty-three [Compromise Tariff Act of 1833] . . . beyond the rate of duty fixed by that act, to wit: twenty per cent. on the value of such imports." 5 *U.S. Stat.*, 453-58, espec. 453-54. President Tyler vetoed two tariff bills in 1842 which would have raised the tariff while keeping intact distribution [Clay to Letcher, Jan. 6, 1842]. When the tariff of 1833 expired on July 1, 1842, Tyler declared its rates still in effect until a new bill was passed and approved. He also ordered that distribution be suspended, because the average rate of duties at the juncture exceeded 20%. Hence, the funds distributed were those accumulated between Jan. 1 and July 1, 1842, the total amount being only $691,117.05 with Kentucky's share standing at $27,776.19. The new tariff, approved on August 30, 1842 [5 *U.S. Stat.*, 548-67], raised duties far above 20% and specifically (sec. 30) suspended distribution so long as the 1842 tariff remained in effect. Congress, however, passed another bill which would have continued distribution despite the rise in tariff rates, but Tyler pocket-vetoed the measure. For a discussion of the political ramifications of the tariff/distribution issue, see Kirwan, *John J. Crittenden*, 162-66; Hibbard, *History of the Public Land Policies*, 184-89; Raymond G. Wellington, *The Political and Sectional Influence of the Public Lands, 1828-1842* (New York, 1914; reprint ed., 1970), 96-117;

Roy M. Robbins, *Our Landed Heritage, The Public Domain, 1776-1936* (Lincoln, Nebr., 1962), 85-89; Stephenson, *Political History of the Public Lands*, 73-96; Thomas Donaldson, *The Public Domain, With Statistics . . .* (Washington, 1884), 753.

To CHARLES FLEMING ROGERS Lexington, June 27, 1842

I should be greatly obliged if you would send me a Check for the balance you owe me, as I have some immediate pressing demands to meet.[1] I think you told me that I should have it before this time.

ALS. KyLx. 1. No evidence concerning this payment has been found.

To ROBERT P. LETCHER Lexington, June 29, 1842

I return Mr. Cs. letter[1] with another[2] giving a different, and I think probably the true, version of the Captain's [Tyler's] intrigue.[3] I wish he would consummate it, I care not with which of the parties. No Whig ought to forbid the bans, altho' it be the work of the devil.

You may destroy Mr. [Nathan] Sargents letter.

ALS. NcD. 1. Probably John J. Crittenden's letter of May 27, 1842, not found, but mentioned in Clay to Crittenden, June 3, 1842. 2. Probably Nathan Sargent's letter, date unknown, which Gov. Letcher was asked herein to destroy. 3. In a letter to Letcher, dated June 23, 1842, Crittenden expressed the opinion that Tyler was "now pluming his wings for a new flight of treachery and folly. Rumors of changes and cabinets and measures fill the city." He concluded that Tyler "must look . . . to the Locofocos," and predicted that he would try to come to terms with the Southern branch of the Whig party, perhaps forming an alliance with Calhoun. Coleman, *Life of Crittenden*, 1:183-84. For Tyler's attempts to form a third party, see Seager, *And Tyler Too*, 170-71.

From William C. Preston, Washington, June 29, 1842. Reports from the Capital that the "British negotiation I believe goes on smoothly in regard to every point except the Maine boundary [Ashburton to Clay, April 11, 1842] which is complicated and embarrassed by the multitude of diplomatists congregated upon it. . . . Our hope is that Abbott Lawrence & Govr. [Edward] Kent will get the ascendency and carry on the matter. The other four—all of them I think are in a train of a very favorable adjustment." Reports also that the separation of Congress and President Tyler has become "wider & wider and the general confusion worse confounded . . . and it is now generally believed (on good ground perhaps) that there is a negotiation on foot to bring in the Locofocos to the cabinet." Says that Virginia's William C. Rives, in a speech in the Senate yesterday, "abused your distribution policy [Clay to Ewing, April 30, 1841; Remark in Senate, June 9, 1841; Clay to Letcher, January 6, 1842; Remark in Senate, January 21, 1842] from begin[n]ing to end. . . . He barely stop[p]ed short of denouncing it as unconstitutional." Laments the death of Samuel L. Southard, whose funeral took place yesterday [Clay to Mangum, June 7, 1842]. Concludes: "Today Tyler sends in his veto of the month tariff [Clay to Letcher, January 6, 1842]. . . . This is downright madness—God preserve us for our condition is most sad—" ALS. DLC-HC (DNA, M212, R5). Printed in Colton, *Clay Correspondence*, 4:460-61.

Maine had appointed Democrats William Pitt Preble and Edward Kavanagh and Whigs Edward Kent and John Otis as commissioners to attend the Webster-Ashburton negotiations, while Massachusetts had appointed Abbott Lawrence, John Mills, and Charles Allen. The commissioners objected to yielding to the British territory on the south side of the St. John River but were ultimately persuaded to concede part of that disputed territory in exchange for free access to the St. John, $150,000 each to Maine and Massachusetts, and a few other minor concessions. See Burrage, *Maine In the Northeastern Boundary Controversy*, 321, 326, 334, 336, 340-41; Baxter, *Daniel Webster*, 339-48, 387; Merk, *Fruits of Propaganda*, 58-75.

From JOHN J. CRITTENDEN Washington, July 2, 1842

I have learned here from a source to be relied on implicitly, that, at the Meeting to be held in Pen[n]sylvania on the 26th of this month for the nomination of a Presidential candidate,[1] it is intended to nominate General [Winfield] Scott, but with a declaration of their intention to support the candidate of the Whig party, whether designated by a National Convention or other evidences of the preference & choice of that party. All these qualifications of their nomination, are understood as having reference to, & as providing for the event of your being the candidate of the party, which all seem to regard as a *set[t]led* matter—It would be better for all parties that the Pen[n]sylvania Convention should at once & directly give you their nomination—And I have had conversations with some of Scotts most confidential friends, to convince them of the correctness of my opinion, especially as it regarded Scott himself,—for that such a nomination of him, in the midst of so universal & ardent a sentiment in your favour, would place him in a very awkward, if not ridiculous attitude before the World, & would beside[s] expose him to much jealousy & prejudice &c—No one that I have conversed with, dissents from this view of the matter, but yet it is doubtful whether any thing can be done to change the course, as above stated, of the Pen[n]sylvania Convention—It is most probable that their nomination will be given to Scott, but it will be regarded by themselves & every body else as merely *nominal*, & the qualifications annexed to it as virtually & substantially a nomination of you—I shall not cease however to attend to the subject & to give it, as far as I can, the best shape and direction. There is but one opinion here, & that is that you are the Candidate of the Whig party—the only man to be thought of—that the *people* have already set[t]led that question,—And I assure you that I have never witnessed on any other occasion, or in any other instance, such a flow of public opinion & feeling as is now going on in your favour—Making all allowances for my own biases, I am sure I can say, that the evidences & progress of this public opinion, have been such as to surprise both your friends & opponents. The force of that public opinion is manifest in all its effects—it decides the doubtful, it encourages the timid, it stimulates the bold, & it alarms your opponents—All this I can see around me. There is no longer any serious thought of a Whig Competitor for you—

I understand that Scott has lost all hope, & I wish he could be saved from all further disappointment or difficulty on the subject—He is a good Whig & a good fellow—And will eventually support you heartily—It is not to be wondered at, if in the first moments of his disappointment, he show some little impatience, & his wounded vanity should not permit him at once to take the most proper or prudent course—In common with the rest of us, he has his portion of Vanity—And that may well be excused on account of his other good qualities—I like him, & am sure he will do right at last.

I have not conversed with him about this Pen[n]sylvania Convention, or his purposes in respect to it—

I have conversed with [William C.] Preston & [William S.] Archer, his most intimate friends, & have left it with them to counsel him—

Both of them fully agree with me as to the folly—the impossibility of bringing him into competition with you, and would be glad to see him rid of the whole affair—And the only question seems to be how he is to get out of it in the most decent & respectable *manner*

I have conversed with [James] Cooper[2] of Pen[n]sylvania, & am to converse with him further—He is a good Whig—convinced that you are the only candidate upon whom we can rely for success—and is well disposed towards you, and will do all he can to give the right direction to the proceedings of their Convention—He is in correspondence with them.

Since I have been writing this [George] Evans of Maine came to my seat to tell me, that he had just heard that the Convention assembled in his State to nominate State officers, a governor &c had nominated you for President, in a most enthusiastic manner—[3]At my request he has promised to write you as soon as he recieves a printed account of the proceedings—Be sure that you answer his letter—All our friends here would be flattered by your correspondence, & you must task yourself a little to please them—

If we can only keep up the feeling that now exists, your election will be certain—Tyler is one of your *best friends*—His last Veto[4] has served us all well—It had just reached the Convention in Maine that nominated you, & denounced him—It has had a fine effect upon our friends here, and will insure the passage of our Tariff bill with a reservation to the States of the proceeds of the public lands—[5]You may set that down as certain—Suppose Tyler vetos that, What then shall we do? Shall we pass the Tariff, giving up the lands, or adjourn, & let all go together?[6] Write me immediately an answer to these questions.

ALS. DLC-John J. Crittenden Papers (DNA, M212, R20). Written from the Senate Chamber. Copy, excerpt, is in NcD. 1. The Democratic State Convention of the Friends of Gen. Winfield Scott was held in Harrisburg on July 26, 1842, with Samuel Park as its president. The approximately 200 delegates adopted 10 resolutions and vowed to support only Scott for president. The Whig State convention, held at Harrisburg on Feb. 22, 1843, endorsed Clay for president. Washington *Daily National Intelligencer*, August 11, 1842; Mueller, *The Whig Party in Pennsylvania*, 88; Poage, *Henry Clay*, 108. 2. For Cooper, a Pennsylvania Whig congressman and later a U. S. senator, see *BDAC*. 3. For Evans, a Whig senator from Maine, see *BDAC*. The Whig State convention had met in Portsmouth, Me., on June 28, 1842, and nominated Edward Robinson for governor and Clay for president. *Niles' Register* (July 9, 1842), 62:304. 4. Of the "provisional" or "little" tariff. See Clay to Letcher, Jan. 6, 1842. 5. *Ibid.*; Clay to Letcher, June 24, 1842. 6. *Ibid.*

From JAMES T. MOREHEAD Washington, July 2, 1842

The late Veto[1] by the President is doing much to unite the party as we were united in 1840. You will have seen the movement of the Baltimore Patriots—running up the flag.[2] I learn today from Brooke, that the New York Express will follow the example.[3] Our friends in the House are acquitting themselves extremely well. The public prints will furnish you the details.

The rumors concerning the difficulties in the Cabinet, I know, were not without foundation.[4] [John C.] Spencer began to put his house in *order*.[5]

The Locofocoes were not content that Webster should remain in office; It was a sine qua non: But to eject *him* without his consent, would render the Senate one compact body; and for the present it has been declined.[6]

[George] Evans, of the Senate, has at length, I think, made up his mind, to abandon Webster to his destiny. I wish you would drop him a line now and then, written with proper caution.

Present indications are as favorable as they could be. If we succeed in disposing of the subject of the Tariff satisfactorily, Congress will adjourn under the most auspicious circumstances. The present determination is to unite the North and South in the support of a good bill, joining the proceeds of the sales of the lands—and if Tyler Vetoes it, as he must, then to fo[r]ce down & pass a rate of duties of 20 per cent with a home valuation—What do you think of these things[7]

The Independent[8] has stopped as you will have perceived. We are now engaged in an effort to revive it. There is some difficulty about it. I retained the money you sent me for Judge [Alexander] Porter's subscription, until the result is known. If the paper is discontinued, I will return it to you or him as you may direct.

The Rhode Island war is again closed.[9] [Thomas W.] Dorr has escaped. The delegation from the State applied to Tyler for aid, after hostilities were renewed. His answer was, that the Legislature had not renewed the application, and in short that he had no power to interpose. The first application he contended, ceased to be authoritative upon the adjournment of the Legislature, and that of the Governor of Rhode Island [Samuel W. King] was not a justification. [William] Sprague is entirely off. Tyler's whole course in respect to Rhode Island was prompted by a wish to conciliate the Locofocoes.

I had a letter today from Epes Sargent,[10] putting some interrogatories to me, some of which I am not able to answer. He enclosed me a letter for you which I forward, which probably relates to the same subjects.

I shall be glad to hear from you often....

ALS. DLC-John J. Crittenden Papers (DNA, M212, R20). 1. Clay to Letcher, Jan. 6, 1842. 2. An editorial in the Baltimore *Patriot & Commercial Advertiser* of June 30, 1842, castigated Tyler for his June 29 veto of the little, or provisional, tariff bill. Editor and publisher, Isaac Munroe, declared that he had long been losing faith in the president's acceptance of Whig beliefs. He also praised Clay's speeches as beautiful and patriotic in comparison to Tyler's veto message. 3. Possibly Francis T. Brooke. 4. Rumors of impending Cabinet changes were rife in 1842. For example, in April, 1842, Alexander Hamilton, Jr., of N.Y. wrote Tyler urging him to drop Webster and John C. Spencer from the Cabinet. There was also speculation that John C. Calhoun might go into the Cabinet. Morgan, *A Whig Embattled*, 74, 166; Coleman, *Life of John J. Crittenden*, 1:183-84, 189-90. 5. Reference obscure. 6. Webster resigned as secretary of state on May 8, 1843. He returned to private law practice until he was reelected to the U.S. Senate in Dec., 1845. Fuess, *Daniel Webster*, 2:129-35, 149. 7. Clay to Letcher, Jan. 6, 1842. 8. Clay to Webb, Feb. 12, 1842. 9. Speech in Lexington, June 9, 1842. 10. Not found, but see Clay to Sargent, Sept. 13, 1842.

To JOHN O. SARGENT Lexington, July 2, 1842

I received your favor communicating your motives for declining the superintendance of the publication of my Speeches. They are entirely satisfactory. I think Mr. [Daniel] Mallory, in whose zeal and friendship I have full confidence, pressed his preemptive right a little too far. The truth is, that I claim no property in the Speeches, which, such as they are, belong to the public; and my intention in my correspondence with him was merely to express my assent, as I have done in other instances, to his publication of them, if he chose to embark in the enterprize; but I thought he had given it up until I heard lately from him.[1]

I have only solicitude on two points, one, that the work should be accurately and neatly executed, and the other, that it should not occasion loss to the publisher. The plan you and I conversed about, of a brief historical memoir in respect to the fate of the measure or question, to which the particular speech related I thought a very good one. . . .[2]

ALS. MHi. 1. In 1843 Daniel Mallory published in New York a two-volume work called *The Life and Speeches of the Hon. Henry Clay. . . .* The following year, John O. Sargent's brother, Epes, published in New York an eighty-page book called *The Life and Public Services of Henry Clay, New ed., rev., enlarged and brought down to the year 1844.* See also Clay to Sargent, June 2, 1841. 2. Clay to Sargent, June 2, 1841.

From WILLIE P. MANGUM Washington, July 4, 1842

I received last night, your favor of the 26th. ult: & some days ago, your Lexington Speech,[1] for which, in Common with the Whole Country, I tender you my most sincere thanks.—No speech ever came, in better time and more admirably adapted to the state of the Country and the condition of public opinion.—You will have perceived, that it has fallen with electrical effect on the North & East; and that its influence, is incalculably enhanced, by going to the public at the same instant, with the late absurd, insolent & extraordinary Veto.—

Its influence at Baltimore was instantaneous & Complete—An entire union of the party, with a zeal & enthusiasm wholly unparalelled.—The [Baltimore] Patriot that has *Tylerized* so long, regained its just position in one night, and with a freshness & energy of spirit will place itself in the front rank of the Whig press.—All accounts concur that the Whig party there will be as one man.—

I saw a letter from Munroe of the Patriot,[2] written in the best spirit & showing obviously, that the occasion which enabled him to right himself if not anxiously desired, was at least, agreeable.—So, in Philada.—& so, in New York.—[James T.] Morehead has gone to Philadelphia to make a dinner Speech &C. &C.—I urged him yesterday, & he is off, this morning, with [John] Sergeant, & will come upon them in the midst of the feast.—He is charged to the Muzzle, & will doubtless, give them a first rate bang-up Speech.—It will do good.—I greatly misconceive the signs of the time, if *this day* shall not give the most unequivocal evidence of the rising, & aroused spirit of the people.—Marked as your life has been, with bright & brill[i]ant epochs, there is none, in my judgment, comparable with the present, in true moral sublimity.—The spectacle of a great party Comprehending more than a moiety of our people, eminently intellectual & patriotic, bursting loose as one man from the man in power, scorning & treading upon, his patronage & bounties, & with, as it were, but one Will, & a fast fealty to their principles, rallying around the Farmer of Ashland, as the leader & best exponent of those principles, with scarce an eye in these multitudinous masses, looking towards any other, though others there be, many, eminent and patriotic!—In respect to the Lexington Speech, there is but one opinion, & that just such, as your best friends would desire.—In respect to the late Veto,[3] the indignation is high, the debate as you will have seen, fiery & pungent, & well sustained.—The outburst was not such as you witnessed last summer, but the scorn & Contempt are perhaps deeper & more abiding.—Its effects elsewhere, I think, much more decisive than the events of the extra session—Here is no case of Conscience—& besides the treachery and apostacy are unequivocal, & no longer seeking disguise.—He is off.—clear off, completely, without condition, reservation or any sort of disguise.—The effects have been fine, exactly at the points where most needed, the North & East.—You have never seen the Whig party *so united* in firm phalanx as they are at present; and the tone is high.

This Yankee is a strange animal, prudent, close & complying *for interest,* to the Verge of servility; but pass with him a certain point, & arouse him, & none are firmer, more obstinate or more to be relied on.—You perceive that we modified the clause repealing the restriction in the land bill.—[4] Of Course, it indicates, no yielding on that point.—It was thought desirable, to avoid the veto on this small affair, & to encounter it, if at all, on a bill around which would be clustered all the great interests of the North & East.—It has come however, producing effects, altogether exceeding our anticipations.—

We shall go on, as if nothing had happened.—We shall pass I trust, a good Tariff,[5] containing a repeal of the land bill restriction (for the lands in *no Contingency* will [be] surrendered,—that is sure) and *that* we suppose, will be vetoed, of Course.—Though the time & labour will be lost, yet this good we promise ourselves—to wit, that our friends to the North & East, seeing us to the South, giving the highest & only guarantee in our power, of good faith, will know their real friends, & the effect must be to knit us in a closer bond of union & Cooperation.—

A third effort will be made, falling back upon 20 pr Ct. & [James F.] Simmons, in that case, will act an important part.[6]

That will be the issue of our efforts.—These things have not been formally settled, yet this will be the Course, I think, with scarce any variation.—

I have been most agreeably surprized to find our new England senators as resolved, apparently as any others on the subject of the lands.—And out of Mass: not a Vote will be lost—Nor do I think, Mass: will give way.—[7]

I hear that Mr [John Q.] Adams will probably speak to day, on the Veto—[8] with all his extravagant notions on that subject, I learn from [Horace] Everett, that he is much excited, & says the Prest. ought to be impeached &C. &C.—[9] A speech from him, if given in that tone, will fix immoveably New England—or rather Mass: where we need aid, & where, I am glad to believe, that Webster has scarcely any effective weight. Abbott Lawrence says openly, that rather than succumb on the land question, let the Tariff be lost, that the manufacturers distressed as they are & will be, cannot be much more so, than will this govt. by its policy.—

The loan would be taken at once,[10] if a good Tariff were passed.—In the present Condition of things, not a dollar more, I presume, will be taken.—With the Confusion at the Custom Houses, not a dollar of revenue paid, except under protest—& that only in cases, where the article is instantly sold;—no money on hand—& the distribution of the land money now due,[11] you can see in what a miserable condition is this weak, miserable, false & utterly incompetent admn.—Sir. Is there not danger, that the system will fall to pieces? Nothing, it seems to me, but the strong & daily brightening hopes, in the future, Can save us.

[Nathaniel P.] Tallmadge is firm.—recent events have had a good effect on him.—With good & true dispositions as I think, Yet with a desire to serve his Conservative friends—(Well enough in itself) & a spice of personal Vanity that overestimated his influence & power in the Whig party, he fell into grievous error on the Exchequer—[12]& He has found that as the party remains firm & uninfluenced—it was easier for one man to turn, than for thousands—Hence he is with us—in good faith—Nor do I think, he was ever Conscious of the opposite.—I have had lately, a long, full & entirely frank Conversation with him—He feels that as man may tamper too far, with impunity—I count fully on his faithful Cooperation in all things.

[William C.] Rives is put where, I have long expected to see him, sitting in this hot weather, under the shade of the Executive, fanning & keeping Comfortably Cool, his & Mr Tyler's Conscience.

I consider him off—off, clear gone, & no one regrets it. [William S.] Archer is in good temper—firm & steady—& will go with us to repeal the restriction in the Land bill, & that settles the question.—Archer you know is a warm personal friend of Gen: [Winfield] Scott, yet with us.—I have spent three or four evenings at Scott's quarters at whist parties &C.—As I play but little, & Scott none at all, I have had much Conversation with the General.—After placing you first & against the world, & in Case of an unhappy Contingency, then looking to him next & decidedly—& exhibiting that as the general sense of our friends, & the anxiety felt, that the imprudence or impetuosity of his friends may not compromise him with his best & only true friends & all that—He takes it kindly, & has evinced a strong sense of the frank & friendly motives that dictate the Conversation—& in a word, seems to be in an amicable temper & not at all disposed to Mischief.—One of these Conversations I had with him, in [the] presence of Gen: Clinch[13] his warm friend, Georgian by residence, No. Carolinean by birth—& found Clinch, who had at first been averse to your nomination in Geo. as *premature*, but gave in cheerfully to the general rush, agreeing entirely.—Scott's Vanity of Course would yield to strong demonstrations in his favor.—Yet he will be passive, & as those demonstrations are not likely to be made, I apprehend nothing adverse from that quarter.—

As to the negotiation between Tyler & [Silas] Wright, but little is known with accuracy.—The amount of it, I suppose, is that Tyler has been making to him, as well as to others, overtures in the most open, bare faced, & almost begging strain of harlotry.—That Wright has played the Amiable—willing to embarrass the whigs, yet too wary to go very far.—Tyler being resolved to Cut loose entirely sought an alliance Comprehending an engagement to push him for the succession.—That of course, they cannot, & will not do—[14]

Yet they flatter him with hopes, that he may get the track, Still the Course must be kept open for all, & that they cannot stipulate for the withdrawal of any.—

That is Tyler's last hope, and as he can do no better, he will play that game. They will use & cajole the poor Creature, & ultimately let down the Wind, him & his infamy with all its rottenness & offensiveness—

I am proud to be able to inform you, that my particular friend, My Lord Bullion [Thomas H. Benton], looks upon all this, with the high scorn & imperturable obstinacy of a goaded bull Bison.—

As to this intrigue, I learned more from Richmond than elsewhere—*the leakings* of that frail vessel the ex-minister [Andrew] Stevenson thereupon.—A very particular account of it has reached here in letters—And the point of difficulty is the Question of Succession.[15]

If Congress were to adjourn at once, I think it very probable, that important Cabinet changes would soon be made.—Forward, Webster & Spencer to go out—[16] Webster must go, as soon as the negotiation on foot, is brought to a close.—He will go voluntarily, & may have anything he desires.—He will probably, take nothing—set up for a persecuted patriot who has borne all things & suffered all things for his dearly beloved Country, such a place in the Whig ranks, & denuded as he is, of popular influence, may yet have power to do much mischief, through others.—These vetoes[17] however, will much circumscribe his power. As to the progress of the negotiation (Lord As[h]burton's,), I know nothing; though I have sought such information, as I might, obtain.—[18]

I infer from the quiet, the apparent cheerfulness & the absence of allusion to dangers on the part of the Capt. [Tyler] & his [Corporal's] Guard, that things are going on Well.—

Calhoun is becoming larger by half than you would readily believe.—The Maine Commissioners [Edward] Kavanagh & [William] Preble are hot Calhoun men—That indicates favorably for pacification—as Calhoun above all things, except to Mr Clay, is most opposed to War.—

I am much surprized at the progress Calhoun had made towards a nomination,[19] and am also, gratified.—

In Congress he is without a rival—more strength than all of them.—He is the very first in the affections of the destructives & butt-enders in the Cities—They are men of sagacity—They see that Mr Calhoun has no conscience to enterpose between them & agrarianism rapine or any other enormity.

He will have strength enough to give much trouble, Yet I suppose, Mr Van Buren will be the man—Benton says, it will be Van Buren, beyond all doubt.—

There is but little defection here—Morriss [*sic*, Calvary Morris] of Ohio—the only certain loss—[Patrick G.] Goode will probably return.—[20] He had the *Animum fugiendi*, but recent events finding him just extending the Wings, he will probably flap them & close them, & stay where he is.—This is the opinion of Everett & others.—

Our valued & worthy friend Gen: Ervine [*sic*][21] has been uneasy—He is deeply in the Iron business, & is much alarmed.—He probably thought business went on too slowly—showed signs of impatience &C. &C. But I regard him as firm, & with no purpose of bad faith. As to the Navy, nothing excessive will be done,[22] I think.—Our friends did not approve the Course of the House, though agreeing generally as to the object sought. They the

Senate got into error however, I think, which will be corrected probably.—

The Army will be retrenched about eight hundred thousand dollars,[23] without touching the staff &C. &C. upon which with time, 2 or 3[24] hundred thousand can be judiciously retrenched.—

We feel the great injury of the protracted Session, Yet it cannot be avoided.—

We work long & steadily each day—But the disposition to vapid debate is annoyingly on the encrease.—We need more energy in the lead to repress this pruriency.—If we had the Dictator,[25] he could do it, like a soldier.—

While the guns & pistols are popping around me, drums beating; & temperance squadrons marching, to say nothing of orations & all that, I have poured out all this inane gossip, that neither your eyes or patience can stand without painful effort.—

You see, I count upon the Dictator having laid aside much of his official impatience, amidst the green lawns & quiet shades of his beautiful Ashland. . . .

ALS. Henry Clay Memorial Foundation, Lexington, Ky. 1. Speech in Lexington, June 9, 1842. 2. Morehead to Clay, July 2, 1842. 3. On June 29, 1842, of the provisional or little tariff. See Clay to Letcher, Jan. 6, 1842. 4. On June 24 the Senate had amended the "provisional" or "little" tariff bill to postpone from July 1, 1842, to August 1, 1842, both the reduction of the tariff rates due under the Compromise Tariff of 1833 and the distribution of public land sales revenues to the states. The House concurred in this the following day. See Clay to Letcher, Jan. 6, 1842. 5. Clay to Letcher, Jan. 6, 1842. 6. On July 1, 1842, Sen. James F. Simmons (Whig, R.I.), chairman of the Committee on Manufactures, made an elaborate report accompanied by a bill fixing a schedule of duties. The report called for a tariff which would provide sufficient revenue for the needs of government with protection as an incidental result. It emphasized the need for home valuation of goods [Clay to Smith, July 10, 1842] and detailed the specific method by which this would be done. In addition, it recommended repeal of the 20% proviso (Sixth Section) of the Distribution Act of 1841 [Clay to Letcher, Jan. 6, 1842]. For the report, which included the proposed tariff bill, see *Sen. Docs.*, 27 Cong., 2 Sess., no. 340, pp. 1-46. 7. The bill entitled "An Act to Repeal the Proviso to the Sixth Section of . . . 'An Act to Appropriate the Proceeds of the Sales of the Public Lands . . . Approved September fourth, 1841,' " was reported in the House by the Committee on Public Lands on August 25, 1842, and passed the House the following day by a vote of 104 to 86. It was reported to the Senate on August 26 and passed on August 30 by a vote of 23 to 19. Tyler pocket-vetoed this bill [Clay to Letcher, June 24, 1842]. Of the 12 New England senators, 7 voted for the bill, while 25 out of 40 representatives from that section voted for it. U.S. Sen., *Journal*, 27 Cong., 2 Sess., 613, 626, 631, 640, 645; U.S. H. of Reps., *Journal*, 27 Cong., 2 Sess., 1409, 1411, 1423, 1468. 8. Adams addressed the House on July 4 "in severe and caustic examination" of Tyler's veto of the provisional tariff (remarks not recorded). *Cong. Globe*, 27 Cong., 2 Sess., 717. 9. For Everett, a representative from Vermont, see *BDAC*. For the impeachment movement, see Clay to Mangum, July 11, 1842. 10. An "Act to Limit the Sale of the Public Stock to Par, and to Authorize Treasury Notes . . ." was reported by the House Ways and Means Committee on August 26, 1842. It was amended and passed on August 29 by a vote of 115 to 38. The Senate received it on August 29 and passed it on August 31 by a vote of 19 to 9; Tyler signed it the same day. This act provided that no stock authorized to be issued for a loan under the Loan Act of 1841 [Clay to Ewing, July 13, 1841] or the Loan Extension Act of 1842 [Remark in Senate, August 18, 1841] should be sold below par. If it could not be sold at or above par, the secretary of the treasury was "authorized to issue Treasury notes in lieu of so much thereof as cannot be thus negotiated, to an amount not exceeding six millions of dollars." U.S. H. of Reps., *Journal*, 27 Cong., 2 Sess., 1424, 1442-43, 1481; U.S. Sen., *Journal*, 27 Cong., 2 Sess., 637-38, 649; 5 *U.S. Stat.*, 581-82. 11. Clay to Letcher, June 24, 1842. 12. Clay to James B. Clay, Dec. 10, 1841; Mangum to Clay, June 15, 1842. 13. For Gen. Duncan Lamont Clinch, oft-time North Carolina Whig congressman, see *BDAC*. 14. Exactly what negotiations Tyler and Wright were conducting at this time is not known; however, they probably involved Tyler's attempt to win the Democratic presidential nomination in 1844. It is known that in March, 1844 the president offered to appoint Wright to the Supreme Court, but Wright, who was himself often mentioned as a compromise candidate for the Democrats, not only refused the offer but also took himself out of consideration for the presidency and subsequently rejected the convention's nomination for vice president because he opposed its stance in favor of Texas annexation. In addition, it was believed by early 1843 that the Calhoun and Tyler forces had struck a bargain to unite in support of Tyler in 1844 and Calhoun in 1848, and some newspapers in Virginia called for a ticket of Calhoun for president and Wright for vice president. Wright remained committed throughout to Van Buren's nomination. John A. Garraty, *Silas Wright* (New York, 1942), 234-40, 263-65, 272-73, 280-81; Charles H. Ambler, "Virginia and the Presidential Succession, 1840-1844," in *Essays in American History Dedicated to Frederick Jackson Turner* (New York, 1910), 177; Mary Cameron Kennedy, "Silas Wright And New York Politics, 1795-1847," Ph.D. dissertation, University of Chicago, 1950, pp. 237-46; Wiltse, *John C. Calhoun: Sectionalist*, 114. 15. While the exact nature of Stevenson's "*leakings*" is not known, Stevenson was working for his own nomination for vice president. In this, he had the support of Thomas Ritchie and the Richmond Junto which at this time favored Van Buren for the presidency. Subsequently, Stevenson, Ritchie, and the Junto turned against Van Buren because he refused to support the annexation of Texas. Francis F. Wayland, *Andrew Stevenson, Democrat and Diplomat 1785-1857* (Philadelphia, 1949), 221; Ambler, "Virginia and the Presidential Succession," 176, 180-81. 16. Walter Forward resigned as secretary of the treasury on March 3, 1843, and John C. Spencer resigned as secretary of war on March 7. The following day Spencer was named to replace Forward as the secretary of the treasury, while James Madison Porter, a Pennsylvania Democrat who had served in the War of 1812 and whose brother was governor of Pennsylvania, was appointed secretary of war. Webster resigned as secretary of state on May 8, 1843, and was replaced by Attorney General Hugh S. Legaré the following day. When Legaré died on June 20, 1843, Tyler moved Secretary of the Navy Abel P. Upshur into the State Department. Kane, *Facts About the Presidents*, 70; Baxter, *Daniel Webster*, 366. For the politics of the J.M. Porter appointment, as well as that of the 1843 Cabinet shuffle in general, see Lambert, *Presidential Politics in the United States*, 87-90. 17. Tyler had vetoed two national bank bills during the previous session of Congress [Tyler to Clay, April 30, 1841], had recently vetoed the "provisional" or "little" tariff bill, and was expected to veto the "great" or "permanent" tariff bill [Clay to Letcher, Jan. 6, 1842], which he did. 18. Ashburton to Clay, April 11, 1842. 19. For Calhoun's attempts to win the Democratic presidential nomination in 1844, see Wiltse, *John C. Calhoun: Sectionalist*, 89-149. 20. For Morris and Goode, both Ohio Whig congressmen who did not seek reelection in 1842, see *BDAC*. 21. For James Irvin (1800-62), a Whig congressman from Pennsylvania, see *BDAC* and *CAB*. 22. Clay to McKennan, May 31, 1842. 23. *Ibid.* 24. The words "three" and "four" have been stricken and the numerals "2" and "3" interlined above. 25. Facetious reference to "Dictator" Clay.

From D. Austin Muir *et al.*, New York City, July 4, 1842. Report that they have been appointed as a special committee of the Democratic Whig Young Men of New York to convey to him news of his "unanimous & enthusiastic nomination" on June 22 for the presidency of the United States, by the Democratic Whig party of New York City and County. State that "so intimately interwoven has your own history been with that of the U. States for the thirty years last past, & so legible upon its pages is the impress of your genius, your patriotism, & your labours, that we feel proud of rallying around the Whig Standard under your guidance, & of pledging ourselves to you and to the world, to do battle manfully in your behalf, 'without surrender and without compromise.' " Describe in detail the many reasons "we desire your elevation to the Presidency," and "solicit your acceptance of the nomination." Ask for a reply. ALS. DLC-TJC (DNA, M212, R10).

Muir was probably the David A. Muir, clerk, who resided at 822 Greenwich in New York City. Thomas Longworth (ed.), *Longworth's American Almanac: New-York Register, and City Directory*. New York, 1840. For the Whig meeting held at New York City's National Hall on June 22, 1842, which nominated Clay for President, see Washington *Daily National Intelligencer*, June 25, 1842.

From Leverett Saltonstall, Washington, July 7, 1842. Acknowledges Clay's letter of June 7 and apologizes for his delay in answering it. Explains that he has been "excessively engaged" in the tariff and other issues which have "required of me great labor. . . . And, after all . . . our labors, it is to be feared, will have been in vain." Continues: "The President seems to be fatally bent on mischief, or *left*, as the good folks in N. E. say, to go on to his own destruction (& what is worse) to do what he can for the destruction of those who shouted him to power. The Revenue bill [Clay to Letcher, January 6, 1842] is in his hands, and we are in a state of agonizing anxiety. What a fate we have had! We are just where we were a year ago, when on Monday, the day after our visit to the Ship Delaware, the great subject of speculation was, whether he would sign the Bank bill [Tyler to Clay, April 30, 1841]. Some think he will sign—the course of duty is so plain—but others—most—think he will return it to the House—yes—that he will veto a *revenue* bill, because he does not like the particular mode in which Congress has thought best to provide the ways & means of carrying on the Government! Monstrous! But what is there to be done?" Says he once thought "Congress would not adjourn without passing some revenue bill," but is no longer optimistic that an agreement can be reached.

Predicts that failure to enact a revenue bill will result in government bankruptcy "and alarm, confusion & embarrassment will be spread over the Country, particularly the N. E. States, & Mass more than any other. If the question was not *vital* to the Govt and the Country, I would not yield a hair's breadth to such infamous executive assumption and abuse of power. Neither would I, if it was Jackson, at the head of a mighty party riding rough-shod over the Constitution—but who is J. T.? A weak—passionate—headstrong vain man, with no party, except such office-holders as dare not say their souls are their own, and a contemptable guard of half a dozen at most, in the house, one of whom, I am sorry to say it, is from Massa[chuset]ts [Caleb Cushing]—Under these circumstances, I cannot but think it the lesser evil, to pass, if we can without division among ourselves, some bill, which will provide for the wants of the Govt, & revive in some degree, the prosperity of our Country. It will be a bitter bill to take. It would be much more agreeable to my feelings to go home at once—but would the people understand that course? Would they not be made to think that it proceeded from our obstinate clinging to the *distribution*, at the expense of a revenue and tariff bill? I fear so."

Congratulates Clay "on being removed from this scene of strife & confusion, & at rest . . . amidst the quiet shades of Ashland—in the beloved circle of family & friends."

Concludes with the observation that the Salem [Mass.] *Register* "was the first to raise that flag, under which I hope we shall go on again to victory." ALS. DLC-John J. Crittenden Papers (DNA, M212, R20).

To James Erwin, July 9, 1842. Expresses "surprize and mortification . . . at the protest of the two acceptances of Mr. Woods for $6000 and $4000." Says he was not prepared for this, because he had "taken the precaution to obtain his acceptances of your bills before I negotiated them." ALS. NcD. Woods not identified.

To OLIVER H. SMITH Lexington, July 10, 1842

I thank you for your kind letter which affords evidence of your friendly recollection. I am delighted to hear of the fine spirit which prevails among the Whigs in Congress, notwithstanding the perfidy of the President.[1] I am also gratified to learn that they will pass a good permanent Tariff.[2] I sincerely hope, in the new aspect which the question has assumed, that is whether laws shall emanate from Congress, or from Mr. Tyler—our Georgia friends will rally around the independence of the Legislature. I think that if this permanent tariff also shall receive the veto, the next step which I understand is in contemplation, that of passing a tariff, limited to 20 per cent. with a provision for a good home valuation is wise and judicious.[3] I think Congress ought not to adjourn until it passes a tariff, or demonstrates to the country that it can not pass one without a surrender of its constitutional independence. You will be threatened with a veto. But disregarding all such threats, I would vote for that measure which according to my own sense of duty, I thought right, whatever may be the opinion of Mr. Tyler: that is the only course by which you can secure your own approbation, and the support of the country. Present my best respects to your colleague, and to your neighbor Mr. [Jabez W.] Huntington, of Connecticut.[4]

Copy. Printed in Oliver H. Smith, *Early Indiana Trials: and Sketches, Reminiscences*, 258-59. 1. Reference to Tyler's June 29 veto of the so-called "little" or "provisional" tariff bill of June 25. See Clay to Letcher, Jan. 6 and June 24, 1842. 2. For the so-called "great" or "permanent" tariff bill of August 5, 1842, vetoed by Tyler on August 9, see *ibid.* 3. Sections 16 and 17 of the 1842 tariff bill [5 *U.S. Stat.*, 548-67, espec. 563-64] provided for home valuation, that is having the value of imported goods ascertained by the United States at the port of entry. See also Clay to Letcher, Jan. 6 and June 24, 1842. 4. For Huntington, see *BDAC*.

To Henry Clay, Jr., Louisville, Ky., July 11, 1842. Sends a "confidential" letter, "the perusal of which may interest and amuse you." Asks if a deposit from "Dr. [Frederick] Gilmer of Missouri" has been made "to my credit at the Bank of K[entucky]." ALS. Henry Clay Memorial Foundation, Lexington, Ky. See Gilmer to Clay, October 6, 1841, and July 29, 1842; also, Clay to Russell, July 27, 1842.

To WILLIE P. MANGUM Lexington, July 11, 1842

I received your agreeable favor of the 4h. If as you characterized it, your letter was full of gossip, I found it instructive, interesting and amusing gossip. I read it, of course confidentially, to Messrs. [Robert P.] Letcher and [Thomas] Metcalfe yesterday, they happening to be here, and they were both highly gratified. Letcher remarked that there was some good reading in that letter.

I hear, with inexpressible satisfaction, that Mr. Tyler's last silly Veto,[1] far from shaking the constancy of the Whigs has only served to excite there indignation and to consolidate their strength. That is its natural effect; and I am delighted that it has been produced. The Whig party bearded the old Lion, amidst his loudest roars. Surely it will not give way, or suffer itself to be frightened by the pranks of a Monkey.

You ought not in my opinion to think of adjourning until a good Tariff be passed,[2] or the House impeaches Mr. Tyler.[3] You need not be apprehensive of popular dissatisfaction on account of the length of the Session. The people will see who has been the cause of it; and one or the other branch of the above alternative will satisfy all.

[John J.] Crittenden and other friends unite with you in assuring me that you will pass a good permanent Tariff, including a repeal of the Land restriction.[4] That is exactly right. It may produce another Veto. No matter. The more Veto's now of right measures the better. And I like also the idea of passing a Tariff with 20 per Cent and a good home valuation,[5] if he should send another Veto. Give my respects to my friend [James F.] Simmons and tell him that I think my praises of R. Island in my Barbecue Speech[6] were worth the compliment of his sending me one of his Reports.[7] I have not yet seen it. In the event of the latter measure being proposed I hope our friends will not divide on what should be the elements of the Home value. Calhoun, if listened to, will theorize you to death. The Home value is the fair cost of an article in the American market to the American Consumer. It is of no consequence what are the component parts of that value—original cost of the fabric, freight, insurance, commissions, duties—all these combined make up the sum of that value, and you can no more exclude one of these items, in the estimate of that value, than you can the others. Least of all, can you exclude duties, which more frequently do not than do incorporate themselves with the value of goods.

Ask [George] Evans, [Horace] Everett, Simmons, if I am not right in this analysis.

Should these Veto's continue, I really think that the House ought seriously to consider what virtue there is in that dormant power of Impeachment in the Constitution. No matter that the Loco's will rally around the President in the Senate & in the House. The more complete the evidence shall be of their thorough identification with him the better for us the worse for them. . . .

ALS. NcD. 1. Of the "little" or "provisional" tariff bill on June 29. See Clay to Letcher, Jan. 6, 1842. For the veto message, see *MPP*, 4:180-83. 2. Clay to Letcher, Jan. 6, 1842. 3. For the Whig movement to impeach Tyler, including the use of the Hitchcock Report [Remark in Senate, June 12, 1841] among the charges leveled against the president, see Lonie E. Maness and Richard D. Chesteen, "The First Attempt at Presidential Impeachment: Partisan Politics and Intra-Party Conflict at Loose," *PSQ* (Winter, 1980), 10:51-62. John Minor Botts (Whig, Va.) spoke in the House on July 11, 1842, in favor of impeaching Tyler (erroneously reported in the July 14th issue of the Washington *Daily National Intelligencer* as occurring on July 10 and subsequently repeated as such in *Niles' Register* and by various historians). Botts revived the matter in Jan., 1843, following his defeat for reelection to the 28th Congress, preferring numerous charges against the president and offering a resolution calling for the appointment of a committee to investigate the charges. The resolution was defeated on Jan. 10, 1843, by a vote of 127 to 83. *Cong. Globe*, 27 Cong., 2 Sess., 742-43; *ibid.*, 27 Cong., 3 Sess., 134; Chitwood, *John Tyler*, 303. For Botts, see *BDAC*. 4. Clay to Letcher, Jan. 6 and June 24, 1842. 5. Clay to Smith, July 10, 1842. 6. Speech in Lexington, June 9, 1842. 7. Mangum to Clay, July 4, 1842.

To HENRY A.S. DEARBORN Lexington, July 13, 1842

I am obliged by your friendly letter; and I am highly gratified to learn that a just conception of Mr. Tyler's perfidy begins to prevail in Massachusetts. There were not wanting persons at a distance who believed that a disposition existed in your State, if not to approve, at least to abstain from all condemnation of his course. Some circumstances seemed to give countenance to this impression. I did not myself entertain such an opinion; and I am rejoiced to learn that unequivocal *demonstrations* are about to be given of its fallacy.[1]

Judging from all accounts that reach me, there will be a cordial and enthusiastic union of the Whig party. I am very grateful for the direction which it is taking towards me; but, instructed by experience, I shall not allow myself to be too much transported, but look on with calm composure.

I received your kind letter early in the Session of Congress, and did not answer it from the cause which you conjectured.

On the question of the Vice Presidency, I do not think it would be proper or right for me to indicate any preference. This reserve does not make it improper for me to say that Govr. [John] Davis is highly thought of by our friends every where, and that I do not see any objections to manifestations of public opinion in his favor.[2]

ALS. ICN. 1. On Sept. 14, 1842, the Massachusetts Whig convention met in Boston and nominated Clay for president and John Davis for vice president. They also declared their "full and final separation" from the Tyler administration. Bartlett, *Daniel Webster*, 181; *Niles' Register* (Sept. 17, 1842), 63:48. 2. Ohio Whigs met at Carthage on August 3, 1842, and nominated Clay for president and John Davis for vice president as did the Ohio State Whig convention when it met in Newark on August 24. See Clay to Ewing, July 24, 1842. Winfield Scott, John McLean, Daniel Webster, and John M. Clayton were among those mentioned as possible Whig vice presidential candidates in 1844. Although Clay refused to endorse anyone publicly, he seems to have preferred Clayton [Clay to Clayton, August 8, 1842] who was nominated by a convention in his home state of Delaware. However, at the Whig National convention a letter was read from Clayton, withdrawing his name from consideration unless there was "a general expression of agreement to its adoption." Those actually nominated at the national convention were John Sergeant [Pa.], Millard Fillmore [N.Y.], John Davis [Mass.], and Theodore Frelinghuysen [N.J.]. With 138 votes required for nomination, the first ballot stood: Sergeant–38; Fillmore–53; Davis–83; Frelinghuysen–101. After the second ballot Sergeant withdrew; and on the third ballot Frelinghuysen was nominated by 155 votes to 76 for Davis and 40 for Fillmore. Van Deusen, *Henry Clay*, 336; Poage, *Henry Clay*, 108-11; Schlesinger, *History of U. S. Political Parties*, 1:421-23. For Frelinghuysen, see *BDAC*.

From H. Hays & Co., Louisville, July 13, 1842. Present Clay with "a plough of our manufacture, as a testimonial of our respect and esteem for the great advocate of protection of domestic manufacturers." State that the form of the plough was a Kentucky discovery "and its manufacture of Kentucky materials." Believe "the people of the United States will, at no distant day, place you in a situation where your eminent abilities will be devoted . . . to the advancement of the three great elements of the prosperity of the nation—agriculture, commerce and manufactures." Copy. Printed in *The Dollar Farmer* (August, 1842), 1:30-31.

Writing from Lexington on July 21, 1842, Clay thanked them for the "beautiful article," saying that "It is the more acceptable . . . because the model of it is a Kentucky invention, and it is wrought from Kentucky materials." Notes that "Among my earliest recollections, is that of having, when a boy, followed the plough." *Ibid.* H. Hays (or Hayes) & Co. was located on the corner of Main and Hancock Streets in Louisville. Louisville *Daily Journal*, June 30, 1842.

From "A True Northern Friend," New York, July 13, 1842. Praises Clay at length, noting that his career has been "too brilliant to escape envy—too patriotic to escape detraction—too fearless to escape opposition—too upright and honest to escape the contumely and bitter hate of those, who love power more than justice—falsehood more than truth—and who would sacrifice to the Shibboleth of party, the best interests of their common Country." Adds: "*All honor to 'the Star of the West'*. I trust it will not long be permitted to revolve in its distant orbit—I trust it will not soon be permitted to set—but may *He* who rules over all yet cause it to rise to our political zenith, and dispel the cloud of darkness which hangs over our once prosperous and happy, but now debased and injured Country; and by its genial influence and mighty power, restore it to its former glorious and proud condition."

Notes that "Ladies, excluded by Law from a voice in the councils of the Nation, have consequently no political influence. It is right that it should be so. Their duties lie in a different direction, and their happiness is drawn from a different source. But Ladies are not excluded from feeling a deep interest in the welfare of their country, and no law, and no physical incapacity, imaginary or real, prevents them from rendering it service by calling upon *Him* who overrules its destinies. . . . This is a *canvassing* which surely can be disapproved by none, and which compromises neither sex nor station. On this great source, then, of Power and Mercy, do I rely; and daily do I offer up my supplications that *God* will open up the eyes of this great Nation of freemen to their true interests, and in good time, cause them to place the Government in the hands of *one* to whom all anxious eyes and honest hearts are now turned." Apologizes for "so long a letter, written by a lady, without any apparent motive," but "I have thought it might possibly tinge a passing moment with a ray of pleasure, to be assured, that although your Country-Women cannot serve you at the Ballot-box, they can, and do, remember you at the Altar." ALS. DLC-HC (DNA, M212, R5). Printed in Colton, *Clay Correspondence*, 4:461-63.

From JOHN J. CRITTENDEN Washington, July 15, 1842

Our friend [John M.] Botts is *passionately* resolved on an Impeachment of the President[1]—I beleive that the very fact of his taking such a lead in the matter, has had the effect of checking or repressing, to some extent, the tendency, that was apparent, to such a result. Bott's ardour, & the strong personal feelings that are ascribed to him, alarm the more timid & prudent, and they do not feel safe or confident in following him in so responsible & delicate an affair.

Besides, it is considered a little premature, at present, when we have another Veto impending[2]—Botts is dissatisfied at not finding all the Whigs concurring with him, and, I am just told has written to you on the subject—His *discretion*, you know, is the least of his vertues, and you should, I think, answer him very *carefully* and very cautiously—He could hardly forbear to use your name and authority as a sanction for his course—And I should consider it as *most unfortunate* and *injurious* to have your name mixed up in this matter.

My feelings against Tyler are strong—But I doubt the policy of impeaching him—He would be aquitted, & his aquital might be considered as an aquital of his *offenses*, by a country that now condemns him. A vote of a *want* of *confidence*[3] amounts almost, to an impeachment in all its moral consequences.

We have just recd intelligence of the election in N. Orleans[4]—It is most cheering, and will serve to increase the confidence of your friends, & to augment the tide that is now running in your favour.

Nothing has occurred to change or disturb my convictions—that we shall pass the permanent Tariff, with a reservation of the land fund to the States, and that Tyler will veto it.[5] "Clouds & darkness" rest upon all beyond that—If our Tariff friends from the North can be reconciled to it, we will as the last alternative, pass a bill, on [James F.] Simmons's plan, with a duty of 20 pr cent. on the home valuation.[6]

I received yesterday your letter of the 10th Inst, and, as the merchants say, its contents are noted—

I have this moment seen our friend Abbott Lawrence, and, happening to tell him I was writing to you, he bids me to say "that there is a sort of a ground swell going on in Massachusetts in your favour"—And as to the negotiation with Ashburton,[7] in which you know he is engaged as a sort of auxiliary, he say[s], "that tho' there have been great difficulties in the way, he sees light ahead, & hopes for favourable results in a *few days*."

With the conclusion of this negotiation I think it very probable, from what I hear, that Webster will retire from the Cabinet, whether into private life, or into some other office, is more doubtful.[8]

Heaven knows when we shall get away from here—The best conjecture is that it will be about the 15th of the next month, but that must depend on contingencies.[9]

ALS. DLC-John J. Crittenden Papers (DNA, M212, R20). Written from Senate Chamber. 1. Clay to Mangum, July 11, 1842. 2. Of the "great" or "permanent" tariff bill of August 5, 1842, which Tyler vetoed, because it contained a distribution clause to which he objected. See Clay to Letcher, Jan. 6, 1842; also Tyler's veto message of August 9, 1842, in *MPP*, 4:183-89. 3. Clay to Mangum, July 11, 1842. There was no subsequent movement for a vote of confidence. 4. In the Louisiana state elections, held July 4, 1842, the Whigs carried New Orleans; however, Democrat Alexander Mouton defeated Whig Henry Johnson for the governorship by a vote of 9,716 to 8,204. *BDGUS*, 2:562. Whigs won control of the state senate by a margin of 9 seats to 8 for the Democrats and the house by 34 to 26. *Niles' Register* (July 30, 1842), 62:342. 5. Clay to Letcher, Jan. 6, 1842. 6 *Ibid.*; also Mangum to Clay, July 4, 1842; Clay to Smith, July 10, 1842. 7. Ashburton to Clay, April 11, 1842. 8. Morehead to Clay, July 2, 1842. 9. Saltonstall to Clay, July 7, 1842.

To JOHN J. CRITTENDEN Lexington, July 16, 1842

Your favor of the 9h. is received. You ask whether there may not be danger, in the event of another Veto upon the permanent Tariff of some of our most ardent friends of a Tariff yielding the distribution?[1] I hope not. Acting together in the passage of the bill; the indignation which another Veto will excite; the public manifestation of disapprobation of the first, & the still stronger disapprobation which will be exhibited of the second; the confusion which has been occasioned in the collection of the Revenue, by the last Veto[2]—all these circumstances combined will, I trust knit you together, consolidate your strength, and prevent desertion.

I think you can not give up distribution, without a disgraceful sacrifice of Independence. The moral prejudice of such a surrender, upon the character of the party and upon our institutions would be worse than the disorder & confusion incident to the failure to pass a Tariff, great as that disorder and confusion would be. It would be to give up the Legislative power into the hands of the President. And would expose you to the scorn, contempt and derision of the People & of our opponents. The disorder & confusion would continue but for a short time, until Congress met again, or were called together, and then let them pass just such another Tariff as he had Veto[e]d. The occasion calls for the greatest firmness. And do not apprehend that the People will desert you, or take part with Mr. Tyler. They will do no such thing.

When the Veto comes back, the Loco's will probably vote with the President.[3] That will identify them still further with him, and as, by their vote, they could enable you to pass the bill against the Veto, they will have to share with him the odium of its defeat.

But, if in the contingency which has been supposed, some few of our friends should desert, let them go. They will find it difficult to sustain themselves against the storm which will raise around their heads.

If they go, they can effect nothing but by an union with the whole Loco party, and thus attempting to pass a good Tariff, without distribution. Now I suppose it will be impractical to carry the whole Locofoco party or enough of them with the deserters to pass such a Tariff.

In every view of it, I think our friends ought to stand up firmly & resolutely to distribution.

The more Vetoes the better now; assuming that the measures Veto'd are right.

The inevitable tendency of events is to impeachment; but nothing ought to be done inconsiderately or without full consultation.[4] I was sorry therefore to see our friend [John M.] Botts allow himself to be drawn out prematurely by Mr. [Caleb] Cushing.[5]

As to a vote of want of confidence,[6] it would be a right thing, if you will resolve to follow it up with more stringent means. The idea of such a vote is drawn from English usage. And there if ministers do not resign, after it is given, the vote is followed by other more efficient proceedings. Here John Tyler & John Jones would laugh at your Vote, if you stopt there. They would pass a vote of want of confidence in you.

It would not do to move such a Vote in the Senate, because it is the Tribunal to try impeachments.

It should be confined, if moved, to the House. I am afraid that you would not effect the object of a more thorough identification between the Locos & Tyler. They would go off upon the ground of its being irregular, & unconstitutional. And would say that you ought to impeach.

If a vote of want of confidence could be carried by the union of the great body of both parties, its effect would be very great. If it can be carried in the House, without any splitting of our party, *and nothing better can be done,* I should think it advisable.

You may shew these views, if you think them worth any thing, to the Speaker [John White] & your Colleague [James T. Morehead] and to Genl. [Willis] Green.

ALS. DLC-John J. Crittenden Papers (DNA, M212, R20). 1. Clay to Letcher, Jan. 6, 1842. 2. Of June 29, 1842. See *MPP*, 4:180-83. See also Clay to Letcher, June 24, 1842. 3. On August 17, 1842, the House, by a vote of 92 for passage and 87 against, failed to override Tyler's veto of August 9 [*MPP*, 4:183-89] of the "permanent" tariff bill. U.S. H. of Reps., *Journal*, 27 Cong., 2 Sess., 1342. 4. Clay to Mangum, July 11, 1842. 5. *Ibid.* In a July 6, 1842, speech in the House defending Tyler's right to submit his reasons for signing the apportionment bill [Clay to Adams, July 24, 1842], Cushing had taunted Botts by saying, "Suppose . . . the gentleman from Virginia [Mr. Botts] should move an impeachment of the President," adding that he presumed this was not an impossible supposition. Botts then replied that "It was not only a supposable, but a certain case." *Cong. Globe*, 27 Cong., 2 Sess., Appendix, 892. 6. Crittenden to Clay, July 15, 1842.

To EPES SARGENT Lexington, July 16, 1842

I transmit to you herewith some memo:[1] hastily made from memory, without any sort of assistance from a diary. I know not whether any part of it can be weaved into your work,[2] with any advantage; but if it can, I can send you more of such trash.[3] Of course it is submitted to you, to use or to suppress, as you please. It is the rough & first draft, of which I retain no copy. I shall be obliged for the return of this, when you want it no longer. I never kept a diary. I never thought the events of my life worthy of such a record.

The State papers which I have composed, in my opinion, possessing the most permanent value, are: My instructions to our Ministers sent to the Congress of Panama, or rather Tacuyba [*sic,* Tacubaya];[4] the Land report in 1832;[5] and the Report on our differences with France,[6] about the non-fulfillment of her treaty, which threatened, during Genl Jacksons Admon, a rupture between the two nations. This last report was so highly approved that it obtained the unanimous concurrence of the Senate—composed as it was of a large part of members bitterly opposed to me.[7]

I say again to you, that I would not be hurried, both on your account and mine.

ALS. KyU. 1. Not found. 2. Clay to Sargent, July 2, 1842. 3. On August 11, 1842, Clay again wrote Sargent, sending "some further memoranda" which will be "the last with which I will annoy you." Has not yet heard "of your reception of my last communications, relating to the Compromise Act [8:604, 619-22, 626-27], Negotiations at Ghent [7:727-28 (index)] &c." ALS. Henry Clay Memorial Foundation, Lexington, Ky. 4. See 5:313-44. 5. For the report and Clay's defense of it, see 8:494, 539-41. 6. See 8:754. 7. For other of his papers which Clay thought important to his 1844 campaign for the presidency, see Clay to Sargent, August 20, 1842.

To NOAH NOBLE Lexington, July 18, 1842

I received your favor of the 12h. You will have seen what I said, in my Speech at the Lexn. Barbecue,[1] about leaving the People to the undisturbed exercise of their choice, in regard to a Chief Magistrate, my resolution to remain passive &c. Now I must bear all that in mind, if I should be, as seems probable, the Whig Candidate.

As to the idea of my traversing the whole Union it would be physically impossible, and if I attempted such a tour it would destroy me physically.

The only ground upon which a visit to Indianapolis can be justified would be my former engagement, the fulfillment of which is desired or insisted on by my friends. And, if such be the fact, I repeat what I said in my former letter that I will go there some time in October.[2] If I do go, I hope it will be promulgated that the visit is made on that ground. And I should also have to require from the goodness of my friends that I should not be expected to visit any other place.

There is time enough to think of the matter, and, if it be finally decided on, to make the necessary arrangements. . . .

ALS. In. 1. Speech in Lexington, June 9, 1842. 2. For Clay's trip to Indiana in Oct., 1842, see Van Deusen, *Henry Clay*, 361-62, and Speech in Richmond, Indiana, Oct. 1, 1842. The latter was the so-called "Reply to Mendenhall." For Hiram Mendenhall (1801-52)—North Carolina-born millwright, carpenter, blacksmith, Quaker, and Abolitionist—see Ebenezer Tucker, *History of Randolph County, Indiana* . . . (Chicago, 1882), 338.

To JAMES B. SWAIN Lexington, July 18, 1842

I have received your letter communicating your purpose of publishing an edition of my Speeches.[1] You are right in supposing that I consider them public property, and that any Citizen has a right to publish them who thinks proper to do so. In the event of an edition of them, I feel a solicitude only on two points: 1st. that they should be accurately published, and 2dly. that the publishers should find in the sale of the work an ample indemnity for their labor trouble and expense.

You are aware that a very cheap but incomplete Edition has been recently published at Cincinnati.[2] Like its predecessor published in Philada.[3] some years ago it does not embrace all the Speeches I had made, at the time of the publication, worth preserving, if indeed any I ever made be worth preserving.

You are not unapprized, I presume, either that Mr. D[aniel]. Mallory of your City [New York] entertains some intention of publishing an Edition.[4] Mr. P[hilip]. R. Fendall[5] of Washington City some years ago contemplated the same object, and made a large collection of copy and material with that view. Having delayed the execution of his design, John O. Sargent Esq., during the last year, embraced the same object and received Mr. Fendalls collection from him; but in consequence of his professional engagements, and in consequence of Mr. Mallory's claiming a prior right to make the publication, Mr. Sargent passed over to him all the collection which he possessed, including that of Mr. Fendall, and Mr. M. has now possession of it.[6]

I think Mr. M. is mistaken in supposing, if he does suppose, that he has any *exclusive* right to make the publication. I, some years ago consented to his publication of them,[7] just as I should have consented to the publication of them by any respectable Citizen, who chose to apply to me for that purpose; but I had no right to give, & certainly did not intend to invest him with, any exclusive priveledge.

But Mr. Mallory is a very good person (at least I always so regarded him) has been long and zealously attached to me and is I believe poor. It would give me pain and mortification, if any collision should arise between him and any other friend about the publication, or if he should experience any loss or disappointment.

I hope therefore that there will be some friendly understanding or amicable arrangement between you and him. There can be no necessity for two Editions, if there be for one, of the work executed in an expensive manner.

I shall be happy to render you any assistance in my power. It would be well for you to obtain, if you can procure them, the Philada. & Cincinnati Editions. In these and in Niles's Register, you will find all you want. In the 32 Vol. page 375 you will see the first speech I made at Lexington;[8] and in the 36 Vol page 399 you will find another Speech that I made there.[9] In the same 36 Vol. page 39 is one I made at a public dinner at Washn.[10]

The Speech I delivered on the Veto during the present Session of Congress was published without my revisal. I should like to correct and revise it before it is published in any durable collection.

ALS. KyU. 1. Swain published in New York in 1842-43 *The Life and Speeches of the Hon. Henry Clay* (2 vols.). 2. Richard Chambers published in Cincinnati in 1842 *Speeches of the Hon. Henry Clay, of the Congress of the United States.* 3. *The Speeches of Henry Clay Delivered in Congress of the United States; To Which is Prefixed a Biographical Memoir. . . .* Philadelphia, H. C. Carey & I. Lea, 1827. 4. Clay to Sargent, July 2, 1842. 5. See 8:252-53. 6. Clay to Sargent, July 2, 1842. 7. See 8:252-53. 8. On July 12, 1827. See 6:763-79 and *Niles' Register* (August 4, 1827), 32:375-80. 9. Speech at Fowler's Garden, May 16, 1829. See 8:41-54 and *Niles' Register* (August 15, 1829), 36:399-405. 10. On March 7, 1829. See 8:4-6 and *Niles' Register* (March 14, 1829), 36:39-40.

To HILAND HALL Lexington, July 19, 1842

I received your[1] favor with a Copy of the "Tribute to my Country," sent to me by the request of its author, Samuel Elliot Esq.[2] I have looked enough into it to satisfy me that it is the production of a good, sensible and patriotic man. I will thank you to communicate to him my respectful acknowledgments for his interesting work.

I wish I could congratulate you upon the close of the present Session of Congress, after the passage of such good laws as the public interest demands. But I fear the Veto[3] will present an insuperable obstacle to such a termination of your arduous labors.

ALS. CSmH. 1. For Hall, a Vermont congressman and later governor, see *BDAC*. 2. For Elliot (1777-1845), a jurist and writer, see William Stewart Wallace, *A Dictionary of North American Authors Deceased Before 1850* (Toronto, Canada, 1951), 136. Elliot's book, *A Humble Tribute to My Country: or, Practical Essays, Political, Legal, Moral, and Miscellaneous, Including a Brief Account of the Life . . . of General LaFayette,* was published in Boston in 1842. 3. Of the "little" or "provisional" tariff bill of June 25, 1842, vetoed on June 29. See Clay to Letcher, Jan. 6, 1842.

To JOHN M. BERRIEN Lexington, July 21, 1842

I intended before to have congratulated you on the ability with which, all accounts concur in representing you as having acquitted yourself, during the progress of the bill, providing for the enforcement of the Public law,[1] and upon the success of that measure in the Senate. What an extraordinary Opposition the Whigs have to encounter from their opponents in Congress! They will agree to nothing; neither to furnish the supplies needed by Government, nor to fulfill its duties towards foreign powers. And, when a law is passed, in spite of them, they threaten disobedience & nullification! Your colleague,[2] I observe, thought your bill a *contemptible* one—a remark which you best answered by the silence of contempt.

This letter will reach you in a *real* crisis—not one of Mr. Calhouns crises. What will become of Congress & you all? Will you succumb to Mr. Tyler? Or assert the dignity and independence of Congress? I shudder at consequences, but most of [all] at the possible degradation of the Legislative branch.[3]

We could get along with a man who was only fool or knave, or mad; but the extraordinary ocurrence of all three of those qualities combined in one person is intolerable. . . .

ALS. NcU. 1. Berrien had introduced on March 8, 1842, a bill to "Provide further remedial justice in the Courts of the United States." It passed the Senate on July 8, 1842, by a vote of 27 to 17 and the House on August 26 by 92 to 84; it was signed into law on August 29. This bill empowered justices of the Supreme Court to grant writs of habeas corpus when subjects of foreign countries were in the custody of the U.S. See U.S. Sen., *Journal*, 27 Cong., 2 Sess., 209, 460, 644; U.S. H. of Reps., *Journal*, 27 Cong., 2 Sess., 1426; 5 *U.S. Stat.*, 539-40. 2. Alfred Cuthbert (Dem., Ga.) spoke in the House against the bill on July 7, 1842, speech not recorded. *Cong. Globe*, 27 Cong., 2 Sess., 734. 3. If Tyler were to veto the "great" or "permanent" tariff bill, which he did on August 9, 1842. See Clay to Letcher, Jan. 6, 1842.

To JOHN J. CRITTENDEN Lexington, July 21, 1842

I received your letter of the 15h. instant. [John M.] Botts has not written to me. If he should, I shall express to him my serious regret at that movement of his about impeachment.[1] It was, I think ill-timed & injudic[i]ous. No such movement ought to be made, if made at all, without full consultation with friends. I am not surprised at its tendency to repress the spirit of Impeachment. There is cause enough, God knows; but it is a novel proceeding, full of important consequences, present and future; and should not be commenced but upon full consideration, not of one mind only (I dare say Mr. Botts has so considered it) but many minds.

Mr. Tyler will probably Veto the Tariff,[2] and dismiss old Jonathan Roberts.[3] If he should do so, and Congress adjourns without settling the Tariff, there will be a state of feeling among the People that may force Congress to impeach him when it reassembles. In the contingency of his Impeachment, I do not think that his aquittal by the vote *exclusively* of the Locos' would have any bad effect.

In my former letter,[4] I wrote you what struck me about a vote of want of confidence. As a *preliminary* measure, confined to the House, I thought well of it. But as a definitive & final proceeding, without any ulterior measures, I was afraid it would not do much good.

We have lost the Govr. in Louisiana.[5] A Comee. of five gentlemen from that State, which they left the 9h. & 10h. inst. who dined with me yesterday, assure me that that result was owing entirely to the predominance of the Creole feeling & other local causes; and that there cannot be a doubt of the State being Whig & for me.[6]

ALS. NcD. 1. Clay to Mangum, July 11, 1842. See also Crittenden to Clay, July 15, 1842, and Clay to Crittenden, July 16, 1842. 2. Clay to Letcher, Jan. 6, 1842. 3. Clay to Sargent, May 31, 1842. 4. Clay to Crittenden, July 16, 1842. 5. Crittenden to Clay, July 15, 1842. 6. In the 1844 presidential canvass, Polk carried Louisiana and its 6 electoral votes by 13,782 to 13,083. McKee, *National . . . Popular and Electoral Vote*, 56-57.

To CLAY CLUB OF RAPIDES PARISH, LA. Lexington, July 23, 1842

I have received, with very great satisfaction, the letter which you addressed to me last month.[1] You inform me of the establishment of a club to which the honor has been done me of attaching my name, in the parish of Rapides; and, in virtue of a resolution of the club, you have communicated very friendly and flattering sentiments of regard, attachment and confidence towards me. I thank you, cordially, gentlemen, for these gratifying proofs of esteem. They are received with feelings of lively gratitude, and will be cherished with unfading recollection in my memory.

I concur with you in the principles of public policy which ought to prevail in the administration of the general government. Whilst it does not surprise me, it affords me great pleasure to learn, that in the fine cotton growing country in which you reside, surpassed by none in the United States, opinions in favor of the protection of the productions of our own country against the competition, within our own limits, of the rival productions of foreign countries, are making rapid progress. I have always believed that "the interests of each division of the union, as well as the interests of every class and condition of society, are identical; and that the prosperity or adversity of any one of them would be, in a greater or less degree, felt by all." And I have looked forward, with confidence, to the arrival of the period when this great truth would become generally impressed upon the American mind.

In acting upon this policy, our experience has shown how important, stability is, to its successful operation. This will be best secured by moderation and firmness. The tariff of 1828, forced through congress by a combination between pretended friends and undisguised enemies, against the wishes of those who sincerely desired to foster and build up American manufactures, was the principal cause of the unsettled and agitated state of the public mind, which ensued.

With a sound currency of uniform value throughout the union, emanating from and guaranteed by federal authority; with a tariff so adjusted as to afford an adequate revenue, and efficient protection to agriculture, commerce and manufactures; and with the withdrawal of the proceeds of the sales of the public lands from the common treasury, where, in consequence of the fluctuating amount, the policy of the government is liable to sudden and frequent disturbance, we may confidently anticipate the restoration of prosperity.

You do me the honor, gentlemen, to express a wish for my election as president of the U. States. On this subject, I have recently expressed myself so fully at a speech delivered at a barbecue near Lexington, (of which I transmit a copy) that I now have nothing further to add.[2] Whether I shall be a candidate or not, or if a candidate, whether elected or not, I pray you and my friends in the parish of Rapides, whom you represent, to accept my thanks for the friendly feelings towards me by which they are animated.

And I beg that portion of you, who have taken the trouble to come, from so great a distance, to present, in person, to me your note, to accept assurances of my profound acknowledgements, and my lasting gratitude. . . .[3]

Copy. Printed in *Niles' Register* (Sept. 3, 1842), 63:4. 1. In a letter, dated only June, 1842, and written from Alexandria, La., the Clay Club of Rapides Parish wrote Clay that "a large portion of the citizens of this Parish" have "associated themselves together" for the purpose of promoting "your election to the Presidency of the United States in 1844." Indeed, they want to express "from the heart . . . of the great Cotton-growing region of the United States" their support "of the Protective Policy which you have always advocated." Note that the South, like the rest of the nation, is suffering "from the derangements of the currency and the depression of industry and enterprise" brought on by "the departure of our Government from the principles" of the "AMERICAN SYSTEM." Believe that "Your accession" to the presidency "will contribute more than any other event to restore an honest, patriotic, and public . . . spirit to the Administration of the Government." Copy. Printed in Lynchburg *Virginian*, August 18, 1842. 2. Speech in Lexington, June 9, 1842. 3. Printed in *Niles' Register* on the same page as this letter is one from Clay to N. & H. Shaw, dated July 16, 1842, thanking them for a white beaver hat which they had sent him. States: "May the head of that man, who would not desire the protection of his own brethren and fellow citizens against the productions of foreign industry, never be covered with such a hat."

To JOHN Q. ADAMS Lexington, July 24, 1842

In what a sad condition has our unfortunate Country been brought by an unhappy series of events, during the last thirteen years! Embarrassment, distress, ruin prevail among the people, throughout the whole land; and division in our councils, with falsehood, treachery and imbecility in our Chief Magistrate! The contemplation of what we are, what we were, and what we might have been is enough to sicken the heart. But it is our duty not to despair, and to carry our Country safely through all the perils which en compass it, if possible. And, in looking upon the gloomy state of things, now existing at Washington, my hopes concentrate more upon you than upon any other man. In the dispensations of an all wise Providence, it has hitherto so happened in our Country, that, upon every great emergency, some man appeared who was adequate to the service of conducting us safely through the impending danger. On the present occasion that noble office is yours! And I feel encouraging confidence that we shall find deliverance from the exertions which you will make in the present crisis.

I regretted Mr. [John M.] Botts's movement,[1] in respect to an impeachment, because I thought it ill timed, and without concert. The tendency of Mr. Tyler's conduct is manifestly towards an impeachment; and if he perseveres in his course, it may become expedient and proper to ascertain if there be any virtue in that dormant power of the Constitution; but the time has not yet arrived for putting it to the test.

I was highly gratified with your motion for a special Comee. in the case of the apportionment bill; and I anticipate much satisfaction from your exposure of Mr. Tyler's proceeding in filing reasons for his approval of a bill. It was manifestly unconstitutional. Your report has not yet reached me. That motion for a special Comee. and the resolution which you have reported were highly proper in themselves, without reference to any ulterior proceeding; but they were also proper as preliminaries to other more grave proceedings, if they should beco[me] necessary.[2]

The patience, firmness, and union which have been exhibited by the Whigs, during the present Session, are as honorable to them as they are satisfactory to the considerate portion of the Country. How admirably does their conduct contrast with that of their opponents in Congress! Whilst these have, when in power, brought upon the Government every financial difficulty, which it now experiences, and upon the people most of the ills, which now afflict them, they perversely oppose every measure of the Whigs which is brought forward for the public benefit. And, when they fail in Congress, successfully to oppose, by reason and argument, those measures, we behold them encouraging the treachery elsewhere, by which they are defeated. As if the misfortunes of their Country and their Government afforded them just cause of joy and triumph!

I hear that the Tariff which you [House of Representatives] have just passed is to receive the Veto.[3] And I learn, with infinite regret, that some of the Whigs think of giving way to Executive dictation. But I am also informed that you are, where I never doubted you would be, firm and immovably fixed in your purpose of upholding the Constitutional independence of Congress.

We want a Tariff. Both the People and the Government greatly need it; and I sincerely hope that the power of the Veto will not be exercised; but, if it should be, deeply important as a Tariff is, it dwindles into utter insignificance in comparison with the just authority, and Constitutional Indepen[den]ce of, Congress, in the passage of a Revenue bill.

Should the Veto be exercised, the occasion will require all the wisdom, experience & firmness of the members of Congress. And I am sure that you will receive in the same friendly spirit in which I offer any suggestions that occur to me.

It seems to me that, in no contingency, ought the land fund to be abandoned. If the President returns the bill, I would vote for no other bill which did not preserve that fund for distribution among the States.[4] Should it be practicable to pass another Tariff (such for example as Mr. [James F.]

Simmons proposes)[5] leaving the Land fund for distribution, it might be well to pass it. Should Congress adjourn, without being able to pass any Tariff which the President will sanction, upon their re assembling, whether upon his convocation, or at the regular Session, I think it would be right to pass again & send to him just such a bill as he had rejected.

Depend upon it, my dear Sir, that Congress will come out triumphantly, in the contest which the President has most wantonly provoked, if it act with firmness, dignity and perseverance. The People will sustain it. The veto of the temporary Tariff has greatly shocked the public sensibility.[6] And if there should be another Veto, I am deceived, if there will not be awakened a spirit of general indignation which has never, in the same degree, been exhibited in this Country.

I feel persuaded that I shall find an apology, for troubling you with this letter, in the patriotism by which I am sure you are animated.

I pray you to present my friendly respects to Mrs. Adams, to whom Mrs. Clay offers her's also. . . . P.S. I mingle my griefs with your's on account of the death recently of two of the members of your former Cabinet.[7]

ALS. MHi. Letter marked "(Confidential)." 1. Clay to Mangum, Feb. 11, 1842. 2. For the Apportionment bill, see Clay to Crittenden, June 3, 1842. On June 25, 1842, Tyler notified the House of Representatives that he had signed the bill and had sent it to the State Department along with a message [*MPP*, 4:159-60] explaining his reasons for signing despite his belief that the provision requiring the states to form geographical districts for the purpose of electing members of the House was unconstitutional. John Q. Adams, arguing that the action of submitting reasons when approving a bill was itself unconstitutional and was in fact a masked veto, moved for the appointment of a House Select Committee to consider the message. In a speech on June 29, Adams noted that one state had already announced its refusal to comply with the district provision of the act and that other states would probably follow. Thus, he concluded that "this protest or paper from the President would stand among the archives of the Government, to justify them in their course." On July 2 the House passed a resolution of the Select Committee directing the secretary of state to turn over to the House a copy of Tyler's reasons for signing the bill, and on July 16 the committee's report was read and ordered to be printed and to lie on the table. The report accused the president of encouraging states to break the law and of having a personal interest in the organization of the House in the next Congress, because it might be called upon to elect the president (for which Tyler might be a contender) if no candidate won an electoral majority in 1844. *Cong. Globe*, 27 Cong., 2 Sess., 689, 693-94; Adams, *Memoirs of John Quincy Adams*, 11:189, 191, 194-95, 198-99, 201, 207, 210; U.S. H. of Reps., *Journal*, 27 Cong., 2 Sess., 1027-30, 1045, 1047, 1080; *Reports of Committees*, 27 Cong., 2 Sess., no. 909, p. 10. In fact, the states of New Hampshire, Georgia, Mississippi, and Missouri refused to follow the law and elected their representatives for the 28th Congress on a general state-wide, rather than a district, ticket. The House, declaring that the act of July 25, 1842, was not constitutionally binding and that the elections were valid, seated the representatives of those states and struck the protest of the Whigs from its journal. Von Holst, *Constitutional and Political History*, 2:505-9. 3. The "great" or "permanent" tariff which Tyler vetoed on August 9. Clay to Letcher, Jan. 6, 1842. 4. *Ibid*. 5. Mangum to Clay, July 4, 1842. 6. The "little" or "provisional" tariff. Clay to Letcher, Jan. 6, 1842. 7. For the death of Samuel L. Southard, Adams's secretary of the navy, see Clay to Mangum, June 7, 1842. James Barbour, Adams's secretary of war, had died on June 7, 1842.

To THOMAS EWING Lexington, July 24, 1842

I recd. your favor from Cincinnati, and being at a loss where to address you, I direct to your residence.

I should have been very happy to have seen you here, and I am sorry that you did not come.

From others as well as yourself I learn that the Whig prospects are good in Ohio.[1] I rejoice at them, and sincerely hope they may be realized.

You will have seen in my Lexington Speech[2] the ground I have taken in respect to mixing in the popular movements. It was assumed after much consideration, & with the advice of friends. There are so many & such strong considerations—of fitness and propriety, health, convenience, physical impossibility of traversing the Union, difficulty of stopping if one began &c &c—that I do not see how I can depart from that ground. It was to remain passive, and to go no where but upon the calls of business or for health.

I have been exceedingly pressed to go to several States; and if my name should be finally presented as a Candidate, I shall be urged to go to all, if I go to any.

Anxious as I am for the success of our friend [Thomas] Corwin, I do not see how I can with consistency or propriety attend any of your Conventions.[3] To that effect I have already written to him & others.

What events may not the next ten days bring forth at Washington! What solicitude must not you and every patriot feel for the preservation of the independance of Congress![4]

ALS. DLC-Ewing Family Papers (Supp. Roll 2). Addressed to Ewing in New Lancaster, Ohio. 1. In the 1842 Ohio state elections Whigs won 12 seats in the senate to 10 for the Democrats, bringing the total in the senate to 20 Democrats and 14 Whigs. Democrats carried the state house by a margin of 40 to 32. In the gubernatorial race, Democrat Wilson Shannon defeated Whig incumbent Thomas Corwin by a vote of 119,774 to 117,902, with Liberty party candidate, Leicester King, polling 5,134 votes. Weisenburger, *The Passing of the Frontier*, 409-10, 435; *BDGUS*, 3:1,201; Edgar Allen Holt, *Party Politics in Ohio, 1840-1850* (Columbus, O., 1931), 98. See also Clay to Bacon, Oct. 27, 1843. 2. Speech in Lexington, June 9, 1842. 3. A number of Whig conventions were held in 1842. On February 22 the Whigs had met in Dayton and nominated Thomas Corwin for governor. On August 3 about 10,000 Whigs assembled at Carthage and nominated Clay for president and John Davis for vice president. The Whig Young Men's convention met at Newark on August 24 and likewise nominated Clay and Davis. Weisenburger, *The Passing of the Frontier*, 407; *Niles' Register* (Sept. 17, 1842), 63:36; Washington *Daily National Intelligencer*, Feb. 28, 1842. See also Clay to Dearborn, July 13, 1842. 4. Allusion is to the fate of the pending "great" or "permanent" tariff bill of August 5 which Tyler vetoed on August 9 because it had a distribution section in it. Clay to Letcher, Jan. 6, 1842.

To CHARLES CROOK Lexington, July 25, 1842

I received your[1] letter of the 16h. inst and thank you for the friendly interest you so kindly take in my welfare. I agree with you that the condition of our Country and of its government is most deplorable. And I believe that we can only be delivered from the evils which encompass us by great & strenuous exertions and the blessing of Providence. I am afraid that you estimate too highly any in my power

The grave subject, which you so fervently recommend to my serious consideration, does not escape my attention. Undoubtedly prayer—earnest, devout and constant prayer—should be offered up to that God, who can best relieve, protect and preserve us; but I think it would be also wise to omit no honorable endeavors which we can make to serve & sustain our Country, in our respective spheres & vocations.

ALS. DLC-HC (DNA, M212, R5). Copy in ICHi. 1. For Crook, who lived in Baltimore's fourth ward, see Maryland Census, Population Schedule of the Sixth Census of the U.S., 1840, vol. 2 (M704, R159). His occupation is listed as "cotton manufacturer" in the 1842 Baltimore City Directory. Information supplied by Donna Ellis, manuscripts librarian, Maryland Historical Society, Baltimore, Md.

To JACOB GIBSON Lexington, July 25, 1842

I received your letter by my neighbour and friend Mr Henry,[1] and the good account he gives me of you induces me to transmit this answer.

My opinion on the subjects of Slavery and Abolition was fully expressed in the Senate of the U. States in Feb. 1839,[2] and I have seen no reason since to change it. The Speech which I delivered on that occasion may be found in a cheap, altho' imperfect, collection of my Speeches, recently published in Cincinnati,[3] and to that I respectfully refer you. I regret that I have no Copy of it by me, detached from the book, or I would send it to you

I regard the existence of Slavery as an evil. I regret it, and wish that there was not one slave in the U. States.

But it is an evil which, whilst it affects the States only or principally where it abounds, each State, within which it is situated, is the exclusive judge of what is best to be done with it, and no other State has a right to interfere in it. Kentucky has no right to interfere with the Slavery of Virginia; and Ohio has no right to interfere with it in either

The jurisdiction of each State, where slavery exists, is among the reserved rights of the States.[4] Congress possesses no power or authority to abolish it. Congress is invested with no power relating to it, except that which assumes its legitimate and continued existence. As to Slavery, with the exception of the conservative representative and taxing powers of Congress, the States are as much beyond the control of Congress as if they were independent nations, unconnected by any confederative Constitution.

Altho' I believe Slavery to be an evil, I regard it as a far less evil than would arise out of an immediate emancipation of the Slaves of the U. States, and their remaining here mixed up in our Communities. In such a contingency, I believe that a bloody Civil War would ensue, which would terminate only by the extinction of the black race.

It results, from those opinions which I entertain, that I consider the movements of the Abolitionists as altogether unauthorized and most unfortunate. I believe them productive of no good whatever, but attended with positive mischief to both the White and the black races. Of all the modes of separating the free blacks from the rest of the population of the U. States, in my opinion, that of colonizing them in Africa is best. They are then in the abode of their ancestors, in a climate congenial with their constitutions, and with boundless Territorial scope before them. For these and other reasons, I think Africa far preferable to Oregon. An emigrant can be sent to Africa much cheaper than he can be to Oregon. He would there be not only in the home of his forefathers, but he might render great service to the natives of Africa by introducing among them the arts of civilization, and the religion of Christ. He would moreover be secure forever against the progress of the White man, which he would be far from being in Oregon.

I have regretted extremely the agitation of Abolition in the free States. It has done no good, but harm. It will do no good. The great body of Abolitionists, like the great mass of every party, I have no doubt is honest, sincere and humane. Their leaders deceive them, and will endeavor to profit by them. They will seek to ride into public office, and to snatch public honors, upon the delusions which they propagate

Abolition is a delusion, which cannot last. It is impossible it should endure. What is it? In pursuit of a principle—a great principle if you please, it undertakes to tread down and trample in the dust all opposing principles, however sacred. It sets up the right of the people of one State to dictate to the people of other States. It arrays State against State. To make the black man free, it would virtually enslave the white man. With a single idea, some of its partizans rush on blindly, regardless of all consequences. They have dared even to threaten our glorious Union with dissolution. And suppose that unhallowed object achieved, would it emancipate the Slaves? What is their next step? Is it to light up a War between the dissevered parts of the Union, and through blood, devastation & conflagration to march forward to Emancipation? Are they at all sure that through such diabolical means they would be able finally to arrive at their object? No, my friend, let each State and the People of each State take care of their own interests, leaving other States and the People of other States to take care of theirs. We have enough to do in our respective and legitimate spheres of action—enough for the exercise of all the charities and sympathies of our nature.

But what is ultimately to become of Slavery? asks the impatient Abolitionist. I cannot tell him, with any certainty. I have no doubt that the merciful Providence, which permitted its introduction into our Country, against the wishes of our Ancestors, will, according to HIS own good pleasure & time, provide for its mitigation or termination.

In the mean time we have had much to encourage us. Our revolution led to the cessation of the African Slave trade with the U. States. It altogether ceased in 1808. Many States emancipated their slaves, not by the perilous process of an immediate liberation, but by the gradual & cautious proceeding of a slow and regulated emancipation, liberating the offspring at mature age, and leaving the parents in slavery; thus making preparation for the proper use of the liberty which their children were to enjoy. Every where a spirit of humanity was, more and more, infusing itself into the Laws for the regulation of the treatment of Slaves, until it was checked in some places by the agitation of abolition. Some States where the proportion of Slaves was not very great, in comparison with the Whites, were beginning seriously to think about the practicability of a gradual emancipation within their limits; but they too have been checked by the intemperate zeal of Abolitionists. The feasibility of African Colonization has been demonstrated, and the Society, with its limited means, has been quietly prosecuting its noble object.

By some of the means indicated and others hidden from our view, by an all-wise Providence, we may cherish the hope that, if violent abolitionists will cease stirring up strife and agitating the passions, we may ultimately alleviate the evils, if not eradicate the existence of slavery in our land.

The generation that established our Independence achieved a great and glorious work. Succeeding generations have accomplished much in advancing the growth, the power and the greatness of this Nation. We must leave some things to posterity, and among others the task of making adequate provision for the institution of slavery.

In spite of slavery, our arms triumphed in the Revolutionary struggle. And it is not too much to assert that, if Abolition had developed itself then, as it since has done, we should have failed. We should have been unable to form the Confederation, or subsequently to have adopted the present Constitution. In spite of Slavery, we were success[f]ul in the second War with Great Britain. And in neither war, it is a gratifying historical fact, was the enemy able, by all his arts of seduction, to withdraw many slaves from their fidelity. In spite of slavery, we have moved onward in our march to power and greatness, augmenting our population, in a period only co-extensive with that of my own life, from 2½ to seventeen million.

If our Country is now sweltering under the agony of extreme pecuniary distress and embarrassment, it has not been produced by slavery, at least not by black slavery. It has been brought about, I think, by the exercise of arbitrary power, but not that which the master exerts over his black slave.

Let us cease to agitate a topic which divides, distracts & inflames the Community; which tends to array man against man, state against State, and section against section; and which threatens the greatest of all possible Calamities which could befal this People, the dissolution of the union of these States. Let us, in place of discord and dissention, cultivate, peace harmony and good will among the people and the States of this confederacy. And let us recollect that we have other duties—far higher duties—to perform towards our Country, towards posterity and towards the world than even the extirpation of African slavery, however much its original introduction among us is to be deplored.

I have thus, in answer to you[r] enquiries, given you a full candid and unreserved exposition of my opinions & feelings, on the several subjects to which they relate. I hope they will be received and examined in the same friendly & frank spirit in which they are communicated.

ALS. DLC-HC (DNA, M212, R5). Printed in Colton, *Clay Correspondence*, 4:463-66.
1. The 1840 census lists 5 Henrys in Lexington and Fayette County. The city directory for 1838-39 indicates a John Henry who owned property on Jack's Creek Pike 11 miles from Lexington. Editors have not been able to determine which of these is the Mr. Henry to whom Clay refers. Ronald V. Jackson *et al.* (eds.), *Kentucky 1840 Census Index*. Bountiful, Utah, 1978; MacCabe, *Directory of the City of Lexington . . . 1838 & '39*, 127. 2. Speech in Senate, Feb. 7, 1839. 3. Clay to Swain, July 18, 1842. 4. Under the tenth amendment to the U.S. Constitution.

To WILLIAM H. RUSSELL Lexington, July 27, 1842

Many thanks for your acceptable present of Buffalo tongues which I have safely received.

The general rule which I have adopted (see my Barbecue Speech)[1] is to make no visits except such as are required by health or business. It was adopted after much consideration, and with the concurrence of discreet friends. I could not make a tour of the U. States or any considerable portion of them. And the difficulty would be where to begin and where to end. I doubt whether I could survive the delivery of a dozen Speeches made in quick succession, and in the open air. And wherever I go there is an irrepressible curiosity to hear me Speak. If I were to visit some places, and not others to which I might be invited, should I not give as much offense as I could possibly achieve good? At this very time, I am urgently pressed to go to several States, but have hitherto declined. It is possible that I may be compelled to visit one or two, in fulfillment of old engagements which are insisted upon.

I really want very much to see St. Louis and Missouri; but this year I cannot have that satisfaction. Perhaps my private interests may render it expedient that I should go there next year. I am greatly obliged by the kind offer of your hospitality & friendly attentions, of which I should be sure to avail myself, if I go.

My friend Dr. [Frederick] Gilmer has not come up to his engagements. He wrote me that he would certainly deposite the first payment to my credit with the Bank of K. at Louisville; but he has not done it.[2]

Don't forget to attend to the payment of the Taxes upon my land opposite to Alton[3] and upon the 40 Acres at the mouth of Grand river.

Are you not afraid of the frowns of Captn. Tyler? If your office be worth holding I don't think that you pursue the most prudent course to retain it. . . .[4]

ALS. MoSHi. Addressed to Russell "near Fulton Missouri." 1. Speech in Lexington, June 9, 1842. 2. Gilmer to Clay, Oct. 6, 1841, and July 29, 1842; Clay to Henry Clay, Jr., July 11, 1842. 3. Russell to Clay, Feb. 26, 1842. 4. Tyler appointed Russell U.S. marshal for the district of Missouri, and he was confirmed on July 22, 1841. He was removed in 1843, and a replacement, Weston F. Birch, was nominated when Congress reconvened in Dec., 1843; however, this nomination was rejected by the Senate. The position was not officially filled until the confirmation of Robert C. Ewing on Jan. 14, 1845. U.S. Sen., *Executive Journal*, 5:389, 410; 6:197, 309, 329, 352, 369, 380.

To James Duane Doty, Madison, Wisc., July 28, 1842. Thanks him "for the specimens of Prairie Grass seed which you have sent me." Would like "to get about a gill" of each of "the two last specimens just received." ALS. WHi. For Doty, see 5:770.

From Frederick G. Gilmer, Auburn, Mo., July 29, 1842. Reports that "Ten days ago I wrote you a letter enclosing two others . . . as evidence of my ability & anxiety to meet my engagements to you speedily." These indicate that "a lot of land which I own near Russellville," Ky., can be sold for $900. States that he has directed that this be done and the money paid "to you immediately." Has heard that Clay has instructed Col. William H. Russell "to sue on the note unless immediate payment was made," and asks that "you defer sueing 'till the 1st of Oct" by which time "I have a fair prospect of paying you $900." Explains that the next court will not be held until the 3rd Monday of October so "that sueing me sooner would not expedite the collection of the debt a moment." ALS. DLC-TJC (DNA, M212, R10). See Gilmer to Clay, October 6, 1841; Clay to Henry Clay, Jr., July 11, 1842; Clay to Russell, July 27, 1842.

To NATHAN SARGENT Lexington, July 31, 1842

I thank you for your favor of the .[1] Mr. [John J.] Crittenden can tell you some thing of young Langhorne,[2] that makes his appointt. of Mid Shipman even more extraordinary than it appears to you to be.

I am glad that the N. E. question is settled,[3] altho' the terms are curious enough, if what I hear of them be true. It will be strange if the right to navigate the St. Johns is limited to a section of the river. And as to the island in Lake Superior, I suppose that was intended as a humbug.[4]

I am waiting with breathless anxiety to learn what the Captain [Tyler] will do with the Tariff, and, if he Veto it, what Congress will then do.[5] I hear that a better & firmer purpose to resist Executive dictation now prevails.

We came very well out of the Louisiana Election.[6] And I have sanguine hopes of N. Carolina.[7]

Our State is blessed with abundant Crops. I am as busy as possible with my occupations on the farm. I am making extensive preparations to Water rot Hemp.

ALS. ViU. 1. Manuscript has a blank space at this point. 2. For John D. Langhorne, who was appointed midshipman on July 6, 1842, resigned from the Navy in 1853, and settled in Lynchburg, Va., where he became a banker, see *NCAB*, 48:297-98. His father owned a hotel in Maysville, Ky., where Crittenden was entertained. Langhorne had apparently been involved in a street fight shortly before his appointment as midshipman. Kirwan, *John J. Crittenden*, 100; Cincinnati *Daily Gazette*, August 1, 1842. 3. Ashburton to Clay, April 11, 1842. 4. The treaty provided that the St. John River be the boundary line and that the river be open to navigation by both parties. The "island in Lake Superior" probably refers to section 2 of the treaty which set as the boundary a line "thro' the river St. Mary and Lake Superior, to a point north of Ile Royale in said Lake, one hundred yards to the north and east of Ile Chapeau, which . . . lies near the north-eastern point of Ile Royale." Parry, *Treaty Series*, 93:416-25. 5. The so-called "great" or "permanent" tariff which Tyler vetoed on August 9, 1842. See Clay to Letcher, Jan. 6 and June 26, 1842. 6. Crittenden to Clay, July 15, 1842. 7. In the 1842 state elections in North Carolina, Democrats won 67 seats in the house to 52 for the Whigs and also carried the senate 30 to 20. *Niles' Register* (Sept. 17, 1842), 63:35. In the gubernatorial race, John M. Morehead, a Whig, defeated Louis D. Henry, a Democrat, by a vote of 37,943 to 34,411. *BDGUS*, 3:1130.

From John J. Crittenden, Senate Chamber, Washington, August 3, 1842. Reports that the so-called great or permanent tariff bill [Clay to Letcher, January 6 and June 24, 1842] is "now under consideration in the Senate," and believes "we shall carry the bill through without any amendment, & that we shall have it before Mr Tyler by Saturday night." Thinks some of the duties it sets are too high, especially the five cents per square yard duty on bagging which is "much complained of by our Southern opponents." Wishes it were four cents rather than five. "But upon a consideration of all circumstances—the exigency for money, the exigency of the time, & the delay & danger of sending the bill back to the House, we concluded, with the probability of a Veto before our eyes, to take & pass the bill as it came to us." Notes that if President Tyler vetoes the bill as expected, "Mr [John Q.] Adams is of opinion, that . . . we ought at once to adjourn, without doing or attempting any thing more—and in that sentiment some of our ardent friends concur—I do not—It seems to me that we should then pass [James F.] Simmons's [Mangum to Clay, July 4, 1842] bill with a duty of 20 pr cent. and immediately adjourn, and that too, with a determination & agreement, to disregard the threatened proclamation of the President to convene us instantly to supply him with Revenue—So far as I can learn Tyler still retains all his delusion, malignity & madness."

Anticipates that the "[Webster-Ashburton] treaty with England will be communicated to us on Saturday next [Ashburton to Clay, April 11, 1842]." Adds that "We expected it sooner, but there have been some difficulties in adjusting the Creole case [Remark in Senate, January 11, 1842]." ALS. DLC-John J. Crittenden Papers (DNA, M212, R20). Copy in NcD.

From Joseph Story, Cambridge, Mass., August 3, 1842. Thanks Clay for sending "the copy of your Lexington Dinner Spe[ech]" which "abounds with passages of great eloquence, & statesmanlike views, & lofty principles [Speech in Lexington, June 9, 1842]." States: "I am a Whig, & although I do not pretend to mingle in the common politics of the day, there are great measures, upon which I have a decided opinion, & which I would not disguise, if I could—I am for a national Bank—a protective Tariff—a Distribution Law of the public Lands—& a permanent Bankrupt Law—All these measures are in my judgment indispensable to the public prosperity & peace of our country." Notes that "In promoting these measures I know no man, who has laboured more perseveringly, or with more zeal, ability, & honorable devotion than yourself at all times—I, as one, feel grateful to you for these labours." ALS. DLC-HC (DNA, M212, R5). Printed in Colton, *Clay Correspondence*, 4:467.

To N. Field Campton, Northern Liberties, Philadelphia, Pa., August 4, 1842. Has "recieved your letter, as President of the Corresponding Committee of the Henry Clay Club, formed by my friends in the unincorporated Northern Liberties, Oxford township." Thanks him for the "sentiments of friendship, of attachment, and of confidence which the club and yourself do me the honor to entertain."

Notes that while he has "resolved to remain passive and leave my fellow-citizens undisturbed to designate such persons and employ such means as they may think proper to secure his election as Chief Magistrate . . . I do not profess to be indifferent to, but . . . am profoundly grateful for the enthusiastic demonstrations which have been made in respect to myself. These have far surpassed any that I ever anticipated." Adds that "Whatever may be the results . . . I shall ever cherish the recollection of these demonstrations," including those made in Northern Liberties. Copy. Printed in Frankfort *Commonwealth*, September 6, 1842.

To John L. Dinimack *et al.*, Boston, August 4, 1842. Compliments them for their statement criticizing the "extraordinary course," the "treacherous course" of President Tyler and also for their endorsement of his candidacy for the presidency at their dinner meeting in his [Clay's] honor on July 4. Thanks them for their invitation to visit Boston. Recalls his last visit to Boston [8:664-66], a pleasant occasion which occurred in the autumn following passage of the Compromise Tariff Act of 1833 [8:604, 619-22, 626-27]. Describes that act as a "timely measure of peace and harmony, whose triple object was to snatch the Protective System from the impending destruction with which it was menaced, by a combination of open enemies and false friends, to preserve the Union from the danger of a Civil War, and to avoid the necessity of placing an immense Military force, in hands [Andrew Jackson's] which I was unwilling to trust, to be employed in deeds of blood and devastation, against our own brethren, and in the bosom of our own Country." Says he was particularly well received in New England in 1833 "among the Manufacturing Class," which well understood his motives in the tariff matter. Admits, however, that a few New Englanders wanted the tariff issue pushed to "an extremity," as they had when the Missouri question [2:669-70, 740-48, 775-77, 785-86, 788; 3:15-50, *passim*] was debated and "amicably adjusted" in 1820. Regrets he will not be able to visit Boston. ALS. MB. Written in Lexington. For the dinner honoring Clay, see Boston *Daily Evening Transcript*, July 2, 1842.

From NATHAN SARGENT Washington, August 6, 1842

I have just receiv'd your obliging favor of the 31st. ulto. and am glad to hear you are so busy on your farm, for it assures me you are in good health.

I do not wonder you wait with such anxiety to hear the fate of the Tariff bill,[1] so much depends on it. The opinion is gaining ground fast that he [Tyler] will sign it, and the fact that [Henry A.] Wise is away, at the Bedford Springs [Virginia], is a favorable circumstance. You have probably been informed that the bill passed the Senate yesterday. The Whigs have screwed their courage to the sticking point, I think, in regard to the Executive dictation. They are prepared for almost any measure. It is said that Genl. [Winfield] Scott & J[ohn]. C. Spencer have strongly urged the Captain to sign the bill—that his veto would certainly give you Penna. I think the Captain [Tyler] is weighing chances, how his signature or veto is to effect a certain quondam freind.[2]

It is not easy to say what Congress will do should the bill be vetoed, but I think they would pass no other.[3] Many of our friends are immoveable on that point while others are extremely desirous that some measure should be adopted. Letters from the country, from every quarter, speak in a firm & manly tone. Most of them advise no flinching, no compromise—no additional bill. [Thaddeus] Stevens, writing to Jas. Cooper, says, "Our Scott convention was rather a slim affair; only about 50 or 60 delegates present.[4] Clay is going at a canter in Pena.; every act of Tyler's helps him & will continue to do so. Poor Tyler is more fool than knave, and that is saying a great deal. Die with the land bill rather than record your vote in submission to a tyrant. I shall suffer much for the want of a tariff, but I had rather be a bankrupt than a slave." I can assure you Pa. is waking up, and what is more, I fully believe we can carry the state in 1844.[5]

A publishing House in Phila. are about to issue a Clay Almanac containing on the calendar pages songs, annecdotes, poetry &c, & connects with it a brief popular biography.[6] I have been enlisted & am preparing the matter. I have got you down as far as your Tariff speech of 1824; but as I am limited to 16 pages I write with my arms pinioned, and have constantly to go back & strike out to make room for what seems more important. I have dwelt more upon your boyhood & orphanage than has been done by any one before. An edition of 50.000 is to be issued immediately, it will be sold at 15$ or 20$ a thousand.

I communicated your friendly regards to Jona. Roberts and rec[e]ived a long letter from him to day expressing his gratification at the interest you take in his welfare, and his full appreciation of your motives of delicacy in not holding direct intercourse with him at this time.[7] He is undisturbed as yet, and I am not sure that he will not remain so. Mr. Tyler has got such a kick from the Van Buren portion of the Locos, through the Demo. Review, (see the extract in the Nat. Intelligencer of this morning,)[8] that, he will I think begin to look about him again & see what he is to gain by warring upon the Whigs. The rumor is rife that Mr Webster will soon retire from the cabinet and come into the Senate[9] in the place of [Rufus] Choate, to resign—I look for Congs. to adjourn on the 15th—possibly a week later.[10] Till then I will endeavor to keep you advised, daily, of the movements & prospects, so far as I shall be able to inform myself of them. [P.S.] Mrs Edwards & her daughter, Georgiana,[11] of your place, have been boarding here (at Mr Cudlips [*sic*, Cudlipps]) for some weeks, & are a verry agreeable addition to our mess. Do you see the Cincinnati Gaz? L.M.C. & Oliver Oldschool are one & the same.[12]

Have you an extra copy of your "Appeal to the people of the U.S." Dec. 1827?[13] I had a copy but it is missing. Augt. 7—Nothing new to day—*Veto* stock rather more firm.

ALS. DLC-John J. Crittenden Papers (DNA, M212, R20). 1. Clay to Letcher, Jan. 6, 1842. 2. Reference obscure. 3. Clay to Letcher, Jan. 6, 1842. 4. Crittenden to Clay, July 2, 1842. 5. In the 1844 presidential election, Democrat James K. Polk carried Pennsylvania over Clay by a margin of 167,535 popular votes to 161,203, winning all 26 of its electoral votes. McKee, *National . . . Popular and Electoral Vote*, 56-57. 6. Grigg & Elliott published *The Henry Clay Almanac for 1844* in Philadelphia in 1843. 7. Clay to Sargent, May 31, 1842. 8. An article from the *Democratic Review*, reprinted in the Washington *Daily National Intelligencer* of August 6, 1842, charged that "between the two parties, Mr. Tyler *falls to the ground like lead*," and that his attempts to organize "a middle party for his support" for the presidential succession has resulted in "suspicion of the disinterestedness of his motives [Clay to Sloane, Oct. 23, 1841]." It also argued that Tyler should have declared his allegiance to the "one-term principle" and that his handling of such issues as the national bank, the Dorr Rebellion in Rhode Island, and the apportionment bill had cost him any chance of winning the support of the Democratic party. This reprint was accompanied by another article in the *Intelligencer* which pointed out that while Tyler had received much flattery from the Richmond *Enquirer* and other Van Buren papers for his actions against the Whig party, "Let the Locofocos read the honest confessions of the Democrats' organ." 9. For Webster's 1843 resignation as secretary of state, see Mangum to Clay, July 4, 1842. 10. Congress adjourned on August 31. 11. Possibly the wife of John Edwards who lived on Todds Road in Fayette County. MacCabe, *Directory of the City of Lexington . . . 1838 & '39*, p. 123. 12. Oliver Oldschool was a pseudonym used by Nathan Sargent himself. See the entry on Sargent in the *DAB*. His column in the Cincinnati *Daily Gazette*, signed "L.M.C.," reported on political events in Washington and the proceedings of Congress. See, for example, the *Gazette* of August 1 and 2, 1842. 13. See 6:1394-96.

To PIERCE M. BUTLER — Lexington, August 8, 1842

I received your friendly letter.[1] Perhaps your criticism on the last paragraph of my Barbecue Speech is just.[2] One of my sons made a similar one before it was published. We see from different positions. You think well of Mr. Tyler as a man. I think ill of him both as a man and officer. He has betrayed his friends and violated his word and his honor. It is impossible for me to regard such a person, either in his individual or his official character with any other feelings than those of detestation. I cannot believe that the respect which belongs to office should screen him. Besides I was addressing a popular audience, composed among others of the hunters of K. accustomed to the rifle. After all, you may be right.

You give a flattering account of Whig prospects in the South. My information from other sources corresponds with yours. From N. York and N. England my intelligence is also encouraging.

They write me from Washington that Mr. Calhoun is the favorite with the greater number of the Democrats. The leaders however are opposed to him and say that Van [Buren] will be their man. We shall see.[3]

We have passed the only shoal that was fraught with some little danger ahead—that is the Anti masonic Convention in Pennsa. I understand it was an entire failure; there being only some five or six Counties represented and they did nothing.[4]

I anticipate the pleasure of meeting you in Louisiana the approaching winter.

ALS. ScU. 1. For Butler, see *DAB*. 2. The last paragraph of the speech charged that President Tyler had betrayed the Whig party. See Speech in Lexington, June 9, 1842. 3. The Democratic National convention met in Baltimore on May 27-29, 1844, and nominated for President James K. Polk of Tenn. on the ninth ballot. Silas Wright of N.Y. was nominated for vice president on the first ballot but declined the nomination. The following day, May 29, George M. Dallas of Pa., was nominated for vice president on the first ballot and accepted. For Van Buren's showing in the balloting for president, see Clay to Berrien, Sept. 4, 1843. For other proceedings of the convention, see McKee, *National . . . Popular and Electoral Vote*, 47-49. 4. Crittenden to Clay, July 2, 1842.

To JOHN M. CLAYTON Lexington, August 8, 1842

I received to day your favor of the 31st. Ulto. and I also received that to which you refer, recommending Drs' McClellan and Bird for Professors Chair in the Medical School of Transylvania University.[1] I should have been very happy to have served them both on account of their own merits, and *your* recommendation; but upon enquiry I found that every Chair was filled, and it was thought well filled. And as the principles of our friends, as well as our own, are opposed to proscription, no vacancies could be produced. I request you to make this communication to them, with my respects, and assurances of the pleasure it would have afforded me to have found myself able to serve them.

My information is that Tyler will veto the permanent Tariff.[2] In that event, I sincerely hope that the Land measure[3] will not be sacrificed. Important as a Tariff undoubtedly is, it dwindles into insignificance when compared with the independence of the H. of R. on a Revenue bill. I think you and all our prominent friends ought to strengthen the Whigs in Congress as much as possible. They ought at all hazards to insist upon the distribution of the Land fund. And if Congress is compelled to adjourn, without passing any Tariff, when they reassemble, whether at the regular or a called Session, in my opinion they ought to pass again the same Tariff, which he will have Veto[e]d, and let the Loco's have Veto and Ditto! A point of attack upon them should be, after the return of the bill with the Veto, that they failed to vote for it, and by their failure prevented the Country from getting the benefit of the protection it wants.

I do not agree with you in the wish that our adversaries should have a majority in the next H. of R.[4] I doubt whether they will; but if they should, we shall derive some consolation in the embarrassment of their condition.

I read with great pleasure the proceedings of your Convention in Delaware.[5] I agree with it entirely that, if the parts of the [1833] Compromise act, intended for the benefit of the Manufacturers, and especially that in respect to the Home valuation, are not faithfully executed, the act ought to be abandoned.[6] You and I know positively that the act could not have passed without that principle.

I wish to say some thing to you on a delicate subject. If I were at liberty to indulge my personal feelings and preferences, in regard to the Vice Presidency,[7] you well know what direction they would promptly take. But, under all the circumstances of my situation, I have thought it most delicate & proper that I should abstain from giving any indication of my particular choice or wishes. I have therefore most cautiously avoided even whispering any preference. Lately Genl [Erastus] Root of N.Y. wrote me that he had seen, as he thought, an *insinuation* of my preference for [Winfield] Scott. I instantly wrote him that he was entirely mistaken, and that I had foreborne altogether from interfering in that question.

If, as seems probable, the People will honor me with a nomination, I presume there will be a National Convention,[8] not to nominate a Candidate for the Presidency, but *to concert measures to give effect to the popular nomination, and to nominate a Candidate for the V. P.* The nomination then made will be acquiesced in.

Why can't you go to the H of R in the next Congress?[9] Many of the older & more experienced members are quitting. The Whigs will be greatly in need of a Leader of tact and talent and who will possess general confidence. Thou art the man. A glorious field lies before you; and if I were in your place I would enter it and gather the laurels which await you. Think of this seriously and favorably.

You are wrong and I am right about the restriction on the dividends of a Bank of the U. S. It was not the precise limit of seven per Ct but the principle of *a restriction* that I commended in my Barbecue Speech[10]—a restriction coupled with a guarranty that the dividend should always reach the prescribed amount. Seven per Cent would have done at the Extra Session.[11] Perhaps eight, perhaps nine might now be necessary. Recollect too that the limitation was to supersede any bonus.

I am constantly and agreeably occupied at Ashland. I am executing here, in epitome, all my principles of Internal improvements, the American System &c. I am making an *enormous* Canal a quarter mile long three feet wide at the bottom, six at the top, and 2½ deep, to drain some low ground, and to enable me to construct Vats to water rot Hemp. I am going to rig the Navy with Cordage made of American Hemp—Kentucky hemp—Ashland Hemp. I should be most happy to see you here, the only place where I have a chance of seeing you.

ALS. DLC-John M. Clayton Papers (DNA, M212, R20). Letter marked in margin "Confidential." 1. For George McClellan and Robert M. Bird, see *DAB*. 2. Clay to Letcher, Jan. 6, 1842. 3. *Ibid.* 4. Clay to Crittenden, June 3, 1842. 5. The Delaware State Whig convention met in Dover on July 5, Dr. William Burton presiding. Dr. Robert M. Bird reported a series of resolutions condemning Tyler, nominating Clay for president, recommending John M. Clayton for vice president, and approving the distribution of the proceeds of public land sales. *Niles' Register* (July 23, 1842), 62:336. 6. The tariff act finally passed in 1842 did provide for home valuation. See Clay to Letcher, Jan. 6, 1842, and Clay to Smith, July 10, 1842. 7. Mentioned in 1842-44 as possible Whig vice presidential nominees in the coming election were: John M. Clayton (Del.), Henry A.S. Dearborn (Mass.), John Davis (Mass.), Millard Fillmore (N.Y.), Theodore Frelinghuysen (N.J.), Francis Granger (N.Y.), John Sergeant (Pa.), Winfield Scott (N.J.). 8. For the Whig National convention, held in Baltimore on May 1, 1844, see McKee, *National . . . Popular and Electoral Vote*, 49-50, and Schlesinger, *History of U.S. Political Parties*, 1:420-25. Ambrose Spencer presided at this convention which nominated Clay for president by acclamation and Theodore Frelinghuysen for vice president on the third ballot. 9. Clayton returned to the U.S. Senate in 1845. *BDAC*. 10. Speech in Lexington, June 9, 1842. 11. For a discussion during the 27th Congress, 1st Session on limiting the dividends of the B.U.S., see Speech in Senate, June 21, 1841.

To JAMES WATSON WEBB Lexington, August 9, 1842

I send you enclosed a Lexington Intellr. of this day containing an article headed "Mr Clay—Ultra abolitionist" the facts and statements of which may be relied upon. Perhaps you may think it worth while to copy it in your paper or to take some other notice of it.[1]

LS. CtY. 1. Webb printed the article in his New York *Morning Courier and Enquirer* on August 23, 1842. It consisted of a handbill issued by the Rev. Abel Brown announcing a lecture in Albany, N.Y., on July 18 in which Brown would tell "why that notorious *Sabbath-breaker, Swearer, Gambler, Duellist, Thief, Robber, Adulterer, Man-stealer, Slave-holder*, &c., HENRY CLAY! should never be President of these United States." It was accompanied by an editorial defending Clay as a slaveholder and with a report that the proposed lecture never took place, since Brown failed to show up, apparently because he learned of the arrival of a mob, armed with an "abundance of wrath and cabbages, sheep-plucks and rotten eggs, swearing and vowing vengeance on Abel Brown." The article also included another handbill in which Brown accused Clay of "Selling Jesus Christ!" by trading in slaves. Webb added his own editorial in Clay's defense, and printed deeds of emancipation which Clay had issued to several of his slaves. The *Courier and Enquirer* identified Abel Brown as the corresponding secretary of the New York Anti-Slavery Society.

From JOHN J. CRITTENDEN Washington, August 12, 1842

We are in a state of great embarrassment here, & as yet no course has been determined upon to lead us through the confusion & difficulty resulting from the last Veto.[1] The great difficulty is in adopting such a course as will satisfy those who are bent on resistance to the usurpations of Tyler, & those who fear the effect of our adjourning without an *adequate* Tariff. Our friends of the North seem to be very seriously & sincerely apprehensive that their constituents will be disconcerted to such an extent as to be fatal in their coming elections, if we should adjourn without doing or attempting something more. We had several meetings on the subject, with but little success, and are to have another this evening—In the midst of these differences of opinion, a kind & conciliatory spirit prevails, and all agree & say that *union* is the greatest interest of us all, & that we will not allow that to be shaken in any event. This is the only auspicious sign that remains in the dark prospect before us.

Tomorrow I may be able to write you more distinctly. And you may be assured that, whether wisely or not, we will act considerately.

Mr [John Q.] Adams as chairman of the Committee is preparing a report[2] on the last Veto—We look for an able & stir[r]ing Report, & take care to stimulate him by letting him know that our expectations are high.

The Treaty with England[3] was laid before us—There has been no action or indication of opinion about it, but I presume it will be approved by the Senate.

ALS. DLC-John J. Crittenden Papers (DNA, M212, R20). Copy in NcD. Written from Senate Chamber. 1. On August 9, Tyler had vetoed the "great" or "permanent" tariff bill. Clay to Letcher, Jan. 6, 1842. 2. The committee to consider Tyler's August 9 tariff veto was appointed on August 11 and issued its report on August 17. The report mentioned the possibility of impeachment but concluded that such an attempt might prove abortive. *Reports of Committees*, 27 Cong., 2 Sess., no. 998, pp. 28-36. 3. Ashburton to Clay, April 11, 1842.

To JOHN M. BERRIEN Lexington, August 15, 1842

I received your favor of the 3d. inst. I have been fully apprized of the delicacy of your situation in respect to the Land question, the embarrassment of which was increased by the course of your Colleagues in the House. Perhaps you took the wisest course, under all circumstances.[1] Whilst I regard as confidential your communication respecting your consultation with your Colleagues, I embrace the occasion to say that what took place affords additional proof of the expediency of the District system.[2] The effect of the General system is to impair individual independence, and to induce too great a desire to act in concert.

I am not surprized at the want of counsel & concert among the Whigs generally, which you describe. The proper course for them to pursue is not so perfectly clear as to be free from great difficulty. After I was in bed last night, intelligence of the Veto reached me.[3] And I presume you are all now in a state of the greatest excitement and perplexity. I infer that you will pass no revenue bill. The difficulty of acting on Mr. [James F.] Simmons's,[4] embracing such an infinite variety of prices of articles, is almost insuperable; and, what with a feeling of just indignation, the extraordinary length of the Session, and the nigh approach of the next, I presume you will conclude to go home.

If I had any advice to offer, it would be too late to communicate it. So much depends upon local circumstances, upon the temper of the two houses &c. That no person at a distance can judge of what is best to propose. Of one thing I feel confident that if you adjourn, without adopting any revenue measure, the blame will attach to Mr. Tyler, and that more will be due to the Democrats than to the Whigs. They have encouraged Mr. Tyler, and they by uniting with the Whigs might have neutralized his Veto. . . . [Marginal addendum: "I think that the number of those who agree with us about the Veto must increase considerably, from its recent exercise."]

ALS. NcU. 1. Berrien voted against the "little" or "provisional" tariff and failed to vote on the "great" or "permanent" tariff [Clay to Letcher, Jan. 6 and June 24, 1842], both of which provided for distribution. The final tariff bill (without a distribution clause), which ultimately became law was passed by resolution so there was no roll call, but Berrien voted nay on its third reading. He also failed to vote on the continuation of distribution, even though the tariff was over 20% and the Distribution and Preemption Act of 1841 required suspension of distribution when the tariff level exceeded that percentage [Clay to Letcher, June 26, 1842; 5 *U.S. Stat.*, 453-58]. Tyler subsequently pocket-vetoed the continuation bill. All of the Georgia congressmen, as well as the other Georgia senator, Alfred M. Cuthbert, either voted against these bills or failed to vote. On August 2, 1842, Berrien explained in Congress his position on the tariff and distribution issues. *Cong. Globe*, 27 Cong., 2 Sess., 679, 828-29; U.S. Sen., *Journal*, 418-19, 427-28, 544, 629, 631-32; U.S. H. of Reps., *Journal*, 27 Cong., 2 Sess., 1019-20, 1051-52, 1108-9, 1342-43, 1386-87. 2. For the new law directing that congressmen be elected by districts rather than at large, see Clay to Crittenden, June 3, 1842. 3. Clay to Letcher, Jan. 6, 1842. 4. *Ibid.*; Mangum to Clay, July 4, 1842.

To Curtis H. Shockley, August 15, 1842. Has received the letter "communicating your wish to procure a Milch cow of the most approved breed." Notes that the "breed which is most approved here is the Short Horn Durham" whose price has previously ranged from $500 to $2,500 but is now only $200 to $250 for a full-blooded, three-year-old heifer. However, notes that while he has no purebreds, he has "a number of heifers two and three years old, very deep in the blood, 7/8 hs. 15/16h. & c. and some of them very promising Milkers." Prices two of the heifers plus one calf at $150, but suggests that Shockley buy two heifers with their calves. Adds: "Should you conclude to take them, it must be understood that their delivery at Augusta must be at your own expense & risk; but I would endeavor to engage a faithful person on the best terms in my power." ALS. NcU.

Shockley, a lawyer from Columbia County, Ga., served in the state house of representatives in 1845, 1847, 1863-64 Extra Session, 1864-65 Extra Session, and as a delegate to the state constitutional convention in 1865. Information supplied by Joanne Smalley of the Georgia Dept. of Archives and History.

To JOHN S. LITTELL[1] Lexington, August 17, 1842

I received your obliging letter[2] with its inclosure. The arrangement, by which Mr. Epes Sargent has undertaken to compose a biography of me,[3] was made by the young men of New York, prior to my learning, through Mr. [Henry] Toland, your friendly wishes. It would have been, otherwise, very agreeable to me to have acceded to them.

Mr. Sargent's work, I presume, from what I have heard of its progress, is now nearly ready for the press. I wish he had a better subject for his pen; and I fear that it may be with him, as it has been with many of the artists, who have taken my portrait, that, owing to the defects of the original, nothing very striking or interesting will be produced. I am sure that it will be no more his than it was their fault. I have perused your song[4] with lively interest, and I cordially thank you for it. If my judgment is not biased by the flattering expressions and sentiments towards me, which it contains, I think it will be found to be extremely well adapted to the popular use for which it was intended.

Accept, my dear sir, my grateful acknowledgements for your friendly views and intentions toward me; and assurances of my esteem and regard.

Copy. Printed in Colton, *Clay Correspondence*, 4:467-68. 1. John S. Littell (1806-75) was president of the Clay Club of Germantown, Pa. He published in New York in 1842 a book, *The Clay Minstrel; or, National Songster to Which is Prefixed a Sketch of the Public Services, and Character of Henry Clay*, which was enlarged and revised in 1844. For Littell, see *NCAB*, 5:355. 2. Littell had written Clay from Philadelphia on August 1, 1842, saying that he "felt very great regret" when informed by Mr. [Henry] Toland that someone else was already writing Clay's biography. Adds, however, that knowing "the agreeable and patriotic duty was in much abler hands than mine, reconciled me, in a measure, to the disappointment, and . . . I commenced *singing*." Encloses a copy of his song [not found]. ALS. DLC-HC (DNA, M212, R5). 3. Clay to Sargent, July 2, 1842. 4. *The Clay Minstrel* contains a number of songs written by Littell, so it is impossible to tell which of these he may have sent Clay.

To JOHN J. CRITTENDEN Lexington, August 18, 1842

The contrary views in the two letters enclosed[1] indicate more. Chaos seems to be piling on chaos. You will have seen the dissolution of the Ohio Legislature,[2] by resignation of members, a *bold* but I am inclined to think a right measure.

Wont you go to the Blue Licks? I think I will go for a few days

Copy. DLC-John J. Crittenden Papers (DNA, M212, R20). 1. Not found. 2. The Apportionment Act of 1842 [Clay to Crittenden, June 3, 1842] caused the Ohio legislature to meet in special session in the summer of 1842 for the purpose of redistricting the state. The Whig minority accused the Democratic majority of attempting to gerrymander the districts, and on August 9 twenty-eight members resigned in order to prevent a quorum and thereby to defeat the passage of the redistricting bill. Weisenburger, *The Passing of the Frontier*, 410; Washington *Daily National Intelligencer*, August 16, 1842; Holt, *Party Politics in Ohio*, 98-99, 353.

To EPES SARGENT Lexington, August 20, 1842

I received your letter informing me of your having engaged to prepare for Mr. [Daniel] Mallory a Biographical sketch of me, to precede my Speeches, which he is about to have edited.[1] Since he perseveres in his undertaking, of the success of which I entertain fears, I am glad that I have fallen into your hands.

With respect to the Valedictory[2] which I pronounced in the Senate last Spring, the most accurate copy is that which was published on satin.[3]

I do not wish my Speech on the Veto published, until that which has run the circuit of the News papers is corrected by me. It was first published in the [Washington *Daily*] Nat. Intellr. without my revisal, and it contains some inaccuracies which I wish to be corrected.[4] I will transmit a correct copy whenever it is needed.

I do not know how there came to be omitted, in the Cincinnati Edition of my Speeches, the most important one I ever made on the Tariff—that of March 1824.[5] In 1823 I was in very ill health—so low that my life was despaired of both by my friends and myself. I had attended the Olympian Springs, in the summer, in this State, had been placed on a strict regimen, and had been subjected to a long use of the blue pill for the despapsia. In spite of all remedies, I felt a gradual decline, and feared a speedy dissolution. In November, I was to start for Washington, and fully anticipated that, after reaching it, if I should reach it, I should be obliged to fly to the South, as the last resort. I procured a small travelling carriage, a saddle horse, threw aside all the prescriptions of the Physicians and commenced my journey. Each day, I walked on foot, rode in the carriage, and on horse back. I arrived at Washington quite well, was elected Speaker, and went through more labor than I ever performed in the same Session, except perhaps the last Extra Session.[6] That Speech of March 1824—the most elaborate I ever delivered, was part of it.

Several of my communications to you, addressed to Boston and Albany remain to be acknowledged.

I hope you found in some of the periodicals of the day, my letter to Jonathan Russell, in relation to transactions at Ghent, and which he published in 1828—or 9, in violation of private correspondence.[7] If you did, I should be glad to know how I can get a sight of it.

ALS. DNA, RG59, General Records of the State Dept., Appointment Papers, 1861-69. Addressed to Sargent in New York City. 1. Clay to Sargent, July 2, 1842. 2. Speech in Senate, March 31, 1842. 3. Clay to Sargent, May 31, 1842. 4. Speech in Senate, August 19, 1841. It was published in the *Intelligencer* on August 26, 1841. 5. See 3:683-730. 6. 27th Congress, 1st Session. 7. It was published on Oct. 23-24, 1828. See 3:219-26, 252-57, 269-72, 282-84; 7:533.

To EPES SARGENT "Blue Licks," Nicholas Co., Ky., August 22, 1842

Your favor of the 16h found me at this watering place. You are right in your conjecture that the letter of the 9h. July 1822,[1] in Prentice's appendix to the second Edition of his Biography[2] is the one to which I alluded. You will think the fact strange but I have never seen that second Edition.

The vindication of me agt the Libeller Abel Brown[3] is Editorial and contained in a number of the L[exington]. Intell[igence]r which I sent you, headed "Mr. Clay & ultra abolitionists" It has been republished in the Eastern papers.[4]

I should think it might be well for you to take notice of it in your Biography.[5] The facts stated in the article are incontestible. P.S. I do not intend to take any formal notice of Abel Brown's libel, under my own signature H.C.

ALS. DLC-Breckinridge Long Papers (DNA, M212, R21). Addressed to Sargent in New York City. 1. Clay to Jonathan Russell. See 3:252-57. 2. The 1st and 2nd editions of George D. Prentice's *Biography of Henry Clay* were published in Hartford and New York, respectively, in 1831. 3. Clay to Webb, August 9, 1842. 4. *Ibid.* 5. This does not appear in Sargent's *Life of Henry Clay.*

To BUCKNER S. MORRIS Lexington, August 27, 1842

I received your[1] favor, and thank you for the friendly sentiments and purposes which it communicates.

In respect to the enquiry, which you make, as to a suitable Candidate for the Vice Presidency, I have thought that, if I had any decided preference, considerations of delicacy and propriety ought to restrain me from disclosing it. I should have full confidence in the fidelity of either Genl. [Winfield] Scott, Govr. [John] Davis, Mr. [John M.] Clayton, Mr. Sargeant [*sic*, John Sergeant] or Mr. [Francis] Granger.

I think it not unlikely that a National Convention may ultimately be called to designate a Candidate for the V.P. and to adopt measures of concert to secure success to the popular nomination of a Candidate for the Presidency[2] In the mean time, I see no objection to public manifestations of the preferences which may be entertained in different parts of the Union.

You will perceive from the tenor of my letter that it is not intended for publication.

ALS. ICHi. Addressed to Morris in Chicago, Ill. 1. Morris had served in the Ky. legislature as a representative from Bracken County before moving to Chicago in 1834. He was elected mayor of Chicago in 1838 but lost his 1844 bid for a seat in Congress. Bessie Louise Pierce, *A History of Chicago*, 3 vols. (New York, 1937), 1:178, 207, 421, 423; Collins, *History of Kentucky*, 2:772. 2. Clay to Clayton, August 8, 1842.

From William Price, Hagerstown, Md., August 27, 1842. As "presiding officer" of the Maryland Whig convention, "which assembled in the city of Baltimore on the 24th instant" and "unanimously nominated you for the office of President of the United States," forwards "a copy of their address to the Whigs of Maryland, with a full account of their proceedings." Notes the "deep, thundering and long-continued acclamations with which" the nomination was received, adding that "it was but the echo of a voice coming up from the Whig population of Maryland, by whom you were virtually nominated before the Convention was thought of." States further that the Whigs of Maryland "go for measures, not men," but "they entertain no misgivings as to the course you will pursue in the event of your election. Your life has been no sealed book to them or to the world; and your constancy to the great principles for which they have been so long contending, they have learned to value the more highly from the accumulated perfidy and fraud of a high existing functionary of their own appointment." They are now confident of success, because they united "their long cherished principles" with the cause "of the man they love and admire." Copy. Printed in Washington *Daily National Intelligencer*, September 27, 1842. Clay carried Maryland in 1844 by a vote of 35,984 to 32,676 over Polk with James G. Birney, Liberty party candidate, getting 3,308. McKee, *National . . . Popular and Electoral Vote*, 56-57.

Clay replied on September 13, 1842, tendering "my grateful acknowledgements for the honor done me in presenting my name to the consideration of my countrymen as a candidate for the highest office in their gift." Agrees with "the sentiment that the paramount object in the selection of a candidate . . . should be the public measures, and not the men, to be promoted; and that individual qualifications should only be regarded in reference to the ability and fidelity with which the public interests may be advanced." Although thankful "for the numerous demonstrations of confidence and attachment towards me," feels he should "postpone a definitive decision of the question of yielding my consent to the use of my name as a candidate." Concludes: "I have no wish again to embark on the tempestuous ocean of public affairs but from a high sense of duty, and in conformity with the command of an authority which I should feel bound to obey." Copy. Printed in Washington *Daily National Intelligencer*, September 27, 1842.

To John Woods, Hamilton, Ohio, August 27, 1842. Rejects an invitation "to visit Hamilton and Ohio," saying that "the ground which I have taken, in the circumstances under which I find myself, will not allow me to contract any new engagements. I have thought it best not to leave home but in the pursuit of health or business or to fulfill old promises to visit places which I have never seen." Hopes "that the Whigs may triumph at the approaching election in your state [Clay to Ewing, July 24, 1842]." Copy. OClWHi. Original owned by Helen L. Arnott, Cleveland, Ohio. For Woods (1794-1855)—a lawyer, editor, and former Ohio congressman—see *NCAB*, 3:510; *BDAC*.

From Anson G. Henry *et al.*, Springfield, Ill., August 29, 1842. Writing as the executive committee of the Clay Club of Springfield, report having heard that "you are to visit Indianapolis, Indiana, on the 5th of October next." If so, "we hope you will not deny us the pleasure of seeing you in our State." Add that "You have never visited Illinois, or at least this portion of it; and should you now yield to our request, we promise you such a reception as shall be worthy of the man on whom are now turned the fondest hopes of a great and suffering nation." Copy. Printed in John G. Nicolay and John Hay (eds.), *Complete Works of Abraham Lincoln . . .*, 12 vols. (New York, 1894), 1:231-32. Clay declined this invitation on September 6, 1842. *Ibid.* Abraham Lincoln was among the nine signers of the letter of invitation.

For Dr. Henry (1804-65), see Harry E. Pratt, "Dr. Anson G. Henry, Lincoln's Physician and Friend," *LH* (October and December, 1943), 45:3-17, 31-40.

To PETER B. PORTER Lexington, August 29, 1842

Enclosed I transmit a part of a Pittsburg[h] paper containing two articles respecting my servant Charles [Dupuy] and me. In one of them it is asserted that he ran away from me, when I was at the Falls three years ago, and that I offered $50 to a colored man to recover him. This you know to be absolutely false. It was by your nephew P. B. Porter Esq. that I was cautioned against the seductive practices of some abolitionists to prevail on him to quit my service. I am sure he will recollect it.

I do not know whether it is worth while to correct the tale of his elopement and my offer of fifty dollars to recover him; for the refutation of one falsehood seems to be but the parent of another. But if it be worth the contradiction, it could no where come with so much propriety as from the Falls themselves. Perhaps your nephew might think it proper to address a note to the Editor of the Pittsburg[h] paper contradicting the story, and confirming what he communicated to me about the endeavors of certain abolitionists to seduce him from my service. Some times it may be expedient for friends to do what a man would not himself be expected to do.

I am enjoying some quiet & much agreeable occupation on my farm.

Congress has, I presume, and I think wisely, passed a Tariff,[1] altho' with the sacrifice of much indignant & outraged feeling.

Should the result of the elections in Ohio[2] and N. York[3] realize our hopes, the Whigs will have easy work hereafter. . . .

ALS. NBuHi. Addressed to Porter at the Falls of Niagara, N.Y. 1. Clay to Letcher, Jan. 6, 1842; Remark in Senate, Feb. 3, 1842. 2. Clay to Ewing, July 24, 1842. 3. In the New York elections of 1842, 24 Democrats and 10 Whigs were chosen for the U.S. House. *Guide to U.S. Elections*, 577. Democrat William C. Bouck was elected governor over Whig Luther Bradish by a vote of 208,072 to 186,060. *BDGUS*, 3:1078. Those elected to the state legislature were: senate—22 Democrats, 10 Whigs; assembly—92 Democrats, 36 Whigs. *Niles' Register* (Dec. 3, 1842), 63:212.

To JOHN Q. ADAMS Lexington, September 1, 1842

I cannot better execute the request of Govr. [Thomas] Corwin than by transmitting to you, his letter, containing it, addressed to me; and adding my fervent wishes that you would make the visit which he suggests.[1] You would be every where received with the utmost cordiality. The Whigs of the West, as far as I know their sentiments, are unanimous and enthusiastic in their admiration of your firm and manly stand, in the H. of Representatives, against a weak and wicked Executive.[2]

You would find the journey, especially in an Extra Stage, an easy one. The whole way from Washington to Dayton the road is excellent; the greater part of it being the Cumberland National road.

You would make Mrs. Clay and me extremely happy if you would extend your visit to Ashland; and we should be delighted to entertain Mrs. Adams also, if she should accompany you.[3]

The months of September & October, and November, until about the middle of it, may be perfectly relied upon for good weather.

I expect to go to Dayton, and on the 5h. Oct. to Indianapolis, in fulfilment of an old engagement which they will not absolve me from.[4]

Mrs. Clay unites with me in warm regards to Mrs. Adams. . . .

ALS. MHi-The Adams Papers. 1. On this same day, Sept. 1, Clay answered a letter from Gov. Thomas Corwin of Ohio, dated August 27, reporting that he had accepted speaking invitations from Dayton and Indianapolis and that he would write John Q. Adams, as Corwin had suggested, urging him to visit the West. The Dayton speech was scheduled for Sept. 29; that in Indianapolis for Oct. 5. LS. OCHP. 2. See, for example, Mangum to Clay, July 4, 1842, and Crittenden to Clay, August 12, 1842. 3. For Adams's regrets that he could not visit Ohio and Kentucky at this time, see Adams to Clay, Sept. 20, 1842. He did, however, visit Ohio and Northern Kentucky in 1843 [Clay to Adams, Nov. 19, 1843]. 4. Clay to Crane, Sept. 1, 1842.

To Joseph H. Crane *et al.*, Dayton, Ohio, September 1, 1842. Acknowledges and accepts an invitation to a barbecue given by the Whigs of Ohio to the Whigs of Kentucky, to be held in Dayton on September 29. Feels that "no where else" in Ohio "have I warmer, more steadfast, or more faithful friends." Copy. Printed in Frankfort *Commonwealth*, September 13, 1842. Also addressed to Samuel Forres, H.G. Phillips, Richard Green, Daniel A. Haynes, and Charles Anderson.

On this same day, September 1, Clay received and answered a letter from Robert C. Schenck, dated August 27, informing him that plans for a huge barbecue in Dayton, to honor all Kentucky Whigs, had been made by Ohio Whigs and that he was to be invited. Says he "should attend it." Clay agrees. LS. ODa.

For the Dayton barbecue of September 29, 1842, sponsored by the Ohio Whig State Central Committee, which attracted some 100,000 to 200,000 people (the estimates vary considerably), and at which Clay gave a major political speech lasting an hour and a half [Speech in Dayton, September 29, 1842], see John Pfeifer, "Henry Clay and the Great Dayton Barbecue," *The APIC Keynoter* (Spring, 1984), 84:16-17. Schenck served as grand marshal of the event, at which John J. Crittenden also spoke, and at which resolutions nominating Clay for president, Gov. John Davis of Mass. for vice president, and Thomas Corwin for a second term as governor of Ohio, were passed.

To JOHN M. BERRIEN Lexington, September 4, 1842

I received your obliging letter of the 28h Ulto. I think we ought to be satisfied with the general results of the protracted Session of Congress, which I suppose is now terminated. There should be no reproaches between the Whigs who voted for and against the Tariff.[1] Their condition was one of such extreme embarrassment, that I can see high motives of public duty for either course.

I regret that you did not obey the dictates of your own good judgment, although I can justly appreciate the desire which you naturally had that Messrs. [William S.] Archer, [Willie P.] Mangum, & [John] Henderson should unite with you, in voting for the Tariff. For myself, I certainly should have prefer[r]ed the adjustment of that question upon the principles which I indicated lately in the Senate;[2] but it appears that both friends and foes of the protective policy conceived, I think erroneously, that the Home valuation could not be enforced.[3] Without the enforcement of that, all the other parts of the Compromise[4] could not be justly insisted upon; for I *know* that the Compromise never could have been carried without the promise, which it contains, of Home valuation.[5]

The Tariff, which has passed, is for Revenue, with protection as its incident. The measure of protection may, in some instances be too high; but the great difficulty always, in granting it, whether incidentally or independently, is the proper fixation of that measure. And such ultraists as [John C.] Calhoun, [Levi] Woodbury &c. will always be sure to denounce, as extravagant, any protection whatever may be its degree. Except in a few instances, if I understand the bill, the general rate of duties is less than by the act of 1832.[6] If a Tariff had been passed, in proper time, by the V. Buren administration, in contemplation of the arrival of the period when the Compromise was to have full effect; and if the Government had not destroyed the Nat. currency I have no doubt that a much less amount of protection would have been sufficient than is perhaps now necessary.

It is now manifest that the foes—I mean the ultra foes, of the protective policy intend to take the ground that it cannot be constitutionally granted, even as an incident to Revenue. For more than 30 years after the establishment of the present Constitution no one presumed to controvert the power to protect the manufacturing interest. And when it was questioned, a clear concession was made of the right to afford that protection in the form of laying duties for Revenue. But now this is to be contested. Such is the perversity of men, goaded by ambition, or surrendering themselves to prejudice passion or partizanship!

Now, I am sure that you can not take that ground. Hence my regret that you did not at once avow your principles & take your position. Sooner or later you will be compelled to do it, and the sooner the better. What I fear, for our friends in Georgia, is the difficulty of opposing the Tariff, and at the same time maintaining their Whig connection. I hope my apprehensions may not be realized.

In the mean time, I do believe that the people are greatly ahead of their representatives at Washington, in sustaining Protection either as a principal or an incident. See what was done at the largest meeting recently held at Nashville; which ever assembled in Davidson Co.[7] See what is passing in Virginia, N. Carolina, Louisiana and even in your own State.[8] In this State the number of dissentients is very few.

I congratulate you on the general aspect of the Whig cause. Our success, if I am rightly informed, in N. York & Ohio,[9] is almost certain. . . .

ALS. NcU. 1. Clay to Letcher, Jan. 6 and July 24, 1842. 2. Clay to Letcher, Jan. 6, 1842; Remark in Senate, Feb. 3, 1842. 3. Clay to Smith, July 10, 1842. 4. Compromise Tariff Act of 1833. See 8:604, 619-22, 626-27. 5. Section 3. See 4 *U.S. Stat.*, 630. 6. See 8:443, 445, 455-56. For a comparison of the 1832 and 1842 tariff bills, see Frank W. Taussig, *The Tariff History of the United States* (New York, 1888), 103-14. 7. The Nashville and Davidson Co. Whigs held a meeting on August 13, 1842, in which they nominated Clay for president. They also denounced Tyler as belonging "In heart and purposes . . . to our adversaries," and endorsed a one-term presidency, a national bank, distribution of the proceeds of public land sales, and a tariff for revenue which would also protect American "agriculture, commerce, manufactures and all the mechanic arts." Franklin (Tenn.) *The Western Weekly Review*, August 19, 1842. 8. In the spring and summer of 1842 there were various meetings in all these states endorsing a tariff with at least incidental protection. For Virginia, see Lynchburg *Virginian*, July 28, August 22, 1842. For North Carolina, see Raleigh *Register & North Carolina Gazette*, March 15, 1842. For Louisiana, see New Orleans *Bee*, April 22, May 10 and 11, 1842. For Georgia, see Raleigh *Register & North Carolina Gazette*, July 1, 1842. 9. Clay to Ewing, July 24, 1842; Clay to Porter, August 29, 1842.

To Thomas W. Duffield, Jr., Frankford, Pa., September 6, 1842. Thanks him for a copy of an address he had delivered to the literary club of Oxford [Pa.], and suggests that in the future the members might usefully debate such topics as the presidential veto power, free trade vs. tariff protection, distribution of the proceeds of public land sales, a currency consisting exclusively of precious metals, establishment of a Bank of the United States, and the power of the president to dismiss appointed federal employees from office. Thinks that such debates "might be made highly instrumental in propagating truth & dispelling error." ALS. ViU.

To John W.G. Simrall *et al.*, Madison, Ind., September 8, 1842. Explains his decision to accept no invitations to attend public meetings on his trip to Indiana, via Cincinnati and Dayton, save the gathering at Indianapolis [Clay to Adams, September 1, 1842]. Notes the necessity of his stop at Dayton because of "the Barbecue being given to my State & not to me." Asserts, however, that if his return trip to Kentucky takes him through Madison, "it would afford me pleasure, without ceremony or parade, and without any public entertainment, to exchange friendly salutations" with various citizens of Madison and Jefferson County. ALS. ICHi.

From Amos P. Granger *et al.*, Syracuse, N.Y., September 10, 1842. Have learned that Clay has ordered a shipment of Onondaga County salt for use at "Ashland." Report that he and his committee are sending Clay, free of charge, 23 barrels of salt because of "the high estimation in which your character and public services are held." The shipment will go via A.M. January & Son in Maysville, Ky. They comment on the quantity and quality of Onondaga salt and note that the protective tariff on salt had produced a situation whereby "capital was profitably employed, and thousands of laborers in this and other dependent branches of industry, received a comfortable subsistence." Regret, however, that the level of protection of salt "under the late existing laws" has declined, and complain that "the war-cry of repeal" of the tariff on all foreign imports "has already been sounded." Therefore, "The eyes of the nation again turn to you." Copy. Printed in Colton, *Clay Correspondence*, 4:468-69.

On September 22, 1842, A.M. January & Son of Maysville wrote Clay that they had received 23 barrels of salt from Syracuse, N.Y., and that the barrels would be transported to Ashland free of charge. ALS. DLC-TJC (DNA, M212, R14). See also Clay to Spencer, September 13, 1842, and Clay to Granger, September 24, 1842.

To Thomas Ewing, Lancaster, Ohio, September 11, 1842. Makes reference to a mutual legal problem and says he will soon be traveling to Indianapolis via Dayton. Concludes: "I am happy to receive from you a communication of the flattering prospects of the Whigs in Ohio, of which I receive concurring testimonies from other friends. Success in Ohio and in N. York this fall will be decisive." ALS. DLC-Ewing Family Papers (Supp. Roll 2). For Whig political fortunes in Ohio and New York, see Clay to Ewing, July 24, 1842; Clay to Porter, August 29, 1842.

To THURLOW WEED Lexington, September 12, 1842

I am very sorry that I cannot accept the invitation which you did me the favor to transmit, and to which the enclosed is an answer.[1] My friends in Indiana would take no denial to their demand that I would fulfill an old engagement to visit the Capital of their State to which I go on the 5h. of October. And in the meantime the Whigs of Ohio have fixed one of the two days of your Fair for a Barbecue to the Whigs of K[entucky]. at Dayton, which I have promised to attend, as an humble Citizen of the latter State.[2]

They are very confident of success in Ohio in Oct. & I think with much ground of hope.[3] Should the Whigs achieve a triumph there, and your anticipations are realized in New York,[4] the victory of 1844 will eclipse that of 40.

Do me the favor to present my respects to Govr. [William H.] Seward.

ALS. NHi. 1. In a letter to James Wadsworth *et al.*, dated Sept. 12, 1842, Clay declined with regret an invitation to attend the Albany Cattle Show and Fair on Sept. 28-29, sponsored by the New York Agricultural Society. He urged the society to continue working to improve the breeding of cattle even though the general depression in the national economy persists. ALS. NRU-Wadsworth Papers. 2. Clay to Crane, Sept. 1, 1842; Speech at Dayton, Sept. 29, 1842. 3. Clay to Ewing, July 24, 1842. 4. Clay to Porter, August 29, 1842.

To JAMES D. DOTY Lexington, September 13, 1842

I received your favor and the grass seed, for which I thank you.

I am afraid that I can offer you no advice of any value, respecting the admission of your Territory,[1] as a State, into the Union. My opinion was truly & freely expressed, in regard to the mode in which new States should be admitted, at the Lexington Barbecue.[2] I think it a necessary preliminary that an act of Congress should pass, defining the limits and prescribing the mode of forming a Constitution of the new State. And I am of opinion that the extent of your Territory is entirely too great for one State. If the Ordinance present any difficulty about its division, the requisite authority ought to be obtained by an appeal to those with whose consent it can be procured. To incorporate any portion of the Territory, within the present limits of Illinois, in the new State will only lay the foundation of future dispute. There are some things which, although wrong when done, must be acquiesced in; and perhaps the Northern extension of the boundary of Illinois is among them.[3]

It is probable that sectional considerations will weigh in Congress in the decision of the question of your admission; one favoring and the other opposing your division. In their conflict it is not easy to anticipate the result. And the question may be further complicated by political motives.

I should be glad to see you admitted, with suitable limits and in a regular way. . . .

ALS. WHi. 1. Doty was at this time governor of Wisconsin Territory. 2. Speech in Lexington, June 9, 1842. 3. Four times during the governorship of James Doty (1841-44), Wisconsin residents rejected a referendum for statehood. One reason for this was that Doty insisted on a boundary as far south as Lake Michigan in accordance with the Ordinance of 1787. This would have included approximately 8,500 square miles which had been given to Illinois when it had become a state in 1818 so that it could have access to the Great Lakes. If northern Illinois were incorporated into Wisconsin, it would bring with it a proportionate share of Illinois's large public debt. Furthermore, Doty, a Whig, was constantly at odds with the Democratic territorial legislature. When Henry Dodge was made governor in 1845, Democrats and Whigs united in taking steps toward statehood. A referendum in April, 1846, resulted in a vote of nearly 6 to 1 in favor of statehood. The enabling act [9 *U.S. Stat.*, 56-58] which passed Congress and was signed by President James K. Polk on August 6, 1846, set the final boundaries of Wisconsin and did not include the northern Illinois land. After two constitutional conventions, Wisconsin was finally admitted to the Union on May 29, 1848. Over the years its size had been reduced not only by the land incorporated into Illinois, but also by land given Iowa, Michigan, Minnesota, and to Great Britain under the 1842 Webster-Ashburton Treaty. William F. Raney, *Wisconsin, A Story of Progress* (New York, 1940), 124-36; Robert C. Nesbit, *Wisconsin, A History* (Madison, Wisc., 1973), 209-24.

To EPES SARGENT Lexington, September 13, 1842

I have to thank you for the N. World containing your Biography of me,[1] which I have hastily perused. You have made the most of the poor subject of which you had to treat. I think it extremely well adapted to the popular use for which it was designed. After having performed its temporary office, it will serve as a basis for a more permanent Biography,[2] should that ever be required; and in that some of the partizan character of the work might be modified or expunged.

There are a very few mistakes in it; but there is one of importance sufficient to deserve correction. You make, or rather, I suppose, the setter of the types has made Gottingen the place of negotiation for peace with G. Britain. It was Gottenburg in Sweden, where the respective Comm[issione]rs were to have met and not Gottingen. And I did go to Gottenburg in the Spring of 1814. The seat of the negotiation was afterwards changed to Ghent, where the peace was concluded.[3]

What progress are you making in your sketch for Mr. [Daniel] Mallory?[4] I mentioned to him that my Veto Speech was published from the notes of the Stenographers, without any examination of it by me; and that there are some corrections which I desire to be made before it is published.[5]

ALS. DNA, RG59, General Records of the State Dept., Appointment Papers, A. and R., 1861-69. 1. *The New World, A Weekly Journal of Popular Literature* was published in New York City by Jonas Winchester and edited by Park Benjamin. Hudson, *Journalism in the United States*, 587-89. Although the issue containing Clay's biography has not been found, the *New World* (Sept. 3, 1842), 5:162 contained an announcement that it would publish the biography "in a single Extra Number of the New World on a beautiful new type" and that it would be "furnished to clubs." 2. Clay to J.O. Sargent, July 2, 1842.

3. See subject index entries in 7:727. 4. Clay to J.O. Sargent, July 2, 1842; Clay to E. Sargent, August 20, 1842. 5. Speech in Senate, August 19, 1841. See Clay to E. Sargent, August 20, 1842. The August 19 speech with very minor changes appears in Daniel Mallory's *The Life and Speeches of the Hon. Henry Clay . . .*, 4th ed. (New York, 1844), 2:485-507.

To NATHAN SARGENT Lexington, September 13, 1842

I thank you for your favor of the 2d. inst. and the paper containing the account of the reception of the Whig Members of Congress in Philada.[1] It was richly merited by their labors, by their sacrifices and by what they finally accomplished.

We are all perfectly satisfied in this quarter with the passage of the Tariff;[2] whilst there is no disposition felt to censure those of our friends who voted against it upon the high motives by which they were actuated. It was a case of extreme embarrassment; and acquiescence, if not praise, is due to the course of both sections of our friends.

In compliance with an old engagement, the performance of which is insisted on by my friends, I go to Indianapolis on the 5h. prox.[3] And as the Whigs of Ohio give a Barbecue to those of K. on the 29h. inst. at Dayton,[4] in consequence of a pledge made in 1840, I shall attend that on my way to Indianapolis. . . .

ALS. ICHi. 1. On August 25, 1842, a meeting of Philadelphia Whigs appointed a committee to invite the Whig members of Congress to visit Philadelphia for the purpose of increasing enthusiasm and promoting a victory for the party in Philadelphia city and county. A steamship picked up the congressmen in Washington on Sept. 1 and took them to Philadelphia where a reception was held at the Museum Building. That evening a mass meeting took place at the Exchange. Resolutions adopted included one endorsing Clay for president. The meeting concluded with nine cheers for Clay. Washington *Daily National Intelligencer*, August 29, Sept. 3 and 5, 1842. 2. Clay to Letcher, Jan. 6 and June 24, 1842. 3. Henry to Clay, August 29, 1842. 4. Clay to Crane, Sept. 1, 1842.

To THOMAS SPENCER Lexington, September 13, 1842

I have received your favor of the 29h. Ulto. I am greatly obliged to my friends for the Salt, although I have some doubts whether I ought to accept so valuable a present It has not yet arrived, nor the communication from the Comee. to which, when I receive it, I shall make a respectful reply. I thank you for your description of the contents of the several barrels.[1]

I am glad that the Tariff passed.[2] It was a concession due to a suffering people and to an empty treasury. With regard to the public lands, the suspension of the distribution of their proceeds will only be temporary, if the Whigs retain power, and if they lose it, the other party will repeal the law.[3] During the suspension the receipts will not be large. But whilst I think that the passage of the law is to be approved, I do not think that those of our friends who voted against it are to be censured. It was a case of extreme embarrassment, and one in which all reproaches and criminations between differing friends should be avoided. In expressing these views, I must say that I am not sure how I should have voted, if I had been in Congress. In this quarter, what has been done is entirely approved.

We must cherish hopes of the future in devising ways against the shocking abuses of Executive power.

ALS. ICU. 1. Granger to Clay, Sept. 10, 1842. When the 23 barrels of New York salt were sent to Clay he was told which barrels and how many barrels contained either common, solar, ground, or refined dairy salt. 2. Clay to Letcher, Jan. 6 and June 24, 1842. 3. The Distribution Act of 1841. See Clay to Ewing, April 30, 1841; Remark in Senate, June 9, 1841; 5 *U.S. Stat.*, 453-58.

To JACOB STRATTAN[1] Lexington, September 13, 1842

I received your favor communicating the patriotic purposes and views of the young men of Philadelphia; and I take pleasure, in compliance with your request, in stating some of the principal objects which, I suppose, engage the common desire and the common exertions of the Whig party, to bring about, in the Government of the U. States. These are:

A sound National currency, regulated by the will and authority of the Nation

An adequate Revenue, with fair protection to American industry

Just restraints on the Executive power, embracing a further restriction on the exercise of the Veto.

A faithful administration of the Public domain, with an equitable distribution of the proceeds of Sales of it among all the States

An honest and economical administration of the General Government, leaving public officers perfect freedom of thought and of the right of suffrage; but with suitable restraints against improper interferance in elections

An amendment of the Constitution, limiting the incumbent of the Presidential office to a single term

These objects attained, I think that we should cease to be afflicted with bad administration of the Government

ALS. KyBgW. 1. For Strattan, a merchant whose business was located at 153 High and who resided at 425 Sassafras in Philadelphia, see *M'Elroy's Philadelphia Directory for the Year 1842*, 5th ed. (Philadelphia, 1842).

To Lewis D. Campbell *et al.*, Hamilton, Ohio, September 14, 1842. Thanks them for their kind invitation to pass through Hamilton enroute to Dayton, but regrets that neither his route to Dayton via Lebanon, Ohio, nor his route home from Indianapolis will take him near Hamilton. ALS. KyU. For Campbell, sometime (1831-35) publisher of a pro-Clay newspaper in Hamilton and later (1848-58; 1870-72) a member of the U.S. House, see *BDAC*.

To ROBERT P. LETCHER Lexington, September 15, 1842

I have been prevented from going to Frankfort this week by bad weather and not very good health.

I think you or the Lieut. Governor[1] ought to go to Dayton. The Barbecue is given to the State.[2] The State ought therefore to be represented by some of its highest dignitaries. It will be an excursion only of a week's duration if you return from Dayton. True dignity will be manifested in going, not in staying away.

Copy. OHi. 1. For Manlius V. Thomson—a Scott County lawyer, lieutenant governor, and colonel in the Mexican War—see William H. Perrin, *History of Bourbon, Scott, Harrison and Nicholas Counties* (Chicago, 1882), 77; Collins, *History of Kentucky*, 1:45, 55, 350, 364, 369-70. 2. Clay to Crane, Sept. 1, 1842.

To Whigs of Hamilton County, Ohio, September 15, 1842. Has received with "profound gratitude and respect" the resolution adopted by "a large meeting of the citizens of Hamilton County, by which they have done me the honor to nominate me as a Candidate for . . . President of the United States." Notes that in his Barbecue speech [Speech in Lexington, June 9, 1842], he expressed his "feelings and views, without reserve, in respect to the association of my name with the office of President." Adds that the distant date of the election and the "developement of the opinion and wishes of the people now in progress, would seem to indicate the propriety of postponing a definitive decision of the question of yielding my consent to the use . . . of my name." Copy. Printed in Cincinnati *Daily Gazette*, September 23, 1842. Addressed to "J.C. Wright, John P. Foote, Wm. D. Gallagher, & c., & c." Wright was editor of the Cincinnati *Daily Gazette*.

To ABRAHAM JONAS Lexington, September 16, 1842

I received your friendly letter. It is my purpose to visit Indianapolis,[1] in compliance with an old engagement, on the 5h. prox. but I shall not be able to extend my journey West of it. I have determined not to leave home, except in pursuit of business or health, or to comply in a few instances with former promises. I have no expectation at present of having the gratification of visiting Illinois.

I am very glad to perceive from your election to the Legislature that you enjoy the same consideration which was entertained for you in Kentucky;[2] and I hope that you will never have any cause to repent your emigration. We however miss you very much.

I anxiously hope that your opinions may prove correct of the ultimate political character of Illinois.

ALS. IHi. Addressed to Jonas in Columbus, Adams County, Ill. 1. Henry to Clay, August 29, 1842. 2. Jonas, born in Devonshire, England, in 1801 came to the U.S. in 1815 and settled in Grant County, Ky., where he later practiced law. He served in the Kentucky house of representatives in 1828, 1829, 1831, and 1833. He subsequently emigrated to Adams County, Ill., where he was elected to the lower house of the state legislature in 1842 and the state senate in 1844. His son, Benjamin F. Jonas, served as a U.S. senator from Louisiana. See the son's entry in *BDAC* and in *NCAB*, 4:544; see also Theodore C. Pease, *Illinois Election Returns 1818-1848* (Springfield, Ill., 1923), 362, 380, 526.

From JOHN Q. ADAMS Quincy, Mass., September 20, 1842

Towards the close of the recent Session of Congress and at a very critical period of its deliberations I had the pleasure of receiving your letter of 24. July; and since my return home I have received your very kind invitation[1] enclosing that of Govr [Thomas] Corwin to the barbacue at Dayton Ohio on the 29th. of this month—[2]

During the Administrations of Genl Jackson and of Mr Van Buren, I served as a member of the House of Representatives of the United States because the People of my native Congressional District were pleased to assign to me that Station—I did not consider it a debasement to serve in it after having occupied even the highest seat of honour and of power, but I was aware that it would no longer become me to undertake to lead in the Councils of the Nation—From the time of our conclusion of our Negotiations at Ghent[3] I had considered the cardinal points of the policy of the general Government were— 1. The extinction of the National debt— 2. The application of the resources of the Union to the improvement of its condition—physical, moral, intellectual, political—To promote the general welfare was so far in my estimation from being in the Constitution words of no meaning that they constituted the great end for which *all* the powers vested in the National Government were confided to them, and that the non-uses of the powers granted to the Government for that purpose was a dereliction of duty to the constituent people, not less culpable in those entrusted with them than the usurpation for unworthy purposes of powers never conferred—The idea, that a Nation destined by the Creator to be the mightiest that ever existed on the face of the Globe, entering upon the theatre of human action with a proclamation of principles investing man in the name of his maker, with all the powers bestowed upon him by nature, for the improvement of his condition, and enjoining it upon him as the summary of all his duties—that such a Nation should with deliberate purpose have so constituted itself as to cripple all its own powers of self improvement, has always appeared to me a Doctrine the depravity of which is instigated only by its stupidity—That the power to incorporate a company of brokers, or to levy a turnpike toll, should be denied to a Legislative body, able to annex millions of square miles of territory, and millions of population to the community, argues such an incongruity of theory, such an unnatural combination of the sublime and the base, that I can never think of it with patience, or attribute it to any other source than political knavery—From the day of the Peace of Ghent and the final provision made for the extinction of the National debt, *internal improvement*, was at once, my conscience and my treasure—It was at once the divine law of our Nature and the inexhaustible mine of our wealth; and the system of Government for the Union, founded on that or a congenial principle, chiefly by your agency was making its way gloriously against the perverting and crafty Jeffersonian paradoxes of State rights and Nullification, at the close of Mr. Monroes Administration and when the Act of 1824 making the annual appropriation of 30000 of dollars for progressive surveys passed,[4] I fondly indulged the hope that the system was established—How this hope has been blasted is well known to you—I had abandoned it altogether when a transient glimpse returned on Harrisons election, with the prospect of your success in carrying through your combined Bank, Land, and Tariff System[5]—The extra Session brought back all my apprehensions, and that which has just closed has left me desponding though not yet despairing of the rescue of our Country from the deepest and most indelible disgrace—

The most extraordinary feature in the phenomenon of Mr. Tylers career since his accession as he calls it to the Presidency is not the capacity of his ambition for a genuine election to that office but the means upon which he has fallen to obtain it—Like the Kingdom of Heaven he seems to think it can be taken only by violence—There is an absurdity in his pretensions to Legislative powers and his appeals to the people to support him, (that is, to elect him) because he is without a party, which savours more of bedlam than of the white House at Washington—

There is a consolation in the reflection that his term of service is drawing to a close—Hitherto his Administration has consisted only in desperate struggles to prevent the enactment by Congress of usual and beneficial Laws—In this work of destruction he has been too successful, and I look forward with great solicitude to the next Congress—Were it possible that this should harmonize with him—who could fortell the consequences?—

I am greatly obliged to you, and to Govr. [Thomas] Corwin whose letter you [were] so good as to enclose to me, for your and his invitation to me, to attend the great barbacue meeting at Dayton on the coming 29th. of this month—but were there no other obstacle in my way, I am at this moment entangled with engagements here among my own late Constituent[s], which confine me till the ensuing Session of Congress, entirely to this region—I say my late Constituents because all our Congressional districts of the last ten years, are already dissolved by our State Legislature, and their number has been reduced in conformity to the new apportionment act, from twelve to ten—[6]The district which I have represented is broken up; and that of which I am now a Resident is so differently composed that it is altogether uncertain whether I shall be a member of the next Congress or not—

You will have been informed that the recent Whig Convention of this State,[7] made an unanimous nomination of candidates for the Offices of President and Vice President of the United States at the election of 1844. I can scarcely dare look so far in advance of time, as to expect to witness the issue of that election, but whether in this, or in another world, I shall not cease to feel an intense interest in the event, nor to pray that its result may prove a blessing to our Country. . . .

Copy. MHi-Adams Papers. 1. Clay to Adams, Sept. 1, 1842. 2. Clay to Crane, Sept. 1, 1842. 3. For relevant references, see subject index entries in 7:727. 4. For the act which empowered the president to spend $30,000 a year employing civil engineers to survey and plan any roads of national importance, see 3:568-69, 572-93, 619-27, 632-33; and 4 *U.S. Stat.*, 22-23. 5. See, respectively, for bank—Clay to Porter, April 29, 1841, Clay to Ewing, April 30, 1841, Speech in Senate, June 21, 1841; for land—Clay to Ewing, April 30, 1841, Remark in Senate, June 9, 1841, Clay to Letcher, Jan. 6, 1842, Remark in Senate, Jan. 21, 1842, Clay to Letcher, June 24, 1842; for tariff—Clay to Letcher, Jan. 6 and June 24, 1842, Remark in Senate, Feb. 3, 1842. 6. Clay to Crittenden, June 3, 1842; see also Clay to Adams, July 24, 1842. 7. Clay to Dearborn, July 13, 1842.

To NICHOLAS O. BRITTON Lexington, September 23, 1842

I received your obliging letter, & candidly thank you for the sentiments of regard & friendship towards me, which it communicates, and I am extremely happy to receive from you such strong expressions of confidence in the Whig character of your State. The apathy which you nevertheless describe as the cause of the loss of your legislature is greatly to be deplored.[1] Besides depriving the country of the services of one able & upright Senator,[2] it inspires our adversaries with fresh hopes, & will stimulate them to make invigorated exertions. It is to be regretted, that the force of the truth, that the price of liberty is eternal vigilance, is not more generally felt

With respect to my becoming a candidate for the high office to which you refer, I can add nothing to what I said in a public speech delivered at a Barbecue near this place, in June last.[3] I have no wish to be forced upon the people; no desire that my name should be used, unless I am fully persuaded that it is wanted by a majority of my countrymen. The prevalence of the apathy noticed by you, makes it difficult to comprehend their real wishes; & there is certainly some danger that the road to victory may be lost by the Whigs from the defeats which they suffer. There is, however, ample time yet to form some satisfactory opinion as to the probable views of the majority of the people of the U. S. If we have our troubles, our adversaries are not free from theirs.

The course of Mr Tyler has been such as to produce disgust & dis[s]atisfaction. But if he has been faithless, our friends in Congress have been true & faithful. Why should they be abandoned because of his perfidy? Why, when their defeat is precisely what he desires? For there can be no longer a doubt that he is wielding all the power & influence of his office for the benefit of those who opposed his election, against those whose exertions & suffrages secured it.

I wish I could see any near prospect of the restoration of a sound currency. If Mr Tyler adheres to the opinions on which he has acted, there is none. As to his Exchequer,[4] it would make such a fearful addition to the already enormous power of the Executive, that I have never, for a moment, thought it ought to be adopted

I suppose that the only alternative left to the country is to hobble on as well as it can, with the State Banks, incompetent as I am obliged to regard them to supply a general currency of uniform value.

I am unable to say when I shall have the gratification of visiting your state. I shall seize with eagerness the first occasion I can to enjoy it. . . .

Copy. DLC-HC (DNA, M212, R5). Printed in Colton, *Clay Correspondence*, 4:470-71, with variations in punctuation and capitalization and with elimination of ampersands. Addressed to Britton [not identified] in Petersburg, Va. 1. Clay to Crittenden, June 3, 1842. 2. Reference obscure. 3. Speech in Lexington, June 9, 1842. 4. Clay to James Brown Clay, Dec. 10, 1841.

To NATHANIEL SILSBEE Lexington, September 23, 1842

I am grieved, my dear friend, to learn through your letter, that your health has been bad. I sincerely hope that you may soon find it perfectly reestablished.

The proceedings of your Convention[1] are worthy of your State and the renown of the Hall where they transpired. I do not, of course, speak of those which relate to myself; but for them I am truly grateful. . . .

ALS. DLC-HC (DNA, M212, R5). Addressed to Silsbee in Salem, Mass. 1. Adams to Clay, Sept. 20, 1842.

To AMOS P. GRANGER *et al.* Lexington, September 24, 1842

I have the pleasure to acknowledge the receipt of your friendly letter of the 10th instant, transmitting an invoice of twenty-three barrels of salt and one box, embracing all the varieties manufactured at Syracuse, and a list of my friends who have done me the favor to contribute it. In consequence of my experience of the superiority of the Onondaga salt, in the preservation of meat, and in all other uses to which that article is applied, I requested my friend, Mr. [Ambrose] SPENCER, to have forwarded me a small supply. I had not the slightest expectation that my request would have attracted any other than the usual attention, much less that it should have elicited a present so liberal, and which comes recommended to me by so many flattering and friendly circumstances. I am advised this morning of the safe arrival of the salt at Maysville,[1] and it will reach this place in a day or two.

I know not how to express, in terms corresponding with my feelings, my great obligations for this acceptable present. I request you to offer for it, to those who contributed it, collectively and individually, my cordial and grateful acknowledgments.

They have done me the honor to send it to me as a testimonial of their confidence and esteem, and especially in consequence of my devotion to our American and domestic interests. I can never cease, gentlemen, to regard it as a duty, not to be neglected by the General Government, to afford efficient protection to those interests. The form of that protection is a question of subordinate consequence. That is best which commands the most satisfaction and promises the greatest durability. I had supposed that no man would controvert the power and the duty of Government, in imposing duties for revenue, to make liberal discrimination for the benefit of domestic industry. About the period of 1824, when the power of affording direct protection was first strenuously contested, that of incidental protection was freely and unreservedly conceded.[2] But nothing can conciliate or appease the spirit of visionary Free Trade. And we now behold the dawn of opposition to all protection, either direct or incidental. The tariff of 1832[3] was framed under the hope that it would quiet all discontents and produce general reconciliation. It moderated the pre-existing duties. The tariff of 1842,[4] recently passed, provides a scale of duties generally lower than that of 1832. Yet it is scarcely passed before the war-cry of Repeal is raised against it.

The party opposed to the Whigs, during the progress of the bill, with the land clause, through Congress, professed to be animated only by opposition to that clause. The bill passed, and then the Veto was applied. A majority of the Whigs adopted the painful but patriotic resolution to make a temporary sacrifice of the principle of distribution to secure the passage of a measure demanded alike by the necessities of the People and of the Treasury.[5] How did their opponents meet them? Here was a fine opportunity to manifest the truth and sincerity of their profession that the land clause was the exclusive cause of their dissatisfaction with the bill. But when stript of that clause we find them, with but few exceptions, as unrelenting and determined in their opposition as ever. And when they cannot invoke the aid of Veto and ditto, they fulminate denunciations of Repeal!—as if the country were to be kept in a state of perpetual agitation, and no repose or security was to be allowed to its great business concerns!

I trust that the cooler reflection of these gentlemen will prompt them to abstain from any attempt totally to repeal the law, and limit their exertions to its improvement, by suitable amendments, if any shall be found necessary. But, if they should persevere in their announced purpose, the People are competent to apply the proper corrective.

In my humble opinion there is no just objection to the salt tax. Its equality is undeniable. All consume it, and pay in proportion to their consumption; the rich who use most paying the most. Its tendency, moreover, is to equalize the price of the article between the inhabitants of the seaboard who use marine or foreign salt, and those of the interior who use that of our salines. And the competition between the two descriptions is sure to keep the price within reasonable limits.

Wishing a revival and long continuation of the prosperity of the salt manufacture of your town, and health and happiness to yourselves and those whom you represent....

Copy. Printed in Washington *Daily National Intelligencer*, Oct. 12, 1842. 1. Granger to Clay, Sept. 10, 1842. 2. For Clay's principal speech on the 1824 tariff, delivered March 30-31, 1824, see 3:683-730; also see 4 *U.S. Stat.*, 25-30. 3. See 8:443, 445, 455-56. 4. Clay to Letcher, Jan. 6 and June 24, 1842. 5. *Ibid.*

To PETER B. PORTER Lexington, September 24, 1842

I recd. your favor and along with it the Pittsburgh paper containing the statements of your nephew and yourself, for which I am greatly obliged.[1]

The resolution which you sketched in respect to the Call of a Nat. Convention for the nomination of a Candidate for V.P. &c. was very happily worded.[2] Perhaps the disposition made of that question by the Syracuse Convention was well enough.[3] Public opinion in favor of some Candidate may be so manifested as to lessen the necessity for such a convention, which however I think under that state of case would have a stirring and beneficial effect.

I hope you will succeed at your approaching Election,[4] the loss of which would have a damping effect on the Whigs, and increase the difficulties in a final triumph.

I am called by business to N. Orleans this winter and shall leave home for that purpose about the 15h. of Novr. Can you not come here before then? I should be most happy to see.

I start tomorrow for Indianapolis via Dayton.[5]

ALS. NBuHi. 1. Clay to Porter, August 29, 1842. 2. Clay to Clayton, August 8, 1842. Porter's resolution has not been found. 3. The Syracuse Whig convention of Sept. 7, 1842, passed a resolution calling for a national convention to nominate a candidate for vice president. They specified that it would be held in Baltimore at a time to be chosen by Whig members of Congress. Washington *Daily National Intelligencer*, Sept. 13, 1842. 4. Clay to Porter, August 29, 1842. 5. Clay to Crane, Sept. 1, 1842; Henry to Clay, August 29, 1842.

Speech in Maysville, Ky., September 26, 1842. According to the Maysville newspaper, "Upon reaching the Eagle Hotel, Mr. CLAY addressed the crowd which assembled to greet him, expressing his gratitude and thanks for the attention paid him, and congratulating the country, that the same spirit which achieved the great victory of 1840, was now abroad in the land, eager for another contest, and as he believed ominous of another triumph." Copy. Printed in Maysville (Ky.) *Western Star*, September 29, 1842.

Speech in Dayton, Ohio, September 29, 1842. With reference to the resolutions "just adopted, connecting my name with a high and exalted office," states that he would have preferred it "if on this occasion any association of my name with that office had been altogether omitted." Reminds his audience that they are present today to celebrate the great victory of the Whigs in 1840. Claims that for "Twelve long years, the Whigs had struggled against the mal-administration of government" prior to that victory. Laments the death of President Harrison. Announces that his purpose today is to present the "leading principles" of the Whigs, who, in 1839-40, were accused "of having no principles common to us as a party."

Notes that the "first great principle" of the Whigs is to provide the nation with a "sound currency of uniform value," and thinks this can best be accomplished through "a bank of the United States, emanating from the will of the whole people, sanctioned by the general authority." Condemns the Democrats for their opposition to "any bank of the United States—they are opposed to any bank of any description," and for their support, exclusively, of "hard money." The Whig doctrine, Clay says, is "give us money and in sufficient quantity; give us hard money and soft money—if convertible into that which is hard." Discusses his reasons for believing in the inferiority of specie as the sole circulating medium and states the advantages of having instead a uniform currency based on both specie and paper money.

Asserts that another Whig principle is a tariff adequate to protect the nation "against unequal and ruinous foreign competition with other Countries." Harks back to his authorship of the Compromise Tariff Act of 1833 [8:604, 619-22, 626-27] and explains that his motives for offering it were "First, to preserve the Tariff, and the system of protection, for the space of nine years certain. Next, to avert the calamity of a civil war; and next, to prevent the necessity of placing a vast military force at the control, and in the hands of General Jackson, the consequences of the use of which, I feared, might be perilous to our free institutions. I would say nothing disrespectful of that distinguished man. I simply express my opinion of him in his public character, in which he had not my confidence. I was unwilling to place him at the head of an army to march through our country and spread desolation and devastation. To prevent a civil war—to prevent the placing at the command of General Jackson, vast military means, the effects of which I could not foresee; and to preserve the great manufacturing interests from impending destruction, induced me to propose, and my friends to second the proposition, to pass the compromise act. That act would have achieved all—up to 1839-40—all that it promised, or could have been desired, if the currency had been sound; if exchanges had been such as they would have been in a sound state of the currency, under the compromise act." Is certain the compromise tariff could never have been passed had not the promise of home valuation [Clay to Smith, July 10, 1842] after June 30, 1842, been included in the legislation. Believes that in the last session of Congress the unsuccessful tariff bill offered by Sen. James F. Simmons of Rhode Island [Mangum to Clay, July 4, 1842] contained a more effective balance between protection and the need for revenue than the bill finally passed [Clay to Letcher, January 6, 1842; Remark in Senate, February 3, 1842] and signed by Tyler. Asserts, however, that he supports the act that was passed because "it possesses, therefore, that quality of stability, which I consider so essential to the successful prosecution of business. A tariff arranged upon those principles, after unexampled difficulties, was passed at the last session of Congress, and I am glad that it did pass. I respect equally the motives of those of our friends who voted against and for the act. The first were, unwilling to submit to executive dictation in any form—and there is enough in the arrogance and abuses of executive power as developed within the last year to alarm all true patriots. The last, no less indignant at the presumptuousness of the executive department, were unwilling that Congress should adjourn without provision for the treasury, and protection for the people. Both, I believe, were animated by the purest motives, and neither ought to be reproached by the other or by the country at large." Feels, further, that until the nation abandons "all parental legislation for the great interests of this country," it is the "duty of the government to afford protection to all the great interests of the country." Condemns at length the anti-protectionist tariff policy of the Democrats in Congress, tracing their votes on the tariff bills debated in the recent session. "I say, in presence of this vast multitude, that, as a party, they are opposed to all protection. They would let your grain wither in your barns—they would let mechanics and manufacturers sink in an unequal contest with the pauper labor of Europe—

they would let your country be drained of all its specie—they would let this republic revert to its ancient, colonial, and vassal condition, rather than grant protection, direct or incidental, to American industry. Is this not their doctrine? ['*It is*,' resounded from the multitude.]"

Supports, in an aside, the gubernatorial candidacy of Thomas Corwin [Clay to Ewing, July 24, 1842] in a series of quips and anecdotes that produced "[great laughter]."

Returns to the tariff legislation recently enacted, admitting that while he wished there had been a "land clause" [i.e., distribution to the states of public land sales receipts] in the bill that was passed, "the embarrassment of the treasury and of the country was so great, that there ought to be no criminations or recriminations between those of our friends, who, under those trying circumstances, yielded to what they believed a stern necessity, and those who thought that no necessity, however great, would justify them in surrendering the independence of Congress to executive dictation. I know not how I should have voted if I had been a member; but I approve of the passage of the bill, without thinking that the slightest censure ought to attach to our friends who voted against it. I rejoice that it passed. I have no doubt of the purity of the motives which animated the one portion, and the other, of the Whig party."

Attacks the Jackson administration's banking and currency policies for having plunged the nation into a severe depression that continues yet. Having done this, the Democrats have since opposed Whig measures designed to bring back prosperity, especially by means of a new bank of the United States. Charges that these obstructionist Democrats "set about wooing the President" during the 27th Congress, 1st Session, and in so doing persuaded him to veto two bills reestablishing a bank of the United States [Tyler to Clay, April 30, 1841; Remark in Senate, August 16, 1841; Speech in Senate, June 21 and August 19, 1841; Remark in Senate, August 24, 1841]. As for Tyler himself, Clay charges that his first bank veto was evidence of his "execrable perfidy to the party whom he has deceived and betrayed!" His second bank veto was of a compromise bill he had privately approved before it was sent to Congress. But what happened? "Don't you think we had some little cause to suppose that Mr. Tyler would sustain his *own* child? Don't you think we had some right, when we sent it to him, in that unaltered state in which it came from his own hands, to suppose that it would obtain his signature? I should have supposed that, among Christians, among honest men, among Ohio farmers and mechanics, it would not have been an unreasonable expectation. It was sent to him, and notwithstanding his prior approbation, it received his *veto*!! . . . Here, again, the cry of exultation and triumph was heard from the leaders of our opponents. The welkin was made to ring with their shouts of joy, at the veto of that bill—at the veto of a measure virtually decreed by the People in their majority of 1840!"

Charges also that the Democrats had earlier attempted "to replenish the public coffers by the issue of treasury notes—a dangerous and, I think, improper mode. It was a measure for which I did not vote, not because I was unwilling to aid them in any of their laudable efforts, but because I thought the treasury might be replenished by duties on foreign commerce. I did not vote for the bill, because it went to create government paper. I had a little historical knowledge upon the subject of government paper." Admits, however, that the Whigs in Congress had generally supported this legislation when it was proposed by the Van Buren administration.

Sharply assails President Tyler's abuse of Executive power, especially his proscriptions of Whigs in public office, calling attention specifically to his removal of Jonathan Roberts [Clay to Sargent, May 31, 1842] as collector of the port of Philadelphia. Argues also that limiting the presidential veto ("one of the leading objects of the Whigs in 1840") is necessary, even though "The Democrats—the lovers of the people, love the veto power, every exercise of which is to crush the will and judgment of the people." Recalls his earlier effort [Speech in Senate, January 24, 1842], while in the Senate, "to limit and restrain the executive power—to check the veto power by a majority in both houses; and I ascertained that not a Democratic vote would be given for it. And when the same proposition was submitted to the House of Representatives—out of one hundred Whigs, ninety-eight voted for the reduction of executive power, and only two, adversely. But every Democrat voted for this Aristocratical, this anti-Democratical, and Monarchical feature." Given the fact that under the new apportionment law there will be 223 members of the House of Representatives [Clay to Crittenden, June 3, 1842], and that two-thirds of this number is 148 (the number needed to override a presidential veto), Clay poses a hypothetical case "in which one hundred and forty-seven are in favor of passing a law, and the President opposed to it—ought it to pass, or not? [Yes, yes, yes, from thousands of tongues.] Mr. Tyler thinks one way—the one hundred and forty-seven think another way. Who shall prevail? ['*The people, the people,*' from the surrounding mass.] Then you are the *true Democrats*, and snatch from the brow of your opponents a designation which they have no longer a right to wear: for we find them arrayed, in the contingency supposed, of supporting Mr. Tyler's opinion, against the voice of one hundred and forty-seven, and against the opinion of thirty-five senators. Are they the Democrats at heart, who think that the opinion of Mr. Tyler should prevail against one hundred and forty-seven representatives of the people, and thirty-five representatives of the states? ['*No, no.*'] That is the question, and the whole question, respecting the veto power, and nothing more nor less." Explains that if both houses override a presidential veto by a simple majority vote, the veto should be set aside.

Asserts with pride that while the Van Buren administration during its four-year tenure, had averaged annually an expenditure of $28,000,000, the Whigs, "during the very first year of [their] ascendency in Congress" had reduced that figure to $25,000,000. Argues, too, that the cynical Democrats cling to public office with far more tenacity than do Whigs. Indeed, witness the fact that Tyler "is now hurling out of office every Whig; and, as we see, by the papers, daily removals—almost as uniformly we hear and see that locofocos (I use the term not in reproach, but as one in popular use) are appointed in their places." Asks rhetorically: "Do you think these Democrats mean to be faithful to Mr. Tyler? Do you think that Mr. Van Buren, our friend Colonel Johnson, Buchanan, Benton, Cass, Calhoun, and others, down the entire alphabet, mean to waive their various and conflicting pretensions, and support the present incumbent?"

Concludes with the observation that the Democrats "have reproached us with having no principles. What are their's? They have made relentless opposition to all our measures of relief; and when fairly beaten in the halls of Congress, they have fled for refuge to Mr. Tyler and the Veto. What do they propose for this suffering country? If not responsible for existing embarrassments, they would be bound, as statesmen and patriots, to contribute all in their power to the deliverance of their country from them. But if their unwise policy occasioned them, are not they doubly bound? What, I respectfully again ask, is their remedy? If it be not the condemned Sub Treasury, Hard Money, Free Trade and Direct Taxes—what is it?" Copy, printed pamphlet. *Speech of Henry Clay at Dayton, Ohio, September 29, 1842.* As Reported by Marcus T.C. Gould, stenographer. Cincinnati, 1842. 24 pp. No manuscript version has been found.

According to Gould, the "multitude" to which Clay spoke was "variously estimated from one hundred thousand to two hundred thousand." See also Clay to Crane, September 1, 1842. The Dayton event was sponsored by Ohio Whigs for

Whigs residing in "her sister Kentucky" to see which of the two groups was supreme "in Whig principles." The formal invitation is in J. Ridgway, Jr., *et al.* (i.e., the Ohio Whig State Central Committee) to Kentucky, dated Columbus, Ohio, August 23, 1842, printed in *Speech of Henry Clay at Dayton, Ohio, September 29, 1842*, p. 24. The invitation is signed also by John A. Lazell, John Greenwood, A.F. Perry, Lewis Heyl, C.H. Wing, and S.Z. Seltzer.

A House Select Committee, chaired by John Q. Adams, had made a report on August 17, 1842, which concluded with a resolution calling for a constitutional amendment which would have allowed Congress to overrule a presidential veto by a simple majority of both houses rather than a 2/3 majority. The resolution was lost, however, when the House voted 99 in favor and 90 against, thereby failing to give it the two-thirds majority necessary in each house for the passage of a constitutional amendment. U.S. H. of Reps., *Journal*, 27 Cong., 2 Sess., 1352.

From HIRAM MENDENHALL[1] *et al.* Richmond, Ind., October 1, 1842

We, the undersigned, citizens of Indiana, in view of the declaration of rights contained in the charter of American independence; in view of that justice which is due from man to his fellow men; and in view of those noble principles which should characterize the patriot, the philanthropist and the Christian; ask you, most respectfully, to unloose the heavy burdens and that you let the oppressed under your control, who call you "master" go free. By doing so you would give liberty to whom liberty is due, and do no more than justice to those under your charge, who have long been deprived by you of the sacred boon of freedom; and set an example that would result in much good to suffering and debased humanity; and do an act altogether worthy of a great and good man.[2]

Copy. Printed in Leonard S. Kenworthy, "Henry Clay at Richmond in 1842," *IMH* (Dec., 1934), 30:355. For an account of Clay's visit to Richmond, Ind., see *ibid.*, 353-58. 1. Clay to Noble, July 18, 1842. 2. See Speech in Richmond, Ind., Oct. 1, 1842.

SPEECH IN RICHMOND, INDIANA October 1, 1842

I hope that Mr. [Hiram] Mendenhall may be treated with the greatest forbearance and respect.[1] I assure my fellow-citizens here collected, that the presentation of the petition [that Clay free his own slaves] has not occasioned the slightest pain, nor excited one solitary disagreeable emotion. If it were to be presented to me, I prefer that it should be done in the face of this vast assemblage. I think I can give it such an answer as becomes me and the subject of which it treats. At all events, I entreat and beseech my fellow-citizens, for their sake, for my country's sake, for my sake, to offer no disrespect, no indignity, no violence, in word or deed, to Mr. Mendenhall.

I will now, sir, make to you and to this petition such a response as becomes me. Allow me to say that I think you have not conformed to the independent character of an American citizen in presenting a *petition* to *me.* I am, like yourself, but a private citizen. A petition, as the term implies, generally proceeds from an inferior in power or station to a superior; but between us there is entire equality. And what are the circumstances under which you have chosen to offer it? I am a total stranger, passing through your State, on my way to its capital, in consequence of an invitation with which I have been honored to visit it, to exchange friendly salutations with such of my fellow-citizens of Indiana as think proper to meet me, and to accept of their hospitality. Anxious as I am to see them, and to view parts of this State which I had never seen, I came here with hesitation and reluctance, because I apprehended that the motives of my journey might be misconceived and perverted. But when the fulfillment of an old promise to visit Indianapolis was insisted upon, I yielded to the solicitations of friends, and have presented myself among you.

Such is the occasion which has been deliberately selected for tendering this petition to me. I am advanced in years, and neither myself nor the place of my residence is altogether unknown to the world. You might at any time within these last twenty-five or thirty years, have presented your petition to me at Ashland. If you had gone there for that purpose, you should have been received and treated with perfect respect and liberal hospitality.

Now, Mr. Mendenhall, let us reverse conditions, and suppose that you had been invited to Kentucky to partake of its hospitality; and that, previous to your arrival, I had employed such means as I understand have been used to get up this petition, to obtain the signatures of citizens of that State to a petition to present to you to relinquish your farm or other property, what would you have thought of such a proceeding? Would you have deemed it courteous and according to the rites of hospitality?

I know well, that you and those who think with you, controvert the legitimacy of slavery, and deny the right of property in slaves. But the law of my State and other States has otherwise ordained. The law may be wrong in your opinion, and ought to be repealed; but then you and your associates are not the law-makers for us, and unless you can show some authority to nullify our laws, we must continue to respect them. Until the law is repealed, we must be excused for asserting the rights—aye, the property in slaves—which it sanctions, authorizes, and vindicates.

And who are the petitioners whose organ you assume to be? I have no doubt that many of them are worthy, amiable, and humane persons, who, by erroneous representations, have been induced inconsiderately to affix their signatures to this petition, and that they will deeply regret it. Others, and not a few, I am told, are free blacks, men, women, and children, who have been artfully deceived and imposed upon. A very large portion, I have been credibly informed, are the political opponents of the party to which I belong—democrats, as they most undeservedly call themselves, who have eagerly seized this opportunity to wound, as they imagine, my feelings, and to aid the cause to which they are attached. In other quarters of the Union, democrats claim to be the exclusive champions of southern interests, the only safe defenders of the rights in slave property, and unjustly accuse us whigs with abolition designs wholly incompatible with its security. What ought those distant democrats to think of the course of their friends here, who have united in this petition?

And what is the foundation of this appeal to me in Indiana, to liberate the slaves under my care, in Kentucky? It is a general declaration in the act announcing to the world the independence of the thirteen American colonies, that all men are created equal. Now, as an abstract principle, there is no doubt of the truth of that declaration; and it is desirable, in the original construction of society, and in organized societies, to keep it in view as a great fundamental principle. But, then, I apprehend that in no society that ever did exist, or ever shall be formed, was or can the equality asserted among the members of the human race, be practically enforced and carried out. There are portions of it, large portions, women, minors, insane, culprits, transient sojourners, that will always probably remain subject to the government of another portion of the community.

That declaration, whatever may be the extent of its import, was made by the delegations of the thirteen States. In most of them slavery existed, and had long existed, and was established by law. It was introduced and forced upon the colonies by the paramount law of England. Do you believe that, in making that declaration, the States that concurred in it intended that it should be tortured into a virtual emancipation of all the slaves within their respective limits? Would Virginia and the other southern States have ever united in a declaration which was to be interpreted into an abolition of slavery among them? Did any one of the thirteen States entertain such a design or expectation? To impute such a secret and unavowed purpose would be to charge a political fraud upon the noblest band of patriots that ever assembled in council; a fraud upon the confederacy of the Revolution; a fraud upon the union of those States, whose Constitution not only recognized the lawfulness of slavery, but permitted the importation of slaves from Africa, until the year 1808. And I am bold to say, that, if the doctrines of ultra political abolitionists had been seriously promulgated at the epoch of our Revolution, our glorious independence would never have been achieved—never, never.

I know the predominant sentiment in the free States is adverse to slavery; but, happy in their own exemption from whatever evils may attend it, the great mass of our fellow-citizens there do not seek to violate the Constitution, or to disturb the harmony of these States. I desire no concealment of my opinions in regard to the institution of slavery. I look upon it as a great evil, and deeply lament that we have derived it from the parental government, and from our ancestors. I wish every slave in the United States was in the country of his ancestors. But here they are, and the question is, how they can be best dealt with? If a state of nature existed, and we were about to lay the foundations of society, no man would be more strongly opposed than I should be, to incorporate the institution of slavery among its elements. But there is an incalculable difference between the original formation of society and a long existing organized society, with its ancient laws, institutions, and establishments. Now, great as I acknowledge, in my opinion, the evils of slavery are, they are nothing, absolutely nothing, in comparison with the far greater evils which would inevitably flow from a sudden, general, and indiscriminate emancipation. In some of the States the number of slaves approximates toward an equality with that of the whites; in one or two they surpass them. What would be the condition of the two races in those States, upon the supposition of an immediate emancipation? Does any man suppose that they would become blended into one homogeneous mass? Does any man recommend amalgamation—that revolting admixture, alike offensive to God and man; for those whom he, by their physical properties, has made unlike and put asunder, we may, without presumptuousness, suppose were never intended to be joined together in one of the holiest rites. And let me tell you, sir, if you do not already know it, that such are the feelings—prejudice, if you please (and what man, claiming to be a statesman, will overlook or disregard the deep-seated and unconquerable prejudices of the people?)—in the slave States, that no human law could enforce a union between the two races.

What then would certainly happen? A struggle for political ascendancy; the blacks seeking to acquire, and the whites to maintain, possession of the government. Upon the supposition of a general immediate emancipation in those States where the blacks outnumber the whites, they would have nothing to do but to insist upon another part of the same declaration of independence, as Dorr and his deluded democratic followers recently did in Rhode Island; according to which, an undefined majority have the right, at their pleasure, to subvert an existing government, and institute a new one in its place, and then the whites would be brought in complete subjection to the blacks! A contest would inevitably ensue between the two races—civil war, carnage, pillage, conflagration, devastation, and the ultimate extermination or expulsion of the blacks. Nothing is more certain. And are not these evils far greater than the mild and continually improving state of slavery which exists in this country? I say continually improving; for if this gratifying progress in the amelioration of the condition of the slaves has been checked in some of the States, the responsibility must attach to the unfortunate agitation of the subject of abolition. In consequence of it, increased rigor in the police, and further restraints have been imposed; and I do believe that gradual emancipation (the only method of liberation that has ever been thought safe or wise by any body in any of the slave States), has been postponed half a century.

Without any knowledge of the relation in which I stand to my slaves, or their individual condition, you, Mr. Mendenhall, and your associates, who have been active in getting up this petition, call upon me forthwith to liberate the whole of them. Now let me tell you, that some half a dozen of them, from age, decrepitude, or infirmity, are wholly unable to gain a livelihood for themselves, and are a heavy charge upon me. Do you think that I should conform to the dictates of humanity by ridding myself of that charge, and sending them forth into the world with the boon of liberty, to end a wretched existence in starvation? Another class is composed of helpless infants, with or without improvident mothers. Do you believe as a Christian, that I should perform my duty toward them by abandoning them to their fate? Then there is another class who would not accept their freedom if I would give it to them. I have for many years owned a slave that I wished would leave me, but he will not. What shall I do with that class?

What my treatment of my slaves is you may learn from Charles [Dupuy], who accompanies me on this journey, and who has traveled with me over the greater part of the United States, and in both the Canadas, and has had a thousand opportunities, if he had chosen to embrace them, to leave me. Excuse me, Mr. Mendenhall, for saying that my slaves are as well fed and clad, look as sleek and hearty, and are quite as civil and respectful in their demeanor, and as little disposed to wound the feelings of any one, as you are.

Let me recommend you, sir, to imitate the benevolent example of the society of Friends, in the midst of which you reside. Meek, gentle, imbued with the genuine spirit of our benign religion, while in principle they are firmly opposed to slavery, they do not seek to accomplish its extinction by foul epithets, coarse and vulgar abuse, and gross calumny. Their ways do not lead through blood, revolution, and disunion. Their broad and comprehensive philanthropy embraces, as they believe, the good and the happiness of the white as well as the black race; giving to one their commiseration, to the other their kindest sympathy. Their instruments are not those of detraction and war, but of peace, persuasion, and earnest appeals to the charities of the human heart. Unambitious, they have no political objects or purposes to subserve. My intercourse with them throughout life has been considerable, interesting, and agreeable: and I venture to say, nothing could have induced them, as a society, whatever a few individuals might have been tempted to do, to seize the occasion of my casual passage through this State to offer me a personal indignity.

I respect the motives of the rational abolitionists, who are actuated by a sentiment of devotion to human liberty, although I deplore and deprecate the consequences of the agitation of the question. I have even many friends among them. But they are not monomaniacs, who, surrendering themselves to a single idea, look altogether to the black side of human life. They do not believe that the sum total of all our efforts and all our solicitude should be abolition. They believe there are duties to perform toward the white man as well as the black. They want good government, good administration, and the general prosperity of their country.

I shall, Mr. Mendenhall, take your petition into respectful and deliberate consideration; but before I come to a final decision, I should like to know what you and your associates are willing to do for the slaves in my possession, if I should think proper to liberate them. I own about fifty, who are probably worth about fifteen thousand dollars. To turn them loose upon society without any means of subsistence or support would be an act of cruelty. Are you willing to raise and secure the payment of fifteen thousand dollars for their benefit, if I should be induced to free them? The security of the payment of that sum would materially lessen the obstacle in the way of their emancipation.

And now, Mr. Mendenhall, I must take respectful leave of you. We separate, as we have met, with no unkind feelings, no excited anger or dissatisfaction on my part, whatever may have been your motives, and these I refer to our common Judge above, to whom we are both responsible. Go home, and mind your own business,[2] and leave other people to take care of theirs. Limit your benevolent exertions to your own neighborhood. Within that circle you will find ample scope for the exercise of all your charities. Dry up the tears of the afflicted widows around you, console and comfort the helpless orphan, clothe the naked, and feed and help the poor, black and white, who need succor; and you will be a better and wiser man than you have this day shown yourself.

Copy. Printed in Colton, *Clay Correspondence*, 6:385-90. Often titled "Reply to [Hiram] Mendenhall." For an account of Clay's visit to Richmond, Ind., in Oct., 1842, see Leonard

S. Kenworthy, "Henry Clay at Richmond in 1842," *IMH* (Dec., 1934), 30:353-58. 1. Mendenhall to Clay, Oct. 1, 1842. 2. An earlier version of this sentence apparently read: "Go home and slop your hogs." Kenworthy, "Henry Clay at Richmond," *IMH*, 30: 353.

Speech in Indianapolis, October 5, 1842. Speaking of his "enthusiastic reception" in Indiana during the past few days, notes that he could not help but contrast it with his situation 15 years ago, at the time of the so-called "corrupt bargain" with President Adams. Then, he recalls (raising his voice), "it appeared all mankind conspired against me [4:48, 53-54, 73-74, 80-85, 113-14, 144-50, 157-59; 7:716-19; Beverley to Clay, February 8, 1842]. My motives were traduced, my character aspersed and vilified; but I was strong *here*, HERE (striking his breast) in honesty and fidelity to my country. I said then—and thank God the people of Indiana are sustaining the declaration!—that 'truth is omnipotent, and public justice certain.' " Does not believe, however, that he personally is worthy of the grand reception he has received. "No, no! *It is the cause*—THE GLORIOUS CAUSE—the system of national policy, of which I have long been an humble advocate, that calls forth this exhibition of feeling—this display of sensibility."

Outlines his principles, viz:

"1st. 'A currency of uniform value springing from the will of the nation.'

"2d. 'The duty of the national legislature to give protection to the industry of the people of the U. States.'

"Mr. Clay said he would not quarrel with any one about *forms*. The bill would meet his approbation which afforded satisfaction to the greatest numbers. He looked to the substance rather than to the form. He should prefer that the principles of the compromise act be adhered to as closely as possible. The *home* valuation provision should have been insisted upon, though some gentlemen of the south deemed it impracticable. Mr. Clay differed with them on this subject. He knew that the compromise act of 1833, never could have received the sanction of congress but for the incorporation of this most salutary principle; and if it cannot now be carried out, the compromise should be abandoned. He was for a tariff for revenue to the government and protection to the manufacturers.

"3d. The curtailment of the arbitrary use of the executive power, and especially the resistance of the monarchical feature, the veto, transferred from foreign governments, and engrafted on our own.

"4th. The distribution of the proceeds of the public lands, which, though now suspended by the exercise of executive power, he hoped would not be longer than the suspension of some of the banks in the redemption of their notes.

"5th. Upon the subject of internal improvements, Mr. Clay said that although he did not doubt the power of the general government to carry out a system of public improvements, as heretofore expressed in the Senate, he would be willing to abandon that power, in exchange for the one of distribution, except as it related to Lake Harbors, the commerce of the seaboard, and national roads. These ought to be prosecuted under authority of the general government."

Lauds President Tyler and Secretary of State Webster for their work in securing the Webster-Ashburton treaty [Ashburton to Clay, April 11, 1842] with Great Britain ("all credit is due them for this negotiation" even though Tyler "deserves so little commendation in other respects"), and proclaims it a fair and balanced solution to the northeastern boundary issue which Jackson had failed signally to solve. Sees it as assurance of permanent Anglo-American peace ("experience teaches that those treaties are most enduring where *neither* party has secured any undue advantage"), and says he would have voted for ratification had he been in the Senate.

Discusses the domestic issues faced in the so-called "extra session" of Congress [27th Congress, 1st Session], which he had urged "the lamented Harrison" to call, and during which the Whigs had attempted to write into legislation the will of the people as expressed in the election of 1840. Explains the fate of the national bank bills during that session. Asks: "Fellow citizens . . . what did *you* mean by the victory of 1840? Did you mean only to change one tenent of the white house for another? Was it to be a barren victory? No! no! The object *you* had in view was to produce a radical change in the policy of the government. *You* wish to see the currency restored, disordered exchanges rectified, a revival of business secured, and all the great measures decreed by the will of the nation established. Forty years had attended the utility of a national bank, in establishing a national currency. At that extra session, a bank bill was introduced and contrary to the general expectation, vetoed by the president. So anxious, however, were the whigs to carry out the will of the nation, that some of them (I was not of the number) wished to ascertain from Mr. Tyler *what kind* of a bank bill would meet *his* approbation. He (Mr. Clay) could not go and ask any executive a question of that sort. The president did tell them. They exhibited the draft of a bill and with his own hand and his own pen he altered the title. He told *them* he would sign it—he told his secretary of state [Webster] that it would be approved by him. This was one of the occasions on which (contrary to his [Clay's] general practice and the habits of his life), he 'kept dark.' He felt sure that if he favored it, that very favor would be likely to prejudice the measure in the estimation of the executive. . . . We passed the bill in the senate in the same shape in which it came from the house, and as exhibited to the president—body, head, and tail. Would you suppose it possible that a bill thus prepared would receive his veto? Singular as it must appear, it was vetoed, and on such principles, too, as left us no hope of establishing any bill calculated to correct the currency of the country."

Defends himself against the recurring "corrupt bargain" charge as it related to his guidance from the Kentucky general assembly on the matter: "Here . . . let me correct a mistake which seems to be abroad in some quarters, resembling an old story of many years standing. When I voted for Mr. Adams, it was said that I violated *instructions. Not so*! When I gave that vote, I represented the Lexington district, and it is a well known fact, that at no period since that vote was cast, has the Lexington district reversed it, in any manner. The counties which composed it never gave a majority for Gen. Jackson. The legislature had no power over members of congress. Both are equally the servants of the people—elected by the people—and subject alone to their correction. I was sustained by the people who elected me, and to them I dare appeal for my justification. In regard to the bankrupt bill I was never instructed. The house passed resolutions to that effect; they were sent to the senate, amended, returned to the house, the amendment not concurred in, and the matter fell between the two branches of the legislature."

Explains that in hard money countries and areas like England, Ireland, Scotland, France, Portugal, Spain, and Cuba the people are miserable and wretched; and adds that many Democrats and "some of the whigs too" who favor a hard money economy "are in the same condition. They cry for hard money, when they have not a dollar's worth in the world." Assures his audience that the Democrats are not necessarily democrats and that they have no "exclusive claim . . . to that title." Reminds them, further, that "I was myself born a democrat—rocked in the cradle of the revolution—and at the darkest period of that ever memorable struggle for freedom. I recollect in 1781 or '82, a visit made by [Sir Banastre] Tarleton's troops to the house of my mother, and of their running their swords into the new made graves of my father and grandfather, thinking they contained hidden treasures. Though then not more than four years of age, the circumstance of that visit is vividly remembered, and it will be to the last moment of my life. I was born a democrat—was raised and nurtured a republican—and shall die a republican, in the faith and principles of my fathers." Summary from New York *Express* as reprinted in *Niles' Register* (October 29, 1842), 63:135.

On the subjects of free trade, protectionism, and hard money, topics not included in the *Niles' Register* version of the Indianapolis speech, Clay had this to say: "The Whigs don't want to destroy commerce, or to prohibit the introduction of foreign fabrics—that would be uncivilized; but they wish to secure a system of National *Independence*, which will enable the American people to live more upon their own resources. This is Whig policy. What do the Democratic leaders say at Washington?—They are in favor of 'free trade' and would have no duties levied, but admit foreign fabrics, regulated only by the wants of the country. It is true, they don't profess that this is their object, but it is the inevitable result of their doctrine. By their 'free trade' notions, if practically carried out, our country would be impoverished—drained of the hard money which our Democratic leaders are so anxious to establish as the standard value of our productions. While our money would be thus drawn from us to support the pauper labor of Europe, they would not buy a cents worth from us not needed by their direct necessities. A state of things like this would not fail to drive us back to our colonial condition before the Revolution, when coon-skins and peltries formed the currency. While they are thus recommending to us the adoption of light duties and free trade, or no duties at all, they are submitting to the most enormous duties, imposed by foreign Governments, on their own productions, amounting to nineteen hundred per cent on the article of tobacco alone! This is 'reciprocity!' —the reciprocity of American 'free trade' politicians and British manufacturers! Let me ask which party is the wisest and most patriotic—the one which protects the industry of the country from the rivalry of foreign governments, or that which consigns to the control of such rivalry the most vital interests of this great nation?" Copy, excerpt. Printed in William G. Brownlow, *A Political Register . . . With the Life and Public Services of Henry Clay* (Jonesboro, Tenn., 1844), 67-68. Brownlow misdates the Indianapolis speech as November 5, 1842.

The Indianapolis *Indiana State Sentinel*, October 18, 1842, a Democratic party paper highly critical of Clay, reported that "The speech of Mr. Clay, made here, is not come-at-a-ble; and we give his friends credit for suppressing it." The *Sentinel* notes, however, that "Mr. Clay took strong grounds for a National Bank" and "took special pains to attack General Jackson." The paper also points out that Clay's "change of attack from Gen. Jackson to John Tyler was a good move for him; but it was made too late. Henry Clay is a 'used up man.' " Unable to obtain a copy of or a reporter's summary of Clay's speech in Indianapolis, the editor of the *Sentinel* ran instead, on October 18, excerpts from Clay's speech in the Senate on January 28-29, 1841, dealing with preemption, this with a view toward demonstrating Clay's hostility to Jackson's public land policy in general and his contempt for squatters in particular. This information courtesy of Mr. John Miller, Indiana Historical Society, Indianapolis.

For Clay's recollection of the Tarleton raid in Spring, 1781, see Bernard Mayo, *Henry Clay, Spokesman of the New West* (Boston, 1937), 5-6.

The Ky. house had adopted resolutions on January 5, 1842, by a vote of 76-21 instructing her U.S. senators and requesting her representatives to use their exertions to have the Bankruptcy bill repealed. The resolutions then went to the Ky. senate where they were passed 22 to 7 with amendments on January 18. The senate amendments changed the wording from "instructing" the senators to "requesting" them and also changed the emphasis from working for repeal of the Bankruptcy bill to supporting a public land sales distribution bill. On January 19 the house rejected the amended resolutions, 82 to 5. The following day the senate insisted on its own amended version; on January 24 the house "adhered" to the original resolutions and on the 28th the senate again "adhered" to its amendments. There the matter rested. Ky. H. of Reps., *Journal* . . . 1841-1842, pp. 11, 48, 61-63, 66, 143, 150-51, 158, 204, 223; Ky. Sen., *Journal* . . . 1841-1842, pp. 48, 56, 113-17, 123, 167.

Speech in Columbus, Indiana, [*ca.* October 6-9], 1842. Clay was introduced to the crowd at the courthouse at Columbus by former (1837-39) Indiana Whig Congressman William Herod, who had fought for his country under General Jackson and was at this particular moment in what a reporter present termed a state of "*peculiar excitement.*" Indeed, Herod began his introduction with the shout "Hurra for Jackson." Clay, also "evidently in a state of high excitement, from what cause we are unable to say," emphatically replied: "Hurra for Jackson, you say. Where is your country? I say hurra for my country, and the man that says hurra for Jackson, deserves not the name of a freeman, but he ought to be a subject of the autocrat of Russia, and have the yoke of tyranny placed upon his neck till he was bowed down, down to the very dust." Copy. Printed in Indianapolis *Indiana State Sentinel*, November 1, 1842. This information courtesy of Mr. John Miller, Indiana Historical Society. Save for this single quotation, Clay's speech in Columbus has not been found. For Herod, see *BDAC*.

To TRUSTEES OF TRANSYLVANIA UNIVERSITY

Lexington, October 12, 1842

By an agreement between you and me as the Exor of Col. James Morrison, I was to be chargeable & have accordingly been charged with interest upon the assumed sum of fourteen thousand dollars. That agreement bears date the 24h. Nov 1822.[1]

Mrs. [Esther Montgomery] Morrison, by the will of Col. Morrison, was impowered to dispose of fifteen thousand dollars, and she has by her last will executed that power.[2] Consequently I became bound, upon her death, to pay that sum in conformity with her will; and hold myself chargeable accordingly.

Adding that sum to the advances for the Estate of Col. Morrison, made since the last settlement of account with the County Court of Fayette, and the result is that his Estate now stands indebted to me.

I have deemed it proper therefore to notify you that I consider myself absolved from the payment of interest, agreeable to the above agreement from the day of Mrs. Morrisons death,[3] or from such other day as according to law I stand absolved.[4]

ALS. DLC-TJC (DNA, M212, R10). 1. Not found. 2. In his will James Morrison had left his wife $15,000 in land and $15,000 in money, as well as five slaves of her choice. In her will she freed five slaves and divided the land and money among her sister, nephew, niece, and other relatives with some of the money going into a trust fund. Fayette County Will Book, P, 1841, pp. 280-82. 3. Mrs. Morrison's will was probated in the Oct., 1842 session of the Fayette County Court. 4. On Oct. 12, 1842, Clay gave an Executor's Bond for $70,000 to the Fayette County Court, pledging to inventory and distribute the estate of Esther Morrison "*to such person or persons as shall be entitled to the same by law or the provisions of said will*" and to "*execute all trusts and powers with which* he *shall be invested by the provisions of said will.*" DS. Fayette County Executor's Bonds, No. 4 (1838-52), p. 108.

To JOHN SLOANE

Lexington, October 28,1842

I thank you for your friendly letter communicating your view of the causes of the result of the recent election in Ohio.[1] It came upon us with a considerable shock, as we had confidently anticipated a different event. Its effect will however I think be only temporary. Whenever the Whigs shall recover from the disappointment produced by Mr. Tyler's course, and especially when our opponents shall designate their Presidential Candidate, we may I hope look for success with confidence. As for myself I have reached a time of life, and have so often had occasion to regret the success of erroneous systems and principles of public policy, that I shall be prepared for any issue of the struggle in which we are engaged. . . .

ALS. MH. 1. Clay to Ewing, July 24, 1842.

From AMBROSE SPENCER Lyons, N.Y., October 28, 1842

I have read with deep mortification a letter addressed by my son, John C. Spencer, to certain persons in Rochester.[1] Among the first ideas suggested by this letter, was this; whether you would not naturally infer, a coincidence on my part, in the general sentiments of the letter. I feel impelled by self respect, & the sincere regard I have for you personally, as well by my admiration of your brilliant & patriotic career through your life time, to remove from your mind any erroneous opinions on points affecting my own consistency & honor. I then assure you, that my son has not spoken my opinions, in several & indeed in the main points of his letter. I have held no counsel with him, nor even attempted to controul him, but have left him free to act without any advice of mine. I heartily concur with my whig brethren throughout the nation, that Mr. Tyler has acted most perfidiously towards those who have elevated him to power; & I feel for him that contempt, which his duplicity & perfidy ought to inspire in honorable bosoms. Altho' I can not think my son would knowingly mistake facts, yet the advice he imputes to Mr Tyler's first cabinet, is so extraordinary, that it seems to me improbable if not impossible.

When I last saw you in Washington it was my wish to have a full conversation with you, but it was a period, which forbid that gratificat[ion.]

I have now disburthened my mind from what would have weighed upon it, & altho' I should object to any publicity being given to this letter thro' the press, I have no objection to your communicating its contents to discrete friends—

What will be the issue of our election is impossible in this great state, to be foretold with any certainty[2]—Every thing depends on a full poll, if it be a full one I think we shall succeed. I do not believe, that Webster's speech[3] or Cushings,[4] or the letter will have any material effect. . . . P.S. I shall leave this [place] in a few days for Albany where I shall spend the winter

ALS. DLC-HC (DNA, M212, R5). Printed in Colton, *Clay Correspondence*, 4:472. 1. On Oct. 19, 1842, John C. Spencer had written a letter in response to one from "The friends of the administration of President Tyler in Western New York." The letter analyzed and explained Tyler's messages to Congress and was, in general, a long and detailed defense of Tyler's leading policies, including his foreign policy and his vetoes of the various national bank and tariff-distribution bills, as well as his counter proposal for a Board of Exchequer bank plan. He also lauded Tyler's reorganization of his Cabinet, and criticized Clay's attacks on the president. He offered these "views and sentiments . . . in explanation of my position, and in defense against the reproaches which have been cast upon me for not resigning the office I hold." These reproaches, he opined, stemmed from his "best exertions to prevent the nomination of Mr. Clay, at the Harrisburg Convention

[Porter to Clay, Nov. 14 and Dec. 30, 1837]" in Dec., 1839. In the letter Spencer also claimed that when Tyler had returned the second bank bill with his veto [Tyler to Clay, April 30, 1841], he had asked the advice of the Cabinet on whether or not he should include in his veto message a statement promising that he would retire from public life at the end of the existing presidential term. Spencer said the Cabinet dissuaded him from this action, arguing that no one had the right to expect such a promise and that, since he had not himself been elected president, he had no obligation to abide by the one-term pledge which Harrison had made. Washington *The Madisonian*, Oct. 27, 1842. 2. Clay to Porter, August 29, 1842. 3. On Sept. 30, 1842, at a public dinner in his honor at Faneuil Hall celebrating the conclusion of the Webster-Ashburton Treaty, Webster spoke at length defending the Tyler administration and criticizing those in Congress who "seem more desirous to make out a case against the President, than of serving their country to the extent of their ability, vetoes notwithstanding." He called the idea of a national bank "obsolete" and endorsed Tyler's Exchequer plan [Clay to J.B. Clay, Dec. 10, 1841]. He attacked the Compromise Tariff of 1833 [8:604, 619-22, 626-27] charging that the motive of the act was "to impose for all time a restriction upon the Legislature in regard to levying duties without any changes in the Constitution." He concluded by declaring his willingness to "act with sober men of any party and of all parties." James W. McIntyre (ed.), *The Writings and Speeches of Daniel Webster in Eighteen Volumes. National Edition* . . . (Boston, 1903), 3:116-40; Washington *Daily National Intelligencer*, Oct. 31, 1842. 4. On Oct. 7, 1842, at Temple Street Church in Newberryport, Mass., Caleb Cushing spoke to his constituents, giving an account of his "stewardship" in the House of Representatives. He defended President Tyler and charged that the issue of the national bank "made by Henry Clay and by him forced upon the Harrison Cabinet is the source of all subsequent political and party evils." He also argued that premature discussion of a Whig presidential candidate for 1844 would further fragment the Whig party. Claude M. Fuess, *The Life of Caleb Cushing*, 2 vols. (reprint ed., Hamden, Conn., 1965), 1:365-66.

To EPES SARGENT Lexington, October 29, 1842

My frequent absences from home during the last few weeks have delayed my acknowledge[ment] of the receipt of your several favors transmitting the memoranda with which I had supplied you for the biography.[1] I have received them all in safety and thank you for the punctuality with which you have returned them.

We are all looking with anxiety to New York to compensate at the approaching election[2] for disappointments which have existed elsewhere.

LS. MB. 1. Clay to Sargent, July 16, 1842. 2. Clay to Porter, August 29, 1842.

To James B. Watkins, Owensboro, Ky., October 31, 1842. Reports that while he is going to Louisiana "for business and health" this fall, he is not inclined to make a public appearance in Owensboro en route, because "it is inexpedient for me to present myself, any where, under circumstances which might seem to indicate that I was soliciting the popular suffrage." ALS. DLC-HC (DNA, M212, R9).

To JOHN M. CLAYTON Lexington, November 2, 1842

A thousand thanks for your noble defense of me and the Compromise Act, in your Speech at Philada.[1] and in Vindex.[2] It was worthy of you, and is entitled to my lasting gratitude.

Was ever man so fallen as Mr. Webster? His Faneuil Hall Speech is the most vulnerable production, from beginning to end, that any sensible man ever put forth.[3] There is not a paragraph in it which might not be seriously and justly animadverted upon. I at one time thought of making a formal reply to it. You have relieved me from that office, and perhaps considerations of policy were opposed to it; for there will be a few adhering to a man, who once stood so high even in his present prostrate condition.

And there is [John C.] Spencer too![4] What a tryo [*sic*, trio], Tyler, Webster and Spencer!

I am glad that Vindex brought forward that resolution of Mr. W. which I had almost forgotten.[5]

Be of good cheer, my true friend, all will be right yet. Depend upon it, the elections of this year are no test of public opinion.[6] With the divisions of the other party; with the high handed measures which they will endeavor to push when the majorities are with them, in the State Legislatures; and with the approach of the day of deliverance from fate, perfidious and weak counsellors, we shall, by the blessing of God, achieve a glorious triumph.

My franking privilege has not yet expired, or I should not have troubled you with this brief letter; for whether you hear from me or not, I am sure that your confidence will be unshaken in the affection & attachment of. . . .

ALS. DLC-John M. Clayton Papers (DNA, M212, R20). 1. Clayton had spoken at a Whig meeting in Philadelphia on Oct. 5, 1842, attacking especially the portion of Webster's Faneuil Hall speech of Sept. 30 which impugned the motives of Henry Clay in bringing forward the Compromise Tariff of 1833 [8:604, 619-22, 626-27]. Clay had, said Clayton, stepped forward with the compromise tariff in order to save the manufacturing interests of the country as well as to save the nation from the consequences of nullification. Washington *Daily National Intelligencer*, Oct. 8. 1842. 2. An article signed "Vindex" appeared in the Washington *Daily National Intelligencer* on Oct. 31, 1842. It pointed out "gross inconsistancies" between Webster's Faneuil Hall speech and his former opinions on banks and the currency. It also accused him of "gross injustice to Mr. Clay" in impugning the motives of the compromise act itself and denied that the motive of the act was to restrict the power of Congress to pass a protective tariff. In fact, Vindex noted, John M. Clayton had expressly declared in 1833 that the act was no more binding on subsequent legislatures than any other act. 3. A. Spencer to Clay, Oct. 28, 1842. 4. *Ibid.* 5. In 1833 Webster had introduced a resolution in the Senate which said, in part, that "The annual revenues of the country ought not be allowed to exceed a just estimate of the wants of the Government." Washington *Daily National Intelligencer*, Oct. 31, 1842. 6. Clay to Crittenden, June 3, 1842.

To AMBROSE SPENCER Lexington, November 9, 1842

I duly received your friendly letter of the 28h. Ulto. My knowledge of your character, and my great confidence in your honor and probity would have prevented my indulging, for a single moment, the supposition that you coincided in the views feelings and opinions of the Secretary of War [John C. Spencer], as disclosed in his late letter,[1] without any communication from you. The only occasion, therefore, for that, with which you have favored me, is that which you have assigned, to disburthen your own mind. I needed no such testimony to your fidelity. Without it, I should have known that an intelligent mind and an upright heart, like yours, must necessarily have felt and thought of the conduct of Mr. Tyler as you do.

I respect the delicacy of the relation between the Secretary and you too highly to admit of my making any public use of your letter. I shall rarely, if ever, shew it confidentially.

The fate of the Empire State for one year was decided yesterday.[2] I am prepared to hear of the defeat of the Whigs. But such a result cannot change our principles nor alter our duty to our Country. Nor will it lead me to despair of an auspicious issue of the contest of 1844. When the question is reduced to a competition with only two men, with their well known respective principles; and when the patronage of Mr. Tyler shall have lost its potent influence, and the Whigs see distinctly, nigh at hand, a deliverance from weakness folly and treachery, I am greatly deceived if they do not achieve a victory as glorious as that of 1840.

ALS. PHi. 1. Spencer to Clay, Oct. 28, 1842. 2. Clay to Porter, August 29, 1842.

To JOHN S. LITTELL Lexington, November 11, 1842

I received your favor of the 28th ultimo, with the small volume accompanying it, containing your Biographical Notice of me.[1] Amid preparations for my departure for Louisiana, where I propose passing at New Orleans a portion of the ensuing winter, I have not yet given it the deliberate perusal to which, I have no doubt, its merits entitle it, although I have looked a little into it with much satisfaction. But I can not delay conveying an expression of my grateful thanks for the interest which you take in me, and of which I have received many strong proofs. I appreciate these, the higher, because I am quite sure that they have been rendered from disinterested and patriotic motives. I pray you to accept my cordial acknowledgments for them all.

I am now in the hands of a Philadelphia artist, Mr. Neagle,[2] who has advanced me so far in his portrait of me, and with so much success, that I feel authorized to say that I think he will make a faithful and spirited likeness of me. . . .

Copy. Printed in Colton, *Clay Correspondence*, 4:473. 1. Littell to Clay, August 17, 1842. 2. For John Neagle (1796-1865), a well-known Philadelphia portrait painter, see *DAB*. The painting Neagle was working on hangs in the Union League Club in Philadelphia. See Amyx, "Portraits of Henry Clay," typescript, University of Kentucky, vol. A, for Neagle's various portraits of Clay; also Clay to Neagle, May 29, 1842.

To OLIVER H. SMITH Lexington, November 11, 1842

I have this moment received your friendly letter. Your suggestions as to the cause of our defeat at recent elections are I think weighty and just. There is good reason to believe that when there is a single and direct contest between two candidates and only two, a different result will happen; we shall then be aided too by all intervening measures of our opponents, in States where they have acquired the Legislative ascendency.

I am truly concerned that any doubt should remain of your election.[1] When I left you, I had other hopes and impressions, and shall trust that your apprehensions may not be realized; although I agree with you that at present, a private station is the post of honor and profit.

I expect to go in eight or ten days to Louisiana, where I expect to remain the greater part of the winter, and where I shall be glad to hear from you at Washington. . . .

Copy. Printed in O.H. Smith, *Early Indiana Trials: and Sketches, Reminiscences* (Cincinnati, 1858), 260. 1. On Jan. 24, 1843, the Indiana legislature elected Democrat Edward A. Hannegan to the U.S. Senate over Smith by a vote of 76 to 69, 5 votes scattered. Riker and Thornbrough, *Indiana Election Returns*, 134.

Deed of Trust For "Ashland," November 15, 1842. Conveys to Madison C. Johnson, in trust, for the consideration of one dollar "a certain estate or tract of land, called Ashland . . . containing five hundred and fifteen acres of land." The conveyence of "Ashland" was to provide and support $20,000 in negotiable notes to satisfy possible creditors injured by the collapse of Thomas Hart Clay's hemp bagging and rope business. These notes were drawn for a period of five months from date November 15, 1842, or during the period of Clay's expected absence from Lexington on a trip to Natchez and New Orleans to raise money needed to manage his debts [Clay to Lucretia Hart Clay, December 9, 1842]. The security placed in Johnson's hands was in the form of four promissory notes of $5,000 each, all bearing date of November 15, 1842, to be held by Clay himself, Henry Clay, Jr., John Brand, and H. T. Duncan; all were endorsed by Clay, save his own note which was endorsed by Henry Clay, Jr. "It is the intention of this deed," explained Clay, "to secure perfectly the payment of the said four . . . promissory and negotiable notes, as they may respectively become due [on April 15, 1843]." If, however, "the said H. Clay shall pay the said four notes, or any other that may be substituted for them, in whole or in part . . . then this deed and every thing herein contained shall cease and determine. But if the said Clay shall fail in all or any of the particulars aforesaid, then the said Johnson, upon the request of the parties to the said four notes, or any one of them, shall proceed, after advertizement of sixty days in two of the News papers published in Lexington, to sell the tract of land hereby conveyed or so much thereof as may be sufficient to raise the necessary sum to pay off and discharge the said four notes. . . . But the said Johnson shall first sell such part of the said tract of land hereby conveyed as the said Clay may request him first to sell; and in default of such request the said Johnson shall sell that part thereof which lies on and adjoining the Tates Creek Road, or so much thereof as may be necessary for the purposes aforesaid." ADS, by Clay. KyU. For the failure of the firm of Thomas H. Clay and Waldemar Mentelle, see Clay to Lucretia Hart Clay, December 9, 1842. For the eventual payment of these notes, see Eaton, *Henry Clay and the Art of American Politics*, 76-77; see also Bond to John Jacob Astor, August 17, 1843, and Van Deusen, *Life of Henry Clay*, 359.

Partial Statement of Debts, Lexington, November 23, 1842. Clay estimates that his debts, including his "little debts" of $50, come to $19,391. Not all the figures listed herein can be clearly identified. The sum of $5,294 is carried over from "the other side," which is missing. The sum of $3,588 is carried down from "Above," which is also missing. Clearly stated are debts to Curd & Hunt [John W. Curd, E.W. Hunt], Lexington woolen manufacturers of "(say) 6000," and $4,568 to the Lexington branch of the Bank of Kentucky; also $1,650 to Eliza Jane Weir. On this day he paid the $1,650 owed Miss Weir [Prenter to Clay, January 16, 1837], and $85 owed James Erwin. These payments reduced his outstanding debt from $21,126 to $19,391. AD, in Clay's hand. DLC-TJC (DNA, M212, R19). Part of document missing.

To LUCRETIA HART CLAY Natchez, December 9, 1842

I arrived here the 5h. very much fatigued and out of sorts by the Voyage, and I am far from being well now. During the passage, at all the principal places of stopping, crowds assembled around the Boat and the Wharves to greet & welcome my arrival; but an indiscribable state of feeling prevented my having any agreeable excitement by these demonstrations. At this place arrangements were made to entertain me, free of expense, at a public hotel; but I prefered lodging at the house of Mr. Elliott [*sic*, William St. John Elliot], where I am comfortably situated, and where Mr. & Mrs. [Daniel] Vertner[1] are.

I have found the depression in every department of business, and the reduction of prices of every thing greater than I anticipated. Owing to these causes, the low price of Cotton, the low price of Bagging & Rope, and the uncertainty of the future, I shall not be able to make any contracts for those articles. I have had interviews with Dr. [Stephen] Duncan and other planters, and I find them unwilling to contract. The Louisville Co. has offered to deliver bagging at a price to be fixed by the N. O. market between now & the first of July, *but which was in no event to exceed 15 Cents* and the offer has not been accepted. I have therefore relinquished all hopes of making any contracts. And I lament that I see no alternative but the sale of Thomas' property as was understood before I left home.[2] Indeed, if contracts could be made here, the sale would be still necessary. I wish you would communicate this to him, as it will render it unnecessary for me to write him from this place.

I shall go from here to Judge [Alexander] Porters,[3] and shall not get to N. Orleans until about Xmas.

I stopt at Vicksburg, and was at Mr. [William C.] Smedes.[4] They were well.

This letter will be sent to Mr. [John J.] Crittenden at Washington, as I fear the Ohio river is closed. If it closes by ice, letters from home had better be put under cover to Mr. Crittenden or Mr [James T.] Morehead at Washington for me at N. Orleans. I have not heard from home since I left it. I hope that some of the family (James [Brown Clay] & Thomas [Hart Clay] especially) will write to me.

Should the cattle not be sent to Louisville before the 1st. Feb. I think it will be best not to send them until my return.

I wrote you a long letter, which Charles,[5] to whom I handed it to dry the superscription, by mistake burnt.

Such was the severity of the weather when I left Louisville that I am afraid you have suffered with the cold at Ashland. When I got here, it was so moderate that fires were unnecessary but it is otherwise to day.

Every body is very friendly & kind to me; but life appears cheerless and uncomfortable. I hope it is otherwise with you—God bless you, my dear wife; give my love to all.

ALS. Josephine Simpson Collection, Lexington, Ky. 1. For Elliot, long-time president of the Natchez Protection Insurance Co., see James, *Antebellum Natchez*, 211, 219, 243, 280; Kane, *Natchez*, 194, 198-202. For Vertner, see 1:108. 2. The hemp bagging and rope manufactory of Thomas Hart Clay and his brother-in-law, Waldemar Mentelle, failed sometime during the late summer or early fall of 1842. Clay's attempts to keep it afloat with his own resources, "upwards of $30,000 under the hope that the markets would improve" were unsuccessful. To recover whatever was possible from the debacle, perhaps enough to revive the business on a smaller scale, the family decision was to auction off the equipment. This was done on March 8, 1843. When the liquidation was accomplished, his son still owed him "about $20,000 [Clay to Silsbee, March 18, 1843]." To provide collateral partially to cover the Clay-Mentelle disaster and other debts, Clay, prior to departing on a fund-raising trip to New Orleans in early Dec., 1842, had, on Nov. 15, 1842, mortgaged "Ashland," for $20,000 for a period of five months [Deed of Trust, Nov. 15, 1842]. As it turned out, Clay's trip to New Orleans in Dec., 1842-Feb., 1843 to collect notes due him and to raise additional funds from among his political friends and business associates there sufficient to resurrect the Clay-Mentelle firm was unsuccessful. Several of his business associates in Natchez and New Orleans had stored in their warehouses Clay-owned bagging and rope, earlier shipped down-river, that was being held off the hemp market in the hope of higher prices. These stores were sacrificed at existing market prices. For Clay's financial activities in New Orleans in Dec., 1842-Feb., 1843, see Memorandum of Remittances From New Orleans, *ca.* April 29, 1843. See also Van Deusen, *Life of Henry*

Clay, 359; Poage, *Henry Clay*, 120. Clay managed to pull together in collections, sales, and loans in New Orleans only about $8,600, not enough to make feasible the revival of Clay & Mentelle. Thomas Hart Clay remained his father's debtor in the amount of $20,000 [Clay to Silsbee, March 18, 1843]. 3. Porter lived in Attakapas, near Franklin, La. See Francis P. Burns, "Henry Clay visits New Orleans," *LHQ* (July, 1944), 27:737. 4. For Smedes, a Vicksburg lawyer and partner of S.S. Prentiss, see Dallas C. Dickey, *Seargent S. Prentiss; Whig Orator of the Old South* (Baton Rouge, 1945), 49, 231, 280, 285, 346. 5. Charles Dupuy, Clay's slave and body servant.

To THOMAS HART CLAY Natchez, December 12, 1842

I have been here a week, and I have seen many of the prominent planters. I regret to inform you that I have found no disposition among them to contract for bagging & rope. The low price of those articles, the low price of Cotton, and the uncertainty & depression of all business are such as to disincline all of them to enter into contracts. The Louisville Manufacturing Co. offers to supply bagging at a price to be fixed by the market at N.O. between the 1st. Jan. & 1st July next, but in no event to exceed 15 Cents, and this offer has not yet been accepted. I have relinquished therefore my hope of contracting. I shall still endeavor to sell what you will have on hand at the end of the year.

How matters stand at N.O. I have not particularly heard. Mr. [Thomas] Smith writes me that the markets are very vascillating W. & Foreman[1] remitted the bal. in their hands, as they had been directed, to N. York— You may therefore tell James [Brown Clay] that he may use the check I sent him from Louisville to take up my acceptances for K.S. & Co.[2]

I go tomorrow to Judge [Alexander] Porters & shall not get to N.O 'till about Xmas. I hope to find something in the hands of Payne & Harrison;[3] and if I do, I will make a remittance to meet your negotiable note to Coleman Graves[4] & perhaps something beyond it.

I see no alternative, I lament my dear Son to say, but the sale which you contemplated of your property.[5] I hope that may pay the debts expected. So far I find the state of things here worse than I anticipated. I shall be agreeably disappointed if I find it any better at N. Orleans.

I wrote to your Mother & sent my letter via Washington, fearing that the navigation of the River was stopt at onc[e]. This letter I shall commit to the chances of the river.

I feel more than I can express for you, for the Messrs. [Elijah & D.M.] Craigs & for myself. I wish I had the means of relieving them immediately. If I had they should be applied. I hope those to whom they are bound for you will wait until the Sale & until I go up, if God should spare me to get up.

Mr. Heron, connected with Hewitts [*sic*] manufactory[6] at Louisville told me on my voyage, that they could manufacture bagging at 1 Cent & 9/10 hs. of a Cent per yard, and that they were going to put up 10 new looms.

My health has not been good.

Give my love to Mary [Mentelle Clay] & your children.[7]

ALS. DLC-HC (DNA, M212, R5). 1. [Charles] Worsley & [George] Forman, commission merchants were located at 44 Poydras Street, New Orleans. *New Orleans City Directory, 1842*, courtesy of Collin B. Hamer, Jr., City of New Orleans Public Library. For Worsley's obituary, see New Orleans *Daily Delta*, Feb. 3, 1855; for Forman's, see New Orleans *Commercial Bulletin*, March 29, 1854. 2. Not identified. 3. [J.W.] Payne,

Harrison & Co., commission merchants, were located at 38 Gravier St., New Orleans. *New Orleans City Directory, 1842.* 4. For Graves (1806-74), see *RKHS* (Oct., 1936), 34:368 and (April, 1938), 36:136-37. 5. Clay to Lucretia H. Clay, Dec. 9, 1842; Clay to Silsbee, March 18, 1843. 6. Probably Hewit, Anderson & Co., bagging factory, located in 1848 at the corner of Market and Sixth Streets in Louisville. *Louisville and New Albany Directory for 1848*, courtesy of Dr. Thomas Owen, University of Louisville Archives. Heron has not been identified. 7. Little is known of these children save their names, viz: Lucretia Hart Clay (1838-60); Henry Boyle Clay (d. after 1906); Thomas Hart Clay (d. 1907); Rose Victoire Clay (n.d.); Mary Russell Clay (n.d.). For Lucretia H. Clay, see James C. Klotter, "The Breckinridges of Kentucky, Two Centuries of Leadership," Ph.D. dissertation, University of Kentucky, 1975, p. 175.

To THOMAS HART CLAY New Orleans, December 25, 1842

I have found the state of affairs here[1] not very different from what I expected. K. & Connyngham [*sic*, Kelly & Conyngham] have made sales only to the amt of $4444:77, against which they have charges, $1964:64. They will pay those acceptances given to James [Brown Clay], but that will leave them creditors to an amt that will nearly absorb the proceeds of the bag. and rope when sold, if sold at present prices.[2] They have on hand 538 pieces of bag. & 639 coils of rope; and at Mobile 60 of each. They have sold 363 pieces & 192 coils.

The sales of Payne & Harrison amt to $1139:81. I have not yet recd. their a/c of charges. They have sold 106 pieces of the 200 Clay & Mentelle, and 7 of the Arrow brand. They could have sold all of the latter at 14 but misunderstood us. They were offered 11 Cents Cash for the former, but did not feel authorized to take it. It is now doubtful whether it can be got; such is the downward tendency of all prices. All unite in praising the Arrow brand.

I shall receive what cash is on hand with Payne & Harrison, after deducting their charges, and will remit it to meet the negotiable note given to Coleman Graves, in a few days.

I have nothing to add to what had passed before I left home in regard to a sale of your property.[3] I lament that there is no other alternative. I wish it could relieve from all embarrassments. I have made no effort yet to take up a loan; and such is the extreme pressure of the times that I fear I shall not be able to effect it.

You will advise me when a sale is to be made by your Trustees. I shall wish to get there if I can.

The pair of horses and your mothers hams have arrived. We can get them sold at abt ten Cents.[4] I wrote to her yesterday via Washn. This letter I send by the river. My health remains the same, not very good. My love to Mary and the children. I recd. your letter of the 7h.

ALS. DLC-HC (DNA, M212, R5). 1. For an account of Clay's visit to New Orleans, Dec. 22, 1842, to Feb. 16, 1843, with a brief side visit to Mobile in early February, see Francis P. Burns, "Henry Clay Visits New Orleans," *LHQ* (July, 1944), 27:736-47. See also Clay to Lucretia Hart Clay, Dec. 9, 1842. 2. Clay to James B. Clay, Dec. 24, 1841. 3. Clay to Lucretia Hart Clay, Dec. 9, 1842. 4. Lucretia's hams sold at 12½¢ per pound. See Clay to Lucretia Hart Clay, Jan. 3, 1843.

From LUCIUS C. DUNCAN[1] New Orleans, December 27, 1842

Application has been made to the Board of Directors of the Society for the Relief of Destitute Orphan Boys, established near this city, by the agents of the Shakers residing at South Union, Kentucky, for a number of the lads under the care of the Society, to be apprenticed to them until they obtain the age of majority.

The agents, among other references, have informed us that you had visited their institution and were acquainted with their tenets, habits and principles.[2]

I had the pleasure of holding a short conversation the other evening with you on the subject, which I mentioned to the Board of Directors yesterday, and I was instructed by them to ask of you the favor to state in writing your opinion of the propriety of our placing a number of our boys under the care of that Institution.[3]

Several persons here, who are partially acquainted with the Institution, strongly recommend us to comply with the application which has been made, and we should feel specially obliged if, at your leisure, you would address us a line on the subject.[4]

I write this note by the direction of the Board. . . .

Copy. Printed in New Orleans *Daily Picayune*, Jan. 7, 1843. 1. Duncan, a lawyer at 15 Royal Street in New Orleans, was originally from Kentucky. He died August 9, 1855. For his obituary, see New Orleans *Bee*, August 11, 1855. 2. Clay had visited the Shakers at South Union as early as 1829 and had promised his assistance in case of persecution. Julia Neal, *By Their Fruits; The Story of Shakerism in South Union, Kentucky* (Chapel Hill, 1947), 97; Marguerite F. Melcher, *The Shaker Adventure* (Cleveland, reprint ed., 1960), 184-85. 3. Clay replied to Duncan on Dec. 27, 1842, saying that he considered the Shakers to be "a religious, sober, industrious and economical community, worthy of all respect and confidence. I do not know what other disposition you may be able to make of the boys under the care of the Society . . . but I should entertain a confident belief that any of them placed under that of the Shakers at South Union would be properly attended to." Copy. Printed in New Orleans *Daily Picayune*, Jan. 7, 1843. 4. In Jan., 1843, eighteen boys were apprenticed by the orphan society to the Shakers. Neal, *By Their Fruits*, 169.

To SEARGENT S. PRENTISS New Orleans, December 29, 1842

I received your[1] obliging letter of the 27h. I have borne in mind your friendly invitation to visit you and Mrs. Prentiss on my return to Kentucky, and I hope that circumstances will be such as to admit of my enjoying that satisfaction. At present I am not able to fix the period of my sojourn here, which will depend upon the private objects and purposes which brought me hither; but when I am able to see its termination, if I return [to Kentucky], as I now expect to do, by the River route, I will inform you some days beforehand of that on which I shall hope to get to Vicksburg.

I am to see the Comee. from Jackson tomorrow.[2] I have been so far successful in my endeavors to prevent my voyage assuming the aspect of a political tour; and, if they will agree to that indispensable condition, I think, when with you, I will go to your seat of Government. . . .

ALS. DLC-HC (DNA, M212, R5). 1. For Prentiss, see *BDAC* and Dickey, *Seargent S. Prentiss*. 2. W.C. Richards *et al.* wrote Clay from New Orleans on Dec. 29, 1842, inviting him to visit Jackson, Miss. Copy. Printed in Jackson (Miss.) *The Southron*, Jan. 5, 1843. Clay replied to them in a letter, dated Dec. 30, 1842, saying that when he reached Vicksburg, "I will make an excursion to Jackson, and shall be most happy to meet there any of my friends and fellow-citizens, without ceremony and without parade." *Ibid.*

To FRANCIS T. BROOKE New Orleans, December 30, 1842

I recd your favor by Mr. [Alexander] Porter, as I had recd. your previous letters to which it refers. I should have before written to you but that I really possessed nothing to communicate, and I wish now only to assure you of the receipt of your favors, and of my constant regard.

My Voyage has been distinguished by enthusiastic demonstrations wherever I have been. My effort has been rather to repress than to excite them. So far I have succeeded in avoiding my tour being given a political aspect. I expect to remain at the South until some time in February. I feel already benefitted by the climate, altho my health was not bad when I left home.

Your sources of political information are so much better than mine that I can add nothing to the stock which you possess. Every where I find great confidence prevailing among the Whigs of their success in 1844. All the elections of the past fall, which have been lost by them,[1] have been lost not by the increased strength of their opponents, but by voters remaining absent from feelings of mortification and disgust created by the acting President.[2] Such is the view which I find every-where taken. The problem to be solved is whether the Whigs can be rally'd in 44. I hope and believe they will be.

I have seen a Mr. Carter[3] and his lady here, near relatives of Mrs. [Mary Champe Carter] Brooke, and promised them to say so. They were well and I believe doing well. . . .

Copy. DLC-TJC (DNA, M212, R14). Printed in Colton, *Clay Correspondence*, 4:473-74.
1. Clay to Crittenden, June 3, 1842. 2. A reference to President Tyler. 3. Mrs. Brooke had numerous brothers, nephews, etc. For the Carter family, see Edgar Woods, *History of Albermarle County in Virginia* (Charlottesville, Va., 1901), 163-66; *VMHB*, 30: 70-79.

To John R. Grymes *et al.*, New Orleans, December 30, 1842. Declines with regret the invitation to dinner by the members of the New Orleans bar. Explains that he is in New Orleans on private business and that he "had prescribed to myself the rule of avoiding, as far as I possibly could, public entertainments, if any should be offered on my account." Says he must conform to his rule in this instance, but hopes he will have many opportunities to meet with members of the local bar in other social settings while he is in New Orleans. Copy. Printed in New Orleans *Daily Picayune*, January 4, 1843.

On December 28, 1842, Grymes had extended the invitation, signed also by Ádolphe Mazureau, George Eustis, Pierre Soulé, Isaac T. Preston, Christian Roselius, Levi Pierce, Judah P. Benjamin, and other prominent local lawyers. *Ibid.*; see also Burns, "Henry Clay Visits New Orleans," *LHQ*, 27:740. For Benjamin, Roselius, and Soulé, see *DAB*.

To LUCRETIA HART CLAY New Orleans, January 3, 1843

I was glad to hear through letters from James [B. Clay] and from Nan[n]ette [Price Smith] to Mr. [Thomas] Smith that your health was much better than it was when I left home. I pray that it may continue to improve & that you may be long spared. My health has improved since my arrival here, and if it were not for the embarrassments of my family I should be much better.

There is no improvement but rather a decline in the price of bagging and rope. In other respects, I have found affairs as well as I expected. I shall make all the collections that I expected, and I think I will gather about

$10,000 to assist in meeting my engagements. I have not yet attempted to effect any loan, and I am almost afraid to make the experiment of attempting one. If I should endeavor to effect it, it will be in consequence of some encouragement which I have not yet seen.[1]

Your hams are sold at 12½, except half a dozen that I gave to [Nathaniel] Watkins. What would you like the proceeds invested in? Desire James to write me. I believe I have also sold my pair of horses at $350, the expences will bring them down to $300.

I enclosed to Thomas [Hart Clay] the other day $750 to meet some engagements. [J.W.] Payne and Harrison [& Co.] & R. J. Cunningham are making little sales occasionally at reduced prices.

I shall be glad to learn whether Thomas executed his deed of trust and whether the Trustees have fixed on a day of Sale.[2]

I see Mr. [James] Erwin every day almost, and he seems more cheerful than I expected. He continues to say that he will get through without any great sacrifices.

Nothing can exceed the kindness I experience at Dr. [Hugh L.] Mercers, and from the inhabitants generally. I shall pass two days of this week in the Country, and three of the next at Baton Rouge.

During my stay here the weather has been generally good—not very cold, but cold enough to make a fire comfortable.

I went to day to the Supreme Court to look into the suit against Mr. [John B.] Humphreys' Estate. Whilst there, a man fired a pistol in the Court, and you may hear that it was fired at me.[3] It was done by a cracked man. It is possible that my presence may have occasioned it; but I do not believe that the man had any design against any body. The ball was lodged in the ceiling of the Court room.

I hope that Mr. [Albert] Florea[4] will take care of my Stock and every thing on the farm. I fear that you will have a very severe winter. Give my love to James and John [Morrison Clay] & our grand children.

And may God bless & protect you, my dear wife.

ALS. DLC-TJC (DNA, M212, R10). 1. Clay to Lucretia Hart Clay, Dec. 9, 1842. 2. *Ibid.* 3. For Clay's visit to the Louisiana Supreme Court on Jan. 3 to examine the lower court record of the case of *Preston* v. *Humphreys*, and the shooting incident there that day, see Burns, "Henry Clay Visits New Orleans," *LHQ*, 27:742-45. For Clay's argument in the case on Jan. 28, see, below, Argument in the Supreme Court of Louisiana, Jan. 28, 1843. 4. Overseer of "Ashland" plantation.

To JOHN J. CRITTENDEN New Orleans, January 14, 1843

I received your favor of the 30h. Ulto. which I was very glad to get, as I have obtained but little intelligence from Washn. since my arrival here.

You will have heard of [Alexander] Porter's Election.[1] It has given very general satisfaction, there being but one regret accompanying it, and that is that Mr. [Charles M.] Conrad has been sacrificed in consequence of a faithful discharge of his duty. But Judge Porter has had no agency in brin[g]ing about the result, and members of the Legislature were even assured, prior to the election, that he approves of Mr. C[onrad]s. course about the fine.[2] The judge was not & is not here, and some doubt is entertained of his acceptance; but I think he will accept.

I do not think I shall go to Cuba, but return to K. in Feby.

The papers have not exaggerated the enthusiasm of my reception every where; and I find a good & confident feeling prevailing with the Whigs.

What of a Whig Nat. Convention?[3] When will that assemble of the Loco's?[4] Let me hear from you fully.

My health has been benefited by my sojourn here.

How do you find the Whig Senators? Is there any want of fidelity among them?

Give my respects to [James T.] Morehead.

ALS. DLC-John J. Crittenden Papers (DNA, M212, R20). 1. The election for U.S. senator took place in the Louisiana legislature on Jan. 9, 1843. The Democrats announced they would not make a nomination but would vote for a member of the Whig party "who had once before filled the office," while the Whig ranks were divided. The vote stood: Alexander Porter-45; Charles M. Conrad (the incumbent)-22; John Slidell-5; blank-2. New Orleans *Daily Picayune*, Jan. 10, 1843. 2. Democrats supported Porter because they disliked Conrad. The latter had played a significant role in Congress on the bill to pay back to Andrew Jackson the $1,000 fine which had been imposed on him in New Orleans for his actions in reimposing martial law in the city following his victory over the British there in 1815. On May 18, 1842, in a speech in the Senate, Conrad had attacked Jackson's actions in New Orleans and had said that, although he did not object to refunding the money, he did not want it remitted either on the grounds that it had been imposed by error of the Louisiana courts or "to wipe a stain from Gen. Jackson's character" as some Democrats had put it. After his speech, the Senate adopted an amendment which specified: "That this act shall not be construed as an expression of the opinion of Congress upon any judicial proceeding or legal question growing out of the declaration of martial law by General Jackson during the defence of New Orleans." This amendment was adopted on May 19 by a vote of 23 to 22, with Whigs voting in favor and Democrats voting against. Because of the amendment, Democrats voted against the bill, and it was defeated 17 to 24. *Cong. Globe*, 27 Cong., 2 Sess., 373-74, 376, 515. When the bill to repay the $1,000 finally passed and was approved on Feb. 16, 1844, it did not contain that provision. See 5 *U.S. Stat.*, 651. For the Jacksonian view of this matter, see Bassett, *Correspondence of Andrew Jackson*, 6:143-46, 154, 156-57, 165-66, 184-85, 190-200, 203, 206-8, 259-60. For Jackson's declaration of martial law in New Orleans and the fine imposed by the court, see Robert V. Remini, *Andrew Jackson and the Course of American Empire, 1767-1821* (New York, 1977), 308-15. 3. Clay to Clayton, August 8, 1842. 4. Clay to Butler, August 8, 1842.

To LUCRETIA HART CLAY New Orleans, January 18, 1843

Since my arrival here, my health has improved but I have had my usual share of bad colds, of which one now confines me to the House.

I have made all the collections which I expected here, and have converted the funds into bills on N. York, which I shall take home with me to meet my engagements as far as they will go. I have brought suit for the fee which was engaged to be paid me for the Mississippi negro case;[1] but a proposal has been made to me to arbitrate it, to which I shall assent, if it can be done.

Tell Thomas [Hart Clay] that Payne and Harrison have now sold all the Arrow brand bagging at from 12½ to 14. They think they can sell on a credit that with Clay & Mentelle's brand at 13 which I have authorized them to do.

I have seen the advertisement of his property, and I hope to get home by the time of the Sale.[2] I wish his expectations may be realized as to getting $50 for his land, as that would pay all his debts except mine.

The price of bagging & rope continues low; and yet I wish he had it in his power to try another year, as I cannot help thinking that with the low price of hemp, and hands something might be made.

Your hams were all sold at 12½ and Mr. [Thomas] Smith is purchasing with the proceeds some white and brown sugar, coffee and rice. There will be something left. Do you wish any thing bought with it? I think that, as your hams are much praised, there will be no difficulty of selling next fall those you now have on hand.

I sold the horses for $350, netting about $300, which is more than I could have got for them at home.

Lewis arrived with the Cattle, in very bad order, as I learnt. They were left where I wished. I saw him but for a moment as I was going to Baton Rouge. He returned, I suppose, in the Steam boat.

Nat. Watkins came down a few days ago. He tells me that his brother John is settled on his farm.[3]

I have to go to Mobile on the 30h. expecting to return by the 4h. Feb. My aim will be to get back to Louisville about the last of that month.

Mr. [James] Erwin has been absent from the City near a fortnight. He went up to the neighbourhood of Henry Johnsons', with what purposes I do not know.[4]

[Martin] Duralde looks very well. I see him & [W.C.C., Jr.] Claiborne frequently, and I have seen Mrs. [Julie Duralde] Clay, who is also in good health.

Mr. Smith is here, attending to his business, and I have found him very useful to me. I should think that he will promote the interests of his house by remaining here.

I have been trying to get the cause with [John B.] Humphreys Estate so arranged that I may argue it; but I am not sure that the other side will accommodate me. If they do not agree that I shall argue it orally I will do it in writing.[5]

Every body is kind to me, even many of the Locofocos'. One of them gave me a barrel of sugar the other day, which I have directed to be sent up to you.

At Baton Rouge they gave me a very costly Saddle which was exhibited at the Fair.

Give my love to all our children & Grand children, and god bless you my dear wife. . . .

ALS. DLC-TJC (DNA, M212, R10). 1. Clay to Slaughter & Ballard, Jan. 9, 1841. 2. Clay to Lucretia Hart Clay, Dec. 9, 1842. 3. Nathaniel W. Watkins [2:892] and John Watkins [1:190] were Clay's half brothers. Nathaniel, a lawyer, lived in Missouri, while John, a farmer, lived most of his life in Woodford County, Ky., but died in Missouri in 1845. See Smith & Clay, *The Clay Family*, 19, 20, 26, 28. 4. James Erwin married Henry Johnson's daughter, Margaret, at "Chatham" in Washington County, Miss., on Feb. 21, 1843. Thomas S. Erwin, "Clay and Erwin Families," *FCHQ* (April, 1929), 3:114-15. 5. Clay to Lucretia Hart Clay, Jan. 3, 1843; Argument in Supreme Court of Louisiana, Jan. 28, 1843.

To John Gayle, Mobile, Ala., January 18, 1843. States that he has "resolved to have the satisfaction of seeing your city, and . . . I intend to leave New Orleans on Monday the 30th instant, and expect to reach Mobile the next morning." Asks that his "reception should be as quiet, and attended with as little display as possible." Copy. Printed in New Orleans *Daily Picayune*, January 25, 1843. For Gayle, governor of Alabama, see *NCAB*, 10:427.

To THOMAS HART CLAY New Orleans, January 22, 1843

I received your favor of the 11h. inst. I do not know whether the arrangement can be made or not for mailing the advances you propose, on the faith of shipments of bagging and rope; but I will endeavor to effect it. Considering the low price of hemp, and of hands, I am satisfied that, even at present reduced prices, something may be made *if good articles are manufactured,* and the greatest economy is practised. And I wish that you could now re-embark in the business on a reduced scale.[1] Could you hire hands now, at the price you mention, and start, say, three looms? Should your factory be sold,[2] you would probably be able to make some arrangement with the purchaser for the residue of this year. My crop of hemp would serve to begin with, and perhaps some arrangement might be effected to purchase hemp, if no person can be found to make advances in this Country.

You can make inquiries and ascertain the practicability of recommencing business, on the moderate scale, above mentioned, by the 8h. March. I shall endeavor to reach home before that day.

If you should again enter on the business, it is absolutely indispensible to make your fabrics—of the best quality; and it is quite, perhaps more, important to attend to the quality of the rope than the bagging. Morrison[3] makes the best rope that comes here. It is small, even, & neat. It commands readily one cent, or one cent and a half, more than any other.

You had better keep quiet and say nothing out of the family about your resuming business.

I wrote to your mother that Payne & H[arrison]. had sold all of the Arrow brand, which all unite in saying is good; and that I had authorized them to sell on a credit what remained on hand of the C[lay]. & M[entelle]. brand. I have not seen K. & C.[4] for some days; but their sales are slow owing to the inferior quality of what they have.

I have succeeded better than I expected in making collections; and I hope to carry back with me funds to pay off the Morrison legacies, or most of them, and to pay for the hemp due in March.[5] I sent you a check for $750 to pay Coleman Graves.[6]

You have not informed me whether your good friends the Craigs[7] have been annoyed; and how they got along with the note in the branch bank.

My general health is improved; but I cannot regain my spirits entirely....

ALS. DLC-HC (DNA, M212, R5). 1. Clay to Lucretia Hart Clay, Dec. 9, 1842. On Feb. 8, 1843, Clay wrote Goodhue & Co. in New York City, importers of gunny cloth and gunny bags, asking the "probable amount of them now on hand in N. York," how much more importation of these commodities is expected in 1843, and what is the "ordinary price of those articles at the ports of exportation." Explains that "I desire this information for the benefit of some of my Kentucky friends who have been engaged in the manufacture of Cotton bagging, and who, notwithstanding the discouraging state of the market, feel obliged to persevere in their business." Asks them to address their answers to Sen. John J. Crittenden or Rep. Willis Green in Washington "who will know where to transmit" this information. ALS. NNS. For [Jonathan] Goodhue & Co., see Bonner, *New York*, 709. 2. Clay to Lucretia Hart Clay, Dec. 9, 1842. 3. Probably Richard Morrison, rope and bagging manufacturer, located at E. 5th Street near Upper in Lexington. MacCabe, *Directory of the City of Lexington . . . 1838 & '39*. 4. Kelly & Conyngham, commission merchants. 5. Clay to Lucretia Hart Clay, Dec. 9, 1842. 6. Clay to Thomas Hart Clay, Dec. 12, 1842. 7. Probably E.W. & D.M. Craig. See Clay to Silsbee, March 18, 1843, note 1.

To Richard Henry Wilde *et al.*, Augusta, Ga., January 26, 1843. Regrets that he will be unable to accept the "hospitalities" offered by "a public meeting in Richmond county inviting me to visit Augusta." Explains that "I now feel constrained, by private considerations, to ascend the rivers which brought me here [New Orleans]" and will therefore not return to Kentucky via Georgia. Copy. Printed in Washington *Daily National Intelligencer*, February 14, 1843.

Argument In Supreme Court of Louisiana, New Orleans, January 28, 1843. Thanks the court for the privilege of addressing it [in the matter of *Preston* v. *Humphreys*] and apologizes for his "want of knowledge of the peculiar civil code of laws of Louisiana." Knows, however, that "this case was governed by general principles with which all lawyers must be familiar—by common sense principles, which are recognized throughout Christendom." Summarizes the facts of the case which turn on the sum of $9,000 paid by John B. Humphreys to James Brown in 1830 for part interest in a sugar plantation near New Orleans, a transaction which later became an issue when the will of Mrs. James Brown was probated. Extols the laws of Louisiana which so well and wisely protect the property rights of women and regrets that other states have not such laws. "Women," he concludes, "are the pillars—aye, the Corinthian pillars—that adorn and support society; the institutions that protect women throw a shield also round children; and where women and children are provided for, man must be secure in his rights. He admitted those laws were, in some instances, open to abuse—as what human laws were not?—still he looked on them as monuments that perpetuated the wisdom of those who framed them, and did honor to Louisiana." Copy. Paraphrase printed in the New Orleans *Daily Picayune*, January 29, 1843. The New Orleans *Picayune* incorrectly rendered Humphreys's name as "Thomas" rather than "John."

Mrs. Lucretia Hart Clay was one of the heirs of Mrs. Brown's estate. See 8:739-40, 771-72, and Clay to Ingersoll, September 30, 1837. In July, 1843 the Louisiana Supreme Court overturned a lower court decision and ordered the heirs of Humphreys to pay $9,000 to the estate of James Brown. For details of the case, see Burns, "Henry Clay Visits New Orleans," *LHQ*, 27:741-45, and Merritt M. Robinson, *Reports of Cases Argued and Determined in the Supreme Court of Louisiana* (New Orleans, 1845), 5:299-313.

To LUCRETIA HART CLAY New Orleans, February 10, 1843

I returned from Mobile on tuesday. I had a very boisterous passage going there, and fear some unfavorable accounts of the fate of the Boat may have reached you. We were not in fact in any danger. There, as every where else that I have been, nothing could exceed the Kindness of my reception and entertainment. I staid at the house of Mr. Ledyear [*sic*], the gentleman who married a daughter of John P. Erwin that was in Kentucky.[1] The public demonstrations towards me were friendly and enthusiastic. Mr. [Thomas] Smith went and returned with me.

I have done now all the business that I expect to accomplish before I go home. I have not been able to bring my case with [Rice C.] Ballard[2] to a close, and must leave it to be decided by the Court. The case, which I argued, against the Estate of Mr. [John B.] Humphreys,[3] was not to be decided until the cause was reached on the call of the docket, and it has not been yet reached. I think we cannot lose it. I have not yet made any application for a Loan, and feel great repugnance in doing it. I am not sure that I shall.

I shall leave this City next thursday. I am obliged to stop at two or three points on the river; but still it will be my earnest aim to get home before Thomas's [Thomas Hart Clay] Sale;[4] and I hope and believe I shall.

Mr. [James] Erwin has not yet got through his troubles; but still seems confident of finally doing so. The amount due to his children is upwards of Fifty two thousand dollars, and he has determined to execute an additional security for its payment, which I have prepared for him.

Dr. [Hugh L.] Mercer and his family have treated me with a degree of kindness and friendly attention, which I shall ever remember with gratitude. I think he would be very likely to assist me,[5] if I were to ask him; but I cannot think of such an abuse of his liberal hospitality.

There is no improvement in the prices of Bagging and Rope—But I cannot help thinking that there must be in the course of the year.

Mr. Williams tells me that my Stock was received in a terrible condition. They must have been neglected after I or they left home.

I wish that the old man would be told to feed the white bull calf and the Orozimbo's[6] heifers roan calf well on meal and hay.

My love to all at home; and God bless you, my dear wife.

ALS. DLC-HC (DNA, M212, R10). 1. William J. Ledyard married Lara Erwin, daughter of John P. Erwin and niece of James Erwin, on April 14, 1834. For John P. Erwin, see 3:868. For the Ledyard-Erwin connection, see Thomas C. DeLeon, *Belles Beaux and Brains of the 60's* (New York, 1907), 190-92. 2. Slaughter and Ballard to Clay, Jan. 9, 1841. 3. Argument in Supreme Court of Louisiana (*Preston* v. *Humphreys*), Jan. 28, 1843. 4. On March 8. See Clay to Lucretia Hart Clay, Dec. 9, 1842. 5. In the matter of a personal loan. See *ibid.* 6. See 8:804.

To John J. Crittenden, Washington, February 10, 1843. Reports that "The fate of the Exchequer has reached us; but not that of its offspring in the Senate and the House. I presume they will neither of them secure a majority." Adds that "I shall leave here next week; but do not expect to get home until a few days before you in March." ALS. DLC-John J. Crittenden Papers (DNA, M212, R20). Written from New Orleans.

For Tyler's Exchequer plan, initially introduced in the 27th Congress, 2nd Session, see Clay to J.B. Clay, December 10, 1841, and Mangum to Clay, June 15, 1842. In Tyler's Annual Message of December 6, 1842 [*MPP*, 4:194-209, espec. 204-7], he again recommended a Board of Exchequer. On December 12 Millard Fillmore introduced a resolution referring all financial matters, including the Exchequer plan, to the House Ways and Means Committee. This committee reported on January 10, 1843, recommending that "the plan of an exchequer presented . . . at the last session . . . ought not to be adopted." This resolution passed on January 27 by a vote of 193-18. U.S. H. of Reps., *Journal*, 27 Cong., 3 Sess., 24, 39, 156-57, 168, 171, 173, 246-47, 253, 256, 260, 265. The Exchequer plan was also revived in the Senate as part of SB 3, introduced by Nathaniel P. Tallmadge (N.Y.) on December 13, 1842. It was last debated on February 7, 1843, with no vote on it ever taking place. U.S. Sen., *Journal*, 27 Cong., 3 Sess., 27, 53, 114, 153.

SPEECH IN MEMPHIS — February 25, 1843

Mr. CLAY arrived at Memphis[1] on Saturday 25th ult., and was greeted with a warm, hearty and enthusiastic welcome from thousands of men of all parties, a splendid parade of the military, and the sunny smiles of the ladies, whom we are happy to say are almost all friends of the distinguished Statesman of the west.

We have only room for the following extracts from his remarks upon the occasion, in reply to the eloquent welcome of Le Roy Pope, Esq.

Mr. CLAY proceeded to allude to the striking contrast exhibited in the past and present condition of the country, and to state briefly the causes of the public distress and the proper measures of relief. The unsoundness and scarcity of the circulating medium was a chief cause of the disastrous state of the country. A sound and sufficient circulating medium, one of uniform value at every point of the Union, was as essential to the health of the body politic, as a sound, sufficient and uniform circulation of blood to the human body. No more could the currency of the country be corrupted and unnaturally diminished and the country be prosperous, than could the blood of the human body be disordered and excessively diminished and the body continue in vigor and health. Corrupt the currency and abstract one half of it from circulation, and nothing but pecuniary prostration and distress must follow. He declared himself opposed to the hard money doctrine. Hard money and hard times go together—Banks are unavoidable. Some of the States will have them, and the others must therefore do the same, or be tributary for their currency to those which have them, and thus be subject to all their evils without enjoying any of their benefits. If there be local banks, a National Bank is indispensible, not the abortive, miscalled Bank of the United States of Pennsylvania, powerless for good and prolific of evil,[2] but an old fashioned, time tried Bank of the United States—a Bank of the Union not of one State. If there were defects in it, in the organization of another avoid those defects and provide guards and penalties against their recurrence. No one would abandon the great Father of Waters which sweeps past your city, because wrecks occur on its bosom, and the engines of steam produce occasional destruction of property and life. Multiply the guards and increase the precaution, not abandon the use, is the dictate of common sense and wisdom.

Another cause of the disjointed condition of the country, he said, was the excessive abuse of the powers of the Executive Department of the Government, not only of the President but of the entire Executive department—Widely without its sphere had that department extended. Had there been no power to veto, there would have been no prevention of the charter of a National Bank—no removal of the Deposites—no treasury circular—no multiplication of State banks—no inflation of paper currency—no stimulating of excessive enterprises and mad speculations—no consequent explosion, collapse and the universal ruin which overspreads our noble land. Such is the history of our career. The providences of God have been as kind and bountiful throughout the entire progress of our career as at any other period of our history. The refreshing rains have fallen upon the earth, the kindly sun has poured out upon the fields his genial influences with the same bountiful copiousness which have blessed our former times—but the work of man, the hand of those that direct our earthly government, has neutralized all these blessings, and overspread our land. . . .

Of the remedies which Mr. Clay proposed for our evils, one he deemed paramount and essential. Industry and Economy must be practiced in all things—we must make more, and buy less—we must produce at home, on our own farms and plantations more than we need to consume—our wives and daughters must ply their own needles more, and employ the mil[l]iners less. Be not alarmed my friends he said, at the words I say—this is the American System—it is the long and short of the System—Industry and Economy—Make at home what we have been buying abroad—and in that way we will get out of debt, and keep so, and keep our money.—A moderate and reasonable tariff was all we ever desired—one sufficient to stimulate and sustain our own American, domestic industry and economy.—Stability and uniformity were the great necessities of the system. It should be equal and uniform in its operations on the great interests of the country.

Copy. Excerpts summarized and printed in the Franklin (Tenn.) *Western Weekly Review*, March 10, 1843. Final sentences, beginning with "Be not alarmed," printed in Brownlow, *A Political Register . . . of Henry Clay*, 67. 1. On Feb. 8, 1843, Clay wrote a committee of Memphis Whigs accepting an invitation to visit their city but declining a public dinner in his honor. Copy. Printed in Jonesboro (Tenn.) *Whig*, March 1, 1843. 2. Eyre to Clay, Feb. 12, 1841.

From Henry Bry, Monroe, La., February 26, 1843. Discusses several aspects of *Preston* v. *Humphreys* [Argument in Supreme Court of Louisiana, January 28, 1843], and asks if Clay can use his help in the case. He would "feel proud to do all in his power for Henry Clay, for the Statesman who I trust will be called by the American People to arrest the torrent of demoralisation which began to overflow the Sand under the administration of a military chieftain [Jackson] and continued under that of a———would-be-fox [Van Buren]." In a postscript, Bry's daughter, Hannah L. Bry, thanks him for the "Daguerreotype of 'Henry Clay' " which she regards as a "most precious" possession. ALS. DLC-TJC (DNA, M212, R14).

Bry was a Swiss immigrant and farmer who had served in the Louisiana house of representatives, and as a judge in Ouachita Parish. In 1846 he became clerk of the Louisiana Supreme Court at Monroe. Clarence E. Carter (ed.), *The Territorial Papers of the United States* (Washington, 1940), 9:869, 871; *The Celebration of the Centenary of the Supreme Court of Louisiana* (New Orleans, 1913), 59.

On April 27, 1843, Bry reported his success in concluding a "deed of conveyance as you desire" in the matter of the land owned by the late James Brown. ALS. DLC-TJC (DNA, M212, R14).

Bry again wrote on July 14, 1843, giving a detailed report of his title search on the property. *Ibid.*

To JOHN M. BERRIEN Lexington, March 13, 1843

I owe you an apology for my omission to answer your obliging letter of the 21st Jan. received at N. Orleans.

I congratulate you on your safe return to the bosom of your family, which I hope you found in good health.

With the general action of Congress at its late Session the Country has reason to be satisfied. No part of that of the Senate has afforded more satisfaction than the rejection of [Henry A.] Wise and [Caleb] Cushing.[1] It would have been increased if [John C.] Spencer and [William W.] Irwin had shared the same fate.[2]

My trip to the S. Western States below was full of personal gratification. I was received & treated by both parties with the greatest enthusiasm & hospitality.

Louisiana may be regarded as certain for the Whig cause; and there are divisions, on local subjects and on the Presidential Candidates, among the

Democrats,[3] that I do believe will give it not only Mississippi but even Alabama! We have great and just reason to count upon Tennessee.[4]

Of our prospects elsewhere, I will say nothing, as you are probably better informed than I am. . . .

ALS. NcU. 1. Tyler had nominated Wise to be minister to France on Feb. 27, 1843. The Senate rejected the nomination with 12 yeas and 24 nays on March 3. Twice more on the same day, March 3, the president renominated Wise and the Senate rejected him by a margin of 8 to 26 and 2 to 29. Later, on Jan. 18, 1844, Tyler nominated Henry A. Wise to be minister to Brazil. He was confirmed on Feb. 9 by a vote of 30 to 10. U.S. Sen., *Executive Journal*, 6:175, 186-87, 189, 220, 234. On March 2, 1843, Tyler had nominated Caleb Cushing to be secretary of the treasury. The Senate rejected him 19 to 27 on March 3. When he was twice more renominated the same day, they again rejected him 10 to 27 and 2 to 29. He was subsequently appointed commissioner to China on Dec. 15, 1843, and confirmed, 22 to 19, on June 17, 1844. *Ibid.*, 178-79, 186-87, 189-90, 192, 352. 2. After Cushing's rejection as secretary of the treasury, Tyler nominated Spencer for the post. He was confirmed 22 to 20 on March 3, the same day as his nomination. *Ibid.*, 190-91. Irwin was nominated on March 2, 1843, and confirmed the following day as chargé to Denmark, no vote given. *Ibid.*, 179, 182. For Irwin, see *BDAC*. 3. Clay predicted a conflict between the Van Buren and Calhoun factions of the Democratic party that would benefit the Whigs. See Clay to Leigh, March 17, 1843. 4. Polk beat Clay in Alabama, 37,740 to 26,084, took Louisiana by the slim margin of 13,782 to 13,083, and carried Mississippi by 25,126 to 19,206. Clay carried Tennessee by 60,030 to 59,917. McKee, *National . . . Popular and Electoral Vote*, 56-57.

From Randolph R. Gurley, March 16, 1843. Encloses an American Colonization Society deed for Clay's signature, and reports that a number of life membership certificates in the society, also requiring Clay's signature, had been mailed to him, under frank, a few days ago. Hopes Clay has returned from his southern [New Orleans] tour in good health and that his "invaluable life may be long preserved." ALS. DLC-Records of the American Colonization Society (DNA, M212, R20). At this juncture Gurley was again, though briefly, secretary of the society.

To JAMES B. SWAIN Lexington, March 16, 1843

I received your letter requesting a sketch of this place ["Ashland"] for the embellishment of my Life and Speeches which you are publishing.[1] It is not very easy to procure such a sketch, in an interior place like Lexington; but I will endeavor to engage Mr. Nagle [*sic*, John Neagle], or some other artist to prepare one in the course of a few weeks, and when completed I will transmit it to you.[2]

I regret that your efforts to make an amicable arrangement with Mr. [Daniel] Mallory were not more successful; but from your account of the matter, I do not see that any blame justly attaches to you. I am extremely sorry that your indemnity for the publication was injuriously affected by that gentleman;[3] but I hope that the course of events may be such as to make it ultimately full and ample.

My Speech on the Veto[4] was published in the papers without any correction or revisal of mine; and it has some inaccuracies, which I should be glad to have set right, before it takes the more durable form, which it will assume in your book. If you could, under cover to the honble J.J. Crittenden, Frankfort, (K) transmit to me a copy of it, in your proof sheet or other print (for I have no copy of it) I would have the corrections made. . . .[5]

ALS. NcD. 1. Clay to Swain, July 18, 1842. 2. There was no picture of "Ashland" in Swain's book; and although Neagle had recently done a portrait of Clay [Clay to Neagle, May 29, 1843], it did not appear in Swain's book either. The portrait that was included was an engraving by J.F.F. Prud'homme from an original painting by George Linen. Also included was a sketch of Clay's birthplace in Hanover Co., Va., drawn by

J. Bingley and engraved by J.N. Gimbrede. 3. Apparently Mallory claimed a "preemptive" right to publish certain Clay speeches. See Clay to Sargent, July 2, 1842, and Clay to Swain, July 18, 1842. 4. Clay to Sargent, August 20, 1842. 5. See Swain, *Life and Speeches . . .*, 492-517.

To BENJAMIN W. LEIGH Lexington, March 17, 1843

Col. W R. Johnson,[1] passing through Lexington a few days ago, gave me the agreeable information that your health and spirits were good. Mine were improved by my Southern jaunt, from which I have just returned. If pomp and parade, and displays of extravagant enthusiasm, by Democrats as well as Whigs, by women as well as men and boys, could afford me gratification, I had enough of it, God knows. I was gratified, although often much wearied.

Should I be alive, and be the Candidate of the Whigs for the Presidency, (to which I have never yet consented) the vote of K. is not more certain than that of Louisiana.[2] I went to Alabama and Mississippi with not the most distant expectation of those States (the former especially) voting for the Whigs. I came away with strong hopes, and a pretty confident belief, that we shall get both of them.[3] This will be the result, if realized, of local causes, and of an implacable difference between the respective partizans of Mr. V. B. [Van Buren] & Mr. Calhoun. The local causes, in the former, are the basis of the White population for representatives in Congress, and the question of putting an end to their vicious local bank system; and in the latter, repudiation & the currency. A most bitter schism exists on the bank question in Alabama, and on repudiation in Mississippi, in the Democratic party, and in both on the Presidency, altho' I rather think that Mr. V. B has the major part with him. In Tennessee our friends (and John Bell, whom I saw, among them) are very confident of success.[4]

But I had another object in writing to you now. It was to say that I have just perused the address of the Whig Convention of Va to the People of the old dominion,[5] and that I have risen from its perusal with the highest admiration of the ability candor and good temper which characterizes its composition. With very slight modifications, I heartily concur in its principles and general reasoning. I was rejoiced to find that it boldly announces the attachment of the Whigs of Virginia to a Bank of the U. S. and to a Tariff for Revenue mainly, and for protection, incidentally. There is no other ground to be conscientiously taken. Never, until in these days of tergiversation and corruption, was it questioned that, in arranging a Tariff for Revenue, protection might be incidentally secured. Look at the debates in Congress, especially from 1820 to 24. And it is only now questioned because it belongs to M[r]. Calhoun's system of ultraism to controvert it.

The silence or brief notice with which Mr. Tyler is treated in the Address was wise. He is sufficiently cast off from the Whigs, by his treachery and their repudiation of him, and henceforward we shall have the gratification and the amusement of witnessing his quarrels with the Democratic party which has contributed to his prostitution, and with which he is now to be regarded as fully identified.

There is one omission in the Address, which I regret. I mean Executive power & the Veto. To the Veto, in the form in which it now is in the Constitution, I am utterly opposed. With good Presidents, it may not be attended with mischief; with bad ones, as we have seen, it may inflict incalculable injury upon the Nation. Like the principle of hereditary succession, too much is left to the chapter of accidents, in the personnal character of the Chief of the State.

You may not gain your Cause in Virginia, and I do not expect it;[6] but the Address shews (of course I do not mean to speak of that part of it which so kindly relates to me) that you deserve success. At all events, it cannot fail to do good in Va. and every where. Present my best regards to Mr. C[hapman]. Johnson, to Judges [Francis T.] Brooke and [Robert] Stanard, and, altho' last not least in my friendly recollection, to Mrs. [Julia Wickam] Leigh.

ALS. ViU. Addressed to Leigh in Richmond, Va. 1. Probably William Ranson Johnson of Petersburg, Va. See *DAB*. 2. Clay carried Ky. in 1844 by 61,255 to Polk's 51,988 but lost La. by 13,782 to 13,083. McKee, *National . . . Popular and Electoral Vote*, 56-57. 3. Clay to Berrien, March 13, 1843. 4. *Ibid.* 5. The Va. Whig convention was held in Richmond on Feb. 22-23, 1843, with Benjamin W. Leigh serving as president. The address, produced by a committee appointed by the convention, supported a national bank, distribution to the states of the public land sales fund, a one-term presidency, a tariff for revenue but also with incidental protection, and Henry Clay for president. They opposed federal assumption of state debts and absolved the Whigs from any fault in the failure of the Bankruptcy Act. Lynchburg *Virginian*, March 6, 16, 20, 1843. 6. Polk carried Virginia's 17 electoral votes by a margin of 49,570 to 43,677 over Clay. McKee, *National . . . Popular and Electoral Vote*, 56-57.

To James Bleakley, New York City, March 18, 1843. Regrets that he was unable to attend the celebration of the ratification of the Treaty of Ghent sponsored by the Henry Clay Club of the Eighth Ward. Comments: "My colleagues and I, in the session which negotiated that treaty, earnestly endeavored to secure all the rights of the nation which we could, under actual circumstances, and to sacrifice none. It is highly satisfactory that the nation . . . approved, and has continued to be contented with its terms." Catalogue copy, excerpt. Printed in The Rendells, Inc., *The American Frontier*, vol. 1. Letter written from Lexington.

Bleakley, secretary of the club, does not appear in the 1842-43 *New York City Directory*, nor has he been otherwise identified.

From George M. Davis, Alton, Ill., March 18, 1843. Reports that Clay's land [680 acres] lying across from Alton at the juncture of the Mississippi and Missouri rivers [Clay to James Brown Clay, October 30, 1840] has been much trespassed upon and "large quantities of wood" have been stolen from it by "vagabonds who deem it *a virtue* to steal the timber from the land of Nonresidents." Explains that because the land is periodically inundated, its "only value consists in the timber." In response to Clay's inquiry about the possible value of that land, states that "At the present depressed period of affairs in this section of the west, I do not believe you could sell for over Ten Dollars per acre." Asks Clay for "the numbers of legal designation of your tract" so he can make a personal examination of it and thus better evaluate its value. ALS. DLC-TJC (DNA, M212, R14). Davis was an Alton attorney.

To NATHANIEL SILSBEE Lexington, March 18, 1843

I venture to address you on a subject of some delicacy on which there are but few friends I have in the world that I would approach. The general pecuniary pressure, owing mainly to the folly at Washn., which prevails in the U. States, has reached some of our interests in Kentucky, and especially that of the manufacture of Hemp into bagging and rope. My son Thomas [Hart Clay] was engaged in that business; and owing to the low prices and slow sales of the fabric became embarrassed.[1] I advanced him a large sum, upwards of $30.000 under the hope that the markets would improve; but they declined still further instead of advancing. The consequence was that he had to assign his property for the equal benefit of all his creditors. I allowed myself to be postponed to all of them, and they will be all paid but me. He will remain my debtor about $20.000.

That advance to him has subjected me to momentary embarrassment. I am not in any danger of being sued for any thing I owe, and my property is ample, not merely to pay any debts, but to leave me a full competency. In the present universal depression, I should be unwilling to bring any valuable property into market.

Under these circumstances, I should feel greatly relieved, if I could effect a loan of $10.000, in the course of a few months, for a year and a half or two years. I would engage to pay the interest half yearly in Boston or N. York, and give ample security, if it be required.

I have supposed it possible that it might not be inconvenient to you to render me the friendly service of loaning me that sum; but I should be unwilling to accept it, if it occasioned you the slightest inconvenience, or if you entertained the least doubt of ultimate indemnity.

That sum would put me quite at ease.

I returned about ten days ago from N. Orleans. Political prospects are far better in the S.W. than I anticipated. Should I be the Candidate for the Presidency, Kentucky is not more certain than Louisiana; and, owing to divisions on local and general politics in Alabama and Mississippi, I do believe the Whigs will obtain those States. Our friends count with great confidence, and I think with reason, on Tennessee.[2]

What will become of the old Bay State?[3] I suppose that the result of the last fall's Election,[4] so unexpected & so distressing to us all, is to be attributed to Messrs. Webster & [Caleb] Cushing.[5] But will their influence be allowed to continue her in her present unnatural position?

ALS. MH. Letter marked "(Confidential)." 1. Clay to Lucretia Hart Clay, Dec. 9, 1842. By June, 1843, Thomas was having difficulty meeting interest payments on his notes. A payment of $74.40 on a note for $3,600 at the Lexington Branch of the Bank of Kentucky, due March 1, 1843, was finally paid on June 24. Receipt. DS, by D. M. and Elijah W. Craig. DLC-TJC (DNA, M212, R19). 2. For the 1844 presidential election results in La., Miss., Ala., Tenn., and Ky., see Clay to Berrien, March 13, 1843; Clay to Leigh, March 17, 1843. 3. Clay carried Mass. by 67,418 to Polk's 52,846, with James G. Birney, Liberty party candidate, polling 10,860 votes. McKee, *National . . . Popular and Electoral Vote*, 56-57. 4. In the 1842 Mass. congressional elections, Democrats won 2 seats and Whigs won 8 seats. *Guide to U.S. Elections*, 577. In the gubernatorial race Democrat Marcus Morton won 56,491 votes to 54,939 for Whig John Davis and 6,382 for Liberty party candidate Samuel Sewell. Because no candidate received a popular majority, the election went to the state legislature where Morton was chosen. *BDGUS*, 2:698. The legislature also chose Democrats for other state offices such as secretary of state and treasury, indicating that the Democrats controlled the state legislature. *Niles' Register* (Jan. 28, 1843) 63:339; Richard H. Sewell, *Ballots for Freedom: Antislavery Politics in the United States, 1837-1860* (New York, 1976), 85-86. 5. For Webster's and Cushing's activities, see Spencer to Clay, Oct. 28, 1842.

To LUCRETIA C.[1] ERWIN Lexington, March 24, 1843

During my absence from home last winter, a letter from you addressed to me came there [Lexington]. Your brothers[2] read it but have omitted yet to give it to me.

From other sources, I have learnt your removal from Columbia [Tenn.]

to Nashville. I hope the change will prove both agreeable and beneficial. You will now see more frequently your Aunts, and have the advantage of their good advice, which I hope you assiduously follow. I trust too, my dear Grand daughter, that you will be diligent in your studies, obedient to your instructors and to the rules of the school, and careful in all your deportment. Should you now neglect your studies, you will never cease in all after life to regret it.[3]

You will have heard of your father's marriage.[4] I hope the event will conduce to his happiness and to that of all his children & relatives.

Let me hear from you occasionally, and be assured that nothing will be more gratifying to your grandmama and me than to hear of your improvement & success in your Education.

All are well at the Woodlands & here ["Ashland"]. My respects to your Aunts & uncles.[5]

ALS. MHi. 1. For the young lady's correct middle name, see Clay to Lucretia Hart Clay, May 21, 1838. At this time she was 12 years old. 2. Henry Clay Erwin (1827-59); James Erwin, Jr. (1828-48); Andrew E. Erwin (1830-63); Charles E. Erwin (1835-60). 3. Clay to Lucretia Hart Clay, May 21, 1838. 4. Clay to Lucretia Hart Clay, Jan. 18, 1843. 5. James Erwin's sister, Jane Erwin Yeatman Bell, and his brother, John P. Erwin, lived in Nashville.

Speech in Lexington, April 10, 1843. According to the Lexington *Intelligencer*, as reported by the Raleigh *Register* of May 2, 1843, Clay discussed Tyler's proscriptive patronage policy in this address as well as the bank, tariff, and distribution issues; also, the Bankruptcy Act [Remark in Senate, April 22, 1840], and limitation of the veto power of the president. He again explained why he had shifted his stance on the national bank issue in 1816 [2:200-205, 210, 216-19].

Clay's critical views on Tyler's patronage policy, as quoted by *Niles' Register* of April 29, 1843 from an account of this speech carried in the Lexington *Observer and Reporter*, were introduced by Niles' as follows: "We regret that we cannot present to our readers the whole of Mr. Clay's speech; but there was one part of it relating to the administration of the patronage of the government, so very important as to require that it should be published, and we think we can present it in the precise language of that gentleman."

The substantive part of Clay's remarks on Tyler's patronage practices continued in summary form, viz:

"After having shown, that the present administration had totally abandoned the principles and the party which brought it into power; had identified itself with the democratic party, with which it was now one and indivisible; and was systematically and corruptly administering the patronage of the government to buy up the people of the United States, or rather to buy up the democratic party to the support of Mr. Tyler, Mr. Clay proceeded to say: 'that he had no hesitation to express his opinion, as an humble and private citizen, that no man who had any feelings of self-respect or honor or patriotism could take or hold any office, the tenure of which depended on the president's will, subject to the degrading and disgraceful conditions which were imposed upon its possession; and that it would be the bounden duty of the next president elected, be he whig or democrat, to purify the public service by promptly discarding all such contaminated incumbents. He hoped there were many, he knew there were some, now in office, who disdained to submit to any such disgraceful conditions, and they ought, and he doubted not would receive just and full consideration, and be judged according to their capacity, honesty and fidelity to their country.'

"Mr. Clay went on further to say, 'that, in his opinion, if a whig president should be elected, it would be his imperative duty to do ample justice, in the administration of the public patronage, to the great whig party of the country—which he verily believed for years had embraced a majority of the people of the United States. That party, for upwards of fourteen years, with the exception of one month, had been systematically proscribed and excluded from all public employments. Not only from original appointments, but, when they held office, they have been hurled out to make way, often for unworthy persons, of opposite politics. And so far is Mr. Tyler now pursuing this practice that he is dismissing men whom he put in, not only without charge, without fault, without any species of trial, but with a full knowledge that the duties of their offices have been diligently, honestly and faithfully executed, and putting back in their places men whom he had himself dismissed.—Every consideration of equality, of equity, and of justice demands, . . . that the most full and complete reparation of the injuries done to the whig party should be hereafter made. Nor would that be proscription. It would be the severest rebuke of proscription. On the contrary, to continue in office men, who had been put there by the dismission of other and better men, for political reasons, would be to sanction, consummate and perpetuate proscription. But if it could be regarded as proscription, who is to be justly reproached with beginning proscription in this country?'

"No man felt more profoundly than he did, the evils which were likely to grow out of struggles for the prize of government, with the distribution of all its honors and offices exclusively confined to the successful party. He doubted whether our system could long endure the consequences of such struggles. But he hoped that a remedy would be hereafter found, either in the amendment of the constitution or the law, to guard against these evils."

On the failed attempt of the Whigs in the summer of 1841 to reestablish a national bank [Tyler to Clay, April 30, 1841; Speech in Senate, June 21, 1841], Clay emphasized the constitutionality of such a bank and explained at length what he considered to be the widely misrepresented or generally misunderstood section 10 of the second bank bill [Tyler to Clay, April 30, 1841] which provided both the mechanism for establishing branches in the several states and the limitations thereon [Porter to Clay, mid-July, 1841; Crittenden to Clay, August 16, 1841; Remark in Senate, August 24, 1841]. "The question of the assent of the States," the Lexington *Intelligencer*, as reported by the Raleigh *Register*, quoted him as saying, "was one of expediency alone, and did not involve the constitutional power of Congress to establish a Bank. That power was claimed and exercised in the establishment of the Bank—the privilege of branching was a matter entirely distinct, and might be conferred, subject to any restrictions, upon the Directors, Congress might see fit to impose, and those restrictions could not, by any fair construction, be understood as a concession on the part of Congress, or an abandonment of its constitutional power. But the last clause of the section, Mr. C. affirmed, rendered the matter beyond all dispute, that Congress, so far from yielding, or even seeming to yield, its constitutional power to establish branches in the several States, expressly asserted the power to exist and declared its intention to exercise it whenever it might become, in the words of the Constitution, 'necessary and proper for carrying into execution any of the powers granted to Congress' by that instrument. The charter, in this form, was not such as he himself, or the mass of the Whigs, would have preferred, but they have regarded it as a question of expediency, and not as a matter of principle, and as the bill could only be passed by retaining this feature, the great body of the Whigs were willing to yield this minor consideration for the sake of securing the passage of the bill and furnishing to the country a sound and uniform currency."

The Lexington *Intelligencer*, as quoted by the Raleigh *Register*, also adds: "Upon the question of the Tariff, and the Distribution of the proceeds of the Public Lands, Mr. C. conclusively showed that the Whigs in Congress had done every thing that could be expected of them. They had succeeded in passing a Tariff which, while it affords sufficient revenue to meet the wants of an economical administration of the Government, at the same time furnishes adequate incidental protection to American Industry. The Whigs had been censured for the clause which was attached to the Distribution Bill as originally passed, providing that whenever the rate of duties should exceed 20 per cent. the distribution should be suspended. In this way only could the Bill have passed at that time, and believing that, in the adjustment of the Tariff, it would not be necessary to exceed that rate, or that if it should, the postponing clause might be afterwards repealed, the Whigs, rather than lose the Bill entirely, gave a reluctant consent to its introduction. At the next session that clause was repealed, and the Distribution law stripped of all clogs or impediments, which would prevent its free and full exercise, but Mr. Tyler interposed his veto and thwarted Congress in this measure.

The rapid and alarming increase of executive power, and the means proposed for restricting it, were ably and eloquently treated of, and a conviction of the necessity of a limitation of the veto power, we believe, was fastened upon every unprejudiced mind. A more finished, conclusive, irresistible argument upon any subject we have never listened to.

"In conclusion, Mr. Clay made an eloquent appeal to the Whigs to stand firm in defence of their principles, and declared his sincere and unwavering confidence in the success of those principles in the approaching contest. And as that patriot voice, which has lost none of its rich fullness and sweet melody—and that has so often rallied the drooping spirits of his desponding comrades, and nerved their arms to deeds of daring valor—fell upon the ear, it sent a thrill of joy and hope through every breast, and awakened in each heart new hopes and new resolves for the future. Each Whig buckled on his armor closer and felt his strength re-invigorated and his confidence in the justice and success of the cause in which he battled, greatly increased. May the same spirit animate our friends every where, and may continued, uninterrupted health and happiness be vouchsafed to the gallant chief, upon whom the hopes of the Whigs of America are now, centered, until the consummation of that victory, which will assuredly crown the efforts of the Whig party in 1844." Copy. Printed in the Lexington *Observer and Reporter* as quoted and printed in *Niles' Register* (April 29, 1843), 64:136-37; Lexington *Intelligencer* as quoted and printed in Raleigh *Register*, May 2, 1843. Neither of the Lexington, Ky., newspapers are available for 1842 and 1843.

In a 1910 biography of Henry Clay, Thomas Hart Clay included an excerpt from a speech by his grandfather, which he dated "May, 1843," but which was probably part of the elusive speech of April 10, 1843. According to this excerpt, Clay also said on this occasion: "Fellow citizens—I am now an *old man—quite* an old man. . . . But yet it will be found . . . that I am not too old to vindicate my principles, to stand by my friends, or to defend myself . . . I feel like an old stag which has been long coursed by the hunters and the hounds, through brakes and briers, and o'er distant plains, and has at last returned to his ancient lair to lay himself down and die. And yet the vile curs of party are barking at my heels, and the bloodhounds of personal malignity are aiming at my throat. I scorn and defy them as I ever did." Copy, extract. Printed in Thomas Hart Clay, *Henry Clay*. American Crisis Biographies (Philadelphia, 1910), 399-400. This biography was started by Thomas H. Clay who died in 1907 before completing it; it was finished by Ellis Paxton Oberholtzer.

To DANIEL ULLMANN Lexington, April 13, 1843

I received your favor, transmitting a letter from Mr. [Edward] Gamage which satisfactorily explains his motives in accepting a foreign appointment.[1]

I saw that you had been pronouncing a discourse on my poor life and poor services.[2] I wish that you had had a better subject; but I have no doubt that you made the most of that which you selected. I presume I shall see the discourse when published.

From a survey of the whole ground of the Union, I feel great confidence that the Whigs will achieve a victory in 1844 that will eclipse that of 1840. I think the reaction has begun, altho' the result of the Connecticut election has not quite come up to my hopes.[3] Should you triumph in the City it will tell most powerfully throughout the Union.[4]

I lately addressed the People at home,[5] and declared the principles which, in my opinion, ought to regulate the administration of the patronage of the General Governmt. I invite your attention to them as published.

AL. NHi. Signature removed by recipient for gift autograph. Addressed to Ullmann in New York City. Printed also in Colton, *Clay Correspondence*, 4:474. 1. Gamage, a South Carolinian, was nominated by Tyler on August 24, 1842, to be consul at Florence in the Grand Duchy of Tuscany. He was confirmed by unanimous consent of the Senate on August 26. U.S. Sen., *Executive Journal*, 6:137, 139. For Gamage, see *SCHGM*, 43:48; 59:115; 67:157. 2. On March 23, 1843, Ullmann had delivered an oration of two hours upon "The Life and Services of Henry Clay" to the Democratic Clay Club of New York's tenth ward. New York *Weekly Courier and Enquirer*, March 25, 1843. 3. In the 1843 Connecticut state elections the Whigs carried five of the 21 senatorial districts; in the house the Democrats won a majority of about 30. Hartford *Daily Courant*, April 6, 1843. In the gubernatorial race, Democrat Chauncey F. Cleveland defeated Whig Roger S. Baldwin by a vote of 27,416 to 25,401. *BDGUS*, 1:168. Democrats also won all four congressional seats in Connecticut. *Guide to U.S. Elections*, 578. 4. In the New York City charter election, held on April 12, 1843, Democrat Robert H. Morris defeated the Whig candidate for mayor, Robert Smith, by a majority of 6,000 votes. Democrats also won 12 alderman and 14 assistant seats out of 17 on each board. Washington *Daily National Intelligencer*, April 14, 1843; Nevins, *Diary of Philip Hone*, 655. 5. Speech in Lexington, April 10, 1843.

To JOHN M. CLAYTON Lexington, April 14, 1843

I transmit to you enclosed a part of a Lexington paper giving some account of a Speech which I made last monday to the People, in Lexington.[1] In the course of that Speech I stated the principles on which, in my opinion, the patronage of the Genl Government ought to be administered. With the exception of one or two unimportant ingrammaticisms, which your eye will readily detect, in the article, it correctly represents my language, so far as respects those principles. Mr. Tyler, having thrown off the mask, and come out an unblushing democrat, I thought the time a suitable one to make a declaration of those principles. Two good effects I hoped might result from such an annunciation. 1st. It might deter, as far as any thing coming from me could deter, the acceptance of office, upon the dishonorable conditions now prescribed to encumbents. And 2dly. It would animate the Whigs by an assurance that, if successful, justice would be done to them. Your opinion as to the expediency of such a declaration strengthened my own convictions.

The public papers did not exaggerate the enthusiasm which marked my reception every where at the S. West. I should not be surprized if we carry the whole of the S. West, including Alabama & Mississippi.[2] My friends assure me that Tennessee[3] is perfectly safe.

The recent elections in Massach[use]tts and Connecticut,[4] altho' not terminating as we could have wished, demonstrate that the *reaction* has commenced. With a good cause; with perfect union on our side, and perfect distraction & division on the other side; and with the traitor Tyler now fully identified with them, I think we cannot fail of achieving a glorious victory. What, say you, guilty or not guilty?

What do you think of a young man like me resuming the practice of the Law?

I was induced to do it to assist my son James [Brown Clay] and to be at my office, in Lexington, more accessible to perfect strangers who might be prompted by mere curiosity to see me. But I am not at all unwilling to receive liberal fees.[5]

ALS. DLC-John M. Clayton Papers (DNA, M212, R20). 1. Speech in Lexington, April 10, 1843. 2. Clay to Berrien, March 13, 1843. 3. *Ibid.* 4. Clay to Silsbee, March 18, 1843; Clay to Ullmann, April 13, 1843. 5. On May 31, 1843, for example, Clay was engaged by D.L. Price to represent him in a case involving a contested will. He agreed to pay Clay $500, "one hundred to be paid on the establishment of the said will, and four hundred on the first day of April next, and nothing if the will be not established." DS, in Clay's hand. DLC-TJC (DNA, M212, R10).

To JOHN M. BERRIEN Lexington, April 23, 1843

I received today your obliging letter of the 11h. and who do you think dined with and have just left me today? Govr. [Robert P.] Letcher, [William S.] Archer, [John J.] Crittenden and Speaker [John] White. We were glad to meet each other and should have been greatly delighted to have had you with us; but you were not forgotten, and I was much gratified with the high testimony borne by the three members of Congress to your ability zeal and fidelity.

I agree with you that all personal considerations are merged in the superior importance to the Union; to self government, to order, law and morality, of the present political contest. Its magnitude is such that I sometimes tremble in contemplating our possible failure. And yet, looking at all the existing causes in operation, notwithstanding our recent discomfiture in the City of N. York,[1] I cannot but believe that we must prevail.

You must have shared with me in satisfaction that the recent Whig address in Va.[2] has taken boldly the ground for a Nat. Bank, and a Tariff for revenue, with incidental protection. On that ground, I think you can stand at the South, and Georgia has the merit of having preceded Va. in assuming it.

In regard to a Candidate for the V. P. I have really formed no conclusive opinion;[3] and if I had I should take no measures to promote it. *Personally* I like [John M.] Clayton better than any who have been talked of for it. But it is a grave question, and should be well considered. I think Mr. [Millard] Fillmore deserves the high estimate in which he was held by the Whigs of the last Congress. I think him able, faithful, and with uncommon business habits.

I perceive that Tyler has dismissed Mr. [James] Hunter. I hope he will bear it like a man. I am sure Mrs. Berrien will.[4] Most certainly no man can retain office and consent to the disgraceful conditions which are now imposed on incumbents. To this sentiment I recently gave a public expression, and I shall be happy to know that it meets your approbation.

I am afraid that it will not be in my power to visit Georgia at the time you kindly propose. And yet I fondly cherish the hope that I shall be able, at no distant day, to surprize my friends there.

My information from Tennessee,[5] Indiana[6] & Ohio[7] continues to be very encouraging. It is not so of Illinois; and therefore I indulge no expectation of a Whig successor to Mr. [Samuel] McRoberts.[8] I have just however seen a statement that [Oliver H.] Smith of Indiana means to contest the seat of [Edward A.] Hannegan, and upon ground, if the statement be correct, that may be successful....[9]

ALS. NcU. 1. Clay to Ullmann, April 13, 1843. 2. Clay to Leigh, March 13, 1843. 3. Clay to Clayton, August 8, 1842. For the Whig vice presidential nomination, see Clay to Dearborn, July 13, 1842. 4. In July, 1833 Berrien had married Eliza C. Hunter, daughter of Col. James Hunter of Savannah. On June 16, 1841 (at Berrien's request) Tyler nominated James Hunter to be collector of the port of Savannah, and the Senate confirmed him on June 23. In 1843, however, President Tyler removed all those whom he had appointed to federal offices at Berrien's request. Subsequently, William B. Bullock was nominated to be collector at Savannah but was rejected by the Senate. Edward Hardin finally received the post in 1844. U.S. Sen., *Executive Journal*, 5:383, 393, 6:309, 340; Royce C. McCrary, Jr., "John MacPherson Berrien of Georgia (1781-1856): A Political Biography," Ph.D. dissertation, University of Georgia, 1971, pp. 213, 247-48, 272; Alexander R. MacDonell, "John MacPherson Berrien," *GHQ* (March, 1933), 17:1-12, espec. 10. 5. Clay to Berrien, March 13, 1843. 6. Polk beat Clay in Indiana in 1844 by 70,181 to 67,867, with James G. Birney, running on the Liberty party ticket, receiving 2,106 votes. McKee, *National . . . Popular and Electoral Vote*, 56-57. 7. Clay carried Ohio over Polk in 1844 by 155,057 to 149,117, with Birney getting 8,050 votes. *Ibid.* 8. Sen. Samuel McRoberts had died in office on March 27, 1843. James Semple, also a Democrat, was appointed to the seat in August, 1843 and was subsequently elected to it by the Illinois legislature on Dec. 11, 1844. He occupied the seat until March 3, 1847, when he chose not to seek reelection. *BDAC*; Springfield *Illinois Register*, August 25, 1843. Polk beat Clay by 57,920 to 45,528 in 1844 with James G. Birney receiving 3,570 votes. McKee, *National . . . Popular and Electoral Vote*, 56-57. 9. Clay to Smith, Nov. 11, 1842.

To N.W. HATCH Lexington, April 26, 1843

I received, some days ago, the four trees of the species of Magnolia Makrophylia, in good order which you did me the favor to send me.[1] I have planted them, and they promise to do remarkably well. I request your acceptance of my thanks for them. They are a beautiful variety of Magnolia, of which I have several species growing here. I consider the acquisition of them very valuable, especially if, as I hope, they will bear our winters. But I should not express my grateful sense of the obligation under which you have placed me if I did not also tender my acknowledgements for the friendly and flattering motives which prompted you to offer me a present so very acceptable. Engaged as you are, in one of the most innocent, useful and agreeable pursuits of man, the voluntary testimony which you have done me the honor to render to my public services is highly appreciated, and will be gratefully remembered by me....

Copy. Printed in Boston *Daily Evening Transcript*, July 19, 1843. 1. Identifying himself as a "hortoculturist by profession," Hatch had written Clay from Vicksburg, Miss. on April 11, 1843 in conjunction with presenting him four trees "of the genus Magnolia, and species Makrophylia." He noted that the magnolia "Like yourself . . . is purely American. . . . The purity of its spotless bloom is an emblem of your reputation, and its unrivalled foliage, but a type of your well earned honors." *Ibid.*

To SEARGENT S. PRENTISS Lexington, April 27, 1843

I think you have the political game in your hands in Missi. if you play your cards well. The goodness of our cause; the badness of that of our opponents; the dishonesty of repudiation;[1] the divisions both on local and general questions among our opponents; the moral action within and without the State, in regard to the obligations of honor and good faith; the flight of Graves and the suicide of his less guilty confederate,[2]—all these causes must give you victory at your next election.[3] When I had the pleasure of being with you,[4] you thought it would be the best policy, if the Democratic Convention would nominate a bond paying Democrat,[5] to make no opposition but support the nomination, and you said as much to some of the delegates to that Convention. But they did not make such a nomination, and their failure absolves you from all obligation in the matter.

And now what is best to be done? Will you pardon me for making a suggestion? It appears to me that it would be the wisest to run Whig Candidates, who are in favor of paying the State debt, for all the important offices. If you attempt to run Democrats, who are for paying the bonds, many Whigs, some from principle, some upon pretexts, will refuse to vote for them because they are democrats. It is easier to draw to the Whigs, the honest democrats, than it is to carry the mass of the Whigs to them; because there is less difficulty in moving a few than many. And I must say that, I think, it has been the vice of the Whig party, frequently[6] manifested, during the last eight or ten years, that it has too often sought to ally itself to the odds and ends of other parties, instead of resting upon the strength of their own numbers and their own patriotic principles. What sacrifices have they not made to gain Anti Masons, even abolitionists &c &c?

I wished to bring this view of the matter to your consideration. At the same time, I know that your superior knowledge of local causes and circumstances makes you much more competent to judge than I am.

I recollect with great pleasure the agreeable hours I recently passed under your roof. I hope your own happiness has been augmented by an event in your family, which I presumed was not distant.[7] Trusting that it has been fortunate, on that supposition, I venture to offer you my congratulations. . . .

ALS. NcU. Letter marked "(Confidential)." Apparently addressed to Prentiss in Vicksburg, Miss. 1. At issue in all of Mississippi's political campaigns from 1840 to 1852 was the question of whether or not to redeem or to repudiate the state's bonded debt. Whigs generally were in favor of paying off the bonds, while Democrats were split between those in favor of paying and those advocating repudiation. Repudiators won majorities in all the state elections during the period, because the poorer people were convinced that redeeming the bonds would necessitate higher taxes. For more on this issue, see Dickey, *Seargent S. Prentiss*, 198-228; Reginald C. McGrane, *Foreign Bondholders and American State Debts* (New York, 1935) *passim*. See also Remark in Senate, Feb. 18, 1840, and Speech in Lexington, June 9, 1842. 2. Richard S. Graves, treasurer of Mississippi, had received a draft for $165,079 in U.S. treasury notes from the federal government, made out to himself personally rather than to the office of state treasurer. In March, 1843, Graves was charged with embezzling these funds, and he escaped to Canada. Mrs. Graves subsequently delivered to the state $69,232.68 in Mississippi treasury warrants, $92,000 in U.S. treasury notes, and $2,749.68 in foreign gold, leaving $44,838.46 unpaid. On March 31, 1843, Col. W.H. Shelton of Jackson, Miss., president of the Brandon Bank, drowned himself in the Pearl River. He had allegedly made a large loan to Graves, and his suicide was assumed to be as a result of his involvement in the Graves affair. Lowry & McCardle, *A History of Mississippi*, 299-302; Washington *Daily National Intelligencer*, April 17, 1843. 3. In the Nov. 6, 1843, gubernatorial race in Mississippi Democrat Albert G. Brown, who favored repudiating the state's bonds, defeated the Whig candidate, George H. Clayton, who opposed repudiation, by a vote of 21,035 to 17,322. *BDGUS*, 2:808. All four seats in the U.S. House were won by anti-redemption, or repudiation, Democrats. The Whigs did not offer candidates in this race, because Mississippi had refused to conform to the districting provision of the apportionment act [Clay to Crittenden, June 3, 1842; Clay to Adams, July 24, 1842]; therefore, the Whigs considered the election illegal. *Guide to U.S. Elections*, 578; *Niles' Register* (Nov. 25, 1843), 65:208. In the state senate Whigs elected 5 members and retained 6 old members, giving them a total of 11 seats. Democrats won 10 seats and continued to hold 10 seats, giving them a total of 20. In the state house the Whigs won 35 seats, the Democrats won 59, with 1 "unknown." These elections constituted a victory in all branches for the repudiation Democrats. Jackson (Miss.) *The Southron*, Nov. 17, 1843; Jackson *The Mississippian*, Nov. 18, 1843. 4. In Vicksburg in Feb., 1843. 5. The Mississippi Democrats had held a state convention on Feb. 23, 1843, and nominated Albert G. Brown for governor; however, the convention refused to commit itself on the issue of state bonded debt repudiation and failed to nominate a candidate for the U.S. Senate. Because of dissension on these and other issues, Brown resigned as a candidate in May and called for a new convention. A second convention was held on July 10, 1843, and it, too, nominated Brown, a repudiator, for governor. James B. Ranck, *Albert Gallatin Brown, Radical Southern Nationalist* (New York, 1937), 27-32. 6. The word "often" is struck through and "frequently" is substituted. 7. Mary Williams Prentiss gave birth to their first child, Jane, on April 14, 1843. Dickey, *Seargent S. Prentiss*, 200.

MEMORANDUM OF REMITTANCES FROM NEW ORLEANS

[Lexington, *ca.* April 29, 1843]

Bills purchased or remitted for H. Clay—N. Orleans. By [Charles] Worsley & Foreman [*sic*, George Forman] remitted a check to the Bank of Commerce[1] N. York, drawn by S. Roberts[2] on J. C. Harris,[3] Philada. the 19h. Novr at 30 days sight recd. at N.Y. by B. of C. 3d. Decr 42 (see letter)	$2000.
" Do Robb and Hodge[4] check on Nevins Townsend & Co. of N. York[5] at 30 days sight recd at N.Y. 3 Decr 42 by B. of C (see letter)	1716.40
× Saml. Nicholson[6] on Brown Brothers & Co.[7] dated 24h. Decr. 1842 at N. Orleans, payable seventy days after date for . . .	3109:59
√ Do. Do. dated 27h Decr 1842 do do for	823:55
× Alexr. Porter on Dunlop, Moncure & Co.[8] Richmond Va. payable in N York seventy days after date dated 27h. Decr 1842 for	460:-
× Sam. Nicholson on Brown Brothers & Co payable in N. York, seventy days after date (29h. Decr 1842) for ———	2041:99.
√ Gardner, Sayers & Co. on Mess[rs]. W.C. Pickersgill[9] & Co. in N. York, seventy days after date (5 Jan 1843)	2150 "
√ Sam. Nicholson on Brown, Brothers & Co. of N.Y. dated 18 Jan. 1843 payable seventy days after date—	955:10.
√ Do. Do. Do. Do ———	1000.
Geo. Lee on [Jonathan] Goodhue & Co. N. York,[10] dated 21st. Jan. 43 payable 70 days after date ———	1000.
Sam. Nicholson on Brown, Brothers & Co. of N. York, dated 25h. Jan. 1843, payable 70 days after date ———	767:26.
delivered K. S & Co. Adams & Whitall on K. Smith & Co.[11] at sight dated 30h. Jan. 1843———	320.
Those marked thus X forwarded the first numbers for collection to the Bank of Commerce, N. York. H.C.[12] Saml Nicholson on do. (B.B. & Co.) dated 15 Feb 1843 pay[a]ble 70 days after date for ———	175:25
Robb and Ho[d]ge on Nevins Townsend & Co. N. York payable 70 days after date of 15 Feb 1843 for	203:43

[Second page]

	Checked on the funds on the first page		
Nov. 42.	Drew in favor of J[ames]. B[rown]. Clay on the Bank of Commerce to be applied to paymt. of my accept[an]ce. for K. Smith & Co.		$2000.
Decr 29.	Drew in favor of Tho[mas]. H. Clay on Bank of Commerce [N.Y.C.] for		$750
10 Mar. 1843	Drew in favor of R[ichard]. Pindell for ——		416:90
11 Mar.	Drew in favor of Mr. J. Pickett[13] a check for —		500.
18h		do. Mr. Audubon[14] ——	27.
	do.	do in favor of the Lexn. B[ranch]. B[ank].	3000
	do.	do. in favor of the Northern Bank [of Kentucky] ————	1500
3d. April.	do	do in favor of J[ohn]. J. Astor[15] ——	221:32
	Bal. yet to be drawn for $912.76 [interest on Astor loan].		
29h. Apl	Check in favr of R. Pindell ————————		750

Recd. to be credited to Clay & Mentelle[16]

From Worsley & Foreman (see other side) 3 Jan. 1843—— $3716 40

To be credited to Tho. H. Clay & Co.[17]

From the honble A[lexander] Barrow 4 Jan 1843 —— 1361:6.

" K. Smith & Co. on Dr. Percy[18] 23 Decr. 1842 —— 1026:15

" Do. on Pope & Wilkins[19] do do —— 607:8

" Payne & Harrison 16 Jan. 1843 . . . . 1488:37

" Flower & Finley[20] ———— 422:74

[Endorsed on verso by Clay:]

1842-3

Memo. of remittances from
N. Orleans

AD. DLC-TJC (DNA, M212, R19). 1. Hereafter abbreviated as "B. of C." 2. Not identified. 3. J.C. Harris, broker, was located at 55½ Walnut Street in Philadelphia. *Philadelphia City Directory 1842.* 4. Robb and Hodge, merchants, were located at Camp Street & Gravier in New Orleans. Information courtesy of Collin B. Hamer, Jr., City of New Orleans Public Library. 5. Nevins Townsend & Co. does not appear in the *New York City Directory* for 1842-43. 6. Samuel Nicholson was located at 182 Perdido Street, New Orleans. Information supplied by Collin B. Hamer, Jr. 7. For Brown Brothers, New York City merchants and financiers, see Bonner, *New York*, 423, 471, 481. 8. Not identified. 9. Gardner, Sayers & Co. has not been identified. William C. Pickersgill, merchant, was located at the corner of Exchange & Hanover streets, while his home was at 28 Washington Square in New York City. John Doggett, Jr., *The New York City Directory for 1842 and 1843. . . .* New York, 1843. 10. George Lee has not been identified. 11. Adams & Whitall have not been identified. K. Smith & Co. possibly refers to Kempton D. Smith, auctioneer, located at 195 William Street, New York City. Doggett, *New York City Directory for 1842 and 1843.* 12. This sentence inserted by Clay at this point in the listings. 13. Not identified. 14. Probably John J. Audubon. 15. For the annually renewed Astor loan of $20,000 @ 6%, see 8:763; also Clay to James B. Clay, Oct. 30, 1840, and Clay to William B. Astor, Oct. 30, 1841. 16. Clay to Lucretia Hart Clay, Dec. 9, 1842; Clay to Silsbee, March 18, 1842. 17. *Ibid.* 18. Not identified. 19. Not identified. 20. [William] Flower and [L.A.] Finley, commission merchants, Natchez Street, New Orleans. Gibson, *Guide and Directory . . . of New Orleans.*

To SOLOMON VAN RENSSELAER Lexington, May 1, 1843

Prior to the receipt of your favor of the 22 ult.—I had heard of your removal from the P.O. at Albany, and I largely shared in the indignation which that malevolent and wanton act of a Traitor and a tyrant [John Tyler] excited. You will bear it, I have no doubt, as a Veteran and a Patriot ought to do.

With respect to the proper time of laying before the public the proofs which you possess of the declared sentiments of Tyler, in favor of a Nat. Bank, I think, whenever it suits your convenience to publish them, that is the proper time. The public has already possession of evidence that ought to Satisfy any unbiased mind; but that which you have may serve to clench the fact. I am glad to feel authorized to infer from the tone of your recent letter, that your health is good, and your Spirits unsubdued. May you live to see our common Country delivered from the base and faithless hands that now sully and dishonor it! That is the prayer of . . .

Copy. Printed in Catharina Van Rensselaer Bonney (comp.), *A Legacy of Historical Gleanings*, 2 vols. (Albany, N.Y., 1875), 2:183-84. Addressed to Van Rensselaer in Albany, N.Y.

From Thomas J. Campbell, Athens, Tenn., May 7, 1843. Thanks Clay for sending him, on request, a copy of the pamphlet dated December 29, 1827, rebutting the corrupt bargain charge [6:1394; 7:716-19 (index references); Beverley to Clay, February 8, 1842], and notes that John White had also sent him a copy. Assures Clay that "the falsehoods and calumnies propagated on the occasion to which the pamphlet refers, will *not* have the slightest influence on the elections, in this section of Tennessee." Says that the main political issues in East Tennessee are national bank [Tyler to Clay, April 30, 1841; Speech in Senate, June 21, 1841], tariff [Clay to Letcher, January 6 and June 24, 1842], distribution to the states of public land sales receipts [Clay to Letcher, January 6, 1842; Remark in Senate, January 21, 1842], and the bankruptcy law [Remark in Senate, December 28, 1841; Speech in Senate, January 28, 1842]—that these "are the weapons of attack now, and the subjects upon which *you* are assailed." Adds that "The *three* first are our Whig tenets" and are quite popular, and that only the bankruptcy law "is unpopular here, but will have no influence whatever on our elections." Reports that prospects of his own election to Congress are "decidedly flattering" and his success "is considered as certain." Believes the Whig margin of victory in the 1844 presidential canvass will be not less than 3,000 in East Tennessee and 5,000 in the state as a whole [Clay to Berrien, March 13, 1843]. Is confident that at least three Whigs from East Tennessee will be elected to the lower house of the state legislature in the coming [August] statewide elections. Notes that East Tennessee Whigs parry the unpopularity of the Bankruptcy Act of 1841 by citing support for it by Andrew Jackson and Martin Van Buren. Observes that the inability of Tennessee to fill either of its U.S. Senate seats [Clay to Brooke, March 12, 1841], has hurt the Democrats. Assures Clay that he is so popular in East Tennessee as a presidential possibility in 1844 that "sundry of our Iron factorys have his name already emblazoned, in my District, upon the doors of their shops and workhouses." ALS. DLC-John J. Crittenden Papers (DNA, M212, R20).

For Campbell, a Tennessee congressman from 1841 to 1843, see *BDAC*. Campbell was defeated for the U.S. House in 1843 by Democrat Julius W. Blackwell by a vote of 5,793 to 5,700. In Tennessee's congressional races in 1843 Democrats won 6 seats in the House to 5 for the Whigs. *Guide to U.S. Elections*, 579. In the gubernatorial race Whig James C. Jones defeated Democrat James K. Polk by 58,307 votes to 54,470. *BDGUS*, 4:1474. The Whigs won a majority of 3 seats in the state senate and a majority of 5 seats in the house. Jonesboro (Tenn.)

Whig and Independent Journal, August 30, 1843. In the 1844 presidential race, Clay carried East Tennessee over Polk by 18,986 votes to 15,716. Clarksville *Jeffersonian*, November 30, 1844.

To WILLIAM H. RUSSELL Lexington, May 11, 1843

I have this moment received your favor, with the Buffalo tongues,[1] for which accept my thanks.

I am glad to see that you bear your removal, as I anticipated you would, with scorn and contempt for its author.[2] But really Mrs. Russell (with the perusal of whose letter you favored me) has displayed more than Roman spirit in her treatment of that event. I think that Capt Tyler has placed you under very heavy obligations for the opportunity he has afforded you of enjoying more of the conversation and company of such an estimable wife.

Never for a moment did I doubt the correctness of your statement of the amount of the arrears of taxes due on my land near Alton.[3] I thank you for your attention to the preservation of the timber upon it. By the bye, I believe James [Brown Clay] has made some arrangement with a Frenchman to settle and clear 50 Acres of it.[4]

I hardly know what to say about a visit to St Louis. I am apprehensive of the excitement, fatigue and exhaustion which would be incident to it. But I will hold it under advisement, altho' I fear I shall not be able to undertake the journey this year.

I shall be most happy to see you here, and hope you will come; and my satisfaction would be increased if you would bring with you your Lady, whom I have long had reason to esteem and admire. I am happy to tell you that, from all I have heard, I think your brother will be elected with ease.[5] We are all delighted with his manly avowal of his principles, and his resolution to follow wherever they will carry him. . . .

ALS. KHi. Addressed to Russell at Bluffton, near Fulton, Mo. 1. Clay to Russell, July 27, 1842. 2. *Ibid.* Tyler had removed Russell from his job as U.S. marshal for the District of Missouri. 3. *Ibid.* 4. Clay to James Brown Clay, Oct. 30, 1840. 5. Thomas A. Russell (1797-1846) was elected to the Kentucky house of representatives for the 1844 term. Anna Russell Des Cognets, *William Russell and His Descendants* (Lexington, Ky., 1884), 77-78.

To JAMES K. POLK Lexington, May 20, 1843

I have received information, through so many concurring channels, public and private, that, although loth to believe, I am constrained to conclude, that you have made my conduct and motives, in the Presidential election by the House of Representatives of 1825, a frequent topic of discussion, in your public addresses to my fellow Citizens of Tennessee, during the political canvass now in progress in that State; reviving and propogating the charge, which originated against me at that epoch.[1] Now, Sir, I recognize your clear and indisputable right to controvert any system of public policy which I ever supported, to animadvert upon any public measures which I may have sustained, or to question the correctness of any opinion on public affairs, which I ever expressed, in any terms of language you may think proper to use; but I do not admit your right to assail my honor and probity, or the purity of my character, behind my back, and at a distance from me.

And, if you choose to indulge in such a theme, I claim the right to be heard by the same tribunal before which you have arraigned me. I regret that it is impracticable for me to appear before every popular assembly which, I understand, you have addressed on the subject of my character and conduct, on the occasion alluded to. But I can present myself, upon the theatre which you have selected, to a portion, at least, of the People of Tennessee. My reputation is dear to me. After a long service in the public Councils, I have but little else to leave my descendants; and, according to the usual course of nature, I cannot expect to remain long with them.

The high offices which you have filled—member and Speaker of the H. of Representatives of the United States and Governor of the Commonwealth of Tennessee—and those to which you aspire,[2] give to your charges a grave consideration, and demand a notice of them, to which, coming from any other source of less prominence, I should not deem them entitled.

I repose great confidence in the zeal and ability with which Governor [James C.] Jones[3] and other friends in Tennessee will, I am sure, defend me; but they have other objects to attend to, of far greater public importance than my vindication, and I have no right to impose on them entirely the burthen[4] of defending my character.

I have, therefore, to request that you will agree to meet me at such time and place in Tennessee, as may be mutually designated, and publicly discuss the charge which you have revived against me.[5] I disclaim, explicitly, [al]l intention to interfere or influence, in the slightest degree, the approaching election in Tennessee.[6] I have no such desire or purpose. My sole and exclusive object is, to repel charges, deeply affecting my honor and the purity of my public conduct, which you have voluntarily renewed. And, whilst I may have this opportunity of self-vindication, before my neighbours of Tennessee, you will have an equal opportunity of sustaining your charges, without being longer liable to the reproach of seeking an advantage from the absence of a fellow Citizen, residing in another State.

With these views, and with that single purpose, on my part, I propose that we meet at Nashville, Knoxville, or the seat of Justice of the County of your residence, at such time, during the months of June or July next, as you may deem most comformable to your own convenience, and publicly discuss the charge which you have revived against me, of improper conduct in the Presidential election of 1825. And, as I have full confidence in the intelligence, love of truth and justice of the great body of my fellow Citizens, of both political parties, in Tennessee, I further propose that twenty four of them shall be selected, embracing twelve whigs and twelve democrats (you to choose the Whigs and I the Democrats) to whose final decision shall be submitted the question, whether you have or have not revived and propogated against me an exploded and groundless calumny; and whether you are—or are not bound to make any and what reparation.

Entertaining a just and confident hope that your sense of propriety and justice will prompt you cheerfully to accede to these proposals, through the same or a similar public channel to that which is the medium of this note,[7] I remain. . . .

ALS. DLC-HC (DNA, M212, R5). 1. For Clay's so-called "corrupt bargain" with John Quincy Adams in Jan., 1825, see 4:48, 53-54, 73-74, 80-85, 113-14, 144-50, 157-59; 7:716-19.

Polk frequently mentioned this charge against Clay during his 1843 gubernatorial race. See reports of his speeches in Nashville *Republican Banner*, April 10 and 28, and May 19, 1843. 2. At this time Polk was running for governor. For the 1843 Tennessee elections, see T.J. Campbell to Clay, May 7, 1843. 3. For Tenn. Gov. James C. Jones, see *DAB*, *BDAC*, and *NCAB*, 7:209. 4. The word "duty" is struck through and "burthen" substituted in its place. 5. Clay and Polk did not meet in debate; indeed, Clay may never have mailed this letter. See Charles G. Sellers, *James K. Polk, Jacksonian, 1795-1843* (Princeton, 1957), 477. 6. T.J. Campbell to Clay, May 7, 1843. 7. Editors have found no publicly printed version of this letter.

To Alonzo James Madison Hudson *et al.*, Mercersburg, Pa., May 25, 1843. Solicited by students of Marshall College in Mercersburg to contribute money to the building fund of their Goethean Society, Clay responds with a "small note" as well as the observation that "you have *resolved* to raise too large a sum for your object, in one year, considering the hard state of the times. Every body is or ought to be practising economy, and there is a necessity for it. The period is exceedingly inauspicious for large & liberal contributions towards any object not of prime necessity. Under such circumstances, would it not be well for the Society to put up a little longer with the rooms, which they have hitherto occupied, and which are only rather small and inconvenient, and endeavor through several years, instead of a single one, to collect a sufficient sum to erect a new Hall?" ALS. PLF. Addressed also to E[rnest]. W. Reinscke and F[ranklin]. B. Shuford.

The Goethean Society was a literary and debating society whose members were usually of German extraction. The cornerstone of Goethean Hall was laid on August 28, 1844, and the building was dedicated August 28, 1846. Information supplied by Charlotte B. Brown, College Archives, Franklin & Marshall College, Lancaster, Pa.

To JOHN M. CLAYTON Lexington, May 27, 1843

I duly received your favor of the 25h. Ulto. and I was gratified to receive your coup d'oeil of the Presidential contest. I had thought, with you, that Mr. V. Buren would obtain the nomination of the other party; but I begin to believe that his rivals will break him down.[1] They are now playing the same game towards him that was practiced in my case in 1839. All the other aspirants are pushing at him, and they have driven him from Novre. to May, and I should not be surprized if they pushed him off the course. His only safety, perhaps, lies in the difficulty of settling among themselves who shall have the nomination.

We cannot fail to profit by these divisions, and the postponement of their Convention to May [1844] is so much the better for us.[2] Already at the S[outh]. & S. West it is not uncommon for the Calhoun men to declare that they will go for the Whig Candidate in preference to V. B. At the North I presume the reverse is said by the V. Buren men. [William C.] Preston thinks that So. Carolina will throw away her vote if Calhoun does not get the nomination.[3]

To run different Democratic Candidates would be fatal to them, altho' you may be right in supposing it to be their best chance. I think the effect of such a course would display their weakness; and the People would not be willing to run the risk of an election by the House. You have seen what the Globe says.[4]

I cannot undertake the Tour you propose. It would kill me. And I cannot affect ill health, when my health was never better. Such a journey would have an adequate motive, if I desired to be ill.

I think we shall do well in New England, with the exception of Massachusetts and N. Hampshire.[5] In the former State, Mr. Webster has just enough left to introduce confusion, and perhaps to render that State doubtful. But we shall see how the Whigs will rally there the ensuing fall.

I think you are too despondent. I believe we shall beat them in 1844 worse than in 1840. I never entertained any hope of Virginia until after their recent election. Now, I am inclined to think we shall get the State.[6] We shall send you a strong Western breeze this summer and fall. The confidence of our friends in Tennessee, and their *exertions* are daily encreasing.[7]

What I apprehended, in the event of a Nat. Convention,[8] is about to be realized—intrigue to supplant the favorite Whig Candidate. [John] McLean, [Winfield] Scott, Webster &c will be, have been, all approached.[9] I have it from pretty good recent authority that M[c]Lean has, however, said that any Whig who would allow himself to be taken up against me must be a fool. And yet I am not sure that he might not be prevailed upon to countenance his own nomination.

You have seen Webster's Balto Speech.[10] He appears desirous to avert his eyes from the U. S. and to cast them abroad. He talks of an *arrangement* with Foreign powers about the Tariff. The only *arrangement* we ever made, without treaty, was of the Colonial trade with England, and a very bad one it was.[11] He speaks of the injury to our Navigation by the Reciprocity treaties, the great interest of the Country which has been constantly flourishing, amidst the depression of all other great interests. Instead of looking with the eye of a Statesman to the whole system of Reciprocal navigation, like a pleader, he selects the single case of poor Bremen![12] Suppose to establish the opposite position, the success of our navigation with the Brazils were held up to conspicuous view?[13] By the bye, he attributes to our treaty with that Empire (inequality in the Tariffs of the respective Countries) a defect which flows from our own separate legislation, in omitting to tax Coffee &c.

If you were here and saw my lawns, trees, flocks and herds—this paradise of a Country (and why can't you come here?) you would not be so unreasonable as to propose that I should be sweated to death, in the Atlantic Cities, this summer.

I am not sure that I shall leave home at all before winter. If I do, it will be to go to the W. Sulphur Springs in Va.[14] You must recollect that I am a young attorney, seeking to establish a character for industry &c.[15] I have already made my debut in the Courts.

ALS. DLC-John M. Clayton Papers (DNA, M212, R20). 1. Clay to Butler, August 8, 1842. 2. *Ibid.* 3. South Carolina (where presidential electors were chosen by the state legislature rather than by the people) cast its nine electoral votes for Polk in 1844. McKee, *National . . . Popular and Electoral Vote,* 57. 4. An editorial in the Washington *Globe* of May 3, 1842, said that Democratic failure to organize a national convention to nominate a candidate for the presidency, or failure of one or more candidates to submit to the convention's decision, would result either in a Whig victory or in throwing the election into the House. A Whig president would be preferable, the editorial concluded, to having an election by the House which would satisfy no one. 5. Polk beat Clay in Maine (9 electoral votes) in 1844 by a margin of 45,719 to 34,378 with James G. Birney's Liberty party getting 3,308; in New Hampshire (6) Polk won 27,160 to 17,866 with Birney polling 4,161; in Vermont (6) Clay won 26,770 to 18,041 with Birney getting 3,954; in Massachusetts (12) Clay beat Polk by 67,418 to 52,846, Birney polling 10,860; Clay carried

Connecticut (6) by 32,832 to 29,841 with 1,943 for Birney; and in Rhode Island (4) Clay outpolled Polk 7,322 to 4,867 with Birney getting 107. In sum, New England gave Clay 22 of its 37 electoral votes and a popular margin over Polk of 186,586 to 178,474. Birney polled 65,608 votes nationally, 24,333 in New England. McKee, *National . . . Popular and Electoral Vote*, 56-57. For the Liberty party and Birney candidacy, see Clay to Porter, Sept. 17, 1843. 6. In the Virginia elections of April 27, 1843, Democrats won 20 seats in the state senate to 12 for the Whigs and 75 seats in the house to 59 for the Whigs. Richmond *Enquirer*, May 12, 1843. Democrats won 12 U.S. House seats to 3 for the Whigs. *Guide to U.S. Elections*, 579. The state legislature had previously elected James McDowell, a Democrat, to serve a term as governor from Jan. 5, 1843, to Jan. 1, 1846. See *BDGUS*, 4:1640-41 (which erroneously identifies McDowell as a Whig) and Charles H. Ambler, *Sectionalism in Virginia From 1776 to 1861* (New York, 1964), 207, 209, 223, 226, 255-57. See also McDowell in *BDAC*. 7. Clay to Berrien, March 13, 1843. 8. For the 1844 Whig national convention, see Clay to Clayton, August 8, 1842. For the choice of a vice presidential nominee, see Clay to Dearborn, July 13, 1842. 9. For McLean's prospects, see Clay to Leigh, June 20, 1843; for Scott's, see Crittenden to Clay, July 2, 1842; for Webster's, see Sydney Nathans, *Daniel Webster And Jacksonian Democracy* (Baltimore, 1973), 216-17. 10. In his Baltimore speech of May 18, 1843, Webster argued that the U.S. should attempt to regulate commerce and set duties (especially with England) by an "arrangement" worked out between the executives of the two countries and enacted into law by their legislatures. This would neither increase the treaty-making power, nor would it violate the U.S. constitutional stipulation that bills involving money for the support of government must originate in the House of Representatives. This method would effectively promote commerce and would not provoke tariff retaliation as a unilateral tariff would do. Webster also pointed out the short-comings of previous reciprocity treaties, citing specifically the 1827 treaty with Bremen and its detrimental effect on the U.S. carrying trade. McIntyre, *Writings And Speeches of Daniel Webster*, 13:150-71. 11. Probably a reference to the Jackson administration's controversial commercial reciprocity agreement with Great Britain in 1830. For the failure of the administration of John Quincy Adams to secure a commercial arrangement with Great Britain that would permit direct U.S. trade with her colonies, especially with the British West Indies, see 2:839; 3:729; 4:180, 417, 941-42; 5:629-32, 831-35, 913; 6:316. Related aspects of the complex Anglo-American colonial trade and tariff struggle during Clay's tenure as secretary of state (principally its British West Indian dimension) are subject-indexed in 7:666-67, 729-30. A thorough analysis of the problem is found in Mary Wilma Hargreaves, *The Presidency of John Quincy Adams* (Lawrence, Kan., 1985), 89-112. Still quite useful is Benns, *The American Struggle for the British West India Carrying Trade*, 87-162. See also Clay to Kennedy, April 17, 1839, notes 3 and 4. For the background, negotiation, and content of the Anglo-American reciprocity agreement of 1830 (which conditionally reopened the B.W.I. to U.S. shipping), as well as the domestic partisan politics attendant upon negotiation of the accord, see Benns, *American Struggle for the British West India Carrying Trade*, 163-88; also, Munroe, *Louis McLane*, 286-87, 290-91. 12. See 4:116, 644, 931; 5:504, 911; 6:392, 517, 1370-71. 13. For Brazil's constant harassment of U.S. ships, shipping, seamen, and other U.S. nationals in 1825-27, see 7:639 (index references, col. 2). 14. He did not go to White Sulphur Springs in the summer or fall of 1843. 15. A facetious remark. See Clay to Clayton, April 14, 1843.

To JOHN NEAGLE Lexington, May 29, 1843

In returning to the City of Philadelphia, you[1] will naturally desire to carry with you, along with the full length portrait of me, which you have taken at this place, some evidence of the opinion which is entertained of it in Kentucky. I know that you took the greatest pains to produce a perfect likeness, studying thoroughly your subject, and carefully examining all the previous pictures of it, which were accessible to you. And it is the judgment of my family and friends that you have sketched the most perfect likeness of me that has been hitherto made. My opinion coincides with theirs. I think you have happily delineated the character, as well as the physical appearance, of your subject.

I cannot part from you as an Artist, without expressing the satisfaction which I have derived from your acquaintance and conversation, as a gentleman. During your short sojourn here, you have made friendly impressions upon myself and my family, of which we shall long retain a lively recollection. And you take with you the cordial wishes for your fame success and happiness of all of us.

ALS. DLC-Ainsworth R. Spofford Papers (DNA, M212, R22). 1. For Neagle, see Clay to Littell, Nov. 11, 1842.

To ROBERT S. OAKLEY Lexington, May 30, 1843

I received your letter and thank you for the friendly motives which prompted it. You describe a recent journey in New England and tell me that my imprudence was every where a theme of conversation. I should have been glad to have learnt what instances of my imprudence were dwelt upon. I know I have my full share of the infirmities common to our nature but I cannot comprehend those who are pleased to associate my "imprudence" with Mr. Webster's "mistakes."

I hear with patience and consider with respectful attention the counsels of my friends; but, at last, I must rely mainly on my own judgment in the direction of my conduct. You appear to think that if I were to announce an opposition to the annexation of Texas to the U. States, I should be benefited by it in N. England. Now, I must say, in the first place, that I do not believe that there is a serious purpose in any section of the U. S. nor a considerable number of American Citizens who think of proposing to effect such an annexation. During my visit last winter to the S. West, I do not remember to have heard any opinion expressed in favor of it. In a correspondence several years ago with the late Revd. Mr. [William E.] Channing, I expressed myself opposed to the annexation.[1] My opinion, far from being changed, is strengthened and confirmed by subsequent reflection & subsequent events.

But then I could not reconcile it to my feelings of propriety to publish my opinion for the purpose indicated by you.

As to the practice of Duelling, if you will take the trouble to examine my address to my Constituents, published in March 1825, you will find that I express a strong condemnation of it.[2] I could not now express a more emphatic denunciation of the practice. That address may be found in Niles Register,[3] and other contemporaneous periodicals, and in some of the Editions of my Speeches.

My Dear Sir, I am no Candidate for any office, and I am much less desirous of issuing from the retirement, which I have voluntarily sought, to fill even the highest office of the Country, than the world imagines. If I should ever consent to be a Candidate, I shall wish the Country to decide impartially upon my pretensions, without any bias from any opinions I might express, or any thing I could now do.

If I were to comply with the numerous letters I receive, scarcely a week would elapse, without my expressing *opposite* opinions upon all the political questions of the day, and many of the moral ones too.

At my age, my character and my opinions are too well formed to admit of my altering the one or lightly changing the other. In one respect indeed I hope for improvement but that is on a subject between me & my maker, which no mortal has a right to interfere with.

I pray you to consider this letter as addressed to you only & not for the public.

ALS. KyU. 1. Channing to Clay, August 1, 1837; Clay to Porter, Jan. 26, 1838. 2. Dated March 26, 1825. See 4:146. 3. *Niles' Register* (April 2, 1825), 28:71-79.

To ANDREW BROADDUS, JR. Lexington, June 5, 1843

I received your letter informing me that a new objection is started to a National Bank, arising out of the fact that the Convention, which formed the Constitution of the U. S., refused to grant to Congress the power to create Corporations, and requesting my views of that objection.

I have delayed transmitting an anwer to your letter until I could again examine carefully the Journals of the Convention,[1] which I have accordingly done. I find that, on the 18h. August 1787, a proposition was submitted to the Convention, to vest in Congress a number of enumerated powers, in addition to those which had been previously agreed upon by the Convention. Among the powers so enumerated, one was, "to grant charters of incorporation, in cases where the public good may require them, and the authority of a single State may be incompetent." Another was, "to grant charters of incorporation." This proposition was referred to a Committee, which does not appear to have ever reported. Consequently the Convention itself never expressed any opinion as to the propriety of the proposed powers being vested in Congress.

But on the 14h. September 1787, it was proposed to add, to the eighth section of the first article of the Constitution, which contains an enumeration of the powers granted to Congress, a clause, "To grant letters of incorporation for canals &c," and that clause was rejected by a vote of the Convention, Pennsylvania, Virginia and Georgia voting for the clause.

Such is the state of the fact as it appears in the Journals of the Convention.

I would remark, in the first place, that the Constitution ought to be interpreted by its own language; but I admit that, in doubtful questions, contemporaneous expositions of it, and votes on propositions made, and decided by the Convention, may serve to elucidate its meaning. With respect to the first, many members of the Convention, with General Washington at their head, concurred, shortly after its adoption, in the establishment of the first Bank of the U. States. But, the immediate object of your enquiry relates to the effect which the proceedings of the Convention ought to have on the power of Congress to incorporate such an institution; and to that, in the second place, I intend now to invite your attention.

It has been seen that the Convention expressed no opinion on the two first propositions submitted to it, to invest Congress with power to create corporations; and that it rejected the proposal to invest it with power "to grant letters of incorporation for canals &c"

These were proposed grants of general powers, with slight modifications. If they had been made, Congress would have been authorized to grant charters for any conceivable purpose. And if I had been a member of the Convention, I would have voted against all of them.

The power in Congress to establish a Bank is derived from that clause in the Constitution which delegated to Congress the power "to make all laws which shall be necessary and proper for carrying into execution the foregoing powers and all other powers vested by the Constitution in the Government of the U. States, or in any department or officer thereof." Is a Bank a necessary and proper instrument for executing powers granted to Congress? If it be, Congress has power to establish one; if it be not Congress has not the power. That was the question decided by the first Congress of the U. States; decided by Genl. Washington; decided by the Congress which established the second Bank; and decided unanimously by the Supreme Court of the U. States. Mr. Madison opposed the first Charter; but, acquiescing in repeated decisions against his opinion, sanctioned the law establishing the second Bank.

If the Convention had refused to grant to Congress the *specific* power to establish a Bank of the U. S. its refusal would have had decisive weight with me. But it did not act upon any such specific proposal. It only rejected a general proposition to give to Congress the power to grant letters of incorporation for canals &c.

When in 1811 the question of the renewal of the Charter of the B. of the U. S. came up in the Senate, believing, as I then did, that such an instrument was not necessary and proper to enable Congress to execute powers vested in it by the Constitution, I voted against the renewal. The experience of the War, the suspension of the local banks, and the derangement in the currency, which ensued, convinced me that I was wrong. And accordingly when, in 1816, it was proposed to establish a second Bank of the U. States, I supported it.[2] All subsequent reflection and experience have satisfied me of the correctness of that support.

It has been said that, previous to the election of Genl. Harrison, I had abandoned or modified my opinion in favor of a Bank of the U. S. Such is not the fact. I stated, I think, on more than one occasion in the Senate, that I would not urge or desire to see a Bank established against the sense of a majority of the people of the U. S.[3] I say so now. I expressed my conviction, in my speech in Hanover,[4] that a Bank was necessary and that I did not see how it could be dispensed with. I added that it was not the thing itself, but its objects and purposes that appeared to me desirable; and that if they could be accomplished by State Banks, or in any other safe way, for one I should be satisfied. All this I repeat now.

I believed that the People of the U. S., by the election of Genl Harrison and the House of Representatives, had manifested a wish to have a Bank of the U. S. Accordingly, at the Extra [First] Session in 1841, I proposed one.[5] It was carried in that house by a majority of thirty; and that majority would have been still larger but for the fact that several gentlemen voted against the charter, because it did not, in their opinion, make the Bank strong enough, in its branching power. That vote, in the judgment of impartial men, I think ought to be regarded as satisfactory evidence of public opinion.

You ask permission to use this letter publicly. I have no other objections to your doing so but that there is really nothing new in it, and that I have a great repugnance to appearing in the public prints, unless when it is absolutely necessary. But there is nothing in the letter about which I desire any concealment.

ALS. NcD. Addressed to Broaddus at Sparta, Caroline County, Va. For the genealogy of Andrew Broaddus, Jr. (*ca.* 1815–*ca.* 1895), pastor of Salem Baptist Church in Sparta, Va., for some 40 years, see Marshall Wingfield, *A History of Caroline County, Virginia, 1827-1924* (Richmond, Va., 1924), 325-27, 338-41. 1. *Journal of the Federal Convention, Kept by James Madison. Published under direction of the U.S. government from original manuscripts.* Washington, 1840. 2. For Clay's shift on the bank issue in 1816, see 2:200-205, 216-19; 8:900, col. 1; also Speech in Senate, March 10, 1838; Remark in Senate, July 10, 1841; and Speech in Lexington, June 9, 1842. 3. See, variously, Speech in Senate, Sept. 25, 1837; Comment in Senate, Sept. 26, 1837; Speech in Senate, May 21, 1838; Speech in Senate, Jan. 20, 1840. 4. Speech . . . Hanover County, Va., June 27, 1840. 5. Speech in Senate, June 21, 1841; also Speech in Senate, August 19, 1841.

From J.W. Heard, Jefferson City, Missouri, June 10, 1843. Informs Clay, by deed, that William H. Russell has straightened out Clay's tax dispute with the state of Missouri by producing duplicate tax receipts for 1836 through 1842. Explains that the issue turned on the non-payment by Clay of the 1836 tax due on his 680 56/100 acres in St. Charles County, and the subsequent (in 1840) seizure of that property by the state. Notes that given his payment of $62.96, the tax and penalty due for 1836, Clay has recovered full possession of his property. DS, partly printed deed of release. DLC-TJC (DNA, M212, R19). Heard was register of lands for Missouri.

To WILLIAM B. CAMPBELL Lexington, June 14, 1843

Other Tennessee friends have obliged me by communicating their opinions of the probable result of your pending Election,[1] and they give me cheering accounts; but I should like to be favored with your's, on which I know I could place great reliance. I regretted extremely your retirement from Congress,[2] of which I had heard, but continued to hope that circumstances might be such as to induce you to continue in the public councils.

The information of our political prospects, which reaches me from all quarters is very encouraging. Judging from it, from the goodness of our cause, and the badness of that of our opponents, from our perfect union, and their thorough distraction and division, I think we may anticipate in 1844 a triumph even more brilliant than that of 1840. Such an event would inspire increased admiration of the retributive justice of Providence. It would be a deserved rebuke for the countenance and support which the Democratic party has given to the treason of Tyler. A just punishment for their exultation over the defeat of the measures of the People by the exercise of the Veto! . . .

ALS. NcD. For Campbell, a Tennessee Whig congressman in 1837-43, see *BDAC*. Addressed to Campbell in Sparta, Tenn. 1. T.J. Campbell to Clay, May 7, 1843. 2. Effective on March 3, 1843.

To BENJAMIN W. LEIGH Lexington, June 20, 1843

I wrote you a letter several weeks ago, in answer to a previous one which I had received from you, enquiring into the origin of Mr. Wise's alienation, and his present enmity to me.[1] It required no reply, but as I know your punctuality in conducting your correspondence, and as I have received no acknowledgment of it, I have apprehended its miscarriage.

The result of your elections both surprized and gratified me.[2] It demonstrated that with confidence and spirited exertions the Whigs may finally succeed in Virginia[3]

I continue to receive encouraging information from almost every quarter. In Tennessee[4] and Indiana[5] the most animated canvass is in progress and in both our friends are very confident of success. P.S. I ought to add that I am informed from N. York that some of the Intriguers of 1839[6] are again engaged in active machinations. They talk of J[ohn]. McLean of Ohio,[7] and employ all their old topics. It is chiefly the Webster clique. H.C.

ALS. ViU. 1. According to Wise and his biographers, the disruption of his friendship with Clay began soon after Congress convened following the election of 1840. It grew worse as Clay and his supporters in Congress attempted to enact their legislative program and reached its zenith in the Clay-Tyler disputes of 1841-42 when Wise sided with Tyler. See Wise to John B. Coles *et al.* in Washington *The Madisonian*, Dec. 14, 1841; Simpson, *A Good Southerner*, 49-53; Wise, *Seven Decades of the Union*, 171-73. 2. Clay to Clayton, May 27, 1843. 3. Clay to Leigh, March 17, 1843. 4. T.J. Campbell to Clay, May 7, 1843. 5. In the Indiana state elections of August 7, 1843, the Democrats won 27 seats in the state senate to 23 for the Whigs and 55 seats in the house of representatives to 45 for the Whigs. *Niles' Register* (Sept. 16, 1843), 65:37. In the congressional race, the Democrats won 8 seats to 2 for the Whigs. *Guide to U.S. Elections*, 578. James Whitcomb, a Democrat, was elected governor by a vote of 60,784 to 58,721 for Whig Samuel Bigger and 1,683 for Liberty party candidate, Elizur Deming. *BDGUS*, 1:400. 6. Reference is to the small group of men, "The Intriguers of 1839" (Thurlow Weed, William H. Seward, Francis Granger *et al.*), who had deprived Clay of the Whig presidential nomination at Harrisburg in Dec., 1839 with such tactical devices as a diversionary stalking horse (Winfield Scott) and a state-delegation unit rule, coupled with the insistence that Clay simply could not be elected. Porter to Clay, Nov. 14 and Dec. 30, 1837; Van Deusen, *Life of Henry Clay*, 323-34. 7. Since many Whigs felt that a Clay candidacy would lead to defeat in 1844, a group of Ohio congressmen initiated a movement for native-son John McLean believing that he could win the votes of Clay supporters as well as those of the Calhounites and Tylerites. But after it became apparent that Clay would win the Whig nomination for president, McLean rejected the related suggestion that he become the candidate for vice president on the Clay ticket. Francis P. Weisenburger, *The Life of John McLean, A Politician on the United States Supreme Court* (Columbus, Ohio, 1937), 103-5.

To JOHN M. CLAYTON Lexington, June 21, 1843

I read with satisfaction your letter in respect to Tariff treaties, which is copied into the Lexn. paper of this day.[1] The proposition to negotiate such a treaty will pass off with as little favor as the Exchequer[2] so warmly recommended from the same quarter.

You will see an article in the Louisville Journal of Saturday the 17h. which treats of the same subject, and which coincides in some of your views.[3] In the Observer and Reporter of this day, published in Lexn. there is an editorial article, on Reciprocity treaties to which I invite your attention.[4] It suggests matter for reflection rather than aiming at a full developement of the subject.

I learn from the City of N. Y. that a few of the persons (Mr. Grinnell[5] and the Custom House clique of Webster's remaining partizans) who were concerned in the intrigue of 1839,[6] are actively employed in playing the same game. They claim to be Whigs, full of ardent devotion to the cause, and expressing unbounded admiration of me; but, with grief and sadness, declaring that I cannot be elected, and that John McLean of Ohio ought to be brought out![7] Measures have been adopted there to counteract these machinations. I thought it right to apprize you of this new movement.

ALS. DLC-John M. Clayton Papers (DNA, M212, R20). 1. Clayton responded to Webster's Baltimore speech [Clay to Clayton, May 27, 1843] in a letter published originally in the Philadelphia *Inquirer*. Calling Webster's proposal for a "commercial arrangement" by treaty with England "one of the wildest and most Utopian visions that ever bewildered the imagination of a practical statesman," Clayton contended that Webster's "only real object" in making the proposal was to throw the votes of southern agriculturalists against the candidate of protection in the 1844 presidential election. Moreover, Clayton believed that such an arrangement would be impossible to obtain for a variety of reasons, including the problem of obtaining England's agreement to lower her own duties, the doubtful constitutionality of a tariff by treaty, and difficulty in obtaining congressional approval. Reprinted in Louisville *Daily Journal*, June 30, 1843. 2. Clay to James B. Clay, Dec. 10, 1841; Mangum to Clay, June 15, 1842; Clay to Crittenden, Feb. 10, 1843. See also *MPP*, 4:82-87; Chitwood, *John Tyler*, 291-93. 3. The Louisville *Daily Journal* editorial of June 17 called Webster's Baltimore speech the twin of his Faneuil Hall speech of Sept. 30, 1842 [Spencer to Clay, Oct. 28, 1842], saying that at Faneuil Hall he recanted on his long commitment to a national bank; and in the Baltimore speech he recanted on his commitment to the tariff. The editorial also charged that he was attempting to divert attention from the corruption at Washington of which he had been a part while serving in Tyler's Cabinet. 4. The article noted that the reciprocity treaties which had been negotiated with foreign powers provided that American and foreign vessels would be placed on an equal footing in the assessment of all maritime charges, fees, duties, etc. It surveyed the effect of such treaties, saying that it was unfair to point out one instance, such as the treaty with the Hanseatic towns (or Bremen), in which reciprocity had worked unfavorably to U.S. interests while ignoring advantages gained by the pact in trade with some larger powers. The editorial concluded that if the U.S. "cannot sustain our navigation in a free and equal competition with foreign powers, how can we the manufacturers of the United States [compete]?" Reprinted in Washington *Daily National Intelligencer*, June 28, 1843. 5. Probably Moses H. Grinnell, a close friend of Webster and a member of the "Wall Street Clique" which advised William H. Seward while he was New York's governor. Van Deusen, *William Henry Seward*, 58; Moser, *Papers of Daniel Webster, Correspondence*, 5:189, 215-16. 6. For the "Intriguers of 1839," see Clay to Leigh, June 20, 1843. 7. *Ibid.*

To Jessie L. Williams *et al.*, Fort Wayne, Ind., June 23, 1843. Turns down an invitation to participate in ceremonies in Fort Wayne, on July 4 celebrating the opening of the Wabash and Erie Canal because "I cannot leave home in this busy season of the year, the growing crops on my farm being very much behind, in consequence of the extremely unfavorable Spring which we have just passed." ALS. InHi.

The Wabash and Erie Canal joined Toledo, Ohio, and Lafayette, Ind. Williams was a civil engineer who was active in canal building and served as engineer-in-chief of the Wabash and Erie Canal for many years. *DAB*.

To THOMAS WORTHINGTON[1] Lexington, June 24, 1843

I received your favor of the 24h. Ulto. accompanying an invitation to attend the Convention which is to assemble on the 4h. prox: at Cincinnati, on the subject of the immediate occupation of Oregon.[2] Whilst I agree with you fully as to the validity of our title, and should be ready to concur in measures to assert and maintain it, by even War, if peaceful means should prove incompetent, I regret that I cannot agree in the expediency of its immediate occupation by the authority of the Government, and still less without its sanction. It is hardly necessary to go into all the considerations which have brought my mind to this conclusion; but I will briefly state some of them. It could not be occupied with out great expence. A line of forts would be necessary from the State of Missouri, across the Rocky mountains to the Pacific. A naval establishment and a permanent naval force would be necessary there. These would subject the Nation to a heavy present & permanent expenditure, at a time when it is pressed by financial embarrassments. I think our true policy is to settle and populate our immense territory on the East of those mountains and within the U. States, before we proceed to colonize the shores of the Pacific; or at all events postpone the occupation of the Oregon some thirty or forty years.

If we are true to ourselves, I have no fears of the power of England on this Continent. Twenty five years hence, our population will be near 35 millions, greater than at that time will be her own in the United Kingdom.[3] What can she do with us, when we have grown to that size? She is destined to lose all her present possessions in North America, in probably less than half a century, either by their Independence or conquest.

Under these circumstances I think it wisest to cultivate and preserve our resources; to avoid foreign War whilst it can be honorably avoided; and to abstain from remote and expensive enterprizes.

I do not understand that England is attempting to settle and occupy the territory on the Pacific which we claim. And from my recollection of what has passed in former negotiations between the Governments of the two Countries, I believe that a boundary heretofore proposed by ours will be finally agreed to by G. Britain.[4]

Entertaining these views and opinions, I could not with propriety attend the Convention at Cincinnati; and I have not thought it necessary to transmit a formal answer to the invitation which I have received.

Of the recent act of a British officer, in seizing the principal of the Sandwich Islands,[5] there can be but one opinion of the nature of that outrage. If sanctioned by the Government of G. Britain, it will be an additional evidence of her grasping ambition, and I trust will meet with suitable opposition from the U. States & other powers.

ALS. NHi. Letter marked "(Confidential)." Addressed to Worthington at Logan, Ohio. 1. For Thomas Worthington (1807-84), son of Ohio Governor Thomas Worthington, see USMA, *Register*, 180; Sears, *Thomas Worthington*, 162, 172, 234. 2. A convention of delegates from states in the Mississippi Valley was held at Cincinnati July 3-5, 1843, to consider the propriety of taking immediate control of the Oregon territory. Col. Richard M. Johnson served as president. The convention passed resolutions calling for an Oregon boundary of 54°40′ and encouraging migration to that region. *Niles' Register* (July 22, 1843), 64:327. 3. U.S. population in 1870 was 38,558,000, while that of the British Isles in 1871, including Scotland, Wales, and Ireland, was 31,484,200. Morris, *Encyclopedia of American History*, 443; Brian R. Mitchell (ed.), *Abstract of British Historical Statistics* (Cambridge, Eng., 1962), 12-14. 4. The Convention of 1818 had set the northwestern boundary at the 49° parallel from the Lake of the Woods to the crest of the Rocky Mountains. No boundary was established west of the mountains, but the U.S. and Britain agreed to joint occupation of the Oregon territory (between the 42° parallel and 54°40′) for a period of ten years. This was extended in 1827. Beginning with the John Q. Adams administration, the U.S. made repeated offers to fix the boundary at the 49° parallel. As American settlement in the region grew, Congress began in the early 1840s to receive petitions asking for the creation of a territorial legislature. The "Oregon Question" was injected into the 1844 presidential campaign when the Democratic platform called for the "reoccupation" of Oregon. Expansionists increasingly called for a northern boundary of the area to be fixed at 54°40′. In his first annual message, Polk called for ending joint occupation, and the British were so notified on May 21, 1846. A treaty was signed June 15, 1846, and proclaimed on August 5, establishing the 49° parallel as the boundary [Parry, *Treaty Series*, 100:40-42]. For more on the Oregon problem, see Reeves, *American Diplomacy under Tyler and Polk*, 190-264; Wilbur D. Jones, *Lord Aberdeen and the Americas* (Athens, Ga., 1958), 26-31, 56-62, 77, 79-82; Frederick Merk, *The Oregon Question, Essays in Anglo-American Diplomacy and Politics* (Cambridge, Mass., 1967), espec. 395-417. 5. Ostensibly in an effort to protect the interests of British residents, Lord George Paulet, commanding the British warship *Carysfort*, assumed control of the Hawaiian Islands on Feb. 25, 1843, by a provisional cession from King Kamehameha III. Paulet seems to have acted to forestall seizure of the islands by the French Pacific fleet. The U.S. applied what became known as the "Tyler Doctrine" to the situation, declaring that the nation seeks no "peculiar advantages, no exclusive control over the Hawaiian Government," that the U.S. supports Hawaiian independence and "anxiously wishes for its security and prosperity," and that the U.S. would make "a decided remonstrance against the adoption of an opposite policy by any other power." The British rejected Paulet's action as unauthorized, and on July 31, 1843, Rear Adm. Richard Thomas restored rule to the native king. Sylvester K. Stevens, *American Expansion in Hawaii 1842-1898* (Harrisburg, Pa., 1945), 3-20; Ralph S. Kuykendall, *The Hawaiian Kingdom 1778-1854* (Honolulu, 1947), 206-26.

To ROBERT P. LETCHER Lexington, June 26, 1843

What are your present terms of exchanging six year for thirty year State bonds? If they are not too jewish I believe I will exchange the few I have. Do you pay the accrued interest or insert it as part of the principal in the new bond.[1]

A letter which I have received from N. York informs me that the intrigue of 1839 is renewed there by [Moses H.] Grinnell[2] and a few others (I suppose the Custom House and Webster clique) and they renew also all their old topics. Such as that they are inflexible Whigs, full of admiration of Clay, but he can't be elected &c &c.[3] Their present aim is J[ohn]. McLean of Ohio, and I *suspect* Burnett & Wright have gone to the Eastward on that errand.[4] The Bunker Hill celebration will afford an opportunity and a cover for concocting their machinations.[5] I understand that the above clique is active, artful and insidious. Measures of counteraction have been adopted in N. York.

ALS. NcD. 1. The Ky. General Assembly in March, 1842 had passed "an act authorizing the exchange of thirty year State Bonds for six year State Bonds." It authorized the governor to issue state bonds payable in not less than thirty years, and at an interest not exceeding six percent per annum, payable semi-annually in the City of New York, in exchange for six years bonds; no bond to be issued for less than $1,000, and the terms of exchange to be set by the governor and to be "equitable and just . . . Provided, that the Governor shall not give more than dollar for dollar." Ky. H. of Reps., *Journal* . . . 1841-1842, pp. 637, 658, 675, 678; Ky. Sen., *Journal* . . . 1841-1842, pp. 393, 418, 422; Ky. Gen. Assy., *Acts* . . . 1841-1842, p. 104. 2. Clay to Leigh, June 20, 1843; Clay to Clayton, June 21, 1843. 3. *Ibid.* 4. John C. Wright, editor of the Cincinnati *Daily Gazette*, and Jacob Burnet had traveled to Boston and were reportedly saying they would support Clay, if nominated, but that he would certainly be defeated. Burnet, however, wrote a letter denying this and saying that Clay was his own choice and also was McLean's choice. He did admit that he doubted any slave state candidate could win. Frankfort *Commonwealth*, July 18, 1843. 5. The Bunker Hill celebration in Boston on June 17, 1843, was held to lay the cornerstone of a monument commemorating the fiftieth anniversary of the battle. Webster was the principal speaker. Curtis, *Life of Daniel Webster*, 1:248-50.

From Count Alexandre de Bodisco, Georgetown, D.C., June 27, 1843. Thanks Clay for the kindness shown him when he first arrived in Washington as Russian minister (in 1838), and regrets that he must now return to Europe [4:520], "leaving here as a pledge of our return two fine boys and two Nephews, under the Care of Mrs B: [Harriet Williams Bodisco's] parents [Clay to Lucretia Hart Clay, April 12, 1840]." Adds: "The Diplomatic Corps has been rather amused by all the great discoveries lately made about tarif[f] treaties and by the attempt to make out of Mr. Rumph [*sic*, Vincent Rumpff] a very smart man. The best treaty he ever negociated was his mar[r]iage with one of [John J.] Astors daughters. Bremen is one of the two great outlets of your important and growing trade with the german league [6:1370-71], to disturb that trade for the sake of the few Ships she employs, would be a hazardous experiment. If your Government would succeed by reciprocity stipulations to have your grains & provisions admitted in England, We in Europe, would soon enough outbid you in cheapness and furnish all that could be required, corn not excepted at 48 hours notice. I have read with great attention Mr [John M.] Claytons able article in the Ph[iladelphia]: Inquirer [Clay to Clayton, June 21, 1843], it put me in mind of the opinion on this subject of one of the great men of my Country He used to say, that the best commercial treaty is not worth a System of permanent and moderate protective duties at home and full liberty for the trading community to provide herself at the cheapest markets." Hopes the "young giant [United States]" fares well in the future. As for the coming presidential election, "I'll follow with undiminished solicitude the coming events with the hope that the contest will be settled according to our wishes." ALS. DLC-HC (DNA, M212, R5). Printed in Colton, *Clay Correspondence*, 4:474-75. Bodisco remained Russia's minister until his death in Washington on January 23, 1854. For eulogies to Bodisco in the Senate and House on January 24, 1854, and the adjournment of both on January 25 out of respect to the departed Russian, see *Cong. Globe*, 33 Cong., 1 Sess., 242-43, 247. For Rumpff, see 6:276.

To JOHN M. CLAYTON Lexington, June 28, 1843

Before I received your letter of the 21st inst. as you will have been apprized by a letter from me which will have reached you before this does, I had read your published letter on Commercial treaties, and it had been published in our K. papers.[1] Its effect has been capital and electric. It will put an end to that heresy, which only wanted to be exposed to insure its general rejection. I observe that Gales and Seaton have been constrained to notice & publish the greater part of it.[2]

You will also have seen the two brief notices inserted editorially in the Journal of Louisville and the Observer of Lexington on Commercial & Reciprocity treaties.[3] Should Mr. Webster reply to you and any suggestions shall occur to me I will transmit them to you.

I have read your letter declining the nomination for V. P.[4] The motives of it cannot fail to make for you a highly favorable impression on our friends every where. The question of selecting a Candidate for that office is not free from difficulty and should command the serious attention of the party. The feeling for Mr. [John] Davis is considerably abated, and should Massachusetts, infected by Websterism, be unable to shake off Locofocoism, I should not be surprized if the Whig Convention turned its attention in some other direction. Besides the Latimer case to which you refer,[5] I understand that there is extant a Speech of Mr. Davis, made during or about the time of the last war with G. B. containing some very exceptionable sentiments, susceptible of being turned to our injury, if he should be our Candidate.[6] I have never seen it, but I have been informed that there is no doubt of its existence, and that it will be brought forth, in that contingency.

You have not a higher opinion of the merits of Mr. Sargeant [*sic*, John Sergeant] than I entertain. What effect would his nomination have in Pennsa.? Harrison declined appointing him to a place in his Cabinet, or taking any Cabinet officer from that State, in consequence of the division of the party which gave him [Harrison] its vote into Antimasons and Whigs.[7] Is there any thing in that consideration?

Towards the close of the last Session of Congress, I learn that a pretty strong feeling sprang up among the Whigs in favor of Mr. [Millard] Fillmore as a Candidate for the V. P.[8] It arose from the fidelity, zeal and ability with which he discharged the duties of the Chairman of the Come. of Ways & Means. But I have heard nothing of it since, and have seen no popular movement for him.

My opinion of Mr. V. Buren being selected as the Candidate of the other party weakens daily.[9] All the other aspirants seem opposed to him, and I begin to think that they may break him down. I am sure they would, but for the difficulty of agreeing who should have the nomination, were he put hors de combat. In that lies only any chance for him.

I believe we shall beat them, and more signally than we did in 1840.

ALS. DLC-John M. Clayton Papers (DNA, M212, R20). 1. Clay to Clayton, June 21, 1843. 2. Washington *Daily National Intelligencer*, June 21, 1843. 3. Clay to Clayton, June 21, 1843. 4. Clayton wrote a letter on June 17, 1843, to the editors of the Wilmington *Delaware Journal* announcing that he would not be a candidate for vice president. Washington *Daily National Intelligencer*, June 23, 1843. 5. Police officers from Norfolk, Va., had served papers from the governor of Virginia asking Gov. John Davis to return fugitive slave George Latimer. Davis refused and transmitted a document to Virginia's governor giving his reasons for refusing the warrant. The owner of Latimer was eventually compensated $400 for his loss of property and expenses in attempting to get Latimer returned. A citizens' committee from Norfolk appointed to investigate the incident reported that the action of Massachusetts indicated a lack of decency and a disregard for the Constitution. *Niles' Register* (Jan. 14 and 28, 1843), 63:320, 341-43. Davis's action on this matter and his abolitionist views were seen as crucial elements in making him unavailable as a vice presidential candidate. See Davis article in *DAB*. 6. Probably Davis's speech of July 4, 1816, which was highly critical of the War of 1812 and very complimentary to the Federalists. It was printed under the title *An Oration Pronounced at Worcester, (Mass.) on the Fortieth Anniversary of American Independence* (Worcester, 1816), 3-20. 7. In 1838 the Antimasons in Philadelphia had nominated Harrison for president; in 1839 the Whigs in Harrisburg had followed suit. Vaughn, *The Antimasonic Party*, 180-81. As for slighting Sergeant in 1840-41, Harrison evidently had not wanted to offend one faction of his supporters in Pennsylvania by appointing a Cabinet officer from the other faction. Mueller, *Whig Party in Pennsylvania*, 66-67. 8. Fillmore's popularity increased as a result of his actions as chairman of the Ways and Means Committee in steering the Tariff of 1842 through the House. The Poughkeepsie *Eagle* began to tout him for vice president as early as June, 1842. Eventually, Thurlow Weed made a deal to support Fillmore, and Horace Greeley placed his name on the masthead of the New York *Tribune* as the Whig vice presidential candidate. Robert J. Rayback, *Millard Fillmore, Biography of A President* (Buffalo, N.Y., 1959), 141-51. 9. Clay to Butler, August 8, 1842.

To DANIEL ULLMANN Lexington, July 7, 1843

I am obliged by your friendly letter of the 23d Ulto. I think with you that, looking to all the causes now in operation, we have good prospects of achieving in 1844 a more signal victory than that of 1840.

I am thankful for your friendly offer to supply me with information as to the course and conduct of individuals in your quarter. That which I already possess is quite extensive, but I will if necessary avail myself of your kind offer.

I do not know that I can point out any sources of information, in respect to my career and conduct, other than the Biographies which have been published.[1] There are doubtless many anecdotes, preserved by tradition, but these would be better told by others than me.

Was your eulogy of me ever published?[2] I have not seen it.

ALS. NHi. Addressed to Ullmann at Fort Hamilton in New York City. 1. Clay to Ullmann, April 13, 1843. 2. Ullmann's oration seems not to have been published.

To ROBERT L. CARUTHERS Lexington, July 9, 1843

I thank you for the copy of your excellent reply to Mr. Cave Johnson, which you did me the favor to send me.[1] It is prepared with great ability, and, I should think, can not fail to exert a decided influence wherever it is read. The whole campaign, in Tennessee, as far as I am able to judge, has been conducted with uncommon tact, skill, and vigor. And our friends will have richly merited the [victo]ry which, I trust, they will achieve.[2] Information has [con]stantly been pouring in upon me from all parts of your S[tate,] and from its general tenor I can not doubt your success. Still, so much depends upon the issue of the contest in Tennessee, that I shall feel the greatest solicitude until I hear what it positively is. Mr. Speaker [John] White, who has recently been to those Counties of his District which border upon Tennessee, yesterday told me that, from what he learnt whilst there, he apprehends the struggle will be very close. I hope you are in no danger of any erruption into Tennessee by the K. democrats from the adjoining Counties.

From all quarters of the Union I receive the most encouraging accounts. The public mind seems to be settling down in a firm conviction that the Whigs will succeed next year. That is a favorable state of it, if it should not lead to any relaxation of exertion.

ALS. NcU. For Caruthers (1800-82), at this time fresh from service in the 27th Congress as a Whig, see *BDAC* [spelled Caruthers] and *NCAB*, 8:126 [spelled Carruthers]. 1. For U.S. Rep. Cave Johnson, soon to be President Polk's postmaster general, see *DAB* and *BDAC*. On June 6, 1843, Caruthers had answered a letter of Cave Johnson's which blamed the public debt on the Whig party. Caruthers's letter was published in the Nashville *Republican Banner*, June 19 and 21, 1843. 2. T.J. Campbell to Clay, May 7, 1843.

To B.F. Moore *et al.*, Raleigh, N.C., July 10, 1843. Responds to their invitation, extended as representatives of the Whig delegation in the North Carolina state legislature, to visit North Carolina. Says he has not abandoned his intention to do so, especially since their state was "the first to denounce the unparalleled treachery which has marked the career of the acting President [John Tyler] of the United States." Lauds the patriotic North Carolinians because they were the first to "declare the Independence of the Colonies [8:774-75]," and "will be among the last to abandon the support of the Union." Promises to visit the state next spring but cannot now set the precise date. Copy. Printed in Knoxville *Register*, August 23, 1843.

Moore's Committee of 13 had written Clay in June, 1843. They reminded him of his promise in 1842 to visit North Carolina some day, and also of the fact that in April, 1842 the state's Whigs had been the first to endorse his presidential candidacy [Clay to Porter, January 22, 1842], "without qualification or condition," and they had done this at a time when Whigs were disgusted and dismayed by the "then recent defection of the President [Tyler] from the great party to whom he owed his elevation." Assert their conviction that Clay can restore the nation to a "glorious and happy state" by ending the "misgovernment and corruption . . . treachery and selfishness" that has characterized Tyler's administration. Copy. Printed in Raleigh *Register and North Carolina Gazette*, July 21, 1843.

Clay's travel took him from Lexington to New Orleans on business in December, 1843. He arrived there on December 23 and departed by steamer for Mobile on February 24, 1844. He reach Mobile *ca.* February 26, 1844, and departed there on March 5 for Montgomery. He was in Columbus, Ga., on March 13, in Macon on the 17th, and Milledgeville on the 19th. He arrived in Savannah on March 21 and remained there until March 25. He was in Augusta, March 26-April 2. He proceeded to Columbia, S.C., by rail, arriving on the evening of April 2. He departed Columbia for Charleston on April 6. He then continued north to Raleigh, N.C., arriving there on April 12. He reached Petersburg, Va., on April 19, and left there for Portsmouth and Norfolk, arriving in the latter on April 21. He remained in Norfolk until April 25 then departed for Washington where he arrived *ca.* April 29. He remained in the capital until *ca.* May 10, and was back in Lexington by May 18. As he told one correspondent of his anticipated travel through Alabama, Georgia, South Carolina, North Carolina, and southside

Virginia, "I shall throughout the whole journey be moving on ground which I never trod before [Clay to Bayard, November 10, 1843]."

To ALBERT G. BOONE[1] Lexington, July 11, 1843

Our friend Col. [William H.] Russell delivered to me the Indian Hunting shirt which you did me the honor to present me, and for which I pray your acceptance of my cordial thanks. I shall carefully preserve it as a valuable token of the esteem of the grand son of the distinguished Pioneer [Daniel Boone], who led the way to the fine Country which we inhabit, and as a curious memorial of an interesting and unfortunate race of men.

I reciprocate your friendly wishes for my happiness and hope you may enjoy a length of life as great as your famous Grand sire.

ALS. ICHi. Addressed to Boone in West Port, Jackson County, Mo. 1. For Albert Gallatin Boone, see Hazel A. Spraker (comp.), *The Boone Family* ... (Rutland, Vt., 1922), 189.

To JOHN M. BERRIEN Lexington, July 17,1843

I received your favor communicating a very interesting account of the proceedings of your [Georgia] State Convention.[1] I congratulate you on the prominent part which you bore in it; and I have perused with great satisfaction the address you made on assuming the duties of the Chair. After the vile attacks made upon you,[2] your nomination for the V. Presidency was a compliment well deserved, whatever may be the final decision of the National Convention. With you I suppose that, if the Candidate for the first office should be taken from a Slave State, the Candidate for the second will be designated in a free State, altho' there is a contrary precedent. All this, however, will be matter for the consideration of the Nat. Convention.[3] The harmony which marked the deliberations of the Convention, and the complete union which you have brought about in the Whig press of Georgia are highly auspicious circumstances.

I am greatly obliged by your friendly agency in suppressing the resolution which proposed inviting me to a Mass meeting; and I have occasion for your further friendly offices. A Committee of the General Assembly of No. Carolina recently renewed their invitation to me to visit that State, reminding me of a promise I made to that effect more than two years ago, and *insisting* upon its fulfillment.[4] My repugnance to making any thing which bears the aspect of a political visit would have induced me to have foreborne or postponed the pleasure of visiting that State, if I could have offered any legitimate excuse, but I could not, and therefore returned an answer that I would go to N. Carolina next Spring, if my life and health should be spared. My plan is this: Business carries me to N. Orleans this winter, and I intend to proceed thence, via Mobile and the Southern route, through Georgia and So. Carolina to the North State [North Carolina].

Thus I am brought into your State. Now what I desire is, to avoid visiting too many places. Waiving other considerations, I should distrust my physical ability to go to more than one or at most two places in any one State meeting large concourses of my fellow Citizens. I am sure that it would be injurious to my health. I think it will be in the month of March, possibly from the middle to the end of it; but I am to fix the time at N. Orleans and notify, beforehand, the N. Carolina Commee. of it. I hope you will employ your friendly exertions to prevent my being pressed to attend at many points and to reconcile our friends to such an arrangement as I have suggested.

The ground on which I place my acceptance of this invitation is that of the fulfillment of a positive engagement. Other grounds may be taken by my friends, such as that I have never seen the three Southern States, that I shall be enjoying the benefit of a Southern winter and spring &c. My escape from the severity of a Northern winter, during the last, was of essential service to me.

From Massachusetts, I receive encouraging information of the probable restoration of the Whig ascendancy this fall, whatever *course* Mr. Webster may take.[5] From Pennsa. I am assured that the prospects of success next year are decidedly superior to those which existed in 1840.[6] I am afraid our friends have not done well in Louisiana at their late election;[7] but if the confident calculations of the Whigs in Tennessee[8] and Indiana[9] shall be realized it will neutralize any unfavorable result in Louisiana. If I were to credit the intelligence from Missouri,[10] and Illinois,[11] of which I receive a great deal, we shall carry those States. But experience has taught me the uncertainty of previous speculations about elections. By the by, there is no truth in a statement which may have met your eye of a meeting between Col. [Thomas Hart] Benton and me. I did not see him at all, nor have I spoken to him for ten years. . . .

ALS. NcU. 1. The Georgia Whig convention met in Milledgeville on June 19-20, 1843. Berrien chaired the convention and was also delegated to write an address which was subsequently published in Savannah in 1843 under the title *Address to the People of Georgia, of the Whig Convention, assembled at Milledgeville, in June, 1843*. The convention nominated George W. Crawford for governor and selected a slate of delegates to attend the Whig National convention in 1844, instructing them to vote for Clay as president and Berrien for vice president. McCrary, "John MacPherson Berrien," Ph.D. dissertation, Univ. of Georgia, 1971, pp. 273-76. 2. After the special session of the 27th Congress, John H. Howard, "a Calhounite Democrat," presented a series of resolutions to the Georgia state legislature in late 1841, calling for the censure of Berrien because of his objections to Tyler's vetoes, castigating the national Whig party program, and instructing Berrien and other Georgia representatives in Congress to vote against any national bank bill and to support repeal of the distribution and bankruptcy acts. These resolutions passed the legislature after Berrien's party boycotted the final vote, an action which thus allowed his party to claim that the resolutions were illegal since a quorum was not present when they were adopted. *Ibid*., 256-57; Paul Murray, *The Whig Party in Georgia, 1825-1853* (Chapel Hill, 1948), 100-101. 3. Clay to Clayton, August 8, 1842. 4. Clay to Moore, July 10, 1843. 5. The 1843 Massachusetts state elections resulted in the Whigs controlling the lower house over the Democrats by 50 seats and the state senate by 28 seats. The state government in all its branches was thus controlled by the Whigs. *Niles' Register* (Jan. 27, 1844), 65:340. In a special election for the U.S. House in the 10th district, Whig Joseph Grinnell defeated Sampson Perkins (no party given) by a vote of 4,943 to 3,927. *Guide to U.S. Elections*, 578. In the gubernatorial election on Nov. 13, 1843, Whig George Briggs defeated Democrat Marcus Morton by 57,899 to 54,242 with Liberty party candidate Samuel Sewell receiving 8,901 votes. Since no one had a majority, the election was thrown into the senate, and Briggs was elected on Jan. 3, 1844. *BDGUS*, 2:698. 6. Sargent to Clay, August 6, 1842. 7. Louisiana congressional elections took place on July 4, 1843, for the 28th Congress. Democrats won all 4 seats. Washington *Daily National Intelligencer*, July 10, 15, 17, 19, 1843. *Guide to U.S. Elections* (p. 577) erroneously indicates this election as taking place in 1842. 8. Campbell to Clay, May 7, 1843. 9. Clay to Leigh, June 20, 1843. 10. Polk beat Clay in Missouri, 41,369 to 31,251 in the 1844 presidential election. McKee, *National . . . Popular and Electoral Vote*, 56. There were no state or congressional elections in Missouri in 1843. 11. In the 1843 congressional elections in Illinois, Democrats won 6 seats to 1 for the Whigs. *Guide to U.S. Elections*, 578. For the 1844 presidential election in Illinois, see Clay to Berrien, April 23, 1843.

To THOMAS B. STEVENSON[1] Lexington, July 19 [?], 1843

The news from Louisiana is bad enough.[2] From Tennessee I daily receive the most satisfactory and cheering accounts.[3] I agree with you, that on the result of that election much of the future depends. From Pennsylvania,[4] from Georgia,[5] North Carolina,[6] and Massachusetts,[7] I get good accounts.

An editorial article will appear to-day in the *Observer*, on [Jacob] Burnet's letter, which may be worth copying in the *Commonwealth*.[8]

I think we shall not do as badly in Fayette as you apprehend.[9]

Copy. Printed in Colton, *Clay Correspondence*, 3:457. 1. Stevenson, who at various times served as editor of newspapers in Maysville, Ky., and in Cincinnati, was at this time editor of the Frankfort *Commonwealth*. He also served as president of the Maysville and Big Sandy Railroad and as a judge in the New Mexico Territory. Collins, *History of Kentucky*, 2:560-61. 2. Clay to Berrien, July 17, 1843. 3. Campbell to Clay, May 7, 1843; Clay to Berrien, March 13, 1843. 4. In the 1843 U.S. congressional elections in Pennsylvania, Whigs won 13 seats to 11 for the Democrats. *Guide to U.S. Elections*, 579. Democrats won 58 and Whigs 42 seats in the lower house of the state legislature. In the state senate the Democrats won 9 of 12 seats, giving them an overall dominance of 22 to 11. *Niles' Register* (Oct. 12, 1843), 65:128. For the 1844 presidential election in Pennsylvania, see Sargent to Clay, August 6, 1842. 5. Two Whigs were chosen in a special election in 1843 to the U.S. House in Georgia. *Guide to U.S. Elections*, 578. In the gubernatorial election, Whig George W. Crawford defeated Democrat Mark A. Cooper by a vote of 38,813 to 35,325. *BDGUS*, 1:294. Whigs also elected a majority in both houses of the state legislature with a net gain of 11 in the senate and 37 in the house. *Niles' Register* (Oct. 14, 1843), 65:112. In the 1844 presidential election, Polk carried Georgia by a popular vote of 44,177 to 42,106 for Clay, thereby winning all 10 electoral votes. McKee, *National . . . Popular and Electoral Vote*, 56-57. 6. In the congressional elections in North Carolina in 1843, 5 Democrats and 4 Whigs were chosen; however, Whigs claimed victory because their total popular vote in all districts exceeded that of the Democrats by several thousand votes. *Guide to U.S. Elections*, 578; Raleigh *Register and North Carolina Gazette*, August 25, 1843. In the 1844 presidential election in North Carolina, Clay won 43,232 popular votes to 39,287 for Polk, thereby receiving the state's 11 electoral votes. McKee, *National . . . Popular and Electoral Vote*, 56-57. 7. Clay to Berrien, July 17, 1843; Clay to Clayton, May 27, 1843. 8. The footnote subtending this statement, written by Stevenson, which appears in Colton, reads: "The Hon. Jacob Burnet, of Ohio, had published a letter in the *Cincinnati Gazette*, saying that while he and Judge McLean would vote for Mr. Clay, the *Abolitionists* would vote for no resident of a slave State, which was probably meant as a slant to favor Judge McLean's presidential aspirations. The article in the *Observer and Reporter*, a newspaper at Lexington, which he sometimes wrote *Observer*, and sometimes *Reporter*, defined the true grounds of selecting the candidate to be such as regarded sound national principles, without reference to his residence, etc. The *Commonwealth* newspaper, published at Frankfort, was then edited by me.—T.B.S." Burnet's letter of June 10, 1843, which had been published in the Cincinnati *Gazette* on June 11 was printed by Stevenson in the Frankfort *Commonwealth* on July 18, the day before the date given in Colton for Clay's letter to Stevenson suggesting that it be published. This would seem to indicate either that Clay had not seen the *Commonwealth* of the previous day or that this letter to Stevenson is misdated. The Lexington *Observer & Reporter* is not available for this period, but the Frankfort *Commonwealth* reprinted the *Observer's* editorial concerning Burnet's letter on July 25, 1843; however, it does not give the date on which it originally appeared in the *Observer*. See also Clay to Letcher, June 26, 1843. 9. In the congressional race in the 8th district, Whig Garrett Davis carried Fayette County over Democrat C.A. Wickliffe by 1,342 votes to 920. Lexington *Gazette*, Sept. 2, 1843. See also Clay to Davis, August 21, 1843. Whigs won all 3 Fayette County seats in the state house of representatives as well as the senatorial seat in the district which included Fayette County. Frankfort *Commonwealth*, August 15 and 22, 1843. In the 1844 presidential race, Clay carried Fayette County over Polk by 1,695 votes to 824. Kentucky *Gazette*, Dec. 7, 1844.

To WILLIAM B. CAMPBELL Lexington, July 21, 1843

I received your favor of the 12h. and thank you for the very full and satisfactory information which it contains. The evil which you describe of the multitude of Whig Candidates[1] is felt by us,[2] and will endanger two or three Congressional districts, and several County elections; but we are so strong that I do not apprehend any very serious injury.

Now that Louisiana has behaved so badly,[3] our anxiety is greatly increased as to the result in your State.[4] If Tennessee, Indiana[5] and No. Carolina[6] shall realize our hopes and expectations, the Whig cause will be placed on high and impregnable ground. One of the best informed men in Pennsa. writes me that our prospects there[7] are far better than they were in 1840. And I receive cheering accounts from Georgia[8] N. York[9] and Massachusetts.[10]

Do not trouble yourself to write me until after the election.[11] Then I shall be obliged by a line of early information as to the issue of it in your quarter of the State. . . .[12]

ALS. NcD. Addressed to Campbell in Carthage, Tenn. 1. For the 1843 Tenn. congressional elections, see T.J. Campbell to Clay, May 7, 1843. 2. For the 1843 Ky. congressional elections, see Clay to Anderson, July 23, 1843. 3. Clay to Berrien, July 17, 1843. 4. T.J. Campbell to Clay, May 7, 1843. 5. Clay to Leigh, June 20, 1843. 6. Clay to Stevenson, July 19, 1843. 7. *Ibid.* Specific correspondent not identified, but see Nathan Sargent to Clay, August 6, 1842. 8. Clay to Stevenson, July 19, 1843. 9. New York had no gubernatorial or congressional elections in 1843, but in the election for the state legislature on Nov. 7, Democrats won 91 seats in the lower house to 37 for the Whigs. In the state senate, 9 seats were contested in the election. The Democrats won 8 of these and the Whigs 1, bringing the overall numbers in the senate to 20 for the Democrats and 6 for the Whigs. *Niles' Register* (Nov. 18, 1843), 65:192. 10. Clay to Berrien, July 17, 1843. 11. In Tennessee on August 1, 1843. See T.J. Campbell (no kin to W.B. Campbell) to Clay, May 7, 1843. T.J. Campbell lived in Athens, in eastern Tenn. 12. *Ibid.* W.B. Campbell lived in Carthage, in central Tenn.

To James A. Campfield, Hanover Neck, Morris County, N.J., July 21, 1843. Thanks Campfield for his friendly sentiments, but doubts he will be able to visit New Jersey. Explains: "If I could overcome the objection, on principle, to political tour's, I should find it very difficult to decide where to begin or where to end in this widespread Confederacy." Assures him, however, that "I share with you fully in the disappointment in the Country's not realizing its just expectations from the issue of the great victory of 1840. The causes are as obvious as they are mortifying." ALS. Courtesy of Mrs. Oscar N. Torian, Sewanee, Tenn.

To George Washington Anderson, Louisville, July 23, 1843. Regrets that Anderson and his wife, Eleanor, have just lost a small child. Mentions the fact that Anderson [3:117-18] owes him some money from the Hart estate. Adds: "I regret extremely your misfortunes, of which I have had also my full share, and can therefore cordially sympathise with you. Twice in my life have I been nearly ruined by responsibilities for others, and it will require some years of unremitted exertion to disembarrass myself. I have experienced moments of very great depression, but they have been succeeded by firm resolves to struggle and bear up to the last." Concludes with the observation that "The aspect of our K. elections is far from being gratifying. We are in danger of defeat in three or four Congressional Districts." Is pleased, however, to learn that William Poindexter Thomasson's election is likely. ALS. KyU.

In the Kentucky state elections of August 7, 1843, Democrats won 24 seats in the lower house to 16 for the Whigs. In the state senate the Whigs won 26 seats to 12 for the Democrats. Frankfort *Commonwealth*, August 15 and 22, 1843. There was no gubernatorial election in 1843. In the elections for the U.S. House, the Democrats and the Whigs each won five seats. In the 7th district, composed of the counties of Jefferson, Shelby, Oldham, Henry, Trimble, and Carroll, Whig William P. Thomasson [see *BDAC*] defeated Democrat Joseph Lecompte by a vote of 4,900 to 4,497, with Whig James C. Sprigg winning 1,152 votes. *Guide to U.S. Elections*, 578. For the counties comprising each of Kentucky's congressional districts, see *Niles' Register* (October 7, 1843), 65:89.

To JOEL BRANHAM & ROBERT BLEDSOE Lexington, July 23, 1843

I duly received your favor of the 13th inst.[1] in which you inform me that conflicting opinions prevail in your State in regard to my opinions on the policy of protecting domestic manufactures, and you request of me information in relation to them. I take pleasure in complying with your request.

My opinion is, that the revenue necessary to an economical administration of the General Government ought to be derived, in a season of peace, exclusively from duties imposed on our foreign imports, and that a tariff for that purpose ought to be so adjusted as to afford a reasonable encouragement to our domestic manufactures. I am opposed to direct taxes and internal duties except in time of war, when they may be necessary to give vigor and success to our arms. I am opposed to the doctrine of free trade with foreign Powers, all of whom subject our commerce with them to restrictions, often very great and burdensome.

These opinions I have always entertained and still entertain. I never was in favor of duties being so high as to amount to a prohibition of articles on which they were laid. I have thought it best for all interests that there should be competition. I think it of great importance that a tariff should possess stability, as frequent changes affect injuriously all our great interests. To impart to it that character it should be moderate, reasonable, and certain.

I voted for the tariffs of 1816, 1824, and 1832.[2] I think they were all reasonable and moderate at the times they were respectively passed. In the infancy of manufactures, the object being to acquire the skill and accumulate the capital necessary to their successful establishment, a greater degree of protection is expedient than is requisite after they have made a considerable progress. The difficulty lies in fixing that degree. In 1816 we were without much experience, and failed to make in all cases a proper adjustment of the measure of protection. Eight years' experience, in 1824, enabled Congress to fix it with more equity and precision. Eight years of progress in our manufactures, in 1832, justified some reduction in the amount of duties, and generally the tariff of 1842[3] is more moderate than that of 1832. As our manufactures advance and become perfected, less and less protection will be needed, until many articles will be able to compete with the foreign rival articles without any protection at all in the form of duties.

I was not in Congress in 1828, and therefore did not vote for the tariff of that year.[4] The duties in many instances imposed by that tariff were extravagantly high, and other duties were imposed which were not called for by any interest. That tariff was a fraudulent production: it was framed by a combination of some members from the South and some from the North, who were afraid openly to vote against a tariff, and yet wished to obtain credit for being favorable to support Southern interest. It was shaped with the design of defeating the passage of any tariff; because it was believed that it was so injurious to the manufacturing interest in many respects that the honest and true friends of that interest would not vote for it. Had it been defeated those Northern members who united in concocting it would have returned home and asserted that they were the true friends of protection, and that its really honest friends were inimical to it. But it was not defeated. The genuine friends of manufactures resolved not to be cheated by such a combination, and determined to take the bill for the sake of the good that was in it, notwithstanding the bad which was put there against their consent. The scheme not having succeeded as was designed, the Southern members, who were concerned in it, afterwards bitterly reproached their Northern confederates for the disappointment.

I have more than half a dozen times expressed, within the last two or three years, on public occasions, the opinion which I now communicate as to a combination of the principles of Revenue and Protection in a tariff. I send you herewith the last speech on that subject which I made in the Senate of the United States,[5] and also a brief sketch of the principles of the Whig party, as I understand them, which I prepared.

I have no other objection to the publication of this letter but that it would imply a sensitiveness in regard to my opinion which I do not feel, and I think it has been already sufficiently promulgated. . . .

Copy. Printed in Washington *Daily National Intelligencer*, Nov. 30, 1843. See also Clay to Meriwether, Oct. 2, 1843. 1. Branham and Bledsoe were Democrats residing in Eatonton, Ga. On July 13, 1843, they had written Clay requesting him to clear up doubts as to whether his views on the tariff "have undergone if not an entire change, at least some modification." Ask him flatly: "Are you in favor of a tariff for the protection of American manufactures? Have your principles in reference to this subject undergone change or modification?" Copy. Printed in Washington *Daily National Intelligencer*, Nov. 30, 1843. 2. For these tariffs, see, successively, 2:138, 178-80, 182-85; 3:683-730; 8:443, 445, 455-56. 3. Clay to Letcher, Jan. 6 and June 24, 1842; Remark in Senate, Feb. 3, 1842. 4. See 6:876-77; 7:449-51, 660 (index entries); 8:94-95. 5. Either his Speech in Senate of March 1 or March 23, 1842.

To Chambersburg Clay Club, Chambersburg, Pa., July 25, 1843. Thanks club members for their willingness to support him for the presidency but informs them he has not yet decided to be a candidate for that office. Responds at length to the club's query of how it can be possible that this nation, which possesses a constitution adapted to human welfare concerns, which has enormous natural resources as well as an excellent transportation system and a tradition of vigor and enterprise, has sunk into an economic depression so deep that capitalists can find no outlet for investments and laborers can find no employment. Explains: "It is impossible to contemplate the administration of the Government during nearly the last fifteen years without feelings of the deepest regret and bitterest mortification. That long period has been marked by relentless proscription, similar in spirit, if not attended with the same effusion of blood as that which is recorded in Roman history to have been perpetrated by Marius and Sylla [*sic*, Sulla]; by reckless experiments and the over throw of valuable institutions, by the destruction of the best currency in the world, and consequent derangement in all the business of society; by extensive and scandalous peculation on the part of public functionaries; by extravagant and profligate expenditure of the public money; by attempts to subvert the long-cherished policy of the country under which it had eminently flourished and prospered; by relaxation in the respect and authority due to the law and Cons[titu]tion; by widespread and alarming demoralization; by a fearful growth and corrupt use of the power of the Executive branch of the Government; and, finally, by a degree of perfidy in the head of that branch, of which no equal example can be found in this or any other country, in this or any other age. At the commencement of the administration of the present acting Chief Magistrate the leaders of our political opponents, with a few honorable exceptions, assiduously courted and caressed him, flattering and praising him for his violation of the just expectations of a confiding people. They marched up in solid column, arm in arm, along Pennsylvania avenue to the Presidential mansion, to thank and congratulate him for exercising a royal prerogative to defeat the wishes and hopes of the people. Men, under the abused name of Democrats, loudly exulted in the failure of a measure demanded by the urgent wants and voice, and essential to the promotion of the interests of the people, exulted in the perverse and corrupt will of one man overruling the will of a large majority of the nation! In the dispensations of an all-wise Providence retributive justice is sure to come sooner or later. The acting President, so much wooed by political leaders in the beginning of his administration, now, as its end approaches, in his turn, and very much to their annoyance, exercises all his blandishments upon their party. Nor is their danger or regrets diminished by the fact that, whilst their instruments of seduction were honeyed words, his are the lucrative offices of Government."

Recalls that in the 1840 presidential election the Whigs had promised "a radical improvement in public policy." Thus, given the "unexampled and overwhelming majority" the Whigs had then received, the "manly, liberal and patriotic" course for the opposition Democrats to have followed at that time would have been cheerfully to acquiesce in the peoples' will. "They should have said 'The people disapprove of our system. They require a sound currency of uniform value. They are opposed to the Sub-Treasury. They demand a distribution of the proceeds of the sales of the public lands among all the States. They insist upon an honest and economical administration of their public affairs. They are opposed to the encroachments of the Executive department, and require salutary restraints upon its power. We shall continue, by free discussion and fair arguments, to recommend our measures, and to expose those of our political opponents; but they are entitled to a fair trial of their system of policy, and we will make no factious opposition, nor throw any unreasonable obstacles in their way. Above all, we scorn to employ any arts to seduce from the path of his duty the man who has reached his elevated station, in spite of our strenuous exertions against him, by the confidence which they generously reposed in his honor and fidelity.' " All this they refused to do. Instead, they identified themselves closely with "the acting President [Tyler]." Reminds club members that internal dissention during the War of 1812 had taught the "patriotic lesson" that only through unity can success be achieved. Is confident, however, that the low state into which the nation has fallen since 1828 can be changed, because "It is our peculiar good fortune to have in the ballot box a remedy." Is certain, therefore, that "a great and glorious deliverance awaits us, and that the People will in 1844 nobly vindicate their rights, and manifest anew their capacity for self government by a triumph more brilliant, more decisive, and I hope more auspicious than that of 1840." Copy. Printed in Washington *Daily National Intelligencer*, August 30, 1843. Addressed to Samuel Seibert *et al.* An undated excerpt of their letter to Clay is in *ibid.*

To Thomas E. Mittag, Hagerstown, Md., July 25, 1843. Expresses in a written endorsement on the front cover of "The Ashland March," a piece of music composed and dedicated to him by Philip Burgheim, "(Professor of Music)," his acceptance and appreciation of said dedication. Copy. KyBgW. The sheet music was published in 1843 by Frederick D. Benteen in Baltimore. The original sheet music, scored for piano, is in KyU.

For Mittag, one of the owners and publishers of the Hagerstown *Herald and Torchlight*, see Thomas J.C. Williams, *A History of Washington County Maryland . . .* (Baltimore, 1968), 434.

To JOHN O. SARGENT Lexington, July 29, 1843

I received your favor of the 15h. and was gratified to learn from it that Mr. [Daniel] Mallory has brought his labors to a close, and that his book would soon make its public appearance.[1] I hope he may be fully remunerated by the sale of his work, for the cost and trouble which it has occasioned him.

The strong and abiding faith, which seems to prevail every where, in the success of the Whigs next year, is not the least remarkable circumstance of the times. It is a faith against facts. For the election last year and this year have gone against us. Nevertheless I partake of the faith, and verily believe that the victory of 1844 will by its brilliancy eclipse that of 1840.

Your account of M[atthew]. L. Davis amuses me. He preserves his character to the last, and much better, I apprehend, than he will his office. But that he does not care about. Should you see him present him assurances of my warm esteem.

Mr. Webster's course has shocked and afflicted me.[2] I predicted and told him his fate at the close of the Extra Session. I then said to him "If you mean to continue in Mr. Tylers Admon for the purpose of closing any incomplete business, to which your attention and services are necessary, the public will approve your conduct. But if you identify yourself with it and remain indefinitely the public will condemn you."

I consider the betrayal of the public confidence, on the part of eminent men, as one of the greatest misfortunes of the times. It tends to engender universal distrust, to confound the true and faithful with the false and perfidious, and to disable the People from making just discriminations.

I am glad to hear that you are pleased with your profession and succeed in it. It is an honorable pursuit.

ALS. MHi. 1. Clay to Sargent, July 2, 1842. 2. For example, see Clay to Clayton, May 27, 1843.

To Robert Garrett & Sons, Baltimore, July 31, 1843. Has learned that the speciman of hackled [cleaned and combed] hemp he recently sent for evaluation and sale has been sold for 8½ cents per pound, but wants to know what [rope] manufacturers in Baltimore think of the unhackled speciman he also sent. Believes that "our water retted hemp, when properly prepared, is equal to the best Russia hemp, and ought to command as high a price. If there be a difference I should be glad to know what it is." ALS. DLC-HC (DNA, M212, R21). This letter was printed in the Baltimore *American*, from which it was reprinted in *The Dollar Farmer* (September, 1843) 2:41. *The Dollar Farmer, A Monthly Publication Devoted to Practical and Scientific Agriculture* was published in Louisville from 1842-46 by George Prentice and George W. Weissinger. Demaree, *American Agricultural Press*, 394.

On June 28, Clay had sold to Messrs. Croxall & Browning, through Robert Garrett & Sons, 16 bales of hackled hemp totaling 4,239 lbs. @ 8½ cents, or for $360.31. On July 13-14, he sold 11 bales of unhackled hemp, totaling 2,958 lbs. @ 7½ cents, or for $221.85. Subtracted from his gross total of $582.16 were charges of $5.18 for freight, $2.25 for advertising and labor, $14.02 for interest, and $29.11 for the agents' commission of 5%. Total overhead: $50.56. Net sale: $531.60. Account of Sale of Hemp, June 28, 1843. DS. DLC-TJC (DNA, M212, R19). Enclosed in Garrett to Clay, August 7, 1843 (see below).

Garrett & Sons answered Clay's July 31 inquiry on August 7, telling him that they had procured "for the 'hackled' [hemp] the highest price that an article of American growth has commanded in our market." Report also that "The Manufacturers inform us that y[ou]r. belief is correct, that y[ou]r. W.R. [water-rotted] Hemp, when properly prepared, is equal to the *best* Russian. They state that in *brightness* & *strength*, this parcel has proved fully equal, if not superior to prime Russian; the objection however is that it is not sufficiently cleaned. . . . [and] should be in larger hands. . . . For an article similar . . . [and] properly cleaned, we feel assured, from the present test, that the full price of Russian can be realized. This lot has proved more satisfactory in manufacturing &, we are advised, is the best of American [hemp] that has ever appeared in this market." ALS. DLC-TJC (DNA, M212, R19). A slightly altered excerpt of this letter was printed in the same issue of *The Dollar Farmer* as Clay's July 31 letter and also in the Nashville *Republican Banner*, August 25, 1843.

R. Garrett & Sons wrote Clay again on August 23 reporting that the difference in value between the hackled and the unhackled hemp was but one cent per pound, and that the latter, at the lower price, "would suit quite well." Add: "You are aware that the greatest degree of brightness attainable is highly desirable." Inform him that Croxall & Browning, rope manufacturers, had purchased his parcel of the hackled hemp. Conclude: "Our market is at present bare of prime water Rotted & Such would sell readily." ALS. DLC-TJC (DNA, M212, R14).

To CAMERON & FALL[1] Lexington, August, 1843

I duly received your letter, requesting my present views as to the station that the mechanical portion of our population should occupy in the United States, and also as to the subject of home industry and manufactures. Although I have often had occasion publicly to express my opinions on these matters, I take pleasure in communicating them to you.

It has always appeared to me, gentlemen, that the task of administering our common Government would not be very difficult, if honesty, liberality, and reasonable information, were carried into the public councils. It was instituted to promote the general prosperity, by a faithful exercise of the powers granted by the Constitution. All parts of the Union, and all the great interests of the country should, therefore, receive the parental care and attention of the Government. No one section, and no one interest should desire or expect to engross its exclusive regard.

The main pillars of society are agriculture, commerce, including navigation, and manufactures, including the mechanic arts. Owing to the peculiar position of the United States, agriculture requires but little protection, and that confined to a few branches of it. It is otherwise with the other two interests. They require some protection against the selfish legislation and the rivalry of foreign powers, which, to make it beneficial and effectual, should possess two qualities, moderation and stability, intimately connected with each other. Without moderation, other interests would feel that they had been unjustly dealt by, dissatisfaction would ensue, and that stability in legislation so desirable in all business and pursuits, would not be served.

Protection to manufactures and commerce is in fact, whatever it may be in form, encouragement to agriculture. The cultivator of the soil is conscious of the great advantage of having along side of him the blacksmith, the wheelright, the saddler and harnessmaker, the tailor, the hatter, the shoemaker, the cabinet-maker, and masons and carpenters. His comforts and theirs are both increased by such proximity, and they are enabled to augment their respective productions. But of what avail would it be to multiply them, without commerce, foreign and domestic, whose office is to distribute the surplus produce of agriculture and of the fabrics of the mechanic and manufacturer?

I am so far a friend of free trade as to think that, within the limits of the Union, it should be entirely unfettered, and perfectly equal between all interests and all parts of our country. But to that free trade which would throw wide open our ports to foreign productions, without duties, theirs remaining closed to us, or our admission allowed only upon the condition of high duties and severe restriction, which would compel a resort to direct taxation instead of the custom-house, to supply the wants of the Federal Treasury; and which would leave our domestic industry unprotected and exposed in an unequal contest with the rival productions of foreign powers, I am utterly and irreconcilably opposed. I had hoped, and supposed, that all would have cheerfully rallied around a tariff which, seeking to supply the treasury with an adequate revenue, for an honest and economical administration of the Government, should at the same time, incidentally, by proper discrimination, extend reasonable protection to such branches of our domestic industry as needed it. That is all which is now asked or insisted upon. But even that moderate and equitable basis, for the final settlement of this great and vexed question, encounters strong and decided opposition.

The mechanic arts, from the commencement of the operation of our present Constitution, have constantly enjoyed some degree of protection from Government in the form of duties imposed on fabrics of foreign mechanics; and I think it ought to be continued.

With respect to the station which that portion of our population engaged in mechanical pursuits ought to occupy in the United States, I think that all citizens, native and naturalized, without any regard to their respective vocations, should enjoy such consideration in society, as is due to their virtue and intelligence, their industry, sobriety, and general deportment....

Copy. Printed in *The Dollar Farmer* (Sept., 1843), 2:44-45, reprinted from *The Agriculturist*; also printed in the Portsmouth (N.H.) *Journal of Literature and Politics*, Sept. 2, 1843; *Niles' Register* (August 19, 1843), 64:397; and Nashville *Republican Banner*, August 9, 1843. 1. John Fall and either Donald or William Cameron, or both, were publishers of *The Agriculturist* which was the organ of the Tennessee state and county agricultural societies and was published in Nashville from 1840-45. Demaree, *American Agricultural Press*, 364-67. John Fall and Donald and William Cameron were also publishers of the Nashville *Republican Banner*. David Kaser, *A Directory of the Book and Printing Industries in Ante-Bellum Nashville* (New York, 1966), 24, 29.

To WILLIAM L. HODGE Lexington, August 10, 1843

I only received yesterday your obliging letter communicating the causes which produced the defeat of the Whigs in La.[1] and assurances that the State, notwithstanding, is thoroughly Whig.

I thank you for the friendly motives which induced you to address me.

For the last twenty years I have been assured that the State of La. was friendly to me. It never voted for me; and, if my name should be presented as a Candidate, I do not expect its vote.[2] I nevertheless saved the Sugar duty for it in 1824, and under like circumstances should feel myself bound in duty to save it again. But if any man suppose that the principle of protection will be extended to Sugar and nothing else, he must be very ignorant or a fool or knave. The reverse is much more probable, that it may be applied to other articles, to the exclusion of Sugar.

Notwithstanding the inauspicious result of the Election in Louisiana, the more to be depreciated for its exterior influence than any direct bearing it has, I am happy to assure you of my conviction that the triumph of the Whigs next year will eclipse that of 1840.[3] This opinion is founded upon extensive information derived from all quarters of the Union. The elections have just taken place in this[4] and two or three surrounding States. In this we may loose two or three members by divisions; but I shall be greatly disappointed if the general result is not highly encouraging.

Entertain no fear of N. England.[5] Mr. Webster cannot control a solitary Electoral vote in it. Should he come out for Mr. Calhoun, it will complete his political annihilation.

ALS. KyLoF. For Hodge, see 4:599. Hodge, formerly a Philadelphia merchant, had moved to Louisiana and subsequently became the owner of the New Orleans *Commercial Bulletin*. *LHQ*, 22:1099. 1. Clay to Berrien, July 17, 1843. 2. Clay to Berrien, March 13, 1843. 3. In 1840, Harrison carried Kentucky over Van Buren by an impressive margin of 58,489 to 32,616. In 1844, Clay carried Kentucky over Polk by 61,255 to 51,988. McKee, *National . . . Popular and Electoral Vote*, 44, 56. 4. Clay to Anderson, July 23, 1843. 5. Clay to Clayton, May 27, 1843.

To ROBERT P. LETCHER Lexington, August 15, [1843]

I did not receive your favor of the 13h. until this morning. I should be very glad to accept your kind invitation for wednesday, but I am so busy at home with my vats for water-retting hemp &c that I cannot conveniently leave it. I shall not communicate your invitation to the friends named in your letter as I presume it was contingent. I did not know until yesterday that you were in Lexn. on sunday last. As the Court of Appeals will now soon be in Session I shall have frequent opportunities of seeing you and other friends at Frankfort.

We have done very badly in our K. elections.[1] In Tennessee however our friends have achieved a glorious victory.[2] The losses we have sustained here in themselves are not so important, as the H. of R. will contain a large majority against us in any event;[3] but they shew division and a want of concert, for which a remedy must be found, or we may apprehend more fatal disasters.

The worst news is from Indiana,[4] where we have, I fear, met a tremendous defeat. I have received no explanation of it. And I did not anticipate it.

We had no Eastern mail yesterday, and I have not yet seen that of today. The very partial returns which had reached me from N. Carolina looked favorably;[5] and I hope they may continue so.

What we most want is a system of general organization. There ought to be at N. York or Philada. a Central Comee. for the whole Union; a State

Comee. for each State, and local Comees. in every County & Township. And there should be an active correspondence carried on between all parts of this system. With such an organization we would, I think, be certain of victory.

ALS. NcD. 1. Clay to Anderson, July 23, 1843. 2. Campbell to Clay, May 7, 1843. 3. The 29th Congress, 1st Session had 143 Democrats and 77 Whigs in the House, plus 6 others. This represented a significant shift from the 27th Congress which had counted 133 Whigs, 102 Democrats and 6 others, but not much change from the 28th Congress which numbered 142 Democrats, 79 Whigs and 1 other. Morris, *Encyclopedia of American History*, 406; McKee, *National . . . Popular and Electoral Vote*, 46, 57. See also Clay to Crittenden, June 3, 1842; and Adams to Clay, July 24, 1842. 4. Clay to Leigh, June 20, 1843. 5. Clay to Stevenson, July 19, 1843.

To JAMES SIMPSON Lexington, August 15, 1843

I received your friendly letter of the 4h. instant, in which you inform me that representations have been made at Memphis that the Whigs are opposed to the Catholic Irish; and that in the event of my election as Chief Magistrate, the Naturalization laws would be repealed. And you request from me my own views on these subjects. I take pleasure in a prompt compliance with your request.

It is to be regretted that emigrants from Foreign Countries should not seek[1] information of the views of a political party from the most reliable and authentic sources. It is always unsafe to take them from the adverse party. I know of no opposition, on the part of the Whig party, to the Catholic Irish. I entertain no such feeling myself. Without regard to Country or their particular Religion, I judge of men by their conduct & character. I have many friends among the Catholics, and some that I highly esteem among their clergy. I voted for the grants of land to the French and to the Poles,[2] without ever inquiring or thinking whether they were Catholics or Protestants. I espoused the Independence and Liberty of Spanish America,[3] altho' it is Catholic, with quite as much ardor as if it had been protestant. And, in supporting the Cause of Greece,[4] it never occurred to me, whether its inhabitants belonged to the Greek, the Catholic or the Protestant Church. It was enough, to engage my sympathies and exertions, that they were struggling against oppression for deliverance and Liberty. During my public career, and especially during the last War with G. Britain, I contended for the protection, security and rights of our naturalized fellow Citizens, with as much zeal and earnestness as I ever did for those of Native born.

The Repeal of the Naturalization laws[5] constitutes no part of the creed of the Whigs. My opinion is that it is a Constitutional duty of Congress always to keep in force a law prescribing an uniform mode of Naturalization, upon such conditions as, in the judgment of Congress, ought to be imposed. There may be abuses under our system of Naturalization. Unworthy persons of bad character may be sometimes naturalized. If such abuses exist, as I believe they do, they ought to be checked and prevented, by a due execution of the existing laws, or if they be incompetent, by the enaction of supplemental laws. It is a high privilege to be an American Citizen, with all the rights and immunities which are attached to the character. We deprive Native born Citizens, who shew their unworthiness, by perpetrating certain crimes, of the Elective franchise, which ought not to be granted to persons of bad character born in foreign Countries.

These are my sentiments upon the subjects contained in your letter, which you are at liberty to shew to any person you may think proper. At the same time, having great repugnance to appearing unnecessarily in the News papers, I have not written this letter for publication.

ALS. RPB. For Simpson, distinguished Kentucky jurist, see 4:414 and Levin, *Lawyers and Lawmakers of Kentucky*, 78-79. 1. The word "always," preceding "seek" is struck through. 2. For Clay's vote on granting lands to the French, see 2:318-19. An "Act Granting Land to Certain Exiles from Poland" passed the Senate on May 12, 1834, Clay voting yea, and was approved on June 30, 1834. U.S. Sen., *Journal*, 23 Cong., 1 Sess., 1834; 4 *U.S. Stat.*, 743. 3. For Clay's long and fervent advocacy of independence movements in Spanish America, see relevant subjects indexed in 7:762-64; see also 2:512-62. 4. See 3:597-99, 608-9; 5:388-89. 5. The naturalization law in effect at this time was that of May 24, 1828, which specified that "a free white person" who had been a resident for five years could be naturalized. Remaining in effect was the stipulation from the 1802 law that the person to be naturalized must be of good moral character. See 4 *U.S. Stat.*, 310-11. For a comparison of naturalization laws from 1802-48, see William J. Bromwell, *History of Immigration to the United States . . .* (New York, 1855; reprint ed., New York, 1969), 189-225. For the relatively rapid growth of immigration in the period, see *ibid.*, 89-152, 174-79, and Carl Wittke, *We Who Built America, The Saga of the Immigrant* (rev. ed., Cleveland, Ohio, 1964), 101-439. For Irish immigration to the U.S., see Potter, *To the Golden Door, passim.*

Bond To John Jacob Astor, Lexington, August 17, 1843. Clay, together with Henry Clay, Jr., and James Erwin, acknowledge a collective debt to Astor in the amount of $40,000. Bond witnessed by John Morrison Clay. The condition of Clay's personal obligation to Astor of $20,000, states that "whereas the said Astor heretofore made a loan to the said Henry Clay of Ashland of the sum of Twenty thousand dollars, to be reimbursed, principal and interest, in the City of N. York, which loan, having become due on the first day of May last, the said Astor, at the instance of the said obligors, hath agreed to extend the same until the first day of May 1845: Now, if the said Henry Clay of Ashland shall well and truly pay to the said Astor the said sum of twenty thousand dollars in the City of New York, on the first day of May 1845; and, in the mean time, shall pay the interest thereon, at six per Cent. per annum, also in the City of N. York, the said interest to be paid semi annually, on the first day of November and May of each year, then this obligation is to be void, otherwise it is to run on in full force and virtue." ADS, by Clay, Henry Clay, Jr., and James Erwin. DLC-HC (DNA, M212, R6).

By May 8, 1845, interest in the amount of $2,094.16 had been paid, but only $6,500 had been paid on the $20,000 principal. On this document is written, not in Clay's hand, "Cancelled by a New Bond for $13,500 payable June 23/1847." Written across the face of this note, in Clay's hand, is the single word "Cancelled," but he gives no date. For Clay's running indebtedness to Astor, beginning in 1835, see 8:763; see also Van Deusen, *Life of Henry Clay*, 379-80, and Clay to January, October 6, 1838.

To WILLIAM B. CAMPBELL Lexington, August 19, 1843

I received your favor of the 12h. and cordially congratulate you on the auspicious result of your Election,[1] which it communicates, and of which I had heard through various friendly channels. The election in Tennessee was by far the most important of the year,[2] & its successful issue more than compensates for any partial defeats which we have sustained elsewhere. It was important as deciding the character of the U. States Senate, as being the residence of Genl. Jackson, and as rebuking the Revolutionary course of your Senate.[3] Such an event cannot fail to exert a powerful and salutary influence throughout the whole Union. I am glad that the resolution exists to have Tennessee represented in the Convention of May next;[4] and I shall be rejoiced to learn that you will be able to attend it.

I am ashamed to speak of my own State, it has done so badly.[5] We ought to have elected nine, but have elected only five members to the H. of R. And yet the State has not lost any of but has probably increased its Whig strength. We lost two members by running two Whig Candidates against one Loco. in each of two Districts. We lost two others by unfortunate and unsatisfactory Candidates With this shameful issue of the Congressional Elections, we have carried two thirds of the members of the General Assembly.

They have done very badly in Indiana, where we have lost our Governor by about two thousand of a majority & a large majority of members of Congress.[6] I have been informed, altho' reluctant to credit, that this result has been in part produced by the co-operation of some Whigs, the friends of a Judge of the Supreme Court,[7] who were desirous of reviving against me the old plea of unavailability!

On the other hand, the old North State has done nobly.[8] This year, the mother and the daughter have fairly won the prize.

We shall not have a fair canvass and a fair field until the Candidates of the respective parties are designated & announced. When that is done the contest and the comparison will be circumscribed. We have a right to count largely upon the divisions and dissentions already operating, and those which the next Session will disclose among our opponents. Looking to these, and to the inherent strength of our Cause, we have every ground of hope and confidence.

ALS. NcD. 1. That is, the Tenn. state elections, since Campbell himself was not a candidate for office. See Campbell to Clay, May 7, 1843. 2. *Ibid.* 3. Clay to Brooke, March 12, 1841. 4. The Whig national nominating convention in Baltimore. See Clay to Clayton, August 8, 1842. All 26 states sent Whig delegations to Baltimore. 5. Clay to Anderson, July 23, 1843. 6. Clay to Leigh, June 20, 1843. 7. John McLean. See Clay to Leigh, June 20, 1843. 8. Clay to Stevenson, July 19, 1843.

To ROBERT L. CARUTHERS Lexington, August 21, 1843

I duly received your favor of the 12h. and tender to you cordial congratulations on the glorious issue of your Election. Of all the elections of the current year that of Tennessee was decidedly the most important.[1] The political character of the Senate depended upon it.[2] [It] was the State of Genl. Jackson's residence. And I will add, wi[th g]reat pleasure, that, during the Canvass, our friends openly an[d b]oldly avowed their principles, and declared their preferen[ce] . . . or individuals. Considering what a powerful agency Tennessee had in the original election of Genl. Jackson, her patriotic denunciation of the policy, to which that event gave rise, cannot fail to exert a great and salutary influence throughout the Union. I feel inexpressible gratitude for the success[f]ul vindication of my name, and the generous support which was given to me.

I hope your fears, as to any difficulty in the Election of Mr. [Ephraim

H.] Foster to the Senate,[3] will not be realized. He has displayed so much zeal, activity and ability in the Canvass, that I hardly think any obstacles can be thrown in his way from the quarter to which you allude.

We have done badly in K.[4] We have lost two members of Congress by running in each of two Districts two Whig Candidates against one Loco. And we lost two others by injudicious & unsatisfactory selections of Candidates. And yet I feel perfectly sure that our strength is as great as it ever was. This is proven by the fact that we have elected two thirds of the members of the Genl Assembly, . . . an increase of the majority of last year.[5] We shall profit by this reverse hereafter. Relying on our great strength, we had no organization, which our friends are now resolved to effect for future operations.

On the other hand, the old North State has done nobly.[6] The prize of patriotic exertion this year must be awarded to the Mother and the Daughter.[7]

ALS. NcU. 1. T.J. Campbell to Clay, May 7, 1843. 2. Clay to Brooke, March 12, 1841. 3. *Ibid.* For Foster, see *BDAC*. 4. Clay to Anderson, July 23, 1843. 5. Clay to Davis, August 21, 1843. 6. Clay to Stevenson, July 19, 1843. 7. North Carolina and Tennessee.

To JOHN DAVIS Lexington, August 21, 1843

Mr. Dinimack, not being able to proceed as far West as this place, transmitted to me from Richmond [Va.] the letter which you gave him to me, and I received it yesterday. I was sorry that he could not deliver it personally as it would have afforded me pleasure to extend to him or any other friend of your's any civilities in my power.

I was very glad to hear directly from you. The newspapers will have anticipated my answer to some of your inquiries. You will have seen from them that, in Tennessee, our most fervent hopes have been realized.[1] In Indiana we have lost our Governor by about 2000 majority, and a large majority of the members of the H. of R.[2] And I am mortified to say that we have done badly in K.[3] having lost four members whose elections we ought to have carried. This was owing to their being run in each of two Districts two Whig candidates against one Loco; and in two other Districts our selection of Candidates was unfortunate and unsatisfactory to our party. Yet I feel perfectly sure that our strength is as great as it ever was. This is proven by the fact that we have elected two thirds of the members of the Genl. Assembly, an increase on the majority of last year.[4] In the District in which I reside there was an animated contest.[5] Here Col. [Richard M.] Johnson & his family live, and also the Wickliffes and the Marshalls. These defections acting in concert with the Locos' proper and the Johnsons concentrated all their exertions upon the election of young [Charles A.] Wickliffe. It was a formidable combination; but it was beaten down by a majority of near a thousand. Our representation will stand equally divided in the House, several of the members of the other party being however committed to vote for me should the election of President devolve on the H[ouse]. This is of no consequence, but I mention it as shewing one of the means which were employed to secure these elections.

I have not yet heard from the other States which held their elections this month; but in Illinois[6] and Alabama,[7] owing to the shameful manner in which those States have been Gerrymandered, I presume we shall elect only two or three members.

My opinion is, that the Whigs will carry in the Presidential election Ohio, Kentucky, Tennessee, Indiana, Mississippi, and, if I am to credit the most confident assurances, Louisiana.[8] They have also a good chance for Illinois and Missouri.[9] In this latter State the division between the friends of [Richard M.] Johnson & V. Buren, among the Locos', I am assured has prostrated Col. [Thomas H.] Benton. It is manifest that he considers himself in great peril.

I think we have much to count upon from the divisions among our opponents; and not less upon the developements of their policy at the next Session. The respective partizans of Free trade and Incidental protection must come in conflict. Altho' the doctrines of Free trade have made extraordinary progress with the other party, I presume that they are not all prepared to sustain them. The Northern friends of Mr. V. Buren, I suppose, will not all be ready to renounce the principle of protection, under the incidental form which is now contended for.

By the bye, nothing has surprized me so much as the fate of the principle of protection. Judging from the results of elections and other manifestations of public opinion, it has lost ground at the North and in N. England, and even in Massachusetts. Whilst that would seem to be the case in those quarters, incidental protection has made great and encouraging progress in the Southern & South Western States. In No. Carolina, in Georgia, in Virginia & in Tennessee that principle has been boldly proclaimed by State Conventions and other organs of public sentiment. In Tennessee on the stump, in the press, on all public occasions, by our friends that principle was openly avowed and boldly sustained. The canvass has been conducted, and the election won; on the ground of incidental protection, along with the other principles of the Whigs.

I have not been able to comprehend the cause of the decline in favor of that principle in your State especially and should be glad to meet with a satisfactory solution of it.

I have known and appreciated all your difficulties in Massachusetts, and am rejoiced to hear from you that "those who have sought to distract us are powerless." I who know how great has been your deference, and that of other public men of your State; and how often you have been ready to waive or decline honors which were offered to you, that honors might visit another, or at least that there might be no interference with him, can well comprehend what your feeling must be. And I sincerely hope, for our Country our Cause and for your sake, that Massachusetts will at her approaching Election,[10] break the spell by which she has been too long bound, and resume once more her proud position among the Whig States.

I am glad to find that we concur so fully as to the folly of regulating our Tariff by Commercial treaties.[11]

ALS. MWA. 1. T.J. Campbell to Clay, May 7, 1843. 2. Clay to Leigh, June 20, 1843. 3. Clay to Anderson, July 23, 1843. 4. In the 1842 state elections in Kentucky, Whigs won control of the lower house over the Democrats by a majority of 57 to 43. In the state senate, 6 Whigs were elected to 4 Democrats, giving the Whigs control over the senate by a majority of 27 to 11. *Niles' Register* (Sept. 17, 1842), 62:35. 5. In the 1843 election in Kentucky's 8th congressional district—composed of Bourbon, Fayette, Jessamine, Woodford, Scott, Franklin, and Owen counties—Whig Garrett Davis had defeated Democrat C.A. Wickliffe by 5,788 votes to 4,916. (C.A. Wickliffe was the son of Tyler's postmaster general, Charles A. Wickliffe.) *Guide to U.S. Elections*, 578. The Wickliffe's switched from the Whig to the Democratic party about this time. 6. Clay to Berrien, July 17, 1843. 7. In the 1843 elections in Alabama, Democrats won 6 congressional seats to 1 for the Whigs. *Guide to U.S. Elections*, 578. Democrats also controlled the state senate by a margin of 19 to 14 over the Whigs and the house by 62 to 38. *Niles' Register* (Sept. 2, 1843), 65:16. 8. For the 1844 presidential election results in these six states, see Clay to Berrien, March 13 and April 23, 1843; also Clay to Leigh, March 17, 1843. 9. Clay to Berrien, April 23 and July 17, 1843. 10. Clay to Berrien, July 17, 1843. 11. Clay to Clayton, May 27 and June 21, 1843.

From F.S. Bronson, La Grange, Ga., August 22, 1843. Reports that he is launching a newspaper to be called the La Grange *Herald*, that there is also a newly organized Clay Club in town "consisting of a large number of our citizens," and that he needs to know "*precisely*, in what manner I am to meet Democracy in their numerous modes of attack." Asks about Clay's view of the tariff issue at the present time and, specifically, if he would support "a bill as protective in its principles as was the Tariff Act of 1832 [8:443, 445, 455-56]." Copy. Printed in Raleigh *Register & North Carolina Gazette*, October 20, 1843. For Clay's answer to Bronson's query, which was published in the Raleigh *Register* on October 20, 1843, see Clay to Bronson, September 13, 1843.

Bronson's newspaper, launched as a weekly in 1843, subsequently became the La Grange *News*. Clifford L. Smith, *History of Troup County* (Atlanta, 1933), 143.

From Harriet Martineau, Tynemouth, England, August 23, 1843. Recommends to Clay's personal attention and kind offices "my friend Mr. Macready, known to you as our great Actor, and no less distinguished among *us* as a Scholar, a gentleman, & a great public Moralist." Regrets, however, that in America there exists an "extraordinary prejudice against the Stage, and want of taste for the Drama as even a literary portrait, by which, in my opinion, even the most enlightened part of your Community suffers so much privation. The truth is, I do sadly fear Mr. Macready not being appreciated, whereas, if he presented himself as a divine or a lawyer, or merely on the ground of his literary tastes, there would be no fear of his missing his deserts. You are one of the few to whom I look, not only to appreciate him yourself, but to introduce him advantageously." Mentions her illness, now so serious as to necessitate her use of an amanuensis. Assures Clay of her "unspeakable interest in your country and its concerns," and notes that "My American friendships are a chief solace of my life." LS. NcD. For William Charles Macready, see *DNB*.

To Messrs. Belrose, Son & Blanchard, Portsmouth, N.H., August 28, 1843. Proclaims the "perfection" of the company's brand of wallpaper, a box of which had been sent him in Lexington. Adds: "As you supposed, gentlemen, it affords me inexpressible delight to witness the progress of the arts and manufactures in our country, and the realization of hopes and opinions which I formed more than a quarter of a century ago. Believing that the prosperity of the nation greatly depends upon their continued success and advancement, I trust that nothing may occur to check their prosecution. Nations will find, just as certain as individuals, that, if they purchase abroad a greater amount in value than they sell abroad, for any considerable length of time, embarrassment and ultimate impoverishment are the inevitable consequences." Copy. Printed in Portsmouth (N.H.) *Journal of Literature and Politics*, June 8, 1844. Courtesy of Richard E. Winslow, III.

To HENRY T. LLOYD Lexington, August 29, 1843

I have duly received your friendly letter, and the box to which it refers, containing half a dozen bottles of American Cologne water, all in good order, and I tender you my warm thanks for the acceptable present, and the friendly sentiments toward me, which induced you to offer it. Mrs. Clay, who is a better judge of its quality than I am, pronounces it equal to the best German or French Cologne Water, and my opinion coincides with her's.

It was long ago remarked that any man who made a blade of grass grow, where one did not before, was a public benefactor. That citizen is an equal benefactor, by whose skill and industry an article of consumption is produced at home, and the necessity of sending abroad the money to purchase it, is avoided. To ensure the prosperity of our country, and to escape those afflicting revulsions, which are so ruinous, we must learn and practice the invaluable truth, to sell as much, and buy as little as possible, abroad. Every prudent planter and farmer acts on that principle, and what is wise in individuals, is wise in nations. I congratulate you on the perfection to which you have brought the manufacture of a very agreeable article, in extensive use, and tender you cordial wishes for your success, prosperity, and happiness.

Copy. Printed in Colton, *Clay Correspondence*, 4:475-76.

To THOMAS B. STEVENSON Lexington, August 29, 1843

I recd your favor, but I have not yet seen in the Journal the article to which you refer.[1] I am surprised that it should have excited any thing like anger in Mr [John J.] Crittenden. The use of his name in connection with the office of Governor was founded upon his great & just popularity and certainly ought to excite any other feelings than those of dissatisfaction.[2] He has only emphatically to say no, and I suppose he would not be further urged.

I sincerely hope that a good selection of a candidate may be made; but whether it be Mr Ousley [*sic*, William Owsley][3] or any other I think that a new Election of Delegates in Oct is a desirable proceeding.[4] Without prompt and general concurrence however in that course it cannot succeed.

My letters from *Eastward* continue to breathe a good spirit and great confidence. I do not think that our proverbially bad luck in Ky[5] has produced as much discouragement as we feared.

As I expect to see you next week in Frankfort I must reserve for that occasion further communications.

Copy. OCHP. 1. An editorial in the Louisville *Daily Journal* of August 25, 1843, suggested that Crittenden be brought forth as the Whig candidate for governor in 1844. The article noted, however, that it would entail a great sacrifice for him to consent to be the candidate. 2. *Ibid.* 3. In the 1844 gubernatorial election in Kentucky, William Owsley, the Whig candidate, defeated Democrat William O. Butler by 59,680 votes to 55,040. Whig Archibald Dixon was elected lieutenant governor. *BDGUS*, 2:519; Lexington (Ky.) *Observer & Reporter*, August 28, 1844. Whigs won 19 of the 32 seats up for election in the state house of representatives, while the Democrats won 13, giving the Whigs a total of 64 seats, the Democrats 35, and 1 neutral. In the state senate, Whigs won 7 seats to 2 for the Democrats, giving the Whigs an overall majority in the senate of 26 to 12. Lexington *Observer & Reporter*, August 14, 17, 1844; Louisville *Morning Courier*, August 28, 1844. 4. The Whig state convention was held in Louisville on Nov. 13, 1843.

It nominated William Owsley and Archibald Dixon for governor and lieutenant governor, appointed electors for president and vice president, and chose delegates to the Whig national convention [Clay to Clayton, August 8, 1842]. The convention also appointed three central committees of five members each—one in Lexington, one in Louisville, and one in Hopkinsville—to organize the Whig party for the 1844 election. *Niles' Register* (Nov. 25, 1843), 65:199; Frankfort *Commonwealth*, Nov. 21, 1843. 5. Clay to Anderson, July 23, 1843.

To CALVIN COLTON Lexington, September 2, 1843

Allow me to suggest a subject for one of your Tracts which, treated in your popular and condensed way, I think would be attended with great and good effect, I mean Abolition.[1]

It is manifest that the ultras of that party are extremely mischievous, and are hurrying on the country to fearful consequences. They are not to be conciliated by the Whigs. Engrossed with a single idea, they care for nothing else. They would see the administration of the Government precipitate the nation into absolute ruin before they would lend a helping hand to arrest its career. They treat worse and denounce most those who treat them best, who so far agree with them as to admit slavery to be an evil. Witness their conduct toward Mr. Briggs and Mr. Adams, in Massachusetts,[2] and toward me.

I will give you an outline of the manner in which I would handle it. Show the origin of slavery. Trace its introduction to the British Government. Show how it is disposed of by the Federal Constitution. That it is left exclusively to the States, except in regard to fugitives, direct taxes and representation. Show that the agitation of the question in the free States, will first destroy all harmony, and finally lead to disunion. That the consequences of disunion—perpetual war—the extinction of the African race—ultimate military despotism.

But the great aim and object of your Tract should be to arouse the laboring classes in the free States against Abolition. Depict the consequences to them of immediate abolition. The slaves being free, would be dispersed throughout the Union; they would enter into competition with the free laborer; with the American, the Irish, the German; reduce his wages; be confounded with him, and affect his moral and social standing. And as the ultras go for both abolition and amalgamation, show that their object is to unite, in marriage, the laboring white man, and the laboring black man, and to reduce the white laboring man to the despised and degraded condition of the black man.

I would show their opposition to colonization. Show its humane, religious and patriotic aim. That they are to separate those whom God has separated. Why do the Abolitionists oppose colonization? To keep and amalgamate together the two races, in violation of God's will, and to keep the blacks here, that they may interfere with, degrade, and debase the laboring whites. Show that the British nation is co-operating with the Abolitionists, for the purpose of dissolving the Union, the World's Convention, etc.

You can make a powerful article that will be felt in every extremity of the Union.

I am perfectly satisfied it will do great good.

Let me hear from you on this subject.

Copy. Printed in Colton, *Clay Correspondence*, 4:476-77. 1. Colton produced *Political Abolition by Junius* (New York, 1844, 16 pages) in the Junius tracts no. 5, Nov., 1843. 2. The Liberty party in Massachusetts fielded candidates in 1843 against both John Q. Adams, who was up for reelection to Congress, and George N. Briggs, who was running for governor, although both men were known to oppose slavery. The Liberty party candidate for governor garnered enough votes to prevent a majority, thus throwing the election to the state legislature [Clay to Berrien, July 17, 1843]. Adams defeated his Democratic opponent, Isaac H. Wright, by 8,089 votes to 5,340 with Liberty party candidate Appleton Howe winning 733 votes. *Guide to U.S. Elections*, 581. For Briggs, see 5:945, *BDAC*, and *DAB*. See also Clay to Bacon, Oct. 27, 1843.

To NATHAN SARGENT Lexington, September 2, 1843

I recd. to day your favor of the 26h. Ulto. I wish you would ask Mr. [Josiah] Randall to shew you a letter I wrote to him, suggesting a plan of organization. Our friend Jonathan Roberts used to be a capital worker. I think if you, he, Mr. Badger[1] & Mr. Randall would go to work together you might put Pennsa. in a state of complete organization. Wherever the plan has been put into operation its effects have been wonderful. I have known the minority in a County to carry the election.

I am not surprized at your mortification by having imputed to you the epithet old politician. If I had yielded to similar feelings, I should a thousand times have abandoned politics for ever. But we must recollect that it is *our Country* that we have to serve, and that it is our duty to serve it, altho' treated unjustly.

Your account of prospects in Pennsa. is quite encouraging. If our friends, the Whigs & Anti Masons, can carry the Legislature at the ensuing election,[2] the whole Nation will resound with joy. I am very glad that our friend Mr. Cooper consents to run for Adams.[3] He is among the cleverest men that I have ever known in Congress.

Mr. Geo. W. Miller[4] writes me a very friendly letter full of kind feeling and sentiment. He tells me you know him. Do me the favor to express to him my thanks for his letter, and make my respects also to Mr. Christopher.[5]

ALS. ViU. Addressed to Sargent in Philadelphia. 1. Probably William Badger, a Philadelphia lawyer. See 8:30-31. 2. Clay to Stevenson, July 19, 1843. 3. Reference is probably to James Cooper, a Whig from Gettysburg who served in the U.S. House in the 26 and 27th Congresses and who was elected to the Pennsylvania house of representatives in 1843 from Adams County. He was reelected in 1844, 1846, and 1848 and served in the U.S. Senate from 1849-55. *BDAC*. 4. Miller served in the Pennsylvania general assembly in 1858 and 1860. Information supplied by Henry E. Brown, associate archivist, Pennsylvania Division of Archives & Manuscripts, Harrisburg, Pa. 5. Christopher has not been identified.

To JOHN M. BERRIEN Lexington, September 4, 1843

I sympathise with you in your suffering under the Tyler Grippe. I too have had it, and I found it as mean & insidious as its detestable name implies.

You have sketched for me a route, in my Southern trip, very kindly, and I suppose a very good one, if I proceed, as I expect to do, from Mobile. I am alarmed at the receptions &c of which you speak. I can perform it all, if I am not forced to make public Speeches. I never had any taste for them, intellectually, and they are physically very prostrating. I hope to escape them.

The elections of the summer have not all gone as well as we could have wished. We lost Indiana by only 2000 votes, however, and from local causes, and possibly unfair means.[1] I am told that a clique was formed last winter at Indianapolis for Judge [John] McLean,[2] and that they worked against us, to lay the foundation of an argument of unavailability against me. I do not vouch for this information but I have received it. The Judge himself speaks outright & well.

Illinois was against us in 1840. I am assured that wherever a contest was made we reduced their majorities of that year. The number elected to the H. of R. is the result of Gerrymandering; and our friends in that State are far from being discouraged.[3]

We did badly in K. in the Congressional Elections, whilst we increased our majority in the Legislature.[4] Our loss is attributable to our great strength, which led to too much confidence, no general organization, and, what was worse than all, running too many Candidates. In this District, where are concentrated all the influences of Col. [Richard M.] Johnson & his numerous connection, of the Wickliffe defection[5] and that of the Marshalls, the Whigs fought manfully and achieved a brilliant victory.

But No. Carolina and Tennessee—the mother & the daughter—have won the prize of the year.[6] Considering that in this latter State Jackson resides, that he has been beaten & his policy repudiated in the State at large, and in the County & in the precinct in which he dwells; and considering also as another fruit of the victory that the Whig ascendancy in the Senate has been preserved,[7] we cannot too highly appreciate the victory.

You ask who will be the nominee of the Locofoco Convention? I think Mr. V. Buren. He may not at first, probably will not, have a majority, but he will have a plurality. And then they will settle down upon him because, if put aside, they could not agree upon another.[8] Passion too, very often, decides the course of parties. And as they were beaten with him, they will wish now to triumph with him.

I received & perused with much interest the Address to the people of Georgia.[9] What a monstrous picture of mal-administration it displays!

I read too with great pleasure Mrs. B[errien]s. song. Present her my respects and thanks. Tell her that the Muses have been kind to her on the occasion of her first wooing them, and considering that she had selected a bad subject.

My respects also to Col. [James] Hunter,[10] whose letter I have recd. and will hereafter acknowledge.

ALS. NcU. 1. Clay to Leigh, June 20, 1843. 2. *Ibid.* 3. For the 1843 Illinois elections, see Clay to Berrien, July 17, 1843. For the 1844 presidential election in Illinois, see Clay to Berrien, April 23, 1843. 4. Clay to Anderson, July 23, 1843. 5. Clay to Davis, August 21, 1843. 6. Campbell to Clay, May 7, 1843; Clay to Stevenson, July 19, 1843. 7. Clay to Brooke, March 12, 1841. 8. The total number of votes at the Democratic national convention in early May, 1844 [Clay to Clayton, August 8, 1842] was 266, with 178 needed to secure the presidential nomination. Van Buren's vote on the first eight ballots was, successively, 146, 127, 121, 111, 103, 101, 99, 104; that of Lewis Cass was 83, 94, 92, 105, 107, 116, 123, 114; the Richard M. Johnson vote was 24, 33, 38, 32, 29, 23, 21, 0; James Buchanan polled 4, 9, 11, 17, 26, 25, 22, 0. Polk received no votes on the first seven ballots, got 44 on the eighth ballot, and all 266 on the ninth. McKee, *National . . . Popular and Electoral Vote*, 47. 9. Clay to Berrien, July 17, 1843. 10. For Hunter, Berrien's father-in-law, see Clay to Berrien, April 23, 1843.

From Alfred Beckley *et al.* (Clay Club of Fayette County, Virginia), September 8, 1843. Express their "profound mortification at the unparalleled treachery of the acting President." Also invite Clay to visit their congressional district, the 14th in western Virginia, on his way to or from North Carolina. State that "they see not why, from their mountain peaks, they should not raise the rallying cry to the Whig forces scattered, but not defeated; and that cry will be HENRY CLAY of Kentucky *to the rescue*! who will at the call of his countrymen sacrifice that long coveted but briefly enjoyed repose of Ashland, and step forth to carry out the great principles he has ever advocated with a oneness of motive, a lofty persuasive eloquence, and a manly intrepid frankness that challenges, and has met the admiration of his country!" Copy, excerpt. Printed in Raleigh *Register and North Carolina Gazette,* November 10, 1843. For Clay's response, see Clay to Beckley, September 25, 1843.

To MATTHEW L. DAVIS Lexington, September 12, 1843

I received with pleasure your favor of Ulto.[1] and was happy to learn from it that your health continued good. We all had great fears about it. As to your fidelity to your political principles, I never doubted. We have much to hope from the future. Considering the extraordinary unanimity among the Whigs, both as to measures and their Candidate, and that the condition of their opponents is directly the reverse, there being no agreement among them, either as to measures or men, I do not see how we can fail. But nous verrons.

I regret the difference among our friends in N.Y. on the point of making battle this fall, and I am unable to advise them. All that I would say is that defeat will have a bad effect, whether with or without a fight; worse however with than without one.[2] In the general I think it is best to contend all along, and never suffer these judgments by default, as you call them. If you submit to repeated defeats, the danger is that they become habitual, and you can't bring your forces into the field, when you want to fight a general battle. The exterior discouragement too is to be deprecated. Whereas, if you constantly fight, if you are always harnessed, you are ever ready to move.

There is a state of things in the City which may require much discretion. If the V.B. and Calhoun parties should each run a ticket, the question would be, whether the Whigs might not, by their divisions, elect their own ticket.[3] If that should be improbable, then the Whigs ought to decide which of the two other tickets is best for them to support. May not the exasperation be such between them, that either would prefer the Whigs to the other? All these are matters requiring a degree of local information which I do not possess.

We did badly in K. at our late election; but it was owing to causes implying no diminution of Whig strength.[4] Next year we will give our majority of 1840.[5]

I am glad that the Revenue is improving; but I hope it will not exceed the wants of the Treasury.

ALS. PHi. 1. Date not given in manuscript. 2. Clay to W.B. Campbell, July 21, 1843. 3. The Van Buren and Calhoun parties did not field separate tickets. The Democrats, Whigs, and Native American parties all presented tickets in the state legislative election in New York City. Twelve Democrats and one Whig were elected to the state assembly. The Democrats also won the New York City seat in the state senate, but only by a 29 vote margin. The Native American party polled 8,265 votes in the city. *Niles' Register* (Nov. 11 and 18, 1843), 65:176, 192. 4. Clay to Anderson, July 23, 1843. 5. Clay to Hodge, August 10, 1843.

To F.S. BRONSON Lexington, September 13, 1843

I received your favor, addressing some inquiries to me[1] in respect to the policy of protecting American interests. On that subject I have very frequently publicly expressed my sentiments, within the last two years. In the Senate of the United States, early last year, I fully expressed my views, and what I said was published.[2] About the same time, I communicated them in the answer which I transmitted to a letter, addressed to me, by a Committee of the Legislature of New York, which was also published.[3] I again expressed my opinion, in reply to a letter which I received from a fellow citizen of Philadelphia, requesting me to state the principles of the Whig party.[4] A statement of them as understood by me, was accordingly made, and it is now conspicuously published at the head of many newspapers. The last expression of my opinion is contained in a letter which I recently addressed to Nashville, and of which I now transmit you a copy.[5] If you had seen these various expressions of the opinions which I hold on the subject of your letter, I presume you would not have deemed it necessary to address me.

The sum and substance of what I conceive to be the true policy of the United States, in respect to a Tariff, may be briefly stated. In conformity with the principle announced in the compromise act,[6] I think, that whatever revenue is necessary to an economical and honest administration of the General Government, ought to be derived from duties, imposed on Foreign imports. And I believe that, in establishing a Tariff of those duties, such a discrimination ought to be made, as will incidentally afford reasonable protection to our national interests.

I think there is no danger of a high tariff being ever established; that of 1828[7] was eminently deserving that denomination. I was not in Congress when it passed, and did not vote for it: but, with its history, and with the circumstances which gave birth to it, I am well acquainted. They were highly discreditable to American legislation, and I hope for its honor, will never be again repeated.

After my return to Congress in 1831, my efforts were directed to the modification and reduction of the rates of duty contained in the act of 1828. The act of 1832[8] greatly reduced and modified them; and the act of 1833, commonly called the compromise act, still further reduced and modified them. The act which passed at the Extra Session of 1841, which I supported, was confined to the free articles.[9] I had resigned my seat in the Senate when the act of 1842 passed.[10] Generally, the duties which it imposes, are lower than those in the act of 1832.—And without intending to express any opinion upon every item of this last tariff, I would say, that I think the provisions, in the main, are wise and proper. If there be any excesses or defects in it, (of which I have not the means of judging) they ought to be corrected.

My opinion, that there is no danger hereafter of a High Tariff, is founded on the gratifying fact, that our manufactures have now taken a deep root. In their infancy, they needed a greater measure of protection; but, as they grow and advance, they acquire strength and stability, and, consequently, will require less protection. Even now, some branches of them are able to maintain, in distant markets, successful competition with rival foreign manufactures.

Hoping that this letter may be satisfactory to you, and afford all the information you desire, and tendering my grateful acknowledgements for the friendly feelings and sentiments entertained by you towards me. . . .

Copy. Printed in Raleigh *Register and North Carolina Gazette*, Oct. 20, 1843; also in Knoxville *Register*, Nov. 1, 1843. 1. Bronson to Clay, August 22, 1843. 2. Speech in Senate, March 1, 1842. 3. Clay to Bradish, April 15, 1842. 4. Reference obscure. 5. Possibly, Clay to Cameron & Fall, August, 1843. 6. See 8:604, 619-22, 626-27. 7. See subject index entries on the so-call "Tariff of Abominations" of 1828 in 7:660. For Clay's view of it at the time see, especially, 7:449-51. 8. See 8:443, 445, 455-56. 9. Clay to Ewing, April 30, 1841; Remark in Senate, July 16, 1841. 10. Clay to Letcher, Jan. 6 and June 24, 1842; Remark in Senate, Feb. 3, 1842.

To PETER B. PORTER Lexington, September 17, 1843

It is very true, as mentioned in your favor of the 6h. inst., that it is a long time since I received a letter from you or addressed one to you; but I have occasionally had the satisfaction of hearing of you. I should have written you if I had any thing interesting to communicate. Our election in K. owing to running too many Whig Candidates &c &c. turned out badly; but there is no diminution of our strength, and next year we shall give as large a majority as in 1840.[1] The young Duke [C.A. Wickliffe] was beaten handsomely; and, what do you think? both he and his father [Charles A. Wickliffe] have since openly joined the Loco's![2]

I concur with you in thinking that Mr. V. Buren is the strongest of the Candidates of the other party, and I have always supposed that he will obtain the nomination.[3] I hope that the opinion so often expressed by my N. York friends will be found, in the sequel, to be correct, that is that it is easier to beat him *in N. York* than any other of the Locofoco Candidates. But it strikes us strange, at a distance, that you will make no general battle this fall.[4] Is there not danger that you will be so habituated to defeat, that you will be unable to triumph when you attempt it?

I am surprized that Genl. [Lewis] Cass should have ever been thought formidable. I am sure that opinion was confined to New York. I am equally surprized that it should have been seriously believed by any one that we could get the votes of the Ultra abolitionists. I have always believed that they would only vote for an abolitionist; and that is now manifest.[5]

My information from Massachusetts corresponds with yours, that Mr. Webster is now powerless. John Davis writes me to that effect.[6]

I have heard very lately of Judge [John] McLean. He is open and unreserved in my support; but I believe that he & some of his friends indulge the hope that I will decline the nomination. If I should not, I think they will cordially sustain it. By the bye, I suppose he has given a mortal offense to the abolitionists by a late judicial decision.[7]

I am committed to a visit next Spring to No. Carolina. I purpose passing the winter at the South & proceeding from N. Orleans, via Mobile and Georgia to No. Carolina. I do not expect to go to the North, but to return home through Washington City.

I was greatly grieved by the condition of our friend [Willis] Hall, and I fear, from the nature of his attack, that we can not expect his complete recovery.[8]

I observed you announced in the City; but I address this letter to you at your residence.[9]

ALS. NBuHi. 1. For the 1843 Kentucky elections, see Clay to Anderson, July 23, 1843; for the 1844 Kentucky presidential vote, see Clay to Leigh, March 17, 1843. 2. Clay to Davis, August 21, 1843. 3. Clay to Berrien, Sept. 4, 1843. 4. The Whigs did field candidates in the 1843 New York state elections. See Clay to Campbell, July 21, 1843. 5. On August 30, 1843, the Liberty party, which sought to attract abolitionists of various hues, had nominated James G. Birney of N.Y. (formerly of Ky.) for president and Thomas Morris of Ohio for vice president at its convention in Buffalo. At this convention were 148 delegates representing 12 states. McKee, *National . . . Popular and Electoral Vote*, 51-55. Fladeland, *James G. Birney*, 225-26, 246. Birney polled 15,812 votes in New York in the November 1844 election. This, according to some historians, caused Polk to carry New York's 36 electoral votes and Clay to lose the election. 6. Clay to Davis, August 21, 1843. 7. In April, 1843, John Van Zandt had met nine Negroes on a road outside Cincinnati and had allowed them to ride in his wagon. Seven of these blacks had escaped from Kentucky. During the journey they were seized and taken back across the Ohio River. Wharton Jones of Kentucky then sued Van Zandt for damages resulting from his "harboring and concealing a slave." This case was heard by McLean in the U.S. Circuit Court of Ohio where Van Zandt was ordered to pay Wharton $1,200. This decision was later upheld by the U.S. Supreme Court. See Weisenburger, *John McLean*, 192-93, which erroneously dates the case as 1842. See also Washington *Daily National Intelligencer*, July 24, 1843. 8. For Hall (1801-68), at this time a member of the New York general assembly, see *CAB*. 9. As was the custom, Porter had announced in a local newspaper his arrival in the city (from his upstate residence in Black Rock, Erie County) for a visit.

To NATHAN SARGENT Lexington, September 19, 1843

Your favor of the 10h. is received. Your dream was not altogether unfounded. I have been slightly indisposed but I am nearly recovered. I am ashamed to say it was with the Tyler Grippe.

Your account of prospects in Pennsa. is truly encouraging.[1] I fervently hope they may be realized. I should be delighted to hear of your Election,[2] and that of the injured Mr Badger.[3]

We shall think about a Comee. at Frankfort, here or Louisville. Those at Nashville and Cincinnati were, however, I think not very advantageous to Jackson & Harrison. We have a Convention in November, which can easily appoint a suitable Comee.[4] But I expect to be absent from home from Decr. until May. Business will take me again to N. Orleans, from whence I shall proceed via Mobile to Georgia and N. Carolina. I do not wish this however to get into the News papers.

ALS. ViU. 1. See Sargent to Clay, August 6, 1842, for the 1844 presidential election results in Pennsylvania; for the 1843 state election, see Clay to Stevenson, July 19, 1843. 2. Sargent was defeated in his bid for a seat in Congress from Pennsylvania's 3rd district. He received 3,162 votes to 3,997 for Democrat John T. Smith. Philadelphia *United States Gazette*, Oct. 16, 1843. 3. Probably William Badger. See Clay to Sargent, Sept. 2, 1843. 4. For the Ky. Whig convention, see Clay to Stevenson, August 29, 1843.

To John Quincy Adams, Quincy, Mass., September 21, 1843. Has learned that Adams has consented to visit Cincinnati in the fall. Invites him and his wife to visit "Ashland" while he is west of the mountains. Adds: "The route I would suggest is, to proceed, by the Ohio river, from Cincinnati to Louisville, thence to Frankfort, at your option, by land or by the Kentucky river, thence to Lexington, and from here to Maysville on the Ohio river. The whole route is made on Steam boats, a Rail road, and the best McAdamized roads. At Maysville, you will have the choice of ascending the Ohio river, or passing through the State of Ohio by land." ALS. MHi.

Adams replied on October 17 that Mrs. Adams's health would not permit her to accompany him to Cincinnati and that his "own age and infirmities have admonished me that the engagement which I have contracted is at least as much as I can expect to perform with impunity." ALS. DLC-HC (DNA, M212, R5).

Adams arrived in Cincinnati on November 8, 1843, visited Covington, Ky., on November 13 and stopped in Maysville on November 14. Adams, *Memoirs of John Quincy Adams*, 11:423-31.

To JOHN M. BERRIEN Lexington, September 22, 1843

I have received your favor, of the 12h. inst. and share with you in the gratification of your triumph in Savannah.[1] I hope it may prove the prelude to your success in Georgia next month.[2]

I have attentively perused the Whig Address to the People of Ga. prepared by you.[3] It is temperate, able, and with candid men ought to be conclusive. It has the merit also of great perspicuity, in the division and treatment of its topics. As President of the Colonization Society, I only protest against the classification of that institution with "any other bubble".

Every days developement makes more manifest that Mr. V. Buren is to be the Candidate of our opponents. It is now possible that Mr. Calhoun may get up another Convention, organized on the District plan,[4] and that we may have two Democratic Candidates. In such a course I think we have nothing to apprehend.

Col. [Richard M.] Johnson has left us on a political tour to the East and North. *He expects* V. B. to be nominated, and the belief in K. is that he will consent to be placed in his old position as a Candidate for V.P.[5] He is extremely needy & has an insatiable thirst for office.

It so happened that the very morning I received your letter, communicating the opinion of your N. Y. correspondent that, in the event of Mr. V. Bs. nomination, the Irish in that State would go against him. I received a similar assurance from an Irish lecturer of some note now in Lexington.[6]

ALS. NcU. 1. The Savannah municipal election for aldermen had been held on Sept. 4, 1843. Whigs had won 11 seats to 3 for the Democrats. Raleigh *Register and North Carolina Gazette*, Sept. 15, 1843. 2. Clay to Stevenson, July 19, 1843. 3. Clay to Berrien, July 17, 1843. 4. No separate Calhoun convention was held. For the various strategies used during the spring and summer of 1843 in an attempt to secure Calhoun's nomination for president, see Wiltse, *John C. Calhoun: Sectionalist*, 134-49. Calhoun withdrew from the race on Dec. 21, 1843, and his reasons for doing so were published in the Charleston *Mercury* on Jan. 27, 1844. 5. Clay to Berrien, Sept. 4, 1843. 6. Editors have found no evidence in extant newspapers of the period concerning the visit of an Irish lecturer to Lexington.

To Alfred Beckley *et al.*, Lexington, September 25, 1843. Declines with regret their invitation of September 8 to visit "the Mountain Region of Kanawha" in western Virginia during his southern tour next year. Explains that the geography of his planned route does not permit such a visit.

Clay agrees with them, however, in their assessment of the "treachery" of John Tyler which they mentioned in their letter of invitation. Indeed, the "treachery . . . of the acting President . . . is mortifying to us as Americans." Further,

"Considering the youth of our Republic, and the virtuous and illustrious men who have filled the office of Chief Magistrate of the Union, it is painful, in the extreme, to behold such an example of utter abandonment of all the obligations of honor, of duty and of fidelity. But, far from allowing that degrading fact to throw us into a state of apathy and despondency, it ought to stimulate every American freeman to redouble his energies, in rescuing his Government from the impure hands into which it has accidentally fallen. Against Mr. Tyler no exertion is necessary. He will soon retire with the contempt and amidst the scoffs of all honorable men. Our efforts should be directed against those who first seduced and then profited by him; those who, after having won him to their uses, now affect to shrink from the contaminating association; those who, after his complete identification with them, and at the moment when he is appropriating to their exclusive advantage the whole patronage of the Government, unjustly upbraid us with the failure of measures, the adoption of which was prevented by his perfidy and their countenance and support of him." Moreover, Whigs cannot rest "until the Government is purified and once more confided to honest and faithful hands." ALS. PHi.

To J.H. CLAY MUDD Lexington, September 25, 1843

I received your favor transmitting a number[1] of the Lee County [Iowa] Democrat, containing a copy of what purports to be a speech of mine delivered on the preemption bill, in the Senate, on the 29th of January, 1838. It is a gross caricature of what I said, and I so pronounced it in the Senate. I regret that I have no copy of the correction by me, but it was published at the time in the National Intelligencer.[2]

I was opposed to the pre-emption policy by itself. I believed it fraught with injustice to the public, that it occasioned great irregularity in the settlement of the public lands, and engendered controversy and dispute among the settlers. When, without the authority of law, the public lands were settled, I considered and treated such settlements as trespasses on the public property. So did President Van Buren in his message to Congress.[3] But I never used the epithets, which were put into my mouth, against the pre-emptioners themselves, many of whom I knew to be respectable and my friends. I was willing, on a general adjustment of the land question, to combine the pre-emption and distribution principles together. And accordingly you will find in the Senate's Journal of 1840, 1841, (page 155-6) that I voted for such a combination. Again: I voted for the distribution bill of the extra session of 1841, in which the pre-emption principle is incorporated, and large and liberal grants of land are made to the new States. . . .[4]

Copy. Printed in Knoxville *Register*, May 8, 1844. 1. This letter was printed by the editors of the Knoxville *Register* to counter charges in the "Locofoco press" that Clay's characterization of settlers on the public land as "land pirates and squatters" revealed his basic "hostility to the West." Mudd was a resident of Burlington, Iowa. 2. It was, in fact, Clay's speech of Jan. 27, rather than the 29th, which had been printed in the Washington *Daily National Intelligencer* on Feb. 5, 1838, and corrected on Feb. 7, 1838. Clay had not used the phrase "land pirates and squatters," as charged by Democrats, in his Jan. 27 speech attacking abuses in the preemption and distribution of the public lands; however, he did refer in that speech to "armed intruders," "grasping speculators," and a "lawless body of armed men" in describing the squatter problem. For other pungent language, characterizing the squatters, see Comment in Senate, Dec. 16, 1837, and Jan. 26, 27, and 29, 1838; Remark in Senate, Jan. 9, 1839. Clay's charge that the Democrats misquoted his remarks about the squatters for political gain is detailed in Clay to Estes, June 1, 1839. 3. Annual Message of Dec. 5, 1837, *MPP*, 3:388-89. Van Buren employed the words "encroachment" and "intrusion(s)," rather than "trespass." See also Clay to

Estes, June 1, 1839, footnote 1. 4. Clay to Ewing, April 30, 1841; Remark in Senate, June 9, 1841; also Clay to Estes, June 1, 1839, footnote 1.

From Peter B. Porter, City Hotel, New York City, September 25, 1843. Reports that he has learned from "a confidential friend of Mr. Webster," since arriving in New York, that Webster has given up his quest for the Whig nomination and has also abandoned his efforts to defeat Clay's nomination by "interposing the name of McLean, Calhoun, or some other Candidate." He has "come to the conclusion that his best, and only remaining course will be, to re unite with the Whig Party, effect a reconciliation with you, and [secure] a nomination as vice President, on the same ticket with you as president—provided your friends will consent to receive him in that capacity—and with a further understanding also, that the proposition for this arrangement shall come from your friends to his—and they have gone so far as to name Judge Burnett [*sic*, Jacob Burnet] of Ohio, & myself as the two friends by whom it shall be made." Says he told his informer that "it was the height of folly & absurdity to suppose that either you or your friends would ever commit such an act of degradation as to come forward and ask a reconciliation or any future concert of action with him—Altho' there was every reason to believe that a proposition of this kind from him or his friends, to you or your friends, might be favourably regarded if accompanied with proper explanations." States that he also informed Webster's friend that the Whig nominating convention will choose the party's vice presidential nominee, and that Clay is expected to honor its selection. Concludes with the observation that he will remain in New York ten or twelve days "during which time some efforts will be made to arrest the jealousies & petty quarrels that now exist among the leaders of the Whig Press in this City, & place it in a better condition to meet the approaching elections." ALS. DLC-John J. Crittenden Papers (DNA, M212, R20).

A number of Daniel Webster's friends such as James Watson Webb, Nicholas Biddle, and Hiram Ketchum, conceding that Clay would win the Whig presidential nomination in 1844, began in 1843 to promote Webster as Clay's vice presidential running mate. Neither Webster nor Clay seem to have favored or encouraged such a move, although by the fall of 1843 Webster was indeed beginning his return to the mainstream of the Whig party. Moser, *Papers of Daniel Webster, Correspondence*, 5:315-17, 321-23; Fuess, *Daniel Webster*, 2:136-46; Baxter, *Daniel Webster*, 368-71.

For the quarrels between the Whig editors and Clay's attitude, see Clay to Webb, November 8, 1843.

To EPES SARGENT Lexington, September 26, 1843

I duly recd. your favor of the 20h. Ulto. and the paper containing your Biography of me.[1] I am very well satisfied with it, and do not know that I can make any suggestions that would improve it; but if I had any, I could not make them on the margin of the paper you sent, in consequence of its blotching so much. There is now and then a trifling error in grammar, which your own eye will readily detect.

Lively anecdotes relieve very much the tediousness of this species of composition, and I will relate one which, if you think it worth while, you may interweave in your story: Whilst Mr. Van Buren was V. President, I dined with him, in company with the Heads of Department, the Judges of the Supreme Court, and some of the Foreign ministers. Mr. V. Buren, Mr. Forsythe [*sic*, John Forsyth] (who was present) and I had been abroad. The conversation turned upon the treatment of the U. States, by the Governments of Great Britain and France. We all agreed that they fared better with Tory Ministries in England and France than Whig ministries. The reason we supposed to be, that the Tories, who were not apprehensive of the imputation of favoring Republican institutions, were more inclined to do us justice than the Whigs, who were fearful of that imputation. After that point was settled, I turned rather suddenly to Mr. V. Buren, and remarked that, with his permission, I would give a toast. With great pleasure, he replied, and asked the Gentlemen to fill their glasses. I proposed, Tory Ministries in England and France and a *Whig ministry* in the U. States. It occasioned a hearty laugh at the table, with evident confusion on the part of the V. President, who had no tact in warding off a sally or joke.

The course of Mr. Webster has ceased to surprize or afflict me. On his own account, I regret it, as I always regret that any great man (for such he is in some respects) should be wanting in self respect and dignity. I presume, from what I hear from Massachusetts, that even there he has become powerless. His treatment of you, as described in your letter, was mean and contemptible.

The policy of not holding a State Convention of the Whigs this fall in N. York seems to be definitively settled.[2] Those can judge of its wisdom best who possess more local information than I do. I hope it may turn out well. For myself, I am for fighting, always, eternally, until we are rid of the alliance of Locofocoism and Tylerism.

Poor Willis Hall! How much have I been afflicted by the serious attack which he has experienced. He is a man of truth honor and fidelity, and I hope God will yet spare him to us.

The aspect and the progress of our cause are highly encouraging. With right on our side, agreement as to measures and union as to men; with wrong on the other side, disagreement as to measures, and discord as to men, I do not see how we can fail to achieve a glorious triumph. Of that there appears to be an abiding confidence, among the Whigs, in all parts of the Union, amounting to a sort of political faith. If they will only super add good works, the Nation will be saved.

ALS. MCM. 1. Clay to Epes Sargent, Sept. 13, 1842. 2. There was no Whig state convention held in New York in 1843.

Speech at the Bourbon County (Ky.) Agricultural Fair, *ca.* September 28, 1843. Having been presented with a pair of wool blankets made by Mrs. James Hutchcraft of Bourbon County, Clay expresses his "peculiar gratification" at seeing the "excellent and tasteful articles" of home manufacture which are exhibited at the fair. Adds: "You are in the right course—dismiss your merchants—supply your own family; for, with such fabrics as have been spread out to our view to-day, we need no merchants but our own fair countrywomen. . . . This is a proper occasion for declaring the great American maxim that it is both our interest and our duty to make as much *at home* as we can, and to buy as little as possible abroad. The family or nation that acts upon this principle will never become bankrupt." Expounds on the similarity between nations and families, saying that "a nation is no more than a large collection of families." Continues: "That man or nation is not free or independent that is always in debt, or that lives mainly upon the labor of others. To make ourselves, to make the American nation, independent, we must furnish our own necessaries, our own comforts, our own luxuries, principally. And why can we not, why should we not do it? . . . Let us foster and uphold our own industry, and it will enrich individuals and the nation; but neglect that, and prefer the labor of foreigners, and both individually and nationally we become poor." Concludes with the hope that, "if spared in health," he will be at the next and "many succeeding Fairs." Copy. Printed in Washington *Daily National Intelligencer*, October 18, 1843.

To JAMES A. MERIWETHER Lexington, October 2, 1843

You are right, so far as the record is concerned, in your statement that I did not vote for the tariffs in 1816[1] and 1824,[2] but I supported their principles, and have always admitted that I was in favor of them.

I did not vote for the tariff in 1828,[3] for which, however, Mr. Van Buren, Col. [Thomas H.] Benton, Col. [Richard M.] Johnson, Mr. [Silas] Wright, and others of our present opponents, did vote. And it is remarkable that from that period my exertions in Congress have been directed to the reduction and moderation of tariffs. Thus, in 1832 I supported that tariff[4] which greatly modified and reduced the tariff of 1828, insomuch that it was supposed by reasonable men that it would or ought to satisfy the nullifiers of South Carolina. The next year, 1833, I brought forward the compromise.[5] In 1841 I supported the tariff of that year, which was limited to the free articles.[6]

I never was in favor of what I regarded as a high tariff. And my present opinion is in perfect coincidence with that of the whole Whig party of the United States, including Georgia, as I understand it. We believe that the revenue from the General Government should be derived from the foreign imports, to the exclusion of direct taxes and the proceeds of the sales of public lands; and that no more revenue should be levied than is necessary to an economical administration of the Government; but that, in levying it, such discriminations ought to be made as will afford moderate and reasonable protection to American interests against the rival and prohibitory policy of foreign Powers.

I should have preferred that the Compromise in all its parts (including the home valuation) could have been adhered to. But you well know from what quarter the opposition came to the home valuation, without the incorporation of which in the compromise act that act never could have passed.

I think the present tariff, in the main, is right, and working much good.[7] There may be excess or defects in it of which I have not here the means to judge; and, if there be, they ought to be corrected by supplemental legislation.

Copy, extract. Printed in Washington *Daily National Intelligencer*, Nov. 30, 1843. For Meriwether, a Whig congressman from Eatonton, Ga., see *BDAC*. He had written Clay to protest the misuse by some Democrats of Clay's letter to Branham and Bledsoe of July 23, 1843, charging that they had published distorted and misleading extracts of the full letter. 1. Clay, then Speaker of the House, did not vote on the Tariff Act of 1816 which passed the House on April 8, 1816, by a vote of 88 to 54. *Annals of Congress*, 14 Cong., 1 Sess., 1352. 2. Again, as Speaker Clay did not vote when the House approved the Tariff of 1824 on May 22 by a vote of 107 to 102. *Annals of Congress*, 18 Cong., 1 Sess., 2430. See also 3:683-730. 3. See 6:876-77; 7:449-51, 660 (index entries); 8:94-95. 4. See 8:443, 445, 455-56. 5. See 8:604, 619-22, 626-27. 6. Clay to Ewing, April 30, 1841; Remark in Senate, July 16, 1841. 7. Clay to Letcher, Jan. 6 and June 24, 1842; Remark in Senate, Feb. 3, 1842.

To PETER B. PORTER Lexington, October 3, 1843

From your favor of the 25h. Ulto. received today, I presume you had not recd. a letter which I addressed to you at the Falls in answer to a previous one from you.[1] I lose no time in replying to your last.

The communication received by you from the friend of Mr. Webster is remarkable.[2] On the very 25h. Ulto. on which your letter bears date, I recd. a letter from Willis Hall at Albany of the same date, in which he says: "Webster passed through a few days since on his way to Rochester. He is for Calhoun, and may give you some trouble in New England but none in N. York. His plan is to unite New England & N. York, but it is no go."; "Give yourself no uneasiness[3] about the State of N. York—I am satisfied that it will go for you."[4]

I approve in the main of the answer you gave to Mr. Websters friend. I have done him no wrong, and therefore I have no reconciliation to seek. His course since Mr. Tyler's accession, but especially since the Extra Session, has deeply surprized me. I told him the last day of that Session "If you mean to remain in Mr. Tyler's Cabinet to finish some business not yet completed (alluding to the McLeod affair[5]) the public will justify you; but if you mean to remain there permanently it will condemn you."

I defended him when his nomination as Secy of State was before the Senate and was nigh getting into a personal affair with Mr. [Alfred] Cuthbert about it.[6]

Should I be a Candidate for the Presidency, I shall be glad to receive his support or that of any other American Citizen; but I can enter into no arrangements, make no promises, offer no pledges to obtain it. It is impossible that I can be any party to any arrangement by which Mr. Webster, or any body else, is to be run as the Candidate for V. President with me. I have declined all interference in behalf of [John] Davis, Sargeant [*sic*, John Sergeant] or [John M.] Clayton or any body else, and must continue to do so. My duty is to remain perfectly passive until the nomination is made, and after that to give to the nomination of whoever may be proposed such support as I can consistently with honor, delicacy and propriety.[7]

Mr. Webster's enmity may be somewhat prejudicial, but I believe much less so than some apprehend. I am not sure that we should not profit more by his enmity & total alienation from our party than we should be benefited by any strength which he, becoming again united to us, could bring to our cause.

Be that as it may, if he choose again to support the Whig Cause, he must take his chance with every body else, upon a full consideration of all circumstances, without any previous promises or pledges whatever, at least from me.

As to my making advances to him—as to my approaching him, whom I have never injured, and seeking with him a reconciliation, when, if there be any alienation, he has voluntarily, without cause, alienated himself, the thing is impossible, and must not be thought of much less talked of.

The proposition to refer to you and to Mr. Burnett [*sic*, Jacob Burnet] is itself a proof to me of purposes not perfectly fair. I need not say to you that I have all confidence in you and would refer any matter whatever to you; but it is otherwise with Judge Burnett. I have very little confidence in his judgment. He was mainly instrumental in supplanting me at the Harrisburg Convention;[8] and he is now the friend of Judge [John] McLean. And I have no doubt that he and Mr Webster have been earnestly laboring to push me aside, & substitute Judge McLean [for] me.[9] This desire, if yet abandoned, has been only recently abandoned.

I should think it unwise to hold out any expectations to Mr. Websters friends of his being nominated as V.P. I do not believe that there is the remotest probability of such an event, altho' I am wholly unable to say who will be nominated.

My opinion, upon the whole case presented in your letter, is that you should treat the parties with perfect politeness, and leave them to take their own course, as they may, with perfect freedom. . . .

ALS. NBuHi. Letter marked "(Confidential)." 1. Not found, but see Clay to Porter, Sept. 17, 1843. 2. Porter to Clay, Sept. 25, 1843. 3. The word "trouble" is struck through and replaced with "uneasiness." 4. Clay to W.B. Campbell, July 21, 1843. 5. Porter to Clay, Jan. 4, 1841. 6. For Clay's defense of Webster, see Remark in Senate, Feb. 22, 1841. See also Fuess, *Daniel Webster,* 2:89-90; Moser, *Papers of Daniel Webster, Correspondence,* 5:100. 7. Clay to Dearborn, July 13, 1842; Clay to Clayton, August 8, 1842. 8. Porter to Clay, Nov. 14 and Dec. 30, 1837. 9. Clay to Stevenson, July 19, 1843.

From Henry [illeg.], Philadelphia, October 5, 1843. Recalls their acquaintance 31 years ago. Congratulates Clay for recently trying to straighten out a poorly governed nation, the economy of which is recovering by the sole force of production and in spite of the acts of the central government. Opines that "Such another revolution and fall in property, may not again be witnessed in 1000 years." Asks him to make a clear statement that he will run for president in 1844. Assures him that he will be "most triumphantly elected" and that Van Buren's certain nomination by the Democrats "will be the signal for the most desperate feuds amongst the friends of the other [Democratic] candidates." Confesses that he is "very sensible that I have committed great political errors, but I intend to atone for them as much as possible, by using every exertion to restore the public honor and happiness, by electing you to the Presidency." Believes that Clay's election will bring the nation many years of prosperity and tranquility, but that "I cannot shut my eyes to the belief, that great organic changes" must occur in the present organization of the government "within 20 or 30 years." ALS. DLC-HC (DNA, M212, R5).

To JOHN L. LAWRENCE Lexington, October 5, 1843

I received your favor of the 28h. Ulto. and I had previously received a letter from Genl. P.B. Porter of a similar purport to which I promptly replied.[1] It might be well for you to confer with him. On the subject of Mr. Webster's becoming a Candidate for the V.P. on the ticket with me, I must observe that I have declined all interference on that question in behalf of Mr. [John] Davis, Mr. Sargeant [*sic,* John Sergeant], Mr. [John M.] Clayton, Mr [Nathaniel P.] Tallmadge or Mr. [John M.] Berrien, or any body else. I cannot interfere for Mr. Webster. My duty is to be perfectly passive. I shall render such support, as, with honor delicacy and propriety, I can give to whoever may be nominated by the Whig Nat. Convention.[2]

But I must further add that, in my humble opinion, before the pretensions of Mr. Webster could be properly even considered, he ought to give some public and unequivocal testimony of adherence to the Whig cause.

And in perfect candor I must say to you that, under no circumstances, in my opinion, ought Mr. Webster's name to be used as a Candidate for the V.P. What would every one of the gentlemen above mentioned think of being put aside and Mr. Webster being substituted? What would the Whig party generally think of it? What would all men of honor truth and fidelity think of it? Ask your own heart and your own feelings. You can have no better criterion.

The Whig party, and I, if I should be their Candidate, will be glad to have the support of Mr. Webster & his friends. But that support, to make it desirable and estimable, must be spontaneous and unbought. For one, I must say that I will make no promises or pledges, nor enter into any engagements to obtain it. If it be voluntarily rendered Mr. W. must take all the chances for preferment, like all other men.

Mr. Webster has doubtless some friends who may be influenced by his course and his fortunes. But, if I were to strike a balance between those whom we should *gain* or *lose*, by his accession to our cause, I am strongly inclined to believe that I should have to assign a decided preponderance to the loss.

All I write now is in strict confidence. I should have preferred that the subject had not been broached to me; but as it has been, I cannot conceal from you any opinions I entertain.

The treachery of Mr. Tyler ought to inspire the greatest caution with the Whig party. They will endeavor to avoid a similar rock. No candidate for the V.P. will add much, if any, strength to the Candidate for the first office; but a bad selection might be of great prejudice.

ALS. ViU. Letter marked "(Confidential)." 1. Porter to Clay, Sept. 25, 1843; Clay to Porter, Oct. 3, 1843. 2. Clay to Dearborn, July 13, 1842; Clay to Clayton, August 8, 1842.

From David Francis Bacon, New York City, October 7, 1843. Encloses [not found] a copy of the response of the Whigs of New York to the "insulting and outrageous" article in James Watson Webb's *Courier and Enquirer* of October 5 [*sic*, 4] supporting the nomination of Daniel Webster to the vice presidency [Porter to Clay, September 25, 1843] on Clay's presidential ticket. Says he has since "made it my sole business" to warn Whigs in the city that the nomination is "treason to our cause." Characterizes the act as a "re-concoction of the old vile [1839] Harrisburg plot coming from the same authors, [Edward] Curtis, [Moses H.] Grinnell, [Richard M.] Blatchford, [William H.] Seward and the whole of the united Webster, Scott, Seward and Harrison cliques." Identifies Curtis as the ring leader of the conspirators. States that when Webster was last in the city, a dinner was given him at the home of James G. King "to which were invited all the old Webster aristocrats, such as P[hilip] Hone, [James Watson] Webb, John A. King, and others whom I have mentioned; and there, over the wine this thing was settled by these 'Old Hunkers' of the Whig party." Speculates upon how news of this conspiracy will strike various leaders of the Whigs. What will they say "to our nomination of the man who says 'a United States Bank is an obsolete idea [Spencer to Clay, October 28, 1842],' and that our Tariff must be destroyed, and readjusted by assent of the British Parliament [Clay to Clayton, May 27, 1843], to be afterwards modified only by that assent? The coadjutor of John Tyler in his whole war on Congress and the Distribution [Clay to Letcher, January 6 and June 24, 1842], the Districting clause of the Apportionment bill [Clay to Crittenden,

June 3, 1842], and all Whig measures,—now taken back to the bosom of those whom he has thus injured. . . . What besotted folly! What delirious madness! What hideous treason!" Reports, however, that Charles King is still loyal to Clay and the Whig cause. Says he will offer resolutions in each of the four congressional district conventions that will soon meet in New York City to nominate delegates to the coming Whig convention in Baltimore. These resolutions "will pledge New York to sustain the course of the resigning Members of the Harrison Cabinet, to maintain the course of the Whig Congress on the Distribution, the District clause and *all* their measures, against John Tyler and his Cabinet, and to approve the action of the Whig Senate in rejecting his nominations. We will also resolve that a U.S. Bank is *not* 'an obsolete idea',—that the present Tariff is good enough, and that we do not want the help of the British Parliament to mend it. We shall also nominate Honest John Davis for the Vice Presidency, mainly on the ground that, in 1842, he was betrayed, opposed and sacrificed to Marcus Morton and the Massachusetts Locofocos [Clay to Silsbee, March 18, 1843], for having allowed his name to be used as Vice President under Henry Clay,—thus sacrificed by the very man who now claims to put his name in that very place under that same Presidential candidate." Says he had personally favored Millard Fillmore for vice president but that the Webster movement "has taken away from me all power of choice. The friends of Daniel Webster have made John Davis Vice President [Clay to Clayton, August 8, 1842; Clay to Dearborn, July 13, 1842]." Names a few friends of Clay in the city "who have some glimmers of sense left" and who "have labored with me unceasingly to crush this plot at its inception [Porter to Clay, September 25, 1843]." Regrets that the "organization of our great Central Whig Agency for political correspondence throughout the Union" has not been completed. Blames this on the illness of Willis Hall who has appointed him [Bacon] secretary and agent of the organization. Says he will have ample time to carry out his assigned tasks in the great Whig cause as soon as his "African book" is published. Asserts he will not accept a proffered salary for his political services. "My trade is bookmaking," a pursuit he says he will resume in January, 1845 and continue in unless and until "the demon of misrule shall rise again and call forth the recluse, the student and man of business again to such a war as we are now so soon to close in glorious victory."

Assures Clay that he need not worry about the anti-colonization dimension of his coming book. "I shall blow the whole Colonization scheme to atoms with it; but I shall not do you any hurt. It will give me the ear and the heart of all the honest Anti Slavery men to such an extent that by the same blow of the same weapon I shall also annihilate all political Abolitionism. I will show that I am entitled to be heard on that subject by all that I have seen and said and been and done and suffered. Read it, if you have time. . . ."

Explains his plan for organizing the 1844 Whig presidential campaign, viz: "In the course of this winter, I want to set in motion a system of organization throughout New York, New England,—and afterwards, on the same model, through Pennsylvania, Ohio, &c. This is to form a Whig local association, with *weekly* meetings, in each village and each School district of the State, with weekly addresses, weekly pecuniary contributions, and weekly distributions of pamphlets, documents, papers, &c. The fundamental idea is borrowed from the religious organizations of the day. The model of my primary local association is the Christian Church. The officers, the exercises, the exhortation, the singing, the weekly meetings (on *Wednesday* night,) the enrolment of members, the contributions, and all—are to be on the primitive apostolic model as nearly presented in the Congregational churches of New England. Then I want itinerant lecturers, political preachers going about in regular circuits all next spring and summer, on the Methodist plan,—changing from village to village and from county to county and from State to State, alternating with each other so as to keep each place regularly supplied with a new speaker, and thus making a small original stock of ideas *go a great ways.* The officers of each local association to be a President, Secretary, Registrar, Treasurer and Marshal,—a choir of regular singers to be also kept up. These little unit associations are to be mutally fraternized, and affiliated to County, District and State Central Associations, with regular and definite means of communication, for the concentration and diffusion of political intelligence, public and private. General County meetings or mass meetings to recur at stated times as a part of the system, monthly, quarterly &c as may seem best,—each association then appearing in emulous display of strength and zeal, marshaled and led, each by its own marshal. Each of all the hundreds of thousands of members of these associations will also make a weekly contribution of *one cent* to the great cause of our 'church militant,'—*one cent* weekly, *no more* and no less, rich and poor all to be on one level, with no invidious display of difference in means,—and each one receiving a noble equivalent in the distribution of papers. We had last fall 186.000 Whig votes in the State of New York. We have really 220.000 Whig voters. But 200.000 cents weekly will go far towards paying expenses. I am also a-going to get up a Clay button, to be brought into fashion first at Baltimore May 1, [1844] & to be worn on every Whig coat in the United States. We shall then have by the 4th of July 1.500.000 men in the Clay uniform."

Concludes with the observation that "These are great secrets with me yet. I think I may trust you with them, though [Clay to Bacon, October 27, 1843]." ALS. DLC-HC (DNA, M212, R5).

For David F. Bacon (1813-66), a New York City physician who had worked for the American Colonization Society as the principal colonial physician in Liberia, see *CAB*. Bacon's book, *Wanderings on the Seas and Shores of Africa*, was published in New York in 1843. It presented a negative view of the colonization experiment, presenting Bacon's conclusion that blacks born into slavery were not capable of self-government and that conditions in Liberia were much worse than writers had generally described them to be.

For Richard M. Blatchford (1798-1873), a New York City lawyer who had served as financial agent for the Bank of England and the B.U.S., see *DAB*.

For the complete text of Webb's article in the New York *Courier & Enquirer* advocating Clay for president and Webster for vice president, which was published the following day by Horace Greeley, see New York *Tribune*, October 5, 1843.

Ward meetings were held on October 6, 1843, to select delegates to the four congressional district conventions scheduled for October 16. The latter meetings would then choose delegates to the Whig national convention. Although Bacon's name was not mentioned in newspaper accounts, resolutions similar to those he proposed were adopted at the various ward meetings. New York *Tribune*, October 5, 7, 24, 1843; New York *Herald*, October 7, 10, 1843.

No "Central Whig Agency for political correspondence throughout the Union" was organized for the 1844 race.

To JOHN M. CLAYTON Lexington, October 10, 1843

An occasion has arisen which calls for a few words from me to you. I received a few days [ago] communications from two particular friends[1] that Mr. Webster was desirous of returning to us and running as Candidate for V. P. I promptly replied,[2] that we should be glad to receive his support &c; that I had declined to interfere in behalf of yourself, John Sargent [*sic*, Sergeant] or J[ohn]. Davis; and that I could not be expected to interfere in his favor. But I felt it to be my duty to say more, confidentially of course.

I said that the idea of running Mr. W. would be shocking to the moral sense of our friends; that I believed our gain was greater than our loss by his alienation from us; and that I was positively certain that the acquisition of himself and his friends would form no compensation for the certain losses which would accrue from putting him on our ticket. I said further that there were higher considerations than any political calculations or results opposed to his nomination—considerations founded in justice to the true and faithful men who had been constant in their devotion to our cause and to honor; and I asked what must they think of being superseded by Mr. Webster, after all that has recently occurred?

I think it right that *you* should have the views which I thus entertain.

ALS. DLC-John M. Clayton Papers (DNA, M212, R20). Letter marked "(Confidential)." 1. From Peter B. Porter, dated Sept. 25, and from John L. Lawrence, dated Sept. 28 (not found). 2. Clay to Porter, Oct. 3, 1843; Clay to Lawrence, Oct. 5, 1843.

From Peter B. Porter, New York City, October 11, 1843. Thanks Clay for his letter of October 3. Reports that Webster has recently been twice in the city, first on his return from Rochester, second on his return from Washington, and that he has just departed New York for Boston. Says Willis Hall was "right in saying to you that Mr Webster had resolved to support Calhoun [Clay to Porter, October 3, 1843]—That *was* his determination after he had given up [John] McLean—but he has now changed his course again, and the following facts, which have been confidentially communicated to me by his confidential friend, may be relied on: viz. That Mr Webster, on leaving here two days ago, assured this friend, that he should return to Massachusetts with a determination to reconcile himself to the whig party, and give it his best support—That, although there were some things in your course which he did not entirely approve, yet that he had a high respect for you and should give you his vote & support for the presidency—That, some few weeks since (probably when on his way to Rochester) he wrote [August 29, 1843] a long letter to President Tyler expostulating with him in the freest & most severe terms, upon the wickedness & folly of his late official course, and advising him to stop at once his wild career, or he would damn himself and ruin his country; asking no reply to his letter, but requesting that it might be carefully put on file, as a subject of future reference & reflection—That, in his recent visit to Washington, he dined twice with the President—once alone & in private when their whole political creed was canvassed & reviewed—and once in company with the whole Cabinet, when not a word was said on politics—and that Webster had a confidential interview with Mr Upsher [*sic*, Abel P. Upshur], Secretary of State, in which their political views in regard both to the present & the future were found on comparison to be perfectly harmonious, and moreover that they were *thoroughly whig.*"

Remarks that as soon as James Watson Webb learned of a possible Clay-Webster ticket [Porter to Clay, September 25, 1843], he had rushed to support such an arrangement in his newspaper [Bacon to Clay, October 7, 1843], mainly because "his vanity to be considered the leader of every important political movement could not be restrained." Believes, however, that the movement to place Webster on a Whig ticket headed by Clay "is likely to operate favourably for us, as Mr Webster & his friends have committed themselves so fully that they cannot now recede, and they have no alternative but to give their support to the legitimate whig ticket, and whether this support shall prove to be earnest or feeble, is of no great consequence."

Reports that the "Van Buren & Calhoun men are at present in a state of glorious warfare in this City. Their nominating Committee, composed of delegates from both sections, have held nightly meetings for nearly a week past for the purpose of forming a legislative ticket, but without having agreed, as yet, on a single candidate [W.B. Campbell to Clay, July 21, 1843]. Last night, or rather at 2 OClock this morning, they closed their deliberations by a row & a fight—Mike Walsh being the leader of one of the hostile parties. And it is more than probable that they never will be able to agree on a joint ticket [Clay to Davis, September 12, 1843], on which their success must wholly depend."

Concludes that Whig "political prospects are uncommonly bright & promising," citing as evidence the "cheering & unexpected result of elections in Maryland & Georgia [Clay to Stevenson, July 19, 1843]." ALS. DLC-HC (DNA, M212, R5).

For Webster's "long letter" to Tyler, dated Boston, August 29, 1843, see Moser, *Papers of Daniel Webster, Correspondence,* 5:311-13. Webster had arrived in Washington on September 29 and had left by October 10. New York *Herald,* October 2, 10, 1843.

In the 1843 U.S. congressional elections in Maryland, Whigs won all 6 seats. *Guide to U.S. Elections,* 578. Legislative elections in Maryland in 1843 were held only for the house of delegates, and Whigs won 47 seats to 35 for the Democrats. Washington *Daily National Intelligencer,* October 9, 1843.

For Mike Walsh, professional political street fighter and gang leader (Spartan Club), see Mushkat, *Tammany,* 208-10; Seager, *And Tyler Too,* 234-35.

From Peter B. Porter, New York City, October 13, 1843. Remarks that the movement to put Webster on Clay's presidential ticket [Porter to Clay, September 25, 1843] is "favourable to you—for although the project meets but with very little countenance from the whig papers, it puts it out of the power of the Webster Men to act against you hereafter!"

Says he has read, in confidence, to John L. Lawrence, James Watson Webb, and "one or two other whig friends" paragraphs three, four, and five of Clay's letter to him of October 3. Reports that "Our friends were delighted with this reply, and even the Webster men were obliged to acknowledge that it was perfectly correct and proper—altho' they, and especially Mr Webb, would have been glad to find some expression of personal good will toward Mr Webster, which he (Col. Webb) said was all that was wanting to secure the zealous cooperation of his friends in your election. He was anxious that I should allow him to take a copy of what I had read, thinking, as he said that he could turn it to some usefull account in promoting your election. But as I wholly declined this, he said it was not important, as he had written to you himself [on October 4] & should soon expect a reply [Clay to Webb, October 27, 1843]."

Encloses a copy of the Buffalo *Commercial Advertiser* of September 27, calling attention to an article therein, written by his nephew, George W. Holley, on the "details of the movements of our great men" in attendance at the New York State Agricultural Fair in Rochester the previous week. ALS. DLC-HC (DNA, M212, R5). For Webster's speeches at the Rochester fair, see Fuess, *Daniel Webster,* 2:135-36; Moser, *Papers of Daniel Webster, Correspondence,* 5:313-14.

From John Davis, Worcester, Mass., October 14, 1843. Wonders "how deeply" Calhoun must feel the results of recent elections in Tennessee [T.J. Campbell to Clay, May 7, 1843], North Carolina [Clay to Stevenson, July 19, 1843], and Georgia [*ibid.*]. Asks, "How much astonished must he be to see the doctrines of a protective tariff and distribution of the proceeds of the public lands prevail against his theory of politics and his scheme of nullification?"

Thinks Clay's pending candidacy for president has helped unify the Whig party. Warns, nonetheless, that "We have difficulties and embarassments to contend with—The abolitionists who appear to be disinclined to all connexion with the Whigs have strength enough which they take from us to put us in some peril. We can however do nothing with them except to let them alone which is the wisest course—You are however the object at which they aim most of their shafts and whom the leading members of the party are most desirous of defeating—We take pains to circulate your life and speeches published by [Horace] Greeley as the best method of placing your character fairly before the public and of refuting the calum[n]ies to which the press gives birth—Many abolitionists, though by no means all, are conscientious men who view slavery as a sin and reason to the consequences which follow—with them it constitutes the Alpha & Omega of politics and morals and it is in vain to discuss the topic with such—" Explains, further, that the appearance of the abolitionist Liberty party in the Massachusetts state elections in November, 1842 [Clay to Silsbee, March 18, 1843] had "no doubt occasioned our defeat." But while "Subsequent events . . . have left this third party as they styled themselves almost barren of strength," a "new movement . . . is started at this moment to embarrass us—I allude to an article in the New York Courier and Inquirer proposing Mr. Webster for the vice presidency [Porter to Clay, September 25, 1843]." Believes that Webster probably fears pending political exile and would therefore like to be placed on the Whig ticket with Clay. This is, however, a movement that cannot be made "without exciting great dissatisfaction even here," and "it may be the means of throwing us into some confusion but we shall I think pass over it by adopting his [Webster's] own doctrine that it ought to be and is all refered to the convention."

Is confident that, aside from the Webster matter, "things look very favorable"; but the Whigs must win control of the Massachusetts legislature, because "in case we fail to elect the governour we may also in the end fail to elect Electors for 1844 in which events the choice of both will devolve upon the legislature—The importance of this is felt and I think we shall suceed as the Locofoco administration has done little to recommend itself to the people."

Laments that in the state elections in New Jersey on October 10 things did not go well for the Whigs. Blames this on the behavior of former U.S. Navy Captain Robert F. Stockton—once "a decent man"—during the contest. Asks: "What more glaring proof can a past Captain give of his unfitness than to attach himself to the rotten corrupt administration of Tyler—Corruption & Tyler & Tyler & corruption will stick together as long as Cataline & Treason—He it was either by his voluntary act or by the advice of others that ratified the bargain and paid down the thirty pieces of silver to the traitor Collins by whose apostacy & desertion the whigs were defeated in the legislature and the govt. thrown into the hands of the locoes—it was openly said by Every body as soon as the treachery appeared that the keepership of a light house was to be the reward and when the work was done, in the face of all this it was bestowed—The name of Tyler will stink in the nostrils of the people; for the history of our government affords no such palpable example of the prostitution of Executive patronage to the wicked purposes of bribery—The loccoes of this state are equally criminal and it will be hard for them to wipe off the stain." ALS. DLC-HC (DNA, M212, R5).

The Life and Speeches of Henry Clay, edited by James B. Swain in two volumes, was published by Horace Greeley in New York in 1843.

In the 1844 Massachusetts elections, Whig George N. Briggs defeated Democrat George Bancroft by 69,570 votes to 54,714, with Liberty party candidate Samuel Sewell winning 9,635. *BDGUS*, 2:702. Whigs also won all 10 congressional seats and all 27 of the vacancies in the state senate, as well as carrying the lower house of the state legislature by a decisive majority. *Guide to U.S. Elections*, 580;

Niles' Register (November 16 and 30, 1844), 67:176, 196. For Stockton, see *DAB*. Stockton was a strong defender of President Tyler, arguing, for example, in a speech at Trenton, N.J., on May 19, 1843, that the victory of 1840 was not a Whig victory, but "a triumph of the people—of Conservative Democracy" and that "Tyler was a Conservative Democrat when he was elected. . . . [and] Such I believe him to be now." This speech was printed under the title *Speech of Capt. R.F. Stockton, in Defence of the Administration of President Tyler* (Trenton, 1843), 4-10.

In the New Jersey state elections of 1843 the Democrats won control of the state senate by a margin of 12-6 over the Whigs and of the lower house by 36-22. *Niles' Register* (October 14, 1843), 65:112. Democrat David Haines was elected governor by a secret session of the state legislature. *BDGUS*, 3:1018. The Democrats won 4 seats in the U.S. House to 1 for the Whigs. *Guide to U.S. Elections*, 578.

No one named Collins, "traitor" or not, received a patronage appointment from Tyler.

To DAVID FRANCIS BACON Lexington, October 27, 1843

I received your favor,[1] which I have perused with much interest. I have thought it most proper to leave to the Whigs of the U.S. the selection of a Candidate for the V.P. unbiased by any wishes or preferences which I might be supposed to have. I shall be content with whatever choice they make. And I have no doubt that they will give deliberate consideration to the whole subject.

You have magnificent projects in view. Can't you spare the Colonization Society, and direct your energies to some others of them? You will find all wooing of the Ultra-abolitionists vain and useless. They hate most those who, without adopting their principles, make some approximation towards them. They opposed Tom Corwin;[2] will not vote for [George N.] Briggs, and denounce Mr. [John Q.] Adams,[3] Mr. [Joshua R.] Giddings and Mr. [Seth] Gates![4] In short they give more support to the Locos', directly or indirectly, who have never spared them, than to the Whigs who have treated them generally with respect.

I appreciate highly your zeal, ability & disinterestedness, and should be happy to see you here. I shall always be glad to hear from you; but I shall have need of all your indulgence for the brevity with which I may write; such is the extent of my correspondence.

ALS. CtY. 1. Bacon to Clay, Oct. 7, 1843. 2. Thomas Corwin, an anti-slavery Whig, had been defeated for reelection as governor of Ohio in 1842 by a margin of 117,902 votes to 119,774 for Democrat Wilson Shannon. Liberty party candidate, Leicester King, demonstrated that he held the balance of power by winning 5,134 votes. *BDGUS*, 3:1202 and Weisenburger, *The Passing of the Frontier*, 409-10, 435. 3. For Briggs and Adams, see Clay to Colton, Sept. 2, 1843. 4. Joshua R. Giddings of Ohio and Seth Gates of New York had been elected to the U.S. House in 1838 as anti-slavery men. They soon joined John Q. Adams in the fight against the proslavery gag rule. Although Giddings and Gates left the Whig party in the late 1840s, at this time they were still being severely castigated for supporting both William Henry Harrison for president and slaveholder R.M.T. Hunter for Speaker of the House in 1840. Gates was not reelected for the 28th Congress. Giddings, however, was reelected on Oct. 10, 1843, with 10,048 votes to 5,287 for his Democratic opponent, Samuel Starkweather, and 1,312 for Edward Wade of the Liberty party. See *BDAC* for Gates and *Guide to U.S. Elections*, 581; also Weisenburger, *The Passing of the Frontier*, 377, 383 and Richard H. Sewell, *Ballots for Freedom: Anti-Slavery Politics in the United States 1837-1860* (New York, 1976), 47-48, 63-64, 66, 138-39, 166, 202-3; also Clay to Ewing, July 24, 1842.

To JOHN M. BERRIEN Lexington, October 27, 1843

Absence from home has delayed my acknowledgment of your favors respecting the Georgia Election.[1] Yes! Georgia does proudly stand alongside of "the mother and daughter".[2] I congratulate you on her patriotic position. She has realized all our fondest hopes. There may she always nobly stand!

But we must not confine our congratulations to the three Southern associates. Pennsa.[3] Maryland, and her monumental City [Baltimore][4] and Ohio[5] and Vermont[6] have all—all acquitted themselves nobly.

I enclose for your perusal and subsequent destruction a letter about the Key Stone State [Pennsylvania] from one of its northeast sons (Mr. J. Cooper, late of the H. of R) himself a leading Antimason, the friend of Mr. Thad. Stevens.[7] From that you will perceive that we have reason to hope for a perfect co-operation between the Whigs and Antimasons hereafter. For the want of it we lost the Legislature, if loss it can be regarded; but I am inclined to think that it is better that the Locofoco's should have the perilous responsibility which their ascendancy for the present gives them in the Legislature.

The victory of next year will dim the splendor of that of 1840. That is my *cool* judgment. You know I am never warm.

The affair of running Mr. Webster as Vice President had a still birth,[8] and that without any aid from me. I wrote a letter[9] declining to make any engagements, to hold out any promises, or to give any pledges, and taking the ground of entire passiveness. An extract from it was read to his friends,[10] and they were *perfectly satisfied* with it. . . .

ALS. NcU. 1. Clay to Stevenson, July 19, 1843. 2. North Carolina and Tennessee. See *ibid.*, and T.J. Campbell to Clay, May 7, 1843. 3. Clay to Stevenson, July 19, 1843. 4. Porter to Clay, Oct. 11, 1843. In Baltimore the Whigs elected James O. Law mayor by a vote of 7,630 to 7,298 for his Democratic opponent. Whigs also won 4 of 5 Baltimore seats in the house of delegates. In the 1st branch of the city council, Whigs won 15 seats to 13 for the Democrats. (The 2nd branch of the city council had been chosen the previous year when a Democratic majority of 23 to 5 was elected). *Niles' Register* (Oct. 21, 1843), 65:116-17; Columbus *Ohio State Journal*, Oct. 10, 1843. 5. Clay to Sloane, Oct. 27, 1843. 6. In the 1843 elections in Vermont, Whigs won 3 seats in the U.S. House to 1 for the Democrats. *Guide to U.S. Elections*, 579. In the state senate Whigs won 21 seats to 9 for the Democrats and also carried the state house by 120-90 seats. Washington *Daily National Intelligencer*, Sept. 18, 29, 1843. Columbus *Ohio State Journal*, Sept. 26, 1843. In the gubernatorial election Whig John Mattocks won 24,405 votes to 21,982 for Democrat Daniel Kellog and 3,766 for Liberty party candidate, Charles Williams. Since no candidate received a majority, the election was thrown into the state legislature where Mattocks was chosen. *BDGUS*, 4:1572. 7. For James Cooper, see *BDAC*. For Stevens and the end of Anti-Masonry in Pennsylvania in 1843, see Vaughn, *The Anti-Masonic Party*, 185, 189. 8. Porter to Clay, Sept. 25, 1843. 9. Clay to Porter, Oct. 3, 1843. 10. Porter to Clay, Oct. 13, 1843.

From John R. Nelson *et al.*, State House, Nashville, October 27, 1843. Nelson, writing for the "entire Whig delegation" from East Tennessee serving in the state's general assembly, invites Clay to visit their region next spring when he sets out for his scheduled trip to North Carolina. Explains that the road he must travel will take him through East Tennessee and that "a slight deviation will take you to Knoxville, the centre of that division of the state." Points out that the people of the region wish to honor him for his great patriotism, sterling political principles, individual worth, etc. Copy. Printed in Knoxville *Register*, November 15, 1843. Signed by five state senators and twelve state representatives.

On November 3, Clay answered from Lexington, declining the invitation and noting that his route to North Carolina would be via New Orleans, Alabama, Georgia, and South Carolina. Thanks them profusely. *Ibid.*

To JOHN SLOANE Lexington, October 27, 1843

I have recd. your obliging letter, and share with you largely in the gratification which the result of your Election affords.[1] It is perhaps better than if you had secured both branches of the Legislature, since having the popular one you are secure against any further Gerrymandering; and if you had both no positive good could be effected next winter.

I fully concur with you in thinking that no good is to be accomplished by wooing the Ultra abolitionists. They hate most those who make any approximation towards them. They opposed [Thomas] Corwin,[2] will not vote for [George N.] Briggs, and denounce Messrs. [John Q.] Adams,[3] [Joshua] Giddings, [Seth] Gates &c.[4] They would nullify the Constitution. The day will come, if they are not checked in their progress, when the free States will have to decide on the alternative of repudiating them or repudiating the Union.

The laboring classes in the free States will sooner or later be aroused against these Ultras; for what is their plan? emancipation and amalgamation. Emancipation would lead to competition and low wages, anticipating the march of time and the progress of population. Amalgamation would Africanize the whites (that is the laboring classes) who might, if any did concur in it.

I have been well advised of the schemes of Judge [Jacob] B——— [Burnet] and his associates.[5] I presume they are now abandoned. The spontaneous manifestations of the People have given them the coup de grace. I am sorry that you should have incurred the Judges displeasure; but I presume it will not annihilate you. He said to me in Washn. with his own lips, after the nomination in 1839 at Harrisburg:[6] "You were the choice of 99 out of a hundred of the Whigs of the U. States." Believing that, how could he consistently go for another? Or does he think that the wishes of the many should always yield to the desire of the few?

I should be most happy to have that interview to which you refer; and I hope we may both live to meet at no distant day. . . .

ALS. MH. 1. In the 1843 congressional elections in Ohio, Whigs won 12 seats to 9 for the Democrats. *Guide to U.S. Elections*, 578-79. Of the 18 seats to be filled in the state senate, the Whigs and the Democrats won 9 each, giving the Democrats a total of 20 seats to 16 for the Whigs. In the lower house 55 Whigs, 50 Democrats, and 3 Independents were elected. Columbus *Ohio State Journal*, Oct. 21, 1843. 2. Clay to Bacon, Oct. 27, 1843. 3. For Briggs and Adams, see Clay to Colton, Sept. 2, 1843. 4. For Giddings and Gates, see Clay to Bacon, Oct. 27, 1843. 5. Clay to Stevenson, July 19, 1843; Porter to Clay, Sept. 25, 1843. 6. Porter to Clay, Nov. 14 and Dec. 30, 1837.

To JAMES WATSON WEBB Lexington, October 27, 1843

An absence of two weeks from home has delayed my acknowledgment of your favor of the 4h. instant, refer[r]ing to an article in the Courier and Enquirer upon the subject of the Vice Presidency, and to Mr. Webster's name in connection with it.[1]

Considering the relation in which I stand to the Whig public, I have thought it my duty to abstain from any intimation of a preference for any particular friend for the office of V. P. I have accordingly foreborne to give the slightest intimation of any such preference, if I had it. The Convention of May next will doubtless weigh justly all pretensions and designate some person who will be satisfactory to the party.[2] I am prepared, not merely to acquiesce in their nomination but, to give to it all the support I can consistently with honor and propriety.

Prior to Genl. Harrisons Election, I had thought Mr. Websters case one of the hardest among our eminent public men. He had worked long and well, without ever having received any appointment under the General Government. I had indeed suggested his name, during Mr. Adams' administration, for Minister to England,[3] but he could not then well be spared from Congress, and for that and some other reasons he was not appointed.

About four years ago, after it was known that Genl. Harrison was elected, several leading papers (I believe your's among them) took the ground that neither Mr. W— nor I ought to form a part of his Cabinet unless *both* did. I met Genl Harrison in November 1840 at Frankfort and had a long interview with him at the Governor's. After declining to accept the tender which he made to me of any place that I might select, under his administration, I remarked that I did not see how he could avoid offering Mr. Webster some *distinguished* place; and that, if I had been elected President, in deference to public opinion, I should have felt bound to make such an offer to him.[4] I was informed that Genl Harrison either that or the next day addressed a letter to Mr. W. inviting him to a seat in his Cabinet. I will not say that this was in consequence of my remark; but I will say that Genl. Harrison was evidently greatly pleased with my suggestion, and lavished on me afterwards many praises for it, and for what he chose to call my magnanimity.

I was not unaware at that time of the part which Mr. Webster and his friends had taken to prevent my nomination at Harrisburg in 1839.[5]

When his nomination came before the Senate as Secy of State, the defense of it rested chiefly with me. And afterwards, in open Senate, in defending him, I was nigh getting into a personal difficulty with a Southern Senator.[6]

I advert to these circumstances to shew that, up to the commencement of Genl. Harrisons administration, the relations between Mr. W. and me, so far as I was concerned, were certainly not inimical. Nor were they, during the Extra Session of 1841, altho' they were marked by some coolness and distance on his part. Nevertheless he concurred, as I understood from his colleagues, in the Compromise clause which I offered in the Senate to the first bank bill, touching the branching power,[7] which I never should have proposed but under a firm conviction, which they entertained and impressed me with, that it would secure Mr. Tyler's approval of the bill.

I said to Mr. Webster on the last day of the Extra Session, in substance: "If you mean to remain in Mr. Tyler's Cabinet to complete any unfinished affair (thinking of the McLeod case)[8] the public will justify you; but if you intend to continue there indefinitely, it will condemn you"

I have been greatly surprized and shocked by Mr. Webster's course, since the conclusion of the Treaty of Washington. Had he then left Mr.

Tyler, he would have repaired all injury which his character had sustained, by his continued association with him. But he went to Boston, made his Faneuil Hall Speech and lost the Whigs the Massachusetts Election.[9]

There could be but one interpretation given to that Speech, and there was but one. Mr. Webster asked himself "where am I to go"? And I confess, with pain & regret, that I have not since seen where he has gone.

You tell me that he assures you that he is a Whig. and could be nothing else. I am rejoiced to hear it. He has talents of the highest order, and could render service much good service to our Country. But has he given any *public* evidence of his adherence to the Whigs? If he has, I have not seen it. His recent letter expressing his intention to support the nominations of the Whig Candidates in Masstts. for Governor and Lt Governor,[10] places that support exclusively upon one ground, a very just, though probably not a very popular one, but certainly one which he might take, without reference to political parties.

I have thus candidly written you on a delicate subject. I send you my feelings and sentiments as I have thrown them off, in the first rough sketch, without even retaining a Copy. Confident in your honor and fidelity, I am sure that no improper use will be made of it.

I have only time to add one word of congratulation on the bright political prospects which beam all around us. The victory of 1844 will dim the lustre of that of 1840.

ALS. KyU. Letter marked "(Confidential)." 1. Probably the editorial mentioned in Bacon to Clay, Oct. 7, 1843; see also, Porter to Clay, Sept. 25, 1843. 2. Clay to Dearborn, July 13, 1842; Clay to Clayton, August 8, 1842. 3. See 4:203, 230. 4. Harrison to Clay, Nov. 2, 1840; Clay to Porter, Dec. 8, 1840. 5. Porter to Clay, Nov. 14 and Dec. 30, 1837; Clay to Leigh, June 20, 1843. 6. For Clay's clash with Sen. Alfred Cuthbert (Ga.) on Webster's appointment as secretary of state, see Remark in Senate, Feb. 22, 1841. 7. Porter to Clay, mid-July, 1841. 8. Porter to Clay, Jan. 4, 1841. 9. A. Spencer to Clay, Oct. 28, 1842. 10. Webster had written William Davis of Plymouth, Mass., on Oct. 16, 1843, indicating his support for Whig candidates for governor and lt. governor, George N. Briggs and John Reed. For the letter, see McIntyre, *Writings and Speeches of Daniel Webster*, 16:408-13; see also Clay to Berrien, July 17, 1843.

To THOMAS EWING Lexington, October 29, 1843

I received your favor and share with you in gratification at the result in your Election.[1] It is good in itself but better in its future promises, from the circumstances detailed by you. It will secure a fair ap[p]ortionment of the Representation in the next Legislature. I most fervently hope that your anticipations about Fairfield[2] may be realized.

You will have seen the movement to make Mr. Webster our Candidate for V. P. The project was communicated to me. I stated in reply that I took no part in the designation of the Whig Candidate for V. P.[3] It was the affair of the Convention of May.[4] I should be glad if the Whigs could receive the support of Mr. W. & his friends; but I could enter into no engagements, make no promises, give no pledges &c.

ALS. DLC-HC (DNA, M212, R21). Letter marked "(Confidential)." 1. Clay to Sloane, Oct. 27, 1843. 2. Fairfield County, Ohio, which usually went for the Democrats, elected a Whig to the U.S. House in 1843. *Guide to U.S. Elections*, 579. The county chose two "Independent Bank Currency" Democrats to represent it in the lower house of the state legislature. Columbus *Ohio State Journal*, Oct. 14 and 21, 1843. 3. Porter to Clay, Sept. 25, 1843; Clay to Porter, Oct. 3, 1843; Bacon to Clay, Oct. 7, 1843; Clay to Bacon, Oct. 27, 1843. 4. Clay to Dearborn, July 13, 1842; Clay to Clayton, August 8, 1842.

To THOMAS H. BAIRD Lexington, November 1, 1843

I must confess that I should have been mortified with your letter, if I did not know your fidelity and attachment to me.[1] That, at this time of day, any doubts should be entertained of my devotion to the policy of cherishing our manufactures, or that any impression should be made upon a friend, by a perversion of my meaning, by an enemy, amazes me.

In my letter to Mr. [F.S.] Bronson,[2] I refer to various recent expressions of my sentiments and opinions, and among them to a sort of Whig creed, which is now at the head of many news papers, one article of which is An adequate revenue, with *fair protection to* manufactures. If these be consulted, they will dispel any doubts which might be created, by tearing a sentence, or phrase, of my letter from the residue of the context.

But to the letter itself. What does it say? 1st. That Revenue is to be derived from the Imports. That excludes the proceeds of the public lands, which are left for distribution. 2dly. That in laying a Tariff, *such a discrimination* ought to be made as will incidentally afford reasonable protection &c. I do not say that we should establish a Tariff, shut our eyes to our manufactures, make no discriminations for their benefit, and give them no protection but such as would incidentally arise from a purely Revenue, or horizontal tariff. That is the doctrine of some of the other party. But I say that, whilst we are seeking after Revenue, we should think also of, and provide for, our manufactures, by discriminations in their favor. And 3dly. I express myself in favor of the present Tariff.[3]

Our manufactures want a certain amount of protection, in the form of duties laid upon foreign rival articles. Is it of any sort of consequence to them, if the amount required be obtained, whether it be granted as protection per se, or as incidental protection by proper discriminations for their benefit in the adjustment of a Tariff for Revenue? If you attach vital importance to forms, you must recollect that other people may also think there is something in forms. And that it would be unwise to lose the substance by a pertinacious pursuit after the form.

Our Government is in debt. To pay that debt and to meet its current expenses, excluding the proceeds of the public lands, will require, for some years to come, an amount of Revenue so large that, in adjusting a Tariff to raise it, with proper discriminations, every degree of reasonable protection can be afforded. What more is wanted? I need hardly observe that, by discriminations, I mean that a higher rate of duty should be put upon a foreign fabric, coming into competition with a similar American fabric, than upon another foreign fabric which does not compete with any American one.

I write this letter purely for your own satisfaction. I can not and will not consent to its publication. Such a publication would make me appear ridiculous. I should have to pile letter upon letter until they reached a Mountain height, if I were to write to correct every perversion of my meaning and misrepresentation of me that are made.

ALS. ViU. Letter marked "(Confidential)." 1. For Baird (1787-1866), prominent banker, lawyer, jurist, road builder, and manufacturer of Washington, Pa., later of Pittsburgh, see 4:383-84 and, especially, Boyd Crumrine, *The Courts of Justice, Bench and Bar of Washington County, Pennsylvania* (Washington, Pa., 1902), 51-53. 2. Clay to Bronson, Sept. 13, 1843. See also Clay to Branham & Bledsoe, July 23, 1843; and Clay to Meriwether,

Oct. 2, 1843. 3. Clay to Letcher, Jan. 6 and June 24, 1842; Remark in Senate, Feb. 3, 1842.

From THOMAS EWING Lancaster, Ohio, November 1, 1843

The whigs have much to forgive Mr Webster—More I apprehend than they will readily forgive him, & yet his name[1] would give us in some sections a little strength & possibly in places where we would greatly need it—I have personally much cause to object to, & distrust him—I could easily excuse his note to the Intelligencer after the dissolution of the Cabinet,[2] for that indicated merely a bluntness of moral perception on his part—but he also got up a report,[3] which he knew to be false, & caused it to appear in several papers devoted to his interest, namely, that the resignation of the cabinet was an intrigue, got up & arranged on consultation with you & to advance your interests—I am confident, from circumstances that the slander originated with him, & he well knew that while our course was yet undetermined, all the members of the cabinet studiously avoided conversation with you on the subject—not because we did not desire the aid of your experience & judgment in the emergency, but because we knew the use that would be made of such consultation, by the common enemy—However I am content to let all this pass if the good of the cause require it—But great & important reform is necessary on his part before we can touch him without injury. Much less with advantage—1st He must shew himself a whig, by strict adherence to the cause & earnest efforts to advance it—2nd. He must drop all *exhibitions* of personal hostility toward yourself—& this he ought to do—not negatively merely, but by some affirmative expression, sufficiently public & emphatic—But there would still be difficulties—Mr Webster is generally understood to be an intemperate man—It is also said that his open & gross immorality has become in the highest degree offensive to the strict community in which he lives & among whom he ought to have most weight—I doubt exceedingly whether we could make him useful to us—If I were satisfied we could I would be willing to waive all objections to him & put him on the ticket—Every thing must be very carefully weighed & the wisest steps taken to secure large masses of men, & we must take care not to lose on one hand in trying to gain on another—Much of our success this year in Ohio is to be attributed to the German & Irish laborers, most of them Catholics—They think all Boston was concerned in burning the Charleston [*sic*] convent[4] & they have especially a strong feeling agst Mr Webster—we should probably lose many of their votes if he were on the ticket—The only difficulty with John Davis lies in this [quarter][5] We cannot consent to lose these men for we rely upon them to make up what shall be taken from us by the Liberty party which is becoming exceedingly troublesome[6]

By the way, what shall we do with these Liberty men?—If we could break up their organization next year our way would be smooth—Their leaders might be operated upon—their organization temporarily broken—in which event their votes would be cast *next year* with the whigs—but they are moved by a violent spirit of enthusiasm which we cannot permanently control, & unless they hasten into excesses which will disaffect their more moderate adherents we shall at least have trouble with them—There is one of their party—a bold & eloquent young man, whose good will I have taken pains to secure—who feels kindly toward yourself, through whom I think much can be done, if we think the effort not hopeless—If we cannot neutralize we must try & divide the party into *moral* & *political* abolitionists & then reduce the numbers of those who are for mischief—We have the means in our power of electing you, & we shall do it if we commit no blunder

ALS. DLC-HC (DNA, M212, R5). Letter marked "(Confidential)." 1. As vice presidential nominee on the Clay ticket. Porter to Clay, Sept. 25, 1843. 2. In a letter, dated Sept. 13, 1841, to Gales & Seaton, editors of the Washington *Daily National Intelligencer*, Webster explained his reasons for refusing to join the other Cabinet members in resigning from Tyler's administration [Speech to Whig Caucus, Sept. 13, 1841]. This letter was printed in the Washington *Daily National Intelligencer* on Sept. 14, 1841, and is reprinted in Moser, *Papers of Daniel Webster, Correspondence*, 5:151-52. 3. No report that can clearly be ascribed to Webster, blaming Clay for the Cabinet resignations, has been found; however, at this time a number of newspapers printed unsigned editorials which made this accusation against Clay. Among these were *The Madisonian* on Sept. 18, 1841, and the Washington *Daily National Intelligencer* of Sept. 18 which reprinted an accusatory editorial from the New York *Express* while itself denying Clay's culpability. On Sept. 25, 1841, *The Madisonian* also published an unsigned editorial, presumably written by Webster, attacking Ewing, Badger, Bell, and Crittenden for their resignations. See Moser, *Papers of Daniel Webster, Correspondence*, 5:160-61; McIntyre, *Writings and Speeches of Daniel Webster*, 15:137-39. 4. On August 11, 1834, a mob, composed primarily of brickworkers, had sacked and burned the Ursuline Convent in Charlestown, Mass. Richard Hofstadter and Michael Wallace, *American Violence* (New York, 1970), 298-301. 5. The word "quarter" is struck through, but no alternate word is provided. 6. Clay to Porter, Sept. 17, 1843. The Liberty party polled 8,050 votes in Ohio in 1844, enough to have given Polk victory there had 5,945 of that number gone to the Democrats. McKee, *National . . . Popular and Electoral Vote*, 56.

From Z. Barton Stout, Allen's Hill, Ontario County, N.Y., November 2, 1843. Mentions his letter from Clay of October 31 [not found] in response to an earlier letter of his own which had given Clay an account of the proceedings of the Ontario County Whig convention of 1842. Encloses herein an article from the Canandaigua Ontario *Repository* of November 1 which gives an account of the proceedings of the recent convention of the Whig party in the 29th congressional district (Ontario and Livingston counties). Reports that this convention had selected him as its delegate to the coming Whig national convention [Clay to Clayton, August 8, 1843; Clay to Berrien, September 4, 1843]. Thinks it most "fitting" that the appointment was "given to one, who has never been any thing else politically but a National Republican and Whig, rather than to one, however zealous in our cause, of more modern date." Informs Clay that he had been a delegate to the Whig national nominating convention in Baltimore in December, 1831 [8:418, 915], had supported "Harry of the West" there, and now has an opportunity to do so once again. Says the men most talked about for vice president [Clay to Dearborn, July 13, 1842; Clay to Clayton, August 8, 1842] at the 29th district convention were John Davis (Mass.), Millard Fillmore (N.Y.), John Sergeant (Pa.), and John Clayton (Del.). Thinks them all men of "capacity and fidelity to Whig principles," and warns that "The Harrisburg blunder of nominating such a creature as John Tyler is a lesson not soon to be forgotten." Asks what Clay's preference is as to a Whig candidate for vice president, noting that his "wishes and opinion" in the matter would have "great weight with me." Says he is "most decidedly and earnestly opposed" to the New York *Courier and Enquirer*'s support of Webster for the vice presidency [Porter to Clay, September 25, 1843]. Confesses that he was once a warm friend of this "eminent statesman," but now he cordially hates "every thing at all contaminated with or by the arch traitor Tyler."

Recounts a conversation he had with John Quincy Adams at the train station in Canandaigua when Adams was recently enroute to Cincinnati, viz: "I said, 'Well Mr. Adams, we have lately had Mr. Webster among us, and in his speech at the Rochester Agricultural Supper [Porter to Clay, October 13, 1843], he paddled back somewhat from the position he had placed himself in, by his Baltimore speech [Clay to Clayton, May 27, 1843].' 'O yes,' replied Mr. A., 'and since then, he has paddled still further back, he has come out in support of the Whig nominations in Massachusetts.' 'Yes,' rejoined I, 'but Mr. Webster is a citizen of the nation as well as of Massachusetts.' 'True,' said Mr. Adams, 'and he will paddle back all the way yet, he is soon to make a speech at Salem.' 'But,' I asked, 'does he not entertain a feeling of asperity towards our Candidate Mr. Clay?' 'O Yes,' said Mr. A., 'but he is a politician and can get over that.' He added, 'That feeling arose from their position of rivalship—and from Mr. W_______'s not being able to see why he should not have been the preferred candidate instead of Mr. Clay.' So you see Mr. W. is about to answer his Faneuil Hall [Spencer to Clay, October 28, 1842] question, '*Where shall I go,*' by returning step by step to the Whig fold."

Sends Clay the lyrics of a "Clay Song" written by Mrs. Stout and published in the New York *Daily Tribune* of August 21 last. Remarks that it may be sung to the tune of "Auld lang syne." ALS. DLC-HC (DNA, M212, R5).

To EPES SARGENT Lexington, November 3, 1843

I am greatly obliged by your favor of the 28h. Ulto. I am rejoiced to hear of our friend Willis Halls improvement. I have been much and deeply concerned with his affliction, and sincerely pray that God may spare him to his friends and Country.

Mr. [John W.] Dodges painting of me is very excellent. Nagles [*sic,* John Neagle], and that and [*sic,* of] [Trevor T.] Fowlers are the best portraits that have been taken of me.[1]

I do not interfere on the question of the selection of our Candidate for the V. Presidency. It does not I think become me. I regret however to see so much warmth excited among our friends in regard to Mr. Webster, in N. York.[2] I think it may be safely left to the Balto. Convention to nominate a suitable person.[3]

The confidence in the success of the Whig cause next year is great and general. I share it. My belief is that the victory of 1844 will transcend that of 1840.

ALS. MCM. 1. For John W. Dodge, a New York City miniaturist, and Trevor T. Fowler, a well-known portraitist, see Groce, *Dictionary of Artists in America.* 2. Porter to Clay, Sept. 25, 1843. 3. Clay to Dearborn, July 13, 1842; Clay to Clayton, August 8, 1842.

To IVERSON L. HARRIS[1] Lexington, November 4, 1843

Many thanks for your obliging favor and the agreeable tidings which it conveyed. The success of the Whigs in Georgia, I find, has even exceeded your expectation.[2]

I also received the two numbers of the Georgia Journal which you were good enough to transmit, by desire of one of the Editors, to whom I request you to offer my acknowledgments. The accession of so worthy and distinguished a gentleman as Mr. McCombs to the Whig cause is highly gratifying. Thousands and tens of thousands of the party, to which he recently belonged, seeing the ruinous course of its measures, and the dangerous tendency of its principles, will follow his patriotic example before the circle of another year is completed.

ALS. Courtesy of J. Winston Coleman, Jr., Lexington, Ky. Addressed to Harris in Milledgeville, Ga. 1. Harris was born in Watkinsville, Ga., in 1805 and moved shortly thereafter to the family plantation "Pamona" near Milledgeville. Anna M.G. Cook, *History of Baldwin County, Georgia* (Anderson, S.C., 1925), 359-61. 2. Clay to Stevenson, July 19, 1843.

From JOSEPH SMITH Nauvoo, Ill., November 4, 1843

As we understand you are a candidate for the Presidency at the next election, and as the Latter-Day Saints (sometimes called Mormons, who now constitute a numerous class in the school politic of this vast republic) have been robbed of an immense amount of property, and endured nameless sufferings by the State of Missouri, and from her borders have been driven by force of arms, contrary to our national covenants, and as in vain we have sought redress by all constitutional, legal, and honourable means, in her courts, her executive councils, and her legislative halls, and as we have petitioned Congress to take cognizance of our sufferings without effect,[1] we have judged it wisdom to address you this communication, and solicit an immediate, specific, and candid reply to *What will be your rule of action relative to us as a people*,[2] should fortune favour your ascension to the chief magistracy? . . .[3]

Copy. Printed in Henry Mayhew, *The Mormons: Or Latter-Day Saints* . . . (3rd ed., London, 1852), 137. 1. For the expulsion of the Mormons from Missouri in 1839 and for Joseph Smith himself, and their petition to Congress, see Remark in Senate, Jan. 28, 1840. 2. For Clay's answer to Smith's inquiry and Smith's reply, see Clay to Smith, Nov. 15, 1843, and Smith to Clay, May 13, 1844. 3. Smith also wrote identical or similar letters to John C. Calhoun, Lewis Cass, Richard M. Johnson and Martin Van Buren. Smith, *History of the Church*, 6:64-65.

To George W. Varnum, Philadelphia, November 4, 1843. Assures him he has no "*private* opinion respecting a National Bank" that differs from his various public speeches on the subject either in the Senate [8:434, 443, 552, 558, 640-41] or in Hanover County, Va. [Speech at Taylorsville, June 27, 1840]. AL, signature removed. KyU.

To DANIEL ULLMANN Lexington, November 5, 1843

I received your favor of the 14h. Ulto. and share with you in the satisfaction which recent elections have produced. I suppose however that we shall have some drawback in that of N. York. I am eager to hear the result whatever it may be.[1]

I have taken no part in the selection of a Whig Candidate for the V. Presidency. So far as I am concerned, I think it proper to leave that matter exclusively to the Whigs and their Convention in May next.[2] But I regret to see more excitement than appears to me necessary in regard to Mr. Webster.[3] It is however chiefly confined to your City.

ALS. NHi. 1. Clay to W.B. Campbell, July 21, 1843. 2. Clay to Dearborn, July 13, 1842; Clay to Clayton, August 8, 1842. 3. Porter to Clay, Sept. 25, 1843.

From Peter B. Porter, New York City, November 6, 1843. Reports that the urinary complaint which brought him to the city has responded well, albeit slowly, to treatment and that he will be leaving for home in a few days. Discusses his attempts to end the "senseless bickerings & quarrels" among Whig newspaper editors in town. Notes that he has written several articles for the New York *Express*, in one of which he mentioned John Quincy Adams as a possible Whig vice presidential candidate ("intended as a damper to Webb's proposition to run Webster"). Thinks the *Express* is now the soundest Whig newspaper in the city; says it also has the greatest circulation, and "is looked to as the best index of whig politics." Summarizes the unsettling effect James Watson Webb's *Courier and Enquirer* had on local Whig politics when it proposed Webster for vice president on the 1844 Whig ticket [Porter to Clay, September 25, 1843; Bacon to Clay, October 7, 1843]. Believes that the subsequent decision of Webb to avoid a divisive fight on the Webster issue at the public meeting of Whigs in New York City a week ago has brought harmony to the party. Says Porter of Webb's surrender: "The meeting was accordingly held when it was at once apparent that Webster's friends were greatly in the minority—But in the mean time some of our more considerate friends, had prepared a set of resolutions which were promptly adopted, in which Webster & his friends were treated with great respect, but indicating in terms not to be misunderstood that he could not be the candidate of New York for the vice presidency. Webb & his friends, perceiving the position in which they stood very thankfully received the modified resolutions & the meeting closed in harmony, instead of a quarrel, and all now seem cordially united in promoting the great cause." Reports, further, that Webster himself, who was in New York a few days ago, declared "to his most intimate friends in this city—that the proposition to make him vice president did not originate with him, nor had it received his sanction—but that he was going home, and thence to *Andover*, where, on thursday next, he should make the greatest speech that he had ever made in his life—in which he should show himself to be a good whig by explaining & sustaining all the great whig measures of Tariff, U.S. Bank, public Lands internal improvements &c &c and would moreover shew why he did not sooner resign the office of Secretary of state—and further that he did actually resign it the very moment he had accomplished the several objects which induced him to retain it, and which were not only to complete the Treaty with great Britain [Ashburton to Clay, April 11, 1842], but to explain to Sir Robert Peel & the British Parliament certain matters connected with the Negociation which they had not properly understood—and furthermore to make in his official character an appropriate reply (as he certainly did) to the protests of Gov. [Lewis] Cass, on the occasion of his quitting the office of minister to France."

Believes that the Whigs will probably be beaten in the N.Y. state elections tomorrow [Clay to Campbell, July 21, 1843], because we have "made but very little preparation for the Contest." Adds that their old friend Peter R. Livingston predicts Clay will carry N.Y. state in 1844 by 20,000 votes if his opponent is Martin Van Buren. Feels, however, that Cass will likely get the Locofoco nomination, not Van Buren. ALS. DLC-HC (DNA, M212, R5).

The Whig meeting at National Hall in New York City, held on October 31, 1843, adopted resolutions, some of which were brought forward by Webb, declaring for Clay as their presidential candidate but also stating (without mentioning Webster by name) that in selecting a vice presidential candidate the national convention should "evince a spirit of conciliation toward the minority in our ranks." Another resolution, brought forward by Dudley Selden and adopted by the group, added that the vice presidential candidate should possess "that high integrity and fidelity to his principles and party, which, in the event of the death of the President, will ensure" that the party's principles will be carried out. New York *Herald*, November 1, 1843.

Webster, without apologizing or explaining his previous statements [Spencer to Clay, October 28, 1842; Clay to Clayton, May 27, 1843], reaffirmed in his November 9 speech at Andover his committment to the Whig position on such issues as the tariff and the national bank and declared his loyalty to the Whig party. He also explained his reasons for staying on so long as Tyler's secretary of state. For the speech, see McIntyre, *Writings and Speeches of Daniel Webster*, 3:159-85. See also Nathans, *Daniel Webster*, 218; Fuess, *Daniel Webster*, 2:138-39; Baxter, *Daniel Webster*, 368-69.

Lewis Cass wrote a violent protest of the Webster-Ashburton treaty to Secretary of State Webster on October 3, 1842, complaining that the treaty had not disavowed the right of the British to search American vessels. Because he had indicated to the French that the U.S. would oppose the right of search, he felt the treaty gave the appearance that he was not supported by his government. He therefore resigned his post and, not waiting for his resignation to be accepted, embarked for home in mid-November. This set off a bitter correspondence between Cass and Webster. Frank B. Woodford, *Lewis Cass: The Last Jeffersonian* (New Brunswick, N.J., 1950), 211-14; Curtis, *Daniel Webster*, 2:187-204.

By 1843 Cass was considered one of the leading contenders for the Democratic presidential nomination. In fact, he ran second to Van Buren on the first ballot at the Democratic national convention and was first by the seventh ballot before the swing to Polk began on the eighth. Woodford, *Lewis Cass*, 215-28.

Peter R. Livingston had served as secretary to John Armstrong when he was minister to France and had also served as speaker of the house and president pro tem of the senate of New York State. In 1836 he became a Whig, and he gave the keynote address at the 1839 Whig national convention. See 3:422; Hammond, *History of Political Parties in . . . New York*, 2:106, 265; Henry N. MacCracken, *Blithe Duthcess, The Flowering of An American County From 1812* (New York, 1958), 27, 30-31.

To John S. Richards, [near Egg Harbor, N.J.], November 6, 1843. Agrees with Richards that too often his letters to various correspondents find their way into print. Complains that "My letters have several times been published without my previous expectation, and I have been sometimes mortified with the parade of letters from me acknowledging small presents &c, of which I am made the almost involuntary recipient. It is easier to see the evil than to prescribe a remedy for all this. Altho' my correspondence is excessively oppressive I cannot decline returning a civil answer to a kind and friendly letter. The frequent publication of my letters imposes however an inconvenient restraint upon the freedom of correspondence. Instead of writing for the eye only of a friend one feels that he is writing for all the eyes of all the Arguses; or rather he sometimes forgets that he is doing so, and may thus appear less advantageously." States, further, that he is particularly pleased with the outcome of the recent state elections in Pennsylvania [Clay to Stevenson, July 19, 1843], because "No State has been under greater delusions or more deceived by Demagogues than Pennsylvania." Copy. Printed in *PMHB*, No. 4 (1908), 32:507.

Richards (1784-1871) at this time operated Gloucester Furnace, an iron manufactory, near Egg Harbor, N.J. He subsequently operated the Carbon Furnace at Mauch Chunk (now Jim Thorpe), Pa., before retiring to Patterson, Pa., in 1854 where he spent the remainder of his life. Arthur D. Pierce, *Family Empire in Jersey Iron* (New Brunswick, N.J., 1964), 255-56.

To WILLIAM E. ROBINSON Lexington, November 6, 1843

. . . . I yield to no one in this Country in ardent feelings for Ireland, and for her happenings; but I am not satisfied as to the propriety of any American Statesman taking part on the mere question of Repeal.[1] All our wisest men, and all our policy, have been adverse to our making ourselves parties to mere domestic questions in Foreign nations. How can we do that without recognizing a foreign right to interfere in ours? If Ireland had declared her Independence, and had manifested a capacity to maintain it, and to conduct the necessary relations with Foreign powers, her case would then be like those of the Spanish American Republics and Greece,[2] and would fall within the scope of our long established policy, which is to recognize a Government de facto. But I do not understand the present aim of Mr. [Daniel] O'Connell & his friends to be Independence,[3] but a mere alteration of the conditions of the connection between Ireland and England. Have the people of the U. States any legitimate right to intervene on such a domestic question?

ALS. IaU. Copy printed in Louisville *Courier Journal*, June 24, 1889. 1. The Irish, led by Daniel O'Connell, were seeking repeal of the Act of Union which in Jan., 1801, abolished the Irish parliament and merged the kingdoms of England and Ireland. O'Connell formed the National Repeal Association in 1840 which was dedicated to restoring the Irish parliament. For O'Connell (1775-1847), see *DNB*. For the repeal movement, see Thomas N. Brown, *Irish-American Nationalism* (New York, 1966), 4-10; George M. Trevelyan, *British History in the Nineteenth Century (1782-1901)* (New York, 1923), 218-21, 287-89. 2. See, for Spanish America, 2:512-62; 7:764-65; for Greece, 3:597-99, 603-14. 3. They were seeking home rule rather than independence. See note 1 above.

To GIDEON B. SMITH Lexington, November 7, 1843

I received your favor, and the copy of your address[1] on the culture of silk, for which accept my thanks. It contains many valuable suggestions. I have long entertained the opinion that the culture and manufacture of silk may be beneficially incorporated among the objects of our national industry.— They require only patience, perseverance, and a careful attention to minute details. There is no just cause for the apprehension, entertained by some, that we may so multiply the proceeds of our domestic industry as to leave no subjects of exchange in foreign commerce. Our difficulty is, not that there will be too little, but too much foreign commerce. In any conceivable state of civilized society, there will always be, in the infinite variety of the productions of different soils and climates, and varied human industry, and in the tastes, caprices, and wants of man, ample scope for foreign commerce. Of this truth, there are many obvious examples in the European nations.

Copy. Printed in *Niles' Register* (Nov. 18, 1843), 65:179. Printed also in Raleigh *Register & North Carolina Gazette* of Dec. 9, 1843, showing a date of Nov. 6. 1. Smith, a Baltimorean, had given a lecture on the introduction of silk culture in the U.S. before the National Silk convention, sponsored by the American Institute, in New York City on Oct. 13, 1843. In it, he had stated that "It is a good maxim for any people, individually or collectively, to buy only that which they cannot themselves produce." Smith was a noted entomologist, as well as a physician and a patron of John J. Audubon. At various times he edited the *American Turf Register and Sporting Magazine*, the *Penny Magazine*, and the *Journal of the American Silk Society*. J. Thomas Scharf, *The Cronicles of Baltimore* . . . (Baltimore, 1874), 92, 94; *MHM* (June, 1939), 34:139.

To PETER B. PORTER Lexington, November 8, 1843

Absence from home and ignorance where to address you have delayed my acknowledgment of your favors of the 11h. & 13h. Ulto. I am perfectly contented with the address and judgment with which you conducted the delicate affair to which they relate.[1] It is very manifest that the idea of running

Mr. Webster, as the Whig Candidate for V.P. does not take with the Whigs, and I presume will be abandoned. The affair went off very well at the recent public meeting,[2] both parties thinking they gained a victory, but the friends of Mr. Webster being pleased that matters were no worse.

I expect to hear of our defeat yesterday in your State, but I shall hear it without discouragement.[3]

You are I believe apprized of my trip to the South. I go about the middle of next month on business to N.O. Remaining there during the winter, I shall proceed via Alabama Georgia & So. Carolina to North Carolina early in the Spring, and expect to reach Washn. in April.

Will these Southern trips create any jealousy at the North? You know I have never been in those States.

I hope to hear that your health is improved. . . .

ALS. NBuHi. 1. Porter to Clay, Sept. 25, Oct. 11 and Oct. 13, 1843. 2. Porter to Clay, Nov. 6, 1843. 3. Clay to Campbell, July 21, 1843; Clay to Davis, Sept. 12, 1843.

To JAMES WATSON WEBB Lexington, November 8, 1843

Altho' my correspondence is exceedingly oppressive, I cannot deny myself the satisfaction of a prompt acknowledgement of the receipt this day of your favor of the 1st. You must have received about its date an answer which I transmitted to your previous favor.[1] In the movements which you have made, in regard to the association of Mr. W[ebster]s. name with the V.Py,[2] I never doubted your good intentions and upright purposes. I have had too many proofs of your fidelity and ardor in the Whig cause, and in relation to myself personally, to distrust you. And I sincerely hope that the harmony, which you sought to bring about at the public meeting may have been secured, as would seem probable from Mr. Grinnel's declaration.[3] That gentleman has uniformly avowed his attachment to and confidence in me.

As to Mr. Webster's nomination, my former letter will have informed you that I intend to take no part in the designation of the Whig Candidate for V.P.[4] That, so far as I am concerned, is the exclusive affair of the Convention of May.

I lament the discord among the Whig Editors in N. York. Is there nothing that can be done to heal it?[5]

Will you allow me to say, that I think forbearance would be wise towards those who concurred in or were instrumental in the nomination of Genl Harrison? Many of them, no doubt, acted under honest convictions and are now heartily with us. I must always think that the Convention of Harrisburg[6] violated a great principle (that of conforming to the *known will* of their Constituents) but I have ever believed that the large majority of it acted on patriotic motives. I think therefore all reproaches had better be spared.

I am prepared to hear of our defeat this week in your City and State.[7] Such an event will not, however, shake my confidence in the issue of the contest next year.

ALS. CtY. 1. Clay to Webb, Oct. 27, 1843. 2. Porter to Clay, Sept. 25, 1843. 3. Possibly Moses H. Grinnell; however, no "declaration" has been found. For the Whig meeting, see Porter to Clay, Nov. 6, 1843. 4. Clay to Webb, Oct. 27, 1843. 5. Porter to Clay, Sept. 25, 1843. 6. Porter to Clay, Nov. 14 and Dec. 30, 1837; Clay to Leigh, June 20, 1843. 7. Clay to Campbell, July 21, 1843; Clay to Davis, Sept. 12, 1843.

To CALVIN COLTON Lexington, November 9, 1843

Do not imagine that I am forgetful of you, or insensible to your exertions for the public, and for me. I have been absent from home, my correspondence is excessively oppressive, and not until this afternoon have I been able to read your life of me.[1] In the main, its facts are correct. It is a good outline, well-adapted to its purpose. There are a few inaccuracies, and too much commendation and panegyric. I do not know that it is worth while to point out the errors. I would do it if I could write on the margin.

You are unjust toward the Compromise Act.[2] It saved our manufactures, gave them stability, and they did well, until the disorders in the currency, and consequent revulsions, affected them, and every thing, and every body else. Up to 1840, it worked well, and afforded a sufficient measure of protection. It was the duty of a Van Buren Congress to provide for the period beyond that, but it would not perform its duty.

Copy. Printed in Colton, *Clay Correspondence*, 4:481-82. 1. Colton's "Life of Henry Clay" appeared in Sept., 1843 as no. 4 of the Junius Tracts. These tracts were all combined and published in one volume by Greeley & McElrath in New York in 1844. See also Clay to Colton, Sept. 2, 1843. 2. See 8:604, 619-22, 626-27.

To RICHARD H. BAYARD Lexington, November 10, 1843

. . . . The political prospects of the Whigs are very encouraging, even if New York has gone against them this week,[1] as I am prepared to hear. But they ought not to be enduced, by them, to relax in their future exertions. Undismayed by adversity, and unintoxicated by brilliant, but partial triumphs, I hope they will persevere, with untiring energy, until the Country and its Government are redeemed Should they act on this principle they will achieve a victory next year which will dim the lustre of that of 1840.

Whilst I entertain as high an opinion of our friend [John M.] Clayton as you or any other of his friends do, I have felt it due to my situation to take no part in the designation of a Candidate for the V. Presidency. Delicacy and propriety, it seemed to me, enjoined this forbearance.

I have argued a number of important causes this year with as much zeal and ardor as I ever did at any period. Next month I go to N. Orleans on business, and towards the Spring I shall proceed, through Alabama, Georgia and So. Carolina, to North Carolina, and shall throughout the whole journey be moving on ground which I never trod before. . . .

ALS. DLC-James A. and Richard H. Bayard Papers (DNA, M212, R20). 1. Clay to Campbell, July 21, 1843.

To JOHN MINOR BOTTS Lexington, November 10, 1843

I have perused your letter to the Whig[1] and am greatly obliged by the friendly motives which dictated it By this time, however, you will have learned, from a card published by Mr. Giddings,[2] that it was no letter of mine, but one of a name sake,[3] which has excited Mr. Ritchie. I do not write letters for different latitudes. I have but one heart, and one mind; and all my letters are but copies of the original, and if genuine will be found to conform to it, wherever they may be addressed.

Copy, extract. Printed in Raleigh *Register and North Carolina Gazette*, Dec. 19, 1843. 1. Botts had written the Richmond *Whig* denying a charge by the Richmond *Enquirer* (edited by Thomas Ritchie) that Clay had written Rep. Joshua R. Giddings, anti-slavery Whig of Ohio, supporting the abolitionist views of Giddings. See Clay to Giddings, Nov. 10, 1843. 2. *Ibid.* On Nov. 6, 1843, Giddings wrote editor Ritchie, explaining that Clay's support of his [Giddings's] anti-slavery view's were those of Cassius M. Clay, not Henry Clay—views to which Henry did not subscribe. Printed in Raleigh *Register and North Carolina Gazette*, Dec. 19, 1843. 3. Cassius M. Clay, a distant cousin of Henry Clay, was a leading emancipationist who became minister to Russia in the 1860s. See David L. Smiley, *Lion of Whitehall*. Madison, Wisc., 1962.

To LEVI FAHNESTOCK Lexington, November 10, 1843

I duly received your favor, as chairman of the Whig Banner Committee of Baltimore, requesting a Staff to be cut, by my hands, at this place, for the elevation of the Banner, to be presented, in behalf of the Whigs of Baltimore, to such State Delegation to the Young Men's Whig Committee of Ratification[1] as shall have the largest proportionate number of Delegates in attendance.

I shall take great pleasure in complying with this request.[2] A stick of white or blue ash, (the best description of timber, I think, of all the kinds that grow in our forests,) has been already cut, and is in progress of preparation for the Staff.—When completed, I will forward it through such channel as will ensure its safe arrival.

The conception of a plan of a Young Men's Convention, to ratify the nominations previously made by the Whig National Convention was very fortunate, and it will be productive of the best effects. Nor could any place be more suitable, for the assembling of such a convention, than the Monumental City, which covered itself with glory during the last war, and has recently again won imperishable laurels. Long may they continue to grace its patriotic brow!

Copy. Printed in Washington *Daily National Intelligencer*, Nov. 22, 1843; reprinted in Newburyport (Mass.) *Daily Herald*, Nov. 24, 1843. 1. The National Whig Convention of Young Men, held at Baltimore on Sept. 21, 1843, formed the Young Men's Convention of Ratification which was to meet at Baltimore on May 2, 1844, to ratify the national convention's nominations for president and vice president. This was to be modeled on the Young Men's Convention of May 4, 1840. The ratification convention did, in fact, assemble on the assigned day and proceeded to ratify the nominations of Clay and Frelinghuysen. Delaware was awarded the banner for having the largest delegation present. *Niles' Register* (Sept. 30, 1843), 65:74; *ibid.* (April 27 and May 18, 1844), 66:132, 149, 180-87. 2. On Oct. 19, 1843, Fahnestock had written Clay asking for a "staff for said banner to be cut by the honored hands of the farmer of Ashland from the growth of the soil of his own home." Assured him that a Whig victory was likely and that "the Republic is on the eve of a great and glorious though bloodless revolution." Copy. Printed in Washington *Daily National Intelligencer*, Nov. 22, 1843.

To JOSHUA R. GIDDINGS Lexington, November 10, 1843

I received your friendly letter, and thank you for the kind notices which prompted it.[1]

I have been so often before the public, frequently involuntarily and unexpectedly of late, that I should regret the necessity of my again presenting myself. I hardly think it can be deemed necessary by any fair and reasonable Abolitionists. My opinions have been long deliberately formed; and have been extensively published. I should have to refer to the evidences for them. I have now before me a letter from Georgia, requesting a letter on that subject for publication. I shall decline furnishing one.

After having seen you, Mr. [John Q.] Adams and Mr. [Seth] Gates[2] denounced by the ultra Abolitionists, I am quite sure that nothing which I could say would satisfy them.

You will have seen that a letter to you from Mr. Cassius M. Clay, which was read at some public meeting, has been attributed to me. I saw your explanatory card, which will put that matter right.[3]

I congratulate you on your election,[4] and upon the bright prospects of the Whigs.

Copy. OHi. 1. Not found, but see Clay to Botts, Nov. 10, 1843 2. Clay to Colton, Sept. 2, 1843; Clay to Bacon, Oct. 27, 1843. 3. Clay to Botts, Nov. 10, 1843. 4. Clay to Bacon, Oct. 27, 1843.

To WILLIAM SCHOULER Lexington, November 10, 1843

Dr. Bartlett delivered me your friendly letter of the 29h. September, and the three volumes of the Lowell offering which accompanied it. Accept my cordial thanks for both. My burthensome correspondence, my professional engagements, and the occupations of an extensive farm have not yet allowed me leisure to peruse the whole of Miss Farley's work;[1] but a member of my family, who had previously read it, speaks favorably of it, and from the glances which I have given it, I think that is merited testimony.

I take a deep interest in Lowell. I consider it, in respect to Manufactures, what the U. States are in respect to self-Government. Lowell will test whether the Manufacturing system is compatible with the social virtues; and the U. States whether Man can wisely govern himself.[2] I hope and believe that both experiments will succeed; but both have shewn that they are not perfect, and therefore not always free from error. When I visited Lowell ten years ago, the decorum, order, fulfilment of religious duties, and general deportment of the working classes, male and female, made a favorable and agreeable impression on me. I have often urged that fact in combating the doctrines of Free trade. Looking at the subject in this view of it, what great responsibility is attached to the population of Lowell!

I am greatly obliged by the friendly opinions which you have expressed of me. It is such opinions that, throughout life, [have] always been a stimulating motive with me to merit. And they have sustained me amidst the many trials to which I have been exposed.

The prospects of the Whig cause are very encouraging. I look forward to their realization with the deepest anxiety—an anxiety less on my own account, if my heart do not deceive me, than on account of my Country; for I verily believe that on their success greatly depends the fate of that other experiment so interesting not only to the people of the U. States but to mankind.

I shall eagerly look for the result in your State next week.[3] The threats of the Abolitionists, as mentioned by you, prove how little confidence belongs to the Ultras' of that party. For of all the Delegations in Congress, whose conduct I have observed, that of Massachusetts (and Mr. [George M.]

Briggs among them)[4] has made the greatest sacrifices to conciliate them. Yet he is denounced by them!

ALS. MHi. 1. For William Schouler (1814-72), Elisha Bartlett (1804-55), and Harriet Farley (1817-1907), see *DAB*. Schouler was a cloth printer, newspaper editor, and sometime member of the Mass. house of representatives. Bartlett was the first mayor of Lowell, Mass. (1836) and taught at a number of medical schools, including Transylvania University and the University of Louisville. Farley was a mill hand in Lowell who became the editor, along with Harriot Curtis, of *The Lowell Offering*, a periodical made up of contributions from female workers in Lowell. For a year they employed Schouler to publish it. The periodical ended in 1845, but Farley revived it in 1850 under the name *New England Offering*. 2. For the Lowell experiment in developing a model cotton mill community, see Thomas Bender, *Towards An Urban Vision* (Lexington, 1975), 21-51; George F. Kenngott, *The Record of a City, A Social Survey of Lowell, Massachusetts* (New York, 1912), 1-27; Margaret T. Parker, *Lowell a Study of Industrial Development* (New York, 1940), 118-210. 3. Clay to Berrien, July 17, 1843. 4. Clay to Colton, Sept. 2, 1843.

To Alexander William[s] ***et al.***, Greeneville, Tenn., November 10, 1843. Thanks them for their invitation of October 10 to visit Greene County next spring, while enroute to Raleigh, North Carolina, an invitation he regretfully declines since his proposed journey will not take him through eastern Tennessee. Appreciates this particular invitation, however, because it includes a "frank exposure of the prejudices which once existed against me, in the minds of many of my fellow-citizens of Tennessee, their causes and their final removal as described in your letter. These prejudices, gentlemen, were not peculiar to Tennessee. When they raged, in their greatest violence, conscious of their injustice, I felt convinced that the day would come when my countrymen would be fully persuaded that I had served them with zeal, integrity and fidelity. That day has come, and I rejoice that a merciful Providence has permitted me to survive the calumnies that were put forth to crush me. And I rejoice also that magnanimous Tennessee stands preeminent in devotion to truth, to justice and to the separation of unmerited injury." Copy. Printed in Knoxville *Register*, December 6, 1843; also in the Jonesboro (Tenn.) *Whig*, December 13, 1843. Written in Lexington.

In the invitation, dated Greeneville, Tenn., October 10, 1843, William[s] notes that Jacksonian leaders in Tennessee, "solicitous for his [Jackson's] advancement to the Presidency," had earlier launched against Clay "the most savage crusade that ever disgraced the meridian of an enlightened country." Adds that a "deadly hatred" of Clay was fanned by "a combination of presses, wholly enlisted in the war against you." Assures him, however, that many honest men have recently abandoned the Jacksonians, having discovered that the true welfare of the nation "can have no affinity with Locofocoism"; they have thus "turned from it with disgust, and are now the zealous advocates of the leading measures of the Whig party." Copy. Printed in the Jonesboro (Tenn.) *Whig*, December 13, 1843.

To WILLIAM C. PRESTON Lexington, November 12, 1843

I received your favor of the 3d. It was my intention to pass through Columbia and pay my respects to Mrs. P. & yourself.[1] Your hospitable invitation strengthens the previous motives to do so. I desire during the whole of my Southern tour to avoid all parade, and *especially* in my transit through So. Carolina, for obvious reasons. I hope you will assist me in conforming to that desire. I anticipate the necessity of going from Augusta to Savannah, where I have some business to transact.

I think, with you, that Virginia is within the reach of the Whigs.[2] An admirable spirit is getting up there, and, what is no less important, an efficient organization. I suggested a plan which I am assured is in progress of execution.[3] The theatre which you have selected for a Campaign is the best in the whole State for successful operations. The next would be from Botetourt down the Roanoak [*sic*, Roanoke], and its tributaries.

I thank you for your suggestion about Dr. Bronson. I knew nothing of him. He wrote to me about the Tariff;[4] and, as I have but one original on that or any other subject, I thought I would send him a Copy. I am glad that you approve it. It is also generally approved at the North. The same person has written to me on the subject of Abolition and Slavery;[5] but I have declined giving any answer for publication; refering him to my Speech in the Senate, the resolutions I offered there in Jany 1838 as an amendment to Mr. Calhouns[6] &c &c. . . .

ALS. NjMoHP. 1. Clay to Moore, July 10, 1843. 2. Clay to Leigh, March 17, 1843. 3. Not clear to whom or when Clay proposed a Whig campaign plan specifically for Virginia, but see his larger plan for organizing nation, states, and counties in his letter to Letcher, August 15, 1843. 4. Bronson to Clay, August 22, 1843. 5. Bronson letter not found. 6. Speech in Senate, Jan. 9, 1838.

To John S. Littell, Germantown, Pa., November 13, 1843. Thanks the Clay Club of Germantown for their "fair and very able exposition of Whig principles" and for "the songs, which appear to be well calculated to excite and stimulate that spirit, which is all that is needed to insure a great and glorious triumph." Copy. Printed in Colton, *Clay Correspondence*, 4:482.

To PETER B. PORTER Lexington, November 13, 1843

I received today your favor of the 6h the most agreeable part of the contents of which is the assurance of your restored health, about which I had entertained apprehensions; but you term its gossip has much interest. Under an impression that you had gone home, I addressed you lately at the [Niagara] Falls.

I observe you entertain a high opinion of the "Express"[1] I have not seen much of it lately, but I had thought the Tribune unexcelled in efficiency, and surpassing all others in its Statistics & general information in regard to localities.

The quarrels among our Editors in N. York are provoking.[2] I have remonstrated to [James Watson] Webb against them.[3] He does not perceive the inconsistency of attacking Greeley[4] &c for their course at the Harrisburg Convention, and at the same time supporting Mr. Webster.

I shall hear tomorrow of your Election.[5] I anticipate a defeat but without discouragement.

ALS. NBuHi. Addressed to Porter in Niagara Falls, N.Y. 1. Porter to Clay, Nov. 6, 1843. 2. Porter to Clay, Sept. 25, 1843. 3. Clay to Webb, Nov. 8, 1843. 4. Horace Greeley, editor of the New York *Tribune*. Porter to Clay, Sept. 25, 1843. 5. Clay to Campbell, July 21, 1843.

To JOSEPH SMITH Lexington, November 15, 1843

I have received your letter,[1] in behalf of the Church of Jesus Christ of Latter day Saints, stating that you understand that I am a Candidate for the Presidency, and enquiring what will be my rule of action relative to you, as a people, should I be elected.

I am profoundly grateful for the numerous and strong expressions of the People, in my behalf, as a Candidate for President of the U. States; but I do not so consider myself. That must depend upon future events, and upon my sense of duty.

Should I be a Candidate, I can enter into no engagements, make no promises, give no pledges, to any particular portion of the people of the U. States. If I ever enter into that high office, I must go into it free and unfettered, with no guarantees but such as are to be drawn from my whole life, character and conduct.

It is not inconsistent with this declaration to say, that I have viewed, with a lively interest, the progress of the Latter day Saints; that I have sympathised in their sufferings under injustice, as it appeared to me, which has been inflicted upon them; and that I think, in common with all other Religious Communities, they ought to enjoy the security and protection of the Constitution and the Laws.

ALS. USlC. 1. Smith to Clay, Nov. 4, 1843.

To JAMES T.B. STAPP Lexington, November 16, 1843

I received your friendly letter, and thank you for the information which it communicates.

I should be extremely happy to see Illinois added to the Whig States;[1] and with the Clubs which you have formed and a system of organization, extending to all the Counties, I do not see why that desirable object might not be accomplished.

I am glad to see that you are appointed a delegate to the Balto. Convention;[2] and I should be very glad to receive and entertain you under my roof; but I expect to leave home for the South in three or four weeks, and not to return until the month of May. Should you pass this way at any time when I am here I hope you will give me a call.

The elections of this fall are very encouraging to the Whig cause. They shew that the party is recovering from the disappointment produced by Mr. Tyler's extraordinary course, and authorize a confident belief of a signal triumph next year.

ALS. IHi. For Stapp, see 5:481. Addressed to him in Vandalia, Ill. 1. Clay to Berrien, April 23, 1843. 2. Clay to Clayton, August 8, 1842.

To John Quincy Adams, [Washington], November 19, 1843. Hopes he has arrived safely home in Washington following his "Western journey." Regrets he could not visit Lexington [Clay to Adams, September 21, 1843] while in northern Kentucky. Thanks him, however, for "the friendly testimony which you bore, at Covington and at Maysville, towards me. It was eminently kind, considerate, and well timed." Reports that Governor Robert P. Letcher was also "very happy" with the compliment Adams paid him and the friendly letter he addressed to him. ALS. MHi-Adams Papers, Letters Recd., 527.

Adams toured Ohio and Northern Kentucky in November, 1843, but did not visit Lexington. In a speech in Covington, Ky., on November 13 he fulsomely praised Clay. He did the same at Maysville on November 14. Washington *Daily National Intelligencer*, November 22, 1843; Adams, *Memoirs of John Quincy Adams*, 11:430-31.

From [J.W.] Payne & Harrison, New Orleans, November 22, 1843. Report that the sale of Clay's bagging and bale rope, up to November 20, shows a credit in his favor of $2,209.68, and that the firm has on hand 182 coils of his rope which is being held pending his further instruction. Note that "the best rope in the market now" is selling for but 5¢ cash per pound and that the price will not likely advance this season. Remark that other business decisions can be made when Clay arrives in New Orleans in December. ALS. DLC-TJC (DNA, M212, R14). Enclosed in this letter were copies of the New Orleans *Price Current, Commercial Intelligencer,* and *Merchants' Transcript.* Clay arrived in New Orleans on December 23, 1843.

To EMANUEL C. REIGART[1] Lancaster, Pa., November 25, 1843

I have duly received your letter requesting me, at the instance of several respectable gentlemen of the anti-masonic party in Pennsylvania, to state what are my existing relations to freemasonry.

I entertain great repugnance to appearing before the public at all, on any subject, and especially upon one which, according to my humble apprehension, is not necessarily connected with the administration of the general government; but the respectful terms in which you have been pleased to address me, and the conscientious motives by which I presume you to be actuated, entitle you to a frank and full answer to the inquiry contained in your letter; and I now have the pleasure of accordingly transmitting such an answer.

I became a mason in early life, from youthful curiosity and a social disposition. But I never had any taste for or was much skilled in the mysteries of the order. All the professed objects of the institution as developed to me (and I knew no other) were charitable and benevolent. I never did contract, and never would have contracted, any obligations whatever incompatible with my duty to my country or to society. I have always regarded the constitution and laws of the land as supreme, and my obligations and duties to my country as paramount to all other earthly obligations and duties.

Official evidence of my retirement from the lodge upwards of nineteen years ago has been published; and I have not since been a member of any lodge,[2] nor held any office, place, or appointment of any kind in the institution. Nor do I believe that I could, upon my own knowledge or recollection of its rites and ceremonies, obtain admission at this time in any lodge of any degree whatever. I never in my life voted for or supported any man, for any civil or military or other appointment under government, because he was a mason; nor against any man because he was not a mason. In 1825 I voted for Mr. Adams as president of the United States, although, as I have understood, he was not a mason, and against General Andrew Jackson, notwithstanding he was a distinguished member of that order; but it is proper to state that I was not at all influenced by that fact. Among my most determined political opponents in Kentucky are masons, who now or lately held, according to the newspapers, eminent stations in the lodge.

Such is a faithful account of my relations to masonry, an institution which has comprised some of the most eminent men of our country, dead and living. I presume that the experience of many men has been, like my own, that as we advance in life we cease to take any interest in attending such institutions.

In the sentiments of love of country, of obedience to its laws, of acknowledgment of their paramount obligation, and of devotion to our free institutions, by which all ought to be, and I understand anti-masons are animated, I most heartily and cordially concur.

Copy. Printed in *Niles' Register* (Dec. 16, 1843), 65:244. Written in response to a question in Reigart to Clay, Lancaster, Pa., Nov. 14, 1843, in *ibid.* 1. For Reigart, a lawyer who had been elected to the Pennsylvania legislature as an Anti-Mason (1834) and subsequently became a Native American candidate for Congress (1846) and for governor (1847), see Alexander Harris, *A Biographical History of Lancaster County* (Lancaster, Pa., 1872), 477-79. 2. Clay had left the Lexington Masonic Lodge on Nov. 18, 1824. The secretary of the lodge published a notice to this effect in *Niles' Register* (Jan. 7, 1832), 41:346.

To Charles L. Crockett *et al.*, Wythe County, Va., November 27, 1843. Expresses his desire to visit their county, but doubts he will be able to do so next spring. Rejoices "to learn that the people of my native State, and the people of the whole Union, have become sensible of the great advantages of fostering our national industry." Predicts that "the day will come—it is nigh at hand—when all will be surprised that there should ever have been any difference of opinion about the policy of just and reasonable encouragements to the interests of our own country, against the rivalry, the selfishness, and the prohibitory policy of foreign nations, who are indifferent to our welfare." Copy. Printed in Washington *Daily National Intelligencer*, December 25, 1843.

To LEWIS D. CAMPBELL[1] Lexington, November 29, 1843

Since the date of your favor of the 17th. inst., which I duly received, you will have seen, on the subject of it, several letters of mine published, which, with my previously publis[h]ed opinions, on the Tariff, will afford all the information you desire. Indeed I do not know how I could be more full or explicit. If the Government shall authorize a Distribution of the proceeds of the Public Lands, and make adequate provisions for the payment of the National debt there can be no doubt that, in a Tariff laid on foreign imports, by proper discriminations, in behalf of our domestic interests, all just and reasonable encouragement can be extended to them. I do not think it at all necessary to look forward to the improbable event, when a just combination of the principles of revenue and protection, would not afford that reasonable and proper encouragement: but if, contrary to my expectations, such an event should happen, the Government will be no doubt guided by the state of public opinion, the state of our domestic interests, and by all other lights existing at the time of its occurrence.

I pray you not to subject me to the mortification of again seeing my name in print upon this threadbare subject. I am only induced to write to you from the respect which is entertained for you . . . .

LS; also revised by Clay. Courtesy of J. Winston Coleman, Jr. 1. For Campbell, see *BDAC*.

To JOHN PENDLETON KENNEDY Lexington, December 3, 1843

I duly received your favor, and the Copy of the Colonization Report,[1] for which I thank you. I am very glad to possess that highly valuable document, embodying so much interesting information, in regard to one of the most benevolent, and one of the greatest projects that ever engaged National enterprize.

I hope you will not forget to send me a Copy of your Defense of the Whigs.[2] To three points I trust[3] you will direct your special attention. 1st. That the Whigs at the Special and succeeding Sessions of Congress labored honestly to carry out all the measures which they had promised. 2. That they were prevented by the perfidy of Tyler, and make that perfectly clear. 3d. That he was aided and encouraged by the Leaders in Congress of our opponents; and that, after having seduced him, he has finally incorporated himself with them, administering the patronage of the Government to their exclusive advantage. The true use now to make of Tyler is to lash our adversaries. In my Chambersburg letter[4] I indicated that employment of him.

I presume the idea of running Mr. Webster as the Whig Candidate for V.P. will not be persisted in.[5] If it had been expedient to use his name in connection with that office, it was unwise to have made any movement to that effect, before he had given some public evidence of his adherence to Whig principles.

Upon the whole, we may be well satisfied with the political events of the year which is drawing to a close. If the result in N. York be apparently against us,[6] it ensures the nomination of Mr V Buren and is so far satisfactory; for I think the Whigs will lick him next year worse than they did in 1840. Against him all the documents are prepared and ready, and we have nothing to do but to publish another Edition of them, without revisal or correction, organize, and go ahead. . . .

ALS. MdBP. 1. The report of Feb. 28, 1843, entitled "African Colonization, Slave-Trade, Commerce, Report of Mr. Kennedy of Maryland, from the Committee on Commerce of the House of Representatives . . . on the Memorial of the Friends of African Colonization, Assembled in Convention, in the City of Washington, May, 1842. . . ." was published in *The African Repository and Colonial Journal* (Dec., 1843), 19:357-79. Clay was president of the American Colonization Society from 1836-49. Staudenraus, *The African Colonization Movement*, 187. 2. Kennedy's book did blame Tyler for deserting the Whig party and for the failure of the Whigs to enact their program. He also attacked the Democrats for giving so much support to the Tyler administration but added that the Whig quarrel was with Locofocoism rather than the president, because only the Democratic party presented a threat to the Whigs in the 1844 election. J.P. Kennedy, *Defence of the Whigs, By a Member of the Twenty-Seventh Congress* (New York, 1844), 147-48. 3. Word "hope" is struck through and "trust" substituted in its place. 4. Clay to Chambersburg Clay Club, July 25, 1843. 5. Porter to Clay, Sept. 25, 1843. 6. Clay to Campbell, July 21, 1843.

To THOMAS WILLIAMS *et al.* Lexington, December 3, 1843

[Thanks the Clay Club of Pittsburgh for the invitation to visit their city on his return home from North Carolina next spring. Says he would like to see Pittsburgh again because, with the possible exception of Lowell, Mass., it best "manifests the wisdom of cherishing our own domestic and American interests." Continues:]

Now, throughout the whole extent of the Union, the whig party is happily united in a remarkable degree as to the wisdom of that policy. All members of it believe that the revenue necessary to an economical administration of the government, should not be extorted by harrassing systems of direct and internal taxation, but should be raised exclusively by duties on foreign imports, and that in arranging a tariff of those duties, reasonable, moderate and certain protection should be extended to our domestic interests. Such a tariff will possess permanency and stability, a quality far more essential and important than a high tariff, producing dissatisfaction, fluctuation and uncertainty.

And it is a matter of high gratification, that although there are great divisions in opinions amongst our political opponents, as to the wisdom of this policy, vast numbers of them realizing its indisputable benefits from actual experience, coincide in opinion with us. I think, therefore, we have much reason to anticipate that the events of next year will establish this policy upon a satisfactory basis, reconciling all interests, and all parts of the Union. I hope that they will also settle other great and interesting questions, and leave the Nation once more in quiet, to pursue successfully all the branches of its varied business in full confidence and tranquility.

[Regrets he cannot accept their kind invitation, pleading probable fatigue at that stage of his proposed journey].

Copy. Printed in Frankfort *Commonwealth*, Dec. 26, 1843.

To EDWARD CHURCH[1] Lexington, December 4, 1843

I duly received your favor of the 23d. ulto., and share largely with you in the gratification, produced by the successful issue of the Massachusetts election,[2] and I sincerely hope that the Whigs will maintain, in that State, the ground which they have so nobly won.

I have hitherto thought, and still think for the present, that it is best to abstain from any determination on the question, whether I shall or shall not give my consent to the use of my name as a candidate for the president of the United States. The next five or six months may bring forth events that ought to influence my judgment one way or the other. I shall nevertheless take care to decide in time, as far as I can to prevent any embarrassments to the Whig cause.

LS. Written by an amanuensis, signed by Clay. 1. Church, a native of Massachusetts, had once resided in Lexington. It was he who introduced Robert Fulton's steamboat to Europe in the 1820s; see also 1:559. Addressed to Church in Northhampton, Mass. 2. Clay to Berrien, July 17, 1843.

To RICHARD PETERS, JR. Lexington, December 4, 1843

I have received your favour, transmitting to me a programme of a complete edition of the laws of the United States, which you propose to collect and publish, and to sterotype.[1] I believe the wants of the community, of the courts, and of the bar, require such a work; and the plan of executing it which you propose can have no higher recommendation than that which Judge Story has given it. I would add my individual wish that your index may be as full and perfect as that which is contained in the judge's edition of the Statutes.[2]

Copy. Printed in 1 *U.S. Stat.*, xiii. 1. Richard Peters, *The Public Statutes at Large of the United States of America From the Organization of the Government in 1789, to*

March 3, 1845. . . . Boston, 1848. 2. Joseph Story, *The Public and General Statutes Passed by the Congress from 1789 to 1836.* . . . 4 vols., Boston, 1827-37.

To LEVERETT SALTONSTALL Lexington, December 4, 1843

[Regrets he had not seen Saltonstall's daughter Anne when he was in her vicinity in Louisiana last winter. Continues:]

I am rejoiced at the deliverance of Massachusetts from the Locofoco party;[1] but that Liberty party has trouble for you ahead. You will all in the end open your eyes to its tendency. The mass is honest, but, as too often happens, its leaders are selfish, ambitious, and seeking to profit themselves. It is in vain to attempt to conciliate them. See how they have treated Mr. [George N.] Briggs, Mr. [John Quincy] Adams, Mr. [Joshua R.] Giddings &c![2] They will finally, that is, the corrupt portion of them, coalesce with the Loco's. Birds of a feather &c. The Loco's have always denounced them more and treated them worse than the Whigs; but what of that, say their profligate leaders, who have fat offices in their teeth. I have been informed that, in one of their Conventions at Troy, an Abolition orator openly supported Mr. V. Buren because, as he urged, he was more flexable and managable than I am![3]

I am surprized that Texas should occasion you so much uneasiness at the North. In the whole circle of my acquaintance in K. I do not remember to have heard lately a solitary voice raised in favor of or against Annexation. Let Mr. Tyler recommend it, if he please, and what of that? The whole world will see the motive, and the impotency of the recommendation.[4] Every body knows that annexation could only be effected by treaty, and where are two thirds of the Senate to be got to ratify such a treaty? Such a recommendation would be the last desperate move of a despicable traitor.

By the by, are you acquainted with the Representatives of the late Revd. Mr. [William E.] Channing? If you are, you will oblige me by procuring from them a copy of a confidential letter I addressed to him some years ago on the project of annexation.[5] I do not wish to make or encourage new issues, as I regard this to be; but, in the progress of events, it may become necessary for me to make some public expression of my opinions on this project, in which case I should prefer availing myself of that letter.

Mr. Tyler has not deceived me since the Extra Session. Its events convinced me that he was utterly devoid of principle, and that he would finally embrace Locofocoism. I lamented that all our Massachusetts friends did not see as clearly as you did. But we both well know one of the causes of their blindness. Mr. Webster (for his name naturally associates itself with this subject) seems at last to have found out where he is to go, but he moves slowly and with studied dignity. But the Whigs are good Christians, and ought to open their doors to all who knock at them.

We shall beat our opponents next year terribly. There is no mistake about it. We shall get States that did not go with us in 1840.

I hope to start next week for N. Orleans, where I shall pass the larger part of the winter,[6] and thence go to Raleigh. . . .

ALS. DLC-Leverett Saltonstall Papers. 1. Clay to Berrien, July 17, 1843. 2. Clay to Colton, Sept. 2, 1843; Clay to Bacon, Oct. 27, 1843. 3. For the history of the Liberty party, see Fladeland, *James Gillespie Birney*, 175-88, 207-66; Aileen S. Kraditor, "The

Liberty and Free Soil Parties," in Schlesinger, *History of U.S. Political Parties*, 1:741-881; Sewell, *Ballots For Freedom*, 43-169; John R. Hendricks, "The Liberty Party in New York State," Ph.D. dissertation, Fordham University, 1959. 4. For Tyler's political problems with Texas annexation as a campaign issue in 1843-44 and his motives in urging annexation, see Seager, *And Tyler Too*, 209-42; Chitwood, *John Tyler*, 343-66. 5. Not found, but see Channing to Clay, August 1, 1837; Clay to Porter, Jan. 26, 1838; Clay to Crittenden, Dec. 5, 1843. 6. Clay to Moore, July 10, 1843.

From James Tallmadge, New York City, December 4, 1843. Chides Clay for his past political errors of omission and commission, specifically "the incident of 1826, when apprehensions were entertained you might not have been correctly informed as to the particulars of certain occurrences which had happened in this state & an explanation being proffered, your reply was, 'I want no information about it.' " Assures Clay that he [Tallmadge] never believed that Clay had prevented him from securing a patronage post from President John Quincy Adams [5:173-74, 764]. Says these are all "by-gone matters," however, and that "The present condition of the country requires that every good man & patriot shall unite to redeem the nation from bad men & the degradation & revulsion consequent on several years of misrule." Thinks the Whigs will carry New York in 1844 [Clay to Campbell, July 21, 1843] because of "policies which you have so long and so ably maintained." ALS. DLC-HC (DNA, M212, R5). At this time Tallmadge (1778-1853), who had been lt. governor of New York in 1824-26 (when DeWitt Clinton was governor), was president (1830-46) of New York University. See *BDAC*.

To JOHN J. CRITTENDEN Lexington, December 5, 1843

I received your favor of the 29th. ulto.[1] On the subject of Texas, or rather its annexation to the United States, I had received a letter from Mr Child, the editor of an abolition paper in New York,[2] to which I returned no answer, not that I was unwilling to announce my opinion upon that subject, but that I did not think it right, unneccessarily, to present new questions to the public. Those which are already before it are sufficiently important and numerous, without adding fresh ones. Nor do I think it right to allow Mr Tyler, for his own selfish purposes, to introduce an exciting topic,[3] to add to the other subjects of contention which exist in the country. How is he to present it? Texas can only be annexed to the United States by treaty or by conquest. If the former, it is Mr Tyler's duty, if he thinks it right to annex it, to conclude a treaty for that purpose, if he can and, lay it before the Senate.[4] Nobody I presume would propose to acquire it by war and conquest. But let me suppose that he limits himself to a simple recommendation of the annexation, without having negociated any treaty for that purpose, what could Congress do upon such a recommendation? They could pass no act to effect it. He might as well recommend the annexation to the United States of Mexico itself or of any other independent Power. Indeed a recommendation of any other *independent* country would be less irrational than the annexation of Texas, because to Texas Mexico asserts a title, which she is endeavouring to enforce by the sword. We could not therefore incorporate Texas into the Union without involving the United States in war with Mexico, and I suppose nobody would think it wise or proper to engage in war with Mexico, for the acquisition of Texas. We have, it is true, acknowledged the independence of Texas, as we had a right to do, for the sake of our commercial and other intercourse with Texas, but that acknowledgment did not extinguish or in any manner affect the rights of Mexico upon Texas. What has the House of Representatives to do with the treaty making power prior to its exercize by the president and the Senate? Considered as a practical question, every man must be perfectly convinced that no treaty, stipulating the annexation of Texas, can secure for its ratification a constitutional majority in the senate. Why then present the question? It is manifest that it is for no other than the wicked purpose of producing discord and distraction in the nation

Taking this view of the matter I think, if there be such a recommendation, it would be best to pass it over, if it can be done, in absolute silence. Should a discussion of it, in spite of your wishes, be forced then, I think, it would be better to urge some such topics as I have suggested above and to treat it as a question with which Congress has nothing to do, and which has been thrust upon it, by one, who has neither the confidence of the Nation or either of the great parties in it, with the evident view of promoting his own personal interests, by producing dissension, discord, and distraction. If there be no formal application from Texas itself, it might be urged that to discuss the question of annexing it to the United States, would be derogatory from the respect due both to Texas and Mexico, and would violate the dignity and the character of our own government.

I think in some of the modes which I have suggested or in some other, which may present itself to our friends at Washington, the mischievous designs of Mr Tyler may be averted.

Should however a question be actually forced upon you, in such manner, that you will be compelled to express an opinion, for or against annexation, I do not know what yours may be, but I should have no hesitation myself in voting against it. And here are some of my reasons. First, the territory of the United States is already large enough. It is much more important that we should unite, harmonize, and improve what we have than attempt to acquire more, especially when the acquisition would be inevitably attended with discord and dissatisfaction. 2d. It is wholly impracticable to accomplish the object of annexation, if it were desirable, for reasons already stated. And, in the third place, if Texas were annexed to the United States the motive with those who are urging it would not be fulfilled. It would not now, or ever, give to the slaveholding portion of the Union a preponderating weight[.] The other portion would continue to retain the ascendancy, which would be ultimately increased, by the annexation of Canada, to which there could be no objection, if Texas were admitted into the Union.

I might add that there is great reason to doubt whether Texas could be admitted consistently with the constitution of the United States. But I do not dwell upon that point, because of the force of the examples of Louisiana and Florida.

Some six or seven years ago I addressed a confidential letter to a distinguished friend communicating my opinion adverse to the annexation of Texas.[5] I placed it, at that time, upon the ground that we already had quite as much, if not more, territory than we could govern well. That I had no desire to see a new element of discord introduced into the Union, and that it was far more important, to the happiness of the people of the United

States, that they should enjoy in peace, contentment, and harmony what they have than to attempt further acquisitions of territory, at the hazard of destroying all those great blessings. I have no copy of that letter but I hope it is in existence, and, if it be, I shall endeavour to procure a copy of it to be used hereafter if rendered necessary by the progress of events instead of any further expression of my opinion. I shall regret very much, should the proposition come to a formal question, if the Whig Party should, in a *body*, vote in the affirmative. Such a vote would be utterly destructive of it, without the possibility of securing Texas. The best use to make of Texas, perhaps, is to hold out to our Northern friends that, if, by the unhappy agitation of the question of slavery, they should force a separation of the slave from the free states, in that contingency, the former would be prompted to strengthen themselves by the acquisition of Texas.

Texas is destined to be settled by our race, who will carry there, undoubtedly, our laws, our language, and our institutions, and that view of her destiny reconciles me much more to her independence than, if it were to be peopled by another and an unfriendly race. We may live as good neighbors, cultivating peace commerce and friendship. I think you will find that it will turn out that there is not the smallest foundation for the imputation of a design on the part of Great Britain to establish a colony of Texas.[6] Such an attempt, on her part, would excite the hostility of all the great Powers of Europe, as well as the United States. But, odious as such a design, on the part of Great Britain, would be as she would cover it probably under the pretext of emancipation, her conduct would not be regarded with so much detestation, by the civilized world, as that would be of the United States, in seeking to effect annexation, since the motive which would be attributed to her and with too much justice would be that of propagating instead of terminating slavery.

I send you this letter, in its rough draught, just as I have dictated it to my son John, who has been kind enough to act as Amanuensis for me.

When the message arrives,[7] I may write you again, if there is any occasion in that document for my doing so. I am very glad to hear of the faith which our friends entertain in our success next year, but I hope they will add good works, which I cannot help thinking important both in religion and politics

LS. Dictated to John Morrison Clay with two interlineations in Clay's hand. Letter marked "Private and Confidential." 1. In which Crittenden had warned Clay of Tyler's forthcoming annual message, which would likely include a statement on Texas. Kirwan, *John J. Crittenden*, 173-74. In his Third Annual Message to Congress, in Dec., 1843, Tyler demanded that Mexico recognize the independence of the Republic of Texas and cease her sporadic attempts to reconquer that nation. While he stopped short at this time of recommending the annexation of Texas, he did state that "Texas is separated from the United States by a mere geographical line," and noted that "her territory, in the opinion of many, down to a late period, formed a portion of the territory of the United States." *MPP*, 4:261-62. 2. David Lee Child for a time assisted his wife Lydia Maria Child in editing the *Weekly National Anti-Slavery Standard* in New York City. Sewell, *Ballots for Freedom*, 26, 35, 287-88, 341-42; *DAB*. 3. Texas annexation. See Clay to Saltonstall, Dec. 4, 1843. 4. Tyler laid such a treaty, signed April 12, 1844, before the Senate for ratification on April 22. On June 8 it was rejected by a vote of 35 to 16, or 28 votes short of the necessary two-thirds margin. Chitwood, *John Tyler*, 349-56; Seager, *And Tyler Too*, 209-19, 229. 5. Letter to William E. Channing not found; but see Channing to Clay, August 1, 1837, and Clay to Porter, Jan. 26, 1838. 6. For the pros and cons on the question of British interests in Texas—commercial, territorial, and anti-slavery—see, variously, Seager, *And Tyler Too*, 209-19; Chitwood, *John Tyler*, 342-66; Justin H. Smith, *The Annexation of Texas* (corrected ed., New York, 1941), 301-5, 381-413; Pletcher, *Diplomacy of Annexation*, 113-49; Ephraim D. Adams, *British Interests and Activities in Texas, 1838-1846* (Baltimore, 1910), *passim*; Reeves, *American Diplomacy Under Tyler and Polk*, 116-36, 146-56. 7. Tyler's Third Annual Message. *MPP*, 4:260-63.

To JOHN M. BERRIEN Lexington, December 9, 1843

I received today, on the eve of my departure to New Orleans, your favor of the 30th. ulto. The diploma and volumes of collections of the historical Society, of which you have kindly taken charge for me to Washington, I will thank you to retain until I receive them from you at that city, or give other directions concerning them. My voyage to New Orleans and my journey afterwards to the Southern Atlantic States, may be attended with so many contingencies that I cannot even yet fix the time when I shall reach Georgia. I hope it will be about the 20th. of March.

I wrote a confidential letter to Crittenden, about Texas,[1] which, if he does not show it to you, I will thank you to ask him to let you see.

The Senate will have a most delicate and important duty to perform in passing upon the appointments made by the President in the recess. And I take the liberty of saying to you that, whilst a spirit of liberality should be exercised, where party politics are concerned, I think there are high principles involved in regard to some of those appointments. One class of them comprehends persons, who have been sent abroad manifestly to elude the action of the Senate. In those cases, it seems to me that the Senate owes to its own character and dignity to vindicate its just constitutional authority and to rebuke the defiance or meanness of the President. Nor would pecuniary considerations weigh a feather with me, in asserting the proper participation of the Senate[2] in the appointing power. There is another class of appointments, embracing persons who have basely abandoned their principles, with an understanding, express or implied, that the Executive should pay for their treachery in the public appointments of the Government. Sound morality, political justice, and precedent all seem to me to concur in rejecting both of these classes of appointments. It will be asked how are they to be filled? I would say that I would continue to reject, as long as the names of persons should be offered who fall within the principles I have stated. The truth is, that the public interest would not suffer, if the places which persons have been recently sent abroad to fill, were to remain unoccupied, during the residue of Mr Tyler's term. The acting President leaves vacant foreign appointments as in the instance of the French mission whenever he pleases.[3] The Senate has an equal right to decide when, in their judgment, temporary vacancies may be allowed. It is better that these vacancies should exist than be filled in the manner they are likely to be in the present administration. I request that you will do me the favor when you next write to Mrs Berrien to communicate my respects to her and my congratulation upon her recovery from her recent indisposition.

LS. NcU. Written by an amanuensis but revised slightly and signed by Clay. Letter marked "(Confidential)." 1. Clay to Crittenden, Dec. 5, 1843. 2. The word "President" is struck through and "Senate" substituted. 3. Lewis Cass left his post in Paris on Nov. 12, 1842; the nomination of Henry A. Wise to replace Cass was made on Feb. 27, 1843, but the Senate rejected it on March 3; William R. King was appointed to the Paris post by Polk on April 9, 1844. Richardson Dougall and Mary Patricia Chapman, *United States Chiefs of Mission, 1778-1973* (Washington, 1973), 56, 58; U.S. Sen., *Executive Journal*, 6:174-75, 189.

To James B. Everhart, West Chester, Pa., December 12, 1843. Reports he is about to depart Lexington for New Orleans. Regrets he cannot visit West Chester, because "both on the score of principle and policy, I am averse to making visits which would wear the aspect of electioneering tours." Regrets also that he cannot take Everhart on as a law student since he will be away from home for the next four or five months and is "unable to conjecture" what he will be doing after that. Recommends instead "an excellent Law school in Lexington [Transylvania]." ALS. MH.

Everhart, an 1842 graduate of Princeton, studied law in West Chester under Joseph J. Lewis, then spent one year at Harvard Law School and another studying in the office of William A. Meredith in Philadelphia. He later practiced law in West Chester and served in both houses of the Pennsylvania legislature. *NCAB*, 3:125.

To E.P. Pitts *et al.*, [Accomac County], Va., December 12, 1843. Hopes circumstances will permit him to visit Accomac County when he is in nearby Norfolk next spring, because "There are two places in the United States which, more than almost any other I am desirous of seeing!" Explains that "one is the Eastern Shore of Virginia, and the other the Island of Nantucket; in both of which, the primitive manners customs and hospitality of the early emigrants to them from Europe, I understand, are admirably preserved." Copy. Printed in *Niles' Register* (January 20, 1844), 65:331. For Clay's itinerary through the South in December, 1843-May, 1844, see Moore to Clay, July 10, 1843.

From John H. Beall, Hancock, Md., December 22, 1843. Answers an interrogatory from Clay, dated November 29 [not found], in which Clay had enclosed a deposition by one Jane Rankin pertaining to his [Clay's] executorship of the James Morrison estate. Beall, in this letter, encloses [not found] "Information about the negroes, suing for their freedom." Thanks Clay for allowing him to render this personal service and hopes that "the whole American people" will call him into their service. ALS. DLC-TJC (DNA, M212, R14). Endorsed by Clay: "Co. Morrison's Estate. [Information about the negroes, suing for their freedom]." *Ibid.*

Just which Morrison slaves were suing for their freedom is not known. There were, however, two slaves, William and Peter, whose emancipations had been provided for in the will of Esther Montgomery (Mrs. James) Morrison; both boons were subsequently revoked in codicils to the will. Fayette County Will Book P, 1841, pp. 280-82. See also Clay to Trustees of Transylvania University, October 12, 1842.

From P.W. Barbour, Charlestown, Ind., December 27, 1843. Asks Clay to continue to pursue his claim in Georgetown, Ky., and give him an estimate of what his chances are. Informs Clay that he is now living in Charlestown because he had "Promised to Give you a coppy of that Bond for a deed to my house But having lost my Tittle [title] all at a Gambling i was Obliged to Leave town and thereby was not able to Go after it." Adds: "Please Do not treat me the way you did in the summer and not answer this Request But Let no one Know where i am." Asks Clay to write him at Harmony Landing, Ky., rather than Charlestown, since he does "not want every Bodey to know of my Buisiness." ALS. DLC-TJC (DNA, M212, R14). Harmony Landing once stood 2.5 miles east of Goshen (on the Ohio River) and 9.5 miles west of La Grange.

To James Brown Clay, Lexington, Ky., December 27, 1843. Encloses a draft for $2,611.91 to meet a debt of $2,500 to the Messrs. [Elijah W. & D.M.] Craig of Lexington, payable in Philadelphia on the 9th or 12th of February, 1844. Instructs his son to handle the details of the payment and to apply the balance "to the uses of the family or of Thomas's factory [Clay to Silsbee, March 18, 1843]." Adds that "I shall be very anxious to hear what Thomas [Hart Clay] may do in the hiring of hands [Clay to Lucretia Hart Clay, December 9, 1842; Clay to Silsbee, March 18, 1843]." Reports that in New Orleans "Prospects for the present are not good on the Sale of bagging and rope. The shortness of the Cotton Crop is the cause." ALS. DLC-TJC (DNA, M212, R10). Written from New Orleans. See Clay to Thomas Hart Clay, January 22, 1843.

To Catherine Walker, New Orleans, December 29, 1843. Wishes he could help the son of "my late friend," Mr. G. Walker, with a loan; but regrets he has "no pecuniary means other than are necessary to my [own] indispensible wants." ALS. KyU. Written in New Orleans to Mrs. Walker who lived in Frenchman St. there.

To James Brown Clay, Lexington, Ky., December 30, 1843. Repeats his instructions of December 27 relative to paying off the $2,500 note held by the Messrs. [Elijah W. & D.M.] Craig. Reports that the 44" wide hemp bagging he had sent to Savannah sold for 16¢ per yard and that more than a third of the bale rope sent there had sold for 8¢ per pound. Has been told that Georgia planters would "cheerfully" pay 2¢ more per yard for bagging more closely woven, and that they prefer a 46" width for securing square packages and 44" for round. "Mention this to Thomas [Hart Clay]." On the other hand, laments that only half of the bale rope sent to Memphis had been sold, most of it "at 5 Cents only." ALS. DLC-TJC (DNA, M212, R10). Written from New Orleans.

To Thomas J. Johnston, Natchez, December 30, 1843. Volunteers his legal assistance, without compensation, in the continuing case of Henry de la Francia's $11,850 claim [7:82, 233] against the U.S. government for compensation for arms sold Reuben Kemper, agent of the West Florida revolutionary convention during its uprising against Spain in 1810. Believes, however, that while Johnston has taken some additional evidence, the Francia claim seems no more solid now than it appeared when it was reviewed and denied back in 1817 and again in 1828. The question of whether Francia actually owned the arms he sold Kemper remains an open one, Clay notes. Further, the West Florida convention had never listed a debt owed Francia in its formal catalogue of claims against the U.S. ALS. KyU. Written from New Orleans.

To John J. Crittenden, Washington, December 31, 1843. Reports his arrival in New Orleans "a week ago" and his intended departure for North Carolina "towards the close of February." Says his health is very good, but that "our friend" Judge Alexander Porter is dying. ALS. NcD. Clay arrived in New Orleans on December 23 and left on February 24, 1844. Porter died on January 13, 1844.

From ADAM BEATTY N.p., *ca.* 1843[1]

An intimate acquaintance of more than forty years; and the many evidences of kindness, and friendship experienced, during that long period; together with a knowledge of your devoted attachment to the interests of Agriculture; and of the great benefits you have conferred upon the agriculturists of the United States, by your pre-eminent and successful efforts, in the National Councils, to rear up a home market for agricultural products, emboldened me to ask your permission to dedicate to you this first effort, as far as I know, at a treatise, in book form, on the important subject of agriculture, by a Kentuckian.

I am conscious that the volume, now presented to the public, has defects, which I would have gladly removed. I humbly hope, however, that it will be found to contain some practical information, which will prove beneficial to the farming community; and that it may induce some abler writer to give to the public a more perfect treatise on the most important of all human occupations.

With a deep sense of gratitude, for the many acts of kindness and friendship received, I assure you of my most cordial friendship and esteem.

Copy. Printed in Adam Beatty, *Southern Agriculture, Being Essays on the Cultivation of Corn, Hemp, Tobacco, Wheat, Etc. and the Best Method of Renovating the Soil* (New York, 1843), 3. 1. This letter was printed in Beatty's book as a dedication to Henry Clay. The book was copyrighted on Feb. 24, 1843, and published in New York sometime thereafter. An 1844 edition was published in Maysville, Ky. For its place in the history of agriculture, see Hopkins, *Hemp Industry in Kentucky*, 21, 42; Demaree, *American Agricultural Press*, 102.

CALENDAR OF UNPUBLISHED LETTERS AND OTHER DOCUMENTS

Letters deemed to have slight historical importance to an understanding of Henry Clay and his career are listed below. Copies of them are on file in the offices of *The Papers of Henry Clay* at the University of Kentucky, Lexington, and may be consulted by interested persons. The locus of the original manuscript of each letter has been included below, as has an indication of the general subject matter of each. Subject classification code numbers have been employed as follows:

1 Requests for general assistance and government assistance, information, documents, reports, correspondence, books and other printed materials.

2 Transmission of routine information, and documents, including that between the Executive and Legislative branches.

3 Applications, recommendations, appointments, and resignations pertaining to government employment and political office.

4 Correspondence and transmission of information relating to the claims of private citizens against the U.S. and foreign governments:
 a. United States
 b. Great Britain
 c. France
 d. Spain
 e. Holland
 f. Other European nations
 g. Latin American nations.

5 Correspondence and transmission of information relating to land grants, pensions, and related legal actions.

6 Routine correspondence relating to:
 a. Forwarding of mail
 b. Interviews and audiences
 c. Introductions & character references
 d. Invitations, acceptances, regrets, condolences
 e. Appreciation, gratitude, social pleasantries
 f. Subject matter not clear
 g. Application, recommendations pertaining to private employment.

7 Routine legal correspondence and documents relating to:
 a. Clay's law practice as counsel or executor
 b. Cases in which Clay was plaintiff, defendant, witness, or deponent

c. James Morrison Estate management
d. Eliza Jane Weir guardianship
e. James and/or Ann Hart Brown Estate management.

8 Routine correspondence and documents (including deeds, agreements, leases) relating to Clay's land purchases and sales, livestock transactions and breeding, and investments.

9 Routine bills, receipts, checks, bank drafts, promissory notes, loans, payments, rents, mortgages, tax documents.

10 Correspondence relating to routine political and professional services rendered constituents, colleagues, friends, other politicians.

11 Miscellaneous.

JANUARY 1837
1837 From Thomas S. Redd, DLC-TJC, 9.
3 From James Whitcomb, DNA, 8.
7 From Benjamin F. Crutchfield, DLC-TJC, 9.
11 From Moore, Morton & Co., DLC-TJC, 8, 9.
16 From Crutchfield & Tilford, DLC-TJC, 9.
26 From Enoch Clark, DLC-TJC, 9.
27 From William Shumbert, DLC-TJC, 9.

FEBRUARY 1837
nd From H.I. Bodley, DLC-TJC, 7a, 9.
1 From Samuel Lambdin & E.R. Bennett, DLC-TJC, 6c.
4 From James B. Longam, DLC-TJC, 9.
16 From Josiah Downing, DLC-TJC, 9.
21 From Joseph Boulanger, DLC-TJC, 9.
22 From Horace B. Hill & Co., DLC-TJC, 9.
25 From Virgil Maxcy, DNA, 1.
25 To Virgil Maxcy, DNA, 2.

MARCH 1837
nd From H.I. Bodley, KyLxT, 7d.
2 From E. Dyer, DLC-TJC, 9.
3 From Joseph Boulanger, DLC-TJC, 9.
3 From Duff Green, DLC-TJC, 9.
7 From S.M. Books, DLC-TJC, 9.
8 From P. Mauro & Son, DLC-TJC, 9.
8 To R.K. Richards *et al.*, KyU, 6d.
17 To Edward Everett, MHi, 6f.
21 From Thomas Smith, DLC-TJC, 9.
23 From James Downing, DLC-TJC, 8, 9.
30 From Hamilton Jenkins, DLC-TJC, 9.

APRIL 1837
8 From William B. Astor, MH, 9.
15 To John Forsyth, DNA, 2, 6a.
20 With S.S. Nicholas, DLC, 7c.
21 From John J. Astor, DLC-TJC, 9.
25 From Isaac Burnet, KyLxT, 6g.
27 From William B. Astor, MH, 9.

MAY 1837
1 *Clay* v. *Commonwealth of Ky.*, Ky, 7b.

8 From Henry Clay, Jr., DLC-TJC, 9.
10 From Layton & Headington, DLC-TJC, 9.
15 From Nimrod L. Finnell, DLC-TJC, 8, 9.
23 From D.L. Myers Trimble, DLC-HC, 9.
29 From L.D. Stockton, DLC-TJC, 7a.
31 From Thomas Broaddus, DLC-TJC, 9.

JUNE 1837
8 From H.B. Hill & Co., DLC-TJC, 8, 9.
16 From January & Huston, DLC-TJC, 9.
21 From Robert Wickliffe, DLC-TJC, 8.
26 From Browning & Headley, DLC-TJC, 9.
26 From W.P. Browning, DLC-TJC, 9.
29 To Bank of Ky.-Lex. branch, DLC-TJC, 9.
29 From Thomas McCracken, DLC-TJC, 9.
30 From P.G. Hunt, DLC-TJC, 8.

JULY 1837
26 From A. & B.H. Hall, DLC-TJC, 9.
26 From Thomas Rankin, DLC-TJC, 8.

AUGUST 1837
7 From John Anderson, DLC-TJC, 9.
7 From Athey & Lewis, DLC-TJC, 9.
7 From Porter & Butler, DLC-TJC, 9.
10 From City of Lexington, DLC-TJC, 9.
15 From John Headley, DLC-TJC, 9.
17 From Spencer M. Grayson, DNA, 7a.

SEPTEMBER 1837
nd From John Hunter, DLC-TJC, 9.
8 From Duff Green, DLC-TJC, 9.
11 From Thomas Broaddus, DLC-TJC, 9.
12 From Stuart & Brothers, KyLxT, 7d.
15 From A. Fuller & Co., DLC-TJC, 9.
18 From A. Fuller & Co., DLC-TJC, 9.
21 From J.W. Ware, Dr. Thomas D. Clark Collection, Lexington, Ky., 6d.
22 From William Walker, DLC-TJC, 9.
27 To Bank of Ky.-Lex. branch, DLC-TJC, 9.
30 From John J. Astor, MH, 9.

OCTOBER 1837
nd From Jacob Swigert, DLC-TJC, 7b.
4 To Unknown Recipient, CtY, 11.
13 From Enoch Tucker, DLC-TJC, 9.
19 From Henry Shepherd, DLC-TJC, 9.
24 To William Sullivan, MB, 6e.
25 From John W. Hunt, KyLxT, 9.
26 From January & Huston, DLC-TJC, 6e, 9.
26 From January & Huston, DLC-TJC, 9.
30 To Bank of Ky.-Lex. branch, DLC-TJC, 9.

NOVEMBER 1837
nd From William Rankin, DLC-TJC, 9.
11 To Middleton Rawlings, Fleming Co. Deed Book U, 7a.
16 From Silas Evans, DLC-TJC, 7a, 9.
18 From Adams & Hogan, DLC-TJC, 9.
18 From Albert Florea, DLC-TJC, 9.
21 From William Barlow, DLC-TJC, 9.
21 To H. Fisk *et al.*, Newark (N.J.) *Daily Advertiser*, Dec. 7, 1837, 6d.

22 From D. Warner, DLC-TJC, 9.
25 To Bank of Ky.-Lex. branch, Mary Clay Kenner Collection, Rogersville, Tenn., 9.
25 To Bank of Ky.-Lex. branch, Mary Clay Kenner Collection, Rogersville, Tenn., 9.

DECEMBER 1837
4 From Enoch Tucker, DLC-TJC, 9.
5 From William Gunston, DLC-TJC, 9.
10 From William Byrd Chamberlayne, DLC-HC, 7b.
13 To James Whitcomb, DNA, 1, 2.
14 From Henry Baldwin, DLC-TJC, 7a.
14 To David Hoffman, TNV, 10.
16 From James Whitcomb, DNA, 2.
21 From E.C. Davis, DLC-TJC, 9.
28 From Beverly Allen, DLC-TJC, 2.
28 From Robb Winebrener & Co., DLC-TJC, 9.
31 From Thomas A. Russell, DLC-TJC, 9.

JANUARY 1838
1838 From H.I. Bodley, KyLxT, 7d.
1838 From Robert S. Todd, DLC-TJC, 7c, 9.
3 From E.H. & C.H. James, DLC-TJC, 9.
8 To Friends of Henry Clay, Washington *Daily National Intelligencer*, Jan. 16, 1838, 6d.
9 To Samuel J. Peters, ViU, 6e.
11 From John Miller, DLC-TJC, 9.
11 To Thomas A. Russell, Henry Clay Memorial Foundation, Lexington, Ky., 9.
15 From Thomas Powell, DLC-HC, 4g.
20 From James Whitcomb, DNA, 2.
25 To Ralph R. Gurley, DLC, 2.
25 To L.J. Koger, KyLoF, 10.
29 From James Whitcomb, DNA, 2.

FEBRUARY 1838
2 To Bank of Ky.-Lex. branch, Mary Clay Kenner Collection, Rogersville, Tenn., 9.
9 From Joseph George, DLC-TJC, 9.
22 From Thomas Allen, DLC-TJC, 9.

MARCH 1838
8 From James Whitcomb, DNA, 2.
19 To Thomas McKane, KyHi, 2.
21 To C.R. Gold, MSaE, 10.
23 From Henry Peyveux, DLC-TJC, 9.
27 From James B. Clay, DLC-TJC, 9.
29 To Joseph Cowperthwait, DLC-HC, 9.
30 To J.T. Irwin *et al.*, GU, 6d.

APRIL 1838
4 To Unknown Recipient, PHi, 6e.
7 To Whom It May Concern, J. Winston Coleman, Jr., Collection, Lexington, Ky., 6c.
11 To Joseph Lancaster, Kunglige Biblioteket, Stockholm, Sweden, 11.
12 From Joshua M. Grundin, DLC-TJC, 9.
21 To U.S. Bank of Pa., DLC-TJC, 9.
23 To U.S. Bank of Pa., DLC-TJC, 9.
24 From William B. Astor, MH, 9.

MAY 1838
nd To J.W. Thomson, DLC-TJC, 8.
19 To U.S. Bank of Pa.-Wash. branch, DLC-TJC, 9.
22 From J. Gayles, Jr., DLC-TJC, 9.
23 To U.S. Bank of Pa., DLC-TJC, 9.

25 From James B. Clay, DLC-TJC, 9.
28 From M. Burns, DLC-TJC, 9.

JUNE 1838
nd From Jacob Swigert, DLC-TJC, 7b.
nd To Whom It May Concern, DLC, 6c.
1 From John Headley, DLC-TJC, 9.
4 From W.P. Browning, DLC-TJC, 9.
6 To Ann E. White, KyU, 6e.
8 To U.S. Bank of Pa., DLC-TJC, 9.
16 *Clay & Craig* v. *Hart* and *Hart* v. *Clay & Craig*, *Reports of . . . Court of Appeals of Ky.* (Spring, 1838), 7b.
18 To Whom It May Concern, Raleigh *Register & North Carolina Gazette*, June 18, 1838, 11.
19 To City of Washington, D.C., DLC-TJC, 9.
20 From January & Huston, DLC-TJC, 9.
20 From J. Howard March & Co., DLC-TJC, 9.
20 From J. Howard March & Co., DLC-TJC, 9.
20 To U.S. Bank of Pa.-Wash. branch, DLC-TJC, 9.
30 From J. Dunham, DLC-TJC, 9.

JULY 1838
2 To Joseph Gales, DLC, 11.
2 To Edward Poinlois, ViU, 6c.
2 From Nelson Thompson, DLC-TJC, 9.
4 To William Clay, MH, 6c.
4 From Enoch Tucker, DLC-TJC, 9.
5 To U.S. Bank of Pa., DLC-TJC, 9.
6 From William Thumblet, DLC-TJC, 9.
7 To Jonathan Meredith, DLC-HC, 6c.
7 From Frank Taylor, DLC-TJC, 9.
8 From S.A. Hill, DLC-TJC, 9.
9 From Hamilton & Denham, DLC-TJC, 9.
18 To U.S. Bank of Pa., DLC-TJC, 9.
21 To J. Liggett, Washington *Daily National Intelligencer*, August 24, 1838, 6d.
23 From M. & R.H. Sweeney & Co., DLC-TJC, 9.
23 To U.S. Bank of Pa., DLC-TJC, 9.
24 From Finnell & Zimmerman, DLC-TJC, 8, 9.
24 To U.S. Bank of Pa., DLC-TJC, 9.
25 From January & Huston, DLC-TJC, 9.
26 To U.S. Bank of Pa., DLC-TJC, 9.
26 To U.S. Bank of Pa., DLC-TJC, 9.
27 From January & Huston, DLC-TJC, 9.
27 To U.S. Bank of Pa., DLC-TJC, 9.
28 To Citizens of Woodford County, Frankfort *Commonwealth*, August 15, 1838, 6d.
28 From January & Huston, DLC-TJC, 9.

AUGUST 1838
1 To U.S. Bank of Pa., DLC-TJC, 9.
4 To U.S. Bank of Pa., DLC-TJC, 9.
15 To U.S. Bank of Pa., DLC-TJC, 9.
15 To U.S. Bank of Pa., DLC-TJC, 9.
21 From Albert Florea, DLC-TJC, 9.
21 To Bank of Ky.-Lex. branch, Mary Clay Kenner Collection, Rogersville, Tenn., 9.
21 To U.S. Bank of Pa., DLC-TJC, 9.
21 To U.S. Bank of Pa., DLC-TJC, 9.
21 To U.S. Bank of Pa., DLC-TJC, 9.
25 To U.S. Bank of Pa., DLC-TJC, 9.
30 From March & Benson, DLC-TJC, 9.

SEPTEMBER 1838

11 To Bank of Ky.-Lex. branch, Mary Clay Kenner Collection, Rogersville, Tenn., 9.
12 To Bank of Ky.-Lex. branch, Mary Clay Kenner Collection, Rogersville, Tenn., 9.
13 From Washington & Hamilton, DLC-TJC, 9.
19 From Thomas Rankin, DLC-TJC, 9.
20 To John W. Allen, NcD, 6c.
20 To Richard Biddle, NcD, 6c.
20 To Jacob Burnet, NHi, 6c.
20 To Peter B. Porter, NBuHi, 6c.
21 From Robert Fisk, DLC-TJC, 9.
22 To James Erwin, MB, 2.
24 To U.S. Bank of Pa., DLC-TJC, 9.
24 To U.S. Bank of Pa., DLC-TJC, 9.
25 With Robert Wickliffe, DLC-TJC, 11.
28 To U.S. Bank of Pa., DLC-TJC, 9.

OCTOBER 1838

1 From Buchanan & Gray, DLC-HC, 9.
1 To U.S. Bank of Pa., DLC-TJC, 9.
5 From A. Logan, DLC-TJC, 9.
6 From John M. Moore, DNA, 5.
8 To Bank of Ky.-Lex. branch, Mary Clay Kenner Collection, Rogersville, Tenn., 9.
8 From John W. Hunt, DLC-TJC, 9.
13 From William Hardman, DLC-TJC, 9.
18 From J. Anderson & Co., DLC-TJC, 9.
18 From Joseph Cowperthwait, DLC-TJC, 9.
20 To U.S. Bank of Pa., DLC-TJC, 9.
22 From Joseph Ficklin, DLC-TJC, 9.
26 From Bank of Ky.-Lex. branch, DLC-TJC, 9.
26 From Thomas Broaddus, DLC-TJC, 9.
27 To Bank of Ky.-Lex. branch, Mary Clay Kenner Collection, Rogersville, Tenn., 9.
27 From Albert Florea, DLC-TJC, 9.
28 From John J. Astor, MH, 9.
31 From James Whitcomb, DNA, 5.

NOVEMBER 1838

5 To U.S. Bank of Pa., DLC-TJC, 9.
6 To U.S. Bank of Pa., DLC-TJC, 9.
9 From George Poindexter, DLC-TJC, 9.
10 To Bank of Ky.-Lex. branch, Mary Clay Kenner Collection, Rogersville, Tenn., 9.
12 To Bank of Ky.-Lex. branch, Mary Clay Kenner Collection, Rogersville, Tenn., 9.
13 To Bank of Ky.-Lex. branch, DLC-TJC, 9.
17 From Stephen Duncan, DLC-TJC, 9.
18 From John Kirkpatrick, DLC-TJC, 9.
20 To Bank of Ky.-Lex. branch, Mary Clay Kenner Collection, Rogersville, Tenn., 9.
21 To Bank of Ky.-Lex. branch, Mary Clay Kenner Collection, Rogersville, Tenn., 9.
21 To Bank of Ky.-Lex. branch, Mary Clay Kenner Collection, Rogersville, Tenn., 9.
23 To Bank of Ky.-Lex. branch, Mary Clay Kenner Collection, Rogersville, Tenn., 9.
29 From Coleman Rogers, DLC-TJC, 8.

DECEMBER 1838

5 To Robert Swartwout, NN, 6d.
10 From Richard Graham, MoSHi, 10.
11 To John Minor, NjMoHP, 7a.
21 To Col. Clive & Mr. Bonvesie, Dr. Thomas D. Clark Collection, Lexington, Ky., 6c.

JANUARY 1839

1839 To William Fitzhugh, MHi, 6d.
1839 To Nathaniel P. Tallmadge, WHi, 10.

15 From Richard Graham, DLC-TJC, 5, 8.
21 To Samuel L. Southard, NjP, 6d.
23 To Unknown Recipient, NN, 6d.
25 To Unknown Recipient, KyLoF, 6e.
26 To Levi Woodbury, DNA, 1.
28 From Levi Woodbury, DNA, 2.

FEBRUARY 1839
nd From H.I. Bodley, KyU, 7b.
nd From H.I. Bodley, KyU, 7c.
nd From H.I. Bodley, KyU, 7a.
11 To Nicholas Biddle, TKL, 6c.
13 To John J. Milligan, TNV, 6d.
18 To Lewis Cass, MiU-C, 6c.
22 To Chevalier Gustave de Nordia, Kunglige Biblioteket, Stockholm, Sweden, 2.

MARCH 1839
11 To Christopher Hughes, MiU-C, 6e.
19 From Benjamin F. Crutchfield, DLC-TJC, 9.
21 To Thomas Jones, Fleming Co. Deed Book U, 8.

APRIL 1839
nd To Daniel B. Price, DLC-TJC, 7c.
1 To J.E. McDowell & J.H. Thomas, Fleming Co. Deed Book V, 8.
3 From H.B. Hill & Co., DLC-TJC, 9.
4 To Bank of Ky.-Lex. branch, DLC-TJC, 9.
6 To Bank of Ky.-Lex. branch, Henry Clay Memorial Foundation, Lexington, Ky., 9.
9 From Joel R. Poinsett, DNA, 5.
9 From R.B.J. Twyman, DLC, 9.
9 To R.B.J. Twyman, Henry Clay Memorial Foundation, Lexington, Ky., 9.
20 From H.B. Hill & Co., DLC-TJC, 9.
22 To J. Blunt *et al.*, NHi, 6d.
22 From John W. Hunt, KyLxT, 8.
28 To John W. Hunt, KyU, 2.
30 From Joseph Cowperthwait, DLC-TJC, 9.

MAY 1839
3 To Bank of Ky.-Lex. branch, Mary Clay Kenner Collection, Rogersville, Tenn., 9.
4 From Montmollin & Cornwall, DLC-TJC, 9.
5 To James Taylor, OCHP, 7a.
16 To Bank of Ky.-Lex. branch, Mary Clay Kenner Collection, Rogersville, Tenn., 9.
21 From Thomas Bradley, DLC-TJC, 9.
22 *Brown* v. *Humphreys*, DLC-TJC, 7e.

JUNE 1839
nd From J.C. Rodes, KyLxT, 7d.
3 To Bank of Ky.-Lex. branch, Mary Clay Kenner Collection, Rogersville, Tenn., 9.
4 To Peter B. Porter, NBuHi, 6c.
10 To Bank of Ky.-Lex. branch, Mary Clay Kenner Collection, Rogersville, Tenn., 9.
12 Farm Memoranda, Josephine Simpson Collection, Lexington, Ky., 8.
15 To Bank of Ky.-Lex. branch, Mary Clay Kenner Collection, Rogersville, Tenn., 9.
21 To William F. Dunnica, KyLoF, 7c.
26 From A. Safts, DLC-TJC, 9.
29 To Bank of Ky.-Lex. branch, DLC-TJC, 9.

AUGUST 1839
ca. 9 From John W. Taylor, NHi, 6e.
12 From George Stevens, DLC-TJC, 9.
15 To Samuel L. Southard, NjP, 6d.

SEPTEMBER 1839

13 From Madison C. Johnson, KyLxT, 7c, 9.
14 To John Andrews, RPB, 9.
22 To James Erwin, MCM, 2.
23 From John Andrews, DLC-TJC, 9.
23 To Bank of Ky.-Lex. branch, DLC-TJC, 9.
23 From U.S. Bank of Pa., DLC-TJC, 9.

OCTOBER 1839

ca. 19 From J.B. Tilford, DLC-TJC, 9.

DECEMBER 1839

20 From Alfred Warner, DLC-TJC, 9.
23 From Moore, Morton & Co., DLC-TJC, 9.
31 From Peter B. Porter, OHi, 6c.

JANUARY 1840

1840 From H.I. Bodley, KyLxT, 7d.
1840 From Exchange Hotel, DLC-TJC, 9.
1840 From R.M. Rhea, DLC-TJC, 9.
1840 From Thomas A. Russell, DLC-TJC, 9.
7 To Thomas H. Clay, Dr. Thomas D. Clark Collection, Lexington, Ky., 11.
13 To Mrs. Aaron Vail, Mme. Jacques de Bon Collection, Geneva, Switzerland, 6d.
15 To E.N. Drury, KyU, 6e.

FEBRUARY 1840

nd From H.I. Bodley, DLC-TJC, 7a.
4 From A. Rockwell, DLC-TJC, 9.
4 From Philemon Thomas, DNA, 3.
8 From William Emmons, DLC-TJC, 9.

MARCH 1840

11 To F.A. Ripley, KyLoF, 10.
12 From Joseph Gales & William W. Seaton, DLC-TJC, 9.
13 From John J. Astor, DLC-TJC, 9.
22 To James K. Paulding, DNA, 2.
23 From William Thumblet, DLC-TJC, 9.
28 To William Coffin, ViU, 6e.
28 From John C. Noble, DLC-TJC, 8, 9.
30 To John H. McMillen, WHi, 10.
30 To James Taylor, NN, 10.

APRIL 1840

3 To Daniel Brent, MH, 6c.
4 To James K. Paulding, DNA, 2.
7 From James K. Paulding, DNA, 2.
8 To Samuel L. Southard, NjP, 6d.
16 From Tucker & Son, DLC-TJC, 9.
18 To Anthony Drane, NcD, 10.
18 From D.S. Vigers, DLC-TJC, 7c, 9.
22 To Thomas P. Ray, Dr. C. Percy Powell Collection, Washington, D.C., 6d.
29 To Mr.— Onderdonk, ViU, 10.

MAY 1840

2 To Joseph Cowperthwaite, KyU, 9.
12 To James N. Barker, DNA, 2.
12 From Peter Hagner, DNA, 5.
22 From James W. Moncreiff, KyHi, 5.
26 From Thomas Allen, DLC-TJC, 9.

JUNE 1840
1 To Mrs. Henry Atkinson, George R. Loeb Collection, Philadelphia, Pa., 6e.
18 From Richard Thompson, DLC-TJC, 9.

JULY 1840
1 From Samuel Hazard, DLC-TJC, 9.
1 From Alfred Warner, DLC-TJC, 9.
3 From Joseph Boulanger, DLC-TJC, 9.
4 To Mary Cutts, MHi, 11.
6 To R.H. Armistead *et al.*, DLC, 6d.
6 To James Caldwell, ViHi, 6c.
6 From William Fisher, DLC-TJC, 9.
6 From Tucker & Son, DLC-TJC, 9.
7 To Daniel Gardner, ViU, 11.
9 To N.F. Cabell *et al.*, Richmond (Va.) *Whig and Public Advertiser*, August 28, 1840, 6d.
11 From Henry S. Fox, DLC-HC, 2.
11 To S. Lawrence, ViU, 6c.
13 From Peter Hagner, DNA, 2, 5.
21 From Thomas Huggins, DLC-TJC, 9.
27 From John B. Tilford, DLC-TJC, 9.
29 From W.P. Browning, DLC-TJC, 9.
30 To Northern Bank of Ky., DLC-TJC, 9.

AUGUST 1840
4 To Bank of Ky.-Lex. branch, DLC-TJC, 9.
5 From Kennedy, Smith & Co., DLC-TJC, 9.
6 From John Hart, DLC-TJC, 9.
18 From Morgan Lewis, KyHi, 2.

SEPTEMBER 1840
7 From L'Hommedieu & Co., DLC-TJC, 9.
7 From Thomas S. Theobald, DLC-TJC, 9.
9 To Bank of Ky.-Lex. branch, DLC-TJC, 9.
10 To Bank of Ky.-Lex. branch, DLC-TJC, 9.
16 To Robert P. Letcher, NcD, 9.
21 From William P. Browning, DLC-TJC, 9.
23 To Bank of Ky.-Lex. branch, DLC-TJC, 9.
26 To Bank of Ky.-Lex. branch, DLC-TJC, 9.
26 To Bank of Ky.-Lex. branch, DLC-TJC, 9.
28 To Bank of Ky.-Lex. branch, DLC-TJC, 9.

OCTOBER 1840
5 From John W. Hunt, KyLxT, 9.
7 From Porter & Butler, DLC-TJC, 9.
8 From John M. Hunt, DLC-TJC, 9.
29 From Alexander Caldwell, DLC-TJC, 9.
30 From Smith, Jeter & Co., DLC-TJC, 9.

NOVEMBER 1840
nd From H.I. Bodley, DLC-TJC, 7e.
2 To Bank of Ky.-Lex. branch, DLC-TJC, 9.
3 From Alexander Campbell, DLC-TJC, 9.
4 To Bank of Ky.-Lex branch, DLC-TJC, 7c, 9.
4 From Enoch Clark, DLC-TJC, 9.
4 To Esther Morrison, DLC-TJC, 7c, 9.
7 To Esther Morrison, DLC-TJC, 7c, 9.
7 To Esther Morrison, DLC-TJC, 7c, 9.
10 From John Wirt, DLC-TJC, 9.
11 From Jesse Bayles, DLC-TJC, 9.
13 From John Anderson, DLC-TJC, 9.

14 To Bank of Ky.-Lex. branch, DLC-TJC, 9.
14 From A. Logan, DLC-TJC, 9.
14 From Robert Wickliffe, DLC-TJC, 7b.
18 From J.B. Johnson, DLC-TJC, 9.
20 To Edmund H. Taylor, KyHi, 1.
24 From Albert Florea, DLC-TJC, 9.
25 From Alexander Campbell, DLC-TJC, 9.
26 From Stephen Duncan, DNA, 3.
28 From Lyman Potter, DNA, 3.

DECEMBER 1840
ca. 1 From Citizens of Brownsville, Pa., DNA, 3.
1 From William B. Rose, DNA, 3.
2 From Joseph Smith *et al.*, DNA, 3.
3 From Thomas Washington, DNA, 3.
4 From James L. Armstrong, DNA, 3.
7 From Joseph Miller, DNA, 3.
8 From R.K. Chamberlayne, DNA, 3.
9 From Athey & Lewis, DLC-TJC, 9.
10 From David Hoffman, DNA, 3.
13 From William Gilliam, DNA, 3.
14 From Henry H. Snelling, DNA, 3.
15 From Thomas Chilton, DNA, 3.
18 From Jacob Acker *et al.*, New York *Morning Courier & Enquirer*, Dec. 29, 1840, 6d.
18 From Richard W. Colfax, DNA, 3.
18 From Joel Crawford, DNA, 3.
18 From Benjamin Silliman *et al.*, Washington *Daily National Intelligencer*, Dec. 28, 1840, 6d.
19 From H. Hill, DNA, 3.
21 From Waddy Thompson, Jr., DNA, 3.
22 To Jacob Acker *et al.*, New York *Morning Courier & Enquirer*, Dec. 29, 1840, 6d.
22 To Benjamin Silliman *et al.*, KyU, 6d.
23 From William H. Garland, DNA, 3.

JANUARY 1841
1841 From Willard Phillips *et al.*, DNA, 3.
1 From Edward Church, DNA, 3.
1 From Joseph Francis & Co., DLC-HC, 11.
1 To L.A. Morgan, NRU, 1.
1 From Zebedee Ring, DNA, 3.
1 From Alfred Warner, DLC-TJC, 9.
7 From Samuel Penn, DNA, 3.
11 From Adoniram Chandler, DNA, 3.
11 From A.M. Porter, DNA, 3.
12 From Washington Barrow, DNA, 3.
12 From J.H. Craven, DNA, 3.
15 From James W. Shaw, DNA, 3.
16 From John W. Treadwell, DNA, 3.
17 To William D. Lewis, NN, 9.
17 From Pierre Van Cortlandt, DNA, 3.
18 From Robert M. Harrison, DNA, 3.
19 From Arthur S.C. Nichols, DNA, 3.
20 From Thomas T. Swann, DNA, 3.
20 From James W. Webb, DNA, 3.
21 From Isaac Thomas, DNA, 3.
23 From William H. Teagarden, DNA, 3.
23 From J.C. Wilkins, DNA, 3.
24 From Washington Barrow, DNA, 3.
24 From D.W. Dickinson, DNA, 3.
25 From Jesse R. Burden, DNA, 3.
25 From J.H. Craven, DNA, 3.

25 From Preston W. Farrar, DNA, 3.
25 From William M. Murrey, DNA, 3.
25 From Samuel J. Peters, DNA, 3.
26 From James Erwin, DNA, 3.
26 From B.R. McIlvaine, DNA, 3.
27 From Arthur F. Hopkins, DNA, 3.
27 From J. Morris, DNA, 3.
28 From John Marland *et al.*, DNA, 3.
28 From Joseph L. White, DNA, 3.
29 From J. Phillips Phoenix, DNA, 3.
29 From John Kelly Smith, DNA, 3.
30 From Thomas M. Cory, DNA, 3.
30 From Samuel Hermann, DNA, 3.

FEBRUARY 1841
1 To Mr. de Bacourt, MH, 6d.
1 From Jacob Burnet, DNA, 3.
1 From Solomon Cohen, DNA, 3.
1 From Arthur W. Magill, DNA, 3.
1 To Roger B. Taney, MdHi, 6b.
2 From William F.J. Elliot, DNA, 3.
2 From Gideon Lee, DNA, 3.
3 From Edward Bates, DNA, 3.
3 From J.S. Hastings, DNA, 3.
4 From William Browne, DNA, 3.
4 From Ephraim M. Ewing, DNA, 3.
4 From Samuel A. Purviance, DNA, 3.
5 From John R. Grymes, DNA, 3.
6 From Thomas M. Allen, DNA, 3.
6 From Benjamin Cheves, DNA, 3.
6 From William Hogan, DNA, 3.
6 From Gideon Lee, DNA, 3.
6 From Etienne Mazareau, DNA, 3.
6 From André B. Roman, DNA, 3.
7 From Hamilton C. Jones, DNA, 3.
7 To James W. Webb, CtY, 3.
8 From Bellamy Storer, DNA, 3.
8 From Charles H. Test *et al.*, DNA, 3.
9 From Samuel Peters, DNA, 3.
10 From J. Curd *et al.*, DNA, 3.
10 From Edward Robinson, DNA, 3.
10 From William F. Thornton, DNA, 3.
12 From John F. Fairbairn, DNA, 3.
12 From William L. Lyons, DNA, 3.
14 From Richard W. Ferguson, DNA, 3.
15 From Luther Bradish, DNA, 3.
15 From Thomas Culbreth, DNA, 3.
16 From Jacob Livingston, DNA, 3.
16 From Joshua Wingate, DNA, 3.
18 From Gavin S. Rose, DNA, 3.
18 From Nathaniel Silsbee, DNA, 3.
19 From Edward Sacket, DNA, 3.
20 From H. Hill, DNA, 3.
20 From A.F. Hopkins, DNA, 3.
20 From Alfred Ingraham, DNA, 3.
20 From L.D. Pinckard, DNA, 3.
21 From J. Phillips Phoenix, DNA, 3.
22 From J.M. Allen, DNA, 3.
22 From Albert J. Kidd, DNA, 3.
22 From Washington Morton, DNA, 3.
22 From Robert S. Rose, DNA, 3.

23 From Jeremy L. Cross, DNA, 3.
23 From P.W. Engs, DNA, 3.
23 From Charles S. Ridgley, DNA, 3.
23 From Jonathan Roberts, DNA, 3.
24 From William Gilliam, DNA, 3.
24 From William D. Wassler, DNA, 3.
25 From D. Graham, DNA, 3.
25 From George F. Hopkins, DNA, 3.
26 From Robert McNair, DNA, 3.
27 From James S. Barbour, DNA, 3.
27 From A. Beebe, DNA, 3.
27 From Samuel McCleane, DNA, 3.
ca. 28 From Mark H. Sibley, DNA, 3.
28 From John A. Spencer, DNA, 3.

MARCH 1841
1 From Jacob Burnet, DNA, 3.
1 From John A. Collier, DNA, 3.
1 From John L. Lawrence, DNA, 3.
3 From William B. Rose, DNA, 3.
4 From Robert Gilmor, Jr., DNA, 3.
5 From James Garland, DNA, 3.
5 From Charles Perrow, DNA, 3.
6 From Peter Hepburn, DNA, 3.
8 From S. Newton Dexter, DNA, 3.
9 From John Ald[?]le, DNA, 3.
15 From A.M. Green, DNA, 3.
17 To Conquest W. Owens, Mason Co. Deed Book, v. 50, pp. 77-78, 7c.

APRIL 1841
1 From John H. Lusby, DLC-TJC, 9.
22 From John B. Tilford, DLC-TJC, 9.
26 From William B. Astor, DLC-TJC, 9.
29 From Thomas S. Theobald, DLC-TJC, 9.

MAY 1841
3 From John Bell, DNA, 3.
9 From Waller Rodes & George Norton, KyLxT, 7d.
10 From D.L. Vigus, KyLxT, 7d.
15 From Robert M. Harrison, DNA, 3.
17 From Robert M. Harrison, DNA, 3.
18 From Enoch Clark, DLC-TJC, 9.
18 From John J. Dudley, DLC-TJC, 9.
19 From John J. Dudley, DLC-TJC, 9.
20 From Robert Lee, DNA, 3.
24 From Robert C. Wetmore, DNA, 3.
28 From John L. Lawrence, DNA, 3.

JUNE 1841
nd From Martin Duralde III, DLC-TJC, 9.
nd From James C. Rodes, KyLxT, 7d.
3 From J. Phillips Phoenix, DNA, 3.
7 From Luther Loomis, DNA, 3.
9 To Mrs. Taylor, NHi, 3.
12 To Thomas Ewing, DLC, 6c.
12 From Richard Graham, MoSHi, 1, 3, 5.
12 From Robert C. Wetmore, DNA, 3.
23 To Franklin Knight, Mary Clay Kenner Collection, Rogersville, Tenn., 11.
30 From George L. Welcker, DNA, 3.

JULY 1841

1 From Thomas Ewing, DNA, 2.
1 From Samuel Hazard, DLC-TJC, 9.
2 From George E. Badger, DNA, 3.
2 From Thomas H. Rochester, DNA, 3.
3 To Unknown Recipient, J. Winston Coleman, Jr., Collection, Lexington, Ky., 6f.
15 From Thomas Ewing, DNA, 2.
23 From T.W. Day *et al.*, DNA, 3.
23 From Thomas D. Gilson [?], DNA, 3.
24 From Nathan Perry *et al.*, DNA, 3.
26 From B.P. Voorhies, DNA, 3.
27 To Samuel L. Southard, NjP, 2.
31 To John Bell, DNA, 3.

AUGUST 1841

3 From George L. Welcker, DNA, 3.
11 From Elisha Huntington, DNA, 5.
11 From John Wirt, DLC-TJC, 9.
12 To Charles A. Davis, NcD, 6c.
17 From Thomas Ewing, DNA, 2.

SEPTEMBER 1841

3 From George L. Welcker, DNA, 3.
25 To Richard E. Stilwell, NcD, 6e.

OCTOBER 1841

nd From James C. Rodes, KyLxT, 7d.
1 To Bank of Ky.-Lex. branch, DLC-TJC, 7c, 9.
6 *Henry Clay* v. *Transylvania University*, Ky, 7c.
12 To Samuel Wilkeson, DLC, 6c.
17 To C.F. Rogers, KyLx, 7a.
20 From Thomas M. Allen, NcD, 3.
22 From Ogle & Watson, DLC-TJC, 7c, 9.
23 From D.M. & E.W. Craig, DLC-TJC, 9.
30 To J. O'Fallon, MoSHi, 6c.

NOVEMBER 1841

3 From John Wirt, KyLxT, 9.
9 From Frederick G. Gilmer, DLC-TJC, 9.
15 To J. Hulme, KyU, 6e.
17 From John W. Hunt, DLC-TJC, 8, 9.
17 From John W. Hunt, KyLxT, 8, 9.
18 To William Burns, KyHi, 7c.
23 From William George, DLC-TJC, 9.
24 From Albert Florea, DLC-TJC, 9.
24 To Esther Morrison, DLC-TJC, 7c, 9.

DECEMBER 1841

15 From John C. Spencer, DNA, 3.
15 From George L. Welcker, DNA, 3.
17 From Walter Forward, DNA, 2.
26 To Nathaniel P. Tallmadge, WHi, 6d.
30 To Abel P. Upshur, Dr. Thomas D. Clark Collection, Lexington, Ky., 3.

JANUARY 1842

4 From Abel P. Upshur, DNA, 3.
18 From N.W. Watkins, DNA, 5.
31 To William C. Rives, DLC, 6d.

FEBRUARY 1842
5 To Elisha M. Huntington, DNA, 1.
7 From Elisha M. Huntington, DNA, 2, 5.
8 From George L. Welcker, DNA, 3.
19 From Francis Markoe, Jr., DSI, 10.
24 To Abbott Lawrence, MH, 6c.
24 To Benjamin O. Tayloe, NN, 9.
25 To Virgil Maxcy, DLC, 6c.

MARCH 1842
3 To Daniel Webster, DNA, 1.
5 From Daniel Webster, DNA, 2.
7 From Elisha M. Huntington, DNA, 5.
7 To Margaret Bayard Smith, DLC, 6d.
7 To Abel P. Upshur, DNA, 1, 10.
9 From Abel P. Upshur, DNA, 2.
28 To Jonathan Tinney, ViU, 11.

APRIL 1842
2 To Edward Everett, MHi, 6c, 10.
2 To Dudley Selden, KyU, 6c.
14 To Peter Force, DLC, 7c.
[?]15 To Mrs. John Q. Adams, MHi, 6d.
15 To Edward Everett, MHi, 6c.
22 To John L. Graham, CSmH, 6a.

MAY 1842
6 To James Caldwell, ViHi, 6c.
10 To Miss Payne, J. Winston Coleman, Jr., Collection, Lexington, Ky., 11.
26 To January & Huston, DLC-HC, 11.
26 To Unknown Recipient, ViU, 10.

JUNE 1842
3 From H. Munday, DLC-TJC, 7c.
26 To Joseph Alderson, KHi, 10.

JULY 1842
14 To Edward Everett, MHi, 6c.
22 From John J. Dudley, DLC-TJC, 9.

AUGUST 1842
31 From Carter & Conant, KyLxT, 9.

SEPTEMBER 1842
3 To J.H. Wheeler, CtY, 6c.
5 From Kennedy, Smith & Co., DLC-TJC, 9.
9 From Kennedy, Smith & Co., DLC-TJC, 9.
11 To James Madison Cutts, ICHi, 6e.
15 To Edward Everett, NcD, 6c.
15 To D. Warner, KyLxT, 7d, 9.
18 To Committee of Memphis Whigs, N.Y. *Daily Tribune*, Nov. 1, 1842, 6d.

OCTOBER 1842
12 To William Seawell *et al.*, N.Y. *Daily Tribune*, Dec. 2, 1842, 6d.
16 To Thomas H. Clay, DLC-HC, 9.
31 To Benedict & Coburn, NUtHi, 11.

NOVEMBER 1842
16 From Richard Pindell, KyLxT, 7c.

17 To James B. Clay, DLC-TJC, 9.
23 To E.W. Hunt *et al.*, PPPrHi, 6e.

DECEMBER 1842
3 From George Curtis, DLC-TJC, 9.
7 To James C. Wilkins *et al.*, Duncan Tavern Historic Center, Paris, Ky., 6d.
10 From E.B. Baker, DLC-TJC, 9.

JANUARY 1843
15 To John J. Crittenden, DLC, 2, 7a.

MARCH 1843
17 From George Curtis, DLC-TJC, 9.
20 To Whom It May Concern, NNPM, 6c.

MAY 1843
15 To A.M. January & Son, Paxton Inn, Washington, D.C., 9.
15 To Robert P. Letcher, OCHP, 6c.

JUNE 1843
5 To William Williams, MdHi, 6e.
14 To John Henry Staats, NHi, 6d.
18 To Joseph Vance, IGK, 2.

JULY 1843
1 To William A. Leavy, DLC-TJC, 9.
12 From John J. Dudley, DLC-TJC, 9.
24 To Edward Everett, MHi, 6c.

AUGUST 1843
5 To William Williams, MdHi, 6d.
15 To Thomas Ewing, DLC, 6c.
18 To J.H. Hedges, NN, 6c, 7a.
22 From George W. Dobbin & Beverley C. Sanders, DLC, 7a.
28 To James Norcom *et al.*, Washington *Daily National Intelligencer*, Sept. 18, 1843, 6d.

SEPTEMBER 1843
4 To W.E. Robinson, NcD, 6d.
13 To John M. Berrien, NcU, 2.
22 From Henry Clay, Jr., DLC-TJC, 9.
22 To Henry Clay, Jr., DLC-TJC, 9.
23 To J.K. Tefft, GHi, 6e.

OCTOBER 1843
3 To T.L. Dunnell, KyU, 6d.
ca. 3 From R.S. Gaither *et al.*, Raleigh *Register and North Carolina Gazette*, Dec. 8, 1843, 6d.
6 From Mr. Bertrand, DLC-HC, 6d.
20 From Henry Clay, Jr., DLC-TJC, 9.

NOVEMBER 1843
7 From J. Phillips Phoenix, ICN, 2, 6e.
8 To Edward Everett, MHi, 6c.
8 To A.B. Quinby, ViU, 2, 6e.
10 To R.S. Gaither *et al.*, THi, 6d.
27 To Adoniram Chandler, NcD, 2, 6e.

DECEMBER 1843
1 From John Orrick, DLC-TJC, 8, 9.
5 To John H. Hewitt, GEU, 6e.
12 To Alexander Anderson, ViU, 6d.

NAME & SUBJECT INDEX: VOLUME 9

Abolition and Abolitionism. *See* Slavery and Anti-Slavery
Accomac County, Va., 645, 901
Adam (slave), 52
Adams, John, 502
Adams, John Quincy: from, 768-70, 859; to, 524, 741-42, 761, 858-59, 891; role in *Amistad* case, 382; on returning runaway slaves from Canada, 382; House effort to censure, 641; fights "gag rule," 872; and the Graves-Cilley duel, 643-45, 662-65 (*see also* Duels and Dueling); C. on administration of, 710; on impeachment of Tyler, 725, 755; on Tyler and 1842 reapportionment act, 724-43, 761, 770; on tariff of 1842 and Tyler's vetoes, 725, 728, 749, 755; on overriding presidential veto by majority vote, 776-77; trade policy toward Great Britain during administration of, 821-22, 831-32; on nationalism vs. states' rights, 768-70; speeches in Ohio and northern Kentucky, 858-59, 891; praises C. in Kentucky speeches, 891; on Webster's return to Whig party, 880; 1843 reelection to House, 852-53; condemned by Liberty party, 896; invited to visit "Ashland," 761, 768, 858-59, 891; mentioned, 71, 98, 146, 159-60, 175, 193-95, 229, 235, 254, 256, 329, 343, 349, 370, 407, 436, 439-40, 453-54, 470, 502, 544, 611, 629, 666, 679, 709, 777, 782-83, 819, 829, 872, 874-75, 882, 888, 892, 897
Adams, Louisa (Mrs. John Quincy), 743, 761, 859
Adams County, Ill., 768
Adams County, Pa., 853
Adams-Onis Treaty, 118, 126-29, 289
Adams & Whitall (not identified), 815-16
Adlard, George: to, 398
African Civilization Society, 526-27
The African Repository and Colonial Journal, 894
Agg, John: to, 183-84
Agricultural Bank of Natchez, 242, 396, 631
The Agriculturist, 843
Alabama: support for C. for president in, 65; political weakness of Harrison and Webster in, 65; 1838 state elections in, 225, 230-31; 1840 state elections in, 444-45, 447; 1843 state and U.S. House elections in, 849-50; outcome of 1844 presidential election in, 805-6, 811-12; gerrymandering in, 849; governor of calls for convention of slave states, 477; support in for C. policies in 27 Cong., 1 Sess., 604; C. visits Mobile, 798, 800; mentioned, 18, 21, 153, 195, 222-23, 226, 232, 263, 329, 369, 410, 425-26, 489, 513, 526, 542, 583, 634, 647, 650, 652, 673-74, 804, 807, 833, 874, 885
Albany, N.Y., 43, 60, 94, 96, 114-15, 120, 123, 127, 136, 142, 154, 167, 173, 175, 181, 204, 256, 258, 262-63, 276-77, 292-93, 312, 320, 330, 334-35, 355, 360, 366, 485, 503, 614, 631, 634, 640, 660, 707, 714, 754, 758, 764, 786, 817, 864
Albany (N.Y.) *Argus*, 288
Albany (N.Y.) *Evening Journal*, 123
Alexander, James M. (not identified), 716-17
Alexander Brown & Sons (not identified): from, 11
Alexandria, La., 741
Alexandria, Va., 422, 548, 696
"Algernon Sidney Hampden" (pseud.), 658
Alien and Sedition Acts: C. opinion of, 161, 249; mentioned, 131, 440, 716
Alison, Archibald, 685, 687
Allegheny College, 29
Allegrante (mare), 150, 184
Allen, Mr. ——— (not identified), 241
Allen, Charles, 720
Allen, James D.: to, 425
Allen, John W.: to, 617-18; mentioned, 375
Allen, Lewis F.: to, 219-20, 309; mentioned, 92
Allen, Stephen, 715-16
Allen, Thomas: from, 246-47; to, 170; mentioned, 89, 546
Allen, Thomas M. (not identified): from, 456
Allen, William, 27, 198, 206, 388, 490, 494, 504, 550-51, 568, 571, 578, 603, 674, 679
Alton, Ill., 108, 450, 678, 748, 806, 818
Alvarez, Manuel, 659
Amelia (slave), 52
American Anti-Slavery Society, 102, 111-12, 182, 199-200, 246, 297
American Colonization Society: C. on goals and successful work of, 103; financing and bequests of, 52-53, 240; use of C. franking privilege by, 804; emancipation of slaves by agency of, 506-7; C. lauds report of, 894; C. speech to, 103-4; C. work for (*see* Clay, Henry: slaves and slavery); mentioned, 18, 21, 28-29, 45, 47-48, 81, 134, 169, 182, 256-57, 259, 295-98, 310, 453, 526-27, 859, 868, 872
American Fur Company, 510
American Indians: slavery among Florida tribes, 128; impact of preemption on land titles of, 134; Miami tribes sell lands to U.S., 149-50; U.S. treaties with various tribes, 131-32, 145, 149-50, 265, 415; Jackson's war against Black Hawk, 146; Seminole question, 122, 146; U.S. use of bloodhounds in Second Seminole War, 289; legal test of Seneca treaty, 415; high cost of moving to west, 683; C. opinion of, 834; mentioned, 128-29, 145, 168, 181, 278, 284, 400, 415, 475, 492, 500, 510, 544, 605, 683, 834, 501. *See also* Seminole Wars; various Indian tribes
American Institute, 884
American Peace Society, 478
American Revolution, 98, 136, 265, 337, 427, 447, 491,

American Rev. (continued): 524, 637, 746-47, 779, 783-84
American Silk Society, 375
American System: C. lauded as founder of, 151; definition of by C., 803; mentioned, 158-59, 356, 376, 562, 686, 711, 741, 754
American Temperance Union, 218
American Turf Register and Sporting Magazine, 884
Amherstville, 276
Amistad (vessel), 382
Anacostia River, 153
Anderson, ——— (not identified), 372
Anderson (slave), 10
Anderson, Alexander O., 514
Anderson, Charles: to, 761
Anderson, Eleanor (Mrs. George Washington), 837
Anderson, George Washington: to, 837
Anderson, J.B. (not identified), 169
Anderson, Simeon H., 404
Andover, Mass., 882-83
Andre, John, 608
Andrews, John W., 157
Andrews, Landaff W., 308
Anglican Church, 431, 449
Anglo-American Convention of 1827, 406
Anglo-American Treaty of 1830, 307, 822
Annapolis, Md., 141, 275
Anne (schooner), 276
Annis (slave), 52
Antigua, 200
Anti-Masonic party: role in Pennsylvania in 1840 election, 94, 305-6; role in New York in 1840, 123; role in Pennsylvania in 1844 election, 752; collapse of, 252-53, 283; patronage efforts of in Harrison administration, 471; C. withdrawal from Masonic lodge, 892-93; mentioned, 39, 91, 106-7, 117, 151, 157, 173-74, 257-58, 261-63, 273-74, 287, 290, 295, 320-21, 327-28, 362, 366, 474, 503, 509, 752, 831-32, 853, 873. *See also* Election, presidential, of 1840: Anti-Masonic role in; *and* nominating conventions
Anti-Slavery. *See* Slavery and Anti-Slavery
Antonio (not identified), 328
Arbuckle, Mathew (or Matthew), 544
Archer, William S.: opposes Tyler on land bill restriction issue, 726; votes against 1842 tariff, 762; mentioned, 533, 556-57, 592-93, 639, 650, 674-75, 718, 722, 812
Arcturus (journal), 630-31
Arguelles, Mrs. E.T.: from, 386, 517; mentioned, 66, 510
Arkansas: public land grant to Little Rock, 27; 1819 bill to organize as territory, 394; mentioned, 8, 21, 153, 183, 263, 290, 329, 369, 372, 391, 402-4, 410, 425-26, 445, 489-90, 513, 526, 542, 544
Armstrong, Mr. ——— (not identified), 290
Armstrong, John, 227, 375, 883
Armstrong, Robert, 71
Arnold, Benedict, 343, 608
Aroostook War, 119, 291, 404, 507
Arthur, Sir George, 105
Articles of Confederation, 491, 637, 645-46, 686, 689, 747
Ashburton, Lord (Alexander Baring): from, 697; mentioned, 683-84, 727, 734
"Ashland": deed of trust for, 789-90; mentioned, 27, 48, 50, 52, 84, 125, 133, 192, 204, 217, 227, 233, 238-39, 251, 311-12, 320, 342, 347, 362, 383, 389, 395-96, 409, 454, 465, 481, 536, 613, 622, 635, 677, 680-82, 688, 700, 702, 724, 728, 730, 754, 761, 763-64, 778, 791, 796, 804, 808, 846, 855, 858, 887
Astor, John Jacob: from, 131-32, 510; to, 846; C. loans from, 238, 450, 618, 816, 846; on paper money, 82; interest in U.S. treaties with Indians, 131-32; C. recommends friend for loan from, 402; makes patronage recommendation to C., 510; fur trading of, 510; recalls *Tonquin* disaster, 510; mentioned, 238, 830
Astor, William B.: from, 82, 618
Ashtabula, Ohio, 330
A.T. (not identified): from, 611
Athens, Ga., 164
Athens, Tenn., 837
Atherton, Charles G., 255
Atherton Resolutions, 254-55, 261
Atlantic Insurance Co., 231
Atlantic Ocean, 339, 343, 404, 499, 646
Attakapas, La., 792
Atwill, ———, 624
Auburn, N.Y., 334-35, 631
Audubon, John J., 816
Augusta, Ga., 391-92, 756, 800, 833, 889
Augusta, Ky., 532
Augusta, Me., 154
Austin, Elbridge Gerry, 460
Austin, James T.: to, 460
Austin, John M.: from, 507
Austin, Tex., 481
Austria, 236, 330
Avery, John C., 240
Avon, N.Y., 320

Babcock, James F.: to, 423-24
Baber, Hiram H. (not identified): from, 450
Bacon, David Francis: from, 866-68; to, 872
Badger, George E.: appointed to Harrison Cabinet, 499-500; C. opinion of, 509; mentioned, 460, 505, 612, 879
Badger, William, 853, 858
Bagby, Arthur P., 477
Bahama Islands, 406, 630-31
Baine, A.C. (not identified), 484
Baird, Thomas H.: to, 877
Baldwin, Cornelius C.: to, 222-23
Baldwin, Henry, 82-84
Baldwin, Joseph, 223
Baldwin, Roger S., 811
Balearic Islands, 53
Ball, James V., 375
Ballard, Rice C., 475-76, 800
Baltimore, Md.: Whig defeat in 1837 House election in, 66; Whig support for C. in, 106; C. speech to Whig convention in, 315-16, 410-11; C. pre-Harrisburg speeches in, 338-39, 410; Maryland Whig nominating convention in, 759-60; Webster anti-Whig speech in, 821-22, 827-28, 866-67; city and state 1843 election returns in, 873; Whig Young Men's ratification convention planned in, 887; C. sells hemp in, 841-42; C. serious illness in, 518, 521, 557; mentioned, 11, 40, 111, 222, 274, 330, 375, 414, 427, 478, 498-99, 506, 517, 585, 609, 622, 629, 644, 652, 676, 679, 707, 724, 744, 752, 754, 773, 840, 847, 868, 879-80, 884, 887, 891
Baltimore *Chronicle*, 132
Baltimore and Ohio Railroad Company, 419
Baltimore *Patriot & Commercial Advertiser*, 25, 722-24
Baltimore, Tom (slave), 42, 52

Bancroft, George, 871
Bangor, Me., 291
Banjo Bill (horse), 539
Bank of America, 421
Bank of Commerce (N.Y.C.), 392, 478, 673, 815-16
Bank of the Commonwealth, 31, 57
Bank of England, 2-3, 45, 76, 177, 339, 380, 868
Bank of Kentucky: to, 52; mentioned, 57, 59, 372-73, 677, 731, 748, 790, 799, 807, 816
Bank of Louisville, 719
Bank of Pennsylvania, 498
Bank of the United States: C. explains his 1816 shift in attitude on, 560, 712, 716, 824-26 (*see also* 2: 200-205, 216-19); mentioned, 4-5, 12-13, 29, 49, 54, 56-58, 63, 75-76, 79, 93, 97, 100-101, 140, 143, 145-47, 155, 159-60, 162-63, 175-77, 183, 187-88, 191, 193, 195, 203-4, 207, 210-11, 213, 222, 230, 239, 243, 257, 304, 321, 323, 339, 346, 357, 378-82, 388, 427-28, 433, 453, 465, 468-69, 484, 498, 500, 503, 510, 513, 519-20, 522-24, 530-31, 533-37, 540-41, 543, 545, 549-62, 565-66, 571-76, 578, 581-82, 584-93, 597-601, 607-9, 613-14, 617, 619-20, 628, 637, 660, 687, 707, 711, 729-30, 752, 754, 763, 769-70, 774-75, 783-84, 787, 802, 805, 808-9, 812, 817, 835, 866-68, 875, 881-83. *See also* United States Bank of Pennsylvania
Banks, Linn, 473
Baptist Church, 195, 215, 387
Barbados, 200
Barbour, James S.: C. buys valuable horse from, 184-85; mentioned, 743
Barbour, P.W. (not identified): from, 901
Barbour County, Ala., 560
Barcelona, Spain, 95
Bardstown, Ky., 368, 452
Baring Brothers & Co., 45, 309, 683
Barker, Jacob: from, 533-34
Barker, James N., 652
Barnard, Daniel D., 628
Barrow, Alexander: from, 688; to, 688; mentioned, 435, 539, 584, 606, 816
Bartlett, Elisha, 888-89
Bascom, Henry B.: to, 520, 532
Bates, Isaac C., 502, 717, 719
Batavia, N.Y., 320
Baton Rouge, La., 539, 544, 796, 798
Battle, J.A. (not identified): from, 343
Battle of Leipzig, 98
Battle of New Orleans, 49, 398, 431
Battle of River Raisin, 375
Battle of the Thames, 444
Battle of Waterloo, 98
Battle of Yorktown, 98
Baxter, John B., 453
Baxter, Thomas: from, 10, 11
Bayard, Caroline, 417
Bayard, Mary Sophia Carroll: from, 311-12; mentioned, 417
Bayard, Richard H.: to, 886; family of, 417; returns to Senate, 466; opposes expunging resolution, 469; stance on tariff, 479-80; loses election as president pro tem of the Senate, 707-8, 718-19; mentioned, 121, 468, 535, 559
Beal, William H., 385-86
Beall, John H. (not identified): from, 901
Beardsley, Samuel (not identified), 61
Beasley, Reuben G.: from, 2, 44, 140; mentioned, 20, 23, 30, 40
Beatty, Adam: from, 902-3; dedicates book to C., 902-3
Beaver County, Pa., 399
Beck, Mrs. George, 457
Beckley, Alfred: from, 855; to, 859-60
Bedford Springs, Va., 750
Beers, Joseph D., 241
Beers, Seth, 196
Beirne, Andrew, 494
Belfast, Ireland, 11
Belgium, 28, 39
Bell, David: from, 51
Bell, Jane Erwin Yeatman (Mrs. John): to, 529-30; mentioned, 41-42, 317, 431, 808
Bell, John: from, 316-17; C. defends principles and character of, 235; explains Tennessee political scene to C., 316-17; low opinion of Charles Hammond, 317; opinion of Andrew Jackson, 316-17; reelected to 26 Cong., 316-17, 344; on C.'s electoral prospects in Tennessee, 344-45; opens Nashville home to C. friends, 439; appointed to Harrison's Cabinet, 474-75, 499; mentioned, 42, 220, 330, 361, 442, 454, 460, 510, 530, 544, 612, 805, 879
Belmont County, Ohio, 399
Belrose, Son & Blanchard: to, 850
Benedict, Lewis, 321
Benjamin, Judah P.: from, 795; to, 795
Benjamin, Park, 765
Bennett, James Gordon: from, 538; mentioned, 342-43
Bennett, Sanford S.: to, 53-54
Bennett & Hardy, 54
Benteen, Frederick D. (not identified), 840
Benton, Thomas Hart: seven resolutions on Treasury Department operations, 535-37, 541, 546-47; on permanent preemption system, 463-64, 486-90 (*see also* Congress of the United States: 26 Cong., 2 Sess.); condemns hissing in Senate gallery, 586; C. clash with on Senate floor, 649; a Democrat defects from leadership of, 655; C. does not speak to, 835; mentioned, 3, 5, 12, 14, 20, 269, 285, 289, 376-77, 390, 410, 456, 511, 545, 559, 562, 570, 572-73, 577-82, 600, 603, 605, 626, 718, 727, 776, 849, 863
Berrien, Eliza Hunter (Mrs. John M.), 812-13, 854, 900
Berrien, John M.: to, 521, 612, 739, 755-56, 762-63, 803-4, 812-13, 834-35, 853-54, 859, 873, 900; C. accepts position of, on distribution issue and 1842 tariff act, 755-56, 762-63; nominated for vice president by Georgia Whigs, 834-35; movement in Georgia legislature to censure, 834-35; C. discusses 1844 presidential election with, 834-35, 854; chairs 1843 Georgia Whig nominating convention, 834-35; his "Address to the People of Georgia," 834-35, 859; on American Colonization Society, 859; Tyler removes father-in-law of from federal office, 812-13; wife of composes song, 854; mentioned, 535, 542, 572, 593, 671, 865
Bertrand (horse), 150, 168, 185
Betsy (slave), 52
Betts, Thaddeus, 301, 404
Beverley, Carter: from, 648-49, 696-97; to, 659; apologizes to C. for role in "Corrupt Bargain" issue, 648-49, 659-60, 696-70, 709-10

Beverley, Mackenzie: from, 311
Beverley, Maria Carter, 311
Beverley, Robert, 311
Biddle, Nicholas: from, 29, 36, 91, 138-39, 139, 144, 182, 191, 193-94, 226-27, 231; to, 33, 36, 111, 139, 148-49, 179, 193, 227, 228-29, 234; on conversion of Bank of the United States to United States Bank of Pennsylvania, 29-30; on bank issue in 1836 election, 29-30; on Whig victory in 1837 New York state elections, 91; lends money to C. friends, 36; works to defeat Sub-Treasury proposal, 138-39, 144, 182, 191; attacks resumption of specie payments by New York banks, 175, 182; sees C. as compromiser of bank crisis, 182; C. explains his new Bank of the United States strategy to, 193; bank of resumes specie payments, 193-94; letters to J.Q. Adams on resumption of specie payments, 175, 193-95; cooperation with U.S. Treasury, 243, 258; on loans to Republic of Texas, 226-27, 229; lauds U.S. and Pennsylvania for paying foreign debts, 446; on C.'s financial situation, 231; C. seeks loan from bank of, to buy horse, 227, 231, 234; mentioned, 57, 79, 177, 187, 195, 237-38, 253, 303, 379, 498, 500, 861
Bidwell, Marshall S., 105-6
Bienniel Register, 448
Bigger, Samuel, 436, 827
Bingaman, Adam L., 123
Bingley, J., 805
Binney, Horace, 328
Birch, James H., 456
Birch, Weston F., 748
Bird, Robert M., 753-54
Bird, William A., 455, 459, 503
Birney, James G.: from, 111-13; to, 244-45; discusses slavery and abolition with C., 111-13, 244-45; on abolition in Kentucky, 112-13; candidate of Liberty party in 1840, 356-57; votes cast for in Ohio in 1840 election, 450-51; votes cast for in New England in 1844, 821-22; mentioned, 199-200, 246, 306, 410, 447, 452, 759, 807, 813, 858
Black, John, 36, 123
Blackburn, ——— (not identified), 186
Blackburn, George: from, 231
Blackburn, Robert: from, 231
Blackford, William M., 110
Black Hawk, 146
Black Rock, N.Y., 104, 228, 455, 503, 858
Blackwell, Julius W., 817
Bladensburg, Md., 645
Blair, Francis P.: controversy over reappointment as printer to Senate, 501-2, 510-11; C. attacks, 511-12; mentioned, 86, 89, 454, 513, 516, 643
Blatchford, Richard M., 866, 868
Bleakley, James (not identified): to, 806
Bledsoe, Robert: from, 839; to, 838-39; mentioned, 863
Blennerhassett, Harman, 679
Blennerhassett, Margaret (Mrs. Harman): from, 680; to, 678; mentioned, 679
Bliss, Leonard, Jr., 189
Bloomfield, R. (not identified): to, 432
Blue Book, 448
Blue Licks, Ky., 757
Bluffton, Mo., 818
Blythe, Calvin, 704
Blythe, James, 450
Board of Exchequer Bank plan, 598, 617, 623-25, 628-29, 631, 639, 718-19, 726, 771, 786-87, 801, 827
Bob (slave), 11
Bodisco, Alexandre de: from, 830-31; wedding of, 404; mentioned, 236, 403
Bodisco, Harriet Williams de, 404, 830
Bodley, Harry I.: to, 702
Bolivar, Simon, 412
Bomford, George, 84
Bonaparte, Napoleon, 146-47, 343
Bond, William K., 386
Boone, Albert G.: to, 834
Boone, Daniel: C. characterizes, 354; mentioned, 834
Boone County, Mo., 450
Bonneau, Anthony, 196
Boonville, Mo., 241
Bordeaux, France, 95
Borras, Joseph, 95
Boston, Mass.: temperance in, 269; reaction to Harrison nomination in, 368; Harrison political organization and activity in, 425; collector of customs appointment in, 462; Bunker Hill celebration in, 830; anti-Catholic violence in, 878-79; mentioned, 130, 154, 179, 183, 207, 222, 248, 255, 443, 460, 568, 733, 750, 758, 807, 869, 876
Boston *Atlas*: attacks C. and Webster candidacy, 229-30, 232-34, 237, 239-40, 245, 247, 250-52, 260-64, 269, 274; mentioned, 156, 271, 290, 522
Boston *Courier*, 269
Boston *Daily Advertiser*, 264
Boston *Morning Post*, 656-58, 663
Boston Temperance Society, 269
Botetourt County, Va., 890
Botts, John M.: from, 686; to, 688, 886-87; C.'s messmate in D.C., 386; bank branching clause amendment of, 566; leads move to impeach Tyler, 732, 734-36, 742; C. accepts invitation from to farewell dinner, 688; defends C. against anti-slavery charge, 886-87; mentioned, 299, 429-30, 609, 739-40
Bouck, William, 357, 455, 761
Boudet, Othon: from, 89
Boulanger, Joseph: from, 181
Bouligny, Dominique, 312
Bouligny, Ursin, Jr.: to, 354, 377; C. sells calves to, 354, 377; mentioned, 312, 372
Bourbon (horse), 585
Bourbon County, Ky.: speech at agricultural fair of, 862-63; mentioned, 850
Bourbons, 147
Bourtoulin, Dmitrii Petrovich de, 328-29
Bowman, Thomas: to, 36
Boyd, Linn, 51, 333-34
Boydton, Va., 433
Boyle County, Ky., 334
Bracken County, Ky., 759
Bradish, Luther: from, 690-91; to, 362, 698-700; mentioned, 151, 234, 238, 243, 249, 761
Bradley, ——— (not identified): to, 443
Bradley, William A., 596
Bradley, William C., 233
Branch, John, 167
Brand, John, 790
Brand & Macalester, 314
Brandon Bank (Miss.), 814
Brandywine (vessel), 383
Brandywine, U.S.F., 311
Branham, Joel: from, 839; to, 838-39; mentioned, 863
Braxton, Corbin, 473, 521
Brazil, 685, 804, 821-22
Breckenridge, John (or Breckinridge), 263
Breckinridge family, 218
Bremen (Germany), 821-22, 828, 830

Brenan, ——— (not identified), 439
Brent, Daniel, 353
Bridgeport, Conn., 372
Bridgeport, Va. (W. Va.), 494
Briggs, George Nixon: condemned by Liberty party leaders, 896; mentioned, 835, 852-53, 871-72, 874, 876, 888-89
Briscoe v. *The Bank of the Commonwealth of Kentucky*, 31
Bristo (slave), 52
British Parliament: House of Commons, 579; House of Lords, 680; mentioned, 244, 281, 545, 597, 867, 882
British Queen (vessel), 10
Britton, Nicholas O. (not identified): to, 770-71
Broaddus, Andrew, Jr.: to, 824-25; mentioned, 826
"Broad Seal War," 248
Brockenbrough, John, 177
Broglie, Duc de (Achille Leon Victor), 407
Bronson, F.S. (not identified): from, 850; to, 856-57; mentioned, 877, 890
Bronson, Isaac Hopkins, 333
Brooke, Ann Shee, 313
Brooke, Catherine L.: from, 313; to, 313-14
Brooke, Ella Ambler, 110
Brooke, Francis E., 110
Brooke, Francis T.: to, 26-27, 39, 100-101, 110, 129-30, 172, 198-99, 224, 239, 245-46, 257-58, 261-62, 266-67, 272, 275-76, 298-99, 436, 457-58, 473, 497, 513-14, 534, 557, 617, 641, 722, 794-95; C. briefs on events in Congress, 26-27; value to C. as political informant, 298; C. advises on Whig presidential electoral strategy in Virginia, 298-99; marriages of children of, 110; C. advises on military land warrants, 198-99; illegible handwriting of, 239; C. visits home of, 409; asks C. for patronage favor, 497; declines presidency of Virginia court of appeals, 641; mentioned, 723, 806
Brooke, Margaret Lyle, 110
Brooke, Mary Champe Carter (Mrs. Francis T.), 27, 101, 110, 795
Brooke, Robert, 110, 709
Brooke, Robert, IV, 313
Brooklyn, N.Y.: Mechanics Institute in, 700, 702; mentioned, 134, 141, 357, 707
Brooklyn *Star*, 134
Brothers in Unity, 546
Brown, Abel, 754-55, 758
Brown, Albert G., 123, 814-15
Brown, Ann Hart (Nancy), 82, 800
Brown, Bedford, 269-70
Brown, Charlotte B., 820
Brown, Henry E., 853
Brown, James: settlement of estate of (*see espec.* 82-84), 202, 302-3; C. role in *Preston* v. *Humphrey* estate case, 796, 798, 800-801, 803; mentioned, 42, 373, 386
Brown, John W., 476
Brown, J.P.W. (not identified): from, 343
Brown, Mason: to, 82, 83
Brown, Samuel, 83
Brown, William O. (not identified): from, 509
Brown Brothers & Co., 815-16
Brown Shipley & Co., 11
Browne, William: to, 437-38
Browning, W.P., 454
Brugger, Robert J., 362
Brunswick, Mo., 171, 450
Brush, Mary (not identified), 382
Bry, Hannah L., 803
Bry, Henry: from, 803
Bryan, George, 295
Bryan, George S.: from, 61-62
Bryant, Edwin, 98, 309, 531-32
Buchanan, James: from, 446-47; sponsors rights of children to public lands, 18, 22-23; on Calhoun's six resolutions on slavery, 127-29; defends "Resurrection Notes" bill, 176-77; amends Webster's substitute bank/currency bill, 209-10; legislative instructions to on Sub-Treasury bill, 139, 583-84; denies harsh language about C., 446-47; C. questions loyalty of to Jackson, 483; on preemption of public lands, 483; on Whig proscriptions of public employees, 551; ridicules C. references to slave Charles, 583-84; role in "Corrupt Bargain" issue, 649; chided on bachelorhood, 673, 676; mentioned, 14, 30, 35, 80, 136, 140, 148-49, 154, 171, 209, 211, 377, 383, 396, 422, 437, 488, 511, 545, 547, 553, 558-59, 561, 569, 571, 574, 597-98, 601, 653, 660, 686, 776, 854
Buchanan (Va.) *Advocate and Commercial Gazette*, 223
Buckingham, Joseph T., 269
Buckingham County, Va., 586
"Buckshot War," 253
Buel, Jesse, 614
Buffalo (steamship), 216
Buffalo, N.Y.: uprising at, 105-6, 120; Indian treaty signed at, 145; C. speech in, 331-32; mentioned, 60, 104, 113, 201, 273, 320, 324, 330, 336, 451, 455, 503, 592, 858
Buffalo *Commercial Advertiser*, 273, 288, 870
Buffalo *Journal*, 273
Buford, William, 150
Bullock, James M. (not identified), 181
Bullock, William B., 813
Bulwer, Edward George Earle Lytton, 26, 118
Bunker Hill: convention held at, 438, 443; celebration of battle at, 830
Burch, James K., 305-6
Burgheim, Philip (not identified), 840
Burgoyne, John, 240
Burgoyne, John (General), 98, 337
Burlington, Iowa, 860
Burlington, Vt., 333
Burnet, Jacob: ambivalence of toward C. for president, 836, 864-65, 873; involvement in Webster vice presidential bid, 861, 864-65, 873; C. distrust of, 865; proposed intermediary in C.-Webster conciliation, 861, 864-65, 873; mentioned, 115, 830, 874
Burnett, Alexander S., 38
Burnley, Albert T.: to, 407; mentioned, 226-27
Burr, Aaron, 442, 679
Burr, Samuel J., 375
Burton, Robert M., 317
Burton, William, 754
Bush, Joseph H.: from, 719
Bush, Lewis D.P., 214
Butler, Benjamin F., 21, 31, 290
Butler, Pierce M.: to, 752
Butler, William O., 851
Buxton, Thomas F., 526-27

"Cabell's Dale," 218
Cabiness, John M.: to, 48-49
Cadiz, Spain, 118
"Cadmus" (pseud.): from, 118
Cahoon, John C.: from, 302; to, 318-19
Caldwell, James: to, 296
Caldwell, Sir John B., 417
Calhoon, John, 16-17, 334
Calhoun, John C.: opposes American Colonization Society, 18; nullification and presidential ambitions of, 65, 158-62; respect for

Calhoun, J.C. (continued): and support of C. by, 62, 283; description of, 125, 163, 208, 596-97; on C.'s late awareness of abolitionist threat, 209-10, 283; on 1837 public land bill, 21, 25-26, 137-38, 152-53; as railroad company director, 224; clash with Jackson on public land speculation, 25, 27; on land bill of 1840 (*see* Congress of the United States: 26 Cong., 1 Sess.); opposes Whig distribution-preemption bill, 567-68; clashes with C. in Senate, 147-48, 158-62, 369-70, 389, 562-63, 568; "Edgefield Letter" of, 147, 158-62; legal tender amendment to Sub-Treasury bill, 77-79; bill to regulate the deposits and reduce (redistribute) treasury surplus, 34-35 (*see also* 8:813); supports Sub-Treasury bill, 138, 147-48, 158-62; six resolutions on slavery (*see espec.* 121), 123-29, 131, 137, 178, 890; links political interests with slavery, 129; switches from States' Rights and Anti-Jackson (Whig) parties to Democrats (*see espec.* 147), 106, 159, 230-31; C. break with (*see espec.* 147), 209, 369-70; rumored return to Whigs in 1839, 301; rapprochement with Van Buren and Democrats, 369-70; offers substitute for administration's preemption/land bill, 369-70, 464, 481-82, 489-94; fights Whig bank bills, 536-37; fights Whig loan bill, 566-68; on C. advocacy of national bank and American System, 562; C. designates as originator of American System, 376; on free trade vs. tariffs, 646; blocks formation of anti-Van Buren group, 39; alludes to C.'s "Corrupt Bargain" with Adams, 369-70; attempts to trap C. on Texas annexation issue, 129, 136; on distribution and disunion, 567-68, 673-75; on right of petition, 387; attacks British on *Enterprise* case, 406; on Maine boundary settlement, 727; purchases Georgia gold mine, 718-19; 1844 presidential candidacy of (*see* Election, presidential, of 1844: John C. Calhoun candidacy and role in); mentioned, 17, 32, 70, 80, 85, 106, 109, 130, 149, 151, 155, 166-67, 194-95, 216, 222, 296, 326, 393, 410-11, 423, 429, 437, 477, 508, 512, 522, 540-41, 543, 547-48, 550, 552, 561, 569, 571, 578-80, 582, 592-94, 598, 600, 603-5, 629-30, 655, 659-60, 666, 676-77, 682-83, 685-86, 720, 723, 727, 729, 732, 739, 752, 762, 776, 804-5, 820, 827, 835, 844, 855, 859, 861, 864, 869, 870, 881

California, 383, 481

Call, Richard K., 290

Cambreleng, Churchill C.: named as minister to Russia, 414; mentioned, 715

Cambridge University, 467

Camden, Gideon Draper, 494

Camden, S.C., 497

Cameron, Donald: to, 842-43

Cameron, William: to, 842-43

Campbell, David: from, 456-57; to, 460-61; mentioned, 296

Campbell, Lewis D.: to, 767, 893

Campbell, Thomas J.: from, 817-18

Campbell, William B.: to, 826, 836-37, 846-47

Campfield, James A. (not identified): to, 837

Campton, N. Field (not identified): to, 750

Canada: revolt against Great Britain, 104-6, 113-14, 119, 293-94; *Caroline* case, 119 (*see also Caroline*); role of U.S. citizens in rebellion of, 104, 113; C. on Anglo-French conflict in, 387; mentioned, 129, 140-41, 232, 242, 255, 276, 278, 284, 291-92, 312-13, 320, 326-28, 330-31, 333-34, 340, 382, 405, 417, 471-72, 780, 814, 898

Canadian Refugee Relief Association, 255

Canandaigua, N.Y., 60, 320, 330, 332, 880

Canandaigua, Ontario *Repository*, 879

Canby, Samuel, 213-14

Canning, George, 654

Cannon, Newton, 71, 316-17

Carey, Henry Charles: to, 543; mentioned, 259

Carey, John L.: to, 372; authors book on slavery, 372; mentioned, 315

Carey, Mathew: to, 259; sends C. his book, 259; mentioned, 543

Carey & Lea, 689

Carlin, Thomas, 216

Carlisle, Pa., 315

Carolina Watchman, 412

Caroline (vessel), 119, 126, 130, 331, 471, 474, 508, 523, 529, 684

Caroline County, Va., 473, 826

Carpenter, Thomas F., 445, 716

Carroll, Charles, 311

Carroll County, Ky., 837

Carroll County, Mo., 171, 450

"Carrollton," 311

Carter, ——— (not identified), 795

Carthage, Ohio, 733, 744

Carthage, Tenn., 837

Caruthers, Robert L.: to, 832-33, 847-48

Carver, Jonathan P. (not identified): to, 425-26

Carysfort (vessel), 829

Cass, Lewis: resigns as U.S. minister to France, 882-83; mentioned as Democratic presidential candidate in 1844, 882; attacks Webster-Ashburton treaty, 882; mentioned, 290, 375, 680, 776, 854, 857, 881, 900

Castle County, Dela., 214

Catholic Herald, 24

Catron, John, 39

Cayuga Bridge, 647

Cayuga County, N.Y., 335

Cayuga Indians, 145

Cazmon (brig), 231

Centre College, 320

Chalmers, John G., 556

Chamber of Commerce, 485

Chambers, John, 394

Chambers, Richard, 738

Chambersburg, Pa.: to Clay Club of, 839-40; mentioned, 306, 327, 894

Chandler, Adoniram: from, 68; to, 66-68, 257

Channing, William (not identified): to, 155

Channing, William E.: from, 65; to, 103-4; and Texas annexation, 65, 135-36, 823-24, 896-99; opposes C.'s anti-abolitionist speech, 283; C. on arrogance of, 314-15; mentioned, 155, 387

Charles I (Great Britain), 381

Charles II (Great Britain), 381

Charleston, S.C., 52, 62, 222, 391-92, 406, 539, 645, 686, 833

Charleston and Cincinnati Railroad Company, 224-26

Charleston *Mercury*, 62

Charlestown, Ind., 901

Charlestown, Mass., 878-79

Charlotte (slave), 52

Charlotte, N.C., 407
Charlottesville, Va., 299
Charter party, 714
"Chatham," 798
"Chaumiere," 88
Chesapeake and Ohio Canal Company, 419, 497
Cheviot, Ohio, 393
Chicago, Ill., 759
Chickasaw Indians, 265
Child, David Lee: to, 178-79; mentioned, 897, 899
Child, Lydia Maria, 899
Children of Unidentified Friend: to, 144-45
Childs, C.G., 624
Childs, Joseph: from, 144; to, 143-44; mentioned, 182
Chillicothe, Ohio, 53, 198, 640
Chilton, Robert S.: to, 353, 365
China, 804
Chinn, Richard, 42, 397-98
Chinn, Thomas W., 386
Chippewa Indians, 131-32, 510
Choate, Rufus: reveals Tyler will veto first Whig bank bill, 556; C. insults and apologizes to, 556-57; mentioned, 535, 609, 717, 719, 751
Christian Statesman, 169
Christopher, ——— (not identified), 853
Christopher, Jesse M. (not identified): to, 460
Christy, Garland: from, 11; to, 52
Church, Edward: to, 895
Cilley, Jonathan: killed in duel (*see* Duels and Dueling); mentioned, 153, 157, 164-65, 334, 643-45, 648, 656-58, 661-65
Cincinnati, Ohio: 1838 U.S. House and local elections in, 239-40; newspaper in blames C. for 1838 Whig defeat in, 250, 252, 262-63; meeting in nominates Harrison for president, 163-64; C. writes to ladies of, 448; support for Harrison candidacy in, 448; anti-bank sentiment in, 550-51; 1843 convention in, favoring occupation of Oregon, 828-29; C. to Committee of Whigs in, 703; mentioned, 115, 216, 248, 342-43, 375, 393, 424, 484, 576, 641, 671, 737-38, 743, 745, 758, 763, 836, 858-59
Cincinnati *Daily Gazette*, 300, 408, 484, 751-52, 768, 830, 836
Cincinnati *Republican*, 250
Cincinnatus, 700
Citizens Bank of New Orleans, 397
"Civitas" (pseud.), 342
Claiborne, John F.H., 174
Claiborne, William C.C., Jr., 312, 798
Clark, Aaron: from, 477, 595-96; mentioned, 43, 174, 301
Clark, James, 7, 180-81, 242-43, 245, 299
Clark, James C., 429
Clark, John B., 445
Clark County, Ohio, 424, 640
Clarke, A., 341
Clarke, John Freeman: from, 307
Clarke, Matthew St. Clair, 539, 672
Clay, Anne (granddaughter): birth of, 31; mentioned, 365, 392, 396, 626
Clay, Anne Brown (daughter). *See* Erwin, Anne Brown Clay
Clay, Cassius M.: C. confused with on abolition advocacy, 886-88
Clay, Clement C., 169, 195, 230, 251, 265-66, 400-401, 406, 408, 417, 423, 478-79, 482-83, 486, 561-63, 572, 581, 584
Clay, Henry
— economic views and personal financial affairs: stances on Bank of the United States, 158-62; British advise on banks, 6; supports rights of congressmen to borrow from proposed new Bank of the United States, 559-60; on free trade vs. protection, 666-70, 682-87, 699-700, 772, 851; on future of U.S. manufacturing, 888; on law of supply and demand, 266; on national economic self-sufficiency, 862-63; on economic state of the nation, 40-41, 43, 45-46, 48-50, 54, 63, 65-66, 372, 402; exposed to writing of W.M. Gouge, 63-64; on collapse of cotton prices in South, 43, 669; on European sugar and cotton prices, 42; Frankfort Bridge Company investments of, 451; hemp sales to U.S. Navy, 577, 754; interest in hemp prices and tariff on, 24, 706; interest in tariff on hemp bagging, 430-31, 706, 749; interest in hemp prices and shipping costs (*see espec.* 73, 185), 90, 101, 123, 168, 186, 196, 213, 236, 242, 285, 302-3, 470; hemp production and sales (*see espec.* 841-42), 364, 397, 412-13, 470, 498, 521, 529, 539, 623, 698, 705, 791, 892, 902; sales and prices of bale rope and bagging, 330, 470, 583-84, 604, 795, 892, 902; interest in foreign hemp, 23-24, 577, 841-42; competition from Russia and India hemp, 236, 706, 841-42; Astor loan (*see* Astor, John Jacob); seeks Biddle loan, 227, 231, 234; business transactions in New Orleans, 42, 372, 395, 791, 795-96, 799, 815-16; land owned in Illinois (*see* Illinois); land owned in Missouri (*see* Clay, James Brown; Missouri); land owned in Ohio, 115, 368-69; property in Lexington, 155, 238, 301, 303, 312; debts, bad loans, and poor judgment as co-signer (*see espec.* 837), 42, 179, 238, 372, 413, 450, 624-25, 652, 688, 790, 799, 806-7; continuing financial difficulties of (*see espec.* 789-90, 837), 231, 238, 372, 386, 388, 392-93, 395, 397, 400, 450, 624-25, 643, 650-52, 703, 730-31, 795-96, 806-7, 902; impact of rumored Erwin bankruptcy on, 385-86, 395; tries to collect money owed him, 155, 720, 730, 748, 799, 837; franking privilege of, 788; loans repaid to, 719; deceived by debtor, 652; summary of C. debts, 790, 806-7; major sale of "Ashland" livestock, 613; forgets deposit in Natchez bank, 698; attempts to borrow money, 796, 800, 807; friends assist financially, 801, 846; size of estate and income, 231, 238; views on tariff (1818-42), 838-39, 856, 863 (*see also* Election, presidential, of 1844: issues, charges, and countercharges in campaign); on Tariff Act of 1824, 772-73, 863; on Tariff Act of 1832, 772-73, 863; on Tariff Act of 1833, 31-32, 172, 370, 374, 582, 660, 750, 753, 774, 863, 886; on his tariff voting record, 863; on specific vs. ad valorem tariffs, 525-26
— farm, farmer, and home—

Clay, Henry (continued):
"Ashland": purchase of English cattle, 1, 309; purchase of European asses and mules, 2, 20, 23-24, 30, 40, 44-45, 53-54, 94, 140, 621-22; purchase of horses, 23, 234, 481, 584-85, 592; breeding and care of swine, 309, 623; sale of bulls, cows, and heifers, 186, 218, 236, 257, 312, 318, 354, 372, 377, 383, 756; sale of asses and mules, 388, 584-85, 610, 621-22, 624, 704-5; sale of horses, 796, 798; sale of sheep, 364; major sale of "Ashland" livestock, 613; slaughter of livestock, 72; cattle breeding, 174, 213-14, 219, 309; breeding and breeding fees for asses, 46, 53, 179, 204; breeding and stud fees for horses, 94, 150, 168-69, 184-85, 522, 673; quality of "Ashland" horses, 539; veterinary services at, 54; love of "Ashland" and life there, 49-50, 409; number and value of slaves on, 238, 781; additions to land at, 84; pictures of, 536; purchase of equipment and furniture for, 610; purchase of vegetable, flower, and grass seed for, 241, 385, 390, 673, 677, 748, 764; Kentucky bluegrass, 219, 241, 821; purchase of plants and flowers for, 538; purchase of salt for, 362, 763-64, 766-67; gift of magnolia trees to, 813; gift of plough to, 733; Albert Florea as overseer, 90; quality of management at, 192-93; Lucretia manages milk business at, 383; construction of drainage canal at, 754; ice houses at, 652; crops expected and realized at, 46, 90, 192-93, 231, 239, 318, 749, 828; cultivation of hemp, 671-72, 749, 844; interest in tariff on foreign hemp bagging, 430-31, 706, 749; prices and sales of "Ashland" hemp products (bale rope, bagging), 73, 184-85, 470, 577, 706, 791-92, 795, 801, 841-42 (*see also* Clay, Henry: economic views and personal financial affairs); C. on a U.S. silk industry, 884; C. on sugar from beets, 178-79; wool shipments and prices, 325; mortgage on "Ashland," 789-90; beauty of "Ashland," 821; prominent visitors entertained at "Ashland," 330, 454, 680-81, 700, 702-3; student boarders at "Ashland," 457

— health: on C.'s health generally, 87, 150, 401, 521, 792, 795, 797, 805; daily health and exercise habits, 557-58; illnesses, 31, 144, 184-85, 299, 305, 352, 383, 411, 417, 430, 468, 518, 521, 557, 624-25, 652, 688, 758; importance of, to Whig prospects, 717

— lawyer and law practice: work on Morrison estate, 42 (*see also* Morrison, Esther Montgomery; Morrison, James); Eliza Jane Weir estate, 8-12; *Briscoe* v. *Bank of Commonwealth of Kentucky*, 31; *James Blythe* v. *Henry Clay*, 450; *United States* v. *Nathaniel Cox*, 42; land claims, 196; general practice, 448; mediates Marshall v. Woolley dispute, 247; *Groves* v. *Slaughter* ("The Mississippi Case"), 475-76, 800-801; association with Webster in *Groves* case, 475-76; *Watson* v. *Clay*, 506-7; *Preston* v. *Humphreys*, 796-98, 800, 803; refuses Seneca treaty case, 415; resumes law practice in 1843, 812, 821, 901-2; turns down prospective law student, 901; slavery issue in practice, 51-53, 901 (*see also* Clay, Henry: slaves and slavery); C. on Story's and Peters's volumes of U.S. statutes, 895. *See also* U.S. Supreme Court

— personal items, attitudes, and activities: on his Virginia birth and boyhood, 353, 395, 426, 709, 733, 783; migrates to Kentucky, 693-94, 698, 709, 751; as ploughboy, 733; inadequate education, 693; lack of ambition, 710; as young debater, 131; advice to children, 144-45; takes care of grandchildren (*see espec.* 396), 40, 42, 50; advice to grandchildren, 187, 808; disappointment in sons' behavior, 132-33; maternal grandparents of, 395-96, 810; portraits and busts of, 196-97, 371, 385, 475, 536, 700, 702, 789, 803-4, 822-23, 880; knowledge of history books, 108; books, journals, pamphlets, and newspapers read or acquired, 63-64, 74-75, 108, 142-43, 150, 309, 372, 415, 531, 623-24, 630-31, 685, 888-89; on newspapers, 206; children named for, 460; ships named for, 220, 700; township named for, 507; post office named for, 612; book dedicated to, 902-3; on age and aging, 401, 823; "grand climacteric" (63rd birthday), 401; interest in phrenology, 475; purity of personal motives, 693; on food, wine, and gambling, 181, 231, 318, 487, 498; on temperance and prohibition, 218, 275, 472, 708-9; addiction to snuff, 117; visits to springs and spas, 72, 757-58; on anecdotes, 861-62; anger and temper, 514; on semantics and grammar, 584, 811; on women, 342-43, 673, 709, 777-82, 800; on women in politics, 448, 709; on Daniel Boone, 354, 834; on human nature and opinion of mankind, 218; on foreign immigration, 218; on Catholic immigration, 16; on Irish, 478; linked to Graves-Cilley duel (*see* Duels and Dueling); birthday ball in Washington, 688; public dinner for in Washington, 688; most important papers and documents of, 736-37; keeps no diary and seldom retains copies of speeches and letters, 69, 71, 104, 382, 415, 736; objects to letters printed without his permission, 883; on newspaper treatment of himself, 206; burden of personal correspondence and his amanuenses, 139, 142, 152, 513-14, 532, 872, 883; involved in steamboat and carriage accidents, 216, 226, 251-52, 254, 311; friends fear for safety of C.'s life, 151; rumored assassination attempt on, 796; accused of contradictions on squatter issue, 114, 134-36, 214; gifts to, 206, 517, 621, 697, 702, 733, 741, 818, 834, 851

— politics, political activities, and views: Whig principles, 773-76; on Democrats, 378-81, 426-29; on political views of Kentuckians, 484-85; on Declaration of Independence, 715; on revolution, 249, 715; on compact theory of the constitution, 341-42; on origin of the constitution, 123-24; on constitutional precedents, 143; Virginia and Kentucky Resolutions, 161, 440, 492; broadening of franchise, 248; on suborning the rural vote, 437; on definition of Jeffersonian democracy and true democrats, 492-93; on doctrine of instructions, 140; on nullification, 713, 750; on union vs. disunion, 81, 124, 203-4, 713; on nationalism of, 203-4; on Jackson's proclamation to South Carolina, 341; on Force Bill, 341; on right of petition, 24, 109, 124, 387; on European immigration, 136, 218, 444, 472; British political system, issues, and parties, 691-92, 712, 957; U.S. Senate filled with blackguards, 14; compares Senate with European bodies, 691-92; degredation of Congress, 27; use of power as House Speaker, 568; denies being a dictator, 694; political consistency of, 710; "Corrupt Bargain" charge (*see* Election, presidential, of 1840: issues, charges, and countercharges in campaign; Election, presidential, of 1844: issues, charges, and countercharges in campaign); should not have accepted post as secretary of state, 709-10; on the public, 65; South's dislike of C., 33; daily work habits in Senate, 172; length of speeches, 563-64; politicians as normal people, 162; his difficult career as public servant, 65; dislike of public speeches, 411, 853; on political betrayal, 841; on his compromises, 30, 102; on the history of his 1833 tariff compromise (*see* Clay, Henry: economic views and personal financial affairs); ceases patronage recommendations, 309; on recess patronage appointments, 900; on limiting the veto power of the president, 608-9, 775-76; on one-term presidency, 312-13; would "rather be right" than president, 283, 302; on sectionally balanced presidential and vice presidential tickets, 834; on free press, 423; on newspapers in politics, 208, 415, 423; low opinion of newspaper reporters, 423; political publications, 86; party platforms in presidential elections, 416; on party press, 371; importance and strategy of organized political parties, 299; on urban vs. rural political virtues, 248, 314; on history of his distribution bill, 374; on public land squatters (*see espec.* 321-22), 134-36, 267-68; as father of American System, 102-3; hailed as national benefactor, 41; on U.S. expansion to Pacific, 383; desire to withdraw from public life, 401, 458-61, 466. *See also* Election, presidential, of 1840; Election, presidential, of 1844; Clay, Henry: personal items, attitudes, and activities

—religion and religious views: on Catholic immigrants, 16; on Roman Catholicism, 16, 24, 845-46; Free Masonry, 892-93; C. on nature of Jesus, 145; seeks divine assistance in opposition to Sub-Treasury bill, 145; supports *Christian Statesman* newspaper, 169; on coercion in religion, 218; on religious persecution, 890-91; on God and race, 257; on God and slavery, 64, 744; anti-Catholic violence in Boston, 878-79; colonization and Christianity in Africa, 745-47; God in U.S. history and politics, 745-47; spiritual preparation for death, 697; on prayer, 747; Quakers and abolition, 781; Irish Catholics, 845-46; Shakers, 793-94; Mormons, 384, 881, 890-91

—slaves and slavery: views on solicited, 1, 41, 223; personal transactions in (1837-43), 43, 51-53, 388; on best defense of, 223; slavery damages master and slave, 43, 64; on evils of, 103, 223; caught in middle of slavery issue, 246; on slavery, Christianity, and God, 128, 278-83, 744; God and racial amalgamation, 256-57, 278-83, 852; slavery and American party system, 124-25, 278-83; C. on books on, 372; work for American Colonization Society, 18, 21, 28-29, 43, 45, 47-48, 52-53, 80-81, 103, 240, 256-57, 279, 310, 506-7, 804, 852, 859, 867, 894; on abolitionist appeals to slaves, 56; abolition retards improvement of African race, 64, 80-81, 212; growth of abolitionist societies, 56, 111-12, 246; spread of abolitionism, 246; C. on history of abolitionism in United States, 279-82, 319, 778-79, 852; colonization vs. abolition, 256-57, 745, 852, 867-68; on right of petition to abolish (*see espec.* 8:817-18, 833; 9:109), 124, 278; on "gag rule" in House, 641; attitude toward abolitionists, 43, 64, 212, 244, 278-83, 319, 509, 747, 852, 874; on constitutional dimensions of, 278-83, 319, 745-47, 852; abolitionist arguments, 467; abolition in D.C. (*see espec.* 279-80), 109-10, 125-27, 246, 279; criticisms of C. stance on abolition, 209-10, 467; advice to C. on slavery, abolition, dissolution of Union, 259-60, 467; on immediate vs. gradual emancipation, 64, 244, 280-81, 747, 779-80, 852; legal work for emancipation, 506-7 (*see also* U.S. Supreme Court); on civil war and race war in United States, 281-82, 387, 852; on compensated emancipation, 126, 244, 278-79; on emancipation, abolition, and free and white wage levels, 282, 323, 780, 852, 874; on Negro inferiority, 282; on dangers of racial amalgamation, 874; on African slave trade, 508, 684; on interstate slave trade, 504, 508; on how to end slavery peacefully, 323; on recovery of fugitive slaves, 242-43, 319; on emancipation of his own slaves, 583-84, 777-81; views of self as slavemaster, 583, 780; relations with slave Charles, 583-84, 760, 773, 780; number and value of slaves on "Ashland," 238, 781; on slaves as property, 281, 314, 319,

Clay, Henry (continued): 406; prices of slaves, 685-86; pros and cons of colonization, 779-81, 867-68; economics of abolition in Kentucky, 112; slavery in Kentucky, 244, 281; abolitionism slows emancipation in Kentucky, 244, 281; British advice on abolition, 467; abolition of slavery in British West Indies, 244, 279, 467; on British searches of American ships in slave trade, 508; on *Creole* case, 629-30 (*see also* Great Britain; *Creole*); on *Enterprise* case, 406; on Texas annexation, 64 (*see also* Texas, Republic of); on popular sovereignty concept, 124-25. *See also* Slavery and Anti-Slavery.
— war, peace, and foreign policy views: support for Canadian revolution in Buffalo, 113-14; U.S. claims against Mexico (*see* Mexico); threatened war with Britain over *Caroline* issue, 126 (*see also* Great Britain; *Caroline*); on immigrants and immigration restriction, 96-97, 136; on U.S. continental expansion, 383; evaluation of his most important policy documents, 736-37; on ideal treaties, 782; opposition to free trade, 838-39 (*see also* Clay, Henry: economic views and personal financial affairs)
Clay, Henry, Jr. (son): from, 507-8; to, 20, 23, 30, 73, 152, 250-51, 272-73, 365, 388-89, 391, 481, 584, 599, 607-8, 625-26, 731; imports European livestock, 23, 46; business and financial transactions with C., 23, 30-31, 46; in Kentucky legislature, 152, 285; death of infant daughter Martha, 217-18; death of wife Julia, 391-92, 395-96, 398, 400, 409, 411; eye trouble of, 373, 388; C. transfers slave to, 388; hemp crop on his "Maplewood" farm, 389; visits C. in Washington, 409, 411; sells his property, 678; debt to Astor, 846; children of, 626; mentioned, 45, 324-25, 383, 413, 461, 606, 652, 688, 790
Clay, Henry, III (grandson), 24, 365, 392, 396, 626
Clay, Henry Boyle (grandson), 624, 793
Clay, James Brown (son): to, 45, 87, 88, 90, 108, 121-22, 132-33, 165, 238, 257, 303, 317-18, 334, 347, 450, 480-81, 585, 623, 624-25, 672-73, 902; farms C. land in Missouri (*see* 8:801), 40, 45-46, 48-49, 87-88, 90, 818; C. sends slave and cattle to in Missouri, 88, 90, 165; C. plans to visit in Missouri, 40, 48-49; homesick and unhappy in Missouri, 121-22, 132-33, 317-18; C. urges him to come home from Missouri, 88, 165; problems with livestock on Missouri farm, 87-88, 108, 165; assists C. in sale of Missouri lands, 88, 108, 122, 238, 450; buys land near St. Louis, 303; manages "Ashland" for C., 72, 539; sells Kentucky cattle, 303; accident on horseback, 334; illnesses of, 72, 317-18; C. advises on moral and social life, 121-22, 132-33, 165, 317-18; C. recommends history books to, 108; C. assists financially, 122, 165; debts of, 672-73; business setbacks of, 624-25; asks C. to build him a house, 165; accompanies C. on trip to New York and Canada, 324-25; love affair of in Natchez, 392; studies law, 673; C. joins in practice of law, 812; visits to and prospects in New Orleans, 623, 652; handles C.'s notes and drafts, 902; mentioned, 84, 312-13, 400, 404, 610, 650, 678, 705, 791-93, 795-96, 816
Clay, John (father): Tarleton outrages grave of, 783-84; mentioned, 396
Clay, John (brother), 310
Clay, John Morrison (son): proposed trip to Europe, 23; attends Princeton, 73, 133, 186-87, 196; attends Washington College, Pa., 308; returns to Lexington from Missouri, 383, 386; tension with H.C. Duralde, 325; in Washington with C., 538; health of, 538; as amanuensis to C., 899; mentioned, 72, 347, 389, 392, 395-96, 400, 404, 409, 439, 481, 508, 585, 673, 678, 796, 846
Clay, Julia Prather (daughter-in-law): gives birth to daughter Anne, 31; family of, 90-91; death of daughter Martha, 217-18; death of, in childbirth, 388-89, 391-92, 394-96; mentioned, 24, 73, 152, 365
Clay, Julie Duralde (sister-in-law): shops for Lucretia Hart Clay in New Orleans, 42; mentioned, 798
Clay, Lucretia Hart (wife): to, 72, 187, 383-84, 385-86, 389-90, 392, 394-96, 400-401, 403-4, 409, 430-31, 439, 538-39, 652, 677-78, 688, 790-91, 795-96, 797-98, 800-801; health and illnesses of, 59, 89, 299, 795; milk business of at "Ashland," 383, sells hams in New Orleans, 793, 796, 798; beneficiary of will of Ann Hart (Mrs. James) Brown, 82-84; on cologne water made in the United States, 851; mentioned, 42, 50, 52, 66, 90, 101, 150, 174, 185, 241, 301, 312, 324, 330, 389, 435, 531-32, 534, 673, 680, 704, 743, 761, 792, 808
Clay, Lucretia Hart (granddaughter): birth of, 398; mentioned, 585, 624, 793
Clay, Marie (Mary) Mentelle (wife of Thomas H.), 84, 87, 169, 186, 396, 398, 504, 585, 624, 792-93
Clay, Martha (granddaughter): death of, 217-18; mentioned, 392
Clay, Mary Russell (granddaughter), 793
Clay, Matilda (granddaughter), 392
Clay, Porter (brother): recommends land purchase to C., 318; mentioned, 133, 310
Clay, Rose Victoire (granddaughter), 793
Clay, Theodore Wythe (son): C. pays board for in Lunatic Asylum, 453
Clay, Thomas Hart (son): to, 84, 131, 150, 155, 168-69, 179, 184-85, 186, 187, 196, 204, 257, 285, 335, 352, 364, 392-93, 397-98, 411, 413, 477-78, 504, 584-85, 624, 643, 650-51, 792, 793, 799; marries Mary Mentelle, 87-88; C. advice to on managing "Mansfield," 131, 150, 168-69, 179; children of, 792-93; asked to board Duralde boys, 150; C. gives power of attorney to, 155; on personal behavior of, 87, 187; hemp crop and bagging business of (*see espec.* 412-13), 168-69, 184-

86, 204, 285, 397, 411, 430-31, 529, 539, 624, 789-90, 797-98; debts and financial problems of, 624-25, 643, 673, 790-93, 806; loans of, 131, 394-95, 411, 477-78, 624, 650-51; oversees "Ashland" for C., 168-69, 184-85, 204, 285, 397-98; handles C. financial obligations in Lexington, 395, 643, 650-51; sale of bagging business of (*see espec.* 791-92, 806-7), 792-93, 795-97, 799, 801, 902; business collapse of, 806-7; mentioned, 383, 386, 388-89, 396, 404, 583, 585, 606, 610, 623, 652, 688, 705, 816
Clay, Thomas Hart, Jr., 793, 810
Clay, Thomas Julian (grandson): birth of, 388-90; mentioned, 392, 396, 626
Clay, William, 6
Clay & Mentelle, 792-93, 797, 799, 816
Clay County, Mo., 172
The Clay Minstrel, 757
"Clay's Prairie," 432
Clayton, George H., 814
Clayton, John M.: from, 501; to, 184, 204-5, 205, 416, 465-66, 468-69, 479-80, 499-500, 505-6, 509-10, 513, 619-20, 753-54, 787-88, 811-12, 820-21, 827, 868-69; in carriage accident, 184; on Calhoun and nullification, 159; mentioned for Harrison Cabinet, 466, 468-69, 474, 480, 499-500, 505-6; fails to get Harrison or Tyler Cabinet post, 501, 505-6, 620; urged to run for U.S. House, 416, 753-54; urged to run for U.S. Senate, 505-6, 513; good opinion of Tyler, 620; as possible 1844 vice presidential candidate, 733, 753-54, 759, 812, 831-32, 864-65, 886; defends C.'s tariff views, 787-88; pessimistic about Whig prospects in 1844, 820-21; attacks tariff reciprocity treaty concept, 827-28, 830-32; mentioned, 27, 161, 530, 879
Clayton, Thomas M.: as U.S. Senator, 505-6; health of, 505-6; mentioned, 27, 469
Clay Village, Ky., 612
Clear Creek Academy, 150
Clear Creek Polemic Society, 150
Clements, M.A., 17
Cleveland, Chauncey F., 707, 811
Cleveland, Ohio, 177, 320, 324, 424
Clifton (vessel), 499
Clinch, Duncan Lamont, 726, 728
Clinton, DeWitt, 503, 897
Clinton, George, 503
Clinton, N.Y., 335
Cobb, Sanford (not identified), 321
Cochran, Mrs. ——— (not identified), 386, 417
Cochran, John W.: to, 399
Coddington, J.I., 596
Coffin, Samuel (not identified): to, 421
Colborne, John (1st Baron Seaton), 333
Coleman, Henry: to, 671-72
Colfax, Schuyler: from, 321
Collegiate Institute of Louisville, 386-87
Collier, James: to, 437
Collins, ——— (not identified), 871-72
Colombia, 110, 412
Colton, Calvin: to, 852, 886; writes pamphlet attacking abolition, 315; C. urges him to write anti-abolitionist tract, 852-53; writes biography of C., 886; mentioned, 493, 652
Colton, Walter, 624
Columbia, Ark., 302
Columbia, Mo., 450
Columbia, S.C., 327, 481, 833, 889
Columbia, Tenn., 807
Columbia County, Ga., 756
Columbia River, 141, 510
Columbia University, 697
Columbus, Ga., 833
Columbus, Ill., 768
Columbus, Ind.: C. speech in, 785
Columbus, Ohio, 157, 192, 194, 243, 245, 320, 342, 368
Columbus *Journal and Register*, 173
Combs, Leslie: from, 362-63; to, 330, 359-60
Combs, Mrs. Leslie, 439
Commercial Bank of Natchez, 698, 719
Committee of Gentlemen: to, 434
Committee of New York City Whigs: to, 66-68
Compromise Tariff of 1833. *See* Tariff of 1833
Concord, N.H., 122, 421
Congregationalist Church, 415, 867
The Congressional Globe, 86, 176, 590
Congress of Panama, 736
Congress of the United States
— 22 Cong., 2 Sess. (Dec. 3, 1832—March 2, 1833): C.'s Compromise Tariff of 1833 in, 172
— 23 Cong., 1 Sess. (Dec. 2, 1833—June 30, 1834): Gold Coinage act in, 76, 79
— 24 Cong., 2 Sess. (Dec. 5, 1836—March 3, 1837; beginning in this volume at Jan. 1, 1837): C. major speeches on Specie Circular, 2-5 (*see also* 8:861; Specie Circular); repeal of Specie Circular (*see espec.* 8:861; 9: 2-5, 155-56), 7, 15, 18; public land (preemption and graduation) bill and amendments to (*see espec.* 8:873; 9:6-7), 15-18, 21-23, 25-26, 34-37; investigation of public land frauds in, 22; expunging resolution (*see espec.* 8:735; 9:12-14), 20 (*see also* Expunging Resolution); Bank of the United States, 68 (*see also* Bank of the United States); Catholic immigration, 16, 24 (*see also* Roman Catholic Church); recognition of Texas independence (*see* 8:838-39, 848; Mexico; Texas, Republic of); prepayment of French and Neapolitan spoliation indemnities, 15-16 (*see also* 2:846; 3:52-53, 312-13; 5:29-31; 6:113; 8:448, 754); Cumberland Road bill, 28 (*see also* Cumberland Road); bill jointly to regulate Treasury deposits and reduce (distribute) the surplus (*see espec.* 8:813), 34-35; C. on spoliation claims of New York City and Philadelphia mercantile community, 15; remission of duties on New York City fire losses, 28; C. private bills and petitions, 1-2, 17; American Colonization Society charter, 18, 21, 28-29 (*see also* American Colonization Society); tariff reductions, 18-19, 30-33; disputed 1836 electoral vote, 19; Senate vote for vice president, 19; challenge to 1833 tariff compromise in, 31-32 (*see also* 8:604, 619-22, 626-27; Tariff of 1833); copyright protection for foreign authors (*see espec.* 22, 44), 23, 26,

Cong. of the US (continued): 28-29, 43; trade reciprocity legislation, 28; purchase of Madison manuscripts, 29; fortifications bill, 34-37; national economic crisis, 4-6; Wise committee investigation of Jackson administration, 20; schism in Democratic party during, 20; administration control over House declines during, 37-38; C. friends depart Senate, 27; publication of C. speech in, 68; C. reelected to U.S. Senate during (*see espec.* 8:871; 9:7-8), 14, 20, 27, 29, 33, 38
— 25 Cong., 1 Sess. (Sept. 4, 1837–Oct. 16, 1837): Van Buren message to, 73, 89; early call for 1st session, 45-46, 48-49; party strengths in (*see espec.* 39), 50-51, 58-59, 73, 78; "Conservatives" in, 20, 80 (*see also* Conservative Democrats); appointment of Senate standing committees, 73; U.S. economy on eve of (*see espec.* 3-6), 46, 48-50, 63-65; Van Buren administration plans to cope with economic depression, 55, 59, 63, 68, 73-74; suspension of specie payments on eve of, 47; on resumption of specie payments, 55, 101-2; C. on banking legislation to be considered, 49, 63, 74, 85; Sub-Treasury bill debate in (*see espec.* 75-80, 155-56), 80-81, 84-85, 87, 93, 101 (*see also* Sub-Treasury System); act to relieve Deposit Banks, 101-2; Treasury note bill, 74, 78-79, 85; C. on establishment and structure of a new national bank (*see espec.* 75-79), 57-58, 68, 75-81, 183, 187-88 (*see also* Bank of the United States); warehouse bill, 75, 85-86; bill to delay fourth installment, 74; level of U.S. attorneys' fees in New York City, 84-85; Mexican claims issue, 86, 104, 171, 180, 286; abolition of slavery in the District of Columbia, 109; Texas annexation and slavery extension, 56 (*see also* Texas, Republic of); Dolley Madison relief bill, 86-87; publication of C. speeches in, 81
— 25 Cong., 2 Sess. (Dec. 4, 1837–July 9, 1838): first annual message to, 93, 117, 136, 141, 170; death of member of, 96; Senate committee appointments, 97; District of Columbia bank bill, 104, 111, 113-15; post office issues, 102, 154, 167; abolition of slavery in the District of Columbia and right of petition (*see espec.* 109), 110-13, 124-27, 137 (*see also* "Gag rule"); copyright protection for foreign authors (*see espec.* 22), 104, 118, 130, 134, 196; state taxation of certain public lands, 114; C. attack on squatters, 114, 135-36, 214, 267-68, 321-22, 860; preemption bill (*see espec.* 133-34, 136), 135, 137-38, 149-50, 206, 214, 264-65; public land price graduation bill (*see espec.* 167, 170-71), 169, 214, 264-65, 270; administration's Sub-Treasury (Independent Treasury) bill (*see espec.* 75-80, 130, 145-48), 96-97, 108, 117, 130-31, 136, 138-40, 142-44, 148-49, 153, 155-56, 158-66, 168, 170, 176-77, 179, 195, 203, 205, 208, 210-11 (*see also* Sub-Treasury System); relationship of currency resolution of 1816 to Sub-Treasury and specie payment resumption issues (*see espec.* 165-66), 156, 176, 191-92, 195; modification of Scrip Act of 1830, 198-99, 213; Treasury note bill (*see espec.* 74, 78-79), 155-56, 187; "Resurrection Notes" bill, 175-77; repeal of Specie Circular (*see espec.* 8:861; 9:3-7, 182-83, 190, 193), 165-66, 185, 189, 191-93, 198, 202-3; resolution to accept notes of specie-paying banks (*see espec.* 179-80), 176, 182-83, 185-86, 188-93; specie shortages and shinplasters, 154, 167; establishment of a new national bank (*see espec.* 80, 187-88), 97, 140, 150, 176, 183, 191-93, 195, 203-4, 207, 210-11, 213, 304-5 (*see also* Bank of the United States); bill to amend the Deposit Act of 1836, 209-11; Cumberland Road bill, 167; Washington monument project, 206; bill to establish board of claims commissioners, 178; copying fee for Senate claims materials, 208; Senate rules changes, 212; creation of surveyor general's office for Michigan, 205; controlling growth of executive patronage, 155; petitions about inventions, 211; imprisonment for debt, 206; naval, harbor, and coastal appropriations, 130, 212-13; Seminole question, 122 (*see also* Seminole Indians; American Indians); "Corrupt Bargain" accusation, 159-60 (*see also* "Corrupt Bargain" charge); C. on foreign immigration, 136; naturalization legislation, 96-97; Steamboat Safety Act of 1838, 253; Graves-Cilley duel, 153, 157-58, 164-65; Meade and Menard relief bills, 117-18, 131, 209; neutrality legislation, 154-55; U.S. occupation of Oregon, 141; C. clash with Senator Niles, 195-96, 204, 207-8, 210; C. response to Calhoun's six resolutions on slavery (*see espec.* 121, 123-26), 127-31, 137, 215, 890; claims and Texas annexation tensions with Mexico (*see* Mexico; Texas, Republic of); Maine boundary issue (*see* Great Britain; Northeastern boundary); *Caroline* incident (*see* Great Britain, *Caroline*); session fatigues C., 187; adjournment date, 208; printing of C. speeches in session, 178
— 25 Cong., 3 Sess. (Dec. 3, 1838–March 3, 1839): Whig political mood in, 264, 272, 274, 296; procedural issues in, 263-64; Sub-Treasury bill, 241, 243; Bank of the United States issue, 243 (*see also* Bank of the United States); postponement of fourth installment of distribution of surplus, 253-54; tariff changes, 253, 263; tariff on hemp, 276; C. recollections of Compromise Tariff bill of 1833, 285; national economic depression, 253-54; relationship of U.S. Treasury to U.S. Bank of Pennsylvania, 243, 257-58; bill to make secure customs house receipts, 290-91; Mexican claims issue in,

286; public land price graduation bill (*see espec.* 251), 262, 264-72, 274-75; C. attacked for remarks on squatters (*see espec.* 136), 267-68, 321-22; peace resolutions in, 253, 263, 265, 275; Gold Coinage Act of 1834, 276; international copyright bill (*see espec.* 22), 253, 257, 271; regulation of steamboats, 253; Cumberland Road bill, 273; naturalization issues, 276; North Carolina instruction of senators (*see* North Carolina); Menard, White, and Tudor relief bills, 274, 284; civil appropriations bill, 306-7; armed occupation and settlement of Florida bill, 288-90; defalcation of Swartwout and Price (*see espec.* 253-54), 256, 560; Atherton resolutions on slavery, 254-55, 261; C. speech on abolitionism and reactions to (*see espec.* 278-83), 285-86, 290-93, 295-98, 300, 302, 305, 317-19, 745-47, 890; *Caroline* incident (*see* Great Britain; *Caroline*); U.S. role in Canadian revolt, 255 (*see also* Great Britain)

— 26 Cong., 1 Sess. (Dec. 2, 1839–July 21, 1840): party strengths in (*see espec.* 241, 329), 266, 346, 348, 378; evaluation of performance of, 396-97; agrarian leveling spirit in, 388; C. tired of service in Congress, 401; contest for House Speaker, 361, 365, 368; slow to begin business, 367; on appointing its own reporters, 423; Sub-Treasury (Independent Treasury or "Divorce") bill (*see espec.* 75-80, 263, 378-82), 373-74, 376-77, 382-83, 391, 396, 437 (*see also* Sub-Treasury System); poor state of U.S. economy, 377-82, 407; new Bank of the United States advocated, 378-82 (*see also* Bank of the United States); District of Columbia banking legislation (*see espec.* 422), 430, 432; general bankruptcy law (*see espec.* 408-9, 418-20), 399, 414, 417; treasury notes issued during, 397, 401; branches for U.S. Mint (*see espec.* 8:763), 407; international copyright bill (*see espec.* 22, 372), 369-71, 398; land grants to "new states" for internal improvements, 406, 423; cession of public lands to states in which they lie, 369-70, 389, 423; Cumberland Road bill, 400-402; Louisville and Portland Canal, 385; St. Marie Falls, Michigan, Canal subsidy bill, 402, 405, 408; public land price graduation bill, 265-66, 409; land office for Michigan, 413; supplement to Preemption Act of 1838 (*see espec.* 133-34, 137-38), 406-8; public land claims issues, 402-4; debate on repudiation of state debts and possible U.S. assumption of, 376, 390-92, 396, 492; discussion of tariff modifications, 372, 375-76, 388-89, 397, 399, 406, 409; tariff on hemp bagging, 430-31; removal of tariff on salt, 388-89; tariff-collection reform bill, 429-30; domestic silk industry problems, 375-76, 384, 389, 397, 399, 404, 417, 430; discussion of U.S. postal rates, 385; Smithsonian legacy, 387; fishery subsidies, 388; right of petition to abolish slavery, 387-88; Clay-Calhoun clash in, 369-70, 389; Seneca Nation treaty, 145, 415; use of bloodhounds in Second Seminole war, 397 (*see also* Seminole Wars); publication of U.S. treaties and laws, 431; U.S. emigration to Oregon, 372; Maine boundary crisis (*see* Great Britain; Northeastern boundary); annexation of Texas, 399 (*see also* Texas, Republic of); recognition of Haiti, 399; War of 1812 bounty-lands claims, 413; Kentucky request for compensation for arms supplied U.S. in War of 1812, 398, 431; militia reorganization proposal (*see espec.* 421), 422-23, 427; interference of federal officials in elections, 426-27; Mormon redress petitions, 384; international congress petitions, 384, 389; mileage allowance and stationery bill, 421-22, 431-32; date of adjournment of, 396, 400, 404

— 26 Cong., 2 Sess. (Dec. 7, 1840–March 3, 1841): attempt to repeal Sub-Treasury (Independent Treasury) Act of 1840 (*see espec.* 464-65), 469, 502, 504 (*see also* Sub-Treasury System); debate on calling "Extra Session" of 27 Cong. (*see espec.* 453-54), 484, 495-96, 510; public land price graduation bill (*see espec.* 265-66, 369-70), 486-94, 546; cession of public lands to states in which they lie, 477, 484, 489-91, 493; distribution of public land sales proceeds to all states (*see espec.* 486-94), 469, 477, 484, 782; proposed permanent preemption system (*see espec.* 463-64, 482-83, 486-94), 472, 477-81, 484, 496; relief laws of 1830 and 1831 for public land purchasers, 480; tariff issue (*see espec.* 479), 465-66, 480, 496; home valuation of dutiable articles (*see espec.* 479), 465, 480; general bankruptcy law, 478, 485, 497; reestablishment of Bank of the United States, 484, 498; U.S. assumption of state debts, 492; international copyright bill, 486; debate on Blair and Rives as Senate printers, 501-2 (*see also* Congress of the United States: 27 Cong., Special Session of Senate); C. defense of Webster on interstate slave trade, 504, 508-9; administration plan to handle deficit, 479; C. clash with Cuthbert, 504, 508-9; New Hampshire militia compensation bill, 472; abolition of grog ration in Navy, 472; peace petitions, 478; C&O Canal stock transfer to Maryland, 497; rights of children born to U.S. citizens abroad, 507; Maine boundary arbitration (*see* Great Britain; Northeastern boundary); *Caroline* crisis (*see* Great Britain; *Caroline*); recognition of Haiti, 495; U.S. settlements in Oregon, 493

— 27 Cong., Special Session of Senate (March 4, 1841–March 15, 1841): party strength in, 514; C. presents

Cong. of the US (continued): Morehead's credentials, 510; debate on dismissal of Blair and Rives as printers to Senate (*see espec.* 501-2), 510-13; on calling "Extra Session," 511, 514-16; appointment of sergeant-at-arms, 511; patronage appointments, 514; C. confrontation with King and Smith, 512, 516
– 27 Cong., 1 ["Extra"] Sess. (May 31, 1841–Sept. 13, 1841): party strengths in (*see espec.* 416-17, 514), 538, 544, 570, 615; splits and tensions in Whig party, 539, 543-44, 553; Whig morale, 538; Democratic filibusters in, 547-48, 550; the calling of the "Extra" session (*see espec.* 446, 453-54), 484, 495-96, 511, 513-16; Tyler message to, 530-31, 534; C. and Whig legislative agenda for and program in (*see espec.* 468, 513, 538), 461, 464-65, 484-85, 519, 523-26, 533-34, 539-40, 605, 692, 694; C. seen as leader in, 456, 462, 604; C. on limiting subjects to be discussed in, 538-39; C.'s plan for a new national bank (*see espec.* 548-50), 523-26, 533, 543-44, 553, 587-92, 607 (*see also* Bank of the United States); reports of Select Committee on Currency on proposed banks (*see espec.* 535-36, 593), 537, 545-46, 548; repeal of 1841 Sub-Treasury Act (*see espec.* 527-29, 582-83), 513, 530-31, 533-37, 539-43, 545, 581, 604 (*see also* Sub-Treasury System); Ewing's bank plan in, 530-31, 535-36, 539-40, 542, 545-50; debate on first bank (Fiscal Bank of U.S.) bill (*see espec.* 528, 535-36, 548-50), 453, 468, 503, 510, 513, 519-26, 533-37, 539-41, 543, 545-48, 550-62, 565-66, 569-76, 578, 580-83, 587-92, 597-98, 730; debate on amendments to Fiscal Bank of United States bill (*see espec.* 554-56, 558, 565-66, 572-73), 552-53, 559-63, 570-71, 574-75; debate on branching power of first bank bill (*see espec.* 549-50, 565-66), 533-34, 543, 554-57, 573, 575-76, 587-92, 875; debate on second bank (Fiscal Corporation) bill (*see espec.* 528-29, 593-94), 587-92, 598-602, 604, 636-39, 775-76; debate on branching power of second bank bill, 585-86, 809; comparison of Fiscal Bank bill and Fiscal Corporation bill, 593-94; Tyler's vetoes of Whig bank bills (*see espec.* 528-29, 549-50, 586-92), 556, 581, 584-85, 593-99, 604, 607, 610, 612, 618, 620; C. on Tyler's veto of second bank bill, 594, 604, 608-9, 738, 757, 765-66; Tyler's bank (Board of Exchequer) bill, 623; role of 1836 Deposit Act in national bank debate (*see espec.* 540-41), 562-63, 582-83; Bankruptcy bill (*see espec.* 408-9), 418-20, 533, 544, 547, 550, 552, 562, 569, 573, 581, 590, 594, 605; renewal of District of Columbia bank charters (*see espec.* 422, 548), 544, 551, 574; national financial problems faced by, 515-16, 566-68, 580-81, 602-3; Treasury Department estimates and expenditures, 535, 546-47; inquiries on Treasury Department operations (*see espec.* 535), 536, 541-42, 546, 552, 580-81; Loan bill (*see espec.* 560-61, 566-68), 563, 569-70, 580, 602-3, 605; assumption of state debts, 582; public land (distribution, preemption, internal improvements) bill and act (*see espec.* 525-26, 542), 513, 523, 528-29, 541, 558, 563, 566, 568, 578, 581-83, 586, 590, 592, 594, 598, 603-6; debate on tariff bill and act (*see espec.* 525-26, 566-67), 547, 577, 580-82, 587, 592-94, 596-99, 602-6; restructuring U.S. government, 461; copyright bill, 532; discussion of C. body-slave Charles, 583-84; payment of claims for liberated slaves (*see* Great Britain); *Caroline* incident (*see* Great Britain; *Caroline*); C. clash with Cuthbert in, 875-76; C. clash with Choate in, 556-57; nativism in, 553; C. motion to limit debate, 542, 545, 547, 561, 563, 568; discussion of open executive sessions in Senate of, 578; proscriptions attributed to Whigs, 551; C. on annual budgets, 582; Post Office appropriations, 599; Smithson fund investment, 605-6; fortifications bill, 577-78, 596, 602; Navy appropriations bill, 576-77, 606; Virginia military land warrants, 617; frauds involving army and Indian bureau, 544; debate on Senate procedures, 578-82; election of House clerk and Speaker, 522, 539, 543; election of Senate secretary and president, 539, 547; pressure on C. during, 539; C. on retiring at end of, 616, 618-19, 691-96; adjournment date, 553, 557, 585, 606-7; C. trip home from (*see espec.* 607-8), 553, 557, 606, 609-10, 612, 618; C. evaluation of work of, 609-10, 614-16, 618, 692, 696; Whig election losses following, 620-21
– 27 Cong., 2 Sess. (Dec. 6, 1841–August 31, 1842): Whig legislative plans and pledges, 615, 619, 627; Whig party behavior in, 742-43; party strength in, 619, 652; great measures supported by C. in, 692-95; Mangum as Senate president pro tem, 707-8, 717-19; Tyler's relations with (*see* Tyler, John); C. resignation from (*see espec.* 612, 656), 616-22, 636, 641, 652-53, 677-78, 688, 690-91, 696, 701-3; Tyler's bank (Board of Exchequer) bill (*see espec.* 623, 801), 619-20, 624-25, 629, 631-32, 639, 771, 786; empty U.S. Treasury, 625, 726; Treasury note bill (*see espec.* 634-35, 725-26, 728), 587, 602-3, 654, 665-66; extension of Loan Act of 1841 (*see espec.* 587), 602-3, 665-66, 725-26, 728; Pope's bank plan, 614; District of Columbia bank bill, 676; tariff bills of June 1842 ("little" or "provisional") and August 1842 ("great" or "permanent") (*see espec.* 628, 719-20), 703, 708, 725, 728; Tariff Act of 1842 (*see espec.* 628, 646-47, 719-20), 660, 706-8, 731-32, 742-43, 760-63, 766, 772, 775, 863; Tyler veto of the "provisional" tariff bill (*see espec.* 628, 719-20), 646-47, 717, 722-23, 725,

728, 730-32, 735, 739-40, 742-43; Tyler veto of the "permanent" tariff bill (*see espec.* 628, 719-20), 725, 728, 730, 734-35, 739-40, 742-44, 748-56; home valuation of imports for tariff purposes (*see espec.* 730-31), 667-68, 725, 728, 734-35, 753-54, 762-63; Simmons' substitute tariff proposal (*see espec.* 725, 728), 742-43, 749, 755-56, 774; C. retrospect on Compromise Tariff of 1833, 660, 667-68; 1833 tariff limitations (20% clause) on 1842 tariff proposals, 646, 668, 682-83, 708, 719-20, 753-54; distribution element in 1842 tariff debate (*see espec.* 719-20), 668, 682-83, 686, 717, 719, 722, 725, 728, 730-32, 735, 742-43, 753, 766, 772; repeal of distribution provision in Distribution and Preemption Act of September 1841 (*see espec.* 628, 634-35, 719-20), 648-50, 673-75, 679, 689-90, 717, 719, 725, 728; voluntary vs. involuntary distribution (*see espec.* 628), 634-35, 673-75; protection of American labor, 636; public opinion on tariff, 636, 681; repeal or postponement of Bankruptcy Act of 1841 (*see espec.* 626, 641-43), 629-36, 640, 650, 652-53, 655, 689, 694; constitutional amendments to curb power of president (*see espec.* 636-40), 626-27, 650, 653, 659, 672, 694, 776; House of Representatives reapportionment (*see espec.* 706-7, 742-43), 708, 753, 770, 776; "gag rule" in House, 641; attempt in House to censure J.Q. Adams, 641; C.'s eleven resolutions on national economy (*see espec.*, 654-55, 665-70, 689-90), 671, 676-77, 679, 682-87; copyright bill (*see espec.* 22), 629-30, 689; New York City custom house investigation (*see espec.* 595-96), 650, 653; C. on Dorr Rebellion, 714-16, 723, 731, 780; repudiation of state debts, 640, 660; regulation of river pilots, 629; harbor improvements, 645-46; Senate printing, 625-26, 671; C. eulogy for Representative Williams, 660-61; C. role in Graves-Cilley duel (*see* Duels and Dueling); Blennerhassett claim, 678-80; Army and Navy expenditures, 703-4, 706, 727; War of 1812 bounty land claims, 617; *Caroline* case and McLeod issue (*see* Great Britain; *Caroline*); *Creole* issue and crisis (*see* Great Britain); Webster-Ashburton treaty (*see* Great Britain; Webster-Ashburton Treaty); U.S. claims againt Mexico (*see* Mexico); C.'s farewell speech in Senate, 691-98, 704, 757; public dinner and ball for C. during, 688; C. trip home from, 677-78; adjournment of (*see espec.* 650, 655, 730), 735, 739

— 27 Cong., 3 Sess. (Dec. 5, 1842–March 3, 1843): Tyler's bank (Board of Exchequer) proposal, 623, 718-19, 726, 801 (*see also* Board of Exchequer Bank Plan); tariff issue in, 849; failure to confirm appointments of Wise and Cushing, 803-4; C. assessment of, 803

— 28 Cong., 1 Sess. (Dec. 4, 1843–June 17, 1844); 2 Sess. (Dec. 2, 1844–March 3, 1845): party strengths in, 706-7, 753-54, 844-45; impact of 1842 reapportionment act upon, 706-7, 742-43, 770; treaty for annexation of Texas, 896-900

— 29 Cong., 1 Sess. (Dec. 1, 1845–August 10, 1846); 2 Sess. (December 7, 1846–March 3, 1847): party strengths in, 844-45

Connecticut: 1837 state and U.S. House elections in, 43; Whig campaign in 1837 elections, 207-8; 1838 state legislative elections in, 195-96; 1838 U.S. Senate election in, 196, 210; support for C. nomination for president in, 204-5; 1839 state and U.S. House elections in, 301, 303-6; 1838 and 1839 Whig nominating conventions in, 205; 1840 state elections in, 403-4, 423; Whig rally in New Haven, 423; 1841 governor and U.S. House elections in, 519, 521; 1842 state elections in, 707; 1843 state elections in, 811-12; mentioned, 199, 232, 263, 362, 424, 547, 604, 822

Conover, James F.: to, 518

Conrad, Charles M., 796-97

Conservative Democrats, 39, 73, 88-89, 91-93, 96-97, 116-17, 127, 174, 182, 190, 195, 216, 220, 224, 233, 239, 242-43, 247, 257-58, 261-63, 266, 272, 296, 299, 305, 351, 357, 449, 473, 872

"Constans" (pseud.), 264, 269, 274

Constantinople, 668

Constitution, U.S.S., 310-11

Constitution of the United States: expunging resolution in relation to, 12-13; C. on origin and nature of, 123-25; C. on powers and clauses in, 165, 215, 279-80, 429, 476, 487-89, 491; implied power of an implied power, 177; established interpretations of, 143, 709, 713-14, 716; varying views of, 645-46; amendment limiting presidential term, 214; three-fifths clause of, 491; regulation of slavery in, 476 (*see also* Clay, Henry: slaves and slavery); general welfare clause in, 489; support of land sales distribution to states in, 488-91; tariff-distribution relationship in, 488; amendment to limit federal judges' terms, 431; and pocket veto, 489; proposal to limit presidential veto power, 610, 636-39, 775-77, 805-6; amendment to limit president's powers of appointment and removal, 636, 640; and internal improvements, 645-46; presidential power as commander-in-chief, 544; Madison's interpretation of, 709, 716; and protective tariff, 762; enumerated and implied powers in, 824-26; and annexation of Texas, 897-99; and tariff by treaty, 827-28

Conyngham, David, 625

Cook, Bates, 288, 307-8

Cook, Noah: from, 68; to, 66-68; mentioned, 105-6

Cooke, George, 371

Cooper, James, 722, 751, 853, 873

Cooper, Mark A., 836

Cooper, Samuel, 181

Coos County, Me., 472

Corbin, Robert B., 473, 521

Corbit, Henry C. (not identified): to, 577
Cordes, Samuel, 506
Cornwallis, Lord Charles, 93
"Corrupt Bargain" charge, 95-96, 146, 159, 224, 349, 370, 442, 648-49, 709-10, 782-83, 817, 819
Corwin, Thomas: bid for reelection as Ohio's governor, 744, 775, 872, 874; mentioned, 185, 436, 450-51, 621, 761-62, 768-69
County Antrim, Ireland, 186
Court of St. James's, 309
Covington, Ky., 450, 859, 891
Cowles, Frederic, 187
Cowperthwait, Joseph: from, 10; to, 10
Cox, John, 334
Cox, Nathaniel (not identified), 42
Crabb, George W., 386
Craig, D.M.: from, 807; mentioned, 792, 799, 902
Craig, Elijah: from, 807; mentioned, 643, 650, 792, 799, 902
Cramer, John, 463
Crane, Joseph H. (not identified): to, 761; mentioned, 164
Cranston, Robert B., 60
Crawford, George W., 835-36
Crawford, William H., 160, 166, 407
Crawford County, Ohio, 424
Creighton, William, Jr.: to, 47; mentioned, 198
Creole (vessel), 625, 629-30, 659-60, 680, 684, 749
Crittenden, Alexander Parker, 481
Crittenden, John J.: from, 585-86, 721-22, 734-35, 749, 755; to, 706, 735-36, 739-40, 757, 796-97, 801, 897-99, 902; joins C. in Supreme Court case, 386; campaigns for Whig ticket in 1840, 439; amends state debt-assumption resolution, 390; sponsors bill to limit role of patronage appointees in elections, 426; appointment as attorney general in Harrison Cabinet, 458-62, 466, 470, 473, 499; reelected U.S. senator, 477; attempts to amend Van Buren administration preemption bill, 322, 463-64, 481-82, 486; problems of nephew A.P. Crittenden, 481; urges extra session of 27 Cong., 484; called a federalist, 473; sees Tyler as true Whig, 522; urges compromise on Fiscal Corporation branching issue, 585-86; replaces C. in Senate, 656, 696; declines candidacy for president pro tem of the Senate, 717; advises C. on 1844 campaign strategy, 721-22; opposes impeachment of Tyler, 734; attacks Tyler's treachery to Whigs, 720; on "permanent" tariff bill of 1842, 749; role in Graves-Cilley duel, 657-58; urged to run for governor of Kentucky in 1844, 851; mentioned, 17, 19, 21, 40, 65-66, 83, 87, 112-13, 141, 150, 160, 166, 181, 185, 190, 194, 216, 226, 231, 247, 251-52, 267, 278, 342, 398, 408, 417, 420, 429, 451-52, 463-64, 468, 491, 494, 507, 524, 532, 535, 609, 625, 642, 644-45, 650, 652, 663, 695, 716, 718, 731, 748, 761, 791, 799, 804, 812, 879, 899-900
Crittenden, Maria Innes Todd (Mrs. John J.), 706
Crittenden County, Ark., 633
Crockett, Charles L.: to, 893
Crockett family, 469
Crook, Charles: to, 744
Crook, James, 414
Crook, William, 414
Cross, James C., 233
Crowell, David: to, 220
Croxall & Browning: from, 841-42
Crump, John C.: from, 302; to, 318-19
Cuba: C. rejects idea of trip to, 797; mentioned, 289-90, 440, 525, 783
Cudlipps, Mr. ——, 751
Cuevas, Luis G., 171
Culpeper County, Va., 411-12
The Cultivator, 613-14
Cumberland County, N.C., 682
Cumberland Gap, Tenn., 443
Cumberland Road, 27-28, 167, 251-52, 273, 331, 400-402, 761
Cumming, William, 62
Curd, John, 152, 790
Curtis, Edward: to, 88; appointed collector of port in New York City (*see* Harrison, William Henry and administration of); leans toward C. for president in 1844, 485-86; opposition to C. nomination in 1839, 485, 595-96; influence of over Webster, 485-86; damages Whig party in New York City, 595; and investigation of New York City custom house, 595-96; supports Scott's presidential candidacy in 1839, 675-76; mentioned, 89, 216-17, 313, 456, 463, 471, 474, 495, 497, 502-3, 514, 516-17, 562, 866
Curtis, Gwen, 701
Curtis, Harriot, 889
Cushing, Caleb: member of Tyler's "Corporal's Guard," 730; Senate turns down nomination of as secretary of the treasury, 803-4; attacks Botts on Tyler impeachment issue, 736; defends Tyler administration, 786-87; Senate confirms as commissioner to China, 804; mentioned, 261, 375, 522, 736, 807
Cuthbert, Alfred: C. clashes with, 504, 508-9, 876; mentioned, 79, 165-66, 578-79, 600, 641-42, 739, 756, 864
Cutts, Anna Payne, 86
Cutts, Dolley Madison: to, 86
Cutts, Richard, 86

Dabney (slave), 10
Dahlonega, Ga., 407, 539, 719
Dallas, George M., 39, 752
Dana, Judah, 13-14
Dangerfield, Oliver (not identified): from, 65
Daniel, Peter V., 299
Danville, Ky., 306, 320, 383-84, 396
Davidson, James, 622
Davidson County, Tenn., 316-17, 763
D'Avignon, Francis, 536
Davis, Charles A.: to, 162-63
Davis, Mrs. Charles A., 163
Davis, Garrett, 609, 836, 850
Davis, George M.: from, 806
Davis, James, 174
Davis, John: from, 870-71; to, 848-49; as possible vice presidential candidate in 1844, 732-33, 754, 759, 761-62, 831-32, 864, 867-68; opposition to War of 1812, 831-32; effect of Latimer fugitive slave case on career of, 831-32; on abolition, 871; mentioned, 213, 744, 807, 857, 865, 878-79
Davis, Matthew L.: from, 60-61, 62-63; to, 54-55, 66-68, 85, 89, 307-8; on Whig presidential tactics in 1840 in New York City, 60-63; C. opinion of, 841; C. discusses New York politics with, 855; mentioned, 107, 348, 457

Davis, Reuben, 123
Davis, William, 876
Dawson, Moses, 375
Dawson, William C., 361, 522, 612
Day, Mahlon: from, 467
Dean, Nicholas: to, 354
Dayton, Ohio: C. to citizens of, 621; C. campaign speech in, 761; mentioned, 154, 164, 744, 763-64, 766-68, 770, 773, 776
Dearborn, Henry A.S.: to, 462, 732-33; mentioned, 754
Declaration of Independence, 128, 200, 311, 420, 486, 637, 715, 777, 779-80
DeKalb, Johann, 136
Delavan, Edward C.: to, 218
Delaware: carried by Harrison in 1836, 204; legislative movement for C.'s presidential nomination in 1839-40, 204-5; 1838 state elections in, 416; quality of representation in Congress, 469; 1842 state Whig convention in, 733, 753-54; mentioned, 112, 188, 214, 263, 311, 374, 462, 466, 501, 887
Delaware (vessel), 730
Delaware River, 213, 701
Delphine (mare), 481
Deming, Elizur, 827
Democratic party (Jacksonian, Locofoco, Van Buren): 1844 nominating convention of, 752, 797, 821, 894; potential vice presidential candidates in 1844, 726, 728-29, 752, 859; factionalism and schism in, 20, 61, 70-71, 389, 424, 751-52, 788, 803-4, 813-14, 820, 826, 831-32, 847, 855, 862 (*see also* Conservative Democrats); blamed for economic depression and currency problems, 55, 57-58, 66-67, 143, 196, 338-39, 377-78, 403, 410, 427-28, 440, 487, 489-90, 553, 570, 705, 710-11, 742, 753, 775-76; C. characterizes, 379, 381, 425, 433, 462, 487, 492, 496, 502, 537, 600, 715, 742, 783, 839-40; relations with Tyler, 543, 591, 597, 600-602, 620, 625, 681, 720, 732, 735, 751-52, 756, 805, 808, 811, 826, 840, 894; Tyler's rumored return to, 543, 594, 615-16, 646, 735, 805, 808, 811, 894, 896; filibusters of in 27 Cong., 1 ["Extra"] Sess., 547-48, 550, 563; members of convert to Whig cause, 70-71, 261, 263, 553, 655, 814; mentioned, 1, 29, 37-39, 43, 48, 50-51, 59, 64, 69, 76, 79, 88-89, 91, 95, 100, 106, 122-23, 139, 147-52, 157, 159, 162, 166-67, 174, 182, 195, 210, 213, 216, 220, 223-26, 228, 230-31, 233, 237-41, 243, 248-51, 253, 256, 271, 273, 296, 299-302, 308, 314, 317, 323-24, 330, 333-34, 346-47, 353, 357, 361, 380, 387, 396, 401, 404, 409, 416-17, 435-36, 438, 444-45, 449, 451, 454-55, 457, 463, 469, 473, 488, 495, 503, 505, 511-12, 514-15, 519, 521, 524, 536, 542, 545, 551, 557, 567-68, 571, 573, 575, 578, 592-93, 596, 599, 608, 612, 618, 636, 638, 647, 652-53, 666, 673, 683, 686, 704, 706-7, 712-14, 716, 718, 722-23, 736, 740, 744, 749, 757, 761, 765, 774, 778, 780, 784, 789, 798, 800, 807, 815, 817, 822, 827, 829, 833, 835-37, 845, 851, 853, 855-60, 863, 865, 867, 870-76, 879, 882-83, 889
The Democratic Review, 751-52
Democratic Whig Young Men of New York, 729
Denmark, 804
Denny, Mrs. ——— (not identified), 386
Derby (horse), 46
Des Moines River, 169
Detroit (steamship), 216
Detroit River, 276
Devon (cow), 318
Devonshire, England, 768
Dick, A.L. (not identified), 536
Dick, N. & J. & Co., 41-42, 302-3
Dickerson, Mahlon, 31, 285
Dickerson, Philemon: to, 95
Dickins, Asbury, 539, 624
Dickinson College, 36, 315
Dillon, John B.: to, 214
Dinimack, John L. (not identified): to, 750; mentioned, 848
District of Columbia: American Colonization Society chapter incorporated in, 18; size of notes issued and resumption of specie payments by banks of, 104, 111 (*see also* 25 Cong., 2 Sess.); abolition of slavery in, 109-10, 121, 123-27, 278-83; monument to George Washington in, 206; proposed bank in, 422; recharter of banks of, 548, 551; mentioned, 21, 44, 78-79, 112-14, 128, 137, 153, 169, 178, 182, 186, 215, 222, 246, 255, 260, 292, 297, 315, 321, 353, 382, 387, 430, 432, 504, 528, 533, 535, 539, 543, 549, 554-55, 558, 574, 590, 593, 639, 642, 676. *See also* Washington, D.C.
Dixon, Archibald, 851-52
Dixon, Nathan F., 608-9, 640, 688
Dock Ward (Phila.), 701
Dod, Albert B.: to, 196
Dodge, Henry, 765
Dodge, John W., 880
Dodge, J. Turner: from, 274; to, 284
Doherty, William, 157
The Dollar Farmer, 841-42
Donaldson, Samuel J.: from, 506
Donoho, Thomas (not identified), 178
Doran, John L.: from, 115
Dorr, Thomas, 714, 716, 723, 780
Dorr Rebellion, 707, 714-16, 723, 752
Dorsett, Fielder R. (not identified), 413
Dorsey, ——— (not identified), 165
Doty, James D.: to, 748, 764-65; mentioned, 386
Dougherty, Addison: from, 315
Douglas, Stephen A.: loses U.S. House race, 228
Douglass, George L., 532
Dover, Dela., 204-5, 416, 754
Downing, Jack (pseud.), 462
Downing, Josiah: to, 481; mentioned, 59, 169, 480-81, 522, 584-85, 623
Downing, Richard W., 59, 169
Downing, Samuel, 59, 169
Dromore, Ireland, 9-10, 556
Duane, William J., 12, 313
Dudley, Benjamin W., 450, 481
Dudley, Edward B., 167
Dudley, Peter: from, 21, 451; to, 451
Duels and Dueling: aborted Marshall-Woolley duel, 247; Graves-Cilley duel (*see espec.* 153), 157, 164-65, 334, 656-58, 661-65; C. opinion of and involvement in, 164-65, 643-45; Webb-Marshall duel, 648; C.C. Clay bill to end in D.C., 169
Duffield, Thomas W., Jr. (not identified): to, 763
Duke, James K., 481
Dumont, John, 38
Dun, Walter, 53

Duncan, Alexander, 239-40, 393-94, 451
Duncan, Garnet, 439
Duncan, Henry T., 413, 610-11, 790
Duncan, Lucius: from, 793-94; to, 794
Duncan, Stephen: from, 90, 101-2, 123, 213, 236-37, 242, 303, 698; on banks and specie payments, 101-2; hemp business with C., 73, 90, 411-13, 504, 698, 791; on national politics, 101; kinships, 413; finds "lost" C. deposit in Natchez bank, 698; mentioned, 168, 186, 302-3, 623, 631
Dunham, Josiah (not identified): from, 89
Dunlap, Thomas, 9, 227
Dunlap, William, 155, 168
Dunlop, Moncure & Co. (not identified), 815
Dunnica, William F.: from, 520; mentioned, 238, 450, 453
Dupuy, Aaron (slave), 52, 90
Dupuy, Charles (slave): burns C. letter, 791-92; alleged happiness of as slave, 583-84, 780-81; rumored at runaway, 760, 773; travels with C., 386; mentioned, 52, 86-87, 270
Dupuy, Charlotte "Black Lotty" (slave): to, 52
Dupuy, Mary Anne (slave): to, 52
Duralde, Henry Clay (grandson): education of, 89-90, 150; attends Lafayette Seminary, 89-90; attends James Such School in Jamaica, New York, 431, 449, 452, 463, 471, 555; C. visits in New York, 452, 459, 466-67; attends Washington College in Pennsylvania, 308, 325, 347; character of, 347, 513; attends school in Danville, Kentucky, 383-84, 396; mentioned, 50, 52, 508, 678, 688
Duralde, Martin, Jr. (son-in-law): Tyler appoints to patronage job in New Orleans, 529; C. visits, 798; mentioned, 42, 396
Duralde, Martin, III (grandson): education of, 89-90, 150; attends Lafayette Seminary, 89-90; naval career of, 310-11, 383-84, 396; C. buys clothes for, 538-39; mentioned, 50, 52
Duralde, Susan Clay (Mrs. Martin, Jr.), 50, 396
Durfee, Amos, 120
Durham, John George, 387
Dyer, Edward, 511

East India, 498
Eaton, John H., 95
Eatonton, Ga., 839, 863
Eclipse (horse), 185
Edenton, N.C., 323
Edgar County, Ill., 432
Edmiston, Sidney: from, 478; to, 478
Edward Livingston v. *Benjamin Story*, 40
Edwards, Cyrus, 216
Edwards, Georgiana, 751
Edwards, Henry W., 43
Edwards, John, 752
Edwards, Mrs. ———, 751-52
Edwards, Ogden, 486
Edwards, William: to, 532; mentioned, 533
Egg Harbor, N.J., 883
Egypt, 207
Election, presidential, of 1828: Harrison mentioned for vice presidential nomination, 343
Election, presidential, of 1832: Rhode Island supports C. in, 143-44; C. on strategy and tactics used in, 299; "Corrupt Bargain" issue in, 348-49
Election, presidential, of 1836: disputed vice presidential electoral vote in, 19; why C. was not nominated, 25, 33; bank issue in, 29-30; tariff issue in, 33; C. on Whig defeat in, 48, 220-22; Webster as candidate in, 65, 221; Harrison candidacy in, 106-7, 220-22, 393-94; White candidacy in, 221, 316; campaign in Delaware, 204
Election, presidential, of 1840
— general: outcome of, 263; alliance of Whigs and Conservative Democrats (*see espec.* 20), 127, 190, 242-43, 261-62, 304-5; National Republican and Anti-Masonic alliance, 509; Liberty party role in, 356-57; C. reaction to and analysis of, 451, 453-54, 773, 839-40; role of women in, 448, 709; impact of 1837 state elections on, 98-100; impact of 1838 elections on, 225-26, 242-43, 245-46; impact of 1839 state elections on, 346-47; impact of 1840 state elections on, 448; financing the Whig campaign, 207, 344-45, 421; financing the Democratic campaign, 345, 351; campaign dirty tricks, 60-61; Democratic party campaign strategy and tactics, 426-29; Democrat-Locofoco role and influence in, 216, 231, 438; splits in Democratic party during, 389, 424
— Anti-Masonic role in: 91, 94, 106-7, 123, 157, 173-74, 273-74, 287-88, 295, 305-6, 327-28, 362-63, 366-67, 509
— issues, charges, and countercharges in campaign: C. delineation of issues, 304-5; C. asked to state views on, 321; national economic collapse and depression, 55, 66-67, 196, 337, 356-57, 373, 377-81, 410, 426-29, 433, 440-41; banking and specie payment problems, 55-56, 143-44, 284, 303, 321, 356-57, 427-29, 433, 437, 440-41; Sub-Treasury proposal and legislation, 73-80, 154, 168, 190, 338-39, 351-52, 356-57, 389, 530-31 (*see also* Sub-Treasury System); Livingston default and defalcation, 443; reestablishment of the Bank of the United States, 239, 323, 427-29, 433-34, 530-31; U.S. assumption of state debts, 440-41; public land price graduation and reduction, 267, 274, 284, 336-37, 356-57, 373, 428-29; distribution of public land revenue to states, 331-32, 428-29; American System, 356-57; tariff, 100-101, 304-5, 322, 331-32, 356-57; internal improvements, 100-101, 304-5, 331-32, 346, 433-34; C. as slaveholder and views on slavery and abolition, 102-3, 119, 127, 131, 135-36, 164, 173-74, 191, 194-95, 199-200, 222-24, 241, 244-48, 254-55, 262-63, 269, 272-73, 278-83, 286, 290, 295-96, 300, 302, 314-15, 318-19, 321-23, 339-40, 356, 393-94, 429; J.B. Mahan case, 242, 245-46; C. earlier stance on Missouri Compromise, 339-40; power usurpation by Jacksonians, 185-86, 336-39, 403, 410, 421, 425, 433-35, 447; C. campaign "platform," principles, policies, and stances (*see espec.* 222-24), 230-31, 278-83, 318-19, 336-39, 416,

433-34; lack of Whig party platform and principles, 416, 773-76; C. unpopularity, 232-33, 250; proscriptions and patronage policies of Democrats, 235-36, 314-15, 341-42, 364, 425-27; charges of Democratic corruption, 203-4, 245-46, 314-15, 319, 338-39, 351-52, 425, 437-38, 441-43; Swartwout-Price scandal in New York (*see espec.* 253-54), 255-56; C. "Corrupt Bargain" with Adams, 95-96, 98, 160, 349-50, 370, 439-40, 442; C. connection with Aaron Burr, 442; misuse of "Democrats" as party label, 433; temperance legislation, 269, 275; expunging resolution, 410; dueling, 157; moving seat of U.S. government to western state, 321; one-term presidency (*see espec.* 312-13), 325-26, 342, 349, 428; presidential veto power, 223, 428; abolition of Electoral College, 321; direct election of senators, 321; militia reorganization, 421-23, 427; Boston *Atlas* article controversy (*see* Boston *Atlas*); Jackson Proclamation to South Carolina and Force bill, 341-42, 393; agrarian aims of Jacksonians, 314; extravagance of Van Buren administration, 338-39, 410-11; Van Buren character, 215, 302; Jackson choice of Van Buren as successor, 447; New England vs. South tensions, 247-48; Harrison military career and militarism, 422, 440; Harrison health, 424, 438, 519; alleged stupidity of Harrison, 438; Harrison on slavery and abolitionism, 393-94, 424; Harrison "Sandusky Affair," 375; C.'s earlier relations with Harrison, 412; annexation of Texas (*see espec.* 127), 119, 135-36, 228-29; Northeast boundary crisis, 291, 404-5, 295-96 (*see also* Great Britain; Northeastern boundary); *Caroline* issue, 119, 126, 331 (*see also* Great Britain; *Caroline*); war against Seminoles in Florida, 295-96

— newspapers, journals, biographies, pamphlets, and other printed matter involved politically in campaign: 8, 62, 69-71, 86, 89, 95-96, 100, 106-7, 109-10, 127, 130, 137, 151, 166, 177-78, 183-84, 191, 194, 207, 229-30, 234, 237, 239-40, 245-47, 250-52, 262-63, 269, 273-74, 286-87, 290, 295-96, 300-301, 339, 371, 429-30, 448

— nominating conventions: 1838 Anti-Masonic national nominating convention (*see espec.* 251-52), 258, 261-63, 283, 290, 362-63; 1839 Whig national nominating convention (*see espec.* 92, 115-16), 66-67, 70-71, 106-7, 119-20, 131-32, 141-42, 150-51, 166-67, 172, 194-95, 201-2, 225-26, 247-48, 251-55, 272-73, 275, 286-88, 290, 327, 349, 352-56, 359-63, 365, 416, 473, 885; nominating convention of Whig Young Men, 315-16; C. reaction to nomination of Harrison, 337-38, 360, 363-67, 373, 377, 382-83, 388-89, 410, 473; on the "intrigue" against C. at Harrisburg convention (*see espec.* 826-27), 359-63, 365-67, 389, 462-63, 874, 885; analyses and reactions to C. defeat at Harrisburg convention, 362-63, 382, 384, 462-63, 473; reactions to Harrison nomination, 362-63, 365-68, 411-12, 437-38; Whig opposition to a nominating convention, 120; changing dates of Whig nominating convention, 275-76; vice presidential nomination at Harrisburg, 362-63

— James G. Birney candidacy and role in: 365-66, 450

— Clay candidacy and role in: analyses of C. prospects, 60-61, 66-67, 69-71, 91, 105-7, 150-51, 156-57, 166-67, 179, 189-90, 215, 229-30, 232-33, 262-63, 272-73, 286-88, 316-17, 341-42, 344-45, 348-49, 355-57; C. campaign participation (after Harrisburg convention), 386, 390-92, 395, 411-12, 425-26, 429-30, 433-36, 438-43, 708-16; C. major campaign speeches for 1840 Whig ticket, 410, 426-29, 439-43, 708-16; C. analyses of his own candidacy, prospects, and role in, 57-58, 63-64, 69-71, 110, 114-15, 120, 122, 127, 130, 133, 141-42, 152-54, 164, 172-74, 186, 191-92, 194, 197-98, 202-5, 212-13, 230-33, 250-52, 259, 262-63, 290-92, 296, 298, 300, 312-13, 324-25, 327-28; advice to C. on campaign strategy and tactics, 8, 60-63, 65, 81-82, 91-92, 106-7, 115-17, 119, 131, 156-57, 189-90, 320-21, 344-45, 348-49, 355-57, 454-55; C. analysis of Whig party prospects, 327-28, 350; strategy and tactics of anti-Clay Whigs, 156-57; early interest in C. candidacy, 46, 54-55, 62, 65-68, 91, 106-7; C. resistance to his early nomination, 46, 54-55, 58, 63, 66, 69-71, 143; possibility of C. withdrawing from, 246-48, 332, 335-36, 347-48, 350; C. urged to withdraw in favor of Harrison and/or Scott, 348-49, 358; abolitionist support of and opposition to C. during, 173-74, 181-82, 194-95, 244-45, 356-57; Whigs copy Jackson campaign tactics, 437; C. appeal to South, 62, 65, 120, 166-67; C. campaign trips and speeches prior to Harrisburg convention (*see espec.* 312-13, 330), 235, 315-16, 320, 324, 328, 331-39, 342-43, 347, 350; rumored Harrison-Webster alliance against C. (*see espec.* 251-53), 254-56, 273-74, 287-88, 292, 298, 362-63; Clay-Harrison ticket suggested, 355; Clay-Webster ticket suggested, 106-7; Webster supports shift to C., 320-21; C. feels his support eroding, 245-46; C. will support nominee of Harrisburg convention, 354, 357-58; C. on lack of Whig party platform in 1840, 416

— W.H. Harrison candidacy and role in: prospective candidacy of, 91, 106, 120, 142, 156-57, 163-64, 167-68, 192, 194, 212-13, 216, 230, 232, 247-48, 275, 287, 342-43, 346, 348-50, 354-55, 410, 448; C. urged to withdraw in favor of, 349, 358; the "Secret Circular," 157, 163-64; Harrison strategy and tactics to secure nomination, 157, 163-64, 172, 194, 424-25, 437-38; C. doubts about Harrison, 437-38; C. advice to Harrison on

Election of 1840 (continued): campaign matters, 424; Harrison's stump campaigning, 424, 438; C. analyses of prospects of 1840 Whig ticket, 368, 373-75, 377, 383-84, 388-89, 402-3, 407, 410, 415, 421, 424-26, 430, 433-37, 444-45
– Winfield Scott candidacy, prospects, and role in (*see espec.* 277-78, 288): 334, 350, 355-58, 360; C. urged to withdraw in favor of, 358
– Martin Van Buren candidacy, prospects, and role in: 70-71, 191, 194-95, 230-31, 349, 410, 434, 436-37, 443-45, 447-48
– Daniel Webster candidacy, prospects, and role in (*see espec.* 48): 54-55, 58, 60-63, 65-66, 69-71, 91, 94, 105-7, 114, 118-20, 123, 142, 154, 189-90, 194, 198, 204, 212-13, 225-26, 229-30, 232-33, 252-53, 260-61, 264, 269, 287, 290, 292, 326; Clay-Webster conflict in New York City, 189-90, 212-13, 216-17, 225-26, 237
– campaign and related political activity in specific states and sections: Alabama, 65, 230-31, 444-45; Connecticut, 204-5, 403-4, 423; Delaware, 204-5; Georgia, 65, 70; Illinois, 307-8, 444, 448, 455; Indiana, 37-38, 163-64, 172-73, 340, 348-49, 436, 438, 444-45; Kentucky, 119-20, 130, 132, 135, 150, 152-53, 232-33, 272-73, 434-36, 438, 447; Louisiana, 65, 70, 299-300, 435, 444; Maine, 154, 204-5, 443-44; Maryland, 132, 135, 141-42; Massachusetts, 130, 154, 164, 212-13, 252, 260-61, 269, 298, 425; Missouri, 444, 453; New Hampshire, 122, 421; New Jersey, 119, 132, 135, 153, 190, 204; New York, 60-63, 66-71, 82, 85, 91, 94, 105-7, 115-20, 127, 142, 156-57, 167-68, 173-75, 189-90, 192, 195-98, 202-3, 205, 207, 213, 215-17, 234, 262-63, 273-74, 277-78, 286-88, 291-92, 312-13, 320-21, 351, 366, 415-16, 447, 451-52, 455, 471, 509; North Carolina, 166-67, 194, 272-73, 444-45; Ohio, 70-71, 115, 120, 132, 154, 157, 164, 172, 203, 246-47, 249-50, 373-75, 389, 424, 436, 438, 448, 450-51, 454; Pennsylvania, 91, 172, 194, 373, 389, 449; Rhode Island, 143-44, 157, 444; South Carolina, 62, 65, 69-70, 233-36, 316-17, 344-45, 351-52, 432, 434-35, 439, 445; Vermont, 120; Virginia, 174, 239, 257-58, 261-63, 272, 277, 296, 300, 326, 346, 351-52, 426-29, 433, 451; New England, 69, 212-13, 248, 272; North, 69, 286, 291-92; South, 61-62, 65, 120, 154, 166-67, 233, 248, 263, 290; Southwest, 120, 154, 263; West, 89, 216, 219-20, 435-36
Election, presidential, of 1844
– general: Whig divisions in, 861; Whig unity in, 724, 767, 786, 826, 855, 862; Democratic disunity in, 803-4, 820, 826, 831-32, 847, 859, 862, 869-70; Anti-Masonic role in, 853, 873, 892-93; abolitionist vote as factor in, 857; C. on general issues for debate, 763, 766, 808-10, 842-43; role of women in, 709, 734; rumored Webster-Calhoun alliance in, 844; prospect of election going into House of Representatives, 820, 848; importance of sectionally balanced tickets in, 834; impact of 1842 and 1843 state and mid-term national elections on, 706, 788-89, 795, 817, 835, 837, 841, 847-49, 853-55, 876, 881, 891
– issues, charges, and countercharges in campaign: Whig campaign issues, 762-63; C. attack on squatters on public lands, 135-36, 268, 321-22, 860-61; C. role in Graves-Cilley duel, 164-65, 643-45, 648, 754; C. on dueling, 823; "Corrupt Bargain" charge against C., 649, 659, 696-97, 710, 782, 817-19; C. connection with Masons, 892-93; C. morals, 754; C. as slaveowner, 754, 760, 778-81, 871; C. as political loser, 830, 847, 854; C.'s simple background, 751; C. performance at Ghent, 758; C. tariff and trade policies as secretary of state, 821, 830; American System, 803; Bankruptcy Act and its repeal, 633-35, 655, 750, 808-9; Sub-Treasury concept, 774-76, 839-40; national economic depression, 705, 710-13, 741-42, 775, 839-40; state debt repudiation, 805, 814; need for uniform currency and national bank, 711-13, 741, 751, 762-63, 766-67, 773-75, 782-84, 802-3, 805, 808-10, 824-25, 840, 881; economy in government, 767, 774, 805, 839-40; issuance of Treasury notes, 775; tariff (*see espec.* 838-39, 863), 690, 698-700, 740-41, 750, 755, 758, 762-64, 766, 772, 774-75, 788, 805, 809-10, 821, 827, 842-44, 849-50, 856-57, 877, 880, 884, 893, 895; incidental tariff protection, 762, 838-39, 863, 877; reciprocity treaties, 821, 827, 849; abuses of executive power, 766-67, 771, 775-76, 782, 840; restriction of veto power, 767, 775-76, 805, 808-9, 840; single-term presidency, 767; Jacksonism in 1830s, 711-12, 775, 785, 808; public land policy, 711-12, 741, 766-67, 809-10, 860; distribution of public land sales receipts, 711, 750, 753, 763, 775, 805, 808, 840, 863, 877, 893; reapportionment of U.S. House, 776; domestic manufactures, 842-43, 850-51; immigration and naturalization, 845-46; John Tyler's personality, character, political principles, and ambition, 681, 726-27, 730, 742-43, 751, 771, 775-76, 789, 795, 805, 811-12, 817, 833, 855, 859-60, 871, 891, 894; Tyler's vetoes, 722-23, 731-32, 735-36, 738, 750-51, 755-57, 775, 805-6, 826; Tyler's patronage policies and actions, 775, 808-9, 812, 840, 871, 900; Tyler maladministration, 705; Texas annexation issue, 680-81, 823, 896-900; Dorr Rebellion, 714-15, 731, 751-52; U.S. occupation of Oregon, 828-29; persecution of Mormons, 384, 881, 890-91; slavery, abolition, and colonization, 745-47, 754-55, 758, 778-81, 836, 852, 867, 871, 874, 879, 887-89, 894
– newspapers, journals, biographies, pamphlets involved in campaign: 493, 536, 651-52, 655-56, 670, 697, 722-23, 730, 736-37, 751-52, 754-55, 757-58, 787-88,

804-5, 832, 841, 859, 861, 879-81, 890, 894; campaign slogans, 636
— nominating conventions: 1844 Democratic national nominating convention, 752, 797, 821; Democratic vice presidential possibilities mentioned, 726, 728-29, 752, 859; 1843 Liberty party nominating convention, 857-58; 1844 Whig national nominating convention (*see espec.* 754-55), 733, 759, 773, 821-22, 834, 847, 865-66; Whig vice presidential possibilities mentioned, 301, 326-27, 351, 466, 524, 732-33, 754-55, 759, 773, 812, 821, 831-32, 834, 861, 864-70, 872-83, 885-87, 894; C. on choice of vice presidential running mate, 732-33, 861; C. on revival of "intrigue" against him at 1839 Whig convention, 633, 820, 827-28, 830 (*see also* Election, presidential, of 1840: nominating conventions); Young Men's Whig Convention of Ratification in Baltimore, 887; C. provides banner staff for Ratification convention, 887; state legislature nominations of C., 636, 718-19, 759-60; Philadelphia nomination of C., 766
— James G. Birney candidacy and role in: 857-58
— John C. Calhoun candidacy and role in (*see espec.* 859): 718-19, 727, 729, 752, 820-21, 844, 864, 870
— Lewis Cass candidacy and role in: 854, 882-83
— Henry Clay candidacy and role in: early interest in and anticipation of, 454-55, 633-34, 636, 649, 651, 654, 675, 681; support for and endorsements of, 698, 700, 750, 765, 767-68, 803; C.'s conditions for running, 651, 747; as reluctant candidate, 768, 805, 823, 839, 891, 895; on his own candidacy, 701-2, 710, 753, 768, 797, 803, 805, 820-21, 823; prospects in election, 718, 721, 751, 878; C. platform planks and principles for 1844, 811; C. on Whig prospects, 764, 773, 786, 788-89, 804-5, 811-12, 820-21, 826, 831-33, 839-41, 843-44, 846-49, 855, 857-58, 862, 876, 880-81, 885-86, 891, 894-95, 897; Whig strategy and tactics in (*see espec.* 841, 844-45), 633-34, 636, 759, 767, 813-14, 851, 853, 855, 858, 866-68, 887, 889-91, 896-900; health of as factor in campaign, 820, 834; perils of C. letter-writing habit, 883; Democrat converts to C., 655; C. hopes Democrats will nominate Van Buren, 894; C. principal campaign speeches, 665-70, 691-97, 708-16, 724-25, 737, 741, 744-45, 747, 749, 752, 760-61, 763-64, 766-67, 770, 773-85, 801-3, 808-10; campaign appearances, speeches, and dinners turned down by, 703, 760, 794, 820, 837, 853, 901; C. campaign trip through South (*see espec.* 833-34), 853, 857-60, 873, 885-86, 889, 896, 900-902
— John McLean candidacy and role in (*see espec.* 827, 836): 821-22, 828, 830, 847, 854, 865
— James K. Polk candidacy and role in: 818-20
— Winfield Scott candidacy and role in: 647-48, 721-22, 726, 751, 753, 821
— John Tyler candidacy and role in: within Democratic party (*see espec.* 615-16), 736, 805, 862, 896-900; Tyler's third party movement, 615, 751-52
— Martin Van Buren candidacy and role in (*see espec.* 752): 680-81, 727, 820, 831-32, 854, 857-59, 894; C. hopes for Van Buren nomination, 894
— Daniel Webster candidacy and role in (*see espec.* 861): 787-89, 821, 827, 830, 844, 857, 862, 864-66, 868-70, 874-76, 878-80, 882-83, 894
— campaign and related political activity in specific states and sections: Alabama (*see espec.* 804), 805-6, 849-50; Connecticut (*see espec.* 821-22), 706-7, 811; Delaware, 732-33, 753-54, 887; Georgia (*see espec.* 836), 718-19, 834-37, 859, 870, 880-81; Illinois (*see espec.* 813), 835, 891; Indiana (*see espec.* 813), 827, 835, 848; Kentucky (*see espec.* 805), 837-38, 844, 848-49, 858; Louisiana (*see espec.* 804), 734-35, 740, 749, 805-7, 835-36, 843-44, 849-50; Maine, 722, 821; Maryland, 759, 869-70; Massachusetts (*see espec.* 821-22), 732-34, 770-71, 807, 835-36, 849-50, 852-53, 867; Mississippi (*see espec.* 804), 805-6, 849; Missouri, 835, 849; New Hampshire, 706-7, 821; New Jersey, 871; New York (*see espec.* 837), 631, 633-34, 636, 675-76, 729, 752, 760-61, 764, 773, 787-89, 811, 857, 862, 866-70, 879, 886; North Carolina (*see espec.* 836), 636, 670, 718-19, 749, 833-36; Ohio (*see espec.* 813), 732-33, 743-44, 760-62, 764, 768, 785-86, 849, 874; Pennsylvania (*see espec.* 751-52), 721-22, 750, 766, 836, 853, 858, 890; Rhode Island, 822; South Carolina, 820-21; Tennessee (*see espec.* 804), 763, 805, 811-13, 817-19, 821-22, 826, 835-36, 847-48, 889; Vermont, 821; Virginia (*see espec.* 805-6), 706-7, 812-13, 821-22, 826-27, 889-90; New England (*see espec.* 821-22), 752, 823-24, 844; South, 752, 803-5, 820, 847-49; Southwest, 803-4, 811, 820-21
Electoral College, 19, 23
Eliza (slave), 52
Elliot, Samuel, 739-40
Elliot, William St. John, 790-91
Elliott, Jesse Duncan: from, 241
Ellis, Donna, 744
Ellis, Powhatan, 33, 171, 716-17
Ellsworth, William W., 43, 196, 199, 301, 404, 519, 707
Elmore, Franklin H., 199-200, 244-45
Ely, ——— (not identified), 411, 413
The Emancipator, 191, 194
Embry, Jacob, 364
Emerson, Caleb: from, 102-3
Emilius (horse), 585
Emmett, Robert: from, 678
England. *See* Great Britain
Engs, Philip W.: to, 444
Enterprise (vessel), 406
Episcopal Church, 81, 315, 431
Episcopal Seminary, 187
Erie, Pa., 447, 600, 634, 640-41
Erie Canal, 198, 405
Erie County, N.Y., 92, 355, 858
Erie County Savings Bank, 455
Erwin, Andrew: from, 461; asks patronage of C., 461

Erwin, Andrew Eugene, 40, 50, 303, 312, 396
Erwin, Anne Brown Clay (daughter): C. mourns, 50; children of, 312; mentioned, 41, 187, 303, 391-92, 396, 461
Erwin, Charles Edward (grandson): health of, 302-3; mentioned, 40, 50, 312, 396
Erwin, Henry Clay (grandson): C. advises on education of, 431; attends James Such School in Jamaica, New York (*see espec.* 449), 431, 452, 459, 463, 513; mentioned, 40, 50, 312, 395-96, 439, 808
Erwin, James (son-in-law): from, 303; to, 40, 41-42, 52, 302, 312, 372, 385, 397, 730; assists C. with New Orleans business matters, 40-42, 302-3, 372, 400, 650; C. helps rear children of, 40, 42, 187; children of, 312; tombstone for wife's grave, 41; C. advises on commodities speculations, 41-42; debt owed C., 372, 463, 650, 672-73, 677, 688; buys pine trees for his "Woodlands" farm, 312; rumored failure of his New Orleans business, 385-86, 390, 395, 400, 403, 677, 796, 801; education of daughter Lucretia (*see* Erwin, Lucretia Clay); C. advises on education of sons Henry C. and James, Jr., 431; as a poor correspondent, 672; reaction to economic crash in New Orleans, 677, 796, 801; indebtedness to John Jacob Astor, 846; money borrowed from his children, 801; marriage to Margaret Johnson, 798, 808; mentioned, 71-72, 90, 231, 241, 377, 392, 396, 439, 449, 452, 461, 530, 538-39, 623, 625, 643, 790
Erwin, James, Jr. (grandson): C. advises on education of, 431; attends James Such School in Jamaica, New York, 431, 449, 452, 459, 466-67, 513; mentioned, 40, 50, 312, 385, 396, 439, 452, 808
Erwin, John P., 235, 800-801, 808
Erwin, Lucretia Clay (granddaughter): to, 807-8; education of, 187, 808; mentioned, 40, 42, 50, 312, 396
Erwin, Margaret Johnson (Mrs. James), 798
Essex, N.Y., 335
Essex County, Va., 311
Estes, Alston B.: to, 321-22
Etter & Bayne: to, 169
Eustis, George (not identified): from, 795; to, 795
Eustis, William, 375
Evans, David: from, 610-11
Evans, George: from, 688; to, 688; mentioned, 579, 593, 682, 722-23, 732
Everett, Edward: appointment as minister to Great Britain, 604; mentioned, 100, 199, 269, 353
Everett, Horace, 725, 727-28
Everhart, James B.: to, 901
Ewing, Robert C., 748
Ewing, Thomas: from, 530, 541, 558, 878-79; to, 449, 524-26, 535, 546, 547, 548, 552, 558, 561, 563, 580-81, 743-44, 764, 876; opinion of on 1840 election, 424; appointed secretary of the treasury by Harrison, 458-61, 466, 470, 473; C. instructs on new Bank of the United States bill, 524-25; advises C. on Tyler administration options, 530; calls for repeal of Independent Treasury and for new Bank of the United States, 530; message of June 6, 1841, to Congress, 535-36, 539-40; plan for "Fiscal Bank of the U.S." (*see espec.* 535, 549-50), 524-25, 539-40, 545-46, 548, 555, 565-66, 589-90; C. seeks advice from on Benton-Woodbury amendment on the authority of the secretary of the treasury, 547; C. transmits Woodbury resolution to, 552; on foreign ownership of stock in Fiscal Bank, 558; recommends legislative tactics to C., 558; on Webster as vice presidential candidate in 1844; 878; on Liberty party in 1844 election, 878-79; on anti-Catholic violence in Boston, 878; mentioned, 2, 4, 6, 22, 27, 47, 463, 468, 499, 542, 547, 553, 562, 572, 612, 621
Expunging Resolution, 12-14, 20, 68, 77, 261, 269-70, 410, 469, 588, 590, 714
Eyre, Manuel: from, 500

Fahnestock, Levi: from, 887; to, 887
Fairfield, John, 233, 377, 444
Fairfield County, Ohio, 876
Fall, John: to, 842-43
Falls of St. Marie, 402, 405, 408
Farley, Harriet, 888-89
Farmers and Planters Bank of Baltimore, 622
Farnsworth, Benjamin F.: from, 386-87
Farrar, Preston W.: from, 501
Farrow, Col. ——— (not identified), 439
Fauquier White Sulphur Springs, Va., 339
Fauquier County, Va., 578-82
Faulkner, William: from, 655-56
Fayette, Miss., 45
Fayette County, Ky.: 1838 state legislative elections in, 193, 250-51; 1838 vote in for Kentucky constitutional convention, 224; C. to county court of, 785; 1839 election of state senator from, 251; 1844 presidential election results in, 836; 1843 U.S. House elections in, 836; mentioned, 152, 224, 238, 301, 310, 439, 450, 531, 610, 702, 747, 752, 785, 850. *See also* Lexington, Ky.
Fayette County, Pa., 385, 507
Fayette County, Tenn., 350
Fayette County, Va., 855
Fayetteville, N.C., 682, 696
Fayetteville letter, 649, 659, 696
Featherstonhaugh, George W.: from, 418; to, 196, 236, 284-85; mentioned, 474
Federalist party, 162, 195, 393, 424-25, 427, 433, 473, 832
Fendall, Philip R.: to, 68, 240; Harrison promises job to, 533, 604; contemplates editing C. speeches, 738; mentioned, 536
Ficklin, Joseph, 529, 531
Fillmore, Millard: from, 688; to, 688; mentioned as 1844 Whig vice presidential nominee, 733, 754, 812, 831-32; role in passage of 1842 tariff, 832; mentioned, 262-63, 274, 628, 801, 867, 879
Finley, James: from, 612
Fiscal Bank of the United States (bill), 526, 545-46, 548, 569, 572, 707, 729
Fiscal Corporation bill, 602, 611-12, 620, 707, 729-30
Fisher, Charles, 412
Fishkill, N.Y., 330

Flagg, Azariah C., 61
Fleur de Lis (mare), 585
Flint, Joshua B.: from, 307
Florea, Albert (overseer), 90, 389-90, 796
Florence, Italy, 329, 811
Florida Territory: slavery in, 125-29; 1810 uprising in West Florida, 902 (*see also* 7:82, 233; Seminole Wars); sectionalist tension within, 475; on ceding land in East Florida to Seminoles, 475; mentioned, 122, 163, 168, 280, 288-90, 295, 347, 391, 397, 637, 640, 666, 683, 898
Flower, Frank A., 41
Flower & Finley, 816
Folsom, Joshua: to, 368
Foote, John P. (not identified): to, 767-68
Force bill, 163, 341
Forks of the Wabash, 150
Forres, Samuel (not identified): to, 761
Forsyth, John (not identified): from, 95, 189; to, 95, 189; mentioned, 13, 31, 33-34, 291, 294, 414, 418, 861
Fort Delaware, 213
Fort Gibson (Okla.), 544
Fort Hill, S.C., 158
Fort Meigs (Ohio): to Committee for a Fort Meigs Celebration, 399; mentioned, 400, 424, 438
Fort Snelling (Wisconsin Territory; now Minnesota), 131
Fort Wayne, Ind., 828
Forward, Walter, 614, 623, 626, 727, 729
Foster, Ephraim H., 345, 378, 442, 514, 647, 847-48
Fowler, Orson S., 475
Fowler, Trevor T., 880
Fowler, Wiley P., 627-28
Fox, Henry S.: from, 39-40; money owed C., 39-40; mentioned, 291, 377, 418, 471, 474, 547
Franca, Manuel Joachim De, 700, 702
France: assassination attempt on king of, 2; financial problems in, 2; tension with and blockade of Mexico, 210-11, 228-29; spoliation claims crisis and settlement of with U.S., 2, 33; U.S. unfavorable trade balance with, 487, 490; recognition of Texas independence, 414; interest in Hawaii, 829; mentioned, 13, 15, 45, 53, 118, 128, 140, 146-47, 177-78, 206, 227, 265, 304, 343, 387, 399, 402, 407, 622, 637, 691-92, 737, 783, 804, 845-46, 862, 882-83, 900
Francia, Henry de la, 902
Francis, John B., 182
Frankfort, Ky.: smallpox epidemic in, 88; mentioned, 11, 90, 120, 130, 189, 227, 272-73, 342, 449-52, 454, 516, 522, 524, 530, 622, 632, 767, 804, 844, 851, 858, 875
Frankfort Bridge Company, 451
Frankfort *Commonwealth*, 130, 229-30, 836
Franklin, Benjamin, 200, 295, 380
Franklin, La., 792
Franklin County, Ky., 49, 850
Frederick (bull), 236
Frederick the Great, 289
Fredericksburg, Va., 110, 409, 717
Fredericksburg *Political Arena*, 100-101, 110, 429
Fredericton, New Brunswick, 291, 295
Freeman, Frederick: to, 80-81
Frelinghuysen, Theodore: wins 1844 Whig vice presidential nomination, 733, 754; mentioned, 119, 887
French, Richard, 51, 301, 435
French Revolution, 637
Frenchtown, Mich., 375
Fulton, Robert, 895
Fulton (steamboat), 399
Fulton, Mo., 612, 748, 818

Gadsby's Hotel, 66, 163, 199, 372, 386, 510, 569, 571, 644
"Gag rule," 255, 399, 544, 599, 641, 872
Gaines, Edmund P., 21, 34, 122
Gale, Anthony (not identified), 1
Gales, Joseph: from, 177-78; to, 295, 332, 447-48; *Register of Debates* of ceases publication, 86; son of serves as amanuensis to C., 139, 152; prints C. speeches, 177-78; Senate printer to Adams administration, 502; motion to purchase the *Register* of, 511; mentioned, 81, 429, 604, 652, 658, 672, 831, 879
Gallagher, William D. (not identified): to, 767-68
Gallatin Albert: as possible president of a new national bank, 191; pamphlet by on Northeastern boundary, 474; mentioned, 14, 177
Gallatin, Tenn., 439
Gallitzin, Demetrius A.: to, 24
Gamage, Edward, 810-11
Gardner, Sayers & Co. (not identified), 815-16
Garland, Hugh A., 539
Garland, James: to, 300
Garland, Rice, 36, 184, 386, 421, 429
Garlick, Theodatus: to, 385
Garnett, John M. (not identified): from, 52
Garrett, Robert & Sons: from, 842; to, 841
Gates, Seth, 872, 874, 888
Gatewood, Peter: to, 481
Gayle, John: to, 798
Gaylord, Willis, 614
Genesee County, N.Y., 509
Genesee River, 320
Geneseo, N.Y., 332
Geneva, N.Y., 60
Gentry, M.P. (not identified): from, 688; to, 688
George (slave), 51
Georgetown, D.C., 334, 371, 404, 422, 548
Georgetown, Ky., 306, 386, 901
Georgetown College, 386-87
Georgia: C. presidential support in, 65, 164; political weakness of Harrison and Webster in, 65; 1837 election for governor in, 62; 1841 state elections in, 612; 1842 States' Rights Whig convention in, 718-19; 1843 Whig presidential nominating convention in, 834-35; 1843 Whig victory in Savannah local election, 859; 1843 state elections in, 836, 859, 870, 873, 880-81; C. campaigns in, 834-35; resident of requests C.'s views on abolition, 888; mentioned, 18, 70, 263, 290, 328, 425, 522, 644, 647, 726, 730, 743, 756, 762-63, 800, 812, 824, 833, 837, 849, 854, 857-58, 863, 874, 885-86, 900, 902
Georgia *Journal*, 880
German, Obadiah, 320-21
German language, 159, 852, 878
Germantown, Pa., 757, 890
Gettysburg, Pa., 853
Getz, George: to, 109-10
Ghent, Belgium: treaty, 769; mentioned, 33, 622, 659, 737, 758, 765, 768
Gholson, Thomas S.: to, 433-34
Gibson, Jacob (not identified): to, 745-47
Gibson, John, 501
Giddings, Joshua R.: from, 278; to, 330, 887-88; denies

Giddings, J.R. (continued): charge that C. supports his anti-slavery views, 886; C. thanks for political courtesy, 887-88; condemned by Liberty party leaders, 872, 896; 1838 election to U.S. House, 872; mentioned, 385, 874
Giles (slave), 52
Gilmer, Frederick G.: from, 611-12, 748; mentioned, 731
Gilmer, George R., 62
Gilmer, Thomas W., 409
Gilmor, Robert: to, 354, 609-10
Gimbrede, J.N., 805
Glasgow, Ky., 49
Glenham, N.Y., 330
Gloucester County, N.J., 109
Godwin, Thomas H.P.: from, 302; to, 318-19
Goode, Patrick G., 727, 729
Goodhue & Co. (not identified): to, 799; mentioned, 815
Goodrich, William: to, 443
Gorostiza, Manuel Eduardo de, 33-34
Goshen, Ky., 901
Gosport, Va., 564
Gottenburg, Sweden, 765
Gottingen, 765
Gouge, William M.: sends C. pamphlet on banking and currency, 63; mentioned, 64
Gould, Marcus T.C., 776
Grace Episcopal Church, 431
Graham, James (not identified), 476
Graham, John L., 596
Graham, Richard: to, 48; mentioned, 46, 108
Graham, William A., 535, 552
Grand River, 171-72, 450, 748
Granger, Adele, 332
Granger, Amos P.: from, 763-64; to, 771-73
Granger, Francis: as 1836 vice presidential candidate, 19; C. doubts political motives of, 173; views of C. campaign strategy for 1840, 106; appointed postmaster general in Harrison Cabinet, 474, 499; C. asks for patronage appointments and removals, 531-32; as possible 1844 vice presidential candidate, 759; mentioned, 157, 174, 238, 394, 460, 596, 754, 827
Grant County, Ky., 768
Grason, William, 248
Grattan, Thomas C.: to, 478
Gratz, Benjamin: from, 449, 498; to, 387; reports safe arrival of C. grandsons at school in New York, 449; seeks patronage job for brother Jacob, 498; discusses impact of "gunny bags" on hemp manufactures, 498; mentioned, 413, 450
Gratz, Jacob, 498
Graves, Coleman, 792-93, 799
Graves, Richard S., 814
Graves, Mrs. Richard S., 814
Graves, William J.: from, 656-58; kills Cilley in duel (*see* Duels and Dueling); recollection of origin of duel with Cilley, 656-58; mentioned, 153, 157, 164-65, 172, 185, 334, 644-45, 648, 661-65
Gray, J.W., 506-7
Greala[?], Samuel (not identified), 425
Great Britain: authors from seek copyright protection in U.S., 22, 44; financial problems in, 2, 45; political crises in, 44; Anglo-Irish tension in, 883-84; emancipation of slaves in British West Indies, 199-200; perpetual allegiance law of, 689; corn law politics in, 597, 685; suppression of slave trade by, 684; reaction to default of state bonds in U.S., 391; mentioned, 1, 4, 6, 23, 42, 46, 53, 75-77, 118, 151, 177-78, 193, 219, 227, 229, 232, 244, 279, 284, 309, 319, 343, 371, 377, 379-80, 382, 384, 387, 399, 427, 430, 452-53, 455-57, 459, 467, 478, 480, 491, 527, 529, 550, 579, 584, 596, 604-5, 608, 637, 645-46, 654, 669, 678, 691-92, 699, 708, 710, 712, 747, 779, 783-84, 797, 821-22, 827, 830-31, 845, 852, 866-67, 875, 899
— U.S. relations with: recognition of Texas independence, 407 (*see also* Texas, Republic of); ambitions in Hawaii, 829; Canadian rebellion against, 255; Anglo-American convention of 1827, 405; 1830 U.S. reciprocity treaty with, 14, 306-7; population of compared with U.S., 828-29; Tory vs. Whig foreign policy toward U.S., 862; free trade and tariff policies of, 684-85; war scare over Northeast Maine-New Brunswick boundary (*see espec.* 291, 293-94, 404-5), 119, 206-7, 211, 278, 292-95, 301, 303-4, 306, 400, 403, 474, 507-8 (*see also* 7:666-67, 729-30); U.S. wars with, 295; arbitration of Northeast boundary, 404-5, 508, 683-84; Howard report on Northeast boundary, 472; Mudge report on boundary, 418; C. on British presence in Maine, 13; Webster-Ashburton negotiations (*see espec.* 697), 683-84, 720, 727, 734, 748, 755, 765, 782, 882; C. on eventual collapse of British empire, 685; decline of British power in North America, 828-29; *Enterprise* case, 406; *Caroline* incident (*see espec.* 119, 126), 129-30, 140, 255, 331, 471, 474, 508, 523, 529, 684; McLeod case (*see espec.* 471), 474, 508, 523, 617, 619, 864; *Creole* case (*see espec.* 629-30), 659-60, 680, 684, 749; C. wine shipment in *Creole*, 625; C. on threat of war with, 680, 683-84; C. reflection on Treaty of Ghent, 33, 365, 806; liberation of American slaves by, 541; impressment issue, 365, 684; maritime claims questions, 414; U.S. role in Canadian revolt against, 104-5, 119, 255-56, 276; U.S. tension with on Oregon issue, 141, 828-29
Great Lakes, 326-28, 330, 564, 646, 765
Great Western (steamboat), 403-4
Greece: Greek language, 539; C. on independence of, 884; mentioned, 205, 845
Greeley, Horace: from, 68; to, 66-68; supports C. for 1840 presidential nomination, 68; C. opinion of, 371; writes campaign biography of C., 871; conflict with Webb, 890; supports Webster for vice president in 1840, 890; mentioned, 832, 868
Green, C.P. (not identified): from, 670; to, 670
Green, Duff: causes C. defeat in 1836, 25; mentioned, 543, 672
Green, Jones: to, 411
Green, Richard (not identified): to, 761
Green, Willis, 334, 386, 512, 706-7, 736, 799

Greenbrier County, Va. (W. Va.), 533
Greene, Edward: to, 249
Greene County, Tenn., 889
Greeneville, Tenn., 889
Green-Hill Female Seminary (Lexington), 353
Greenhow, Robert, 171
"Greenoch," 412
Greenough, Horatio, 328-29
Greenupsburg, Ky., 206
Greenville, Ohio, 438
Greenwood, John (not identified): from, 777
Gregory, James M., 342
Greig, John, 332
Grider, Henry, 333
Griffiths, R.C. (not identified), 500
Grimball, John, 148
Grinnell, Joseph, 835
Grinnell, Moses H.: member of "Wall Street" clique, 827-28; mentioned, 217, 830, 866, 885
Grinnell, William P. (not identified): to, 574
Griswold, Rufus W.: to, 215
Groves, Moses, 475-76
Groves v. *Slaughter*, 52, 475-76
Groesbeck, John, 321
Grundy, Felix: amends public land (graduation) bill, 169-71; character of, 163; phrenological analysis of, 163; attacks continued circulation of Bank of the United States notes, 163, 175; resignation from and election to Senate seat, 236; service as U.S. attorney general, 236; allegedly buys votes for Democrats, 352; mentioned, 19, 97, 140, 176, 180, 316, 440, 514-15
Grymes, John R.: to, 795
Gulf of Mexico, 228, 564-65, 568
Gurley, Ralph R.: from, 526-27, 804; leaves American Colonization Society, 527; on slave trade, 526-27; on colonization vs. emancipation, 527; mentioned, 47, 169, 256-57, 298
Gurney, James G.: from, 467
Guyandotte, Va. (W. Va.), 72

Hagerstown (Md.) *Herald and Torchlight*, 841
The Hague, 414
Haines, David, 872
Haiti (Hayti): U.S. recognition of, 399, 495; mentioned, 645
Hale, Salma: to, 122
Hall, Allen A.: from, 344-45; mentioned, 341
Hall, David A.: to, 54
Hall, Hiland: to, 738-39
Hall, James, 375
Hall, Sarah, 52
Hall, Willis: from, 68, 196, 254-56, 355-56; to, 66-68; analyzes New York presidential politics, 254-56, 355-57; supports C. for president, 355; serious illness of, 858, 862, 867, 880; mentioned, 196, 864, 869
Hallett, Benjamin, 269
Hamer, Collin B., Jr., 625, 792, 816
Hamilton, Alexander (Secretary of the Treasury), 5, 47, 362
Hamilton, Alexander [Jr.]: to, 46-47, 63-64, 69, 88-89, 96-97, 176, 191, 225, 242, 291, 303-4; mentioned, 723
Hamilton, James, 57, 59, 62, 227, 407
Hamilton County, Ohio: to Whigs of, 767-68; mentioned, 164, 240, 393, 424, 450-51, 640, 760, 767
Hammond, Charles: from, 382; to, 300; attacks C. stance on abolition, 300, 317; John Bell's low opinion of, 317; on U.S. interstate slave trade, 300; death of and disposition of correspondence with C., 407-8
Hammond, Judah, 357
Hampshire County, Va. (W. Va.), 154, 167
Hampton, Wade: from, 592; mentioned, 481, 504, 539, 584, 606
Handy's, Mrs., 66
Hannegan, Edward A., 789, 813
Hanover County, Va., 353, 395-96, 408-9, 426, 429-31, 461, 591, 636, 804, 825, 881
Hanseatic League, 828, 830
Hardeman, Thomas, 484
Harden, Edward: to, 164
Hardin, Benjamin, 614
Hardin, Edward, 813
Hardin, Mark: from, 333-34, 678-79; opposes Sunday mail, 678-79; on God and Bible, 678-79
Hardin County, Ky., 334
Hargous, Luis C., 717
Harlan, James: to, 11-12, 538; mentioned, 113
Harmony Landing, Ky., 901
Harper & Brothers, 689
Harper's Ferry, Va. (W. Va.), 578
Harriman, Edwin: from, 24-25; to, 33
Harris, Carey A., 180-81
Harris, Iverson L.: to, 880-81
Harris, J.C., 815-16
Harrisburg, Pa.: 1839 Whig National convention in, '92, 116-17; mentioned, 120, 138-39, 144, 148, 167, 172-74, 190, 192, 194-95, 251-53, 256, 288, 292, 306, 308, 340, 342, 345-46, 349, 353-55, 357-62, 364-68, 373, 377, 382, 384, 388, 410-11, 416, 438, 455, 462, 473, 588, 630, 633, 675, 710, 712, 722, 786, 827, 832, 865-66, 874-75, 879, 885, 890. *See also* Election, presidential, of 1840: nominating conventions
Harrison, Anna Symmes, 552
Harrison, Benjamin (brother), 450
Harrison, Benjamin (son), 424-25
Harrison, Henry, 517
Harrison, William Henry
— general: from, 342-43, 343, 374-75, 393-94, 410, 424, 438, 450-51, 452, 514; to, 515, 516-17; on Missouri Compromise and admission of Arkansas, 394; friends of support C., 61; political strength of in Pennsylvania, 91; feels awkward running against C., 343; 1828 vice presidential candidacy of, 343; asks favor of C., 343; asks C. about imported jackasses, 343; campaigns in Lexington in 1836, 221; biographers of, 375; military career of, 375, 399-400, 440; as minister to Colombia, 412; views of slavery and abolition, 393-94, 424, 477; on S.C. nullification, 393-94; on his 1840 campaign, 410, 424-25, 438 (*see also* Election, presidential, of 1840: W. H. Harrison candidacy, prospects, and role in); personal mail of, 410; asks C. for political advice, 389; land claims of in Kentucky, 450-51; barely carries home county, 450-51; death of son of, 424-25; meetings in Kentucky with C., 450-52, 454, 457-60, 462, 465-66, 468, 516-17, 875; C. on character and qualities of, 462, 468, 518; militia training, 423; health of, 424, 454, 458; death of (*see espec.*

Harrison, W.H. (continued): 518), 517, 519-20, 692; bill for relief of widow of, 552, 582
– administration: hopes for his administration, 374, 470; offers C. post of secretary of state, 454, 463; C. as power behind throne in, 367, 384, 456, 466, 471; C. credited for victory of, 456; C. plans legislative program of, 416, 453, 461, 492, 495-96, 514; party strength in Congress during, 416-17, 514; patronage appointments and practices of, 454-60, 462, 471, 474, 476-77, 481, 484-86, 494, 498, 500-501, 506, 509-10, 514, 518, 524, 595-96, 604; Cabinet of (*see espec.* 458-59), 460-63, 465, 468-70, 473-74, 480, 499-500, 505; C. detaches self from patronage decisions of, 495, 497-98, 505, 516-17; appointment of Edward Curtis as collector of Port of New York (*see espec.* 456), 463, 471, 474, 485-86, 495, 497-98, 514-17, 595-96; C. seeks patronage from, 461; C. relations with, 458, 499-500, 514-17; importance of Whig unity during, 470-71, 499-500, 503; Indian policy of, 500-501; mentioned, 62, 65, 69-71, 81, 106-7, 115, 120, 142, 156, 163, 167, 172-73, 192, 194-95, 204, 212, 216, 220, 222, 230, 232-33, 239, 247, 250-52, 255, 263-64, 269, 272-77, 287-88, 292, 298, 306, 308, 313, 320, 330, 341, 345-46, 348-51, 354-55, 357-58, 361-62, 364, 366, 368, 373, 383, 402-3, 407, 421-22, 426-28, 434, 436-37, 443-45, 447-49, 483, 488, 511, 523, 526, 529, 533, 588, 611, 619, 647, 667, 705, 710, 769, 773, 782, 787, 825, 831-32, 844, 858, 866-67, 872, 885
Harrison Almanac, 429-30
Harrison County, Va. (W. Va.), 494
Harrodsburg, Ky., 301, 351, 702
"Harry of the West" (Clay), 119, 308, 636, 879
Hart, Anna Marie Allee, 185
Hart, Eleanor Grosh (Mrs. Thomas Hart, Jr.), 185
Hart, Henry Clay: from, 82; to, 82; mentioned, 400
Hart, John S. (wife's nephew): C. anger with, 184-86; gives C. power of attorney, 202; hemp bale rope business of, 184-86, 204; lineage of, 184-85; death of, 184-85
Hart, Thomas, Jr., 185, 837
Hart, Thomas Pindell (wife's nephew): from, 202; C. criticism of, 184-85; gives C. power of attorney, 202; opens a business in Louisville, 202
Hartford Convention, 249
Harvard University, 901
Harvie, J.B., 299
Hatch, N.W.: from, 813; to, 813
Haughton, Richard: from, 156; newspaper of attacks C. (*see espec.* 229-30), 232-34, 237, 239-41, 245-48, 250-52, 260-61, 264, 269, 274-75; explains political position to C. (*see espec.* 251-52), 260-61, 264
Haverhill, Mass., 645
Havre, France, 20, 23, 45, 461
Hawaiian Islands, 829
Hawes, Albert G., 51
Hawes, Richard, Jr., 152, 179, 185, 251
Hayes, Samuel L., 495
Hayne, Robert Y.: as railroad president, 224; death of, 224; mentioned, 669, 711
Haynes, Daniel A. (not identified): to, 761
Haywood, William H., Jr., 39
Heard, J.W.: from, 826
Helm, John B., 301
Helmuth, Henry (not identified): to, 338
Healy, John P. (not identified), 313
Hemp: measurements, packaging, sale, cost of (*see espec.* 73), 470, 498, 706, 841; C. sales of to U.S. Navy, 577, 754; C. compares Kentucky variety with Russian, 841; prices of in Lexington, 42. *See also* Clay, Henry: farm, farmer, and home–"Ashland"
Henderson, James P., 414
Henderson, John: from, 498; mentioned, 364, 386, 417, 554, 762
Henderson, Julia, 417
Henderson, Louisa Fourniquit Post (Mrs. John), 417
Hendricks, William, 37
Henry, ——— (not identified), 745, 747
Henry (slave), 52
Henry, Anson G.: from, 760; to, 760
Henry, Gustavus A.: from, 454
Henry, John, 747
Henry, Louis D., 749
Henry, Patrick, 403
Henry Clay (vessel), 220, 700
The Henry Clay Almanac of 1844, 751-52
Henry County, Ky., 837
Henry County, Tenn.: to Committee of Whigs in, 234-36
Henson, Henry (not identified): to, 444-45
"The Hermitage," 49, 72, 99, 160
Herod, William, 785
Heron, ——— (not identified), 792-93
Hertford County, N.C., 323
Hessians, 136
Hewit, Anderson & Co., 793
Hewitt's Manufactory, 792
Heyl, Lewis (not identified): from, 777
H. Hays & Co.: from, 733; to, 733
Hicks, Beverley A.: from, 89-90, 150
Hiernecke, Samuel (not identified), 534
Higbee, Elias, 384
Higgins, Richard, Jr. (not identified), 633
Hildreth, Richard, 375
Hill, Isaac, 122
Hill, Mrs. S.A., 66, 185, 199
[H.B.] Hill & Company (not identified), 40, 303, 312
Hillis, David, 38
"Hills of Santee," 680
Hines, Richard: from, 681; to, 681
Hinton, J.J. (not identified): from, 343
Hise, Elijah, 334
Hitchcock, Mrs. ——— (not identified), 373, 439
Hitchcock, Ethan Allen, 544, 732
Hoboken, N.J., 190
Hodge, William L.: to, 843-44
Hoffman, David, 458
Hoffman, Josiah Ogden, 89, 216-17, 473
Hogan, John: to, 448
Holland. *See* The Netherlands
Holland Land Company, 145
Holley, George, 870
Holley, John Milton, 91, 474
Holmes, John: to, 309
Hone, Philip, 866
Hopkins, Arthur F.: from, 476-77
Hopkinson, Joseph, 82
Hopkinsville, Ky., 852
Hoppin, William W.: to, 151
Horace, 307

Horn, W.H. (not identified): from, 343
Howard, Benjamin C., 472
Howard, John H., 835
Howard, Tilghman A., 436
Howard County, Mo., 352
Howe, Appleton, 853
Hoxie, Joseph, 61
Hoy, John: from, 12; to, 12; mentioned, 11
Hoyt, Jesse, 653
Hubbard, Henry, 112-13, 129, 390, 472, 707
Hudson, Alonzo James Madison (not identified): to, 820
Hudson, Elizabeth Jennings (maternal grandmother), 395-96
Hudson, George (maternal grandfather), 395-96
Hudson, N.Y., 60
Hudson River Railroad Co., 250
Huey, Daniel: from, 45; to, 47-48
Hughes, Christopher: to, 49-50, 117, 622, 629; sense of humor of, 50; fears recall by Van Buren administration, 49; seeks promotion from Van Buren, 414; sends C. cask of wine, 50; love of wine, 622; claims role in French recognition of Texas independence, 414; private papers of, 414; daughter of shipwrecked, 499; death of wife of, 499; returns to the United States from Stockholm, 622; C. on diplomatic service promotions, 629
Hughes, George Augustus, 622
Hughes, Laura Sophia Smith (Mrs. Christopher), 499
Hughes, Margaret Smith: to, 499; mentioned, 629
Hume, Joseph, 525-26, 597
Humphreys, John B., 302, 796, 798, 800
Hunt, A.D. (not identified): from, 10
Hunt, Catherine Grosh, 185
Hunt, E.W., 790
Hunt, John Wesley, 184-87, 453
Hunt, Memucan, 227, 302-3, 312
Hunter, James, 812-13, 854
Hunter, Robert M.T., 330, 361, 368, 473, 521, 872
Huntington, Elisha M., 341, 455
Huntington, Jabez W., 502, 535, 593, 731
Huron County, Ohio, 640
Huston, William, 309
Hutchcraft, Mrs. James (not identified), 862

Ile Chapeau, 749
Ile Royal, 749
[Illeg.], Henry: from, 865
Illinois: C. land in (*see espec.* 432), 56, 524; 1838 state and U.S. House elections in (*see espec.* 216), 217, 220, 224-25, 228; 1839 state elections in, 307-8; proposed colony for freed slaves in, 45, 47; 1839 state Whig convention in, 308; 1840 state elections in, 444-45, 448; unnaturalized voters swing state to Van Buren in 1840, 444; 1840 Whig presidential political activity in, 448; boundary problem with Wisconsin Territory, 764-65; 1843 state and U.S. House elections in, 835, 848-49, 854; gerrymandering in, 849, 854; 1844 U.S. Senate election in, 813; Whig organization in for 1844 presidential election, 891; outcome of 1844 presidential election in, 813, 835; mentioned, 2, 28, 49, 153, 155, 167, 216, 226, 232, 263, 273, 322, 362, 369, 391, 400-402, 410, 425-26, 455, 489, 513, 526, 542, 760, 768
Imported mare, 168
India, 669, 706
Indiana: 1836 state legislative elections in, 50-51, 70, 72; 1837 elections in, 37-38, 50-51, 59, 70, 72, 98; acquisition of Miami Indian lands, 149-50; canal development in, 149-50, 828; support for C. in 1840 in, 127; 1838 state elections in, 220, 225; internal improvements as political issue in, 346, 348; Harrison popularity in, 349; 1839 state elections in, 307-8, 317, 341, 346, 348-49; 1840 state elections in, 436, 438, 444-45; Battle of Thames celebration in, 444; 1842 U.S. Senate election in, 789; 1843 U.S. Senate election in, 813; C. speech in Richmond, 737, 777-82; visit to and speech in Indianapolis, 737, 760-61, 763-64, 766, 773, 782-85; C. speech in Columbus, 785; 1843 state elections in, 827, 835, 837, 844, 847-48, 854; mentioned, 28-29, 115, 135, 153, 163, 167, 172-73, 214, 224, 226, 232, 263, 273, 322, 368-69, 391, 393, 400-402, 410, 425, 436, 438, 469-70, 481, 489, 513, 524, 526, 542, 609, 763, 849
Indianapolis, Ind.: speech in, 782-85; mentioned, 172, 444, 737, 760-61, 763-64, 766-68, 773, 778, 784, 854
Indians. *See* American Indians; various Indian tribes
Ingersoll, Charles: to, 82, 83, 84
Ingersoll, Joseph R.: to, 327-28
Iowa: Des Moines bridge in, 169; farming potential of, 200; mentioned, 280, 765
Ireland, 11, 276, 478, 689, 691, 783, 829, 845-46, 852, 859, 878, 883-84
Irvin, James, 727, 729
Irving, Washington, 689
Irwin, William W.: chargé to Denmark, 803-4
Isle of Wight County, Va., 582
Italy, 328

Jackson, Andrew
— general: European views of, 2: alleged speculation in public lands, 25; C. sees as warmonger, 146, 750; vulgarity of, 145-46; criticized for attack on Seminoles in Florida, 163; campaigns for Democrats in 1839 Tennessee state elections, 317; C.'s views of, 329, 441-43; reimbursed by Congress for fine paid in New Orleans, 681, 796-97
— administration: policy failures of, 41, 49, 99; deterioration of Congress during, 99, 329, 637; lawlessness and executive usurpation of, 99; recess appointments of, 99; foreign policy of, 306, 821-22; Kitchen Cabinet of, 489; threats of, against South Carolina, 750; mentioned, 3-5, 8, 12-13, 20-21, 31, 37, 39, 50-51, 58, 71, 76-77, 79, 91, 95, 100, 135, 137, 139, 147, 151, 156, 159-61, 183, 185, 222, 233, 236, 254, 268-69, 274, 289, 299, 302, 313-16, 331, 349, 357, 366, 370, 380, 382, 393-94, 401, 407, 413, 424-26, 428, 436-37, 440, 454, 456-57, 462, 473, 483, 491, 502, 505, 508, 528, 531, 537, 540, 551, 553, 560, 588, 590, 623, 640, 655, 659-60,

Jackson, Andrew (continued): 686, 710-11, 730, 737, 768, 774-75, 782-85, 803, 817, 847, 854, 858, 889, 892
Jackson, Daniel (not identified), 466-67
Jackson, Hamilton: from, 700; to, 702
Jackson, Mortimer M.: from, 457
Jackson, Miss., 794, 814
Jackson County, Mo., 834
Jackson County, Ohio, 604
Jacob Faithful (novel), 501
Jacocks, Jonathan: from, 203-4
Jamaica, N.Y., 195, 431, 449, 459, 463, 466-67, 471
James I (Great Britain), 39
James, C.H.: to, 431
James Blythe v. *Henry Clay*, 450
James City, Va., 342
James Henry & Co.: from, 325
James River Company, 419
Jam Jehan Nima, 86
Jane (slave), 52
Janissaries, 455
January, Andrew M.: from, 764; mentioned, 309, 763
January & Huston: from, 73, 185, 412; to, 185; mentioned, 168, 688
January, Thomas T.: to, 238
Jarnagin, Spencer, 514, 647
Jarvis, Edward, 189
Jaudon, Samuel: to, 576; mentioned, 227
Java, 525
Jefferson, Thomas: C. on democracy of, 338, 492; C. quotes on Bank of the United States, 557; mentioned, 200, 245, 403, 426, 440-42, 500, 533, 579-80, 639, 715, 769
Jefferson, N.Y., 335
Jefferson County, Ind., 763
Jefferson County, Ky., 435, 837
Jefferson County, Ohio, 399
Jenifer, Daniel, 372-73
Jennison, Silas H., 233
Jessamine County, Ky., 439, 850
Jesup, Thomas S., 122, 290
Jesus Christ, 297, 745, 754
Johnson, Cave: attacks Whigs, 832-33
Johnson, Chapman, 224, 806
Johnson, Francis, 303, 531-32
Johnson, Jeromus, 61, 64
Johnson, Henry, 111, 798
Johnson, Joel, 111
Johnson, Joseph, 494
Johnson, Madison C.: from, 12, 450; to, 233, 450; mentioned, 320, 789-90
Johnson, Reverdy: from, 644; role in Graves-Cilley duel, 661-65 (*see also* Duels and Dueling); mentioned, 645
Johnson, Richard Mentor: elected vice president, 68-69; C. supports loan application of to Biddle, 111; work as president of U.S. Senate, 509; C. son-in-law marries niece of, 808; seeks vice presidential nomination on 1844 Democratic ticket, 859 (*see also* Election, presidential, of 1844: nominating conventions); on U.S. occupation of Oregon, 828-29; mentioned, 19, 51, 97, 180-81, 494, 776, 848-49, 854, 863, 881
Johnson, William Cost, 178, 522
Johnson, William Ranson, 805-6
Johnston, Edward N., 652
Johnston, Josiah S., 32
Johnston, Thomas J. (not identified): to, 902
John W. Brown, Moses Groves, R.M. Roberts, and James Graham v. *Robert Slaughter*, 475
Jonas, Abraham: to, 768
Jonas, Benjamin F., 768
Jones, Charles L., 475
Jones, George W. (Tenn.), 658
Jones, George Wallace (Wisc.), 153, 658, 665
Jones, Hamilton C.: to, 412
Jones, J.: from, 43-44
Jones, James C., 515
Jones, John A. (not identified): from, 218
Jones, John Beauchamp: as editor of *The Madisonian* newspaper, 718-19; mentioned, 736
Jones, John C., 817, 819-20
Jones, John W., 330, 361, 522
Jones, Wharton, 858
Jones, William, Jr.: from, 98; to, 373
Journal of the American Silk Society and Rural Economist, 375, 884
Julius Clarke & Co., 309

"Kalorama," 627
Kamehameha III, 829
Kanawha, Va. (W. Va.), 362, 859
Kane, John K., 353
Kavanagh, Edward, 720, 727
Keats, John, 307
Keats, George: from, 307
Keeler, A.T. (not identified): to, 569
Keene, Richard R., 83, 373, 386
Keene v. *Brown*, 83-84, 373
Kelley, Alfred, 596
Kellog, Daniel, 873
Kelly, Alexander D., 625
Kelly & Conyngham, 624-25, 793, 799
Kemper, Reuben, 902
Kendall, Amos, 31, 243, 245, 322
Kennedy, John (not identified): to, 415
Kennedy, John Pendleton: from, 688; to, 306, 314-15, 688, 894; attacks Jackson and Van Buren, 306-7, 314-15; defends Jackson's economic foreign policy, 306; sends C. report of American Colonization Society, 894; writes "Defense of the Whigs" for 1844 campaign, 894; mentioned, 616
Kenney, John B. (not identified): to, 338
Kent, Daniel, 373
Kent, DeWitt, 373
Kent, Edward, 148, 233, 444, 720
Kent, James: to, 310; C. praises legal career of, 310
Kent, Joseph, 96, 101, 372-73
Kentucky: C. to general assembly of, 656; troops raised in for Mexican border duty, 21; hemp prices and production in, 24, 470, 706 (*see also* Clay, Henry: economic views and personal financial affairs; Clay, Henry: farm, farmer, and home–"Ashland"; Hemp); reaction of to distribution of surplus, 34-35; proliferation of banks in after Bank of the United States veto, 57, 76; impact of Specie Circular on, 4; C. on reasons to emigrate to, 38; slaves and slavery in, 200 (*see also* Clay, Henry: slaves and slavery; Slavery and Anti-Slavery); land costs in, 38; sells improvement bonds to United States, 180-81; agriculture, climate, diseases in, 38; impressions of, 41; public education in, 627; Historical Society of, 189, 307; railroad development in, 224, 226; production of salt in, 362; Bank of Kentucky defrauded, 372-73, 449-50; need for agricultural college in, 387; ladies' academies and seminaries

in, 368; attempt to recover value of arms given U.S. during War of 1812, 398, 431; loan sought for, 445-46, 449-50; C. on possible tax sources for, 446; controversy with Trust Co., 462; depth of economic depression in, 705-6; inconvenience of handling bonds of, 622-23; seeks share of land sales proceeds, 719-20; manipulation of state bonds in, 830; reaction to tariff on hemp bagging in, 706; home manufactures in, 733, 862-63; C. migration to and acceptance in, 693-94; mentioned, 1, 8, 11, 17-18, 25, 32, 40, 49, 53, 57, 73, 76, 88, 103, 111-12, 121, 133, 140, 160, 165, 174, 195, 207-8, 218, 231-34, 241-42, 249, 259, 263, 285, 309-10, 313, 319-20, 337-38, 340, 359, 361, 385, 402, 404, 425, 433, 436, 439-40, 442-43, 451-52, 456, 461, 467, 477-78, 489, 498, 501, 508, 510, 512, 522, 531, 567, 577-78, 591, 612, 628, 632, 658, 663, 680, 698, 707, 709, 716, 745, 752, 754, 759, 761, 763-64, 766, 768, 777-78, 783-84, 794, 797, 799-800, 805-7, 818, 822, 830-31, 833, 838, 846, 859, 891-92, 903

– politics: C. reelected to U.S. Senate, 7, 14, 20, 27, 29, 33, 38; disputed U.S. House election in, 14 (*see also* 8:638-39); 1837 U.S. House elections in (*see espec.* 50-51), 58-59, 68-72, 98; presidential election of 1832 in, 299; Whig presidential preference in (*see espec.* 119-20, 130), 127, 132, 135, 141-42, 150, 152; Fayette County general assembly election in, 193, 250-51; 1838 U.S. House and state legislative elections in, 152, 216-17, 219-20, 224-26; proposed convention in to discuss emancipation, 244-45, 281; 1839 U.S. House and state legislative elections in (*see espec.* 299), 307-8, 315, 333-34; 1839 Whig state convention in, 301-2, 326-27; 1840 gubernatorial elections in, 301, 329-30, 351, 435; 1840 state legislative elections in, 435, 438, 444-45; legislature of opposes Calhoun public land plan, 399; legislature of wants fugitive slaves returned from Ohio, 272-73; support for new Bank of the United States in state legislature of, 453, 484; comparison of 1840 and 1844 presidential vote in, 844, 855-58; 1840 presidential election in, 434, 447; legislature of supports C. on bank and public land issues, 484-85; 1841 U.S. House elections in, 446, 521, 524; opposition in to repudiation of state debts, 640; C. on political character of Kentuckians, 484-85; opposition in to federal bankruptcy legislation, 628, 633-34, 636, 642; C. campaign speech in Maysville, 773; 1842 state legislative elections in, 848-50; 1843 state legislative and U.S. House elections in (*see espec.* 837), 836, 844, 847-50, 854-55, 857-58; poor Whig organization in, 848, 854; defeat of Wickliffe for U.S. House and "Wickliffe defections," 848-50, 854; 1844 state legislative elections in, 851; 1843 Whig state convention in, 851, 858; disinterest in Texas annexation in, 896

Kentucky, General Assembly of: to, 7; mentioned, 14
Kentucky Historical Society, 189, 307
Kentucky State Agricultural Society, 387
Kentucky and Virginia Resolutions, 249, 393, 440, 716
Kentucky River, 858
Kerr, John Leeds: to, 188
Ketchum, Hiram, 60-61, 572, 861
Key, Francis Scott: role in Graves-Cilley duel, 663; mentioned, 362, 644
Key West, 565
Kimball, Joseph Horace, 199-200
Kimberly, Dennis, 196
King, Charles: from, 644; doublecrosses C. in 1840 campaign, 237; attacks C.'s anti-abolition speech, 288; role in Graves-Cilley duel, 643-45, 648, 662-65 (*see also* Duels and Dueling); mentioned, 463, 573, 661, 867
King, Henry, 25
King, James G.: from, 622-23; mentioned, 866
King, John A., 362, 866
King, John P., 78, 80, 177-78
King, Joseph L., 443
King, Leicester, 744, 872
King, Rufus, 61
King, Samuel W., 445, 714, 716, 723
King, Thomas B., 564
King, William R.: C. personal confrontation with in Senate, 512, 649; mentioned, 396, 516, 535, 547, 567-68, 575, 578, 600, 648, 674, 719, 900
Kinkead, William B., 251
Kinsey, Charles: from, 118-19; mentioned, 123
Klinefelter's Syndrome, 362
Knight, Franklin (not identified), 169
Knight of Malta (jackass), 622
Knox, Henry, 421
Knox County, Tenn., 443
Knoxville, Tenn., 222, 443, 819, 873
Knoxville *Register*, 860
Kremer, George, 160
K.S. & Co. (not identified), 623, 792, 815
K. Smith & Co., 815-16

LaBranch, Alcee, 39
Lacock, Abner, 163
Lafayette, Marquis de: family gives C. copy of memoirs of, 215; mentioned, 136
Lafayette, George W.: from, 215
Lafayette, Ind., 828
LaFayette Seminary, 89-90
LaGrange, Ky., 901
LaGrange (Ga.) *Herald*, 850
LaGrange (Ga.) *News*, 850
Lake Champlain, 331, 335
Lake Erie, 320, 434
Lake George, 331
Lake Huron, 402
Lake Michigan, 645, 765
Lake of the Woods, 829
Lake Ontario, 414
Lake Superior, 402, 748-49
Lambdin & Bennett: from, 73, 102, 330; mentioned, 411, 413
Lambert, David: to, 382-83, 518
Lanarkshire, England, 687
Lancaster, Ky., 66
Lanckart, Mentelle & Co., 413
Lane, Henry S., 609
Langhorne, John D., 748-49
Langtree, S.D., 86
Lardner, A.: from, 9
Latham, Francis S.: from, 8, 95-96
Latham, W.H. (not identified): from, 73
Latimer, George, 831-32
Latter Day Saints, 384, 881, 890-91

Laurel Hill, Pa., 507
Law, James O., 873
Lawler, Joab, 185
Lawrence, Abbot, 207, 213, 233, 404, 629, 720, 725, 734
Lawrence, Abraham R.: from, 455-56
Lawrence, John L.: from, 196; to, 518-19, 865-66; mentioned, 455-56, 463, 573, 870
Lawrence, John W., 573
Lawrence, Joseph, 703
Lawrence, William A. (not identified): from, 68; to, 66-68
Lazell, John A. (not identified): from, 777
Leath, J.T.: to, 647
Leavenworth, Elias W.: to, 249-50, 362
Lebanon, Ohio, 767
Lebanon, Tenn., 317
Lecompte, Joseph, 837
Ledyard, Lara Erwin (Mrs. William J.), 801
Ledyard, William J., 800
Lee, George (not identified), 815-16
Lee, Gideon, 242-43, 594
Lee, R.H. (not identified), 104
Lee, Richard Henry: from, 347; to, 308, 325
Lee County, Iowa, 860
Leeds, England, 597
Lee's Sulphur Springs, Va., 337
Legare, Hugh S., 506, 614, 729
Leigh, Benjamin W.: to, 346, 805-6, 826-27; rumored death of, 101; C. discusses presidential politics with, 346, 805-6; role in Whig nominating convention in Staunton, Va., 351; inquires about H.A. Wise's hatred of C., 826; mentioned, 27, 246, 276
Leigh, Julia Wickam (Mrs. Benjamin W.), 806
Leigh, William (not identified), 362
Letcher, Robert P.: to, 14, 48, 66, 445-46, 449-50, 451, 452-53, 462, 484, 543-44, 628, 719, 720, 767, 830, 844-45; U.S. House bill for relief of, 14-15; knowledge of background of 1833 Compromise Tariff, 329; C. opinion of, 329; elected governor of Kentucky, 301, 329, 351, 435; C. advice to, 445-46, 449-51; first message as governor, 446; C. social relations with, 329; C. warns of special session of Congress, 484; Adams compliments, 891; mentioned, 623, 627, 716, 731, 812
Letcher, Samuel M.: from, 51
Letcher mare, 169
Levis, Hosea J., 373
Lewis (not identified), 798
Lewis, Joseph J., 901
Lewis, W. (not identified), 536
Lewis, William D.: from, 555-56
Lewisburg, Va. (W. Va.), 27, 533
Lexington, Ky.: schools in, 314, 353, 457; law school in, 901; lunatic asylum in, 453; livestock fair in, 53; price and value of land in, 38, 41-42, 301; hemp prices in, 42; value and extent of C. property in, 238; C. sells city lot in, 301-2, 312; county court day in, 303; newspaper in, 309, 754; public lectures in, 859; price of slaves in, 52; railroad investment and promotion sentiment in, 224-27; state legislative elections in (*see* Fayette County, Ky.); 1843 U.S. House elections in, 826; attempt to remove postmaster of, 529, 531; C. assists townspeople of, 478; C. declines public dinner in, 610; welcomes C. home in May 1842, 702; C. 1842 "Barbecue" speech in (*see espec.* 708-16), 724, 731, 752, 754, 764, 770; Harrison visits, 222; Van Buren visits, 680, 704; Webster visits, 40, 46-47; C. 1843 campaign speech in, 808-11; mentioned, 8, 10-11, 59, 65, 71, 90, 96, 187, 193, 196, 218-19, 231, 234, 254, 263, 299, 308, 313, 315, 320, 328, 330, 343, 364, 368, 372, 387, 398, 412, 435, 442, 447, 458, 498, 530, 534, 576, 608, 613, 616, 673, 678, 688, 696, 700, 706, 708-9, 737-38, 741, 744, 747, 749-50, 783, 790, 799, 804-5, 807, 812, 816, 827, 833, 836, 844, 850, 852, 858, 874, 891, 893, 895, 902
Lexington Cemetery, 696
Lexington Female Academy, 314
Lexington Fire, Life and Marine Insurance Co., 9-11
Lexington (Ky.) *Intelligencer*, 98, 309, 481, 754, 758
Lexington *Observer & Kentucky Reporter*, 251, 827, 831, 836
Lexington (Va.) *Gazette*, 223
L'Hommedieu, Richard, 407
L'Hommedieu, Steven S.: from, 407-8
The Liberator, 353
Liberia, 240, 453, 527, 868
Liberty party: origin in New York, 357; in Massachusetts, 871, 896; C. on selfish leadership of, 896; coalition with Democrats predicted, 896; history of, 896-97; prospects in 1844 election, 878-79; in New York politics, 858; mentioned, 452, 744, 759, 807, 813, 821-22, 827, 835, 853, 872-73
Lieber, Francis: to, 74-75, 108, 142-43, 319-20, 327, 369; sends C. manuscript on "Political Ethics," 74-75, 327; C. lauds books by, 108, 142-43, 327; C. recommends Kentucky education experts to, 319-20; C. explains copyright problems to, 327, 369; writes on penal reform, 369
Lilly (cow), 213
Lincoln, Abraham: from, 760; to, 760; connection with C., 760; supports C. in 1844 elections, 760; mentioned, 49, 399
Lincoln, Levi, 386, 462
Lincoln County, Mo., 88, 450, 520, 612
Linen, George, 371, 804
Linn, Lewis F.: urges settlements in Oregon, 493; mentioned, 141, 268, 289, 538, 563, 577-78, 600, 635, 642, 649, 659, 662, 665-66
Littel, John S.: from, 757; to, 756-57, 789, 890
Little Rock, Ark., 27
Livell, Morgan (not identified), 680
Liverpool (vessel), 313
Liverpool, England, 11, 499, 557, 667
Livingston, Edward: C. attacks as defaulter, 440-42, 447-48; responsibility for 1803 defalcation in New York City, 443
Livingston, Peter R.: speaker at 1839 Whig National convention, 882; mentioned, 883
Livingston County, N.Y., 879
Lizzy (Watson slave), 53, 506
Lloyd, Henry T. (not identified): to, 851
"L.M.C." (pseud.), 751-52

Lockport, N.Y., 255, 320, 330, 332
Logan, Stephen T.: to, 48-49
Logan, Ohio, 829
Logan County, Ohio, 368, 495
Logansport (Ind.) *Canal Telegraph*, 214
The Log Cabin, 371
Log-Cabin Anecdotes, 429-30
London, England, 45, 227, 309, 313, 327, 453, 605
Long Island, N.Y., 382, 470-71, 523
Lorain County, Ohio, 641
Lord Nelson (vessel), 414
Louis XIII (France), 13
Louis XIV (France), 455
Louisiana: Harrison and Webster political weakness in, 65; C. support for president in, 65, 300; ethnic tensions in, 387; 1838 state elections in, 225-26; Whig state legislators endorse C. for president, 300, 307; 1840 state elections in, 435, 444; 1842 state elections in, 734, 740, 749; C. Club of Rapides Parish, 740-41; 1843 U.S. Senate election in, 796-97; 1843 state and U.S. House elections in, 835-37, 844; outcome of 1844 election in, 740; state's land claim bill in U.S. Senate, 650; C. protects 1824 sugar duty for, 844; C. visits Baton Rouge, 796, 798; C. argues case before state supreme court of, 796-97, 800; mentioned, 22, 70, 83, 94, 153, 164, 227, 260, 263, 299, 318, 347, 369, 377, 397, 402-4, 421, 425, 476, 489, 501, 542, 641, 647, 752, 763, 768, 787, 789, 803-7, 843, 849, 896, 898
Louisiana Purchase: treaty, 226; mentioned, 128, 324
Louis-Philippe, 2
Louisville, Ky.: smallpox epidemic in, 88; home of C.'s nephew in, 202; planned lecture series in, 307; canal tolls issue in, 385; origins of university of, 386-87; mentioned, 40, 46, 53, 71, 90, 150, 189, 231, 236, 303, 312, 325, 334, 354, 377, 392, 413, 424-25, 450-52, 461, 507, 526, 529, 531-32, 576, 627, 659, 663, 678, 700, 702, 733, 748, 791-93, 798, 841, 851-52, 858
Louisville Bank of Kentucky, 59
Louisville College, 387
Louisville, Cincinnati & Charleston Railroad, 224, 227, 285
Louisville *Daily Journal*, 456, 659-60, 827-28, 831, 851
The Louisville Manufacturing Company, 791-92
Louisville and Portland Canal, 385
Love, James: from, 481
Low, ——— (not identified), 519
Lowell, Mass., 888-89, 894
The Lowell Offering, 888-89
Lowndes, William, 164
Lowrie, Walter, 672
Lumpkin, Wilson, 390, 431
Lunatic Asylum of Kentucky: to, 453
Lynchburg, Va., 749
Lyman, Samuel P.: to, 93
Lyon, Lucius, 19, 136, 206
Lyons, James, 424-25
Lyons, N.Y., 425-26

McAfee, Robert, 375
McArthur, Duncan, 375
McCarty, Jonathan, 51
McCarty, William M., 409
McClellan, George, 753-54
McCombs, ——— (not identified), 880
McDonald, Charles J., 612
McDowell, James, 822
McDuffie, George: C. opinion of, 329; on background of 1833 compromise tariff, 329; mentioned, 65, 330
McGuire, D.J., 341
McIntire, Rufus, 291
McKean, Samuel: to, 305-6; mentioned, 138-39
McKennan, Thomas M.T.: to, 703
McKenzie, William Lyon, 105-6
McKinney, Frances: from, 301
McKinney, James G.: from, 301
McLain, William, 506-7
McLane, John (not identified), 2
McLane, Louis: distrust of Van Buren, 70-71; mentioned, 12, 14
McLean, John: mentioned for 1844 Whig presidential or vice presidential nomination, 827, 830, 847, 854; opinion in *Jones* v. *Van Zandt* offends abolitionists, 857-58; supports C. in 1844 election, 830, 854, 857; mentioned, 183, 733, 821-22, 836, 861, 865, 869
McLeod, Alexander, 120, 471, 474, 508, 523, 529, 547, 617, 619, 864, 875
McMahon, Edward: from, 52
McNab, Allan, 126
McNair, John (not identified), 84
McNairy, Boyd: from, 343; to, 343, 432; mentioned, 439
McNutt, Alexander, 148, 300, 716
McRoberts, Samuel, 543, 551, 813
Macalester, Charles, 314
Macalester, Mr. and Mrs. E., 314
Macedonian (vessel), 311
Machiavelli, 302
Mackinac, Mich., 510
Macomb, Alexander, 290, 552
Macon, Ga., 833
Macready, William Charles, 850
Madeira wine, 231, 487
Madison, Dolley (Mrs. James), 29, 86-87, 110
Madison, James: supported American Colonization Society, 18, 47-48; relief bill for widow of, 86-87; widow publishes papers of, 110; supports national bank, 520, 825; offers C. posts as secretary of war and as U.S. Minister to Russia, 710; C. lauds report of, interpreting constitution, 709; mentioned, 29, 160, 200, 245, 403, 428, 436, 555, 557, 587-88
Madison, Ind., 763
The Madisonian, 44, 89, 246-47, 662, 665, 718-19, 879
Madison *Wisconsin Enquirer*, 383
Madrid, Spain, 95
Magnum Bonum (jackass), 46
Mahan, John B., 242-43, 245, 248
Maher, James, 539
Maid of Baltimore (cow), 174
Maine: failure of 1838 Whig legislative caucus to nominate C. for president, 154, 204-5; impact of Graves-Cilley duel in, 157 (*see also* Duels and Dueling); 1837 state elections in, 98, 100, 147; 1838 state elections in, 232, 252; invades British territory, 295; 1840 state elections in, 444, 447-48; 1842 Whig state convention in, 722; mentioned, 13-14, 148, 229, 233-34, 252, 255, 257, 263, 291-94, 329, 334, 377, 384, 404-5, 445, 507, 539, 720, 727, 821
Major (slave), 383, 388
Majorca, 53
Mallory, Daniel: writes and

Mallory, Daniel (continued): edits C. 1844 campaign materials, 536, 723-24, 738, 757-58, 765-66, 804-5, 841; conflict with Swain on C. campaign biography, 804-5; completes biography of C., 841
Malta, 53, 94
Malthus, Thomas, 687
Mangum, Willie P.: from, 166-67, 688, 717-18, 724-28; to, 92, 194, 688, 707-8, 731-32; on Whig prospects in North Carolina in 1840, 166-67; on North Carolina participation in 1839 Whig National convention, 166, 194; runs for North Carolina legislature, 166; C. discusses his own candidacy with, 194; moves to dismiss Blair and Rives as Senate printers, 510-11; elected president pro tem of the Senate, 707-8, 717-18; on Tyler administration failures, 717-18, 725-27; on Whig cause in 1842-44, 718, 726-27; votes against 1842 tariff, 762; mentioned, 27, 502, 509, 606, 616, 641, 648, 719
Manila hemp, 24
"Mansfield," 24, 52, 72
"Maplewood," 396, 678
March & Benson (not identified): from, 231
Marcy, William L., 151, 249
Marechal, Wenzell Philipp de, 330
Marengo County, Ala., 521
Marion, Ohio, 54
Marion County, Ohio, 54
Marryat, Frederick: to, 232; mentioned, 501
Marseilles, France, 500
Marshall, John, 163, 245, 588
Marshall, Thomas F.: from, 247; mentioned, 648, 665
Marshall College, 820
Marshall family, 848, 854
Marshfield, Mass., 415
Martin, Alexander, 612
Martineau, Harriet: from, 44, 850; thanks C. for copyright legislation support, 44; on problems with literary pirates, 44; on British domestic politics, 44; antislavery views of, 44; asks social favor of C., 850; on anti-theater bias in the United States, 850; on cultural backwardness of the United States, 850
Maryland: legislature of causes C. defeat in 1836, 25; 1837 state and U.S. House elections in, 59, 147-48; 1838 Whig caucus in general assembly of, 132, 135-36, 141-43; 1838 state elections in, 247-48; 1839 U.S. Senate election in, 275-76; 1839 U.S. House elections in, 346-47; attempt to subvert government of, 713, 716; 1842 state Whig convention in, 759; 1843 state and U.S. House elections in, 870, 873; mentioned, 18, 50, 60, 103, 113, 125, 127, 153, 188, 219, 263, 279, 297, 391, 426, 497, 591, 632, 744
Mason, Samson, 609
Mason, Stephen T., 148
Mason-Dixon line, 564
Masonic Order, 119, 893
Massachusetts: 1837 state elections in, 98-99; Whig caucus in legislature nominates Webster for president, 154, 157, 232-33, 252, 298; C. support in legislature of, 252; unpopularity of Harrison and Van Buren in, 232-33; abolitionist movement in, 112, 164, 261, 269, 888-89; temperance legislation in, 269, 275, 360; General Court of endorses Webster for 1840 presidential nomination, 264; legislature of elects Webster to U.S. Senate, 269, 274-75; 1839 state and U.S. House elections in, 352-53, 360-61, 387-88; 1840 state Whig convention in, 438, 443; 1840 U.S. House elections in, 454; anti-Tyler sentiment in, 732-33; pro-C. sentiment in, 734; 1842 Whig presidential nominating convention in, 732-33, 770-71; impact of 1842 reapportionment act in, 770; 1842 state and U.S. House elections in, 807, 811-12, 871, 876; Liberty party in, 852, 871, 896; 1843 state and U.S. House elections in, 835-37, 852-53, 874, 888-89, 895; 1844 state elections in, 871; C. on Lowell Cotton mills in, 888-89; C. wants to see Nantucket Island, 901; mentioned, 24, 27, 69, 100, 113, 130, 156, 160, 199, 213, 239-40, 253, 263, 283, 454, 478, 502, 632, 720, 725, 730, 762, 821, 831-32, 849, 857, 862, 867, 869, 876, 880
Massillon, Ohio, 216
Mathews, Cornelius: to, 630-31
Matteawan, N.Y., 330
Mattocks, John, 873
Maumee, Ohio, 115
Mauch Chunk (Jim Thorpe), Pa., 883
Maury, Ann: to, 557
Maury, James, 557
Maxcy, Virgil, 39
Maxwell (bull), 214
May, John F.: from, 1
May, William L.: from, 455; mentioned, 185
Mayer, Charles F.: to, 458
Maysville, Ky.: C. speech in, 773; mentioned, 72-73, 87, 168, 179, 185, 241, 262, 309, 330, 624, 688, 749, 763-64, 771, 836, 859, 891, 903
Maysville-Lexington Turnpike, 401
Maysville and Big Sandy Railroad, 836
Maysville Road, 100, 401
Mazureau, Adolphe: from, 795; to, 795
Meade, David, Sr., 88
Meade, Richard W., 17, 117-18, 131
Meade, William (not identified), 362
Meany, John, 529-30
Mecklenburg, N.C., 433, 670
Mecklenburg County, Va., 539
Medina County, Ohio, 640
Mediterranean Sea, 94, 241, 310-11, 538
Medoc (horse), 150, 318, 613
Melbourne, Lord (William Lamb), 44, 597
Memphis, Tenn.: C. to Whigs in, 803; C. campaign speech in, 801-3; C. sells bale rope in, 902; mentioned, 72, 564, 647, 845
Memphis (Tenn.) *Enquirer*, 8, 95-96
Menard County, Ill., 425
Menard, Pierre, 209, 274
Mendenhall, Hiram: from, 777; asks C. to free his slaves, 777; C. speech in response to, 737, 777-82
Mendenhall, J.R., 341
Menefee (or Menifee), Richard Hickman: resigns U.S. House seat to practice law in Lexington, 308, 315; mentioned, 185, 644, 657-58, 663
Mentelle, Augustus Waldemarde, 87
Mentelle, Charlotte, 87
Mentelle, Waldemar: sister marries T.H. Clay, 87; Clay and Mentelle hemp business, 412, 529; Mentelle kinships, 412-13; mentioned, 583, 790-91. *See also*

Clay, Thomas Hart
Mercer, Charles F.: role in Graves-Cilley duel, 662-63 (*see also* Duels and Dueling); mentioned, 409, 452-53, 506, 644
Mercer, Hugh L.: C. loathe to borrow money from, 801; mentioned, 796
Mercer, John Fenton, 506
Mercer County, Ky., 434
Mercer County, Pa., 399
Mercersburg, Pa., 820
Meredith, William A., 901
Meriwether, James A.: to, 863
Merrick, William D., 136, 178, 184, 275-76, 511
"Merry Oaks," 396
Metcalf, Chester G., 94-95
Metcalfe, Thomas: to, 357-58; mentioned, 301, 501, 731
Methodist Church, 195, 242-43, 245, 248, 257, 448, 867
Methodist Episcopal Church, 36, 678
Meunier, 2
Mexican War, 767
Mexico: 1837 threat of war with U.S., 33-34; U.S. claims issue with, 86, 104, 171, 286, 658-59, 684; proposed arbitration of U.S.-Mexican tension, 180; 1839 U.S. arbitration convention with, 286; U.S. recognition of Texas independence, 33-36, 897-900; "Pastry War" with France, 210-11, 229, 265; C. on U.S. purchase of California, 383; attacks on U.S. citizens by, 658-59; Alexander imprisonment issue, 716-17; annexation of Texas and probable U.S.-Mexican War (*see espec.* 124), 110, 135; mentioned, 20-21, 146, 228, 522
Mexico City, 34
Miami Indians, 135, 149-50
Michigan: 1837 presidential electoral vote of challenged, 19; 1839 state and U.S. House elections in, 147; surveyor general's office in, 205; aliens permitted to vote in, 713; mentioned, 148, 153, 230-31, 369, 374, 391, 402, 405, 408, 410, 413, 489, 510, 513, 526, 542, 713, 765
Milledgeville, Ga., 719, 833, 835, 881
Miller, Alexander: to, 402
Miller, Andrew, 353
Miller, George W., 853
Miller, John, 784-85
Milligan, John J., 416
Mills, John, 720
"Millwood," 481
Milton (slave), 52
Miner, John L., 157
Miners and Manufacturers Bank, 443
Minnesota, 132, 765
Minorca, 53
Mississippi: Harrison and Webster political weakness in, 65; C. support for president in, 65; 1837 state and U.S. House elections in, 147, 174; 1838 U.S. Senate election in, 123; 1838 special U.S. House election in, 174; 1838 state elections in, 174, 232; slave emancipation in, 240; 1839 cotton crop in, 236; 1839 state and U.S. House elections in, 299; Agricultural Bank of Natchez problems, 396, 631; 1842 C. visit to Natchez, Vicksburg, and Jackson, 790-91, 794, 814; political corruption in, 813-14; repudiation of state bonded debt by, 714, 813-14; proposed Whig political strategy in, 813-14; 1843 state and U.S. House elections in, 813-14; Democratic nominating conventions in, 814-15; outcome of 1844 presidential election in, 811-12; mentioned, 8, 18, 21, 45, 52, 73, 148, 153, 183, 196, 223, 237, 263, 265, 300, 302-3, 307, 369, 383, 391, 402-4, 410, 425, 450, 457, 475-76, 484, 489, 492, 500, 513, 526, 542, 564, 590-91, 716, 743, 797, 804-5, 807, 849
Mississippi Colonization Society, 240
Mississippi River, 2, 108, 169, 238, 253, 402, 564, 629, 700, 792, 802, 806
Mississippi Union Bank, 237
Mississippi Valley, 829
Missouri: military bounty lands in, 453; C. lands in (*see espec.* 238, 352, 450, 520), 88, 108, 121-22, 171-72, 453, 611-12, 661, 748, 806, 818, 826 (*see also* Clay, James Brown); 1838 state elections in, 216-17, 220, 224-26; 1840 state elections in, 444-45; hemp product prices in, 470; expulsion of Mormons from, 881; outcome of 1844 presidential election in, 835; mentioned, 40, 45, 87-88, 103, 119, 121, 125, 128, 132, 153, 230, 232, 263, 323-24, 329, 334, 339, 369, 383-84, 386, 394, 402-4, 410, 426, 456, 489, 500, 513, 526, 542, 565, 577, 731, 743, 750, 798, 828, 849
Missouri Compromise: C. role in Second, 128, 750; John Randolph role in Second, 128-29; C. opposition to 36°30′ slavery restriction in First, 323-24; effect of on slavery issue, 125; mentioned, 30, 32, 102, 279-80
Missouri River, 108, 171-72, 806
Mitchell, Charles F., 361, 519
Mittag, Thomas E.: to, 840; mentioned, 841
Mobile, Ala., 25, 231, 521, 529, 793, 798, 800, 833-34, 853, 857-58
Mobile (Ala.) *Mercantile Advertiser*, 24-25, 33
Monarch (horse), 480-81, 522, 584-85, 592
Monk, Maria, 24
Monroe, James: offers C. posts as secretary of war and as U.S. Minister to Great Britain, 709-10; mentioned, 128, 245, 367, 375, 769
Monroe, La., 803
Monroe County, Va. (W. Va.), 494
Montcalm, Marquis de (Louis Joseph), 343
Montgomery, Isaac: from, 469
Montgomery, John C., 353
Montgomery, Richard, 342-43
Montgomery, Ala., 833
Montgomery County, Ohio, 120, 154, 164
Montgomery family, 470
Montreal, Canada, 330-31, 334
Moore, B.F. (not identified): from, 833; to, 833
Moore, Morton & Co.: from, 56; mentioned, 432
Moore, Samuel: to, 414; mentioned, 499
Moore, Thomas P., 14-15
Morea, 525
Morehead, James T.: C. presents credentials of as U.S. Senator, 510; favors repeal of 1841 Bankruptcy Act, 634; supports C. for president in 1844, 634; briefs C. on events in Congress, 722-23; mentioned, 60, 273, 435, 593, 706, 724, 736, 791, 797
Morehead, John M., 445, 749
Morgan, Christopher: to, 544
Morgan, S.D. (not identified): to, 434-35
Morgan, Thomas J., 148
Morgan County, Ill., 318
Mormons. *See* Latter Day Saints

Morpeth, Lord (George Howard): from, 700
Morris, Buckner S.: to, 759
Morris, Calvary, 465, 727, 729
Morris, Robert, 486
Morris, Robert H., 519, 811
Morris, Thomas (N.Y.), 486
Morris, Thomas (Ohio), 16-17, 192, 206, 245, 858
Morris Canal Bank, 59
Morrison, Esther Montgomery (Mrs. James): changes will, 383-84; death of, 785; provisions of will of, 785, 901; will probated, 785; mentioned, 352, 478
Morrison, James: land of in Missouri, 450; C. loan from, 238, 799; debts owed to, 703; slaves of sue for freedom, 901; mentioned, 179, 352, 384, 453, 785
Morrison, Richard, 799
Morrison College of Transylvania University, 233
Morton, George W.: from, 84; to, 301
Morton, Marcus, 100, 353, 807, 835, 867
Morton, Samuel C.: to, 701
Moses Groves and James Graham v. *Robert Slaughter*, 475
Mt. Sterling, Ky., 308
Mouton, Alexander, 27, 640-41, 735
Mudd, J.H. Clay: to, 860
Mudge, Richard, 418, 474
Muhlenberg, Henry A., 236
Muhlenberg County, Ky., 354
Muir, D. Austin: from, 729
Munroe, Isaac, 723-24
Murray, John L., 333-34
Muskogee, Okla., 544

Nancy (cow), 318
Nansemond County, Va., 318-19
Nantucket Island, 901
Naples: spoliation claims treaty with, 15; mentioned, 622, 668
Nashville, Tenn., 42, 213, 235, 317, 343-46, 351, 412, 432, 434, 439-43, 445, 763, 808, 819, 843, 856, 858
Nashville *Republican Banner*, 345, 833, 843
Nashville *Union*, 436, 441
Nassau, 541, 630-31
Natchez, Miss.: hemp prices in, 73, 90 (*see also* Hemp); yellow fever in, 73, 90; C. financial dealings in, 698; economic depression in, 790-92; mentioned, 168, 179, 184-85, 237, 392, 401, 411-13, 504, 631
Natchez Protection Insurance Co., 791
National Agricultural Society, 613-14
National Republican party, 509, 879
National Whig Review, 371
Native American party, 96-97, 855-56, 893
Nautilus Insurance Co., 315
Nazareth Academy, 368
Nazareth Literary and Benevolent Institution, 368
Neagle, John: to, 822-23; mentioned, 789, 804, 880
Ned (slave), 52
Nelson, John R. (not identified): from, 873; to, 873
Nelson, Wolfred, 255-56
Neptune (bull), 174
The Netherlands: recognizes independence of Texas, 407; mentioned, 27-28, 309, 629
Nevins Townsend & Co., 815-16
New Albany (steamboat), 312
Newark, N.J., 640, 733
Newark, Ohio, 744
Newberryport, Mass., 787
Newbold, T.R.: from, 186
New Brunswick, Canada, 119, 291, 293, 295, 507
Newburgh, N.Y., 330
New Castle, Dela., 184, 416, 506
New England: abolitionism in, 56; C. reputation in during 1st ["Extra"] Session, 27th Cong., 604. *See also* Election of 1840: campaign and related political activity in specific states and sections; Election of 1844: campaign and related political activity in specific states and sections
New England Offering, 889
New Hampshire: 1837 state Whig convention in, 122; abolition movement in, 112; 1838 state elections in, 122, 232; C. declines invitation to visit Concord, 421; 1842 state elections in, 707; on U.S. compensation for militia of, stationed on Canadian border, 472; mentioned, 163, 230, 255, 263, 329, 410, 445, 743, 821
New Haven, Conn., 204, 423
New Haven Hibernian Society, 689
New Haven (Conn.) *Palladium*, 424
New Jersey: presidential sentiment for C. in, 119, 132, 204; legislature of considers nomination of C., 119, 132, 153, 204; 1838 Whig state convention in, 119; abortive Hoboken barbecue for C. and Whigs, 190, 192; legislature of instructs U.S. senators on Sub-Treasury issue, 149; 1837 state elections in, 98; 1838 state elections in, 247-48; 1840 state elections in, 449; 1841 state elections in, 713, 871; 1843 state elections in, 871; C. will not campaign in, 837; mentioned, 135, 183, 263, 361, 632, 872
New Lancaster, Ohio, 744
New Madrid, Mo., 196, 520
New Mexico, 836
New Orleans (vessel), 2
New Orleans, La.: soaring currency exchange rates in, 54; bank failures in, 40-41; economic depression in, 790-91, 793, 795-96, 902; C. investments in, 42, 372, 395, 791, 799; C. importation of European wine and livestock through, 231, 236; hemp product prices in market of, 470, 791, 793, 799, 815-16, 892, 902; C. visits on business, 773, 790-91, 815-16, 892; C. declines public invitations in, 795; rumored assassination attempt on C. in, 796; Whig political prospects in, 807; fine levied by on General Jackson, 681, 797; C. remittances from, 815; mentioned, 5, 18, 20, 23, 30, 53, 83, 94, 222, 241, 286, 303, 312, 317, 354, 383, 385, 390-92, 396-98, 400, 407, 412, 440, 452, 477, 481, 521, 529, 623, 625, 630, 669, 673, 707, 734-35, 773, 789, 792, 794, 798, 800-801, 803-4, 833-34, 857-58, 874, 885-86, 896, 900-901
New Orleans *Commercial Bulletin*, 844
New Orleans *Commercial Intelligencer*, 892
New Orleans *Merchants' Transcript*, 892
New Orleans *Price Current*, 892
New Orleans *True American*, 501
Newspapers: supporting C., 24-25; C. on Washington papers, 206. *See also* Election of 1840: newspapers, journals, biographies, pamphlets involved in campaign; Election of 1844:

newspapers, journals, biographies, pamphlets involved in campaign
Newton, A.O.: from, 9
Newton, John T., 399
The New World, A Weekly Journal of Popular Literature, 765
New York: split in regency ranks in, 60-61; key to Whig hopes in 1840, 88, 91, 105, 207; Whig support for C. in, 61, 92, 105, 114, 118-19, 127, 175, 189, 204, 286-87, 292, 307, 312, 320; Whig political organization in, 93-94; Democratic political organization in, 93; anti-Clay sentiment in, 355; 1837 state elections in, 43, 88-89, 91-94, 96, 98-101, 106, 117; impact of 1837 assembly elections on 1840 presidential election in, 94; role of New York Whig central committee on presidential nominating process, 116-17, 320; Webster presidential prospects in, 94, 118-19; 1837 Albany city election results, 43; Anti-Masonic strength in, 106-7, 287; 1838 and 1839 Whig state legislators' caucus (*see espec*. 92, 115-16), 119-20, 142, 154, 156-57, 173, 175, 258, 262, 276, 286-87, 292-93, 320; New York Whigs support a national convention, 92, 173; 1838 state banking act, 304; banks in resume specie payments, 175; influence of banks in, 117; temperance movement in, 218; abolitionist movement in, 173, 356; salt production and business in, 331, 362; economic depression in, 356; Whigs in urge C. campaign visit, 189-90, 192, 195-98, 201-2; state assembly of on Sub-Treasury issue, 142; Niagara Falls canal proposal, 151; political role of Conservative Democrats in, 91-92, 127, 239; 1838 and 1839 Conservative Democratic conventions in, 242-43, 351; 1838 state Whig convention in, 151, 234, 237-38, 242; state assembly on C. presidential nomination, 273; 1838 state assembly elections in, 151, 174, 207, 216-17, 225, 228, 232, 238-43, 245-50, 256-57, 272, 355; 1838 U.S. House elections in, 216-17; 1839 U.S. Senate elections in, 256, 273, 288; 1839 Whig nominating conventions in congressional districts of, 116, 320; 1839 state and U.S. House elections in, 151, 173-74, 346, 348, 351-55; legal test of removal of Seneca Indians from, 415; 1840 state and U.S. House elections in, 356-57, 455; role of Thurlow Weed in 1840 presidential election in, 287, 320; outcome of 1840 presidential election in, 451-52; 1841 state elections in, 616-18, 620; 1841 Whig state convention in Syracuse, 616-18; Whig rally in Buffalo protesting Tyler bank veto, 592; 1842 Whig state nominating convention in Syracuse, 631, 773; 1842 Whig young men's nominating convention at Auburn, 631; 1842 state elections in, 760, 763-64, 773, 786-88; 1843 state elections in, 837, 855-56, 869-70, 881-82, 885-86, 890, 894; Liberty party activities in, 858; C.'s ignorance of politics of, 897; movement in for Clay-Webster ticket in 1844, 861; mentioned, 27, 39, 54, 56, 58, 62-64, 66, 68-69, 82, 98-100, 111, 141, 145, 147-48, 150, 168, 176, 181-82, 193-94, 203, 205, 215-17, 220, 222, 225, 228, 232, 234, 236-37, 240-41, 245-50, 253, 255-58, 263, 265, 271-73, 278, 283, 288, 293, 298, 302, 305, 308, 326, 334-35, 337, 340, 347, 359, 361, 368, 374, 384, 391, 416, 442-43, 445, 447, 449, 451-52, 455-56, 471, 473-74, 485, 494, 503, 509, 519, 527, 532, 547, 550, 552, 562, 573, 627, 629, 632, 634, 636, 641, 645, 650, 680-81, 690, 723, 752-53, 756, 761, 766, 827-28, 830, 857, 862, 864, 867-68, 872, 880-83. *See also* New York City.
New York Agricultural Society, 764
New York *American*, 286, 288
New York Anti-Slavery Society, 755
New York City: C. support and organization among Whigs in, 60-62, 66-69, 91-92, 118-19, 189-90, 192, 196-98, 200, 202, 301, 333; support for Webster among Whigs in, 54-55, 60; nomination of Webster in, 62, 66, 69; Webster's Niblo Saloon speech in, 48; Clay vs. Webster Whig factions in, 54-55, 67-68, 189-90, 207, 212-13, 216-17, 225-26, 237; 1837 bank convention in on resumption of specie payments by New York banks, 102; 1837 Whig jubilee in, 106, 118-19; political impact of Swartwout scandal in, 255; voter registration reform in, 308; immigrant voting power in, 355; reaction to C. antiabolitionist speech in, 286; 1839 Whig convention in, 320; 1837 state elections in, 88-89; 1838 state elections in, 150, 207, 213, 216-17, 225; 1838 U.S. House elections in, 216-17; 1837 city charter elections in, 43; 1838 city charter elections in, 173-74; 1839 city charter elections in, 301, 304, 306-7, 312, 354-55; C. speech in, 336-37; outcome of 1840 presidential election in, 447; appointment of collector of customs in, 455-56; corruption in customhouse in, 595-96; postmasters and politics in, 596; 1841 customs receipt at, 561; pronational bank sentiment in, 553; as money center of the United States, 380; 1841 city charter elections in, 519, 521, 524; Democratic-Whigs in nominate C. for president, 729; "intrigue" in to deprive C. of 1844 nomination, 827, 830; antagonism of Van Buren and Calhoun Democratic factions in, 855, 869-70; 1843 New York County Whig nominating convention in, 882, 885; quarreling Whig newspapers in, 861, 885, 890; movement in to nominate Webster for vice president, 861, 885 (*see also* Webster, Daniel); Native American party in, 855-56; 1843 state elections in, 855-56, 885; 1843 city charter elections in, 811-12; mentioned, 5-6, 11, 15, 28, 39, 56, 63, 84-85, 88-89, 105, 107, 111, 115, 130, 133, 141, 145, 151, 154, 157, 179-80, 182-83, 231, 241, 247, 250, 254, 260, 285, 287, 291-92, 302, 308, 310-11, 313, 320-21,

New York City (continued): 330, 334, 338, 347, 353, 357, 359-60, 362, 366, 371-72, 383-94, 397-99, 418, 421, 424, 431, 442-44, 449, 457, 459, 463, 466-67, 471, 473, 477-78, 485-87, 495, 509, 514-18, 529, 544, 552-53, 555, 559, 562, 568, 572, 583-84, 597, 599, 630-33, 636, 641, 643, 647, 650, 652-53, 663, 673, 675, 678, 689, 714, 717, 724, 738, 758, 765, 792, 797, 799, 807, 815-16, 832, 844, 846, 858-59, 866-68, 880, 890, 899. *See also* New York
New York City Democratic Whig Association, 274, 284
New York City Young Men's Whig Committee: from, 333; to, 333; mentioned, 315
New York *Commercial Advertiser*, 572
New York *Express*, 722, 879, 882, 890
New York *Herald*, 342-43, 538, 662, 665, 718
New York Institution for the Blind, 260
New York *Journal of Commerce*, 382
New York Life Insurance Co., 315
New York *Morning Courier and Enquirer* (also New York *Weekly Courier and Enquirer*), 55, 69, 107, 234, 271, 449, 645, 648, 661, 665, 676, 754-55, 866, 868, 871, 874, 879, 882
New York Peace Society, 180, 265, 463
New York State Temperance Society, 218
New York State Whig Central Committee, 321
New York *Tribune*, 832, 880, 890
New York University, 897
Niagara County, N.Y., 91, 308, 509
Niagara Falls, 151, 241, 320, 326-28, 330, 581, 634, 760-61, 864, 890
Niagara River, 119
Niblo's Saloon (N.Y.C.), 48
Nicholas, George, 461
Nicholas, Matilda Prather, 461
Nicholas, Robert C., 22
Nicholas, Samuel Smith, 461
Nicholson, Alfred O.P., 502, 514-15, 569-70, 572
Nicholson, Samuel, 815-16
Niles, Hezekiah, 75, 517
Niles, John M.: C. confrontation with in Senate, 195-96, 204; mentioned, 23, 131, 207-8, 210
Niles, William Ogden: to, 75, 81, 517; takes over *Niles' Register*, 75; C. resists patronage appeal from, 517; death of father Hezekiah, 517; mentioned, 375
Niles' Register, 71, 75, 150, 164, 271, 373, 415, 501, 732, 738, 741, 823
Noah, Mordecai M., 61, 157
Noble, Noah: to, 37, 50-51, 737; mentioned, 59
Norfolk, Va., 18, 20, 141, 186, 310-11, 391, 406, 498, 832-33, 901
North America (vessel), 40
North American Review, 478
North American Trust and Banking Company, 241
Northampton, Mass., 179, 895
North Bend, Ind., 450
North Carolina: 1838 state elections in, 166-67, 225; participation of in Whig national nominating convention, 166-67; Whig caucus in legislature of endorses C., 272; 1839 U.S. House elections in, 322-24; on instructions of U.S. senators, 270-71; complains of shortage of specie small change, 276; stances on distribution of public lands proceeds, expunging resolution, Sub-Treasury issue, and Van Buren patronage policy, 269-71; 1840 state elections in, 444, 447; 1840 Whig state convention in, 447; 1840 presidential election in, 167; 1842 Whig nominating convention in nominates C., 636, 647, 670, 681, 833; 1842 Democratic presidential nominating convention in, 718-19; Calhoun nomination effort in, 718-19; 1842 state elections in, 749, 844; "Mecklenburg Declaration" of, 833 (*see also* 8:774-75); 1843 state elections in, 836-37, 844, 847-48, 854, 870, 873; C. campaigns for president in, 833-34; outcome of 1844 presidential election in, 836; C. writes to North Carolina convention, 447; mentioned, 18, 194-95, 204, 232, 263, 273, 276, 302, 324, 425, 434, 445, 499, 505, 584-85, 594, 622, 705, 726, 728, 737, 763, 849, 855, 857-58, 874, 885-86, 894, 902
Northern Bank of Kentucky, 12, 59, 388, 393, 395-96, 613, 651, 816
Northeastern boundary, 14, 119, 206-7, 211, 278, 291-95, 303-7, 404-5, 418, 430, 455, 474, 507-8, 529, 684, 697, 720, 748, 782
Northern Liberties (Phila.): Henry Clay club of, 750; mentioned, 102, 253
North Star (steamboat), 73
Norvell, C.C. (not identified): from, 343
Norvell, John, 19, 172, 400
Norwich (Conn.) *News*, 656
Norwich (Conn.) *Republican*, 655
Nott, Eliphalet, 181
Nourse, Charles: to, 688
Nullifiers and nullification, 249, 393, 440, 484, 508, 660, 713, 769. *See also* States' Rights party
Nuttal, Elijah F., 334
Nye, Arius: to, 618

Oakley, Robert S. (not identified): from, 633; to, 823-24
Oates, Thomas, 354
Oates, William, 354
O'Connell, Daniel, 884
Ogden, David B.: reports probable Webster withdrawal from 1840 presidential campaign, 123; appointed New York City delegate to 1839 Whig national convention, 292; leans to Harrison as Whig candidate in 1840, 292; mentioned, 96, 105, 287, 320
Ogden, James: from, 597-98
Ogden, Thomas L., 145
Ogle & Watson, 478
Ohio: C.'s land in, 115, 368-69; 1837 state elections in, 88-89, 98, 108; advocation in of a Whig national nominating convention (*see espec.* 119-20, 156-57), 70, 132, 154, 192, 194, 203, 247, 275; opposition to Sub-Treasury bill in, 115, 177; support for C.'s land bill in, 115; C. turns down public dinner in, 47; slavery politics in, 240-42, 245, 247-48; Mahan fugitive slave case in, 242, 245; pro-Whig sentiment in Western Reserve of, 154, 164; support for C. in, 115, 127, 154, 164, 621; 1838 state elections in, 239-42, 245, 247, 250, 252, 262; support for Harrison in, 115, 120, 163-64, 275, 424-25; 1839 state elections in, 317, 346; 1840 state

elections in, 436, 438, 447, 449; 1840 presidential vote in Hamilton County, 450-51; 1841 state elections in, 618, 620-21; 1842 dissolution of legislature of, 757; 1842 C. campaign speech in Dayton, 761, 764, 766-70, 773-77; U.S. House reapportionment in, 743, 757; 1842 state elections in (*see espec.* 743-44, 872), 760, 763-64, 874; 1842 Whig conventions in, 742-44; Hamilton County Whigs nominate C. for president, 767-68; German and Irish vote in, 878; abolitionism in, 242, 245, 450-51, 872-73; Liberty party in, 872; 1843 state and U.S. House elections in, 872-73, 876, 888; mentioned, 17, 28, 45, 71, 103, 105, 147-48, 153, 167, 170, 172, 195, 199, 226, 236-37, 243, 249, 257, 263, 272-73, 309, 324-25, 330, 342, 358, 361, 373, 375, 389, 393-94, 399, 401-2, 406, 410, 417, 435, 454, 468, 489-90, 494, 526, 542, 607, 641, 645, 650, 727, 729, 733, 745, 762, 785, 813, 827, 829-30, 836, 849, 858-59, 861, 867, 879, 887, 891
Ohio Canal, 238, 241, 309
Ohio River, 17, 72, 216, 253, 362, 400-401, 629, 678, 791, 858-59, 901
Oldham County, Ky., 837
"Oliver Oldschool" (pseud.), 751-52
Olympian Springs, Ky., 758
Oneal, Charles: from, 54
Oneida, N.Y., 475
Oneida Indians, 145
Onondaga County, N.Y., 249-50, 763, 771
Onondaga Indians, 145
Ontario, Canada, 336
Ontario County, N.Y., 879
Orange County, N.C., 166
Ordinance of 1787, 765
Oregon: U.S. settlements in, 493; C. opposes U.S. occupation of, 828-29; mentioned, 141, 372, 601, 745
Orleans County, N.Y., 679
Orozimbo (bull): progeny of, 801 (*see also* 8:804); death of, 125; mentioned, 174
Orphan Boy (horse), 90
Orphan's Court of Washington County, District of Columbia, 506-7
O'Sullivan, John L., 86
Oswego, N.Y., 330-33, 335
Otis, Harrison Gray: from, 229-30, 260-61, 269, 465; to, 208-9, 212-13, 225-26, 232-33, 247-48, 251-52, 264, 274-75, 290, 298, 360, 368, 467-68; C. differences with, 248; sends C. Boston *Atlas* article, 229-30 (*see also* Boston *Atlas*); role in Hartford Convention, 249; stance on S.C. nullification, 249; definition of Whig party and C. role in it, 465
Otis, John, 720
Ottawa Indians, 510
Ouachita Parish, La., 803
Owen, Thomas, 793
Owen County, Ky., 850
Owensboro, Ky., 787
Owings, Thomas D., 375
Owsley, William, 851-52
Oxford, Pa., 763
Oxford Township, Pa. (Northern Liberties), 750
Pacific Fur Company, 510
Pacific Ocean, 133, 310, 493, 828-29
Palmerston, Lord Henry John Temple, 294, 453
"Pamona," 881
Paoli, Pa., 206
Papinau, Louis Joseph, 255-56, 284
Paris, France, 45, 226, 414, 518, 900
Paris, Ky., 413
Paris (Ky.) *Western Citizen*, 145
Park, Samuel, 722
Parker, Amasa J., 178
Parks, Gorham, 148
Parker, Richard E., 299
"Pastry War," 211
Patrick, Thomas C.: from, 524; to, 432
Patterson, R.S.: to, 431
Paul, Dunbar (not identified), 506
Paulding, James K.: from, 310-11, 311; to, 310, 311; assists naval career of C. grandson, 310-11; accompanies Van Buren on visit to Lexington, 681, 702, 704; mentioned, 706, 708
Paulet, Lord George, 829
Paull, George, 375
Payne, Buckner H.: from, 94
Payne, J.W.: business dealings with C. in New Orleans in hemp, 892
Payne, John Howard: to, 26, 86
Payne, Harrison & Co.: from, 892; mentioned, 792-93, 796-97, 799, 816
Pea Patch Island, 213
Pearl River, 814
Pearson, William H. (not identified): to, 645
Peck, Everard, 262-63, 274
Peel, Sir Robert, 597, 685, 882
Pendleton, John S., 411-12
Pendleton, Nathanael G., 239-40, 450-51
Pennington, William, Jr., 153, 248, 449
Pennsylvania: importance of to 1840 Harrison candidacy, 91; Anti-Masonic strength in, 94, 106, 283, 874, 892-93; role of Anti-Masons in presidential politics, 94, 305-6, 327-28; 1837 state elections in, 98-99, 147-48; emancipation of slaves in, 295; legislature of instructs U.S. senators on Sub-Treasury bill, 138-39, 142, 144, 148-49; 1838 state elections in, 150-51, 173-74, 217, 232, 239-40, 242, 252-53; "Buckshot War" in, 252-53; urban vs. rural political virtue in, 314-15; 1839 Whig convention to choose presidential electors, 305-6, 327-28, 349-50; rump Anti-Masonic/Harrison nominating convention, 305-6; 1839 state elections in, 317, 352-53; Schuylkill Bank fraud against Bank of Kentucky, 372-73; 1841 suspension of specie payments by banks in, 498; 1840 state elections in, 449; 1842 Whig (Scott) state nominating convention in, 721-22, 751-52; 1842 Anti-Masonic nominating convention in, 752; Anti-Masonic/Whig alliance in, 873; 1844 Whig presidential campaign organization in, 853; 1843 state elections in, 836, 853, 858, 873, 883; outcome of 1844 presidential election in, 752, 837; mentioned, 13, 45, 142, 163, 167-68, 177, 194-95, 235-36, 244, 247, 258, 263, 267, 273, 329, 358, 361, 368, 374, 389, 391, 397, 399, 409, 427, 437, 446, 499, 565, 583, 631-32, 641, 660, 673, 679, 689, 711, 729, 824, 831-32, 835, 867, 901. *See also* Philadelphia, Pa.
Pennsylvania College, 532
The Penny Magazine, 884
Penrose, Charles B.: from, 631; to, 631; mentioned, 306
Pensacola, Fla., 565
Percy, Dr. ——— (not identified), 816
Perfect (horse), 168
Perkins, Sampson, 835

Perkins, Thomas H.: to, 240-41; mentioned, 233
Perrin, ——— (not identified), 395
Perrin, Henry, 396
Perrin, Samuel, 396
Perry, A.F. (not identified): from, 777
Perry, J., 341
Perth Amboy, N.J., 220
Peter (Morrison slave), 901
Peters, Richard, Jr.: to, 41, 895
Petersburg, Va., 1, 434, 771, 806, 833
Petigru, James L., 62
Pettigrew, Ebenezer: to, 610, 621-22, 704-5; mentioned, 584-85
Pettrich, Frederick August Ferdinand, 196-97
Peyton, Balie, 624-25, 650, 652, 706
Peyton, Bernard, 514
Peyton, Charles L.: to, 533
Phelps, Jefferson, 69
Philadelphia, Pa.: Whig support for C. for president in, 106-7; C. political organization in, 186; 1839 city and county elections in, 352-53; Tyler removes customs official in, 704; reception for Whig congressmen in, 766; 1842 Whig rally nominates C. for president, 766; mentioned, 9, 11, 15, 31, 33, 36, 82-83, 130, 134, 141, 144, 172, 184-85, 202, 207, 222, 227, 235-36, 242-43, 252-53, 255, 259, 261-62, 275, 283, 285, 313-14, 328, 330, 338, 359, 372, 383-84, 407, 409, 446, 453, 468, 475, 478, 481, 500, 528, 530, 576-77, 583, 627, 633-34, 669, 673, 689, 698, 701, 706, 724, 737-38, 751, 757, 767, 775, 787, 815-16, 822, 832, 844, 853, 856, 901-2. *See also* Pennsylvania
Philadelphia County, Pa., 352-53, 766
Philadelphia Democratic Whig Young Men's General Committee, 338
Philadelphia *Inquirer*, 827, 830
Philadelphia *National Gazette*, 449
Philadelphia *North American*: C. to editor of, 623-24; mentioned, 186
Philadelphia *United States Gazette*, 290
Philips, Stephen C. (not identified), 213
Phillips, H.G. (not identified): to, 761
Phillips, Jonathan, 283, 315
Phoenix, J. Phillips, 519
Phoenix Hotel, 234
Phrenology: analysis of Calhoun and Grundy, 163
Pickett, J. (not identified), 816
Pierce, Franklin, 472, 650, 653
Pierce, Levi (not identified): from, 795; to, 795
Piercy and Reed, 44
Pike County, Ohio, 604
Pike County, Mo., 453
Pindell, Richard: from, 192-93; to, 185, 352; mentioned, 155, 238, 453, 520, 816
"Pine Grove," 301
Pitts, E.P. (not identified): to, 901
Pittsburgh, Pa., 24, 71, 157, 163, 167, 173, 216, 446, 596, 640, 680, 760, 773, 877, 894
Plains of Abraham, 342-43
Plattsburg, Mo., 456
Pleasants, John H., 652
Plymouth, Mass., 876
Poindexter, George, 595-96, 650-51, 653
Poinsett, Joel R.: from, 398; to, 180-81, 398; plan to reorganize U.S. militia, 421, 423, 427; mentioned, 31, 39, 62, 278, 289-90, 422
Poland and Poles, 845-46
Poland (vessel), 499
Polk, James K.: to, 818-19; attacks C.'s "Corrupt Bargain," 818-19; 1843 gubernatorial candidacy of, 819; mentioned, 39, 316-17, 514-15, 740, 752, 759, 765, 804, 807, 813, 817, 820-22, 829, 833, 835-36, 844, 854, 858, 879, 883, 901
Pope, Alexander, 91
Pope, John: national bank proposal of, 614; mentioned, 27, 51, 285
Pope, LeRoy (not identified), 802
Pope, Martha Fontaine, 91
Pope, Patrick H., 334
Pope, Penelope, 91
Pope & Wilkins (not identified), 816
Port Hamilton, Bermuda, 406
Porter, Alexander: wins U.S. Senate election, 796-97; mentioned, 27, 723, 791-92, 794, 815, 902
Porter, Augustus, 474, 574, 629-30
Porter, David R., 151, 397
Porter, James Madison, 729
Porter, Jane Howell, 474
Porter, Peter B.: from, 91, 91-92, 104-5, 115-17, 123, 131, 145, 156-57, 175, 176, 189-90, 195, 238-39, 273-74, 286-88, 320, 334, 365-67, 384, 455, 462-63, 466-67, 471, 485, 485-86, 502-3, 565-66, 572, 573, 592, 633-34, 659-60, 861, 864-65, 869-70, 870, 881-82; to, 94, 96, 113-14, 119-20, 127, 132, 135-36, 141-42, 153-54, 163-64, 173-74, 191-92, 197-98, 202-3, 217-18, 227-28, 241, 262-63, 276-77, 291-92, 312-13, 324-25, 332-33, 347-48, 360-61, 451-52, 458-59, 473-74, 497-98, 522-23, 553, 569, 570-71, 581, 616-17, 631-32, 636, 647-48, 760-61, 773, 857-58, 884-85, 890; service on Northeast boundary commission, 455; on Whig victory in 1837 New York state elections, 91; C. resumes correspondence with, 105, 857; speculates on 1840 Whig presidential candidates, 91; recommends Whig strategy for selecting 1840 presidential candidate, 91-92, 105, 115-17, 119-20, 123, 127, 131, 156-57, 286-88, 882-83; opposes Whig national nominating convention, 131; works for C. nomination in 1840, 91, 123, 366; on why C. was not nominated for president at Harrisburg convention, 365-67; visits C. at "Ashland," 217-19, 227, 238; C. sends bluegrass seed, 241; sends C. pigs, 238, 241; youngest son of attends Such School, 467, 523; favors to C.'s grandsons, 471; nephew (Peter B. Porter, Jr.) in New York state assembly, 91, 474; seeks patronage job for nephew (William A. Bird), 503; on C. anti-abolition speech, 286; recommends patronage appointments to Harrison and C., 485-86, 503-4; reports a conversation with Weed to C., 485-86, 502-3; outlines new national bank plan, 503; sees new fame for C. on bank issue, 503; recommends voluntary branching section in first Whig bank bill, 565-66, 571; on Tyler's veto of first bank bill, 592; C. discusses 1844 presidential politics with, 857-58; on Webster as 1844 vice presidential candidate, 861, 869, 882; health of, 881, 885, 890; mentioned,

69, 203, 242, 630, 865
Porter, Peter B., Jr., 91, 474, 485, 503, 760
Port Gibson, Miss., 310, 413
Portland, Me., 707
Portsmouth, Me., 722
Portsmouth, Ohio, 309
Portsmouth, Va., 833
Portugal, 487, 700, 783
Post Boy (horse), 673
Potomac (vessel), 141
Potomac River, 164, 233, 329, 487
Poughkeepsie, N.Y., 60, 330-31
Poughkeepsie *Eagle*, 832
Powell, Caroline Bayard (Mrs. Henry B.), 417
Powell, Cuthbert, 409
Prather, Catharine, 392, 395
Prather, Matilda Fontaine (Mrs. Thomas), 90, 392
Prather, Thomas, 90
Prather, William: from, 461; mentioned, 90-91, 392
Preble, William Pitt, 720, 727
Preble County, Ohio, 240
Prenter, James: from, 8, 9, 10
Prentice, George D.: to, 69-71; mentioned, 758, 841
Prentiss, Jane, 815
Prentiss, Mary Williams (Mrs. Sergeant S.), 794, 815
Prentiss, Sergeant S.: to, 794, 813-14; mentioned, 148, 174, 302, 792
Presbyterian Church: Board of Foreign Missions of, 263; mentioned, 81, 306
Preston, Isaac T.: from, 795; to, 795; mentioned, 83
Preston, William C.: from, 688, 720; to, 688, 889-90; admires C., 62; supports annexation of Texas, 124, 135-36; mentioned for secretary of the navy in Harrison Cabinet, 466, 499; on bank bill, 565-66, 570, 573; supports Whig positions on bank, tariff, and distribution, 522; C. discusses 1844 presidential campaign with, 889-90; C. hopes to visit home of, 889; attributes to C. the quotation: "I had rather be right than be president," 283; mentioned, 22, 28, 80, 109, 131, 161, 181, 278, 322-23, 329, 393, 422, 431, 486, 556, 572, 607, 609, 645-47, 718, 722, 820
Preston, Mrs. William C., 889
Preston v. *Humphreys*, 796, 800-801, 803
Price, D.L. (not identified): from, 812
Priam (horse), 481
Price, William: from, 759; to, 759-60
Price, William M., 254-55
Prieur, David, 226
Prince Georges County, Md., 404
Princeton, N.J., 196
Princeton University, 73, 133, 186-87, 196, 901
"Proclamation to the People of South Carolina," 341-42, 394
Proffit, George H., 609
Prud'homme, J.F.F., 804
Prussia, King of, 286
The Public: C. to, 441-42
"A Publisher" (pseud.): from, 118
Pueblo, Mexico (N. Mex.), 716
Pulaski, Count Casimir, 136
Pulaski, Tenn., 322

Quakers. *See* Society of Friends
Quebec, Canada, 236, 330-32, 342-43
Quincy, Josiah: to, 467

Rahway, N.J., 673, 676
Raleigh, N.C., 447, 585, 636, 670, 681, 833, 889, 896
Raleigh *Register and North Carolina Gazette*, 273
Randall, Josiah: from, 82, 83; to, 283; mentioned, 328, 853
Randolph, John: role in debate on second Missouri Compromise, 128-29; will of challenged by N.B. Tucker, 361-62, 367; insanity of, 361-62; mentioned, 165, 568
Rankin, Jane (not identified), 901
Rantoul, Robert, 454
Rapides Parish, La.: from Clay Club of, 741; to Clay Club of, 740-41
Rariden, James, 51
Raritan (frigate), 134, 141
Rayner, Kenneth: to, 322-23; mentioned, 324
Reading, Ohio, 45
Red Cow, 72
Redd, Thomas S., 529, 531
Reed, John, 876
Reeder, Benjamin: from, 494
Reese, John James, 532
Reeves, O.T. (not identified), 38
Register of Debates, 86, 341, 511
Reid, Margaret Ross, 240
Reid, Robert R., 290
Reigart, Emanuel C.: from, 893; to, 892-93
Reily, Ellen, 688
Reily, James, 688
Reinscke, Ernest W. (not identified): to, 820
Rensselaer, N.Y., 357
Repplier, C.A. (not identified): to, 338
Reynolds, James C., 417
Reynolds, Jeremiah N.: seeks patronage appointment, 486; C. warned of treachery of, 675-76
Reynoldsburg, Ohio, 417
Rhode Island: 1837 state and U.S. House elections in, 59, 98, 147-48; Whig caucus in legislature nominates C., 143, 157; support of C. in 1832, 143; 1838 state elections in, 181-82; 1840 state elections in, 444; 1842 state elections in, 707, 716; Dorr Rebellion in, 714-15, 723, 731; mentioned, 124, 144, 151, 232, 263, 362-63, 688, 752, 780, 822
Rhodes, William, 152
Richard III (Great Britain), 234
Richards, John S.: to, 883
Richards, W.C. (not identified): from, 794; to, 794
Richardson, Joseph: from, 295-96
"Richland," 88, 108, 122, 133, 165
Richmond, Ind.: C. speech in, 777-82
Richmond, Va., 111, 145, 149, 222, 245-46, 258, 262-63, 267, 272, 275, 277, 296, 299, 386, 390-94, 514-15, 676, 714, 727, 806, 815, 848
Richmond County, Ga., 800
Richmond (Va.) *Enquirer*, 239, 393-94, 473, 752
Richmond Junto, 729
Richmond (Va.) *Penny Post*, 145
Richmond (Va.) *Whig*, 342, 436, 886-87
Richmond (Va.) *Yeoman*, 393-94
Ridenour, Jacob (not identified): from, 239-40
Ridgway, Joseph, Jr., 157
Rigdon, Sidney, 384
Riker, Richard, 174
Rio de Janeiro, 215
Ritchie, Thomas: attacks Harrison candidacy, 393-94; supports Van Buren, 729; newspaper of charges C. with abolitionist views, 886-87; mentioned, 110, 239, 473
Ritner, Joseph, 151, 174, 194
Rives, John C., 86, 454, 502, 510-13, 643
Rives, Landon Cabell, 393-94

Rives, William C.: to, 677; position on Specie Circular, 3, 5, 155-56; supports Walker public land bill, 21-22; proposes state-national dual currency banking scheme (*see espec.* 155-56), 2, 5, 78-80; opposes Sub-Treasury bill, 139; breaks with Van Buren administration, 263; deadlocked with Tyler in Senate election (*see* Virginia); C. opinion of, 261-62; 1839 address to the people of Virginia, 301; supports C. for president, 272; public dinner for, 403; supports Harrison in 1840 election, 393; on bill to reform handling customhouse receipts, 290-91; reelected to U.S. Senate, 473; introduces voluntary branching amendment to national bank bill (*see espec.* 554-55); 556-57, 566, 572, 590; attacks C. compromise bank branching amendment, 554-55, 566, 576; vote on Compromise Tariff of 1833, 677; support of Tyler administration, 689-90, 726; attacks C. distribution policy, 720; mentioned, 4, 20, 174, 198, 224, 239, 243, 247, 257-58, 296, 300, 326-27, 533, 591-92, 599, 602, 609, 618, 634, 687
R.J. Cunningham Co., 796
Roane, William H., 149
Roanoke River, 890
Robb and Hodge, 815-16
Roberts, Jonathan: from, 163; Tyler removes from Philadelphia collectorship, 704, 740, 775; mentioned, 751, 853
Roberts, S. (not identified), 815
Robertson, Duncan: from, 498
Robinson, Edward, 722
Robinson, Solon, 614
Robinson, Thomas, Jr., 416, 469
Robinson, William (not identified), 680
Robinson, William E.: to, 546, 883-84
Rochester, N.Y.: C. visits, 331-33; mentioned, 41, 320, 324, 330, 786, 864, 869-70, 880
Rock Island, Ill., 577
Rocky Mountains, 507, 564, 828-29
Rogers, Charles Fleming (not identified): to, 720
Rogers, Coleman, 165, 257
Rolph, John, 105-6
Roman, Andre B., 226, 377
Roman Catholic Church, 16, 24, 845, 878
Rome and Roman Empire, 205, 637, 694, 839
Root, Erastus, 753
Ron (slave), 52
Rose, W.B. (not identified), 309
Roselius, Christian: from, 795; to, 795
Ross, Isaac, 240
Ross County, Ohio, 47
Royal (horse), 168, 673
Royale (jackass), 46
Ruffin, James F. (not identified): from, 350
Ruggles, John, 22-23, 377, 405
Rumpff, Vincent, 830-31
Rush, Richard: from, 653-54; endorses C. in 1844 election, 654; on C. work for South American independence, 654
Rushville, N.Y., 444-45
Russ, John D.: from, 259-60
Russell, ——— (James B. Clay's overseer), 87
Russell, Jonathan, 758
Russell, Thomas A., 818
Russell, William H.: from, 661; to, 747-48, 818; mentioned, 612, 678, 826, 834
Russell, Mrs. William H., 818
Russellville, Ky., 611, 748
Russia: hemp from competes with U.S. variety, 23, 236; mentioned, 39, 361, 403-4, 414, 483, 710, 785, 830-31, 841-42, 887
Ruter, Martin: from, 29
Rutherfoord, John, 473

Sabine River, 33-34
Sackett, Granville A. ("Alfred"): from, 134
St. Augustine, Fla., 475
Saint Catherine's Female Seminary, 314, 368
St. Charles County, Mo., 520, 661, 826
St. John River, 720, 748-49
St. Joseph, Ind., 645
"St. Julien," 110, 172, 257, 409
St. Lawrence County, N.Y., 335
St. Lawrence River, 336
St. Louis, Mo., 45-46, 49, 88, 90, 108, 122, 133, 165, 172, 206, 303, 318, 324, 547, 748, 818
St. Louis County, Mo., 238, 450
St. Mary River, 749
St. Peter, Wisc., 132
St. Petersburg, Russia, 507
St. Peter's Roman Catholic Church, 52
St. Regis Indians, 145
Salem, Ky., 628
Salem, Mass., 771, 880
Salem Baptist Church, 826
Salem (Mass.) *Register*, 730
Salisbury, N.C., 412
Saltonstall, Anne: to, 417, 697; mentioned, 896
Saltonstall, Leverett: from, 729-30; to, 454, 708, 896; C. social connection with, 417; family of, 417; birthday present to C. from daughter of, 697; mentioned, 386
Saltonstall, Lucy, 417
Saltonstall, Mary Elizabeth Sanders (Mrs. Leverett), 417
Samuel, Edward M.: from, 171-72, 456
Sandusky, Ohio, 320, 324, 375
Sandwich Islands, 829
San Francisco, Calif., 481
Santa Anna, Antonio Lopez de: movements after surrender, 20; mentioned, 684, 716-17
Santa Fe, Mexico (N. Mex.), 659, 717
Santo Domingo, 611. *See also* Haiti
Saratoga (vessel), 231
Saratoga, N.Y., 127, 326, 330-31, 333-35, 337, 342, 497, 631
Saratoga Springs, N.Y., 239
Sargeant, John, 733
Sargent, Epes: to, 130, 736-37, 756-58, 758, 765, 787, 861-62, 880; writes C. 1844 campaign materials, 723-24, 736-37, 756-58, 765-66, 787; supplies biography of C. to Mallory, 765, 861; mentioned, 272, 534, 536
Sargent, John O.: to, 271, 534, 536, 604, 723-24, 841; contemplates doing collection of C. campaign speeches, 536, 723-24, 737-38; C. lauds profession of historian-author-editor, 841; mentioned, 234, 272
Sargent, Nathan: from, 750-51; to, 217, 352-53; 704, 748-49, 766, 853, 858; writes 1844 campaign biography of C., 751; C. advises on presidential campaign strategy in Pennsylvania, 853; advises C. on Whig prospects in Pennsylvania, 858; loses election for U.S. House, 858; mentioned, 515, 720, 752
Satterwhite, Thomas P.: from, 52; mentioned, 616-17

Saugrain, Anthony (not identified), 661
Sauk and Fox Indians, 131
Saunders, R.M., 445
Saunders and Otley, 44
Savannah, Ga., 813, 833, 835, 859, 889, 902
Sawyer, Samuel T., 322-23
Sayre, David A., 450
Sayres, Gilbert H.: to, 697
Schenck, Robert C. (not identified): from, 761; to, 761
Schermerhorn, Henry Van Rensselaer: from, 150-51
Schley, William, 62
Schouler, William: to, 888-89
Schuylkill Bank, 372-73, 462
Schuylkill Navigation Co., 500
Schuzenback, ——— (not identified), 178
Scioto River, 604
Scofield Cassion & Company: from, 509
Scotland, 39, 381, 498, 691, 783, 829
Scott, D.T., 439
Scott, Jefferson: from, 54
Scott, John: from, 703
Scott, Miss ——— (not identified), 439
Scott, Winfield: from, 277-78; role in U.S.-Canadian border crisis, 291-92; on his political prospects and availability, 277-78, 334; dislike of Jackson and Van Buren administrations, 277; will support C. for 1840 nomination, 334, 350; presidential candidacy of, 277, 360, 647, 726, 751-52 (*see also* Election, presidential, of 1840: Winfield Scott candidacy, prospects, and role in; Election, presidential, of 1844: Winfield Scott candidacy and role in); power of in New York state politics, 477; at 1839 Harrisburg nominating convention, 286-88, 675; vanity of, 721, 726; as possible 1844 Whig vice presidential candidate, 753, 759; mentioned, 122, 290, 335, 354-59, 361-62, 364, 367, 595, 676, 722, 733, 754, 821-22, 827, 866
Scott County, Ky., 767, 850
Seaton, Gales, 152, 165
Seaton, William W.: from, 177-78; to, 295, 332; mentioned, 81, 86, 139, 429, 502, 511, 604, 652, 672, 831, 879
Segar, Joseph, 652
Seibert, Samuel (not identified): to, 839-40
Selden, Dudley: from, 68, 196; to, 66-68; mentioned, 70-71, 291, 357, 363, 882
Select Class for Young Ladies, 314
Seltzer, S.Z. (not identified): from, 777
Seminole Indians, 146, 163, 289, 295, 440, 475
Seminole Wars: First, 122, 288; Second, 289-90, 295, 347, 397, 640, 666; C. blames Second on Jackson's militarism, 146; C. solution for ending Second, 168; Congressional debate on prosecution of First, 122; C. criticisms of U.S. involvement in, 288-89, 440, 666; Jackson's illegal raising of troops for Second, 640; economic wastefulness of, 683; U.S. use of bloodhounds in Second, 289, 397; rumored treaty with Seminoles to end conflict, 475
Semple, James, 813
Seneca Indians, 145, 415
Sergeant, John: mentioned for Cabinet post in Harrison administration, 466, 468-69, 474, 480, 831; as possible 1844 Whig vice presidential candidate, 752, 754, 759, 831, 864, 868; mentioned, 328, 612, 724, 832, 865, 879
Seven Years War, 289
Sevier, Ambrose H., 21, 420, 502, 544-45, 569, 600
Seward, William H.: from, 334; to, 347; elected governor of New York, 151, 173-74, 234; supports both Scott and C. for president in 1840, 335, 355; on a C. campaign swing through New York, 335; duplicity of at 1839 Harrisburg convention, 286-88, 455; rumored shift from governorship to U.S. Senate, 477; mentioned, 238, 243, 246, 249-50, 263, 278, 334, 348, 357, 485, 503, 519, 764, 827-28, 866
Sewell, Samuel, 807, 835, 871
Shakers, 793-94
Shannon, Wilson, 237, 436, 451, 744, 872
Shaw, M. (not identified): to, 436-37
Shaw, N. & H. (not identified): to, 741
Shee, Catherine Lawrence, 313
Shee, John, 313
Shelby, ——— (not identified), 372
Shelby, Anthony: from, 457
Shelby, Isaac, 354
Shelby, James, 302-3, 538
Shelby, Nancy, 457
Shelby, Susan, 457
Shelby, Thomas H.: from, 94-95
Shelby County, Ky., 150, 837
Shelbyville, Ky., 612
Shelton, W.H., 814
Shepherd, Henry, 174
Shepherd, James H., 40
Shepherd, Rezin D.: from, 1; livestock transactions with C., 1, 174; mentioned, 2, 40
Shepherdstown, Va. (W. Va.), 174
Shockley, Curtis H.: to, 756
Shreve, Thomas H.: from, 307
Shuford, Franklin B. (not identified): to, 820
Sibby (slave), 52
Sibley, George C.: from, 500-501
Sibley, Henry H. (not identified), 383
Sibley, Mark Hopkins, 151
Sidney (slave), 52
Silsbee, Nathaniel: to, 771, 806-7; C. tries to borrow money from, 806-7; mentioned, 213
Simmons, James Fowler: to, 687-88; introduces tariff bill in U.S. Senate, 725, 728, 742-43, 774; mentioned, 609, 731-32, 734, 749, 755
Simms, Edward: from, 472
Simms, R.E. (not identified), 472
Simpson, James: to, 845-46
Simrall, John W.G. (not identified): to, 763
Singleton, Richard, 702-3
Sioux Indians, 132
Sisters of Charity, 368
Slade, William, 394
Slaughter, Robert: from, 52, 475; mentioned, 476
Slavery and Anti-Slavery: C. transaction in slaves, 51-53 (*see also* Clay, Henry: slaves and slavery); incorporation of District of Columbia chapter of American Colonization Society, 18; support for colonization approach, 45, 47-48, 852; pro-colonization literature, 80-81; Texas annexation as slavery extension issue, 56; Clay-Tappan correspondence on (*see* Tappan, Lewis); C. on slaves as property, 281, 314; growth of abolitionist sentiment, 56; Quakers for abolition, 56, 278; British abolitionist activities in the United

Slavery (continued): States, 852; Negro resistance to colonization, 45; proposed ex-slave colony on northwest coast, 45, 47-48; C. takes Charles Dupuy to Washington as body servant, 386, 583-84; C. on suppressing African slave trade, 684; C. on slavery, abolition, and colonization (*see* Election, presidential, of 1844: issues, charges, and countercharges in campaign); Clay-Mendenhall confrontation, 777-81; slavery in America blamed on the British, 852; interstate slave trade in the United States, 300; constitutionality of, 852; "gag rule" in U.S. House, 641; C. on various perils of abolition, 852, 874; British liberation of American slaves, 541. *See also* Congress of the United States
Slidell, John, 797
Sloane, John: from, 454-55; to, 435, 614-15, 620-21, 785-86, 874
Smallpox epidemic, 88
Smedes, William C., 791-92
Smith, Mr. ——— (not identified), 439, 531-32
Smith, Mrs. ——— (not identified), 439
Smith, Augustine J., 495
Smith, Benjamin Bosworth: from, 627; C. criticism of, 312; as superintendent of public instruction in Kentucky, 627; declares himself a Clay man, 627; mentioned, 187
Smith, Charles, Jr. (not identified), 61, 64
Smith, Francis L.: to, 696
Smith, Francis O.J.: from, 539
Smith, Gerrit: from, 296-98; mentioned, 314, 357, 475
Smith, Gideon B.: to, 884
Smith, Harriet Staples Douglas, 187
Smith, John (N.Y.), 456
Smith, John (N.C.; not identified), 682
Smith, John P., 150
Smith, John Speed, 273
Smith, John T., 858
Smith, Joseph: from, 881; to, 890-91; asks C. his view on Mormon persecution, 881, 890-91; mentioned, 384
Smith, Kempton D., 816
Smith, Larkin B., 152, 193
Smith, Margaret Bayard: to, 196-97
Smith, Nannette Price (Mrs. Thomas), 532, 625, 795
Smith, Oliver H.: from, 348; to, 340-41, 350, 443-44, 730-31, 789; mentioned, 37, 598, 609, 813
Smith, Perry, 208, 512
Smith, Persifor F., 347
Smith, Peter S.: from, 475
Smith, Robert, 357, 811
Smith, Robert N.: from, 150
Smith, Samuel, 49-50
Smith, Sol, 25
Smith, Thomas, 24, 88, 303, 312, 532, 623, 625, 792, 795, 798, 800
Smith, Thomas S., 704
Smith, Truman, 430
Smith, William (Ala.), 19, 39
Smith, William (Va.), 473
Smithson, James, 387, 605
Smithsonian Institution, 387, 605-6
Smock, Jacob, Jr.: to, 434
Snead, John S.: to, 236
Society of Friends (Quakers), 56, 278-79, 467, 737, 781
Society for the Relief of Destitute Orphan Boys, 793-94
Somerville, Tenn., 350
Soule, Peter: from, 795; to, 795
South: abolitionist movement in, 18; supports Texas annexation for slavery extension, 64; Webster unpopularity in, 62
Southard, Henry, 708
Southard, Rebecca Harrow (Mrs. Samuel S.), 66
Southard, Samuel L.: to, 16, 59, 65-66, 80, 123, 185, 449; C. needs his vote on land bill, 16; as head of Morris Canal Bank, 59, 65-66; retains U.S. Senate seat while bank president, 65-66; shares Washington boarding house with C., 65, 185; C. asks about New Jersey politics, 123; vote on Sub-Treasury bill, 149; silent on outcome of 1839 Whig National convention, 473; elected president of U.S. Senate, 547; illness and death of, 708, 717, 720, 743; mentioned, 17, 538, 546, 578-80, 582, 593, 609, 624
Southard, Virginia, 66
South Boston, Va., 434
South Carolina: to Chancery court of, 506-7; Whigs in resist Webster nomination for president, 61-62; Whig support for C. in, 62, 65; Webster and Harrison political weakness in, 65; nullification by, 674, 713, 750; views of slavery in, 223; effect of tariff and free trade upon, 669; mentioned, 18, 52-53, 57, 59, 69, 124, 148, 158-59, 161, 199-200, 224, 230, 249, 263, 290, 370, 410, 445, 537, 540, 565, 567-68, 645-47, 660, 673, 675, 685, 703, 811, 820-21, 833-34, 863, 874, 885-86, 889
Southgate, William W.: connection with Graves-Cilley duel, 656-58 (*see also* Duels and Dueling); mentioned, 69
South Union, Ky., 793-94
Southwick, E. (not identified): from, 339-40
Sovereign (horse), 481, 584-85, 592
Spain, 45, 53, 95, 118, 126-29, 206, 289, 382, 402, 689, 783, 902
Spanish America, 35, 654, 845-46, 884
Sparkman, Henry S., 353
Sparta, Va., 826
Spartan Club, 870
Specie Circular, 2-5, 7, 15, 18, 20, 27, 57, 76-77, 146, 156, 166, 183, 185, 189-91, 193-95, 237, 378, 534, 540, 711-12, 802
Speed, Thomas: from, 613-14; to, 152-53, 453-54
Spencer, Ambrose: from, 786; to, 256, 292-93, 470, 594, 788-89; embarrassed by son John's defense of Tyler, 786; grandson of arrested for forgery, 659-60; mentioned, 288, 425-26, 754, 771
Spencer, Ambrose [II], 660
Spencer, John C.: as New York secretary of state, 293; support of Tyler deemed pro-Scott plot, 675-76; controversial letter of, defending Tyler and his vetoes, 786, 788-89; reports Tyler considered resigning at end of first term, 786; U.S. Senate confirms as secretary of the Treasury, 803-4; mentioned, 157, 238, 288, 503, 614, 659, 722-23, 727, 729, 751, 787
Spencer, Thomas (not identified): to, 766
Sprague, Peleg, 233
Sprague, William, 182, 687-88, 723
Sprigg, James C., 838
Springfield, Ill., 49, 308, 760
Springfield, Mass., 578

Springfield, Ohio, 424
Stamboul (horse), 59, 94
Stanard, Robert, 806
Stanly, Edward, 194-95, 302, 386, 622, 704
Stapp, James T.B.: to, 891
Stark County, Ohio, 399, 641
Starkweather, Samuel: to, 415, 447, 519, 621; mentioned, 416, 872
State Bank of Indiana, 526
State Bank of New York, 467
States' Rights party, 124, 147, 158, 161, 164, 342, 598, 609, 637
States' Rights Whigs, 231, 719
Staunton, Va., 258, 299, 346, 351
Stearns, John: from, 494
Steele, John, 248
Steenrod, Lewis, 494-95
Sterling, Lyne, Jr., 157
Stettinius, Joseph (not identified), 238
Steuben, Baron von, 136
Steubenville, Ohio, 325, 435
Stevens, Enos, 707
Stevens, Samuel, 321
Stevens, Thaddeus, 288, 306, 751, 873
Stevenson, Andrew, 294, 309, 727, 729
Stevenson, Thomas B: to, 836, 851
Stockholm, Sweden, 50, 499
Stockton, Lucius W., 167
Stockton, Robert F.: corrupt role of in 1843 New Jersey state election, 871-72
Story, Benjamin, 40
Story, Joseph: from, 749-50; endorses C. views on national issues, 749-50; mentioned, 72, 895-96
Stout, S.V.D. (not identified): from, 343
Stout, Z. Barton (not identified): from, 879-80
Stout, Mrs. Z. Barton (not identified), 880
Stow, Alexander W.: from, 41; to, 43
Strange, Robert, 27, 152, 269-70, 276
Strattan, Jacob: to, 767
Stringer, Leonard (not identified), 174
Strobel, George, 95
Stuart, David, 510
Stuart, James, 9
Stuart, John T., 228, 384
Stuart, Robert, 510
Stuart, William M., 596
Stuart monarchy (Great Britain), 381
Sturgeon, Daniel, 583
Sublett, G. (not identified), 461
Sub-Treasury System (Independent Treasury), 39, 63, 73, 75-81, 84, 87, 89, 93, 96-97, 101, 108, 115, 117, 130-32, 136, 138-47, 149, 151-52, 154-55, 158, 160, 162-66, 168, 170, 173, 176-80, 190-91, 194-95, 203, 205, 208-11, 235-36, 241-43, 254, 263, 270, 337-38, 351, 356, 373-74, 376, 378, 380-83, 389, 391, 396, 403, 427, 437, 440, 464-65, 469, 488, 494-96, 502, 504, 513, 527, 529-31, 533-37, 539-43, 545, 551, 560, 563, 581-83, 586, 590, 605, 607, 617, 619, 776, 840
Such, James: from, 513, 555; C. sends three grandsons to New York school of (*see espec.* 431), 449, 452, 513, 555; C. provides with letter of introduction, 467; interest of Peter B. Porter in Such School, 467; on health and progress of C. grandsons, 513; mentioned, 466, 471
Suffolk, Va., 302, 434
Summers, George W., 494
Summit County, Ohio, 634
Sumter County, S.C., 680
Surry County, Va., 302
Sussex County, Dela., 469
Sutton, David, 386
Sutton, George W., 386
Swain, James B.: to, 371, 737-38, 804; writes campaign biography of C., 804-5; mentioned, 871
Swartwout, Robert: from, 196; to, 92-93, 167-68, 203, 207, 216, 237, 249, 353-54, 631; C. personal favor for, 207; mentioned, 62, 153, 198, 486
Swartwout, Samuel: involvement in Burr conspiracy, 442-43; defalcation as collector of Port of New York (*see espec.* 254), 442, 653; question of whether or not he was ever nominated for vice president, 653; mentioned, 255, 560
Sweden, 49, 456, 499, 622, 629
Swift, Benjamin, 56, 110
Swift, John, 353
Syracuse, N.Y., 242-43, 334, 351, 357, 362, 616-18, 631, 764, 771, 773

Tacubaya, 736
Tallahassee, Fla., 453
Tallmadge, James: from, 897
Tallmadge, Nathaniel P.: to, 117, 242-43, 301, 304-5, 325-27, 331, 351, 618-19; attacks Van Buren's Sub-Treasury bill, 170; reelected to U.S. Senate, 256, 288; attacks Van Buren's 1837 annual message, 117; rumored as possible Whig vice presidential candidate (*see espec.* 524), 301, 326, 351, 865; Virginia Whig convention endorses for vice president, 258, 351; disinterest in Harrison Cabinet post, 466; supports J.M. Clayton for Harrison Cabinet seat, 480; supports Scott's nomination at 1839 Harrisburg convention, 675; Tyler appoints governor of Wisconsin Territory, 52-54; candidate for president of U.S. Senate, 718; on Tyler's Exchequer bank proposal, 726; mentioned, 20-21, 61, 80, 93, 238, 247, 258, 273, 312, 320, 357, 430, 477, 535, 649, 676, 698, 719, 801
Talman, George F., 61
Talman, James T., 61
Talman, John H., 61
Tammany Hall, 714, 716
Taney, Roger B., 4, 650
Tangier, 534
Tannehill, W.F. (not identified): from, 343
Tannehill, Wilkins: from, 307; to, 307; mentioned, 189
Tappan, Arthur: Tyler criticizes for advocating abolition in District of Columbia, 137; C. criticizes visionary abolitionism of, 314
Tappan, Benjamin, 432, 437, 490, 494, 551, 606
Tappan, Lewis: from, 181-82, 199-200; to, 212; on political future and strength of abolitionists, 181-82; C. to Tappan letters destroyed in fire, 182; implores C. to embrace emancipation, 199-200, 212
Tariff of 1816, 838-39, 863
Tariff of 1824, 509, 751, 773, 838-39, 863
Tariff of 1828, 159, 660, 856-57, 863
Tariff of 1832, 838-39, 850, 856
Tariff of 1833, 19, 30-33, 57, 62, 76, 85-86, 100, 102, 158-59, 161, 172, 222, 230, 285, 306-7, 329, 331, 341, 370, 374, 376, 384, 411, 428-30, 465-66, 468, 479, 487-88, 496-97, 508, 513, 525-26, 542, 582, 592, 603-5, 628, 646, 654-55, 660, 666-69, 677, 682-86, 689-90, 700, 713, 719, 737, 750,

Tariff of 1833 (continued): 753, 762-63, 774, 782, 787-88, 856, 863, 886
Tariff of 1842, 628, 646-47, 660, 706-8, 719-20, 731-32, 742-43, 760-63, 766, 772, 775, 863
Tarleton, Sir Banastre, 783-84
Tarlton, Ohio, 618
Tayloe, Benjamin O. (Va. Gov.), 521
Tayloe, Benjamin O.: from, 521, 604; to, 529, 583, 606; hemp business dealings with C., 583, 604, 606; anticipates second Tyler bank veto, 604; on abolition, 604; mentioned, 584
Tayloe, Edward Thornton, 521, 583
Tayloe, Henry, 521
Taylor, Franck, 372, 387
Taylor, Zachary, 290
Taylorsville, Va., 426, 429, 431, 636
Temperance movement: in Massachusetts, 269; C. opposes coercive approach of, 709
Tennessee: newspaper support for C. in, 7; decline of Jacksonianism in, 7; bank failures in, 41-42; opposition in to Sub-Treasury system, 140; 1837 state and U.S. House elections in, 71; support for C. for president in, 127, 299, 316-17; C. 1840 presidential campaign and prospects in, 8, 233, 316-17, 344-45; 1839 state and U.S. House elections in (*see espec.* 316-17), 299, 307, 344, 346, 351; 1839 Whig rally for C. in Nashville, 343; Democratic and Whig political strategy and tactics in, 344-45; C. urged to campaign in, 343, 345-46, 351-52; C. political speech in Nashville, 343, 412, 432, 434-35, 439-43; 1840 Knox County Whig convention at Cumberland Gap, 443; C. campaign speech in Memphis, 801-3; 1843 state and U.S. House elections in (*see espec.* 817-18), 819-20, 826, 832-33, 836-37, 844, 846-48, 854, 870; outcome of 1844 presidential election in East Tennessee, 818; mentioned, 18, 21, 70, 72, 95, 98, 153, 183, 234-36, 259, 263, 290, 308, 322, 341, 350, 424-25, 445, 454, 461, 489, 504, 514-15, 591, 647, 713, 752, 804-5, 807, 811, 813, 821, 827, 835, 843-44, 849, 873, 889
Tennessee Beacon, 322
Tennessee River, 213
Texas, Republic of: U.S. troops raised for border duty during Texas Revolution, 21; U.S. neutrality in Texas war with Mexico, 34; U.S. annexation of as political issue (*see espec.* 35-36), 64, 110, 124, 135-36, 399, 823, 896 (*see also* Election, presidential, of 1844: issues, charges, and countercharges in campaign); South would annex to strengthen slavery, 64; U.S. recognition of independence of, 85-86; opposition to U.S. annexation of, 65, 110, 897-99; withdraws request to be annexed by the United States, 226-29; Biddle bank loan to, 226-27, 229; U.S. reaction to possible foreign attacks upon, 228; U.S. policy in continuing Texas-Mexico tension, 229; serious financial problems of, 457; attempts of to float European loans, 407; Great Britain recognizes independence of, 407; war with Mexico, 86; Tyler's first treaty of annexation, 897-99; C. arguments against U.S. annexation, 135-36, 897-900; British interests and ambitions in, 899; mentioned, 20, 29, 39, 56, 119, 127, 129, 155, 414, 481, 484, 556, 681, 688, 729
Thayer, John E., 332
Theller, Edward A., 276
Thomas, Richard, 829
Thomas, William: to, 431
Thomasson, William P., 837
Thome, James A., 199-200
Thompson, Benjamin F.: to, 470-71
Thompson, Charles, 409
Thompson, Danielle, 215
Thompson, Jacob, 123
Thompson, Jonathan, 154, 653
Thompson, John R.: to, 584
Thompson, Robert, 321
Thompson, R.W. (not identified): from, 688; to, 688
Thompson, W. (not identified), 53
Thompson, Waddy, Jr.: to, 56-59, 522, 716; U.S. minister to Mexico, 522; reports on C. political strength among Southern Whigs, 647; C. seeks help from on Alexander imprisonment issue, 716-17; role in Graves-Cilley duel, 657-58 (*see also* Duels and Dueling); mentioned, 178, 644
Thompson, Waddy, Sr., 59
Thomson, James W.: from, 213-14
Thomson, Manlius V., 301, 767
Thornton, Harry I.: to, 230-31
Thornton, Lucy Crittenden, 231
Thurston, Benjamin B., 182
Tigert, Mr. ——— (not identified), 108
Tilford, John, 65, 180-81
Tillinghast, Joseph R., 60
Tioga County, N.Y., 618
Tipton, John, 17, 136, 268
Todd, H.B., 353
Todhunter, Parker E., 522, 673
Toland, Henry, 756-57
Toledo, Ohio, 828
Tompkins, Gwin, 53
Tom (slave), 10, 52
Tonquin (vessel), 510
Toronto, Canada, 104-5, 320
Tory party (Great Britain), 597, 862
Townsend, John, 321
Tracy, Albert H., 151, 157, 173, 249, 288
Transylvania University: to trustees of, 785; finances of, 179, 233-34; reorganization of, 234, 386-87; C. interest in and work for, 386-87; C. debt to, 42, 179, 450, 688, 785; C. assists in search for president of, 532; C. on faculty appointments at, 753; Transylvania Institute, 233-34; mentioned, 51, 238, 241, 310, 320, 347, 889, 901
Treaty of Ghent, 365, 405, 630, 806
Treaty of Paris of 1783, 206, 211, 293
Trenton, N.J., 95, 119, 123, 149, 153-54, 204, 872
Trimble, David, 206
Trimble County, Ky., 837
Trinity Episcopal Church (Washington, Pa.), 347
Triplett, Philip, 333-34
Trotter, James Fisher, 123
Trotter, Joseph: to, 498
Trowbridge, Charles C., 148
Troy, N.Y.: C. speech in, 335-36; mentioned, 94, 105, 115, 330, 583, 604, 896
"A True Northern Friend" (pseud.): from, 733-34
The True Whig, 651-52
Tucker, Aaron, 311

Tucker, Elizabeth Henrietta Carroll, 311
Tucker, Henry St. George, 299, 361
Tucker, Luther, 614
Tucker, Nathaniel Beverley: from, 361-62, 367-68, 391; to, 462, 520; asks C. aid in breaking John Randolph's will, 361-62, 367; on Harrison as possible U.S. president, 367-68; plan for new national bank, 520
Tudor, William, Jr., 284
Turkey, 455
Turner, William (not identified): from, 274; to, 284
Tuscany, Grand Duchy of, 811
Tuscarora Indians, 145
Tyler, John
— general: from, 137, 341-42, 527-29, 651; resigns Senate seat in 1836, 588; on abolition and the "gag rule," 137; seeks C.'s opinion on presidential power of removal, 341; on C.'s reaction to Jackson's Proclamation to South Carolina and Force bill, 341-42; supports C.'s distribution plan, 271; supports C. for president in 1840, 342; good relations with C., 518-19, 530; referred to as "vice president" and "acting president," 518, 521, 681, 900; deluded about his popularity, 625; more fool than knave, 751; burned in effigy, 602; said to return to Democratic party, 615-16, 646, 735; as a president without a party, 681, 769; third party movement of, 615-16, 620, 720; attempt to impeach (*see espec.* 731-32), 544, 725, 734, 736, 739-40, 742, 755; attempt to get vote of no confidence in, 734-35, 740
— administration: patronage policies and practices of, 455, 518, 522, 524, 528-29, 532-34, 551, 574, 593, 647, 652, 704, 706, 727-28, 740, 748, 775, 803-4, 817-18; inaugural address of, 520-21, 587; C. anticipates Whig orthodoxy from, 518-26, 529; retains Harrison Cabinet, 519, 588; goals of, 527-29; Ewing analysis of what to expect from, 530; message of June 1, 1841, 530-31; anticipated reaction toward revival of national bank, 522-23, 528, 530-31; veto of Whig bank bills, 528-29, 543-44, 553, 556-57 (*see also* Congress of the United States: 27 Cong., 1 Sess); reaction to the bank vetoes of, 529, 587-92, 604, 608-10, 612, 616-17; C. opposition to and criticism of, 532, 534, 543, 553, 587-92, 608, 620, 631, 641, 646, 696, 739-40, 817, 853, 896; resignation of Harrison Cabinet and appointment of new Cabinet (*see espec.* 614), 609, 612, 616-17, 681, 720, 786, 878-79; Webster remains in Cabinet of, 841, 864; Webster departs Cabinet of, 723, 727-28, 735-36, 751-52; Cabinet changes of, 720, 723, 727-28, 751-52; "Kitchen Cabinet" or "Corporal's Guard" of, 591-92, 619, 730; viewed as "traitor" to Whig party, 543, 557, 591-92, 594, 597-98, 601, 608, 616-17, 619, 625, 647-48, 681, 696, 704-6, 712, 715, 717, 720, 749, 752, 771, 811, 817, 855; attitude of toward distribution, 528-29, 646-47, 689-90; defended by Cushing, Spencer, and Webster, 786-87; C. on "intrigue" of, 704, 706, 720; Whig state election defeats blamed on, 618; U.S. customs receipts during, 561-62, 567; investigation of New York customhouse during, 595-96; maladministration of, 705, 725-27; split with Congress, 696, 720, 730-31; and U.S. House reapportionment bill, 742-43; Democratic support for, 826, 840, 862; Hitchcock report controversy, 544-45; handling of Dorr Rebellion, 714, 723; 1844 reelection prospects of, 522, 722; the "Tyler Grippe" of, 853, 858; abuse of executive power by, 730, 769; C. praises for Webster-Ashburton treaty, 782; on status of Hawaii (Tyler Doctrine), 829; on Texas annexation, 680-81, 823, 896-97, 899 (*see also* Texas, Republic of); mentioned, 19, 44, 89, 224, 258, 327, 364, 368, 414, 456, 462, 510, 548, 550, 555, 561, 563, 570, 573, 577, 582, 586, 600, 607, 611, 623-24, 628, 634-35, 638-39, 653, 670, 676, 707-8, 716, 718-19, 724, 729, 733, 744, 750, 753-54, 756, 763, 774-76, 784, 789, 795, 801, 805, 808-10, 812-13, 828, 833, 835, 841, 850, 859-60, 864, 866-67, 869-72, 875-76, 883, 891-92, 898
Tyler, Lyon Gardiner, 520
Tyler Doctrine, 829
Tyrees Springs, Tenn., 439
Tyrrell County, N.C., 705

Ullmann, Daniel: from, 68; to, 66-68, 473, 810-11, 832, 881
Underwood, Elizabeth Cox, 334
Underwood, Joseph R., 113, 333-34
Union, Va. (W. Va.), 494
Union Bank of Mississippi, 716
Union Canal Company, 498
Union College, 181
Union County, Ky., 311
"Union Jack" (pseud.): from, 564-65
Union Theological Seminary, 697
Uniontown, Pa., 507
Unitarian Church, 307, 672
U.S. Army: C. on size of, 28; C. on national defense costs, 34, 666-67; militia reorganization proposal, 421-23, 427; pay equalization of line and staff officers of, 268; C. on useless fortifications, 34; mentioned, 426, 481, 703, 728
U.S. Bank of Pennsylvania: replaces Second Bank of the U.S., 29, 33; C. doubts usefulness of, 3-4; increases discount rates, 36; abuses of, 140; rumored conversion by Van Buren to national bank, 243, 246, 257-58; second specie-payment suspension of, 252-53, 315; resumption of specie payments by, 446; third specie-payment suspension of, 498; other Philadelphia banks suspend specie payments, 498; closes its doors, 446; scandals and disclosures about, 500, 520, 528, 541; C. attacks corruption in, 802; mentioned, 9-10, 75, 81-83, 111, 175, 177, 187, 191, 193, 227, 303, 379, 400, 403, 478, 611. *See also* Bank of the United States
U.S. Census (1840), 266
U.S. Civil War, 577
U.S. Constitution. *See* Constitution of the United States

United States Internal Improvement and Manufacturing Loan Office, 154
The United States' Magazine and Democratic Review, 86, 371
U.S. Marine Corps, 606
U.S. Military Academy, 310, 481
U.S. Navy: C. on building of naval vessels, 134, 141; C. supports naval preparedness against Great Britain, 508; grog ration abolished in, 472; need for a naval academy, 564; need for naval fortifications, 564-65; C. hemp sales to, 577, 754; 1841 home squadron appropriations bill, 576-77; armed merchantmen in wartime, 564; needs canal link between Great Lakes and Mississippi River, 564; C. on need for revived navy, 684; mentioned, 118, 241, 396, 426, 432, 434, 646, 650, 703, 727, 749
United States v. *Nathaniel Cox*, 42
U.S. Post Office: role in currency-circulation decisions, 183; origin of Cabinet status of, 183; C. complains about service of, 531
U.S. Public Land Office: Tyler removes commissioner of, 455; relief laws of 1830 and 1831 for public land purchasers, 480; terminology used in preemption-distribution debates, 486-94 (*see also* 8:540)
U.S. Senate: question of hiring newspaper employees as recorders of debates in, 538; appointment of reporters for, 423. *See also* Congress of the United States
U.S. Senate *Journal*, 21, 322, 860
U.S. Supreme Court: C. and *Briscoe* v. *Bank of Commonwealth of Kentucky*, 31; C. and *Edward Livingston* v. *Benjamin Story*, 40; C. and *United States* v. *Cox*, 42; C. and *Keene* v. *Brown*, 42, 82-83, 373, 386; *Amistad* case, 382; *Groves* v. *Slaughter*, 52, 475-76, 797; *Cordes and Paul* v. *Clay*, 506; *Jones* v. *Van Zandt*, 858; Van Buren appointees to, 40; mentioned, 26, 39, 52, 254, 415, 588, 728, 739, 825, 847, 861. *See also* Constitution of the United States
University of Georgia, 164
University of Louisville, 307, 889
University of Pennsylvania, 532
University of Virginia, 214, 584
Unknown Correspondent: from, 339
Unknown Recipient: to, 38, 65, 94, 234, 322, 429, 517, 623
Upper Canada, 104, 320
Upshur, Abel P.: low opinion of Webster, 620; mentioned, 614, 703, 729, 869
Urbana, Ohio, 342, 346
Ursuline Convent, 879
Utica, N.Y., 60, 234, 237-38, 334

Van Buren, Abraham, 703
Van Buren, Angelica Singleton, 703
Van Buren, Martin
—general: from, 680-81; to, 680, 702; unpopularity of, 44, 215; manners of, 224; character of, 215; weight of, 704; C. personal attacks on, 76, 78, 141; C. meets at Saratoga, 334-35; visits "Ashland," 680-81, 702, 704, 706, 708; candidacy of for 1844 Democratic nomination, 681, 751-52; C. anecdote on lack of humor of, 861-62; agreement with C. on Texas annexation, 681
—administration: inaugural address of, 44; and Panic of 1837, 2, 45, 48; clone of Jackson administration, 99; Cabinet appointments of, 31-32, 39; impact of 1837 state elections on, 99-100; policies for dealing with economic depression, 55, 59, 68, 73, 479; message proposing a Sub-Treasury System, 73; reactions to Sub-Treasury proposal of, 72-73, 75-80, 89 (*see also* Congress of the United States: 25 Cong., 1 Sess.); first annual message of, 93, 117, 136, 141, 170; pro-South activities and political strategies of, 29; appointments of, 39; Conservative Democrats oppose, 20, 117; opposes abolition in District of Columbia, 44; public land policy of, 136, 170-71; on squatters on the public lands, 322, 860; C. attacks unbalanced budget of, 482-83; tariff policy of, 886; corruption in, 203, 253-54, 256, 560; mentioned, 13, 30, 37, 49-51, 58, 62-63, 71, 74, 81, 88, 96-98, 101, 105, 115, 119-20, 122, 135, 138, 144, 146-47, 149, 155-56, 158-60, 164, 166-67, 175, 177, 182, 191-92, 194, 196, 209, 216, 221-22, 230-31, 233, 236, 239, 241, 243, 245-46, 255, 257-58, 263, 266, 277, 279, 290-96, 301-2, 305-6, 316, 329, 338, 340-41, 344-45, 347, 349, 356-57, 369, 371, 373, 378, 380-81, 403, 407-8, 410, 414, 418, 424, 426-28, 433, 436-38, 440-45, 447-49, 451-55, 458, 464, 466, 473, 484, 486, 495-96, 505, 532, 536, 539, 561, 570, 582, 590, 593, 596, 666, 683-84, 703, 727, 729, 762, 768, 775-76, 803-5, 817, 820, 831, 844, 849, 854-55, 857, 859, 863, 865, 869, 881-83, 894, 896
Vance, Joseph: from, 115, 368-69; mentioned, 237, 240, 242, 245
Vandalia, Ill., 891
Vanderpoel, Aaron, 715
Van Ness, Cornelius P., 95
Van Rensselaer, Rensselaer, 104-5
Van Rensselaer, Solomon: to, 817; mentioned, 104, 151, 355, 357
Van Zandt, John, 858
Varian, Isaac Leggett, 174, 301
Varnum, George W. (not identified): to, 881
Veazey, Thomas, 148
Veracruz, Mexico, 211
Vermont: on statehood for Texas, 110; abolitionism in, 110, 112; Whig legislative caucus of, debates 1840 presidential nominee, 120; Anti-Masonic party in, 106, 283; 1839 Whig state convention in, 120, 215; 1838 state elections in, 232-33; 1843 state and U.S. House elections in, 873; 1844 presidential election in, 821; mentioned, 194, 263, 394, 489, 728, 739
Vernon, William S. (not identified), 461
Verplanck, Gulian C.: from, 68, 196; to, 66-68, 98-100, 200-202; elected to N.Y. state senate as a Whig, 88; supports C. for president, 68; passes "Secret Circular" to Porter and Clay, 157; invites C. to visit New York,

196; mentioned, 190
Versailles, Ky., 150
Vertner, Daniel, 790-91
Vertner, Mrs. Daniel, 790
Vesper (slave), 52
Vicksburg, Miss., 791-92, 794, 813-15
Vienna, 668
Vigus, Damis L.: from, 179
Vincennes, Ind., 393-94
"Vindex" (pseud.), 787-88
Virginia: shortage of specie in, 154; abolitionism in, 1, 302; support for C.'s land policy in, 271; C. seeks endorsement by Whig legislative caucus of, 258, 262-63, 275, 277; 1838 state elections in, 174, 179, 232; U.S. Senatorial election deadlock in (*see espec*. 224, 258), 261, 266-67, 272, 275, 296, 300, 326; C. popularity and support for president in, 302, 311-12; Whig-Conservative Democrat cooperation in, 261, 299; 1839 state and U.S. House elections in, 296, 299, 312, 315, 324-26; 1839 Democratic unity convention in, 298-99; 1839 Whig state convention in, 258, 299, 346, 351; importance of in 1840 presidential election, 272; C. visits Richmond, 386, 390-92, 394-95, 398; C. recalls boyhood in Hanover County, 395, 426; 1840 state and U.S. House elections in, 409; 1840 C. campaign speech in Taylorsville, Hanover County, 426-30, 461, 591-92, 881; Whig barbecue in Boydton, 433; support for Harrison in, 239, 451-52, 459; 1841 state and U.S. House elections in, 473, 494-95, 521; 1841 election of governor in, 473, 521; Rives elected U.S. Senator of, 473; Harrison patronage appointments in, 514; votes of congressional delegation on 1841 bank bills, 533; support in for C. performance in 27 Cong., 1st ["Extra"] Sess., 604; 1842 state elections in, 707, 770; 1843 Whig state convention in, 805-6, 812; 1843 state elections in, 822, 826; pro-Clay sentiment in western Virginia, 855; C. on presidential campaign of 1844 in, 889-90; C. wants to visit Eastern Shore of, 901; mentioned, 2, 18, 21-22, 49, 103, 113, 125, 127, 139-40, 149-50, 160, 199, 213, 219, 239, 249, 254, 259, 279, 297, 301, 313, 322, 327, 342, 353, 361, 374, 393, 403, 410-11, 424-25, 460, 466, 469, 491, 494-95, 506, 520, 528-29, 565, 582, 588, 601, 617, 627, 638, 641, 679, 704, 709, 716, 729, 736, 745, 763, 779, 821, 824, 832, 834, 849, 859
Virginia mare, 150, 318

Wabash-Erie Canal, 149, 828
Waddel, Hugh, 194-95
Wade, Edward, 872
Wadsworth, James: to, 764; mentioned, 320, 332
Wake County, N.C., 670, 681
Wakeman, Stephen (not identified), 61, 64
Walden, Jacob T. (not identified), 509
Wales, 829
Walker, Catherine (not identified): to, 902
Walker, G. (not identified), 902
Walker, G.P. (not identified): from, 698
Walker, Robert J.: stance on public land legislation, 6-7; on U.S.-Mexican relations, 171; mentioned, 15-18, 21-22, 25-26, 35, 81, 114, 129, 134-35, 138, 153, 169, 265-67, 369, 382-83, 423, 437, 474, 559, 570-71, 573-75, 578, 598, 658-60, 719
Wall, Garret D., 109, 149, 165
Wallace, David, 38
Walsh, Mike, 870
War: just war with Britain, 126, 295; U.S. always victorious over Great Britain, 295; Congress of Nations to preserve peace, 180, 253; opposition to U.S. filibustering operations, 154-55; preparedness for possible war with Great Britain, 405; C. on avoiding or accepting war, 684; C. on compulsory military education of American youth, 423; C. recollections of American Revolution, 783
Warden, William (not identified), 174
Warfield, Elisha: from, 610; to, 610
War of the American Revolution. *See* American Revolution
War of 1812: C. role in onset of hailed, 41; taxing of slaves to support, 319; impressment issue in, 365; benefits provided to U.S. by, 331-32; C. pleased with origin and outcome of, 331, 427; C. retrospect on, 331-32, 405; siege of Fort Meigs by British, 399-400; Battle of New Orleans in, 398, 440; Battle of Lake Erie in, 440; Battle of the Thames in, 444; retarded prosecution of, 570; peace treaty ending, 365; C. shifts on bank issue because of, 160, 165, 825; Kentucky seeks recovery of value of arms given United States during, 398; mentioned, 49, 163, 413-14, 434, 508, 560, 567, 617, 630, 646, 661, 673, 686, 699, 704, 729, 747, 831-32, 840, 845
Warren County, N.C., 670
Warrenton, Va., 339
Warrington, Lewis: to, 310; mentioned, 311
Warrington Springs, Va., 412
Warrior (jackass), 54
Washington, George, 47, 206, 245, 338, 403, 428, 588, 622, 700, 824-25
Washington, Thomas: to, 351-52
Washington, D.C.: C. speech in, 363-64; C. boarding and housekeeping arrangements in, 65-66, 68, 185, 386, 417, 509-10; C. social life in, 181, 236, 403-4, 417; C. daily health habits while in, 539, 557-58; lack of ice in, 652; new Whig newspaper needed in, 110, 183-84; C. takes his body slave to, 386, 583-84; C. on slavery in, 279-80 (*see also* District of Columbia; Congress of the United States); C. sees no manacled slaves in, 292-93; Bodisco-Williams wedding in, 403-4; economic depression and unemployment in, 432; routes to and from taken by C., 534, 607; farewell dinner and birthday ball for C. in, 688; mentioned, 6, 13, 17, 20, 26, 34, 45, 47-48, 52-56, 63, 71-72, 77, 83, 87, 89-90, 94, 96, 102, 111, 123, 132, 138, 218, 220, 232, 235, 237, 246, 249, 254-55, 273, 278, 285-86, 296, 298, 308, 311, 343, 346, 352, 354, 372, 377-78, 408, 411, 413, 416, 421-22, 425, 431, 433-35, 437, 453-55, 457, 459, 464, 467-69, 472, 484, 486, 501, 505-6, 511-12,

Washington, D.C. (continued): 516-19, 521-24, 532-33, 538, 544, 546, 548-49, 555-56, 569, 571, 587, 595-96, 611-12, 614, 616-19, 622, 640, 657, 659, 672, 675, 678, 680, 696-97, 700, 703, 705-6, 708, 714, 716, 719, 738, 741, 744, 752, 758, 761, 763, 766, 769, 784, 786, 789, 791-93, 796, 799, 806, 828, 830-31, 833, 857, 869-70, 874, 885, 891, 898, 900
Washington, Miss., 798
Washington, Pa., 308, 347, 703, 877
Washington College (Washington and Jefferson University), 308
Washington County, Pa., 641
Washington (D.C.) *Daily National Intelligencer*, 130, 173, 177-78, 206, 273, 306, 316, 322, 423, 448-49, 524, 531, 568, 651-52, 661, 663, 665, 732, 751-52, 757, 860, 878-79
Washington (D.C.) *Globe*, 89, 130, 206, 321-22, 423, 511-12, 516, 820-21
Washington (D.C.) *Independent*, 651-52, 723
Washington Monument Society, 206
Washington (D.C.) *United States Telegraph*, 25
Washita Lands, 302
Watertown, N.Y., 333
Watkins, Elizabeth Hudson Clay (mother), 396
Watkins, Henry (stepfather), 396
Watkins, James B. (not identified): to, 787
Watkins, John (half-brother): farmer in Woodford County, Ky., 798
Watkins, Nathaniel W. (half-brother): from, 456; lawyer in Missouri, 798; mentioned, 796
Watkinsville, Ga., 881
Watson, Alexander, 52-53, 506-7
Watson, David, 53
Watson, E.C. (not identified), 154
Watson, Edward, 53
Watson, Mary, 52
Watson, Muryar, 53
Watson, Samuel, 53
Wayne, Anthony, 206
Wayne, Isaac: to, 206
Wayne, James M., 506
Wayne County, Ohio, 641
Wayne County, N.Y., 91, 426
Webb, James Watson: from, 81-82, 635-36, 675-76; to, 495, 505, 640, 643-44, 648, 651-52, 680, 754, 874-76, 885; role in 1840 presidential campaign, 54-55, 106-7; on Webster 1840 presidential candidacy, 60-61, 81-82, 106-7; supports C. for president, 61, 69, 80-81, 106-7; hostility to Harrison's candidacy, 69, 81, 106; sees C. victory in 1840 election, 69, 106; advises C. on 1840 campaign tactics, 82, 106-7; advises C. on New York state and city politics, 106, 495; seeks New York City postmastership, 485, 505; warns C. against false friends, 675-76; supports C. 1844 presidential candidacy, 651, 754-55; advises C. on repeal of Bankruptcy bill, 635; role in Graves-Cilley duel, 643-45, 648, 658, 661-62, 664-65; duel with Representative Thomas F. Marshall, 648; on C. as moralist and slaveholder, 754-55; supports a Clay-Webster ticket in 1844 election, 866, 869, 874, 882, 885; advice of on people in Harrison Cabinet, 875-76; vanity of, 869; mentioned, 153, 234, 271, 519, 861, 868, 870, 890
Webster, Caroline LeRoy, 40, 46
Webster, Daniel: from, 518; to, 40; family visits C. in Lexington, 40, 46, 55-56; C. recommends for legal work, 46; defeat of in 1836 presidential election (*see* Election, presidential, of 1836); as possible candidate for nomination in 1840 election, 204-5 (*see also* Election, presidential, of 1840: Daniel Webster candidacy, prospects, and role in); popularity of in West, 55; unpopularity of in South, 61-62; C. supports for U.S. minister to Great Britain, 875-76; 1837 speech in Niblo's Saloon, 48, 81; 1837 mass rally for in New York City, 54-55; will support Whig convention nominee in 1840 election, 107; mentioned for vice presidential nomination in 1840 election, 107, 362-63; will support C. in 1840 if nominated, 81, 123; C. attacks for support of preemption, 137; supports and amends C. bill to discontinue Specie Circular policy, 185, 190, 198, 203; on bill to amend 1836 Deposit Act, 209-11; Whig caucus in Massachusetts legislature nominates for president, 154, 157, 232-33, 252, 298; thinks presidential executive power too strong, 163; criticized for having supported 1833 Force bill, 163; connection with Boston *Atlas*, 229-30, 233-34, 237, 274-75; waffling on public land (graduation and reduction) bill, 274-75; reelected to U.S. Senate, 269, 274-75; political competition with C. in New York City (*see* New York City); not consulted by C. on 1833 Compromise Tariff bill, 285; trip to Europe during 1840 presidential campaign, 312-13, 320; opposes C. nomination by 1839 Harrisburg convention, 875-76; on withdrawing from 1840 presidential race, 123, 212-13, 312, 326-27, 485; on outcome of 1840 election, 298; rumored alliance with Harrison in 1840 campaign, 251-52; attacks Van Buren's 1840 annual message to Congress, 465-66; correspondence with Biddle on U.S. foreign debt, 446; on Cabinet appointments in Harrison administration, 458-59, 461, 463, 466, 470, 473-74, 499, 504, 875; C. defends appointment of as secretary of state, 504, 508; influence of Weed over, 485; on regulation of interstate slave trade by Congress, 504, 508; stance on 1841 bank issues, 572; decision of to remain in Tyler Cabinet, 619-20, 841, 862, 864, 866, 875; defends Tyler administration, 786-87; C. break with, 786-87, 841, 862, 875-76; leaves Tyler Cabinet, 723, 727, 751-52; role in 1844 presidential election, 787-88 (*see also* Election, presidential, of 1844: Daniel Webster candidacy and role in); anti-Whig speech in Boston, 787, 876, 828-29, 880; anti-Whig speech in Baltimore on U.S. trade and tariff policy, 821-22, 827-28, 866, 880; attacks national bank

and C.'s 1833 Compromise Tariff, 787-88, 866; treason of to Whigs, 787-88, 821, 866-67; speeches in Rochester, 870, 880; returns to Whig party, 876, 882-83, 896; rumored corruption, political dishonesty, intemperance, and immorality of, 827-28, 878; rumored support of McLean in 1844 election, 869; rumored support of Calhoun in 1844 election, 844, 864, 869; C. opposes a Clay-Webster ticket in 1844 election, 862, 864-71, 873-76, 878-82, 894; mentioned, 3, 22, 25, 27, 32, 58, 60, 65-66, 68-70, 82, 91, 94, 105-6, 114, 118, 120, 122, 142, 157, 173, 189, 192, 194, 216-17, 221, 225, 232, 239-40, 245, 250, 255, 260, 264, 272-73, 276-77, 287, 290, 292, 295, 315, 364, 394, 420, 454, 456, 462, 468, 475, 480, 486, 493-94, 497, 502-3, 507, 509, 515, 523-24, 547, 609, 658-60, 725, 729, 733, 735, 782-83, 807, 823, 830-31, 835, 857, 861, 885, 890

Webster, Julia, 40, 46

Webster-Ashburton Treaty, 405, 697, 720, 749, 765, 782, 787, 875, 882-83

Weed, Thurlow: to, 764; sees C. as leading Whig candidate for 1840 election, 123, 287-88; power of in Anti-Masonic movement, 123; suggests Whig presidential strategy in New York, 287; shifts support to Scott in 1839 Whig National convention, 301-2, 355; role of in 1840 presidential election in New York, 287, 320; supports Curtis for collector of Port of New York, 485; mentioned, 263, 278, 321, 361, 486, 503, 517, 519, 675, 827, 832

Weekly National Anti-Slavery Standard, 899

Weimar, ——— (not identified), 621-22, 704-5

Weir, Eliza Jane: from, 9, 10, 11; C. handles inheritance of, 8-12; mentioned, 400, 555, 790

Weir, James: to, 9; mentioned, 8

Weir, James (uncle of Eliza and James Weir), 8-9

Weissinger, George W., 841

Welch, G.H. (not identified): to, 28

Weller, B.S. (not identified): from, 343

Wells, Thomas L.: from, 196

West: reception of Webster in, 55; opposition to Sub-Treasury in, 89

West Chester, Pa., 901

Western Reserve (Ohio), 154, 164

West Indies, 199-200, 244-45, 279, 307, 310, 467, 597, 822

Westmoreland County, Va., 211

West Port, Mo., 834

Wetmore, Robert C., 108, 357, 675

Wheatley, Seth: to, 71-72

Wheeling, Va. (W. Va.): C. to citizens of, 87; mentioned, 88, 360, 430, 436, 494, 534, 538, 607, 688

Whig party (Great Britain), 862

Whig party (United States): sectional division on slavery and abolition, 1; divided leadership of, 54-55, 58; must unite on strong single leader, 58; southern Whigs fail to support C. in 1836, 25; defeat of in 1836 presidential election, 48; must encourage converts from Jacksonism, 51, 55; in New York, 88; lacks appeal to the masses, 229; definitions of, 465; threat of explosion in on bank issue, 572; compared to British Tory party, 597; performance in 1841 state elections, 617-18, 620-21; C. speech to congressional caucus of, 608-9; C. blames 1841 state Whig defeats on Tyler, 618; address to nation at end of 27 Cong., 1st ["Extra"] Sess., 616; C. on general weakness of political strategy of, 814; mentioned, 27, 38-39, 43, 47, 49, 59-63, 66, 68-71, 77, 79, 82, 91-95, 97-98, 100-101, 105-8, 110, 115-20, 122-23, 127, 130-32, 135, 142-44, 147-52, 154, 157-58, 163-64, 166-68, 172-76, 179, 182, 190-91, 195-97, 202, 205, 207-9, 215-17, 220, 224-26, 228, 230-43, 245-64, 266, 269, 271-78, 286-88, 290, 292, 296, 298-99, 301-3, 305-6, 308-9, 313, 315-18, 320-21, 323-24, 328-30, 333-36, 340, 343-48, 350, 352-55, 357, 359, 361-68, 371, 382, 384, 389, 393, 403-4, 408-10, 412, 416-17, 421, 423-25, 427, 434-36, 438-39, 441, 443-45, 447-51, 454-59, 462, 464, 469, 471, 473, 484-87, 492, 494-95, 502-3, 509, 511-15, 518-24, 526, 529, 532, 534, 536, 539, 543, 545-46, 550-54, 556-57, 563-67, 571, 573-75, 582, 584, 587-88, 592-96, 598, 600-601, 604-5, 610, 612-15, 625, 628, 631, 636-37, 642, 646-49, 652-53, 666-67, 670, 673, 675-76, 681, 683, 686-88, 696, 703-4, 706-8, 710, 712-13, 715-18, 720-32, 734-35, 737, 739, 742-44, 749, 751-57, 759-67, 770, 772-78, 783-89, 795, 797, 803-13, 815, 817, 819-22, 826-27, 830-41, 843-45, 847-74, 876-83, 885-91, 894-97, 899

Whisker (horse), 481

Whitcomb, James, 455, 827

White, Albert S., 481, 718-19

White, Hugh L.: to, 220-21; political power of in Tennessee, 345; on Harrison's 1836 presidential candidacy, 222; C. does not support in 1836 presidential campaign, 222; supports C. for president in 1840 campaign, 222; mentioned, 18, 236, 316, 378, 401, 514

White, John: elected Speaker of U.S. House in 1841, 522; C. denies involvement in election of as Speaker, 522; predicts close presidential race in Tennessee in 1844, 833; mentioned, 543, 634, 708, 736, 812, 817

White, John Campbell (not identified), 274

White, John Whitney: to, 256-57

White, John Williams, 257

White, Joseph M., 328-29

White, Mrs. Joseph M., 328

White, Seneca: to, 415

White, William Nelson, 90

White Bull Calf, 174, 801

White Cow, 186

White House, 515, 553, 769, 783

Whitesides, ——— (not identified): to, 443

White Sulphur Springs, Va. (W. Va.), 224, 272, 296, 346, 430, 436, 557, 821-22

Whitney, Reuben M., 20

Whitney, Steven: to, 421

Whitney, W.W.: from, 52

Whittier, John Greenleaf: from, 56; to, 64-65; antislavery views of, 56; C. lectures on slavery, 64

Whittle, Conway D., 186

Whittle, Fortescue: to, 185-86

Whittlesey, Elisha: to, 309; C. provides with letter of

Whittlesey, E. (continued): introduction, 309; recommends J.M. Clayton for post in Tyler Cabinet, 620
Whom It May Concern: to, 169, 353, 527
Wickham, A. (not identified): to, 131
Wickham, Selden McClurg (Mrs. John), 275-76
Wickliffe, C.A. (son of Charles A., Sr.): runs unsuccessfully for U.S. House seat, 848, 854, 857; defects from Whig party, 854, 857; mentioned, 836, 850
Wickliffe, Charles (innkeeper), 251
Wickliffe, Charles A., Sr.: from, 398; serves as acting governor of Kentucky, 398; defects from Whig party, 854, 857; mentioned, 299, 450-52, 614, 627, 848, 850
Wickliffe, Robert, Jr., 233-34
Wickliffe, Robert, Sr., 310
Wickliffe, Robert N., 251, 273
Wickliffe mare, 185, 673
Wilde, Richard H.: to, 328-29, 800
Wilkeson, Samuel: to, 310; C. praises for American Colonization Society work, 310
William (Morrison slave), 901
William I (The Netherlands), 309
William C. Pickersgill & Co., 815-16
Williams, ——— (not identified), 801
Williams, Alexander (not identified): from, 889; to, 889
Williams, Charles, 873
Williams, Jessie L.: to, 828
Williams, Joseph L., 316-17, 424-25
Williams, Lewis, 660-61
Williams, Reuel, 206-7, 211, 377, 572
Williams, Sherrod, 404
Williams, Thomas (not identified): to, 894-95
Williamsburg, Va., 342, 391
Williamson, Thomas, 310-11
Wilmington, Dela., 184, 213, 416-17
Wilmington *Delaware Journal*, 832
Wilson, James, Jr., 122
Wilson, John S. (not identified), 271
Wilson County, Tenn., 316-17
Winchester, Jonas, 765
Winchester, Ky., 179
Winchester, Va.: C. to Gentlemen in, 403
Wines, Enoch Cobb: to, 23
Wing, C.H. (not identified): from, 777
Wingate, Thomas S. (not identified): from, 150
Winker, G. (not identified), 622
Winnebago, Indians, 132
Winslow, Richard E., III, 850
Winthrop, Me., 158
Winthrop, Robert C.: to, 438, 443, 629; mentioned, 332
Wirt, John: from, 10, 238; to, 10
Wisconsin: problems with boundary of and entry into Union, 764-65; patronage issues and locofocoism in, 457; relationship of tariff to mining in, 457; mentioned, 41, 132, 255, 280, 518, 524
Wisconsin, State Historical Society of, 41
Wise, Henry A.: from, 661; to, 662-65; investigates abuses in Jackson administration, 20; supports John Sergeant for post in Harrison Cabinet, 480; low opinion of Webster, 619-20; influence on Tyler, 620; role in Graves-Cilley duel, 643-44, 657-58, 661-65 (*see also* Duels and Dueling); near-duel with Representative Edward Stanly, 704; U.S. Senate defeats nomination of as minister to France, 803-4; Senate approves nomination of as minister to Brazil, 804; break with C., 826-27; mentioned, 27, 153, 302, 364, 645, 750, 900
Withers, Reuben, 467
Wolf, George, 236
Wolfe, James, 343
Wolf River, 564
Women: induced to sign anti-slavery petition, 778; C. views as pillars of society, 709, 800; C. eye for, 342; C. courtliness toward, 673, 709; C. on role of in politics, 448; role of in 1840 presidential election, 448, 709; C. wants to appear vigorous to, 411
Wood, Eleazer D., 375
Wood, Samuel, Jr.: from, 157-58; to, 164-65
Woodbury, Levi: from, 397; demands Treasury Department statistics, 552; mentioned, 4, 30-31, 85, 189, 198, 243, 253, 269, 376, 410, 463-64, 479-80, 535-36, 542, 546-47, 550, 560, 568-69, 581, 592-94, 635, 650, 683, 762
Woodford Circuit Court: to, 247
Woodford County, Ky., 439, 798, 850
"The Woodlands," 302, 312, 373, 530, 808
Woodpecker (horse), 185
Woods, ——— (not identified), 730
Woods, John: to, 760
Woolley, Aaron K.: conflict with T.F. Marshall referred to C. and John J. Crittenden for mediation, 247; connection with J.R. Ingersoll, 328; mentioned, 310
Woolley, Sally Howard Wickliffe, 310
Woolson Cutter & Co., 9
Word, Thomas J., 148, 174
Worsley, William W.: from, 470
Worsley & Forman, 792, 815-16
Worthington, Thomas, 435, 829
Worthington, Thomas [Jr.]: to, 828-29
Worthington, William C.: to, 435
Wright, Isaac H., 853
Wright, John C.: to, 483-84, 767-68; mentioned, 830
Wright, Silas: bill to remit tariff duties on goods lost in New York City fire, 28; filibusters bank bill, 545; Tyler's overtures to, 726-27; rejects Democratic nomination for vice president in 1844, 728-29; opposition to Texas annexation, 729; mentioned, 15, 19, 30, 35, 37, 61, 74, 80, 93, 111, 114, 131, 136, 164, 179, 183, 185-87, 190, 210-12, 251, 253, 263, 290, 374, 420, 464-65, 487-89, 491-92, 535-37, 550-51, 560-61, 566-69, 605, 659, 670, 683, 690, 752, 863
Wurtsboro, N.Y., 16
Wycoff, Alexander R.: from, 68; to, 66-68, 250
Wythe, George, 709

Yale University: C. declines to speak at, 546
Yates, John Van Ness: from, 215
Yates, Robert, 215
Yates, Robert C., 215

Yates County, N.Y., 445
Yeatman, Thomas, 41-42
Yeatman, Woods & Co., 41-42
Yellow fever, 73
York, Va., 342
York County, Pa., 682
Young, John C., 320
Young, Richard M., 267-68, 295, 322
Young Ladies' Seminary, 314
Young & Stern (store): from, 52

Zanesfield, Ohio, 368
Zingaree (horse), 302

www.ingramcontent.com/pod-product-compliance
Lightning Source LLC
LaVergne TN
LVHW040202080826
844660LV00001B/80

* 9 7 8 0 8 1 3 1 0 0 5 9 3 *